The
INTERNATIONAL CRITICAL
COMMENTARY
on the Holy Scriptures of the Old and
New Testaments

GENERAL EDITORS

J. A. EMERTON, F.B.A.
Fellow of St. John's College
Emeritus Regius Professor of Hebrew in the University of Cambridge
Honorary Canon of St George's Cathedral, Jerusalem

C. E. B. CRANFIELD, F.B.A.
Emeritus Professor of Theology in the University of Durham

AND

G. N. STANTON
Lady Margaret's
Professor of Divinity in the University of Cambridge

FORMERLY UNDER THE EDITORSHIP OF

S. R. DRIVER
A. PLUMMER
C. A. BRIGGS

THE PASTORAL EPISTLES

A CRITICAL AND EXEGETICAL COMMENTARY

ON

THE PASTORAL EPISTLES

BY

I. HOWARD MARSHALL

Professor of New Testament Exegesis,
University of Aberdeen

IN COLLABORATION WITH

PHILIP H. TOWNER

Translation Consultant, United Bible Societies
Adjunct Professor of New Testament, Regent College, Vancouver

t&t clark

T&T Clark LTD
A Continuum Imprint

The Tower Building	80 Maiden Lane
11 York Road	Suite 704
London. SE1 7NX	New York, NY 10038

www.tandtclark.com
Copyright © T&T Clark Ltd, 1999

First published 1999
Reprinted 2003
This edition 2004
Reprinted 2006

ISBN 0 567 08455 8

British Library Cataloguing-in-Publication Data
A catalogue record for this book is available from the British Library

Typeset by The Charlesworth Group, Huddersfield
Printed and bound in Great Britain by The Cromwell Press, Trowbridge

Coniugis carissimae
memor

CONTENTS

PREFACE

Commentators should be expected to justify their work in adding to the vast number of works already available on a particular book or books of the New Testament by pleading better reasons than simply the requirement to contribute to a series. In the case of the Pastoral Epistles (PE) it is not too difficult to do so. Since the publication of the original volume in the International Critical Commentary in 1924, there has been no detailed critical commentary on the Greek text of the epistles in English apart from the major work of G. W. Knight III (NIGTC) in a series intended primarily for students. There have, however, been numerous treatments of varying length on the English text, several of which stand out by reason of their insight. Only on the Letter to Titus do we have a full-length contribution by J. D. Quinn in the Anchor Bible series. However, at the time of writing this Preface we can look forward to the posthumous work of Quinn (with W. C. Wacker) on 1 and 2 Timothy (Eerdmans Critical Commentary) and to W. D. Mounce's volume in the Word Biblical Commentary.

The situation is different in other languages. The standard German work by M. Dibelius was updated by H. Conzelmann in 1955 (HNT) and is available in English (Hermeneia), but it represents the approach of its time, good on background and philology, but lacking in appreciation of the letters as a whole and their theology. A major step forward was taken by N. Brox (RNT, 1963) whose work is still of great significance as the first major exposition of the theology of the letters as post-Pauline documents. Since then, 1 Timothy has been the subject of a detailed commentary of high quality by J. Roloff (EKK) and all three letters have been treated in the excellent theological commentary by L. Oberlinner (HTKNT).[1] In French, the comprehensive work of C. Spicq remains a monument of learning, especially (but by no means only) in the area of philology. Meanwhile, there has also been a very considerable scholarly contribution to understanding of the letters in monographs and articles, both in English and in German, and the time is ripe for gathering together the fruits of these in commentary form.

[1] I am particularly grateful to Professor Oberlinner for his generosity in making his work available to me as soon as it was published.

In an age when word-processing and data-processing facilities make the production of increasingly lengthy and detailed works so much easier, but when technology has done nothing to enable readers to read them faster, I have felt it necessary to exercise strict discipline in the present enterprise. Therefore, I have not reproduced in detail the philological information and the background materials that are readily available not only in the most recent version of Bauer's Lexicon[2] but above all in the work of Spicq, both in his commentary and in his remarkable *Theological Lexicon of the New Testament*, and in Dibelius-Conzelmann. This leads me to note how W. R. Schoedel in his commentary on the letters of Ignatius comments on the way in which earlier scholars gathered 'a rich collection of parallels that has become the common possession of subsequent scholarship'; he has felt free to continue 'the practice of reporting such items without acknowledgment to avoid endless footnoting'.[3] I have gratefully followed this example, although I have often indicated where parallels are cited in standard works that may be easier for students to get hold of than the original sources.

The text printed in the lemmata is that of Nestle-Aland (which is identical with that of *The Greek New Testament*), and the Gramcord programme was used for printing it out in the typescript. Much of the information on the meanings of words is drawn from the standard lexicons. The textual information is based on that in Nestle-Aland (27th edition). I claim no expertise in textual criticism, but I have attempted to comment on the major variants; here I was greatly helped by the valuable work of J. K. Elliott.[4] The omission of an English translation of the letters is quite deliberate; with a plethora of existing translations available I can see no need to add to their number.

The bibliographies are deliberately selective; it has not been thought worthwhile to include material that is now dated or has little of lasting value to offer.

The chief aim has been the understanding of the flow of the argument and the exposition of the theology which it enshrines, so that the message of the letters emerges with all desirable clarity. At the same time I have commented in some detail on Greek syntax for the benefit of students who may appreciate all the help that they can get with the text.

---

[2] The latest revision of the German edition has been utilised in preference to the English translation of the earlier edition.

[3] Schoedel, W. R., *Ignatius of Antioch* (Hermeneia. Philadelphia: Fortress Press, 1985), xiii.

[4] I am grateful to Professor Elliott for his comments on the Introduction, Section III.

Organising the mass of material in what is now called a user-friendly manner has not been easy, and experiments were made with several formats. In the end it was decided to print the text-critical comments separately from the exegesis, to deal with each section of the letters by means of a general comment followed by comments on clauses or phrases, to discuss some matters that required more extended treatment in excursuses, and to use footnotes for references and other material that would break up the flow of the argument too much. In addition to the main bibliography on general works, there are sectional bibliographies of relevant works.

I am grateful to all who have helped with the production of this volume; to the general Editors of the Series, Professors Charles E. B. Cranfield and Graham N. Stanton, for the invitation to participate and for their counsel along the way; to the type-setters who turned files composed with the aid of Nota Bene into print; and to the staff of T&T Clark for their meticulous care in the publishing of the book.

My chief debt in the writing of the volume is to Dr Philip H. Towner, who completed his doctoral thesis on the theology and ethics of the Pastoral Epistles in Aberdeen. Subsequently he was appointed as a Research Fellow in New Testament in the University of Aberdeen with the specific task of collaborating in the writing of this commentary. In addition to reading critically through the whole of the material and correcting the proofs, he was also responsible for drafting a substantial portion of the text, including parts of the exegesis and also several of the excursuses; in doing so he was able to contribute much from his own research, the fruits of which will be seen more fully in his own forthcoming commentary on the letters in the New International Commentary. Without the stimulus of his cooperation I do not know whether I would ever have reached the end of the project.

Both Dr Towner and myself belong to what may be called the more conservative side of New Testament criticism. We were reared on the Pauline authorship (whether directly or indirectly) of the Pastoral Epistles, and in this connection we remember with affection and respect the name of Donald Guthrie who was not afraid to argue against the growing consensus in scholarship.

This commentary, therefore, is more inclined to question some of the things readily taken for granted by scholars trained in less traditional schools, and part of its aim has been to find an understanding of the origin of the letters which will do justice to their closeness to Paul while recognising the difficulties in attributing them to his pen. At the same time I have not been uncritical of a tradition which I highly value and have constantly attempted to discover the truth and to refrain from dogmatic statements where the evidence is insufficient to justify even that relative probability which is the most that historical and literary criticism can hope to achieve.

This has posed problems for the presentation of the exegesis. I have tried to present the message of the letters as they are ostensibly meant to be understood, as letters from Paul to Timothy and Titus, but I am well aware that right from the beginning of their 'canonical' history the letters were intended to be read for their relevance to the church and its leaders, and it is therefore also on that level that they are interpreted. I am conscious that only to a very limited extent has the commentary attempted to ask questions about the history of exposition or about the significance of the letters for the modern reader, but I hope that the exegesis has been done in such a way that expositors will find it a helpful basis for application. A recent commentator on another epistle has stated that 'commentaries should be a resource for worship rather than a self-indulgent exploration of the biblical text'.[5] Like him I write from a self-consciously Christian set of presuppositions, and it is my hope that this commentary will help readers to appropriate the message of this particular part of Holy Scripture.

Aberdeen, April, 1999   I. Howard Marshall

---

[5] L. Kreitzer, *The Epistle to the Ephesians* (London: Epworth Press, 1997), 13.

ABBREVIATIONS AND BIBLIOGRAPHY

The commentary is based on the Nestle-Aland text (NA^{27}) which is identical with that in *The Greek New Testament* (UBS^4). Translations of Graeco-Roman authors are generally taken from the Loeb edition of their works. Standard abbreviations for ancient texts and modern periodicals are used, as listed in the *Journal of Biblical Literature* 'Instructions for Contributors' (*JBL* 107 [1988], 579–596; updated annually in the October issue of the *Catholic Biblical Quarterly*). Commentaries on the Pastoral Epistles are cited throughout simply by the name of the author. Where a commentator has written more than one volume on the letters (e.g. Oberlinner), the references in the text can be assumed to be to the appropriate volume. An author's name accompanied by the date of publication signifies that the work cited is listed in the general bibliography. An asterisk after an author's name signifies that the work cited is listed in the sectional bibliography.

After a Greek word or list of references one asterisk signifies that all the references in the book in question have been given, two asterisks that all the references in the PE have been given, and three asterisks that all the references in the NT have been given.

ABBREVIATIONS

AF: Apostolic Fathers
AV: Authorised (King James) Version
BGU: Aegyptische Urkunden aus den Museen zu Berlin
CH: Corpus Hermeticum
CIG: Corpus Inscriptionum Graecarum
CIL: Corpus Inscriptionum Latinarum
Cl.: Classical (Greek)
Gk.: Greek
GNB: Good News Bible
Hel.: Hellenistic (Greek)
LA: Luke-Acts
LXX: Septuagint
MT: Masoretic Text
mg: margin (as opposed to text of an edition)

NA: Nestle-Aland, *Novum Testamentum Graece* (Stuttgart: Deutsche Bibelgesellschaft, 1993²⁷).
NEB: New English Bible
NIV: New International Version
NJB: New Jerusalem Bible
NRSV: New Revised Standard Version
ns: new series
PE: Pastoral Epistles
PGM: Papyri Graecae Magicae
REB: Revised English Bible
RV: Revised Version
t: text (as opposed to marginal reading of an edition)
TR: Textus Receptus
UBS (UBS⁴): *The Greek New Testament* (Stuttgart: Deutsche Bibelgesellschaft/United Bible Societies, 1993⁴; occasionally reference is made to the third edition [1975] as UBS³).
WH: Westcott and Hort

PERIODICALS AND SERIES

AnBib: Analecta Biblica
ANCL: Ante-Nicene Christian Library
ATR: Anglican Theological Review
BBB: Bonner biblische Beiträge
BBET: Beiträge zur biblischen Exegese und Theologie
BBR: Bulletin for Biblical Research
BibInt: Biblical Interpretation
BETL: Bibliotheca ephemeridum theologicarum lovaniensium
BFCT: Beiträge zur Förderung christlicher Theologie
Bib: Biblica
BibInt: Biblical Interpretation
BLit: Bibel und Liturgie
BJRL: Bulletin of the John Rylands University Library of Manchester
BK: Bibel und Kirche
BSac: Bibliotheca Sacra
BT: Bible Translator
BZ: Biblische Zeitschrift
CBQ: Catholic Biblical Quarterly
CH: Church History
ConNT: Coniectanea neotestamentica
CQ: Classical Quarterly
CTM: Concordia Theological Monthly
ETR: Études théologiques et religieuses
EvQ: Evangelical Quarterly
ExpTim: Expository Times

FRLANT: Forschungen zur Religion und Literatur des Alten und Neuen Testaments
GCS: Griechischen christlichen Schriftsteller
HTKNT: Herders theologischer Kommentar zum Neuen Testament
HUCA: Hebrew Union College Annual
HUT: Hermeneutische Untersuchungen zur Theologie
IBS: Irish Biblical Studies
Int: Interpretation
ITQ: Irish Theological Quarterly
JAC: Jahrbuch für Antike und Christentum
JBL: Journal of Biblical Literature
JETS: Journal of the Evangelical Theological Society
JSNT: Journal for the Study of the New Testament
JSNTSup: Journal for the Study of the New Testament – Supplement Series
JR: Journal of Religion
JTS: Journal of Theological Studies
LB: Linguistica Biblica
LTP: Laval théologique et philosophique
MTZ: Münchener theologische Zeitschrift
Neotest: Neotestamentica
NovT: Novum Testamentum
NovTSup: Novum Testamentum Supplements
NRT: La nouvelle revue theologique
NTAbh: Neutestamentliche Abhandlungen
NTS: New Testament Studies
NTTS: New Testament Tools and Studies
PRS: Perspectives in Religious Studies
QD: Quaestiones disputatae
RB: Revue biblique
ResQ: Restoration Quarterly
RevExp: Review and Expositor
RevQ: Revue de Qumran
RevThom: Revue thomiste
RHE: Revue d'histoire ecclésiastique
RSPT: Revue des sciences philosophiques et théologiques
RSR: Recherches de science religieuse
RTR: Reformed Theological Review
SBLDS: SBL Dissertation Series
SBM: Stuttgarter biblische Monographien
SBS: Stuttgarter Bibelstudien
SEA: Svensk exegetisk årsbok
SecCent: Second Century
SJT: Scottish Journal of Theology
SNTSMS: Society for New Testament Studies Monograph Series

SNT(SU): *Studien zum Neuen Testament (und seiner Umwelt)*
ST: Studia theologica
TGl: Theologie und Glaube
TLZ: Theologische Literaturzeitung
TQ: Theologische Quartalschrift
TS: Theological Studies
TSK: Theologische Studien und Kritiken
TrinJ: Trinity Journal
TU: *Texte und Untersuchungen*
TynBul: Tyndale Bulletin
TZ: Theologische Zeitschrift
VC: Vigiliae Christianae
WMANT: Wissenschaftliche Monographien zum Alten und Neuen Testament
WTJ: Westminster Theological Journal
WUNT: Wissenschaftliche Untersuchungen zum Neuen Testament
ZNW: Zeitschrift für die neutestamentliche Wissenschaft
ZTK: Zeitschrift für Theologie und Kirche
ZWT: Zeitschrift für wissenschaftliche Theologie

WORKS OF REFERENCE

ABD: Freedman, D. N. (*et al.*), *The Anchor Bible Dictionary* (New York: Doubleday, 1992).

ANRW: Temporini, H., and Haase, W. (eds.), *Aufstieg und Niedergang der römischen Welt* (Berlin: de Gruyter, 1972–)

BA: Bauer, W., *Griechisch-Deutsches Wörterbuch zu den Schriften des Neuen Testaments und der frühchristlichen Literatur*, 6e Auflage, hrsg. von Aland, K., und Aland, B. (Berlin: De Gruyter, 1988). Reference is occasionally made to the English translation (Arndt, W. F., and Gingrich, F. W., *A Greek-English Lexicon of the New Testament and Other Early Christian Literature* [Cambridge: Cambridge University Press, 1957]) as 'BAG'.

BD: Blass, F., and Debrunner, A., *Grammatik des neutestamentlichen Griechisch*, bearbeitet von Rehkopf, F. (Göttingen: Vandenhoeck und Ruprecht, 1979).

Berger-Colpe: Berger, K., and Colpe, C., *Religions geschichtliches Textbuch zum Neuen Testament* (Göttingen: Vandenhoeck und Ruprecht, 1987).

DBSup: Pirot, L. (*et al.*, eds.), *Dictionnaire de la Bible, Supplément* (Paris: Letouzey et Ane, 1928)

Dittenberger, *Or.*: Dittenberger, W., *Orientis Graeci inscriptiones selectae* (Leipzig: Herzel, 1903–5).

Dittenberger, *Syll.*: Dittenberger, W., *Sylloge Inscriptionum Graecarum* (Leipzig: Herzel, 1915–24³).

DPL: Hawthorne, G. F., Martin, R. P., and Reid, D. G., *Dictionary of Paul and his Letters* (Downers Grove: InterVarsity Press, 1993).

EDNT: Balz, H., and Schneider, G., *Exegetical Dictionary of the New Testament* (Grand Rapids: Eerdmans, 1990–3).

Field: 1899: *Notes on the Translation of the New Testament* (= *Otium Norvicense* iii; Cambridge: Cambridge University Press, 1899). (Reprint with additions by the author of *Notes on Select Passages of the Greek Testament Chiefly with Reference to Recent English Versions* [Oxford: Hall & Stacy, 1881]).

FPG: Denis, A.-M., *Fragmenta Pseudepigraphorum Quae Supersunt Graeca* (Leiden: Brill, 1970).

GELS: Lust, J., Eynikel, E., and Hauspie, K., *A Greek-English Lexicon of the Septuagint* Part I (A–I); Part II (K–Ω) (Stuttgart: Deutsche Bibelgesellschaft, 1992, 1996).

Kilpatrick: Kilpatrick, G. D., *The Pastoral Letters and Hebrews. A Greek-English Diglot for the use of Translators* (London: British and Foreign Bible Society, 1963).

LN: Louw, J. P., and Nida, E. A. (*et al.*), *Greek-English Lexicon of the New Testament based on Semantic Domains* (New York: United Bible Societies, 1988).

LS: Lewis, C. T. and Short, C., *A Latin Dictionary* (Oxford, 1879, 1955).

LSJ: Liddell, H. G., and Scott, R., *A Greek-English Lexicon* ed. Jones, H. S. and McKenzie, R. (Oxford: Oxford University Press, 1940).

MG: Moulton, W. F., and Geden, A. S., *A Concordance to the Greek Testament*, fifth edition, revised by Moulton, H. K. (Edinburgh: T. and T. Clark, 1978).

MHT: Moulton, J. H., Howard, W. F., and Turner, N., *A Grammar of New Testament Greek* (Edinburgh: T. and T. Clark, 1906–76).

MM: Moulton, J. H., and Milligan, W., *The Vocabulary of the Greek Testament illustrated from the Papyri and other Non-literary Sources* (London: Hodder and Stoughton, 1914–29).

Moule: 1953: Moule, C. F. D., *An Idiom Book of New Testament Greek* (Cambridge: Cambridge University Press, 1953).

New Docs.: Horsley, G. H. R., Llewelyn, S. R., Kearsley, R. A., *et al.*, *New Documents illustrating Early Christianity* (North Ryde: The Ancient History Documentary Research Centre, Macquarie University, 1981–; Grand Rapids: Eerdmans, 1997–).

NIDNTT: Brown, C. (ed.), *The New International Dictionary of New Testament Theology* (Exeter: Paternoster Press, 1975–8).

NHL: Robinson, J. M. (ed.), *The Nag Hammadi Library in English* (Leiden: Brill, 1977).

NTA: Hennecke, E., *New Testament Apocrypha*, Edited by Wilson, R. McL. (London: Lutterworth, 1963, 1965).

OCD: Hornblower, S., and Spawforth, A., *The Oxford Classical Dictionary* (Oxford: Oxford University Press, 1996³).

OTP: Charlesworth, J. H. (ed.), *The Old Testament Pseudepigrapha* (London: DLT, 1983–5).

PG: Migne, J.-P. (ed.), *Patrologia Graeca* (Paris: J.-P. Migne).

PGL: Lampe, G. W. H. (ed.), *A Patristic Greek Lexicon* (Oxford: Oxford University Press, 1961–8).

PL: Migne, J.-P. (ed.), *Patrologia Latina* (Paris: J.-P. Migne).

PW: Pauly, A., *Real-Encyclopädie der classischen Altertumswissenschaft*, ed. Wissowa, G., *et al.* (Stuttgart: Metzler, 1894–1980).

PWSup: Supplement to PW (Stuttgart: Druckenmüller, 1903–80).

RAC: Klauser, T. (ed.), *Reallexicon für Antike und Christentum* (Stuttgart: Hiersemann, 1950–).

RGG: Galling K. (ed.), *Religion in Geschichte und Gegenwart* (Tübingen: Mohr, 1957–65³).

SB: (Strack, H. and) Billerbeck, P., *Kommentar zum Neuen Testament aus Talmud und Midrasch* (München: C. H. Beck, 1956³).

TDNT: Kittel, G., and Friedrich, G., *Theological Dictionary of the New Testament*, translated by Bromiley, G. W. (Grand Rapids: Eerdmans, 1964–76).

THAT: Jenni, E., and Westermann, C., *Theologisches Handwörterbuch zum Alten Testament* (München: Kaiser/Zürich; Theologischer Verlag, 1971, 1976).

TLG: Thesaurus Linguae Graecae.

TLNT: Spicq, C., *Theological Lexicon of the New Testament*, translated by Ernest, J. D. (Peabody: Hendrickson, 1994).

TRE: Krause, G., and Müller, G., *Theologische Realenzyklopädie* (Berlin: De Gruyter, 1977–).

Wetstein: Wetstein, J. J., Η ΚΑΙΝΗ ΔΙΑΘΗΚΗ *NOVUM TESTAMENTUM GRAECUM* (Amsterdam, 1752), II.

WH *Notes*: Westcott, B. F., and Hort, F. J. A., *The New Testament in the Original Greek* (Cambridge and London: Macmillan, 1892), Volume II, Appendix I. Notes on Select Readings.

COMMENTARIES

(This list includes works in English from about 1900 together with the main recent works in German and French. A full listing of earlier works including others of less importance up to 1969 can be found in Spicq, 11–21.)

Arichea, D. C., and Hatton, H. A., *Paul's Letters to Timothy and to Titus* (UBS Handbook Series. New York: United Bible Societies, 1995).

Barrett, C. K., *The Pastoral Epistles* (New Clarendon Bible. Oxford: Oxford University Press, 1963).

Bassler, J. M., *1 Timothy, 2 Timothy, Titus* (Abingdon New Testament Commentaries. Nashville: Abingdon Press, 1996).

Bernard, J. H., *The Pastoral Epistles* (Cambridge Greek Testament. Cambridge: Cambridge University Press, 1899).

Bratcher, R. G., *A Translator's Guide to Paul's Letters to Timothy and to Titus* (London: United Bible Societies, 1983; now superseded by Arichea and Hatton).

Brown, E. F., *The Pastoral Epistles* (Westminster Commentaries. London: Methuen, 1917).

Brox, N., *Die Pastoralbriefe* (Regensburger Neues Testament. Regensburg: Verlag Friedrich Pustet, 1963).

Calvin, J., *The Second Epistle of Paul the Apostle to the Corinthians and the Epistles to Timothy, Titus and Philemon* (Translated by T. A. Smail. Calvin's New Testament Commentaries. Carlisle: Paternoster Press, 1996²).

Chrysostom, *The Homilies of St John Chrysostom on ... Timothy, Titus and Philemon* (Translated by J. Tweedy. Oxford: J. H. Parker/London: Rivington, 1853; references in the Commentary are to *PG* LXII).

Cramer, J. A., *Catenae Graecorum Patrum in Novum Testamentum* (Oxford: Oxford University Press, 1844; Hildesheim, 1967²), VII, 3–100.

Davies, M., *The Pastoral Epistles* (Epworth Commentaries. London: Epworth Press, 1996).

Dibelius, M., and Conzelmann, H., *The Pastoral Epistles* (Hermeneia. Philadelphia: Fortress, 1972).

Donelson, L. R., *Colossians, Ephesians, First and Second Timothy, and Titus* (Westminster Bible Companion. Louisville: Westminster John Knox, 1996), 115–89.

Dornier, P., *Les Épîtres Pastorales* (Paris: Gabalda, 1958²).

Easton, B. S., *The Pastoral Epistles* (London: SCM Press, 1947).

Ellicott, C. J., *Commentary on the Pastoral Epistles* (London: Longmans, 1861, 1883⁵).

Fairbairn, P., *The Pastoral Epistles* (Edinburgh: T. and T. Clark, 1874; reprinted Grand Rapids: Zondervan, 1956).

Falconer, R. A., *The Pastoral Epistles* (Oxford: Oxford University Press, 1937).

Fee, G. D., *1 and 2 Timothy, Titus* (New International Biblical Commentary. Peabody, MA: Hendrickson, 1988).

Gealy, F. D., and Noyes, M. P., *The First and Second Epistles to Timothy and the Epistle to Titus* (The Interpreter's Bible. Nashville: Abingdon, 1955), XI, 341–551.

Guthrie, D., *The Pastoral Epistles* (Tyndale New Testament Commentaries. London: Tyndale, 1957, 1990²).

Hanson, A. T., *The Pastoral Letters* (Cambridge Bible Commentary. Cambridge: Cambridge University Press, 1966).

The Pastoral Epistles (New Century Bible Commentary. London: Marshall Pickering, 1982; references are to this commentary and not the previous one).

Hasler, V., *Die Briefe an Timotheus und Titus* (Zürcher Bibel Kommentar. Zürich: Theologischer Verlag, 1978).

Hendriksen, W., *New Testament Commentary: Exposition of the Pastoral Epistles* (London: Banner of Truth, 1959).

Holtz, G., *Die Pastoralbriefe* (Theologischer Handkommentar zum NT. Berlin: Evangelische Verlagsanstalt, 1965, 1972²).

Holtzmann, H. J., *Die Pastoralbriefe, Kritisch und Exegetisch Behandelt* (Leipzig: Engelmann, 1880).

Horton, R. F., *The Pastoral Epistles* (Century Bible. Edinburgh: T. C. and E. C. Jack, 1901).

Houlden, J. L., *The Pastoral Epistles* (Penguin NT Commentary. Harmondsworth: Penguin, 1976; reprinted, London: SCM Press, 1989).

Hultgren, A. J., *I–II Timothy, Titus* (and Aus, R., *II Thessalonians*) (Augsburg Commentary on the NT. Minneapolis: Augsburg, 1984).

Jeremias, J., *Die Briefe an Timotheus und Titus* (Das NT Deutsch. Göttingen: Vandenhoeck und Ruprecht, 1934, 1963⁸).

Johnson, L. T., *The Pastoral Epistles* (Knox Preaching Guides. Atlanta: John Knox, 1987).

Letters to Paul's Delegates. 1 Timothy, 2 Timothy, Titus (The New Testament in Context. Valley Forge, PA: Trinity Press International, 1996). (References are to this commentary and not the previous one).

Karris, R. J., *NT Message – the Pastoral Epistles* (Dublin: Veritas Publications, 1979).

Kelly, J. N. D., *A Commentary on the Pastoral Epistles* (Black's NT Commentaries. London: A. and C. Black, 1963).

Knight III, G. W., *Commentary on the Pastoral Epistles* (New International Greek Testament Commentary. Grand Rapids/ Carlisle: Eerdmans/Paternoster, 1992).

Knoch, O., *1. und 2. Timotheusbrief Titusbrief* (Die Neue Echter Bibel. Würzburg: Echter Verlag, 1988).

Lea, T. D., and Griffin, H. P., *1, 2 Timothy, Titus* (New American Commentary. Nashville: Broadman, 1992).

Leaney, A. R. C., *The Epistles to Timothy, Titus and Philemon* (Torch Bible Commentaries. London: SCM Press, 1960).

Lenski, R. C. H., *The Interpretation of St Paul's Epistles to the Colossians, to the Thessalonians, to Timothy, to Titus and to Philemon* (Minneapolis: Augsburg, 1937, 1961), 471–947.

Lock, W., *The Pastoral Epistles* (International Critical Commentary. Edinburgh: T. and T. Clark, 1924, 1952³).

Martin, R. P., '1, 2 Timothy and Titus', in Mays, J. L. (ed.) *Harper's Bible Commentary* (San Francisco: Harper, 1988).

Meinertz, M., *Die Pastoralbriefe des heiligen Paulus* (Die heilige Schrift des NT. Bonn: Hanstein, 1931⁴).

Merkel, H., *Die Pastoralbriefe* (Das Neue Testament Deutsch. Göttingen: Vandenhoeck und Ruprecht, 1991).

Mounce, W. D., *The Pastoral Epistles* (Word Biblical Commentary. Dallas: Word Books, forthcoming).

Oberlinner, L., *Die Pastoralbriefe. Erste Folge. Kommentar zum Ersten Timotheusbrief* (Herders theologischer Kommentar zum NT Band XI/2. Freiburg: Herder, 1994).

Oberlinner, L., *Die Pastoralbriefe. Zweite Folge. Kommentar zum Zweiten Timotheusbrief* (Herders theologischer Kommentar zum NT Band XI/2. Freiburg: Herder, 1995).

Oberlinner, L., *Die Pastoralbriefe. Dritte Folge. Kommentar zum Titusbrief* (Herders theologischer Kommentar zum NT Band XI/2. Freiburg: Herder, 1996).

Oden, Thomas C., *First and Second Timothy and Titus* (Interpretation. Louisville: John Knox, 1989).

Parry, R. St J., *The Pastoral Epistles* (Cambridge: Cambridge University Press, 1920).

Plummer, A., *The Pastoral Epistles* (Expositor's Bible. London: Hodder and Stoughton, 1888).

Quinn, J. D., *The Letter to Titus* (Anchor Bible 35. New York: Doubleday, 1990).

Ramsay, W. M., *Historical Commentary on the Pastoral Epistles* (edited by M. Wilson. Grand Rapids: Kregel, 1996). (reprint of articles in *Expositor* (1909–11) 7:7, 481–94; 7:8, 1–21, 167–85, 264–82, 339–57, 399–416, 557–68; 7:9, 172–87, 319–33, 433–40; 8:1, 262–73, 356–75).

Roloff, J., *Der Erste Brief an Timotheus* (Evangelisch-Katholischer Kommentar zum Neuen Testament. Zürich/Neukirchen-Vluyn: Benziger/Neukirchener, 1988).

Sampley, J. P., and Fuller, R. H., *Ephesians, Colossians, 2 Thessalonians, the Pastoral Epistles* (Proclamation Commentaries. Philadelphia: Fortress, 1978).

Schierse, F. J., *Die Pastoralbriefe. 1. und 2. Timotheus/Titus* (*WB*. Düsseldorf, 1968; not accessible to me).

Schlatter, A., *Die Kirche der Griechen Im Urteil Des Paulus* (Stuttgart: Calwer, 1936, 1962).
Scott, E. F., *The Pastoral Epistles* (Moffatt NT Commentary. London: Hodder and Stoughton, 1936, 1957³).
Simpson, E. K., *The Pastoral Epistles* (London: Tyndale, 1954).
Spicq, C., *Les Épîtres Pastorales* (Études Bibliques. Paris: J. Gabalda, 1948, 1969⁴)
Stott, J. R. W., *Guard the Gospel: The Message of 2 Timothy* (Leicester: Inter-Varsity Press, 1973).
Stott, J. R. W., *The Message of 1 Timothy and Titus: The life of the local church* (Leicester: Inter-Varsity Press, 1996).
Towner, P. H. *1–2 Timothy and Titus* (Downers Grove/Leicester: InterVarsity Press, 1994).
White, N. J. D., *The First and Second Epistles to Timothy and the Epistle to Titus* (Expositor's Greek Testament. London: Hodder and Stoughton, 1910), IV, 55–202.
Wohlenberg, G., *Die Pastoralbriefe* (Kommentar zum NT. Leipzig: Deichert, 1923³).

GENERAL BIBLIOGRAPHY

(A detailed bibliography of books and articles up to 1969 is given by Brox, 78–97; see also Schenk 1987 for the period from 1945)

Allan, J. A., 'The "in Christ" formula in the Pastoral Epistles', *NTS* 10 (1963), 115–21.
Almquist, H., *Plutarch und das NT* (Uppsala, 1946).
Badcock, F. J., *The Pauline Epistles and the Epistle to the Hebrews in their Historical Setting* (London: SPCK, 1937).
Balch, D. L., *Let Wives be Submissive. The Domestic Code in 1 Peter* (Atlanta: Scholars, 1981).
Banks, R., *Paul's Idea of Community* (Exeter: Paternoster, 1980).
Barr, J., *Biblical Words for Time* (London: SCM Press, 1969²).
Barrett, C. K., 'Pauline controversies in the post-pauline period', *NTS* 20 (1973–4), 229–45.
Bartchy, S. S., ΜΑΛΛΟΝ ΧΡΗΣΑΙ (SBLDS 11. Atlanta: Scholars, 1973).
Bartlet, V., 'The historic setting of the Pastoral Epistles', *Expositor* 8.5 (1913), 28–36; 161–7; 256–63; 325–47.
Bartlet, V., 'Titus the friend of Luke and other related questions', *Expositor* 8.13 (1917), 367–75.
Bartsch, H.-W., *Die Anfänge urchristlicher Rechtsbildungen: Studien zu den Pastoralbriefen* (Hamburg: Reich, 1965).
Bauer, W., *Orthodoxy and Heresy in Earliest Christianity* (London: SCM Press, 1972).

Beasley-Murray, G. R., *Baptism in the New Testament* (London: Macmillan, 1962).

Becker, J., *Paulus der Apostel der Völker* (Tübingen: J. C. B. Mohr [Paul Siebeck], 1989).

Beker, J. Christiaan, *Heirs of Paul: Paul's Legacy in the New Testament and in the Church Today* (Edinburgh: T. and T. Clark, 1992).

Berger, K., 'Hellenistische Gattungen im Neuen Testament', ANRW II.25.2 (Berlin: De Gruyter, 1984a), 1031–432.

Berger, K., *Formgeschichte des Neuen Testaments* (Heidelberg: Quelle & Meyer, 1984b).

Binder, H., 'Die historische Situation der Pastoralbriefe', in Fry, F. C. (ed.), *Geschichtswirklichkeit und Glaubensbewährung. Fest. F. Müller* (Stuttgart, 1967) 70–83.

Bjerkelund, C. J., *Parakaleó* (Oslo, 1967).

Bockmuehl, M. N. A., *Revelation and Mystery in Ancient Judaism and Pauline Christianity* (WUNT 2.36. Tübingen: J. C. B. Mohr [Paul Siebeck], 1990; rep. Grand Rapids: Eerdmans, 1997).

Boismard, M.-E., *Quatre hymnes baptismales dans la première épître de Pierre* (Paris: Cerf, 1961).

Bornkamm, G., *Early Christian Experience* (London: SCM Press, 1969).

Bosch, J. S., 'Le charisme des Pasteurs dans le corpus paulinine', in De Lorenzi, L. (ed.), *Paul de Tarse. Apôtre de notre temps* (Rome: St Paul's Abbey; 1979), 363–97.

Braun, H., *Qumran und das Neue Testament.* (Tübingen: J. C. B. Mohr [Paul Siebeck], 1966).

Brooke, A. E., 'The Problem of the Pastoral Epistles', *JTS* 23 (1922), 255–62.

Brown, J. P., 'Synoptic Parallels in the Epistles and Form-History', *NTS* 10 (1963–4), 27–48.

Brown, L. A., 'Asceticism and Ideology: the language of power in the Pastoral Epistles', *Semeia* 57 (1992), 77–94.

Brox, N., 'Die Kirche Säule und Fundament der Wahrheit: Die Einheit der Kirche nach den Pastoralbriefen', *BK* 18 (1963), 44–7.

Brox, N., 'Amt, Kirche und Theologie in der nachapostolischen Epoche: Die Pastoralbriefe', in Schreiner, J. (ed.), *Gestalt und Anspruch des NT* (Würzburg: Echter, 1969a), 120–33.

Brox, N., 'Historische und theologische Probleme der Pastoralbriefe des Neuen Testaments: Zur Dokumentation der frühchristlichen Amtsgeschichte', *Kairos* 11 (1969b), 81–94.

Brox, N., 'Zu den persönlichen Notizen der Pastoralbriefe', *BZ* 13 (1969c), 76–9.

Brox, N., 'Lukas als Verfasser der Pastoralbriefe?' JAC 13 (1970), 62–77.

Brox, N., '*Propheteia im ersten Timotheusbrief*', *BZ* 20 (1976), 229–32.

Bruce, F. F., *The Acts of the Apostles* (Leicester: Apollos, 1990³).

Bultmann, R., 'Pastoralbriefe', *RGG²* (1930), IV, 993–7.

Bultmann, R., *Theology of the New Testament* (London: SCM Press, 1952, 1955).

Butler, C., 'Was Paul a Male Chauvinist?', *New Blackfriars* 56 (1975), 174–9.

Campbell, R. A., *The Elders: Seniority within Earliest Christianity* (Studies of the New Testament and its World. Edinburgh: T. and T. Clark, 1994a).

Campbell, R. A., 'Identifying the Faithful Sayings in the Pastoral Epistles', *JSNT* 54 (1994b), 73–86.

Campbell, R. A., 'Leaders and Fathers: Church Government in Earliest Christianity', *IBS* 17 (1995), 2–21.

Campenhausen, H. von, 'Die Begründung kirchlicher Entscheidungen beim Apostel Paulus', in *Aus der Frühzeit des Christentums. Studien zur Kirchengeschichte des ersten und zweiten Jahrhunderts* (Tübingen: J. C. B. Mohr [Paul Siebeck], 1963a), 8–13.

Campenhausen, H. von, 'Polykarp von Smyrna und die Pastoralbriefe', in *Aus der Frühzeit des Christentums. Studien zur Kirchengeschichte des ersten und zweiten Jahrhunderts* (Tübingen: J. C. B. Mohr [Paul Siebeck], 1963b), 197–252.

Campenhausen, H. von, *Ecclesiastical Authority and Spiritual Power in the Church of the First Three Centuries* (London: A. & C. Black, 1969).

Carson, D. A., Moo, D. J., and Morris, L., *An Introduction to the New Testament* (Leicester: Apollos, 1992).

Childs, B. S., *The New Testament as Canon: An Introduction* (London: SCM Press, 1984).

Cohen, S. J. D., 'Was Timothy Jewish (Acts 16:1–3)?', *JBL* 105 (1986), 251–68.

Collins, J. N., *DIAKONIA. Re-interpreting the Ancient Sources* (New York: Oxford University Press, 1990).

Collins, R. F., 'The Image of Paul in the Pastorals', *LTP* 31 (1975), 147–73.

Cook, D., 'The Pastoral Fragments reconsidered', *JTS* ns 35 (1984), 120–31.

Couser, G., *God and Christian Existence in 1 and 2 Timothy and Titus* (PhD Thesis, Aberdeen. 1992).

Dahl, N. A., 'Formgeschichtliche Beobachtungen zur Christus-verkündigung in der Gemeindepredigt', in Eltester, W. (ed.), *Neutestamentliche Studien für R. Bultmann* (Berlin: de Gruyter, 1954), 3–9.

Dalbert, P., *Die Theologie der hellenistisch-jüdischen Missionsliteratur unter Ausschluss von Philo und Josephus* (Hamburg: H. Reich, 1954).

Danker, F. W., *Benefactor: Epigraphic Study of a Graeco-Roman and New Testament Semantic Field* (St Louis: Clayton, 1982).

Dautzenberg, G., Merklein, H., and Müller, K.-H. (eds.), *Die Frau im Urchristentum* (QD 95. Freiburg: Herder, 1983).

Davies, M., *The Pastoral Epistles* (New Testament Guides. Sheffield: Sheffield Academic Press, 1996).

de Boer, W. P., *The Imitation of Paul: An Exegetical Study* (Kampen: J. H. Kok, 1962).

Deichgräber, R., *Gotteshymnus und Christushymnus in der frühen Christenheit* (Göttingen: Vandenhoeck und Ruprecht, 1967).

Deissmann, A., *Bible Studies* (Edinburgh: T. and T. Clark, 1901).

Deissmann, A., *Light from the Ancient East* (London: Hodder and Stoughton, 1927).

Delling, G., *Paulus' Stellung zur Frau und Ehe* (Stuttgart: Kohlhammer, 1931).

Delling, G., *Studien zum Neuen Testament und zum hellenistischen Judentum* (Berlin: De Gruyter, 1970).

Delorme, J. (ed.), *Le Ministère et les Ministères selon le Nouveau Testament* (Paris: Seuil, 1974).

Dibelius, M., *Botschaft und Geschichte 2* (Tübingen: J. C. B. Mohr [Paul Siebeck], 1956).

Donelson, L. R., *Pseudepigraphy and Ethical Argument in the Pastoral Epistles* (HUT 22. Tübingen: J. C. B. Mohr [Paul Siebeck], 1986).

Donfried, K. P., and Marshall, I. H., *The Theology of the Shorter Pauline Letters* (Cambridge: Cambridge University Press, 1993).

Dornier, P., 'Les Épîtres Pastorales', in Delorme 1974, 94–101.

Dunn, J. D. G., *Baptism in the Holy Spirit* (London: SCM Press, 1970).

Dunn, J. D. G., *Christology in the Making: An Inquiry into the Origins of the Doctrine of the Incarnation* (London: SCM Press, 1980, 1989²).

Easton, B. S., 'New Testament Ethical lists', *JBL* 51 (1932), 1–12.

Edwards, R. B., *The Case for Women's Ministry* (London: SPCK, 1989).

Elliott, J. K., *The Greek Text of the Epistles to Timothy and Titus* (Studies and Documents XXXVI. Salt Lake City: University of Utah Press, 1968).

Ellis, E. E., *Prophecy and Hermeneutic in Early Christianity* (WUNT 18. Tübingen/Grand Rapids: J. C. B. Mohr [Paul Siebeck]/Eerdmans, 1978).

Ellis, E. E., 'Traditions in the Pastoral Epistles', in Evans, C. A., and Stinespring, W. F. (eds.), *Early Jewish and Christian Exegesis: Studies in Memory of William Hugh Brownlee* (Atlanta: Scholars, 1987), 237–53.

Enslin, M. S., 'Once again, Luke and Paul', *ZNW* 61 (1970), 253–71.

Fascher, E., 'Timotheus', PW 2. Reihe 12 Halbbd. (Stuttgart, 1937), Sp. 1342–54.

Fee, G. D., 'Reflections on Church Order in the Pastoral Epistles with Further Reflection on the Hermeneutics of *ad hoc* Documents', *JETS* 28.2 (1985), 141–51.

Fee, G. D., *God's Empowering Presence. The Holy Spirit in the Letters of Paul* (Peabody, MA: Hendrickson, 1994).

Feuillet, A., 'La doctrine des Épitres pastorales et leurs affinités avec l'oeuvre lucanienne', *RevThom* 78 (1978), 181–225.

Fiedler, P., 'Haustafel', *RAC* XIII, 1063–73.

Fiore, B., *The Function of Personal Example in the Socratic and Pastoral Epistles* (AnBib 105. Rome: Pontifical Biblical Institute, 1986).

Fiorenza, E. S., *In Memory of Her: A Feminist Theological Reconstruction of Christian Origins* (London: SCM Press, 1983).

Ford, J. M., 'A Note on Proto-Montanism in the Pastoral Epistles', *NTS* 17 (1970–1), 338–46.

Fowl, S. E., *The Story of Christ in the Ethics of Paul*, (JSNTSup 36. Sheffield: JSOT Press, 1990).

Fridrichsen, A., 'Zu ΑΡΝΕΙΣΘΑΙ im Neuen Testament insonderheit in den Pastoralbriefen', ConNT 6 (1942), 94–6.

Gärtner, B., *The Temple and the Community in Qumran and the New Testament* (SNTSMS 1. Cambridge: Cambridge University Press, 1965).

Gayer, R., *Die Stellung der Sklaven in den paulinischen Gemeinden und bei Paulus* (Frankfurt: Lang, 1976).

Gibson, R. J., 'The Literary Coherence of 1 Timothy', *RTR* 55 (1996), 53–66.

Gielen, M., *Tradition und Theologie neutestamentlichen Haustafelethik* (BBB 75. Frankfurt: Anton Hain, 1990).

Gilchrist, J. M., 'The Authorship and Date of the Pastoral Epistles' (unpublished PhD thesis, Manchester, 1966).

Gnilka, J., *Theologie des Neuen Testaments* (HTKNT Supp. V. Freiburg: Herder, 1994), 350–68.

Goodwin, M. J., 'The Pauline Background of the Living God as Interpretive Context for 1 Timothy 4.10', *JSNT* 61 (1996), 65–85.

Goppelt, L., *Die apostolische und nachapostolische Zeit* (Göttingen: Vandenhoeck und Ruprecht, 1962).

Goppelt, L., *Theology of the New Testament*, Vol. II (Grand Rapids: Eerdmans, 1982).

Goppelt, L., *A Commentary on 1 Peter* (Grand Rapids: Eerdmans, 1993).

Green, J. B. and Turner, M. (eds.), *Jesus of Nazareth: Lord and Christ* (Carlisle: Paternoster, 1994).

Gunther, J. J., *St Paul's Opponents and their Background* (NovTSup 35. Leiden: Brill, 1973).

Guthrie, D., *The Pastoral Epistles and the Mind of Paul* (London: Tyndale, 1956).

Guthrie, D., *The Pauline Epistles. New Testament Introduction* (London: Tyndale, 1961).

Haenchen, E., 'Pastoralbriefe und Gnosis', *RGG* II (1958), Sp. 1654f.

Hainz, J. (ed.), *Kirche im Werden* (München: Schöningh, 1976).

Hainz, J., 'Die Anfänge des Bischofs- und Diakonenamtes', in Hainz 1976:91–108.

Hanson, A. T., *Studies in the Pastoral Epistles* (London, SPCK, 1968).

Hanson, A. T., 'The Domestication of Paul: A Study in the Development of Early Christian Theology', *BJRL* 63 (1981a), 402–18.

Hanson, A. T., 'The Use of the Old Testament in the Pastoral Epistles', *IBS* 3 (1981b), 203–19.

Harrison, P. N., *The Problem of the Pastoral Epistles* (Oxford: Oxford University Press, 1921).

Hartman, L., *Auf den Namen des Herrn Jesus. Die Taufe in den neutestamentlichen Schriften* (SBS 148. Stuttgart: Katholisches Bibelwerk, 1992).

Hasler, V., 'Das nomistische Verständnis des Evangeliums in den Pastoralbriefen', *Schweizerische Theologische Umschau* 28 (1958), 65–77.

Hasler, V., 'Epiphanie und Christologie in den Pastoralbriefe', *TZ* 33 (1977), 193–209.

Haufe, G., 'Gnostische Irrlehre und ihre Abwehr in den Pastoralbriefen', in Tröger, K.-W. (ed.), *Gnosis und NT* (Gütersloh: Mohn, 1973), 325–39.

Haykin, M. A. G., 'The Fading Vision? The Spirit and Freedom in the Pastoral Epistles', *EvQ* 57 (1985), 291–305.

Hegermann, H., 'Der geschichtliche Ort der Pastoralbriefe', in Rogge, J., and Schille, G., (eds.) *Theologische Versuche 2* (Berlin, 1970), 47–63.

Hengel, M., and Heckel, U. (eds.), *Paulus und das antike Judentum* (WUNT 58. Tübingen: J. C. B. Mohr [Paul Siebeck], 1991).

Herr, T., *Naturrecht aus der kritischen Sicht des Neuen Testaments* (München: F. Schöningh, 1976), 34–105.

Hitchcock, F. M., 'Classical Allusions in the Pastoral Epistles', *Theology* 17 (1928), 62–71.

Hofrichter, P., 'Strukturdebatte im Namen des Apostles. Zur Abhängigkeit der Pastoralbriefe untereinander und vom ersten Petrusbrief', in Brox, N., *et al.* (ed.), *Anfänge der Theologie. Festschr. J. B. Bauer* (Graz: Styria, 1987), 101–16.

Horrell, David., 'Converging Ideologies: Berger and Luckmann and the Pastoral Epistles', *JSNT* 50 (1993), 85–103.

Hort, F. J. A., *Judaistic Christianity* (Cambridge and London: Macmillan, 1894), 130–46.

Hort, F. J. A., *The Christian Ecclesia* (London: Macmillan, 1897).

Hort, F. J. A., *The Epistle of James* (London: Macmillan, 1909).

James, J. D., *The Genuineness and Authorship of the Pastoral Epistles* (London: Longmans, 1906).

Jeremias, J., *Abba* (Göttingen: Vandenhoeck und Ruprecht, 1966).

Jewett, R., *Paul's Anthropological Terms* (Leiden: Brill, 1971).

Johnson, L. T., 'II Timothy and the Polemic against False Teachers: A Re-examination', *Ohio Journal of Religious Studies* 6 (1978), 1–26.

Jülicher, A., *Introduction to the New Testament* (London: Smith, Elder, 1904).

Kamlah, E., *Die Form der katalogischen Paränese im Neuen Testament* (WUNT 7. Tübingen: J. C. B. Mohr [Paul Siebeck], 1964).

Kamlah, E., 'ΥΠΟΤΑΣΣΕΣΘΑΙ in den neutestamentlichen Haustafeln', in Böcher, O., and Haacker, K. (eds.), *Verborum Veritas. Festschr. G. Stählin* (Wuppertal: Brockhaus,1970), 237–43.

Karris, R. J., 'The Function and Sitz im Leben of the Paraenetic Elements in the Pastoral Epistles' (Diss. Harvard, 1971).

Karris, R. J., 'The Background and Significance of the Polemic of the Pastoral Epistles', *JBL* 92 (1973), 549–64.

Käsemann, E., 'Ministry and community in the New Testament', in *Essays on New Testament Themes* (London: SCM Press, 1964), 63–94.

Kertelge, K., *Gemeinde und Amt im Neuen Testament* (München: Kösel, 1972), 140–51.

Kertelge, K. (ed.), *Das kirchliche Amt im Neuen Testament* (Darmstadt: Wissenschaftliche Buchgesellschaft, 1977).

Kertelge, K. (ed.), *Paulus in den neutestamentlichen Spätschriften: Zur Paulusrezeption im Neuen Testament* (QD 89. Freiburg: Herder, 1981).

Kidd, R. W., *Wealth and Beneficence in the Pastoral Epistles* (SBLDS 122. Atlanta: Scholars, 1990).

Kittel, G., 'Die γενεαλογίαι der Pastoralbriefe', *ZNW* 20 (1921), 49–69.

Klauck, H.-J., *Hausgemeinde und Hauskirche im frühen Christentum* (SBS 103. Stuttgart: Katholisches Bibelwerk, 1981).

Klöpper, A., 'Zur Christologie der Pastoralbriefe', *ZWT* 45 (1902), 339–61.

Klöpper, A., 'Zur Soteriologie der Pastoralbriefe', *ZWT* 47 (1904), 57–88.

Knight III, G. W., *The Faithful Sayings in the Pastoral Letters* (Kampen: J. H. Kok, 1968).

Knoch, O., *Die 'Testamente' des Petrus und Paulus* (SBS 62. Stuttgart: Katholisches Bibelwerk, 1973).

Kohl, J., 'Verfasser und Entstehungszeit der Pastoralbriefe im Lichte der neueren Kritik' (Diss. Wien, 1962; not accessible to me).

Kowalski, B., 'Zur Funktion und Bedeutung der alttestamentlichen Zitate und Anspielungen in den Pastoralbriefen', *SNT* (SU) 19 (1994), 45–68.

Kramer, W., *Christ, Lord, Son of God* (London: SCM Press, 1966).

Kretschmar, G., 'Der paulinische Glaube in den Pastoralbriefen', in Hahn, F., and Klein, H. (eds.), *Glaube im Neuen Testament* (Biblisch-Theologische Studien 7. Neukirchen-Vluyn: Neukirchener Verlag, 1982), 113–40.

Küchler, M., *Schweigen, Schmuck und Schleier. Drei neutestamentliche Vorschriften zur Verdrängung der Frauen auf dem Hintergrund einer frauenfeindlichen Exegese des Alten Testaments im antiken Judentum* (Novum Testamentum et Orbis Antiquus 1. Freiburg: Universitätsverlag, 1986).

Kümmel, W. G., *Introduction to the New Testament* (London: SCM Press, 1966).

Läger, K., *Die Christologie der Pastoralbriefe* (Hamburger Theologische Studien 12. Münster: Lit, 1996).

Lampe, P. and Luz, U., 'Nachpaulinisches Christentum und pagane Gesellschaft', in Becker, J. (ed.), *Die Anfänge des Christentums* (Stuttgart: Kohlhammer, 1987), 185–216.

Lau, Andrew Y., *Manifest in Flesh: The Epiphany Christology of the Pastoral Epistles* (WUNT 2.86. Tübingen: J. C. B. Mohr [Paul Siebeck], 1996).

Laub, F., *Die Begegnung des frühen Christentums mit der antiken Sklaverei* (SBS 107. Stuttgart: Katholisches Bibelwerk, 1982).

Laub, F., 'Sozialgeschichtliche Hintergrund und ekklesiologische Relevanz der neutestamentlichen-frühchristlichen Haus- und Gemeindeleiterparänese – ein Beitrag zur Soziologie des Frühchristentums', *MTZ* 37 (1986), 249–71.

Le Fort, P., 'La responsibilité politique de l'église d'après les épitres pastorales', *ETR* 49 (1974), 1–14.

Lemaire, A. (ed.), *Les Ministères aux origines de l'Église* (Paris: Cerf, 1971).

Lestapis, S. de, *L'enigme des Pastorales* (Paris: Gabalda, 1976).

Lightfoot, J. B., *Biblical Essays* (London: Macmillan, 1893).

Lindars, B., *New Testament Apologetic* (London: SCM Press, 1961).

Lindemann, A., *Paulus im ältesten Christentum. Das Bild des Apostels und die Rezeption der paulinischen Theologie in der frühchristlichen Literatur bis Marcion* (Tübingen: J. C. B. Mohr [Paul Siebeck], 1979).

Lippert, P., *Leben als Zeugnis. Die werbende Kraft christlicher Lebensführung nach dem Kirchenverständnis neutestamentlicher Briefe* (SBM 4. Stuttgart: Katholisches Bibelwerk, 1968).

Lips, H. von, *Glaube-Gemeinde-Amt: Zum Verständnis der Ordination in den Pastoralbriefen* (FRLANT 122. Göttingen: Vandenhoeck und Ruprecht, 1979).

Lips, H. von, 'Die Haustafel als "Topos" im Rahmen der urchristlichen Paränese. Beobachtungen an Hand des 1 Petrusbriefes und des Titusbriefes', *NTS* 40 (1994), 261–80.

Lohfink, G., *Die Himmelfahrt Jesu* (München: Kösel, 1971).

Lohfink, G., 'Die Normativität der Amtsvorstellungen in den Pastoralbriefen', *TQ* 157 (1977), 93–106.

Lohfink, G., 'Paulinische Theologie in der Rezeption der Pastoralbriefe', in Kertelge 1981:70–121.

Lohfink, G., 'Die Vermittlung des Paulinismus zu den Pastoralbriefen', *BZ* 32:2 (1988), 169–88.

Lohse, E., 'Die Ordination im Spätjudentum und im Neuen Testament', in Kertelge 1977:501–23.

Lohse, E., 'Das apostolische Vermächtnis – Zum paulinischen Charakter der Pastoralbriefe', in Schrage, W. (ed.), *Studien zum Text und zur Ethik des Neuen Testaments* (Berlin: De Gruyter, 1986), 266–81.

Lövestam, E., 'Über die neutestamentliche Aufforderung zur Nüchternheit', *ST* 12 (1958), 80–109.

Lüdemann, G., *Paulus der Heidenapostel. II. Antipaulismus im frühen Christentum* (FRLANT 130. Göttingen: Vandenhoeck und Ruprecht, 1983).

Lührmann. D., *Das Offenbarungsverständnis bei Paulus und in paulinischen Gemeinden* (WMANT 16. Neukirchen: Neukirchener, 1965).

Lührmann, D., 'Epiphaneia: Zur Bedeutungsgeschichte eines griechischen Wortes', in Jeremias, G., *et al.*, *Tradition und Glaube* (Göttingen: Vandenhoeck und Ruprecht, 1971), 185–99.

Lührmann. D., 'Neutestamentliche Haustafeln und antike Ökonomie', *NTS* 27 (1980–81), 83–97.

Lütgert, W., *Die Irrlehrer der Pastoralbriefe* (BFCT 13:3. Gütersloh: W. Bertelsmann, 1909).

Luz, U., 'Erwägungen zur Entstehung des Frühkatholizismus', *ZNW* 65 (1974), 88–111.

MacDonald, D. R., *The Legend and the Apostle: The Battle for Paul in Story and Canon* (Philadelphia: Westminster, 1983).

McDonald, J. I. H., Kerygma *and* Didache. *The articulation and structure of the earliest Christian message* (SNTSMS 37. Cambridge: Cambridge University Press, 1980).

MacDonald, M. Y., *The Pauline churches: A socio-historical study of institutionalization in the Pauline and Deutero-Pauline writings* (SNTSMS 57. Cambridge: Cambridge University Press, 1988).

MacDonald, M. Y., *Early Christian Women and Pagan Opinion: The Power of the Hysterical Woman* (Cambridge: Cambridge University Press, 1996).

McEleney, N. J., 'The Vice Lists in the Pastoral Epistles', *CBQ* 36 (1974), 203–19.

McKay, K. L., 'On the Perfect and Other Aspects in New Testament Greek', *NovT* 23 (1981), 289–329.

McKay, K. L., 'Aspect in Imperatival Constructions in New Testament Greek', *NovT* 27 (1985), 201–26.

Maehlum, H., 'Die Vollmacht des Timotheus nach den Pastoralbriefen' (Diss. Basel, 1969; not accessible to me).

Malherbe, A. J., 'Ancient Epistolary Theorists', *Ohio Journal of Religious Studies* 5 (1977), 3–77.

Malherbe, A. J., 'Medical Imagery in the Pastoral Epistles', in March, W. E. (ed.), *Texts and Testaments: Critical Essays on the Bible and Early Church Fathers* (San Antonio: Trinity University, 1980), 19–35.

Malherbe, A. J., *Social Aspects of Early Christianity* (Philadelphia: Fortress, 1977, 1983²).

Malherbe, A. J., *Moral Exhortation, A Greco-Roman Sourcebook* (Philadelphia: Westminster, 1986).

Malherbe, A. J., *Paul and the Popular Philosophers* (Minneapolis: Fortress, 1989).

Malherbe, A. J., 'Hellenistic Moralists and the New Testament', *ANRW* II.26.1 (Berlin: De Gruyter, 1992), 267–333.

Malherbe, A. J., 'Paulus Senex', *ResQ* 36 (1994), 197–207.

Marshall, I. H., *Kept by the Power of God. A Study of Perseverance and Falling Away* (Carlisle: Paternoster, [1969] 1995³).

Marshall, I. H., 'Faith and works in the Pastoral Epistles', SNT(SU) 9 (1984), 203–18.

Marshall, I. H., 'The Christology of the Pastoral Epistles', SNT(SU) 13 (1988), 157–77.

Marshall, I. H., 'Universal Grace and Atonement in the Pastoral Epistles', in Pinnock, C. (ed.) *The Grace of God, The Will of Man* (Grand Rapids: Zondervan, 1989), 51–69.

Marshall, I. H., '"Sometimes Only Orthodox" – Is there more to the Pastoral Epistles?', *Epworth Review* 20.3 (1993), 12–24.

Marshall, I. H., 'The Christology of Luke-Acts and the Pastoral Epistles', in Porter, S. E., Joyce, P., and Orton, D. E. (eds.), *Crossing the Boundaries: Essays in Biblical Interpretation in Honour of Michael D. Goulder* (Leiden: Brill, 1994), 167–82.

Marshall, I. H., 'Prospects for the Pastoral Epistles', in Lewis, D., and McGrath, A. (eds.), *Doing Theology for the People of God. Studies in Honor of J. I. Packer* (Downers Grove, IL: InterVarsity, 1996a), 137–55.

Marshall, I. H., 'Salvation, Grace and Works in the Later Writings in the Pauline Corpus', *NTS* 42 (1996b), 339–58.

Marshall, I. H., 'Recent Study of the Pastoral Epistles', *Themelios* 23.1 (1997), 3–29.

Martin, R. P., *Carmen Christi. Philippians ii.5–11 in recent interpretation and in the setting of early Christian worship* (Cambridge: Cambridge University Press, 1967).

Martin, R. P., *New Testament Foundations: A Guide for Christian Students Vol. 2* (Grand Rapids: Eerdmans, 1978).

Marxsen, W., *Introduction to the New Testament* (Oxford: Blackwell, 1968), 199–216.

Maurer, C., 'Eine Textvariante klärt die Entstehung der Pastoralbriefe auf', *TZ* 3 (1947), 321–37.

Mayer, H. H., *Über die Pastoralbriefe* (FRLANT 20 [n.f. 3]. Göttingen: Vandenhoeck und Ruprecht, 1913).

Meade, D. G., *Pseudonymity and Canon. An Investigation into the Relationship of Authorship and Authority in Jewish and Earliest Christian Tradition* (WUNT 39. Tübingen: J. C. B. Mohr [Paul Siebeck], 1986).

Meeks, W. A., *The First Urban Christians: The Social World of the Apostle Paul* (New Haven: Yale University Press, 1983).

Meier, J. P., '*Presbyteros* in the Pastoral Epistles', *CBQ* 35 (1973), 323–45.

Merk, O., 'Glaube und Tat in den Pastoralbriefen', *ZNW* 66 (1975), 91–102.

Metzger, W., *Die letzte Reise des Apostels Paulus* (Stuttgart: Calwer, 1976).

Michaelis, W., 'Pastoralbriefe und Wortstatistik', *ZNW* 28 (1929), 69–76.

Michaelis, W., *Pastoralbriefe und Gefangenschaftsbriefe. Zur Echtheitsfrage der Pastoralbriefe* (Gütersloh: W. Bertelsmann, 1930).

Michaelis, W., *Einleitung in das Neue Testament* (Bern: BEG-Verlag, 1946, 1961³).

Michel, O., 'Grundfragen der Pastoralbriefe', in Loeser, M. (ed.), *Auf dem Grunde der Apostel und Propheten, Festgabe für Theophil Wurm* (Stuttgart: Quell, 1948), 83–99.

Morris, L., *The Apostolic Preaching of the Cross* (London: Tyndale, 1955; 1965³).

Mott, S. C., 'Greek ethics and Christian conversion: the Philonic background of Tit. II, 10–14 and III, 3–7', *NovT* 20 (1978), 22–48.

Moule, C. F. D., 'The Problem of the Pastoral Epistles: A Reappraisal', in *Essays in New Testament Interpretation* (Cambridge: Cambridge University Press, 1982), 113–32. Originally in *BJRL* 47 (1965), 430–52.

Moulton, H. K., 'Scripture Quotations in the Pastoral Epistles', *ExpTim* 49 (1937–8), 94.

Munck, J., *Paul and the Salvation of Mankind* (London: SCM Press, 1959).

Munro, W., *Authority in Paul and Peter. The Identification of a Pastoral Stratum in the Pauline Corpus and 1 Peter* (SNTSMS 45. Cambridge: Cambridge University Press, 1983).

Murphy-O'Connor, J., '2 Timothy contrasted with 1 Timothy and Titus', *RB* 98 (1991), 403–18.

Murphy-O'Connor, J., *Paul: A Critical Life* (Oxford: Clarendon, 1996).

Müller, U. B., *Zur frühchristlichen Theologiegeschichte: Judenchristentum und Paulinismus in Kleinasien an der Wende vom ersten zum zweiten Jahrhundert n. Chr.* (Gütersloh: Mohn, 1976), 58–74.

Nauck, W., 'Die Herkunft des Verfassers der Pastoralbriefe. Ein Beiträg zur Frage der Auslegung der Pastoralbriefe' (Unpublished Diss. Göttingen, 1950).

Nägeli, Th., *Der Wortschatz des Apostels Paulus* (Göttingen: Vandenhoeck und Ruprecht, 1905).

Niederwimmer, K., *Askese und Mysterium: Über Ehe, Ehescheidung und Ehrversicht in den Anfängen des christlichen Glaubens* (FRLANT 11. Göttingen: Vandenhoeck und Ruprecht, 1975).

Nielsen, C. M., 'Scripture in the Pastoral Epistles', *PRS* 7 (1980), 4–23.

North, J. L., '"Human Speech" in Paul and the Paulines: the Investigation and Meaning of ἀνθρώπινος ὁ λόγος', *NovT* 37 (1995), 50–67.

Oberlinner, L., 'Die "Epiphaneia" des Heilswillens Gottes in Christus Jesus. Zur Grundstruktur der Christologie der Pastoralbriefe', *ZNW* 71 (1980), 192–213.

Oberlinner, L., 'Zwischen Anpassung und Konflikt. Die Weisungen für die christliche Gemeinde und die Kirche nach den Pastoralbriefen', *BK* 45 (1990), 87–93.

Oberlinner, L., ' "Ein ruhiges und ungestörtes Leben führen." Ein Ideal für christlichen Gemeinden?', *BK* 46 (1991), 98–106.

Oberlinner, L., and Vögtle, A., *Anpassung oder Widerspruch? Von der apostolischen zur nachapostolischen Kirche* (Freiburg: Herder, 1992).

Ollrog, W.-H., *Paulus und seine Mitarbeiter* (WMANT 50. Neukirchen-Vluyn: Neukirchener, 1979).

Ozanne, Charles., *The Pastorals in Perspective* (Norwich: The Open Bible Trust, 1993).

Padgett, A., 'Wealthy Women at Ephesus. 1 Tim 2:8–15 in Social Context', *Int* 41 (1987), 19–31.

Pax, E., ΕΠΙΦΑΝΕΙΑ. Ein religionsgeschichtliche Beitrag zur biblischen Theologie (München: K. Zink, 1955).

Penny, D. N., 'The Pseudo-Pauline Letters of the First Two Centuries' (Diss. Emory, 1979; not accessible to me).

Pervo, R. I., 'Romancing an Oft-Neglected Stone: The Pastoral Epistles and the Epistolary Novel', *Journal of Higher Criticism* 1 (1994), 25–48.

Peterson, E., *HEIS THEOS* (Göttingen: Vandenhoeck und Ruprecht, 1926).

Pfitzner, V. C., *Paul and the Agon Motif* (NovTSup 16. Leiden: Brill, 1967).

Prast, F., *Presbyter und Evangelium in nachapostolischer Zeit* (Stuttgart: Katholisches Bibelwerk, 1979).

Pratscher, W., 'Die Stabilisierung der Kirche als Anliegen der Pastoralbriefe', SNT(SU) 18 (1993), 133–50.

Prior, M., *Paul the Letter Writer and the Second Letter to Timothy* (JSNTSup 23. Sheffield: JSOT Press, 1989).

Prümm, K., 'Herrscherkult und Neues Testament. Ein Beitrag zum sprachlichen Problem der Pastoralbriefe und zur Frage nach den Wurzeln des paulinischen Christusbekentnisses ΚΥΡΙΟΣ ΙΗΣΟΥΣ', *Bib* 9 (1928), 3–25, 129–42, 289–301.

Quinn, J. D., 'The last Volume of Luke: the Relation of Luke-Acts to the Pastoral Epistles', in Talbert, C. H. (ed.), *Perspectives on Luke-Acts* (Edinburgh: T. and T. Clark, 1978), 62–75.

Quinn, J. D., 'The Holy Spirit in the Pastoral Epistles', in Durken, D. (ed.), *Sin, Salvation and the Spirit* (Collegeville: Liturgical Press, 1979), 35–68.

Quinn, J. D., 'Paul's Last Captivity', in Livingstone, E. (ed.), *Studia Biblica 3* (JSNTSup 3. Sheffield: Sheffield Academic Press, 1980), 289–99.

Quinn, J. D., 'Paraenesis and the Pastoral Epistles', in Carrez, M., *et al.*, *De la Tôrah au Messie. Mélanges Henri Cazelles* (Paris, 1981a), 495–501.

Quinn, J. D., 'Ordination in the Pastoral Epistles', *International Catholic Review* 8 (1981b), 358–69.

Quinn, J. D., 'The Pastoral Epistles', *Bible Today* 23 (1985), 228–38.

Rapske, B. M., 'The Widow in the Apostolic Church' (Unpublished MTh. diss., Regent College, Vancouver, 1987).

Redalié, Y., *Paul après Paul. Le temps, le salut, la morale selon les épîtres à Timothée et à Tite* (La Monde de la Bible 31. Genf: Labor et Fides, 1994).

Reed, J. T., 'Cohesive ties in 1 Timothy: in defense of the Epistle's unity', *Neotestamentica* 26 (1992): 131–47.

Reed, J. T., '"To Timothy or not": a discourse analysis of 1 Timothy', in Porter, S. E., and Carson, D. A. (eds.), *Biblical Greek Language and Linguistics* (Sheffield: JSOT Press, 1993), 90–118.

Reiser, M., 'Bürgerliches Christentum in der Pastoralbriefen?', *Bib* 74 (1993), 27–44.

Ridderbos, H., *Paul: An Outline of his Theology* (London: SPCK, 1977).

Robinson, J. A. T., *Redating the New Testament* (London: SCM Press, 1976).

Rogers, P., 'The Few in Charge of the Many. The Model of Ministerial Authority in the Pastoral Epistles as a Positive Norm for the Church' (Diss. Masch. Gregoriana. Rome, 1976; not accessible to me).

Rogers, P., 'The Pastoral Epistles as Deutero-Pauline', *ITQ* 45 (1978), 248–60.

Rogers, P., 'How valid is the ecclesiology of the Pastoral Epistles?', *Milltown Studies* 3 (1979), 1–20.

Rogers, P., 'Pastoral authority then and now', *ITQ* 48 (1981), 47–59.

Rohde, J., *Urchristliche und frühkatholische Ämter. Eine Untersuchung zur frühchristlichen Amtsentwicklung im Neuen Testament and bei den apostolischen Vätern* (Berlin, 1976).

Roloff, J., *Apostolat – Verkündigung – Kirche* (Gütersloh: Mohn, 1965), 236–71.

Roloff, J., 'Pfeiler und Fundament der Wahrheit', in Grässer, E., and Merk, O. (eds.), *Glaube und Eschatologie* (Tübingen: J. C. B. Mohr [Paul Siebeck], 1985), 229–47.

Roloff, J., 'Der Kampf gegen die Irrlehrer. Wie geht man miteinander um?', *BK* 46 (1991a), 114–20.

Roloff, J., 'Der Weg Jesu als Lebensnorm (2 Tim 2, 8–13). Ein Beitrag zur Christologie der Pastoralbriefe', in Breytenbach, C., and Paulsen. H. (eds.), *Anfänge der Christologie (= Fs. F. Hahn)* (Göttingen: Vandenhoeck und Ruprecht, 1991b), 155–67.

Rordorf, W., 'Nochmals: Paulusakten und Pastoralbriefe', in Hawthorne, G. F., and Betz, O. (eds.), *Tradition and Interpretation in the New Testament: Essays in Honor of E. Earle Ellis* (Grand Rapids: Eerdmans, 1987), 319–27.

Rose, H. J., 'The Clausulae of the Pauline Corpus', *JTS* 25 (1924), 17–43.

Rudolph, K., *Gnosis. The Nature and History of an Ancient Religion* (Edinburgh: T. and T. Clark, 1983).

Sand, A., 'Anfänge einer Koordinierung verschiedener Gemeindeordnungen nach den Pastoralbriefen', in Hainz 1976:215–37.

Sand, A., 'Überlieferung und Sammlung der Paulusbriefe', in Kertelge 1981:11–24.

Schenk, W., 'Die Briefe an Timotheus I und II und an Titus (Pastoralbriefe) in der neueren Forschung (1945–1985)', *ANRW* II.25.4 (Berlin: De Gruyter, 1987), 3404–38.

Schierse, F., 'Eschatologische Existenz und christliche Bürgerlichkeit', *Gemeinde und Leben* 32 (1959), 280–91.

Schierse, F., 'Kennzeichen gesunder und kranker Lehre. Zur Ketzerpolemik der Pastoralbriefe', *Diakonia* 4 (1973), 176–86 (not accessible to me).

Schlarb, E., *Die gesunde Lehre: Häresie und Wahrheit im Spiegel der Pastoralbriefe* (Marburg: Elwert, 1990).

Schlier, H., 'Die Ordnung der Kirche nach den Pastoralbriefen', in Kertelge 1977:475–500. (Previously in *Die Zeit der Kirche* [Freiburg: Herder, 1958[2]], 129–47).

Schlosser, J., 'La didascalie et ses agents dans les épîtres pastorales', *RSR* 59 (1985), 81–94.

Schmithals, W., 'Pastoralbriefe', *RGG*[3] (1961), V, 144–8.

Schmithals, W., 'The Corpus Paulinum and Gnosis', in Logan, A. H. B., and Wedderburn, A. J. M. (eds.), *The New Testament and Gnosis* (Edinburgh: T. and T. Clark, 1983), 107–24.

Schnackenburg, R., 'Christologie des Neuen Testaments', in *Mysterium Salutis* (Einsiedeln: Benziger, 1970), III:1, 227–387 (espec. 355–60).

Schnackenburg, R., *The Church in the New Testament* (London: Burns and Oates, 1974).

Schnider, F., and Stenger, W., *Studien zum neutestamentlichen Briefformular* (NTTS 11. Leiden: Brill, 1987).

Schoedel, W. R., *Ignatius of Antioch* (Hermeneia. Philadelphia: Fortress, 1985).

Schöllgen, G., 'Was wissen wir über die Sozialstruktur der paulinischen Gemeinden?', *NTS* 34 (1988a), 71–83.

Schöllgen, G., 'Hausgemeinde, οἶκος-Ekklesiologie und monarchische Episkopat', JAC 31 (1988b), 74–90.

Schrage, W., 'Zur Ethik der neutestamentlichen Haustafeln', *NTS* 21 (1975), 1–22.

Schrage, W., *The Ethics of the New Testament* (Edinburgh: T. and T. Clark, 1988), 257–68.

Schroeder, D., 'Die Haustafeln des Neuen Testaments. Ihre Herkunft und theologischer Sinn' (Unpublished Diss. Hamburg, 1959).

Schulz, S., *Die Mitte der Schrift* (Stuttgart: Kreuz, 1976).

Schürer, E., *The History of the Jewish People in the Age of Jesus Christ (175 BC-AD 135)*. Revised and edited by Vermes, G., Millar, F., Black, M., and Vermes, P. (Edinburgh: T. and T. Clark, 1973–87).

Schürmann, H., ' "... und Lehrer" Die geistliche Eigenart des Lehrdienstes und sein Verhältnis zu anderen geistlichen Diensten im neutestamentlichen Zeitalter', in *Orientierung am Neuen Testament. Exegetische Aufsätze III* (Düsseldorf: Patmos, 1978), 116–56.

Schwarz, R., *Bürgerliches Christentum im Neuen Testament?* (Klosterneuburg: Osterreichisches Katholisches Bibelwerk, 1983).

Schwarz, R., 'Bürgerliches Christentum in den Städten am Ende des ersten Jahrhunderts?', *BK* 47 (1992), 25–9.

Schweizer, E., *Church Order in the New Testament* (London: SCM Press, 1961).

Schweizer, E., 'Two New Testament Creeds Compared (1 Cor xv.3–5; 1 Tim iii.16)', in Klassen, W., and Snyder, G. F. (eds.), *Current issues in New Testament Interpretation: Essays in Honour of O. Piper* (London: SCM Press, 1962), 166–77.

Seeberg, A., *Der Katechismus der Urchristenheit* (München: Chr. Kaiser, 1966 [orig. 1903]).

Sell, J., *The Knowledge of the Truth – Two Doctrines* (Frankfurt: Lang, 1982).

Simonsen, H., 'Christologische Traditionselemente in den Pastoralbriefen', in Pedersen, S. (ed.), *Die paulinische Literatur und Theologie* (Århus: Forlaget Aros, 1980), 51–62.

Skarsaune, O., 'Heresy and the Pastoral Epistles', *Themelios* 20.1 (1994), 9–14.

Skeat, T. C., ' "Especially the parchments": a note on 2 Tim 4.13', *JTS* ns 30 (1979), 173–7.

Souter, A., 'A Suggested Relationship between Titus and Luke', *ExpTim* 18 (1906–7), 285.

Souter, A., 'Did St. Paul speak Latin?', *Expositor* 8.1 (1911), 337–42.

Spicq, C., 'Pastorales', *DBSup* 7 (1961), 1–73.

Stecker, A., 'Formen und Formeln in den paulinischen Hauptbriefen und den Pastoralbriefen' (Diss. Münster, 1966; not accessible to me).

Steimer, B., *Vertex Traditionis. Die Gattung der altchristlichen Kirchenordnungen* (BZNW 63. Berlin: De Gruyter, 1992).

Stenger, W., 'Timotheus und Titus als literarische Gestalten', *Kairos* 16 (1974), 252–67.

Stettler, H., *Die Christologie der Pastoralbriefe* (WUNT 2.105. Tübingen: J. C. B. Mohr [Paul Siebeck], 1998.

Tachau, P., *'Einst' und 'Jetzt'* (Göttingen: Vandenhoeck und Ruprecht, 1972).

Thatcher, T., 'The Relational Matrix of the Pastoral Epistles', *JETS* 38 (1995), 51–62.

Thiessen, W., *Christen in Ephesus. Die historische und theologische Situation in vorpaulinischer and paulinischer Zeit und zur Zeit der Apostelgeschichte und der Pastoralbriefe.* (Texte und Arbeiten zum Neutestamentlichen Zeitalter 12. Tübingen/ Basel: Francke, 1995).

Thomas, J., 'Formgesetze des Begriffskatalogs im NT', *TZ* 24 (1968), 15–28.

Thraede, K., 'Frau', *RAC* VIII, 197–270.

Towner, P. H., *The Goal of our Instruction* (JSNTSup 34. Sheffield: Sheffield Academic Press, 1989).

Towner, P. H., 'The Present Age in the Eschatology of the Pastoral Epistles', *NTS* 32 (1986), 427–48.

Towner, P. H., 'Gnosis and Realized Eschatology in Ephesus (of the Pastoral Epistles) and the Corinthian Enthusiasm', *JSNT* 31 (1987), 95–124.

Towner, P. H., 'Structure and Meaning in Titus' (Unpublished paper, 1994).

Towner, P. H., 'Pauline Theology or Pauline Tradition in the Pastoral Epistles: the Question of Method', *TynBul* 46.2 (1995), 287–314.

Trites, A. A., *The New Testament Concept of Witness* (SNTSMS 31. Cambridge: Cambridge University Press, 1977).

Trummer, P., *Die Paulustradition der Pastoralbriefe* (BBET 8. Frankfurt: P. Lang, 1978).

Trummer, P., 'Corpus Paulinum – Corpus Pastorale. Zur Ortung der Paulustradition in den Pastoralbriefen', in Kertelge 1981:122–45.

Trummer, P., 'Gemeindeleiter ohne Gemeinden? Nach-bemerkungen zu den Pastoralbriefen', *BK* 46 (1991), 121–6.

Turner, N., *Style* (Edinburgh: T. and T. Clark, 1976 [Vol. 4 of MHT]), 101–5.

van Bruggen, J., *Die geschichtliche Einordnung der Pastoralbriefe* (Wuppertal: Brockhaus, 1981).

van der Horst, P. W., 'Macrobius and the New Testament', *NovT* 15 (1973), 220–32, espec. 230–1.

van der Horst, P. W., 'Musonius Rufus and the New Testament', *NovT* 16 (1974), 306–15, espec. 313f.

van der Horst, P. W., 'Hierocles the Stoic and the New Testament', *NovT* 17 (1975), 156–60, espec. 159.

van Unnik, W. C., 'Die Rücksicht auf die Reaktion der Nicht-Christen als Motiv in der altchristlichen Paränese', in *Sparsa Collecta* Vol. 2 (Leiden: Brill, 1980), 307–22.

Vanhoye, A. (ed.), *L'apôtre Paul: personnalité, style et conception du ministère* (BETL 73. Leuven: Peeters, 1986).

Vaughan, C., 'Selected Bibliography for the Study of the Pastoral Epistles', *South Western Journal of Theology* 2 (1959), 7–18.

Verner, D. C., *The Household of God: The Social World of the Pastoral Epistles* (SBLDS 71. Chico: Scholars, 1983).

Vielhauer, P., *Geschichte der urchristlichen Literatur* (Berlin: De Gruyter, 1975).

Vielhauer, P., *Oikodome. Aufsätze zum Neuen Testament. Band 2* (Munich: Kaiser, 1979).

Vögtle, A., *Die Tugend- und Lasterkataloge im Neuen Testament* (*NTAbh* 16, 4/5. Münster: Aschendorff, 1936).

Wagener, U., *Die Ordnung des »Hauses Gottes«: Der Ort von Frauen in der Ekklesiologie und Ethik der Pastoralbriefe* (WUNT 2.65. Tübingen: J. C. B. Mohr [Paul Siebeck], 1994).

Wallis, Ian G., *The faith of Jesus Christ in early Christian traditions* (SNTSMS 84. Cambridge: Cambridge University Press, 1995).

Wanke, J., 'Der verkündigte Paulus der Pastoralbriefe', in Ernst, W. (ed.), *Dienst der Vermittlung. Festschrift zum 25-jährigen Bestehen des Philosophisch-Theologischen Studiums im Priesterseminar Erfurt* (Leipzig: St Benno Verlag, 1977), 165–89.

Warkentin, M., *Ordination – A Biblical-Historical View* (Grand Rapids: Eerdmans, 1982).

Warren, M., 'Commentaries on the Pastoral Epistles', *Theology* 63 (1960), 15–19.

Wegenast, K., *Das Verständnis der Tradition bei Paulus und in den Deuteropaulinien* (WMANT 8. Neukirchen: Neukirchener, 1962), 132–58.

Weidinger, K., *Die Haustafeln. Ein Stück urchristlicher Paränese* (*UNT* 14. Leipzig: Hinrich, 1928).

Weiser, A., 'Die Rolle der Frau in der urchristlichen Mission', in Dautzenberg 1983:158–81.

Weiser, A., 'Evangelisierung im antiken Haus', *Studien zur Christsein und Kirche* (SBB 9. Stuttgart: Katholisches, 1990), 119–48.

Weiser, A., 'Die Kirche in den Pastoralbriefen. Ordnung um jeden Preis?' *BK* 46 (1991), 107–13.

Weiser, A., *Die gesellschaftliche Verantwortung der Christen nach den Pastoralbriefen* (Beiträge zur Friedensethik 18. Stuttgart: Kohlhammer, 1994).

Wendland, P., 'Σωτήρ: eine religionsgeschichtliche Untersuchung', *ZNW* 5 (1904), 335–53.

Wengst, K., *Christologische Formeln und Lieder des Urchristentums* (Gütersloh: Mohn, 1973²).

Wilson, S. G., *Luke and the Pastoral Epistles* (London: SPCK, 1979).

Windisch, H., 'Zur Christologie der Pastoralbriefe', *ZNW* 34 (1935), 213–38.

Witherington III, B., *Women in the Earliest Churches* (SNTSMS 59. Cambridge: Cambridge University Press, 1988).

Wolfe, B. P., 'Scripture in the Pastoral Epistles: Premarcion Marcionism?', *PRS* 16.1 (1989), 5–16.

Wolfe, B. P., 'The Place and Use of Scripture in the Pastoral Epistles' (Unpublished Diss. Aberdeen, 1990).

Wolter, M., 'Verborgene Weisheit und Heil für die Heiden. Zur Traditionsgeschichte und Intention des "Revelationsschemas"', *ZTK* 84 (1987), 297–319.

Wolter, M., *Die Pastoralbriefe als Paulustradition* (FRLANT 146. Göttingen: Vandenhoeck und Ruprecht, 1988).

Young, F., 'The Pastoral Epistles and the Ethics of Reading', *JSNT* 45 (1992), 105–20.

Young, F., *The Theology of the Pastoral Letters* (New Testament Theology. Cambridge: Cambridge University Press, 1994).

Ysebaert, J., *Die Amtsterminologie im Neuen Testament und in der Alten Kirche. Eine lexikographische Untersuchung* (Breda: Eureia, 1994).

Ysebaert, J., *Greek Baptismal Terminology. Its Origins and Early Development* (Nijmegen: Dekker and van de Vegt, 1962).

Zeilinger, F., 'Die Bewertung der irdischen Güter im lukanischen Doppelwerk und in den Pastoralbriefen', *BLit* 58 (1985), 75–80.

Ziesler, J. A., 'Which is the best commentary? XII The Pastoral Epistles', *ExpTim* 99 (1988), 264–67.

Zmijewski, J., 'Die Pastoralbriefe als pseudepigraphische Schriften: Beschreibung, Erklärung, Bewertung', *SNT(SU)* 4 (1979), 97–118.

INTRODUCTION

1. THE UNITY OF THE EPISTLES

Hofrichter 1987; Trummer, P., 'Corpus Paulinum – Corpus Pastorale. Zur Ortung der Paulustradition in den Pastoralbriefen', in Kertelge 1981:122–45.

Despite some dissent,[1] the three letters are by one author.[2] Any differences in character between them are due to the different situations addressed rather than to differences in authorship or thinking.[3] This means that the letters can be considered together as a group of writings. They represent a common outlook with the kind of variations that one would expect to find in any group of writings by one author whose thought was liable to change and development.

So much so is this the case that some scholars insist that they were deliberately composed as a corpus and intended to be interpreted as such (Trummer*). Quinn 1978 thought that they were intended together as the third part of Luke's work.

Theories of this kind are improbable. It remains difficult to understand the composition of Tit as part of a 'corpus' alongside 1 Tim unless Tit is a sort of 'first attempt' which has somehow survived. Even though Tit is much more than a pale imitation of 1 Tim, it is difficult to understand it as part of a group of writings with one and the same destination. It is more probable that the different recipients of the letters indicate that they were meant for more than one situation, although these situations were broadly similar.

It is often assumed that 2 Tim was composed or was intended

[1] Mayer 1913:20–26 drew attention to some differences between 1 and 2 Tim which at least raised the question of identity of authorship. Hofrichter* argued that Tit was structurally based on 1 Pet, and that 1 Tim 1–3, 1 Tim 4–6 and 2 Tim were further developments from Tit by different authors. In a paper given at the SBL meeting in Chicago in 1994 T. W. Martin argued that Tit and 1 Tim represent different fronts in opposition to each other over christology. Murphy-O'Connor 1991 has also defended the view that 2 Tim is by Paul, whereas 1 Tim and Tit are by a later writer; he finds differences in the manner of address, the 'lower' christology of 2 Tim, the understanding of ministry and of the gospel, and the absence of discussion of the false teaching. None of these points seems to me to be strong enough to suggest difference of authorship. Cf. Prior 1989 for a full discussion of 2 Tim.

[2] The use of the phrase 'one author' is not intended to exclude the possibility that a group of people may have been involved in the composition of the letters.

[3] I am indebted to unpublished material by R. Fuchs and G. Wieland who examine the different ways in which the theology is developed in the three letters in order to meet the requirements of different situations.

1

to be read after 1 Tim; its relationship to Tit is less clear. The canonical order arises from placing the longest of the letters first and then naturally following it by the second letter to the same person, with Tit then following automatically. Defenders of the hypothesis that the letters are based on Pauline fragments have argued that the amount of such material in 2 Tim indicates that the author wrote it first and used up most of his genuine fragments in so doing (Easton, 17f.). This order of composition may well be the case and we shall cautiously defend it later. Nevertheless, in the present commentary the letters will be expounded in the order Tit – 1 Tim – 2 Tim. The justification for this order is that Tit addresses a less developed and complex ecclesiastical situation than 1 Tim and may indeed have been composed before it (although there is no way of establishing this point with certainty) and 2 Tim is intended to be read as Paul's last letter (whether or not it was the last to be composed). At the same time by reading the letters in this order we shall rescue Tit from being read, as it tends to be, in the shadow of 1 Tim and given less attention in its own right than it deserves.

2. ATTESTATION AND CANONICITY

The New Testament in the Apostolic Fathers by A Committee of the Oxford Society of Historical Theology (Oxford: Clarendon Press, 1905); Bernard, xi–xxi; Brox, 26–8; Bruce, F. F., *The Canon of Scripture* (Downers Grove: InterVarsity Press, 1988); Campenhausen, H. von, *The Formation of the Christian Bible* (London: Black, 1972); Duff, J., 'P[46] and the Pastorals: A Misleading Consensus?', *NTS* 44 (1998), 578–90; Gamble, H. Y., *The New Testament Canon: Its Making and Meaning* (Philadelphia: Fortress, 1985); Grant, R. M., *The Formation of the New Testament* (London: Hutchinson, 1965); Knox, J., *Marcion and the New Testament: An Essay in the Early History of the Canon* (Chicago: University of Chicago Press, 1942); Maier, G. (ed.), *Der Kanon der Bibel* (Giessen: Brunnen/Wuppertal: Brockhaus, 1990); Metzger, B. M., *The Canon of the New Testament: Its Origin, Development and Significance* (Oxford: Clarendon Press, 1987); Mitton, C. L., *The Formation of the Pauline Corpus of Letters* (London: Epworth, 1955); Quinn, J. D., 'P[46] – the Pauline Canon?', *CBQ* 36 (1974), 379–85; James 1906:5–24; Weninger, F., 'Die Pastoralbriefe in der Kanongeschichte zur Zeit der Patristik', Dissertation, Wien, 1964.[4]

The two general issues that arise here are (a) how soon knowledge of the PE is to be found, and (b) how soon they are recognised as authoritative Pauline documents (and therefore 'canonical'). Two particular questions that arise concern the alleged absence of the PE from the original contents of P[46] and whether they were rejected by Marcion or not known by him. The place of the PE in the later development of the canon of the New Testament does not require any detailed discussion in the present

[4] Listed by Brox, 95; I have not been able to consult it.

context. The question of early knowledge and use of them is more contentious.

With the earlier patristic writers the problem is whether we are simply to see similar phraseology to that of the PE being used, perhaps by writers who belong to the same general period. There is a general absence of deliberate or formal quotations in this period, and the coincidences in language may permit of more than one explanation. Striking phrases common to the PE and other authors may be due to a common stock of language rather than to literary dependence on the PE. Despite the need for caution, we can recognise that there are some examples of dependence.

The committee responsible for *The New Testament in the Apostolic Fathers* found it highly probable that 1 and 2 Tim were known and used by Polycarp, and quite likely that they were known and used by 1 Clement (Tit) and Ignatius (all three), and possible that they were known and used by Barnabas (1 and 2 Tim; Tit) and 1 Clement (1 Tim). We may summarise the evidence in two formats.[5] In Table 1 we have listed for each of the letters in the Pauline corpus the knowledge displayed by the Fathers and have assigned a score to each letter on the basis of A = 3; B = 2 and C = 1. In Table 2 we have listed the NT writings known to each individual writer.

These tables, which are generally recognised to be based on a cautious and careful survey, show that there is no absolute certainty that any of the PE are known to any of the AF, although their individual total scores are no lower than for other letters in the Pauline corpus.[6] The key witness is Polycarp, where there is a high probability that 1 and 2 Tim were known to him. He does not formally cite Paul's letters but has a clear unacknowledged quotation (1 Tim 6.7, 10, cited by Polycarp 4; see commentary below).[7] Polycarp also echoes the typical phraseology of the PE, and in the light of his quotation we may conclude that the PE were known and read at this time. The fact that it is Polycarp who of all the AF furnishes the strongest evidence for use of the Pauline corpus generally strengthens the case that he is also referring to the PE rather than echoing language that was current in the church. The

---

[5] See the table in *The New Testament in the Apostolic Fathers*, 137.

[6] See also the statement and discussion of the evidence in Bernard, xi–xxi, who is rather more positive; similarly James 1906.

[7] Brox 1969b:81f. denies usage by Polycarp. Schenk 1987:3406 n. 9 rightly accepts dependence on the grounds of the combination of allusions.

TABLE 1

PROBABILITY OF USE OF INDIVIDUAL LETTERS IN THE PAULINE CORPUS

	A CERTAIN	B HIGH	C LOW	D UNCERTAIN	SCORE
Romans		Barnabas Polycarp	Ignatius	Hermas ?Didache	5
1 Corinthians	1 Clement Ignatius Polycarp			Barnabas Didache 2 Clement	9
2 Corinthians		Polycarp	?Ignatius	Barnabas 1 Clement	3
Galatians		Polycarp	Ignatius	1 Clement	3
Ephesians		Ignatius Polycarp Hermas	Barnabas	1 Clement 2 Clement	5
Philippians		Polycarp	Ignatius	1 Clement	3
Colossians				Barnabas 1 Clement Ignatius Polycarp	0
1 Thessalonians				?Ignatius Hermas	0
2 Thessalonians		Polycarp		?Ignatius	2
Philemon				?Ignatius	0
1 Timothy		Polycarp	Ignatius	1 Clement Barnabas	3
2 Timothy		Polycarp	Ignatius	Barnabas	3
Titus			1 Clement Ignatius	Barnabas	2

evidence for knowledge by Ignatius is weaker, amounting as it does to similarities in phraseology. In my judgement the evidence for possible knowledge by 1 Clement is somewhat stronger. The Oxford Committee did not discuss Diognetus 11.3, but knowledge here of 1 Tim 3.16 is probable (see commentary).

However, the evidence of Polycarp for the early existence of the letters is controversial in view of the uncertainty regarding the date of his writing. P. N. Harrison argued that Polycarp 1–12 is a separate composition later than Polycarp 13–14 and is to be dated as late as AD 140.[8] His arguments, though accepted

[8] Harrison, P. N., *Polycarp's Two Epistles to the Philippians* (Cambridge: Cambridge University Press, 1936).

TABLE 2

PROBABILITY OF USE OF PAULINE CORPUS BY INDIVIDUAL APOSTOLIC FATHERS

	CERTAIN	HIGH	LOW	UNCERTAIN
Barnabas		Rom	Eph	1 Cor, 2 Cor, Col, 1 Tim, 2 Tim, Tit
Didache				1 Cor
1 Clement	Rom, 1 Cor		Tit	2 Cor, Gal, Eph, Phil, Col, 1 Tim
Ignatius	1 Cor	Eph	Rom, ?2 Cor, Gal, Phil, 1 Tim, 2 Tim, Tit	Col, ?1 Th, ?2 Th, ?Philem
Polycarp		1 Cor Eph, Phil, 2 Th, 1 Tim, 2 Tim	Rom, 2 Cor, Gal	Col
Hermas		1 Cor, Eph		Rom, 1 Th
2 Clement				1 Cor, Eph

by some scholars,[9] have been effectively criticised by Gilchrist 1966 and Macdougall.[10] The hypothesis of Campenhausen 1963b that the PE were composed by Polycarp or somebody closely associated with him as a response to Marcion has not found support. The difference in style from the letter of Polycarp is decisive against composition by Polycarp himself, and the closeness in phraseology is insufficient to justify ascribing the PE to a colleague of his. It remains most plausible that Polycarp is a witness to early knowledge of the PE.

The lack of knowledge of the PE in this period is to be compared with the rather similar state of affairs surrounding several of the accepted Pauline letters. There is nothing unusual about the low degree of proven usage of the PE in the context of the general difficulty of establishing knowledge and use of the accepted Pauline letters.

II. LATER SECOND-CENTURY USAGE

There is no dispute about the knowledge and use of the PE as authoritative documents along with other NT writings later in the second century.[11] They are quoted by Theophilus,

[9] Campenhausen*, 178 n. 157.

[10] Macdougall, D., unpublished thesis, 'The Authenticity of 2 Thessalonians', Aberdeen, 1993.

[11] For the parallels in *Didasc.* to the material in the PE on bishops and widows see the convenient table in Mayer 1913:83–9.

Ad Autolycum, 3.14 who refers to their teaching as 'the divine word'; his work contains clear echoes of 1 Tim 2.2; Tit 3.1, 5 (cf. Athenagoras, *Supplicatio* 37.1 with 1 Tim 2.2). Justin, *Trypho* 47.15 contains a clear echo of Tit 3.4. Irenaeus cites them freely as authoritative works directed against heresy by Paul (*AH* 1 Praef., citing 1 Tim 1.4; 1.16.3, citing Tit 3.10 (cf. 3.3.4); 2.14.7, citing 1 Tim 6.20; 3.3.3 referring to 2 Tim 4.21; 3.14.1, citing 2 Tim 4.10f.).[12] They are expressly included in the Muratorian List, whose second-century provenance remains probable despite recent proposals to date it later.[13]

III. THE PROBLEM OF P[46]

Two areas remain problematic. First, the absence of the PE from P[46] (c. AD 200) has been variously explained. The last seven leaves of the papyrus are missing, and it has been claimed that there would not have been room on them for all of 2 Thes, Philem and the PE. The 'standard' view is that the scribe did not intend to include the PE. Jeremias, 4, proposed either that the scribe intended to include only the letters to churches, or that the omission happened because the scribe had miscalculated the remaining space available to him; he surmises that extra leaves may have been added to the codex. Quinn 1974 develops the former hypothesis, namely that there existed separate collections of Paul's letters to churches and to individuals (cf. the distinction in the Muratorian List), and that P[46] is an example of the former, containing nine letters of Paul to groups of Christians together with Hebrews. In this case the absence of the PE from P[46] says nothing about their canonical status.

However, it is also possible that the PE were included in P[46]. Duff* has followed up the comment by Jeremias that the number of characters per page increases significantly in the second half of the extant papyrus, and argues that the scribe was deliberately compressing his writing in order to accommodate the remaining letters in the Pauline corpus (including Heb). He notes that the same phenomenon of writing increasing numbers of characters to the page is found in P[75]. He then suggests either that the scribe left the MS incomplete or that he added some extra pages to the original quire (a known practice at the time). Either way, the argument that the scribe did not intend to include the PE (for

---

[12] There are echoes of characteristic language in the Epistle of the Churches of Vienne and Lyons (Eusebius, *HE* 5.1.17, 30; 3.2); Hegesippus (Eusebius, *HE* 3.32); Heracleon (Clement, *Strom.* 4.9); Justin, *Trypho* 7.7; 35.3; 47.15.

[13] Hahneman, G. M., *The Muratorian Fragment and the Development of the Canon* (Oxford: Clarendon Press, 1992); see, however, the review by Ferguson, E., *JTS* ns 44 (1993), 691–7.

whatever reason, such as that he did not known them or did not consider them canonical) cannot be sustained.[14] Consequently no conclusions about knowledge of the PE or their authority at this time can be drawn.

IV. THE PROBLEM OF MARCION

The second problem concerns Marcion's knowledge or lack of knowledge of the PE. The discussion is complicated by the suggestion that the PE may have been composed as late as, or even later than, the time of Marcion (possibly even in opposition to him).[15] The only evidence we have is Tertullian's statement, which is made in the context of the fact that Marcion allowed Philemon into his collection:

> Soli huic epistolae [sc. Philem.] brevitas sua profuit, ut falsarias manus Marcionis evaderet. Miror tamen, cum ad unum hominem litteras factas receperit, quod ad Timotheum duas et unam ad Titum de ecclesiastico statu compositas recusaverit. Affectauit, opinor, etiam numerum epistolarum interpolare. (*Adv. Marcionem* 5.21)

According to this statement the PE were not in Marcion's 'canon' of Pauline letters; the debate concerns whether he did not know them or deliberately excluded works that were accepted by other Christians at the time. There should be no dispute that (whether rightly or wrongly) Tertullian regarded Marcion as having rejected (*recusaverit*) the PE, excising whole letters as well as parts of those which he accepted (Metzger*, 159).[16] The problem, therefore, is not about the interpretation of Tertullian's words but about whether he was reliably informed[17] or even interpreting the facts polemically.[18] Bruce*, 131, 138f., is typical of many scholars in stating that probably the copy of the Pauline corpus which Marcion used lacked them, but he offers no evidence for this judgement other than the parallel of P[46] (on which, as we

---

[14] I am indebted to the author for letting me see an advance copy of his article.

[15] This view of the origin of the PE is upheld by Bauer 1972:226f.; Knox*, 73–6; Goodspeed; Campenhausen*, 181; Köster, H., 'Häretiker im Urchristentum', *RGG*[3] III, Sp. 21; Rist, M., 'Pseudepigraphical Refutations of Marcionism', *JR* 22 (1942), 39–62. However, even if the PE should be later than Marcion, it is quite impossible to claim that they were written against him, since the opponents who are attacked attached positive value to the law in the Old Testament and made it the basis of their speculations.

[16] Mitton*, 38f., holds that Tertullian is not sufficiently scathing if Marcion had really rejected them.

[17] Gamble*, 42, holds that Tertullian is mistaken and that Marcion simply did not know the PE.

[18] Schenk 1987:3405f.

have seen, no weight can be placed). Equally, however, it can be said that no concrete evidence for doubting Tertullian's verdict exists.

The whole question of whether Marcion abbreviated an existing canon or rather created a (short) canon whose existence forced the church to produce its own longer canon is disputed, and the wisest verdict may still be that of Kümmel 1966:342f. who states that Marcion's activity 'strengthened the tendency already existing in the church toward a normative evaluation of apostolic writings'.

It can be concluded that the PE were known to Christian writers from early in the second century and that there is no evidence of rejection of them by any writers except for Marcion. Their canonical history sheds no light on the question of their origin and authorship.

3. THE TEXT OF THE EPISTLES

Baillet, M., 'Les manuscripts de la grotte 7 de Qumrân et le Nouveau Testament (suite)', *Bib* 54 (1973), 340–50; Bartlet, J. V., 'A new fifth-century fragment of 1 Timothy', *JTS* 18 (1917), 309–11; Elliott 1968; Elliott, J. K., 'The United Bible Societies Textual Commentary evaluated', *NovT* 17, no. 2 (1975), 130–50; 'A Greek-Coptic (Sahidic) Fragment of Titus-Philemon (0205)', *NovT* 36 (1994), 183–95; (Kilpatrick, G. D.), *The Pastoral Letters and Hebrews. A Greek-English Diglot for the use of Translators*, London: British and Foreign Bible Society, 1963; Metzger, B. M., 'A hitherto neglected early fragment of the Epistle to Titus', *NovT* 1 (1956), 149–50; Nebe, G. W., '7Q4 – Möglichkeit und Grenze einer Identifikation', *RevQ* 13 (1988), 629–33; O'Callaghan, J., '¿1Tim 3,16; 4,1.3 en 7Q4?' *Bib* 53 (1972), 362–7; 'Les papyrus de la grotte 7 de Qumrân', *NRT* 95 (1973), 188–95 (cf. the summary in *Los primeros testimonios del Nuevo Testamento* (Córdoba: Ediciones El Almendro, 1995), 139–42); Puech, É., 'Des fragments grecs de la Grotte 7 et le Nouveau Testament? 7Q4 et 7Q5, et le papyrus Magdalen grec 17 = P⁶⁴', *RB* 102 (1995), 570–84; Quinn, J. D., 'P⁴⁶ – The Pauline Canon', *CBQ* 36 (1974), 379–85; Reicke, B., 'Les deux fragments grecs onciaux de 1 Tim appelés 061 publiés', *ConNT* 11 (1947), 196–206; Schenk 1987:3405; Stewart, R., 'A Coptic Fragment of 2 Timothy', *SPap* 21 (1982), 7–10; Thiede, C. P., *The Earliest Gospel Manuscript? The Qumran Fragment 7Q5 and Its Significance for New Testament Studies* (Carlisle: Paternoster, 1993); Zereteli, G., *Un palimpseste grec du V siècle sur parchemin (Epist. ad Tit. 1, 4–6, 7–9)* (Bruxelles, 1932), 427–32 (not accessible to me).

The text printed as lemmata in this commentary is that of NA²⁷ (=UBS⁴).

We are fortunate to have a detailed, up-to-date study on the text of the Pastoral Epistles by Elliott* 1968. It is of permanent value for its exhaustive collection of textual variants with the evidence for each of them. They are discussed with minute care and great insight. The aim of the work is to establish the text of the letters on the basis of the so-called eclectic method. The approach adopted is to consider each set of variations on its merits, in the light of what the original author is likely to have written in view of his known style (established, as far as is possible, on the basis of textually unassailable evidence) and in the light of the known proclivities of scribes. In this process the external attestation by MSS plays a secondary role, and the original text may be found in only a few sources, or even a single one, and the lateness of a reading is no barrier to its being original. The result is a very individual reconstruction of the text, which follows the general principles behind that constructed earlier by Kilpatrick*[19] but differs considerably in detail.

Critics have claimed that Elliott's eclecticism is questionable as a method when it depends on singular or nearly singular readings, or readings for which there is little or no Greek evidence. One important question is whether the original text, written in Koine Greek, has been subject to Atticising in an Alexandrian recension but preserved in a more pure form in later MSS that have escaped the Atticising process. Many of Elliott's decisions rest on the assumption that this is indeed the case. It is, however, doubtful whether this assumption is true at all points (to put the point no more strongly), particularly when the evidence for the alleged non-Atticistic reading is small in quantity. There is no obvious explanation as to why correct readings should have survived in comparatively obscure corners.

The present commentary cannot compete with Elliott's presentation of the material, and has no need to do so. It has the limited aim of listing and discussing briefly all the variants noted in NA[27] together with the textual evidence given there, along with all other variants listed by Elliott which appeared to merit discussion as possibly enshrining the original text. It should be noted that the variants are all listed from these standard editions and no attempt has been made to check them with original sources. The eclectic text edited by Kilpatrick has also been cited wherever appropriate; it is unfortunate that it has no textual apparatus and no accompanying commentary. Along with Elliott's detailed analysis the brief, selective comments of Metzger are particularly valuable.[20]

---

[19] G. D. Kilpatrick was the editor of a series of booklets prepared for private circulation for the use of translators. His innovative approach to the text failed to win general acceptance and the series reverted to use of a standard text after the first few fascicles had appeared. Fortunately Kilpatrick's work on the PE was published before the moratorium on his pioneering work was imposed.

[20] Earlier discussions of the text and textual problems can be found in Bernard, lxxv–lxxviii; Parry, clv–clxi (list of readings only); Lock, xxxv–xxxviii (mainly discussion of readings); Spicq, 299–311.

According to Elliott, 13f., there are two papyri containing parts of the PE (P³² = P. Ryl. 5, Manchester, c. AD 200, containing Tit 1.11–15; 2.3–8; P⁶¹ = P. Colt 5, New York, c. AD 700, containing Tit 3.1–5, 8–11, 14–15). As is well-known, P⁴⁶ lacks the PE. The same is true of the major uncial B (03), but there are around 25 uncials which contain some or all of the PE, some of them very fragmentary: ℵ (01) A (02) C (04) D (06) E (a transcript of D) F (010) G (012) H (015) (frg.) I (016) (frg.) K (018) L (020) P (025) Ψ (044) 048 (frg. 1 Tim 5.6–6.15; 2 Tim 1.1–2.25; Tit 3.13–15) 061 (frg. 1 Tim 3.15f.; 4.1–3; 6.2–4, 5–8; Reicke*) 088 (frg. Tit 1.1–13) 0205 (frg. Tit 2.15–3.7 in Gk.; 2.11–3.15 in Coptic; Elliott 1994); 0240 (frg. Tit 1.4–6, 7–9; cf. Metzger*) 0241 (frg. 1 Tim 3.16–4.3; cf. Bartlet*) 0259 (frg.) 0262 (frg.);²¹ 0285 (frg 1 Tim 1.1–7); and 056 075 0142 0150 and 0151 (all commentaries).²² In addition there are over 500 cursives, of which Elliott examined about 150.

Considerable interest has been aroused by the claim made by O'Callaghan and others that the Qumran fragment 7Q4 contains a part of 1 Timothy. This identification was regarded as 'certain' by its proposer and as possible by Thiede. There are two tiny pieces of papyrus which contain some 21 letters (three illegible and two or three uncertain), and these have been identified as containing parts of 1 Tim 3.16–4.3. The identification must assume two places where the papyrus contains singular readings together with one otherwise attested variant, and one itacism.

In such a case as this, it is quite impossible to claim a certain identification, since so many assumptions have to be made in order to make it 'work'. Rather one must ask if there is a demonstration of a real possibility, or whether there are considerations which make it less than plausible that this identification is a possibility. In the present case there are two considerations which make the identification unlikely (cf. Puech*). First, the reconstructed reading τὸ πνεῦμα ῥητῶν, 'the Spirit of words', is a very unlikely phrase which does not fit the context. Second, the putative omission of ὅτι ἐν in line 3 to make the stichometry work is unattested elsewhere. It is very debatable whether one can go so far with such assumptions to make an

---

²¹ The text of 0259 (*P. Berl.* 3605), which contains 1 Tim 1.4f., 6f., and 0262 (*P. Berl.* 13977), which contains 1 Tim 1.15–16, is reproduced in *New Docs.* II, 137–9 §91 (12 and 13).

²² Elliott's list has been updated from Aland, K. and B., *The Text of the New Testament* (Grand Rapids: Eerdmans, 1989²), 107–28, 246; Aland, K., *Kurzgefasste Liste der Griechischen Handschriften des Neuen Testaments* (Berlin: De Gruyter, 1962).

identification work. Other identifications for the fragment have been suggested (Nebe*). Since the papyrus does not have to be a copy of a known writing but could be of any (otherwise known or unknown) work, the identification is not 'required'. On the whole, it seems that the possibility of the identification is weak; there is most certainly nothing that demands it.

4. GENRE AND STRUCTURE

Banker, J., *Semantic Structure Analysis of Titus* (Dallas: Summer Institute of Linguistics, 1987); Blight, R. C., *A Literary-Semantic Analysis of Paul's First Discourse to Timothy* (Dallas: Summer Institute of Linguistics, 1977); Bush, P. G., 'A Note on the structure of 1 Timothy', *NTS* 36 (1990), 152–6; Gibson 1996; Miller, James D., *The Pastoral Letters as Composite Documents* (Cambridge: Cambridge University Press, 1997); Quinn 1981a; Reed 1992; Reed 1993; Smith, R. E., and Beekman, J., *A Literary-Semantic Analysis of Second Timothy* (Dallas: Summer Institute of Linguistics, 1981); Towner, P. H., 'Structure and Meaning in Titus', unpublished paper. 1994; Welch, J. W. (ed.), *Chiasmus in Antiquity* (Hildesheim: Gerstenberg, 1981).

There is surprisingly little agreement among commentators as to the structure and nature of the argument in each of these epistles. The problem is not so acute in the case of Titus, but the commentaries on 1 Timothy and even more so on 2 Timothy demonstrate a remarkable lack of agreement. There is a fair degree of unanimity in dividing up the epistles into their constituent small units, but there is little agreement on how to group the smaller units into larger wholes and trace a line of argument, or whether indeed this is the right way to understand the epistles at all. This is all the more surprising given the current concern for the study of structure in literature in general and more especially in the NT. Considerable attention has been devoted to the epistolary genre, but the study of epistolary structure has not been particularly helpful in the case of the PE, since it offers little insight so far into the analysis of the body of letters. Rhetorical analysis, which analyses documents in terms of ancient rhetorical theory, has been applied to some of the NT letters, but there is some doubt as to how far the attempt has been successful.[23] The application of literary-semantic analysis to the NT documents by scholars associated with the Summer Institute of Linguistics (SIL) has been largely ignored by mainstream

---

[23] The most detailed application is Betz, H. D., *Galatians* (Philadelphia: Fortress, 1979). But see Fairweather, J., 'The Epistle to the Galatians and Classical Rhetoric', *TynBul* 45 (1994), 1–38, 213–44; Kern, P. H., *Rhetoric and Galatians: Assessing an Approach to Paul's Epistle* (SNTSMS 101. Cambridge: Cambridge University Press, 1998).

scholarship.[24] We shall use whatever means offer themselves to discover the flow of thought in an argument and so to provide a kind of macrocontext within which the significance of the details can be more clearly seen.

I. GENRE

Throughout this commentary the documents under discussion are referred to as epistles or letters without any attempt to distinguish between these two terms. The three PE each have the ancient form of a letter, as is evident from the opening salutations. They are presented as personal messages from the writer to a single reader. Nevertheless, all three documents end with a benediction couched in the plural form (assuming that the text is correct). In their present form, therefore, they are implicitly overheard by the Christian believers associated with the named recipients, presumably the members of the congregations for which they are responsible.

The Second Letter to Timothy fits most closely into the genre of the personal paraenetic letter, as we know it from elsewhere in the NT and from contemporary sources,[25] in that it commences with an expression of thanksgiving to God for the recipient and closes with specific personal remarks and greetings. It is often thought to have the characteristics of a testament, i.e. a person's last words to his family before dying (Knoch 1973), but it has been rightly observed that 2 Tim has much more the character of a paraenetic letter (Prior 1989:110–12; Johnson, 38–41) and it certainly assumes that the writer and the recipient will have further contact. Titus has more the character of a set of instructions from a superior person to his agent, but like 2 Tim it has a personal conclusion. The one that is least like a letter is 1 Tim which is almost totally lacking in personal touches although it is specifically addressed to Timothy. Both Tit and 1 Tim thus fit into the genre of mandates.

Whether the documents are genuine letters is of course disputed. If the dominant view that they are post-Pauline compositions is correct, then they have been written in the form of letters but in reality are meant for different audiences. Since they purport to be Pauline compositions (or what Paul would have written if he were still alive) they are naturally cast in the only

---

[24] For these approaches see Beekman, J., and Callow, J., *Translating the Word of God* (Grand Rapids: Eerdmans, 1974); Callow, K., *Discourse Considerations in Translating the Word of God* (Grand Rapids: Eerdmans, 1974); see also Louw, J., *Semantics of New Testament Greek* (Philadelphia: Fortress/Chico: Scholars, 1982).

[25] Cf. Quinn 1981a:495–501; Malherbe 1986:124–9; Johnson, 39–41.

form that we know for sure that he employed. They thus maintain the tradition of personal communications from the church leader to his colleagues or congregations.

II. TRADITION AND REDACTION

One possible approach to the question of structure is to consider the building blocks from which a letter is composed. The study of tradition and redaction has been extended by a number of scholars from the Gospels to the Epistles. If we can determine the nature and identity of the materials used by the author, this may help us to understand better what he was doing.

a. Structural elements

In this regard Hanson, 42–7, has made three observations.

1. Types of source materials

First, Hanson makes a list of various types or forms of material which can be detected in the letters. He finds nine types of material, the first six of which can be regarded as source materials while the remaining three represent materials directly composed by the author himself although they depend to some extent on traditional materials.[26] (See Table 3)

2. Interrupted themes

Hanson's second point is that the author has a habit of beginning certain themes, then interrupting himself and then returning to the topic originally begun. (See Table 4)

3. Connective phrases

The third point is that the writer has a set of stock phrases which he uses when switching from one topic to another for no apparent logical or inherent reason. 'He has ... devised a whole series of connecting words or phrases that help to smooth the transition from one [topic] to another. The most remarkable of these is **the saying is sure** which occurs five times' (Hanson, 46f.).

---

[26] Hanson does not give complete lists of the material in each category in his introduction, and the classification of some of the material is obviously open to debate.

TABLE 3

THE SOURCES OF THE PASTORALS (HANSON)

1.	Extracts from a church order	1 Tim 3.1–7, 8–13; 5.3–16, 17–24; Tit 1.5–9.
2.	Domestic codes	1 Tim 2.9–15; 6.1–20; Tit 2.1–10.
3.	Liturgical fragments	1 Tim 3.16; 2 Tim 2.11–13; Tit 2.11–14 + 3.3–7.
4.	Confessional or homiletic statements	1 Tim 2.4–6; 6.11–16.
5.	Lists of sinners or sins	1 Tim 1.9–10; 6.4–5; 2 Tim 3.2–5; Tit 3.3.
6.	Historical details about Paul's life	1 Tim 1.3, 20; 5.23; 2 Tim 1.5, 16; 2.17; 4.9–21; Tit 3.12–13.
7.	Pauline passages transposed	1 Tim 1.12, 20; 2.13–15; 3.15–4.10; 4.12; 5.18, 19; 6.3–5, 12; 2 Tim 1.3–4, 6–8, 8–9, 9–10; 2.1–13, 8–13, 20–21; 3.2–4, 16–17; 4.6–8, 8, 11b.
8.	Midrash or haggada on Scripture	1 Tim 1.13–16; 2.3–4; 3.15; 2 Tim 2.19; 3.7; 4.16–18.
9.	Direct exhortation and instruction	1 Tim 2.1f., 8–9; 5.1–2; 6.6–10, 17–19; 2 Tim 2.2; 3.16; Tit 1.5, 12, 14; 3.10.

TABLE 4

INTERRUPTED THEMES (HANSON)

false doctrine	1 Tim	1.3–7	1.18–20
public prayer		2.1–3	2.8
life style for a church leader		6.6–10	6.17–19
guarding the deposit	2 Tim	1.11–14	2.1–7
movements of colleagues		4.9–15	4.19–21
liturgical fragment	Tit	2.11–14	3.3–7
false teachers		1.10–16	3.9–11
good works		3.8	3.14

4. Evaluation of the observations

The conclusion which Hanson draws from this investigation is that the author writes rather in the manner of some of the OT wisdom literature where logical connections are often simply not there. He says, 'The Pastorals are made up of a miscellaneous collection of material. They have no unifying theme; there is no development of thought.' The author

carefully alternated his materials. It would not have done to put all his church order material, or all his Pauline trans-positions, or all his liturgical material together in one block. That would have looked too like a manual of church order, or an exposition of Paul, or a book of worship, and he wanted to give the impression that he was writing letters. (Hanson, 42)

The result is that, when Hanson analyses the letters, he is content simply to give a list of paragraph headings without looking for any more detailed structure (Hanson, 54, 118, 168.). Hanson is by no means alone in analysing the letters in this way. Essentially the same kind of structure is offered by quite a large number of English commentators (e.g. Scott; Simpson; Barrett; Kelly; Fee). The difference is that he has attempted to place the analysis of the units on a firm basis by a form-critical analysis, whereas they have simply distinguished apparently disconnected units.

However, Hanson's analysis is open to criticism. In particular, his identification of the types of material allegedly used by the author of the PE (see a. above) requires some revision.

There is no problem about recognising the possibility of the use of extracts from a church order and from domestic codes (1 and 2). The second of these patterns is readily traceable elsewhere in the NT. But there are difficulties with the suggestion that these would necessarily be *written* documents which the author took over.[27] For it is clear that the author did not simply take over any such codes verbatim. He felt able to create his own material, to adapt and modify existing material, and to work by analogy with existing material.

The liturgical fragments (3) also raise problems. Here again we need to ask whether the style and content of this material confirm that it is older material taken over by the author. The material agrees stylistically and theologically with the rest of the letters. Nevertheless, traditional language is used; this is particularly obvious in Tit 2.14a which represents tradition which the author has made his own. There is no sharp distinction between the so-called liturgical fragments and category (4), the confessional statements. In both cases it may be better to think

---

[27] Although scholars generally talk about this material as coming from a house code, it seems clear that it is not primarily concerned with relationships within the family but rather with relationships within the church. Traditions related to the domestic codes have been used, but these have been partly replaced by material from a different background; see Schroeder 1959:188–92.

of pieces of traditional phraseology picked up and elaborated by the author himself rather than of actual quotations of any length from existing sources.[28]

Lists of sinners and sins (5) fit into a well-known pattern used by Paul and other writers, but again we may ask whether existing lists are taken over or adapted. Free formulation following a pattern seems to be indicated.

Historical details about Paul's life (6) will be variously evaluated according to our theories of authorship. If the Epistles are not by Paul we still face the question whether the author is using actual fragments of Pauline material, or incorporating known information or simply creating *ab initio*.

Hanson's three remaining categories are of types of material composed by the author himself – his reformulation of passages from the Pauline epistles, his development of midrash or haggada based on Scripture and his use of direct exhortation and instruction and do not require any special comment at the moment, except to note that in all three cases the author is making his own creative use of materials, in some cases written, which were already available.

In the light of this discussion Hanson's conclusion requires some modification. Where he has identified some six types of building block which apparently existed in written form and were taken over by the author, it is more probable that the amount of written material of this kind that was available was quite small, and that the author used considerable freedom in taking up and using traditional materials that were available. In other words, we should attribute more to the creative powers of the author than to the use of pre-formed materials.

b. Coherence or incoherence?

Miller* starts from the observation that it is difficult to find any coherent argument or clear development of thought in the PE such as one would expect to find in works by a single author. He notes that there are many examples in Judaism of religious works which are in effect collections of material gathered together over a period of time; originally independent units have been stitched together, often with little attempt to weave them together into a coherent text. He claims that the same phenomenon is to

---

[28] Holtz, T., ' "Euer Glaube an Gott". Zu Form und Inhalt von I Thess 1,9f.', in Schnackenburg, R. (*et al.*), *Die Kirche des Anfangs. Festschrift für Heinz Schürmann zum 65. Geburtstag* (Leipzig: St. Benno-Verlag, 1977), 459–88, has similarly argued that 1 Th 1.9f. is not a piece of tradition but is composed from traditional phraseology.

be found in early Christian writings. In short, 'in the literary landscape of which the NT documents are a part, we find texts that exhibit clear marks of frequent and substantial editing. In their present form, the majority of these documents cannot be attributed to any single author' (Miller*, 49). Scribes treated texts as living traditions and continued to edit and add to them.[29] Against this background he develops the thesis that the PE are in fact collections of very diverse literary materials which were originally independent but have been loosely strung together in the manner of the Jewish wisdom literature; brief fragments of Pauline letters have thus been filled out to give the present form. The major part of his book is devoted to a 'compositional analysis' of the PE which aims to demonstrate the incoherence of the argument and the likelihood that different units have been edited and strung together without much regard to development of thought. The conclusion is that there was a 'school for Pastors' which possessed some authentic letters from Paul to Timothy and Titus which became the basis for the development of collections of material over a lengthy period of time and resulted in the compilations which are now known as the Pastoral Epistles.

Miller's case is unconvincing. Many of the examples of compositional processes which he cites, especially those from the NT itself, are very controversial and would not be accepted by many scholars. Other examples concern works that have been compiled or whose text has been transmitted over long periods of time, whereas in the case of the PE we are dealing with a comparatively short period. But above all the detailed argument for the incoherence of the PE and for the building up of the text from short units of material is simply not persuasive. The ensuing discussion, especially the exegesis in the commentary, will show that the hypothesis does not do justice to the actual contents of the letters. This is not to say that source material has not been used, but rather to insist that the documents have been composed in a much more coherent manner than Miller allows. In an Appendix to his book which deals with research subsequent to the completion of his thesis Miller notes how various scholars have found much more logic in the PE than he allowed (especially Karris, Fiore, Verner and Donelson) and has to concede that he may have overplayed his hand. Certainly Miller has shown that the author's thought is at times hard to follow, but his proposal

---

[29] Cf. Mayer 1913:68 *et passim* who finds various later additions in the text of the PE (e.g. 1 Tim 3.11, 12; 5.5–7) but without any solid justification.

cannot account for the degree of order and logical structure found by many commentators.

III. THE QUESTION OF A LOGICAL STRUCTURE

The type of view that has just been described is a counsel of despair. However, Hanson himself offers us some hints which may point in a different direction. His second comment, which was about the presence of a 'sandwich' structure at certain points in the letters, indicates that there is at least some elementary arrangement of the material into longer sections. Again, his observation that the author has a habit of concluding one section with language which forms the springboard for a new topic may point to some kind of technique of connected composition in the letters. These two hints, together with the fact that the author was not simply piecing together traditional written sources in alternating blocks, suggest that we may be justified in looking for a greater degree of structure in the letters.

Attempts to do so have been made by many other commentators. What purports to be a new approach has been developed by linguists and translators working with the Summer Institute of Linguistics[30] (Blight*; Smith and Beekman*; Banker*).[31] The novelty of this approach is that it attempts to work in a more scientific and ordered manner by breaking down a text into its smallest semantic components and then considering the internal structure and purpose of each and seeing how they relate logically to one another. Sections are established by looking for signs of coherence and boundaries, and within each section an attempt is made to classify its character, role and purpose. The various types of semantic relationship are classified and used to see how each unit relates to the next. The task is carried out in the smallest detail so that every word and phrase is examined, and the results are depicted in chart form at different levels of detail. As a result a text can be divided up at various levels into parts, divisions, sections and paragraphs, and the semantic relationships between them can be established. The general approach commends itself as sensible and well founded, but it can never be fully objective in its results. An element of subjective judgement is inevitable.

---

[30] The SIL is a group of scholars engaged in translation of the Bible into tribal languages. They have developed their analysis of the progress of thought in the various NT books as an aid to translators.

[31] Banker's work is a revision of the earlier treatment by Kopesec, M., *A Literary-Semantic Analysis of Titus* (Preliminary Edition; Dallas: Summer Institute of Linguistics, 1980).

TABLE 5

ANALYSES OF TITUS

Bernard	Lock	Spicq	Brox	Banker	Quinn
1.1–4	1.1–4	1.1–4	1.1–4	1.1–4	1.1–4
1.5–9	1.5–3.11	1.5–16	1.5–16	1.5–3.14	1.5–3.11
				1.5–3.11	
	1.5–16		1.5	1.5	1.5–16
			1.6–9	1.6–9	1.5–9
1.10–16			1.10–16	1.10–3.11	
				1.10–16	1.10–16
2.1–15	2.1–15	2.1–3.11	2.1–3.7	2.1–14	2.1–3.11
2.1–10		2.1–10	2.1–10		2.1–10
2.11–15		2.11–15	2.11–15	2.15	2.11–14
3.1–7	3.1–8	3.1–11	3.1–7	3.1–8c	2.15–3.11
3.8–11			3.8–11	3.8d–11	2.15–3.2
	3.9–11				3.3–8a
					3.8b–11
3.12–14	3.12–15	3.12–15	3.12–15	3.12–14	3.12–15a
3.15				3.15	3.15b

a. The structure of Titus

If we ignore analyses of the type offered by Hanson, 47, who sees nothing more than 'an ingenious pastiche', we find that other commentators divide up the epistle into two or three main sections or into a larger number, in each case with possible subdivisions. For a comparison of representative analyses of this kind see Table 5.[32]

The identification of the opening and closing epistolary elements causes no problems. All agree that 1.1–4 is the salutation and 3.15 is the closing greeting. 3.12–14 stands on its own as specific information and instruction for Titus. It is obviously not a dispensable part of the letter, but is an integral part of it though not its main point. Banker*, 8f., regards it as a second main division of the letter, coordinate with 1.5–3.11, but this is probably too formal an understanding of it. It is perhaps best

[32] It is recognised that simply tabulating the divisions proposed by a commentator cannot be as helpful as giving the actual headings proposed by them which help to show why the various units have been identified. However, the tables may serve at least the limited purpose of demonstrating the variety of divisions made by scholars.

regarded as an integral element in the letter form separate from the main teaching 'body'.

When we come to the body proper of the letter in 1.5–3.11 the divisions are not so clear. It may be most helpful to frame our remarks in the form of a response to Banker's analysis. Banker divides this into three sections, 1.5; 1.6–9; 1.10–3.11, the last of which is subdivided into 1.10–16; 2.1–14; 2.15; 3.1–8c; 3.8d–11. There are thus essentially seven units in this analysis.

A.	1.5	The theme of the division stated. Titus is to complete what remains to be done in Crete. (This is then developed in the following sections.)
B.	1.6–9	Titus is to appoint leaders.
C.	1.10–16	Titus is to rebuke the harmful leaders.
D.	2.1–14	Titus is to teach believers to live consistent lives.
E.	2.15	Titus is to teach with full authority.
F.	3.1–8c	Titus is to remind believers to behave appropriately towards everyone.
G.	3.8d–11	Titus is to avoid divisions and resist divisive people.

We thus have seven sections which appear to be of equal weight in the analysis, but in fact the first is introductory and the last is summarising. Effectively, therefore, there are five parallel pieces of instruction to Titus in 1.6–9; 1.10–16; 2.1–14; 2.15; and 3.1–7.

This analysis is open to some criticism. We may begin by recognising with virtually every commentator a break of some kind at 1.16/2.1 where a new section on how to instruct the various members of the church begins. Within the preceding section (1.5–16) Banker recognises that in terms of surface structure 1.5 belongs closely with what follows, but he argues that its semantic relationship to what follows justifies us in treating it as a separate division constituent. That is to say, 1.5, 'complete what is lacking', stands as a theme for the whole of the body of the letter and not just for the section on the appointment of elders (Banker*, 32f.). Banker is not working simply in terms of grammatical and syntactical connections; he is also looking for the underlying logic of content, and therefore is prepared to dispense with syntactical considerations where necessary. The crucial point here is whether (a) the author's horizon in 1.5 is confined to the appointment of elders; or whether (b) he had in mind the whole of the following instructions; or whether (c), although the author has not actually intended it, we can in fact regard 1.5 as functioning as a general heading for all the material that follows. Since in general NT writers do not offer headings within their writings, I am tempted to argue that 1.5 is not intended to function as a heading for the body, as Banker takes it, but is rather the introduction to the section about appointing elders; however, the rest of the body can certainly be regarded as further instruction on this broad theme. Banker's analysis is not convincing here because of the assumption that 'a well-structured written communication, *such as is found in the New Testament books* [my italics], consists of *semantic units*, arranged in a *hierarchical system*' (Smith and Beekman 1981:1). The assumption here, which is not defended by argument, is that the books of the NT are necessarily 'well-structured written communication[s]'.[33]

(a) 1.(5) 6–9 form one connected unit (despite a syntactical break). Then 1.10–12 is a unit which explains why the specific instruction in 1.9b is given. In 1.13–16 the author tells Titus himself how to deal with the opponents, and what to say to them, and gives a further description of them. Verses 13–16 go quite closely with the description in 1.10–12. Verses 10–12 serve the double function of explaining why elders with particular qualities must be appointed, namely in order to deal with the false teachers, and then giving the reason why Titus himself must deal sharply with the false teachers. Vs. 13–16 are tightly linked to what precedes, commenting on the citation in v. 12 and developing the theme of how the false teachers are to be treated. This means that the whole of 1.5–16 has a connected theme and should be regarded as a connected unit. Consequently the major break introduced by Banker at 1.9/10 is unjustified.

(b) 2.1–15 is a unified whole indicating what Titus is to teach the believers. It divides up after the general introduction in 2.1 into what he is to say to the old people, the young people and the slaves (2.2–10). This is followed by a general doctrinal backing for what has been said (2.11–14) and a final summing up for Titus (2.15). It is clear that this material all hangs together as one whole. Banker separates off 2.15 as a separate 'propositional cluster' because he thinks that it applies to the whole of 1.10–3.11, but in fact he recognises that the ταῦτα refers to the preceding material. It is thus not clear that it should be separated off to form a separate unit.

It should be noted that 2.10b forms the hook on which vs. 11–14 hang; the question that arises is whether 10b was deliberately inserted in order to form a transition to what the

---

[33] It would appear that the members of this school fall into the opposite error from Miller and assume total coherence in the NT documents. Both ends of the spectrum are vulnerable to criticism, and the truth lies somewhere in between.

writer intended to say or whether vs. 11–14 were added as an afterthought suggested by the theme in 10b. This question frequently arises where we have this kind of catchword connection between sections. Since the three subsections each end with a statement of purpose (2.5b, 8b, 10b), it is best to conclude that the doctrinal digression is quite deliberate and qualifies the whole of 2.1–10 rather than being an afterthought tagged on to v. 10b.

Although v. 15 functions as a return to the point after an apparent digression, it in fact adds some new thoughts about the authority with which Titus is to act; it is thus not simply an empty marker.

(c) The set of instructions might now appear to be complete, but there is a fresh start in 3.1–2, giving instructions to the whole congregation about behaviour towards other people. It is not immediately obvious why this teaching was not included immediately after 2.10, especially when the teaching in 2.1–10 takes into consideration the influence of believers on the society around them. However, it should be noted that in 2.1–8 we have not so much a *Haustafel* as rather a *Gemeindetafel*; it deals with different relationships within the church rather than within the family. Then in 3.1–2 we have instruction about relationships between believers and the world in general. This difference in theme explains the discontinuity and the fresh start. The instruction is grounded in a doctrinal argument in 3.3–7, incorporating traditional material in the form of a trustworthy saying. Then in 3.8[34] there is a return to the theme of exhortation with a positive summing up, and this in turn leads by contrast to a comment to Titus on how to treat opponents (9–11). Thus 3.8–11 is instruction to Titus about how he is to act in the church.

We note how in this ch. there is a doctrinal basis for the ethical teaching introduced in the same way as in ch. 2. In both cases the theme is the gracious action of God, but whereas in ch. 2 the thought is more of living lives that are in accordance with the gospel, in ch. 3 the thought is more of showing graciousness to the sinful world, just as God did to us when we belonged to it. The section closes with a summary in 3.8, similar to that in 2.15 and introducing fresh thoughts. 2.1–15 and 3.1–11 are similarly constructed blocks of material, and are thus separable and of equal weight. The theme in ch. 3 is not very different from that in ch. 2; in both cases we have the instruction that Titus is to give positively to the church. 2.1 could well function as a theme for the whole of chs. 2–3.

---

[34] Commentators differ whether 3.8a and 8b belong with what precedes or with what follows. In any case there is general agreement that a new theme begins in 3.9. It seems much more likely that 3.8–11 form one section with the opening words acting as a bridge with what has just preceded.

We may also note how 3.9–11 are closely connected to 3.8 syntactically and revert to the theme of how Titus is to teach with special reference to the opponents (cf. also 2.15 for an implicit reference to opponents). The pattern is thus like that in ch. 1 in that teaching about what to do in the church in view of the presence of opposition is followed by a justification for the instruction and then by instructions on Titus's own role as church leader. This similarity in pattern confirms our view that 1.5–16 is one connected section.

This analysis may suggest at first sight that we have three main sections of equal weight. But the general similarity in theme between chs. 2 and 3 may rather indicate that they are two parts of one major section. The reference to the opposition in 2.15 and 3.9–11 indicates that the same background can be presupposed for chs. 2 and 3 as for ch. 1. With these points in mind we can offer our analysis of the Epistle (Table 4), which is closest to that offered with variations by Jeremias, Spicq and Brox. Banker's analysis has formed a useful basis, but I would see the relationship between the different divisions somewhat differently from him in terms of coordination and subordination.

It emerges that a simple scheme does not do justice to the writer's pattern of thought. He did not sit down to write a plan for his letter before he wrote it. He appears rather to have had certain topics on his mind and to have taken these up in a somewhat spontaneous manner. There is thus a certain looseness about the organisation of the letter. His style tends to repetitiveness. He gives a set of instructions, offers a basis for them in the facts of the situation or in a doctrinal statement, and then finds his way back to the level of exhortation; this leads to something like an *inclusio* pattern: commands, doctrinal/factual grounding, recapitulation. This is repeated in each chapter.

In the light of this consideration of the structure of the epistle we can comment on its purpose and character. Two points can be made. First the opening theme is the fact of opposition, characterised by empty talk with Jewish connections. This has to be dealt with – by the appointment of sound teachers, by Titus's own rebukes, and by disciplinary action where necessary. The fact of opposition runs right through the letter, and a concrete situation appears to be in mind. Second, there is the need for instruction of the church in what befits sound doctrine.[35] This is conveyed in instructions incorporating what Titus is to teach the various groups in the church, all concerned with

---

[35] Fee in particular has insisted that 1 Timothy is written with one purpose only, namely to deal with false doctrines and false teachers in the church; the same would appear to be true of Titus.

TABLE 6

PROPOSED ANALYSIS OF TITUS

OPENING SALUTATION (1.1–4)

BODY OF THE LETTER – INSTRUCTIONS TO THE CHURCH
LEADER (1.5–3.11)

    I. THE APPOINTMENT OF ELDERS AND THE DANGER FROM
    OPPONENTS (1.5–16)

        a. The appointment and duties of elders (1.5–9)

        b. The rise of opponents and how to treat them (1.10–16)

    IIA. TEACHING FOR THE CHURCH – HOW BELIEVERS ARE TO
    RELATE TO ONE ANOTHER (2.1–15)

        a. Preface (2.1)

        b. To older men (2.2)

        c. To older (and younger) women (2.3–5)

        d. To younger men (2.6–8)

        e. To slaves (2.9–10)

        f. The doctrinal basis for the preceding exhortation (2.11–14)

        g. Recapitulation (2.15)

    IIB. TEACHING FOR THE CHURCH – HOW BELIEVERS ARE TO
    LIVE IN SOCIETY (3.1–11)

        a. General social teaching addressed to all (3.1–2)

        b. The doctrinal basis for such conduct (3.3–7)

        c. Recapitulation; how to deal with the recalcitrant (3.8–11)

PERSONAL INSTRUCTIONS (3.12–14)

CLOSING GREETING (3.15)

behaviour, but all provided with a doctrinal basis. Thus the behaviour springs from the doctrinal teaching, and both are to be taught to the church.

The question which arises is whether the positive doctrine and practical teaching bear any relation to the heresy. Why does the author choose to address the groups of young and old, and slaves? The initial impression is that the writer deals first with the problem of the disruptive influences in the church in ch. 1. Then he turns from this topic to give positive teaching on Christian behaviour which he backs up by reference both to the gospel and to the sinful character of the pre-Christian life in 2.1–3.8. In the final admonition to Titus he stresses the need to concentrate on this positive teaching and to curb the activities of the disruptive elements (3.9–11). Teaching in sound doctrine without entering into controversy is the major antidote to heresy, opposition and disruption. Instruction in sober living and godly behaviour is appropriate over against the demoralising effects of the opposition. If this is the case, then the letter can be seen to have a unified theme. The theme of the letter is thus how Titus is to deal with a defective church situation in Crete. It is primarily about what he is to do in the church and the instruction which he is to give; material on his own personal demeanour as an example to the others (2.7) is mentioned only briefly.

b. The structure of 1 Timothy

Having established as far as possible how the writer's mind works in Titus, we can now advance to the more complex question of 1 Timothy. Here we note the same lack of unanimity among commentators (Table 5) as in the case of Titus.

Again it may be helpful to start with the broad outline of the literary-semantic analysis. Blight divides up the body of the epistle into five main sections.

1.3–20	Deal with the false teachers.
2.1–3.16	Instructions about conduct in the church.
4.1–16	Take heed to yourself as a teacher.
5.1–6.2	How to act towards different groups in the church.
6.3–21a	Follow Christian doctrine and complete your tasks.

This pattern gives an alternation between instructions about the church and instructions for Timothy personally with respect to his duties as a minister and a believer. Within this structure there are four thematic statements (1.18–19; 3.14–15; 6.13–14; 6.20), each of which gives a partial statement of the purpose of the letter. Further, a broad correspondence between 1.3–7 and 6.20–21c can be seen, giving a sandwich structure to the letter (Blight*, 7–11).

A different approach is adopted by Roloff, 48–50. He emphasises the importance of the letter-form and the three-cornered relationship of the writer, the recipient and the congregation. 1.1–20 is concerned with the writer and the recipient and the former's commission to the latter; similarly the concluding section (6.3–21) is concerned with the same relationship (with the exception of 6.17–19) and is in effect a peroration with a concluding recapitulation. The congregation is brought into the central 'body' of the letter. In chs. 2–3 there are general instructions which are meant directly for the congregation but mediated through Timothy. In 4.1–6.2 Timothy is told to place

TABLE 7

ANALYSES OF 1 TIMOTHY

Brox	Spicq	Holtz	Hasler	Blight	Roloff
					1.1–20
1.1–2	1.1–2	1.1–2	1.1–2	1.1–2	1.1–2
	1.3–3.13	1.3–4.11			
1.3–20	1.3–20	1.3–11	1.3–20	1.3–20	1.3–11
		1.12–4.11			1.12–17
					1.18–20
2.1–3.16	2.1–15		2.1–3.16	2.1–3.16	2.1–3.16
					2.1–7
					2.8–15
	3.1–13				3.1–13
	3.14–16				3.14–16
4.1–11	4.1–6.19		4.1–10	4.1–16	4.1–6.2
	4.1–16				4.1–11
			4.11–5.2		
4.12–5.2		4.12–6.21			4.12–6.2
	5.1–6.2b	4.12–16		5.1–6.2	
5.3–6.2		5.1–6.2	5.3–6.2		
6.3–21	6.2c–19	6.3–21	6.3–19	6.3–21	6.3–21
					6.3–10
					6.11–16
					6.17–19
	6.20–21		6.20–21		6.20–21

specific instructions before the congregation and these are concerned with particular problems which require the authority of Timothy to deal with them. Hence there is a difference in character between the two main parts of the body.[36]

We can begin our own analysis by separating off the epistolary greeting in 1.1f. and the closing greeting in 6.21b. There is a remarkable absence (on any hypothesis) of the normal concluding remarks, news and greetings such as we find in Tit and 2 Tim. The letter shares with Titus the absence of an opening thanksgiving.

[36] Oberlinner does not discuss the structure in the introduction to his commentary; his outline (Oberlinner, V–VI) is in essence identical with that of Roloff.

All commentators except Holtz make a major break at 1.20/2.1, and this is fully justified.[37] Within ch. 1 there is essentially teaching on one topic, the commission of Timothy to deal with heresy. There is a 'chiastic' pattern.[38]

A   Reminder to combat heresy, briefly described (1.3–7)
B   Explanatory comment on misunderstanding of the law (1.8–11)
B'   The gospel of grace illustrated by Paul's conversion (1.12–17)
A'   Timothy as a teacher contrasted with the heretics (1.18–20)

With 2.1 there is a clear break and an apparent shift of topic. We propose that here, as in Tit, the writer gives positive instructions regarding practices in the church which are being neglected or carried out in their wrong way because of the disruptive elements. Most commentators see a close connection between chs. 2 and 3, and regard 3.14–16 as a sort of postscript to what precedes.[39] 2.1–7 is about prayer for all people which is either being neglected or carried on in the wrong spirit. Verse 8 returns to the point of prayer after the danger of a digression. 9–15 is about women, their dress and their teaching, and their true way in life. An important question is how 2.8 and 9 are related. The most likely view is that after speaking in general terms about prayer in 2.1–7 (with a doctrinal undergirding in 2.3–7) the author deals with the way in which men must pray in v. 8 and then correspondingly with the way in which women must pray in vv. 9f. This is followed by a digression on the problem of women teaching in the church as a related topic. It seems clear that this teaching, though of general relevance to any church, is motivated by the disruption and unruliness in the church.

---

[37] Holtz takes a highly individual line. He divides the epistle into two main sections, 1.3–4.11, with the theme 'Fellowship in the church and the Lord's Supper', and 4.12–6.21, with the theme 'Preparation for the work of a pastor'. There is, however, no clear reference to the Lord's Supper in the first part of the letter, and some passages (especially 4.1–11) do not readily fall under this heading. Holtz subdivides his first main section at 1.11/12, but this seems to be very artificial.

[38] I use the term 'chiastic' for any type of pattern in which sections correspond in inverse order. Some writers distinguish chiasmus properly so called, in which there is a central pivotal theme (A B C B' A') from inverted parallelism (A B B' A'); cf. Gibson*, 58.

[39] An exception is Gibson*, 63f., who argues that this section is the starting point for the material dealing with how Timothy himself is to behave in the congregation.

Chapter 3 takes up a separate topic, introduced quite abruptly. The two sections on bishops and deacons clearly belong together. The section appears to be an encouragement to the right people to take on responsibility in the church, and, since the qualities desiderated are in general those said to be absent from the opponents the aim is clearly to install the right people. Verses 14–16 are a general comment which goes with the preceding instruction.[40] The emphasis on the function of the church to uphold the truth confirms our view that it provides a rationale for what precedes. It could almost form the conclusion of the body of a letter. Nevertheless, it is surely impossible to read what follows without bearing in mind that this section has just preceded it, and therefore it is justified to see it as in some sense a pivot between the two halves of the letter, even though it belongs more with what precedes.

The themes of chs. 2 and 3 are thus related, in that both deal with church order, but tackle different aspects of it. The question whether these are two subsections of a division dealing with church order or two separate divisions of the letter is probably unanswerable if not meaningless.

There is an abrupt fresh start at 4.1.[41] Some commentators make a further division at v. 10 (11) but others at the end of the chapter (4.16) or at the end of 5.2. Which of these possibilities is best? We see that 4.1–5 predicts a heresy, which is assumed to be already a danger, and offers an answer to it. 4.6–10 is in effect an admonition to Timothy to teach the truth and oppose heresy. Thus it continues essentially the same theme of godliness as opposed to heresy. 4.11 (12)–16 is personal advice to Timothy about how he is to conduct himself as a teacher. Then 5.1 introduces instructions regarding how to deal with specific people. It emerges that there are no grounds whatever for making a break at 4.11 (12) since the same theme of Timothy's personal conduct as a teacher continues.

There is a connection between this section and 5.1–6.2 in that Timothy's attitude toward the congregation is still in mind, but now the thought moves from the general to the particular.

---

[40] Spicq is unusual in dividing up the epistle into three main parts with 3.14–16 as the second of these, separating teaching which is more about the constitution of the church from material which is more in the nature of practical rules. However, the close links in 3.14 and 15a with what precedes show that the section is really the conclusion of the preceding topic rather than a section on its own. Nevertheless, his proposal does bring out the fact that the next part of the letter which deals with the need to oppose false teaching arises from the church's function of upholding the truth.

[41] On Holtz's view, which puts the break at 4.11/12 rather than 3.16/4.1 see above (note 37).

Treatment of the old and young is followed by sections on how to deal with widows (vv. 3–16), with elders (vv. 17–19), and with sinful members of the church (probably elders are primarily in mind, vv. 20–25); 6.1–2 discusses how to teach slaves. 6.3–10 then sum up with comments on the opposition and this slides over into discussion of the rich in general. Hence 5.1 to 6.2 at least forms a connected section.

It is concerned with classes of people who need special treatment and instruction. The chapter can hardly consist of 'standard' teaching set down aimlessly. There must be some motivation for it. We note that the same problem of how to deal with older and younger people also emerged in Tit. The discussion of widows is probably related to this. The implication is that there was a special problem with older people in a church where the leadership may have been in the hands of younger people. The problem of slaves taking undue advantage of their freedom in Christ is not surprising. As for 5.23, the instruction to Timothy about wine, the most probable explanation for its sudden insertion is that the sins of the elders which he was to rebuke included drunkenness (cf. 3.3, 8; Tit 1.7); Timothy himself, acting as an example to them, abstained from alcohol completely, but is advised that medicinal use is permissible.

The reference of 6.2b is most probably to all that precedes, and not just to the directions to slaves, especially since 6.3ff. clearly refers to a wider group than the slaves and in fact slides over into a discussion of the rich. Therefore a fresh section begins in 6.3 with an alternating pattern.

The false teaching, especially on riches 6.3–10;   6.17–19.
Timothy's own attitude and behaviour 6.11–16;   6.20–21a.

This suggests an A B A′ B′ pattern of alternation rather than Hanson's simple A B A′ sandwich. The apparent lack of unity in this section disappears when we note (with Lock and others)[42] that the problem is not the rich as such but the teachers in the church who want to be rich, and whom Timothy must not imitate.

This analysis suggests the structure set out in Table 8. The major difference from that proposed by Roloff and Oberlinner is that they both separate off 1.3–20 and 6.3–21 from the rest of the letter as personal instructions to Timothy. (There is also no break at 4.11/12 such as they make.) It is not a matter of great moment whether we have major or minor breaks at 1.20/2.1 and 6.2/3.

[42] Lock, 4.

TABLE 8

PROPOSED ANALYSIS OF 1 TIMOTHY

OPENING SALUTATION (1.1–2)

BODY OF THE LETTER – A. TEACHERS AND CHURCH LEADERS
(1.3–3.16)

    I. INSTRUCTION TO AVOID FALSE DOCTRINE (1.3–20)

        a. Forbid opponents to promulgate false teachings (1.3–7)

        b. The true purpose of the law (1.8–11)

        c. The source of Paul's power and commission (1.12–17)

        d. Renewal of commission to Timothy (1.18–20)

    II. INSTRUCTION ON PRAYER (2.1–15)

        a. Prayer for all people (2.1–7)

        b. Men and women at prayer and in the church meeting (2.8–15)

    III. QUALIFICATIONS FOR OVERSEERS AND DEACONS (3.1–13)

        a. Qualifications for overseers (3.1–7)

        b. Qualifications for deacons (3.8–13)

    IV. THE CHURCH AND THE MYSTERY OF THE FAITH (3.14–16)

BODY OF THE LETTER – B. THE ATTITUDE OF THE CHURCH
LEADER TO THE CHURCH AND THE GROUPS IN IT (4.1–6.21a)

    I. TIMOTHY'S DUTIES AS A TEACHER IN THE FACE OF
HERESY (4.1–16)

        a. The rise of heresy and the need for sound doctrine (4.1–5)

        b. The need for instruction that leads to godliness (4.6–10)

        c. Timothy as a teacher (4.11–16)

    II. THE TREATMENT OF VARIOUS GROUPS IN THE CHURCH
(5.1–6.2a)

        a. How to deal with the old and the young (5.1–2)

        b. Instructions about widows (5.3–16)

        c. Instructions about elders (5.17–25)

        d. Instructions about slaves (6.1–2a)

    III. TRUE AND FALSE TEACHERS CONTRASTED (6.2b–21a)

        a. Teachers with false doctrines and motives (6.2b–10)

        b. Instructions on true teaching (6.11–16)

        c. What to teach to the rich (6.17–19)

        d. Final warning to Timothy, summing up earlier themes
(6.20–21a)

CLOSING GREETING (6.21b)

The structure proposed here is closest to that of Spicq.[43] The body of the letter basically falls into two main sections 1.3–3.16 and 4.1–6.21a, with remarkably similar themes and patterns. In each case the writer starts with the fact of heresy. In Part I he deals with the heretical teachers and the consequent need to maintain the truth of the gospel. He then goes on to discuss what should happen in the church meeting and the kind of people who should be involved in leading the church. The section culminates in a justification of the instructions based on the character of the church as the pillar of the truth. Then in Part II the writer again starts with the fact of heretical teaching and over against this he again sets the need for exemplary behaviour and teaching by Timothy. This broadens out into a discussion of how to treat the various classes of people in the church including the elders, both good and bad. Finally, he again tackles the problem of how to deal directly with the false teachers, pointing out the errors of their motives and encouraging Timothy to be a true teacher.

This parallelism might suggest that two similarly structured documents (broadly speaking) have been linked together, but there is sufficient unity of theme between the two parts to suggest that they belong closely together.

We must now ask briefly what emerges about the purpose of the letter. We can trace a number of themes which motivate the writer: the need to defend and promote true doctrine; the need for church leaders to live by it themselves, especially the addressee of the letter; the need to administer the church in a way that upholds the truth. Thus the truth of the gospel is the broad theme – Timothy is to defend it against heresy; practise it in his own life; and develop a church order which is in harmony with and promotes it.

It is noteworthy that ch. 1 deals in very broad and vague terms with the doctrinal content of the heresy, though it develops the thought of the law; it is not till 4.1–3 that we get a more detailed account and even there the accent is on its ethical implications. It seems that the writer is more concerned with the practical effects of foolish teaching on Christian living rather than with attacking the teaching on a doctrinal and theoretical level. This may well suggest that there was little intellectual content to the false teaching and that it really was a farrago of nonsense.

---

[43] See the overview in Spicq, 826f.

We may thus identify the theme of the letter as the need to teach and minister and lead the church in such a way as to promote the gospel and to resist heretical teaching. All the sections of the letter lead to this end and serve this theme. Thus the letter has a similar aim to Titus. Moreover, we can see similar structural devices being used. The way in which the author seems to reach a conclusion and then starts again is notable, as is his use of an *inclusio* structure.

c. Chiasmus in 1 Timothy

A number of scholars have suggested the presence of chiasmus in the letter.[44] Bush* finds parallelism between 1.12–20 and 6.11–16, 20, 21 suggesting that these sections form an *inclusio*, and that in the former Paul mediates the gospel to Timothy whereas in the latter God himself is the one to whom Timothy is responsible. He identifies a number of markers in the text and analyses the body of the letter, 1.12–6.21a into 6 sections: 1:12–20; 2.1–3.15; 3.16–4.11; 4.12–6.2; 6.3–10 (+17–19, which is misplaced as a result of scribal error); 6.11–16, 20, 21a. The similarity of themes at the beginning and end of the letter is not surprising, given the fact that the letter as a whole is concerned with opposition and heresy; the proposed divisions, however, break the natural flow of the letter.

A more thorough-going chiastic structure is identified by Welch*:

```
1:1–20
    2.1–3.13
        3.14–4.16
    5.1–6.2
6.3–21
```

The essence of this structure is that a central personal admonition to Timothy is flanked by ecclesiastical and administrative material, which in turn is surrounded by matching introductory and closing sections. It has the merit of recognising the natural divisions in the letter, but the break at 3.13/14 rather than 3.16/4.1 is doubtful.

---

[44] Blight*, 86–95, also records a number of chiastic structures in 1 Timothy which were discovered by R. Smith. These are based on the observation of matching words. They do not affect the structure of thought in the letter and the basis for affirming them is not very convincing.

Gibson 1996 has elaborated on this scheme:

I. 1.1–20
      A 1.1–2
        B 1.3–7
          C 1.8–11
            D 1.12–17
              E 1.18
        F 1.19–20
II. 2.1–3.13
              G 2.1–10
                H 2.11–3.1a
                I 3.1b-13
    III. 3.14–5.2
                  J 3.14–16
                    K 4.1–5
                      L 4.6
                    K′ 4.7–11
                  J′ 4.12–5.2
  II′. 5.3–6.2
              I′ 5.3–25
            H′ 6.1–2
I′. 6.3–21
      F′ 6.3–10
          E′ 6.11–12
        D′ 6.12–16
      C′ 6.17–19
    B′ 6.20–21a
  A′ 6.21b

It will be clear that there are points at which this scheme does not work neatly, notably the fact that section G has no counterpart and the irregularity with the B and F sections. Further, the break at 5.2/3 is unnatural. Various sections do not really match one another (e.g. H and I with their counterparts).

No chiastic structure so far proposed appears to be cogent.

d. The structure of 2 Timothy

2 Timothy is the most difficult of the Pastoral Epistles to analyse, as is evidenced by the way in which the various commentators differ considerably from one another in how they do it (see Table 9). The literary-semantic analysis with its different levels of components is sufficiently complicated to need setting out separately (see Table 10).

TABLE 9

ANALYSES OF 2 TIMOTHY

Bernard	Dibelius	Spicq	Barrett	Brox	Oberlinner
1.1–2	1.1–2	1.1–2	1.1–2	1.1–2	1.1–2
1.3–5	1.3–18	1.3–2.13	1.3–5	1.3–18	1.3–5
1.6–2.13			1.6–18		1.6–14
					1.15–18
	2.1–3.9		2.1–4.5	2.1–4.8	
				2.1–13	2.1–7
					2.8–13
2.14–3.17		2.14–4.8		2.14–26	2.14–21
				2.22–26	
				3.1–9	3.1–9
	3.10–4.8			3.10–17	3.10–17
4.1–8				4.1–8	4.1–8
			4.6–18		
4.9–18	4.9–18	4.9–18		4.9–18	4.9–18
4.19–22	4.19–22	4.19–22	4.19–22	4.19–22	4.19–22

From a survey of the major commentators it can be seen that the main question is whether there are major breaks at 1.18/2.1, 2.13/14, 3.9/10, 3.17/4.1 and 4.8/9.[45] Does 2.1–13 form a section on its own, or does it go more closely with what precedes or with what follows? Strangely none of the commentators has a major break at 2.26/3.1; all put a break at 3.9/10 or have a long section extending both ways.

There is at least agreement that 1.1f. is the salutation and that 4.19–22 constitutes the closing greetings.

The opening greeting is followed by a thanksgiving in 1.3–5. The analogy of other letters shows that this often leads on to a main section with no strong break, and there is no need to regard it as a separate unit.[46] In this case the thanksgiving is because of the strength of Timothy's faith, and it forms the basis for further appeal. The appeal comes in 1.6–8, namely to keep his charisma in full flame and to take his share of suffering in

[45] Oberlinner, VII, follows the pattern found in Hanson of simply dividing up the letter into paragraphs with no hierarchical structure.

[46] Some commentators (Bernard; Guthrie; Barrett; Smith and Beekman*) put a major division at 1.5/6. They appear to be simply recognising that the element of thanksgiving is formally separable from what follows and not necessarily suggesting that 1.3–5 should be regarded as completely separate from 1.6ff.

TABLE 10

LITERARY-SEMANTIC ANALYSIS OF 2 TIMOTHY

1.1–2	Salutation	
1.3–4.18	Body of letter	
1.3–5	Introduction to body	
1.6–4.8	Instructions about Timothy's ministry	
1.6–7	Do your task fervently	
1.8–2.13	Be willing to suffer and teach the truth	
1.8–12	Be willing to suffer	
1.13.14	Preserve the truth	
1.15–2.2	Let God empower you and entrust the message to faithful people.	
1.15–18	Examples of faithlessness and faithfulness	
2.1–2	Provide for continuation of teaching	
2.3–13	Encouragement to endurance and suffering	
2.14–26	Reminders to teachers and to Timothy himself	
2.14–15	Summary	
2.16–19	Avoid foolish talk	
2.20–22	Avoid youthful desires	
2.23–26	Avoid foolish questions and teach truth	
3.1–9	The evils of the last days	
3.10–17	Do not turn away from what you have learned	
4.1–8	Preach the true message	
4.9–15	Do your best to come to me soon	
4.9–13	Do your best to come to me soon	
4.14–15	Be on your guard against enemies	
4.16–18	The Lord is faithful	
4.19–22	Closing greeting	

Christian witness. This appeal is strengthened and grounded (a) by a kerygmatic formula and (b) by a comment on Paul's own suffering and confidence in God. Then in 1.13f. there is a command to hold fast to the truth of the gospel. This is a different theme from that in 1.6–8, but it is closely related to 1.11f. and to 1.7. Holding fast to the truth of the gospel entails suffering for it. It is Paul's gospel, and therefore 1.15–18 follows appropriately. You must hold fast to my gospel because others have forsaken me – though on the other hand Onesiphorus was faithful. It looks as though we have a series of related commands in 1.6–12 and 1.13–18.

The next section, 2.1–6(7), then repeats some of these themes – be strong and take your share of suffering – but there is a new feature in v. 2 – pass on the gospel to faithful helpers. Here is the nearest thing to a mention of church order in the letter, but it is remarkably undeveloped and vague as compared with 1 Tim 3. The main theme is clearly Timothy's own ministry. Verse 3 reverts to the theme of suffering but adds the military metaphor. This is developed in 4, and then followed by two different metaphors in 5 and 6. Verse 7 can be regarded as a comment on what has just preceded or on what follows. With recent scholars I tend to prefer to see it as backward-looking.

It is clear that 2.8–13 belongs together. It starts as a reminder of the gospel, but the point is that it entails suffering for Paul – in accordance with a faithful saying.

The next unit is 2.14–21. In bearing witness to these things Timothy must encourage others not to engage in empty dispute, but to stick to the true word, for strife leads to ungodliness, as exemplified by Hymenaeus and Philetus. Despite their activities God's truth stands firm. It seems that vv. 20f. are linked to this as application. Then in 2.22–6 the theme of 'no strife' is resumed, in relation to opponents. Thus we can see that there is a theme running right through 2.14–26 which would encourage us to believe that this is one section, with some apparent digressions.

Our problem is how far these separate units can be grouped together. There is considerable repetition of basic material throughout them and the writer moves from one component to another in kaleidoscopic fashion. 1.3–14 flows smoothly without any noticeable break. 1.15–18 is a discrete unit and appears to act as a bridge between the preceding and following units. But it tends to belong with what precedes more closely. The matter is discussed further below.

By any account a new section starts at 3.1 with its description of ungodliness in the last days. This is surely a preparation for the following exhortation rather than an addition to what has just been said, and therefore it should be linked with what follows. Therefore the scheme of Dibelius-Conzelmann which puts a major break at 3.9/10 is wrong.

The section 3.10ff. starts with a basis for exhortation in Paul's own example which leads to the general truth that the godly will be persecuted while evil-doers prosper. So let Timothy hold fast to what he has learned, especially to Scripture. Fortified by this, Timothy will then preach faithfully, even though people may not listen (4.1–5). He holds the torch, for Paul's own work is over. Smith and Beekman regard 3.1–9, 10–17 and 4.1–8 as separate divisions, but despite the differences in style between them (description of evildoers; appeal to hold fast to the truth; solemn adjuration to faithful witness and ministry) they belong closely together.

It is clear that 4.9–18 is a section of personal instructions and news similar to Titus 3.12–14 and having a similar function; it makes little difference whether it be regarded as part of the conclusion to the letter or as a separate section at the end of the body.

Opinions differ about 4.6–8 in which Paul moves from exhortation to Timothy to a comment on his own position as one whose life work is finished. Although some scholars would put a break at 4.5/6 and regard 4.6–8 as introducing the material in 4.9ff., this seems improbable. Barrett, 118f., who adopts this division, regards the paragraph as a link between the charge to Timothy and the personal material. However, it seems better to regard the paragraph as primarily strengthening the appeal in the foregoing verses. The best view is that 4.6–8 with its statement that Paul's work is nearly over functions both to underline the importance of Timothy's faithfulness in ministry (4.1–5) and also to prepare for the personal request that follows. So we can make a break at 4.8/9. Clearly there is a sub-break at 4.15/16 where the instructions cease and are followed by personal news.

These considerations suggest the scheme given in Table 11. There are good grounds for dividing up the letter into major divisions rather than simply seeing a series of separate paragraphs.

This structure breaks the main teaching part of the epistle into four sections. Is it is right to go further and group these sections more closely in any kind of way? Possible combinations are:

1.3–2.13; 2.14–4.8 (Spicq)
1.3–18; 2.1–4.8 (Brox)
1.3–2.26; 3.1–4.8

We start from the fact that there is a major break at 2.26/3.1. There is a fresh start at 3.10, but 3.13 clearly refers back to 3.1–9, and 3.1–9 is pointless if it does not form the basis for some kind of exhortation (cf. 1 Tim 4). Therefore, 3.1–4.8 forms a connected series.

Although we have provisionally made a break at 1.18/2.1 (so Dibelius-Conzelmann; Brox; Barrett), there are strong verbal and contextual links between the two sections. But, although there is a smooth link at 2.13/14 (cf. similar links elsewhere), a new theme or stress appears here.

The problematic section for any analysis is 2.14–26. Spicq places a major break after 2.13, and regards 2.1–13 as summing

TABLE 11

PROPOSED ANALYSIS OF 2 TIMOTHY

SALUTATION (1.1–2)

BODY OF THE LETTER – TIMOTHY AS A CHURCH LEADER (1.3 – 4.8)

I. THE NEED FOR TIMOTHY TO SHOW COURAGE AND TO HOLD FAST TO THE GOSPEL (1.3–18)

    a. Thanksgiving for Timothy's faith (1.3–5)

    b. Appeal to Timothy to stir up the gift of the Spirit and not to be fearful (1.6–7)

    c. The need to hold firmly to the gospel which Paul preaches and for which he suffers (1.8–12)

    d. Injunction to hold fast to the gospel (1.13–14)

    e. Paul's foes and friends (1.15–18)

II. EXHORTATION TO BE STRONG AND TO ENDURE SUFFERING (2.1–13)

    a. Be strong and single-minded (2.1–7)

    b. Motivation for endurance (2.8–13)

III. THE CHURCH LEADER AND HIS OPPONENTS (2.14–26)

IV. UNGODLINESS AND THE CONSEQUENT NEED FOR FAITHFULNESS AND TRUTH (3.1–4.8)

    a. Prophecy of increasing ungodliness in the church (3.1–9)

    b. Paul's example and teaching, and the importance of Scripture (3.10–17)

    c. Closing charge to Timothy (4.1–8)

APPEAL TO VISIT PAUL SOON – CLOSING INSTRUCTIONS (4.9–18)

GREETINGS, REPETITION OF APPEAL TO COME, AND FINAL BLESSING (4.19–22)

up the material in ch. 1.[47] He then argues that, having spoken about Timothy's ministry in general, Paul now goes on to tell him how to deal with opponents and gives him a programme of action to deal with them (Spicq, 752). As he has to admit, however, there is a mixture of personal exhortations and official directives. Nevertheless, the tone is more practical here and concerns what Timothy is to do over against other people.

An alternative approach is that of Brox. 1.3–18 is a preface in which Timothy is given basic personal instruction. Then comes the main section of the letter (introduced by the address 'my child' in 2.1) with five sub-sections containing specific instruction on how to act in the church. This raises the question whether

[47] 'Cette section reprend d'une manière plus directe et plus vive les exhortations du chapître précédent et en donne une application concrète' (Spicq, 737).

ch. 1 stands on its own over against 2.1–4.8 and has more of a personal character. The weakness of his analysis lies in 2.1–13 which seems to be more concerned with Timothy's own need to be strong and ready for suffering.

A further consideration may be the possibility of an analogy with 1 Timothy with its twofold division of the main body at 3.16/4.1. I am thus tempted to see the epistle as falling into two main parts with the break at 2.26/3.1. The first part contains three sub-sections with the first and second of these belonging fairly closely together. The second main part is more tightly knit together.

However, it may be safest simply to think in terms of four main sections. There is a danger in trying to force a flowing letter into a rigid scheme, and in this case there is a middle way between establishing a logical development of material and finding nothing more than a loose coupling of related points.

It emerges from this survey that the epistolary situation is the imminent end of Paul's work. Therefore Timothy must replace him and must teach others also to continue the task. It is important that the instructions are not tied to a specific congregation or situation but refer to the church and its situation in the world generally. There is a situation of nominal Christianity in which people (a) reject the Pauline gospel; (b) indulge in wild doctrinal speculations; (c) live ungodly lives; and (d) attack defenders of the truth. In this situation Timothy must (a) live by the strength of the Spirit; (b) remember the gospel and testify to it; (c) not engage in strife; and (d) be strong because this course will involve suffering at the hands of so-called Christians. The whole epistle is dominated by this concern, and it forms a sustained message to Timothy about what he is to do personally. It is his personal bearing and teaching which are of prime importance. Only in 2.2 does the thought of preparing other people to teach come in. The horizon is the church itself, or, more precisely, Timothy's own place in it as a minister, and the world outside is not given a lot of attention, though evangelism is to be carried out.

This reflects a somewhat different outlook from 1 Tim and Tit where there is much more attention to the church and the various groups in it and how they are to behave. The dominant mood here is the 2nd-person imperative addressed to Timothy himself about his personal bearing. There is little or no instruction about what he is to tell others to do or what qualities are to be sought in them. It all remains on the level of general doctrinal and ethical teaching.

A further important question is concerned with the nature of the suffering that Timothy may have to endure. One gains the impression that the suffering is more due to opponents in the church than to the State. Timothy's task is to find faithful men – among a group of unfaithful Christians. Although Paul is admittedly treated as an evildoer (2.9) and is in a Roman prison, yet he has been abandoned by all (namely believers) in Asia (1.15; cf. 4.10, 14f. [?], 16). The dividing line between persecution from inside and outside the church can be at times a thin one. Do the unfaithful Christians line up with the world to persecute believers? It is interesting that there is no thought of persecution and suffering in Tit or in 1 Tim. This is a new feature in 2 Tim; the thought of church life involving suffering for loyalty to the gospel is again peculiar to this epistle – although the idea of the good fight is not peculiar (cf. 1 Tim 6.12).

The structure of the epistle thus confirms the impression that this writing is about the personal demeanour of the church leader as he suffers for the sake of the gospel and has little interest in church order; it thus stands on its own by contrast with the other Pastorals.

The structure too is different in kind. It falls into a series of units whose individual themes and logical relationships are less clear, and the thought is much more convoluted. Whether we are dealing with a real letter or with a carefully constructed artificial one, the structure in fact seems to me to reflect quite impressively the more random thoughts of an older man composing a letter under difficulties (perhaps with frequent interruptions and pauses) and filled with personal concern for his colleague and stands in contrast with the much more orderly, cooler tone of 1 Tim and Tit. It is more personal in character, and there is less impression of an 'official' letter which is really meant for the church; there is much less here than in the other Pastorals which could be regarded as out of place in a letter from a senior leader to a junior colleague with whom he has had close contact over many years.

5. THE OPPOSITION TO PAUL

Brox, 31–42; Dibelius-Conzelmann, 65–7; Donelson 1986:116–28; Dubois, J. D., 'Les Pastorales, la Gnose et L'hérésie', *Foi et Vie* 94 (1995), 41–8; Ford, J. M., 'A Note on Proto-Montanism in the Pastoral Epistles', *NTS* 17 (1970–1), 338–46; Goulder, M., 'The Pastor's Wolves. Jewish Christian Visionaries behind the Pastoral Epistles', *NovT* 38 (1996), 242–56; Haufe 1973; Hengel, M., 'Die Ursprünge der Gnosis und das Urchristentum', in Ådna, J. (*et al.*), *Evangelium Schriftauslegung Kirche: Festschrift für Peter Stuhlmacher zum 65. Geburtstag* (Göttingen: Vandenhoeck und Ruprecht, 1997), 190–223; Holtzmann, 126–58; Karris 1973; Lightfoot 1893:411–18; Lütgert 1909; MacDonald 1983; MacDonald 1988; Oberlinner [1996], 52–73; Rohde, J. 'Pastoralbriefe und Acta Pauli',

Studia Evangelica 5. (TU 103. Berlin: Akademie, 1968), 303–10; Roloff 228–39; Rudolph 1983:302f.; Schlarb 1990:59–141; Schmithals, W., 'The *Corpus Paulinum* and Gnosis', in Logan, A. H. B., and Wedderburn, A. J. M., *The New Testament and Gnosis: Essays in honour of Robert McL. Wilson* (Edinburgh: T. and T. Clark, 1983), 107–24; Spicq, 85–119; Thiessen 1995:317–38; Towner 1987; Wilson, R. McL., *Gnosis and the New Testament* (Oxford: Blackwell, 1968); Wisse, F. 'Prolegomena to the Study of the New Testament and Gnosis', in Logan and Wedderburn, *New Testament and Gnosis,* 138–45; Wolter 1988:256–70; Yamauchi, E. M. *Pre-Christian Gnosticism. A survey of the proposed evidences* (London: Tyndale Press, 1973).

If anything about the circumstances of the PE is clear, it is that their immediate occasion is the development of groups within the churches which are regarded as opposed to the authority and teaching of Paul. From a negative point of view, the PE may be regarded as basically responses to this situation. This evaluation, however, needs to be amended since by itself it may give the impression that the motive of the author is entirely negative and defensive, simply concerned with the refutation of error. It is clear that the main motivation of the author is the positive one of wishing to maintain the purity and truth of the gospel over against what he saw as distortions of it, because of his conviction that the gospel contains the saving truth by which the church stands. The concept of heresy is already clearly formulated.[48]

The identification of the opposition continues to be a matter of dispute, not least because the writer refrains from a direct confrontation with the teaching of his opponents. Nevertheless, the starting point must be to note its characteristics as presented to us in the letters. An immediate problem is whether we are dealing with the same basic phenomenon in all three letters. On the whole, this appears to be the more likely interpretation of the evidence. A further point is whether the writer is dealing with (a) a movement which belonged historically to the time of Paul (or foreseen by him as an impending danger) but which was still a danger to the churches (so Brox, 38f.); (b) a movement which belonged to a later period, presumably that of the writer himself (e.g. early second-century Gnosticism) although it may have had links with, or resemblances to, earlier movements (e.g. Donelson 1986:121); (c) a movement which is not to be linked with other known phenomena but is rather a vague, general description of a broad type of opposition to Paulinism or is indeed fictitious (Dibelius-Conzelmann, 66; this is a most unlikely possibility). In answering this question it will be important to see to what extent the opposition described in the letters can be compared with other known and datable movements.

[48] Marshall, I. H., 'Orthodoxy and Heresy in earlier Christianity', *Themelios* 2 (1976), 5–14; Skarsaune 1994.

I. GENERAL CHARACTERISTICS

a. The opposition is regarded as sizeable, is winning support and is dangerous. It has had considerable success, especially among the women. It does not appear to have become established in the recognised teachers of the church, but it has active proponents within the churches. Its success is so great that the writer considers it necessary to write letters which are largely motivated by the need to deal with it. He has also taken disciplinary action against certain proponents of it. The use of 'some' to refer to the opposition does not allow any conclusions regarding the number of people involved. Rather, the writer is dealing with a powerful movement which has already made serious inroads into the life of the congregations.

b. The opponents are engaged in teaching, both in the church meetings and in private conversations in people's homes. They talk a lot of nonsense and raise foolish controversies (Tit 1.10; 3.9; 1 Tim 6.3–5; 2 Tim 2.14–16; 2.23). This repeated comment may be taken in various ways. First, it may be regarded simply as a put-down without serious content. The writer is endeavouring to combat the heresy not by engaging in refutation of its views but by simply dismissing it as trivial and unimportant. He is pronouncing a value-judgement against it. Second, it may represent a fair judgement upon the views of the opponents. We may compare how it is very hard to see the rationale of much allegorisation and speculation in some modern forms of religion (like certain aspects of the New Age movement). Third, the aim may also be to stress the futility of the speculations, just as one might comment on the foolishness of much of the speculation in some modern sects which may divert attention from more important matters.[49] The effect was to relativise the teaching about the gospel and piety which the writer considered important. He did not want to enter into what he saw as endless argument that could never come to a conclusion and prevent people from coming to terms with what he regarded as central to the gospel. Anybody who has tried to argue with the door-to-door representatives of some modern cults will have no difficulty in appreciating his position. When the writer comments that the opponents deceive people (Tit 1.10; 2 Tim 3.13), he admits that the nonsense is plausible and takes people in; that is why it is dangerous. Nevertheless, the common view that the writer refuses to enter into any kind of discussion with his opponents

---

[49] Closer to mainstream Christianity we may compare the speculations of people like British Israelites or ultra-dispensationalists which divert people, otherwise orthodox, from the gospel.

is an overstatement; rather, entry into foolish and time-wasting speculations is forbidden (Tit 3.9 note).

c. However, when the writer comments that the opponents are deceived or under the influence of Satan (1 Tim 4.1; 2 Tim 2.26; 3.13), he is working on a different level, and drawing a theological conclusion from their false views, based on the accepted belief that Satan is 'the father of lies' and can influence people for evil. The comment tells us nothing about the actual character of the opposition. To attribute teaching to deceit in this way is simply to say that it is wrong without specifying how.[50]

d. Similarly, to say that the opponents reject the truth (Tit 1.14; cf. 1 Tim 6.5; 2 Tim 3.8; 4.4) and Paul himself (as the ostensible author) (2 Tim 1.15; 4.10, 16) may be simply a way of saying that their teaching is different from Paul's. However, the vigour of the remarks makes it more probable that there was active and open opposition to Paul and his teaching, just as there was in Paul's own lifetime. (This raises the question whether we can identify any specific Pauline teaching that was rejected.)

e. A particular criticism of the opponents is directed against their immorality (Tit 1.18; 2 Tim 3.1–5);[51] in particular, they are said to be greedy and to make money out of their teaching (Tit 1.11; 1 Tim 6.5–10). Their conduct is regarded as being similar to that of people who are not Christian believers (Tit 3.3; 1 Tim 1.13, 15), and it is the reverse of that which is commended to the readers and those who hold positions of leadership. Another way of putting the point is to say that their consciences are corrupted (Tit 1.15; 1 Tim 1.19; 4.2); again this is simply to ascribe a 'spiritual' basis for observable conduct and to condemn it.

There need be no doubt that this description is based on observation of the opponents, although some scholars have argued that it is nothing more than a stock blackening of character typical of ancient polemic (Karris 1973; cf. Spicq, 86–8). Some features may belong to this category, but it is difficult to believe that this explains all of the description; even Karris lists a minimum set of characteristics that are specific.

The danger of the opposition is that those who are attracted by it will fall into the same types of conduct. Common to all the letters is the danger of immoral conduct among church members and leaders (Tit 1.6–7; cf. 2.12; 1 Tim 3.1ff.; 5.6; 5.11; 2 Tim 2.22) as they revert to what they were like before their conversion.

---

[50] Spicq, 104–10, detects magical practices in 2 Tim 3.13 (cf. 3.8). While this is possible, the evidence is not strong, and in any case there is no emphasis upon it (cf. Karris 1973:560f.).

[51] The combination of preaching asceticism and practising sexual immorality is well attested (Lucian: *Fugitivi* 18f.; in Karris 1973:554).

II. SPECIFIC CHARACTERISTICS

It is not surprising that hard details about the views of the opponents are difficult to find in the letters. We list four clear points (a.–d.), followed by five others (e.–i.) that are more disputable.

a. The teaching was related to Judaism. All three letters indicate that the opponents held to Jewish myths (Tit 1.14; 1 Tim 1.4; cf. 4.7; 2 Tim 4.4 [the identification as 'Jewish' is admittedly absent here]). In Tit they are associated with circumcision (Tit 1.10), and in 1 Tim they themselves profess to teach the law (1 Tim 1.7).

These elements belong together, and it is therefore plausible that we have a group of Jewish Christians (and/or circumcised Gentiles) who were teaching the Jewish law and developing myths on its basis. Nevertheless, there is no specific attack on circumcision in the letter and no indication that there was a dependence upon 'works of the law' for salvation.

It should be emphasised that in both 1 Tim and Tit this is the first thing that we read about the opponents, and it is presumably intended to colour our reading of what follows.[52]

b. The opponents encouraged ascetical practices. The specific examples named are the forbidding of marriage and the eating of (some) foods (1 Tim 4.3; cf. Tit 1.15; 1 Tim 5.23). The latter refers to permanent abstinence from certain foods on principle rather than to temporary fasting from all foods.[53] It appears to be connected with ritual requirements regarding purity (Tit 1.15). The attractiveness of widowhood to certain women and the probable unwillingness to bear children by others (1 Tim 2.15) may fit into this context.

c. The opponents claimed to know God (Tit 1.16; cf. 1 Tim 6.20 for a knowledge falsely so-called[54]). This is not a particularly specific statement, and it is paralleled in NT Christianity generally. In particular, it is a Jewish claim (Rom 2.20; Thiessen 1995:324). Nevertheless, it may reflect a claim that the only, or the true, way to know God was through acceptance of the teaching and practices of the opponents. 2 Tim 3.7 indicates that teaching played an important part.

---

[52] For this reason the attempt of Roloff* to play down the Jewish character of the movement is immediately open to criticism.

[53] See discussion at 1 Tim 4.3.

[54] To say that this verse explicitly names the heresy as 'Gnosis' (Rudolph 1983:302; Hengel*, 190–2) is mistaken. The reference is rather to the knowledge claimed by the heretics. The term is first attested as the name of a religious movement in the title of Irenaeus' 'Refutation and Subversion of Knowledge falsely so called', which echoes the phraseology here (Hengel, *ibid.*, 193f.).

d. They said that the resurrection was past (2 Tim 2.18).
Various scholars identify this statement as the main key to understanding the position of the opponents. Yet its force is hard
to establish. One possibility is that the spiritual resurrection
associated with baptism in Pauline teaching was understood as
the only resurrection. Another view is that the resurrection of
Jesus meant that the new age had fully come and that believers
must now live the life of the world to come; physical marriage
was no longer appropriate and restrictions on food and drink
may have been tied in. However, the way in which the author
states that this view was upsetting some believers suggests rather
that the stress lay in part, at least, on the denial of a future
resurrection.

e. Arising out of statements about the resurrection being past
is the somewhat speculative suggestion that the opponents were
practising some form of 'enthusiasm'. This term is vague, but
appears to refer to a kind of outlook which ignores the realities
of life in the physical world (illness and death) and/or claims
some kind of special inspiration by the Spirit or other divine
powers.[55] The alleged lack of emphasis on teaching about the
Spirit in the letter has been seen as the author's attempt to play
down the place of the Spirit over against exaggerated claims to
possession of it. However, there is no clear indication of any
special claims to the Holy Spirit, nothing corresponding to
Bishop Joseph Butler's 'Sir, this pretending to revelations of the
Holy Spirit is a very horrid thing.'[56]

f. The opposition may have encouraged the participation of
women in teaching and other forms of church life. They certainly
attracted women by their house-to-house visiting. The implication
that some women were devoting themselves to teaching instead
of to the rearing and upbringing of children is a reasonable one.
One of the reasons for the prohibition of women teaching in
1 Tim 2 is because of their association with the heresy; otherwise, the mention of Eve as the one who was deceived is left
unmotivated.

g. The stress placed upon Paul as a preacher of the gospel to
the Gentiles (1 Tim 2.7; cf. 3.16) and upon the fact that salvation
is available for 'all' (1 Tim 2.4–6; 4.10; Tit 2.11) may indicate
that the opposition was Jewish-Christian in outlook and at least
attached little importance to the Christian mission to Gentiles.
They may have insisted to such an extent on Jewish and ascetical
practices that their form of Christianity had little appeal to
Gentiles.

[55] Cf. especially Schlarb 1990:93–131.
[56] Karris 1973:557f. comments on the lack of clear evidence that the opponents
claimed 'to be prophets or to be especially endowed with the Spirit'.

h. Linked with this is the fact that in the kerygmatic statements in 2 Tim 1.9; Tit 3.5 there is an explicit rejection of human 'works' as the basis for God's gracious saving act in Christ. This rejection is of human works in general, and, while its origin is undoubtedly in Pauline teaching against Jewish 'works of the law', it has here been generalised and there is no specific application to Judaism. It must, therefore, remain questionable whether 'works of the law' are specifically in focus. It seems unlikely that a specific application would not have been made if Jewish works were being made a condition or essential accompaniment of salvation.

i. The reference to the manhood of Jesus (1 Tim 2.5) may be directed against a docetic understanding of his person. The same emphasis has sometimes been identified in 1 Tim 3.16. However, the latter passage is more plausibly interpreted in terms of the universal, cosmic significance of Jesus Christ.

III. IDENTIFYING THE OPPOSITION

The problem now is to identify the character of this opposition and to relate it to other known movements.

a. The Jewish basis[57]

The links of the opposition to some form of Judaism are very clear. They themselves claim to be teachers of the law. Esoteric speculations based upon the OT, and specifically upon the Pentateuch, are known. Asceticism was common in various Jewish groups, including the Qumran sect. Here it is explicitly based on 'commandments' (Thiessen 1995:319). The claim to know God is common and is associated with the accusation that the Gentiles do not know God (Thiessen 1995:320). The lack of openness to the Gentiles could well be Jewish. A Jewish basis for the opposition is thus beyond question. However, this can be only part of the story. Two factors which give pause to identifying the opposition *simpliciter* with some form of Judaising Christianity are the teaching about the resurrection and the freedom given to women. Neither of these is particularly Jewish.[58]

[57] See especially Spicq, 85–119.

[58] The stress on the OT as a source for myths and legends is sufficient in itself to rule out the possibility of Marcion or his followers forming the opposition. Marcion regarded the OT god as a demiurge and presumably downplayed the law. It is thus inconceivable that the opponents here are Marcionites. They are also opposed to Paul; one can hardly claim, therefore, that they are pro-Paulinists (like Marcion) whom the author is trying to detach from their claims to be the true Pauline succession.

b. The Pauline mission and its opponents

We are dealing with Christian groups in an area influenced by Paulinism. Three factors are relevant here. First, throughout the historical Paul's mission he was opposed by groups of Jewish Christians. Second, Paul's own teaching about the death and resurrection of believers with Christ (Rom 6) and about the oneness of men and women in Christ (Gal 3.28) was easily open to misunderstanding. Third, various elements in the pattern of opposition in the PE can be traced earlier. Stress on the law is found in the Judaistic opposition to Paul, especially as reflected in Romans, Galatians, Philippians and Colossians. Misunderstanding of the resurrection in one form or another is seen in 1 Corinthians and Philippians. In Philippians 3 we have people who claim to be already 'perfect', in a context where Paul talks of his own desire to attain to the resurrection. Restrictions on foods are attested in Romans, 1 Corinthians and Colossians, and sexual asceticism is seen in 1 Corinthians.

Consequently, all the factors in the situation can be accounted for in terms of a combination of Jewish and Christian elements. Morever, there is nothing which requires us to postulate a significant difference in time from that of Paul himself. What must be stressed is that the phenomenon is not simply 'judaising', as if the opponents were simply introducing Jewish beliefs and practices into the church. They are, after all, Christians, and it is the combination of a non-Pauline version of Christianity, including perhaps misunderstanding of Paul's teaching, with a Judaising outlook, that creates the unusual character of their teaching. The way in which the PE insist that the Pauline 'deposit' is given to Timothy may suggest that the opposition also claimed to be based on Paul's authority. However, the PE also refer to people who were opposed to Paul and disciplined by him.

c. An early form of Gnosticism?

The most widely supported alternative view is that the opposition is a form of second-century Gnosticism, probably in a relatively undeveloped stage which could have arisen in the late first century.[59]

---

[59] Supporters of this view are legion: cf. Yamauchi*, 49: 'there is near agreement ... that the heresy which was combatted in these books was some form of Gnosticism.' See especially Roloff; Oberlinner; Goulder* for the most recent expositions of this hypothesis. An important early defender was Lightfoot* who argued for the closeness of the heresy to the teaching of the Ophites according to the account in Hippolytus. Lütgert 1909 saw the close resemblances between the situation in the PE and in Corinth and found in both an early form of Gnosticism.

The hypothesis has been defended in detail by Haufe*. He claims that the opponents held to what he calls an enthusiastic soteriology which saw baptism as burial and resurrection with Christ and argues that it must be *assumed* that the motif of redemptive *gnosis* was linked to this understanding of baptism. But this assumption is unfounded and with it the scheme collapses.

Similarly, Schmithals* holds that the basic element is 'an enthusiastic and spiritualistic posture': the resurrection has been spiritualised and the opponents believe that they belong to the limited group who experience the redemption of their bodies and (in the mind of the author) are self-conceited. From this enthusiasm flow their ascetic tendencies and depreciation of creation, and their desire for emancipation from the earthly, and their disinterest in the life of the world. They may have denied the humanity of Jesus. The reference to myths and genealogies may be to an attempt to distance God the Creator from the evil world by postulating intervening aeons.

Roloff, 234, likewise defends a Gnostic basis. For him the crucial factors in a coherent unified package are: the ascetic attitude reflecting a hostile view of the creation; the esoteric, speculative elements in the teaching; and the marginal place of legalistic Jewish elements; the catchword 'Gnosis'. Thus we have a dualistic system offering salvation in the form of deliverance from the evil world. It grew up in the Pauline milieu and had close links to the Colossian 'philosophy' and to the heretical movements in Asia reflected in Rev. Roloff postulates that the opponents saw the Creator of the world as a hostile, destructive power, but this is to go well beyond what the evidence says. He also plays down significantly the Jewish elements in the opposition in a way that does not seem to be justified.

Goulder* holds that the opponents were Jewish Christian Gnostic visionaries. Their asceticism created the capacity to receive visions. The stress on the invisibility of God is taken to be a denial of the reality of their visions. The 'knowledge' to which the opponents laid claim is alleged to have been based on visions. Their principal false belief, however, was a Cerinthian, docetist view of Jesus: Christ was merely a heavenly power who came temporarily upon Jesus. There was no bodily resurrection and presumably no parousia. In short, they were a group closely akin to the earliest Barbelo Gnostics.

In assessing this hypothesis we must start from what we know for certain about Gnosticism, namely its existence as a second-century phenomenon.[60] There is scholarly agreement

---

[60] Wilson* 1968:22.

that, whatever else it is, Gnosticism is 'a unique form of religion found in second-century sects, teaching devolution in godhead leading to creation, a dualistic view of man, [and] salvation by knowledge' (Messina definition). This definition leaves open the possibility that Gnosticism existed in the first century and recognises that it existed in various forms. The problem is how Gnosticism developed and at what stage the developing embryo can be regarded as properly Gnostic.

The usual answer is that Gnosticism is in effect a group of beliefs joined together in a particular constellation, and that it is present where this constellation is needed in order to account for the phenomena in the text. That is to say, the constellation itself need not be explicit, but its implicit presence must be postulated to explain the author's structure of thinking (symbolical universe) as it expresses itself in what he writes. The likelihood of Gnosticism being present is naturally all the stronger when it is known to have been part of the environment of a document.

In contrast to this situation is the presence of various individual elements which formed part of Gnosticism, whether aspects of the fundamental mind-set or specific offshoots from it, but without sufficient evidence for the actual Gnostic package as a coherent whole. Ideas may be present individually which could be part of Gnosticism but which may be part of other systems of thought. Thus the asceticism which is found in the PE could certainly be part of a Gnostic outlook, but it could equally well be found independently; the Gnostics had no monopoly on asceticism.[61] Further, there must have been a period during which some of the elements that came to form the Gnostic package were developing but had not yet assumed their Gnostic identity. It is, therefore, possible that apparent Gnostic elements in the PE belong to this pre-Gnostic period. (We should also remember that the development of Gnosticism in one area of the ancient world does not allow us to assume automatically that it was universally present.)

The difficulty of solving the problem is exacerbated by the persistence of hypotheses regarding the presence of Gnosticism in different areas of the first-century church and as an influence upon some NT writers. The hypothesis of the existence of Proto-Gnosticism, i.e. of 'full' (but as yet not fully developed) Gnosticism in the first century, is still common. It is more likely however, that what we have is rather the presence of 'Pre-Gnosticism', i.e. of elements that later went to make up the

---

[61] Wilson*, 42 notes: 'Here again, then, we have something which may be Gnostic *in a Gnostic context*, but is not necessarily to be employed as a primary criterion for the detection of Gnostic influence.'

Gnostic package but which are not yet themselves compounded together in the characteristically Gnostic fashion.[62]

Thiessen 1995:317–38 has shown convincingly that the characteristics of the opposition in the PE can all be understood in terms of a form of Jewish Christianity without recourse to Gnosticism (similarly, Dubois*). In the case of the PE there is not the slightest evidence that the negative view of creation taken by the opponents was based on a belief in devolution in the godhead. The writer does not have to prove to them that the world was created by God rather than by some demiurge, but simply that all of God's creation is good (1 Tim 4.4). There is nothing especially Gnostic or dualistic about their view of man; the dualism of flesh and spirit is common to the NT. And, although 'knowledge' plays a part, there is no stress on salvation by knowledge.[63] The denial of a future resurrection is already found reflected in 1 Corinthians.

According to Wisse* scholarship has gone astray in trying to define the basic teaching of Gnosticism, and he suggests that we should think simply in terms of their 'élitist, esoteric, syncretistic and anti-authoritarian attitudes ... [their] intense acosmic and ascetic spirit'. Adoption of this definition enables us to include easily the opponents in the PE who were difficult to include on the older principle. Such a broad 'definition' is surely a counsel of despair.

d. An ascetic movement?

Scholars who are dissatisfied with the Gnostic hypothesis have drawn attention to the existence of an ascetic movement in the early church. The *Acts of Paul* is a second-century document which promotes celibacy and assigns a prominent place in the church to women. Continence and asceticism are the path to divine approval. The belief that the resurrection has already taken place in that believers have come to know the true God is attested. What is going on here is more like a radical apocalypticism than Gnosticism.

D. R. MacDonald (1983) has developed the thesis that the PE are directed against the kind of picture of Paul and his teaching which was later gathered together in the *Acts of Paul*.[64]

---

[62] Admittedly, the leading contemporary scholar in this field rejects this distinction (Rudolph 1983:24f.).

[63] The use of ἐπίγνωσις and ἐπιγινώσκω is characteristic of the writer's own understanding of salvation, and is fully in line with pauline thinking. There is, however, a false γνῶσις (1 Tim 6.20) which is to be rejected; it is not, however, linked directly with salvation.

[64] Cf. earlier Mayer 1913:70–4 (cf. Rohde 1968:303).

The thesis is reiterated by M. Y. MacDonald 1988:181–3 and Young 1994:13–23 (cf. Verner 1983). It is questioned by Davies 1996:86f., who notes that the teaching about women in the PE merely reflects standard conservative attitudes in the first century over against the new attitude in the church in which women might serve publicly alongside men. But Davies' argument only explains the teaching of the author of the PE and does not account for the combination of asceticism/celibacy and the role of women which is found in the opponents, and the MacDonald explanation at least provides a parallel to this. But it does not necessarily follow that the PE are to be set as late as this theory may seem to require. Ascetic practices were evidently a problem in the church from an early date.[65]

e. Conclusion

Despite the widespread support which it has received, we conclude that the identification of the heresy in the PE as a form of Gnosticism is not only an unnecessary hypothesis but also a distortion of the evidence. A combination of the Jewish, Christian and ascetic elements suffices to explain the nature of the opposition in the PE. We have to do with a group of Jewish Christians, perhaps travelling teachers with an ascetic streak, who were active within the Pauline mission area. They attached importance to the law, which they interpreted allegorically, and from it they derived a radical set of ascetic restrictions regarding purity. They claimed that they alone possessed true knowledge of God, and they also claimed that Christian conversion was tantamount to a resurrection from the dead which apparently replaced the hope of a future resurrection. It is probable that their teaching appealed to women who were able to enjoy a greater degree of emancipation from married life and domestic duties than in more orthodox forms of Christianity. That they claimed a special endowment with the Spirit and in this sense were 'enthusiasts' is not attested. As Jewish Christians they appear to be have been unenthusiastic for the Gentile mission. The effect of their teaching was to remove Christ from his central position as the Saviour and the mediator between God and humankind. Their religion had become a matter of speculations and discussions which were diverting people from what in the eyes of the author really mattered. He attacks them for their greed for money and for their immorality generally.

---

[65] Rohde*, 303f., supposes that the *Acts of Paul* would need to be earlier than the PE for this hypothesis to work, but the attitudes expressed there could be earlier than the documents in which they appear.

6. THE ECCLESIASTICAL SITUATION

Bartsch 1965; Kertelge 1972:140–51; Lohfink, G., 'Die Normativität der Amtsvorstellungen in den Pastoralbriefen', *TQ* 157 (1977), 93–106; Mussner, F., 'Die Ablösung des apostolischen durch das nachapostolische Zeitalter und ihre Konsequenzen', in Feld, H., and Nolte, J. (eds.), *Wort Gottes in der Zeit* (FS K. H. Schelkle) (Düsseldorf: Patmos, 1973), 166–77; Sand 1976:215–37; Schlier 1977.

The PE are ostensibly addressed to Timothy and Titus who are depicted as having some kind of pastoral responsibility for Christian congregations in Ephesus and Crete respectively. Although these pastors are the nominal recipients of the letters, there is much to suggest that 1 Tim and Tit were intended to be overheard by the local leaders in these congregations and probably by the ordinary members as well. The character of much of the contents, which has been regarded as material that should have been familiar to experienced leaders, suggests that part of the function of the letters was to give instruction ultimately meant for the congregations. This would not be surprising in 'mandates' which state the functions of an agent in relation to the group over which he is placed. Alongside the opposition to Paul, therefore, a second element in the situation is the state of development of the churches depicted in the PE.

Although questions of church 'order' are important in the PE, they are by no means central. Approximately one sixth of the letters is taken up with church order in the strict sense, i.e. the appointment of leaders and related matters.[66] Despite earlier arguments in favour of the suggestion (Bartsch 1965), it is not possible to identify some kind of manual of church order or stereotyped material of this kind behind the letters. There is nothing to prove that an existing church order is being drawn upon in the sections which list the qualities desirable in an overseer or deacon, especially since the style is that of the author of the PE. Clearly there has been some development in the organisation of the church from the period of Paul's *Hauptbriefe*, but nevertheless the picture is one of structures that are still in an early process of development. There are obvious implications for the dating of the letters.

I. LOCAL CHURCH LEADERS

The churches in Crete are represented as being under the supervision of Titus who has the task of appointing elders/bishops in them, apparently for the first time in at least some of the

---

[66] Out of a total of 242 vv., we have 41 vv. (1 Tim 3.1–13; 5.1–22; Tit 1.5–10).

congregations (Tit 1.5–10). What is debatable is whether this is the actual situation or whether it is part of a fictitious representation of an earlier period. If the latter, then the real point of the passage is simply the need to maintain a succession of leaders; how they are to be appointed and by whom is not clear, since *ex hypothesi* there is no Titus or Titus-like figure to do the appointing. But it is not clear on this view why the writer has not spoken in more general terms of appointment rather than of making new appointments where none existed before, and also why, if it was necessary to refer to deacons and 'the women' (female deacons) in 1 Tim, there was no need to do so here. It is, therefore, more likely that, whatever the date of the letter, it is dealing with a real, contemporary situation.

The churches within the ambit of Ephesus evidently have elders and there is a system for the appointment of people as bishops and deacons. Although 1 Tim 3.1–13 is about the kind of people to be appointed, it can be assumed that it is also presenting an ideal to those who already have these positions. It is true that 'new converts' should not be appointed, but the churches in Asia had been in existence for ten years or more by this time, and therefore there were people of some standing in them. The fact that the same leaders can be indifferently called bishops or elders (or that there is some overlap between these two groups) is a further sign that the church order is not far advanced (cf. Acts 20.17 and 28).

Although 2 Tim contains no formal church order, it nevertheless contains the direction to pass on the Pauline gospel to reliable people who can teach others. It is assumed that the recipient knows what the Pauline gospel is. It must also be presumed that there are people corresponding to Timothy and Titus who are in the position to pass on the gospel. That is to say, there must be a personal link between Paul and the recipients as well as the epistolary link. It tends to be assumed by commentators that the direction of this 'succession' is primarily 'vertical' or temporal, i.e. that it is concerned with a future period after the time of Timothy and Titus. But we should not exclude a more 'horizontal' or territorial element in that what Timothy is being instructed to do is to widen the circle of teachers in the local churches for which he is responsible, and it may well be that this is in fact the primary thought.

These points may suggest that the letters were produced in a circle which included the historical Timothy and Titus who collaborated to set down what they had learned from Paul but who were sufficiently their own men not to imitate his speech in detail nor to express their theology in his way but were creative in expressing Pauline thought in a fresh idiom. They were writing for the benefit of the churches in their own time and expressing how they saw their duties as evangelists in the succession to Paul. So we may be dealing with a situation at the shift from Timothy and Titus to the next generation which is based in turn on the shift from Paul to Timothy and Titus. This is more plausible than a vague fourth to fifth generation shift.

II. THE POSITION OF TIMOTHY AND TITUS

The proposed scenario is historically plausible in that Paul himself certainly exercised considerable authority as an apostle over the congregations which lay within his mission field. Moreover, during his exercise of this authority he was able to employ his colleagues to visit the congregations on his behalf and to exercise similar authority (1 Cor 16.10f.; 2 Cor 7.15; 8.23f.). It is entirely likely that Paul envisaged the continuation of this general superintendency of the congregations by his junior colleagues. It is surely less likely that the author of the PE was complicating the issue for his readers by portraying an ecclesiastical setup that bore no relation to reality and which would call in question the whole concept of a 'succession' of Pauline teaching if in fact the vital first members of the 'chain' were non-existent.

In addition to the teaching for and about the local church leaders we also have a considerable amount of teaching given to the nominal addressees of the letters, Timothy and Titus, about their personal conduct as Christian leaders. It is agreed on all sides that the advice is strange if it is directed to people who had been missionaries and trusted companions of Paul for some considerable period of time (again 10–15 years?). Nevertheless, some caution is needed. We need to remember that the kind of instruction given to the members of Christian churches today is not, and cannot be, arranged in clear stages of increasing difficulty and higher knowledge, like instruction in mathematics or stages in learning to play music. Instruction to mature believers can include elementary teaching, and at every stage of their Christian life people need to be reminded of basic doctrines and given basic ethical instruction. Consequently, the point of the letters is not necessarily to tell the recipients what they do not already know but to remind them of what they do know and to reinforce it. (There is an interesting parallel in Ignatius's letter to Polycarp, a mature church leader aged about 40 at the time, in which he instructs him in matters that should surely have been already familiar to him.) At the same time, much of the teaching may be given to Timothy and Titus (or through them to church leaders) in order to provide them with an authoritative expression of what they are to say to the churches. This point is sometimes put by arguing that the instruction is really intended for the churches but it is directed in this fictitious manner to the church leaders (since, if the letters are pseudonymous, the fictitious recipients must be members of the Pauline circle rather than actual churches addressed). It is more accurate to say that the instruction is intended to strengthen the hand of the leaders as they pass it on. What they are to teach is given the stamp of Pauline authority.

In any case the setting of the recipients in Ephesus and Crete makes good sense in the light of what is known about these areas (Thiessen 1995). The characteristics of the Cretans, as known from ancient authors, are reflected in Tit (see commentary) and, while it may be possible to regard the references to their insubordination and lying tendencies as literary clichés, it is more probable that they are mirroring a real situation. The differences between 1 and 2 Tim and Titus further suggest that real situations are being addressed.

III. THE COMMUNAL LIFE OF THE CHURCHES

We can gain a surprisingly full summary of the character of life in the churches as reflected in the letters. The following points are relevant to the question of how far the congregations had developed in their organisation and activities. (For detailed discussion see the appropriate points in the commentary.)

a. Ministry includes a variety of activities – teaching, rebuking and encouraging (e.g. 1 Tim 4.11–14; 2 Tim 4.1–5; Tit 2.1, 15). Prophecy is known (1 Tim 1.18; 4.14; cf. 4.1), although there is dispute as to how far it was practised at the actual date of the PE.

b. There is a particularly strong emphasis on the place of teaching. Timothy and Titus (or persons represented by these figures) have an authoritative teaching role (2 Tim 1.13; 2.2, 24; 3.16; 4.2; Tit 2.1, 15; 3.8), but there is also teaching by people within their own local congregations (1 Tim 5.17; Tit 1.9). Individuals destined for future teaching are themselves taught specially (2 Tim 2.2). Teaching is given to different groups in the church as well as to the congregation as a whole (Tit 2.2–10; 3.1–8). There is reading of Scripture, preaching and teaching (1 Tim 4.13). Discussions and controversies are possible, but not always edifying (2 Tim 2.25; Tit 3.9).

c. The scope of teaching is not confined to matters of faith but also includes behaviour in the family and in society (Tit 2; 3.1f.). The writer can even lay down directives about dress and general decorum (1 Tim 2.9f.).

d. The practice of baptism is implied (Tit 3.5), but there is no mention of the Lord's Supper. People could be appointed to some tasks by the laying on of hands (1 Tim 4.14; 2 Tim 1.6).

e. Discipline has to be exercised (1 Tim 5.20; 2 Tim 3.16; 4.2). The responsibility rests on Timothy and Titus, and it is not clear whether the local congregations shared the responsibility (cf. 1 Tim 1.20). It was possible to bring charges against sinners (1 Tim 5.19).

f. Prayers are to be offered for all kinds of people including rulers (1 Tim 2.1f.).

g. The presence in the letters of material that is capable of being memorised and recited probably implies that congregational participation in church meetings included the use of communal confessions and similar material (1 Tim 3.16; 2 Tim 2.11–13; cf. the 'trustworthy sayings').

h. Hospitality is a duty of the leaders (1 Tim 3.2; Tit 1.8). This may imply that there were still travelling teachers and not merely that the believers provided hospitality for other Christians on their journeys. More broadly, the congregations show practical care for the needy (Tit 3.14), and individuals are expected to use their resources generously to help other people in need (1 Tim 6.18f.).

This is a surprisingly full picture. The significant point for our purpose is that virtually everything in it can be paralleled from Paul's own life time, and there is nothing here that cannot fit into the immediate post-Pauline period.

IV. THE PLACE OF WOMEN

Women played a significant role in the Pauline mission, to judge by the number of favourable references to them in Acts and Romans 16 and (to a lesser extent) elsewhere. This remains the case in the PE. Clearly some women were teaching in some congregations (cf. the teaching of children [2 Tim 1.5; 3.15] and younger women [Tit 2.4]), since otherwise there would be no need for the prohibition in 1 Tim 2. The most probable interpretation of 1 Tim 3.11 is that some women acted as deacons (or at the very least were closely associated as wives with the diaconal tasks of their husbands). It is noteworthy that one of the longest connected sections in the PE is devoted to the provision of charitable care for widows (1 Tim 5.3–16), and they for their part are people who have already been exercising a charitable role in the church.

Problems with women in the church (as also with men) were not new. The quarrel in Philippians 4.2f. was of sufficient moment to cause a disturbance in a local church. 1 Cor 14.33b–35 indicates that at some point women were playing a role in church meetings which was inconsistent with social expectations. It is possible to exaggerate the extent of the problem. It has been claimed that a major purpose of the writer of 1 Tim is to reinforce the position of men in the church and to curb the growing power of women (Wagener 1994). It will be argued below that the restrictions on the women teaching are to be understood against a cultural background and the involvement of some women with the writer's opponents and therefore are related to a particular situation.

The present problem is to place this on the ecclesiastical map/timeline. There is similar material in 1 Clement 1; 21 where the silence of women is commended. For the rest of the AF there is total silence about any teaching or speaking role of women in the church, and for Ignatius women scarcely exist. Only in Hermas does an aged woman play a significant part as the transmitter of revelation.

V. CONCLUSION

This examination of the ecclesiastical situation shows that the PE fit well into the period around the death of Paul and the transition to the period in which he was no longer there to lead the congregations which he had planted. The church situation does not require us to assign the PE to a later date. It is true that we know so little about the life of the church in the 'tunnel period' from c. AD 70 to AD 100 that it could be argued that the PE might fit in anywhere in this period without serious difficulty. On the whole, however, the PE reflect an undeveloped ecclesiology that more naturally belongs to the earlier part of this period.

7. AUTHORSHIP AND RECIPIENTS

The questions of authorship and reception are closely linked together. If the PE are genuine writings of Paul, then it can be taken for granted that they were directed to the historical Timothy and Titus. If they are post-Pauline, then, although they may depend upon some material originally addressed to these historical figures, they are in fact intended for other recipients. In the latter case, it is very unlikely that we can give names to either the author or the recipients. We shall then have to be content to try to say something about the kind of people involved and the areas with which they were associated.

A significant minority of scholars hold that the PE are the work of Paul, whether directly or indirectly by the use of a secretary/amanuensis.[67] Nevertheless, most other scholars now take it almost as an unquestioned assumption that the PE are not the work of Paul. The grounds for this verdict are of two kinds. On the one side, there are the alleged differences from the acknowledged writings of Paul in style and thought. These are regarded as sufficiently great to exclude the possibility of Pauline authorship. On the other side, there is the possibility of developing a plausible scenario for a set of pseudonymous compositions and an explanation of their actual content in terms of such a setting. Indeed, for most scholars the only real point left for debate is the precise identification of such a setting. The general tendency is to place the letters well after the time of Paul, either towards the end of the first century or even well within the first half of the second century, and to argue that they represent the efforts of an individual or group which was attempting to reclaim the situation for a form of Pauline Christianity over against the development of a Gnostic type of religion.

However, we have already seen in the previous section that the nature of the heretical teaching that is opposed and the ecclesiastical background that is reflected in the PE fit comfortably into the time at the end of Paul's life and the period immediately following. We shall have to ask, therefore, whether any of the evidence really demands a later date for them, and whether they are not more plausibly explained as attempts to deal with the situation that arose at or around the time of Paul's death and immediately afterwards. This question is closely related to that of their nature and origin. The reigning hypothesis is that they are pseudonymous documents in the sense that they were written to deceive readers into believing that they contain the actual wording and teaching of Paul and therefore bear Paul's authority. This hypothesis is in danger of uncritical acceptance.

---

[67] Jeremias; Spicq; Simpson; Guthrie; Hendriksen; Kelly, Holtz; Fee; Knight; Lea and Griffin; Johnson; Oden; Towner; Stott; cf. Simpson, E. K. 'The Authenticity and Authorship of the Pastoral Epistles', *EvQ* 12 (1940), 289–311; Ellis, E. E., 'The authorship of the Pastorals: a resumé and assessment of current trends', *Paul and his Recent Interpreters* (Grand Rapids: Eerdmans, 1961), 49–58 (originally published in *RevExp* 56 [1959], 343–54; *EvQ* 32 [1960], 151–61); 'Die Pastoralbriefe und Paulus', *Theologische Beiträge* 22.4 (1991), 208–12; 'The Pastorals and Paul', *ExpTim* 104 (1992–93), 45–7; 'Pastoral Letters', *Dictionary of Paul and his Letters* (Downers Grove: IVP, 1993), 659–66; McRay, J., 'The Authorship of the Pastoral Epistles: A Consideration of Certain Adverse Arguments to Pauline Authorship', *ResQ* 7 (1963), 2–18; van Bruggen 1981; Prior 1989.

See also Porter, S. E., 'Pauline Authorship and the Pastoral Epistles: Implications for Canon', *BBR* 5 (1995), 105–23; Idem, 'A Response to R. W. Wall's Response', *BBR* 6 (1996), 133–8; Wall, R. W., 'Pauline Authorship and the Pastoral Epistles: A Response to S. E. Porter', *BBR* 5 (1995), 125–8.

Discussion of the issue is complicated by the fact that items of evidence are often observed and interpreted differently by scholars who approach them from different angles, and it is sometimes very difficult to find the decisive evidence which will compel the universal adoption of one interpretation rather than another.[68] To what extent we have been unable to avoid a one-sided interpretation of the evidence must be for the reader to judge.

I. FACTORS RELEVANT TO THE QUESTION OF AUTHORSHIP

a. Language and style

Barr, G., 'Scale and the pauline epistles', *IBS* 17 (1995), 22–41; Bird, A. E., 'The Authorship of the Pastoral Epistles – Quantifying Literary Style', *RTR* 56 (1997), 118–37; Carrington, P., 'The Problem of the Pastoral Epistles: Dr Harrison's Theory Reviewed', *ATR* 21 (1939), 32–9; Drake, B., 'Unanswered questions in computerized literary analysis', *JBL* 91 (1972), 241f.; Forbes, A. D., 'Statistical Research on the Bible', *ABD* (1992) VI, 185–206; Gilchrist 1966: 27–61; Grayston, K. and Herdan, G., 'The Authorship of the Pastoral Epistles in the Light of Statistical Linguistics', *NTS* 6 (1959–60), 1–15; Guthrie 1956; Harrison 1921; Harrison, P. N., 'The Authorship of the Pastoral Epistles', *ExpTim* 67 (1955–6), 77–81; Hitchcock, F. M., 'The Latinity of the Pastorals', *ExpTim* 39 (1927–8), 347–52; idem, 'Tests for the Pastorals', *JTS* 30 (1929), 272–9; idem, 'Philo and the Pastorals', *Hermathena* 56 (1940), 113–15; Holtzmann, 84–118; Kenny, A., *A Stylometric Study of the New Testament* (Oxford: Oxford University Press, 1986); Ledger, G. R., 'An exploration of differences in the pauline epistles using multivariate statistical analysis', *Literary and Linguistic Computing* 10.2 (1995), 85–97; Linnemann, E., 'Echtheitsfragen und Vokabelstatistik', *Jahrbuch für evangelikale Theologie* 10 (1996), 87–109; Mealand, D. L., 'Computers in New Testament Research: an Interim Report', *JSNT* 33 (1988), 97–115; idem, 'Positional Stylometry Reassessed: Testing a Seven Epistle Theory of Pauline Authorship', *NTS* 35 (1989), 266–86; idem, 'The Extent of the Pauline Corpus; A Multivariate Approach', *JSNT* 59 (1995), 61–92; Metzger, B. M., 'A Reconsideration of Certain Arguments against the Pauline Authorship of the Pastoral Epistles', *ExpTim* 70 (1958–9), 91–4; Michaelis, W., 'Pastoralbriefe und Wortstatistik', *ZNW* 28 (1929), 69–76; Morton, A. Q., and McLeman, J., *Paul, The Man and the Myth* (London: Hodder, 1966); Neumann, K., *The Authenticity of the Pauline Epistles in the Light of Stylo-statistical Analysis* (Atlanta: Scholars Press, 1990); O'Rourke, J. J., 'Some considerations about attempts at statistical analysis of the Pauline corpus', *CBQ* 35 (1973), 483–90; Robinson, T. A., 'Grayston and Herdan's "C" Quantity Formula and the Authorship of the Pastoral Epistles', *NTS* 30 (1984), 282–8; Roller, O., *Das Formular der paulinischen Briefe* (Stuttgart: Kohlhammer, 1933); Torm, F., 'Über die Sprache in den Pastoralbriefen', *ZNW* (1917–18), 225–43; Turner, N., *Style* (MHT IV), 101–5; Wake, W. C., 'The Authenticity of the Pastoral Epistles', *Hibbert Journal* 47 (1948–9), 50–5.

---

[68] An appropriate example can be seen in Towner's demonstration that passages which express the ecclesiology of the PE can be interpreted rather differently depending on which overall perspective regarding the composition and date of the letters the scholar adopts (Towner 1995).

1. Vocabulary

For most English-speaking scholars the investigation by Harrison 1921 continues to be decisive.[69] He developed three main points.

First, he demonstrated that the PE have a far greater proportion of words per page not found elsewhere even in a thirteen-letter collection of 'Pauline' letters than any other letters in it. The essential point is that the PE have a vocabulary of 902 words (including 54 proper names), i.e. 848 ordinary words. Of the latter 306 are not found in any of the ten Pauline letters.[70] This proportion is much higher than for any other Pauline letter. Conversely, there are some 1635 ordinary words and 103 proper names which occur in one or more of the ten Pauline letters and do not appear in the PE. It is also argued that a number of words which are common to Paul and the PE are used with different meanings.

Second, Harrison argued that the vocabulary was closer to that of second-century writers than to Paul. He observed that of the 175 *hapax legomena*[71] in the PE 93 are found in the Apostolic Fathers and Apologists. Out of 131 other words which are not in the working vocabulary of Paul 118 occur in the second-century authors. Conversely, of 634 words in the ten epistles of Paul which are not found in second-century authors, 595 of them are also not found in the PE.[72]

Third, he showed that the PE especially lack a great deal of the connective tissue found in the genuine letters. Out of a total of 214 'particles' which occur in the ten Pauline letters 112 do not occur in the PE. This is a large number and suggests a comparative poverty of style in the PE.

Critics have shown that there are undoubtedly some serious flaws in Harrison's methodology and presentation. In a thesis that has been undeservedly ignored Gilchrist 1966 showed that many of Harrison's allegedly distinct arguments were variants

---

[69] In the German-speaking world the work of Holtzmann, 84–118, occupies a similar place.

[70] We shall operate here on the basis of the ten letters bearing Paul's name. Scholarship has cast doubts on the authenticity of three of these (Eph; Col; 2 Thes), but even if we include them for purposes of comparison, the unusual character of the PE still stands out strongly. The number of words found only in the PE *and* any or all of Eph, Col and 2 Thes is no more than 30.

[71] I.e. words not occurring elsewhere in the NT.

[72] Harrison's claim must not be misunderstood. He was not arguing that the words were unknown at an earlier date, but rather that the vocabulary of the PE is closer to that of second-century Christianity than it is to that of Paul, and that it is typical of second-century authors in general. Nevertheless, Badcock 1937:115–21, and Guthrie 1956 showed that the *hapax legomena* are virtually all attested in the first century (many in the LXX); there is as much correspondence between the PE and the LXX as there is between the PE and the second-century writers.

of one and the same argument; Harrison is said to provide a 'stage army' in which the same argument is served up several times in different forms. Earlier Michaelis* made much the same point. Linnemann* has argued that there are such differences in vocabulary among the accepted Pauline letters as to make conclusions based on the peculiarities of the PE very dubious.

Later scholars have refined Harrison's methods. His method of calculating words per page has been replaced by more precise counts. Grayston and Herdan* adopted a more sophisticated mathematical approach than Harrison and confirmed his vocabulary argument. However, their approach has been challenged by Robinson*, O'Rourke*, Neumann*, 26–30, and Bird*. At the end of a critique of earlier efforts and his own very complex statistical discussion of a large number of different tests (relating to style as well as to vocabulary) Neumann* concludes that the PE show a non-Pauline character.[73] A further important observation is made by Johnson, 11f., and backed up in the discussion of individual passages in his commentary, namely that the use of non-Pauline words tends to be most evident when the writer is dealing with topics, such as the heresy or the qualifications for church leaders, which are not addressed in the accepted letters of Paul; the unusual vocabulary is thus in some measure due to the unusual subject-matter.[74]

Despite the weaknesses in presenting it, there is some substance in the case developed by Harrison and others: the shape of the vocabulary of the PE is different from that of the genuine Pauline letters.[75] Each of the PE shows a relatively high ratio of vocabulary to total word count. The problem is how this fact is to be interpreted.[76]

2. Syntax

A related approach is the attempt to analyse the syntactical style of the letters by considering such factors as sentence-length, the positioning of words, and the relative proportions of nouns and verbs and other parts of speech. Initial investigations in this area by Morton were severely flawed, but they have been succeeded by more refined methods. They have, however, been subject to considerable criticism (Kenny*; Neumann*), More recently,

---

[73] Neumann's work is unfortunately almost impenetrable for the non-statistician, and I can do no more than report his conclusion.

[74] The 'bunching' of unusual words in specific passages was already noted by Carrington*.

[75] So rightly Fee, 24. Cf. O'Rourke*, 487, who comments that the Pastorals have basically a 'relatively high ratio of vocabulary to total word count'.

[76] See Forbes*, 185–93, for a critical survey of recent studies.

Mealand* 1989 has carried out a number of tests based on the positioning of particles which show that within the Pauline corpus there is homogeneity within only a limited group of seven letters. Mealand included 2 Tim in the ten letters that he tested, but omitted Philemon (too short) and 1 Tim and Titus (presumably assumed to be non-Pauline). In a later and more detailed investigation Mealand* 1995 brought together a variety of tests (in the manner of Neumann) which confirm that the PE stand apart from the rest of the Pauline corpus of letters. Neumann's own comprehensive test is also open to criticism. He appears to regard as valid those tests which support his understanding of the letters and to reject those which do not (cf. Bird*, 135–7). For example, the assumption that 1 Timothy and 2 Timothy are by the same author means that he discounts any tests which place them far apart from each other. Moreover, his test samples do not include Titus.

Most of these approaches involve the use of statistical methods. They are generally open to the criticism that the PE are too short in length to permit of reliable analysis; Bird* has demonstrated that Yule's requirement that texts be of a reasonable length (longer than the individual PE) before stylometric tests can work reliably is fully justified. We should accordingly be cautious about the validity of the tests discussed above.

More weight should be attached to other considerations. Other scholars have been at pains to collect and list individual examples of unusual linguistic phenomena in the PE. For example, Schenk 1987:3408–16 has noted a considerable volume of turns of phrase and the like which distinguish the PE from the letters of Paul, including the use of compound words and stereotyped phraseology. This type of qualitative analysis is much more significant than purely statistical approaches.

With all due caution it is difficult to avoid the conclusion that there are differences in syntactical structure and phraseology between the PE and those letters whose Pauline authorship is not in serious doubt.[77]

3. Rhetorical style

Linked with these two points is the more diffuse element of rhetorical style, i.e. the manner of composition and argument. An analysis of the structure of the letters shows that they are constructed in a different manner from the acknowledged

---

[77] Cf. Turner*, who notes the undoubted differences and explains them partly by some Latin influence on Paul in Rome and in greater part by the use of a different amanuensis who was given a freer hand.

letters of Paul. There is, for example, the lack of an opening thanksgiving in 1 Tim and Tit (admittedly paralleled in Gal). There is also the lack of personal material (except in 2 Tim). More significant is the use of patterns of argument which are not characteristic of Paul. The work of Fiore 1986 on the use of personal example and of Donelson 1986 on the use of enthymemes shows that the manner of argument includes elements that are not found in Paul in the same kind of way. There is a considerable amount of material which is expressed in ways that do not appear to be Pauline.

The writer is fond of using doctrinal material to back up ethical material or exhortation rather than proceeding from doctrine to its application (e.g. 1 Tim 2.3–7; Tit 2.11–14; 3.3–7). His use of the phrase 'the saying is trustworthy' is distinctive. He loves to create (or take over) catalogues of good qualities and vices. He is fond of the head-tail construction whereby the last phrase in one section provides the theme for the next (2 Tim 1.8/9, 10/11; 2.8/9).

To sum up: despite the lack of precision that is inevitable when handling matters of style, there should be no room for doubt that the PE are distinctive in the Pauline corpus in that the three letters share a common shape of vocabulary, style and method of argument which is somehow different from that of the other ten letters in it.

4. Attempts to account for the differences

Already at this point the ways in which these phenomena can be explained need to be set out. Six types of explanation have been offered.

(a) At one end of the spectrum of possibilities is the claim that the differences from the acknowledged letters of Paul are minimal and well within the range of style of a single author, perhaps writing over a long period of time.

This explanation faces several difficulties. First, the differences are considerable. Second, if the basis of the claim is the argument that a writer's style can change over time, it has to be stressed that the available period of time is not very long; no more than some five to ten years can have intervened between the writing of Phil (if it dates from Paul's captivity in Rome) and the earliest of the PE. Third, we do not have the evidence that an individual's style can alter to such an extent and for no very obvious reason.

(b) A variation of the previous explanation attributes the changes to the effects of old age on a writer. Old age is alleged to lead to a different style of writing.

This theory should be abandoned from further consideration. It is based on a false assumption. It also leads to the unwelcome conclusion for those who defend the authenticity of the PE as letters of Paul himself in this way that, while this explanation certainly saves the PE for 'Paul', it is a different Paul from the earlier Paul who writes differently and whose thought may well have aged as well as his style of writing. Consequently, a person writing an account of 'The theology of Paul' would not be able to use the PE as a source for his thought in the same way as the earlier letters. Manifestly, this point is not an argument against the possibility of this explanation, but merely an indication that it does not do what its proponents would like it to do, namely to place the PE in the same category as the earlier letters of Paul. They have to attribute the PE to a senescent Paul.

But it is more important to expose the false assumption that lies beneath the explanation. There simply is no evidence that old age does have these effects in general or the specific effects seen in the PE. We are, *ex hypothesi*, thinking of a person who is old rather than one who has become senile. Observation shows that old age may make people garrulous or less sharp. It does not lead to a significant shift in the way in which they express themselves.

(c) A quite different type of theory is that the PE are by Paul but contain very considerable elements of 'traditional material', and it is in effect the style of the tradition which we are observing.[78]

Again the argument has an 'unhappy' implication for its proponents. It results in assigning a very great deal of the content to tradition rather than to the author, so that again the PE are saved for the name of Paul at the cost of denying him a creative role in their composition.

But in any case the theory will not work. There is a stylistic and theological homogeneity in the PE which makes it difficult to separate tradition from composition. The style is apparently that of the author rather than of his sources (see discussion of Tit 2.11–14 below).

(d) There is the possibility that the details of composition are due to a colleague or 'secretary' who was given a rather free hand by Paul.[79] Here again the effect is to 'rescue' the PE for Paul at the cost of denying that he himself was responsible for their contents. They have his blessing but not his mind. Nevertheless, a faithful secretary would doubtless have attempted to keep as far as possible to the kind of things that Paul would have said.

[78] Ellis 1987:237–53.
[79] Richards, E. R., *The Secretary in the Letters of Paul* (Tübingen: Mohr, 1991). For earlier statements of this position see Roller*; Jeremias, 9f.

The difficulty here is that this procedure is different from that of Paul as we know him; there is a homogeneity about his authentic letters which shows that he dictated them himself and added his signature at the end. However, there is the possibility defended by some scholars that Colossians was produced in this way. There is also the problem that no secretary or co-author is mentioned in the PE, not even a messenger who is responsible for bringing the letters to their destination.

In an interesting inversion of the usual hypothesis it has also been suggested that the other, genuine Pauline writings are the work of 'secretaries', whereas 2 Timothy is an example of what happened when Paul wrote himself without the aid of an amanuensis (Prior 1989:57–9).[80] This theory collapses in view of the essential homogeneity of the authentic letters which can hardly have all been written by one helper but rather reflect the single mind of Paul himself. Roller*, 20–2, has painted a realistic picture of the conditions in a Roman prison which would have prevented Paul from writing 2 Tim by himself.

(e) A different but related theory (developed by Harrison and others) is that the PE contain some genuine fragments of letters written by Paul embedded in the work of a later writer. With this theory we move from attempts to argue that the real or final author is the living Paul (but perhaps using a co-author or amanuensis) to the view that the letters are to be attributed to a later author. The letters, however, remain 'Pauline' to the extent that genuinely Pauline material (whether in the form of epistolary material or even oral material) has been incorporated in them.

The theory has been attacked by Cook 1984 who has demonstrated that the passages in question are written in the same language and style as the rest of the letters. (The same is equally true of the passages which are claimed to be based on 'tradition' in the previous theory of composition.) However, the objection is open to the response that the existence of a uniform style throughout a composition is no argument against the possible use of sources by an author who has recast them in his own style. It may not be possible to separate out sources on the basis of stylistic differences, but this does not mean that sources were not used.

(f) Finally, there is the straightforward conclusion that the PE are fresh compositions by an author other than Paul. The stylistic features observed are regarded as incompatible with authorship by the person who wrote the genuine letters in the Pauline corpus.

---

[80] Prior 1989:168 leaves open the question of the origin of 1 Tim and Tit. On his view 2 Tim envisages a further period of Pauline missionary activity into which these letters, if authentic, could be fitted (Prior 1989:90).

At this point in the discussion the issue between these options cannot be finally settled. Sufficient has been said to indicate that solutions (a) to (c) are opposed by strong arguments, and that the choice appears to lie between solutions (d) to (f). Further considerations must be taken into account in order to decide between these possibilities.

b. The problem of literary dependence

Barnett, A. E. *Paul Becomes a Literary Influence* (Chicago: University of Chicago Press, 1941); Lohfink 1988; Trummer 1978.

If it could be shown that the PE demonstrate literary dependence on the acknowledged letters of Paul, this would be a further argument against authenticity. The case for use of the Pauline corpus was developed especially by Holtzmann, 109–18; Barnett*, 251–77, and Hanson, 28–31, 199, *et passim*. The difficulty is that of deciding whether an echo of Paul is due to literary dependence (whether direct paraphrase of passages in his letters or the influence of passages remembered consciously or unconsciously) or is due to the same person writing fresh material or is simply due to a common fund of Christian vocabulary and ideas within the area of Pauline influence. How can one *demonstrate*, for example, that 1 Tim 1.8 is literarily dependent on Rom 7.16? Lohfink 1988 has examined several passages and finds only one clear case of literary dependence in 2 Tim 1.3–12/Rom 1.8–17. For the rest he argues that a living Pauline tradition is the source of the influence. The echoes are in fact so faint that the theory of literary dependence cannot be used as an argument for post-Pauline authorship, although it may be plausible as an explanation of the echoes for those who hold this view of the letters.

c. The historical setting of the author

Binder 1967; Brooke, A. E., 'The problem of the Pastoral Epistles', *JTS* 23 (1922), 255–62; Duncan, G. S., 'Paul's ministry in Asia: the last phase, Acts 19–22', *NTS* 3 (1956–7), 211–18; idem, 'Chronological table to illustrate Paul's ministry in Asia', *NTS* 5 (1958–9), 43–5; Harrison, P. N., 'The Pastoral Epistles and Duncan's Ephesian Theory', *NTS* 2 (1955–6), 250–61; *Paulines and Pastorals* (London: Villiers, 1964); Hitchcock, F. M., 'The Pastorals and a Second Trial of Paul', *ExpTim* 41 (1929–30), 20–3; Holtzmann, 15–64; Lestapis 1976; Metzger 1976; Murphy-O'Connor 1996; Pherigo, L. P. 'Paul's Life after the Close of Acts', *JBL* (1951), 277–84; Reicke, B., 'Chronologie der Pastoralbriefe', *TLZ* 101 (1976), 81–94; Robinson 1976; van Bruggen 1981.

The problem of historical setting can be addressed on two levels. The first is historical, and consists in enquiring whether there is a possible setting in the career of Paul into which the letters can be plausibly placed. A variant of this view is that the pseudonymous letters contain authentic fragments which can be fitted into a historical framework. The second is literary and asks whether a presumed pseudonymous author was envisaging a particular historical setting in the life of Paul (whether real or imaginary). The problem is bound up with the presentation of Timothy and Titus in their relationships with Paul. The letters do not give a lot of information to enable us to fix them in a specific setting, but there is sufficient material to suggest some possible scenarios which are not directly reflected in our other sources of information.

The material in the letters can be rapidly summarised:

1 Timothy refers back to a journey by Paul to Macedonia, at which time Timothy was associated with work in Ephesus (1 Tim 1.3). The letter anticipates that Paul will visit Timothy (1 Tim 3.13). The situation presupposed in the letter, therefore, is a time when Paul has left Timothy in Ephesus while he himself has gone to Macedonia and intends to pay a visit to Ephesus.

Titus is addressed to Titus who is in Crete, having been 'left' there by Paul. This means that Paul was also there with him and departed leaving him in charge; the implication may be that Paul had worked in Crete but not completed what he intended to do. At the time of writing Paul was to send Artemas or Tychicus to Crete, and thereafter Titus was to proceed to Nicopolis and join Paul there. It is assumed that Zenas and Apollos are/will be passing through Crete.

In 2 Timothy Paul is a prisoner, and the clear impression is that he was in Rome, where Onesiphorus had visited him.[81] A picture is painted of Paul facing the end of his life, having already experienced a judicial hearing, with the implication that a second one is shortly to follow. However soon this may happen, Timothy is urged to visit him and to do so before the winter sets in and travel becomes impossible. Various people are said to have deserted Paul or to have left him to do Christian work elsewhere. Paul has been in Troas and his clothing and books are to be picked up from there and brought to him. It is implied that he had been in Ephesus and Miletus where various companions had

---

[81] Various attempts have been made to reinterpret the *prima facie* evidence of 2 Timothy. (a) Reicke* and Robinson 1976 have argued that the imprisonment and trial were in Caesarea and not in Rome, but this necessitates a highly improbable rendering of 2 Tim 1.17. (b) Prior 1989 has argued that 2 Tim is not about Paul's expectation of martyrdom but his expectation of being released to continue his work; this view rests upon an improbable interpretation of 2 Tim 4.6 (see note). The traditional rendering seems to be required.

been left. Despite the desertions, there are friends and supporters with him.[82]

We can now attempt to relate this material to what we know from elsewhere.

1. The theory of a second imprisonment

The traditional historical reconstruction by defenders of Pauline authorship works with the hypothesis of a period of activity by Paul after a putative release at the end of his two years of imprisonment in Rome (Acts 28).[83] This view has the undoubted advantage over its rivals of placing the three letters together in one period of time, and thus accounting for their stylistic peculiarities *as a group* over against the other letters.[84]

Acts 28 concludes with Paul spending two years in custody in Rome. The argument is that the evidence presented there at the very least allows the possibility that when Paul's appeal came before the court it was successful. The case is supported by the tradition recorded in Eusebius, *HE* 2.22:

> after defending himself the Apostle was again sent on the ministry of preaching, and coming a second time to the same city suffered martyrdom under Nero. During this imprisonment he wrote the second Epistle to Timothy, indicating at the same time that his first defence had taken place and that his martyrdom was at hand.

Eusebius himself comments on the contents of 2 Tim and states that in his view Luke wrote the Acts at this time, and that Paul's martyrdom in Rome did not occur during the imprisonment recorded by Luke.

A third piece of evidence is that according to 1 Clement 5 Paul travelled to the limit of the west. Ellis has argued strongly that this refers to Tartessus in Spain and not to Rome.[85] This tradition reappears in *Acts of Peter* 1.1 (*NTA* II, 279) and the Muratorian Canon. It fits in with Paul's intention in Romans and may be based upon it. There is, of course, no certainty that

---

[82] The information in 2 Tim has been thought to be self-contradictory as regards the envisaged timescale, and especially the presence and absence of friends. It is to be presumed that whoever wrote the letter as we have it intended to be coherent. It is probable that we are dealing with an uncertain legal situation in which lengthy delays were not impossible, and it is likely that there is an implicit distinction between people who served in Paul's missionary work and other believers resident in the area.

[83] Lightfoot 1893:421–37 gives a sober reconstruction.

[84] This is the view of such scholars as Brooke*; Michaelis 1946:262–4; Spicq; Guthrie; Knight. For a full development see Metzger 1976.

[85] Ellis, E. E., ' "The End of the Earth" (Acts 1:8)', *BBR* 1 (1991), 123–32.

Paul's hopes expressed in Romans were ever fulfilled, granted that he did not reach Rome at the time and in the way that he himself had planned. The tradition, if accurate, implies activity by Paul after his imprisonment in Rome (since nothing suggests that he travelled west before that point). The problem is then whether further missionary work in the 'east' can also be fitted into the scenario. It is certainly not impossible. Paul expresses hopes of revisiting Asia in Philemon. There is also the intriguing possibility that Crescens was sent to Gaul (2 Tim 4.10), which would imply a Pauline mission in the western Mediterranean.

These points can hardly *prove* that Paul was released from prison in Rome for a further period of missionary activity, but equally the possibility cannot be disproved.

The hypothesis has been given fresh life by Murphy-O'Connor 1996:356–71, who starts from the evidence of the PE themselves. He argues that 2 Timothy is different in thought from 1 Tim and Tit and that the arguments against its authenticity are essentially based on the difficulties of the latter two letters. He therefore adopts the hypothesis that 2 Tim is authentic and on this basis develops his defence of a second imprisonment. 2 Tim presupposes an imprisonment in Rome under different conditions from those of the first imprisonment when Paul had numerous friends about him. It is very likely that he did go to Spain without the sponsorship of Roman Christians for a short period; the mission was not successful because of the language barrier (Greek was not widely spoken). He returned to Illyricum and then to Asia, travelling via Macedonia to Troas (where he left his cloak and books), then to Ephesus, Miletus and on to Corinth. Meanwhile Timothy had moved from Ephesus (into the interior of the country) where things had become difficult. Timothy had not been successful and Paul kept him from returning there. At some point after the fire of Rome (Murphy-O'Connor is vague at this point) Paul moved to Rome, from where he wrote to Timothy. Here he was known to the authorities and fell a victim to Nero's persecution.

Murphy-O'Connor's hypothesis has the advantage of a comparative simplicity that is possible for him because he does not have to accommodate 1 Tim and Tit in his scenario.[86] A much fuller hypothetical scenario was developed earlier by Metzger 1976. He claims that Paul abandoned his plan to go to Spain in view of more pressing needs in the east (the Muratorian Canon is regarded as being in error). Paul sent Titus to Crete, and then

[86] It should be noted that the theory of a second imprisonment in Rome may not be necessary for scholars who uphold only the authenticity of 2 Timothy (or an underlying authentic letter), although they probably have greater difficulties in explaining the personal data on the basis of only one Roman imprisonment.

instructed him to come to Nicopolis, Timothy went with Paul who intended to send him to Ephesus (from an intended stop at Miletus). Tychicus was summoned from Ephesus to tell Paul on the ship what was happening at Ephesus. Artemas joined Paul and was to be sent to Crete to relieve Titus. Paul then visited Crete to see the existing churches and saw for himself the needs. He sent a messenger from Miletus to Ephesus to say that he was not coming and was sending Timothy instead. The news from Tychicus allowed Paul to write 1 Tim. But Paul still hoped to visit Ephesus. However, he feared arrest in Ephesus in view of past events, and so from Troas he wrote 1 Tim and Titus. Then he journeyed through Macedonia to Nicopolis. From here he sent Titus to Dalmatia. He then went to Corinth. He still wished to see Ephesus and went across to Miletus, where he was arrested as a result of the activity of Alexander, and was sent to Rome. He saw Timothy briefly. Luke and Tychicus went with him, but Trophimus was left at Miletus. He reached Rome, where Onesiphorus travelled separately to meet him (and died). Meanwhile Luke wrote Luke-Acts to defend him and planned a third volume. Here Paul wrote 2 Timothy, and then came the end.

The merit of this type of theory is that it allows the interpreter considerable freedom, since there is no other hard information about what happened during this period, and therefore it is easy to postulate whatever movements by Paul and his companions are required to account for the data in the letters. The proposed scenario is not impossible, but it is unprovable. It should be emphasised that unprovability is not necessarily an argument against a historical hypothesis.

However, objections can be raised to theories of this nature.

(1) There is the basic question whether the postulated release of Paul is capable of proof or is at least defensible against objections.

(2) The theory may contain internal weaknesses or contradictions. More serious is the question whether the evidence on which the theory is based is free from contradictions and whether the picture presented is a realistic one. It has often been claimed that the *personalia* in the PE are internally inconsistent.

(3) It is arguable that the theory requires a repetition of previous events to such an extent as to be improbable (Paul's visits to Ephesus and Miletus; his arrest – on what grounds?).

(4) One may ask whether a scenario which depends upon so much conjecture is at all plausible (Harrison 1921:102–15).

These objections are all capable of being answered.

(1) The evidence of Acts does not require that Paul was executed immediately at the end of the two-year period, even if the author knows that Paul was eventually put to death.

(2) The internal problems are concerned with the consistency and realism of the events described in 2 Tim 1.16–18 and 4.9–22. Why should Onesiphorus not have been able to find Paul? Or why should Paul want a cloak brought all the way to Rome from Troas? Or who exactly was with Paul at the time of writing? These questions can be answered. It can be argued that Paul would be difficult to find in a city of 1,000,000 inhabitants, assuming that he really had few friends and that Onesiphorus did not have any contacts. Again, who are we to know how the mind of a person in the wretched conditions of a prison would work? And for the apparently varied information on the number of people with Paul see the commentary on 2 Tim 4.

(3) There is nothing improbable in Paul revisiting areas in which he had previously worked.

(4) There is in reality very little conjecture in the theory, which simply builds on reported information.

It follows that there is no insuperable obstacle to the historical possibility of the scenario described, whether as part of an authentic letter of Paul or as fragments of an authentic letter (see below 3.).

2. A setting earlier in Paul's career

Other attempts have been made to fit the PE into Paul's missionary career as recorded in Acts.[87]

Lestapis 1976 argues that Tit and 1 Tim were written while Paul was at Philippi in AD 58 (Acts 20.30). He arrived in Rome in AD 61 and shortly after wrote 2 Timothy. The unity of style between the letters is due to the fact that in all three cases Paul had the assistance of Luke in the composition. This conclusion rests basically on a study of the personal references in the PE.

Van Bruggen 1981 in essence takes the same position. He argues that 1 Tim dates from Paul's third missionary campaign before the events described in Acts 20. He does not want to place it later because of the elementary nature of the instruction to the church and the youth of Timothy. The letter is really for the church but is addressed to the responsible leader. Titus is dated to the same period. The captivity letters are assigned to Caesarea,

---

[87] Reicke*; Robinson*; van Bruggen*. See also Badcock 1937:73–158, who argues that Titus was written during Paul's lengthy stay at Ephesus, 1 Timothy was written at Philippi when Paul was en route for Jerusalem (Acts 20), and that 2 Timothy was written from Paul's imprisonment in Caesarea. The letters as we have them, however, have been written up by an editor after Paul's death. This theory involves much conjecture, including the claim that the original reference in 2 Tim 1.16–18 was not to Rome but to Antioch.

except for Ephesians. 2 Timothy belongs to the first and only imprisonment in Rome, which was long.

Much the same line was adopted by Reicke* and Robinson* with the significant difference that they assigned 2 Tim (along with the other captivity letters of Paul) to his imprisonment in Caesarea; this requires that 2 Tim 1.16f. be interpreted to mean that Onesiphorus sought Paul in Rome (on the basis of mistaken information) and then went to Caesarea and found him there.[88] This exegesis is quite unconvincing and its failure makes this part of the hypothesis untenable.

The most recent defender of authenticity, Johnson 1996, is content to claim that there is a good deal of Paul's activity which is not recorded in Acts and that we have in effect no difficulty in recognising this. The PE and the activities recorded in them can equally well form part of this activity over which Acts passes in silence.

Like the theories of a second imprisonment, theories of this kind cannot be refuted by showing that the correlations do not work, since the record in Acts is sufficiently fragmentary to allow for all kinds of reconstructions. They show that the PE as they stand can be fitted into Paul's lifetime. The great difficulty is rather that these three letters, which differ from the *Hauptbriefe* (i.e. Paul's principal writings – Romans, 1 and 2 Corinthians and Galatians) in linguistic and theological style but manifest a close unity among themselves, are interspersed with them over the same period of composition, and we are left wondering how and why the same writer could move so easily from one style to another. The arguments for and against them being Pauline compositions can be settled only by a consideration of other factors. Nevertheless, it would seem that for defenders of the substantial authenticity of the PE, the theory of the second imprisonment affords less difficulties than attempting to place 1 Tim and Tit earlier in his career.

3. Theories based on fragmentary hypotheses

Both of the above scenarios assume that the letters in their present form are authentic, unified compositions. A different possibility is that the PE are artificial compositions incorporating fragments of actual Pauline letters, and when these fragments have been prised away from their present setting, it is possible to devise various hypothetical situations for each of the fragments. Here

---

[88] The problem of Onesiphorus is avoided by Binder*, who regards 2 Tim 4.9–22 as a fragment of a separate letter from 1.1–4.8.

again there are few limits that can be set on the ingenuity of scholars.

Thus arguments against the self-consistency of 2 Tim 4 and therefore against the historicity of the details can be met by assigning different fragments to different situations and allowing that the letters are secondary compositions (cf. Binder*).

The best-known hypothesis of this kind is probably that of Harrison 1921:115–35 who originally suggested the following reconstruction involving five fragments:

(1) Tit 3.12–15, sent from Macedonia after the writing of the severe letter to Corinth;

(2) 2 Tim 4.13–15, 20, 21a, sent from Macedonia after Paul's visit to Troas (2 Cor 2.12f.);

(3) 2 Tim 4.16–18a, sent from Caesarea after Paul's first 'defence' there;

(4) 2 Tim 4.9–12, 22b, sent from Rome to summon Timothy to join Paul;

(5) 2 Tim 1.16–18; 3.10–11; 4.1, 2a, 5b–8, 18b, 19, 21b–22a, sent from Rome to Timothy as Paul's last letter to him.

Later on he revised his theory (Harrison 1964) and cut down the number of letters to three:

(1) Tit 3.12–15, sent from Macedonia;

(2) Combination of fragments 2 and 4, sent from Nicopolis to Timothy;

(3) Combination of fragments 3 and 5, sent from Rome to Timothy.

This reconstruction is open to various criticisms. It has been shown by Cook 1984 that the fragments have the same style as the rest of the PE and therefore cannot be separated out on grounds of a different style. This point may be readily granted, but there is of course no reason why an editor should not have imposed his own style on the sources which were used (cf. the procedure of Luke in Acts). More force attaches to the objection that the hypothesis must assume a complicated process whereby the fragments were joined together into their present form and order. The difficulties are eased somewhat with the later version of the theory, but it is evident that such precision is very dubious. The theory, as advocated by Harrison, also does not explain why the other material in the putative letters was not preserved, especially if there was a strong desire to preserve whatever there was of Paul's writings. Nevertheless, the possibility that fragments of Pauline letters were preserved in later compositions cannot be ruled out as impossible; it is possible that the extent of the underlying Pauline material was greater than Harrison allowed.

4. The fictitious character of the evidence

It will have been seen that the foregoing theories are hard to disprove since there is little in the way of hard circumstantial evidence for or against them. The principal difficulty for anyone who takes any of the first two theories is to offer a convincing explanation of how the PE could have been composed in or around the same time as the other, undoubtedly genuine letters of Paul with their different language and style. The problem is most acute for those who place the letters into the Acts scenario rather than at the end of Paul's life. They have to show how and why the thinking is different in this series of letters from that in the other series with which they are intertwined chronologically.

If the view that the personal details are historical is rejected, they have to be explained as part of the fictional, pseudepigraphic set-up created by the author of the letters. The older generation of scholars (Harrison; Easton; Barrett) was prepared, as we have seen, to accept that genuine fragments were embedded in pseudonymous letters. The contemporary trend is very much to regard the details as fictitious and to explain them as modes of conveying paraenesis in veiled form: Paul is presented as an example to be followed, his opponents reflect current dangers in the church, and so on.[89] It is claimed that such material is part of the stock-in-trade of the pseudonymous writer to give credibility to his deception. Nevertheless, such an explanation is also not without problems, and there is a difficulty for the theory of post-Pauline composition here. The explanations offered for the creation of the various items are artificial and unconvincing. It must also be stressed that paraenetic purpose and authentic composition need not be mutually exclusive possibilities. Moreover, the example of many expository commentaries demonstrates that it is possible to draw paraenesis out of virtually anything that Paul wrote, whether or not he intended it to be paraenetic. In the end of the day, the decisive question is whether there are solid factual grounds for contesting the credibility of the information.[90]

d. The recipients

The difficulty for Pauline authorship here is the nature and manner of the instruction given to colleagues of Paul who have worked with him for many years and should be in no need of

---

[89] In addition to the commentators who argue for a late date for the PE see Becker 1989 for a sceptical verdict on all the putative historical sources for the last days of Paul.

[90] Cf. Reicke 1976:84.

what at times seems elementary instruction that should have been well known to them. There is also a formality and impersonal character which it is hard to envisage between people who have been close colleagues and companions. Defenders of authenticity argue that this material is really meant, or is meant as much, for the congregations of Timothy and Titus who will then know how their leaders are to behave and how they are to respond to them. In support of this view one can point to the plural form of the final blessings in all three letters.[91] This hypothesis might appear to be more difficult to apply to 2 Timothy which bears all the marks of a personal letter intended for Timothy himself. Nevertheless, the instruction to Timothy to convey Pauline teaching to other leaders (2 Tim 2.2) suggests that the contents of the letter were meant to be shared with a wider audience (Reicke*, 89).

The defenders of the authenticity of 1 Tim and Tit have a fairly sound case as regards this point, since the pseudonymous solution is similar. These letters are really for the third/fourth generation churches and their leaders who are directly addressed under the guise of Timothy and Titus. The letters are cast as indirect instruction (by telling Timothy and Titus what to tell their congregations) as a means of showing how the leaders of the readers have their authorisation and theology handed down to them from Paul. Scholars are becoming ever more sophisticated in developing this point.[92]

Both forms of this interpretation emphasise the element of indirect address to the congregations, and there may be a danger of overemphasising it. The letters are addressed to individuals and are concerned with how they are to exercise their ministry. This is clearest in the case of 2 Tim which is essentially instructions for the personal life and witness of the church leader. But it has also been demonstrated that 1 Tim is concerned primarily with the figure of 'Timothy' himself, and the argument could be extended to apply to Tit also (Reed 1993). It follows that the letters, if post-Pauline, are addressed primarily to church leaders, to the people appointed to lead local congregations, and they are in effect given the kind of instruction that Paul gave to his own colleagues who in their turn appointed the readers as their colleagues. The people who would most easily identify with the named recipients are surely church leaders rather than members of the congregation, although the latter were probably intended to overhear instruction and exhortation meant directly or indirectly for themselves.

[91] Admittedly there is textual variation with the sing. form in each case (see textual notes *ad loc.*).

[92] See especially Wolter 1988.

It should also be noted carefully that the letters are addressed to leaders who have some kind of supervision over several congregations and not directly to local church leaders. The ostensible situation is that of Timothy and Titus as members of Paul's missionary team who are responsible for the oversight of the congregations established by the mission. If the letters are not meant for the historical Timothy and Titus, the most plausible understanding is that they are directed to people exercising the same functions as they are presented as doing. If the author's purpose was primarily to address the local leaders of congregations, then it was open to him to write a letter in the style of Philippians addressed to a local congregation with its leaders (sc. bishops and deacons). The later in time the letters are placed, the more likely it is that this procedure would have been followed. It is thus probable that the letters really are addressed to the situation caused by the departure of Paul, the transitional period when oversight by the missionaries was still being practised.

There remains the problem that the letters are giving Timothy and Titus the kind of instruction with which they should already have been familiar and in a way that is surprisingly formal. However, this problem tends to be greatly exaggerated. There are parallels to this situation in both style and content in the letter of Ignatius to Polycarp which gives exhortation and advice on much the same level as that in the PE.

It is sometimes claimed by defenders of authenticity that the differences in style from the earlier letters are due to the fact that here individuals are being addressed rather than congregations. However, we have a clear example of a Pauline letter to an individual in Philemon, and it shows no differences in style or theology from the other letters of Paul. It is not at all obvious why a different style (and – see below – a different way of expressing theology and ethics) should have been adopted by Paul in addressing his colleagues.

The discussion thus indicates that the envisaged readers of the letters are people who can model themselves on Timothy and Titus, and this must include persons like them who were in a supervisory capacity over congregations. It can also include local church leaders, since the line between people with broader and narrower responsibilities will have been a fluid one. But the view that the letters are really addresses to churches disguised as addresses to their leaders will not work. The letters are intended for church leaders as the primary audience, although they are to hear them read, as it were, in the presence of the congregation who are intended to apply some of what is said to themselves.

e. The theological and practical instruction

That the actual content of the letters is different in character from that of the earlier Paul is not to be denied, even by those who would insist that what is said is in theological harmony with Paul. We then face two sorts of question.

1. The ecclesiastical situation

The first question is whether the material on leadership and other aspects of church organisation can fit into a scenario within the lifetime of Paul and is of a kind that he would have written.

Already in the acknowledged writings of Paul we have evidence of a development leading to the existence of 'bishops and deacons' as local church leaders alongside at least two other groups of people. The first of these is people who had charismatic gifts to minister in various ways including prophesying and teaching and more 'tangible' forms of ministry. The second is the group of people like Paul himself and his colleagues who were engaged in a church-planting exercise which included the after-care of new congregations. These three types of activity and personnel can be found at every stage in the early development of the church. In the PE Timothy and Titus perform functions similar to those of Paul himself and his missionary colleagues. The major difference is that there is little about charismatically-endowed individuals other than those who hold some kind of official position (Timothy himself!). There could have been a shift in ministry from the informality characteristic of Corinth, and there has apparently been a development in a more formal type of teaching ministry. But the pattern could vary from place to place and time to time, and the question is whether the variant of it here is credible within a Pauline setting or immediately afterwards and indeed whether this is not the best setting for it compared with other possibilities.[93]

2. The nature of the theology

The second question relates to the differences in theology and theological expression from the acknowledged letters of Paul. Here the issue is not whether the theology has shifted from that of Paul's earlier letters – that is beyond dispute (just as Eph and Col also show undoubted developments from the *Hauptbriefe*) – but rather the direction and manner of the shift: is it the kind

[93] See especially Campbell 1994, who places the developments in the PE close to the time of Paul.

of development that Paul himself might have experienced or does it tend in other directions? That is to say, are the developments such as Paul might have produced himself, just as (for example) his use of the term 'body' has developed from 1 Corinthians to Colossians, or are they more likely to be the work of somebody else? (See below Section 8. for a more detailed discussion of the character of the theology.)

The significant factor here is the way in which the theology of the letters is expressed in new ways. The older critical position saw in the PE a rather tired, pedestrian theology which was a definite decline from the Pauline heights. The comparative disuse of much Pauline theological terminology has often been noted (such as the infrequency and limited range of the phrase 'in Christ'). But at the same time there is clear evidence to show that the PE represent a creative attempt to re-express Pauline theology in new ways for a new situation and to use fresh terminology to do so. It is striking how far the language and ideas of the PE find parallels in the Graeco-Roman world and especially in the Greek-speaking Hellenistic Judaism which had taken over much from the surrounding world.[94] The Christology is newly formulated in terms of epiphany, and the nature of the Christian life is expounded in terms of godliness and sobriety.[95]

Could Paul himself have developed these new forms of expression? It can be argued that there is nothing here that Paul himself could not have done with his broad background in both Palestinian and Hellenistic Judaism. This may be true enough (we have little evidence to settle the issue of Paul's capacity for change), but the real problem is why he has not adopted this medium in his earlier letters and above all why he has felt it necessary to re-express the nature of the gospel and the Christian life in letters ostensibly addressed to close colleagues. This remains a problem if the letters are assigned to the hypothetical period after Paul's first imprisonment in Rome, and it is all the greater if the PE are written during the same period as Paul's other letters.

f. The picture of Paul

De Boer, M. C., 'Images of Paul in the Post-Apostolic period', *CBQ* 42 (1980), 359–80; Collins, R. F., 'The Image of Paul in the Pastorals', *LTP* 31 (1975), 147–73; Wanke 1977; Wild, R. A., 'The Image of Paul in the Pastoral Letters', *Bible Today* 23 (1985), 239–45; Zmijewski 1979.

[94] It is remarkable how frequently Philo provides some of the closest parallels in language and thought. Cf. Hitchcock, F. M., 'Philo and the Pastorals', *Hermathena* 56 (1940), 113–15.

[95] Marshall 1993; summarised in Section 8. below.

Finally, one of the major current arguments against Pauline authorship is the picture of Paul which is reflected or presented in the PE. The argument is that here Paul is made to put himself forward as a saint and martyr and as the sole apostle and authority for the gospel. He is deliberately presented as an example to be followed, or even as the prototype of the Christian convert, and as the person on whom the gospel depends. Succession from him and his message is vital for the continuance of the church. Above all, the kind of statements attributed to Paul about himself are such as the historical Paul could never have made. He is self-consciously a saint and a martyr.[96]

It is probable that the proponents of this argument have pressed their point too hard. Nevertheless, there are some points where the reader may feel that the self-presentation of Paul is more like what other people would have said about him rather than what he himself would have said.

g. Conclusion

The result of these half-dozen points is to show that direct Pauline authorship faces a number of objections of varying strength. The doctrinal and ecclesiastical setting of the letters is compatible with composition during or immediately after the life of Paul, but the way in which the thought is expressed, both linguistically and theologically, poses great problems. There is no great difficulty in envisaging the historical Paul having to deal with the kind of concrete situations envisaged in the PE and writing letters to his colleagues to advise them on what to do in the face of opposition and the need to consolidate the church situation. The problem is the way in which it is done, which seems to make it unlikely that he himself wrote in these terms to trusted colleagues. The difficulty is least acute with 2 Tim.

Although the objections vary in strength, their cumulative effect is to cast doubts on the traditional defence of direct Pauline authorship and to raise the question whether it really belongs within 'the art of the possible'. Is some other hypothesis better founded?

II. THE PROBLEM OF PSEUDONYMITY

Aland, K., 'The Problem of Anonymity and Pseudonymity in Christian Literature of the First Two Centuries', *JTS* 12 (1961), 39–49; Balz, H. R., 'Anonymität und Pseudepigraphie im Urchristentum', *ZTK* 66 (1969), 403–36; Bardy, G., 'Faux et fraudes littéraires dans l'antiquité chrétienne', *RHE* 32 (1936),

---

[96] See especially Wanke 1977; Wolter 1988.

5–23, 275–302; Bauckham, R., 'Pseudo-Apostolic letters', *JBL* 107.3 (1988), 469–94; Brox, N., *Falsche Verfasserangaben. Zur Erklärung der frühchristlichen Pseudepigraphie* (SBS 79, Stuttgart: Katholisches, 1975); idem (ed.), *Pseudepigraphie in der heidnischen und jüdisch-christlichen Antike* (Wege der Forschung 484. Darmstadt: Wissenschaftliche Buchgesellschaft, 1977); idem, 'Pseudo-Paulus und Pseudo-Ignatius', *VC* 30 (1976), 181–8; idem, 'Zum Problemstand in der Erforschung der altchristlichen Pseudepigraphie', *Kairos* 15 (1973), 10–23; Donelson 1986; Hegermann 1970; Hengel, M., 'Anonymität, Pseudepigraphie und "literarische Fälschung" in der jüdisch-hellenistischen Literatur', in Fritz, K. von, *Pseudepigrapha I: Pseudopythagorica – Lettres de Platon – Littérature pseudépigraphique juive,* (Entretiens sur l'antiquité classique, 18) (Vandoeuvres-Genève: Fondation Hardt, 1972), 231–308; Lea, T. D., 'The Early Christian View of Pseudepigraphic Writings', *JETS* 27 (1984), 65–75; Meade 1986; Rist, M., 'Pseudepigraphic Refutations of Marcionism', *JR* 22 (1942), 39–62; idem, 'Pseudepigraphy and the Early Christians', in Aune, D. E. (ed.), *Studies in New Testament and Early Christian literature: Essays in Honor of Allen P. Wikgren* (Leiden: Brill, 1972); Sint, J. A., *Pseudonymität im Altertum* (Commentationes Aenipontanae 15. Innsbruck, 1960); Speyer, W., 'Fälschung, literarische', *RAC* VII, 1969, 236–77; idem, *Die literarische Falschung im Altertum* (München: Beck, 1971); idem, 'Religiöse Pseudepigraphie und literarische Fälschung im Altertum', *JAC* 8/9 (1965–6), 88–125; Stenger, W. 'Timotheus und Titus als literarische Gestalten. Beobachtungen zur Form und Funktion der Pastoralbriefe', *Kairos* 16 (1974), 252–67; Torm, F., *Die Psychologie der Pseudonymität im Hinblick auf die Literatur des Urchristentums* (Studien der Luther-Akademie 2, Gütersloh: Bertelsmann, 1932); Zmijewski 1979.

The reigning alternative hypothesis is that the letters were written much later than Paul by some unknown person who was using Paul's authority to say what he believed that the church of his day needed to know. He chose to use Paul's name and hide himself behind it because for him Paul was the only apostle and the source and foundation of the teaching which he believed that the church needed (Zmijewski*, 110f.)

Those who adopt this view may evaluate the PE in different ways. On the one hand, there is the straight view that the author has a theology which represents a decline from that of Paul into 'early catholicism'. On the other hand, there is the more positive evaluation of the PE as an attempt to maintain Paulinism in a changed situation. These two types of judgement tend to be intertwined with one another, and it would be hard to find either of them in a pure form.[97] On the whole, the current tendency is to argue that the author of the PE did a good job in his own day, even if he did not do it as well as Paul would have done.[98]

This understanding of the composition of the PE is to be carefully distinguished from the way in which heretics created and used pseudonymous writings in order to promote their own

---

[97] Cf. Hanson, 48–51, espec. 50f.
[98] Cf. Young 1994 for a very positive presentation; see further Marshall 1993.

false teachings. Proponents of this view would generally argue that the author of the PE had a profound reverence for Paul (witness the commendatory picture of Paul which the letters convey) and laid the utmost stress on the preservation of the 'tradition' and the teaching given by Paul as the sole authority who is named. The letters are ostensibly concerned above all else to conserve and consolidate, to preserve the Pauline gospel and teaching as the right response to heretical teaching. In doing so, the risk was to ossify the Pauline teaching and to allow no further developments of it. At the same time, to be sure, there is a 'shift' from Paulinism in that the stress on holding fast to the 'deposit' represents a shift from the creative thinking of Paul and in that the author does reformulate Pauline teaching in various ways in response to the needs of his time and as a reflection of his own individual thinking.[99] The author could thus consciously be striving to reproduce Paulinism while at the same time being unconsciously influenced to produce something rather different. Nevertheless, the overall aim is to bring Paul up to date and to preserve his influence for a new generation.

It would be difficult to condemn the *motives* behind such an exercise. The problems arise when we consider the *method* that is alleged to have been employed. The generally accepted explanation invokes the practice of deceptive pseudonymity. That is to say, the letters were written in such a way as to make people believe falsely that they were written by Paul, so that they would accept them as authoritative, apostolic writings. The later the letters were composed, the more likely it is that deliberate deceit was involved. They are pseudonymous in the sense that they were written by somebody other than Paul who was trying to deceive his readers into thinking that they were genuine writings by Paul (which had presumably been 'lost' and had now been rediscovered).

There is now an enormous literature on the phenomenon of pseudonymity in the ancient world. It was a widespread practice in many different areas. According to most writers it involved the attempt to deceive the readers regarding the true authorship of the writing. Scholars who hold that there is a deliberate attempt to deceive in the PE (and other NT writings) attempt to play down the moral disquiet that this procedure may arouse for some modern readers. It is argued that by the standards of the time it was not morally culpable and there was no moral

---

[99] There are, of course, critics who insist that the result is very unpauline. Donelson 1986:60 castigates the author's ignorance of Pauline thinking.

stigma attached to it.[100] It must not be judged by the literary conventions of the modern world.[101]

The weakness of this argument is that it measures the morality of pseudonymity by the standards of the non-Christian ancient world rather than by the standards of Christian teaching. It is a simple and incontrovertible fact that second-century orthodox Christianity objected strongly to it, as practised by heretics or even by the presbyter who wrote 'out of love for Paul' (Tertullian, *De Baptismo* 17; cf. Torm*, 27). According to Donelson 1986:11f. there are no examples of works that were known to be pseudonymous being accepted as authoritative. It is unlikely that first-century Christians differed on the matter. This point has been denied by Meade 1986:206, who claims that there was a discontinuity between the first and subsequent centuries. Meade basically asserts this point rather than offering any solid arguments for it. His reasoning appears to be that the early church began to show an 'increasing rejection of anonymity and pseudonymity' in the second century with the rise of heresy and the need to discriminate more carefully between orthodoxy and heresy and to exercise control over the authors of Christian literature. But this argument fails to take into account the fact that heresy was already a problem in the first century; it assumes that anonymity and pseudonymity were fairly widespread in the first century, which is very questionable, and the telltale phrase '*increasing* rejection' (my italics) indicates that in any case a hard and fast line between the first and second centuries cannot be drawn. Meade's claim is quite unconvincing.[102]

The problem is eased if it can be maintained that the attribution of a writing to an earlier person was nothing more than a claim to continuity of teaching. Thus Bauckham roots the procedure in 2 Peter in 'the conventions of a Jewish literary genre' which the later church no longer understood. Evidently, it was conventional to supplement the writings of earlier authorities with material that stood in the same tradition. The authority of the pseudonymous author of 2 Peter thus 'lies in the faithfulness with which he transmits and interprets for a new situation, the normative teaching of the apostles. ... The pseudepigraphical device is therefore not a fraudulent means of claiming apostolic authority, but embodies a claim to be a faithful mediator of the

---

[100] This view must be carefully distinguished from the view which says that writings were produced under false names but without any attempt to deceive, since the readers knew perfectly well who the real author was. For this view see further below.

[101] 'In short, if one had a cause which was important enough and a lie could assist, then it is "permissible" to employ a lie' (Donelson 1986).

[102] See Wilder, T. L., 'New Testament Pseudonymity and Deception', Unpublished thesis, Aberdeen 1998.

apostolic message.'[103] Here there is a subtle shift from 'claiming to be the apostle' to 'claiming apostolic authority', but it is not obvious that the element of fraud has been eliminated so long as there was any intent to deceive.

The same line is developed independently and in great detail by Meade 1986, who holds that the later writer was not making a claim to authorship but to standing in the same tradition, like the people who added their oracles to the writings of an earlier prophet in the OT. But this hypothesis does not get round the fact that there was intent to deceive, and the apparatus of pseudonymity was used to this end.[104]

The problem that remains, then, is twofold. On the one hand, this type of pseudonymity involves an intent to deceive the readers into the belief that it was the apostle himself who was writing. This conflicts with the fact that there was a high regard among early Christians and in the NT for truth and truthfulness. There is also a strong emphasis, not least in the PE themselves, on the importance of preserving the tradition without perverting it in any way. People so motivated would have been unlikely knowingly to write or accept deceptive, pseudonymous works. The composition of Christian writings and the intent to deceive were not compatible. On the other hand, the demonstrable clear attitude of the orthodox church to pseudonymity in the second century is a powerful confirmation of this thesis. Consequently, it can be argued on the basis of the early church's attitude to truth that the practice of deceptive pseudonymity in the first century by defenders of orthodox Christianity is extremely improbable.

Is there, then, some alternative to deceptive pseudonymity which is free from the objections to which it is open?

III. PRESERVING THE PAULINE TRADITION: AN ALTERNATIVE TO PSEUDONYMITY

a. Theoretical possibilities

Apart from pseudonymity there are various ways in which a named author may not in fact be the actual writer and composer of a document.

(1) An author may use another person as a secretary and delegate powers to them to write on his behalf, and then sign the letter as being in effect from himself. This type of theory has often been suggested for the PE, but it is open to the objections

---

[103] Bauckham, R., *Jude, 2 Peter* (Waco: Word, 1983), 161f.
[104] As Meade has to allow (e.g. 121).

that it attributes to Paul a different procedure from that adopted in his other letters, that it requires one common amanuensis for all three of the PE (despite their different places and times of origin), and that no reference is made to a co-author in the letters.

(2) Again, it is permissible for the work of an author who has died to be posthumously edited and published for future generations, although in the modern world it would be normal for some indication of this fact to be made.[105]

(3) It is not too great a step to a situation in which somebody close to a dead person continued to write as (they thought that) he would have done. An incomplete work can be completed by somebody else, but again in a modern situation this would be made quite explicit.[106] There is a rather fluid boundary between this and the previous possibility, depending on how far the actual words of the deceased are utilised.

In none of these cases does the element of intentional deceit arise. Later generations might forget the facts of the origin, in much the way in which Hebrews appears to have gained access to the canon, humanly speaking, because it was believed to be by Paul and not just because its contents commended it. But this is no argument against the legitimacy of the original enterprise. It is free from the moral stigma that early Christians attached to the practice of pseudonymity. Since the nuance of deceit seems to be inseparable from the use of the terms 'pseudonymity' and 'pseudepigraphy' and gives them a pejorative sense, we need another term that will refer more positively to the activity of writing in another person's name without intent to deceive: perhaps 'allonymity' and 'allepigraphy' may be suggested as suitable alternatives.

Such a scenario can be positively defended for the PE and offers the most plausible solution to the enigma of their origin. It is not a new theory, being upheld by such scholars as Harrison and Easton,[107] but has been too easily dismissed in much recent scholarship.

---

[105] For a rare example in the ancient world see the Prologue to Ecclus.

[106] The example of students attributing their works to the philosopher who taught them may belong here.

[107] Harrison 1921:12; Easton, 19; Dornier, 25, holds that authentic Pauline letters were edited after his death by an unknown follower. This view is traced back to F. C. Baur; see Donelson 1986:9. See further Dunn, J. D. G., 'Pseudepigraphy', in Martin, R. P., and Davids, P. H. (eds.), *Dictionary of the Later New Testament and its Developments* (Downers Grove: InterVarsity Press, 1997), 977–84. Dunn essentially follows Meade (his student), but claims: 'the charge of deceit and falsehood leveled against these writings becomes inappropriate; what we have rather is a legitimate speaking in and use of the great teacher's name, recognized as such by the churches that first used the letters in question' (984).

b. The composition of the PE

1. The destination

It is most reasonable to associate the letters with the leaders of the congregations in the two areas mentioned in the PE, Crete and Ephesus/Asia Minor. The plausibility of the connection with Ephesus has been demonstrated in detail by Thiessen 1995:248–341. We know sufficient of the situation in Asia to recognise the likelihood of opposition to Paul there (cf. Acts 20), and placement of the letters close to Paul's lifetime leaves the field free for the activity of John at a still later date. It can be taken for granted that the sort of problems that Paul encountered continued after he ceased to be active in the area, and it is not at all surprising that the kind of doctrinal aberration found in Corinth crossed the Aegean Sea to Ephesus and found its way to Crete. In Paul's own lifetime the same opponents stalked around his mission field generally and followed him into comparatively remote locations such as Galatia.

We can thus propose a general scenario in which the tendencies that can be detected in Paul's lifetime and especially towards the end of it continued and required the same kind of response as he would have given. In this situation somebody produced letters written allonymously in the name of Paul, addressed to his immediate helpers and with the implicit rubric: 'These letters represent the kind of thing that I think that Paul would have to say to our churches today if he were still alive. Consequently, I have not simply repeated the actual things that he said, but I have had to think how he would have reacted to present circumstances.'[108] If Paul had in fact written letters (possibly Col and Eph) in his own lifetime in collaboration with others who had a major share in their composition, this could have afforded a precedent to encourage such further writing.

2. The key role of 2 Timothy

The starting point is the enigmatic character of 2 Timothy. It may not be too much of an exaggeration to say that, if it were not for the existence of its two companions, it would be possible to develop a plausible case for the Pauline authorship of 2 Tim. The Pauline character of the content of 2 Tim is patent. There

---

[108] This point is, of course, also made by those who regard the PE as deliberately pseudonymous. Zmijewski 1979:118 emphasises that the aim was not merely saying what Paul would say if he were still present but rather that he presented what he really believed was Pauline tradition in order to make it effective for his own time.

are scholars who are prepared to defend its substantially Pauline character, whatever they make of the other two letters. Thus it has been argued that 2 Tim is substantially the work of Paul whereas 1 Tim and Tit are the work of an imitator (Murphy-O'Connor 1991).

What this amounts to is saying that the last known letter of Paul to Timothy has been preserved but has been written up by an unknown compiler. The composition of Tit and 1 Tim could then have been a second step in the process of presenting Pauline teaching to deal with the growing opposition to Paul in some of his congregations.[109] The same person[110] accordingly proceeded to write two further letters incorporating Pauline material and other traditional material for the benefit of church leaders in Crete and Ephesus respectively. The similarities between these two letters render one of them unnecessary if they are both written to the same location, and therefore separate destinations are plausible. Thus it was 2 Tim which provided the spur for the writing of the subsequent two letters. The homogeneity of style demands that all three PE are by one and the same author (or the same team of authors).[111] It is perfectly possible that this composition was done in concert with the historical Timothy and Titus who remembered what Paul had said to them as well as what he had written.[112] We must not forget that the actual persons named in the New Testament existed, travelled and talked to one another!

Various things fall into place on this supposition. It explains the very general character of 2 Tim which is concerned primarily with the personal life and qualities of Timothy. The emphasis falls on suffering for the sake of the gospel and the need for courage. It reflects the fact of dispute and opposition within the church,

---

[109] Cf. Easton, 17–19, who argues for the sequence 2 Tim–Tit–1 Tim. He argues that Tit 1.1–4 condenses 2 Tim 1.1–10; that 1 Tim 1.1f. uses 2 Tim 1.1f. and Tit 1.1–4; that 1 Tim 3.2–5 uses Tit 1.5–8; and that a development can be seen in the treatment of the opponents (2 Tim 2.17; Tit 3.10f.; 1 Tim 1.20). He also claims that the author was not perpetrating deceptive forgery, but dates the composition at the turn of the century.

[110] It is possible that a group was involved, but the similarities in style between the PE favour the view that one person was responsible for the actual drafting. The modern analogy would be the report based on discussion by a working party but drafted by one of their number.

[111] At this point our hypothesis differs from that of Murphy-O'Connor in that he apparently regards 2 Tim as genuine and 1 Tim and Tit as imitations. Our view is that all three PE are the work of the same author and all may incorporate Pauline material. The differences which Murphy-O'Connor claims to find between 2 Tim and the other two letters are not sufficient to rule out common authorship, although they may show that 2 Tim stands closer to Paul.

[112] Cf. Bauckham*, 492–4, who comments that, unlike other postapostolic documents, 1 Tim 6.14 appears to assume that Timothy will survive to the parousia.

but the description remains fairly general apart from the references to specific opponents of Paul, the specific teaching that the resurrection has already taken place, and the behavioural consequences of the idiosyncratic teaching. The need to broaden the circle of orthodox teachers is emphasised. But the thought is centred much more on the personal opposition to Paul which was already a characteristic in his lifetime (2 Cor; Rom 15). In short, 2 Tim was written less as a response to a specific situation of opposition and more as a general exhortation to Timothy. This fits in well with the situation of Paul himself in imprisonment. The stress on suffering for the gospel is better explained as reflecting Paul's own position than that of church leaders at a later date elsewhere. The more detailed discussion of the heresy and church order in 1 Tim and Tit then reflects the growing concern with these problems and the need for practical solutions to them.

3. Attempts to identify the author

Can we identify a possible author? 2 Tim 4.11 states that only Luke was with Paul. Was Luke the person responsible for the composition of the PE? Despite the advocacy of this view by a number of scholars, it is indefensible on grounds of style and theology.[113]

The style of the PE is no closer to that of Luke than it is to that of Paul. It can hardly be argued that the distinctive style of the PE, as compared with that of LA, is due to the author attempting to copy the style of Paul or incorporating material written in a Pauline style, since, as we have seen, it is precisely the differences from Paul which lead us to posit a different author. No convincing explanation can be given as to why the author of LA should have adopted this specific style in writing the PE.

Although some similarities in thought can be perceived, perhaps reflecting composition around the same period in the same kind of ecclesiastical situation, the way in which the theology is expressed is significantly different. This is particularly true of the lack of attention to the Holy Spirit in the PE. As for the situation,

[113] For earlier attempts see Moule 1982 (originally 1965); Strobel, A., 'Schreiben des Lukas? Zum sprachlichen Problem der Pastoralbriefe'. *NTS* 15 (1968–9), 191–210; Feuillet 1978; and especially the full defence in Wilson 1979. Against this view see Brox 1970; Schenk 1987:3421–3; and my review of Wilson in *JSNT* 10 (1981), 69–74. See also Kaestli, J.-D., 'Luke-Acts and the Pastoral Epistles: The Thesis of a Common Authorship', in Tuckett, C. M. (ed.), *Luke's Literary Achievement: Collected Essays* (Sheffield: Sheffield Academic Press, 1995), 110–26. It is, of course, a possibility that Luke was responsible for transcribing Paul's actual letter to Timothy and that another person was responsible for a later revision of it.

the concern with opposition and heresy in the PE is central in a way which is certainly not the case in Acts (although the danger is not entirely absent). Luke's manifest unconcern about the internal organisation of the congregations is also rather different from the attitude in the PE. The hypothesis of a Lucan origin for the PE should be dropped from consideration.[114]

Another suggestion is authorship by Timothy or Titus (Bauckham*, 492–4). Timothy has also been claimed as the author of Colossians, written within Paul's lifetime.[115] If correct, this would set a precedent for co-authorship with the co-author taking the main share in the composition. But the differences between Colossians and the PE are as great as between the PE and the Pauline corpus generally, so that the difficulties for the hypothesis that a single person, whether Timothy or anybody else, was directly responsible for both are on a level with the difficulties surrounding straight Pauline authorship. If Timothy were not the author of Colossians, this would free him for the PE. If we attribute Colossians to Timothy, then Titus becomes a candidate for authorship of the PE. The hypothesis would then be that Timothy himself (or Titus) recast material originally received from Paul. All of this is highly speculative, even if it cannot be regarded as impossible.

But in fact other people are named in 2 Tim as being with Paul. Attention has been drawn to Tychicus (2 Tim 4.12), but he can hardly be intended as the author of 2 Tim. Eubulus, Pudens, Linus and Claudia are mentioned at the end (2 Tim 4.21). Here there is a small circle of local friends, out of whom Linus has been associated with the leadership of the church in Rome. Is there a hidden signature of a writer here who has deliberately kept him/herself out of the limelight? It is not implausible that somewhere in this circle lies the origin of 2 Tim.[116] Although they were apparently local people, to be distinguished from the group of Paul's earlier missionary companions named earlier in 2 Tim 4, they were closely associated with him and in effect were replacing the missionary companions who were no longer with Paul for good or not so good reasons.

Such writings, then, may have rested on actual communications by Paul. Thus 2 Timothy can very well be based on an authentic last letter of Paul to Timothy, and 1 Tim and Tit can reflect in

---

[114] Nevertheless, it is possible that Luke was the amanuensis to whom the original letter to Timothy that forms the basis of 2 Tim was dictated by Paul.

[115] Schweizer, E., *Der Brief an die Kolosser* (Zürich: Benziger/Neukirchen: Neukirchener, 1976), 20–7; Dunn. J. D. G., *The Epistles to the Colossians and to Philemon* (Grand Rapids: Eerdmans/Carlisle: Paternoster, 1996), 35–9.

[116] For the hypothesis of a circle round Timothy, one of whom composed 1 Timothy see Carrington*, 37.

part what Paul wrote or said to them on earlier occasions.[117] In view of the homogeneity of style it is virtually impossible to sort out material that may be derived from genuine Pauline letters to his colleagues from material that is drawn from other sources or is the author's own creation. Nevertheless, Johnson has demonstrated that the non-Pauline features in the PE tend to fall into distinct sections separated by passages which are more Pauline in vocabulary and character. No more than in the case of Acts does our inability to recreate the sources mean that there were no sources.

The probability that some Pauline material was used and the impossibility of identifying a named author should not obscure the fact that we are dealing with a person of considerable theological skill who was capable of putting his own stamp on his material and producing a set of documents marked by a unified and fresh exposition of Pauline theology. He was evidently in touch with the thought of Hellenistic Judaism and able to present the Christian message in the language and categories of the Hellenistic world.

4. The place of origin

Questions concerning the place of origin and the destination of the NT writings can sometimes be confused with each other. Establishing that the letters to Timothy have to do with Ephesus does not of itself locate the author there. 2 Tim is meant to be read as emanating from Rome, and this will be the actual place of origin of the hypothetical Pauline letter which underlies it. It was perfectly possible for a person in Rome to have knowledge of the situation in Ephesus or elsewhere and to write in a relevant way to it. 1 Clement shows knowledge of the church situation in Corinth. There is, of course, no trace of concern by another *church* for the recipients of the PE; they are couched as if from an individual church leader. In this respect, if the PE emanate from Rome, it is not the Rome of 1 Clement. Rather we have the work of a person (or perhaps a person with a supporting group) who is concerned to keep alive the influence of Paul in churches which were in danger of slipping away from the Pauline gospel, and the geographical location is somewhat irrelevant. But this Pauline circle was composed of people who were prepared to travel, and therefore they cannot necessarily be tied down to one specific location. They may have had associations

---

[117] Although the letters were not, on this hypothesis, written during Paul's third missionary campaign, they may have been composed to reflect this setting and may reflect the kind of things that Timothy and Titus were instructed to do at that time.

with Rome, but it could also be claimed that they reflect the Ephesian situation and that this is the more likely place of origin. The fact is that we know so little about them that it is pointless to speculate further.

5. *Considerations favouring this solution*

This general dating and situation for the PE is supported by the following considerations:

1. The opposition which is allegedly directed against the Pauline understanding of Christianity within the general area in which he had evangelised and founded churches is most plausibly situated in the period immediately after Paul's decease, and the method of reply fits that period more aptly. There is considerable stress on the way in which the opposition is directed against Paul personally, and this ties in with the situation during his own lifetime.

2. The heresy is in many respects undeveloped and it shows little relationship to second-century Gnosticism. Its closest links are with the teaching that circulated in Corinth and Colossae, and its rise is due in part to misinterpretation of Paul's own teaching. The 'new' feature is the speculative use of the Old Testament, and this could have developed at any time.

3. The structures of church leadership are still undeveloped. The existence of elders/bishops is not yet taken for granted in some of the churches, and the picture of successors to Paul still makes sense. It is increasingly difficult to understand the centrality of the persons taking over Paul's role as the overseers of congregations planted during the Pauline mission the later the PE are dated.

4. Early catholic features are absent. The church is not an institution dispensing salvation. Rather it is the apostolic tradition which enshrines the gospel and it is the activity of preaching and teaching which conveys the gospel to the people. The church as an institution is scarcely mentioned; the emphasis falls rather on the people who lead it as individuals who must be faithful to the gospel and upright in their lifestyle.

5. The theology is close to that of Paul, but there is no clear evidence for use of his earlier letters as literary sources. Echoes of their phraseology are inevitable on any theory of authorship. It is true that Pauline theology is expressed in other non-Pauline documents, but the verdict of Jeremias, 8, still stands: 'nowhere in the whole of the non-Pauline literature does Pauline teaching appear so clearly as in the Pastoral Epistles.'[118]

---

[118] Jeremias accepted that Eph and Col were genuine letters of Paul and did not belong to 'the non-Pauline literature'.

6. This hypothesis accounts for the elements which point to a possibly later date and setting than that of Paul's own life. At the same time, it recognises that the concerns for the preservation of doctrine and the consolidation of church structures in existing congregations are exactly what would be expected from Paul himself as he foresaw the end of his own ministry and supervision.[119] What we are witnessing is the broad transition from the period of Paul's personal leadership to that of his successors rather than a later period of succession from the second to the third or even a fourth generation.

7. The writing of orthodox works in the name of early Christians is most likely to have taken place soon after their deaths. It ceased thereafter. The orthodox Christian writings which survive from the end of the first century and the beginning of the second are without exception anonymous[120] or are by persons whose names they bear; none of the writings of the Apostolic Fathers or the Apologists claim to be by figures of the past.[121] It is only in less orthodox circles that real pseudonymity arises.[122] It was there that deceit was necessary in order to claim apostolic authority for dubious teaching.

8. This understanding of the composition of the PE solves the problem that the theory of pseudonymity fails to solve. It offers a solution to the problem of how letters ascribed to Paul could be produced in a church which laid a high regard on truth and truthfulness and which is not likely to have produced or accepted pseudonymous works. Theories of deliberate deceit assume far too easily that the practice was acceptable in the early church.

9. The hypothesis explains why there is no elaborate attempt at creating verisimilitude. The writer does not imitate Pauline style closely, nor does he cite from Paul's acknowledged letters, although there are inevitable echoes of them. There is a striking

---

[119] The work of Campbell 1994:176–9 strongly supports this *Sitz im Leben* for the composition of the letters.

[120] It should perhaps be stressed that anonymity and pseudonymity are two quite different phenomena, although they are frequently confused or equated. In any case the assumption that various NT books are anonymous in the sense that their first readers did not know who their authors were because they had concealed their identity is unfounded; it is clearly false for the writings of Luke and the Fourth Gospel which imply that the dedicatee and the writer's companions respectively knew who was the author. It is equally unlikely that the authors of Mt and Mk were unknown to their readers (or to at least some of them).

[121] The *Didache* of 'the Twelve Apostles' claims no more than that its teaching 'is in accordance with the witness and teaching of the apostles'; only in later documents are explicit pseudepigraphical claims to authorship by the apostles made. See Bradshaw, P., *The Search for the Origins of Christian Worship* (London: SPCK, 1992), 104f.

[122] *3 Corinthians* and the *Epistle to the Laodiceans* are later, clumsy forgeries and do not affect the point.

economy of personal details of the kind that would create a (fictitious) setting that would favour authenticity. The personal details in 2 Tim are most probably drawn from actual Pauline notes. The material cited as 'tradition' is not especially Pauline. On the contrary, the author was free to write in his own style. These points show that the author was not trying to deceive his readers into thinking that these were genuine Pauline works.

c. Conclusion

Our hypothesis, then, is that the indications are that the PE belong to the period shortly after the death of Paul. They, especially 2 Tim, are based on authentic Pauline materials whose extent cannot now be traced precisely, and they may well have been produced in a group which included Timothy and Titus themselves. The stimulus came from the existence of the authentic letter behind 2 Tim, which was already beginning to face up to the problems of the opposition, and led to the composition of 1 Tim and Tit to deal more explicitly and fully with the problems caused by opposition and heresy in Ephesus and Crete. The letters were intended to give Pauline backing to Timothy and Titus and associated church leaders in their work of calling the congregations back from false teaching and practices. They are examples not of pseudonymity but of allonymity. Their composition was accordingly in no sense deceptive, in that it was known that these were fresh formulations of Pauline teaching to take account of the changing situation. Nevertheless, with the passage of time the origins of the letters were forgotten and they were assumed to be from Paul himself.

8. THE THEOLOGY OF THE EPISTLES

Brown 1992; Davies 1996; Holtzmann, 159–90; Horrell 1993; Sand, A., '"Am Bewährten festhalten". Zur Theologie der Pastoralbriefe', in Hainz, J. (ed.), *Theologie im Werden. Studien zu den theologischen Konzeptionen im Neuen Testament* (Paderborn: Schöningh, 1992), 351–76; Towner 1989; Young 1994.

In the final part of this Introduction we shall attempt to offer a preliminary evaluation of the nature of the theology that is expressed in these documents.[123] In a famous comment on the Pastoral Epistles Denney stated: 'St. Paul was inspired, but the author of these epistles is sometimes only orthodox'.[124] Although

---

[123] No attempt is made here to give a complete account of the theology of the PE; see especially the **Excursuses** for more detailed discussion of individual motifs.

[124] Denney, J., *The Death of Christ* (London: Hodder and Stoughton, 1903), 203. Cf. Jülicher 1906:200.

Taylor remarked that 'Denney's sally ... is more brilliant than just,'[125] the characterisation continues to find supporters. Bultmann 1955:II, 186 referred to 'a somewhat faded Paulinism' in the PE. Rather more forcefully Hanson, 50, comments: 'Certainly the author of the Pastorals falls far short of Paul in almost every aspect.' Schweizer insists, 'As long as one compares them to the Pauline letters, one can only ascertain that everything is paler and sounds weaker than with Paul and not nearly as creative and progressive. The message is repeated in "orthodox" fashion, but it is no longer discussed with those who reject it; they are simply dismissed.'[126]

I. SOME CHARACTERISTICS OF THE PASTORAL EPISTLES

Various characteristics of the PE appear to support this rather negative verdict on the quality of their Christian thought. The letters can be seen as the work of somebody trying to do his best and remaining loyal to the faith, but nevertheless lacking the fire and vitality of the real Paul, and saying what he has to say in an inferior manner.

a. The lack of understanding of doctrine

Above all, there is said to be a lack of concern with doctrine, which is generally thought to reflect a less sure and insightful grasp of it. 'No possible change of circumstances or rise of fresh problems could have made Paul thus indifferent to such cardinal truths of his gospel as the fatherhood of God, the believing man's union with Jesus Christ, the power and witness of the Spirit, the spiritual resurrection from the death of sin, the freedom from the law, and reconciliation.'[127] The implication is that, if Paul had been granted a longer lease of life and had still been in his prime at the date forty or more years after his actual death when the PE were written, he would still have made a better job of it than his anonymous successor. Similarly, Vielhauer drew a contrast with the writer of Ephesians (which is assumed to be post-Pauline) and stated: 'One cannot speak of taking Pauline

[125] Taylor, V., *The Atonement in New Testament Teaching* (London: Epworth Press, 1945[2]), 47 n. 2.
[126] Schweizer, E., *A Theological Introduction to the New Testament* (London: SPCK, 1992), 99. The list of such comments can easily be lengthened. Schrage, W., (*The Ethics of the New Testament* [Edinburgh: T. and T. Clark, 1988], 257) says that in comparison with Paul the PE are 'much more prosaic, pedestrian, bourgeois, moralistic'; cf. Verhey, A., *The Great Reversal: Ethics and the New Testament* (Grand Rapids: Eerdmans, 1984, 126–9).
[127] Moffatt, J., *Introduction to the Literature of the New Testament* (Edinburgh: T. and T. Clark, 1918[3]), 42.

theology further, as for example happens in Ephesians, if we take this to mean a development even in a single direction, but rather of a reduction despite the accompanying acceptance of new concepts, images and traditions.'[128] On this view, the Epistles belong to that period of the church which is sometimes called 'early catholic' – a third generation period of consolidation in which there were few new insights into the faith and tradition was handed down in a rather wooden fashion. This period in particular is characterised in two further ways:

b. The loss of charisma and its replacement by office

There was a growing stress on appointment to office with prayer for the gifts of the Spirit to be granted in association with the laying on of hands in the place of the earlier exercise of varied ministries by people who were already the recipients of charismatic gifts. Appointment was of people who fulfilled various definable requirements as regards their character and natural abilities. The implication is that the gifts of the Spirit to ordinary members of the congregation, enabling them to exercise various ministries in the manner of 1 Cor 12–14, were no longer present, and that the church had to make do with the gifts of the Spirit given to people of good spiritual character in response to ordination. If the writer was not a Paul, the churches for which he was writing were equally far removed from the lively, charismatic congregations known to Paul. As Banks 1980:198 comments:

> Not only are the divergences between the Pastorals and other Pauline correspondence (including Ephesians) *greater in number*; they also move *in another direction*. It seems unlikely that Paul's thought and practice would turn aside into shallower waters, rather than move further in a more profound direction, in the period of time between the last of the Captivity letters and the first of the Pastorals – especially when only two or three years can have passed.

c. The bourgeois lifestyle and ethics

At the same time, the church was settling down to become an institution within Graeco-Roman society, and therefore it was

---

[128] Vielhauer, P., *Geschichte der urchristlichen Literatur* (Berlin: De Gruyter, 1975), 232. Similarly, von Campenhausen referred to 'the completely different bland speech' of the PE (Campenhausen, H. F. von, *Aus der Frühzeit des Christentums* [Tübingen: Mohr, 1963], 200f., as cited by Childs, B. S., *The New Testament as Canon: An Introduction* [London: SCM Press, 1984], 379).

striving to fit in with that society by the adoption of a moral
code and lifestyle which were in harmony with those of the
surrounding culture. Since it was very much a 'middle-class'
type of institution, the character of its life was what has been
labelled 'bourgeois'.[129] Perhaps unconsciously, the church was
becoming more like its neighbours and losing its cutting edge
in society.

d. The concern with organisation rather than theology

The result of this trend is that the PE are largely taken up with
matters affecting the organisation of the church rather than with
the development of its theology, and with laying down rules for
conduct rather than tackling the principles of Christian living.
One might indeed argue that what is wrong with the PE is that
they are trying to deal with spiritual problems not by offering
spiritual solutions but by means of ecclesiastical joinery.

e. The uninspired and uninspiring style

Finally, in this brief list of characteristics is the fact that the
writer lacks the literary verve of Paul in expressing his theological
and ethical teaching. His writing is turgid, and the pattern of
thought is often not clear. He is unimaginative. When he has to
deal with points of view that differ from his own, his method is
not to enter into constructive debate but to dismiss alternative
views without argument as being not worthy of serious attention
and to denigrate their protagonists in the stereotyped forms of
ancient polemical literature. By contrast, Paul is alleged to enter
into dialogue with his opponents and doctrinal understanding is
advanced through the cut and thrust of argument.

II. ORTHODOX LETTERS FOR AN UNENTHUSIASTIC CHURCH?

One way of explaining the character of the letters is offered by
Donelson 1986:200f. He claims that what we see in the PE is a
church which is coming to terms with the fact that the lively
Christianity, characterised by the spiritual presence of Christ
and the gifts of the Spirit, which we find in Paul and John no
longer works, if it ever did. Experience speaks otherwise. In this
situation two solutions are possible. One is the way that was
possibly taken by the opponents of the author of the PE; they
'may have believed in a more aggressive version of the spirit'

---

[129] For the classic statement of this position see Dibelius-Conzelmann, 39–41.
(The German original has 'Christlicher Bürgerlichkeit', which is translated as
'good Christian citizenship'.)

and so would be 'the true heirs of Pauline thought'. But the writer of the PE was apparently a realist. Since the kind of Christianity espoused by Paul and John does not work because 'Jesus is not accessible and ... the spirit keeps relatively quiet', he provides 'clear ethical norms and reliable authorities' for 'a version of Christianity which is reasonable and moral. This version is actually closer to what mainline western churches practice today than anything in Paul and John.' Although Donelson is somewhat ambiguous in expression, he appears to be suggesting that the PE offer an approach which has been corroborated by the experience of a church which does not know whatever it was that Paul and John experienced. They offered 'a non-threatening lens through which orthodoxy could read Paul' and which could stand over against Gnostic heresies.[130] Thus the author grasped Paul's authority to promote a system of orthodoxy which did not reflect Paul's complexity. In effect the PE are an expression of the typical Christianity of their time and presumably were acceptable in a rather bland, lifeless church.

The general tendency in modern scholarship has in fact been to take the direction suggested by Donelson. Scholars who took the PE as genuinely Pauline, as also some of those who did not, regarded them as being among the latest writings of the NT, and consequently held that they represented the peak of development rather than stages in a decline to a more mediocre type of Christianity. Therefore, the rather formal understanding of church structure which was found in them, with suitable people being appointed to hold office on the basis of fulfilling a set of definable characteristics and then ordained in a ritual which involved prayer and laying on of hands so that they might receive the appropriate gifts of the Spirit, was regarded as the 'proper' way to do it. At the same time, the rather haphazard church organisation which is found in the earlier letters of Paul could be dismissed or played down as being an elementary, *ad hoc*, and undeveloped stage in a church which was still finding its way. Indeed, it could be argued that the growth of the church in size and complexity demanded a more orderly type of ministry, and the PE happily provided it. In this way, one could be happy with 'mere orthodoxy' and appreciate the PE from this point of view.

The strong stress on tradition was also important, for it meant that the church remained firmly tied to what it saw as its historical roots in the theology of the apostles, and thereby protected from the threats posed by Gnostic and other heresies, which were a

---

[130] Contrast Johnson 1987:1–3 who argues that the PE can and do threaten the contemporary church!

hotbed of speculation. With the Spirit confined to those ordained in a succession that could be traced back to the apostles, it would have been easy to deny the authority of people who indulged in theological speculation. What matters, then, is orthodoxy, in the sense of holding fast to tradition and the provision of an organisation that will ensure this. Anything that goes beyond it is of the devil! There is no place for fresh, creative thinking. Thus the PE basically hold on to the past, understood as the standard of orthodoxy. They represent either a failure to come to terms with the needs of the new generation or a more realistic response to the needs of a church which could not live indefinitely on the high level of Spirit-inspired enthusiasm which Paul had envisaged. Either way, there has been a loss of vitality compared with Pauline Christianity.[131]

III. TOWARDS A MORE POSITIVE EVALUATION

There are one or two different threads entangled in this estimate of the PE. One is the question of the theological and rhetorical style of the author which is admittedly different from that of Paul himself in his prime. The style is less lively, although the PE are not without their high points. The other question is whether the theology, differently expressed as it is, represents a decline from that of Paul.

One way of assessing the matter is to recognise that the times demanded a different approach from that of Paul; it was a time of consolidation rather than of advance. The writer of the PE did what was needed in the circumstances, not necessarily entirely successfully, by refuting the heresy, by setting up or consolidating a church structure that would exclude it, and by encouraging the existing church leaders to stand firm despite temptations to be slack. This was the third or fourth generation, and it demanded appropriate measures. 'Not theological inferiority but the passage of time, the transition of Christianity into the post-apostolic generation, brings this decisive change in perspective' (Brox, 55).[132]

Young 1992 raises the question of 'The Pastoral Epistles and the Ethics of Reading'; she asks whether it is possible to have an ethically responsible approach to texts which are pseudonymous. In brief her answer is that we can and must deal fairly with the

---

[131] Roloff, 388, comments that this type of understanding was congenial to some Roman Catholics, but that it was condemned – too harshly – by Protestant critics who saw anything that was 'early catholic' in the NT as a dreadful lapse from Pauline theology.

[132] For similar affirmations see (for example) the commentaries by Hultgren 1984; Karris 1979; and, above all, Barrett 1963.

PE as documents which were composed to deal responsibly with the problems caused for the community by the death of its founder or authority. We can then see them as inspirational documents for that particular situation rather than regretting that they do not look like documents of the calibre of Paul himself. We should respect them for what they are, while also respecting ourselves and therefore being aware of the differences between the original readers and ourselves. They must then be read in the light of the three facts: (a) that the surface text-type is not the implied text-type; (b) that the implied readership (the community) is not the stated readership (Timothy/Titus); and (c) that the implied author (an anonymous disciple of Paul) is not the stated author (Paul). There is also of course the fact (d) that we are not the original readers and the differences between us and them must be taken into account. Questions can then be asked about the past meaning and future potential of the texts. In this way, the PE can be understood more positively (cf. Young 1994).

Yet another attempt to cope with the problem posed by the PE is that of Meade 1986 who develops the concept of *Vergegenwärtigung*. His understanding is that the tradition which has been handed down in the church has to be revitalised and reapplied to new situations. Thus the PE maintain the continuity with Paul and emphasise his authority but interpret him for a new generation. Meade is primarily concerned with the 'shape' of the PE, to see how they function as letters making a claim to stand in an authoritative tradition. He does not work out in detail how the traditions are contemporised by the author. But he significantly notes that there is an important element of revitalisation going on and not simply consolidation.[133]

IV. COHERENCE AND CONTINGENCY

Beker has argued that in the genuine writings of Paul the clue to understanding lies in the concepts of coherence and contingency. Paul's thought has a coherent centre which is expressed contingently in his responses to the different human situations with which he is faced. Thus 'he was able to bring the gospel to speech in each new situation without compromising either the wholeness of the gospel or the specificity of the occasion

---

[133] There is also of course the not insignificant group of commentators who cannot be dismissed as 'fundamentalists' but regard the PE as the work of Paul himself and who would insist on their inspirational quality in warm terms. See Johnson (1987; reiterated in Johnson 1997); Kelly (1963); Fee (1988); Oden (1989).

to which it was addressed.'[134] Beker then applies this thesis to the authentic letters. He argues for a specific coherent centre in apocalyptic: the centre of Pauline thought is the future triumph of God which he has inaugurated in the Christ-event, rather than, say, the 'righteousness' or 'justification' which has been identified especially by scholars in the Lutheran tradition as the key to Paul.

For Beker himself there was also a literature in which the insights of Paul were ignored, misunderstood or trivialised, and the PE belong in this category.[135] Paul emerges as an 'institutional organizer and implacable dogmatician'. Although the resulting picture is distorted, nevertheless, it can be seen somewhat more positively when the changed circumstances of the church in the author's time are taken into account.[136]

Beker's basic approach can be developed in a somewhat different manner to make sense of the PE as contingent examples of the application of the central coherent core of Paul's thought to their particular situation, on the basis of a modified characterisation of that core. If this thesis can be demonstrated, then it follows that the PE display a more creative use of the Pauline gospel to face up to new situations and provide a fresh approach to them.

a. The coherent core

In his identification of the core of Paul's theology Beker appears to identify the characteristic set of structural categories within which Pauline theology is formed with the content of the theology. Apocalyptic is properly the source of the categories used by Paul rather than being the content. Beker is correct to see that the apocalyptic *mode* or *idiom* determines to some extent the materials of Paul's theology, such as the future triumph of God, and he also rightly sees that the cross and resurrection are of great importance. However, it seems to me to be a confusion of categories when he claims that apocalyptic is the central *theme*

[134] Beker, J. C., *Paul the Apostle: The Triumph of God in Life and Thought* (Edinburgh: T. and T. Clark, 1980), 34.

[135] Op. cit., 250f., with reference to the understanding of the law. More fully see Beker 1992:36–47, 83–6, 105–8.

[136] Beker 1992:36–47 holds that the Paul portrayed in the PE has become a static authoritative figure who stands on his unique authority and does not have to argue for his views. The coherent core of the gospel is no longer flexibly integrated with its contingent expressions, but there is constant appeal to a fixed body of dogmatic teaching and instructions. There is no longer any dialogue with his readers or opponents. Pauline terms lose their freshness and are used in a rather tired and worn-out way. The whole outlook is pragmatic and the writer is concerned to safeguard the church from the possibly hostile attitude of the state if it upsets social norms.

of Pauline theology; the result is a tendency to over-accentuate the future triumph of God. It is doubtful whether Beker quite does justice to the fundamental significance of Jesus and the present effects of his work.[137]

Ridderbos claims that the centre of Paul's theology is 'the saving activity of God in the advent and the work, particularly in the death and the resurrection, of Christ', and that this theme is developed in a redemptive-historical, eschatological framework.[138] If we adopt this identification of the centre of Pauline theology and amend Beker's thesis in the light of it, the question will then be whether the PE represent a valid contingent application of this central coherency to a specific situation, or whether they represent a misunderstanding of it, or even a simple repetition of it that does not carry us any further.

Two preliminary points must be offered. First, in a situation characterised by opposition and heretical teaching, the PE demonstrate that same *building of practice upon doctrine* which lies at the heart of Pauline thinking and which is indeed characteristic of much of the NT. This is seen clearly in Romans with its careful structure of doctrine (chs. 1–11) followed by practice (chs. 12–15), but also in other letters where there is a more intricate blending of doctrinal principles used to prepare for or to back up ethical instruction. This same structure of thinking prevails in the PE, where teaching is often based on doctrinal buttressing – e.g. 1 Tim 2.1f./3–7. There is the way in which 1 Tim 3.16 functions as the hinge of the letter. The faithful sayings act as the warrants for ethical instruction. Similarly, the function of Tit 2.11–15 and 3.4–7 is to act as the basis of instruction. Thus Towner 1989:255 can conclude: 'Theology and ethics come together in the author's thought to form a coherent structure.... He articulates his theology in such a way that the Christ-event and salvation form its interrelated focal point or center of gravity.'[139] Thus we can see how the doctrine is used to form the basis for the specific instruction.

Second, an important role is occupied by traditional material in the PE. This is seen conspicuously in the so-called 'faithful sayings', but there is other material which is generally regarded as being based on tradition. What is important here is that *the tradition is used creatively*, as in the genuine letters of Paul, rather

---

[137] Cf. Marshall, I. H., 'Is Apocalyptic the Mother of Christian Theology?', in Hawthorne, G. F., and Betz, O. (eds.), *Tradition and Interpretation in the New Testament: Essays in Honor of E. Earle Ellis* (Grand Rapids: Eerdmans, 1987), 33–42.

[138] Ridderbos, H., *Paul: An Outline of his Theology* (London: SPCK, 1977), 39.

[139] Cf. Merkel, 14f.

than being simply wooden repetition.[140] One indication of this is the language. It is notable that the traditional material is generally not betrayed as such by a distinctive vocabulary and syntax which would indicate that the writer was quoting material which he himself had not composed. On the contrary, it is significant that time and again the traditional material is couched in the typical vocabulary and style of the PE and that it applies very directly to the situation which is being addressed. Thus 1 Tim 2.4–6 is plainly based on tradition (Mark 10.45) but it has been elaborated and expanded in such a way that it bears very specifically on the theme of salvation for all sorts and conditions of people which is appropriate to the context; moreover, the same tradition reappears in Tit 2.14 where the material is developed somewhat differently to suit the context of godly living expressed in good works. It should also be noted that the faithful sayings and other material that can be classified as tradition are not word-for-word repetitions of material in the Pauline letters. Rather it is presented as material which Paul himself would have regarded as tradition. In these ways we can see that the doctrinal basis for the practical paraenesis is itself being reshaped creatively in the light of the current situation.

From these considerations regarding the general parameters of the teaching in the PE we now turn to consider where the coherence, the core of Christian understanding in the letters, is to be seen. Naturally, we have to look for it in statements that are expressed contingently in relation to the specific situation of the letters. At the heart lie Christology and soteriology. The *Christology* of the PE goes beyond that of the genuine Pauline epistles in various ways. It is firmly rooted in tradition, but at the same time it takes up and develops the concept of 'epiphany' in a vigorous new way. The concept is one which would have been particularly effective in the Hellenistic world, although the roots of the idea probably lie in the OT and Judaism.[141] It is used to speak to new readers and it develops the concept that Jesus has appeared as God manifest and will reappear. The hope of the parousia is always present and alive. The common view that there is a weakening of eschatological expectation is unjustified (cf. rightly Johnson, 95f.). The writer ties together God and Jesus in a fresh, new way, and thereby makes clear the position of Jesus as the agent of salvation.

The PE thus express the understanding of Jesus Christ found in Paul, whereby he is placed firmly alongside God the Father as the source of grace and peace, yet understood as the Man

---

[140] The treatment by Wegenast 1962:132–58 is not satisfactory in its discussion of the PE.
[141] Marshall 1988:157–77.

whom God gave to redeem humankind by his death. When the PE claim that he is God manifest in the flesh, this is essentially what Paul had said in Galatians 4.4, but it is being expressed in a new way.

The *soteriology* of the PE is again firmly rooted in tradition, as we have already noted. The writer makes it clear that grace has been revealed in the appearance of Jesus, who gave himself for sinners to redeem them, and that he is thus the mediator between God and humankind. He understands the effectiveness of the work of Christ in terms of justification. Where he is distinctive is in the stress on the universal scope of the work of Christ. Paul is, of course, quite certain that salvation is given on the same terms to both Jewish and Gentile believers (Rom 3), but this point is emphasised in the PE. The concept of 'not by works of the law' is enlarged to make it clear that human works in general do not contribute to justification. The reason for this stress must lie in some kind of limitation of salvation on the part of the opponents, although just exactly what kind of limitation is not apparent.

In the light of these considerations it is clear that the PE share the same coherent core of theology as the Pauline letters.

b. The contingent response

We now consider the way in which the core finds expression in the contingencies of the new situation. Church order and ethics are the two main areas to be discussed.

The detailed discussion of *church order* has often seemed to represent a going-back on Paul, a retreat from the freedom of the Spirit exercising his gifts throughout the congregation into an orderly, tightly constricted structure in which ordination and office are all-important. On the contrary, it is important to note that alongside the undoubted stress on charismatic ministries in Paul there are also the beginnings of a system of leadership, apparently based on such considerations as 'the first converts' or 'the older men', which existed and developed alongside the charismatic ministries. With the passing of the first converts and with the development of the church, there was increasing need for adequate local leadership. This was attained in a number of ways.

First, the need was seen to develop a Pauline kind of leadership in the several parts of the Pauline mission field, specifically in Ephesus and Crete. Timothy and Titus represent the second-generation of leadership, functioning in a way similar to Paul himself. They are examples of how the concept of 'apostleship' is remodelled to cope with a new situation. 2 Tim, in particular, shows how the character of apostleship, as developed especially in 2 Cor, is to be preserved in the next generation of Christian leaders.

Second, within the local churches the system of eldership was carried further. There was no longer a haphazard recognition of the older people, in years or membership, as the obvious leaders, and in place of this there was choice among people who possessed the qualities and character for leadership, as these were understood in the Hellenistic world in the light of the gospel. This implied, for instance, that younger people might be appointed to leadership, certainly so in the case of Timothy and probably so in the case of Titus.

Third, there is a further development in the process of relating the charismatic and the appointed ministries. The problem inherent in charismatic ministries, right from the beginning, was that of discriminating between the true and the counterfeit; both Paul and John testify to the need to test the spirits. The solution in 1 Cor appears to lie in the discriminating activity of the congregation itself, but what do you do when a congregation itself goes astray? The criterion of discrimination is probably to be regarded as faithfulness to the kerygma, love, and edification of the congregation, in short, a christological criterion.[142] In the difficult situation faced by the PE we find the same stress on the importance of conformity to tradition, but it appears that the teaching is largely (if not exclusively) in the hands of the elders. A radical situation required radical measures. Where false teaching was being presented, it was necessary that the faithfulness of the teachers to the centralities of the gospel should be safeguarded.

Finally, it should be noted that the PE deal with a situation where local church leaders already existed, and therefore their author should not be criticised for introducing a new system. Rather, where church leaders exist, it is necessary to address them and discuss their character and functions. (Even in Titus, where Titus is to appoint elders in every town, this represents the extension of an existing system rather than the creation of a new one.) What is happening in the PE in part is that there is an important understanding of the charismatic gifts of the Spirit as being necessary for church leadership as well as for ministry in the church. Leadership does not belong automatically to the older men, but to those people to whom the Spirit points and whom he equips.

The question of *ethics* now arises. The letters introduce new concepts to describe the nature of Christian conduct. The most

---

[142] Cf. Dunn, J. D. G., *Jesus and the Spirit* (London: SCM Press, 1975), 293–7.

important of these is εὐσέβεια, which expresses a proper attitude to God and to other people for whom respect is appropriate. Here we have a fresh term with a history in Judaism and in the Hellenistic world.[143]

A comparison with 1 Peter may be fruitful at this point. There is a considerable similarity in the way in which Peter urges his readers to live responsibly and positively in the world despite its hostility. What Peter has done has been assessed as highly positive in that he was encouraging Christians to live responsibly in the world and so to commend the gospel.[144] The PE should be similarly assessed.

One specific area of concern is wealth. The problem is not raised in the Pauline letters, although there is teaching on Christian giving. When it is addressed here, the author faces up to the fact that some people are rich; he does not yet know the concept of total renunciation of property practised by the monks. Rather he is concerned with the responsible use of wealth. (Nor does he envisage a situation in which slavery ceases to exist, however much Philemon may point in that direction when taken to its logical conclusion.) But the question of how a rich person can be saved still arises. The writer speaks radically enough about the dangers of wealth and the love of money. He therefore counsels 'living as though one had none' by zeal in generosity to the needy and so laying up treasure in heaven.

c. The apparent lack of some Pauline emphases

So far we have argued that we can see the coherent centre of Pauline theology being applied to a contingent situation in the PE. But it would be a valid objection to our case if it could be shown that there are other items, central and integral to Pauline theology, which have been neglected, or if the theology of the PE is expressed in such a way as to make these emphases ineffective or indeed to oppose them. Various motifs were noted earlier as missing from the PE.

1. The fatherhood of God

There is a notable lack of explicit reference to God as Father, the description being found only in the epistolary salutations. However, this omission must be seen in context. It is important to analyse what actually happens in the authentic letters of Paul. We can classify the contexts in which the term is used by Paul

---

[143] For a detailed discussion see **Excursus 1**.
[144] See especially Goppelt 1982:II, 161–78.

as: opening salutations; liturgical material including prayers for the readers; references to God as Abba and as the father of Jesus Christ; and traditional formulations.[145] It then emerges that it is above all the non-use of the language of prayer, especially the absence of prayer-reports, in the PE that is responsible for this omission. Where there is an opening prayer-report, it is addressed to 'God' (2 Tim 1.3), exactly as Paul can also do in 1 Th 1.2; 2 Th 1.3.

If the actual term is rare, the theology expressed in the concept of God as Father is present. It is often said that the concept of God in the PE is remote (cf. 1 Tim 1.17; 6.15f.), but in fact the PE stress his gracious epiphany in Christ. The rich care of God for his people is seen in the development of the use of the term Saviour. Thus an alternative terminology has been used to express the same theological themes as are conveyed by the term 'Father'.

2. The power and witness of the Spirit

This concept is also at first sight strangely absent. However, in a discussion of the references which are present Haykin 1985 argues, first, that a high regard for the Spirit's activity in prophecy is evident in the way in which the author cites prophecy as an authoritative commentary on various events (1 Tim 4.1), second, that the Spirit is undoubtedly poured out on all believers – and poured out 'richly' (Tit 3.5f.) – and, third, that the Spirit working in the lives of such as Timothy is likened to a burning fire (2 Tim 1.6f.).[146] Nothing warrants the conclusion that the working of the Spirit was confined to church leaders or that prophecy was a thing of the past. On the contrary, the language of Tit 3.5f. is as powerful as anything elsewhere in Paul. Moreover, as we have observed, nothing indicates that the 'opposition' claimed charismatic gifts and that the author was deliberately playing down the role of the Spirit to curb their excesses.

3. Union with Jesus Christ and spiritual resurrection from death in sin

Union with Christ is expressed by Paul in a variety of ways, including being 'in Christ' and 'with Christ'. The concept of

---

[145] a. Opening salutations – as in the PE. b. Material that is 'liturgical', such as prayers for the readers (2 Cor 1.3; 1 Th 3.11; 2 Th 2.16); doxologies (Phil 2.11; 4.20); prayer to God (cf. Rom 15.6) or teaching about prayer (Eph 2.18; 3.14; 5.20; Col 3.17). c. References to God as Abba (Rom 8.15; Gal 4.6). d. Reference to God as Father of Christ (Rom 6.4; 15.6; 1 Cor 15.24; 2 Cor 11.31). e. Other traditional material (1 Cor 8.6; cf. Eph 4.6).

[146] Haykin 1985:291–305.

dying with Christ is also fairly widespread in Paul. It is part of a fairly complex group of ideas in Paul which includes the thought of suffering and dying with Christ, the hardships faced by the servants of Christ, and the new life in the Spirit. The 'in Christ' language is rare in PE, and the range of constructions is limited compared with Paul, but it is not entirely absent (2 Tim 2.2, 11; 3.15). There is, however, rather more stress than is sometimes noticed on the fact that the missionaries and faithful servants of Christ are called to suffering (2 Tim 2.3), and there is a faithful saying about dying and living with Christ. The thought of union with Christ is thus clearly present, and the lack of development is because the author is not dealing with the doctrinal basis for spiritual living except in relation to Timothy himself.

4. Freedom from the law

Finally, the suggestion that the PE are not concerned with freedom from the law, especially in view of what has been said about the Jewish-Christian nature of the congregations, overlooks the comments on the law in 1 Tim 1.8–11 which see the law more as a bulwark against evil-doers. Paul himself valued the law positively, and his complaints were against its use as a means of salvation. Hence his teaching was determined and called forth by polemic against salvation by the law. Tit 3.5 insists more broadly on salvation apart from works, and preserves the principle of 'by grace and not according to works' which is foundational to Paul's own understanding.[147]

5. Conclusion

The total impression given by the PE remains one in which grace controls the Christian life. The verdict of Bultmann 1955:II, 186 may be a trifle grudging, but he recognised clearly enough that the heart of Pauline theology is to be found here when he wrote: 'Nevertheless, for all its plodding one-sidedness, it is a legitimate extension of Paul's thinking to understand grace as a power that molds everyday bourgeois living; and when this everyday living is placed under the light of grace something also remains of Paul's "as if ... not" (I Cor. 7:29ff. I, p. 351f.).' Today the description of the PE as 'bourgeois' has effectively been abandoned, and this may suggest that the closeness to Paul is rather greater than Bultmann was prepared to allow.[148]

[147] See in more detail Westerholm, S., 'The Law and the "Just Man" (1 Tim. 1.3–11)', ST 36 (1982), 79–95; Marshall 1996b.
[148] See Jeremias, 8; Towner; Schwarz 1983; Kidd 1990; Reiser 1993.

From this discussion it is clear that the author of the PE is his own man and not a mere repeater of Paul's ideas. Nevertheless, there is enough material here to rebut the view that the PE neglect central aspects of Paul's theology. Various significant features of the teaching of the PE are discussed at greater length in the commentary (see especially the relevant excursuses); what has been attempted here is nothing more than a trial probe which has suggested that there is a fresh, creative expression of a theology that is based on Paul in these letters.

A somewhat different type of critique of the PE has been mounted by Horrell. He is concerned with the way in which the PE, while claiming to call the readers back to Pauline theology, do so to a Pauline theology with a difference. The theology is being used in the interests of an ideology. The letters defend an understanding of society in which certain groups, notably women and slaves, are firmly kept in their place of subordination and theological arguments are brought in to enforce this position. Anything which opposes the dominant social order is seen as a threat and is strongly attacked (cf. Brown*). There is no attempt to criticise the situation of those who are in power. The result is a social ethos which is not that of Paul himself.

Horrell raises important questions which should not be ducked. On the one hand, it is certainly the case that in their situation the PE do reinforce some existing attitudes which are no longer acceptable in the modern world, and it is true that the desire to commend the faith and to avoid persecution may have had something to do with this. There is also the very difficult question of how far people can be expected to see the long-term, wider effects of their attitudes and policies and how far they are responsible for results that they could not foresee. Could the author of the PE have foreseen that the degree of structure which he was forced to promote in order to deal with the contingent problem of what he saw as dangerous opposition to the gospel would have been taken as an absolute, unchanging requirement by later generations of Christians who found a rigid hierarchical structure to be a congenial way of running the church? Or could Paul have foreseen how his words would be used by nineteenth-century slave-owners to justify the status quo?

On the other hand, within the acceptance of the social structures in the PE there are some elements which could turn out to be subversive, such as the characterisation of slaves as benefactors of their masters, and the recognition that even the lowest in society can bring fresh lustre to the gospel. It follows that the modern Christian must not take over first-century assumptions regarding society uncritically, any more than one would take over first-century natural science, but must assess them in the light of the underlying theology. Even if the actual application in the first century is culturally determined and needs revision, the underlying theology and the sense of its relevance to ethical behaviour and spiritual life may be regarded as perennially valid and as imposing an ongoing hermeneutical task on those who believe that the PE contain the Word of God.

THE LETTER TO
TITUS

THE LETTER TO TITUS

OPENING SALUTATION
(1.1–4)

Berger, K., 'Apostelbrief und apostolische Rede: Zum Formular frühchristlicher Briefe', *ZNW* 65 (1974), 190–231; Hegermann 1970:47–64; Lieu, J. M., ' "Grace to you and peace": the apostolic greeting', *BJRL* 68 (1985), 161–78; Prior 1989:37–59; Roloff, 55–7 (cf. 1965:255f.); Schnider and Stenger 1987; Stenger 1974:252–67; Vouga, F., 'Der Brief als Form der apostolischen Autorität', in Berger, K., *Studien und Texte zur Formgeschichte* (Tübingen: Mohr, 1992), 7–58; Wolter 1988:82–90; Zmijewski 1979:97–118.

The opening salutation follows a pattern which is familiar from the earlier letters in the Pauline corpus. The Pauline pattern in its turn represents a Christianisation of a secular form of epistolary greeting. The typical form found in Jewish letters named the writer and the recipients and expressed a greeting, e.g.: 'A to B: greeting and good peace' (2 Macc 1.1; cf. 1.10). The Pauline form expands all three parts to indicate the Christian standing and authority of the writer, the Christian character of the recipients, and the Christian nature of the greeting expressed. The Christian gospel thus comes to brief and concentrated expression together with an indication that the presentation of it which will follow in the letter rests ultimately on divine authority.

Titus has the fullest salutation of the three Pastorals. As typically in the Pauline letters, this section sets the tone and introduces the concerns that the letter will later address. Its formality and fulness of content suggest that it is meant not only for Titus but also for the churches for which he is responsible.

The description of the sender is especially developed. Paul is presented as a slave and apostle, a combination of titles which expresses both his position under divine authority and his commission with divine authority to function in the church. His task is to forward faith and knowledge of the truth among God's elect. This task derives its impetus from the hope of eternal life which (a) has been promised by God since time immemorial; (b) has been revealed at the appropriate time as the word which is made known in the church's proclamation; and (c) has been entrusted to Paul by the commandment of God in his role as Saviour. Thus the characterisation of Paul's role develops into a brief statement of the gospel with which he has been entrusted, and the emphasis in the salutation lies upon God's purpose of salvation.

Titus is addressed as his genuine 'child' who shares the same faith and therefore stands in the service of the same gospel by virtue of his fellowship with and appointment by Paul.

Paul sends greetings to him, praying for him to receive spiritual blessings from God the Father and Christ the Saviour.

The function of the salutation is therefore to set the tone of the letter at its outset by stressing (a) the authority which Paul has received from God, (b) the nature of his ministry, and also (c) the content of the gospel which is at the base of his ministry. The material is developed in terms of the nature and goal of Paul's apostleship which is in effect shared by Titus who is the appointed representative of the apostle Paul.[1] It thus serves in effect to state the authorisation which Titus has for his task in the church.[2]

In length and complexity the salutation stands closest to Romans, with which it has some links in content (Holtzmann, 116, 462), and Galatians.[3] It forms an introduction containing elements or themes that will receive further development in the course of the letter (but which are common to the PE): for example, πίστις (1.1, 4, 13; 2.2, 10; 3.15), εὐσέβεια (1.1; 2.12), ἐλπίς (1.2; 2.13; 3.7); ζωὴ αἰώνιος (1.2; 3.7), σωτήρ/σῴζω/ σωτήριος (1.3, 4; 2.10, 11, 13; 3.4, 5, 6), and the concept of divine disclosure (1.3; 2.11; 3.5). The salutation thus to some extent lays the doctrinal foundation for the practical teaching which is about to be given (Johnson, 217–19). The stress is particularly upon the doctrine of salvation. God's gift of eternal life is grounded upon the foundation of God's promise, and has been revealed in the approved (apostolic) preaching which was entrusted to Paul.

Proponents of pseudonymity especially detect in this emphasis on Paul the claim by a Pauline community or student that the 'Pauline' message alone is to be regarded as the standard for the church. Only Paul is named as the author of the letter (in contrast to those genuine letters where others are associated with him). No mention is made of other apostles (contrast 1 Cor 9.5; Eph 2.20; 3.5). The effect is to place him on a pedestal over against the recipients, Titus and Timothy, who are described in

---

[1] Cf. the excursus on the theology of apostleship in Spicq, 595–9.

[2] On the assumption of authenticity Dornier, 118, holds that Titus needed especial affirmation of his position in view of his delicate task.

[3] Quinn, 19f., has argued that its length and elaborate nature (compared with 1 and 2 Tim) suggest that it serves as a 'preface to the collection'. This hypothesis depends completely on prior assumptions about the literary nature of the PE, for there is nothing in Tit 1.1–4 that suggests it bears this relationship to 1 and 2 Tim.

decidedly subordinate terms as compared with earlier mentions of them (Houlden, 46). He is presented as the sole channel of the message or guarantor of salvation, a role which he then delegates to his colleagues. Bühner claims that this motif is closer to Luke-Acts than to Paul.[4] Paul and his successors are thus in effect the only commissioned preachers of the message and the other apostles have vanished from the scene.[5]

However, Paul writes in his own name in Rom and Gal (and possibly Eph); the language used here is no more exclusive than that which occurs in the openings of the undisputed Paulines (Rom 1.1; 1 Cor 1.1; 2 Cor 1.1; Gal 1.1) and elsewhere (1 Cor 4.15); and Paul's references to 'my gospel' (Rom 2.16; 16.25; cf. Gal 1.11–12) were not claims to a higher degree of authority (cf. 1 Cor 15.8–9). There was a message which had been entrusted to Paul, and the implication is that this was an existing entity before it was entrusted to him. Furthermore, since the Paul of the earlier letters considered himself to be the only apostle in his own particular mission-area (cf. Gal 2.7–9), and deliberately refrained from entering the territory of other missionaries (2 Cor 10), the absence of reference to other apostles or missionaries need not indicate a limitation of authority to Paul himself. To see in this salutation, then, elements of an exclusive claim to apostolic authority depends more on the assumption of pseudonymity than on the text. The emphasis that the author creates in these verses reflects more the concern to protect the truth of the gospel and the authority of the messenger in the churches where Titus is active. It is true that, so far as the present passage is concerned, there is stress on the entrusting of Paul with the message that God has revealed (1.3), but this is no different from the apostolic self-consciousness in 1 Cor 4.1f. For Paul the proclamation of reconciliation was an integral part of God's initiative in reconciling the world to himself in 2 Cor 5.18–21; God's saving act is twofold: his action in Christ and the commissioning of the messengers of reconciliation. (See further 1 Tim 1.1 note.)

The line followed in the salutation thus establishes the authority of the Pauline apostolate and the necessity of its ministry of

---

[4] Bühner, J., *EDNT* I, 145. However, it is difficult to see how a stress on Paul as the archetypal holder of the office who is responsible for preserving the teaching of the gospel could be thought to place the PE nearer Luke than Paul.

[5] Brox, 72–4, 280f.; Roloff, 56; Wegenast 1962:143–50; Wanke 1977:174–6; Wolter 1988:82–95. See also Läger 1996, 91, *et passim*, for the developed view that salvation is so much tied to Paul that soteriology is almost turned into 'Paulologie'. This verdict seems to be due to a confusion between the importance of Paul as the preacher of salvation, which is a thoroughly Pauline concept (Rom 10.8–15; 2 Cor 5.18–6.1; Gal 2.7), and the claim that in this capacity he is virtually a saviour.

proclamation within God's salvation plan without suggesting that Paul is the only apostle. The argument aims to reclaim the authority of Paul in a Pauline church in which it has been challenged by opponents. This authority is transferred to or shared by Titus in his status as 'true child'; the salutation establishes the authoritative basis upon which Titus will teach and correct the community.

a. The sender and his message (1.1–3)

The self-description of Paul consists of his name followed by two phrases which describe his position as God's servant and apostle in the mission established by Jesus.[6] Following the apostle's self-designation comes a densely structured combination of prepositional phrases and relative clauses. Two prepositional phrases define further the nature and goal of Paul's apostleship. The second then becomes the basis for a detailed explanation of the nature of the eternal life, the hope of which is determinative of apostleship, and this is rounded off with a repeated reference to Paul's own commission. The structure is:

1a (ἀπόστολος...)
1b <u>κατὰ</u> πίστιν ἐκλεκτῶν θεοῦ
      καὶ ἐπίγνωσιν ἀληθείας
          τῆς κατ᾽ εὐσέβειαν
2a <u>ἐπ᾽</u> ἐλπίδι ζωῆς αἰωνίου,
2b   ἣν ἐπηγγείλατο ὁ ἀψευδὴς θεὸς
          πρὸ χρόνων αἰωνίων
3a   ἐφανέρωσεν δὲ
          καιροῖς ἰδίοις
          τὸν λόγον αὐτοῦ
          ἐν κηρύγματι,
3b   ὃ ἐπιστεύθην ἐγὼ
          κατ᾽ ἐπιταγὴν τοῦ ... θεοῦ.

The relative clause commences a revelation scheme in which three moments in God's plan of salvation come into view and the major thought of the section emerges. The pattern here is that of promised/revealed which in effect is a combination of hidden/revealed and promised/fulfilled.[7]

In comparison with the schema as it appears in Romans, 1 Corinthians, Colossians and Ephesians, however, the argument here and in 2 Tim 1.9–10 concentrates less on concealment and more on revelation, and it views the results from the perspective

---

[6] For the double designation cf. Rom 1.1; 2 Pet 1.1.
[7] Cf. 2 Tim 1.9f.; Rom 16.25f.; 1 Cor 2.7–10; Col 1.26; Eph 3.4–7, 8–11; Dahl 1954:4f.; Lührmann 1965:124–33; Wolter 1987.

of salvation and specifically eternal life without explicit mention of the Christ-event. The shape of the schema and the argument here make Paul's ministry central to the revelation and fulfilment of the promise, but this is entirely natural in the context of a salutation which is introducing Paul to the reader(s) and does not imply that he is presented as the only guarantor of salvation.

The schema consists of two balanced clauses (2b, 3a) followed by an expansion (3b).

(2b). On the one hand, God's promise was made 'before time began'. It is, therefore, his settled will and purpose which is unchanging and cannot be thwarted.

(3a). On the other hand the fulfilment of his promise took place when 'he revealed his word at the right time' (ἐφανέρωσεν; cf. 1 Tim 3.16; 2 Tim 1.10). The fulfilment implicitly substantiates the claim that God is ἀψευδής. But the concern of the argument here is not specifically to uphold the character of God, but rather to emphasise the divine purpose fulfilled in the revelation which determines salvation and the relation of Paul's apostleship to it.

(3b). This activity is what was committed to Paul himself. His commission came by way of a divine command (cf. Quinn, 70), and he and his colleagues can issue authoritative commands to the congregations. If one can be an apostle only by the direct command of God, the appointment entitles the apostle to respect and obedience from the congregation (see Fee, 35).

Where is the stress in this description? (a) It could be on the *responsibility and office* of Paul. He refers to himself as a κῆρυξ in 2 Tim 1.11 in a similar context. The phrase could thus be a means of indicating the greatness of the responsibility which he feels as he stands under the compulsion of divine command. (b) But more probably, in view of the challenge posed by heresy, the stress is rather on his *consequent authority* and the indispensable role of the (in this context, 'his') apostolic preaching ministry in the salvation plan of God (hence the emphasis on ἐν κηρύγματι). He is, then, the authoritative channel of the message, and what he says is to be accepted as God's truth within the churches for which he is responsible. Hence the instructions which Paul gives for life in the church and which arise out of the gospel possess the highest authority (cf. Brox, 281).

TEXT

1. Ἰησοῦ Χριστοῦ Χριστοῦ Ἰησοῦ (A 629 1175 a b vg^mss sy^h Ambst; WH t; Kilpatrick); Χριστοῦ (D*; cf. WH mg Χριστοῦ [Ἰησοῦ]). It has been suggested that the words appear in the order Χριστοῦ Ἰησοῦ (or Χριστοῦ Ἰησοῦ) so that the case may readily be apparent (since Ἰησοῦ could be gen. or dat.); this is not entirely satisfactory as an explanation, but a better one has yet to be given (see the full discussion in Elliott, 198–205). Similar problems arise at Tit 1.4; 2.13; 3.6; 1 Tim 1.1, 15; 2. 5; 4.6; 5.21; 2 Tim 1.1, 10; 2.3; 4.1. Despite the weight of MS attestation for the text (for which cf. 1 Pet 1.1; 2 Pet 1.1), the variant should probably be accepted.

κατ' εὐσέβειαν κατὰ εὐσέβειαν (F G). Elliott, 232, apparently accepts the variant, despite expressing hesitation elsewhere, 119. The external evidence is surely too weak.

2. ἐπ' ἐν (F G H 365 *pc*; omitted by 33 *pc*). The variant is weakly attested; there is no firm example of the phrase ἐν ἐλπίδι in the NT: Elliott, 172f.

ἐπηγγείλατο προεπηγγείλατο (1908) is defended by Elliott, 173, despite the lack of attestation on the grounds that it is not Classical and that scribes objected to compound verbs followed by the same preposition. The external attestation is too weak.

ἀψευδής ἀψευστός (F G). The form ἀψευδής is Classical, and Elliott, 173, defends the variant, but this reading could be due to assimilation to the form in 1.12.

1a. Παῦλος δοῦλος θεοῦ All the Pauline letters begin in this way with Παῦλος, the name which he regularly used; Σαῦλος is confined to Acts (cf. 1 Tim 1.1; 2 Tim 1.1). 'Paul' was almost certainly his Roman surname (*cognomen*).[8] As apostle to the Gentiles, working in a Gentile environment, his tendency to refer to himself as 'Paulus' rather than, in Hebrew fashion, 'Saul' is not surprising. The habit of using only the *cognomen* was not particularly unusual.

Nine of the thirteen letters attributed to Paul follow his name closely with a reference to his apostolic office (2 Cor; Eph; Col; 1 Tim; 2 Tim are identical; cf. Rom; 1 Cor; Gal; Tit). This, however, is the only place in the Pauline writings in which 'slave of God' occurs as a self-designation of the apostle, 'slave of Christ' being much more common.

δοῦλος, 'slave' (in the literal sense 2.9; 1 Tim 6.1), expresses the lack of freedom of the individual rather than the service rendered (*TLNT* I, 380f.). The term is often applied to Christians in general as 'slaves of Christ' (2 Tim 2.24 [Κυρίου]**; 1 Cor 7.22; Eph 6.6; Col 4.12; Rev 2.20), and Paul uses this as a self-designation (Rom 1.1; Gal 1.10; Phil 1.1; cf. 2 Pet 1.1 of Peter; Jude 1 of Jude). Occasionally Christians are designated 'slaves of God'.[9] For the application to leaders see Jas 1.1: 'servant of God and the Lord Jesus Christ'.

---

[8] Cf. Acts 13.7; see BA *s.v.*; Hemer, C. J., 'The Name of Paul', *TynBul* 36 (1985), 179–83; Hengel 1991:193–208; Cranfield, C. E. B., *The Epistle to the Romans* (Edinburgh: T. and T. Clark, 1975), 1:48–50.

[9] Acts 16.17; 1 Pet 2.16; Rev 7.3 (Rev 1.1 is ambiguous); cf. 'your' or 'his servant(s)' in Lk 2.29; Acts 2.18; 4.29; Rev 10.7; 11.18; 19.2, 5; 22.3, 6.

Behind the expression δοῦλος θεοῦ lies OT and Jewish usage reflected in Rev 15.3, which names Moses '*the* servant of God'. The phrase is used of Israel as the servant of Yahweh but also of specific individuals, especially kings and also prophets as the recipients of divine revelation.[10] In view of this pattern, it would not be out of place as a designation for an apostle; an apostle is on a level with them. Cf. the use of ὁ τοῦ θεοῦ ἄνθρωπος of Timothy in 1 Tim 6.11; 2 Tim 3.17.[11]

As a framework for understanding the relationship between God and his messenger or people, the social institution of slavery contained elements that were readily identifiable. In the OT or NT cultural settings, slavery implied servitude, submission, obedience, absence of rights, and the complete authority of the master. A slave was the property of his or her master, and in principle a slave's existence depended upon the master and upon pleasing the master.[12] The religious usage in the OT was a natural development. Even if 'slave(s) of God' would develop later into a title of honour within the church (with a subsequent loss of meaning), some of these original implications were meant to be understood. The OT, which portrays Yahweh's representatives as his slaves/servants and therefore as bearers of his authority, provides the essential background for the NT use of the theme. In particular, the articulation of Christ's incarnation with the same imagery (Phil 2.7) provided a significant model for his followers. At the same time, the exaltation of Jesus as 'Lord' led to the substitution of 'Christ' for 'God' in the phrase, and this became Paul's preferred usage.

It is not immediately clear what motivates the return here to the form 'slave of *God*' as opposed to the more usual form. Several explanations have been offered: (a) It might have better suited a Jewish-Christian audience (cf. Jas 1.1; Quinn, 61). (b) The tradition in Acts 16.17 provided the model for the author's designation of Paul (Holtzmann, 462). (c) The phrase could have been chosen to get rhetorical balance with the next phrase. (d) In any case, one effect of the designation is to bring out the parallel with the OT servants of God, which some see as the author's main intention (cf. Lock, 125). Hasler, 85, thinks that, whereas 'slave of Jesus Christ' expresses subordination, 'servant

[10] David (2 Sam 7.4, 8; Ps 77 [MT 78].70; 88 [MT 89].4); Moses (Ps 104 [MT 105].26; cf. Rev 15.3); Abraham (Ps 104 [MT 105].42); Zerubbabel (Hag 2.24); the prophets (Jer 7.25; 25.4; Amos 3.7; Zech 1.6).
[11] Cf. Rengstorf, K. H., *TDNT* II, 261–80; Weiser, A., *EDNT* I, 349–52; *TLNT* I, 380–6; Couser 1992:138–49.
[12] See Bartchy 1973; fuller bibliography in Weiser, A., *EDNT* I, 349.

of God' expresses more his function as God's representative like the prophets and other bearers of divine revelation (cf. Rev 1.1; 10.7; *et al.*). (e) But the whole sentence is concerned with what *God* has done (note the five occurrences of θεός) in election, promise, manifestation and commissioning; as 'saviour' he is seen as the author of salvation (though the vital role of Christ is also affirmed; v. 4). Therefore, the designation 'slave *of God*' is adopted mainly to conform to the dominant line of thought. Hence the next phrase is added hardly as a contrast (δέ) but as additional information ('and besides'; cf. Jude 1).

ἀπόστολος δὲ Ἰησοῦ Χριστοῦ ἀπόστολος is used throughout the NT as a Christian technical term for the authorised representatives of Christ or the churches who are engaged in particular tasks, usually connected with missionary work, including the establishment and supervision of churches, and who have delegated authority for the purpose.

The term ἀπόστολος Ἰησοῦ Χριστοῦ occurs as the apostle's self-designation in 1 Cor 1.1; 2 Cor 1.1; Eph 1.1; Col 1.1 1 Tim 1.1; 2 Tim 1.1 (cf. 1 Tim 2.7; 2 Tim 1.11**),[13] and the same identification is formed in slightly different ways in Rom 1.1 and Gal 1.1. Paul does not use it in 1 and 2 Th (though cf. 1 Th 2.7), where apparently there was no need to stress his authority in this way, in Phil, where he links himself with Timothy (who was not an apostle) as δοῦλοι of Christ, and in the more personal letter to Philemon, where he makes his requests as a δέσμιος of Christ. Even in Phil and Philem, however, the terms used express the authoritative position which springs from being in the service of Christ (cf. the use of δοῦλος in Rom 1.1 alongside ἀπόστολος). Here the inclusion of the term may be because the church is intended to overhear the letter or (in the case of post-Pauline authorship) to stress the authority of Paul for later generations. The change of order to 'Jesus Christ' (*si vera lectio*; cf. 1 Tim 1.1; 2 Tim 1.1) has no apparent significance.[14] Apostles are always apostles of Christ rather than of God the Father, although the latter appoints them; they are in the service of Christ. They are also in the Pauline corpus never apostles or servants simply of Jesus; the official designation 'of Christ [Jesus]' is used (Holtzmann, 370f.)

For Paul the term ἀπόστολος expressed his calling, given at an appearance to him of the risen Christ, to be a missionary, a calling which carried with it the authority to be an agent of divine revelation and to exercise a position of leadership over the congregations which he founded. This sense of Paul's being

---

[13] The order is typically Χριστοῦ Ἰησοῦ. See textual note.

[14] On the problem in general see Karrer, M., *Der Gesalbte. Die Grundlagen des Christustitels* (Göttingen: Vandenhoeck und Ruprecht, 1991), 48–69.

a missionary and agent of revelation is still alive in the PE, where 'apostle' is closely linked with 'herald' and 'teacher' as words that bring out its meaning (1 Tim 2.7*; 2 Tim 2.ll*). An apostle is thus an authoritative witness and preacher of the gospel.[15]

1b. κατὰ πίστιν ἐκλεκτῶν θεοῦ The first of the two pre-positional phrases that qualify the concept of servanthood and apostleship contains two co-ordinated phrases. Paul's activity takes place in relation to the faith of God's elect and [their] knowledge of the truth that is in accordance with godliness.

Basically Paul as apostle is charged with the task of 'promoting and furthering the faith of God's people' ('the elect'). It includes evangelism but goes beyond this to developing the faith of Christians through the teaching of correct doctrine. The notion of salvation in the 'elect' concept must be taken in the widest sense to include not simply entry into salvation, but also the working out of and maintaining of salvation in the context of membership in God's people (cf. 1 Tim 4.16). The apostle's ministry is by definition concerned with the entire process of salvation (cf. 1 Tim 2.7; 2 Tim 1.11; Col 1.28 ; Phil 2.12).

κατά occurs four times in vv. 1–4 (cf. 1 Tim 1.1; 2 Tim 1.1). Its force here is uncertain.[16]

(a) 'In accordance/in keeping with the faith held by God's elect and the truth as known by them'.[17] The point will then be to characterise the way in which Paul's service is determined by the authentic faith rather than by the Jewish religion or heretical ideas. In an epistle that is concerned with truth over against false teaching this would be appropriate. Yet the link is a difficult one: how is 'apostleship' in accordance with the faith? In fact, it is not Paul's doctrine but his commission which would here be said to be in accordance with the faith of God's people (cf. Parry, 72).

(b) 'In regard/with reference to the faith', referring in a general way to the sphere of apostleship (cf. NIV 'for the faith'; Kelly, 226). Lips 1979:32 n. 33, draws attention to the parallel between κατά and ἐν in Tit 1.4 and 1 Tim 1.2, and concludes that κατά here has the same sense as ἐν in 1 Tim 2.7; it expresses a connection or relationship.

---

[15] See Rengstorf, K. H., *TDNT* I, 407–47; Bühner, J. A., *EDNT* I, 142–6; Roloff 1965; *idem.*, *TRE* III, 430–45; *TLNT* I, 186–94.

[16] Hanson, 169, thinks that the sense is quite vague.

[17] Holtzmann, 185, 462; Lock, 125; Scott, 149–50; Dibelius-Conzelmann, 131; Simpson, 94; Barrett, 126; Houlden, 140; Hasler, 85; REB 'marked as such by the faith...' is meaningless. Oberlinner, 4, holds that the point is to bring out the fellowship between Paul and the people of God insofar as they agree in believing the (true) gospel.

(c) Narrowing the focus of (b), the meaning may be more 'in the service of/to further the faith of the elect'.[18] The thought would then be similar to that in Rom 1.5: 'apostleship [leading to] the obedience of faith among the Gentiles'. The purpose of apostleship is to bring about faith, here probably to strengthen and develop the faith already held by Christian believers (White, 185).

Brox, 279, and Holtz, 204, hold that both senses (a) and (c) can be present simultaneously (*contra* Holtzmann, 462). A comparison of the openings of each of the Pastorals may shed some light on the intention of the phrase. In 1 Tim 1.1 a κατά phrase (κατ' ἐπιταγὴν θεοῦ) is used to ground Paul's apostleship and ministry in God's action. 2 Tim 1.1 achieves this with the phrase διὰ θελήματος θεοῦ. However, the corresponding phrase here is in v. 3. where the same κατά phrase as is used in 1 Tim 1.1 is found in connection with the entrusting of the 'preaching' to Paul. In 2 Tim 1.1, following the grounding of Paul's calling in God's will, the κατά phrase 'according to the promise of life' explains something more about this calling; the thought is probably 'that Paul's apostleship springs from God's promise and is intended to bring it to fruition'. This is close to the thought here and therefore the κατά phrase is best understood as an expression of the goal or purpose of Paul's apostleship (view c).

πίστις 'faith' (1.4, 13; 2.2, 10; 3.15*; 1 Tim 1.2 *et al.*; 2 Tim 1.5 *et al.* See **Excursus 4**) can be either the content of the faith (fitting (a) above) or the subjective act of believing (fitting (b) and (c) above).[19]

ἐκλεκτός is 'chosen' and hence 'of special value' (of the Messiah, Lk 23.35; cf. 1 Pet 2.4, 6); most commonly of persons chosen by God[20] and made members of his people.[21] Behind the usage here lies the frequent use in the OT for God's people.[22] The reference of the term here is disputed. If we exclude Spicq's unlikely suggestion (592) that it was a local designation of Christians in Asia Minor, there are three possibilities.

[18] 'For the sake of' (NRSV); 'for the purpose of' (BA *s.v.* II.4). So BD § 224; GNB; Ellicott 167 (citing Theophylact 'so that the elect may believe through me'); Bernard, 155; Parry, 72; Dornier, 119; Kelly, 226; Spicq, 591f.; Knight, 283; Quinn, 62; Merkel, 88; Arichea-Hatton, 262; Moule 1953:59; Towner, 218; Wolter 1988:82 n. 3.

[19] Cf. Bultmann, R., and Weiser, A., *TDNT* VI, 174–228; Barth, G., *EDNT* III, 91–7, especially 97; Marshall 1984; *TLNT* III, 110–16.

[20] For the anarthrous use here with θεοῦ see Rom 8.33; Col 3.12. Cf. Schrenk, G., *TDNT* IV, 179–92; Eckert, J., *EDNT* I, 417–19.

[21] Cf. Mk 13.20, 22, 27; Rom 8.33; 16.13; Col 3.12; 2 Tim 2.10; 1 Pet 1.1; 2.9; 2 Jn 1, 13; Rev 17.14; 1 Clement 1.1; *et al.*; the word is used of angels in 1 Tim 5.21 (cf. *1 Enoch* 39.1).

[22] E.g. 1 Chr 16.13; Ps 104 (MT 105).6; 105 (MT 106).6; Isa 42.1; 43.20; 45.4; 65.9, 15, 23; Ecclus 46.1; 47.22.

(a) It could refer to those people previously chosen by God to become believers and so receive salvation, but who are not yet believers. Paul's task is then to bring such elect people to faith (NJB; Spicq, 592; given as a possibility by Holtzmann, 462). The stress is then primarily on the *evangelistic* nature of Paul's task. This understanding is strengthened by the following reference to 'knowledge of the truth' which normally refers to 'coming to know the truth'. But since there is no clear evidence elsewhere for ἐκλεκτοί signifying those chosen to believe *before* they have believed, and since alongside any stress on salvation there is at least an equal (if not greater) stress on orthodoxy and truth, this reference should be excluded.

(b) The view that the term refers to all whom God has chosen for salvation, whether they have yet believed or not, is open to the same objections as (a).

(c) More probably, therefore, the term refers to those who truly belong to God's people, with the implication that the faith which they hold is the *true* faith.[23] This view fits in with the normal usage of 'elect' to refer to those who are members of the people of God (see Fee, 168: the term is OT, showing the continuation of the OT people of God in the NT church). The Pauline congregations, insofar as they hold fast to Paul's gospel, are truly the people of God.

καὶ ἐπίγνωσιν ἀληθείας τῆς κατ᾽ εὐσέβειαν The second part of the goal statement explains 'the faith of God's elect' (the connective καί is epexegetic) in terms of 'the knowledge of the truth which is in accord with godliness'.

ἐπίγνωσις*, 'knowledge', generally has the stress on the activity of getting to know (Rom 1.28; Col 2.2; Philem 6), but sometimes more on the content of what is known (Col 1.9f.)[24] In the PE it is found only in the combination ἐπίγνωσις ἀληθείας (1 Tim 2.4; 2 Tim 2.25; 3.7; Heb 10.26).[25] In the PE this formula describes salvation from the perspective of one's rational perception of 'the truth'. It may view salvation from the standpoint of conversion, particularly when it appears in the form εἰς ἐπίγνωσιν ἀληθείας ἐλθεῖν (1 Tim 2.4; 2 Tim 3.7; cf. 2 Tim 2.25). But in other contexts it is clearly a way of referring more broadly to salvation as the state of existence characterised

---

[23] Holtzmann, 462; White, 185; Brox, 279, draws the implication that it is only the orthodox, therefore, who can appeal for support to Paul.

[24] Cf. Bultmann, R., *TDNT* I, 689–714. On the question whether ἐπίγνωσις is synonymous with γνῶσις see Simpson, 66, who argues that the former signifies full recognition or discernment.

[25] Cf. ἐπιγινώσκειν τὴν ἀλήθειαν, 1 Tim 4.3; see also Col 1.6; Philo, *Prob.* 74; Epictetus 2.20.21; Diogenes Laertius 7.42; see also the Qumran texts listed below; Lips 1979:32, 35–8; Wolter 1988:70–7; Quinn, 276–82; Dibelius-Conzelmann, 41.

by the actual grasp of 'the truth' (cf. 1 Tim 4.3; Heb 10.26) rather than to the process of coming to know it. Such knowledge may be a growing consciousness that develops after the initial act of faith (Dornier, 121).

ἀλήθεια, 'truth' (1.14*; see 1 Tim 2.4; 2 Tim 2.15; cf. ἀληθής, Tit 1.13**), was used of speech which refers to things as they really are, and in Biblical Greek it acquired some of the associations of Hebrew אמת, 'faithfulness'.[26]

In the Qumran writings several passages employ the phrase דעת אמת (1QS 9.17–18; 4Q Sir Sabb 1.1, 18; 1QH 10.20, 29). 'Truth' by itself occupies an important place in the community's self-identity (1 QS 6.15; 2.25), for 'knowledge of the truth' determined one's standing in the community and in the covenant. It was the community's belief that it possessed 'the truth' that marked it off from corrupt temple Judaism. The terminology thus had a polemical purpose.

Within the early church, 'truth' language was developed in the context of the Pauline missionary ministry (2 Th 2.10, 12, 13–14; Col 1.5–6; Eph 1.13; Wolter 1988:71). Here the key words λόγος, ἀλήθεια, εὐαγγέλιον, πίστις come together, along with various words denoting perception and acceptance of God's message (ἀκούω, πιστεύω, δέχομαι, ἐπιγινώσκω). In this evangelistic dialogue this terminology served a polemical or apologetic purpose as it stressed the untruth of idolatry and pagan religion.

In the PE ἀλήθεια refers to the authentic revelation of God bringing salvation. Its content is in effect summarised in 1 Tim 2.3–6 (Oberlinner, 5). Already in the early Paulines 'the truth' had become one of several terms to describe God's saving revelation. Both its content and its polemic thrust are evident in the contrast which is made (often with a characteristic verb) with the false teachers and their message in a number of passages (especially 1 Tim 6.5; 2 Tim 4.4; Tit 1.14 [ἀποστρέφω]; 2 Tim 2.18 [ἀστοχέω]; 2 Tim 3.8 [ἀνθίστημι]; see also 2 Tim 2.15; 2.25; 3.7). In view of this pattern and the strong statement in v. 14 below, 'knowledge of the truth' does not define 'the faith of God's elect' simply as the embracing of God's revelation, but as commitment to it and rejection of all competing messages. Salvation is thus inextricably bound to the apostolic doctrine and a right decision about it.

Whether or not the Qumran or the earlier NT usage of 'truth' language stands behind the language of the PE,[27] the two bodies of literature share in common both the belief in the necessity of

[26] Cf. Quell, G., and Bultmann, R., *TDNT* I, 232–47; Hübner, H., *EDNT* I, 57–60; *TLNT* I, 66–86; Lips 1979:33–40.

[27] See Trummer 1978:119–22 for the view that the PE are dependent on language developed in Ephesians.

possessing the truth for 'salvation' and the polemic application of the language. It may have been a polemical interest or need that occasioned the use of ἐπίγνωσις in the PE (as elsewhere in the Pauline corpus), which might be offered to counter the opponents' claims to possess or teach a special knowledge (γνῶσις) of God.[28] This interest is certainly evident in the frequent use of the term ἀλήθεια in reference to the apostolic message (see below).

For εὐσέβεια*, 'piety, godliness' see **Excursus 1**. The addition τῆς κατ' εὐσέβειαν[29] further defines 'the truth' and, therefore, the nature of the faith of the elect. We have the same ambiguity with κατά as earlier in the verse. The phrase can indicate: (a) the truth that is 'in accordance with godliness' (NRSV; cf. REB; GNB; Holtzmann, 463; Spicq, 592–3; Fee, 168; Oberlinner, 1); (b) the truth that 'furthers/leads to godliness' (NIV; NJB; Calvin, 353; Ellicott, 167). (c) the truth that is 'closely connected with godliness' (Bernard, 155). It is strange for the criterion of the truth to be godliness unless there is a contrast with false claims to possess the truth (Holtzmann, 463). It is perhaps more likely that the truth is commended because (among other things) it leads to godliness, though even in this there lies an implicit challenge to the claims of the heretics.

Consequently, whether κατ' εὐσέβειαν means that εὐσέβεια is the criterion (or test) of 'the truth' or its goal, 'godliness', as the all-embracing term for genuine Christianity, is directly related to 'the truth'. Lack of godliness disproves competing claims, while a positive expression of it is the visible emblem of one's genuine relationship to God. The qualification here indicates that there is a concern for 'right faith', expressed elsewhere in the concern for sound teaching (cf. 1.13f.). This is a development in the usage of the term from Paul necessitated by the growth of heresy.

2a. ἐπ' ἐλπίδι ζωῆς αἰωνίου The connection of the second prepositional phrase is disputed: (a) It may stand in parallel with κατὰ πίστιν ... and thus further qualify ἀπόστολος. In 2 Tim 1.1 Paul is an apostle 'according to the promise of life'; since God has promised life, therefore he has called apostles to proclaim the good news (Holtzmann, 464f.). So here Paul's apostleship rests on the hope of eternal life and derives its impetus from

[28] Tit 1.16; 1 Tim 6.20; cf. Col 1.6, 9f.; 2.2f.; 3.10; Bultmann, R., *TDNT* I, 707; Sell 1982:3–29.
[29] The phrase ἀληθείας τῆς κατ εὐσέβειαν is an example of an anarthrous noun followed by the article and a qualifying phrase (1 Tim 1.4, 14; 3.13; 4.8; 6.3; 2 Tim 1.13, 14; 2.10; 3.15); the alternation between use and non-use of the article with ἀλήθεια seems arbitrary (Moule 1953:112). Cf. 1 Tim 1.4 note.

it.[30] (b) Or Paul's apostleship is intended to promote hope in eternal life (Spicq, 593; Kelly, 227). (c) Far less likely is the view that it qualifies πίστιν ... καὶ ἐπίγνωσιν: 'the faith and knowledge which are based on hope'.[31] View (a) gives the best sense. The phrase is most probably a further qualification of Paul's apostleship, for it is the character of Paul and his apostolic ministry and message which are at issue in vv. 1–3. It establishes the present basis of Paul's work in the certain expectation, based on what God has done in the past, of eternal life, to which he himself looks forward and to which his message invites his hearers (cf. Oberlinner, 6).

ἐπί with dat. conveys the sense of rest upon some object, 'on', 'upon'. It is used only figuratively in the PE, 'of that upon which a state of being, an action, or a result is based' (BA). It is especially used with verbs of believing and trusting (1 Tim 1.16; 4.10; 6.17a, 17b), but is also used to express purpose, goal, or result ('leading to', 2 Tim 2.14**).[32] The preposition here may introduce another goal of Paul's calling (see 2 Tim 2.14). But here the force of ἐπί is more 'resting on the basis of'.[33]

For ἐλπίς, 'hope', see 1 Tim 1.1; Tit 2.13; 3.7** (cf. ἐλπίζω 1 Tim 3.14; 4.10; 5.17; 6.17**). In the NT generally it is a firm conviction concerning what will happen in the future based on knowledge or experience of what God has already done or is doing (this may well be the case even in 1 Tim 3.14). In this theological context it is thus a much more positive term than secular 'hope' which conveys the nuances of longing and uncertainty whether the longing will be fulfilled (Acts 27.20). Biblical hope is a function of faith in God, and consequently he himself (or Christ, 1 Tim 1.1) is the object of hope (1 Tim 4.10; 5.5; Acts 24.15; Eph 2.12; Col 1.27) in strong contrast to such uncertain bases as wealth (1 Tim 6.17). In the present context the hope is based on the unalterable promises of God (v. 2b). The word can also be used by metonymy for the object of hope (Tit 2.13; Col 1.5). That object is eternal life (Tit 3.7; cf. Barnabas 1.4, 6; Hermas, *Sim.* 9.26.2).[34]

ζωή, 'life' (3.7; 1 Tim 1.16; 4.8; 6.12, 19; 2 Tim 1.1, 10**), is used in the NT for both ordinary physical existence (1 Cor 3.22; 15.19; Phil 1.20) and also (in the vast majority of cases) for the spiritual life, both now and in the next world, which is the gift

[30] Cf. Dibelius-Conzelmann, 131; Brox, 280; Merkel, 88; Knight, 284; Oberlinner, 6.

[31] NIV; cf. White, 185; Parry, 72f.; Fee, 168f. ('which lead to hope').

[32] For ἐπί with gen. see 1 Tim 5.19; 6.13**; with acc., Tit 3.6 *et al.*

[33] For the phrase ἐπ' ἐλπίδι cf. Acts 2.26; 26.6; Rom 4.18b; 5.2; 8.20; 1 Cor 9.10a, 10b.

[34] Cf. Bultmann, R. and Rengstorf, K. H., *TDNT* II, 517–33; *TLNT* I, 480–92; Nebe, G., *'Hoffnung' bei Paulus* (Göttingen: Vandenhoeck und Ruprecht, 1983).

of God. The word can be used by itself with this sense (e.g. Phil 2.16; Jn 3.36b), but in the PE there is always some qualifier to make this clear. It is 'real life' (1 Tim 6.19); 'life in Christ Jesus' (2 Tim 1.1); life 'now and in the future' (1 Tim 4.8); it is linked epexegetically with ἀφθαρσία (2 Tim 1.10). But most frequently it is, as here, 'eternal life' (3.7; 1 Tim 1.16; 6.12).[35]

αἰώνιος, 'eternal' (with ζωή, 3.7; 1 Tim 1.16; 6.12; with other nouns, 1.2b; 1 Tim 6.16; 2 Tim 1.9; 2.10**), generally has the sense of 'everlasting'. It is used with reference to the exceedingly long periods of time (χρόνοι) before the present age (1.2b; 2 Tim 1.9; Rom 16.25). It is also used as a qualification of God (Rom 16.26), or of his attributes, such as κράτος (1 Tim 6.16), or the δόξα which is his and which he shares with his people (2 Tim 2.10). Through its association with God and with the world to come, the word gains a stronger meaning; eternal life is not only everlasting but also shares the qualities of the life of God himself, its indestructibility and its joy.[36]

2b. ἣν ἐπηγγείλατο ὁ ἀψευδὴς θεὸς πρὸ χρόνων αἰωνίων It is very common in the PE (and elsewhere in the NT) that a term which has been introduced at the end of a phrase becomes the basis for an expansion which assumes major importance in its own right. So here the mention of eternal life leads into a statement of God's activity as the one who promised and revealed it. Thus the certainty of the hope is given an impregnable basis in the purpose of God.

ἣν[37] refers back to eternal life, the substance of the promise. ἐπαγγέλλομαι is 'to promise'; also 'to profess, claim expertise in' (1 Tim 2.10; 6.21**; cf. ἐπαγγελία (1 Tim 4.8; 2 Tim 1.1**). There is no real Hebrew equivalent in the OT, but the words came into use in the LXX and are used of God in 2 Macc 2.18; 3 Macc 2.10 (cf. also *Ps. Sol.* 12.8; *T. Jos.* 20.1; 4 Ezra 5.40; 7.119; *2 Apoc. Bar.* 57.2; 59.2). The belief that God makes promises to his people is well attested in early Christianity.[38]

The same thought is found in 2 Tim 1.1 but without a clear allusion to time past. Here the reference may be to promises made in Scripture (cf. Rom 1.2; 9.4) (Parry, 73) but more probably to a premundane period (cf. the following phrase).

---

[35] Cf. Rad, G. von, Bertram, G., and Bultmann, R., *TDNT* II, 832–72.

[36] To be sure, the word can also qualify such concepts as 'destruction' (2 Th 1.9) and 'fire' (Mt 18.8). The point is that what is 'eternal' is associated with or created by God, and therefore falls outside human possibilities. Sasse, H., *TDNT* I, 208f., surprisingly overlooks this qualitative character of the word.

[37] Note the lack of relative attraction; cf. 1 Tim 4.3.

[38] For the verb see Acts 7.5; Rom 4.21; Gal 3.19; Heb 6.13; 10.23; 11.11; 12.26; Jas 1.12; 2.5; 1 Jn 2.25; the noun is much more frequent. Cf. Schniewind, J., and Friedrich, G., *TDNT* II, 576–86.

Admittedly, this interpretation has to recognise that no recipient of God's promises comes into the picture; the promise is more a statement of intent by God for his own sake. All the stress lies on the fact that God's purpose is eternal and unchangeable.

ἀψευδής***, 'free from deceit, truthful', is Classical and Hellenistic (BA) and is found in Hellenistic Judaism,[39] but the thought is biblical.[40] That God is ἀψευδής may be a deliberate contrast with the lies of the heretics (1.12); the gospel of Paul is true because it is based on the promise of God.

χρόνος usually refers to a period of time rather than a point (Mt 2.7, 16; Acts 1.6). Here it is virtually equivalent to αἰών and refers to the long periods into which time is divided.[41]

The phrase πρὸ (2 Tim 1.9; 4.21**) χρόνων αἰωνίων indicates the time of the promise (cf. 2 Tim 1.9). It may mean: (a) 'before the ages', i.e. 'in eternity past';[42] or (b) 'before ancient times', i.e. 'a very long time ago [sc. in OT times]'.[43] If Barr 1969:75 is correct, then a reference to χρόνοι αἰώνιοι would be to the whole period beginning with creation. In this case, the addition of πρό makes this a reference to the period before time began, just as in 2 Tim 1.9. The tendency to anchor the eschatological salvation in the premundane decision of God may have developed, alongside Israel's growing consciousness of being God's elect, as an antidote to insecurity (cf. 2 Apoc. Bar. 57; 4.3; 1 QS 3–4; b.Pes 54a). The church converted such themes for its own use, as it established a line of continuity back to Israel (cf. Mt 25.34; Acts 3.20; Rom 9.23; 1 Pet 1.20). Within the revelation pattern, the premundane 'time' element accentuates God's part in devising the plan of salvation, which in turn helps to underline the certainty of salvation (cf. Wolter 1988:85–90) and the fact that it depends wholly upon God (Oberlinner, 9).

3a. ἐφανέρωσεν δὲ καιροῖς ἰδίοις τὸν λόγον αὐτοῦ ἐν κηρύγματι The second clause of the promised/revealed scheme is notable for placing the revelation in the gospel rather than in the Christ-event itself. φανερόω is literally 'to cause what is unseen/hidden to be seen' (Mk 4.22), but also figuratively 'to make known', especially of God making known (Rom 3.21).

---

[39] Wis 7.17 is the only LXX reference; Philo, Ebr. 139; cf. Ignatius, Rom. 8.2; M. Poly. 14.2.

[40] Num 23.19; 1 Sam 15.29; Rom 3.3f; 2 Cor 1.19f.; 2 Tim 2.13; Heb 6.18; cf. 1 Clement 27.2; cf. Conzelmann, H., TDNT IX, 594–603.

[41] Cf. Delling, G., TDNT IX, 581–93.

[42] Cf. 1 Cor 2.7; Col 1.26; Eph 1.4; Rom 16.25; Bernard, 155; Jeremias, 60; Hanson, 170 – 'the timeless, eternal world'; Quinn, 65.

[43] Hübner, H., EDNT III, 488; Calvin, 353f.; Ellicott, 168; Holtzmann, 465; Parry, 73; Lock, 126; Dornier, 122; against this interpretation see Nielsen 1980:12–14.

The latter sense can include the former, as in 1 Tim 3.16 which refers to the making known of Christ in a visible manifestation. The word is rare outside the NT and (apart from Herodotus 6.122.1) appears only in Hellenistic Greek; it was not used in a religious context. It is often said to be a synonym of ἀποκαλύπτω, but this is questioned by Bockmuehl who claims that the accent lies on making visible rather than on revealing.[44] It was used in a variety of contexts,[45] but especially of God/Christ revealing himself, his attributes (Rom 1.19; 1 Jn 4.9), his word (Col 1.26, which Hanson, 170, regards as the basis for the present passage), or the 'mystery' (Rom 16.26). It is used of the revelation in Christ, both past (see especially Rom 3.21)[46] and future (Col. 3.4; 1 Pet 5.4; 1 Jn 2.28; 3.2). Paul speaks of God revealing his message or his qualities in and through believers (2 Cor 2.14; 4.10f.).

Against this background the use of the aorist here (cf. 2 Tim 1.10**) might lead to the expectation of a specific reference to the Christ-event. But here the event is viewed from the perspective of its proclamation, through which its relevance is continued: Christ and the message concerning him are seen as one, unified event. There are similar indirect references to the Christ-event in 2.11 where God's grace appears and teaches mankind, and 3.4 where God's goodness and kindness are manifested. Eternal life is revealed in the coming of Christ and in the experience of it enjoyed by believers who have accepted the proclamation about it (cf. 1 Jn 1.2).

The construction of the sentence encourages the reader to think that the object is still ἥν (sc. eternal life), but there is anacolouthon, and a fresh object, τὸν λόγον αὐτοῦ, is added after the verb.[47] It is possible that the fresh object is added loosely in apposition to the clause (Parry, 73). But it is better to assume that the relative clause has been unconsciously replaced by a main clause at this point (Holtzmann, 465).

What has happened is that the reference needed to be made more precise. The promise/fulfilment argument required the content of the promise (ἥν = eternal life) to be expressed in some fashion. But the addition of the new object (with the resultant anacolouthon) was necessary to make the link with eternal life in a way that brought into sharp focus the role of the gospel

[44] Bockmuehl, M. N. A., 'Das Verb φανερόω im Neuen Testament. Versuch einer Neuauswertung', *BZ* 32 (1988), 87–99. Cf. Lührmann, 1965:160; Bultmann, R., and Lührmann, D., *TDNT* IX, 3–6.
[45] E.g. to make clear in speech (Col 4.4); to reveal aspects of one's character (2 Cor 7.12).
[46] Cf. 1 Pet 1.20; 1 Jn 1.2; 3.5, 8; of the resurrection appearances Jn 21.1, 14.
[47] Cf. BD §469; see 1 Tim 6.12 for a similar anacolouthon in a relative clause. White, 186, inclines to the suggestion that περὶ ἧς be supplied before the verb.

ministry in fulfilling God's promise of eternal life. Not the gift as such but the message is revealed (White, 186). Thus 'his word', understood as the gospel message, is a dual-reference to the promise *and* fulfilment of eternal life (Kelly 1963:228; Towner 1989:128; cf. Lips 1979:43).

Hasler, 85f., concludes that the author is not concerned with a historical realisation of salvation in Christ; the hope remains beyond history, and therefore it is only the message which begins to be active in history in and through Jesus. Thus the gospel is Hellenised into *teaching* about salvation and morality. This existential interpretation comes to grief on 1 Tim 2.5f.; 3.16; 2 Tim 1.10, passages which indicate quite clearly the historical facts which lie at the heart of the message. What has happened is rather that the promise/fulfilment schema has been modified from its original reference to promise/historical fulfilment of the promise to contrast the promise of God and the *declaration* that he has fulfilled his promise. The context of false teaching required that the emphasis should lie on the way in which God has manifested the true message about the salvation-event in contrast to the false teachings of the opponents.

λόγος, 'word', 'saying',[48] has a variety of references in the PE:

(a) An individual saying, (3.8; 1 Tim 1.15; *et al.*);

(b) In the plural, it may possibly refer to sayings of Jesus (1 Tim 6.3);[49]

(c) Specifically of the speech of Christians, their message and manner of speaking (2.8; 1 Tim 4.12; 5.17; [of heretics] 2 Tim 2.17); what is to be preached (2 Tim 4.2); plural of what has been said or preached (2 Tim 4.15); ʹ

(d) As here, the 'word of God' as the divine revelation and the standard and content of Christian proclamation (1.3; 2.5; 1 Tim 4.5; 2 Tim 2.9). It is tantamount to the gospel message and the ensuing instruction for converts (2 Tim 4.2).[50] Almost certainly λόγον is not to be understood as the 'Logos'.[51]

Within this framework of contrast between the secrecy of the promise and the openness of the present revelation (cf. Col 1.26), the present time of fulfilment (Mk 1.15; Rom 5.6; Gal 6.9) is indicated by καιροῖς ἰδίοις (see 1 Tim 2.6; 6.15; cf. 1 Tim 4.1; 2 Tim 3.1; 4.3). The term corresponds to νῦν in 2 Tim 1.10 but

---

[48] 1.9; 2.5, 8; 3.8; 1 Tim 1.15; 3.1; 4.5, 6, 9, 12; 5.17; 6.3; 2 Tim 1.13; 2.9, 11, 15, 17; 4.2, 15**.

[49] See discussion *ad loc.* whether the reference is to sayings of Jesus or to teaching which bears his authority.

[50] Cf. Kittel, G., *TDNT* IV, 100–41; Ritt, H., *EDNT* II, 356–9. See especially Schlarb 1990:206–9.

[51] This was the view of Jerome and Oecumenius; cf. Walder, E. 'The Logos of the Pastoral Epistles', *JTS* 24 (1923), 310–15.

brings out the fact that it is the time appropriate in God's plans for the revelation (cf. Gal 4.4 for the same thought). While it might be tempting to take the plural both here and in 1 Tim 2.6 of a continuing time of revelation (Hasler, 86), its use in 1 Tim 6.15 in reference to a single point in time (the future epiphany of Christ) rules this out. More probably it is an idiomatic use of the plural for the singular, and whether the apostolic ministry or the parousia is in view, the term καιροῖς ἰδίοις views it as a development in God's redemptive history.

Like χρόνος, καιρός* can be used of a point of time (2 Tim 4.6) or a period of time (2 Tim 4.3). The older view that it specifically meant the former and especially time considered as opportunity (e.g. 'the decisive moment') has now been finally laid to rest by the work of Barr 1969. When it is used in the plural in the PE, it always has a qualifying adjective (ἴδιος, as here; 1 Tim 2.6; 6.15; ὕστερος, 1 Tim 4.1; χαλεπός, 2 Tim 3.1**). The plural is used of periods of time, similar to the plural ἡμέραι (Acts 3.19; 17.26; Eph 1.10).[52] The dat. expresses the period of time within which something happens (cf. Rom 16.25).

Originally ἴδιος had a stronger sense than the possessive pronoun and signified what was 'one's own' possession by contrast with what belonged to the community (Acts 4.32) or another person.[53] The force of the word grew weaker, especially in the LXX, and it is often no stronger than the personal pronoun (1 Tim 4.2; 2 Tim 4.3). It is used of the individual husbands/ masters to whom wives/slaves are to be subject (2.5, 9; 1 Tim 6.1; 1 Cor 14.35; Eph 5.22; 1 Pet 3. 1, 5) or the individual areas over which people have authority (1 Tim 3.4, 5, 12; 5.4). A person's 'own people' are his relatives (1 Tim 5.8). In 1.12 the force is that the prophet is actually one of their people. In 2 Tim 1.9 God's own plan stands over against human works.

In the present phrase (cf. 1 Tim 2.6; 6.15) the problem is whether the referent of ἴδιος is God or the nearest noun (λόγον). It is more likely that the reference is to 'God's own time', fixed and established by himself and suitable for his purpose (Lock, 126; cf. Acts 1.7).[54] The promise of salvation is brought to fulfilment at the time which he himself sets. The sing. form in Gal 6.9, however, is taken by some to mean idiomatically 'at the appropriate moment' (sc. for reaping; Bernard, 156), but this is unlikely to be the force here.

---

[52] Cf. Lock, 126; cf. Barr 1969:65; Delling, G., *TDNT* III, 455–64, especially 461; Baumgarten, J., *EDNT* II, 232–5.

[53] Cf. Bartsch, H.-W., *EDNT* II, 171f.; *TLNT* II, 205–11.

[54] Cf. Diodorus Siculus 1.50.7 (Johnson, 124). In Josephus, *Ant.* 11.171 καιρὸς τούτου ἴδιός ἐστιν means 'the time is favourable for this task'. Cf. 1 Clement 20.4 of the earth producing harvests 'at the proper seasons'.

The revelation takes place in and through the preaching, more specifically Paul's preaching. It follows that this is the message which Titus (and church leaders generally) must also preach. κήρυγμα can express both the activity and the content of the message, but generally the accent is on the former (2 Tim 4.17; Mt 12.41 par. Lk 11.32; Rom 16.25; 1 Cor 1.21; 2.4; 15.14***).[55] This language is very similar to Rom 16.25–26, where Paul links the revelation of the mystery to his preaching ministry which is continuous with the OT revelation through the prophets. The task is accordingly preaching the divinely authorised message, and κήρυγμα thus combines the ideas of the activity and content (Friedrich, G., *TDNT* III, 716–17). The proclamation would be useless if it did not communicate the intended message.

3b. ὃ ἐπιστεύθην ἐγὼ κατ᾽ ἐπιταγὴν τοῦ σωτῆρος ἡμῶν θεοῦ
A third element is added to the promised/revealed scheme; strictly speaking it is an indication of the place of Paul within the act of revelation, and it serves to bring the sentence back full circle to the person of the missionary who has been commissioned by God. Using the same language as 1 Tim 1.11 (cf. 1 Cor 9.17; Gal 2.7; 1 Th 2.4), the passive ἐπιστεύθην ἐγὼ, with its object, depicts the divine commissioning as the entrusting of the gospel to Paul.[56] ὅ is acc. of respect with the passive verb ἐπιστεύθην. πιστεύω is most frequently 'to believe', 'to trust in' (3.8; 1 Tim 1.16; 2 Tim 1.12), but it can also mean 'to entrust' (Lk 16.11; Jn 3.24), and the passive is used with the sense 'to be entrusted with'.[57]

ἐπιταγή 'command' is used only in the Pauline corpus in the NT (2.15; 1 Tim 1.1; 1 Cor 7.25; with κατ᾽ in 1 Tim 1.1; Rom 16.25; 1 Cor 7.6; 2 Cor 8.8***). It is a strong word for a command by a superior person; it can be used for a decree by a ruler (1 Esdr 1.18; Wis 14.16; Dan 3.16; 3 Macc 7.20) or for divine instructions (Wis 18.16; 19.6), and in the NT it refers either to God's, the apostle's or his delegate's command and authority. Paul expresses the same idea by reference to the 'will' (θέλημα) of God in the earlier epistles (1 Cor 1.1; 2 Cor 1.1; Col 1.1; Eph 1.1; cf. 2 Tim 1.1). The thought of divine command and consequent authority is somewhat stronger than in 1 Tim 1.11.

---

[55] Cf. Friedrich, G., *TDNT* III, 714–17.

[56] The use of the pass. to express a divine action is found in 1 Tim 1.11, 13, 16; 2.7, 13; 3.16; 4.14; 6.12; 2 Tim 1.11; 4.16, 17. Nauck 1950:17–20, holds that this usage is Jewish to avoid actually mentioning God. This may be true of some of the examples, but hardly of them all.

[57] 1 Tim 1.11; Rom 3.2; 1 Cor 9.17; Gal 2.7; 1 Th 2.4; cf. Ignatius, *Philad.* 9.1; in 1 Tim 3.16 it has the force 'to be believed'; cf. πίστις, 1.1 note.

The whole phrase has close parallels in 1 Tim 1.1; Rom 16.25–26 (κατ᾽ ἐπιταγὴν τοῦ αἰωνίου θεοῦ).[58]

Wolter (1988:149–52) argues that the characterisation of the Pauline apostolate as κατ᾽ ἐπιταγὴν θεοῦ here and in 1 Tim 1.1 intends something entirely different from the διὰ θελήματος θεοῦ characterisation of 2 Tim 1.1, on the basis of which 1 Tim and Tit can be distinguished from 2 Tim and their pseudepigraphical nature becomes obvious. Seeing the apostle's call as arising from the will of God connects the person-as-apostle with the Christ-event and salvation and separates his call from any human authority; the person, and his position, is thus legitimated. The language of 'command', however, strikes a different note, that of a royal order; the emphasis is now on legitimating the mission, and the interest in preserving or reviving the authority of the mission (and message) associated with Paul is evident. While the two phrases may indeed intend different nuances, and may correspond to the purposes of the respective letters (i.e. 2 Tim being more personal in tone, 1 Tim and Tit more official), to conclude more than this is difficult.

The addition of 'our Saviour God' indicates that the keynote of the letter is the salvific purpose of God who is the source of all blessings (cf. Hasler, 11, who, however, regards the salvation as future). σωτήρ is 'saviour' in the sense of 'deliverer, preserver' from illness and calamity. The term was used of human deliverers and guides (e.g. philosophers such as Epicurus), but was especially applied to gods (including the supreme god Zeus but also many others as the protectors of cities and the helpers of the distressed, such as Asclepius, the god of healing) and to deified rulers. Behind the NT usage lies that of the OT/LXX in which God is designated some thirty times as the deliverer of his people from danger and the bestower of benefits.[59] The term appears mostly in the later books of the NT where, as here, it is a designation of God[60] or of Christ.[61] In the PE it is primarily God who is Saviour, but this leads directly to the naming of Jesus Christ as Saviour (1.4) inasmuch as God's plan is effected through him. It emerges that the term is especially characteristic of Tit, and its use in 1.3f. sets the theological tone of the letter

[58] Cf. Delling, G., *TDNT* VIII, 36f.; Grimm, W., *EDNT* II, 41; Horsley, *New Docs.* II, 86 § 49.

[59] E.g. Deut 32.15; Pss 23 (MT 24).5; 24 (MT 25).5; 27.9 (MT 28.8); 41 (MT 42).6; Isa 12.2; 17.10; 43.3; 60.16; 1 Macc 4.30; Wis 16.7; Ecclus 51.1; Bar 4.22; Jth 9.11; Fee 1988:36; of other deliverers, Judg 3.9.

[60] 2.10; 3.4; 1 Tim 1.1; 2.3; 4.10; Lk 1.47; Jude 25; 1 Clement 69.3.

[61] 1.4; 2.13; 36; 2 Tim 1.10; Lk 2.11; Jn 4.42; Acts 5.31; 13.23; Eph 5.23; Phil 3.20; 1 Jn 4.14; 2 Clement 20.5; Diognetus 9.6; Ignatius, *Smyr.* 7.1; *Eph.* 1.1; *Magn.* Inscr.; *Poly.* Inscr; *Philad.* 9.2; *M. Poly.* 19.2.

as a whole. The use of the term in the NT is obviously linked with the early development of the use of other words from the same stem to denote the content of Christian experience and hope (cf. Ignatius, *Eph.* 1.1; *Philad.* 9.2).[62]

The use of ἡμῶν emphasises the reality of the purpose of God as it is experienced by his people and is not meant in any kind of exclusive manner (2.11; 1 Tim 2.4; 4.10). There may even be a polemical note against any (enthusiasts) who may have used this term in an exclusive sense, denying the universality of God's saving purpose (cf. Fee, 64).

b. *The recipient (1.4a)*

Τίτῳ γνησίῳ τέκνῳ κατὰ κοινὴν πίστιν After the lengthy description of Paul which has established the foundation for the instructions to be given in the letter, the recipient is introduced. Τίτος (2 Tim 4.10; Gal 2.1, 3; 2 Cor 2.13; 7.6, 13, 14; 8.6, 16, 23; 12.18***) is described, like Timothy, as Paul's child, more specifically as his 'true' child. For the metaphorical use of τέκνον (1.6*) see 1 Tim 1.2; 2 Tim 1.2; 1 Cor 4.17; Phil 2.22; Philem 10; 1 Pet 5.13. γνήσιος, 'genuine', was originally used of legitimate as opposed to bastard children, hence metaphorically 'true, authentic' or 'dear' (1 Tim 1.2; 2 Cor 8.8; Phil 4.3***; adv. Phil 2.20***). Here the former sense is dominant, but the latter is also present. Such sons might be expected to serve their fathers faithfully (Philo, *Cont.* 72). The use of γνήσιος to designate the authorised interpreters of philosophers (so of Aristotle in relation to Plato), the transmitters of revelation (*CH* 13.3) and the helpers of ruling shepherds (Philo, *Spec.* 4.184; *Virt.* 59) may be relevant.[63]

The force of the expression is debated, and may not be the same as in the cases of Timothy, Onesimus or John Mark.

(a) It is possible that Titus was Paul's own convert (Holtzmann, 467; Bernard, 156; Dornier, 123; Knight, 63–4; *pace* Hasler, 86).

(b) He may have been 'ordained' by Paul (Jeremias, 68f.). Neither of these views does justice to γνήσιος.

(c) The phrase may express the relation of the younger to the older man, and thus be expressive of affection (Spicq, 594) or perhaps of subordination.

---

[62] For σώζω see 3.5 note; for σωτηρία 2 Tim 2.10; 3.15**; for σωτήριος.see Tit 2.11**. See further Foerster, W., and Fohrer, G., *TDNT* VII, 1003–21; Schneider, J., and Brown, C., *NIDNTT* III, 216–21; Schelkle, K. H., *EDNT* III, 325–7; *TLNT* III, 344–57; Wendland 1904:335–47; Dibelius-Conzelmann, 74–7; Easton, 229–32; Brox, 232f.; Marshall 1996b; Läger 1996:119–26.

[63] Cf. Büchsel, F., *TDNT* I, 727; *TLNT* I, 136–8, 296–9.

(d) The decisive factor is surely the phrase 'according to a common faith'. κοινός** is 'common' in the sense of being 'shared' between two or more people (Acts 2.44; 4.32; Jude 3).[64] The whole phrase κατὰ κοινὴν πίστιν corresponds to ἐν πίστει in 1 Tim 1.2 (cf. 2 Tim 1.5) and expresses that in respect of which the metaphorical relationship exists. κοινός is similarly used by Jude to make a bond between himself and his readers (Jude 3; cf. 2 Pet 1.2). The qualification indicates that the relationship is a spiritual one between people of different ages who are now like members of a family to one another.[65]

(e) The phrase may then be pressed to indicate the full agreement in doctrine between Paul and Titus (Quinn, 72), and so to authenticate Titus to the church and indicate that he is to receive the same respect and obedience as Paul (Hasler, 86; *TLNT* I, 138). But it does so on the level of the text by means of reassuring Titus of his position in the eyes of Paul.

c. The greeting (1.4b)

TEXT

4. καί ἔλεος (A C² TR syʰ boᵐˢ); ὑμῖν καί (33); om. (1739 1881 *pc*). The substitution of the noun for the conjunction is by assimilation to 1 and 2 Tim (Metzger, 584; Elliott, 173f.).
Χριστοῦ Ἰησοῦ Ἰησοῦ Χριστοῦ (1739 1881); κυρίου Ἰ. Χ. (D² F G TR sy; κυρίου Ἰησοῦ (1175)). Elliott, 201, 232, accepts the text as the normal word order in PE. The form with κυρίου is assimilation to the normal Pauline formula. See 1 Tim 1.1 note.

EXEGESIS

4b. χάρις καὶ εἰρήνη ἀπὸ θεοῦ πατρός καὶ Χριστοῦ Ἰησοῦ τοῦ σωτῆρος ἡμῶν The background of the formula 'grace and peace' lies in Judaism, particularly in non-epistolary settings, and Paul's use of it is not confined to epistolary salutations; rather it reflects an apostolic mode of oral discourse and thus may be connected with the church's meetings (Knoch, 19).[66] In any case, the form had become standard by the time of composition of

[64] Elsewhere it is used in the sense of 'ordinary, impure'; cf. Hauck, F., *TDNT* III, 789–97.
[65] Cf. *Acta Carpi et Papyli*, 30, cited by Lock, 128; Quinn, 72. Some commentators have found in the phrase an allusion to the bond between Paul as a Jew and Titus as a Gentile (Grotius [according to Ellicott, 169]; Parry, 73; Barrett, 127) or to the common faith of all Christians (Quinn, 72f.; Holtzmann, 467f.; Spicq, 594f.), but these ideas are present only marginally, if at all.
[66] See further Berger 1974 and the criticisms by Schnider and Stenger 1987:25–33; Lieu*.

the PE, and the interest lies in the theological significance of the formula as it is used here and in the peculiarities which it demonstrates.[67]

The wording here resembles the normal Pauline form of greeting in omitting ἔλεος (contrast 1 Tim 1.2; 2 Tim 1.2). No specific reason for the omission, as compared with 1 and 2 Tim, can be seen (Spicq, 595 claims that it is unnecessary in the context). The greeting resembles the form in 1 and 2 Tim in the transfer of ἡμῶν from its normal position after πατρός to the end of the whole phrase.[68]

Originally the word χάρις meant 'graciousness, attractiveness' (cf. Lk 4.22; Col 4.6), but it developed the sense of 'favour, goodwill, loving care, grace'. This use is found in secular Gk. of the gods and rulers, but is especially developed in the LXX where it refers to the loving favour of God extended to his people.[69] The term occurs thirteen times in the PE. It is used twice in the idiomatic formula χάριν ἔχω ('to thank'; 1 Tim 1.12; 2 Tim 1.3). It is used six times, as here, in opening salutations and closing greetings; this usage is traditional and stereotyped, but none the less meaningful. This leaves a total of five occurrences (2.11; 3.7; 1 Tim 1.14; 2 Tim 1.9; 2.1) in the body of the letters, compared with some seventy times in the remaining ten letters of the Pauline corpus, i.e. once per 696 words compared with once per 412 words; this comparative infrequency is not significant in letters largely concerned with church order (see further on 1 Tim 1.14).

εἰρήνη, originally in the sense of 'peace' as opposed to war, developed the broader meanings of 'harmony' and well-being in general. In the OT it came to stand for the total wellbeing which comes from God, and which is then in the NT identified with Christian salvation. Apart from the salutations (1 Tim 1.2; 2 Tim 1.2), it is found in the PE only in 2 Tim 2.22** as a Christian virtue or quality (cf. Gal 5.22).[70]

The greeting follows the usual Pauline form in linking God the Father and Christ together as the source of Christian blessings (cf. 1 Tim 1.1 note), though here Christ is designated as τοῦ σωτῆρος ἡμῶν instead of 'our Lord' (as in 1 Tim; 2 Tim). πατήρ (human father, 1 Tim 5.1) is used of God in the PE only in the formal language of the epistolary salutations (1 Tim 1.2;

---

[67] Lieu*, 170–2, comments that the changes from the standard Pauline form are indicative of a later writer.

[68] The omission of ἡμῶν with πατρός is hardly significant; see, for example, 1 Th 1.1.

[69] Cf. Conzelmann, H., and Zimmerli, W., *TDNT* IX, 372–402. especially 397f.; Berger, K., *EDNT* III, 457–60; *TLNT* III, 500–6.

[70] Cf. Rad, G. von, and Foerster, W., *TDNT* II, 400–17; *TLNT* I, 424–38.

2 Tim 1.2**).[71] This lack of use is viewed by some as a divergence from the characteristic Pauline mode of expression, and in the PE it is set alongside a tendency to stress the transcendence and unapproachability of God (cf. 1 Tim 1.17; 6.15–16; Simonsen 1980:61). However, the theological functions of 'father' are here in effect taken over by σωτήρ (1.3), a title that was better suited to the theme of salvation developed throughout the PE and especially in Tit.

The description of Jesus as Saviour replaces the use of 'Lord' found in other NT epistolary salutations.[72] The use here anticipates that in 2.13 and 3.6 and expresses a key theme. The writer can thus use σωτήρ of God the Father and of Jesus in adjacent or almost adjacent verses (1.3; 2.10; 3.4). This interchangeability closely associates God, as the ultimate source or originator of the plan of salvation, and Christ, as the means of executing this plan.[73] The past appearance of Christ made salvation a possibility (2.11–14; 3.6; cf. 2 Tim 1.10). The future appearance will mean the final accomplishment of salvation (2.13; cf. Phil 3.20).

EXCURSUS 1

εὐσέβεια in the Pastoral Epistles

MM, 265f.; Bertram, G., *TDNT* III, 123–8; Brox, 174–7; Dibelius-Conzelmann, 39–41; Fiedler, P., *EDNT* I, 85; Foerster, W., *TDNT* VII, 175–85; idem., 'ΕΥΣΕΒΕΙΑ in den Pastoralbriefen', *NTS* 5 (1958–9), 213–18; Günther, W., *NIDNTT* II, 91–5; Kaufmann-Bühler, D., *RAC* VI, 985–1051; Lips 1979:80–7; Mott 1978:22–48; Roloff, 117–19; Quinn, 282–91; Spicq, 482–92; Spicq, C., *TLNT* II, 196–9; Towner 1989:147–52; Wainwright, J. J., '*Eusebeia*; Syncretism or Conservative Contextualization?', *EvQ* 65 (1993), 211–24.

The concept of εὐσέβεια is of major significance in the interpretation of the PE because of its importance for an understanding of the author's view of the Christian life and ethics. This can be seen immediately from its frequency of occurrence. In the NT this word-group is confined to Acts, 2 Peter and the PE, and it is found chiefly in the PE (εὐσέβεια: 1 Tim 2.2; 3.16; 4.7–8; 6.3, 5, 6, 11; 2 Tim 3.5; Tit 1.1; Acts 3.12; 2 Pet 1.3, 6, 7; 3.11; εὐσεβέω, 1 Tim 5.4; εὐσεβής Acts 10.2, 7; 2 Pet 2.9;

---

[71] Cf. Quell, G., and Schrenk, G., *TDNT* V, 945–1014; Michel, O., *EDNT* III, 53–7.

[72] κύριος is completely absent from Tit but is used frequently in 1 and 2 Tim.

[73] Knoch, 19, argues that this sharing indicates the divine equality of God and Christ.

εὐσεβῶς, 2 Tim 3.12; Tit 2.12).[74] It is one of a number of terms whose currency in pagan ethical thought has suggested to many the adoption of a secular morality indicative of a compromise with the world, the so-called 'bourgeois' ethic.

1. History of interpretation

The history of modern interpretation of εὐσέβεια in the PE can be divided into two stages, the first being up to and including the work of W. Foerster, and the second consisting of subsequent interpretations.

Foerster* 1959 identified three previous approaches to an understanding of the term:

(a) Schlatter, 176, and Spicq, 482–92, argued that in a purely religious manner it designates conduct and an attitude that honours God.

(b) For Holtzmann, 176–9, the author's use of εὐσέβεια was a reflection of developments in the church's thinking about 'Christian' or 'religious' living related to the development of the church's identity and ecclesiology into that of a monolithic institution in the world. What emerged, described as εὐσέβεια, was an uninspired but 'churchly' morality. It is not a manner of life that stems from any theological notion. It is rather a combination of good works and blameless living (i.e. morality, or a 'religious' way of life) which conforms to the ecclesiastical and practical shape of the church in the world.

(c) Dibelius defined 'godliness' as 'that behaviour which is well-pleasing to God and men' (Dibelius–Conzelmann, 39). But what he meant by this is understood clearly only when it is seen in the light of the broader term that he coined for the author's ethical teaching, 'good Christian citizenship' (*christliche Bürgerlichkeit*). By this he understood a life lived in harmony with the orders of the world, peaceful coexistence (1 Tim 2.2), a Christian version of secular morality. The delay of the parousia forced the church to come to terms with life in a hostile world. If this life were lived in Pauline terms, the church's continued existence would be doubtful. If, however, the church adapted itself to secular ideas of respectability, its longevity might be ensured. Εὐσέβεια, then, drawn from the pagan environment, became the foundation stone of this ethic of Christian citizenship.

(d) Foerster's own view combines several elements.[75] One of the most significant of these is the importance he places on secular Greek usage. The term in its Graeco-Roman context

---

[74] Cf. also θεοσέβεια (1 Tim 2.10).
[75] See also Trummer 1978:230; Bartsch 1965:40f.

referred to a general attitude of reverence or respect to various persons, gods and the orders of society, which were created or sanctioned by the gods. In popular usage 'piety' came to mean, not an attitude of respect towards the gods, but the actual worship paid to them in cultic acts. Yet this outward action was understood to be the result of the inner attitude. 'Piety' in both Greek and Roman thinking[76] was a highly regarded virtue and a duty.[77]

Taken from this thought world into the Christian dialogue, εὐσέβεια served to describe a manner of life characterised by respect for world orders (such as marriage, family, creation). In the churches addressed by the PE these were being undermined by false teachers with their Gnosticising ascetic practices. This is seen above all in 1 Tim 2.2 and 5.4, which govern his interpretation of the concept throughout the PE. But, in contrast to Dibelius, Foerster emphasised that Christian εὐσέβεια is not a virtue, for it is grounded in πίστις, the Christ-event (1 Tim 3.16) and God's will (1 Tim 4.10). Nevertheless, as it is absent from the list of qualities in 2 Tim 2.22, εὐσέβεια is clearly not on a level with faith and love, nor is it central or indispensable within the thought of the PE. Ultimately, despite efforts to ground the concept theologically, adoption of the word-group would have negative consequences for the church. Its lack of a built-in christological norm (which is present in πίστις) and its primary reference to orders of the world and the conduct of man in relation to them would lead inescapably to moralism.

(e) Beyond Foerster. Each of the preceding interpretations suffers from certain limitations in approach. Holtzmann and Dibelius overlooked or minimised the theological dimension of 'godliness'. Although Foerster attempted to correct this error, he followed Dibelius into the cul-de-sac created by making one or two occurrences of the term determinative for his interpretation. Then, in each case the Graeco-Roman usage of the word-group, in which εὐσέβεια plays the role of a virtue, was allowed to colour the understanding of the concept as it occurs in the PE.

Brox, 174–7, was one of the first to react to Foerster and his predecessors. His more thorough treatment of the word-group in the PE took him beyond the narrow conclusion of Foerster. Εὐσέβεια is more than 'respect for the natural orders'. Drawn from the secular Greek environment, the term gains a new sense through being used for the behaviour of Christians. Despite

---

[76] The Latin equivalent is *pietas*; a temple was consecrated to *Pietas* as a goddess in 191 BC in Rome.

[77] For references see Kaufmann-Buhler*; Foerster, W., *TDNT* VII, 168–96; Bertram, G., *TDNT* III, 123–8.

its appearing in a list as one virtue among others, more than respectable, reverent behaviour is meant; it is the response of faith, but that which is more appropriate in the later church's post-charismatic situation (cf. Bultmann 1952:II, 184–6).

With the work of Lips (1979:80–7) and Roloff (1988) the discussion advanced one step and then stalled. Lips introduced into the discussion the relation between 'godliness' and 'knowledge', which he demonstrated both from Hellenistic Jewish and Graeco-Roman sources, though clearly he sees the Greek background to be determinative (82–3). Secondly, he attempted to interpret εὐσέβεια on the basis of all of its occurrences in the PE. Passages such as 1 Tim 6.5–6; 2 Tim 3.5 and Tit 1.16 led him to conclude that the term describes the Christian life from the standpoint of the two interrelated aspects of religious knowledge (*Glaubenserkenntnis*) and corresponding conduct. Although Roloff, 117–18, agrees that Foerster's interpretation of εὐσέβεια as a virtue is too narrow, he does not take up Lips' idea that 'godliness' encompasses knowledge and conduct. It describes a visible life lived by the grace of God in all of its directions (118). But while observing the Christian element that has been inserted (especially Tit 2.12), it remains for him a concept of life which conforms to Graeco-Roman ethical categories, and which therefore functions within the Christian dialogue to justify the church's place in the world (see Schlarb 1990:29f.; Wainwright*, 221).

2. The Hellenistic and Jewish background

In the Greek world εὐσέβεια connotes an attitude of reverence which can be directed to a wide range of persons and objects. In Classical Greek piety could be directed towards deceased relatives, living relatives, the ruler, especially the emperor, judges, aliens, oaths and the law generally. Thus the word referred to '"respect" for the orders of domestic, national and also international life'. Since all these were under the protection of the gods, it is understandable that the words came to refer more and more to the gods.[78] Thus, according to W. Foerster, the concept had a broad sense but it became restricted to one's proper attitude to the gods, namely piety. On occasion it is specifically defined as being shown towards the gods. Foerster documents the distinction between piety towards the gods and righteousness towards one's neighbour and self-control as right conduct towards oneself (Xenophon, *Mem.* 4.8.11). In popular usage the

---

[78] It is associated with the cult of Artemis at Ephesus in an inscription (*New Docs.* II, 82 § 19 [AD II]).

terms came not to mean a reverent attitude to the gods but the actual worship paid to them in cultic acts. However, an inner attitude is always expressed in the outward act. Foerster sums up: 'the true content of εὐσέβεια for the educated Greek is reverent and wondering awe at the lofty and pure world of the divine, its worship in the cultus, and respect for the orders sustained by it. It is not being under the unconditional claim of a personal power.'

The corresponding concept in the Roman world was *pietas*. It has been defined as 'dutiful respect toward gods, fatherland and parents and other kinsmen'.[79] According to Cicero, 'piety is justice directed towards the gods (*Est enim pietas iustitia adversum deos*, Cicero, *De Nat. Deorum* 1.116); 'they refer to what happens in fear and worship of the gods as religion and the tasks which duty tells us to perform towards our native land or to parents or others linked to us by blood relationships as piety' (*Religionem eam quae in metu et caerimonia deorum sit appellant, pietatem quae erga patriam aut parentes aut alios sanguine coniunctos officium conseruare moneat*, Cicero, *In. Rhet.* 2.66). Some Romans adopted the cognomen *Pius*; Virgil's 'Pius Aeneas' expresses the Roman ideal.

The concept was very much at home in the Graeco-Roman world. The word-group had an eminently positive air to it.[80] Piety was a highly regarded virtue. It was essentially religious, being concerned with respect for the gods, shown in worship, but at the same time it included respect for the orders of society sanctioned by the gods. Sometimes the word was used narrowly for attitude to the gods in distinction from a righteous attitude towards human institutions and people.

Until recently the importance of the usage in Hellenistic Judaism has been rather overlooked. The fruitfulness of this

---

[79] Greene, W. C., and Scheid, John, *OCD*, 1182, on which this paragraph is based.

[80] The word-group was very frequent in inscriptions, especially in referring to people's virtues. We may supplement earlier collections of material by mentioning the references recently gathered together in *New Docs*: I, 78f. §27 (but late AD V); II, 55f. §16 (AD II/III epitaph of a woman who did good 'with a view to piety' but as an invalid proved that 'mortals' fortunes are not in proportion to their piety'); IV, 35–8 §10 (AD III or IV, epitaph on a judge 'who even among the dead had the judgment of piety'); IV, 74–82 §19 (c. AD 162–4 Inscr. from Ephesus – 'the proconsul has regard for the reverence of the goddess [Artemis]'. The same inscr. contains other words found in the PE); IV, 259–61 §127 (a late Imperial Inscr. from Nikaia refers to a man as 'father of the church of the pious' trans. as 'the orthodox church' [see *PGL, s.v.* 5]); VII, 233–41 §10 (an inscription from Kyme in Asia Minor [c. 2 BC–AD 2] honouring the piety of a civic benefactor displayed in a variety of generous deeds in the community).

area has been demonstrated by Quinn, 282–91. In particular, we find that the word-group is important in certain strata of the LXX. Here the noun εὐσέβεια occurs 59 times. Four of these occurrences are in the canonical books, five in the Apocrypha, three in 3 Macc and 47 in 4 Macc.[81] Where it occurs with a Hebrew equivalent the noun translates יִרְאַת יהוה, 'the fear of Yahweh' (cf. Prov 1.7; Isa 11.2; 33.6). Connected to such ideas as loyalty to the covenant, moral response and devotion to the law, this is the Hebrew term coming closest to 'religion'. The word θεοσέβεια is used in the same manner (Gen 20.11; Job 28.28; cf. Ecclus 1.24; Bar 5.4; 4 Macc 7.6, 22 *v.l.*; 15.28 *v.l.*; 16.11). The opposite attitude is ἀσέβεια which translates words expressive of rebellion against God. It is clear that εὐσέβεια was well-fitted to translate the Hebrew phrase, although the more literal translation was preferred in the LXX, and it is a good question why it was not adopted more widely.

The adjective εὐσεβής is found ten times in the canonical books (Judg 8.31; Job 32.3; Prov 12.12; 13.19; Eccles 3.16; Mic 7.2; Isa 24.16; 26.7 [2 times]; 32.8); for θεοσεβής see Exod 18.21; Judg 11.17; Job 1;1, 8; 2.3; 4 Macc 15.28 *v.l.*; 16.11). It also occurs 28 times in the non-canonical books (2 Macc 1.19; 12.45; Ecclus 15 times; 4 Macc 11 times). It translates 'righteous' (Prov 12.12; Isa 24.16; 26.7).

The verb εὐσεβέω is found only in the non-canonical books (Sus 64; 4 Macc 5 times; cf. *Sib. Orac.* 4.187) and the adverb εὐσεβῶς likewise (4 Macc 7.21).

The literature of Hellenistic Judaism reflects the attempt to translate traditional OT concepts into the Greek language. While it is certainly possible that in the process certain ideas were diluted, transformed or overpowered by Greek concepts, it is not accurate to conclude that this was unavoidably the case. In fact the concepts which the εὐσέβεια word-group converts remain thoroughly biblical. 'Piety' in Isa 11.2 and 33.6 brings together 'knowledge' of and 'the fear of the Lord' (cf. Prov 1.7). Elsewhere (e.g. Prov 13.11; cf. Wis 10.12) εὐσέβεια comprehensively describes a kind of behaviour that pleases God. Applied in these ways, there is no reason to think that the word-group introduces an idea completely at odds with traditional Jewish teaching. Much more it sets the stage for the building of a significant bridge between the Jewish religion and the Greek culture. As Quinn suggests, modern languages would describe this interplay of the knowledge of God and appropriate conduct with the one term, 'religion', a term lacking in Greek and

[81] Prov 1.7; 13.11; Isa 11.2; 33.6; 1 Esdr 1.23; Wis 10.12; Ecclus 49.3; 2 Macc 3.1; 12.45; 3 Macc 1.9; 2.31, 32; for 4 Macc see below.

Hebrew. Εὐσέβεια appears to gather together into one comprehensive idea the knowledge of God and the appropriate response (fear of the Lord).

Similarly, the integration of the word-group into the theology of piety expressed in Ecclesiasticus is natural and does not dilute traditional Jewish teaching in any way. Essentially, its use here describes 'the pious' in terms of categories which are thoroughly traditional (they are the opposite of sinners, 13.17; 33.14; they have a knowledge of God, 43.33; they show obedience to the commandments, 37.12; they are holy and wise in speech, 23.12; 27.11; they are the recipients of divine blessing, 11.22). Εὐσεβής often translates forms of 'righteous' (צדק), and in 49.3 εὐσέβεια stands for the huge concept of Israel's appropriate response to God's covenant (עשׂה הסד; LXX: ἐν ἡμέραις ἀνόμων κατίσχυσεν τὴν εὐσέβειαν).

In 4 Maccabees the word-group plays a role in the argument designed to defend 'devout reason' (ὁ εὐσεβὴς λογισμός) over all human emotions. In this line of thought, εὐσέβεια (meaning the Jewish faith) is the measure of reason and not vice versa, and reason determines appropriate human conduct, which includes worship (see especially 5.22–24).

Philo appears to have been closely in touch with Greek usage; for him εὐσέβεια is the queen and source of the virtues (*Spec.* 4.135, 147; *Abr.* 270; *Decal.* 52, 119; cf. Mott 1978:22–48). However, his interest in the OT and the law is also clear. Consequently, the commandments are related to 'piety' (*Deus* 69), and 'piety' is a matter of one's relation to God (Foerster, *TDNT* VII, 180–1). Similarly, Josephus understands piety as an attitude towards God which is expressed in keeping his laws (Josephus, *Ap.* I.60; Foerster, *TDNT* VII, 180).

Rather than seeing the emergence of this word-group with its distinctive place in Greek thought as evidence that the traditional faith of at least certain groups of Diaspora Jews was becoming weakened through hellenisation (Foerster, *TDNT* VII, 182; Bertram, *TDNT* III, 123–8), Quinn argues that despite certain limitations, 'the *euseb-* language ... offered the Hellenistic Jew a means for explaining and expressing himself to contemporary society' (287f.). What was needed was a term that would be able to bring together into one concept the related ideas of 'the fear of the Lord', 'the knowledge of God' and response or conduct. The εὐσέβεια language met this need because, although in Greek thinking it was a virtue and tied to cultic acts, it was nevertheless broad enough in scope, with the necessary inner and outer dimensions and connotation of loyalty to God, to express adequately an OT/Jewish concept of 'piety' or spiritual life.

3. The New Testament usage

In the light of the usage of the word-group in Hellenistic Judaism and the NT, the interpretation of εὐσέβεια as a virtue, part of a bourgeois moral attitude characteristic of secularisation, is mistaken. The word-group functioned in Hellenistic Judaism to describe 'the fear of the Lord' and the practical conduct which proceeded from it. It combined knowledge of God and behaviour. Evidence of this dynamic equivalence is equally apparent in the NT, though 'piety' develops further along specifically Christian lines. The use of the word-group outside of the PE is confined to Acts and 2 Peter.

In Acts 17.23 the verb denotes the actual exercise of religion, which, with the religion of Athens in view, must be understood in cultic terms. The adjective (meaning 'pious') describes the 'God-fearers', Cornelius and one of his soldiers, in Acts 10.2, 7. Worship of the God of the Jews is meant and the visible evidence of 'piety' is seen in such activities as almsgiving and prayer. The combination of knowledge of God and conduct seems obvious here (cf. the summary in 10.35 which brings together 'fear of the Lord' and appropriate behaviour). Acts 3.12 implies that Peter and John have a Christian 'piety', though it is not, in and of itself, the source of the healing miracle being discussed. Although Acts 17.23 may well use the term as those in Athens would have understood it, the 'Christian' usages conform to the very biblical notion of 'godliness' consisting of reverent knowledge of God and conduct shaped by that knowledge.

In 2 Peter we appear to have both a broad usage of the word-group, i.e. to describe the entire life of a Christian as 'godliness', and a narrower usage, i.e. a type of action (a virtue) to be practised by Christians (1.6f.; 3.11). The author comments that God's power grants us all that we need for life and 'godliness' (1.3) – i.e. eternal life and the way of life that goes along with it. In 2.9, much the same as in Ecclesiasticus, the word-group describes the 'godly' (after the pattern of Noah and Lot), whom God will rescue from trial, in contrast to the 'ungodly' (ἀσεβής, vv. 5f.; after the pattern of fallen angels, the sinners of Noah's day, Sodom and Gomorrah) for whom judgement awaits. But 3.11 uses the plural (εὐσεβείαι) to denote deeds (which reflect piety), and 1.7 lists 'godliness' as one of several aspects of behaviour to be pursued.

4. The usage in the Pastoral Epistles

The PE contain the greatest concentration of the word-group in the NT. In Tit 1.1; 2.12; 1 Tim 2.2; 3.16; 4.7f.; 6.3, 5f.; 2 Tim 3.5,

12 the word-group functions to describe the life (noun), or the manner of life (adverb) which is true Christianity (cf. θεοσέβεια in 1 Tim 2.10 which is synonymous). Several other connections are also clear. 'Godliness' has a theological basis in the Christ-event (1 Tim 3.16; 2 Tim 3.12; cf. Tit 2.12), and it is integrally related to the knowledge of God (or of the gospel, the truth, etc.; Tit 1.1; 1 Tim 6.3, 5, 6, 11). It presupposes a knowledge of God's requirements. Thus, in contrast to the superficial 'form' of godliness of the false teachers (2 Tim 3.5), genuine godliness proceeds out of commitment to God and the orthodox teaching of the faith. 'Godliness' to some extent means 'teaching/ knowledge about what godliness involves'. It does not consist narrowly of cultic acts, even congregational worship; rather it is concerned with the whole of Christian behaviour.

Moreover, it is a thoroughly dynamic description of life, one which the individual must actively (1 Tim 4.7f.) and consciously decide to pursue (Tit 2.12). It is a comprehensive term for the Christian life, combining inner and outer dimensions, and is no more a virtue than are faith and love which are equally comprehensive terms for the characteristics of Christian living. It implies a serious approach to life and religion by contrast with the frivolous disputations of the opponents (1 Tim 2.2). The practice of piety can be seen in very specific ways, such as in honouring parents (1 Tim 5.4). In 1 Tim 6.11 and Tit 2.12 godliness describes one of several aims that the Christian is to pursue or one characteristic of the Christian life. To argue from this, however, that it is simply one of the virtues (cf. Mott 1978:22–48) is to ignore the much stronger tendency to characterise the whole of life in Christ with 'godliness'. It is worth comparing the way Gal 5.22–23 subordinates πίστις in its list of characteristics of the Spirit-controlled life.

Finally, the word-group plays a significant role in the polemic which develops throughout the letters. This polemic was directed against the godless (ἀσέβεια) in the Hellenistic Jewish writings (e.g. Prov 1.7; 3 Macc 2.31–32). The same contrast occurs in the PE, though here the godless are specifically false teachers (see especially Tit 2.12; 1 Tim 1.9; 2 Tim 2.16; cf. 2 Pet 2.6). There can be a counterfeit piety consisting of apparently religious acts divorced from upright living.

Why did the word-group reach such prominence in the PE? Some have argued from 1 Tim 6.5 and 2 Tim 3.5 that the author lifted a concept which figured prominently in the heretics' vocabulary, in order to redefine it and correct misunderstandings about the Christian life introduced by their teaching (Fee, 63; cf. Lips 1979:82–3). But the usage in Acts and 2 Peter suggests a wider currency, and it seems to be used easily throughout the

PE and is not confined to polemical passages. Others have seen in the choice of the term the possible influence of Luke on Paul (Knight, 118; Moule 1982; Wilson 1979:31, 50–2). It remains puzzling, however, why the historical Paul should have felt it necessary to adopt this vocabulary in letters addressed to his immediate colleagues rather than in letters addressed to a Hellenistic audience.

Quinn concluded that the occurrence of the εὐσέβεια word-group in the PE reflects 'the attempt of Roman Christians to identify themselves in terms of the society in which they lived, a city that had temples to personified Pietas ... The values grounded on *pietas* in pagan Rome offered a point of departure for showing what Christians meant by *eusebeia*, and they took the **seb/m-* language to explore that area' (Quinn, 289; cf. Simpson, 40). While Roman influence (or destination) may not be relevant, the observation that the word-group may have been chosen because it provided a contact point with pagan society (Greek or Roman) is worthy of consideration. Ironically, it may well have been the currency of the language in Graeco-Roman thought that delayed and then limited its use in the early church's vocabulary. In any case, as employed in the PE, εὐσέβεια expresses a strongly Christian concept of the new existence in Christ that combines belief in God and a consequent manner of life.

BODY OF THE LETTER – INSTRUCTIONS TO THE CHURCH LEADER (1.5–3.11)

The body of the letter consists of instructions on how Titus is to act as leader of the church, both on what he is to do and also on what he is to say to the church. Thus instruction is indirectly given to the church.

The instruction falls into two main parts. In the first (1.5–16) directions are given regarding the appointment of elders (1.5–9), followed by warning against the presence of opponents who would subvert the sound teaching which it is the task of the elders to provide (1.10–16). In the second part (2.1–3.11) Titus is instructed regarding the teaching that he is to give the church. This can be subdivided into teaching regarding the relationships of believers to one another within the congregational setting (2.1–15) and teaching regarding the way in which they are to live in society (3.1–11).

The indirect character of the instruction has given rise to the feeling that it is remote from the actual situation of the congregations and rather general in content by contrast with the very specific and concrete paraenesis in Paul (Gilchrist 1967). But it should be needless to say that if the PE are primarily written to individual church leaders, then the indirect form of the instruction for the churches which they oversee is inevitable.[1]

This somewhat official character of the letter, like 1 Tim, is reflected in the lack of a thanksgiving or prayer report which is characteristic of the Pauline letters (cf. Jas; 2 Pet).

In the situation presupposed in the letter, a certain urgency in carrying out the instructions arises from the fact that Titus himself was expected to leave Crete (3.12) and must therefore ensure the healthy continuation of the church after his departure (Holtz, 207).

I. THE APPOINTMENT OF ELDERS AND THE DANGER FROM OPPONENTS (1.5–16)

The churches in Crete are represented as lacking in certain respects and as being menaced by unauthorised teachers with

---

[1] 'He is not so much advising Titus for his own sake as commending him to others so that none may hinder him' (Calvin, 356).

false doctrines. The first part of the answer to the problem lies in the appointment of good local leaders who will be able to give proper teaching to the church and to deal with the opponents. The first subsection (1.5–9) gives directions about the need to appoint good leaders and the kind of people to appoint. The second subsection (1.10–16) gives the basis for this command.

a. The appointment and duties of elders (1.5–9)

Bartsch 1965:82–111; Dodd, C. H., 'New Testament Translation Problems II', *BT* 28 (1977), 112–16; Emmet, C. W., 'The Husband of One Wife', *ExpTim* 19 (1907–8), 39f.; Frey, J.-B., 'La signification des termes μόνανδρος et *univira*', *RSR* 20 (1930), 48–60; Holtzmann, 233–8; Lattey, C., 'Unius uxoris vir (Tit 1,6)', *VD* 28 (1950), 288–90; Lightman, M. and Zeisel, W., 'Univira: an Example of Continuity and Change in Roman Society', *CH* 46 (1977), 19–32; Lyonnet, S., '"Unius uxoris vir" in 1 Tim 3.2,12; Tit 1.6', *VD* 45 (1967), 3–10; Page, S., 'Marital Expectations of Church Leaders in the Pastoral Epistles', *JSNT* 50 (1993), 105–20; Potterie, I. de la, ' "Mari d'une seule femme": Le sens théologique d'une formule paulinienne', in *Paul de Tarse: Apôtre du Notre Temps* (Rome: Abbaye de S. Paul, 1979), 619–38; Trummer, P. 'Einehe nach den Pastoralbriefen', *Bib* 51 (1970), 471–84. See also bibliography to **Excursus 2**.

There seem to be two (interrelated) dimensions to Titus's task. He is, generally, to complete the work in the Cretan churches, and related to this is the specific task of appointing leaders in local churches. The main interest is in the qualities of the people to be appointed so that they can adequately carry out their functions. The reason for the appointment is given in vv. 10–16 and lies in the presence of opponents of the writer in the churches who are promoting teaching that he regards as false in itself and as having deleterious moral effects. Therefore, the basic requirement for the elders is faithful adherence to the accepted teaching of the church and the ability to expound it positively and refute error. The preceding requirements are concerned basically with moral character and are fairly general.

The situation envisaged is different from that in 1 Tim 3, where elders already exist. The qualities required are also listed in greater detail with the ability to teach being spelled out. This suggests that the church situation in Crete is portrayed as being in a less developed state. There is no mention of the exclusion of new converts or the need for a good reputation in society at large. On the other hand, the ideal elder is the head of a Christian family. Fee, 171, notes that compared with 1 Tim 3 the list has a more orderly appearance.[2]

---

[2] The pattern found here continued to be used in the church. See the requirements for deacons and presbyters in Polycarp 5; 6.

The main part of the section (vv. 6, 7–9) has the form of a *Pflichtenlehre* (duty code), more specifically a *Berufspflichtenlehre* (duty code for a specific occupation). This listing of qualities appropriate to a specific office or status is a specific category within the more general genre of lists of virtues and vices. Such lists are highly characteristic of the PE; for the former see 2.2, 3, 5, 7f., 9f.; 1 Tim 3.2–4, 8, 11; 4.12; 6.11, 18; 2 Tim 22, 24; 3;10; for the latter see 3.3; 1 Tim 1.9f.; 6.4f.; 2 Tim 3.2–4. They take a variety of forms, lists of adjectives or nouns, lists of negatives, and they may be developed in various ways to incorporate longer phrases. They can be used to describe the evil state of believers before conversion and the good qualities which they should show afterwards, or the evil qualities of those who fall away from the faith and give false teaching. They are used to describe the characteristics that should be found in believers in general, or, as here, of church leaders or particular groups within the church. The use of such lists was already well-established in the early church, especially in the writings of Paul.[3] The question of their origin has been much debated, since they are rare in the Old Testament although common in Judaism. They are, however, common in Graeco-Roman ethics as well as being found in Iranian sources.[4]

There are examples of similar lists of qualities in Greek sources for specific occupations.[5] (They bear some relation to lists of virtues and vices, since the qualities may be the same.) They are often very general but adapted to specific offices.[6]

In the present case there are clear indications that traditional material is being employed and then adapted for use in 1 Tim 3 (or vice versa) (Cf. Verner 1983:103–6).

First, an identical form is used to introduce some of the material:

Tit 1.7   δεῖ γὰρ τὸν ἐπίσκοπον ἀνέγκλητον εἶναι
1 Tim 3.2   δεῖ οὖν τὸν ἐπίσκοπον ἀνεπίλημπτον εἶναι

The connecting particles differ because of context. In 1 Tim 3.2 the statement is preceded by the faithful saying, which describes

---

[3] Rom 1.29–31; 1 Cor 5.11; 6.9f.; Gal 5.19–21; Eph 2.1f.; Col 3.5–9.
[4] See Easton 1932; Vögtle 1936; Wibbing, S., *Die Tugend- und Lasterkataloge im NT unde ihre Traditionsgeschichte* (Berlin, 1959); Kamlah 1964; McEleney 1974; Berger 1984a:1088–92; 1984b:148–54. There are useful brief surveys by Fitzgerald, J. T., *ABD* VI, 857–9; Kruse, C. G., *DPL*, 962f.
[5] Cf. the description of the qualities of the ideal military leader in Onasander, *De imperatoris officio* 1 (Dibelius-Conzelmann, 158–60; like Wetstein, they spell his name as 'Onosander', but 'Onasander' is the preferred spelling of his name in *OCD*). See further **Excursus 3**.
[6] See especially Dibelius-Conzelmann, 158–60; Easton, 197–202; Roloff, 150f. and notes; Schwarz 1983:88–95.

the office of the overseer/bishop[7] as a good work, and the qualities that follow are introduced as a logical and necessary consequence of the faithful saying (thus οὖν). However, in the present setting of Titus 1 the statement is given in substantiation of the initial set of standards.[8] The predicate adjectives, ἀνεπίλημπτος and ἀνέγκλητος, are synonymous, with the selection of ἀνέγκλητος in the present passage perhaps determined by the term's appearance in v. 6. (Cf. further Verner 1983:104–6.)

Second, although the independent nature of v. 6 may suggest that it is an abbreviated or adapted form of a longer code, the conjoining of the two qualities at the head of each set of instructions points to a traditional configuration (cf. Trummer*, 473f.; Schwarz 1983:76–8; Verner 1983:70, 72).

| Tit 1.6 | ἀνέγκλητος, | μιᾶς γυναικὸς ἀνήρ |
| 1 Tim 3.2 | ἀνεπίλημπτον ... | μιᾶς γυναικὸς ἄνδρα |

Third, the qualities in the two lists which are commended or prohibited are generally comparable (cf. Dibelius-Conzelmann, 133). However, the differences in the list in Titus are not necessarily incidental; they may reflect sensitivity to the more rudimentary level of Christianity that prevailed in Crete (see below).

The list is regarded as very general and lacking in specificity by Dibelius-Conzelmann, 99; but this is a verdict typical of Dibelius, who tends to see the general rather than the particular right through the NT. What can be said is surely that the desired qualities are those which are expected in all church members, but it is recognised that people often fall short of the ideal and that leaders should be chosen from those who come closest to it. At the same time, there are specific qualities which are particularly associated with leadership which also appear in such lists, and some of the qualities may have been selected for their suitability to a more primitive Cretan church situation. Vögtle 1936:54 and Brox, 285, comment that the lists are incomplete, but this is characteristic of *all* ethical lists.

Various commentators have argued that the contents of the lists in the PE are often 'secular' in nature and not specifically church- or leader-related, and that the requirements are in some

[7] Since the term 'bishop' carries such a load of meaning which may or may not go back to the NT concept, it has seemed best to translate ἐπίσκοπος by a more neutral term. Although 'overseer' (NIV t; NRSV mg) is not entirely satisfactory, it has been adopted as the usual rendering, but on occasion 'bishop' has been retained, especially with reference to post-NT usage. GNB 'church leader' is too general; NJB 'presiding elder' is misleading.

[8] Most commentators find the use of two lists, with perhaps an independent shorter tradition (Quinn, 85) given in v. 6; thus γάρ is a more suitable connector than οὖν. See, however, Oberlinner, 90f.

cases 'banal' (Brox, 283). Kelly, 232, rightly responds that the latter criticism betrays 'an extraordinary lack of realism' over against the temptations faced by church officials in every age. The former comment is substantially correct, but perhaps fails to recognise that a good deal of the concern is for the reputation of the church in the eyes of outsiders. In general, this verdict fails to take sufficiently into account (a) the fact that qualities of leadership would be similar in the church and the secular world and (b) the amount of specifically Christian colour in the lists.

The main problem posed by the material is the curious way in which the passage begins by discussing the appointment of elders and describes the kind of people to be appointed (vv. 5–6) but then proceeds to describe the character of the overseer at considerably greater length (vv. 7–9). The generally accepted solution to this apparent duplication is that two broadly similar lists of qualifications have been run together, one for elders and one for overseers. It is also generally agreed that for the author elders and overseers are two names for the same functionaries, and that the duplication may be due to the amalgamation of two types of church order. The later emergence of monarchical bishops out of the group of elders has not yet taken place. See **Excursus 2**.

This solution is not entirely satisfactory. There is clear evidence that the function of the elders was seen as the oversight (*episkopé*) or pastoral care of the congregation; this is proved by Acts 20.17, 28 and 1 Pet 5.1, 2 (where the participle ἐπισκοποῦντες is almost certainly original). What we have in the present passage is the same phenomenon. The writer begins by affirming the need for elders to be blameless, and he then details the two areas of marriage and family life in which this must be true. Then he proceeds to explain *why* it is necessary. In his capacity as an overseer the candidate must be blameless inasmuch as he is acting on behalf of God in his household. Then he continues his description, but with a syntactical change necessitated by the inclusion of v. 7a. The composition is similar to that in 1 Tim 3.2–7 where the whole description is set up in the 'an overseer must be...' form, but there is equally a parenthetical justification of the requirements in v. 5, after which the list of requirements continues.[9] Understood in this way, the appearance of two lists in Tit 1 is illusory and what we have is simply a parenthetical explanation of the first requirement followed by a change of style in the form of the list.

---

[9] The justification for the qualities required in deacons in 1 Tim 3.13 comes at the end of the brief list and so does not disturb the sequence.

TEXT

5. ἀπέλιπον (א* D* Ψ 81 365 1505 1739 1881 *pc*; WH mg; Holtzmann, 468; Kilpatrick; Elliott): ἀπέλειπον (A C F G 088 0240 33 1175 *pc*); κατέλιπον (א² D² TR; cf. Acts 18.19; 24.37); κατέλειπον (L P 104 326 *al*). Confusion of -ι- and -ει- is very common in MSS. The aor. is required here by the sense. Elsewhere the PE use ἀπολείπω rather than καταλείπω. Hence the text should be retained (Elliott, 162f.; cf. 2 Tim 4.13, 20 for similar variations).

ἐπιδιορθώσῃ ἐπιδιορθώσῃς (A (D* F G) Ψ 1881 *pc*) is by assimilation to the following verb (Elliott, 174)

8. ἐγκρατῆ ἐνκρατή (A D F G I). Elliott, 175f, adopts the variant spelling (for a similar problem see 2 Tim 2.3, 11); he argues that ἐν- was used for etymological clarity, but assimilation took place in pronunciation. MHT II, 104f. appears to prefer the assimilated form.

9. ἐν τῇ **διδασκαλίᾳ τῇ ὑγιαινούσῃ** τοὺς ἐν πάσῃ θλίψει (A); assimilation to 2 Cor 1.4.

There are lengthy additions here and in 1.11 in a trilingual XIII cent. MS (460) (Elliott, 176f.; Metzger, 584); cf. 2 Tim 4.19.

EXEGESIS

5a. Τούτου χάριν ἀπέλιπόν σε ἐν Κρήτῃ Τούτου χάριν, 'for this reason' (Eph 3.1, 14) points forwards to the following ἵνα clause.[10] ἀπολείπω can mean 'to leave behind' (2 Tim 4.13, 20),[11] but it is possible that the meaning intended here is closer to 'dispatched', 'deployed' or 'assigned'.[12] Wolter (1988:183f.) develops this most extensively to show that both ἀπολείπω and καταλείπω functioned as technical terms for the installation of official deputies or representatives or royal governors; he concludes that Tit 1.5 (and 1 Tim 1.3) may consciously employ this literary device. If this is the case, it may be (as Wolter maintains) simply another element of the pseudepigrapher's fiction, or it may be yet another reflection of the transference of apostolic authority to the appointed delegate.

The island of Κρήτη (Acts 27.7, 12f., 21***; cf. Κρῆτες, 1.12; Acts 2.11***) is located south of the Aegean sea at a strategic navigational point in relation to the winds (Acts 27.7) for the maritime trade. Its location and importance for trade meant that it would be influenced by philosophies and religious teaching from all parts of the Mediterranean world. The people were adherents of a number of religions and cults, including the

[10] χάριν is the acc. of χάρις used as a prep.; it generally follows the word qualified (in non-literary works it could precede the noun, Simpson, 96) and can express goal or reason (1.11; 1 Tim 5.14; Lk 7.47; Gal 3.19; 1 Jn 3.12; Jude 16***).

[11] Also 'to desert', Jude 6; pass. 'to be left over, remain', Heb 4.6, 9; 10.26***; *TLNT* I, 183f.

[12] Cf. 1 Macc 10.79; 2 Macc 4.29; so the synonym, καταλείπω, of military troops in Josephus, *Ap.* 1.77. For synonymous use of the two verbs cf. Josephus, *Bel.* 1.259 and *Ant.* 14.346 (van Bruggen 1981:39f.; *contra* White, 186, who states that the verb is used for leaving behind temporarily, whereas καταλείπω refers to something permanent).

worship of Zeus, Leto, Apollo, Artemis, Aphrodite, Asclepius and Hermes (Dietrich, B. C., in *OCD* 408). There were communities of Jews (Tacitus, *Histories* 5.11; Josephus, *Ant.* 27.327; *Bel.* 2.103; Philo, *Leg. Gai.* 282) and by this time possibly Jewish Christians (Acts 2.11).

ἵνα τὰ λείποντα ἐπιδιορθώσῃ The purpose clause outlines Titus's commission in Crete. He is to set right what was lacking in the churches. The participle τὰ λείποντα signifies 'the things remaining to be done', which had not been included in previous activity (λείπω [trans. 'to leave behind'] is used intrans. in the NT, 'to lack, be in need of', 3.13; Lk 18.22; Jas 1.4f.; 2.15***).[13] Quinn, 83, regards the combination of the participle with its cognate verb, ἀπέλιπον, as part of a stylistic device, which, along with the emphatic change to the second person in this verse, signals the transition from the salutation to the instructions in the body of the letter. This is not very convincing.

ἐπιδιορθόω*** (here aor. mid.) is an extremely rare verb, unattested in Cl., the LXX and Fathers, with the sense 'to set right, to correct in addition'. The use may reflect some local colour, since its only other occurrence is apparently in an inscription on Crete dating to the second century BC (*CIG* 2555, 9, in BA). The related term, διορθόω, occurs in legal contexts discussing lawmaking and treaties with Cretans (c. 200 BC; Dittenberger, *Syll.* 581.85).[14] The term may thus express (in a way sensitive to Cretan nuance) the idea of authority to act (to make appropriate and needed reforms) such as might be given to lawmakers or by an apostle to his delegate.

In this the accent may fall on *completing* a task, the implication being that Paul himself or a colleague had begun to set up the churches and organise their structure, but had departed before the task was completed (cf. Fee, 172). This would accord with the nascent condition of the churches in which leaders have yet to be selected. Or the accent may be on correction and restoration of a good situation that had deteriorated, which makes sense in light of the need to deal with the false teachers and the damage they have caused (1.10–16; 3.9–11; Hanson, 172). In any case, the effect of the instruction is to tie in Titus's present task with the broader commission that had been already given to him (Wolter 1988:180f.) The effect is that Titus is given authority to do more than the specific instructions in the letter (Oberlinner, 19).

---

[13] For the phrase cf. Polybius 13.2.2 (Parry, 74); cf. Hermas, *Vis.* 3.1.9; *Sim.* 9.9.4. Spicq cites an instance of τὰ λείποντα = 'the backlog' (*TLNT* I, 375–7 [377 n. 12]).

[14] It occurs in 1 Clement 21.6. Cf. διόρθωμα, Acts 24.2; διόρθωσις, Heb 9.10 in the sense of reform, reformation; cf. also Philo, *Flacc.* 124, περὶ τὴν τῶν λειπομένων ἐπανορθωσέων; 2 Tim 3.16.

5b. καὶ καταστήσῃς κατὰ πόλιν πρεσβυτέρους, ὡς ἐγώ σοι διεταξάμην Among these tasks that of selecting elders is particularly emphasised.[15] The fundamental nature of this task in completing all that needs to be done in the churches is clear from the immediate attention given to it (vv. 6–9). The implication is that Titus is to take the initiative.

καθίστημι** (here aor. act.) is used here in the technical sense of the appointment of officials.[16] Some scholars hold that the task was to be carried out primarily by Titus himself (Lock, 129, hesitantly; Spicq, 601; Holtz, 207); no weight, however, should be placed on the change to the active voice following the middle form ἐπιδιορθώσῃ (*pace* Bernard, 157, who regards the middle as expressing action to be taken by Titus himself!). However, 'the fact that Titus is told to institute them does not mean that the congregation was to play no part' (Barrett, 128f.; Parry, 74; cf. Acts 6.1–6). Knight, 288, argues that the verb refers to the actual induction or ordination of the leaders as the final stage in choosing and appointing them (cf. Lips 1979:182).

The actual scope of the project is difficult to determine; the impression gained from the letter is of a rather disorganised and immature church, and this may suggest some limits to the extent of the spread of Christianity on the island. Nevertheless, the geographical reference 'in each city' suggests that there were at least several different towns with house churches. κατά has distributive force (cf. Luke 8.1; Acts 15.21, 36; 20.23). Hence the phrase means 'in every city' (i.e. where there was already a congregation [cf. Acts 15.36]; it is less likely that Titus was to set up new congregations with elders).

Crete was proverbial for its 'hundred' cities (Homer, *Iliad* 2.649; [or 'ninety'] *Odyssey* 19.172–9; Horace, *Carm.* 3.27.33f.). During classical and Hellenistic times about thirty-five city states are attested. This number was reduced to about twenty in the Roman period as some were taken over by more powerful neighbours. Gortyna was the capital under Roman rule, but each city retained its own administration. They were notorious for their fierce rivalries, and only Roman jurisdiction ended the frequent inter-city wars. While the distribution of the population may mean that house churches had been planted throughout the

---

[15] καί probably has the epexegetic force 'and especially', 'namely' (Holtzmann, 468; Spicq, 601).

[16] Exod 2.14; 1 Macc 10.20; 4 Macc 4.16; Lk 12.15; Acts 7.10, 27, 35; of church officials (Acts 6.30); of the high priest (Heb 5.1); 1 Clement 42.5; 43.1; *et al*; elsewhere it means 'to take somebody somewhere' (Acts 17.15); 'to cause someone/something to become' (Rom 5.19; Jas 3.6; 4.4; 2 Pet 1.8). Cf. Oepke, A., *TDNT* III, 444–6.

island, the force here is to emphasise the thoroughness with which Titus is to attend to the task.

It is theoretically possible that the meaning is that elders are to be appointed one per city with oversight over several groups (Hasler, 87f.). But the picture that emerges from relevant passages (Phil 1.1; Acts 20.17, 28; 14.23; 16.4) suggests a plurality of leaders in a church (Fee, 21–2; Knight, 175–7, 288; Spicq, 601). Perhaps if 'church' (cf. 1 Cor 1.2) is a collective term for a number of house fellowships in a particular locale, then oversight of the smaller unit by a single leader is possible. One factor to be borne in mind is that the imagery of the steward may well imply one leader per group (Merkel, 90).

The appointments are to be made in accordance with instructions previously given by Paul. The reference is presumably to oral instruction. Thus the letter backs up earlier instructions. This refutes the objection by Merkel, 89, that Paul would not have left off giving instructions to Titus about church organisation until after he himself had left the area.

πρεσβύτερος is 'old man', hence 'elder'. In this context, as also in 1 Tim 5.17, 19, the word refers to elders rather than 'old men' (*pace* Jeremias, 41f.; cf. 1 Tim 5.1; Titus 2.2). The term came into the early church's vocabulary naturally by way of the Jewish synagogue (cf. Acts 11.30; 15.2, 4, 6, 22, 23; 16.4; 21.18; Jas 5.14; 1 Pet 5.1), and has a traditional connection with the missionary activity of Paul (Acts 14.23; 20.17). See **Excursus 3**.

ὡς (1.7; 1 Tim 5.1a, 1b, 2a, 2b; 2 Tim 2.3, 9, 17; 3.9**) could simply mean 'in accordance with the fact that I told you to do so' or 'in the manner in which I told you to act'. The latter rendering is better, since it is followed by a list of specific instructions for the way in which the appointments are to be made.[17] ἐγώ (1.3) is possibly intended to be emphatic; if so, the intent is to underscore the apostolic authority of the instructions (Spicq, 601; Knight, 289; cf. 1.3). Proponents of pseudonymity view this as designed to associate Paul with the system of eldership (Merkel, 89–90; cf. Wolter 1988:180f.; Oberlinner, 18). διατάσσω* is frequent in Paul (1 Cor 16.1; cf. 7.17; 9. 14; 11.34; Gal 3.19) and Luke-Acts (9 times; Mt 11.1***). It can be used of instructions given by civil and military officials, masters, laws or fathers. It is one of the group of terms used in the PE to express authoritative instructions (cf. ἐπιτρέπω, 1 Tim 2.12; βούλομαι, 1 Tim 2.8; 5.14; Tit 3.8).[18]

---

[17] GNB links the clause closely with what follows ('Remember my instructions: an elder must be...'), whereas most scholars assume that it is more closely attached to what precedes.

[18] The usage thus coincides with that in Paul; the active and middle forms are used synonymously. White, 187, holds that the word is used where there

6. εἴ τίς ἐστιν ἀνέγκλητος, μιᾶς γυναικὸς ἀνήρ, τέκνα ἔχων πιστά, μὴ ἐν κατηγορίᾳ ἀσωτίας ἢ ἀνυπότακτα The main thrust of the instruction concerns the kind of people to be appointed as elders. On the whole, the code enumerates qualities that are to characterise the life of any Christian. The assumption to be made from Tit 2.12 is that such qualities have a basis in genuine faith (cf. Schwarz 1983:96–8); the officeholder is to model this life. The general quality (a) of being blameless is elaborated in terms of (b) being the husband of one wife; and (c) being the father of children who are of good Christian character.

The syntax is slightly obscure. This has led to the suggestion that a source is being incorporated here (Quinn, 84–5).[19] An εἴ τις clause normally precedes the main clause (1 Tim 3.1, 5; 5.4, 8, 16; 6.3). This could be the case here with anacolouthon resulting from the insertion of the justifying clause in v. 7. The missing main clause would have been something like, 'let him be appointed'. Alternatively, the clause has been added loosely to what precedes: 'appoint elders ... if anybody is blameless...'. In any case, the sense is clear enough.

ἀνέγκλητος, 'blameless' is repeated in 1.7 and used in 1 Tim 3.10 of deacons; it is synonymous with ἀνεπίλημπτος (Vögtle 1936:55), used of an overseer in 1 Tim 3.2. It is a term limited to the Pauline corpus in the NT (1 Cor 1.8; Col 1.22***).[20] It identifies a basic requirement of the elder – that there be no accusation against him. The legal connotation present in judgement contexts (1 Cor 1.8; Col 1.22) is still present in this setting of less formal assessment. A good reputation both inside and outside the church is required, and one's behaviour forms the basis upon which the reputation is evaluated. Needless to say, there is a difference between living a life which should not lead to accusations and facing unfounded accusations. The elder should as far as possible be able to carry out his task without fear of being denounced for misdemeanours.

Two qualities that should prevent accusations of misdemeanour are listed, each having to do with family life. They are paralleled in 1 Tim 3.2, 4 which is based on the same traditional teaching. The first is best interpreted as faithfulness in marriage. Our own age illustrates forcibly how the slightest suspicion of sexual

---

are a number of commands (Acts 24.23). Cf. Delling, G., *TDNT* VIII, 34f.; Oberlinner, L., *EDNT* I, 313f.

[19] The theory that there has been a later interpolation into the letter in the interests of the monarchical episcopate is no longer seriously considered by scholars.

[20] Cf. 3 Macc 5.31; Josephus, *Ant.* 10.281; 17.289; Epictetus 1.28.10. Cf. ἔγκλημα (Acts 23.29; 25.16; Josephus, *Bel.* 7.45). Cf. Grundmann, W., *TDNT* I, 356–7; Vögtle 1936:55.

irregularity is seized upon as a ground for accusation against Christian leaders.

μιᾶς γυναικὸς ἀνήρ (1 Tim 3.12; see the female equivalent in 5.9)[21] is literally 'the husband of one wife' and expresses a requirement not found elsewhere in ancient sources; this is thus a specifically Christian requirement. The sense is much disputed.[22] There are five main interpretations:

(a) *A person who has not committed polygamy.*[23] This would presumably refer to polygamy before conversion. The fact that polygamy was banned at Qumran (CD 4.20–5.6) implies that it was considered a possible practice in some Jewish circles (cf. Josephus, *Ant.* 17.14).[24] However, such a ban would not have been a necessary requirement in the Christian community (Hanson, 78). Moreover, and decisively, this theory would require that polyandry is meant in 1 Tim 5.9, which is not known to have been a practice in that culture and therefore would not have needed to be addressed.[25]

(b) *A married man as opposed to a celibate.* On this view the requirement could be a response to the heretical prohibition of marriage in 1 Tim 4.3: the leader must set a good example (see the discussions in Roloff 155; Holtz, 76). But it leads to a tautology in 1 Tim 5.9, and the emphatic position of μιᾶς is strongly against it.

(c) *A person who has not remarried after the death of his wife.*[26] This ruling would *a fortiori* also prohibit any who remarried after divorce from becoming elders. According to Knoch, 29, this shows that marriage is binding both in this world and the next. Support for this interpretation has been drawn from the frequent references on inscriptions to women who did not remarry after the death of their husbands as being *univira*

---

[21] ἀνήρ is used for 'husband' (1.6; 2.5; 1 Tim 3.2, 12; 5.9) or for 'male' (1 Tim 2.8, 12**). Cf. Oepke, A., *TDNT* I, 360–3; Bauer, J. B., *EDNT* I, 98f.

[22] See bibliography at head of section. Most translations have 'husband of one wife' (NJB; REB; NRSV mg; similarly GNB t); cf. 'the husband of but one wife' (NIV); has 'married only once' (NRSV t; GNB mg).

[23] Calvin, 223f., 358; Lock, 36f. (polygamy is included in the prohibition); SB III, 647–50; Simpson, 50. Chrysostom, to whom Calvin refers for support, comments that the Jews allowed second marriages and having two wives at once (*PG* LXII, 547).

[24] The possibility of levirate marriage existed among Jews (SB III, 647f.), but was presumably a dead letter. See further Justin, *Dial.* 134.

[25] See Quinn, 85; *pace* SB III, 648, who think that the cases of the man and woman are different, and that repeated marriage and divorce in quick succession are meant in the latter case.

[26] Bernard, 52f.; White, 111f.; Parry, 16; Kelly, 75f., 231; Holtzmann, 233–8; Dornier, 58–60; Spicq, 430–1; Hasler, 27; Verner 1983:130f. It is implied that marriage after divorce is equally forbidden. This was a common view in the early church (Tertullian, *Ad Uxorem* 1.7; Clement, *Strom.* 2.145.3; cf. Page*, 112). Dodd*, 114, calls this 'the dominant view in early times'.

and *monandros* (see Frey*; Lightman and Zeisel*; cf. Anna [Luke 2.36f.] and the widows in 1 Tim 5.9, though there is no way to know whether the latter had been married only once). However, the *univira* inscriptions cited refer to women, the Greek phrase μιᾶς γυναικὸς ἀνήρ (or rather ἑνὸς ἀνδρὸς γυνή) was not used in this connection, and remarriage was certainly not regarded as being sinful (1 Cor 7.8f., 39f.; Rom 7.1–3). Emmet* states that celibacy after the death of one's partner was a virtue in women but was not expected in men. Furthermore, in the light of 1 Tim 5.14, where young widows are encouraged to remarry, such a condition may be contradictory. If correct, it would suggest two standards in the church (so explicitly Holtzmann).

(d) *Anyone remarried after divorce.*[27] (This interpretation would permit remarriage after the death of the first wife.) Cf. Mt 5.32; Mk 10.11 where remarriage is prohibited. If this total ban was relaxed (cf. Mt 19.9; 1 Cor 7.15; Collins 1992), then there could have been a higher standard for leaders. More narrowly, the phrase might identify a person who had not married a non-Christian wife, then divorced her and remarried a Christian – i.e. who had not availed himself of the so-called 'Pauline privilege' (1 Cor 7.10–16; Easton, 212–15). Jeremias, 24, draws attention to the Qumran Scroll 11Q Temple 57.17–19, where the king is not permitted a second wife unless he has been widowed. However, the limitation to remarriage after divorce is by no means obvious from the wording, and such a prohibition is not supported elsewhere in the NT.

(e) *A person who is faithful to his wife.* It is more widely held that the phrase refers to marital fidelity.[28] Some scholars take the term in a very broad sense as consciously intending to prohibit all forms of sexual immorality, including polygamy, successive divorces and remarriages, and marriage by those of forbidden degrees of kinship (Brox, 142; cf. Merkel, 30; Roloff, 156).

The root of the problem is that there is no evidence for use of the phrase outside the PE, and the basis of the interpretation is therefore extremely dubious. Quinn, 86, even doubts that the phrase has sexual morality in mind because other terms (cf. 2.4–5; 1 Tim 5.10–14; πορνεία) might easily have been used.

The limits of interpretation are set (i) by the use of the parallel phrase in 1 Tim 5.9 and (ii) by the improbability that the phrase

---

[27] Jeremias, 24; Oepke, A., *TDNT* I, 362 n. 11, 788; Hanson, 77f.; Lattey*; Bartsch 1965:130. On this view, remarriage by widowers would have been permitted.
[28] Scott, 31; Barrett, 58f.; Houlden, 77f.; Karris, 75; Fee, 80f.; Oberlinner, 22f.; cf. Oberlinner [1 Tim], 118–21; Dodd*; Lyonnet*; Trummer*; Page*; Wagener 1994:172–7.

envisaged a specific form of unacceptable behaviour that was either too well known or sufficiently infrequent to have warranted the special notice given to it here. The latter control rules out a reference to polygamy and remarriage after divorce (and even more specific versions of this sort of remarriage). Equally, the specific cases of remarriage after death of one's partner and prohibition of celibacy are ruled out by 1 Tim 5.9: the *univira* and *monandros* epithets are unlikely to be equivalents of the phrase here, and the permission and even encouragement to younger widows to remarry after the death of a spouse raises considerable doubts. Since the assumption is that the overseer/ elder is married with children (v. 6; 1 Tim 3.4), a statement with regard to a candidate's behaviour within marriage is appropriate (see especially Trummer*, 477–82). It can undoubtedly be assumed that the marriage would have to conform to the standards of acceptability within the church (i.e. monogamous and if a remarriage, then a legitimate one). What is stated is the ideal for all Christians but is prescribed for leaders (cf. Lyonnet*; Wagener 1994:173f.). Nothing is said about a second marriage. It is best to follow Theodore of Mopsuestia, II, 103 (Swete): ὃς ἀγαγόμενος γυναῖκα σωφρόνως ἐβίω μετὰ ταύτης, προσέχων αὐτῇ καὶ μέχρις αὐτῆς ὁρίζων τῆς φύσεως τὴν ὄρεξιν.[29] Oberlinner, *1 Tim,* 120, comments that the author is here not concerned with legal rules to be observed but with the quality of conduct displayed by the church leader within the marriage relationship.

The second quality has to do with the conduct of the elder's children; the phrase τέκνα ἔχων assumes that he will normally be a father with children still under his control, but it would be pedantic literalism to argue that childless men could not be appointed. They are to be πιστά, 'believing', 'faithful' (especially with reference to 'trustworthy' sayings 3.8; 1 Tim 1.15; 3.1; 4.9; 2 Tim 2.11; cf. Tit 1.9; cf. 2 Tim 2.13 of Christ). This word is used as a general term for Christians (as an adjective, 1 Tim 6.2a, 2b; 2 Tim 2.2; as a substantive, 1 Tim 4.3, 10, 12; 5.16). It refers to a quality shown by Christians and Christian leaders (1 Tim 1.12; 3.11). But the sense here is disputed: (a) 'believing';[30] (b) 'trustworthy' (1 Cor 4.17).[31] The former view implies that if a person cannot teach the faith to his own family, he is ill-suited to nurture the church in the faith (so Chrysostom and Jerome,

---

[29] Cf. Theodoret, *PG* LXXXII, 805 (cf. Trummer*, 483; Dodd*, 113).

[30] BA; most Eng. versions; Bultmann, R., *TDNT* VI, 215 n. 311; Barth, G., *EDNT* III, 97–8; Calvin, 358f.; Holtzmann, 469; most commentators.

[31] Schwarz 1983:67; Lock, 130; Knight, 289f., refers to examples where the word is applied to servants in the sense 'submissive, obedient'.

cited by Spicq, 602). The latter view is thought to explain better the prohibited behaviour that follows and to correspond better to the parallel in 1 Tim 3.4, where the overseer's children must be 'obedient' (ἐν ὑποταγῇ). In this case the point is that, if the elder cannot keep his family in subjection, how will he care for the church? But it is hard to see why 'trustworthiness' should be singled out for special mention in this context, and it is not synonymous with 'obedience'. Furthermore, the behaviour described next would be as much a sign of unbelief as of dis-obedience. It should also be remembered that in a patriarchal society the children would be more likely to accept the father's religion than in modern western society.

It is further required that as the outcome of their faith the children should live soberly and in obedience within the family. The point is made by describing the opposite type of character, which demonstrates unbelief. μή is used because the adjective is virtually a participle (Moule 1953:155f.). κατηγορία, 'accusation', is a legal term (Jn 18.29; 1 Tim 5.19***; cf. Lk 6.7 *v.l.*; Josephus, *Ant.* 2.49; *Ap.* 2.137), and the phrase ἐν κατηγορίᾳ with gen. of content is idiomatic, meaning 'not open to the charge of'. ἀσωτία, 'debauchery' (Eph. 5.18; 1 Pet. 4.4***), is a broad term which can have a number of nuances, such as drunkenness (Eph 5.18; Athenaeus 11, p. 485a), excessive behaviour with regard to money (cf. Aristotle, *EN* 4.1; cf. ἀσώτως, Lk 15.13; cf. Lock, 130), gluttony (cf. Prov 28.7 MT), and fornication (2 Macc 6.4). A general lack of self-control and moderation is implied. Foerster comments that in the NT wild, disorderly living is in mind, but in the secular world this manner of life in itself would not have been considered as ἀσωτία, which was rather wasteful dissipation of one's resources. The word here, then, 'combines the spendthrift and the rake' (Simpson, 97; cf. Foerster, W., *TDNT* I, 506f.; *TLNT* I, 220–2). The younger son in the parable of Jesus is a vivid example of the character. ἤ (3.12*) here has the force of 'and'. ἀνυπότακτος, 'insubordinate, rebellious' is a Hellenistic term.[32] It is also used to describe the writer's opponents (1.10; 1 Tim 1.9; cf. Heb 2.8***) and in such cases envisages something more serious than simply 'contrariness'. Here the reference is probably immediately to disobedience towards parents, but the link with 1.10 may be intentional, with the thought being that disrespect for authority at this level has wider implications (cf. Lock, 130).

The condition calls for leaders to be chosen from among those whose families in entirety had turned from pagan religions to

---

[32] It is not found before 200 BC and is not used in the LXX; of Josephus, *Ant.* 11.217, Cf. Delling, G., *TDNT* VIII, 47.

embrace the Christian faith. The adherence of the children to the father's religion would probably have had implications for the father's reputation as a respectable patron both inside and outside the church. The implication is that the father has demonstrated in his own family life the qualities which will enable him to lead effectively in the church (so explicitly in 1 Tim 3.5), but at this point the emphasis is more on the blamelessness of his reputation.

7. δεῖ γὰρ τὸν ἐπίσκοπον ἀνέγκλητον εἶναι ὡς θεοῦ οἰκονόμον, μὴ αὐθάδη, μὴ ὀργίλον, μὴ πάροινον, μὴ πλήκτην, μὴ αἰσχροκερδῆ The first part of this verse appears to begin a parenthetical explanation of why the choice of an elder must be of a blameless person. It thus picks up the first part of v. 6 rather than the latter part. But the clause then continues to give a further list of qualities in the same syntactical form rather than resuming the syntax of the previous clause; in other words, what appears to begin as a parenthesis is never terminated but becomes a further list of qualifications in its own right. This anacolouthon has suggested that in fact a second alternative list of qualities for leaders has been loosely attached to the previous one, a view that may be strengthened by the fact that different words for church leaders are used in each. See above, however, for the proposal that the author is now thinking more of the functions of the elder and therefore switches to this term before continuing with his traditional list of required qualities.[33]

The statement begins with repetition of what has preceded about the need for the church leader to be blameless. The leader is here referred to generically as 'the overseer' (ἐπίσκοπος). The identity of the elder with the overseer is patent (Calvin, 359f.), and the more functional designation (cf. Barrett, 129) indicates the character of his task in broad terms. The need for a blameless reputation is grounded in the fact that he is God's authorised agent who must be free from any ground for suspicion that he is unfit for this task.

The metaphor of stewarding introduces the conception of the church as a household in this letter (cf. 1.11; 2.2–10), complementing the dominant theme in 1 and 2 Timothy (1 Tim 3.15; 2 Tim 2.20–21; cf. Quinn, 88; Hasler, 88). The rest of the verse is a list of five negative qualities which, along with the positive qualities that follow and the requirements listed in v. 6, serve to explain in detail the meaning of ἀνέγκλητος (cf. the mixture of positive and negative in 1 Tim 3.2–7). The negative qualities create a conscious contrast with the image of the trustworthy οἰκονόμος (cf. Quinn, 89).

---

[33] So Hort 1897:190f.

γάρ as a connective gives the justification for choosing people who are blameless.[34] The verb δεῖ (1.11a, b) is used similarly in 1 Tim 3.2, 7; 2 Tim 2.24 where it is also stated what church leaders must be.[35] The basis for the statement lies in the character of the overseer's function as God's steward, but no such basis is given in 1 Tim 3 and 2 Tim 2 where it is stated as a simple matter of what is 'obvious'. According to Popkes the statement is tantamount to a divine decree: 'God's will and nature are the norms of ethics and piety.' Nevertheless, the present passage spells out the underlying basis. The representative of God must be worthy of his master by having the kind of moral character which is worthy of him and which commends rather than condemns him.

τὸν ἐπίσκοπον is clearly a generic phrase; it cannot refer to a specific, singular church leader who is to be distinguished from the elders;[36] a monarchical overseer, in the sense of a single leader to a congregation, is a possibility if it is to be assumed that Titus is to appoint one elder/overseer per city. In fact, the logic of the connection demands the identity of the two offices.[37] The change to the singular is entirely natural, especially after v. 6 has already been phrased in the singular. Thus the equivalence of the two designations demands the repetition of the ἀνέγκλητος requirement in v. 7. The reason why the overseer should be ἀνέγκλητος is that he is θεοῦ οἰκονόμος.

οἰκονόμος indicates the office of a steward (the Scottish 'factor'), a person appointed by (e.g.) a landowner to administer his estates and oversee his workers, representing the master and having full powers granted by him, and answerable (only) to the master for his conduct of the property (cf. Luke 12.42; 16.1, 3, 8; cf. Rom 16.23 of a town official; Gal 4.2 of a child's guardian). The designation contains an emphasis on faithfulness and trustworthiness (cf. 1 Cor 4.2). The word is used metaphorically of a Cynic preacher as a servant of Zeus (Epictetus 3.22.3).[38] The metaphorical use of church leaders assigns to them a position of authority under God (1 Cor 4.1f.); the description extends to all who exercise spiritual gifts (1 Pet 4.10***; Ignatius, *Poly* 6.1). The designation is appropriate for leaders in the οἶκος θεοῦ who

---

[34] The PE are fond of backing up a statement or exhortation in this way (1.10–12; 2.11; 1 Tim 2.5, 13; 4.8; 5.18; 6.10; 2 Tim 1.7).

[35] For the use of δεῖ cf. 1 Tim 3.15; 5.13; 2 Tim 2.6**; Plutarch, *Mor.* 4B, 7C (Almquist 1946:125); Grundmann, W., *TDNT* II, 21–5; Popkes, W., *EDNT* I, 279–80.

[36] Brox 1969b:89f.; *pace* Spicq, 602; Holtz, 208; Houlden, 142; See **Excursus 2**.

[37] Oberlinner, 17, 20f., refers to presbyters and overseers as two separate types of leader, although he notes that their tasks are identical.

[38] Cf. Michel, O., *TDNT* V, 149–53; Kuhli, H., *EDNT* II, 498–500; TLNT *II*, 568–75. See on 1 Tim 1.4.

act on his behalf (1 Tim 3.15; Lips 1979:145–50). Holtzmann,
470, claims that in Paul people are stewards of the divine mysteries,
not of the church as a whole, and that in Paul the description is
applied only to apostles. This generalisation is, however, made
on the basis of only *one* passage, and in fact it applies to Apollos
who is not an apostle. 1 Cor 4.1–2 indicate that a church may
have several persons fulfilling this function.

Five negative qualities are now listed the first two of which
deal with personal character and the remaining three with
relationships (Oberlinner, 25).

(a) αὐθάδης ranges in meaning from the narrower 'self-willed'
and 'stubborn' to the broader 'arrogant' (BA *s.v.*; for 'arrogant'
see Josephus, *Bel.* 6.172; *Ant.* 1.189; Parry 75; Quinn 80).
According to Field 1899:219 it is 'not one who *pleases himself*,
but who *is pleased with himself*, and holds other people cheap, in
one word, *self-satisfied*'.[39] Here and in 2 Pet 2.10*** it describes
behaviour characteristic of false teachers (cf. Prov 21.24), which
inclines to that of the brutal unbeliever, an application found
suitable elsewhere (1 Clement 1.1; cf. 30.8; 57.2). As in *Didache*
3.6 this rude indifference to the feelings of others should not to
be found in Christians or Christian leaders. It is a brutal, hateful
and arrogant attitude characteristic of unbelief and spiritual
death.[40] The fact that it is not paralleled in the list of 1 Tim 3 may
suggest that the list in Titus 1 addresses a far more rudimentary
level of life such as was commonly believed to be typical of
Crete.[41]

(b) ὀργίλος***, 'inclined to anger', 'quick-tempered', perhaps
of 'explosive anger' (see Schwarz 1983:69f.), represents a vice
that belongs equally to the basest of human characteristics. It
was especially viewed as a threat to human relationships
(Epictetus 2.10.18; Prov 21.19; cf. Aristotle, *EN* 4.5), a quality
unfitting in a king (Dio Chrysostom, 2.75 [verb]), and thus in
the biblical tradition it aptly characterises an aspect of unbelief
(Ps 17.49; Prov 22.24; 29.22; *Didache* 3.2).[42]

(c) πάροινος is 'addicted to wine', hence 'drunkard'
(1 Tim 3.3***; not attested in LXX). Literally it refers to being
drunk, to whatever extent (e.g. 'tipsy, slightly drunk');[43] but the
word-group can also refer to the rowdy behaviour and loss of

[39] Note the connection with 'self-pleasers' (Hermas, *Sim.* 9.22.1), inflexibility
(Philo, *Mos.* 1.139; *Leg. Gai.* 301) and quarrelsomeness (Philo, *Abr.* 213; *Her.* 21;
Sacr. 32). Cf. Bauernfeind, O., *TDNT* I, 508f.; *TLNT* I, 229f.

[40] αὐθάδεια figures in the list of vices in *Didache* 5.1; cf. Barnabas 20.1;
Prov 21.24; Josephus, *Ant.* 4.263 (wilful rebellion of a youth towards parents).

[41] Polybius 28.14; Strabo 10.49; Josephus, *Bel.* 2.356; 4.94;

[42] Cf. Stählin, G., *TDNT* V, 382–447, espec. 420f.

[43] In Aristotle, *Problemata* 871ᵃ 9, it is equated with ἀκροθώραξ (Simpson, 51.)

self-control characteristic of drunkenness.[44] The metaphorical force 'not behaving like a drunkard' is adopted here by Holtzmann, 470–1; Lock, 130, in view of the following contrast; but it is not as likely to have this sense here as νηφάλιος in 1 Tim 3.2. The context here describes the roughest behaviour, and drunkenness fits best. For the thought cf. Luke 12.45; *T. Jud.* 14.4.[45]

(d) πλήκτης, 'bully, pugnacious person' (1 Tim 3.3***; not attested in LXX and early fathers), describes ruffians who engage in physical violence,[46] but the term may extend also to ideas of anger and violence and verbal abuse (Roloff, 158 n. 246). The word is applied to wine in Plutarch (*Mor.* 132D; cf. Quinn 80; Schwarz 1983:54), which might suggest that the combination μὴ πάροινον, μὴ πλήκτην here and in 1 Tim 3.3 reflects a traditional association between drunkenness and bullying abuse. Otherwise it is not found in the secular vice lists (cf. Vögtle 1936:241).

(e) αἰσχροκερδής is 'fond of dishonest gain', 'shamefully greedy' (with reference to deacons, 1 Tim 3.8***).[47] It envisages generally 'dishonest gain' (Philo, *Sacr.* 32 [vice list]; αἰσχροκερδία, *T. Jud.* 16.1). The reference may be to teaching for profit, whether the false teachers are immediately in mind (cf. Tit 1.11; Lock 131; cf. 1 Tim 6.5), or whether the emphasis is more generally on the danger of allowing financial compensation to become the chief motivation for ministry (cf. 1 Pet 5.2; Goppelt 1993:346; Knoch, 29). Equally possible, however, is a reference to faithfulness in managing the church's finances (Holtzmann, 471); or it may have in mind elders who engage in discreditable and dishonest trades. Probably the term is broad enough to cover all of these senses as needed. Holtzmann, 471, suggests that the idea is not so much of making money dishonestly as of being fond of gain in a situation where gain is wrong in itself (similarly, Barrett, 129; Fee, 174). αἰσχροκέρδεια was one of the legendary flaws of the Cretans (Polybius 6.46), and this might account for the inclusion of the related term in reference to the overseer in this code (cf. ἀφιλάργυρον in 1 Tim 3.3).

8. ἀλλὰ φιλόξενον φιλάγαθον σώφρονα δίκαιον ὅσιον ἐγκρατῆ
The list of negative qualities is followed by a listing of six desirable qualities, followed by a seventh which is developed at some length and provides a transition to the instructions

---

[44] παροινέω in Josephus, *Ant.* 4.144 appears to mean behaving abusively like a drunkard (cf. ἐμπαροινέω, Aristides, *Apol.* 14, cited by Lock, 130). Cf. MM 496.
[45] *Pace* BA the word itself is not used in *T. Jud.* 14.4.
[46] BA; Ps 34.15 Sym; cf. *Apost. Const.* 8.47.27; cf. ἐπιπλήσσω, 1 Tim 5.1.
[47] The word is not used in LXX; cf. the cognate adverb in 1 Pet 5.2; cf. ἀφιλάργυρος of overseers (1 Tim 3.8; φιλάργυρος, Lk 16.14). Cf. *TLNT* I, 45–8.

regarding the false teachers in vv. 10–16. No particular order is discernible in the list, except that the last one develops a point of especial importance. The other six qualities are such as might be expected in any Christian and all the more in leaders.

(a) φιλόξενος, 'hospitable' (1 Tim 3.2; 1 Pet 4.9***), refers to a virtue which was to be evident in all Christians,[48] and which the duty code applies specifically to the church leader. In the ancient world this virtue was widely extolled.[49] Philo held Abraham up as a model of hospitality, which he describes as a practical outworking of θεοσέβεια (*Abr.* 114). But it was largely practical circumstances that dictated the need for hospitality. In the Roman Empire the dangers of travel, poor conditions of inns, and pressures on Christians who often existed as refugees made hospitality indispensable for the church (cf. Quinn, 90–1; Spicq, 432–3). Furthermore, as Goppelt says, 'hospitality was to a large extent a presupposition for the Christian mission' (1993:299; cf. Mt 10.11; Acts 16.15; 21.7; 28.14; Rom 16.4; *Didache* 11.2, 4). For worship to take place, homes had to be opened and provisions made (Rom 16.5; 1 Cor 16.19; Col 4.15). Consequently, the application of this virtue to the church leader is natural, since the burden of providing hospitality to travellers and those in need would fall on him (cf. 1 Clement 12.3; Hermas, *Mand.* 8.10; *Sim.* 9.27.2).[50]

(b) φιλάγαθος*** is 'loving what is good' or 'loving good people' (cf. ἀφιλάγαθος in 2 Tim 3.3***). Aristotle contrasted it with love of self (φίλαυτος; *Mag. Mor.* II.14.3.1212b, 18ff.) which is a trait of unbelief in 2 Tim 3.2. This suggests the meaning of a selfless attitude and desire for what is inherently good, hence 'fond of doing good' (Parry, 75). It was used widely as a title of honour and as a description of an aspect of royalty (*Ep. Arist.* 124, 292) and of the law-giver (Philo, *Mos.* 2.9). These connections made it a natural selection as a quality describing a model leader. Elsewhere in the biblical tradition it is linked to wisdom (Wis 7.22).[51]

(c) For σώφρων, 'self-controlled' (2.2, 5; 1 Tim 3.2), see **Excursus 3**.

(d) δίκαιος (1 Tim 1.9; 2 Tim 4.8**) does not appear in the list in 1 Tim 3, but the word-group plays an important role, alongside other terms prominent in Greek ethical thought, in the

---

[48] φιλοξενία, Rom 12.13; Heb 13.2; see further 1 Tim 5.10; 3 Jn 5ff.; 1 Pet 4.9; 1 Clement 1.2; 10–12; cf. Job 31.32.

[49] Cicero, *De officiis* 2.64; Epictetus 1.28.23; Josephus, *Vita* 142; cf. Aristides, *Apol.* 15; cf. Malherbe 1983:222–32.

[50] Cf. Stählin, G., *TDNT* V, 1–36; *TLNT* III, 454–7.

[51] Cf. Grundmann, W., *TDNT* I, 18; *TLNT* III, 437–9; *New Docs.* I, 87 §46; III, 40–43 §11.

author's conception of the Christian life.[52] The common meaning is uprightness of conduct and justice in dealing with people. However, in the PE, primarily through 2.12 (cf. 2 Tim 3.16), behaviour that is δίκαιος transcends the secular notion of a cardinal virtue. Its orientation is the Christ-event.[53] Justification by faith in the Pauline sense is meant in Tit 3.5 (δικαιοσύνη; cf. 2 Tim 4.8: 'crown of righteousness') and 3.7 (δικαιόω), and the passive ἐδικαιώθην in 1 Tim 3.16 means vindication (see 1 Tim 3.16 note).[54]

δίκαιος was often paired with the preceding σώφρων and the following ὅσιος word-groups.[55] This pattern depends upon the duty-code, and the grouping of virtues and the virtues chosen suggest some sensitivity to secular thought; nevertheless, through 2.12 and developments in the LXX, the network of virtues has been applied to define Christian conduct.

(e) ὅσιος, 'pure, holy, devout' (1 Tim 2.8**), is likewise absent from the code of 1 Tim 3, and does not occur elsewhere in the Pauline corpus (except for the adverb in 1 Th 2.10). It comes in OT quotations in Acts 2.27; 13.34f. (applied to Christ) and in descriptions of God (Rev 15.4; 16.5) and Christ (Heb 7.26***; for the noun ὁσιότης see Lk 1.75; Eph 4.24***). In Classical Greek the word means 'clean, godly, bound to the obligations (established by the gods)'; it can allude to the practice of washing hands on entry to a sanctuary (cf. 1 Tim 2.8; Exod 30.17–21). The thought is of outward cultic purity and the inward piety expressed by it (Knoch, 26). The term generally characterises a person as a worshipper (Aristophanes, *Ranae* 327, 336; Thucydides 5.104; Xenophon, *Anab.* II 6.25), and it is basically in this sense that it describes a requirement of the people of Yahweh (equivalent to חָסִיד; Deut 33.8; 2 Kgs 22.26; Ps 11.2; 17.26; 31.6; a condition of the heart, Prov 22.11; of the soul, Wis 7.27; cf. Deut 32.4; Ps 144.17 of God). Hauck claims that the background to the usage here does not lie in the Hebrew concept of the covenant but in the 'general Gk. use for "what is right and good before God and man"'.[56] Clearly the form in

---

[52] For δικαιοσύνη see 1 Tim 6.11; 2 Tim 2.22; 3.16; cf. 2 Tim 4.8; Tit 3.5**; for δικαίως see 2.12**.

[53] For the analogous OT religious orientation, see Gen 6.9; Job 1.1, 8; 12.4; 22.19; Pss 31 (MT 32).11; 33 (MT 34).16; 36 (MT 37).12, 21, 25; Tob 13.10; Wis 3.1; Josephus, *Ant.* 12.43; cf. 1 Tim 1.9: δικαίῳ νόμος οὐ κεῖται; 2 Tim 4.8: ὁ δίκαιος κριτής.

[54] Cf. Schrenk, G., *TDNT* II, 182–91; Schneider, G., *EDNT* I, 324f.; Towner 1989:163; *TLNT* I, 318–47, especially 320–6.

[55] With σώφρων: 2.12; Aeschylus, *Sept.* 610; 4 Macc 1.6, 18; 2.23; 15.10; Wis 8.7; with ὅσιος/ἅγιος: Deut 32.4; 1 Sam 2.2; Ps 144 (MT 145).17; Lk 1.75; 1 Th 2.10; Eph 4.24; Philo, *Prob.* 83.

[56] Cf. Plato, *Gorg.* 507B, for justice being towards other people and holiness being towards God.

which the term appears in this list suggests affinity with the use
in Hellenistic literature (cf. Philo, *Prob.* 83), but the meaning
'holy, pure or devout' was readily adaptable to the Christian
situation (cf. 1 Th 2.10; Eph 4.24; Heb 7.26).[57]

The absence of the last two extremely basic qualities from the
list in 1 Tim 3 raises the question of their presence here. It may
simply be a desire on the part of the author to shape the code
according to the fundamental virtues of secular ethics. It is also
possible that the emphasis on the elementary qualities, just as
the prohibition of certain behaviour patterns that would have
seemed too obvious to mention, spoke to an immature church
struggling to break free from depraved patterns of behaviour,
such as were widely associated with Crete.

(f) For ἐγκρατής***, 'disciplined' see **Excursus 3**.

9. ἀντεχόμενον τοῦ κατὰ τὴν διδαχὴν πιστοῦ λόγου The preceding qualities were fairly general, but included ones specific to
church leaders (hospitality). This seventh requirement, which is
related more directly to the ministry of the word, is specific and
essential for the church leader (for similar material cf. 2 Tim 3.14f.).
He is to hold fast to the trustworthy word according to the
teaching, in order that he may be able positively to 'exhort' and
negatively to 'refute' error.

The stress on teaching ability and the specific positive and
negative (corrective) purposes give a fuller form of the brief
and general διδακτικός in 1 Tim 3.2. It is possible that the
greater detail corresponds to a more urgent need in this community (Brox, 285; Scott, 156), possibly because the heresy was
more virulent. But, however urgent the situation was, v. 9 forms
the transition to the direct discussion about confronting the
opponents in vv. 10–16; the immediate application of the duty
code to the confrontation with the false teachers may provide
the reason for the greater attention given to the overseer's
commitment to and use of the word (cf. Herr 1976:81).

ἀντέχομαι (act., 'to hold against', 'hold out') is used in the
middle voice: (a) 'to take hold of, cling to, hold fast';[58] (b) 'to
take an interest in, concern oneself with, help' (1 Th 5.14, in the
sense of 'holding fast to' and not neglecting needy people). The
second meaning is preferred by BA (*s.v.*; see also Dibelius-
Conzelmann 133), but there appears to be some misunderstanding of the LXX references; in the case of entities like the

[57] Cf. Hauck, F., *TDNT* V, 489–93; Balz, H., *EDNT* II, 536f.; Seebass, H.,
NIDNTT II, 236–8.
[58] The verb has perhaps the nuance 'despite opposition', White, 188. Cf.
Deut 32.41; Prov 3.18; 4.6; Isa 56.2, 4, 6; 57.13; Jer 2.8; 8.2; 51 [44].10;
1 Macc 15.34; Josephus, *Bel.* 4.323; Mt 6.24 = Lk 16.13; Hermas, *Vis.* 1.1.8.

Torah 'holding fast to' and 'concerning oneself with' are much
the same thing. The first meaning is surely appropriate here,
with the threat posed by heresy and the thought of the possible
capitulation of the church's leaders in view.[59]

τοῦ κατὰ τὴν διδαχὴν πιστοῦ λόγου designates that to which
the overseer is to hold fast or about which he is to be concerned.
The sense could be either: (a) 'the sure word as taught', 'the
sure word which accords with *the* doctrine', i.e. a reference to
the *content* of the proclamation (NRSV; Holtzmann, 472;
Kelly, 232–3; cf. for the idea Phil 2.16; 2 Th 2.15); or (b) 'the
preaching which is reliable as regards doctrine', i.e. a reference
to *participation* in the preaching ministry (cf. 1 Tim 5.17 for zeal
in preaching; Dibelius-Conzelmann, 133; cf. Brox, 285). The latter
sense will require ἀντεχόμενον to mean 'have a concern for'
(Dibelius-Conzelmann, 133). In the former case, the content of
the proclamation is emphasised, to which the overseer is to 'hold
firm'. However, the following purpose clause is decisive: the
purpose is that the overseer should be 'able' in exhortation and
'sound' (accurate) in correction and rebuke of false teachers.
This makes a reference to the doctrinally pure Christian message
much more suitable, and ἀντεχόμενον means 'holding firm'. In
any case, the assumption is that the overseer preaches and teaches
(as explicitly in 1 Tim 3.2). But perhaps we should go further
and ask whether the text does not require that people who are
to be appointed to this office have already demonstrated their
ability to teach; in that case, teaching would not be confined to
those who held the office of presbyter/elder (Stott, 95).

The presence of heresy determines the emphasis on the approved
doctrine and commitment to it; the 'word' is to be trustworthy
in accordance with (κατά, 1.4) the standard contained in the
'teaching' (cf. Brox 285–6).

διδαχή can refer to the activity of teaching (2 Tim 4.2**; cf.
1 Cor 14.6), but also, as in this context, it can denote that which
is taught. According to Rengstorf, the word tends to mean the
whole of what is taught by a teacher. It thus takes on the sense
of a normative body of doctrines and precepts (in the same
sense, Rom 6.17; 16.17; 2 Jn 9–10; cf. Heb 6.2; 13.9; Lk 4.32;
Jn 18.9; *et al.*). The present context requires this formal meaning.[60] Teaching is an important function in the PE, as the use
of the word-group indicates (διδάσκω, 1.11; 1 Tim 4.11; 6.2;

---

[59] Cf. Aelius Aristides 36, 112K = 48 p. 484D: ἀληθείας ἀντέχεσθαι; Isa 56.6:
ἀντεχομένους τῆς διαθήκης; cf. Brox, 285; Quinn, 81, 92. Cf. Hanse, H.,
TDNT II, 827f.

[60] Cf. Dibelius-Conzelmann, 134; Brox, 285f., although in the PE διδασκαλία
normally serves this purpose (see below); cf. Rengstorf, K. H., *TDNT* II, 163–5;
Weiss, H.-F., *EDNT* I, 319f.

2 Tim 2.2**; διδάσκαλος 1 Tim 2.7; 2 Tim 1.11; 4.3**; διδασκαλία, Tit 1.9 note; διδακτικός, 1 Tim 3.2; 2 Tim 2.24***). Paul identifies teaching as one of the essential gifts to the church, given for its maintenance and edification (Rom 12.7; 1 Cor 12.28–29; Eph 4.11). The task of teaching was apparently limited to those persons who had the appropriate charismatic endowment (see Towner 1989:215), and this seems to hold for the PE (cf. 2 Tim 2.2).

λόγος in effect picks up on 1.3 and refers to Christian proclamation in a broad sense. πιστός (1.6 note) is here 'trustworthy, sure' (3.8; 1 Tim 1.15; 3.1; 4.9; 2 Tim 2.11**; cf. Dibelius-Conzelmann, 134); not 'which is to be believed' (*pace* Quinn, 92). The adjective is almost unnecessary in view of the κατά phrase, except to emphasise that the 'trustworthiness' of the gospel is measured only by the approved (apostolic) doctrine. It is highly unlikely that the whole phrase here refers to any specific 'trustworthy saying' of the type mentioned in 3.8; *et al.*

ἵνα δυνατὸς ᾖ καὶ παρακαλεῖν ἐν τῇ διδασκαλίᾳ τῇ ὑγιαινούσῃ καὶ τοὺς ἀντιλέγοντας ἐλέγχειν δυνατός is 'able, capable' (2 Tim 1.12** of God's power).[61] The double καί ... καί ... expresses the positive and negative tasks. Both are among the tasks assigned to Timothy in 2 Tim 4.2. But they are also the functions of the Paraclete in John, which may suggest that the picture of the Paraclete was modelled on that of the church leader (so Hanson, 174).

(1) The first task is to encourage. παρακαλέω can express a command in the form of a request; Spicq, 321, suggests that it is equivalent to βούλομαι but not as strong as διατάσσω (1.5). It is frequently used of commands by church leaders (Paul to Timothy: 1 Tim 2.1; Timothy and Titus to the churches: 2.6, 15; 1 Tim 1.3; 5.1; 6.2; 2 Tim 4.2**). The word is used broadly for giving encouragement; it suggests instruction with a practical bent, something more than simply detailing facts and doctrines, and it carries an element of persuasion and even command (cf. 2.6, 15). It is linked with διδάσκω in 1 Tim 6.2; cf. 2 Tim 4.2.[62]

The exhortation is to take place 'in the sphere of doctrine'.[63] διδασκαλία covers both the activity and the content of teaching (2.1, 7, 10; 1 Tim 1.10; 4.6, 13, 16; 5.17; 6.1, 3; 2 Tim 3.10, 16;

---

[61] Cf Lk 14.31; Acts 7.22; 11.17; 18.24; Rom 4.21; 9.22; 11.23; Jas 3.2; of people, Rom 12.18; 15.1; 1 Cor 1.26. ἱκανός is also used in this sense by Paul and in 2 Tim 2.1; cf. Grundmann, W., *TDNT* II, 284–317.

[62] Cf. Schmitz, O., and Stählin, G., *TDNT* V, 773–99; Thomas, J., *EDNT* III, 23–7. See further Bjerkelund 1967; Lips 1979:132–5, 273f.; Grayston, K., 'A Problem of Translation. The meaning of παρακαλέω, παράκλησις in the New Testament', *Scripture Bulletin* 11 (1980), 27–31.

[63] So Holtzmann, 472; and most commentators; ἐν is less probably instrumental, 'with doctrine' (*pace* Quinn, 93).

4.3; plural of false teachings, 1 Tim 4.1**). The frequency shows that this is a favourite word of the author. The thought is probably of a fixed body of teaching. It is synonymous with διδαχή (1.9; 2 Tim 4.2).

While the concept of a fixed body of approved (apostolic) teaching is not completely lacking from earlier writings in the NT, it becomes a dominant feature in the PE in the context of heresy. This comes to expression through other related terms ('the faith', 'the truth', 'the deposit'), but the preferred term seems to be διδασκαλία. Attempts to distinguish rigidly between the contents of, e.g., κήρυγμα, εὐαγγέλιον, λόγος on the one side and διδασκαλία on the other (cf. 1 Tim 5.17) have been largely unconvincing (cf. the discussion in Schlarb 1990:196–206; McDonald 1980). The author differentiated between them in some way (1 Tim 5.17), but decisions about contents and the relation to 'the gospel' must bear in mind the connection established in 1 Tim 1.10f., where τὸ εὐαγγέλιον is the standard (κατά) of 'sound teaching'. This implies a close relationship in terms of content, with distinctions probably implied with regard to audience or perhaps purpose; the 'gospel' is the message turned to missionary purposes and the 'teaching' is for the edification of the community (cf. Rom 15.4; Quinn, 94; Lips 1979:47–53). But even this distinction should not be imposed inflexibly (cf. 1 Tim 2.7: Paul is διδάσκαλος ἐθνῶν). In any case, teaching has now become a major function in the church, and the content of the teaching is both doctrinal and ethical.

As with the term ἡ ἀλήθεια as used in the PE (see 1.1 note), διδασκαλία intends a polemical contrast with the teaching of the opponents (cf. Brox, 107; Roloff, 78). This is particularly evident when the modifier ὑγιαίνουσα is present (1 Tim 1.10; 2 Tim 4.3; Tit 1.9; 2.1), but its frequent comparison with the false teaching (1 Tim 4.6; 6.1, 3; 2 Tim 3.10, 16) produces the same effect. ὑγιαίνω is 'to be healthy, sound', physically (Lk 5.31; 7.10; 15.27; cf. 3 Jn 2) and spiritually (1.13; 2.2). The participle is used with words expressive of doctrine and teaching (2.1; 1 Tim 1.10; 6.3; 2 Tim 1.13; 4.3***; cf. ὑγιής, 2.8**). The description implies that there is another kind of teaching abroad which is unhealthy and deleterious. It is propagated by a group called the 'opponents'. As Malherbe 1980 has shown, the ὑγιαίνω-ὑγιής language often played a part in the polemical debates of the secular philosophers. Sometimes the imagery provided simply an assessment of the logic or rationality of one's teaching.[64] But in other cases the language carried the full sense of sickness and disease (Philo,

---

[64] Epictetus 1.11.28; Polybius 28.17.12; Philo, *Cher.* 36; *Det.* 10, 12; Plutarch, *Aud. poet.* 4 (20F); so Dibelius-Conzelmann, 24f.; Roloff, 78; Luck, U., *TDNT* VIII, 308–13 of the PE.

Abr. 223, 275). The graphic imagery of health and disease in relation to the apostle and his opponents seems to be applied in the PE in view of such counter descriptions as ὁ λόγος αὐτῶν ὡς γάγγραινα νομὴν ἕξει (2 Tim 2.17) and νοσῶν περὶ ζητήσεις καὶ λογομαχίας (1 Tim 6.4), which follows immediately upon the conscious distinction – εἴ τις ἑτεροδιδασκαλεῖ καὶ μὴ προσέρχεται ὑγιαίνουσιν λόγοις τοῖς τοῦ κυρίου ἡμῶν (1 Tim 6.3). Elsewhere the imagery is applied to the apostolic 'word' (2 Tim 1.13; Tit 2.8), and describes a believer's soundness of faith (Tit 1.13; 2.2). The close relation between correct teaching and authentic Christian conduct throughout the PE (see **Excursus 3**; cf. 1.13; 2.1–14; 2 Tim 3.10–17) suggests the possibility that the imagery of health and illness does not imply simply that the false teaching is unreliable, irrational or illogical, but that it is palpably destructive in nature, damaging the faith and corrupting the life-style of the one affected (1 Tim 1.4–10; 19b; 4.1–3; 6.3–5; 2 Tim 2.17f.; cf. Quinn, 93–7).[65]

(2) The second task is negative: τοὺς ἀντιλέγοντας are the opponents. ἀντιλέγω is 'to speak against, contradict'; hence more generally 'to oppose' (2.9**; Luke 2.34; 20.27; 21.15; Jn 19.12; Acts 4.14; 13.45; 28.19, 22; Rom 10.21 [LXX]; cf. Thucydides 8.53.26; for the noun see Heb 6.11; 7.7; Jude 17; *TLNT* I, 128). In this context (cf. esp. vv. 10–17) it has actually been debated whether the false teachers 'stand in opposition' to the sound teaching (cf. Rom 10.12) or 'contradict' it (Ecclus 4.25; Josephus, *Ant.* 3.217). Such distinctions are over-subtle: the 'opposition' was doubtless expressed through 'contradiction'.

ἐλέγχω is 'to bring to light, set forth' (2.15); 'to cross-examine, question', hence 'to prove, refute' (cf. Ecclus 20.2; 31.31; Prov 9.7 *et al.*; *Didache* 2.7); but successful refutation may imply or include actual 'rebuke' of one's opponent (1.13; 1 Tim 5.20; 2 Tim 4.2**; Lk 3.19; cf. ἐλεγμός, 2 Tim 3.16***; Knight, 294). In the context of mission, the term denoted both exposing and convicting of sin (Jn 3.20; 16.8 [cf. 8.46]; 1 Cor 14.24; cf. Eph 5.11, 13; Jas 2.9; Jd 15). But it also became a traditional part of the vocabulary of church discipline (Mt 18.15; 1 Tim 5.20; 2 Tim 4.2; Barnabas 19.4), and the ideas of correction and punishment (especially using fatherly imagery) may be implied (Wis 1.8; 12.2; Job 5.17; Prov 3.11 [cited Heb 12.5]; Ecclus 18.13; Rev 3.19). Since engagement with the false teachers seems to have come under the category of church discipline (1.13; 3.10; 1 Tim 1.20; 2 Tim 2.14f., 25f.; cf. 1 Tim 5.19–25;

[65] See further Brox, 107f.; Spicq, 115–17; Roloff, 77–9; Oberlinner, 28f.; Lips 1978:38–53; Malherbe 1980:19–35; Donelson 1986:165f.; Schlarb 1990:196–206, 274–99.

2 Tim 4.2–4), it is within this context that the term is probably to be understood here of refutation on a more intellectual level (cf. διακατελέγχομαι, Acts 18.28). The reproof or rebuke itself can be a punishment. Spicq, 605, sees in this reference an indication that the ability to argue is required of the overseer; it seems more likely that the ability to teach (v. 9a) was understood broadly enough to include both the positive and negative dimensions of ministry.[66]

EXCURSUS 2

Overseers and their relation to elders

Beyer, H. W., *TDNT* II, 608–22; Beyer, H. W., and Kapp, H., 'Bischof', *RAC* II, 394–407; Bornkamm, G., *TDNT* VI, 651–83; Brown, R. E., *'Episkope* and *Episkopos*: The New Testament Evidence', *TS* 41 (1980), 322–38; Brox, 147–52; Campbell 1994a; 1995; Campenhausen 1969:76–123; Cousineau, A., 'Le sens de «Presbuteros» dans les Pastorales', *ScEs* 28 (1976), 147–62; Dassmann, E., 'Hausgemeinde und Bischofsamt', *JAC* 11 (1984), 82–97; Dibelius-Conzelmann, 54–7; Dornier, 163–75; Floor, L., 'Church order in the Pastoral Epistles', *Neotest.* 10 (1976), 81–91; Gnilka, J., *Der Philipperbrief*, Freiburg: Herder, 1968, 32–9; Goppelt 1962:121–38; Hainz 1976; Harvey, A. E., 'Elders', *JTS* ns 25 (1974), 318–31; Hatch, E., *The Organisation of the Early Christian Churches* (London, 1892[4]); Jay, E. G., 'From Presbyter-Bishops to Bishops and Presbyters', *SecCent* 1 (1981), 125–62; Holtzmann, 207–12; Karrer, M., 'Das urchristliche Ältestenamt', *NovT* 32 (1990), 152–88; Kertelge 1972; Kertelge 1977; Knoch, O., 'Charisma und Amt: Ordnungselemente der Kirche Christi', *SNT(SU)* 8 (1983), 124–61; Lemaire, A., 'Les Épîtres Pastorales. B. Les ministères dans l'Église', in Delorme 1974:102–17; Lips 1979; Lohfink 1977; Lohse, E. 'Entstehung des Bischofsamts in der frühen Christenheit', *ZNW* 71 (1980), 58–73; Meier 1973:323–45; Merkel, 90–3; Nauck, W., 'Probleme des frühchristlichen Amstverständnisses', *ZNW* 48 (1957), 200–20 (=Kertelge 1977:442–69); Osten-Sacken, P. von der, 'Bemerkungen zur Stellung des Mebaqqer in der Sektenschriften', *ZNW* 55 (1964), 18–26; Powell, D. *'Ordo Presbyterii'*, *JTS* ns 26 (1975), 289–328; Prast, F., *Presbyter und Evangelium in nachapostolischer Zeit* (Stuttgart: Katholisches Bibelwerk, 1979), 387–416; Roberts, C. H., 'Elders: A Note', *JTS* ns 26 (1975), 403–5; Rohde 1976; idem, *EDNT* III, 148f.; Roloff, 169–89; Schlier 1977; Schweizer 1961:77–88 (ch. 6); Spicq, 65–83, 439–55; Thiering, B., 'Mebaqqer and Episkopos in the light of the Temple Scroll', *JBL* 100 (1981), 59–74; Towner 1989:223–41; Young 1994:97–111; Young, F. M., 'On ΕΠΙΣΚΟΠΟΣ and ΠΡΕΣΒΥΤΕΡΟΣ', *JTS* ns 45 (1994), 142–8; Ysebaert 1994:60–123.

The PE represent a stage in the history of the church when the contours of organisation are becoming more pronounced. In the earlier Pauline letters we have glimpses of a situation in which the founder of the churches is still in close personal contact with them, through visits, correspondence and the activity of colleagues in the apostolic mission. Ministry of all kinds is carried out by any member of the congregation who has the appropriate

---

[66] Cf. Büchsel, F., *TDNT* II, 473–6; Prosch, F., *EDNT* I, 427f.

spiritual gifts for the different functions. At the same time leadership is exercised by a groups of individuals who are entitled to respect by virtue of their work. It is probable that house-groups are led by the head of the family, and that the older men in the congregation are the natural leaders. There is thus an interesting combination of 'charismatic' ministry and leadership by the older people, especially the first converts (cf. Harvey*, 329f.). It is significant that the list of 'charismatic' ministries in 1 Cor 12.28f. can include both apostles and local ministers; the 'mix' is even more apparent in Rom 12.6–8. The term 'elder' is not attested in the earlier Pauline letters in this sense. Only in Phil do we read of 'overseers and deacons' as local church leaders. Paul and his itinerant colleagues are co-workers and brothers, and the concept of 'service' (διακονία) is fairly elastic.

By the time of the PE the situation has begun to change with the growth of the church and the consequent need for a firmer structure, and with the shift to a situation in which the apostles (in particular, Paul) are no longer there to exercise their former close supervision; the development of doctrines and practices that are not in accordance with Paul is beginning to cause serious problems. The PE, however, stand at the beginning of this process, and what we see is the beginning of a co-ordination of the organisation and ministry of the congregations (Sand 1976). We are far from the developed hierarchy of the second century (Meier*). Various points indicate that there is still a considerable degree of flexibility and informality.

The PE know nothing of a continuation of the apostolate, which indeed would have been impossible on the Pauline understanding of the apostles of Christ as eye-witnesses of the risen Lord (1 Cor 9.1; 15.8f.; Gal 1.1, 15f.). Nevertheless, they assume that Paul has passed on his authority and the sacred trust of the gospel to Timothy and Titus who are his trusted colleagues. They are related to him as junior colleagues but to the congregations they have the same authority as his own. The PE are addressed to them rather than to the congregations as part of the process whereby they are shown to be effectually his successors. Timothy has been appointed to his task by the laying on of hands by elders. He is younger than them, and yet they must recognise his authority. The same circumstances may be presumed in the case of Titus. No specific designation is given to them, unless 'evangelist' (2 Tim 4.5) is to be understood in this way. There is certainly no indication that the term 'overseer' was applied to them.[67] The tendency in recent scholarship has been

[67] To construe the lack of a title as being due to the fact that they are to be understood 'als Idealtypen gemeindlicher Episkopen' (Roloff, 179) is unjustifiable.

to argue that both they and their roles are fictitious, and that there never were persons acting as Paul's assistants or successors in this kind of supervisory role. This claim underestimates the importance of the Pauline concept of the apostolic missionaries, a body of people charged with the creation, establishment and ongoing care of local congregations but who remained essentially separate from them. The terms in which they are addressed and their ministry is described do not diverge significantly from the picture of the apostolic coworker that emerges in the main Pauline letters (cf. Ollrog 1979:23).

Reference is made to elders and overseers as the leaders of local congregations, and 1 Tim also refers to deacons and women (deacons). The appointment of these people is motivated by the need to teach the gospel faithfully and to oppose opponents and their false teaching. Consequently, all the emphasis falls on their character and qualities, including their faithfulness to Pauline doctrine and their competence to teach, and virtually nothing is said directly about their actual duties and functions. Lohfink 1977 is correct in arguing against Schlier 1977 (originally published in 1948) that the PE do not lay down a normative structure of ecclesiastical offices but rather emphasise the normativity of the apostolic deposit and teaching, i.e. the gospel and the practical paraenesis based upon it.

1. The nature of 'elders'

The exercise of authority in a community by the older men is characteristic of Judaism. Campbell has shown that elders are the senior men in a community, the leaders of the influential families, and their position is one that is recognised by custom and wont, and not by any kind of official appointment to a definable office. 'Elders' is generally used as a collective term. It 'does not so much denote an office as connote prestige' (Campbell 1994a:65). Such recognition was generally correlated with age but younger men may have gained this prestige because of the prestige of their families. Similar respect for older people as community leaders is found in Graeco-Roman society, but here the actual term πρεσβύτεροι is rare and οἱ γέροντες (ἡ γερουσία) is normal. Harvey* has stressed that there is no evidence for elders forming a council or governing body of any kind in the OT. The Sanhedrin was composed of a wider group of leaders. Nor do elders appear to have responsibilities with regard to the worship and organisation of the synagogue, although they had administrative responsibilities with regard to the broader life of local Jewish communities. Consequently, there does not appear to have been a Jewish model for a council of elders in Christian groups (cf. Powell*, 302–4).

According to the evidence of Acts the early Christians in Jerusalem were led from an early date by a group of elders (Acts 11.30) who were associated with the apostles (Acts 15.2; et al.). For Campbell this group consisted of (or, we may say, at least included) the leaders of the individual house groups in the Jerusalem church. In the Pauline mission the local church leaders are called 'elders' (Acts 14.23; 20.17).

Harvey argues that the term 'elders' was used for the older men in Christian congregations who were regarded as leaders. The older men in question were the senior members of the congregation in that they were or included the first converts to the faith (cf. Powell*, 305). They did not form an organised council with a chairman or president.

It follows that the term had some flexibility and could refer to the older men in general or to those who were especially regarded as leaders. The objection has been raised that if people are elders by virtue of their age/seniority, then it is not possible or necessary to 'appoint' them. Campbell meets this objection by arguing that Acts 14.23 describes the laying on of hands to claim God's blessing upon those who were already in effect the local church leaders.

The term is not used in the earlier Pauline letters; even if this silence implies that it was not actually used in the churches, there is no reason why Luke should not have referred to their leaders by the term with which he was familiar. In any case he is aware that the function of the elders is oversight (Acts 20.28).[68]

Elders are found in the PE only in Tit 1.5 and 1 Tim 5.1, 17, 19. In 1 Tim 5.1, the parallelism with the feminine form in v. 2 clearly indicates that older men in general are meant.[69] In 1 Tim 5.17 reference is made to elders who perform leadership functions well. This may mean that some of the senior men acted as leaders (including teaching functions) or that some of the elders carried out fuller duties than the others. Here the word is more nuanced to the sense of 'elder' (= 'leader') and in v. 19 it is probable that it is the leaders who are in mind. Tit 1.5 is concerned with the appointment of elders in local churches, and

---

[68] Elsewhere the term is found in Jas 5.14; 1 Pet 5.1, 5; 1 Clement 44.5; 47.6; 54.2; 57.1; 2 Clement 17.3, 5; Ignatius, Mag. 2; 3.1; 6.1 et al.; Polycarp inscr.; 5.3 (linked to deacons).

[69] The term πρεσβύτης found in Tit 2.2 means 'old man'. However, the use of this term in no way requires that πρεσβύτερος cannot also be used to mean 'old man'.

here again the word is nuanced to mean 'leaders'.[70] We are, therefore, dealing with a term which is somewhat flexible in its usage and is in course of transition from a general to a more technical meaning (Barrett, 78f.). The apparent equation of these elders with overseers (Tit 1.7) raises the fundamental question of the relationship between two sets of terminology.

2. The source of the term 'overseer'

In secular Greek society ἐπίσκοπος was a term that meant 'overseer', in one sense or another, and described supervisors or leaders in a variety of contexts.[71] It was adopted in the LXX in reference to civil and military supervisors[72] and for those involved in religious oversight (Num 4.16; 2 Kgs 11.18). There is certainly ample correspondence between this broad secular use and 'official' church use to suggest an origin in secular supervisor models, or to see the term as one that presented itself to the Greek-speaking church through the LXX.

It, therefore, seems likely to many scholars that the Christian adoption of the term resulted from the church's interaction with Hellenistic culture,[73] and that the application of the term in the LXX may well have paved the way for this adoption.[74] In any case, the earliest attested use of the term in the Christian church is in Phil 1.1 (on the assumption that it was composed before Acts).[75]

But it is also possible that the early church's adoption of the title is to be linked with the development of the title *mebaqqer* (מבקר) in Jewish sectarian circles, as reflected in the Dead Sea

[70] It has been argued that the term consistently means 'old man' rather than 'elder' in the sense of a church 'official' throughout the PE (Jeremias, 41f.). Against Jeremias see Campbell 1994a:184–6.

[71] For Cl. usage (sometimes in reference to an office) see Beyer, H. W., *TDNT* II, 608–14. There is reference to a religious group in the temple of Apollo at Rhodes (*Inscriptiones Graecae* XII 1.731.8; Deissmann 1901:230–1). The term was used of Cynic and Stoic preachers. Cf. Josephus, *Ant.* 10.53; 12.254; Philo, *Her.* 30 so describes Moses.

[72] Num 31.14; 2 Kgs 11.15; 2 Chr 34.12; Judg 9.28; Neh 9.11, 14; Isa 60.17; 1 Macc 1.51.

[73] Acts 20.28; Phil 1.1; 1 Tim 3.2; Tit 1.7; *Didache* 15.1; Hermas, *Vis.* 3.5.1; *Sim.* 9.27.2; Ignatius, *Eph.* 1.3 and freq. See Brox, 151; Trummer, 215; Schwarz 1983:43.

[74] Schnackenburg 1977:422. On the whole question see further Beyer, H. W., *TDNT* II, 611–14; Gnilka*, 38f.

[75] The claim that there is next to no relationship between the overseers and deacons of Phil 1.1 and the PE (e.g. Oberlinner, 88) and that there was not a 'system' of 'overseers' before the PE (Oberlinner, 93) seems quite unjustified.

Scrolls.[76] The basic similarity is quite clear (stressed by Spicq, 448f.). Critics claim that it is hard to see how (or why) the connection would have been made and note that the title seems to be connected with the church in Asia Minor and Europe rather than in Palestine (though cf. *Didache*).[77] Nevertheless, there is a good case that the functions of the *mebaqqer* would have been required in the earliest Christian house groups, and it is possible that this functional term came into use via this route (Campbell, 158).

3. The duties of the overseer

According to Hatch*, 39–55, in earliest times the function of the overseer was basically economic (cf. the warnings against misuse of money, Tit 1.7; 1 Tim 3.3, 8), including the care of the poor and perhaps duties with cult and correspondence. First, from the standpoint of the relation between spiritual gifts and office, it is thought that logically these routine types of duties would have been outside the territory of the free gifts of the Spirit. This hypothesis accordingly distinguishes fairly sharply between the overseer's office (as technical and administrative) and the charismatic positions of ministry in the church. A second material proof is held to be the traditional connection in 1 Tim 3 and Phil 1.1 of this office with that of the deacon, whose tasks are assumed to have been mainly economic in nature (cf. Hermas, *Sim.* 9.27.2 of overseers). Third, support is sought from the use of the title for financial officers in Greek society (cf. Gen 41.34; Dibelius-Conzelmann, 54f.).

Although it need not be doubted that the finances of the congregations would have been handled by its leaders, it is highly questionable whether these were their main responsibilities. The overseers in the PE were concerned with the teaching given in the congregation and with the refutation of false teaching (Tit 1.9; 1 Tim 3.2; cf. 5.17 of the elders; 2 Tim 2.2 probably also applies to the same group). Nothing is said about so-called 'cultic' duties. They are also given authority which involves both care and discipline of the congregation. Young 1994:102f., has stressed the significance of the description of the overseer as θεοῦ οἰκονόμος, which is a term used of slaves placed in charge of a household and acting on behalf of the head (i.e. God).

The need for them to have a good reputation generally does not require the view that they were the congregation's link with

---

[76] CD 9.18, 19, 22; 13.6, 7, 16; 14.8, 11, 13, 20; 15.8, 11, 14; 1QS 6.12, 20; cf. Thiering*, 59–74; Goppelt 1962:128f.; Nauck*, 207; Quinn 16, 88; Campbell 1994a:155–9.

[77] Cf. Roloff, 173; Osten-Sacken*; Lohse*, 70f.

the secular world; the point is surely that leaders in particular are exposed to the public gaze and therefore must be all the more transparently upright in character.

The tasks of the overseer need to be considered in relation to the tasks of ministry and leadership described in the earlier letters of Paul and also in relation to the problem of the nature of the elders, who are mentioned in Tit 1.5; 1 Tim 5.17; cf. 4.14.

The functional 'charismatic' terms used by Paul to characterise ministry (διακονία, Rom 12.7; προΐστημι, Rom 12.8; ἀντίλημψις, κυβέρνησις, 1 Cor 12.28; *et al.*) obviously overlap with the functions of the overseer, but this is by no means evidence that the office had entirely superseded or absorbed 'charismatic' ministry. It has become increasingly clear that the distinction sometimes drawn between an earlier charismatic ministry and a later institutional system of 'office' is inappropriate and should be dropped from the discussion.[78] Both 1 Th 5.12 and 1 Cor 16.15f. clearly presuppose the existence of local church leaders whose position of authority is recognised by the other believers. There are overseers and deacons in the church at Philippi, but the tasks of ministry are not confined to them. In terms of development, the PE appear to be at roughly the same stage as the church envisaged in *Didache* 15.1 (cf. Eph 4.11; Dibelius-Conzelmann, 55). What is reflected in Titus 1 is different from the missionary practice of Paul as described in Acts (14.23) only in terms of the detail of the description. Oversight is clearly the domain of the overseer, as the term itself, the household management parallel and the term προΐστημι (cf. 1 Tim 5.17) in 1 Tim 3.5, and the authority *vis-à-vis* the false teachers in Tit 1.9 suggest. Suggestions that the Holy Spirit is no longer active except in those appointed to office represent an argument from silence; those who adopt them have to find ways of explaining away the reference to prophets in 1 Tim 4.14. The existence of false teachers (both male and female), however objectionable they may be to the writer, is a further sign that the holding of office was not a precondition for such ministry. (The writer never requires that teaching be confined to those holding an official position,[79] and the description of the qualities required in overseers and deacons is most naturally understood to indicate that they exercised their teaching gifts before their appointment.)

---

[78] This is the lasting contribution of Campbell's work.

[79] Roloff, 178f., frames the question whether there was a place for a '*Lehramt*' that was not directly linked to the '*Leitungsamt*'. But why does the question have to be framed in terms of *Amt*?

4. The relation of overseers to elders

The question of the relation of overseers and elders in the PE has yet to be answered in a final way.

Since elders are not mentioned in the earlier letters of Paul, it has often been argued that a distinction should be made between two basic forms of early leadership models – a Pauline set-up of overseer-deacons and a non-Pauline one of elders – and that the PE represent a blending of these two systems.[80] There would then be different models of church organisation in different areas. Certainly different patterns appear in the Apostolic Fathers (cf. Jay*). Overseers and deacons appear together in 1 Clement 42.4f.; overseer, elders and deacons in Ignatius, *Mag.* 6.1; *Trall.* 2.2–4; 3.1; *Philad.* inscr.; *Smyr.* 12.2; *Poly.* 6.1; elders and deacons in Polycarp 5.3; apostles, overseers, teacher and deacons in Hermas, *Vis.* 3.5.1. In 1 Clement there is clear attestation of a plurality of overseers and their equivalence with elders (1 Clement (42.4; 44.1 with 44.4–5; 47.6; cf also Clement, *Quis Dives* 42). The evidence of Acts 20.17, 28 suggests plurality and inter-changeability, as well as a knowledge of the nomenclature in use in Ephesus; but the sequence and time of this development remain uncertain. One point that needs to be stressed is that in view of the variety of developments in the Apostolic Fathers it is not necessary to interpret the PE as a stage on the way to the explicit three-tiered organisation of Ignatius' letters where a single overseer presides over the elders and deacons.[81]

In the light of Acts 20 it is plausible that the title 'overseer' views the leader from the general perspective of function (over-sight) and 'elder' is more to be associated with office or status (cf. Schweizer 1961:71; Towner 1989:223f.). If it is correct to identify elders and overseers in Tit 1.5–7, then the same would be true here. There may then have been a development which led to the overseers becoming a group distinct from the elders. But the interpretation of the evidence in the PE continues to be disputed.

[80] A theory of this kind can be developed in various ways; see Beyer and Kapp*, 403; Brox 1969b:91; Kertelge 1972:147f.; Prast 1979:400f.; the survey in Campbell 1994a:188–93, and especially Roloff, 169–89. If, however, the view of eldership developed above is correct, then the theory falls to the ground.

[81] It is of course possible that the church order of the PE provided a paradigm for the development of the monarchical episcopate (cf. Sand 1976:215–37), and that within the letters the role played by Timothy and Titus might later have been perceived as in some sense paradigmatic (Trummer 1978:76–8; Lips 1979:108; Stenger 1974:252–67; Campenhausen 1969:108; Roloff 1965:251, citing Theod. Mops. II, 121 Swete; cf. Dibelius-Conzelmann, 57). But that this was part of an intentional fiction on the part of the author (so e.g. Roloff, 179–81; Dibelius-Conzelmann, 56f.; Hanson, 32–4) is only one possible reading of the evidence.

(a) Although the tasks of the overseers and elders seem identical, the term 'overseer' is always in the singular. Some argue, therefore, that the pattern of rule assumed is a monarchical bishop, ruling over the local church, who is distinct from the elders, but chosen from their number.[82] For Oberlinner, 90f., this pattern is the author's ideal, not necessarily the actual reality in the situation with which he was dealing.

(b) Others maintain that a singular overseer is closely related to a college of elders; he may have been chosen, elected or appointed to preside over the college and over the church. According to Lips (1979:113f.), this explanation best accounts for the singular overseer and his close relation to the elders.[83] Hanson, 173, holds that the writer is dealing with monarchical bishops as they were in his own day, but retains a traditional formulation dating from a time when they did not yet exist as a separate office from the elders. Merkel, 90, comments that against the 'household' background only one overseer would have been able to act as the 'householder/steward'.

On either of these scenarios, it would be necessary to interpret Tit 1 to mean that Titus was to appoint one elder = overseer per town. In line with this suggestion it would be tempting to interpret the evidence in 1 Tim similarly, with the plural 'elders' referring to the leaders of the different churches for which Timothy had oversight. However, this is an unnatural rendering of 1 Tim 5.17–20 which presupposes a plurality of elders in any given congregation; otherwise there could be congregations lacking in teachers, and the reference to rebuking the sinful elders (plural!) before everybody (plural) likewise is most naturally understood of several elders in one congregation.

(c) It is more common to view the singular ἐπίσκοπος as a generic reference, belonging to the traditional code cited, similar to the singular elder of 1 Tim 5.1 and widow of 5.9.[84] Two possibilities arise.[85] The first is that the term is simply

---

[82] Cf. Bartsch 1965:107; Roloff, 154, 175f.; Campenhausen 1969:107f.; Prast 1979:402–14 sees a tendency for the overseers to develop out of the elders and become more and more separate from them.

[83] Cf. Dibelius-Conzelmann, 56; Spicq, 439–55; Merkel, 92; Lohse 1980:67. It is not easy to be sure how far different scholars would see this hypothesis as distinct from the previous one.

[84] Oberlinner, 90f., contests this view of the history of the passage; although some of his arguments rest on questionable assumptions, he is right to note that the language used is the author's own. The view that the singular is to be attributed to a later interpolation is generally rejected; see the discussion in Dibelius-Conzelmann, 56; Bartsch 1965:83–5.

[85] Towner 1989:223–7 leaves the options open.

regarded as basically equivalent to 'elder'.[86] Within the local church, therefore, there was a body of leaders known in terms of their function as overseers and in terms of their status as elders.

(d) The other possibility is that there was a plurality of overseers who formed a subset of the larger group of elders (i.e. the 'double honour' elders of 5.17).[87] Related to this view is the hypothesis of Harvey that some of the first converts (i.e. the 'elders' or 'seniors') were appointed as overseers and deacons.

(e) A different route is followed by Campbell 1994a:176–209. He argues that originally the leaders of house-churches each acted as ἐπίσκοπος in their own households and were collectively the πρεσβύτεροι in that local area. What was happening was that Titus was to set up *one* overseer as leader in each of these local areas (κατὰ πόλιν); these people were the 'elders worthy of double honour' in 1 Tim. Thus the reference of 'overseer' was being shifted from the individual leaders of household groups to the overseers of town churches (each composed of several house groups),[88] and the reference of 'elders' was being shifted from the house-church leaders as a group to those of them who were not town overseers. The use of 'overseer' in the sing. in Tit 1.7 is then to be explained not as a generic use,[89] but as a particularisation for each individual appointment (town by town; cf. above). The PE accordingly reflect the development of monepiscopacy and the separation of the roles of overseer and elder.

Campbell's view is not free from difficulty. The postulated terminological distinction does not become clear until the time of Ignatius, which for Campbell is considerably later. The hypothesis requires a difficult understanding of Tit 1.5 where 'appoint elders' is a curious phrase for 'appoint overseers'.[90] It is more

---

[86] This view has a distinguished pedigree; Campbell 1994:183 cites Jerome and Lightfoot in favour of it. See also Schweizer 1961:85; Schwarz 1983:41–3; Kelly, 13, 73f.; Fee, 22; Ysebaert 1994:69–73. Brox, 151, and Schwarz [1983:38] suggest that the author himself is accustomed to the term 'elder', while the term 'overseer' belongs to the duty-code that is being adopted.

[87] Brox, 150f. (cf. 1969:91); Kertelge 1972:147; Bornkamm, G., *TDNT* VI, 668; Beyer, H. W., *TDNT* II, 617; Meier*, 324–9.

[88] Cf. Roloff, 176.

[89] Originally it may have been meant this way, if the hypothesis is correct that a piece of pre-formed tradition, perhaps originally meant for the overseer of a household church, has been incorporated (Campbell 1994a:199).

[90] Campbell is well aware of the problems surrounding the phrase, but does not really face up to the difficulty that 'appoint elders [one each] per city' can hardly be construed to mean 'appoint one of the elders in each city to be *the* elder (i.e. overseer) for that city'. The earlier suggestion by Harvey*, 330f., that the passage means 'Appoint (to positions of responsibility) those of your elders (i.e. older members) who have such and such a character', is rightly criticised by Roberts*, 404.

likely that the phrase refers to the appointment of a group of leaders for each individual town. Or it may be that individual households grouped together to form churches and it was necessary to appoint those who should be the leaders in them (rather than automatically have all heads of households as leaders). A further problem is that the qualities desiderated in the overseer have to do with the leadership of a household and may suggest a junior position compared with that of a leader of a group of congregations. Finally, this view leaves us with the problem of the place of Timothy and Titus or 'Timothy' and 'Titus' if these are in effect 'ideal' figures. There does not appear to be room for a monarchical bishop alongside them (especially with Timothy in Ephesus), and the view that they are meant to represent the overseers is unlikely.

(f) A view somewhat inverse to that of Campbell has been proposed by Young 1994:97–111. She postulates that what is happening in the PE is a shift in the self-perception of the church from 'God's household' to 'God's people'. With this shift came a certain assimilation of the pattern of church life to that of the synagogue, and this led to the development of a group of elders alongside the overseer who was now increasingly seen as equivalent to the *archisynagogos* or official in charge of the synagogue. On this view the overseer and the elders are separate from one another, and the 'deacons' correspond to the synagogue attendants. The attractiveness of this suggestion lies in its recognition that for the PE the household structure of the church is not the last word. The weakness lies in the fact that again a satisfactory explanation of the apparent identification of elders and overseers in Tit 1.5–9 is not provided.

5. Conclusion

Given the complexities regarding the possible use of traditional materials and the general uncertainty about the development of church order, any solution offered must be tentative. The following points are relevant:

(a) A factor that needs to be stressed is our uncertainty about the degree of organisation of the churches at this time. We do not know whether in a given locality (e.g. a town) there was one local congregation, or a set of independent house congregations, or a local congregation that consisted of smaller house congregations, and we do not know whether there was any organisation that brought different localities together in larger groupings. Nor again do we know whether a house congregation consisted of one household or several (as in a modern house fellowship, so called because it meets in a house rather than an ecclesiastical building). It would appear that Titus was responsible for several towns in Crete, but Timothy may have been responsible only for Ephesus, and nothing suggests that they bore the designation of 'overseer'. There is no evidence for the use of the term 'overseer/bishop' for a leader covering a wider area than a town (and its hinterland) at this time.

(b) The period is one of transition and the PE reflect both the existing situation and the author's attempts to regulate it. The slightly different pictures that we get from 1 Tim and Tit may well reflect different stages in development.[91]

(c) Tit 1.5–7 is concerned with the appointment of people to be elders and who are to act as overseers and stewards of God's people.

The best explanation is that each recognisable Christian group has a group of senior persons out of which is crystallising a leadership group. The term 'older men' or 'elders' is in process of coming to mean the latter group and expresses their status. The term 'overseers' is also coming into use; it expresses their function. Some of the 'seniors' are active in leadership, specifically in preaching and teaching, but others are not. Some groups may have had only one overseer/elder because of their size, and if the household metaphor is pressed, this may well be the case. The situation in Crete, where no elders had been appointed previously, is anomalous. The closest analogy is in Acts 14.23 where Paul and Barnabas do not appoint elders in the new churches on their initial visit but only on their return visit. This may suggest that earlier organisation was informal and that the rise of heresy meant that some more formal procedure was required. There is a tendency to encourage the overseers to be active in teaching, since sound teaching is so important over against the rise of heresy. It may be presumed that these people are among the 'faithful people' to whom Timothy is to commit what he has heard from Paul (2 Tim 2.2).

Alongside the overseers were the 'deacons' who are described in 1 Tim 3. They appear to have had less responsible positions than the overseers, and it is likely that they too were largely appointed from the 'seniors' (see **Excursus 10**). (Nevertheless, in the Ignatian set-up the term 'elders' has come to be used for a group distinct from both the overseer/bishop and the deacons.)

On the significance of this conclusion for the nature of the church in the PE see **Excursus 11**.

---

[91] Cf. Cousineau*, 162, who argues that in Tit the presbyters are identical with the overseers, whereas in 1 Tim the latter are a special group developing within the former group.

EXCURSUS 3

The σώφρων word-group and related concepts

The character of the instruction in the PE regarding Christian life-style is largely set by the presence of an extensive vocabulary which conveys the ideal of self-control and moderation. Some eight words and word-groups are used in a total of 26 references; these are curiously distributed with twelve in Tit, thirteen in 1 Tim, and only one in 2 Tim (1.7). It would seem that the author did not picture Timothy as being in need of encouragement to develop this quality of character. They are found principally in the descriptions of the characteristics that should be seen in different groups of people. It is perhaps especially this emphasis which has led to the claim that the PE reflect the morality of the secular world and have lost the eschatological fervour of earlier Christianity.[92]

1. Self-control

Luck, U., *TDNT* VII, 1097–104; Quinn, 313–15; Schwarz 1983:49–51; *TLNT* III, 359–65; Wibbing, S., *NIDNTT* I, 501–3; Zeller, D., *EDNT* III, 329f.

This word-group is the most strongly represented in the PE. The primary word-group includes: σωφροσύνη, 1 Tim 2.9, 15; Acts 26.25***; σώφρων, 1 Tim 3.2; Tit 1.8; 2.2, 5***; σωφρονέω, Tit 2.6; Mk 5.15; Lk 8.35; Rom 12.3; 2 Cor 5.13; 1 Pet 4.7; σωφρονίζω, Tit 2.4***; σωφρονισμός, 2 Tim 1.7***; and σωφρόνως, Tit 2.12***. This gives a total of sixteen occurrences in the NT, of which ten are in PE. It is thus both characteristic and distinctive of the PE.

In Classical Greek σωφροσύνη is related to αἰδώς. Originally referring to a sound mind, it represented the virtue of restraint of desire, hence the sense of 'rational', intellectually sound, free from illusion, purposeful, self-controlled, with prudent reserve, modest, decorous.[93] It represented the opposite of ignorance and frivolity, and it was exalted as one of the four cardinal virtues (with σοφία, ἄνδρεια and δικαιοσύνη). In Plato, *Rep.* 427–434 these are listed as wisdom, courage, temperance and justice (σοφία, ἀνδρεία, φρόνησις, δικαιοσύνη), but the group was somewhat flexible, and σωφροσύνη is included in Stoic writers. Applied to women (especially in funerary inscriptions), it suggests chastity, self-control (*moderatio cupiditatum rationi*

---

[92] Harvey, A. E., *Strenuous Commands* (London, SCM Press, 1991), 13f., draws a strong contrast with the teaching of Jesus in the Sermon on the Mount.
[93] Cf. Aristotle, *Rhet.* 1.9 (cited by Holtzmann, 312).

oboediens, Cicero, *de Fin.* 2, cited by Simpson, 46), and purity, not giving in to passion.[94] It is thus close to ἐγκράτεια.

Wetstein drew attention to the work of Onasander, a philosopher (AD I) who wrote a treatise on the military commander (*De imper. off.*; Dibelius-Conzelmann, 158–60). It contains a description of the kind of person to choose as a general in the army. The list is remarkably general in character and is really more ethical than military. Because of this it is not surprising that it contains a set of qualities that were highly thought of at the time and that one might hope to find in a person in a leadership role. The general is to be chosen not on grounds of noble birth or possession of wealth but because he is 'temperate, self-restrained, vigilant, frugal, hardened to labour, alert, free from avarice, neither too young nor too old, indeed a father of children if possible, a ready speaker, and a man with a good reputation'. Onasander explains what he means by 'temperate': it is in order that the general 'may not be so distracted by the pleasures of the body as to neglect the consideration of matters of the highest importance'. Of the eleven qualities which he lists seven (or their close equivalents) are found in the PE. Other lists of qualities desired in rulers and the descriptions of occupations also contain this one (Vögtle, 73–81).

Although the word-group is very common in Hellenistic Greek (including honorific inscriptions), it has no Hebrew equivalent and is consequently rare in the LXX, being found only in Greek texts in which it is often one of the somewhat elastic list of cardinal virtues (e.g. 4 Macc 1.6, 18; 5.23; 15.10; Wis 8.7) or is extolled as a key to control of the emotions (e.g. 4 Macc 1.3, 6, 30, 31; 2.2, 16, 18; 3.17 5.23; 35). However, the dynamic in σώφρων/σωφροσύνη thus conceived is not simply the power of reason or the mind. 4 Macc 5.23 states clearly the conviction that the law teaches 'self-control'. The connections are clearer still in 4 Macc 2.21–23: God has given the mind (νοῦς) to govern the emotions, and to the mind he has given the law, which teaches 'self-control' (among other qualities) to make ruling the emotions possible (cf. Wis 9.11).[95] Thus self-control is closely tied to the law and thus 'baptised' into Judaism.

The cardinal virtues are never listed as a group in the NT. Justice is important, as is prudence (Tit 3.8; cf. Lk 1.17; Eph 1.8); but bravery (1 Cor 16.13) and wisdom (Eph 5.13; Jas 3.13) are not so significant. Nevertheless, Mott 1978 has argued that it was possible to use three of the virtues to stand

[94] For sexual purity see Philo, *Spec.* 1.102; 3.51; Josephus, *Ant.* 18.66–80; cf. Musonius Rufus 14, 12–14 Hense (van der Horst 1974:313).
[95] See also *T. Jud.* 16.3 *v.l.*; *T. Jos.* 4.2; 9.2f.; 10.2f.; *T. Benj.* 4.4; Josephus, *Ap.* 2.170, *et al.* Philo, *Mos.* 1.154; *et al.* (*TDNT* VII, 1101f.).

for all four, and that this is what happens in Tit 2.12. The same thing happens in Philo. Thus it is not necessary to suppose that here the PE are taking over ideas directly from Greek thought; Hellenistic Judaism has probably provided the bridge.

Elsewhere in the NT the word-group is used of normal sobriety and restraint, but it describes a Christian virtue in 1 Pet 4.7 and in the PE. It is a virtue of Timothy himself (2 Tim 1.7), overseers (Tit 1.8; 1 Tim 3.2), young men (Tit 2.6), and women (Tit 2.4, 5; 1 Tim 2.9, 15); it is in fact a fundamental characteristic of the Christian life (Tit 2.12). Its presence here, as with a number of other ethical terms in the author's vocabulary, has probably been influenced by the language of popular Hellenistic philosophy. In this respect, it communicates in readily understandable terms the idea of 'a suitable restraint in every respect', a self-control which leads to behaviour appropriate to the situation, and is to be seen as a positive virtue as the Christian faces the realities of life in the world.

As with εὐσέβεια (see **Excursus 1**), the author has consciously adjusted the aspect of behaviour expressed by the σώφρων word-group by relating it to the Christ-event. This is seen most clearly in Titus 2. In 2.2, 4, 5 and 6, the word-group functions to describe the respectable and acceptable Christian behaviour of older men, young women and young men (in v. 4 σωφρονίζω refers to the activity of 'training' in which the older women are to be engaged). Following the paraenesis, vv. 11–14 reflect back consciously on the life just described: Ἐπεφάνη γὰρ ἡ χάρις τοῦ θεοῦ ... παιδεύουσα ἡμᾶς, ἵνα ... σωφρόνως καὶ δικαίως καὶ εὐσεβῶς ζήσωμεν ἐν τῷ νῦν αἰῶνι (vv. 11f.). The material employed here clearly grounds the life described (in very Greek fashion) in the grace of God (cf. 2 Tim 1.7: ... ἔδωκεν ἡμῖν ὁ θεὸς πνεῦμα ... σωφρονισμοῦ). Moreover, this same passage indicates a moral change from the old way of life (ἀρνησάμενοι τὴν ἀσέβειαν καὶ τὰς κοσμικὰς ἐπιθυμίας; cf. Tit 3.3–7) which the grace of God in Christ effects (παιδεύουσα). In so doing, the author takes up the language and the theme of *moral* change familiar especially to Hellenistic Judaism (4 Macc; Philo) and establishes the basis for communicating the Christian message effectively in the new environment (cf. Quinn, 314f.).

Thus σώφρων in its relation to the Christ-event depicts a balanced demeanour characterised by self-control, prudence and good judgement. Whatever be the source of this teaching, the theological foundation for life articulated in Tit 2.11–14 requires that it be understood as a quality which faith in Christ produces (see above on εὐσέβεια; cf. further Schwarz 1983), and throughout the PE it stands for one of the marks of the genuine Christian life.

2. 'Discipline'

W. Grundmann, *TDNT* II, 339–42; Baltensweiler, H., *NIDNTT* I, 94–7; Goldstein, H., *EDNT* I, 377f.

A closely related idea is that of 'discipline' (NIV, ἐγκράτεια); the noun occurs in Acts 24.25; Gal 5.23; and 2 Pet 1.6***; and the verb in 1 Cor 7.9; 9.25***; the adjective comes in Tit 1.8***.

The word-group was used for a recognised and important virtue in Greek thought. In the sense of self-control, the word occurred as one of the cardinal virtues in Greek writers[96] and is found frequently in lists of virtues.[97] 'Self-control' may be exercised in relation to specific appetites[98] or in a general sense it may apply to self-control over all of the sensual desires (Ecclus 26.15; Acts 24.25; 1 Cor 9.25). 4 Macc 5.34 links ἐγκράτεια to the law. It is a quality required in military leaders (Onasander 1.3).

The word-group is rare in the LXX (Ecclus 18. 15, 30; Wis 8.21). Josephus, *Bel.* 2.120, 138, speaks of self-control as a quality highly valued by the Essenes. In Philo it signified the power to overcome other desires (*Abr.* 24). It could become a virtue in itself, where asceticism is practised for its own sake.

The references in Paul show that the idea was current at an early stage in the development of the church and its ethics. Self-control is part of the fruit of the Spirit in the normal life of the Christian (Gal 5.23; cf. 2 Clement 4.3), and its significance can be appreciated by thinking of the corresponding negative list of the works of the flesh which include giving way to various sorts of bodily passions. In Paul the word is used of restraint upon one's sexual desires (1 Cor 7.9) or of an athlete who has to exercise self-control over his body and his habits if he is to be fit to run a race; so too there is a spiritual self-control which must be exercised by the believer over his body so that he may not fail the spiritual test (1 Cor 9.25). In Acts 24.25 Paul addressed Felix about justice and self-control, the implication being that he was liable to partiality and corruption and also that his private morality did not bear too much inspection. Self-control in this sense is very much concerned with the restraint of bodily passions. When the use of the vocabulary of σωφροσύνη was developed in the PE, it was thus being used to express a concept that was already at home in the early church.

---

[96] Xenophon, *Mem.* I.5.4; Aristotle, *EN* VII.1–10; *M.M.* II.4–6.
[97] Philo, *Mos.* 1.154; *Prob.* 84; *Virt.* 182; Plutarch, *Amat.* 767E (linked to σωφροσύνη); Epictetus, 2.10.18.
[98] Food or wine, Xenophon, *Oec.* 9.11; the sexual drive, Philo, *Jos.* 54; 1 Cor 7.9.

Grundmann argued, however, that the concept was not developed in Christianity because it was 'so essentially ethical' and that in biblical religion 'there was ... no place for the self-mastery which had a place in autonomous ethics ... belief in creation cut off the way to asceticism. It saw in the world with its gifts the hand of the Creator. Finally, the gift of salvation in Christ left no place for an asceticism which merits salvation' (*TDNT* II, 342). True as these comments on the nature of Christianity are, it is not clear that they are correct with regard to the use of this concept. It can be argued with greater plausibility that responsibility under the God who creates and saves requires the development of a self-control that frees the believer to serve God in love.

In the PE it is important to resist a false asceticism (contrast the thematising of 'continence and the resurrection' in *Acts of Paul and Thecla* 5 [*NTA* II, 354]), but this does not remove the need for self-control of the body and its desires. This is the focus of this word, whereas σωφροσύνη would appear to be more concerned with sobriety in one's thinking and in the resulting behaviour. It has more the nuance of acting thoughtfully and wisely. Perhaps through the influence of the PE, it became an essential quality of Christian leaders (Polycarp 5.2; Hermas, *Vis.* 1.2.40).

3. Sobriety

Bauernfeind, O., *TDNT* IV, 936–41; Budd, P. J., *NIDNTT* I, 514f.; Lövestam, E., 'Über die neutestamentliche Aufforderung zur Nüchternheit', *ST* 12 (1958), 80–109.

A further quality associated with self-control is being 'sober'. νηφάλιος is 'temperate' (in use of wine), 'sober' (Tit 2.2; 1 Tim 3.2, 11***; νήφω, 2 Tim 4.5**; ἀνανήφω, 2 Tim 2.26***). In Cl. Gk. the word is used (mainly) of cultic materials, but implies sobriety on the part of those who use them; the word is not found in the LXX. Philo uses τὸ νηφάλιον for sobriety (*Sobr.* 2; *Ebr.* 123), and according to Bauernfeind it is he who first applies the word to people (*Spec.* 1.100; IV.191[99]); it is certainly so used in Josephus, *Ant.* 3.279 (cf. νήπτης in Onasander).

The clear command against overindulgence in alcohol in Tit 2.3, in reference to older women, strongly suggests that νηφάλιος addresses the problem of drunkenness among older men in traditional Greek culture (Quinn, 130f.). Although the language may reflect a proverbial stereotype, there is ample evidence that the problem was a very real one. There are several references to the prevalence of drunkenness and similar excesses in the

---

[99] But see F. H. Colson's note in the Loeb edition on the latter passage.

New Testament world and their incidence in the church. Paul's description of the church meal at Corinth is relevant here (1 Cor 11; cf. 1 Cor 6.10; *et al.*), as is also the reference to pressure to join with non-Christians in the way of life that they once followed (1 Pet 4.3f.; cf. Spicq, 616f., 619; Hanson, 179f.). The language, then, has a literal application to avoidance of the effects of alcohol in intoxication and other, unrestrained behaviour. Both overseers and female deacons must be temperate (1 Tim 3.2, 1 1) and it is the first characteristic mentioned for the older men in Tit 2.2. Further commands to avoid over-indulgence in alcohol are found in 1 Tim 3.2, 8; Tit 1.7 (all of church leaders) and Tit 2.3 (of older women).

A different way of life was exemplified by Timothy himself, who had to be counselled that he might take a little wine for his stomach's sake and his frequent ailments (1 Tim 5.23), the so-called medicinal use.

The presence of these literal prohibitions against drunkenness raises the question whether the commands to sobriety are simply redundant and repetitive or whether they are to be taken more generally. The adj. in Tit 2.2 and elsewhere may then be intended in its metaphorical sense as 'sober, alert, watchful',[100] and certainly the verb νήφω is used elsewhere in eschatological contexts to encourage expectancy of the parousia (2 Tim 4.5; 1 Th 5.6, 8; 1 Pet 1.13; 4.7; 5.8; cf. ἀνανήφω, 2 Tim 2.26; ἐκνήφω, 1 Cor 15.34; Schwarz 1983:48f.). Nevertheless, the command coincides with the strong disparagement of drunkenness in the biblical tradition,[101] and the literal sense is clearly important. Bauernfeind claims that 'the use here is figurative, though with a hint of the literal sense'. The reference is thus probably to the freedom from dissipation and stupor which goes (for example) with abstinence from alcohol and keeps the person alert and active for the service of God.

4. Dignity

Fiedler, P., *EDNT* III, 238; Foerster, W., *TDNT* VII, 191–6; Günther, W., *NIDNTT* II, 91–3; *TLNT* III, 244–8; Schwarz 1983:61f.

A further set of words that played a significant role in Greek ethical thought is rather characteristic of the ethical descriptions in the PE. σεμνότης occurs in 1 Tim 2.2; 3.4; Tit 2.7***; and σεμνός in 1 Tim 3.8, 11; Tit 2.2; and Phil 4.8***. The English

---

[100] Cf. Jerome, *PL* XXVI, 598; Brox, 292; Knight, 305.

[101] Prov 20.1; 23.20f., 29–35; Ecclus 19.1f.; 35.25–31; Tob 4.15; 1 Macc 16.15f.; 4 Macc 2.7; Rom 13.13; 1 Cor 5.11; 6.10; 11.21f.; Gal 5.21; Eph 5.18; 1 Pet 4.3; 1 Clement 30.1; Hermas, *Mand.* 6.2.5; 8.3; *Sim.* 6.5.5.

versions display an extraordinary variety of translations (for the adj. 'worthy of respect; serious; dignified; a good character'; for the noun 'holiness, proper respect, dignity, proper conduct', etc.).

Frequently in the classical writers the adj. means 'lofty, august, majestic, great'; it is used of the gods and of objects which are worthy of veneration, splendid, magnificent and noble whether aesthetically or morally. It described the honourable character of holy things (2 Macc 3.12; *Ep. Arist.* 171). Both outward and inward dimensions are noticeable.[102] But it comes to be a dominant term to refer to the outward splendour and dignity of men, reflecting seriousness of purpose and solemnity which are visible in one's conduct and speech.[103] Some scholars have associated the term with Stoicism, but it was apparently used much more widely. It was a standard expression of eulogy in the secular world; a son is commended 'because of the dignity of his character and the nobility he inherited from his forebears', and a wife likewise is described as 'most reverent, known for her restraint and dignity' (*TLNT* III, 248).

It is used in a religious sense in Judaism. It is found twice in the Greek version of Proverbs to refer to things associated with God (Prov 8.6; 15.26; the force in 6.8 is uncertain). Then it is applied to things instituted by God, such as the law and the Sabbath day. The temple is likewise designated.[104] The word-group refers rather to what calls forth veneration, worship and wonder. There is thus a dignity about these things or people; they command respect. In particular, 2 Macc and 4 Macc use the term of the Jewish martyrs whose manner of witness and death was such as to call forth respect (2 Macc 6.28; 4 Macc 5.36; 7.15; 17.5). In this way there is some basis for Foerster's suggestion that the force of the word is expressed by 'holy' (*TDNT* VII, 194). In effect the word may have two nuances, being used either of the quality which commands the respect or to describe people as 'worthy of respect'. When people are told to be 'dignified', the thought is that they should do the things or practise the characteristics which deserve respect.

[102] Outward of a beard (Epictetus, 1.16.9–14); inward of respectability (*Ep. Arist.* 5); cf. Dittenberger, *Syll.* 807, 13 of a physician (AD I); Philo uses it in reference to the spiritual world in contrast to the sensual, *Spec.* 1.317; *Decal.* 133; Foerster, W., *TDNT* VII, 194.

[103] Herodotus 2.173; Philo, *Leg. Gai.* 296; Ps-Plato, *Def.* 413e; Josephus, *Ant.* 6.332; Prov 8.6; 15.26.

[104] Objects designated in this way include: the Temple (2 Macc 3.12; Philo, *Leg. Gai.* 198); the high priest (Philo, *Leg. Gai.* 296; Josephus, *Bel.* 4.319); the Law (2 Macc 6.28; Philo, *Opif.* 2; *Spec.* 4. 179; 4 Macc 1.17; *Ep. Arist.* 5, 171, 313; cf. 1 Clement 7.2); the Sabbath (2 Macc 6.11); sacred songs (Philo, *Cont.* 29); the singers themselves (Philo, *Cont.* 88); the white-garbed Therapeutae 'with faces in which cheerfulness is combined with the utmost seriousness' (ibid., 66); and the life of the religious group (ibid., 25).

In Phil. 4.8 σεμνός is one in a list of qualities of things which are commended to the thoughts of Christians. Although these might appear to be aesthetic qualities – that we should fill our minds with what is beautiful – they are in fact basically moral qualities. The interesting thing is that σεμνός, here translated 'noble', comes second in the list after 'true'.[105] In the PE the word-group signifies serious, dignified behaviour that is worthy of respect. It is a quality especially expected in church leaders (1 Tim 3.4 [unless this refers to their children], 8, 11), but from 1 Tim 2.2 (alongside εὐσέβεια) and in Tit 2.2, 7 it is clear that the writer requires it of the congregation generally (cf. 1 Clement 1.3; 48.1). A Christian's behaviour should be such as to win respect from other people because they take life seriously and devoutly and do not trifle. The outward orientation is especially evident in the ἵνα clause of Titus 2.8, and the contrasting kinds of behaviour (dishonesty, drunkenness, slander, 1 Tim 3.8, 11, Tit 2.2) make the visible dimension all the more clear. 1 Tim 2.2 implies that the Christian's expression of this quality (or the freedom to express it) can be affected by external conditions; but the inner dimension of σεμνός/σεμνότης and its grounding in the Christ-event suggest that the quality is to find expression consistently regardless of circumstances.

Other terms used with much the same significance are αἰδώς (1 Tim 2.9***); ἱεροπρεπής (Tit 2.3***), and κόσμιος (1 Tim 2.9; 3.2; cf. κοσμέω, 1 Tim 2.9; Tit 2.10; 1 Pet 3.5; Rev 21.2).

5. Conclusion

The piling up of terms which are not found earlier in the NT and which are more at home in Greek culture indicates a significant change in vocabulary in the PE. Clearly they are using the language of Hellenism, but equally clearly they are doing so to make points that were made in Judaism and in the early church in other ways. For example, criticism of female show and adornment is as much at home in the OT and in Judaism as in Hellenism (Isa 3!). At the same time the sheer concentration on this particular aspect of character may raise questions as to whether the life-style in the PE is over-concerned with a dull respectability. Nevertheless, there are sufficient indications that the author faced a situation in which frivolity and a failure to take matters seriously were problems.

We have a picture of people engaging in foolish discussions about trivialities. The speculative concerns of the opponents,

---

[105] The thought and the language is regarded as so odd in a Pauline letter by Fiedler, P., *EDNT* III, 238, that he does not hesitate to draw the extraordinary conclusion that the verse is an intrusion into the letter by a later editor!

their myths and genealogies, and the resulting controversies
(1 Tim 1.3f.; Tit 3.9) were a diversion from the serious business
of Christian theology and action. Much of it is characterised as
being simply foolish and stupid talking (2 Tim 2.23) that was
not edifying (1 Tim 1.6f.). Church leaders are warned not to be
tempted to waste their own time in tackling these people on their
chosen level of empty arguments. Timothy is counselled against
people who delighted to listen to lots of teachers teaching
them what they wanted to hear (2 Tim 4.3). The same thing
was happening in the churches for which Titus was responsible
(Tit 1.10f.). Quarrels went on that produced all kinds of evil
talking (1 Tim 6.4f.). Godless chatter, as the author calls it, was
leading people away from the faith (1 Tim 6.20f.; 2 Tim 2.16, 25f.).
There were people who paid no attention to what conscience
should have said to them (1 Tim 1.19).

Some of the women in the congregations are singled out for
special mention. We hear of women gadding about instead of
getting on with their duties. Some were concerned with extravagance in dress and hairstyles (1 Tim 2.9); some of them were
teaching to the neglect of their other tasks. The writer talks
about 'silly women' who are easily led astray. Godless myths
and old wives' tales circulated (1 Tim 4.7). There were widows
who lived for pleasure (1 Tim 5.6), and the younger ones are
said to have gone around acting as tale-bearers and busybodies
(1 Tim 5.13).

The rise of people who were lovers of pleasure rather than lovers
of God is seen as a characteristic of the last days (2 Tim 3.4).
Other people were intent on making wealth for themselves and
were falling prey to the attendant temptations (1 Tim 6.9f.).

The sum total of all this is that the churches were in danger
of becoming hotbeds of useless discussion which diverted people
from the gospel and indeed was liable to lead them into error;
it was accompanied by time-wasting activities. There were people
whose minds were set on activities that were empty and useless
in comparison with the service of God.

We should further note that the writer was concerned that the
church should be taken seriously by people outside it and not
become the object of ridicule or contempt because its members did
not take their religion seriously or were engaged in undignified
behaviour (1 Tim 3.7; Tit 2.8).

It is not surprising, then, that in this situation we have a call
to the church to sober up. It may be concluded that to some
extent at least the concentration on this concept was due to the
pastoral situation. The writer wanted to see churches where
the gospel and Christian living were taken seriously. He used
language that was already at home in Hellenistic Judaism and the

Hellenistic world generally to emphasise his point; its prominence in the letters is not a sign of a falling away from earlier expressions of Christian spirituality and morality but is rather due to the specific needs of the situation.

b. The rise of opponents and how to treat them (1.10–16)

Findlay, G. G., 'The reproach of the Cretans', *Expositor* II:4 (1882), 401–10; Folliet, G., 'Les citations de Actes 17,28 et Tite 1,12 chez Augustin', *Revue des Études Augustiniennes* 11 (1965), 293–5; Haensler, B., 'Zu Tit 1,15', *BZ* 13 (1915), 121–9; Harris, R., 'The Cretans always liars', *Expositor* VII:2 (1906), 305–17; Harris, R., 'A further note on the Cretans', *Expositor* VII:3 (1907), 332–7; Harris, R., 'St Paul and Epimenides', *Expositor* VIII:4 (1912), 348–53; Harris, R., 'St Paul and Epimenides', *Expositor* XV:1 (1915), 29–35; Heyworth, S., 'Deceitful Crete: *Aeneid* 3.84. and the *Hymns* of Callimachus', *CQ* 43/1 (1993), 255–7; Lee, G. M., 'Epimenides in the Epistle to Titus (I 12)', *NovT* 22 (1980), 96; Lemme, L., 'Über Tit 1,12', *TSK* 55 (1882), 113–44; Plumpe, J. C., 'Omnia munda mundis', *TS* 6 (1945), 509–23; Pohlenz, M., 'Paulus und die Stoa', *ZNW* 42 (1949), 69–104; Riesenfeld, H. 'The meaning of the Verb ἀρνεῖσθαι', ConNT 11 (1947), 207–19; Stegemann, W., 'Antisemitische und rassistische Vorurteile in Titus 1,10–16', *Kirche und Israel* 11 (1996), 46–61; Thiselton, A. C., 'The Logical Role of the Liar Paradox in Titus 1.12,13. A Dissent from the Commentaries in the Light of Philosophical and Logical Analysis', *BibInt* 2 (1994), 207–23; Winiarczyk, M., *Euhemeri Messenii Reliquiae* (Stuttgart/Leipzig:Teubner, 1991), 2–4; Zimmer, C., 'Die Lügner-Antinomie in Titus 1,12', *LB* 59 (1987), 77–99.

This section gives the reason why elders apt at teaching are required. There are many active rebels in the church spreading human teaching with a Jewish basis; they are upsetting the whole church. Therefore the church leaders must attack falsehood as well as commend the truth. What we have here, then, is concerned with the problem that church leaders need to face and with the way in which they must deal with it, and, although the writer addresses his injunction directly to Titus in v. 13b, he envisages that Titus will instruct the new elders accordingly (cf. Oberlinner, 32). The theme reappears in 3.9f.

The structure of the section is fairly complex. Verses 10f. give the basic reason why the opponents are to be rebuked: there are many bad people (who must be muzzled) who are causing the upset of households of believers, all for the sake of gain. In vv. 12–13a, the writer appeals specifically to a 'Cretan' testimony to demonstrate their bad character and thus support the command to Titus. The command is then repeated in vv. 13b-14: Titus must rebuke them, so that the opponents might return to a sound faith and the congregation will not give heed to their false teaching. Verses 15f. identify and respond to the false teaching and teachers: As a general principle there are people with pure and impure minds; the latter (= the opponents) are false professors of the faith and unteachable. Any claim to possess exact knowledge of God is refuted by the behaviour of the false teachers themselves.

The denunciation of the false teachers and their followers is extremely harsh. The apostolic invocation of the Cretan stereotype brands the heretics and perhaps attempts to get the attention of those who would follow their lead. In this way, the author categorises the movement as one which will take believers back into an extremely ungodly ('Cretan') life which is the antithesis of genuine Christianity and from which faith in Christ has freed them.

The false teachers are described as having denied the knowledge of God that they profess to have by lives which show no evidence of genuine knowledge of God and faith. Adherence to extreme ascetic practices designed to help them guard their purity reflects ignorance of 'the truth' and the apostle's sound teaching of the faith. Life so marked is antithetical to the Christian life with its fruit of 'good works'.

The heresy described is similar to that in 1 Tim 1.3–11; 4.1–7; 6.5 (cf. Knight, 296). Attention is drawn to its Jewish origin and to the specific character of the Cretans. Although the same terminology is used to describe the heresy ('myths', 1.14; cf. 1 Tim 1.4; 4.7; 2 Tim 4.4; 'genealogies', 3.9; cf. 1 Tim 1.4), and a 'Jewish' character ('Jewish myths', 1.14; cf. 'teachers of the law', 1 Tim 1.7) and tendency towards asceticism are indicated (1.15; cf. 1 Tim 4.3), separate (perhaps closely analogous) developments are probably envisaged. There is no mention of the over-realised belief in the resurrection of believers at work in Crete (cf. 2 Tim 2.18), nor, apparently, has marriage been banned.

It has been suggested that the whole description of the opponents is fictitious, partly because of an alleged lack of coherence in vv. 13f. (see note there). It is said to be simply a part of the fictional 'Pauline' paradigm of the PE, which here employs the traditional picture of the Jews or Judaisers as the opponents of Paul (cf. Wolter 1988:263; Houlden, 144). However, the Jewish (and presumably, therefore, Jewish Christian) presence in Crete is extremely well attested, and if indeed the heretics were Jewish-Christian, the designation is to be expected.[106]

---

[106] Josephus, Philo and other ancient sources confirm the existence of a sizeable Jewish community in Crete (Josephus, *Ant.* 17.327; *Bel.* 2.103; *Vita* 427; Philo, *Leg. Gai.* 282; 1 Macc 15.23; Acts 2.11; cf. Tacitus, *Hist.* 5.2; cf. inscriptions in Schürer III.1, 68–72). The community dated at least to the second century BC, as is confirmed by the letter recorded in 1 Macc 15.15–24 concerning Jews which passed from Rome to Ptolemy VIII Euergetes II in Alexandria and then finally to officials in Gortyna (the authenticity of the letter is suspect [Schürer I, 194f.] but the information may be correct). Josephus's description (*Ant.* 17.324–27)

This tendency to regard the heresy in the PE as part of the pseudepigrapher's fiction is not warranted by the descriptions provided by the letters. Differences in description and local colour suggest analogous heretical movements which resulted from the combination of judaising and widespread (dualistic) influences and shaped to some degree by local settings. Since most of the more bizarre teachings show affinity with developments in Corinth and Colossae, there is no need to claim that these kinds of opponents have no historical precedents (cf. Towner 1987:94–124; and Introduction).

A keynote in the description of the opponents is insubordination and refusal to submit to authority. It contrasts with the subordination expected of the elder's children. Oberlinner, 33f., observes that in essence Titus is summoned to call them summarily to obedience rather than to enter into discussion with them. He sees here the danger of an attempt to deal with heresy by powerful suppression: the opponents are simply to submit to authority, and submission can become more important than faith and good works. The problem is resolved by a struggle for power rather than by 'speaking the truth in love'. 'What ought not to be taught' (v. 11) is determined by the church leader's fiat. The temptation to use one's position to settle disputes by fiat is certainly a danger, but it may be unwise to blame the author of Titus for yielding to it, since we do not know the precise circumstances and since there is a danger of failing to reckon with cultural differences between the world of the commentator and the world of the PE.

TEXT

10. [καί] (D F G I K Ψ 33 1739 1881 TR d g vg Lcf Spec; [WH]; Kilpatrick). The conjunction seems pleonastic after πολύς, but BD §442[11] notes that the construction is Cl.; Metzger, 584f., explains the construction as hendiadys. Elliott, 211, also retains the conjunction (cf. 1 Tim 6.9 *v.l.* ; cf. Acts 25.7, but there it is a case of two adjs. with a noun) and comments that it could also be a Semitism (cf. Gen 47.9); it seems most likely that it was dropped by scribes who thought it unnecessary.

ματαιολόγοι praem. καί (F G P *et al.*). The variant is accepted by Elliott, 211, who argues that scribes tried to reduce the frequency of καί in the verse.

τῆς Omit (A[1] D[2] F G Ψ TR; Tisch.); Elliott, 177, argues that the NT prefers anarthrous nouns after ἐκ and other prepositions. This particular phrase is anarthrous elsewhere in NT. Contrast, however, Rom 3.1; 1 Cor 7.19; Col 2.11. It seems more likely that it is scribes who have omitted the article to conform to the idiom.

11. For the addition in 460 see 1.9 note.

gives the impression of a well-to-do but easily deceived community; a man pretending to be a relative of Herod managed to win the confidence and financial support of the Cretan Jews. On the strength of Acts 2.11 it seems likely that some Jews had become Christians.

12. εἶπεν δέ (א* F G 81 *pc*); γάρ (103). The conjunction was probably added to make a smoother connection.

13. ἐστὶν ἀληθής inverted order (D 823 it vg sa). Elliott, 178, argues that ἀληθής followed by the verb is the normal NT word order, whereas the majority reading here is a rare order. He therefore prefers the variant. However, the evidence for the variant is decidedly scanty.

ἐν Omit (א* *pc*; cf. [WH]). Scribes tended to avoid use of prepositions, Elliott, 178.

14. ἐντολαῖς ἐντάλμασιν (F G) is a word found in LXX, not Classical and therefore possibly original, the usual text being an Atticistic correction (cf. Mt 15.9; Mk 7.7; Col 2.8; Elliott, 178). The evidence for the variant is very weak. γενεαλογίαις (075 1908 *pc*) is assimilation to 1 Tim 1.4.

15. πάντα πάντα μέν (א² D ¹ Ψ TR syʰ); πάντα γάρ (syᵖ boᵖᵗ). See BD §447⁵; MHT III, 331; Elliott, 179. Probably these are simply attempts to remove asyndeton.

16. καὶ πρός Omit καί (א* 81 Ambst). Elliott, 211, retains the text.

ἀγαθόν Omit (א* 81); a case of homoioteleuton (Elliott, 143; cf. 2 Tim 2.21).

EXEGESIS

10. Εἰσὶν γὰρ πολλοὶ [καὶ] ἀνυπότακτοι, ματαιολόγοι καὶ φρεναπάται, μάλιστα οἱ ἐκ τῆς περιτομῆς The reason for selecting leaders who are properly equipped to teach is given in vv. 10f. There is a widespread attitude of insubordination in the churches; those infected by it are characterised by foolish talk and deceitfulness. Those responsible are identified as being largely or exclusively Jewish Christians.[107] The present tense is used of an actual heresy; contrast the use of the future tense in prophetic contexts (1 Tim 4.1; 2 Tim 3.1f.; 4.3; cf. Brox, 286). πολλοί (2.3*) indicates the strength of the opposition and the threat it poses. In 1 Tim 1.3 the reference to 'some people' is vaguer.

The opponents are characterised in three ways. First, the repetition of ἀνυποτακτός (1.6 note) introduces a deliberate contrast between the behaviour typical of the opponents and that of the Christian teacher (Brox, 287; Merkel, 93) and of mature Christians in general (ὑποτάσσεσθαι, 2.5, 9; 3.1; cf. Quinn 105–6). It identifies the heretics' refusal to submit to (apostolic) authority. Spicq (606) contrasts receiving the word with meekness (Jas 1.21).

Second, their teaching is empty in content. ματαιόλογος***, 'idle talker', 'empty prattler', and related words[108] are used to denounce the speculative teaching of the opponents in a way that suggests that the term has almost a technical function in

---

[107] εἰσὶν γάρ recurs in 3.9, but there with the sense 'for they are...', rather than, as here, 'for there are...' (see another variant in 2 Tim 3.6).

[108] The word is Hel.; cf. ματαιολογία (1 Tim 1.6); μάταιοι (Tit 3.9); ματαιότης (2 Pet 2.18); cf. Bauernfeind, O., *TDNT* IV, 524.

the author's polemical vocabulary.[109] Generally in the NT the word-group classifies pagan and unregenerate beliefs (idolatry, Acts 14.15; legalism, Jas 1.26; 1 Pet 1.18) and behaviour (Rom 1.21; Eph 4.17) as futile.

Third, the teachers are deceitful.[110] In context (esp. v. 11), the reference would seem to be to the propagation of a false doctrine by which others are deceived.[111] It is not impossible that the thought of 'deceivers' is meant to tie in with the 'Cretan' stereotype under construction, already introduced through the overseer code and coming fully into view in the quotation of v. 12: 'Cretans are liars...'. There is a tendency to regard the whole of this description as nothing more than polemical language without concrete reference, designed to prejudice the readers' minds against the opponents. This is unjustified; at least from the writer's point of view the problem with the opponents was precisely that they talked attractive nonsense.

Finally, the source of the opposition is identified. μάλιστα usually means 'especially', which would emphasise one part of a larger, more diverse group (BA s.v.), but it may mean 'namely', which would simply make the preceding general reference specific (1 Tim 4.10; 5.8, 17; 2 Tim 4.13**; cf. Skeat 1979:173–7; Knight, 297). Given the 'Jewish' tinge of the heresy (1.14; 3.9), the latter use seems probable here. περιτομή is 'circumcision', both the rite and the resulting state.[112] In Paul the word can refer to Jews outside of the Christian faith (Gal 2.7–9) and figuratively to Christians (Phil 3.3; Col 2.11–13). The phrase here with ἐκ, however, is used mainly of Jewish Christians (Acts 10.45; 11.2; Col 4.11), who were secondarily 'Judaisers' (Gal 2.12), and once of Jews (Rom 4.12).[113] Since activity in the church is implied, the reference must be to Jewish Christians.[114] The phrase thus identifies the opposition. It does not necessarily imply that circumcision was an issue in the situation.[115] Nor are racial

---

[109] See note on 1 Tim 1.6; cf. Schlarb 1990:59–73.

[110] Holtzmann, 473, thought that the word φρεναπάτης*** (from φρένα ἀπατάω) was coined by the author or taken from the colloquial language; the latter view has turned out to be the correct one (BA; Dibelius-Conzelmann, 135; cf. φρεναπατάω, Gal. 6.3).

[111] But cf. BD § 119² for 'self-deceived' = 'conceited'.

[112] Cf. Meyer, R., *TDNT* VI, 72–84; Betz, O., *EDNT* III, 79f.

[113] Here ἐκ περιτομῆς designates physical circumcision and could conceivably include Gentile converts to Judaism.

[114] See Ellis 1978:116–28 (= TU 102 [1968], 390–9); Holtzmann, 473; Quinn, 98.

[115] The extent of Jewish-Christian influence in the opposition is played down by Roloff and also by Oberlinner, 35f., but against them should be noted the fact that the references are found significantly at the points where the false teaching is introduced for the first time, here and implicitly in 1 Tim 1.4, 7–11, and also in the closing recapitulation in Tit 3.9.

discrimination and anti-Semitism present (*pace* Stegemann 1996).

11. οὓς δεῖ ἐπιστομίζειν, οἵτινες ὅλους οἴκους ἀνατρέπουσιν διδάσκοντες ἃ μὴ δεῖ αἰσχροῦ κέρδους χάριν The crux of the problem is identified here as being false teaching which has penetrated the church to a dangerous extent. Consequently, action must be taken to prevent the trouble going any further. The phrase οὓς δεῖ ἐπιστομίζειν is almost parenthetical syntactically in the description of the opponents, but it contains the main practical point of the section: the opponents must be silenced in view of their subversive effects on the congregations.[116] It is usually assumed that argument and discussion with them are not envisaged. However, Simpson, 99, thinks that 'silencing by force of reason' is meant, and this possibility should not be entirely excluded (see 2 Tim 2.14 and note), even though the means to be used is apparently an authoritative 'rebuke' (ἔλεγχε, v. 13; cf. v. 9; 2.15; 3.10 [παραιτοῦ]). In view of the procedure envisaged in 3.10, it is unlikely that the force here is tantamount to 'excommunicate' (*pace* Hanson, 175).

The false teachers are to be withstood because they have already in some sense disturbed 'whole households'.[117] The households are assumed to be Christian, and it is probable that the household would have been the place in which the local church gathered for worship and instruction. The combination of ὅλος** (whole) and οἶκος ('household', 1 Tim 3.4, 5, 12, 15; 5.4; 2 Tim 1.16; 4.19**) occurs also in Acts 2.2; 7.10; 18.8; Heb 3.2, 5. The emphasis is on completeness, and here the dangerous extent of the heresy is stressed. ἀνατρέπω is 'to upset', hence 'ruin, destroy' (2 Tim 2.18; Jn. 2.15***), here with reference to the 'faith' or the people who hold it.[118] The view that this statement indicates that the opponents demonstrated a Gnostic disregard for institutions of the world, i.e. here the family (Schmithals 1961:145; Haufe 1973:330), is speculative without further indication. It is also not clear that the tactic of going from house to house preying on

---

[116] ἐπιστομίζω*** is 'to place something on the mouth', either a gag or a bridle, hence: (a) 'to stop the mouth, gag, silence' (cf. φιμόω, Mt 22.34; φράσσω, Rom 3.19; Heb 11.31); (b) 'to bridle, hinder, prevent or curb' (Josephus. *Ant.* 17.251; Philo, *Det.* 23; *L.A.* 3.155; *Her.* 3; cf. Jas 3.3). The verb is unknown in the papyri (MM, 244) but belongs to literary Greek and was used of silencing opponents in debate (Demosthenes, 7.33; see *TLNT* II, 61f.)

[117] οἵτινες, 'who', 'inasmuch as they' (1 Tim 1.4; 3.15; 6.9; 2 Tim 1.5; 2.2, 18**), has a somewhat uncertain sense in NT Greek. Here it may signify that they *belong to* a class of people who do something, or that they belong to this group of heretics *inasmuch as* they do something, or it may be equivalent to a *simple relative pronoun* (so BA here).

[118] For the combination of ἀνατρέπω with οἶκος see BA *s.v.*; Athenaeus 13 (560c) (Klauck 1981:68).

defenceless women in homes (2 Tim 3.6; cf. 1 Tim 5.13) is implied here.[119] The 'upset' in mind is almost certainly the defection of entire families to the false teachers, or the destruction of the faith once professed by members of a household by the false teaching such as 2 Tim 2.18 and 1 Tim 1.20 envisage. Alternatively, since it was typical for the church to meet in houses, it is possible that the reference is to the capitulation of whole house churches.[120]

The activity of the opposition is teaching. διδάσκω 'to teach' (1 Tim 2.12; 4.11; 6.2; 2 Tim 2.2; cf. Tit 1.9 note) occurs here only in the PE in reference to the opponents (but cf. νομοδιδάσκαλοι, 1 Tim 1.7). The present participle διδάσκοντες indicates the means by which the destruction is occurring and indicates an actual situation. Brox, 287, thinks there is a contrast between the secret activity of the heretics in houses compared with the open teaching of the truth in the church; however, this is a false contrast, especially if house churches are in mind (cf. Quinn, 106f.). ἃ μὴ δεῖ refers to 'what ought not to be taught' rather than 'what they have no right to teach' (cf. τὰ μὴ δέοντα, 1 Tim 5.13).[121] As in 1 Tim 1.7, the indefinite reference to the doctrines of the opponents is pejorative and stands in vivid contrast to the descriptions of the apostolic teaching as τοῦ κατὰ τὴν διδαχὴν πιστοῦ λόγου and τῆς διδασκαλίαν τὴν ὑγιαινούσην in v. 9 (cf. Quinn, 106). This may correspond to the technique of referring to the opponents vaguely as τινες (see 1 Tim 1.3 note).

The content of the teaching is not specified. The similarity of expression to 1 Tim 5.13 (see note) leads some to think this is an allusion to magic arts (Holtz, 212; Kelly, 234, and Spicq, 608, allow the possibility). Surrounding references to the apostolic teaching, however, suggest the general meaning of false teaching (Roloff, 298; Hanson, 175); what can be known of its content is described in vv. 14f. below.

Greedy motives mark the heresy as deceptive and contrary to the apostolic ministry (cf. v. 7).[122] For the proper attitude to wealth see 1 Tim 6.17–19. αἰσχρός, 'shameful' (1 Cor 11.6; 14.35; Eph 5.12***), is applied to the thing instead of

[119] So Müller 1976:62–4; Brox, 287; Spicq, 607; Haufe 1973:331f.; Lütgert 1909:20f.; but see Schlarb 1990:83 (n. 37), 314–56.

[120] Cf. Acts 2.46; 5.42; 8.3; 20.20; 2.2; the usual reference in Paul in greetings is to ἡ κατ' οἶκον αὐτῶν/αὐτῆς/σου ἐκκλησία (Rom 16.5; 1 Cor 16.19; Col 4.15; Philem 2).

[121] The neuter plural relative pronoun ἃ has no antecedent (2.1; 1 Tim 1.7). μή is used for οὐ (MHT I, 171, 239f.; III, 284; BD §428⁴; cf. 2 Macc 12.14; Ecclus 13.24).

[122] For χάριν see 1.5 note.

the person.[123] κερδός is 'gain, profit' (Phil 1.21; 3.7***).[124] The phrase is devised to give a contrast with the true teacher who should not be αἰσχροκερδής (1.7; cf. 1 Tim 3.3, 8; 6.10f.), and at the same time brings the 'Cretan' stereotype to bear on the false teachers' behaviour.

With different and more allusive language, the same motive is attributed to the heretics in 1 Tim 6.5. But the Cretan quotation that follows in this case suggests that this criticism is more than simple adherence to a heresy topos,[125] or at least that the geographical factors called for this aspect of the polemic to be expressed in Cretan terms (though many view this as simply an attempt to provide 'local colour' as part of the fiction). Greed and dishonest gain were well-known elements in the traditional criticism of Cretan behaviour.[126]

There was a general suspicion that teachers of philosophy and religion had financial motives (Dio Chrysostom, 32.10; Sophocles, *Ant.* 1055f.), and actual cases of exploitation made a similar impact in the early church (cf. 2 Pet 2.3; Rom 16.17f.; cf. Lips 1979:81f.), so that Paul himself had to give answer to such a charge (1 Th 2.5; cf. Acts 20.33). As to the actual situation, it has been suggested that by gaining the confidence of church members, the opponents managed to draw support meant for itinerant missionaries and prophets from the church's very limited resources.[127] Without legitimate authority and teaching false doctrine, this would constitute 'dishonest gain', but so would trading unauthorised teaching for food and shelter (Quinn 106), or accepting gifts from pupils (Holtzmann, 474).

12. εἶπέν τις ἐξ αὐτῶν ἴδιος αὐτῶν προφήτης Proof of the low character of the Cretans is now offered. It comes in the shape of a self-testimony by a Cretan, who is of course offering an opinion on the rest of his fellow-countrymen in general. τις ἐξ αὐτῶν is a typically vague reference (cf. 1 Tim 1.3, 19) which might suggest that it should be to one of the heretical teachers (so Findlay*, 403–10; cf. Quinn, 109). This identification was

[123] Cf. 'unjust mammon' (Lk 16.9, 11). Cf. Bultmann, R., *TDNT* I, 189–91.

[124] Cf. Philo, *Spec.* 3.154; Josephus, *Bel.* 4.102; cf. Schlier, H., *TDNT* III, 672f.

[125] *Pace* Karris 1973:549–64; Dibelius-Conzelmann, 5–8; Trummer 1978:163–6; Brox, 288; Wolter 1988:260f.

[126] Polybius 6.46.3: ὁ περὶ τὴν αἰσχροκέρδειαν καὶ πλεονεξίαν τρόπος οὕτως ἐπιχωριάζει ὥστε παρὰ μόνοις Κρηταίευσι τῶν ἁπάντων ἀνθρώπων μηδὲν αἰσχρὸν νομίζεσθαι κέρδος; Cicero, *Rep.* 3.9.15: *Cretes et Aeoli latrocinari honestum putant*; Livy 44.45.13: *Cretenses spem pecuniae secuti*; cf. *Anth. Pal.* 7.657.1; for Gnostic teachers taking fees, see Irenaeus, *AH* 1.4.3.

[127] Cf. 1 Cor 9.4, 12, 14; Gal 6.6; Lips 1979:81f.; cf. Theissen, G., *The Social Setting of Pauline Christianity* (Philadelphia: Fortress, 1982), 27–67; but cf. Hengel, M., *Property and Riches in the Early Church* (Philadelphia: Fortress, 1974), 35–41.

suggested by Lemme*, who thought that a Christian prophet might be meant, and it has been defended by Thiessen 1995:327f. The difficulty with this hypothesis is that it leaves unexplained why the prophet should have attacked the Cretans in this way, but it is just possible that he was building on their well-attested reputation and perhaps even citing or echoing a proverbial saying. But the connection is loose and most commentators assume that the reference of αὐτῶν is determined by the following plural Κρῆτες and the implied originator of the quotation, Epimenides.[128] On this view, προφήτης is used here for a non-Jewish person.[129] The prophet is not named but is usually identified as Epimenides, who (like some other Greek poet-philosophers) was regarded as a prophet by Plato, Aristotle, Cicero and others.[130] The language may therefore simply reflect his common reputation. Nothing requires us to think that the author of the epistle regarded him as prophet in the biblical sense. But the point might be that, like Caiaphas (Jn 11.51), this man spoke the truth without realising that he was God's mouthpiece (Spicq, 609; Barrett 131–2; Fee, 179; *contra* Hanson, 177, who asserts that Paul could not have used the term of a pagan poet).

Epimenides was a religious teacher and wonderworker in Crete (see below). In Plato, *Leg.* 1.642D–E, he was active as a priest and prophet in Athens c. 500 BC, but Aristotle, *Ath. Pol.* 1, dates him about a century earlier. According to Diogenes Laertius, 1.109–12, the Athenians sent for him during a pestilence; he is said to have purified the city after the slaughter of Cylon's associates and to have sacrificed to the appropriate god (as a result of which altars to unnamed gods were to be found in various places in Attica; cf. Acts 17.22f.). There are legends of his great age (as much as 157 or 299 years) or of a miraculous sleep for 57 years, and stories of his wanderings outside the body.[131]

Κρῆτες ἀεὶ ψεῦσται, κακὰ θηρία, γαστέρες ἀργαί The quotation forms a hexameter line.[132] The thought is similar to Hesiod,

---

[128] ἴδιος (1.3; 1 Tim 2.6), which was becoming a weak adjective, is strengthened by the addition of αὐτῶν (cf. MHT I, 141; III, 191; Dibelius-Conzelmann, 136; for the omission of the article see 2 Tim 1.9, *et al.*; BD § 286²).

[129] Cf. Irenaeus *AH* 4.33.3: *accusabit autem eos Homerus proprius ipsorum propheta*, probably an echo of this verse (Lock, 134).

[130] In Plato, *Leg.* 1.642D–E he is an ἀνὴρ θεῖος; in Aristotle, *Rhet.* 3.17.10, p. 1418a, 23 (text in Dibelius-Conzelmann, 136) he is a μάντις; cf. Cicero, *De Div.* 1.18 [34]; Plutarch, *Sol.* 12.4.

[131] Griffiths, A. H., *OCD*, 546; Spicq, 608f.

[132] It is also quoted in Tatian, *Orat. ad Graec.* 27; Athenagoras, *Suppl.* 30; Origen, *C. Cels.* 3.43. For detailed references on this point and much besides see Winiarczyk* (I am indebted for this reference to Dr J. L. North).

Theog. 26: ποιμένες ἄγραυλοι, κακ᾽ ἐλέγχεα, γαστέρες οἶον (Dibelius-Conzelmann, 136).

The source of the quotation is disputed.

(a) Its attribution to Epimenides is found in Christian writers, Clement of Alexandria[133] and Jerome;[134] it is said to come from a book variously called Θεογονία or περὶ χρησμῶν (Pohlenz*, 101). Harris* (1906:305–17; 1912:348–53), following a statement recorded by the ninth-century Syrian commentator Isho'dad, which he attributes to Theodore of Mopsuestia, suggested that the quotation might be from another poem by Epimenides, Περὶ Μίνω καὶ ῾Ραδαμάνθους.[135] However, Isho'dad's accuracy has been questioned (Pohlenz*, 101–4). MHT I, 233, notes that the dialect of the phrase is Attic and not Cretan, but reminds us that Epimenides did visit Athens and might have written his verse there.

(b) Quinn, 108, cites the view of Huxley that the association of the saying with Epimenides is mistaken, and that originally it was a Delphic criticism of Epimenides (who claimed too much for Crete), which was gathered into a collection of Epimenides' sayings.[136]

(c) The first phrase of the quotation is found in Callimachus (300–240 BC), *Hymn to Zeus*, 8 (Κρῆτες ἀεὶ ψεῦσται· καὶ γὰρ τάφον, ὦ ἄνα, σειο/Κρῆτες ἐτεκτήναντο· σὺ δὲ οὐ θάνες· ἐσσὶ γὰρ ἀεί).[137] Pohlenz*, 102, and Bruce 1990:384f. follow the suggestion of Epiphanius and Jerome that Callimachus was 'adapting' Epimenides.[138] At least two Christian sources maintained that Callimachus was the author of the quotation (Theod. Mops. II, 243 Swete; Theodoret,' III, 701 Schulze = *PG* LXXXII, 861). The problem is complicated by the statement in Acts 17.28a which appears in combination with the present citation in Isho'dad.

(d) Lemme* (see above) argued that the evidence for Epimenides as the author is flawed. It rests merely on the assumption that the writer was quoting a Cretan poet. He proposes that the 'prophet' was a member of the Jewish-Christian group opposed to the writer, and that the writer uses the term 'prophet' sarcastically and turns his prophecy against his group (rather

---

[133] *Stromata* 1.59.1f; Dibelius-Conzelmann, 136.

[134] *Comm. in Ep. ad Titum*, p. 707, Vallarsi = *PL* XXVI, 572f.

[135] The two poems are mentioned in Diogenes Laertius 1.111, 112.

[136] Huxley, G. L., *Greek Epic Poetry from Eumelos to Panyassis* (London: Faber and Faber, 1969), 81f.

[137] The quotation is cited by Chrysostom (*PG* LXII, 676f.), but he attributes it to Epimenides.

[138] See also the note on Tit 1.12 in the Euthalian apparatus of the NT in Codex Laura 184: Ἐπιμενίδου Κρητὸς μαντέως χρησμός. κέχρηται δὲ καὶ Καλλίμαχος τῇ χρήσει ἐν τῷ ὑπ᾽ αὐτοῦ ῥηθέντι εἰς τὸν Δία ὕμνῳ.

than against Cretans in general). On this view the term prophet is not applied to a pagan source, and the wholesale condemnation of the Cretans disappears.

We are left with some uncertainty regarding both the origin of the material cited and the source from which the saying of Tit 1.12 derives. But the probability is that the author thought that he was citing Epimenides (Oberlinner, 38f.).

Three separate criticisms are contained in the statement, and it is likely that it was quoted primarily for the sake of the first comment, namely the proverbial deceitfulness of the Cretans, which was widely attested. The second characteristic of the Cretans is stated to be boorish, wild behaviour. Again, this was a long-standing description of Cretan behaviour. The third comment concerns their laziness and gluttony, and this is perhaps to be taken as a reference to the desire of the writer's opponents to make money easily by duping their pupils.

For Κρῆτες (Acts 2.11***) see 1.5 note. The nub of the accusation lies in the first of the three descriptive phrases. ἀεί**, 'always', means here 'from time immemorial'. For ψευστής, 'liar', cf. 1 Tim 1.10**.[139] The basis for the accusation contained in the first phrase is that the Cretans claimed that Zeus was buried on their island and erected a tomb as proof.[140] While Greeks in general could be accused of being liars (Spicq, 610), the reputation of the Cretans for lying was such that κρητίζειν meant 'to lie'.[141]

The second phrase accuses the Cretans of wild behaviour, like animals. κακός, 'evil' (cf. 1 Tim 6.10; 2 Tim 4.14, of deeds), can be used of inanimate things.[142] Used with θηρίον, '[wild] animal',[143] it gives the sense 'beast of prey'. The word was often applied to rude, coarse people.[144]

According to Pliny, Nat. Hist. 8.83, and Plutarch, Mor. 86C, Crete was known for its lack of wild beasts. It is therefore possible that the line is mildly ironic in alluding to the wild and

[139] Cf. ψευδολόγος (1 Tim 4.2); Conzelmann, H., TDNT IX, 594–603.

[140] So Callimachus, Hymn to Zeus 1.1–9; Anth. Pal. 7.275, 746 (in Paton, W. R., The Greek Anthology [Loeb edition], II, 150, 396); Lucian, Timon 6; Lucian, Philopseudes 3; Theodoret III p. 701; Lucan, Pharsalia 8, 872; Philostratus, VS 569; cf. Minucius Felix, Octavian 23.13. For fuller references see Winiarczyk*.

[141] Hesychius; Plutarch, Aem. 23.6; Lysander 20, II p. 343; Zenobius IV 62; I 101; Ovid. Ars. Amat. 1.298: quamvis sit mendax Creta negare potest; Amores 3.10.19.

[142] P. Oxy. 1060.7 (AD VI), ἀπὸ παντὸς κακοῦ ἑρπετοῦ; cf. Grundmann, W., TDNT III, 469–81; Lattke, M., EDNT II, 238f.

[143] Mk 1.13; Acts 11.6; 28.4f; Heb 12.20; Jas 3.7; Rev 6.8 and freq.; cf. Foerster, W., TDNT III, 133–5.

[144] Cl; Philo, Abr. 33; Josephus, Bel. 1.624, 627; Ant. 17.117, 120; Ignatius, Smyr. 4.1.

barbaric behaviour of Crete. Behind this aspect of the Cretan reputation was a history of inter-city wars,[145] piracy[146] and selfishness.[147] Some religious rites local to Crete which sanctioned homosexuality were despised as coarse.[148] All of this made Crete a place well-known for rough and dangerous behaviour.

The third phrase accuses the Cretans of sensuality. γαστήρ**, literally 'stomach' (1 Clement 21.2; cf. Prov 20.27) or 'womb' (as elsewhere in NT), is used in the figurative sense of glutton.[149] ἀργός is 'lazy', here in the sense 'lazy, not wanting to work'.[150] For the combination γαστέρες ἀργαί, 'lazy gluttons', cf. Juvenal, Sat. 4.107, 'venter tardus'. For the thought see Phil 3.19.

Brox, 288, and Merkel, 94, hold that the citation is used purely as a means of discrediting the heresy (cf. Findlay*; Fee, 179), and that it is most unlikely that it would have been used in a genuine letter to a church in Crete, since it would also be regarded as derogatory of the church-members in general.

However, as to the saying's applicability to Crete, it is surely taken for granted that the converted members of the church would be regarded as delivered from the sins of their race, and that the attack is on those who were never converted or have fallen away. The earlier Paul spoke in equally strong terms (Gal 5.12), and the application of his words to the congregations addressed was similar (cf. 3.3; 1 Cor 6.9–11; Gal 5.19; Spicq, 611). For this reason (and possibly for the reason that the saying was so common that it had lost its original barb), there would be little danger of hurting the Cretan fellowship's collective feelings. If the religious lie behind the first part of the saying were invoked (see below), then the most obvious application is to the false teachers and any that would follow them. Nevertheless, the broad 'Cretan' stereotype that has been employed may suggest that the Cretan believers in general are to understand the precarious nature of their situation – that they are liable to fall easily if they are not careful. Spicq (611) warns against taking the verse too literally (cf. the positive evaluation in Plato, Leg. 1.635).

[145] Polybius 6.46.9; Plutarch, Moralia 490B; 761D; Diodorus Siculus 30.13.

[146] Homer, Odyssey 19.173ff.; Anth. Pal. 7.654 (The Greek Anthology II, 349).

[147] Polybius 6.47.5; 8.16.4–7; 33.16.4.

[148] Strabo, 10.4.21; see Plato, Leg. 1.636C–D (cf. 8.836B–C) for pederasty on Crete.

[149] Hesiod, Theog. 26; cf. Lucilius 75M; 3 Macc 7.11; Phil 3.19; Philo, Virt. 182; et al.; Epictetus 1.9.26 [κοιλίαι]; Spicq, 610; Suidas, de Sybaritis: γαστέρες ἦσαν καὶ τρυφηταί; Eusebius, Alexander 15, κακὸν δούλων γένος, γαστὴρ ἅπαντα (both cited by Parry 76, from Wetstein). See TLNT I, 293–5.

[150] It can mean more specifically 'idle, having no work to do' (1 Tim 5.13a, 13b; Mt 20.3, 6); 'useless, doing work badly' (Jas 2.20; 2 Pet 1.8; cf. Mt 12.36***); cf. Delling, G., TDNT I, 452.

If it is taken literally, the first part of the quotation contains a famous logical conundrum – namely, whether the saying of a Cretan who testifies that Cretans always lie is itself a lie. The so-called 'liar's paradox', which has traditionally been linked to this statement attributed to Epimenides, was linked by the ancients to Eubulides, an opponent of Aristotle,[151] and Chrysippus.[152] Heyworth*, 256f., argues that the quotation of Epimenides' dictum in Callimachus (*Hymn to Zeus* 1.8) is employed precisely because of the paradox it intends: 'for Epimenides' dictum to have point it must be spoken by a Cretan; at issue here is whether Zeus is a Cretan or not. If he is, he would lie to us: the debate can never be resolved by asking the god himself for information' (257 n. 6).

In any case, the use of the material here gives no evidence of any awareness of a logical problem. There does not appear to be any ancient evidence that the saying was regarded as paradoxical, or as intending a paradox. Its force seems to be that of a self-admission or self-condemnation, as if somehow a Cretan's own testimony (one of Epimenides' stature, that is) on the matter is weightier than that of a (biased) foreigner. Presumably 'always' was not taken *au pied de la lettre*.[153]

13. ἡ μαρτυρία αὕτη ἐστὶν ἀληθής The author affirms the truth of the quotation. The word μαρτυρία characterizes the saying (αὕτη) as a 'piece of evidence' or testimony given by a witness.[154] For the Johannine phraseology cf. Jn 1.19; 5.32; 19.35, *et al.*; 1 Jn 5.9. Paul uses μαρτύριον in this way (1 Cor 1.6; 2 Cor 1.12; 2 Th 1.10; Holtzmann, 475). ἀληθής** (1.1 note) here has the sense of 'veridical', or 'dependable' (BA). Hanson (1982:177) thinks that the comment is necessary lest 1.12 be thought to be self-refuting, but it is doubtful whether the saying would have been taken this way. The confirmation of the

---

[151] Diogenes Laertius 2.108f.; Aristotle, *Soph. Elench.* 180.b.2–7.
[152] Cicero, *Acad.* 2.96; Plutarch, *Moralia* 1059D–E; see note in Loeb edition, XIII, 666.
[153] Hence the complicated interpretation by Thiselton* (cf. Oberlinner, 39f.) would appear to be unnecessary. He holds that the comment 'This testimony is true' must have been intended ironically, since if taken literally it could endorse either the truth or falsity of the liar's assertion. Consequently, the statement was not intended to give information about the Cretans; rather the demonstration of the illogic of the statement is meant 'to demonstrate the self-defeating ineffectiveness of making truth-claims which are given the lie by conduct which fails to match them'.
[154] For μαρτυρία see also 1 Tim 3.7**; cf. μαρτύριον (1 Tim 2.6; 2 Tim 1.8**); μαρτυρέω (1 Tim 5.10; 6.13**); μαρτύς (1 Tim 5.19; 6.12; 2 Tim 2.2**); cf. Strathmann, H., *TDNT* IV, 474–508.

testimony's truth may simply be a way of applying it directly to the false teachers troubling this church.[155]

δι' ἣν αἰτίαν ἔλεγχε αὐτοὺς ἀποτόμως The force of the conjunctional phrase is: 'because of the character of the Cretans, which we know to be a fact'.[156] The author summons Titus himself (like the overseer, 1.9) to refute strongly those who hold to the false teaching. The force of the adverb ἀποτόμως, 'severely, rigorously' is extremely strong.[157] The sharpness is called forth presumably because the opponents talk nonsense and will not listen to reason.

The objects of the reproof (1.9 note) are somewhat unclear.[158] The difficulty arises in part because v. 14b seems to distinguish these people from a further group who twist the truth. The possibilities suggested are that αὐτούς refers to: (a) [only] the false teachers (Quinn, 109); (b) in a slightly broader sense, the opposition, including both the leaders and adherents to the false teaching (Fee, 180); or (c) [only] the people who are deceived by them (Knight, 299f.). If view (a) is adopted, it would be possible to take vv. 13b-14a to refer to the members of the congregation who are misled by the opponents, with an unexpressed change of subject in the ἵνα clause.

The most probable solution is that the lines between the teachers and their followers are rather fluid, and the writer does not sharply distinguish between them. The reference in vv. 10f. and 15f. must at least include the leaders of the heretical movement. Further, there is nothing in vv. 13f. that requires the change of groups that Knight suggests: 3.10 holds out hope for the successful discipline of the 'factious' person, that is, the one promoting divisive teaching;[159] προσέχοντες and ἀποστρεφομένων τὴν ἀλήθειαν in v. 14 are equally suitable to describe both false teachers and followers (1 Tim 4.1; 2 Tim 4.4). Clearly, the first concern is to put a stop to the false teaching and to deal with the leaders of the movement; but the

---

[155] Quinn, 107–9, elaborates a theory that the author was consciously citing two witnesses (cf. 1 Tim 5.19) – Epimenides and himself – to the character of the opponents, but this has no firm basis in the text.

[156] δι' ἣν αἰτίαν is an example of incorporation of the antecedent in a relative clause; here it probably springs from a hypothetical αἰτία δι' ἥν, i.e. '[it is] a reason on account of which refute them', but in effect it functions as a causal conjunction introducing a main clause (BD § 294⁵; § 456⁴; 2 Tim 1.6, 12; Lk 8.47; Acts 22.24; Heb 2.11***); it is equiv. to διὰ ταύτην τὴν αἰτίαν (Acts 28.20) and corresponds to Latin *quamobrem* (cf. Simpson, 122), but this is hardly a sign of Roman influence on the writer, since the idiom was well enough known in Gk.

[157] 2 Cor 13.10***; Plutarch, *Mor.* 131C; Wis. 5.22; cf. ἀποτομία (Rom 11.22); ἀπότομος (Wis 5.20; 6.5; 11.10; 12.9; 18.15, all with reference to God's severe judgement; Polybius 6.1). Cf. Köster, H., *TDNT* VIII, 106–8.

[158] See the detailed discussion in Holtzmann, 478f.

[159] Cf. the redemptive goal of opposing the false teacher in 2 Tim 2.25–26.

problem in the Cretan church is the whole movement, leaders and followers (the teaching and its results), and the broad application of the Cretan quotation suggests a condemnation not just of the false teachers but also of those whose rejection of the faith fulfils the Epimenidean dictum.

There may be more weight in the observation that the description in v. 10 appears to be of a Jewish group, who are giving false teaching and upsetting the faith of others (cf. v. 14). If v. 12 refers to the same group of opponents, their attitude is explained (in part, at least) by being linked to a well-known trait of Cretan behaviour. But would a description of the Cretans as liars be applicable to the predominantly Jewish group who are the main source of the false teaching? The difficulty is partly solved by the suggestion that the people who twist the truth are non-Christian Jews whose false teaching has influenced the opponents (Parry, 77). Barrett, 131, suggests that the Jewish members of the church had been strongly affected by the surrounding Cretan culture. Again, it seems best to suppose that the opponents and those misled by them and the Cretan and Jewish members of the congregations are not sharply distinguished.

ἵνα ὑγιαίνωσιν ἐν τῇ πίστει The purpose of the sharp reprimand is that the people may be healthy in the faith.[160] ὑγιαίνω (1.9 note) can mean 'to become healthy' and so may imply the possible restoration of the heretical teachers (cf. 3.10; 2 Tim 2.25–26).[161] Hence it is not necessary to take the clause to refer to the avoidance of upsetting the faith of the congregation generally. The reference of τῇ πίστει appears to be either to 'the faith', i.e. the Christian religion (cf. 1 Cor 16.13), or to the 'creed' (Lock, 135); see 1.1 note and **Excursus 4**. Thus the purpose of Titus's rebuke will be achieved if the false teachers and those who have gone after them can be restored to an orthodox understanding of doctrine.

14. μὴ προσέχοντες Ἰουδαϊκοῖς μύθοις καὶ ἐντολαῖς ἀνθρώπων ἀποστρεφομένων τὴν ἀλήθειαν The character of a healthy faith is expressed negatively in terms of not adhering to what is false and thus antithetical to belief in 'the truth'. προσέχω, 'to pay attention to' (1 Tim 1.4; 3.8; 4.1, 13**; *EDNT* III, 169f.), has the implication of being interested in it and even believing in it.

The false doctrine is 'Jewish' in nature and characterised in terms of quality and perhaps also content as 'myths and commands of men'. Ἰουδαϊκός** is 'Jewish' (cf. Ἰουδαϊκῶς,

---

[160] ἐν signifies 'with reference to, in the sphere of' (Holtzmann, 476).
[161] Brox, 289; Merkel, 94; MacDonald 1988:172–4; *pace* Malherbe 1980.

Gal. 2.14).[162] Adjectives in -ικός signify 'related to, bearing the nature of something' and are used of derivation, origin, connection; hence the usage need not be derogatory (Gutbrod, W., *TDNT* III, 382f.). The myths in question circulate among Jews, but are not necessarily Jewish by nature.

μῦθος 'myth' (1 Tim 1.4; 4.7; 2 Tim 4.4; 2 Pet 1.16***; 2 Clement 13.3; μύθευμα, Ignatius, *Mag.* 8.1) is always used in the NT in the plural and in a pejorative sense. The word originally meant 'thought' (cf. Ecclus 20.19, the only occurrence in the LXX, but cf. μυθόλογος, Bar 3.23), then thought expressed as a word or account, especially a fairy story or fable, a fabulous account of gods and demigods, the plot of a drama, etc. It could refer to 'a fairy tale or marvel as distinct from credible history'; 'the mythical form of an idea as distinct from the deeper meaning (the kernel of truth) to be extracted from it'.[163] The pejorative nature of the classification, however, goes beyond simply making the judgement of untruthfulness. Greek and Roman critics denounced certain myths because they had been taken as justification for the practice of perverse and immoral kinds of behaviour.[164] Consequently, the label applied here and elsewhere in the PE may target not just the fallacious interpretation of OT passages but also applications of this material to conduct that contradicted traditional patterns of godly behaviour. Manifestly this term was not used by the opponents themselves (Thiessen 1995:321).

Along with 'myths', the phrase 'commandments of men' (ἄνθρωπος, 2.11; 3.2, 8, 10; 1 Tim 2.2 *et al.*; 2 Tim 2.2 *et al.*) classifies the false teaching as human and therefore inferior to the apostle's teaching which is truth from God (cf. Holtzmann, 477–8; Brown 1963:43). In the NT ἐντολή normally refers to divine commands, but here they are qualified as being human.[165] The phrase is traditional for human teaching that is added to (and thus denies or veers from) the teaching of God. Mk 7.7 (Mt 15.9) and Col 2.22 employ the term which derives from Isa 29.13. The application to ascetic teachings in Col 2.22 is perhaps nearest to this passage's intent. It is possible that the phrase also intends to continue the contrast of plural teachings

---

[162] Cf. Dittenberger, *Or.* 543.16; 586.7 (BA *s.v.*); 2 Macc 8.11 *v.l.*; 13.21; *Ep. Arist.* 22, 24, *et al.*; Philo, *Flacc.* 55; *Leg. Gai.* 157, 159, *et al.*; Josephus, *Ant.* 12.34; 14.228; 20.258, *et al.*; Plutarch, *Mor.* 363D.

[163] Cf. Stählin, G., *TDNT* IV, 762–95 (quotations from 770f.); Bruce, F. F., *NIDNTT* II, 643–47; Balz, H., *EDNT* II, 445; Spicq, 93–8 = *TLNT* II, 528–33; Dibelius-Conzelmann, 16f.

[164] E.g. Plato, *Leg.* 1.636C–D; 12.941B; *Rep.* 2.376E–383C.

[165] 1 Tim 6.14**; cf. Schrenk, G., *TDNT* II, 544–56; Limbeck, M., *EDNT* II, 459f.; *TLNT* II, 11–13.

('myths', 'commandments') with the singular 'truth' in the same
way that Mk 7.7–9 contrasts 'the commandments of men'
(διδάσκοντες διδασκαλίας ἐντάλματα ἀνθρώπων, v. 7b; Mt 15.9)
and 'the commandment of God' (τὴν ἐντολὴν τοῦ θεοῦ, vv. 8–9;
Mt 15.3; Quinn, 112; cf. Col 2.8, 22). The allusion may well be
to actual patterns of behaviour (Col 2.22), especially since v. 15
suggests some sort of ascetic food regulations (cf. 1 Tim 4.3;
Brox, 289).

But the teaching is not simply human. Those who promote it
are actively opposed to God and his teaching. ἀποστρέφομαι is
'to desert' (2 Tim 1.15; Mt 5.42) or 'to turn away from, repudiate,
reject' (2 Tim 4.4**). The thought here with the middle voice is
'to turn [oneself] away from', hence reject 'the truth' (Josephus,
Ant. 2.48; 4.135).[166]

In the light of other references[167] the content of 'Jewish myths'
is almost certainly related to the OT. The association elsewhere
with the term γενεαλογία (3.9; 1 Tim 1.4) helps to establish the
reference. Rabbinic interest in creation stories and genealogies
(halakah and haggadah) is probably the most relevant parallel
(Kittel 1921:49–69; Jeremias, 13; Spicq, 322–3; Gunther
1973:78). Philo's use of the term 'genealogies' as a category
pertaining to the OT history (*Praem.* 1–2; *Mos.* 2.46–7) suggests
that it was not limited to the lists of generations, but referred
to OT biographies of famous personages, from whose sacred
histories spiritual lessons might be drawn (cf. 1QS 3.13–15;
1QapGen). This means that the materials in view may well be OT
or OT-related, but further precision is not possible.[168] There
is nothing in this description to suggest Gnostic doctrines
(so rightly Holtzmann, 476f.; *pace* Hanson, 178; Oberlinner, 43f.;
see 3.9 note).

**15. πάντα καθαρὰ τοῖς καθαροῖς· τοῖς δὲ μεμιαμμένοις καὶ
ἀπίστοις οὐδὲν καθαρόν, ἀλλὰ μεμίανται αὐτῶν καὶ ὁ νοῦς καὶ
ἡ συνείδησις** There is no explicit connection with what precedes.
It is likely that the commandments taught by the opposition
included embargoes on certain things as being unclean, such as
foods (cf. 1 Tim 4.3–5; Holtzmann, 479; Spicq, 612; Brox
289–90). In answer to this, Titus reiterates the apostolic principle
governing purity and impurity. Brox, 290, thinks that this goes
beyond Paul who allowed people to live as they wished, but it

---

[166] Cf. Bertram, G., *TDNT* VII, 719–22; for ἡ ἀλήθεια as the authentic
revelation of God, see 1.1 note.

[167] 3.9 (see note), γενεαλογίας καὶ ... μάχας νομικάς; cf. 1 Tim 1.4; 4.7;
2 Tim 4.4.

[168] Quinn, 244–7, refers to the possibility that the allusion is to speculations
about the genealogies of Jesus.

is more likely that some kind of Jewish teaching is being foisted on Gentile believers here.

The saying has verbal parallels in Lk 11.41 (πάντα καθαρὰ ὑμῖν ἐστιν; cf. Mk. 714f.; Mt 15.11) and Rom 14.20 (πάντα μὲν καθαρά ... ἀλλὰ κακὸν τῷ ἀνθρώπῳ τῷ διὰ προσκόμματος ἐσθίοντι; cf. v. 14: οἶδα καὶ πέπεισμαι ἐν κυρίῳ Ἰησοῦ ὅτι οὐδὲν κοινὸν δι᾽ ἑαυτοῦ, εἰ μὴ τῷ λογιζομέν τι κοινὸν εἶναι, ἐκείνῳ κοινόν; cf. Philo, *Spec.* 3.208; Plotinus, *En.* 3.2.6; Spicq, 612). The verbal contact point consists of πάντα καθαρά: nothing is [ceremonially] defiling. Luke adds 'for you', *sc.* the disciples. Paul implies [for everybody], unless you are eating so as to make someone else fall. But although the tradition is articulated differently in different contexts (cf. Acts 10.14f., 28; 11.8–9; 1 Cor 8.4–6; 10.26; 1 Tim 4.3–5; Ps 24.1), the fundamental assertion is that the 'created' nature of foods makes them all 'clean' in principle.

Clearly, then, the tradition is about ritual purity and abstinence from foods. Applied by Jesus, the effect was to abolish the Mosaic law on foods as well as the traditions of the elders. The application here is a reminder that 'Jewish'-type food rules and regulations have already been overturned as irrelevant (cf. Lock, 135; F. Hauck, *TDNT* III, 424; Schlarb 1990:84). The saying moves between different senses of 'clean'. All foods are ritually clean to people who are spiritually clean and cannot defile them in any way. Unbelievers who are spiritually defiled (although they doubtless thought of themselves as ritually clean) in fact make everything they handle spiritually unclean. Their minds and consciences are so incapable of judging in accordance with God's truth that they sin at every turn.

καθαρός can be used of ritual or spiritual purity.[169] The phrase here classifies 'everything' as 'ritually pure', probably in the sense that it applies the traditional interpretation of Jesus which ruled that moral purity is not related to the superficial nature of things, but determined by the condition of the heart. τοῖς καθαροῖς is the peculiar addition of Titus. Merkel, 95, takes it to mean 'the baptised', but a broader moral sense is intended.[170] In view of the contrast that follows (τοῖς δὲ μεμιαμμένοις καὶ ἀπίστοις), the reference is to 'believers' (cf. Rom 14.20). They have been cleansed by the self-offering of Jesus Christ (2.14; Schlarb 1990:84f.; Oberlinner, 45). The parallel in 1 Tim 4.3 suggests that τοῖς καθαροῖς here is equivalent to τοῖς πιστοῖς καὶ

---

[169] 1.15b, 15c; 1 Tim 1.5; 3.9; 2 Tim 1.3; 2.22**; cf. Hauck, F. and Meyer, R., *TDNT* III, 413–26; Link, H.-G., and Schattenmann, J., *NIDNTT* III, 102–8; Thyen, H., *EDNT* II, 218–20.

[170] Thus καθαρά is primarily ritual whereas τοῖς καθαροῖς is primarily moral (Arichea-Hatton, 278f.).

ἐπεγνωκόσι τὴν ἀλήθειαν there. Further, it takes the thought of purity and defilement to a deeper, spiritual level (as references to νοῦς and συνείδησις suggest), and relates them to acceptance or rejection of 'the truth' and genuine knowledge of God (vv. 14, 16). Because believers have been washed from their sins (cf. Acts 15.9), they are clean and are no longer defiled by anything. The dat. indicates either that all things are clean in the opinion of pure people or that all things are clean for their use (so Bernard, 162).

But what did the false teachers regard as being 'defiled'? Was it foods, including Gentile food, regarded as unholy by some kind of religious rules (cf. Col 2.22; 1 Tim 4.3 and note)? Dibelius-Conzelmann, 137f., and Brox, 37f., argue that Gnostic asceticism is in mind, since marriage is also defiling, but this may be to bring an aspect of asceticism into the Cretan setting that does not belong. The 'Jewish' classification is more suggestive of food rules, but the question remains open.

Using anthropological language more typical of the PE (νοῦς, συνείδησις), the contrast introduced at v. 15b locates the source of defilement and purity within the human being in the same way that the Jesus-tradition did (Mt 15.11, 18–20; Mk 7.15). This is a strong attack. The author is saying that people who subscribe to the 'Jewish' views of the false teachers about 'the pure and impure' are not really believers but are still in their old sins (cf. 2 Pet.; Jude for a similar line).

μιαίνω, 'to defile',[171] describes moral defilement in the NT (1.15b; Jude 8; Heb 12.15; cf. the variant reading Acts 5.38D) and ceremonial defilement (Jn 18.28***).[172] The LXX employs the term for ceremonial impurity,[173] but also in a way that connects defilement to immoral behaviour.[174] Elsewhere the term is applied to corruption of the mind (*T. Iss.* 4.4). It belongs to the word field which includes καθαρίζω (e.g. Lev 13.59), ἀκαθαρσία, and ἀκάθαρτος (Lev 13), which makes it at home in this context, contrasted as it is with the preceding τοῖς καθαροῖς.

Defilement and unbelief are linked. The people who are defiled are unbelievers (cf. Rev 21.8: τοῖς δὲ δειλοῖς καὶ ἀπίστοις καὶ ἐβδελυγμένοις καὶ φονεῦσιν καὶ πόρνοις...). Presumably they thought themselves to be pure (cf. 1.1 6), but the author argues that because they are sinners and unforgiven, they

---

[171] For the form τοῖς μεμιαμμένοις, used for Cl. perf. in -ασμένος, see BD §72; MHT II, 223.
[172] Cf. Hauck, F., *TDNT* IV, 644f.
[173] Lev 5.3; 11.44; 13.3, 11, 59; 20.3; Ezek 9.7; Hag 2.13; Jth 9.8.
[174] Num 35.34; Deut 24.4; Ezek 18.6; Job 31.11 cf. *T. Reub.* 1.6; *T. Levi* 14.6.

themselves are impure. For ἄπιστος (1 Tim 5.8**) as a description of unbelievers, see **Excursus 4**.[175]

οὐδὲν καθαρόν could mean: (a) They regard nothing as clean (Hanson, 178); (b) Nothing can make them clean; (c) They make everything they touch unclean (Fee, 181; Knight, 303; Barrett, 133; Dibelius-Conzelmann, 138). If the doctrines of the opponents are being assessed, view (a) would correspond best to the contrast with v. 15a. If, however, the comment addresses their actual condition, then view (c) might be closer. The point would be that since actual pollution comes from an inner source (which will be explained in the remainder of the sentence) nothing used in any way will be pleasing to God. The view that defilement begins with the person, not with the thing, is already widely expressed.[176] As with the next statement, the comment is probably hyperbolical.

ἀλλὰ μεμίανται αὐτῶν καὶ ὁ νοῦς και ἡ συνείδησις explains the implications of the preceding participle, τοῖς μεμιαμμένοις. Actual purity and impurity are matters which depend upon the spiritual condition of the inner person. ἀλλά is not 'but even', but 'but nothing is clean because...' (Holtzmann, 480). The contrast thus states either that their own moral uncleanness causes them to regard everything as unclean and therefore in need of purification, or that it makes it impossible for them to use anything in a way that pleases God. Either way, the comment locates the problem in the condition of the inner person – it is a comment on their morality.

μεμίανται[177] indicates a condition resulting from prior actions or decisions (cf. the perfect participle τοῖς μεμιαμμένοις in v. 15a).

νοῦς, 'mind',[178] is used in the PE only in reference to the false teachers. In each case an appropriate modifier indicates that the νοῦς has become corrupted and ineffective (1 Tim 6.5:

---

[175] BA cite Dittenberger, *Syll*³ 1168, 33 (320 BC) as an example of a religious use. See also Isa 17.10; Prov 28.25 *v.l.*; Philo, *L.A.* 3.164; *Leg. Gai.* 3; 1 Cor 6.6; 7.15; 10; 27; 14.22; Diognetus 11.2; *M. Poly.* 16.1; Ignatius, *Mag.* 5.2. The word can also mean 'unbelievable', Acts 26.8; cf. ἀπιστέω, 2 Tim 2.13; ἀπιστία, 1 Tim 1.13, which imply rather being 'unfaithful'; cf. Barth, G., *EDNT* I, 121–3.

[176] Hag 2.11–15; cf. Philo, *Spec.* 3.208f.; Seneca, *Ep. Mor.* 98.3: *malus omnia in malum vertit*; Seneca, *de Ben.* 5.12 (cited by Lock, 136); Epictetus. 2.5.6–9: 'Are these externals to be used carelessly? Not at all.... They must be used carefully.... the use which I make of them is either good or bad, and that is under my control'; Lucretius, *De Rer. Nat.* 6.17–34; Horace, *Ep.* 1.2.54.

[177] Perf. pass. third pers. sing. (MHT III, 223). αὐτῶν is emphatic by position. καί...καί..., 'both...and...', links the two parts into a whole complex.

[178] 1 Tim 6.5; 2 Tim 3.8**; see Behm, J., *TDNT* IV, 951–60 (the promise of further treatment of the term *s.v.* ψυχή was not fulfilled); Sand, A., *EDNT* II, 478f.; Bornkamm 1969:29–46; Bultmann 1952: I, 211–20.

διεφθαρμένων ἀνθρώπων τὸν νοῦν; 2 Tim 3.8**: ἄνθρωποι κατεφθαρμένοι τὸν νοῦν). Lips 1979:55 describes it generally as the organ of perception (or knowledge, '*Erkenntnisorgan*'), which functions to apprehend and process the revelation of God (ἡ ἀλήθεια, ἡ πίστις; 1979:55f.; cf. Rom 12.2; Ridderbos 1977:117–19). Jewett is perhaps correct to expand the meaning beyond function to include the patterns of thought that determine the direction of the process (1971:450, 358–90). In 1 Tim 6.5 and 2 Tim 3.8, the νοῦς is aligned with ἡ ἀλήθεια in a way that suggests its corrupt condition prevents apprehension or leads to rejection of 'the truth'. In the present passage, the defiled mind (and conscience) lies at the root of rejection of the truth (v. 14) and the specific ascetic regulations that evolve from this rejection (v. 15a). If the perfect tense of the negative modifiers in each case is to be stressed, it would appear that present ungodly behaviour and resistance to the truth are connected to past decisions to reject the apostolic faith (cf. the combination of tenses in 2 Tim 3.8: οὗτοι ἀνθίστανται τῇ ἀληθείᾳ, ἄνθρωποι κατεφθαρμένοι τὸν νοῦν). For συνείδησις see **Excursus 5**.

16. θεὸν ὁμολογοῦσιν εἰδέναι The description of the heretical leaders becomes direct and explicit at this point. Their situation is paradoxical; their claim to know God is cancelled by behaviour in which they deny him. ὁμολογέω, 'to confess, profess' (1 Tim 6.12**), is used of declaring solemnly one's religious adherence and beliefs.[179] In different language 2 Tim 3.5 emphasises the same contrast of profession and reality. The word thus has a religious nuance and goes beyond simple affirmation (*pace* Holtzmann, 480). The phrase 'knowing God' is used here (cf. 1 Jn 2.4) of absolute, complete knowledge (Jn 7.28–29; 8.55; 11.12, 24; 1 Cor 2.2; cf. Spicq, 613).[180] This claim could be Gnostic (Holtzmann, 480; Merkel, 95; Kelly, 237; Schmithals 1983:116), but Parry (77) points out that Gnostics would have claimed a superior and exceptional knowledge of God. It is thus more likely a Jewish (or judaising) claim to more accurate knowledge of God as demonstrated through vigorous ritualism and a better insight into the Torah (cf. Fee, 182f.; Quinn, 114).

τοῖς δὲ ἔργοις ἀρνοῦνται It is assumed that 'knowing God' is evidenced by righteous behaviour. These people deny God by rejecting his good creation (Dibelius-Conzelmann, 104), i.e. by

[179] Jn 9.22; Acts 23.8; Rom 10.9; cf. Michel, O., *TDNT* V, 199–220; Hofius, O., *EDNT* II, 514–17. For the construction with the infinitive see BD §405.

[180] οἶδα, 'to know', is nearly synonymous with γινώσκω in Koine and in the NT (Gal 4.8–9; cf. Seesemann, H., *TDNT* V, 116–19; Horstmann, A., *EDNT* II, 493f.). For the negative see Gal 4.8; 1 Th 4.4–5 (cf. Jer 10.25), where people do not know God (also 2 Th 1.8; Jn 7.28b; 8.19).

asceticism (Knight, 303). But their confession is hollow and false. The contrast actually functions as a challenge to the claims of the opponents. ἀρνέομαι, 'to deny', describes the opposite of confession.[181] Spicq, 614, suggests the force is 'not to take account of', citing 1 Tim 5.8 and 2 Tim 3.5, for the denial is a matter of what can be inferred from their deeds (cf. Fridrichsen 1942:96). However, the contrast it forms with ὁμολογοῦσιν and the implied failure of their consciences in guiding their conduct (v. 15) suggest that the force is that their corrupt behaviour is a tacit denial of God (the object to be supplied), amounting to apostasy from the faith (Lips 1979:85; Riesenfeld*, 215f.).

ἔργον, 'deed', 'action', 'work', 'task',[182] is used in the PE especially to refer to the outward deeds which demonstrate faith or the lack of it. Thus there is frequent reference to good or noble deeds (2.7, 14; 3.1, 8, 14), but it is argued that people who are not [yet] believers are not able to do righteous acts on which they might depend for favour from God. That the deeds in the present verse are evil in character is plain from the context.

Merkel, 95, maintains that the relation between faith and works assumed by the author corresponds to a later tendency (Jas 2.14f.; 1 Jn 2.3–4; 3.6, 10; 4.7–8) which reflects an inversion of the earlier Pauline model in which works are the result of faith. But if the point is (as it seems to be) that corrupted faith produces substandard works, and that the latter are evidence of corrupted faith, Merkel's conclusion is questionable (cf. Gal 5.19–23; 2 Cor 13.5; Mt 7.15–20; Lk 6.43–45; Ecclus 27.6).

βδελυκτοὶ ὄντες καὶ ἀπειθεῖς καὶ πρὸς πᾶν ἔργον ἀγαθὸν ἀδόκιμοι Three sharp phrases sum up the character of the false teachers in relation to God.[183]

First, they are βδελυκτοί***, 'abominable, detestable'.[184] This word is used in Hellenistic Judaism with reference to persons who pervert moral distinctions,[185] and with reference to things.[186] In the LXX, the βδέλυγμα word-group describes things (or people) which God abominates. The verb is frequent, and especially

---

[181] 2.12; 1 Tim 5.8; 2 Tim 2.12f.; 3.5**; Jn 1.20; Josephus, *Ant.* 6.151; cf. Schlier, H., *TDNT* I, 469–71; Schenk, W., *EDNT* I, 153–5; Fridrichsen 1942:94–6; Riesenfeld*; *TLNT* I, 199–205. Simpson, 102, notes that the use with the acc. of a person is Christian.

[182] 1.16b; 2.7, 14; 3.1, 5, 8, 14; 1 Tim 2.10; 3.1; 5.10a, 10b, 25; 6.18; 2 Tim 1.9; 2.21; 3.17; 4.5, 14, 18**; cf. Bertram, G., *TDNT* II, 635–52; Heiligenthal, R., *EDNT* II, 49–51. See **Excursus 6**.

[183] The linking part. ὄντες is appended loosely (as 3.11; 1 Tim 3.10), but the connection with the subject of ὁμολογοῦσιν is clear.

[184] The word is not Cl. Cf. Foerster, W., *TDNT* I, 598–600.

[185] Prov 17.15; cf. Ecclus 41.5 *v.l.*; 2 Macc 1.27; Philo, *Spec.* 1.323.

[186] *T. Gad* 3.2; 1 Clement 2.6; 30.1; cf. use of verb, Rev 21.8.

βδέλυγμα is used for שֶׁקֶץ.[187] It is the typical description of idols and things which are unclean and therefore from which Israel is to keep separate or be defiled (cf. Lev 11.10–42). Thus OT language for cultic and moral pollution is used to describe these people who, ironically, strive to protect their ritual purity (cf. Dibelius-Conzelmann, 138; Quinn, 115).

Second, they are ἀπειθής, 'disobedient',[188] a word used elsewhere of pagans and to describe life out of which believers have come (3.3; Rom 1.30; Lk 1.17). Here and in 2 Tim 3.2 the term forms a connection between pagan disobedience and the behaviour of the false teachers.

Third, they are ἀδόκιμος, 'rejected',[189] a term applied to those who do not pass the test, hence 'rejected', 'below standard', 'useless', 'worthless'. πρὸς πᾶν ἔργον ἀγαθόν shows that the testing ground is human actions. It is here that the test will be passed or failed. The question being asked is, What fruit has their faith (profession of knowledge of God) produced? The conclusion is that the opponents are useless, unfit for good works.[190] The whole phrase is used positively in 2 Cor 9.8 of good people who have abundant resources [to use] for all kinds of good works (cf. Eph 2.10). Equally, in Tit 3.1 (cf. 1 Tim 5.10) the phrase describes people after their conversion. So the heretical teachers have either gone back to their former state or never been converted. The man of God is fitted for good works, 2 Tim 3.17; cf. 2.21; heresy thus leads to and is characterised by a non-Christian way of life which is useless (cf. Plutarch, *Mor.* 4B: πρὸς πᾶσαν πραγματείαν ἄχρηστον). See further **Excursus 6**. The thought here is manifestly of what is approved and commended by God as being morally good and acceptable.

EXCURSUS 4

The πίστις word-group in the Pastoral Epistles

Bultmann, R., and Weiser, A., *TDNT* VI,174–228; Bultmann 1955:II, 183f.; Easton, 202–4; Kretschmar 1982:115–40; Lips 1979:25–93; Marshall 1984:203–18; Marshall 1996b; Merk 1975:91–102; Michel, O., *NIDNTT* I, 593–606; Quinn 271–6; Towner 1989:121–9.

[187] E.g. Lev 11.10, 12, 13, 20, 23, 41, 42; βδελυκτός translates תּוֹעֵבָה in Prov 17.15.

[188] 3.3; 2 Tim 3.2**; cf. Bultmann, R., *TDNT* VI, 10.

[189] 2 Tim 3.8; Rom 1.28; 1 Cor 9.27; 2 Cor 13.5–7; Heb 6.8***; Prov 25.4; Isa 1.22; Philo, *Conf.* 34, 198; Josephus, *Ap.* 2.236; cf. Grundmann, W., *TDNT* II, 255–60; *TLNT* I, 360f.

[190] πρός is 'with reference to' (cf. BD §239⁶).

The vocabulary of faith plays a central role in the PE. The various items occur a total of 57 times, which is almost three times as high as one would have expected in comparison with the use of the word-group in the earlier epistles of Paul. In addition, negative forms occur four times.

πίστις itself occurs 33 times (1 Tim 19 times; 2 Tim 8 times; Tit 6 times). Five main types of usage can be distinguished.

(a) The usage which predominates is the articular form, ἡ πίστις.[191] In this usage the reference is often to the content of what is believed, 'the Christian faith', i.e., a fixed body of doctrine comparable to 'the truth' (cf. 1 Tim 6.21 with 2 Tim 2.18). The usage could lead to the risk of faith becoming merely assent to certain revealed truths (cf. 1 Tim 3.9, 'the mystery of the faith'), but a more active sense is apparent in 1 Tim 6.12; 2 Tim 2.18. In several cases the thought is of apostasy from 'the faith'. This indicates that the subjective attitude of accepting Christian truth is present, i.e. that the point of using πίστις here is that it refers to that which is to be believed and which one is to continue to believe. Similarly, believers are nourished on the words of faith (1 Tim 4.6), a phrase which indicates that more than an intellectual grasp of truth is involved.

The tendency towards an objectification of 'the faith' has been seen as a 'later' development (cf. Lips 1979:29). The tendency, however, is found earlier in Paul (Gal 1.23: εὐαγγελίζεται τὴν πίστιν; 1 Cor 16.13; 2 Cor 13.5; Phil 1.27). Moreover, in the PE the presence or absence of the article alone may not be a clear indication of the objective or subjective meaning. The usage in 2 Tim 3.10 (cf. Tit 2.2; Quinn, 273) shows that the presence of the article does not automatically demand an objective meaning. The anarthrous usage may on a few occasions refer to 'the content of what is believed' (especially in the phrase ἐν πίστει καὶ ἀληθείᾳ, 1 Tim 2.7, but possibly also in 1 Tim 3.13; 2 Tim 1.13). Consequently, the context and the verb or verbal ideas related to 'faith/the faith' will be better guides to meaning.

(b) Faith is associated with conversion (1 Tim 1.14; 5.12; 2 Tim 1.5; 3.15). On several occasions it is a continual activity or process (1 Tim 2.15; Tit 2.10; 3.15; cf. 1 Tim 3.13; Bultmann, R., TDNT VI, 212) and thus a key element in genuine Christian existence. In all these cases the emphasis lies on the continuance of an attitude which began at conversion, just as in 1 Peter where faith is the continuing attitude of the believer rather than the means of conversion (1 Pet 1.5, 7, 9, 21; 5.9).

---

[191] 1 Tim 1.19; 3.9; 4.1, 6; 5.8, 12 (see note *ad loc.*); 6.10, 12, 21; 2 Tim 1.5; 2.18; 3.8; 4.7; Tit 1.13; 2.2.

(c) The phrase ἐν πίστει expresses the new situation brought about by the coming of faith. In 1 Tim 1.2 and Tit 1.4 'faith' (in Christ) is the sphere or basis of the relationship between Christians (cf. Roloff, 58; Fee, 36). The parallel with Paul's use of 'in Christ' in similar statements (Rom 16.3, 9f.; Gal 1.22; Philem 16, 23) is significant; the phrase expresses the nature of being a Christian in active terms and forms a complement to the Pauline objective description 'in Christ'. The usage confirms that for the writer faith is the key characteristic of the Christian (cf. 1 Tim 1.5 [ἐκ]; 2 Tim 3.15 [διά]; Tit 1.1 [κατά]; ἐν πίστει, 1 Tim 1.2, 4; 2.7, 15; 3.13; 4.12; 2 Tim 1.13; Tit 1.13; 3.15).

(d) Faith is one of the qualities promoted by Christian teaching. The objective (1 Tim 2.7) and subjective (1 Tim 2.15) aspects are hard to disentangle (cf. 1 Tim 1.4; 4.12; 2 Tim 1.13; Tit 1.13).

(e) Faith is characteristically linked with other Christian virtues in lists of between two and nine items (1 Tim 1.5, 14, 19, 2.7, 15; 4.6, 12; 6.11; 2 Tim 1.13; 2.22; 3.10f.; Tit 2.2). Here it may appear to be simply 'another Christian virtue' of no greater importance than its companions. Faith is frequently paired with other virtues and is most frequently linked with love. A similar phenomenon is found in Gal 5.22 where it is part of the fruit of the Spirit, but occupies a subordinate position (cf. how it is not even mentioned in 2 Cor 6.4–10, and that here 'Holy Spirit' occupies an odd, subordinate position). In the lists in the PE faith appears each time except in the lists of qualities of church leaders, and in pairs it is generally the first named quality. It is a fair conclusion that faith is the attitude which determines the presence of the other qualities and is not simply one 'virtue' among many.

The verb πιστεύω (6 times) denotes the action and decision of believing in Christ or God (1 Tim 1.16; 2 Tim 1.12) and in the gospel (1 Tim 3.16) and those whose existence is now determined by that belief (Tit 3.8). In all of these cases the element of trust appears to be present, especially in 2 Tim 1.12.

God's entrustment of the gospel ministry to Paul is expressed by ἐπιστεύθην (1 Tim 1.11; Tit 1.3) in a manner reminiscent of Paul (1 Cor 9.17; Gal 2.7; 1 Th 2.4; cf. Rom 3.2). On the use of πιστόω*** see 2 Tim 3.14 note.

The adjective πιστός (17 times) describes a characteristic of believers nine times.[192] In an active sense, the meaning is 'trusting' (or 'believing') and the object is Christ or God (1 Tim 4.3, 10, 12; 5.16; 6.2a, 2b; Tit 1.6); in some of these cases the usage is tantamount to categorising a person as 'Christian'. The

[192] For the formula πιστὸς ὁ λόγος, see **Excursus 9**. Tit 1.9 refers to the gospel as trustworthy.

thought of active belief, expressed in an appropriate way of life, is present (1 Tim 4.10; cf. 1 Tim 3.11; 6.2; Tit 1.6). The term is thus no formal or empty cypher. In the remainder of the occurrences 'faithfulness' in one sense or another is in view. Female deacons are to be faithful in every respect (1 Tim 3.11). πιστός is used once of Christ (2 Tim 2.13) in a context where his faithfulness is a foil to the possible unfaithfulness of Christians. Twice the term is used with special reference to church leaders who will not falsify the tradition and who will stand up to opposition and heresy (1 Tim 1.12 ; 2 Tim 2.2).

The negative forms in the πίστις word-group characterise existence outside of Christ. ἀπιστία is the state of unbelief (1 Tim 1.13**). ἄπιστος (1 Tim 5.8; Tit 1.15**) and ἀπιστέω (2 Tim 2.13**) view that state of existence from the perspective of behaviour that reflects unbelief.

This survey has shown that the usage is not significantly different from that of Paul. Nevertheless, questions persist regarding the trend in the PE. Various scholars have insisted that a form of 'works righteousness' is to be found in the PE, and that faith no longer has the consistently central position which it occupies in Paul.[193] This verdict flies in the face of the evidence. In 2 Tim 1.9 and Tit 3.4–7 we have pivotal statements which assert that the basis for God's saving action lay not in works done by human beings but in his own gracious purpose. The language reflects tradition (cf. especially Eph 2.8–10), but the way in which it is put together is the work of the author himself. Here grace and works are placed in sharp contrast in an opposition which goes even deeper than the faith/works contrast which is characteristic of Paul's *Hauptbriefe*. It has been claimed that there is no mention of faith in these two passages; Easton, 204, went so far as to claim that for the PE faith is not the basis of justification but its result. But faith is so widely present in the PE that its absence from explicit mention in these passages can hardly be regarded as a sign of its unimportance for the writer. In any case, the absence is only apparent, since there is clear reference to it in 2 Tim 1.12 and Tit 3.8. It is to be explained by the thrust of the passages which is not to set up a contrast between faith and works as ways of receiving God's salvation but rather to demonstrate that God's saving action took place quite independently of what we had done (cf. Rom 9.11f., 16). The total disqualification of works is a clear indicator that the only possible response to grace is faith.

[193] Easton, 103, 203f.; Scott, 177; Lips 1979:72, 281. See, however, Lohse 1986:275.

As in Paul, the need for faith to express itself in a new way of life is taught. For the use of the characteristic phrase 'good works' see **Excursus 6**.

EXCURSUS 5

συνείδησις in the Pastoral Epistles

Bultmann 1952:I, 216–20; Chadwick, H., *RAC* X, 1025–1107; Conzelmann, H., *Grundriss der Theologie des NT* (München: Kaiser, 1968), 204–6; Eckstein, H.-J., *Der Begriff Syneidesis bei Paulus* (Tübingen: Mohr, 1983); Gooch, P. W., '"Conscience" in 1 Corinthians 8 and 10', *NTS* 33 (1987), 244–54; Harris, B., 'ΣΥΝΕΙΔΗΣΙΣ (Conscience) in the Pauline Writings', *WTJ* 24 (1961–2), 173–86; Jewett 1971: 402–46; Lewis, C. S., *Studies in Words* (Cambridge: Cambridge University Press, 1967²), ch. 8; Lips 1979:57–65; Lüdemann, G., *EDNT* III, 301–3; Maurer, C., *TDNT* VII, 898–919; Pierce, C. A., *Conscience in the New Testament* (London: SCM Press, 1955); Roloff, 68–70; Spicq, C., *TLNT* III, 332–6; Stelzenberger, J., *Syneidesis im NT* (Paderborn: Schöningh, 1961); Thrall, M. E., 'The Pauline use of ΣΥΝΕΙΔΗΣΙΣ', *NTS* 14 (1967), 118–25; Towner 1989:154–8. Wolter, M., 'Gewissen II' in *TRE* XIII (1984), 213–18.

1. Conscience in the secular world and the earlier Pauline epistles

συνείδησις occurs six times in the PE, four times of the believer, modified by ἀγαθή or καθαρά (1 Tim 1.5, 19; 3.9; 2 Tim 1.3; cf. Acts 23.1; 24.16), twice of the opponents (1 Tim 4.2; Tit 1.15**). It occurs 14 times elsewhere in the Pauline corpus, and altogether 31 times in the NT (including Jn 8.9). It is virtually absent from the LXX (Wis 17.11; Job 27.6 [verb]; the use in Eccles 10.20 is non-technical; cf. Ecclus 42.18 *v.l.*). The older view that the word in its developed moral sense was a technical term of Stoic philosophy has been refuted by Pierce* and Eckstein* who have shown that the usage is much more widespread. Up to the Christian era conscience is always concerned with the consciousness or lack of consciousness of having committed a negative action. Only from the second century AD onwards do we find the 'good conscience' in secular Greek writings, although it can be traced earlier in Philo and Josephus[194] as well as in Latin literature.[195] Over against Pierce* who argued that the effect of conscience was to cause inward pain, Eckstein* claims that its effect is not so much to *cause pain* as rather to *act as a judge* on individual human actions.

---

[194] See Philo, *Praem.* 79–84; *Spec.* 1.203; Josephus, *Bel.* 2.582. These examples use σύνοιδα and συνειδός. See further Lips 1979:61–4, but his examples are all later.

[195] *Ex bona conscientia*, Seneca, *Ep.* 23.7 (cited by Roloff, 68). Cf. *bonae tantum conscientiae pretio ducebatur* (Tacitus, *Agric.* 1.2).

The term may have entered the vocabulary of the NT through Pauline developments in anthropology.[196] According to Eckstein*, 312, in general conscience in Paul is an aspect of human beings, whether Jews, Christians or Gentiles, which has the function of controlling, assessing and bringing to consciousness the conduct of oneself or of other people according to given and recognised norms (cf. Rom 2.13; 9.1; 13.5; 1 Cor 8.7, 10, 12; 10. 25, 27, 28, 29 [twice]; 2 Cor 1.12; 4.2; 5.11). It tends to be a neutral anthropological mechanism; when Paul qualifies it, he does so less directly with an adverbial participle construction (ἡ συνείδησις αὐτῶν ἀσθενὴς οὖσα μολύνεται, 1 Cor 8.7; cf. 8.10), or present participle (αὐτῶν τὴν συνείδησιν ἀσθενοῦσαν, 1 Cor 8.12). It is thus not in itself the source of moral norms but acts in accordance with given norms, and it is common to all people. For Paul the source of such norms is the mind (νοῦς). Consequently, the conscience is not the voice of God nor the mediator of revelation. It is not, as Philo might have it, the voice of God (*Det.* 145f.; *Post.* 59; Maurer, C., *TDNT* VII, 911–13), nor does Paul connect it explicitly with God. Nor is it the source of guidance for conduct.[197] Rather it acts as the judge on individual acts. Although in pre-Christian Greek the concept of the bad conscience predominates, in Paul we also find that conscience can establish his freedom from guilt, and therefore it is not a basically negative judge on human behaviour. Here Eckstein offers a correction to the rather one-sided position of Pierce. He sums up: 'For Paul conscience is a neutral, anthropological judge in human beings which assesses their conduct objectively according to given norms and makes them aware of it correspondingly, whether by criticising it or affirming it, and human beings stand in a relationship of being answerable to it' (Eckstein*, 314).

2. The usage in the Pastoral Epistles

The basis for the use in the PE is disputed. The problem is whether there is development of the earlier Paul's use[198] or a more distinct divergence from Pauline thought.[199]

The term certainly continues to be an anthropological idea in the PE, and clearly functions in relation to norms and behaviour.

---

[196] Cf. Maurer, C., *TDNT* VII, 914; Pierce*; Stelzenberger*, 51–95; Jewett*, 421–46.

[197] Contrast Thrall*, 118–25, who equates the function of conscience among the Gentiles with that of the law among Jews.

[198] Maurer, C., *TDNT* VII, 918; Trummer 1978:236.

[109] Dibelius-Conzelmann, 20; Wilson 1979:52; Roloff, 68–70; cf. also Bultmann 1952:I, 216–20; Thrall*, 118–25.

However, the qualification of the term in each occurrence (good, clean, defiled, seared) and its relation to acceptance or rejection of the faith, shows that it is viewed from a theological perspective and that the interest is in its condition, which is the result of belief or unbelief. Thus the use is not at all neutral, as in the earlier Paul; rather, in the setting of conflict, the writer views behaviour according to the positive possibilities and negative limits which the condition of the conscience permits (cf. Roloff 69). The opponents' consciences are defiled (μεμίανται, Tit 1.15[200]) and seared (κεκαυστηριασμένων [perf. pass.], 1 Tim 4.3).[201] In each case, the context indicates that the condition of the conscience results in some way from rejection of the apostolic faith (1.13, ἵνα ὑγιαίνωσιν ἐν τῇ πίστει; 1.14, ἀποστρεφομένων τὴν ἀλήθειαν; 1 Tim 4.1, ἀποστήσονταί τινες τῆς πίστεως) and that one outworking of this is false teaching and related, extreme behaviour patterns (cf. Lips 1979:58f.). Conversely, the condition of the genuine believer's συνείδησις, described as ἀγαθή (1 Tim 1.5, 19; cf. Acts 23.1; Heb 13.18; 1 Pet 3.16) and καθαρά (1 Tim 3.9; 2 Tim 1.3), is closely related to adherence to the sound teaching of the apostolic faith, which issues in love and service.

Dibelius-Conzelmann, 18–20, comment that in Paul conscience is a general human phenomenon which judges and convicts past wrongdoing (so also in Jn 8.9; Heb 9.14; [10.22]). But they claim that this judging and convicting activity is different from what is expressed by the fixed formula 'good conscience'; this phrase is found only in literature which 'expresses a thought world both more strongly Hellenistic and closer to the vernacular, especially in those instances where one can see the influence of the Hellenistic synagogue and its language'. They further state that the opposite to a good conscience in the PE is not a 'weak' one as in Paul but an 'evil' one. Further, they allege that 'The term here implies the necessarily binding moral alternative, whereas in Paul it expresses the critical possibility of freedom in relation to the alternatives posed.' They then go on to claim that the 'good conscience' 'belongs among the qualities which characterize "Christian good citizenship"'. In a world which has no end in sight and where Christians must come to terms with life in society, 'this view must work out lasting norms for behaviour'. Finally, the possession of a good conscience is 'the best pillow' for enjoying a peaceful Christian life. The whole phenomenon 'is a sign of the transformation of an unbroken eschatological understanding of the world into a view which must reckon with

---

[200] Cf. Dionysius Halicarnassensis, *De Thuc.* 8: μηδὲ μιαίνειν τὴν αὐτοῦ συνείδησιν (Spicq, 613).

[201] For the understanding of this term see note *ad loc.*

the fact that, for the time being, the world is going to remain as it is (and that the Christians are to exist within it)'. No doubt they would be able to back up this interpretation by a contrast with 1 Cor 7.29–31:

> What I mean, brothers, is that the time is short. From now on those who have wives should live as if they had none; those who mourn, as if they did not; those who are happy, as if they were not; those who buy something, as if it were not theirs to keep; those who use the things of the world, as if not engrossed in them. For this world in its present form is passing away.

Although this view is presented as a single comprehensive summing up of what conscience means in the PE, it raises in fact several distinct problems.

The issues may be sharpened by bringing in the verdict of Roloff. His argument is structured around the proposition that the concept of conscience in the PE cannot be seen as a development from the Pauline understanding in view of two deep-rooted differences. He comments:

> 1. The PE speak of a good conscience or of a pure conscience, in the sense of a reality or a positively given possibility, whilst the negative opposing concept (a bad or impure conscience) is significantly missing. The conscience is consequently here not as in Paul the authority that judges human conduct on the basis of previously given norms, but a state of consciousness which presents itself as the result of behaviour that corresponds with previously given norms. This talk of a good conscience stands in a clear tradition-historical continuity with the OT motif of a καθαρὰ καρδία.
> 2. According to this the conscience is not a neutral anthropological entity for the PE but is theologically qualified through God's action. In this it corresponds with πίστις with which it is closely tied up in 1.19: Faith and good conscience appear here as the two characteristics of Christian existence: faith signifies holding fast to the true preaching and teaching, whereas the good conscience signifies correspondence with the previously given norms for conduct (cf. 3.9; 2 Tim 1.3). But this correspondence to existing norms is not the ontological basis but only the cognitive basis for the presence of the good conscience. The PE are controlled by a basis in baptismal theology according to which the good conscience is the fruit of the end-time renewal of the heart given through the Spirit in baptism. The difference from Paul, therefore, consists primarily in the anthropological terminology, not however in

the basic direction of the theological basis. Somewhat simplifying we can say: For the PE the good or pure conscience stands in the place which is taken in Paul by the νοῦς renewed in the end-time by the Spirit or the heart that is cleansed by the action of God. In no way is the good conscience in the PE the expression of an uncritical self-satisfied moralism; to assign it to the qualities which characterise bourgeois Christianity is an inappropriate simplification. (Roloff, 69f.; my translation)

The points raised by these scholars can be summed up as follows:

(a) There is a *significant difference* in the understanding of conscience from that which we find in Paul. For Roloff the shift is of such a kind that we cannot regard it as a simple development from the Pauline view; it is rather the development of a different set of theological ideas.[202] For Dibelius in particular, the understanding of conscience is part of his general theory of a serious deterioration in the dynamic understanding of Christianity that he finds in the PE in comparison with Paul himself. It is linked to the collapse of a living belief in the nearness of the parousia.

(b) The function of conscience is now seen as *prescribing conduct* rather than judging (mainly) past conduct. It corresponds more to the mind in Paul than to the conscience.

(c) Conscience is more a *continuous feeling* rather than an occasional judgement. The PE speak of a good conscience, i.e. a continuing feeling that one is not guilty but rather is pleasing God, instead of the conscience as a seat of judgement which actively condemns or commends specific actions.

(d) Conscience operates *on the basis of fixed norms* rather than acting in some kind of freedom.

(e) For Dibelius the norms for conscience are now developed *on the basis of worldly standards* rather than being based on an eschatological view of the world. Instead of criticising the world, it goes along with its highest standards.

(f) Again for Dibelius the *idea of satisfaction* that one has done one's duty and can go to bed at peace with God and the world has come in. However, Roloff does not go along with this or the previous judgement.

3. Reassessing the evidence

(a) A brief summary of the Pauline material is necessary. Bultmann argued that for Paul conscience involves a knowledge that there is a difference between right and wrong and it judges us for doing what is wrong. Its knowledge 'applies to that which

---

[202] This hypothesis, if correct, would of course exclude any possibility that the PE were later works by Paul himself.

is demanded of man' and the decisive thing is that it knows 'that there is such a thing [sc. a divine demand] at all', for it may err regarding the content of the demand (Bultmann 1952, I, 216–20, citation from 218). It is thus subject to a transcendent source of authority. Hence the question arises as to how conscience is aware of the demands placed upon us. H. Conzelmann comments that for Paul conscience does not set its own norms; 'the content is determined by God's command, i.e. by revelation and not by an autonomous moral code. The conscience is not the source of revelation but the understanding of the concrete requirements of God' (Conzelmann 1968:204). Conscience is common to all people, including non-Christians (Rom 2.15). Thus for Paul conscience acts on the basis of a prior knowledge of God's demands rather than in what Dibelius called 'critical freedom'.

Paul can refer to conscience when he wants to back up something that he has said or done which is right. When he makes a statement that might be challenged as false, he insists that his conscience bears witness in the Holy Spirit that he is telling the truth (Rom 9.1) or his conscience assures him that he has acted in a holy and sincere manner (2 Cor 1.12); in the same way he feels that he can submit himself to the test of everybody's conscience in the church at Corinth that he has not acted deceitfully but has faithfully proclaimed the word of God (2 Cor 4.2; cf. 5.11). The same construction is used in Rom 2.15 where Paul talks of Gentiles who do the works of the law and show the work of the law written in their hearts – in their case their conscience bears witness to them and their conflicting thoughts accuse or even defend them. Here we see clearly that conscience bears witness in accusation or defence on the basis of obedience or disobedience to a knowledge of God's law which is independent of knowledge of the Jewish Torah. Thus conscience does not so much prescribe conduct as evaluate conduct in accordance with given norms.

In Rom 13.5 we have a somewhat stark reference to the Christian duty of submission to rulers 'not only because of the wrath but also because of conscience'. The point is that we should obey not merely because we shall suffer the penalty imposed by the ruler as the agent of God in maintaining justice if we do not do so, but much rather because of conscience. We shall be condemned by our conscience if we do not obey. Paul assumes that conscience will judge in accordance with the principle that rulers must be obeyed, but he does not say whether conscience formulates this principle or is already aware of it. In fact, of course, Paul has already formulated the principles on which conscience operates in this regard.

Finally, in 1 Cor 8–10 we have the discussion of people whose consciences are active in respect of the eating of food sacrificed to idols. The important point which emerges here is that different people's consciences may react in different ways to eating certain types of food. I need not be subject to another person's conscience (1 Cor 10.25–29). Further, some people have a 'weak' conscience (1 Cor 8.7–12). It is hard to distinguish here between the prescriptive and the judging activities of conscience.[203] It should be noted incidentally that there is no suggestion that good and weak consciences are being contrasted, not least because Paul does not use the term 'good conscience' in this context. The weak conscience is to be respected, whereas the evil conscience is something to be condemned.

It seems, then, that for Paul conscience is so bound up with existing norms held by its bearer that there is no question of freedom for the bearer in relation to his own conscience, even if other people's perceptions vary. In other words, conscience is prescriptive in the sense that for the individual its authority is absolute. In effect, conscience says to a person: if that is what you consider to be right, then you are condemned if you do not do it, because you are deciding to do what is not right – even if your perception of what is right is mistaken. Paul commends following conscience in that to do so is to recognise and follow moral principles, even if the principles may be somewhat mistaken.

(b) In the PE the terminology is somewhat different, but it is hard to see any real difference so far as prescriptiveness is concerned. On the contrary, conscience is closely tied to faith (1 Tim 1.5, 19; 3.9; cf. Tit 1.15): it is the knowledge of the faith which forms the basis for the judgements of conscience. Just as conscience is bound to given judgements in Paul, so too in the PE. Moreover, we find that the mind is also part of the psychological framework of the PE. The false teachers are corrupt in their minds (1 Tim 6.5; 2 Tim 3.8) and, most importantly, in Tit 1.15 both the minds and the consciences of the heretics are polluted. This shows that a clear distinction exists between these two organs, and we may suspect that the mind is connected with the knowledge of God and his will which forms the basis for the operation of conscience (Towner 1989:158). Conscience in the PE is thus not the equivalent of the 'mind' in Paul (Rom 12.2). It appears to operate just as much on given principles, and there is the same close connection with the mind or heart or Christian

---

[203] Gooch* suggests that Paul is thinking here of a 'minimal and negative subjective sense' – the weak have 'bad feelings', so that the problem of conflict of consciences does not really arise.

teaching which can lead to the conscience being thought of loosely as the source of moral judgement.

Further, if we ask whether it is the case that conscience is a judge in Paul and a continuing consciousness of not having done wrong in the PE, it can be replied that the line between the two is very thin in 2 Cor 1.12, which expresses a continuing verdict and consciousness; the same is true of Rom 9.1, which is about Paul's standing attitude to his people. Certainly it is a judge on specific actions in 1 Cor 8–10, but this passage deals with a different kind of topic; it is very much concerned with a specific situation, and therefore the judgement on specific actions is to the fore.

We may conclude that there is no great difference between the accepted letters of Paul and the PE as regards the place of moral norms in relation to conscience and as regards the idea of conscience as expressing a continuing state of approval or lack of disapproval of one's actions.

(c) The major problem is the development of the use of attributes with conscience, such as a 'clean conscience'. For Roloff this expression is based on the 'clean heart' in Ps 51.10 (LXX 12) and has been developed in the baptismal theology reflected in Heb 10.22 and 1 Pet 3.21. In Hebrews believers are people whose hearts have been sprinkled from an evil conscience and their bodies washed with clean water, while in 1 Peter baptism is a request to God for a good conscience (or a pledge from a good conscience). Curiously, Roloff makes no reference to Heb 9.14 where the blood of Christ cleanses the conscience from dead works to serve the living God.

The concept of a clean heart is found in 1 Tim 1.5; 2 Tim 2.22. The various interpretations of this phrase include: (i) a heart that has been forgiven and cleansed from guilt at conversion on the basis of the death of Christ; (ii) a heart that has been purified from evil thoughts and wrong ideas; (iii) a heart that is not conscious of guilt. 'Cleansed from past sin and wholeheartedly directed towards God' is F. Hauck's summary (*TDNT* III, 425). These motifs cannot be sharply separated from one another. In 1 Tim 1.5 a good heart appears to be one that has been cleansed from sin and is therefore a source of good motives; it is closely linked to a good conscience which also appears to be one that is in good working order. Similarly in 2 Tim 2.22 the good heart is the cleansed heart that is associated with calling on the Lord in prayer and is the source of right thoughts. It is not necessarily the same thing as a conscience that does not condemn, although they are linked.

We have, then, the concept of heart and conscience being cleansed from sin at conversion as part of the total renewal of

the personality reflected in Tit 3.5. If this is not said explicitly
about the conscience in Paul, it is at least strongly implied by
the reference to the renewal of the mind in Rom 12.2.

Further, it is significant that the writer does distinguish
between the heart and the conscience in 1 Tim 1.5 where they
stand in parallel. When he refers to those who call on the Lord
from a clean heart in 2 Tim 2.22 he is echoing biblical language.
There is no reason to suppose that he could equally well have
used 'conscience' here, as if the two words were synonymous.
This speaks against the view that we have a simple development
from the idea of a 'clean heart' to a 'clean conscience'. Rather
we have what I would call a cross-fertilisation of related ideas.
The concept of conscience has not unnaturally acquired the
concept of goodness/cleanness from the concept of the good/
clean heart. But this does not mean that the use of conscience
here should be disassociated from the Pauline usage. It was a
natural development.

From this it follows that the concept of a good conscience
may include the motif that it is in good working order rather
than simply that it approves of all that I do. Arichea-Hatton,
73, make a careful distinction: 'A good conscience enables a
person to make good judgement. A clear conscience, on the other
hand, is possessed by people who have the conviction that they
have done nothing wrong, and whose actions are not motivated
by selfish desires.' The problem in the PE is opponents whose
consciences do not work at all or are not heeded. It is not that
they have bad consciences which condemn them. It is rather that
they have given up obeying them, and so they fail to register.
The absence of the phrase 'bad conscience' is said by Roloff
to be 'significant'. On the contrary, the problem in the PE is
manifestly that of people whose conscience is a stage worse than
'bad' in that it has been seared and has ceased to operate at all.

It has to be admitted that in other literature a good conscience
appears to be the same as a clean conscience, one that is free
from passing blame because the person has not done wrong. So
Paul talks of his good conscience in Acts 23.1 and makes it his
aim to have a conscience free of offence in Acts 24.16, and the
author of Hebrews says that he and his companions have a good
(καλός) conscience, as they endeavour to live properly in every
way (Heb 13.16).

What we have in the PE would appear to be a development
of this motif. On the one hand, it is essential that the conscience
works in accordance with the norms it gains from the mind or
from faith. The conscience is useless if it has been defiled, so
that it gives wrong judgements, or seared, so that it does not

operate at all. Hence the idea of being in good working order, operating on true norms, is essential to the concept of a good conscience. On the other hand, the believer's aim is that this good conscience will also be 'clean' in that it does not condemn for an inconsistency between faith and action. Both motifs are present, but the emphasis may well shift to and fro between them.

(d) In all of this there is no basis for seeing any deterioration from the teaching of Paul. To be sure, Dibelius insists that he is not making a value judgement when he insists on recognising a difference in the teaching of the PE; rather there was a general change in the church's situation which meant that 'generally acceptable ethical standards' had to be formulated. Even so, it is impossible to avoid a certain pejorative tone in his characterisation of the teaching about conscience, including the suggestion that one can go peacefully to bed without worrying and live 'a peaceful life in blessedness and respectability'. Other scholars have not assented to this view. Roloff is sceptical of Dibelius' view that there is a somewhat debased understanding of conscience and the Christian life in general in the PE. Similarly, C. Maurer comments: 'At this point, then, the Pastorals are not the product of Christian respectability; they are a deliberate echo of the Pauline message of justification out of which they grew' (*TDNT* VII, 918). We should, in other words, trace the origin of the renewed conscience to that renewal by the Holy Spirit of which Tit 3.5 speaks so eloquently.

(e) A final question concerns how the PE see the source of the norms for conscience. The answer lies in such terms as 'the word', 'the teaching', and 'the gospel' which lay down a basis for Christian living in the revelation in Christ and through the apostles. A key verse here is Tit 2.12 which speaks of the educative role of the saving revelation of God: it teaches us to deny impiety and worldly lusts and to live soberly, righteously and piously in this age'. Here we have the clear evidence that the writer saw a very sharp distinction between the ways of life typical of the surrounding world and the way demanded of believers. He had to battle against the asceticism of his opponents who regarded foods and marriage as unclean and against the sinful desires and actions of the non-Christians, and he found the answer in the revelation of divine grace in Christ. P. Towner 1989:156 makes the important point that in each case the failure of conscience to operate was due to 'repudiation of the apostolic faith' and that, correspondingly, conscience 'stands on the line connecting correct belief and corresponding conduct'.

Whether defiled and ineffective or good and clean, the conscience functions to direct, evaluate and control behaviour along lines set by given norms. The connections suggest that correct, morally good decisions leading to godly conduct require acceptance of the apostolic faith ('the truth', 'the sound teaching', etc.), which forms the knowledge and thought patterns of the mind. Rejection of the truth is related to the ineffective conscience, which cannot translate corrupt doctrine into godly conduct.

EXCURSUS 6

Goodness and good works in the Pastoral Epistles

Grundmann, W., *TDNT* I, 10–18; Baumgarten, J., EDNT I, 5–7; Lock, 22f. Marshall 1984:203–18; Grundmann, W., and Bertram, G., *TDNT* III, 536–56; Beyreuther, E., *NIDNTT* II, 102–5; Wanke, J., *EDNT* II, 244f.; White, 101.

In Greek thought the concept of the καλόν refers to what is perfectly good in the moral sphere. The word can be used of what is organically sound, beautiful and morally good, and comes to mean that which has order and symmetry. It is obviously closely associated with ἀγαθός. However, in the LXX the concept of beauty is not important, and καλός is used of what is morally good. Paul uses καλός in the same sense as ἀγαθός.

καλός occurs twenty-four times in the PE, seven times of good works (1 Tim 5.10, 25; 6.18; Tit 2.7, 14; 3.8a, 14), once of a 'good work' (sing. Tit 3.1), and then of things that are pleasing to people (Tit 3.8b) or God (1 Tim 2.3). It can be a general term of approbation (1 Tim 1.8; 3.7, 13; 4.4, 6a; 6.19; 2 Tim 2.3), but it also develops a kind of technical sense to refer to something specifically Christian ('the good teaching', 1 Tim 4.6b; 'the good warfare', 1.18; 'the good fight of faith', 1 Tim 6.12a; 2 Tim 4.7; 'the good confession', 1 Tim 6.12b, 13; 'the good deposit', 2 Tim 1.14**).

By contrast ἀγαθός is found only ten times in the PE (1 Tim 1.5, 19; 2.10; 5.10; 2 Tim 2.21; 3.17; Tit 1.16; 2.5, 10; 3.1**). It is used six times of good work(s) (πᾶν ἔργον ἀγαθόν, 1 Tim 5.10; 2 Tim 2.21; 3.17; Tit 1.16; 3.1; ἔργα ἀγαθά, 1 Tim 2.10), twice of a good conscience (1 Tim 1.5, 19), once of the character of younger women (Tit 2.5) and once of faith (Tit 2.10).

The preponderance of καλός over ἀγαθός is also found in Mt; Mk; Jn; and Heb. Grundmann*, 550, suggests that apart from the phrase καλὰ ἔργα, which comes from Hellenistic Judaism, 'the term derives from the popular usage influenced by Stoic ethics, and that it bears much the same sense as we found in Plutarch'. It thus expresses 'a Hellenistic sense of values' (Beyreuther*, 104), but Grundmann notes that the content of the term is derived from the gospel.

The two terms are, to be sure, largely synonymous. Both are grading terms used of persons, things and conduct. It may be helpful to list the definitions of usage of the two words given by LN. ἀγαθός (a) expresses 'positive moral qualities of the most general nature'; (b) pertains 'to having the proper characteristics or performing the expected function in a fully satisfactory way'; (c) pertains 'to being generous, with the implication of its relationship to goodness' (LN §§ 88.1; 65.20; 57.110). καλός has a wider, overlapping field of meaning. It pertains (a) 'to a positive moral quality, with the implication of being favourably valued'; (b) 'to having acceptable characteristics or functioning in an agreeable manner, often with the focus on outward form or appearance'; (c) 'to providing some special or superior benefit'; (d) 'to being fitting and at the same time probably good'; (e) 'to being beautiful, often with the implication of appropriateness'; (f) 'to having high status, with the possible implication of its attractiveness' (LN §§ 88.4; 65.22; 65.43; 66.2; 79.9; 87.25). According to this analysis ἀγαθός is more expressive simply of inherent goodness and appropriateness and implies a strongly positive feeling of satisfaction, whereas καλός often has the additional element of outward attractiveness and beauty.[204] καλός may thus carry the nuance of 'beautiful' in that the good deeds done by believers are seen as 'attractive'.

The concept of 'good work(s)' plays an important role in the description of the Christian life in the PE. Apart from other usages (1.16a; 3.5; 2 Tim 1.9; 4.14) ἔργον occurs fourteen times in singular and plural expressions, with either ἀγαθόν or καλόν (see above). In the Pauline corpus the singular ἔργον ἀγαθόν occurs most often (Rom 2.7; 13.3; 2 Cor 9.8; Phil 1.6; Col 1.10; 2 Th 2.17). But the plural does occur in Eph 2.10 (cf. Acts 9.36). The idea of 'every good work' (πᾶς with ἀγαθόν) generalises the singular to the point that it approaches a habitual activity. This appears in 2 Cor 9.8; Col 1.10 and 2 Th 2.17. The use of καλόν with ἔργον is unattested in the earlier Paul, but appears in the Synoptic tradition in plural form (Mt 5.16; 26.10; Mk 14.6; cf. Jn 10.32–33). Michel (1948:86) suggested that the Synoptic tradition may lie behind the καλόν configuration in the PE.

'Good works' in the earlier Paul describes the activity of the believer and the result of salvation.[205] The concept in the PE is cast in the Pauline mould, depicting activities or a life of service that results from the experience of conversion and regeneration.

---

[204] See Spicq, 676–84, for a detailed excursus on beauty and its place in Christian morality. The aesthetic element in the word is not to be denied, but it is rather overemphasised by Spicq.

[205] Cf. Bertram, G., *TDNT* II, 652; III, 549; Grundmann, W., *TDNT* I, 16.

The Christ-event is linked closely with 'good works'. Tit 2.14 declares that the self-offering of Christ was designed to create a people zealous for good works. The thought is similar to Eph 2.10, which describes the goal of salvation in terms of a life characterized by 'good works'.[206] The linkage between Christ-event and life-style established in 2.14 and 3.3–7 forms the basis for the implicit command issued in 3.8 – ἵνα φροντίζωσιν καλῶν ἔργων – which applies to those who have placed their faith in God (προΐστασθαι οἱ πεπιστευκότες θεῷ). In 1 Tim 2.10 a similar connection is expressed by linking 'good works' to one's profession to be a genuine Christian (θεοσέβεια = εὐσέβεια; see **Excursus 1**).

The concept of 'good works' is theologically determined. It is a way of characterising the whole of the Christian life as a work of God's grace (the Christ-event) with visible results, the fruit produced by genuine faith (cf. Schwarz 1983:142–5). They manifest themselves in a variety of specific services done for others (1 Tim 5.10, rearing children, showing hospitality, humbly serving other believers; Tit 3.14, meeting practical needs; 1 Tim 6.18, sharing one's wealth).

According to J. Baumgarten, good works have become 'autonomous' in the PE and are 'viewed as the mark of being a good Christian' (*EDNT* I, 7). J. Wanke goes further in asserting that the PE have moved close to Stoic ethics so that 'good works ... refers primarily to good social conduct on the part of Christians'; he claims that the frequency of use, especially as a qualifying adj. (12 times), which is not found in Paul, suggests an altered view of Christianity incorporating the idea of ' "reasonable" and bourgeois conduct' (*EDNT* II, 245). However, while the motif of maintaining a good reputation among people outside the church is present, here and elsewhere the stress is more on the fact that certain things are good because they are ordained or approved by God. To be sure, Wanke concedes that ethical conduct continues to be a consequence of divine grace, and the paraenesis is tied to the gospel. Nevertheless, it may be queried whether this assessment is a basis for asserting that the PE show 'an altered understanding of Christianity'. Concern for the effect of actions on outsiders is found already in Paul (Rom 12.17; 13.1–7; 1 Th 4.12), and he stresses the importance of good works (2 Cor 9.8; Eph 2.10; Col 1.10; 2 Th 2.17) which would be seen as good by outsiders (Rom 13.3; cf. 1 Pet 2.12). It is undeniable that there is a greater stress on good works in the PE, but this is no basis for claiming an 'altered understanding of Christianity'. The difference from Paul is one of degree rather than of kind.

---

[206] Cf. Schwarz 1983:143; Lips 1979:75.

IIA. TEACHING FOR THE CHURCH – HOW BELIEVERS ARE TO RELATE TO ONE ANOTHER (2.1–15)

Padgett, A., 'The Pauline Rationale for Submission: Biblical Feminism and the *hina* Clauses of Titus 2.1–10', *EvQ* 59 (1987), 39–52; Weiser, A., 'Titus 2 als Gemeindeparänese', in Merklein, H. (ed.), *Neues Testament und Ethik. Festschrift für R. Schnackenburg* (Freiburg: Herder, 1989), 397–414.

The whole of 2.1 to 3.11 forms a single instructional unit that may be broken into two sections: 2.1–15; 3.1–11.

2.1–10 addresses the lives of believers according to their social position. The material is concerned not so much with how people should believe in the church but rather with their behaviour in the home and society at large (cf. Johnson, 232). 2.11–14 provides the theological support and grounds for the paraenesis, and is followed by v. 15 which connects the inserted piece of doctrine into the flow of the letter.

3.1–2 and 8–11 take up the Christian's relation to the State and the matter of false teachers respectively; the former instructions seem to be based on traditional material, which circulated independently (cf. Rom 13.1–7) or was attached (perhaps loosely) to one line in the development of the household code paraenesis (cf. 1 Pet 2.13–3.12) to apply it to the Cretan community (see below). In the midst of this last teaching section is another piece of theology (3.3–7), which grounds the practical teaching in a way similar to 2.11–14.

The whole section (2.1–3.11) is not so much teaching (*Lehre*) but rather information, advice, and instruction (*Belehrung*) in the form of instructions about what Titus is to teach others and how he himself is to be an example to them; the material is directed to the church leader, who will then mediate it to the groups (cf. Hasler, 91). Through Titus church leaders are addressed.

At the beginning of the section (2.1) the author intentionally introduces a sharp contrast with the opponents and turns his attention to the believers in the community. The progression from discussing how heretics behave to how Christians/leaders should behave is common in the PE (1 Tim 6.11; 2 Tim 2.1; 3.10, 14; 4.5; cf. Brox, 292). At some points the instructions intentionally contrast Christian qualities with the failings of the opponents. Genuine Christian behaviour, that which results from conversion (2.11–14; 3.3–7; cf. Wolter 1988:130–5; Weiser*, 407), is presented as the antithesis to the behaviour characteristic of heresy. The contrasting picture (σὺ δέ, v. 1) is summed up in the immediate reference to ὑγιαίνουσα διδασκαλία (v. 1; cf. 1.9) which is then filled out with more detailed ethical instructions. Christian behaviour is 'sound in faith' (v. 2, ὑγιαίνοντας τῇ πίστει; cf. 1.13), marked by 'good deeds' (vv. 7, 15; cf. 1.16), and corresponds to and adorns the teaching of God (vv. 5, 7, 10; cf. 1.11, 14). The concluding use of ἔλεγχε (v. 15; cf. 1.9, 13) underlines the connection of this paraenesis to believers with the polemic.

There may be additional points of contrast (cf. Weiser*, 405f.). It is possible that the destructive activity of the false teachers 'in households' is to be counteracted by the 'good teaching' (καλοδιδασκάλους) of older women (2.3). Insubordinate behaviour characterises the opponents (ἀνυπότακτοι, 1.10), but subjection in certain relationships (ὑποτάσσομαι, 2.5, 9; cf. 3.1) is what adorns the gospel.

Within the description of Christian behaviour, the stress is on being σώφρων (2.2, 4, 5, 6, 12), and there is frequent justification of the rules with purpose clauses (2.4, 5, 8, 10; cf. vv. 12, 14). The aim is to avoid outside calumny. The language used indicates a tacit acceptance of the natural and social order, in contrast to revolutionary behaviour (cf. Spicq, 616). Above all, however, the teaching is grounded in the Christ-event. This theological foundation indicates that the life enjoined here transcends a secular lifestyle (Hasler, 91f.; *pace* Brox, 294; Merkel, 97). Conversion is necessary, and respectability serves the gospel ministry.

In view of the contrast thus created and the repetition of key ethical themes, it is extremely unlikely that the teaching was adopted in a haphazard and thoughtless manner. The writer enjoins believers in their respective household and community positions to conduct themselves in ways that will neutralise the deleterious effects of the heresy.

The material is presented in the form of instruction that is to be given by Titus. The general command in v. 1 is developed in terms of four categories of people, older men (v. 2); older women (who are to teach the younger women in their role as wives, vv. 3–5); younger men (vv. 6–8); slaves (vv. 9–10); it is backed up by a doctrinal statement (vv. 12–14) and a final exhortation to Titus to teach with authority (v. 15).

EXCURSUS 7

Household codes and station codes

Balch 1981; Balch, D. L. in *ABD* III (1992), 318–20; Berger 1984a:1049–88; Berger 1984b:135–41; Crouch, J. E., *The Origin and Intention of the Colossian Haustafel* (Göttingen: Vandenhoeck und Ruprecht, 1972); Dunn, J. D. G., 'The Household Rules in the New Testament', in Barton, S. C. (ed.), *The Family in Theological Perspective* (Edinburgh: T. and T. Clark, 1996), 43–63; Easton, B. S., 'New Testament Ethical Lists', *JBL* 51 (1932), 1–12; Fiedler, P., *RAC* XIII,

1063–72; Fitzgerald, J. T., in *ABD* III, 80f.; Gielen 1990; Goppelt 1982:168–71; Goppelt 1993:162–79; Goppelt, L., 'Jesus und die "Haustafel"-Tradition', in Hoffmann, P. (ed.), *Orientierung an Jesus. FS J.Schmidt* (Freiburg: Herder, 1973), 93–106; Hartman, L., 'Some Unorthodox Thoughts on the "Household-Code Form" ', in Neusner, J., *et al.*, *The Social World of Formative Christianity and Judaism: Essays in Tribute to Howard Clark Kee* (Philadelphia: Fortress, 1988), 219–32; Lips 1994:261–80; Lührmann, D., 'Neutestamentliche Haustafeln und antike Ökonomie,' *NTS* 27 (1981), 83–97; Martin, R. P., *NIDNTT* III, 928–32; Motyer, S., 'The relationship between Paul's gospel of "All one in Christ Jesus" (Galatians 3:28) and the "household codes" ', *Vox Evangelica* 19 (1989), 33–48; Müller, K.-H., 'Die Haustafel des Kolosserbriefes und das antike Frauenthema: Eine kritische Rückschau auf alte Ergebnisse', in Dautzenberg, G., *Die Frau im Urchristentum* (Freiburg: Herder, 1983), 263–319; Schrage, W., 'Zur Ethik der neutestamentlichen Haustafeln', *NTS* 21 (1974–5), 1–22; Schroeder, D., 'Die Haustafeln des Neuen Testaments' (unpublished Th.D dissertation, Hamburg, 1959); Strecker, G., 'Die neutestamentliche Haustafeln (Kol 3,18–4,1 und Eph 5,22–6,9)', in Merklein H. (ed.), *Neues Testament und Ethik. FS R. Schnackenburg* (Freiburg: Herder, 1989), 349–75; Thraede, K., 'Zum historischen Hintergrund der "Haustafeln" des Neuen Testaments', in Dassmann, E. (ed.), *Pietas. FS B. Kötting* (Münster: Aschendorff, 1980), 359–68; Towner, P. H., *DPL*, 417–19; Wagener 1994:15–66; Weidinger 1928:53f.

The understanding of the church in the PE is largely based on the concept of the household of God (1 Tim 3.15; cf. 2 Tim 2.20f.). Overseers are to act as God's stewards placed in charge of his household (Tit 1.7), and an analogy is drawn between the human household and the church (1 Tim 3.5). This theological development is partly to be explained by the way early Christian groups met in houses and may have consisted largely of members of individual households. It is understandable that in this context teaching developed on the relationships between the different members of the household.

A carefully structured form of such instruction, commonly referred to as a 'household code', is seen in Col 3.18–4.1 and Eph 5.21–6.9 where the respective reciprocal duties of wives and husbands, children and fathers, and slaves and masters are set out. In both cases the duties of the first-named in each group are expressed in terms of subjection and obedience, while the second-named are to show such qualities as love, care and justice.

A similar, related structure is found in 1 Pet 2.13–3.7. The term 'station code' may be more appropriate here for teaching that is concerned with behaviour appropriate to one's position or 'station' in society generally. Here a general instruction on subjection to human authorities precedes instruction to house-hold slaves (but not masters), wives and husbands, and there is no mention of children and parents. A general instruction to all believers follows. Later in the epistle instruction is given to elders followed by a command to younger people to be subject to the elders (1 Pet 5.1–5). Here a shift in address from the members of the household to the members of the church appears to have taken place.[1]

In the PE relationships within the church and the family similarly appear to be principally in mind.[2] In Tit 2 there is instruction categorised by age and sex. It is addressed first to older men and older women concerning their deportment in general terms. The latter are to instruct the younger women on their marital duties); Titus himself is to instruct the younger men (but no mention is made of their marital situation). Slaves are to be subject to their respective masters and everybody is to be subject to the rulers of the State. There is no instruction given to husbands or to masters of slaves; reciprocity within family relationships is not used as a framework for the instruction. In 1 Tim 2 women are to be in subjection (apparently to their husbands or guardians). In 1 Tim 6.1–2 slaves are to be subject to their respective masters, and this applies whether the masters are non-believers or believers. Again, there is no corresponding instruction to husbands and masters.

The 'codes' in 1 Pet and Tit 2–3 thus differ from those in Col and Eph in significant features: (a) the absence of the parent/child category; (b) the addressing of only slaves and not masters; (c) the absence of instruction to husbands in Tit (here 1 Pet stands with Col and Eph); (d) the teaching on subordination to the State; (e) the preference for ὑποτάσσομαι (used throughout) over ὑπακούω (used in Col and Eph of slave and child) and δεσπόται of the masters (Col and Eph use κύριοι); (f) the care taken to ground instruction with theological material (Tit 2.11–14; 3.3–7; 1 Pet 2.21–24; 3.18–22). The differences are sufficient to justify restricting the term 'household codes' to those which are structured in terms of reciprocal relationships in the household and to use the term 'station codes' for those which are structured in terms of positions in society both within and outwith the household.

The existence and character of this teaching raises a number of problems regarding its origin, development and significance.

A full discussion of the origin lies outside the scope of the present treatment. Weidinger's formative work (1928) stressed the influence of Stoicism[3] and argued that the household code found its way into NT paraenetic teaching through the teaching codes used in Hellenistic Judaism which had been influenced to

[1] See also 1 Clement 21; Ignatius, *Poly.* 4f.; Polycarp 4; *Didache* 4.9–11; Barnabas 19.5–7 for related material.

[2] Lührmann 1980–81:95 sums up the matter by saying that the household tables are becoming community orders.

[3] For an easily accessible example see the discussion of family relationships in Hierocles, *On Duties*, in Malherbe 1986:85–104 (§ 36).

greater or less extent by Stoic duty codes. Crouch* pointed to non-Stoic features and claimed that the household codes were essentially Jewish. Goppelt* and Schroeder* stressed the need to take into account the Jesus tradition and early Christian paraenesis, while not disputing the presence of other influences.

More recent scholarship has shifted attention to the social institution of the οἶκος. The ancient household and the teaching that grew up to regulate and preserve that institution have been thought to provide the most instructive background to the categories and method of instruction of the NT household codes. The use of teaching structured according to household roles and distinctions between persons in the household, as well as the devices of addressing three pairs of people and inculcating reciprocal duties (Aristotle, *Pol.* 1.1253b.1–14), provide a credible background to the structure of the household codes in Ephesians and Colossians (Thraede*; Lührmann*; Balch* 1981; Lips 1994:262f.).

Attention has been drawn to the existence of a 'tract' literature which includes the Neopythagorean letters to wives, stressing the need for subordination (Berger* 1984b:140; cf. Malherbe 1986:82–5 [§§ 34f.]), and this has been taken up critically by Wagener 1994:54–63 who argues for an especially close relationship with the material in the PE.

Nevertheless, the fact remains that there is no exact parallel to the form that has been called a NT household code (Thraede*, 360; Hartman*; Lips 1994:280), and in the NT itself there is a variety of forms of such instruction. The term *Gattung* is thus obviously an inappropriate description of the form. The common features present in Col 3.18–4.1; Eph 5.21–6.9; 1 Pet 2.18–3.7; Tit 2.1–3.2 suggest a relationship perhaps better described with a term like *topoi* (Lips 1994:265).

What may be regarded as the 'purest' household codes are those found in Col and Eph with their discussion of the reciprocal groups found in the typical household. The pattern in Tit and 1 Pet is somewhat different. As Lips argues, the common shape of the tradition in Tit and 1 Pet is not accidental; the addition of the instruction about the State is evidence of a new, common schema. But the way in which this has developed is disputed.

On the one hand, the tendency to drop the reciprocality in addressing only slaves and the absence of the parent and child category in 1 Pet and Tit lead some scholars to the conclusion that the form was developed further, in almost evolutionary fashion from an original form, in the direction of a 'church order' and the content reduced or otherwise altered (e.g. Herr 1976).

On the other hand, Lips regards it as more probable that something like two parallel traditions are indicated rather than one which has suffered loss or been transformed. He argues that the similarities between the household codes in Tit and 1 Pet over and against Col and Eph show that a new form developed along a line different from that followed in Col and Eph, and that the teaching contexts will have determined the resulting forms. When Tit 2 deals not with husbands and wives, parents and children, but rather with older men and women and younger women and men (cf. 1 Pet 5.5 and the structure of the brief instruction to Timothy in 1 Tim 5.1f.), these represent groups in the church on the basis of age, and hence reflect a 'patriarchal' hierarchy in society which formed the framework within which the church had to structure itself. That the process was not without difficulty is seen in the elevation of younger people like Timothy and (in all probability) Titus to office and the resultant difficult relationships with older people who probably resented their position and found it hard to come to terms with it.

There are also differences between 1 Pet and Tit. The theology used to ground the ethical materials is not the same. Tit uses confessional material to emphasise the ethical consequences of the Christ-event. 1 Pet uses christological material that depicts Christ as the model of suffering. The situations are different. 1 Pet addresses a church in the midst of suffering; Tit is dealing with problems caused by heretical teachers, problems which also necessitated laying down careful guidelines for the selection of leaders. These factors influence the form and manner of instruction (e.g. the theological material chosen to ground the ethical teaching).

The codes in 1 Pet and Tit 2 further differ in terms of literary style. 1 Pet addresses the church directly, while Tit, written to an individual, transmits instructions indirectly through the apostolic co-worker to the church (cf. Wolter 1988:156–202). To a much greater degree than in other NT codes, the instructions to various groups in Tit 2.2–3.2 incorporate lists of qualities to be pursued and vices to be avoided. This shape may have been consciously created to conform to the duty code employed in Tit 1.5–9, with the intention being to link the conduct required of leaders with that required of Christians in general and to surround the negative description and denunciation of the false teachers (1.10–16) with a contrasting picture of genuine Christian behaviour.

A great deal of effort has gone into discovering the motives or intentions underlying the NT household code tradition: accommodation to secular ethics (Weidinger*, Dibelius); mission

(Schroeder*, Goppelt); quieting enthusiastic unrest (Crouch*) and the endeavour by some women to practise church leadership and sit loose to family duties (MacDonald 1983; Verner; Wagener); defence-apologetic (Balch* 1981). On the whole, though not exclusively, the NT household codes take up the issue of Christian living at the point of everyday life, for which household roles and the household context provided the typical forum. Lips suggests that the household represents a 'third' unique category within (or alongside) the church. Pauline teaching, he argues, makes a distinction between those within the church, believers to whom the language of 'one another' applies (1 Th 4.9, 18; 5.11, 15), and those on the outside, unbelievers, described as οἱ ἔξω (4.12) or 'all' (5.14, 15). The two categories also appear in Romans; 'one another' in 12.5, 10, 16; 13.8 and 'all' in 12.17, 18; 13.7. The household code represents a teaching formula addressed to a third group, the household, which Paul also identified and addressed as a separate (though not unrelated) entity in the church, consisting of men (husbands)/women (wives) (cf. 1 Cor 7; 1 Th 4.3–5); masters/slaves (cf. Philem). It might be added that in this third group it was possible to have believers and unbelievers existing side by side (cf. 1 Pet 3.1; 1 Tim 6.1).

Goppelt is certainly correct that life lived at this level in the various social roles gave Christians and the church automatic access to unbelievers and daily opportunities to testify to the faith (Goppelt* 1982:170). But whether the household codes were specifically missionary in orientation in every NT application is another question. What can be said is that through them the NT writers reflect sensitivity to the expectations of society at large and seem to encourage Christians to live according to patterns that were widely accepted as respectable. In Tit 2, as also elsewhere, the obvious grounding of a lifestyle described in popular ethical language (σώφρων, σεμνός) in the Christ-event (2.11f.) reveals the attempt to communicate something about Christian values.[4] The writer uses understandable terms, that are by no means arbitrary (*contra* Brox, 292, 297) and works in the context of social roles that are fundamental to society (see **Excursus 1**). The intention of the teaching must be determined from statements of motivation (the ἵνα clauses of 2.5, 8, 10), secular perceptions of the behaviour encouraged and prohibited, and other contextual factors (theological basis, 2.1–14; 3.3–7; the contrasting picture of the false teachers).

---

[4] Wagener 1994:215–18, who is particularly critical of finding the missionary motive in the PE, admits that the traditional interpretation has some justification in Tit 2.

a. Preface (2.1)

The opening sentence is a general instruction to Titus that acts
as a heading for what follows. The pronoun and adversative take
up the contrast motif, which sets apart Titus's ministry from the
activities of the false teachers. Titus is to give the following
teaching, the whole of which represents the antithesis and
apostolic response to the false teaching (1.10–16; Weiser*, 405;
Holtzmann 481; cf. Wolter 1988:134f.). The command also
establishes a connection that is fundamental to the teaching of
the PE, namely, that Christian conduct (which Titus is to address
in this passage) bears a direct relationship to the accepted,
apostolic doctrine of the church. This connection is completed
with the insertion of the theological material in 2.11–14.

EXEGESIS

1. **Σὺ δὲ λάλει ἃ πρέπει τῇ ὑγιαινούσῃ διδασκαλίᾳ** σὺ δέ,
'But you, for your part', is a paraenetic device in the PE for
commanding or commending pursuit of a course that is the
opposite of the false teachers (1 Tim 6.11; 2 Tim 3.10; 3.14; 4.5;
cf. Rom 11.17; 2 Tim 2.1 [σὺ οὖν]).[5] It functions similarly
elsewhere in the NT to distinguish approved behaviour and
responses from those which are disapproved.[6] The device
was widely used in paraenetic materials.[7] λαλέω (2.15; 5.13**)
originally meant 'to babble, stammer', then 'to chatter', and
finally simply 'to speak, talk'. According to Hübner, it differs
from λέγω in that it is rarely used in the NT in the sense 'to say
that...' or followed by indirect discourse. It tends – but it is only
a tendency – to be used more of the ability to speak, and the
accent lies more on the act of speaking than on the content of
what is said; there is the possible implication of more informal
usage than with λέγω (LN I, §33.69–70). In any given case the
context will determine what kind of speaking is meant. Here
the verb is used formally of Christian proclamation, instruction
and teaching (rather than of conversation in accord with wholesome instruction, Parry, 78). For its connection elsewhere with
διδαχή/διδάσκω and other revelatory activities, see Acts 17.19;
18.25; 1 Cor 2.6; 14.6 (cf. 1 Tim 5.13 where the reference is
perhaps to false teaching). The section is closed with a summary

---

[5] For σύ put first emphatically cf. Mt 21.5 (Mic 5.1); Lk 1.76; Acts 1.24;
Lk 11.39 (pl.).
[6] Mt 6.2–6; Lk 9.60; for the pl. form ὑμεῖς δέ, see Jn 14.19; Acts 3.13f.;
1 Pet 2.8f.; cf. the negative accusatory use, Mk 7.10f.; Mt 15.4f.; 21.32; Jn 8.14;
1 Cor 4.10.
[7] Ps-Diogenes, *Epistle* 12 [106, 11 Malherbe]; Ps-Socrates, *Epistle* 7.5; Philo,
Her. 105; Hermas, *Vis.* 3.9.1; *Acts of Thomas* 25; see further Wolter 1988:135f.

using the same verb (2.15).[8] Oberlinner, 105f., suggests that the verb is chosen, however, because the context is what the church members are to do, and Titus is to be an example to those who do not teach but who do converse in ways that are in accord with sound teaching.

ἅ is used without an expressed antecedent, as in 1.11. The content is explained by vv. 2–10 or 2.2–3.11. Ethical conduct that befits orthodox teaching is the theme. πρέπει, 'to be fitting, seemly, suitable', describes actions which are appropriate according to the people or circumstances concerned.[9] τῇ ὑγιαινούσῃ διδασκαλίᾳ (dat. of respect) indicates that in respect of which Titus's teaching is to be 'appropriate'. Thus the apostolic teaching provides the norm. For ὑγιαίνουσα διδασκαλία see 1.9 note. The implication would seem to be that here Titus is to teach people about the kind of behaviour that is in accordance with sound doctrine.

b. To older men (2.2)

The first category of instructions concern older people. They call them to a life that is respectable in every way. There is nothing particularly applicable to older people here, the qualities being those expected in all believers. Rather, the qualities associated with self-control and decorous behaviour alone are singled out as especially important. Four qualities are described, the last of which is developed with the triad of Christian qualities, faith, love, patience. The first three (νηφάλιος, σεμνός, σώφρων) are also used in the duty codes of Tit 1 and 1 Tim 3 of church leaders, who are to exemplify the qualities which typify the normal Christian life. The second and third terms (σεμνός, σώφρων) especially were standard items in the secular description of respectability. The difference lies in the theological grounding of behaviour in the Christ-event (see **Excursus 3**).

TEXT

2. νηφαλίους The spelling is varied (cf. 1 Tim 3.2, 11); see Elliott, 48.

EXEGESIS

2. **Πρεσβύτας νηφαλίους εἶναι, σεμνούς, σώφρονας, ὑγιαίνοντας τῇ πίστει, τῇ ἀγάπῃ, τῇ ὑπομονῇ** In the NT πρεσβύτης, 'old

---

[8] Cf. Debrunner, A., Kittel, G., et al., TDNT IV, 69–136 (especially 76f.; the NT usage of the word is not discussed); Hübner, H., EDNT II, 335f.

[9] πρέπει may have a subject, as here (1 Tim 2.10; Heb 7.26) but is often used impersonally (Mt 3.15; 1 Cor 11.13 [of women]; Eph 5.3 [of speech];

man',[10] always refers to older men rather than to church 'elders', whereas πρεσβύτερος can refer to either group; if the qualities required in them are the same as for elders, it is because the elders would be largely chosen from this group, and in any case there was no double standard for the congregation and its leaders (cf. Fee, 185). The determination of what is meant by 'old' is not clear. The Greeks divided life into various ages. Dio Chrysostom 74.10 gives four ages: παῖς; μειράκιον; νεάνισκος; πρεσβύτης. Philo, Spec. 2.33 follows Lev 27.7 in regarding people over 60 as old; cf. CD 10.7f. which forbids men over 60 from holding office (Nauck 1950:80f.). A more detailed division is given in 'Abot 5.21. According to the rather stylised comment in Philo, Opif. 105, following Hippocrates, human life was divided into seven ages: παιδίον (0–7); παῖς (8–14); μειράκιον (15–21); νεάνισκος (22–28); ἀνήρ (29–49); πρεσβύτης (50–56); γέρων (57–). In terms of this list, the group addressed here would consist of all people over 50. But there was also a rough division into young and old with the boundary set at the age of 40, and the NT writers appear to follow this. There is no doubt that people aged 30 were still 'young' (Polybius 18.125 refers to Flaminius as young at this age; cf. Bernard, 70 n.). Agrippa, aged c. 40 was a 'young man' (Josephus, Ant. 18.197). According to Aulus Gellius 10.28 soldiers are *minores* up to age 46. Irenaeus, *A.H.* 2.22.5, states that one was young up to age 40.

The construction is not clear: the phrase πρεσβύτας εἶναι may be (a) acc. and inf. dependent on λαλεῖ (Holtzmann, 481; Lock, 139; Spicq, 616); (b) dependent on πρέπει; (c) dependent on an implied παρακάλει as in 2.6 (BD § 389; Oberlinner, 104f.); (d) an example of the imperatival inf.[11] Although household tables normally use imperatives, this section with its adjectives has more the appearance of a 'catalogue of duties' than of a set of rules to be obeyed (Dibelius-Conzelmann, 139). Nevertheless, whether a verb of exhortation (in the second person singular to Titus) is to be supplied, or it is dependent on λαλεῖ/πρέπει above, or functions on its own, the force and intention of the teaching is not obscured.

Heb 2.10***); cf. ἱεροπρεπής, Tit 2.3). It is not common in the LXX (Ps 32 [MT 33].1; 64 [MT 65].1; 92 [93].5; Ecclus 32.3; 33.30; 1 Macc 12.11; 3 Macc 3.20, 25; 7.13, 19), but is frequent in Ignatius (*Eph.* 2.2; 4.1; *Rom.* 10.2; *Philad.* 10.1; *Magn.* 3.1, 2; 4.1; *Trall.* 12.2; *Poly.* 5.2; 7.2; *Smyr.* 7.2; 11.2). Cf. the use of δεῖ in 1.11; ἀνήκω, Eph 5.4; Col 3.18; Philem 8; καθήκω, Acts 22.22; Rom 1.28. It is not discussed in *TDNT*, but see Brown, C., *NIDNTT* II, 668f.

[10] Lk 1.18; Philem 9***; *M. Poly.* 7.2; Hermas, *Mand.* 8.10; cf. Bornkamm, G., *TDNT* VI, 683.

[11] Cf. Rom 12.15; Phil 3.16; Knight, 305. The construction is said to be highly probable by MHT I, 179f. Moule 1953:126, lists but notes (a) as an alternative, *contra* Dibelius-Conzelmann, 139.

The first quality required is sobriety. νηφάλιος means 'temperate' (in use of wine), sober' (see **Excursus 3**). Here the term may have the metaphorical sense 'sober, alert, watchful' but the literal command in v. 3 suggests that a literal sense is required here also. A reference to temperate use of wine might also have been an apt rejoinder to the gluttony in 1.12 (Spicq, 617).

The second quality is seriousness. σεμνός is 'worthy of respect', 'serious' (1 Tim 3.8, 11; Phil 4.8***). It is a quality or bearing which is observable, will elicit the respect of other people, and which is exhibited before God and people. It was regarded as a desirable virtue in older men (Cicero, *De Sen.* 4.10, cited by Quinn, 131). See **Excursus 3**.

The third quality is self-control. σώφρων (**Excursus 3**) is 'sensible', showing the proper restraint in all things. It is one of the basic marks of the Christian life in the PE (just as in Greek culture), being a possibility which the author links directly with the Christ-event and conversion (2.12).

ὑγιαίνοντας τῇ πίστει, τῇ ἀγάπῃ, τῇ ὑπομονῇ The fourth requirement indicates that 'soundness', the fourth quality, is to penetrate to the whole of Christian life.[12] For the three qualities being linked (but not necessarily forming a group, so Holtzmann, 482) cf. 1 Tim 6.11; 2 Tim 3.10; 1 Th 1.3; Ignatius, *Poly.* 6.2. Essentially, the traditional triad, faith, hope (for which patience is substituted here), and love is an abbreviated way of referring to the whole of the Christian life. For ὑγιαίνω see 1.9 note; 2 Tim 1.13. It expresses the opposite of being spiritually sick (cf. 1 Tim 6.4). The command is to avoid unsoundness or disease in the Christian life, depicted by the triad of Christian virtues.

The use of the verb (ὑγιαίνω) in the polemic already shows that being healthy in faith means being firm and free from contamination by error (cf. Spicq, 607). πίστις (see **Excursus 4**) with the article may mean the objective content of the faith (the Christian religion), but in view of the link with love and endurance here and of the similar lists of virtues in 1 Tim 4.12; 6.11; 2 Tim 2.22; 3.10, it is more likely the act of believing which then defines the Christian life in terms of loyalty to God and Christ (cf. Bernard, 165; Knight, 306; Quinn, 132).

ἀγάπη is always a quality of Christians in the PE, and is always linked with other qualities, especially faith.[13] 'In love' signifies, negatively, hating evil. Positively, it defines the Christian life in terms of cleaving to the good and expressing that good in selfless service to others (Towner 1989:300 n. 77).

---

[12] The qualities are in the dat. expressing respect (replacing the Cl. acc. of respect; Parry, 78; MHT I, 63, 75; cf. use of ἐν with dat., 1.13).

[13] 1 Tim 1.5, 14; 2.15; 4.12; 6.11; 2 Tim 1.7, 13; 2.22; 3.10**; cf. ἀγαπάω, 2 Tim 4.8, 10. Quell, G., and Stauffer, E., *TDNT* I, 21–55, ignore the PE. See

Of the thirteen occurrences of πίστις in the PE, nine are in connection with ἀγάπη (1 Tim 1.5, 14; 2.15; 4.12; 6.11; 2 Tim 1.13; 2.22; 3.10; Tit 2.2). This combination also occurs eight times in the earlier Paul (1 Cor 13.13; Gal 5.6, 22; 1 Th 3.6; 5.8; Eph 6.23; Col 1.4; 2 Th 1.3; Philem 5), which suggests the use of a Christian paraenetic tradition (cf. Vögtle 1936:51, 171; Lips 1979:79). The Pauline expression in Gal 5.6 reduces Christian existence to the lowest common denominator as πίστις δι' ἀγάπης ἐνεργουμένη – fellowship with God/Christ in the Spirit (Gal 5.22) yielding practical fruit in the form of service to others.[14]

This pair of qualities may have formed the essential combination out of which the threefold (and longer) lists developed. The 'faith, hope, love' triad of 1 Cor 13.13[15] is probably a set paraenetic summary of the essential Christian qualities. But the tendency to expand and develop is readily seen in Paul (Rom 5.1–5; Gal 5.22f.; Eph 6.23), and the influence of the Hellenistic virtue list upon the shape of Paul's teaching is likely.[16]

ὑπομονή, 'endurance, patience' (1 Tim 6.11; 2 Tim 3.10**)[17] is the element of constancy and perseverance which maintains faith and love in the face of opposition and every temptation to discouragement until the believer reaches the end of the long journey. It thus puts up with difficulties caused by other people (often expressed by μακροθυμία, 1 Tim 1.16; 2 Tim 3.10; 4.2) as well as with trying circumstances. It may well be a replacement for 'hope', the traditional element in the triad (1 Tim 6.11; cf. Ignatius, *Poly.* 6.2; 1 Th 1.3), and the reason may be the need to stress the ingredient of patient perseverance in the face of opposition to the faith (Kelly, 240; Fee, 186; cf. Hanson, 179); Radl claims that in the PE the motif is that of not lapsing from the faith but remaining true to Christ throughout the long wait till death or the parousia. The quality is prominent in Heb (10.36; 12.1) and Rev (1.9; *et al.*) as well as being a key term in the earlier Paul (Rom 5.3f.; *et al.*).

Günther, W., Link, H.-G., and Brown, C., *NIDNTT* II, 538–51; Roloff, 66f.; Towner 1989:162f., 165f.; Schneider, G., *EDNT* I, 8–12; *TLNT* I, 8–22.

[14] Cf. Schrage, W., *Die konkreten Einzelgebote in der paulinischen Paränese* (Gütersloh: Mohn 1961), 56, 269.

[15] The combination is attested earlier in 1 Th 1.3 and 5.8, although 1.3 includes ὑπομονή.

[16] Hunter, A. M., *Paul and his Predecessors* (London: SCM Press, 1961²), 33–5; Vögtle 1936:178–88; Kamlah 1964; Gnilka, J., *Der Philipperbrief* (Freiburg: Herder, 1976), 220–2.

[17] In both cases ὑπομονή directly follows ἀγάπη and is part of a list including πίστις; cf. ὑπομένω, 2 Tim 2. 10,12**; cf. Hauck, F., *TDNT* IV, 581–8; Radl, W., *EDNT* III, 405–6. Spicq (*TLNT* III, 414–20) notes that in the LXX it is related to hope in God, in contrast to Stoic and other usage.

c. To older (and younger) women (2.3–5)

Trummer, P., 'Einehe nach den Pastoralbriefen', *Bib* 51 (1970), 471–84.

The next section concerns older women and continues syntactically in the same way as v. 2. Through the purpose statement, vv. 4–5, younger women are indirectly instructed. The qualities required for the older women are very similar to those for the women in 1 Tim 3.11 and those for the younger women match 1 Tim 5.14 (Hanson, 180). The virtues commended are also found in secular writers.[18]

In this household (or community) code paraenesis, the sense is that they are also, like the old men, to exhibit the appropriate qualities. These are described with a general reference to demeanour which is holy, followed by two specific kinds of behaviour to avoid and one to pursue.

The general reference is clearly to holy conduct, as befits God's people. Two activities which are strongly inconsistent with such a demeanour are forbidden; loose talk of a slanderous and scandalous character and addiction to alcohol are linked together in ancient sources and frequently condemned.

The final quality is transitional to the next point: the older women's responsibility to the younger women: they are to be their teachers, largely through example and informal instruction. They are to encourage the younger women to be fully engaged in carrying out their domestic duties as befits Christian women. In view of the authority structure implied by the household code[19] and in view of 1 Tim 2.12, the reference can hardly be to a recognised teaching office (*contra* Trummer*, 476; cf. Theodoret III, 703 Schulze = *PL* LXXXII, 863). The context implies that the primary object of the teaching pertains to conduct that befits a Christian wife (vv. 4–5, including the kind of qualities mentioned in v. 3). This would suggest informal teaching by example and admonition.[20]

TEXT

3. ἱεροπρεπεῖς ἱεροπρεπεῖ (C 33 81 104 *pc* latt sy^p sa Cl.). Elliott, 181, suggests that the variant arose because scribes did not realise that the adjective qualified 'older women'.

μή (2) (ℵ^2 D F G H Ψ 33 TR latt sy^h Cl; WH mg): μηδέ (ℵ* A C 81 1739 1881 *pc* sy^p WH non mg.; Holtzmann, 482; Kilpatrick; Elliott, 137). Elliott, 137,

[18] Musonius Rufus 10.10–17; 14.12–14 Hense (van der Horst 1974:313); Plutarch, *Mor.* 138A–146A (*Conjugalia Praecepta*).
[19] See Weiser*, 410; Lips 1979:141f.; cf. Merkel, 97; Fiorenza 1985:288–94.
[20] Schlarb 1990:334; Dibelius-Conzelmann, 140; Brox, 293; Merkel, 96; Fee, 186; cf. Quinn, 135.

argues that μή is assimilation to 1 Tim 3.8, and cites 1 Tim 2.12; 6.7 for the usage. A similar textual problem arises in 2.10.

σωφρονίζωσιν σωφρονίζουσιν (ℵ* A F G H P 104 326 365 1241 1505 *pc*; Holtzmann, 482) is an orthographical variant, Elliott, 181; cf. 3.8. But it could also be indicative, as in 1 Cor 4.6; Gal 4.17.

5. οἰκουργούς The word is a Hellenistic variant of οἰκουρός (a Cl. word found here as a *v.l.* in ℵ² D² H 1739 1881 TR). The text is preferred by Elliott, 181f.; Metzger, 585. Bernard, 163 and 167, preferred the Cl. word on the grounds that it gave a better meaning in the context, but this argument holds only if the two words had different meanings. See below.

ὁ λόγος τοῦ θεοῦ Add καὶ ἡ διδασκαλία (C *pc* vg^ms sy^h). The addition is assimilation to 1 Tim 6.1; Elliott, 182.

EXEGESIS

3. Πρεσβύτιδας ὡσαύτως ἐν καταστήματι ἱεροπρεπεῖς, μὴ διαβόλους μὴ οἴνῳ πολλῷ δεδουλωμένας, καλοδιδασκάλους πρεσβῦτις*** is 'old, elderly woman'.²¹ ὡσαύτως, 'in the same way' (2.6; 1 Tim 2.9; 3.8, 11; 5.25**), compares a fresh comment with a preceding one, and is used in lists of instructions. This use of ὡσαύτως is peculiar to the PE, but it corresponds to the use of ὁμοίως in the household code of 1 Pet 3.1, 7 (and the instructions to younger men, following elders in 5.5) to mark the transition in the household code paraenesis from one group to another or from one pair of the group to the other (cf. Gielen 1990:329f., 332f.). The verb must be supplied from what precedes (λάλει εἶναι; BA *s.v.* ὡσαύτως).

Four qualities are listed.²² The first is a holiness of character which commands respect. κατάστημα*** is 'condition, state' (Hel.; Josephus, *Bel.* 1.40), hence 'behaviour, demeanour' (3 Macc 5.45).²³ The word does not refer to clothing (*pace* Oecumenius, cited by Holtzmann, 482, although this possibility exists for καταστολή in 1 Tim 2.9). It can be used of general demeanour (*Ep. Arist.* 122, 165, 210, 278), but a corresponding inward dimension that yields outward calm and poise may at times be indicated (cf. Josephus, *Ant.* 15.236; Ignatius, *Trall.* 3.2). Here both are probably meant (cf. Dibelius-Conzelmann, 139f.; Brox, 292).

The choice of the adjective ἱεροπρεπής*** may reflect a liking for compounds and solemn speech. The usual translation is 'reverent'. However, the word properly means 'befitting a holy person, thing', hence 'holy, worthy of reverence'. It was used specifically in relation to temples and their personnel, religious

---

²¹ 4 Macc 16.14; Philo, *Spec.* 2.33; Josephus, *Ant.* 7.142, 186; Hermas, *Vis.* 1.2.2; cf. πρεσβυτέρα, 1 Tim 5.2. See *New Docs.* I, 121 §79.

²² ἐν gives the sense 'as far as X is concerned', 'in the sphere of' (Eph 2.4; Jas 1.8; Heb 13.21; Jas 1.4; BA *s.v.* IV.1).

²³ Cf. Field 1899:220.

processions and cultic ceremonies.²⁴ But there was also a broad use in reference to God, holy things and people (4 Macc 9.25; 11.20; Philo, *Abr*. 101; *Decal*. 60; *L.A*. 3.204); it could also be used more generally of moral life: 'it is ἱεροπρεπέστατον to accustom boys to the truth.'²⁵ It is used in 4 Macc 9.25; 11.20 of the young men who were martyred.

This range of usage leads to several possible nuances here:

(a) 'like a priest(ess)' (BA) with a conscious reference to the narrower usage. A kind of 'priestly dignity' may be specifically in mind: the deportment of Christians should be like that of priests going about their duties in a manner that commands respect.²⁶

(b) 'as befitting people in holy service' (Holtzmann, 482);

(c) 'holy or godly in deportment', in effect summarising 1 Tim 2.10 (Fee, 186; 'as women should who lead a holy life', GNB).

There is nothing in the context to suggest a priestly reference (so rightly Brox, 292f.; cf. Oberlinner, 108), and we should probably interpret it here in this more general way (cf. 4 Macc 9.25; 11.20).²⁷

The demeanour and bearing thus indicated is the counterpart to that required of older men, described with σεμνός/σώφρων. The term at least conveys the idea that the conduct of women is to be holy and 'in relation to God'. Although there is some verbal resonance with 1 Tim 2.9–10 (ὡσαύτως καὶ γυναῖκας ἐν καταστολῇ ... ὃ πρέπει γυναιξὶν ἐπαγγελλομέναις θεοσέβειαν), the choice of ἱεροπρεπής instead of θεοσεβής makes a conscious connection difficult to prove. The bearing and conduct of older women is to reflect dedication to God. It should, therefore, inspire respect on the part of those who observe them. The English term 'reverend', formerly used of persons 'worthy of respect' because of the quality of their lives (but now restricted to a purely formal designation for clergy), may give the sense (Bernard, 166; so Oberlinner: 'ehrwürdig').

The description is followed by commands not to be slanderers and tipplers but to be good teachers. There is presumably nobody less dignified in behaviour than the person who has lost self-control under the influence of alcohol. Slanderers and drunkards

---

²⁴ It is used in inscr. with reference to religious processions (e.g. Dittenberger, *Syll*. 708.24 [II/I BC]; Philo, *Prob*. 75; cf. Josephus, *Ant*. 11.329, of Jaddua the high priest going to meet Alexander the Great; see Dibelius-Conzelmann, 140 n. 6).

²⁵ Plutarch, *Mor*. 11C (*De Lib. Educ*. 14; cited by Seebass, 235). Cf. Schrenk, G., *TDNT* III, 253–4; Seebass, H., *NIDNTT* II, 235; *TLNT* II, 215f.

²⁶ Cf. Tertullian, *de cult. fem*. 2.12: *pudicitiae sacerdotes* (cited by Spicq, 618); Dibelius-Conzelmann, 140; Fee, 186; Merkel, 96; Quinn, 118f.

²⁷ See further **Excursus 3**.

commanded no respect and brought the church into disrepute. We appear to be in a society where these things were not uncommon – and yet were contemptible to informed opinion. διάβολος is here 'slanderous' (1 Tim 3.11; 2 Tim 3.3; Poly 5.2), but is more common in the NT as a noun, 'devil'.[28] This prohibition (Philo, *Sacr.* 32; Menander, *Fragment* 803) fits in with the typical proverbial character of old women in the ancient world.[29] The presence of slanderers in the church among the opposition may also be in mind (v. 5).

The third requirement, μὴ οἴνῳ πολλῷ δεδουλωμένας (equivalent to μὴ πάροινον), is also a requirement of church leaders (1.7; 1 Tim 3.3, 8).[30] Intemperance in language and alcohol were associated in the ancient world (Spicq, 619). The adj. πόλλῳ is emphatic; excess is forbidden (cf. 1 Tim 3.8). δουλόω**, 'to enslave', can be used of passions (2 Pet 2.19; cf. the use of δουλεύω, Tit 3.3).[31] The use of the verb with reference to alcohol is well-paralleled.[32]

Brox, 293, thinks that the mention of addiction to alcohol is not especially relevant and is included rather mechanically from existing lists. However, drunkenness was a serious enough problem to warrant apostolic correction (Eph 5.18; 1 Pet 4.3; cf. Rom 14.21) and even very stern rebuke (1 Cor 11.20–34) in the early church. Furthermore, drunkenness and talkativeness or slanderous talk were common elements in the typical description of old women in Hellenistic culture.[33] In view of these observations, and considering the 'Cretan stereotype' constructed with some care in 1.5–16, it seems more likely that the prohibition is not only relevant but meant to be taken seriously (cf. Quinn, 134–5; Scott 164). As with older men, the instructions here seek to encourage Christian older women to live in a way that makes the stereotype inapplicable to the church. It goes without saying that what is commended here was not required merely of the older women.

---

[28] Cf. Foerster, W., and Rad, G. von, *TDNT* II, 71–81; Böcher, O., *EDNT* I, 297f.
[29] *Anth. Pal.* 7.353, 459 (*The Greek Anthology*, II, 191, 249); Lucretius, *De Rer. Nat.* 4.1165; Cicero, *Pro Caelio* 55.
[30] οἶνος, 'wine', is the normal term for 'fermented juice of the grape' (BA 564; 1 Tim 5.23**; cf. Seesemann, H., *TDNT* V, 162–6).
[31] Cf. Rengstorf, K. H., *TDNT* II, 279.
[32] Cf. Philostratus, *Vita Ap.* 2, 36: δεδουλωμένος ὑπὸ τοῦ οἴνου; Libanius, *Ep.* 316, 3 Förster: δουλεύειν οἴνῳ, cited by BA.
[33] *Anth. Pal.* 7.329; 7.353; 7.384; 7.455–7; Aristophanes, *Clouds* 555; Juvenal, *Sat.* 6.304, 315, 403–11, 432, 440; Dover, K. J., *Greek Popular Morality in the Time of Plato and Aristotle* (Berkeley: University of California Press, 1974), 95–102; Towner: 1989:307. Holtzmann, 482, cites Augustine, *Conf.* 9.8.18, of Monica, but while she was still young.

The fourth and final quality is, typically, developed more fully. καλοδιδάσκαλος*** is a real hapax. There does not seem to be any justification for the translation 'the right teachers', apparently meaning that the appropriate teachers for the younger women are the older women rather than Titus himself (Quinn, 134f.). There would seem to be two possible meanings: (a) 'teaching what is good';[34] (b) 'good at teaching'.[35] The parallel forms κακοδιδασκαλέω (2 Clement 10.5) and κακοδιδασκαλία (Ignatius, *Philad.* 2.1) show that the former meaning is the correct one.

4. ἵνα σωφρονίζωσιν τὰς νέας φιλάνδρους εἶναι, φιλοτέκνους Embedded in the paraenesis to older women is instruction for younger women. The transition comes in the purpose clause that begins in v. 4 and concludes with v. 5. Clearly the older women are to be examples to the younger, and therefore the qualities listed are expected in both age-groups. They are grouped in three pairs concerning their duties at home, their personal piety and their sphere of activity in the home, followed by a seventh characteristic of submission to their husbands (Knight, 308f.). The qualities are largely those which would be recognised and approved by contemporary ancient society.[36] The first pair, stressing love for husbands and children, is often mentioned on commendatory epitaphs. The second pair stress the basic qualities of self-control and moral purity which are a central concern of the writer, and which are specifically applied to the sexual morality of women. Their proper way of life is summed up in the third pair as managing their households and doing so in a spirit of kindness. The final instruction to be submissive to their husbands suggests that there was a danger of Christian freedom and equality leading to behaviour with which the ancient world found it hard to come to terms.[37]

The apostolic instruction thus inculcates a patriarchal structure for this relationship that is consistent with the rest of the NT.[38] Merkel, 97, comments on the lack of any complementary command to husbands or christological motivation and sees this omission as a retrograde step compared with Eph and Col. Even

---

[34] LSJ; BA; *EDNT* II, 244; LN 33.249; and most translations and commentators; cf. Rengstorf, K. H., *TDNT* II, 159–60. 'They must set a high standard' (REB) is an oddity.

[35] Vg, *bene docentes*; see Edwards 1989:80, 85 n. 18.

[36] See (for example) Malherbe 1986:83–5 §§ 34, 35; *New Docs.* VI, 18–23 § 2.

[37] Quinn, 136, suggests that the set of virtues here and the material in 1 Tim 2.13–15 may be linked to a Christian set form of words for a marriage, along the lines of fragments discovered at Qumran (4Q 500, 502).

[38] 1 Cor 11.3; 14.33–35; Eph 5.22–24; Col 3.18; 1 Pet 3.1; cf. Gielen 1990:136–9; Fiorenza 1983:288–94.

so, the middle voice implies willing subjection and makes it the responsibility of the wife to give it rather than for the husband, who has his own responsibilities in the relationship, to take it (cf. Kamlah 1970:241–3; Quinn, 137). No theological basis is given here for the subordinate relationship of the wife (though see Spicq 621, who says that grace sanctions the order of nature, and Knight, 308f.). However, the assumptions of Graeco-Roman society about the relative positions of wives and husbands are clear enough (Plutarch, *Mor.* 142E; cf. Balch 1981:98f., 147); the instruction encourages order in the household at the very point that pagans would be bound to notice innovation or disruption (as the ἵνα μή purpose/motivation confirms).

ἵνα expresses the purpose of their being teachers. νέαι is used as a substantival adj.[39] and is the antonym to πρεσβύτιδες, referring to a defined age group and position in the household and community. σωφρονίζω*** is 'to make somebody sober, bring them to their senses, make of sound mind',[40] hence 'to encourage, advise, urge'.[41] The slang 'wise them up' (Fee, 187) gets close to the force of the Greek word. Perhaps the word was used because the teaching was to be more by personal example than by any kind of 'official' verbal instruction in the church. The sense is to encourage the young women to a like sobriety (as spelled out in concrete, domestic terms) which corresponds to the word of God (cf. Schlarb 1990:334). This suggests that one of the goals of the teaching is to prevent younger women from adopting patterns of careless, flighty living that would attract criticism. The choice of the verb corresponds to the thematic use of σώφρων to describe the authentic Christian life in the PE (2.2, 5; see **Excursus 3**). Thus the specialised meaning in this context is 'to inculcate Christian values'. In view of the prohibition of women teaching in the church meeting in 1 Tim 2 some commentators think that the injunction here implies that the women are to devote themselves to this form of teaching the younger women only and are excluded from other forms (Wagener 1994:92; Oberlinner, 110).

The first pair of qualities have to do with attitudes in the family. The instructions assume that as a rule the younger women are married (Brox, 293) and have children (Holtzmann, 483). φίλανδρος*** is 'loving men' (Cl.), hence 'loving [her] husband'

---

[39] Cf. the more frequent comparative νεώτερος (1 Tim 5.1, 2, 11, 14; Tit 2.6**; Acts 5.6; Polycarp 5.3); cf. Behm, J., *TDNT* IV, 896–9.
[40] Arichea-Hatton, 284; cf. Euripides, *Hipp.* 731, σωφρονεῖν μαθήσεται.
[41] Cf. Luck, U., *TDNT* VII, 1104; *TLNT* III, 362 n. 18; *New Docs.* IV, 10 §1. The verb is not found in LXX but is associated with παιδεύω and νουθετέω in Philo, *Cong.* 172. There are no parallels to the use here with an infinitive.

(cf. 1 Pet 3.1). As the numerous references to this quality show, it was highly prized in Graeco-Roman and Jewish cultures and considered the mark of a good wife.[42]

φιλότεκνος***, 'loving one's children', expresses a quality equally expected and admired in wives[43] and linked with φίλανδρος.[44] Occasionally it is used in a critical sense (e.g. Hermas, *Vis.* 1.3.1: 'indulgent'; cf. BA) but certainly not here.

5. σώφρονας ἁγνὰς The second pair of qualities has to do with the self-controlled and chaste demeanour of the women. σώφρων (**Excursus 3**) signifies the sensible life of balance and restraint and, in the PE, a characteristic of true Christianity. For the quality in women, see 1 Tim 2.9, 15. It is again a quality commended in secular society.[45] ἁγνός is originally 'ritually clean', then with a moral sense, hence '[sexually] pure, chaste' (cf. 2 Cor 11.2; 1 Pet 3.2); more broadly 'pure, sincere' (2 Cor 7.11; Phil 1.17; 4.8; Jas 3.17; 1 Jn 3.3; ἁγνεία is used of women in 1 Tim 5.2; and ἁγιασμός in 1 Tim 2.15; cf. 1 Tim 5.22).[46] Sexual fidelity to the husband is meant.

οἰκουργοὺς ἀγαθάς The third pair of qualities is concerned with status and function in the household. οἰκουργός*** 'working at home, domestic',[47] is a variant of the Cl. οἰκουρός, found as a textual variant here. It is found elsewhere only in Soranus p. 18, 2 *v.l.* οἰκουρός means 'watching, keeping the home'; it can be used of a woman as the housekeeper (Euripides, *Hec.* 1277). It is found as a praiseworthy attribute, being linked with σώφρων and φίλανδρος.[48] However, the word could also

---

[42] It is not found in LXX. Detailed references are given in Spicq, 392 n. 3; cf. BA; Dibelius-Conzelmann, 140 n. 11. The word is linked with other qualities (e.g. Philo, *Praem.* 139, where it is linked with σωφρών and οἰκουρός; cf. οἰκουργός below); for the noun see Josephus, *Ant.* 18.159. Spicq, 620, cites the epitaph ζήσασα φιλάνδρως. It is associated with φίλανδρος, φιλότεκνος, σεμνός and other adjs. in an epitaph from Cairo (AD I/II) cited in *New Docs.* III, 40–3 § 11, where numerous other examples are listed (see further *New Docs.* IV, 37 § 10).

[43] Herodotus 2.66; 4 Macc 15.4–6; Philo, *Abr.* 179; cf. φιλοτεκνία, 4 Macc 14.13. cf. 1 Tim 5.10. See *New Docs.* II, 100f. § 80.

[44] *Inschr. Perg.* II. 604 (Deissmann 1927:314f.; Dibelius-Conzelmann, 140). It is well attested in inscriptions (Spicq, 393f.).

[45] Menander. *Frg.* 610, Xenophon, *Econ.* 7.14; 9.19; Aristophanes, *Lysist.* 473; for inscriptions see Deissmann 1927:315; *TLNT* III, 364f.; Philo, *Praem.* 139; Josephus, *Ant.* 18.180; Spicq, 620f. It is used alongside ἀγαθή in Josephus, *Ant.* 6.296.

[46] Cf. Prov 20.9; 4 Macc 18.7f.; Philo, *Spec.* 2.30; *Praem.* 159; *Jos.* 43; *Cont.* 65.; cf. Hauck, F., *TDNT* I, 122; Balz, H. R., *EDNT* I, 22f.

[47] The word is a compound in which the first part has a locative significance (MHT II, 274); for the verb see 1 Clement 1.3, a possible echo of Tit 2.5 (Parry, 79).

[48] Philo, *Praem.* 139; cf. Cassius Dio 56.3. 3. Lock, 141, cites laudatory Latin epitaphs: 'domiseda'; 'domum servavit, lanam fecit'.

have a pejorative sense when applied to men who were 'stay-at-homes' instead of going to war (Aeschylus, *Agam.* 1225). The verb οἰκουρέω is used in the same senses as the adjective.

Bernard, 167 (following the powerful statement in Field 1899:220–2), suggests that οἰκουργούς is a rather weak term, whereas οἰκουρούς was a recognised term of praise, and therefore prefers to read the latter despite the weaker attestation. Most commentators prefer the text as being better attested, the rarer word, and a Hellenistic form. If the two terms were synonymous, the argument for the Classical word falls. The term envisages efficient running of the household (cf. οἰκοδεσποτέω 1 Tim 5.14) and marks a strong contrast with the peripateticism in 1 Tim 5.13 (cf. Prov 7.11).

ἀγαθάς (1.16) either modifies the preceding word or stands as an independent quality. (a) With the preceding word it means 'good' (NA; GNB; Dibelius-Conzelmann, 141; Hanson, 180); (b) On its own it means 'kind', 'considerate' (so vg *benignas*; Kilpatrick; NJB; NIV; NJB; REB; NRSV; Holtzmann, 483; most commentators; cf. 1 Pet 2.18; 1 Clement 56.16).[49] Normally in the PE ἀγαθός occurs in set combinations.[50] In this case, the rhythm of the sentence and the lack of qualifiers with the other qualities favour view (b) (Arichea-Hatton, 284): the wife is to exhibit kindness towards all those with whom she comes in contact as she applies herself to her domestic duties.

ὑποτασσομένας τοῖς ἰδίοις ἀνδράσιν The final quality is submissiveness by the wife to the husband. Although ὑποτάσσομαι, 'to subject oneself' (2.9; 3.1**; ὑποταγή, 1 Tim 2.11; 3.4) is used variously in the NT (Luke 3 times; Paul 20 times; Heb 5 times; Jas once; 1 Pet 6 times), it has become a fixed part of the household code tradition and of teaching that deals with relationships.[51] Spicq comments that subjection should not be confused with obedience (although it is shown in obedience), and that the concept of reverent submission, involving respect and willingness to serve, has no secular parallels (*TLNT* III, 424–6). Roloff (322) suggests that the adjective ἴδιος is used for emphasis – i.e.

---

[49] Nevertheless, Oberlinner, 112, adopts the previous meaning although regarding it as expressing an independent quality; he translates it as 'tüchtig', i.e. efficient, perhaps hard-working.

[50] συνείδησις ἀγαθή, 1 Tim 1.5, 19; ἔργον ἀγαθόν, 1 Tim 2.10; 5.10; 2 Tim 2.21; 3.17; Tit 1.16; 3.1; cf. πίστιν ἀγαθήν, Tit 2.10.

[51] It is used of wives (Tit 2.5; Eph 5.21; Col 3.18; 1 Pet. 3.1, 5; cf. 1 Cor 14.34); of slaves (Tit 2.9; 1 Pet 2.18); of attitude to government (Tit 3.1; Rom 13.1, 5; 1 Pet. 2.13). ὑποταγή is used in 1 Tim 2.11 of women, and in 3.4 of children. Cf. Delling, G., *TDNT* VIII, 39–46; Goppelt 1993:174–6; *TLNT* III, 424–6; *New Docs.* I, 33–6 §8 (of the attitude expected by a husband from his wife).

'their own husbands (masters)'.[52] The point, in the case of both slaves and wives, is to limit the subordination command to the relationship that exists within the household, rather than applying it to the community in general: the subjection of wives is to their husbands, not to men in general; slaves are to be subject to their specific masters, not to all free men in the community.

ἵνα μὴ ὁ λόγος τοῦ θεοῦ βλασφημῆται Finally, the purpose or motivation behind the life to be pursued by younger women is stated. It is expressed in negative terms as a consequence that may be avoided through godly behaviour.[53] The clause applies to all that has preceded and especially to the command to subordination to husbands (Holtzmann, 484).

ὁ λόγος τοῦ θεοῦ is 'the gospel message which originates with God'.[54] The use of βλασφημέω, 'to blaspheme, revile' (3.2; 1 Tim 1.20; 6.1**), is reminiscent of Isa 52.5; Ezek 36.20–36 (cf. 1 Tim 6.1; Rom 2.24; Jas 2.7; 2 Clement 13.2a), where the concern is that the ungodly behaviour of God's own people will cause the nations to blaspheme God's name.[55] It is possible that the wives of non-Christians are especially in mind, as in 1 Pet 3; but in any case, it is clearly believed that disrespectful behaviour on the part of younger women reflecting insubordination would attract criticism from unbelievers that would undermine the credibility of the Christian message.

As a result of the conversion of the 'subordinate' member, the relationships of wives to husbands and slaves to masters would come under close scrutiny by unbelievers. This may explain why all household codes address wives and slaves without fail (cf. Bartsch 1965:144–59). Women and slaves were held to be particularly susceptible to foreign religions (e.g. Cicero, *Laws* 2.7.19–27), and it was essential to the reputation of the church that an example of godliness be given to unbelievers at this level. In these relationships, particularly if only one member were Christian, the tension set up between believer and unbeliever and belief and practice would be most acute and insubordination or 'emancipation' of any sort would be easily felt. The interest in the reaction of outsiders (cf. 2.8, 10; 1 Tim 3.6–7; 1 Tim 6.1) and the positive motivation of 2.10 suggest that some degree of apologetic-missionary interest may be in view (cf. Quinn, 138; Padgett 1987).

[52] For the use of ἴδιος (1.3) instead of the possessive pronoun ἑαυτοῦ/ἑαυτῶν see 1.3 note.

[53] For the same sentiment, 1 Tim 5.14; 6.1; cf. the positive purpose in 2.10.

[54] The gen. is subjective; cf. 1.3 note; Rom 9.6; 1 Cor 14.36; 2 Cor 2.17; 4.2; Col 1.25). The phrase is unlikely to refer to a specific text such as Gen 3.16 (*pace* Holtz, 220).

[55] Cf. Lindars 1961:22f.; Beyer, H. W., *TDNT* I, 621–5; Hofius, O., *EDNT* I, 219–21.

d. To younger men (2.6–8)

The instruction for young men which follows that concerning older people is at first sight remarkably brief and bland in comparison (cf. the relative lengths of 1 Tim 2.9–15 and 2.8, Brox, 294). But the appearance is deceptive, since, although the statement is rather curt on its own, it is backed up by the qualities which Titus himself is to exemplify for the young men in vv. 7f. Some of these are generally applicable; the others refer more to Titus's own conduct as a teacher, but the character which he manifests as a teacher and the content of his message will influence others by example. Just as the older women are to be an example to the younger, so is Titus to the men (Hasler, 92).

If an existing household table has been taken over, it is arguable that vv. 7–8 (or 7–8a) are an insertion into it (Brox, 295). But the extreme brevity of the basic statement to the young men rather speaks against the hypothesis of use of a source at this point.

Titus himself is regarded as a younger man (Holtzmann, 484) and therefore he can be directly a pattern to this age group. He is thus like Timothy (cf. 1 Tim 4.12; 5.1f.; 2 Tim 2.22). Brox, 295f. thinks that this motif is a further element in the pseudepigraphical framework of the letter, just as in 1 Timothy where it also appears in conjunction with paraenesis and the concept of exemplariness.[56] He also finds it inconsistent that Titus's age is not made explicit. The omission is intelligible. Timothy may well have been younger than Titus (Bernard, 168, thinks that the latter was more of middle-age), and appears to have had a rather timid character, as a result of which people did not readily respect him (1 Cor 16.10f.). Brox overlooks the fact that it is the *authority* of Titus as a leader that is at stake in 2.15.

Instruction to the young as a specific group in the church is not common (1 Pet 5.1; it is possibly implied in 1 Tim 5.1). In the new social relationships within the church it may be that roles were not as sharply defined as elsewhere in society. There was need to emphasise that groups generally regarded as 'subject' in society should not abuse their equality in Christ. The opposite problem is reflected in 2.15 where the youthfulness of appointed leaders was not acceptable to the older generation.

The command here is a very broad one to sobriety of conduct, i.e. the same as to the other members of the church in vv. 1, 5. It is followed by what is in effect a command to Titus himself to exemplify the qualities that should be seen in the young men.

---

[56] Cf. Donelson 1986:61f., 93; Wolter 1988:191–202; Trummer 1978:76–8; Stenger 1974:252–67.

Two areas are specified. The first is the practice of good deeds. This suggests that the writer is again concerned with frivolity in the church, lack of serious purpose in life, and the wasting of time on fruitless discussions instead of aiming to live usefully (cf. 1.16). The second area is more Titus's own responsibilities as a teacher, where three requirements are listed. The first is incorruptibility in his teaching; this apparently refers to its upright quality springing from a pure mind (by contrast with that which comes from depraved people [1 Tim 6.5]). The second is seriousness and dignity, which again suggests that the teachings of the opponents were regarded as frivolous and contemptible. The third is that the actual content is health-giving and free from anything that can be reproached by opponents. The purpose is that opponents may in fact be reduced to silence because there is nothing that they can latch on to and attack in the teaching (cf. Weiser*, 405f.).

TEXT

6. τοὺς νεωτέρους Omit τούς (103, 1739, 424** Theophyl.). The omission is favoured by Elliott, 182, who compares 2.2, 3, 9; 1 Tim 3.8, 12. The MS evidence is too weak.

7. πάντα σεαυτόν (ℵ A C D² F G 1739 1881 TR lat): πάντας ἑαυτόν (Ψ 33 104 326 *pc*); πάντα ἑαυτόν (D*); πάντας σεαυτόν (*pc*); πάντων σεαυτόν (P). Wrong word division is responsible for the variants (Elliott, 182).

ἀφθορίαν ἀδιαφθορίαν (ℵ² D¹ Ψ TR; Kilpatrick); ἀφθονίαν (³² F G 1881 *pc* – transcriptional error). The word is rare and this caused textual problems (see Metzger, 585). The insertion of ἁγνείαν (Ψᶜ 604 326 88 *et al.* vtᵍ vg) is accepted by Elliott, 183, who compares 1 Tim 4.12; 5.2, and argues for loss by homoioteleuton, despite the weak evidence.

σεμνότητα Add ἀφθαρσίαν (D² Ψ TR syʰ). Elliott, 183, includes on analogy with 2 Tim 1.10. arguing that it could have been omitted because of its close similarity in meaning to ἀφθορία, but the meaning does not fit well here.

8. περὶ ἡμῶν περὶ ὑμῶν (A *pc* a vgᵐˢˢ). There was frequent confusion of the pronouns. Elliott, 123, accepts the variant (cf. 2 Tim 1.14), but the evidence is very weak.

EXEGESIS

6. Τοὺς νεωτέρους ὡσαύτως παρακάλει σωφρονεῖν νεώτερος is a comparative form of νέος (2.4), but with little comparative force (but so in Lk 15.13) and often equivalent to the simplex form.[57] The precise identity of the group is disputed. The term refers to age. It contrasts with πρεσβύτερος in a simple twofold classification of young and old with no 'middle-aged' (2.2 note). Behm, J., *TDNT* IV, 897, suggests the range 20–30

[57] 1 Tim 5.1, 2, 11, 14; 1 Pet 5.5; Jn 21.18; Acts 5.6; Polycarp 5.3; equivalent to superlative, Lk 22.26; cf. νεωτερικός, 2 Tim 2.22; νεότης, 1 Tim 4.12.

for the young men. The suggestion that the reference is to newly baptised believers over against the leaders[58] is improbable in the context of 2.1–5 with its reference to young women (Hanson, 181). Nor is there a reference to some kind of association similar to those found in secular contexts (for which see Schürer, III, 103). Earlier, Holtzmann, 238f., argued that the young men stand over against the elders and are in fact deacons (cf. Lk 22.26; Acts 5.6, 10; 1 Pet 5.1); but the young men and the deacons are distinguished in Polycarp 5.2f. Nothing more than the obligation of the younger people to carry out menial duties may be implied in the references (cf. Schneider, G., *EDNT* II, 462f.).

ὡσαύτως (2.3 note) serves to add the next item in a set, but in the present context it may stress the repetition of the concept of σωφροσύνη which is required of each of the groups to be addressed. παρακαλέω (1.9 note) is stronger than λαλέω (2.1) but synonymous. The repetition of a verb instructing Titus what to say is necessary after the lengthy previous instruction (contrast 2.3). σωφρονεῖν** can mean: (a) 'to be of sound mind', as opposed to being insane, mad (Mk 5.15; Lk 8.35; 2 Cor 5.13); (b) 'to be reasonable, serious' (1 Pet 4.7; Rom 12.3[59]). It was used of chaste, virtuous women (1 Clement 1.3; Polycarp 4.3). The basic idea appears to be that of self-control[60] rather than prudence (*pace* Dibelius-Conzelmann, 141; see further **Excursus 3**).

7. **περὶ πάντα, σεαυτὸν παρεχόμενος τύπον καλῶν ἔργων** περὶ πάντα, 'in all respects', is a phrase found here only in NT.[61] Its reference, however, is disputed, as to whether it qualifies (a) what precedes;[62] or (b) what follows.[63] On the one hand, Dibelius-Conzelmann argue that the infinitive in v. 6 is rather bare by itself. One might add that the phrase is not altogether appropriate with the following words. On the other hand, Holtz holds that, if it is linked with what precedes, the phrase forms a conclusion to which nothing should be added, whereas more does follow. This is a subjective opinion. On the whole option (a) is to be preferred.

[58] Elliott, J. H., 'Ministry and Church Order in the NT: A Traditio-Historical Analysis (1 Pt 5,1–5 and plls.)', *CBQ* 32 (1970), 367–91.
[59] Cf. Thucydides 4.60.1; 61.1; 64.4 ('to have judgement'); Xenophon, *Cyr.* 3.2.4; Philo, *Det.* 114; Josephus, *Ant.* 2.296.
[60] Cf. Holtzmann, 484, who notes that it is synonymous with νήφω. Luck, U., *TDNT* VII, 1103, suggests 'a measured and orderly life'.
[61] Cf. περὶ πόλλα, Lk 10.41; Polycarp 4.3.
[62] NA[27]; NJB; REB; Parry, 79 ('perhaps'); Dibelius-Conzelmann, 141; Jeremias, 71; Kelly, 242; Spicq, 622; Brox, 294; Fee, 188; Quinn, 123.
[63] So vg[F]; Chrysostom (*PG* LXII, 684); WH; UBS[3]; RV; GNB; NIV; NRSV; Ellicott, 182; Holtzmann, 484; Lock, 141f.; Easton, 90; Guthrie, 207; Holtz, 220f.; Arichea-Hatton, 286. Knight, 311, is undecided.

παρέχομαι is act. 'to offer, provide' (1 Tim 1.4; 6.17**; Lk 6.29; Acts 17.31; 22.2; 28.2; *et al.*); in Cl. it can also have the force 'to show oneself to be, and the mid. can be used in the same way in Hel.[64] σεαυτόν (1 Tim 4.7, 16a, 16b; 5.22; 2 Tim 2.15; 4.11**) occurs comparatively frequently in the PE because of the amount of exhortation addressed to the recipients. τύπος is 'archetype, pattern, model' (Acts 7.44; Heb 8.5); hence 'moral example, pattern' of a determinative nature.[65] Paul himself functions in this way, and both Titus and Timothy must do so also (1 Tim 4.12; Phil 3.17; 1 Th 1.7; 2 Th 3.9; 1 Pet 5.3.; Ignatius, *Magn.* 6.2f. [cj.]). For the thought cf. 1 Tim 4.15; 1 Cor 4.6; 11.1; 1 Th 1.6; 2 Th 3.7, 9.[66] Wolter 1988:191–5, stresses that Titus (and Timothy in 1 Tim 4.12) are called not so much to be examples to the congregation as rather examples of the ideal believer. It is the older people and the leaders who are given this role in the ancient world, and therefore one is not to deduce from this passage that Titus himself was necessarily a young man (Wolter 1988:192f.; Oberlinner, 116f. contrast 1 Tim 4.12 and see below on 2.15).

ἐν τῇ διδασκαλίᾳ ἀφθορίαν, σεμνότητα (8a.) λόγον ὑγιῆ ἀκατάγνωστον The construction in the rest of the sentence is not clear. Although some scholars have linked ἐν τῇ διδασκαλίᾳ (cf. 1.9; 1 Tim 5.17) with what precedes, with the result that the following accusatives refer to Titus's own character (WH mg; cf. Parry, 79), it appears rather to denote the sphere of the following qualities. It may refer to the manner (Kelly, 242; Arichea-Hatton, 286, since the content comes later) or to the content of the teaching. As for the following nouns in the acc., these may be regarded as (a) the objects of the preceding παρεχόμενος (Holtzmann, 485) or (b) an example of anacolouthon. There would seem to be a case of syllepsis, since the participle is used first with a double acc. ('show yourself as a model of good deeds') and then with plain acc. ('[show] soundness in your teaching'; cf. Brox, 296; Foerster, W., *TDNT* VII, 195). Calvin, 371, took ἀκατάγνωστον to be in agreement with σεαυτόν and λόγον ὑγιῆ as an acc. of respect (cf. Quinn, 142f.).

There are three qualities, the last one being developed more fully. ἀφθορία must mean 'incorruption, soundness', i.e. freedom

---

[64] Cf. BA; BD § 316³; contrast the act. in Josephus, *Ap.* 2.156. The mid. can also mean 'to grant' (Lk 7.4; Col 4.1; cf. Acts 19.24). The use of σεαυτόν with the mid. is redundant but reinforces the personal application of the injunction (Deissmann 1901:254 and Spicq, 622, cite Hellenistic parallels).

[65] Cf. the use of ὑποτύπωσις (1 Tim 1.16; 2 Tim 1.13); ὑπογραμμός (1 Pet 2.21); ὑπόδειγμα (Jn 13.15; Jas 5.10; 2 Pet 2.6; Heb 4.11). Cf. Dittenberger, *Or.* 383, 212 (I bc), τῆς εὐσεβείας (cited by BA); *Sib. Orac.* 1.380; 4 Macc 6.19 [bad]); Fee, 107. Cf. Goppelt, L., *TDNT* VIII, 246–59; *TLNT* III, 384–7.

[66] For καλὰ ἔργα see **Excursus 6**.

from guilt. It is a rare word,[67] but the corresponding adjective ἄφθορος is found with the sense 'uncorrupt, chaste'.[68] The reference is uncertain; Holtzmann, 485, lists: (a) the content of teaching (cf. Spicq, 623: free from any deviation from the truth); (b) the integrity and purity of the teacher's convictions (so most translations; Kelly, 242); (c) the form of the teaching, as corresponding to the essence of the gospel (cf. 1 Cor 2.1f.). Harder holds that the word refers to the 'moral attitude of Titus' over against the false teachers and their teaching. He claims that 'we are not to think in terms of the impregnability against false teaching that Titus is establishing in the churches [Schlatter], nor in terms of doctrine safeguarded by the truth [Wohlenberg], but rather of innocence in the sense of not being, or not able to be, corrupted' (103). Brox, 296, claims that both (a) and (b) are possible (cf. Schlarb 1990:298).

σεμνότης is 'reverence, dignity, seriousness' (1 Tim 2.2; 3.4***; cf. σεμνός, 2.2; 1 Tim 3.8, 11; Phil 4.8***; see **Excursus 3**). Here the idea is of serious and worthy behaviour on the part of the leader. It is not certain whether it refers to Titus's demeanour in general or specifically to a quality of his teaching. If the latter, the reference is hardly to the content of what Titus is to teach, but to the way in which he is to teach. (Spicq, 623, however, thinks that it means the exclusion of all worldly material, such as genealogies and speculations, from the teaching.) It will refer to a seriousness in teaching which contrasts with the crudity and folly of the false teaching, which the writer regarded as contemptible and even laughable. It is a quality which should win respect from other people because the teacher takes life seriously and devoutly and does not trifle. Foerster holds that it is the reputation of the church among outside opponents which is at risk (cf. v. 8b); this would fit in with the general tenor of the passage (2.5b, 10b). But it is more likely that a contrast with the heretics in the church is primarily in view.

8. λόγον (1.3) probably refers here to 'teaching' (cf. Holtz, 221; Lips 1979:40 n. 43), but some commentators think that it may have a broader reference to Titus' speech in general. Again there is a transition in the construction in that the previous noun referred to the manner of the teaching, but this one must refer to its content. Elsewhere in the PE the phrase is in the pl. ὑγιής**, 'healthy', is used here only in the PE instead of the part. of ὑγιαίνω (1.9 note).[69] The metaphorical use of the adjective is common.[70]

---

[67] LSJ give one AD IV reference in Themistius.
[68] Justin, *Apol.* I.15.6; *Dial.* 100.5; Esth 2.2; cf. Harder, G., *TDNT* IX, 93–106.
[69] Cf. ὑγιὴς ὁ λόγος (Hierocles, p. 59, 9, cited by van der Horst 1975:159).
[70] Cf. *Ep. Arist.* 250; Philo, *Spec.* 2.164; Josephus, *Ant.* 9.118; BA.

Quinn, 142f., apparently takes the adjective as descriptive of Titus with an acc. of respect, and similarly with the next adjective. Such a further change in construction is unlikely.

ἀκαταγνωστός*** is 'irreproachable', i.e. 'not open to just rebuke' (Bernard, 169), used of a person who is acquitted (2 Macc 4.47). Here, applied to speech, it must mean 'beyond reproach'.[71]

8b. ἵνα ὁ ἐξ ἐναντίας ἐντραπῇ μηδὲν ἔχων λέγειν περὶ ἡμῶν φαῦλον ὁ ἐξ ἐναντίας [sc. χώρας] is the 'opponent'.[72] ἐντρέπω** here has the Hel. sense 'to make someone ashamed' (1 Cor 4.14); pass. 'to be put to shame, be ashamed'.[73] The hope is that such people will not only have nothing to say against the faith but will be converted (Holtz, 222). περὶ ἡμῶν may refer specifically to Paul and Titus or to Christians generally. φαῦλος**, 'worthless' (Jn 3.20; 5.29; Rom 9.11; 2 Cor 5.10; Jas. 3.16***), is used as a transferred epithet – 'no report of our worthlessness'. For the thought see 1 Tim 3.7; 1 Pet 2.12. The critic is to have no legitimate ground for censure. Bernard, 169, holds that the word is used of deeds rather than words; hence the point is that the teacher's way of life must be above reproach (similarly, Fee, 189). But Quinn, 126, notes that in the LXX four out of the ten uses apply to words.

If specific opponents are in mind, their identity is uncertain. Chrysostom (*PG* LXII, 684) took the sing. reference literally to Satan. Hanson, 181f., draws attention to the sing. form, but seems to think of a plurality of opponents. Three main proposals have been made, and several scholars would hold that more than one group may be in mind: (a) heretical teachers;[74] (b) pagan critics;[75] (c) Jewish opponents (Quinn, 143, on flimsy grounds). Whereas 2.5 and 10 clearly refer to the effect on outsiders, this verse is more concerned with Titus's own conduct within the church, and therefore (a) is to be preferred as the primary reference.

---

[71] The word is found elsewhere mainly in late inscriptions and papyri (cf. Bultmann, R., *TDNT* I, 714f.; Deissmann 1901:200f.; *TLNT* I, 58). Cf. ἀνέγκλητον (1.6f.); ἀνεπίλημπτον (1 Tim 3.2).

[72] Cf. BA; Philo, *Aet.* 7; in Mk 15.39 ἐξ ἐναντίας = 'opposite somebody'); cf. οἱ ἀντιλέγοντες (1.9); ὁ ἀντικείμενος (1 Tim 5.14); οἱ ἀντιδιατιθέμενοι (2 Tim 2.25).

[73] Cf. Ps 34 (MT 35).26; Isa 41.11; 2 Th 3.14; Ignatius, *Magn.* 12.; cf. ἐντροπή, 1 Cor 6.5; 15.34.

[74] Brox, 296; Kelly, 242f.; Fee, 189; Holtz, 221f.; Knight, 313; Oberlinner, 118; Lips 1979:158 n. 278.

[75] Holtzmann, 485, in view of 2.5; 1 Tim 6.1; Lock, 142; Spicq, 623, and Hanson, 181f., include the heretical teachers among them; cf. Foerster, W., *TDNT* VII, 195.

e. To slaves (2.9–10)

This passage should be considered in conjunction with 1 Tim 6.1f. where different teaching is given, but with a similar motive. There are three negative and two positive commands followed by a purpose clause. The first two commands are in the infinitive, followed by three participles. The basic instruction is that slaves are to be subject to their masters, i.e. obedient to their commands. This is followed by two positive and two negative commands stated chiastically. Slaves are to please their masters and not to enter into disputes with them. They are not to steal but to be fully trustworthy. By so doing they will not only avoid outsiders condemning the Christian message because it leads to insubordination (1 Tim 6.1) but they will rather add lustre to the message by showing that it leads to good moral living in society. As pointed out above in connection with younger women (2.6 note on βλασφημέω), slaves were held to be susceptible to foreign religions – exemplary behaviour on their part would demonstrate the validity of the Christian message.

Weiser*, 408f., observes that whereas the first four groups in this section are constituted naturally by age and addressed regarding their duties in the congregation, the fifth group is constituted by their social status and are addressed regarding their household duties to their masters, and the instruction is concerned entirely with subordination (cf. Oberlinner, 119). This sharp distinction is achieved at the cost of underplaying the significance of vv. 4b, 5a and not observing that the qualities to be shown are required both in the congregation and in ordinary life. The boundaries are more fluid than Weiser allows. No hard and fast line can be drawn between the congregation and the household, so long as the congregations met in houses. It must be recognised, therefore, that for all the emphasis on oneness in Christ in the teaching of Paul and the recognition of a brotherly relation between masters and slaves, the church had not yet reached the point of recognising consistently and universally that the new status in Christ posed sharp questions regarding the subordination that was a part of the hierarchical society in which it lived. Modern Christians, members of churches which have been just as slow to recognise the social implications of their oneness in Christ, to say nothing of the ecclesiastical implications, should not be too quick to criticise them.[76]

As, then, with the previous instructions, here the conduct of believers in their own households is a matter on which the

---

[76] On the general problem of how the early Christians related the teaching of Gal 3.28 to the household codes see Motyer*.

Christian leader is to give instruction and exhortation. The evaluations of commentators vary widely.

On the one hand, Brox, 296f. affirms that pagan ethics are simply Christianised by the addition of a Christian motive, but not really questioned. The absence of any reference to possible injustices or to the duties of masters is said to display the danger of upholding the status quo without changing it from within (Merkel, 97). This may be an indication that the churches in Crete did not contain persons sufficiently wealthy to be masters (contrast 1 Tim; Hasler, 93; Holtz, 222). But the lack of reference to masters may be simply because this section is about the duties of 'subject' members. Morever, masters are never told here or elsewhere to make their slaves subject to them, and neither in Stoicism nor in Judaism is there teaching on the duties of slaves (Quinn, 147).[77]

On the other hand, it has been observed that the passage shows that even the lowliest in society can contribute to the splendour of the Christian life (Spicq, 626). According to Hasler, 93, the passage shows that people can live a Christian life within the existing orders of society; they are not displaying servility but rather recognising the will of the Creator within society and seizing the opportunities for living to his glory.[78] This is not a 'bourgeois' transformation of Christian ethics. Similarly, Murphy-O'Connor comments:

> To us there is little striking in what is demanded of the Christian slave – simple honesty and loyalty. It can hardly be said to command respect and admiration. However, in the first century the vast majority of slaves lived in a state of such degradation that it had disastrous effects on their moral character. In this perspective the comportment of a slave who was utterly devoted and scrupulously honest could not fail to provoke wonder that turned to attentive respect when the source of this miraculous change was claimed to be the gospel.[79]

TEXT

9. ἰδίοις δεσπόταις δεσπόταις ἰδίοις (A D P 326 1739 1881 *pc*; Kilpatrick). The variant is adopted by Elliott, 184, on the ground that, when a noun is

---

[77] See *New Docs.* VII, 163–96, espec. 193–6.

[78] Llewelyn, S. R., *New Docs.* VII, 195f. §8, notes that the question of the slave's conflict of loyalties when required by the master to do something that conflicted with God's demands is not raised.

[79] Murphy-O'Connor, J., 'Community and Apostolate. Reflections on 1 Timothy 2:1–7', *BibTod* 67 (1973), 1260–6 (1263).

anarthrous, ἴδιος follows it (1 Tim 2.6; 6.15; Tit 1.3) as a more Semitic construction. This is possible here, as the MS support is reasonable.

10. μή μηδέ (C² D*ᶜ F G 33 *pc* syᵖ WH mg); Elliott, 137, accepts the variant (cf. 2 Tim 2.14; Tit 2.3); Quinn, 127, hesitates.

πᾶσαν πίστιν ἐνδεικνυμένους ἀγαθήν (ℵ² A C D P 81 104 326 365 1505 1739 1881 *pc*). The word order varies: 1–3-2–4 (F G); 1–4-2–3 (629) 2-1-3–4 (Ψ TR); 1–3-ἀγάπην (33 WH mg); 1–3-4 (ℵ*; WH t). Elliott, 185, supports the text. He suggests that πίστιν was omitted because of the awkward position of ἀγαθήν, and notes that πᾶς normally precedes the noun.

τὴν διδασκαλίαν τήν The article after the noun is omitted by 1739 1881 TR, but the PE often have it (1 Tim 1.4; 3.13; 2 Tim 1.1; 2.1, 10), and it should be retained (Elliott, 186).

EXEGESIS

9. Δούλους ἰδίοις δεσπόταις ὑποτάσσεσθαι ἐν πᾶσιν, εὐαρέστους εἶναι, μὴ ἀντιλέγοντας δοῦλος is used in the lit. sense here and in 1 Tim 6.1 (cf. metaphorical use in 1.1; 2 Tim 2.24). The situation of slaves at this time is well summarised in Bartchy 1973:72–82. δεσπότης is the regular term for the 'master, owner' of property (cf. οἰκοδεσποτέω, 1 Tim 5.14); of a vessel (2 Tim 2.21); of slaves (1 Tim 6.1, 2; 1 Pet 2.18; Hermas, *Sim.* 5.2.2).[80] The word was used by Christians as an equivalent to *dominus* as a technical term for human slave masters; κύριος with its sacred meaning tended to be avoided (but see Eph 6.5; Col 3.22). Although Spicq, 625, claims that the plural here is because slaves could have more than one master, it is surely distributive.[81] The infinitive ὑποτάσσεσθαι (2.5 note) is probably dependent on παρακάλει (2.6) understood. It is unlikely to be an imperatival infinitive addressed directly to the slaves (so Spicq, 624), since in this case a nominative would be needed. Spicq, 624, insists that the word connotes not so much obedience as rather 'keeping to one's position and developing attitudes of humility (cf. *Ep. Arist.* 257), respect and love towards every superior authority, whatever it may be' (cf. Delling, G., *TDNT* VIII, 45; Quinn, 147). ἐν πᾶσιν clearly goes with ὑποτάσσεσθαι rather than with the following phrase (*pace* RV; GNB; NRSV); Holtzmann, 486, notes that the phrase always goes with what precedes in the NT; cf. the similar pattern in Eph 5.24; Col 3.20, 22, which is surely decisive.

The situation envisaged is not certain: (a) Christian slaves in Christian families (Fee, 190; Knight); (b) Christian slaves in non-Christian households (Holtz, 222; Hanson, 182; Hasler, 93; mainly non-Christian masters, Knoch, 42). In fact there is no

---

[80] Elsewhere it can be used of God (Lk 2.29; Acts 4.24; Rev 6.10) and Christ (2 Pet 2.1; Jude 4***). Cf. Rengstorf, K. H., *TDNT* II, 44–9.

[81] For ἴδιος see 1.3 note; 1 Tim 6.1; on the omission of the article see BD §286²; §285².

specification (cf. 1 Tim 6.1f. and note), and the duty of slaves in any situation is in mind. There is no reference to the service being really to God or Christ, as in Col 3.23; Eph 6.6; 1 Pet 2.19, but this is compensated for by the purpose clause in v. 10. The general command is developed in four further phrases. There are two positive and two negative commands arranged chiastically. Good service in the broadest sense is expressed by εὐάρεστος, 'pleasing, acceptable'. Although the adv. εὐαρέστως (Heb 12.28) is found in Xenophon, the adj. is Hellenistic.[82] It is used here in a general sense, but elsewhere of pleasing God.[83]

For μὴ ἀντιλέγοντας see 1.9 note; 3 Macc 2.28. In ancient comedy slaves are typically portrayed as having considerable freedom of speech towards their masters (Spicq, 625).

10. μὴ νοσφιζομένους, ἀλλὰ πᾶσαν πίστιν ἐνδεικνυμένους ἀγαθήν Theft was a further standard failing of slaves; cf. *Pesaḥ.* 113b: 'love one another, love theft, love debauchery, hate your masters and never tell the truth' (Spicq, 625). νοσφίζομαι is 'to purloin, pilfer, put aside for oneself, misappropriate' (Acts 5.2f.***; 2 Macc 4.12; *TLNT* II, 546f.); it covers petty larcenies (Simpson, 106).

The positive contrast is expressed in terms of demonstrating utter dependability. ἐνδείκνυμι 'to show, demonstrate', hence 'to do something to somebody', is found almost exclusively in the Pauline corpus in the NT and here is always mid.[84] The verb means not merely to 'prove' but 'to demonstrate' powerfully and visibly (Spicq, 625f.; cf. Roloff, 97 n. 221), with reference to qualities of character, as in 3.2;[85] it is used of demonstrations of the divine character in 1 Tim 1.16 (cf. Rom 9.17, 22; Eph 2.7; cf. ἔνδειξις, Rom 3.25f.). The use of the adj. πᾶς to mean 'in all respects, on all occasions' is common (2.15; 3.2; cf. White, 98). πίστις (1.5 note) is here 'fidelity, faithfulness' shown towards other people.[86] It was a secular virtue.[87] The use of ἀγαθός (1.16) here is odd, and the translators tend towards renderings like 'perfect' (NRSV). The force is not the same as in 'good deeds'

---

[82] Cf. BA; Dibelius-Conzelmann, 141 n. 18; Wis 4.10; 9.10; *T. Dan.* 1.3; Philo, *Jos.* 195; *Spec.* 1.201; *Virt.* 67; cf. Hermas, *Sim.* 5.2.2.

[83] Rom 12.1, 2; 14.18; 2 Cor 5.9; Phil 4.18; Col 3.20; Heb 13.21***; cf. εὐαρεστέω (Heb 11.5f.; 13.16]; ἀρέσκω (2 Tim 2.4); ἀρεστός (Acts 12.3; *et al.*); cf. Foerster, W., *TDNT* I, 456f.

[84] 3.2; 1 Tim 1. 16; 2 Tim 4.14; Rom 2.15; 9.17, 22; 2 Cor 8.24; Eph 2.7; Heb 6.10f.***; cf. ἔνδειξις, Rom 3.25, 26; 2 Cor 8.24; Phil 1.28. Cf. Paulsen, H., *EDNT* I, 449–50.

[85] Josephus, *Ant.* 7.212; cf. 2 Tim 4.14 of evil qualities.

[86] Cf. Mt 23.23; Rom 3.3; possibly Gal 5.22; 2 Th 1.4; see 1 Tim 5.12 and note; 2 Tim 4.7 and note; cf. Bultmann, R., *TDNT* VI, 204 n. 227.

[87] Dittenberger, *Syll.* 727.20 (AD I); see also Philo, *Decal.* 165–7 (Quinn, 148), where slaves are to show 'an affectionate loyalty to their masters'.

or a 'good conscience'. Possibly it means 'true, genuine' (Ellicott, 185). Probably it refers to whatever people would regard as good and praiseworthy in fidelity, and Ellicott's proposal remains the best. Holtz, 223, notes how dictators and tyrants have always demanded utter loyalty from their subjects, and suggests that in contrast fidelity that is good in the sight of God is what is demanded of Christians (Eph 2.10; Col 1.10). Cf. Quinn, 149, for similar comments. In any case, what is required is not bourgeois morality, but heroic (Spicq, 626).

ἵνα τὴν διδασκαλίαν τὴν τοῦ σωτῆρος ἡμῶν θεοῦ κοσμῶσιν ἐν πᾶσιν ἵνα introduces a positive purpose which should act as motivation (cf. 2.5, 8); contrast the negative formulation in 1 Tim 6.1. The aim is to adorn the teaching (διδασκαλία, 1.9) τοῦ σωτῆρος ἡμῶν θεοῦ (1.3; cf. 3.4; 1 Tim 2.3). The reference is to God, not Christ, and the phrase prepares the way for the doctrinal backing in vv. 11–14. The gen. is objective, 'teaching about God our Saviour' (pace Holtz, 224). ἐν πᾶσιν is probably neut. (BA; Knight) rather than masc. (Holtzmann, 486; Easton, 93 ['possibly']). κοσμέω is lit. 'to put in order' (Mt 25.7), 'make beautiful', both physically (Mt 12.44 par. Lk 11.25; Mt 23.29; Lk 21.5; Rev 21.19; of dress, hairstyle, Rev 21.2) and spiritually (1 Tim 2.9; 1 Pet 3.5); hence 'to adorn, do credit to' something or somebody'.[88] Bernard, 170, says that the word was used for setting jewels in such a way as to enhance their beauty, but gives no evidence. It appears rather that the word was used of adding to the beauty of a person or thing by adornment.[89] A good parallel occurs 3 Macc 3.5, where the Jews 'adorned their style of life with the good deeds of upright people'. What is required is a working out of Rom 12.1f. (Knoch, 26). And this can be done even by slaves!

f. The doctrinal basis for the preceding exhortation (2.11–14)

Couser 1992:155–64; Giese, G., 'ΧΑΡΙΣ ΠΑΙΔΕΥΟΥΣΑ. Zur biblischen Begründung des evangelischen Erziehungsgedankens', *Theologia Viatorum* 5 (1953–54), 150–73; Haubeck, W., *Loskauf durch Christus* (Giessen/Basel:Brunnen, 1985), espec. 205–13; Läger 1996:92–8; Lau 1996:150–60, 243–57; Mott 1978:22–48; Schlarb 1990:164–72; Towner 1989:108–11; Trummer 1978:200–2, 232f.; Wilson 1979:17f., 85f.

On the reference of θεός in Tit 2.13: Abbot, E., 'On the construction of Titus II.13', *JBL* 1 (1881), 3–19 (= *The Authorship of the Fourth Gospel and Other Critical Essays* [Boston, 1888], 439–57); Harris, M. J., 'Titus 2:13 and the Deity of Christ', in Hagner, D. A., and Harris, M. J. (ed.), *Pauline Studies:*

---

[88] Of one's πατρίς (Theognis, 947, cited by BA); Eunapius, 456 (of Porphyry: ἐκόσμει τὸν διδάσκαλον; cited by Parry, 80, from Wetstein); further examples in Spicq, 626; cf. Sasse, H., *TDNT* III, 867; *TLNT* II, 330–5.

[89] E.g. Plato, *Ion* 535D; metaphorical in Plato, *Apol.* 17C. Cf. *TLNT* II, 334, n. 21.

Essays Presented to Professor F. F. Bruce (Exeter: Paternoster, 1980), 262–77; Harris, M. J., *Jesus as God: The New Testament Use of Theos in Reference to Jesus* (Grand Rapids: Eerdmans, 1992), 173–85; Wainwright, A. W., 'The Confession "Jesus Is God" in the New Testament', *SJT* 10 (1957), 274–99.

The establishment of ethics on the basis of doctrine is familiar throughout the Bible. The present pattern of exhortation followed by a justification or grounding for it introduced by γάρ is not infrequent in the PE (cf. 1.7 note). Tit contains two extended sections of doctrinal backing for the ethical paraenesis which is given in the letter (2.11–14; 3.3–7), in each case followed by a phrase that integrates the backing into the flow of the letter. Although this passage has been described as the heart of the letter (Spicq, 635), it could be argued that 3.3–7 is equally significant.

The way for the present statement was prepared by the reference to the teaching about God as Saviour which believers are to adorn by their way of life (v. 10), and the passage can be regarded as a statement of this teaching.

In form the passage is a single sentence which can be set out analytically as follows:

Ἐπεφάνη γὰρ ἡ χάρις τοῦ θεοῦ σωτήριος πᾶσιν ἀνθρώποις
    παιδεύουσα ἡμᾶς,
      ἵνα ἀρνησάμενοι τὴν ἀσέβειαν καὶ τὰς κοσμικὰς ἐπιθυμίας
        σωφρόνως καὶ δικαίως καὶ εὐσεβῶς ζήσωμεν ἐν τῷ νῦν αἰῶνι,
        προσδεχόμενοι τὴν μακαρίαν ἐλπίδα
          καὶ ἐπιφάνειαν τῆς δόξης
            τοῦ μεγάλου θεοῦ καὶ σωτῆρος ἡμῶν Ἰησοῦ Χριστοῦ,
            ὃς ἔδωκεν ἑαυτὸν ὑπὲρ ἡμῶν,
              ἵνα λυτρώσηται ἡμᾶς ἀπὸ πασης ἀνομίας
                καὶ καθαρίσῃ ἑαυτῷ λαὸν περιούσιον,
                ζηλωτὴν καλῶν ἔργων.

The initial statement on the appearance of God's grace is extended by a participle which bears the weight of the sentence and stresses that grace has an 'educative purpose'. Thus, the command to teach the believers how to live (2.1) is backed up by a statement which says that, when the grace of God was manifested, its purpose was to educate them in how to live in a godly manner (Lock, 143). The main verb ζήσωμεν is preceded by a participial phrase describing what must be renounced; the renouncing of worldly, sinful desires forms a strong contrast to godly living 'in this age'. It is further flanked by a second participial phrase describing the content of the Christian hope centred on the epiphany of the Saviour; this phrase contains a further contrast between 'this age' and the future hope which believers have while they live in it. Tied to this reference to the coming Saviour by a relative pronoun is a description of his self-giving which leads into a statement of its purpose. Thus doctrine (vv. 12a, 13, 14a) and its ethical consequences (vv. 12b, 14b) are strongly tied together. The nearest parallel in the PE to a sentence of this complexity is 3.4–7.

The picture is not unlike that of pilgrimage in which believers are committed to an ongoing journey or process, and the parameters are similar.[90] The central motif of the guidance is living a life that is characterised by virtue; the qualities inculcated are in fact those approved by the secular world of the time. They are flanked, on the one hand, by a rejection of what should belong to the past, the way of life characterised by irreligion and self-centred desires, and, on the other hand (v. 13), by an attitude of looking forward to the future revelation of the glory of the Saviour. It is at this point that the distinctively Christian element enters which corresponds to the introduction in v. 11 and with it colours the whole statement so that the apparently 'secular' picture of the virtuous life undergoes transformation. The passage then culminates in a kerygmatic statement about the past action of the Saviour which provides the basis for the injunction to godly living and positive goodness. In the same way believers can be exhorted to forget what is or should belong to the past and to run the race with their eyes set on their Saviour who endured for their sakes (Heb 12.1f.; cf. Phil 3.13f.).

The passage thus forms the basis for the preceding instruction on Christian living by reminding the readers that the purpose of God's saving intervention in the world in the self-giving of Christ was to deliver people from evil behaviour and make them into a community characterised by good works; God's grace has an educative transforming effect on people which enables them to turn away from godlessness, to live lives of positive goodness, and to look forward to the final revelation of God's glory in which they will share. Consequently, it is appropriate that they should accept the instructions given to them as part of the educative process in which they have been enrolled.

An interesting question is how far the passage is based on pre-existing material in the form of a Christian confession or hymn. One could certainly envisage the passage being recited as a congregational baptismal or eucharistic confession.[91] Only a minimal use of tradition is allowed by Merkel: an 'old formula' in v. 14 is placed in a 'modern' framework, using contemporary phraseology (Merkel, 98). At the opposite extreme Ellis 1987 views the whole of vv. 2–14 as a reworking of tradition and

---

[90] It is, therefore, not surprising that the thematic discussion of παιδεία (Heb 12.4–11) is found in the epistle of pilgrimage.

[91] Baptismal: Jeremias, 72; eucharistic: Holtz, 224–9; Hasler, 94.

categorises vv. 11–14 in two ways: (a) in terms of topic as 'admonition' (cf. 1 Tim 6.7f., 11f.; 2 Tim 2.11–13); (b) in terms of literary form as 'hymn' (cf. 3.4–7; 1 Tim 2.5f.; 3.16; 6.11f., 15f.; 2 Tim 1.9f.; 2.11–13). He gives as criteria for the recognition of cited and traditioned material: (a) the presence of an opening or closing quotation formula; (b) the self-contained and independent character of the passage; (c) unusual vocabulary and a different idiom, style or theological viewpoint from that of the author; (d) the use of similar material in an independent writing.

Ellis discusses only the first of these points in any detail. The present passage has a closing formula, 'These things speak...' (cf. 1 Tim 4.6, 11; 2 Tim 2.14; cf. 1 Tim 6.2); along with 2.1 ('But as for you speak') this brackets off the whole of the chapter including the 'confessional hymn'.

As for vocabulary and ideas, the notes will show that the only words which do not appear elsewhere in the PE are: σωτήριος, κοσμικός, προσδέχομαι*, λυτρόω, ἀνομία, καθαρίζω, περιούσιος*, and ζηλωτής*. Apart from the words marked with*, the writer uses cognate forms elsewhere, so that the list is drastically reduced. Consequently, it can hardly be claimed that the passage contains vocabulary that is foreign to an author who is characterised by the width of his vocabulary compared with that of Paul. The passage is self-contained, but it has no significant parallels in independent writings (with the exception of v. 14a = 1 Tim 2.6a = Mk 10.45b).

The case for use of tradition thus rests largely on the closing formula (which covers the whole of 2.2–14), on the detachable character of the passage and on its confessional style. But against these points must be placed the set of strong links with the writer's thought elsewhere. Granted that tradition has been used in v. 14, it is difficult to argue that there is a recognisable tradition behind vv. 11–13. The case for the use of formulated tradition as opposed to traditional language here is thus weak.

Another hypothesis is put forward by Hanson 1968:78–96, on the basis of earlier work by M.-E. Boismard.[92] He claims that 2.11–14 and 3.4–7 are two parts of a baptismal, liturgical tradition also used by the authors of Eph and 1 Pet. There are a number of phrases in common between the epistles. The present passage has links with 1 Pet 1.13b–19 (renunciation of ἐπιθυμίαι, holy conduct, hope of the future appearing of Jesus, redemption, and [1 Pet 2.9] God's own people). This would suggest that such themes as these were part of the stock teaching given to converts,

---

[92] Boismard 1961; idem,'Une liturgie baptismale dans la Prima Petri', *RB* 63 (1956), 182–208; 64 (1957), 161–83.

but the links are not sufficient to confirm the existence of a common 'source', still less to reconstruct it.

The passage uses contemporary language from the imperial cult precisely to make the contrast between it and Christian worship (cf. the excursus in Hanson, 186–8). Dibelius-Conzelmann, 145, stress the closeness in tone of the material to what is said about Hellenistic gods and rulers. They argue that the material came to the author via Hellenistic Judaism and that he was able to use formulaic material from various sources without reflection on their differing origins and significance. This procedure is not found in the accepted letters of Paul. Similarly, Hasler, 93f., stresses that the language of Hellenistic ethics is used, precisely in order that Christians might achieve a high moral level in the eyes of the surrounding world and so gain a hearing for the gospel. Yet this morality is given a firm Christian basis in the doctrinal statement into which it is integrated.

One needs to distinguish carefully here between ideas that were at home in Hellenistic Judaism and in Hellenism generally. The explanation offered is not clear at this point.

The thought here is of an educative process giving instruction in how to live. Brox, 298, suggests that the instruction is regarded as actually producing its intended results, since it is the work of grace which has the power to transform lives.

Nevertheless, the concept has aroused negative comment from critics. For Scott, 168: in Paul 'the grace of God consists in a single overwhelming gift which is received in a moment by the act of faith. In the Pastorals it is conceived as working continuously through a steady persistence in Christian belief and practice.' 'In Paul the accent is placed upon justification, here upon education in the faith' (Dibelius-Conzelmann, 142; similarly, Barrett, 137). 'The church appears as an educational institute' (Hasler, 94). 'It is hard to imagine anything more unlike Paul's fervent, far-reaching and profound theology' (Hanson, 184). 'For our writer, the fruit of God's saving grace was less a life of sacrificial suffering than a process of disciplined training' (Houlden, 150).

These comments are wide of the mark. In the context this is but *one* aspect of grace's activity – the one relevant to ethics – which is carried out by 'healthy teaching'. The once-for-all revelation is in view (note again the aorist in v. 11) and the development in v. 14 indicates that salvation is seen in Pauline terms; the thought is clearly paralleled in the importance of persistence in 'faith working by love' in Paul and in the continuing experience of grace in Paul. Nevertheless, the language is fresh and may indicate some influence from the Greek idea that education leads to full attainment of an ideal (Merkel, 99).

Grace is active in the knowledge of the truth and sound teaching, Brox, 298. Cf. 1 Clement 59.3: Ἰησοῦ Χριστοῦ ... δι' οὗ ἡμᾶς ἐπαίδευσας, ἡγίασας, ἐτίμησας. Barrett, 137, notes that grace does not offer a once-for-all deliverance from evil ways but trains people to renounce them.

TEXT

11. γάρ Omit (104 1311 69 460 *et al.*). Elliott, 44, 237, thinks the conjunction may have been added to avoid asyndeton, but it is characteristic of the author's style (1.7; 3.3, 9, 12) and should be retained.

σωτήριος Praem. ἡ ((C³) D² Ψ 33 1881 TR; Kilpatrick). Other variants are the substitution of σωτῆρος (ℵ* t vg^mss); τοῦ σωτῆρος ἡμῶν (F G a b vg^cl ww co Lcf.). Elliott, 186f., holds that 'saviour' is substitution for a rare word or a simple error, and assimilation to the previous verse. He would retain the article, saying that its omission is due to the desire to avoid Semitism. However, in fact it is good Greek. BD §269³ notes that an adj. or part. following after a gen. must have the article if it is attributive (Mt 3.17; 2 Cor 6.7; Eph 6.16; Heb 13.20) unless it is predicative, as here. Holtzmann, 487 takes it as attributive.

13. Ἰησοῦ Χριστοῦ Inverted order (ℵ* F G b; WH mg.; Kilpatrick); so Elliott 201. Omit Χριστοῦ (1739). Cf. 1 Tim 1.1 note.

EXEGESIS

11. Ἐπεφάνη γὰρ ἡ χάρις τοῦ θεοῦ σωτήριος πᾶσιν ἀνθρώποις The basis for the Christian behaviour described in the preceding verses is grounded theologically in the saving epiphany which results from the character of God as Saviour. γάρ introduces the theological basis for 2.1–10 as a whole (Holtzmann, 487) and not just for vv. 9f. Nevertheless, the section is in fact an unpacking of the description of God as Saviour in v. 10. The present section thus gives the content of the 'teaching about our Saviour God' which believers are to adorn by their way of life (Knight, 318; Pax 1955, 239), and it does so by reference to the manifestation of his grace which brings salvation. Four points are made in this opening statement.

First, the content of the Christian message is summed up in terms of God's grace. χάρις (1.4 note) refers to the whole of God's saving act in Christ. Easton, 93f., states that grace here is practically 'the Christian message as a whole', and compares 1 Pet 5.12. The reference must include the historical revelation of grace in the whole event of Jesus Christ and its repeated fresh actualisation in the ongoing proclamation of the gospel (Brox, 298). In the same way we find the inclusion of the act of reconciliation in Christ and the proclamation of the word of this reconciliation in the one action of God in 2 Cor 5.18–21, especially v. 19.

Grace is thus almost personified (cf. *Odes Sol.* 33.1; Spicq, 635f.). For Mott*, 36–46, the passage is an example of the personifying of divine qualities or virtues similar to what is found in Philo. But it is more likely that the personification results from the fact that the essential element in the epiphany is the revelation of Jesus Christ as God's gracious gift to humanity. There is in any case no hypostatising of grace (Dibelius-Conzelmann, 142).

χάρις is a virtue associated with benefactors (cf. Windisch 1935:223–6), described in language which may echo that used of imperial gifts; it is a 'demonstration of a ruler's favour, gift' or the disposition that lies behind the gift.[93] The noun is equivalent to φιλανθρωπία in 3.4. The whole phrase 'the grace of God' is strongly Pauline.[94] Nevertheless, Dibelius-Conzelmann, 144, curiously maintain that the use here does not recall Paul but rather 'the "graces" of the epiphanous gods in their manifestations (as they are praised, e.g. in the cult of the ruler)'. Rather, the author sets the Christian revelation of grace in its traditional sense over against the pagan manifestations.

The grace has been concretely manifested in the world. For ἐπιφαίνω see **Excursus 8**. The statement refers to the appearing of grace rather than of the Saviour himself, but this is similar to the way in which in v. 13 believers await the manifestation of the glory of Christ rather than the manifestation of Christ himself. Nevertheless, the language can equally be used of the manifestation of a person. The passive may imply something sudden and unexpected – of light coming from on high (Holtzmann, 487). The word conveys ideas of the sudden and surprising appearance of light, of its entrance for the first time, and of its effect in illuminating those in darkness (Spicq, 636). Lührmann 1971 shows how the word-group stresses the idea of the helpful appearances of the gods, displaying their virtue and power.

The manifestation of grace conveys salvation – in accordance with the character of God. σωτήριος***, 'saving, with saving power' ('with healing', REB) is found here only in NT as an adj.,[95] but the neut. occurs as a noun (Lk 2.30; 3.6; Acts 28.28;

---

[93] τὰς τῶν Σεβαστῶν χάριτας (Dittenberger, *Or.* II, 669.44, cited by Spicq, 636); cf. Dittenberger, *Syll.* II, 798.7ff. (AD I, of Caligula); Dittenberger, *Or.* I, 383.9f. (of Antiochus I of Commagene) (both quoted by Dibelius-Conzelmann, 144 n. 18). See Conzelmann, H., *TDNT* IX, 375.

[94] Rom 5.15; 1 Cor 1.4; 3.10; 15.10; 2 Cor 1.12; 6.1; 8.1; 9.14; Gal 2.21; Eph 3.2, 7; Col 1.6; 2 Th 1.12; outside Paul see Acts 13.43; 14.26; 20.24; Heb 12.15; cf. Acts 11.23; Heb 2.9; 1 Pet 4.10; 5.12; Jude 4.

[95] The adjective is predicative, giving the translation 'has appeared with saving power' (Moule 1953:114; BD § 269³; *pace* Holtzmann, 487, who takes it as attributive).

Eph 6.17***).⁹⁶ The stress is on God as the source of salvation. The wording may reflect the language of the imperial cult (see note on πᾶσιν ἀνθρώποις), although the adjective does not seem to be attested in this context.⁹⁷

The intended beneficiaries of God's action are 'all people'. For πᾶσιν ἀνθρώποις cf. 3.2; 1 Tim 2.1, 4; 4.10. This phrase must go with σωτήριος (cf. Thucydides 7.64.2 in BA; Holtzmann, 487), not with the verb (AV; NIV); the latter construction would in any case produce a false statement. Similar language was used of emperors.⁹⁸

The motivation for inclusion of this final point is not clear. It may be that it is intended to show that the sphere of grace includes all the different groups in the church mentioned in vv. 2–10. The possibility that the writer's opponents limited the scope of salvation is raised by Brox, 298; Oberlinner, 129. Or it may be that it is simply part of the author's basic belief in the universality of the offer of salvation which he repeats here although it is not essential to his argument (cf. 3.2; 1 Tim 2.3–5; 4.10).

The force is clearly that the salvation is intended for all people (Acts 17.30; 22.14f.; cf. Lk 2.10, 14; 1 Tim 2.4–6). It is not confined to Jews. White, 194, Lock, 143f., and Knight, 319, stress that it is for *all kinds* of people, including even the slaves who have just been mentioned.⁹⁹ However, there is no implied limitation that would exclude any person from the embrace of divine grace, e.g. by suggesting that not all people literally but '[only some individuals from] every class of people' are meant (as Knight, 115). If the provision of salvation is thus universal, it is implicitly affirmed that there is no salvation for anybody anywhere else.

12. παιδεύουσα ἡμᾶς The grace of God is pictured in a somewhat unusual way as a teacher who guides people into a new

---

⁹⁶ The adj. is found in Wis 1.14; 3 Macc 6.31; 7.18 *v.l.*; 4 Macc 12.6 *v.l.*; 15.26; Philo, *Somn.* 2.149. Cf. also *CH* 10.15 ('only the knowledge of God brings salvation to humankind'). The neut. form is used frequently in the LXX for the peace-offering (cf. Spicq, 637), but there is no indication that this nuance is present here. Cf. Fohrer, G., and Foerster, W., *TDNT* VII, 1021–4.

⁹⁷ *salutaris* occurs of Jupiter in Cicero, *De Fin.* 3.20 (66) (Spicq, 637).

⁹⁸ Dittenberger, *Or.* II, 669.7: παρὰ τοῦ ἐπιλάμψαντος ἡμεῖν ἐπὶ σωτηρίᾳ τοῦ παντὸς ἀνθρώπων γένους εὐεργέτου (of Galba; cited by Dibelius-Conzelmann, 144 n.19); Dittenberger, *Syll.* II, 760.7 (Ephesus, I BC, of Julius Caesar): θεὸν ἐπιφανῆ καὶ κοινὸν τοῦ ἀνθρωπίνου βίου σωτῆρα; cf. Spicq, 637).

⁹⁹ 'He does not mean individuals, but rather all classes of men' (Calvin, 373). Cf. Augustine, *De corr. et gr.* 44.

way of life. παιδεύω* here must mean 'to train, educate',[100] although Quinn, 163f., argues that teaching of the young was inseparably linked with corporal punishment on the refractory in the Hellenistic world (cf. 1 Tim 1.20; 2 Tim 2.25 – but note the stress on gentleness here).

The process of education by grace was doubtless understood in practical terms as taking place in part through teaching of the sound doctrine which is part of the content of the Christian message. But education is not confined to formal teaching; it includes elements of persuasion, encouragement, practice and discipline, and a good teacher is able to help his pupils to develop new patterns of thought and behaviour. The Greek term is able to accommodate these various nuances. Dibelius-Conzelmann, 142f., note that παιδεύω shows 'an important change in meaning here' from Paul. The word is certainly used in a different way, but the importance is that this is the first use in this sense of training in Christian spirituality and practice. Bertram demonstrates that the ideas expressed here fit in well with the proverbial wisdom of the OT and the practical piety of Judaism. Fee, 199, notes that the word is already used in the same way as here in Ecclus 6.32; Wis 6.11, 25 (cf. 11.9 for the sense of disciplining). We thus have an example of Christian piety being moulded within the context of ideas already at home in Hellenistic Jewish piety. ἡμᾶς refers to regenerated Christians, not people in general (Spicq, 637f.)

There are three elements in the educative process envisaged, two in this verse and one in the next.

ἵνα ἀρνησάμενοι τὴν ἀσέβειαν καὶ τὰς κοσμικὰς ἐπιθυμίας First, the negative side is seen in the renunciation of ungodliness and a worldly way of life. These two phrases probably refer to such sins as idolatry and impiety on the one hand and selfish and immoral desires on the other.

The clause introduced by ἵνα may be one of purpose dependent on the main verb[101] or on the participle, possibly giving the force 'leading us to' (BA; cf. Holtzmann, 488). But it is better taken as indirect command, giving the content of the 'education' (cf. 1 Tim 5.21).

---

[100] The verb has three senses in the NT: (a) 'to bring up, train, educate' (Acts 7.22; 22.3; note the contrast in Greek education between the ἰδιώτης and the πεπαιδευμένος; Ep. Arist. 287; 1 Clement 59.3; Tatian, Or. 42); (b) 'to discipline by appropriate guidance' (2 Tim 2.25; cf. Hermas, Vis. 2.3.1; 3.9.10; 1 Clement 21.6 = Polycarp 4.2); (c) 'to discipline by punishment' (carried out by fathers, Heb 12.7, 10a; 1 Cor 11.32; 2 Cor 6.9; 1 Tim 1.20; Heb 12.6 [= Prov 3.12; cf. 1 Clement 56.3–5, 16; 57.1]; Rev 3.19); hence, 'to whip, scourge' (Lk 23.16, 22). Cf. Trummer 1978:232f.; Towner 1989:110; in general cf. Bertram, G., TDNT V, 596–625, especially 623.

[101] So Chrysostom (PG LXII, 689) according to White, 194, but the statement seems to be too general to permit this conclusion.

ἀρνέομαι (1.16; 1 Tim 5.8) here has the sense 'to renounce'. Elsewhere it is generally something good or positive which is renounced, so that the word has a negative sense; the use here of renouncing something evil is unusual (cf. however, Lk 9.23). Possibly baptismal language is reflected (Bernard, 171; Jeremias, 72; Dornier, 143; Brox, 298). The aorist may stress the decisive break with the past (Spicq, 638). But Oberlinner, 131f., emphasises that the thought cannot be limited to what should happen at conversion; there must be a continual turning away from godlessness.

ἀσέβεια*, 'godlessness, impiety',[102] refers broadly to ungodly conduct, especially idolatry and the associated behaviour, in contrast to evil conduct towards other people, but this distinction is not always observed. Hence the reference is to the conduct associated with disbelief in God. There may be an intentional contrast with εὐσέβεια (Lock, 144; see **Excursus 1**).

ἐπιθυμία ('desire, longing'; 3.3; 1 Tim 6.9; 2 Tim 2.22; 3.6; 4.3; Tit 2.12; 3.3**) is in itself neutral about the goodness or badness of the desires, but the context may indicate that the objects, and hence the longings, are natural and good or bad.[103] Here the adjective κοσμικός and the link with ἀσέβεια indicate that the latter is meant (cf. 3.3; 1 Tim 6.9; 2 Tim 2.22; 3.6; 4.3). Similarly, ἐπιθυμέω has a good sense in 1 Tim 3.1 and the bad sense 'to covet' in Exod 20.17; Rom 7.7; et al. There was in fact a growing tendency to use the word, as here, of bad desires, temptations, including sexual desire.[104]

κοσμικός** is 'belonging to the world', hence 'earthly, as opposed to heavenly' and hence 'transitory and of lesser worth'.[105] In Christianity the word came to mean 'worldly' as opposed to God and morally reprehensible.[106]

---

[102] 2 Tim 2.16; Rom 1.18 (cf. Deut 9.5); 11.26 (cf. Isa 59.20); Jude 15 (cf. *1 Enoch* 1.9), 18***; *1 Enoch* 13.2; 1 Clement 57.6; ἀσεβής (1 Tim 1.9). Cf. Foerster, W., *TDNT* VII, 185–91.

[103] For the former see Lk 22.15; Phil 1.23; 1 Th 2.17; for the latter see Mk 4.19; Jn 8.44; Col 3.5. Cf. Paul's use of σάρξ in this context (Rom 13.14; Gal 5.16, 24; Eph 2.3). The Stoics, including Epictetus, use it in this way (BA *s.v.*).

[104] In Plato, *Phaedo* 83B, the true philosopher keeps himself free from pleasures, desires, griefs and fears, and 'in Stoicism, with its ideal of "apathy" and complete self-sufficiency,' these four emotions 'became cardinal faults' (Easton, 186f.; examples in BA, including from Judaism 4 Macc 1.22f. [which also adds πόνος]). See also Gen 41.6; Num 11.4; Wis 4.12; Ecclus 23.5; 4 Macc 1.3; 3.2; *et al.*; Philo, *Spec.* 4.93; *L.A.* 2.8; Josephus, *Bel.* 7.261; Josephus, *Ant.* 2.51; 4.143. What 4 Macc attributes to the power of devout reason is here attributed to the effects of divine grace. Cf. Büchsel, F., *TDNT* III, 168–72; Hübner, H., *EDNT* II, 27–8; Easton, 186–8.

[105] Heb 9.1***; cf. 2 Clement 5.6; *M. Poly.* 2.3 of earthly torments; *Didache* 11.11 of the mystery of the church.

[106] 2 Clement 17.3; cf. *T. Jos.* 17.8. The noun is used similarly (e.g. 1 Jn 2.16). Cf. Sasse, H., *TDNT* III, 897f.

σωφρόνως καὶ δικαίως καὶ εὐσεβῶς ζήσωμεν ἐν τῷ νῦν αἰῶνι
Second, the positive side is expressed by three qualities of life.
These coincide with three of the four cardinal virtues (the
missing one is ἀνδρεία) which functioned as ideals in Gk. ethics.[107]
Christians are to live up to worldly standards and impress the
world (Hasler, 94). Nevertheless, Brox, 298f., insists that despite
all the use of Greek terms the thought is genuinely Christian
with its deep orientation to the salvation-event in Christ (cf.
Vögtle, 242 n. 22). Mott argues that the language here is similar
to that of Philo who uses the cardinal virtues to express the goal
of ethical deliverance from vice. The goal of παιδεία is virtue
(ἀρετή), and hence it is natural that the goal of education here
is the development of these cardinal virtues. Interestingly Philo
speaks of παιδεία as being σωτήριος (*Ebr.* 140f.; *Plant.* 144).

Whether by chance or intent, the three adverbs express relations
to self, neighbour and God,[108] but this categorisation should not
be taken too strictly (Brox, 299). For σωφρόνως***, 'soberly'
(Wis 9.11), see **Excursus 3**. The adverb is common in Hellenistic
moral writing (Spicq, 638f. and is found in combination with
ζάω.[109] δικαίως** describes life in accordance with standards of
justice and fairness.[110] The same adverb also forms part of a
series characterising Christian conduct with ὁσίως and ἀμέμπτως
in 1 Th 2.10. εὐσεβῶς*, 'in a godly manner' (2 Tim 3.12***. See
Excursus 1) is likewise common in secular moral writing and
often found in inscriptions.[111] The qualities listed here are often
linked to one another.[112] Righteousness and godliness are also
linked in 1 Tim 6.11.

The sphere of godly living is 'this age/world'. αἰών* (cf.
αἰώνιος, 1.2 note) has three main senses: (a) 'era'; (b) 'universe';
(c) 'world system' (LN). In the first sense it can refer to time up
to the present or to time in the future, in each case conceived as
stretching into eternity. It can also refer, as here, to a specific
period of time, often of the present era and the future era in
contrast to each other. When it refers to the present age it is
often qualified as here (cf. 1 Tim 6.17; 2 Tim 4.10; Polycarp 9.2).

[107] Spicq, 638f. gives secular parallels. See especially Mott 1978 and the
criticisms in Quinn, 167f.; cf. Oberlinner, 126 n. 7.

[108] Bernard, 171; cf. Xenophon, *Mem.* 4.8.11 of Socrates but with ἐγκράτεια
replacing σωφροσύνη; Foerster, W., *TDNT* VII, 176.

[109] Cf. ζήσαντα σωφρόνως (*Inschr. v. Magn.* 162.6, cited in BA); δικαίως καὶ
σωφρόνως βιοῦσι, Heraclides, *Pol.* 39 (BA *s.v.* δικαίως).

[110] Lk 23.41; 1 Cor 15.34; 1 Th 2.10; 1 Pet 2.23***; 1 Clement 51.2; 62.1;
Ignatius, *Eph.* 15.3; *Mag.* 9.2; Barnabas 10.12. See 1.8 note on δίκαιος.

[111] Dittenberger, *Syll.* 772.3 (I BC; linked to δικαίως). Cf. *Ep. Arist.* 37, 261;
Philo, *Aet.* 10; Josephus, *Ant.* 8.300; 1 Clement 61.2; 62.1.

[112] For the combination of the three adverbs here with ἐβίωσε see Socrates,
Ep. 15.1 (BA). For the linking of piety, righteousness and self-control see
Aristobulus, *Frg.* 4.8 (*FPG*, 223).

The phrase may carry connotations of temporariness and of its evil nature in contrast with the age to come, and suggests the idea of a world system which is dominated by evil and opposed to God. But it also emphasises that the Christian life must be lived out in the here and now (Oberlinner, 133).

The phrase εἰς τὸν αἰῶνα is used to refer to the distant future (e.g. Ps 111.9 = 2 Cor 9.9); the rhetorical form εἰς (τὸν) αἰῶνα (τοῦ) αἰῶνος is also found (Ps 44.7 = Heb 1.8). The plural form is used rhetorically in an intensive manner to signify the immeasurable stretch of time whether past (1 Cor 2.7) or future (Lk 1.33); in the latter case the even more rhetorical form εἰς τοὺς αἰῶνας τῶν αἰώνων (Ps 83.5) is found (1 Tim 1.17b; 2 Tim 4.18). In 1 Tim 1.17a** the temporal and spatial aspects of meaning are hard to distinguish.[113]

νῦν* (2 Tim 1.10) is used adjectivally, 'present' (1 Tim 4.8; 6.17; 2 Tim 4.10**).[114] The present age is here referred to in a neutral manner, but stands in contrast with the future age which is characterised by the appearing of the Saviour. Hence there is a certain negative quality about it, and elsewhere it can be regarded as a period of godlessness and evil to which people can be tempted to apostatise (2 Tim 4.10).[115]

13. προσδεχόμενοι τὴν μακαρίαν ἐλπίδα καὶ ἐπιφάνειαν τῆς δόξης τοῦ μεγάλου θεοῦ καὶ σωτῆρος ἡμῶν Ἰησοῦ Χριστοῦ The third element in the new way of life which is 'taught' by grace is expressed by a loosely coupled participial phrase. Life in the present world is accordingly lived in the context of a hope which reaches out beyond it to the new world when the Saviour is fully revealed in glory (cf. 1 Cor 1.7; Jude 21; 1 Pet 1.13); the renouncing of worldliness is thus not asceticism for its own sake but is an aspect of the path to a greater joy than the world can offer. Suggestions that the eschatological outlook is here unemphasised and has a different force from what it had in earlier Christianity where it was the primary factor in determining how believers lived are not convincing.[116] Rather, in conjunction with v. 14 the statement shows that balance of realised and future divine action and salvation which is characteristic of the NT generally.

---

[113] Cf. Sasse, H., *TDNT* I, 197–209; Barr 1969:65ff.; Holtz, T., *EDNT* I, 44–6; Balz, H., *EDNT* I, 46–8.

[114] Cf. ὁ νῦν καιρός (Rom 3.26; 8.18; 11.5; 2 Cor 8.14); ἡ νῦν ζωή (1 Tim 4.8); see also Gal 4.25. The usage is Cl. (e.g. Xenophon, *Anab.* 6.6.13). Paul uses ὁ αἰὼν οὗτος (Rom 12.2 *et al.*).

[115] Cf. Stählin, G., *TDNT* IV, 1106–23; Towner 1989:62.

[116] See Oberlinner, 134. The verdict is due to attributing too great a role to the hope of the imminent return of Christ in the theology of Paul. See Marshall, I. H., 'The Parousia in the New Testament – and Today', in Wilkins, M. J., and

The act of expectation is expressed by the verb προσδέχομαι**.[117] It has two senses: (a) 'to accept, receive, welcome' a person (Lk 15.2; Rom 16.2; Phil 2.29) or thing (Acts 24.15;[118] Heb 10.34; 11.35); (b) 'to await', usually with eager longing, a person (Lk 12.36) or a thing (Mk 15.43; Lk 2.25, 38; 23.51; Acts 23.21; Jude 21). For the present combination with ἐλπίδα there is a close parallel in Job 2.9, προσδεχόμενος τὴν ἐλπίδα τῆς σωτηρίας μου.[119] The usage is thus a Hebraism (Spicq, 639).

The content of the expectation is given in two nouns followed by a lengthy gen. phrase. ἐλπίς (1.2 note; 3.7 note) is used here by metonymy for the content of the hope, its fulfilment (Spicq, 639; cf. Acts 24.15; Rom 8.24; Gal 5.5; Col 1.5). The hope is of something that is confidently expected (Arichea-Hatton, 293).

In a somewhat rare turn of phrase the hope is described as 'blessed'. In Cl. μακάριος* refers predominantly to the state of bliss, free from earthly worries and cares, enjoyed by the gods of the Greeks. This sense is never found in the LXX which uses εὐλογητός in its place and thereby avoids the associations of a word that seems inapplicable to Yahweh. It is, however, found in Philo (*Sacr.* 101) who describes God in Greek terms. The word is also used of people who are free from worries and cares, like the gods. In the NT the word is used of God only in the PE (1 Tim 1.11; 6.15**), but it is frequently used of persons who are the objects of God's favour. Such people are happy or count themselves fortunate on the basis of favourable circumstances (e.g. Acts 26.2), usually on account of some divine action or gift. The LN translation 'happy' is generally inadequate; the traditional translation 'blessed' now sounds archaic but brings out the fact that a person is μακάριος because of the action of the gods or God. To pronounce a person 'blessed' (as in the Gospel beatitudes) is to declare the happiness of somebody who has experienced God's blessing (Rom 4.7f. = Ps 32.1f.) or to declare that people, e.g. mourners (Mt 5.4), who apparently are in a state of misery and deprivation, are really in a fortunate state and should therefore be able to be glad here and now because of some divine action (like the future comfort which

---

Paige, T., *Worship, Theology and Ministry in the Early Church. Essays in Honor of Ralph P. Martin* (Sheffield: JSOT Press, 1992), 194–211.

[117] Paul uses ἀναμένω similarly of eschatological hope (1 Th 1.9f.) and ἀπεκδέχομαι (Rom 8.23, 25; 1 Cor 1.7; Phil 3.20; Gal 5.5; cf. Heb 9.28; 1 Pet 3.20***); cf. ἐκδέχομαι (Heb 10.13; 11.10). Cf. Grundmann, W., *TDNT* II, 57f.

[118] With ἐλπίδα as here; hence Holtzmann, 489, regards it as the basis for this verse.

[119] For the same combination of ideas cf. Isa 25.9 (White, 195).

God will bestow on them). Here only in the NT is μακάριος used of a thing.[120]

There may be more than one nuance in the usage here: (a) The hope is closely associated with the blessed God and therefore itself shares in his incorruptibility and 'blessedness'.[121] Consequently it has a quality about it which is absent from other things that one might hope for in this world. The effect of the use is to bring out the positive character of the hope (Spicq, 639). (b) The word-group can be used of praising people by acknowledging their fortunate state (cf. the use of εὐλογητός), and therefore the thought may be that the hope is one for which thanks should be given to God. (c) The hope is one that confers a blessing on those waiting for it because it is associated with God.[122] It is not clear whether the blessedness is regarded as something already possessed by those who have this hope (cf. the present blessedness of those who look forward to future divine gifts in the Beatitudes) or as the state into which people will enter in the future. It appears to be the latter for Knight, 321, who writes of the hope that 'embodies and brings the blessedness for which Christians hope'; he refers to Rom 5.2 which implies that believers will share in the glory of God (cf. Rom 8.17, 30; 2 Cor 4.17).

The second object of the participle is added without repetition of the article; hence it is probable that we have an epexegetic addition, 'a hope that consists in the revelation of the glory' (cf. Acts 23.6; BD §276³). On the meaning and significance of ἐπιφάνεια* see **Excursus 8**. δόξα* (1 Tim 1.17; 3.16; 2 Tim 2.10; 4.18**), expresses the glorious character of God, originally his splendid shining appearance, and then all that makes him the transcendent God. This could be the reflection of his power and holiness, but in Christian usage the glory of God is more and more seen as the wonder of his grace and love expressed in his saving act in Christ.[123]

The syntax and reference of the whole genitive phrase are matters of debate. As regards the syntax there are four possibilities:

(a) ἐπιφάνειαν is followed by two parallel gen. phrases, 'glory' and 'saviour', i.e. 'the epiphany of the glory of the great God

---

[120] Cf. Dittenberger, *Or.* 383.108: μακαριστὰς ἐλπίδας (cited by BA); Plato, *Rep.* 496C: ὡς μακάριον τὸ κτῆμα. Cf. Hauck, F., and Bertram, G., *TDNT* IV, 362–70; Strecker, G., *EDNT* II, 376–9; *TLNT* II, 432–4.

[121] Cf. 1 Clement 35.1; 2 Clement 19.4; Barnabas 1.2; Bertram, G., *TDNT* IV, 370; Dibelius-Conzelmann, 143; Brox, 299.

[122] Holtzmann, 488; Easton, 94; Fee, 195; Oberlinner, 135. Cf. 1 Clement 35.1 of God's gifts; 2 Clement 19.4 of the age to come; *M. Poly.* 2.1 of martyrdom.

[123] Cf. Kittel, G., and Rad, G. von, *TDNT* II, 232–55; Hegermann, H., *EDNT* I, 344–8; *TLNT* I, 362–79.

and [the epiphany] of our saviour Jesus Christ' (H. Windisch 1935:225). The epiphany of Christ is accompanied by the epiphany of the glory of God (cf. Kelly, 246f.). However, the parallelism of the personal Saviour and the impersonal glory is strange. Further, the phrase 'God and Saviour' is a well-attested pairing, and it is more likely that readers would take the two nouns as being linked together than that they would supply 'epiphany' before the second noun (see below, note on ὁ θεὸς καὶ σωτήρ). The absence of the article with 'Saviour' also speaks against paralleling it with 'of the glory' (cf. Harris* 1980:267; although Moule 1953:109f. states that it is not decisive).

(b) τῆς δόξης is a Hebraic gen. of quality, giving the translation 'the glorious epiphany', and the following genitives are then directly dependent on ἐπιφάνειαν (cf. AV; NIV). The difficulty is whether there is any precedent for the combination of a Hebraic gen. with an ordinary gen. Moreover, the phrase can be taken straightforwardly to refer to the epiphany of the glory of God, just as in v. 11 we have the epiphany of the grace of God; a parallelism between the two phrases is likely.

(c) The two nouns form a hendiadys: 'the epiphany, namely the glory of...'.[124] But this construction gives a second hendiadys, since 'epiphany' is already linked to 'hope' in this kind of way (cf. Ellicott, 187); this is surely impossible.

(d) The straightforward translation, 'the epiphany of the glory of our God...', is surely the correct one. Knight, 322, notes that 'glory' is used elsewhere of the splendour accompanying the parousia (e.g. Mk 13.26); that 'glory' is often followed by a gen. referring to God; and that the phrase is parallel to v. 11 (the epiphany of the grace of God).[125] The parallels in 1 Pet 4.13 (at the revelation of his glory) and 1 Pet 5.1 (the glory to be revealed) strongly favour this view.

As regards the reference, the whole phrase ἡ ἐπιφάνεια τῆς δόξης τοῦ...θεοῦ has been taken here to refer to:

(a) the epiphany of the personal glory of God (gen. of content; Fee, 196);

(b) the epiphany of the Glory of God, namely Christ, who is the glorious manifestation of God (see below);

(c) 'the full manifestation of all that Christ is in Himself and in His saints' (Lock, 144). Believers are changed from one degree of glory to another (2 Cor 3.7–18; 4.4–6) and Christ is glorified in them at the parousia (2 Th 1.10). Since the term 'epiphany' tends to refer to God's saving intervention rather than simply to his manifestation, and in view of the parallelism with hope, this

---

[124] For the association of ἐπιφάνεια and δόξα see Dittenberger, *Or.* 763.19f.; Epictetus 3.22.29 (cited in BA).
[125] See also Harris* 1980:262–77; Harris* 1992:173–85; Fee, 196.

interpretation has much to be said for it. It receives important corroboration from 2 Tim 1.10.

God is described as μέγας*, a word used metaphorically of important things (1 Tim 3.16) and people (e.g. the high priest, Heb 4.14; a prophet, Luke 7.16). It is commonly used of gods and goddesses (Artemis, Acts 19.27f., 34f.; MM 392f.). According to Grundmann, in Classical Greek it is used of almost all the gods, and has its place in cultic epiclesis. It stresses transcendence, majesty, supremacy, and can have a superlative sense ('das schlechthin Überragende, Erhabene und Unvergleichbare', Roloff, 201). It is very frequent in Hellenistic sources and can be used of several gods together.[126] It is equally at home in Judaism with reference to Yahweh[127], his attributes[128] and his name.[129] In the NT it is also used of Christ as Shepherd (Heb 13.20), but this is hardly a parallel to the present use, where it is the title of 'great *God*' that may be used of him. The noun μεγαλειότης is used in 2 Pet 1.16 of Christ. The adjective is not used elsewhere of God in the NT, but the noun is used of him in Lk 9.43; 2 Pet 1.16; Heb 1.3; 8.1; Jude 25.[130] For God as Saviour see 1.3 note.

But to whom is the reference being made? At this point we encounter the major exegetical problem of the verse. It would not be surprising to read of 'our [great] God and saviour', since this is a familiar collocation (see below), although a reference to the epiphany of *God* would be unique in a NT context. The problem arises because of the addition of the words 'Jesus Christ' at the end of the phrase, which forces us to reconsider the question of its syntax: did the writer really intend us to take it as 'our great God-and-Saviour, namely Jesus Christ', or did he mean something else? Is the term 'God' used to refer to 'God [the Father]' alongside Jesus Christ or is it part of a description of Jesus as God and Saviour?[131] There are three main interpretations to be considered.

---

[126] Of Zeus, Pausanias, *Descr. Gr.* 10.12.10. Christians knew and rejected the attribution (Athenagoras, *Supplic.* 23, cited by Spicq, 640). *CH* 13.6, 11 has the superlative τρισμέγιστος.

[127] Exod 18.11; Deut 10.17; 2 Chr 2.4; Ps 47 (MT 48).2; 76 (MT 77).14; 85 (MT 86).10; 94 (MT 95).3; Dan 2.45; 4.20, 30a; 3 Macc 1.9 *v.l.*, 16; 3.11; 5.25; 7.2, 22; *1 Enoch* 103.4; 104.1; Philo, *Cher.* 29; *et al.*; Josephus, *Ant.* 8.319; *Sib. Orac.* 3.19, 71 *et al.*

[128] Exod 32.11; Deut 8.17; Isa 54.7; 2 Esdr 5.8; Neh 4.14; 8.6.

[129] 1 Chr 16.25; Ps 75 (MT 76).2; 98 (MT 99).3; Isa 26.4; 33.22; Jer 39 [32]. 18f.; Mal 1.11; Tob 11.14; Ecclus 39.6; 43.5.

[130] Cf. Grundmann, W., *TDNT* IV, 529–41, especially 538–40.

[131] For the sake of clarity we use the phrase 'God [the Father]' in order to distinguish him from Jesus as God, although the term 'Father' is not used of God in the PE.

(1) The passage refers to two persons.[132]
(2) The passage refers to Jesus as being the glory of God (the Father).[133]
(3) The passage refers to Jesus as 'our God and Saviour'.[134]
Some scholars leave the question open.[135] In any case, the doctrinal implications of these renderings are much the same; if Christ is not explicitly declared to be in some sense 'God', his equality with God is expressed in no uncertain terms.

1. The passage refers to two persons

This interpretation gives the rendering: 'the epiphany of the glory of the great God and [of the glory] of our Saviour Jesus Christ'.[136] The following arguments are offered in favour of this view:

(a) It would be unprecedented in the NT to use θεός as an attribute of Jesus (Winer, 130 n. 2, cited by Knight, 323). To this it may be replied that 2 Pet 1.1 offers a parallel (Harris* 1992:229–38), and the same is probably true of Rom 9.5 (Harris* 1992:143–72). There is, of course, ample precedent in early church writings.[137]

(b) It is unlikely that the word 'God' would be applied to both the Father (v. 11!) and the Son in the same sentence. However, in other places where 'God' is used of Jesus, a differentiation between him and God (the Father) is found in the immediate vicinity (Jn 1.1; 1.18; 20.28–31; Rom 9.5f.; Heb 1.8f.; 2 Pet 1.1f.).

[132] AV; RV mg; NEB mg; GNB mg; NRSV mg; White, 195f.; Jeremias, 64; Schlatter, 196f.; Scott, 169f.; Kelly, 246f.; Holtz, 227f.; Hasler 1977:199–201 (not discussed in his commentary *ad loc.*); Karris, 117; Merkel, 99f.; Oberlinner, 136f.; Johnson, 238; Foerster, W., *TDNT* VII, 1018 n. 70; Abbot*; Windisch 1935:226; Simonsen 1980:55 n. 8; Young, 51–3.

[133] WH mg; Parry 81; Fee, 196; cf. Hort 1909:47, 103f.; Scott, C. A. A., *Christianity according to St Paul* (Cambridge: Cambridge University Press, 1927), 274.

[134] RV t; NEB t; NJB; GNB t; NRSV t; MM 437; Ellicott, 187f.; Bernard, 172f. (with hesitation); Lock, 144–6; Easton, 94f.; Simpson, 108f.; Gealy and Noyes, 540; Guthrie, 212; Hendriksen, 373–5; Dornier, 144; Barrett, 138; Spicq, 640f.; Houlden, 150f.; Hanson, 184f.; Quinn, 155f.; Knight, 322–6; Grundmann, W., *TDNT* IV, 538–40; Pax 1955:242; Towner, 247f.; Harris* 1992:173–85; Lau 1996:243f.; Läger 1996:94–6.

[135] Holtzmann, 490; Dibelius-Conzelmann, 143 (apparently preferring (1). but see 145 n. 29); Brox, 300. Oberlinner, 136, while insisting that a definitive answer is not possible, nevertheless opts for the two-persons interpretation.

[136] See above for discussion of the improbable alternative rendering 'the epiphany of the glory of the great God and [the epiphany] of our Saviour Jesus Christ'.

[137] Ignatius, *Eph.* Inscr; 1.1; 7.2; 15.3; 18.2; 19.3; *Trall.* 7.1 (*v.l.*); *Rom.* Inscr; 3.3; 6.3; *Smyr.* 1.1; 10.1 (*v.l.*); *Poly.* 8.3; *Didache* 10.6 (?); Pliny, *Ep.* 10; *Acts of Thomas* 26; Justin, *Apol.* 1.6.

(c) The use of μέγας is more likely with God than with Christ, since the writer will have used an accepted title of God, never applied elsewhere to Christ, to combat the degrading of the Creator by Gnostic heretics (Klöpper 1904:83). The force of this argument is weakened if the background to the heresy in the PE assumed by Klöpper is absent. Grundmann claims that 'with its cultic and polytheistic background the phrase is better adapted to refer to Jesus Christ as God than to God the Father in the narrower, monotheistic sense' (*TDNT* IV, 540).

(d) In 1 Tim 1.11 there is a reference to 'the gospel of the *glory* of the blessed *God*', where God [the Father] is apparently meant (Holtzmann, 490). However, the writer is so free in saying the same things about God [the Father] and Christ that not too much weight can be attached to this (e.g. the designation of each of them as σωτήρ).

(e) On the analogy of Lk 9.26 there can be one epiphany which is of the glory of God and of the glory of Christ (Holtzmann, 490).

(f) 'Saviour' is a word 'which gradually dropped the article' and became quasi-technical (Bernard, 172). However, in the PE it always has the article except for good grammatical reasons (1 Tim 1.1; 4.10).

Alternatively, it is argued that the addition of ἡμῶν renders the repetition of the article unnecessary, or that the phrase 'our Saviour Jesus Christ' is so similar to 'our Lord Jesus Christ' that it did not require the article (Hasler 1977:200). (See below.)

(g) Since the past and present are determined by the saving activity of God and of Christ, it is likely, indeed necessary, that the consummation similarly will involve the epiphany of God and of Jesus Christ (Oberlinner, 137). Oberlinner goes on to comment that the structure of the section really requires only a reference to God at this point, corresponding with v. 11, but the mention of Jesus as Saviour is included in order to provide a peg for the following soteriological confession. But, as he recognises, a 'double parousia' is an odd concept (cf. Hanson, 184f.)

2. The passage refers to Jesus as being the glory of God (the Father)

On this view 'Jesus Christ' is in apposition to 'glory', giving the translation: 'the epiphany of the glory of our great God and Saviour, [which glory is] Jesus Christ'.[138] In favour of this view it can be argued:

---

[138] Hasler 1977:199–201, adopts this interpretation but adheres to the 'two persons' translation.

(a) The combination θεὸς καὶ σωτήρ is a stereotyped one which is preserved by this interpretation instead of being split up, as in the previous interpretation.[139] However, the phrase was frequently applied both to 'divine beings' and to deified rulers.[140] The combination is equally preserved by interpretation (3) in which it is applied to Christ.

(b) The phraseology reflects the PE usage which refers to God (the Father) as Saviour (1.3; 2.10; *et al.*). But when v. 14 goes on to describe a saving action, it is the work of Christ as Saviour, not God, and in any case 'Saviour' is a title used of him (1.4) as well as of God.

(c) Elsewhere Christ is placed in apposition to the mystery of God (Col 2.2) and is the reflection of God's glory (Heb 1.3). Whereas, however, in Col 2.2 the apposition is quite clear, here it is anything but obvious. The language is ambiguous, and the ambiguity could have been easily removed by inserting ἥτις ἐστιν or the like.

(d) Harris suggests that 'glory of God' may have been a primitive christological title (cf. John 1.14; 12.41; Acts 7.55; 2 Cor 4.6; Eph 1.3 compared with 1.17; Heb 1.3). But in none of the passages listed is δοξά remotely titular.

Moule 1953:109, rightly describes this view as 'highly improbable'.

3. The passage refers to Jesus as 'our God and Saviour'

The third possibility is that the phrase refers to one person: 'the epiphany of the glory of our great God and Saviour, [namely] Jesus Christ'. In favour of this view it can be argued:

(a) 'God and Saviour' is a well-attested formula (see note above), and it is unlikely that it should be split up (Moule 1953:110; Easton, 95). The description of Yahweh as Saviour was common, and it would not be surprising if the appelation of Christ as Saviour led to his closer identification with God the Saviour.

In the context there is a use of semi-technical terms for the royal epiphany of Christ. The author may well be combatting worship of Artemis or human rulers. Thus MHT I, 84, comment: 'Familiarity with the everlasting apotheosis that flaunts itself in

---

[139] The combination 'God Saviour' or 'God the/my/our Saviour' is common enough. Cf. ὁ θεός μου καὶ ὁ σωτήρ μου (Ps 61.3, 7).

[140] For example, Julius Caesar was θεὸν ἐπιφανῆ καὶ κοινὸν τοῦ ἀνθρωπίνου βίου σωτῆρα (Dittenberger, *Syll.* 760.7; Allo, E. B., 'Les dieux-sauveurs du paganisme', *RSPT* (1926), 5–34; Spicq, 640, and 249–51; Dibelius-Conzelmann, 102f.; Harris 1980:266–71; Wendland 1904:335–53). MHT I, 84 refer to the use of the formula for deified kings in Egypt, citing Grenfell, B. P., and Hunt, A. S., *Greek Papyri series II* [London: 1897], §15 (II BC).

the papyri and inscriptions of Ptolemaic and Imperial times, lends strong support to Wendland's contention that Christians, from the latter part of the first century onward, deliberately annexed for their Divine master the phraseology that was impiously arraigned to themselves by some of the worst of men.'[141]

(b) This interpretation gives the best explanation of the omission of the article before σωτῆρος.[142] Other explanations fall short, such as that Σωτήρ was regarded as a proper name and therefore did not need the article (cf. Bernard, 172), or that the article was unnecessary where ἡμῶν is used,[143] or that the distinction of the two persons was so obvious that the article was not needed (Abbot*, 13–16); as Harris notes, elsewhere in the PE σωτὴρ ἡμῶν has the article, and therefore it is the absence here that needs to be explained.[144]

(c) The use of 'great' is better explained if it refers to Christ. Nowhere else in the NT is the adjective 'great' used of God [the Father].[145] Bernard, 172, holds that there must be some special reason for using this unique term here, that it is somewhat pointless if applied to God [the Father], but is significant if applied to Christ, whose epiphany is awaited. Harris argues that the adjective is fitly used of Jesus as 'God and Saviour' and that it is then explained in v. 14. More convincing is Houlden's suggestion (151) that the writer is contrasting 'our deity' with the pagan divinities of surrounding peoples.

(d) Harris claims that this view gives parallelism between the two sections of v. 13, each of which has the structure: article – adjective – noun – καί – anarthrous noun – genitive:

τὴν   μακαρίαν   ἐλπίδα   καὶ   ἐπιφάνειαν   τῆς   δόξης
τοῦ   μεγάλου   θεοῦ   καὶ   σωτῆρος   ἡμῶν

If so, just as the hope *is* the appearance, so the God *is* the Saviour (Harris* 1992:183). This is hardly compelling!

(e) Schnackenburg 1970:357f. holds that the argument points to a christological climax. Just as the grace of God appeared in

---

[141] The reference is to Wendland 1904:335–53.

[142] See BD § 276 – the article is not needed in the second of two words in apposition joined with 'and' (Granville Sharpe's rule). Cf. 2 Cor 1.3; Eph 6.21; Heb 3.1.

[143] Klöpper 1904:82; Holtzmann, 489f.

[144] See the detailed discussion in Harris* 1992:301–3. This argument seems clearly to support one phrase, despite Holtzmann's statement that the use of the article can be arbitrary and subjective (489f.). It has also been argued that the following relative clause implies a single referent, since otherwise the article would be needed with the second noun (Lock, 145; Spicq, 640). But Gal 1.3f. demonstrates otherwise.

[145] μεγαλωσύνη is used of God in Heb 1.3; 8.1; Jude 25; and μεγαλειότης is used of God in Lk 9.43 but of Christ in 2 Pet 1.16.

the first epiphany of Jesus, so the full divine glory will appear in him at his second epiphany. This is more a statement of the implications of this interpretation than an argument for it.

(f) Stauffer commented that the use of ἡμῶν links God and Saviour together so that they both refer to Christ; what was originally a doxology to God has been changed into a doxology to Christ.[146] But he presented no substantiation for his assertion (cf. Turner, N., MHT III, 181). In 2 Pet 1.1, 11 ἡμῶν comes after the first noun rather than the second.

(g) The way in which the PE use the term 'Saviour' both of God and of Christ would help towards the assimilation of the two persons.

(h) 'Epiphany' is a term elsewhere applied to the appearing of the Son, not of God (the Father). Nowhere do we hear of the parousia of the Father (Hanson, 184f.; Schnackenburg 1970:358). To this it can be objected that it is the glory of God, not God himself who is manifested here (cf. Mk 8.38; Abbot*, 4–6). The objection misses the point, however, which is that there is no epiphany of God's glory and grace apart from that in Christ. The NT does not know a future hope of the epiphany of God (the Father). God brings about the epiphany of his Son rather than himself appearing along with him.

(i) Redemption and purification are the work of Yahweh in the OT (Exod 19.5; Deut 7.6; 14.2); in v. 14 these activities are transferred to Jesus and he is therefore appropriately called 'God' here (Lock, 145; Kittel, G., TDNT II, 248).

(j) Post-Nicene writers are said to interpret the phrase as applying to Christ.[147] But Harris notes that the evidence is uncertain and that in any case the major ancient versions distinguish two persons here.[148]

(k) Finally, we must consider the theological arguments against this view, especially when the passage is set in the broader context of the theology of the PE as a whole. Here we find (i) the subordination of Christ to the Father (Dibelius-Conzelmann, 143),

[146] TDNT III, 106, n. 268; New Testament Theology (London: SCM Press, 1955), 324 n. 803.

[147] Clement Alex., Protrep. 1.7 (ANCL II, 173; but see Abbot*, 7); Chrysostom (PG LXII, 690); Theod. Mops. II, 250 Swete, with note admitting that the text is ambiguous, and giving clear citations from Jerome [PL XXVI, 586]; Theodoret III, 706 Schulze = PG LXXXII, 865; Pelagius); Hippolytus, de Antichristo 67 (pace Abbot*, 7f.).

[148] According to Bernard, 172, this is true of the Latin, Syriac, Coptic and Armenian. However, the Latin (adventum gloriae magni Dei et Salvatoris nostri Iesu Christi) and the Syriac are at most ambiguous (in the latter the possessive 'our' has to be attached to one noun, and it is suffixed to 'Saviour', whereas in the Gk. it could be understood to refer to both 'God' and 'Saviour'). Late VII cent. papyri (MHT I, 84) indicate that the phrase was understood to refer to Christ.

and (ii) a stress on the oneness of God. God has the initiative and Christ is only the helper (1 Tim 2.5; 1.17; 6.15f.; Klöpper 1904:83f; Windisch 1935:226). According to Windisch, God is called 'great' precisely to place him above Jesus.[149] The divinisation of Christ in the context of the epiphany idea is said to be impossible (Hasler 1977:200).

These counter-arguments are far from convincing. It can equally be affirmed that the Epistles demonstrate a strong functional equality, if not identity, between God [the Father] and Christ which makes the transfer of the title fully possible. It is difficult to see why the One in whom God is fully manifest should not thereby be entitled to the title of God.

Conclusion

The following points are decisive, and they establish that the third interpretation is the correct one:

(a) the probability that 'God and Saviour' must be treated as one phrase rather than being split in two in view of the absence of the article with 'Saviour' and the attestation of the phrase as a divine attribute;

(b) the improbability that Jesus Christ is in apposition to 'glory' or that two epiphanies are in mind;

(c) the background in the later NT writings and the AF in which the title of 'God' was beginning to be applied to Jesus.

14. ὃς ἔδωκεν ἑαυτὸν ὑπὲρ ἡμῶν A somewhat loosely attached addition to the sentence develops the thought of Jesus as Saviour by describing his action as redeemer and purifier of a people who are to be enthusiastic to do good works. It is thus broadly parallel with vv. 11f. in describing the saving action of God and its purpose in human life. Traditional language is used to refer to the redemptive action of Christ. The fact that the language is traditional does not make it any less meaningful. There is a strong contrast between the glory of the future epiphany of Christ and his self-giving in death (cf. Brox, 300f.). The effect of the whole addition is to strengthen the paraenesis by rooting it once again quite firmly in the past action of God in Christ. The saving effect of grace is described in more concrete terms.

The main (relative) clause is paralleled in Gal 1.4; 2.20; Mk 10.45; 1 Tim 2.6; cf. 1 Pet 1.13–19; 2.9f. for related material. An existing tradition is undoubtedly being used. There are four constant elements in the structure: (a) a verb 'to give/hand over'; (b) 'himself/his soul'; (c) a preposition 'on behalf of/instead of';

---

[149] Holtzmann, 489, however, notes that in 2 Tim 4.18 a doxology elsewhere applied to God (Rom 11.36; 16.27) is applied to Christ.

(d) 'me/us/many/all'. The closest parallel to the formula is found in 1 Tim 2.6, but there it is a much closer rendition of the saying of Jesus in Mk 10.45 in a more Hellenistic form with the Semitisms removed.

ὅς is used to add on what looks like a separate tradition which is appropriate as a motive and basis for Christian behaviour. δίδωμι[150] can be used of giving, dedicating oneself (2 Cor 8.5) or of giving oneself in death as a martyr (1 Macc 2.50; 6.44; cf. Thucydides 2.43.2). For Christ giving himself in death cf. Mk 10.45/Mt 20.28; Lk 22.19; Gal 1.4 (cf. Jn 6.51).[151] The reflexive pron. ἑαυτόν[152] is better Greek for the Semitic τὴν ψυχὴν αὐτοῦ of Mk 10.45, which reflects the absence of a reflexive pronoun in Hebrew and Aramaic. ὑπέρ*, 'on behalf of, concerning' (1 Tim 2.1, 2, 6**), is used in a series of statements about the death and self-giving of Jesus and his priestly activity on behalf of others.[153] The force of the preposition can range from doing something on behalf of others for their benefit (so here, Holtzmann, 491) or as their representative (Heb 6.20) to doing something in place of others, such as dying or bearing a penalty so that they do not need to do so, and so doing it for their benefit.[154] The preposition here is equivalent to ἀντί in Mk 10.45. Linked as it is here with redemption, it suggests that the person gives his life instead of those for whom he dies. It thus expresses representation and solidarity (Spicq, 641f.). According to Harris a possible reason why Paul preferred ὑπέρ to ἄντι was that the former could simultaneously express representation and substitution. ἡμῶν expresses a natural shift to the pl. in view of the following first person.

ἵνα λυτρώσηται ἡμᾶς ἀπὸ πάσης ἀνομίας The stress in the verse lies on this purpose clause which expresses the effects of Christ's self-giving. It has two balanced parts. On the one hand, Christ has redeemed his people from all evil. On the other hand, he has created a new people, i.e. a new Israel, who will do good works. Both of these actions of Christ are antitypical of the

[150] 1 Tim 2.6; 4.14; 5.14; 2 Tim 1.7, 9, 16, 18; 2.7, 25**.

[151] παραδίδωμι is used similarly in Gal 2.20; Eph 5.2, 25. Likewise, God is said to have given his Son (Jn 3.16; cf. Rom 4.25 [passive]; 8.32). Cf. Büchsel, F., *TDNT* II, 166.

[152] 2.14b; 1 Tim 2.9; 3.13; 6.10, 19; 2 Tim 2.13, 21; 4.3**.

[153] Mk 14.24; Lk 22.19, 20; Jn 10.11, 15; 11.50–52; (cf. 13.37f.); 15.13; Rom 5.6, 7a, 7b, 8; 8.32; 14.15; 1 Cor 11.24; 2 Cor 5.15a, 15b, 15c, 21; Gal 2.20; 3.13; Eph 5.2, 25; 1 Tim 2.6; Heb 2.9; (cf. 5.1; 6.20; 9.24); 1 Pet 2.21; 3.18; 1 Jn 3.16a; cf. Simpson, 110–12; Riesenfeld, H., *TDNT* VIII, 507–16; Harris, M. J., *NIDNTT* III, 1196f.; Davies, R. E., 'Christ in our Place: the Contribution of the Prepositions', *TynBull* 21 (1970), 71–91.

[154] E.g. Jn 11.50; 2 Cor 5.15; Gal 3.13; Philem 13; secular examples in Simpson, 110–12.

actions of Yahweh. At the Exodus he delivered the Israelites from slavery and made them his own people. Already in the OT the concept of redemption is spiritualised to refer to deliverance from sin. Thus Christ here has the same roles as Yahweh; the 'high' Christology of v. 13 is maintained. The Christian church is described as his 'Israel'. To the negative deliverance from evil corresponds the positive zeal for doing good.

The first part of the purpose clause is negative in that it is concerned with setting people free from evil. λυτρόω** is 'to set free' – sometimes by payment of a ransom (Lk 24.21; 1 Pet 1.18***). The verb can be used of human action (Exod 13.13; Lev 25.25; 27.13) and of divine, expressing God's deliverance of Israel from Egypt (Exod 6.6; Deut 7.8; 2 Sam 7.23) and his action generally in delivering his people from their enemies.[155] There is only one instance in the LXX of deliverance from sin (Ps 129 [MT 130].8; but cf. Isa 44.22–24; T. Jos. 18.2) and two of deliverance of the individual from death (Hos 13.14; Ecclus 51.2). God's deliverance of his people may involve the exercise of his power (Exod 6.6; Neh 1.10), and in some cases the metaphor of ransom is used, but the idea that God has to pay anything to anybody as the price of setting his people free is rejected (Isa 45.13; 52.3).[156]

The verb is used of the Lord's action on the day of his future epiphany (2 Clement 17.4) and of Christ's action in delivering his people (Barnabas 14.5f., 8) from death (Barnabas 19.2); Ignatius, Philad. 11.1 speaks of the redemption of persecutors of the church through the grace of Christ. Hermas uses it for rescue from a wild beast (Vis. 4.1.7) and of setting people free from their afflictions (Mand. 8.10). The language here echoes Ps 129.8, but what is said there of God is here applied to Christ (cf. Wolfe 1990:48–54).

ἀνομία** is 'lawlessness, iniquity', the opposite of righteousness and synonymous with sin. The word is very frequent in the LXX (228 times) as a translation for עָוֹן and other words. It can refer both to evil intentions and to evil deeds. The relationship with the concept of law is often weak. It is equated with sin in 1 Jn 3.4. Paul uses it rarely.[157] The use of the word here is based on Ps 129.8 LXX, but the word provides a link with

---

[155] Ps 106 (MT 107).2; 118 (MT 119).134; 1 Macc 4.11; Ecclus 50.24; Ps. Sol. 8.36; 9.1.

[156] Cf. Büchsel, F., TDNT IV, 349–51; TLNT II, 423–9; Morris 1965:11–64; Hill, D., Greek Words and Hebrew Meanings (Cambridge: Cambridge University Press, 1967), 49–81; Haubeck*, 205–13.

[157] Rom 4.7 = Ps 31 (MT 32).1; Rom 6.19; 2 Cor 6.14; 2 Th 2.3; Mt 7.23; 13.41; 23.28; 24.12; Heb 1.9; 10.17***; cf. ἄνομος, 1 Tim 1.9; cf. Gutbrod, W., TDNT IV, 1085f.

Ezek 37.23 which has also influenced the next part of the verse
(Haubeck*, 211). Holtzmann, 491, claims that in Paul salvation
is from the power of the law, whereas here it is from the power
of sin (as in 1 Pet 1.18). This assertion neglects Paul's close
linking between the power of sin and the power of the law. To
be delivered from evil may be to be set free from its power or
from its consequences. The context here of the parousia (and
therefore of judgement) suggests that both ideas are included.

καὶ καθαρίσῃ ἑαυτῷ λαὸν περιούσιον, ζηλωτὴν καλῶν ἔργων
The second part of the purpose clause is positive in that it is
concerned more with the creation of a new people characterised
by good deeds. Admittedly, the verb shares the negative quality
of λυτρόω, but it is given a positive character in its context.
καθαρίζω** is 'to make clean', literally (Lk 11.39), cultically
(Heb 9.22), and metaphorically of spiritual cleansing. The last
of these categories can include both the action of God in forgiving
sin and taking away its guilt,[158] and also the action of people in
abstaining from evil deeds (2 Cor 7.1; Jas 4.8).[159] The language
echoes Ezek 37.23, which is used here to fill out the thought
taken from Ps 129.8 (Haubeck*). The thought of cleansing by the
blood of Jesus may be implicit in view of the cultic background
of the phraseology (cf. 1 Jn 1.7; Heb 9.14; 1 Pet 1.2; Lock, 146).
Schlarb 1990:84f. suggests that the use of the language of ἀνομία
and καθαρίζω may be related to false notions of purity held by
the heretics. ἑαυτῷ corresponds to μοι in Ezek 37.23.

The reference of the phrase is disputed. Some find a reference
to baptism (cf. 3.5; White, 196; Lock, 147; Spicq, 642); others
think that the reference is to the sanctification of believers
(Bernard, 174; Guthrie, 213). But much the most likely view is
that the writer is thinking simply of God's total purpose in
creating a new people for himself.

λαός** can be used of a crowd or of a nation, national group,
or of a people as opposed to their rulers. Here it echoes OT
language where Israel was 'the people of Yahweh', the nation
which he had chosen to be the people over whom he would rule
(Deut 7.6; Judg 5.11; 1 Sam 2.24). In the NT the members of
the Christian church are increasingly seen as part of this people,
and they take over to themselves this designation over against
the Jewish people who are regarded as being no longer the people
of God because they have rejected the Messiah, Jesus. Paul takes
over the OT designation of the Jews as the people of God (Rom
10.21; 11.1, 2; 15.10), but he also applies the term to the church

---

[158] Acts 15.9; Eph 5.26; Heb 9.14; 1 Jn 1.7, 9.
[159] For the adjective καθαρός see 1.15a, 15b, 15c, 1 Tim 1.5; 3.9; 2 Tim 1.3;
2.22. Cf. Hauck, F., and Meyer, R., *TDNT* III, 413–26.

of Jews and Gentiles (Rom 9.25f., reapplying Hos 2.25 and 1.10;
2 Cor 6.16, reapplying Lev 26.16). Here also OT language is
reapplied to the new people created by the redemptive action of
Christ; the same point is made even more strongly in 1 Pet 2.9f.
(cf. 1 Clement 64).[160]

περιούσιος***, 'chosen, special', is a word found only rarely
outside the LXX.[161] It is related to the noun περιουσία, 'surplus,
superfluity, abundance', and the verb περιουσιάζω, 'to have
more than enough, abound, be distinguished, eminent'. Hence
the word here conveys the idea of 'a costly possession, a choice
treasure' rather than simply 'a people of possession'.[162] In the
LXX the phrase λαὸς περιούσιος translates עַם סְגֻלָּה (Exod 19.5;
cf. Deut 7.6; 14.2; 26.18; cf. Exod 23.22 [nò Heb. equiv.]).
The Hebrew term occurs also in Mal 3.17; Ps 135.4; Eccl 2.8;
1 Chr 29.3, and refers to private property that one has personally
acquired (Wildberger, H., *THAT* II, 142–4). Cf. 1 Clement 64
and the use of the noun περιποίησις.[163] The concept is also
linked with redemption in Eph 1.14. Spicq, 643, says the phrase
expresses personal possession, choice, preference and privilege.

ζηλωτής** is 'a zealous, enthusiastic person'. The noun is
often followed by an indication of the sphere of the zeal, which
may be a person or a thing.[164] It frequently expresses active
devotion to God (Acts 22.3) and the law in Judaism.[165] The
word can be used absolutely in this sense (4 Macc 18.12; 1 Esdr
8.69 *v.l.*) and came to refer to militant Jewish nationalists
(Lk 6.15; Acts 1.13). However, the language also has 'a good
Gk. ring, denoting the consistent and zealous orientation of
action to a moral ideal'; it is thus expressive of the predominant
Gk. usage for an ethical attitude.[166] It signifies 'eager [to possess]
spiritual gifts' (1 Cor 14.12). The phrase 'eager [to do] good'
(1 Pet 3.13***; cf. Philo, *Praem.* 11) is close to the usage here.[167]
A vigorous, active attitude is indicated (cf. 1 Clement 45.1 where
it is linked to φιλόνεικος).[168]

---

[160] Cf. Strathmann, H., *TDNT* IV, 29–59; *TLNT* II, 371–4; Ridderbos
1975:333–41.

[161] It occurs in *CH* 1.19 and in P. Genève 11, 17 (AD IV, of a married man,
possibly = 'the chosen one' [BA], but might it not mean 'having more than
enough'?).

[162] Cf. Preisker, H., *TDNT* VI, 57f.

[163] 2 Chr 14.13; Hag 2.10; Mal 3.17; 1 Pet 2.9; 1 Th 5.9; 2 Th 2.14; Eph 1.14;
Heb 10.39 (of human obtaining).

[164] See Dittenberger, *Or.* I, 339, 90, quoted by Dibelius-Conzelmann, 143 n. 13.

[165] 2 Macc 4.2; (cf. the use of the verb in 1 Macc 2.24, 50; *et al.*); Philo,
Spec. 2.253; Josephus, *Ant.* 12.271; Acts 21.20; Gal 1.14.

[166] MM, 273; cf. Stumpff, A., *TDNT* II, 882–8, espec. 888.

[167] Cf. also Polycarp 6.3 (ζηλωταὶ περὶ τὸ καλόν).

[168] For καλῶν ἔργων see **Excursus 6**.

EXCURSUS 8

Christology and the concept of 'epiphany'

Brox, 161–6; Deichgräber 1967; Gundry, R. H., 'The Form, Meaning and Background of the Hymn Quoted in 1 Timothy 3,16' in Gasque, W. W., and Martin, R. P., *Apostolic History and the Gospel* (Exeter: Paternoster, 1970), 203–22; Hanson, 38–42; Klöpper 1902; Läger 1996; Lau 1996; Löning, K., 'Epiphanie der Menschenfreundlichkeit. Zur Rede von Gott im Kontext städtischer Öffentlichkeit nach den Pastoralbriefen', in Lutz-Bachmann, M. (ed.), *Und dennoch ist von Gott zu reden. FS H. Vorgrimler* (Freiburg, 1994; not accessible to me), 107–24; Marshall 1988; 1994; Merkel, H., 'Christologische Traditionen in den Pastoralbriefen', unpublished paper given at the SNTS conference, Canterbury, 1983; Metzger, W., *Der Christushymnus 1. Timotheus 3,16* (Stuttgart: Calwer, 1979); Oberlinner 1980:192–213; [1996], 143–59; Roloff, 358–65; Schnackenburg 1970:355–60; Simonsen 1980; Spicq, 245–54; Stenger, W., *Der Christushymnus 1 Tim 3,16* (Frankfurt: Lang, 1977); Stettler 1998; Towner 1989:51–6, 75–119; Trummer 1978:193–208; Wengst 1973; Wilson 1979:69–89; Versnel, H. S., 'What did ancient man see when he saw a god?', in van der Plas, D. (ed.), *Effigies Dei: Essays on the History of Religion* (Leiden: Brill, 1987), 42–55; Windisch 1935.

On ἐπιφάνεια
Bultmann, R., and Lührmann, D., *TDNT* IX, 7–10; Couser 1992:155–64; Dibelius-Conzelmann, 104; Gärtner, B., *NIDNTT* III, 317–20; Hasler 1977:193–209; Lührmann 1971; McNamara, M., *The New Testament and the Palestinian Targum to the Pentateuch* (Rome: Pontifical Biblical Institute, 1978); Mohrmann, C., 'Epiphania', *RSPT* 37 (1953), 644–70; Oberlinner 1980:192–213; Pax 1955; idem, *RAC* V, 832–909; Pfister, F., *PWSup* IV (1924), 277–323; Schlarb 1990:164–72; *TLNT* II, 65–8.

1. Modern study of the problem

(a) *The post-Pauline understanding.* The general consensus among critical scholars in the early part of the twentieth century was to regard the Christology of the PE as something of a declension from that of Paul, hardly an entity worthy of study for its own sake. The PE were thought to have a deuteropauline Christology in that they picked up the Pauline concepts of pre-existence and exaltation, added to them some Johannine insights, and expressed the result with the aid of new terminology drawn from the imperial cult and the syncretistic epiphany theology of the time.[169]

(b) *The pre-Pauline hypothesis.* This consensus was sharply questioned by Windisch*. He argued that the concept of pre-existence is not to be found in the Pastorals. Instead of it he detected, first, the presence of a *Son of man/Messianic* type of Christology which speaks of two stages of existence (2 Tim 2.8; 1 Tim 2.5 (cf. 1 Tim 5.21; 2 Tim 4.1); 1 Tim 6.11–16. Here Jesus

---

[169] Barnikol, E., *Mensch und Messias* (Kiel, 1932; as summarised by Windisch*, 213f.) stressed the living character of the concept of pre-existence in the Pastorals.

is thoroughly subordinate to God. He is a man who is exalted and placed alongside God.

Second, side by side with these statements there are others in which something more like an *incarnation-Christology* is to be found. The texts in question are 1 Tim 1.15; 3.16 and Tit 2.13f. They speak of the 'coming' of Christ and his manifestation in the flesh, but there is no reference to pre-existence. The vocabulary of epiphany is used in this connection, but only in 2 Tim 1.9f. does Windisch find it used specifically of the historical appearing of Christ, and the emphasis there is on the resurrection rather than the incarnation. In fact the epiphany really takes place in the proclamation of the gospel. When we hear of the appearance of our great God in Tit 2.13 the reference, according to Windisch, is to God the Father and not to Christ. Thus it is only with considerable qualification that we can speak of an epiphany-Christology in the Pastorals.

It emerges, then, that Christ is never spoken of as divine, and the phrase Son of God is not used. When Jesus is called Saviour, this occurs in the context of epiphany-theology and here (and here only) we can observe a taking-over of Hellenistic language. Only in the use of *kyrios* do the Pastorals stand near Paul.

Windisch claimed that a similar Christology could be found elsewhere in the NT. In addition to the Synoptic Gospels, he found similar thinking in Acts and 1 Peter, and he also detected it behind the Apostles' Creed. These writings do not develop wisdom, logos and incarnation christologies.

From all this Windisch concluded that the Christology of the Pastorals is basically *pre-Pauline* and draws little from Paul. It is a combination of some Pauline and synoptic/early Christian motifs, with a notable absence of some central Pauline christological concepts. The post-Pauline element lies in the use of the epiphany and saviour terminology. There is no indication that the author is developing his views over against a false, Gnostic Christology. He is *not a systematic theologian* but a purveyor of tradition. The Christology of the Pastorals thus forms an important part of the argument against Pauline authorship, since it represents a throwback to an earlier period.

This position was broadly accepted by subsequent writers who do not add a great deal to what he said.[170] Hanson, 38–42, holds that the author has no consistent Christology of his own but makes use of whatever comes to him in his sources. He does not go back behind Paul but simply picks up titles at random (like 'saviour', taken from the imperial cult). He is a binitarian

---

[170] See the works of Spicq, Brox, Schnackenburg, Trummer and Wilson listed above.

and is in danger of becoming a ditheist. He has no doctrine of the cross.

A more positive view is offered by Merkel*, who claims that the christological texts which appear to incorporate traditional materials derive from sources which lie partly in a Greek-speaking Jewish-Christian church, and partly in Pauline Christianity. The texts have a certain unity in that they show no indication of pre-existence. Nevertheless, the author has taken over a large number of terms from Hellenistic religion and has used these to interpret the salvation event. The author has thus tried to use modern expressions to interpret the content of the old formulae; he is thus modern in expression, but conservative in content.

(c) *The theory of an 'epiphany' Christology*. Merkel is influenced by the work of Hasler, who appears to have been the first to see the key importance of 'epiphany' to the author's Christology. He claims that the author lays aside salvation-historical or apocalyptic ways of thinking and offers a new presentation of Christology in the language and, more importantly, in the thought-forms of the Hellenistic world. Traditional statements are translated into this new set of categories which are associated with the concept of epiphany.

The starting point is the transcendence of God, who is described as the only and the invisible God, the great Creator. He is the source of eternal life and his will is to bestow it on mankind. His gracious will to this end is manifested in Christ who will at a future time appear as the manifestation of the grace of God. He will bestow eternal life on those who, thanks to the grace already revealed in him, have persevered in the faith and in good works, and consequently qualify for it. The hope of salvation is not guaranteed, therefore, by belonging to the church or by being baptised but only by the Holy Spirit who enables believers to do good works that will please the judge. Thus the doctrine of Christ is swallowed up in the doctrine of God. Even the cross has no saving significance of its own but is simply the evidence of the saving will of God. Traditional phraseology loses its original meaning and is made to serve this new conception. The witness of the church now functions as the evidence of eternal life in the future. The practice of Christian virtues will provide the members of the church with integrity at the last judgement; in this way they can be said to be justified by grace. There is thus a unified development of a new Christology in the Pastorals.

Similarly, Oberlinner (1980; 1996) finds a unified christological conception in the Pastorals. He claims that the presentation differs from that of Paul in that the author no longer lives in expectation of the imminent parousia; he has a greater sense of solidarity with the world, and his concept of sin is expressed more in terms of opposition to sound teaching. Christology is embedded in statements about the salvation-event which takes place on three closely linked levels – salvation history, proclamation, and 'surprise' (*Betroffenheit*); the soteriological aspect is thus the point of emphasis. The fundamental framework is provided by the Hellenistic categories of Saviour and epiphany, so that the concepts drawn from other religious settings enable a 'translation' of Christology; into this framework are integrated traditional sayings as well as Pauline material, and the whole has an anti-Gnostic tendency. Oberlinner corrects the picture given by Hasler by insisting that the epiphany of Jesus Christ makes the present time the time of salvation.

Läger 1996 emphasises the contribution made by the author of the PE as a creative theologian although he is careful to present his material as though it were part of the tradition. Her general understanding of the actual Christology is similar to that of Oberlinner, but she notes that the author's interest is more in soteriology. She rightly contests the suggestion that the Christology is particularly subordinationist. Her specific contribution is to argue that the author lays great emphasis on the place of Paul (as he understands him) in soteriology, so that Christology is almost replaced by 'Paulology' and one could say '*extra Paulum nostrum nulla salus*', since salvation is mediated exclusively through his message (see Tit 1.1 note).

2. The use of tradition

The general trend in recent studies to regard the author as a theologian in his own right is fully justified. His work shows signs of a definite literary structure, and he binds theology closely to ethical and ecclesiastical teaching. Although he makes use of traditional material, he gives it his own deliberate formulation.

An important part is played by texts which are based on synoptic traditions (1 Tim 1.15; cf. Lk 19.10; 1 Tim 2.6 and Tit 2.14; cf. Mk 10.45). These stress the coming of Christ in order to ransom people from sin. It is not surprising that these statements stand in the service of a concept of Christ as Saviour.

Side by side with these statements which are basically soteriological are others which deal more with the status of Christ. 2 Tim 2.8 expresses the resurrection of Jesus Christ and his Davidic descent and is related in some way to Rom 1.3f. It is generally held that the author is dependent on Rom at this point, but it is more likely in our opinion that he was using the same traditional material as is incorporated in Rom. The reference to Davidic descent is part of the case for Jesus' status as Messiah (and not simply his humanity); the other part of the case is his resurrection as (implicitly) an act of divine vindication.

Whether or not 1 Tim 3.16 is pre-formed tradition, it is highly enigmatic in its terse presentation. The opening line is clear enough as a depiction of the manifestation of Jesus in this world as a human being. The following lines can be understood as varying depictions of his divine vindication which is spelled out in terms of his being revealed to angels and proclaimed to the nations, his acceptance in this world (by believers) and in the heavenly world of glory (by God) (cf. Lau 1996:91–114).

Both passages are thus concerned with the status of Jesus as the One vindicated by God through resurrection. In both passages, however, the significance of Jesus as Saviour is present: it is brought out explicitly in 2 Tim 2.8 and it is implied in the references to proclamation and belief in 1 Tim 3.16.

A further important feature is the use of the 'in Christ' formula, always (except 2 Tim 3.12) with nouns. Its effect is to put a christological stamp on the gifts of life, grace and salvation (2 Tim 1.1, 9; 2.10) and on the qualities of faith and love to be found in believers (1 Tim 1.14; 3.13; 2 Tim 1.13; 3.1 5). Thereby it is made clear that the saving power of the crucified and risen Saviour, Jesus Christ, continues to be operative in the present era of salvation.[171]

3. Jesus as Saviour

The move towards a less Jewish and a more Hellenistic manner of expression is already apparent in the formulation of the traditional material. The language is generally less Semitic in character. It is also more universal in its scope.

The two main indications that the author has expressed himself by using Hellenistic categories, namely the use of 'Saviour' and 'epiphany', were highlighted by Oberlinner 1980. The characterisation of Jesus as Saviour (2 Tim 1.10; Tit 1.4; 2.13; 3.6) must be seen in the light of three factors.

The first is that it is also used of God (1 Tim 1.1; 2.3; 4.10; Tit 1.3; 2.10; 3.4), and the initial description of him as Saviour in both 1 Tim and Tit sets the tone of both these letters. God is primarily a Saviour. Consequently, the concept of Jesus as

---

[171] Against the view of Donelson 1986:141–54 that the author 'banishes Jesus from the scene' between his two epiphanies see further Lau 1996: *passim*.

Saviour is directly related to this dominant theme. Salvation is the work of God through Jesus.

The second is that the letters contain ten instances of other words from the same word-group. The total salvation vocabulary is found proportionately to a far greater extent than anywhere else in the NT and occupies a major place in the vocabulary of the PE alongside other theological and ethical terms. This vocabulary is used at strategic points in the thought of the letters, both in the opening salutations and also in extended doctrinal passages, so that it is appropriate to describe the author's theology as essentially a theology of salvation (Marshall 1996a). It is within this context that the references to Christ as Saviour are to be understood.

The third factor is the background to the letters. The term 'Saviour' was especially applied to gods and rulers in the Hellenistic world, and the influence of this usage is often held to be decisive for the use in the PE (Brox, 232f.; cf. Oberlinner, 155). Oberlinner draws attention to the paucity of usage in earlier parts of the NT and the evidence of a Hellenistic vocabulary and concepts elsewhere in the PE. He is not unaware of the frequent use of Saviour as a description of God in the LXX. It is true that the term was not used of the Messiah in Judaism. It appears, therefore, that the use of 'Saviour' for the Messiah developed in view of the understanding of his saving function and in the light of the usage for God. At the same time there is the fact that the name 'Jesus' is related to the same root.[172] Moreover, the attestation of the title for Jesus is earlier than the PE (Phil 3.20 ; other NT instances may also well be earlier: Lk 2.11; Jn 4.42; Acts 5.3 1; 13.23; Eph 5.23; 1 Jn 4.14). It appears, therefore, that the PE pick up a designation that was already in use in the church for Christ, but the author does so in close association with his use of the title for God and with an eye to its popularity in the Hellenistic world. The fundamental force of the term is accordingly derived from its Jewish and Christian background.

It has been suggested that the underlying reason for the use of the salvation vocabulary in the PE lies in the significant place which the concept has in Gnosticism and that the PE maintain the Pauline understanding of salvation as redemption over against the Gnostic physical-ontological understanding.[173]

---

[172] Oberlinner, 155 n. 42, disputes the connection on the grounds that the connection between 'Jesus' and 'Saviour' is not attested. But it is surely sufficient that the recognition that 'Jesus' is related to 'save' (Mt 1.21) is found.

[173] M. Hengel (letter of 12 Feb. 1997). However, salvation vocabulary is firmly attested in earlier writings, and if we date the PE around the end of Paul's life, a reaction to Gnosticism is less likely.

4. The concept of epiphany

The noun ἐπιφάνεια means 'appearance, appearing' (2 Th 2.8; 1 Tim 6.14; 2 Tim 1.10; 4.1, 8***; 2 Clement 12.1; 17.4). The word was used of the appearance of something previously hidden (like dawn or an unexpected enemy; LSJ) and especially of the manifestation of gods and divine beings.[174] The term 'epiphany' has come to be used in English for this specialised sense. Lührmann 1971 has shown that in Hellenistic literature ἐπιφάνεια is associated with some kind of help to human beings, e.g. on the battlefield, but has questioned whether there is necessarily a visible manifestation when the concept appears in Hellenistic Judaism. Lau 1996:179–225, has re-examined the evidence for the 'visibility' of the manifestation and concluded that 'the line of demarcation between the ideas of visible appearance and helping intervention is often blurred' (223; cf. Versnel*). 2 Macc in particular offers several examples of visible appearances reminiscent of OT theophanies.

The language is characteristic of Hellenistic religion and the cult of rulers who were regarded as gods or divine beings 'manifest' on earth. But, although the terminology is Greek, the concept is found in the OT (ἐπιφάνεια occurs 12 times in the LXX) and Judaism. The noun ἐπιφάνεια can refer to greatness, majesty (2 Kdms 7.23); to splendour of appearance (Esth 5.1 [15.6]); to the 'appearances' of people sacrificing before God (Amos 5.22 as a result of error); to 'saving interventions of God for his people' involving miraculous signs and visions (2 Macc 2.21; 3.24; 5.4; 12.22; 14.15; 15.27 v.l. ; 3 Macc 2.9; 5.8, 51).[175]

The verb ἐπιφαίνω is used frequently (25 times) in the Gk. Bible. In the active it means 'to show'; the phrase 'to manifest one's face' is frequent (Num 6.25; Ps 30.16; 66.1; 79.3, 7, 19; 118.135; Dan 9.17Θ; 3 Macc 6.18) and indicates the showing of divine favour. The verb is also used intransitively with the sense 'to appear', of what was previously unseen (the heavenly bodies, Acts 27.20), or 'to shine' (2 Macc 12.9 v.l.; Ep Jer 60). In the pass. it means 'to show oneself, make an appearance' (Ezek 17.6). In this sense it is used of divine beings,[176] and expressed the manifestation of God at Bethel (Gen 35.70);[177] the Sinai theophany (Deut 33.2); God's helping intervention (Ps 117.27); and his future manifestation (Jer 36 [29].14; Zeph 2.11; cf.

---

[174] See the discussion in *New Docs.* IV, 80f. §19, in connection with a well-known inscr. in honour of Artemis at Ephesus (AD II).

[175] Cf. Bultmann, R., and Lührmann, D., *TDNT* IX, 9; Lührmann 1971:193–6; Pax 1955:159f.

[176] BA list: Chariton 1.14.1 (Aphrodite); Dittenberger, *Syll.* 557.6 (III BC); 1168.26 (IV BC); Josephus, *Ant.* 5.277; 8.240, 268; 1 Clement 59.4.

[177] Cf. 2 Macc 15.13 of the appearance of Jeremiah in a vision.

Ezek 39.28). It is used of miraculous interventions by God in the temple in 2 Macc 3.30 and in battle in 2 Macc 12.22; 14.15. When God is petitioned to manifest his mercy in 3 Macc 2.19, he does so by a miraculous intervention against Ptolemy in the temple (cf. also 3 Macc 6.4, 9.18, 39). Lk 1.79 describes how the light of God will shine upon those in darkness and the shadow of death.

The adjective ἐπιφανής (13 times in LXX) can mean 'glorious, terrible [in appearance]'.[178] In 2 Macc 15.34 and 3 Macc 5.35 it is used of God as the One who had manifested his supernatural power.

This evidence shows that the concept of God revealing himself both to save and to judge was known in the OT in the tradition of theophanies, and that it was taken over in the LXX. Josephus likewise refers to God's powerful interventions and manifestations, but this usage is absent from Philo.[179] In the secular world the accession of a ruler or his visit to a city could be described as an epiphany (cf. Deissmann 1927:370–4; *TDNT* IX, 9).

In some Jewish literature it is said that the Messiah will be 'revealed' (4 Ezra 7.28; *2 Apoc. Bar.* 29.3; 39.7; cf. Jn 1.31). The same concept is found in the Targums (Tg JI Gen 35.21; PT Exod 12.42; Tg Zech 3.8; 6.12; Tg Jer 30.21; similarly the Kingdom of God will be revealed). This evidence suggests to McNamara*, 246–52, that it is unnecessary to look to Hellenism for the origin of the concept here; although the terminology was familiar in Hellenism, the concept expressed was fully at home in Judaism.

In the NT the noun is used as the equivalent to παρουσία for the future coming of the Lord (Tit 2.13; 2 Tim 4.1, 8; 2 Th 2.8; 2 Clement 12.1; 17.4) (and also as a term for his first coming (2 Tim 1.10***). But whereas the noun is used to refer to the appearance of Jesus Christ or his glory, the verb is used (Tit 2.11; 3.4) for the manifestation of the grace or love of God. The thought is that God's saving purpose is made manifest in that it is put into effect. The thought is broader than simply that of the appearance of Christ and appears to encompass the whole of the saving event including the actual salvation of individuals

---

[178] Of an angel (Judg 13.6); of impressive human appearance (Esth 1.6 *v.l.*; 5.1); of warriors (Hab 1.70; of natural phenomena (Prov 25.14); of a city (Zeph 3.2); of a temple (2 Macc 14.33); of God's name (1 Chr 17.21; Mal 1.14); of the day of the Lord (Joel 2.11, 31 [3.4]; Hab 1.7; cf. Zeph 2.11 *v.l.*; 3.2; Mal 4.5 [3.23]); metaphorically, of a man's dignified way of life (2 Macc 6.23).

[179] For God intervening by providing providential leading see Josephus, *Ant.* 1.255; for miraculous interventions see *Ant.* 2.339; 9.60; 12.136; 18.286; for God's presence in the cloud see *Ant.* 3.310; for a revelation to a prophet, *Ant.* 8.240, 268; for a miraculous appearance of a god in a temple see *Ant.* 18.75, 286.

who experience new birth and justification. It thus becomes possible to speak of a manifestation of grace which trains people to live godly lives. The plan/execution scheme which is expressed in 2 Tim 1.9f. and Tit 1.2f. by the use of the synonym φανερόω is thus implicit in Tit 3.4. At the same time the execution is closely linked to the epiphany of Jesus Christ as saviour (2 Tim 1.10); the thought, however, is not confined to the actual historical event of the life of Jesus but encompasses the ongoing effects that are brought about by the gospel. In this sense there is one epiphany inaugurated by the coming of Jesus and continuing throughout the present and future time.[180] But when the writer uses the phrases 'until the epiphany of our Lord Jesus Christ' (1 Tim 6.14; cf. 2 Tim 4.1, 8) and 'awaiting the epiphany' (Tit 2.13), he is clearly distinguishing a separate event which lies in the future and forms the temporal context for a godly life. To speak, therefore, of the *second* advent of Christ is fully justified (*pace* Oberlinner, 157 n. 48).

When the PE speak of the manifestation of Christ and do so in relation to 'the grace which was given to us in Christ before eternal ages' (2 Tim 1.9f.), the implication is certainly that Christ himself was pre-existent and then revealed in his historical manifestation in flesh. In the light of this passage it is legitimate to assume that the manifestation of a pre-existing being is also intended in 1 Tim 1.15; 3.16. Thus, although epiphany language is not the same as incarnation language, in both cases the pre-existence of Christ is presupposed.[181] The real manhood or humanity or Christ is also a matter of some importance, crystallised in the deliberate use of ἄνθρωπος in 1 Tim 2.5. The intention here is probably to emphasise that Jesus is properly qualified to be a mediator by himself belonging to the human race rather than to make an anti-docetic point.

5. Conclusion

If Jesus Christ shares the designation 'Saviour' with God and is a pre-existent being now made manifest, the implication is that he is a 'divine' being. This is further confirmed by the way in which he is described as the 'Lord' who possesses the divine prerogative of judgement (2 Tim 4.8), and as being alongside

---

[180] So especially Läger 1996:111–19.

[181] Windisch*, 221, claimed that the christology of the PE is adoptionist. It will be clear that this assessment is wide of the mark. Equally, there is no indication of any sort of two-stage Christology. I have argued elsewhere (1994) that the use of the term 'subordinationist' is unhelpful, in that all NT Christology subordinates Christ to God and the PE do not stress this any more than do other NT writings.

God the source of spiritual blessings and the object of service; it is also significant that he can be the object of a doxology (2 Tim 4.18). In this context the interpretation of Tit 2.13 as an application of the title 'our great God' to Jesus Christ is justified.

It emerges that the christological statements in the PE stand fully in line with the traditions which the writer has inherited but employ a new framework which brings out the character of Jesus as the universal Saviour who manifests the saving plan of God in its historical realisation. The saving event comprises three elements, the redemptive death of Jesus, the proclamation of the gospel, and the personal acceptance of salvation by faith, but this structure is firmly attested throughout the NT and should not be regarded as an innovation in the PE. The language used would have aroused echoes in the Hellenistic world, but the concepts used are thoroughly Jewish, Christian, and Pauline.

g. Recapitulation (2.15)

The verse functions to bring the reader back to the point after the doctrinal backing, and to prepare the way for the further instructions that he is to give. Spicq, 643, says that it is very emphatic with its series of three verbs (cf. 2 Tim 4.2). It underlines the importance of the teaching that Titus is to give and offers encouragement in the face of any opposition. The danger is that people will pay no heed to Titus' authority. Probably this was because of his youth, like Timothy. This is not explicitly stated, and Oberlinner, 140, insists that this is too narrow an interpretation at a time when it is more likely that the development of an orderly system of leadership was not universally accepted; but 2.7f. may well point in that direction (though see discussion there; see further Wolter 1988:189–91). Spicq, 644, suggests that the Cretans were especially defiant (cf. above 1.7, 10–13 notes). The comment is apt, since the next section deals again with subordination.

If the letter is inauthentic, the verse can be seen as really addressed to the church, emphasising the importance of the teaching and the need not to ignore or despise it (Brox, 302). For its function cf. 3.8 and 1 Tim 1.18–20.

TEXT

15. λάλει δίδασκε (A) is probably assimilation to 1 Tim 6.2; the variant is possibly due to Atticist objection to a verb which could simply mean 'to chatter' (Elliott, 188).

περιφρονείτω καταφρονείτω (P *pc*) is assimilation to 1 Tim 4.12 (Elliott, 189).

EXEGESIS

15. Ταῦτα λάλει καὶ παρακάλει καὶ ἔλεγχε μετὰ πάσης ἐπιταγῆς ταῦτα refers backwards to the preceding instructions.[182] The doctrine is meant to lead to the moral effort previously described. Three verbs describe the desired action. λαλέω (2.1 note) is the weakest of them; here it must mean 'instruct'. It forms an *inclusio* with 2.1 and this suggests that the reference in the phrase is to the whole of 2.2–14. For παρακάλει see 1.9; 2.6, and for ἐλέγχω see 1.9, 13 and notes (cf. 2 Tim 4.2); the latter has the force (a) 'to refute those who disagree/disobey'. If so, there is a slight shift in construction; ταῦτα no longer functions as direct object, but is taken as acc. of respect or quietly forgotten. Another possibility is that the verb here means 'to expose, set forth, declare' (so BA); since, however, the parallels refer to the exposing of what is evil, this possibility is not likely. μετὰ πάσης ἐπιταγῆς (cf. 1.3) is lit. 'with every kind of command' (Spicq, 644. cf. 1 Cor 7.6). But here the thought is of 'authority', i.e. 'with full authority, with all impressiveness' (BA); ὡς ἐπιτάσσων (Barrett, 139). The reference is to 'the impress of the pastoral word' (Delling, G., *TDNT* VIII, 37). The authority is doubtless to be understood as divine (Knight, 329), but the fact that the word is used elsewhere for divine commands is hardly the basis for taking it in this way here (*pace* Guthrie, 214). Titus's authority to teach and correct the congregation, which is an extension of the apostle's, is established, by way of transference or participation, in 1.1–5. Moreover, all commands to him (1.5, 13; 2.1) grow out of 1.1–4.[183]

μηδείς σου περιφρονείτω The command is similar to 1 Tim 4.12 but with different wording (μηδείς σου τῆς νεότητος καταφρονείτω). Cf. 1 Cor 16.11 (μὴ τις οὖν αὐτὸν ἐξουθενήσῃ), which has been thought to be echoed here, Holtzmann, 493). The third person command is a grammatical curiosity. In 1 Cor 16.11 it is indirectly addressing any of the readers of the letter to whom it applies. Here, although the letter is ostensibly addressed to Titus himself, it may have this force; commentators since Calvin have insisted that this statement is really addressed to the congregation. But the primary force of it is surely an appeal to Titus himself = 'Don't let anybody despise you'; or

---

[182] Cf. 3.8; 1 Tim 3.14; 4.6, 11, 15; 5.7, 21; 6.2, 11; 2 Tim (1.12); (2.2); 2.14. Lips 1979:95 n. 4, argues that the word is used in summarising passages and expressions to refer to what has just preceded. It is not clear whether Quinn, 177f., is arguing for some forward references.

[183] See Lips 1979:149; cf. 122, 132, 138 and Wolter 1988:189–91, who both understand the language as an aspect of the letter's pseudepigraphical function, and as related to the need to underline the continuing authority of the teaching office (cf. also Trummer 1978:137; Brox, 302).

'Don't be put off if anybody despises you'. Kelly, 103, and Fee, 106f., suggest it has both forces. σου is here gen. after the verb, but in 1 Tim 4.12 it may be dependent on the noun ('youth'). περιφρονέω*** is 'to disregard, despise' (with gen.; cf. 4 Macc 6.9; 7.16; 14.1); the verb suggests insolence and lack of respect for authority (Spicq, 644; *TLNT* III, 103f.).

IIB. TEACHING FOR THE CHURCH – HOW BELIEVERS ARE TO LIVE IN
SOCIETY (3.1–11)

This second teaching section consists of three parts: 3.1–2, 3–7, 8–11.[1] An opening set of instructions that culminates in the need for believers to show a gracious attitude to all people is followed by a justification for such conduct in the form of a reminder of how God acted graciously in their lives to save them and give them the gift of the Holy Spirit. With the aid of this theological backing Titus is to encourage good works and to avoid profitless arguments; people who persist in the latter are to be disciplined.

a. General social teaching addressed to all (3.1–2)

Strobel, A., 'Zum Verständnis von Rom. 13', *ZNW* 47 (1956), 67–93.

The section opens with a collection of commands concerned especially with the relations of believers to outsiders. It deals specifically with subjection to the civil authorities, positive good works, avoiding contention with other people, and showing gentleness and courtesy to people in general. Similar teaching on the believers' relation to society is found in 1 Tim 2.1–2; Rom 13.1–7; 1 Pet 2.13–3.17. The passage is analogous to Rom 12.17–13.7, but there is more stress here on meekness and gentleness (Spicq, 645). The qualities required here stand in contrast to the life style of the writer's opponents (Fee, 201).

Unlike the instructions in 2.1–10 which were addressed to different categories of people, the present instructions are to be transmitted to all the members of the church. This fact may be sufficient in itself to explain why the writer makes a fresh start at this point instead of incorporating this teaching in the preceding unit. It may also be the case that the two units are based on separate sets of material that were used in oral instruction in the church.

Underlying the instruction is the realisation by believers that they now form a separate group in society (Spicq, 645). They must take a positive attitude to society as good citizens, both by doing good and by avoiding strife. Their outgoing attitude of

---

[1] Merkel, 100f., draws attention to the parallelism in structure with ch. 2.

patient gentleness to everybody is backed up by the example of God's own patience to them; the unspoken implication would seem to be that this attitude may lead to the conversion of unbelievers, which, if correct, would move the thrust of the text beyond the level of *christliche Bürgerlichkeit.*[2]

Why is this instruction needed here? Rom 13 and 1 Pet 2 show that it was part of Christian moral teaching. According to Lips 1994:267, the combination of this instruction with 2.1–10 links it to the line of development of the household code represented in 1 Pet 2–3 (see note on 2.1). There may, then, be nothing more behind it than the need to emphasise obedience to the State in a context where disobedience was commonplace, much as Christians today may need to be reminded to be law-abiding (cf. Hasler, 95). However, as with 2.1–10, the teaching may have been called forth by a tendency towards insubordinate behaviour somehow associated with the influence of the errorists. Some commentators link the instruction with the alleged reputation of the Cretans as being epecially rebellious (Lock, 151; Spicq, 646). Were the many Jews there '*assidue tumultantes*' as at Rome? Quinn, 183–5, develops the hypothesis that the teaching here, which does not verbally echo Paul, is of Jewish-Christian origin and may have developed in such circles in Rome. However, the fact that Crete was said to be particularly factious may be irrelevant, unless this explains the lack of mention of this motif in 1 Tim.

TEXT

1. ἀρχαῖς Add καί (D² 078 TR lat sy; UBS mg.; Kilpatrick). Elliott, 211f. argues that scribes reduced the instances of καί linking two separate ideas (cf. 1 Tim 2.5, 7; 6.11), whereas it is necessary to the sense (cf. Lock, xxxviii, 152). Metzger, 655, notes that it is omitted by the best Alexandrian and Western MSS. There are also no connections between the immediately following infinitives, which shows that the author is in fact writing very concisely (cf. BD §460¹*; Parry, 82, suggests that in each case the second word has the effect of qualifying the first). Addition of καί by copyists who wished to avoid asyndeton is more likely. Quinn, 178f., holds that the addition was intended to harmonise with Eph 3.10; Col 2.15 where the reference is to angelic powers. Hasler, 95, raises the possibility that the cause of the problem is the addition of ἐξουσίαις as an explanatory gloss (similarly, Quinn, 183f.).

πειθαρχεῖν Praem. καί (F G); or add after verb (A). The variants should be rejected, since the infinitives are asyndetic in the rest of sentence (Elliott, 212).

[2] Brox, 303, comments that obedience to the State is regarded as completely unproblematic – as though this was unusual. But this is so throughout the NT and does not require special mention here. In any case, only 'normal' circumstances are in mind, and worship of the emperor was out of the question (Hanson, 189; Merkel, 101). What is envisaged is rather the ethical infiltration of society (Hasler, 95). In any case, the writer upholds a basic principle of society; there is no thought of revolution (Spicq, 646).

ἐνδεικνυμένους **πραΰτητα** ἐνδείκνυσθαι σπουδήν τά (?) (א*); The variant should be rejected as it is assimilation to Heb 6.11 (Elliott, 189f.). The article may be a remnant of πραΰτη-τα and thus a sign of error.

πραΰτητα πραότητα (אᶜ Ψ D F G 326 88 1908 69 256). Elliott, 100: the text is a late form of Attic πραότης, found in LXX; the variant is probably Atticistic and therefore secondary.

EXEGESIS

1–2. **Ὑπομίμνῃσκε αὐτοὺς** Titus is to remind his congregations of the teaching they already know which needs repetition. αὐτούς must refer in context to all the members of the church (cf. 2.15).[3] The implication is that previous oral teaching had been given. At the same time, the verb[4] functions as a means of formal transition to fresh teaching. For the indirect mode of issuing instructions to the congregation see 2.1–10.

Seven requirements are listed in asyndeton. Cf. Rom 8.35b; 2 Cor 7.11; Heb 11.32; 12.18 for piling up of words like this, with/without connectives. There are five infinitives followed by an adjective (sc. εἶναι) and a participial phrase which forms the climax of the list. These can be analysed in terms of content, however, as expressing four basic requirements arranged in two pairs: subjection to authorities and readiness for good works; non-aggression and showing patience to everybody.

(a) Subjection to authorities
ἀρχαῖς ἐξουσίαις ὑποτάσσεσθαι, πειθαρχεῖν The two nouns together are meant to cover all possibilities, and are probably not to be sharply distinguished.[5] It seems that the combination

---

[3] Quinn, 182–5, limits the reference to Jewish Christians, though without much warrant. Equally unlikely is the view that the intended antecedent is δούλους in 2.9–10 (*contra* Trummer 1978:143, 240). The pronoun lacks an antecedent, but there is no need to suspect copying of 2 Tim 2.14 (Houlden, 152).

[4] ὑπομιμνῄσκω (2 Tim 2.14**; Lk 22.61; Jn 14.26; 2 Pet 1.12; 3 Jn 10; Jude 5***) is 'to remind [somebody of something]', with acc. of person and acc. of thing (3 Jn 10; *T. Levi* 9.6; 1 Clement 62.3) or with a noun clause (Barnabas 12.2) or, as here, with the infinitive in the sense 'to remind somebody to do something' see 1 Clement 62.2. The verb can also mean 'to call to mind, bring up something', (Wis 12.2; 18.22; 4 Macc 18.14) 2 Tim 2.14 (but see note). For the noun see 2 Tim 1.5. Spicq, 645f. (cf. Quinn, 183) takes the pres. imper. as signifying the need for frequent reminders (cf. Plutarch, *Mor.* 786D: ὑπομίμνῃσκε δὲ σεαυτὸν ὦν πολλάκις ἀκήκοας).

[5] ἀρχή means: (a) 'beginning'; (b) 'first place', hence 'authority'. With the latter meaning it can have the sense of 'authority exercised by somebody, rule, magistracy' (Cl.; Lk 20.20; cf Jude 6; Gen 40.13, 21; 41.13; 2 Macc 4.10, 50) or the 'holder of authority, ruler' (Lk 12.11; Cl.; Exod 6.25; Hos 1.11). The word is used in the plural in Thucydides 5.47; 4 Macc 8.7; Josephus, *Ant.* 4.220. Cf. *M. Poly* 10.2. It is used of heavenly powers in Rom 8.38; 1 Cor 15.24; Eph 3.10; 6.12; Col 1.16; 2.10. Cf. Delling, G., *TDNT* I, 479–84.
ἐξουσία means 'power, authority', (Lk 20.20), hence 'office, magistracy' (Diodorus Siculus 14.113.6: τὴν ὑπατικὴν ἐξουσίαν, of the consulate). Hence it can be used of the holders of authority, magistrates (Dionysius Halicarnassensis

was something of a cliché (e.g. Lk 12.11; 20.20). Governmental officials, whether imperial, national or local, are in mind. Although Paul generally uses the two terms with reference to angelic powers, he uses the latter of rulers and magistrates in Rom 13.1–3 (cf. ἄρχων).[6]

ὑποτάσσομαι is used of subjection to political powers, as in Rom 13.1, 5; 1 Pet 2.13; cf. 1 Chr 29.24. It connotes recognition of their authority; this is then developed in terms of obedience. According to G. Delling, 'the primary point is recognition of the existing relation of superordination' (*TDNT* VIII, 44); similarly, Barrett, 139, thinks of recognition of authority without being servile. The pattern is common: see Prov 24.21; 3 Macc 3.3; and cf. the example of Jesus' obedience to the established order (Lk 2.51; Jn 19.11; Spicq, 646). There is an implicit contrast with the attitude which is ἀνυπότακτος (Tit 1.6, 10; 1 Tim 1.9).

The second verb reinforces the point by indicating obedience as the normal pattern. It expresses what being subject means in practice (Holtzmann, 493).[7] Presumably, the concrete application implicit in the use of the verb would correspond to Rom 13.6, where the paying of taxes is introduced as one practical expression of subordination to the State.

(b) Readiness for good works

πρὸς πᾶν ἔργον ἀγαθὸν ἑτοίμους εἶναι Believers are to fulfil the role of good citizens in the context of the preceding instruction about obedience to the authorities,[8] but the thought need not be confined to this (Fee, 201; Knight, 333; Brox, 303, says that there is no link). Cf. 1 Clement 2.7 for the same phrase in a general church context. Trummer suggests that the admonition to Christians to respect the social and political structures becomes most radical in the PE (1978:144), but this view is based on the assumption that the PE are written at a time when the church had already experienced severe persecution at the hands of the

---

8.44; 11.32; P. Oxy. 261.15; Josephus, *Bel.* 2.140; Lk 12.11; Rom 13.1, 2, 3; Hermas, *Sim.* 9.28.4). It is frequently linked with ἀρχαί (Lk 20.20; Eph 1.21; 3.10; 6.12; Col 1.16; 2.10, 15; *M. Poly.* 10.2). Cf. Foerster, W., *TDNT* II, 562–74.

[6] A distinction between the two nouns here, e.g. as references to imperial and local authorities, is scarcely possible.

[7] πειθαρχέω, 'to obey' (Acts 5.29, 32; 27.21***; Bultmann, R., *TDNT* VI, 9f.; *TLNT* III, 63–5), is used of obedience to laws (Josephus, *Bel.* 1.454; *Ap.* 2.293; Philo, *Mos.* 1.164, 329. It can be used without an object (Dibelius-Conzelmann, 147), unless we take both verbs with both nouns (Knight, 332). According to Spicq, 646, the force is 'to let oneself be persuaded, to accept a rule willingly' (Acts 27.21; cf. Philo, *Cong.* 63; noun, Philo, *Mos.* 1.85), hence to be at the service of commandments as prescribed by authority (similarly, Quinn, 185).

[8] Cf. similarly Rom 13.3, where those who do good works have the approval of the rulers; 1 Pet 2.13–15 (Holtzmann, 493; Parry, 82; Scott, 172; Spicq, 647).

State, a situation which the letters themselves do not readily verify.

The presence of this requirement to be ready to 'do good (or 'good works')'[9] in the context of teaching about the church's responsibility to the State reflects a traditional format. Rom 13.3 has οἱ γὰρ ἄρχοντες οὐκ εἰσὶν φόβος τῷ ἀγαθῷ ἔργῳ ἀλλὰ τῷ κακῷ ... τὸ ἀγαθὸν ποίει, καὶ ἕξεις ἔπαινον ἐξ αὐτῆς. 1 Pet 2.14f. has εἴτε ἡγεμόσιν ὡς δι' αὐτοῦ πεμπομένοις εἰς ἐκδίκησιν κακοποιῶν ἔπαινον δὲ ἀγαθοποιῶν· ὅτι οὕτως ἐστὶν τὸ θέλημα τοῦ θεοῦ ἀγαθοποιοῦντας φιμοῦν τὴν τῶν ἀφρόνων ἀνθρώπων ἀγνωσίαν. A statement describing the ruler's responsibility to dispense justice is lacking (though probably assumed) in Titus. The station code is reminiscent of the Hellenistic-Jewish ethos of the State[10] and charges the Christian to exhibit exemplary behaviour within it (cf. Trummer 1978:143f.). The charge may have been given a shape more suitable to the interests of the PE (πρὸς πᾶν ἔργον; cf. 1.16 note).

The reference is to 'good works', not 'any honourable form of work' (REB; Hanson, 189), and the phrase hardly implies a limitation – do only what is good (Holtzmann, 493; *pace* Spicq, 647). Rather, according to the meaning of the term in the PE, 'readiness to do "good works"' is a call to live in such a way that the fruit of the new life in Christ is manifested in tangible ways in this mundane context (see **Excursus 6**; Schlarb, 1990:349 n. 139).

(c) Non-aggression

μηδένα βλασφημεῖν, ἀμάχους εἶναι, ἐπιεικεῖς Three phrases sum up the way in which believers are to avoid causing offence to non-believers[11] but rather to commend their faith by their demeanour.

μηδείς is fairly general in view of the following 'all men' (Holtzmann, 493), although the reference may be more specifically to slander of the civil authorities (Spicq, 647). βλασφημεῖν[12] can be used of slander or speaking ill on a secular level (cf. Rom 3.8; 14.16; 1 Cor 10.30). However, in all these cases it is speaking ill of Christians which is meant and therefore the sense of

---

[9] πρός πᾶν ἔργον ἀγαθόν as in 1.16; 2 Tim 3.17 (cf. εἰς, 2 Cor 9.8; also 1 Tim 5.10; 2 Tim 2.21). ἕτοιμος is 'ready, prepared' (Mt 24.44; 25.10; Lk 12.40; 22.33; 1 Pet 3.15); for the use with πρός τι, see BA; Tob 5.17BA; 1 Pet 3.15. It can signify preparedness and readiness to do what is good. Cf. Ps 56 (MT 57).7; 107 (MT 108).1; Amos 4.12; Mic 6.8. Cf. ἑτοιμάζω, 2 Tim 2.21, and ἐξαρτίζω, 2 Tim 3.17. Cf. Grundmann, W., *TDNT* II, 704–6.

[10] Cf. *Ep Arist.* 240, 279, 280, 291f.; Strobel 1956:84f.; Goppelt 1993:185–7.

[11] Brox, 303, thinks that the heretics are especially in view.

[12] See 2.5 note. For the construction cf. Philo, *Spec.* 4.197: ὅπως μηδεὶς μηδένα βλασφημῇ καὶ κακηγορῇ.

'blaspheme' may be present. Beyer, *TDNT* I, 624, holds that even here 'the predominantly religious connotation is present'. If the reference is to the secular authorities, who are ultimately appointed by God, this may be the case, but it is rather pushing the term. For the danger of Christians committing this sin see also 1 Tim 6.4, where it is one of the results of disputes in the church, and 2 Tim 3.2, where it is characteristic of nominal believers (v. 5) in the last days. Jews were forbidden to blaspheme the gods of other peoples (Josephus, *Ap.* 2.237 with Thackeray's note).

ἄμαχος continues the injunction with the broad sense of being 'peacable', i.e. 'not quarrelsome'.[13] It takes up a motif present throughout the PE. In 1 Tim 3.3*** it is to be a characteristic of the overseer. Cf. the use of μάχη and μάχομαι in 2 Tim 2.23f. and Tit 3.9, where Timothy and Titus are warned against quarrelsomeness; see further Jas 4.1–2 and note the positive commendation of peacableness in Mt 5.9; Rom 12.18; *et al.*

More positively, the believers are to be ἐπιεικής, 'yielding, gentle, kind', i.e. being reasonable, 'conciliatory'. Spicq claims that the word refers to the clemency that should be associated with justice, expressed in moderation and reasonableness.[14] According to Preisker, the word here has less of a Christian or septuagintal accent: 'the literary character of the list, and the schematism of the concepts borrowed from Hellenism, suggest that here, as often enough later, ἐπιεικής bears the general sense of "meek" customary from Attic times.' Preisker argues that elsewhere Christians show this quality in virtue of their heavenly calling and that it is 'an expression of royal or heavenly majesty'; this is true even in 1 Tim 3.3 where it refers to the overseer as a figure of authority 'with eschatological assurance and in virtue of eschatological possession'. This differentiation lacks any real basis; the close similarity of 1 Tim 3.3 and Tit 3.2 makes it very unlikely that the word is used in different senses in the two passages. The 'eschatological' basis for Christian character is, of course, present in 3.3–6, even more so than in 1 Tim 3. The attitude is to be contrasted with that of the author's opponents (e.g. 3.9; 1 Tim 6.3–5; 2 Tim 2.22–26).

[13] In Cl. the word had the force of 'invincible' ('somebody with whom no one fights'; so in Josephus *Ant.* 15.115); but it also had the meaning 'not having fought', i.e. 'taking no part in a battle' or 'disinclined to fight' (*Epigr. Gr.* 387.6; MM 25; LSJ). This is the force here, 'placable, inoffensive' (Fee, 201). Cf. Bauernfeind, O., *TDNT* IV, 527f.

[14] 1 Tim 3.3 of an overseer. Phil 4.5; Jas 3.17; 1 Pet 2.18***; 1 Clement 1.2; 21.7; 29.1; for the etymology see MHT II, 314; Simpson (Homeric ϝείκω, 'to give way, yield' (cf. εἰκός, 'reasonable, fair') with ἐπί. For the noun see Acts 24.4; 2 Cor 10.1 (of Christ's character with πραΰτης); Wis 2.19. See Spicq, 647, and *TLNT* II, 34–8; Preisker, H., *TDNT* II, 588–90.

(d) Showing patience to everybody
πᾶσαν ἐνδεικνυμένους πραΰτητα πρὸς πάντας ἀνθρώπους
After a series of three 'passive' qualities the list climaxes in a
requirement to take the initiative (Spicq, 647) in demonstrating[15]
all manner of[16] good to people in general.[17] The implication
is that the rule is unalterable in all circumstances. The quality
of 'gentleness' or 'meekness'[18] is seen in Christ himself (e.g.
2 Cor 10.1; cf. Mt 11.29; 21.5; cf. Spicq, 642f.) and commended
by him (Mt 5.5, πραΰς). The thought is not so much of sweetness
as of patience, and is depicted in terms of non-retaliation in
Rom 12.14; 1 Pet 3.9. Christians are not to attack their
opponents. Gentleness is to characterise relationships within the
church, especially in disciplinary situations (1 Cor 4.21; Gal 6.1;
2 Tim 2.25); according to Judge it is 'an attribute of those with
authority'. It occurs frequently in catalogues of virtues (Gal 5.23;
Eph 4.2; Col 3.12; 1 Pet 3.15***) and is to be shown especially
to non-Christians (1 Pet 3.15).

The Christian behaviour here described is outward looking;
cf. 3.8b, where ταῦτά (*sc.* the teaching in 3.1–8a) ἐστιν καλὰ
καὶ ὠφέλιμα τοῖς ἀνθρώποις). Brox, 304f., links this universal
scope of Christian courtesy with the thought of God's universal
love in vv. 3f.

b. The doctrinal motivation for such conduct (3.3–7)

Beasley-Murray 1962:209–16; Burnett, F. W., 'Philo on Immortality: A Thematic
Study of Philo's Concept of παλιγγενεσία', *CBQ* 46 (1984), 447–70; Couser
1992:165–76; Dey, J., ΠΑΛΙΓΓΕΝΕΣΙΑ (*NTA* 17:5. Münster, Aschendorff,
1937); Dunn 1970:165–9; Fee 1994:777–84; Flemington, W. F., *The New
Testament Doctrine of Baptism* (London: SPCK, 1948), 101–5; Friedrich, J.,
Pöhlmann, W., and Stuhlmacher, P. (eds.), *Rechtfertigung. FS für E. Käsemann*
(Tübingen: Mohr-Siebeck, 1976); Hartman, L., *Auf den Namen des Herrn Jesus.
Die Taufe in den neutestamentlichen Schriften* (SBS 148. Stuttgart: Katholisches,
1992), 106–11; Holman, C. L., 'Titus 3.5–6: A Window on Worldwide Pentecost',
Journal of Pentecostal Theology 8 (1996), 53–62; Käsemann, E., 'Titus 3, 4–7',
in Käsemann 1960:298–302; Keuck, W., 'Sein Erbarmen. Zum Titusbrief (3,4f.)',
BibLeb 3 (1962), 279–84; Le Déaut, R., 'Φιλανθρωπία dans la littérature grecque
jusq' au NT', *Mélanges E. Tisseront, I* (Civitas Vaticana, 1964), 255–94;
Löning, K., '"Gerechtfertigt durch seine Gnade" (Tit 3,7). Zum Problem der
Paulusrezeption in der Soteriologie der Pastoralbriefe', in Söding, T. (ed.) *Der
lebendige Gott. Studien zur Theologie des Neuen Testaments. Festschrift für*

---

[15] For ἐνδείκνυμι see 2.10 note; the thought in 2 Cor 8.24 is similar.
[16] πᾶς is elative (cf. 2 Pet 1.5; Jude 3 and references in Dibelius-
Conzelmann, 147).
[17] For πρὸς πάντας ἀνθρώπους cf. 2 Cor 8.24; 10.1.
[18] πραΰτης, 'meekness, gentleness', 2 Tim 2.25** (cf. πραϋπαθία [1 Tim 6.11]);
Cl. (πραότης); Jas 1.21; 3.13. Cf. Hauck, F., and Schulz, S., *TDNT* VI, 645–51,
646; Spicq, 647f.; *TLNT* III, 160–71; Leivestad, R., '"The Meekness and
Gentleness of Christ" II Cor. x.1', *NTS* 12 (1965–6), 156–64; Lippert 1968:56f.;
Judge, E. A., in *New Docs.* IV, 169f. §80.

Wilhelm Thüsing zum 75. Geburtstag (Münster: Aschendorf, 1996), 241–57; Luz, U., 'Rechtfertigung bei den Paulusschülern', in Friedrich*, 365–83; Mott 1978:22–48; Mounce, W. D., 'The Origin of the New Testament Metaphor of Rebirth' (Diss. Aberdeen, 1981); Norbie, D. L., 'The washing of regeneration', *EvQ* 34 (1962), 36–8; Quesnel, M., *Baptisés dans l'Esprit* (Paris: Cerf, 1985); Schnackenburg, R., *Baptism in the Thought of Paul* (Oxford: Blackwell, 1964); Spicq, C., 'La philanthropie héllenistique, vertu divine et royale. A propos de Tit 3, 4', *ST* 12 (1958), 169–91; Trummer 1978:173–93.

After this surprisingly short paraenetic section comes a further theological grounding that provides the basis for it.

Holtzmann, 494, expresses a possible connection between this passage and what precedes: 'since we once were what they still are, but were delivered through the kindness of God, so we ought to show kindness to those whom we once resembled' (cf. Löning*, 247). Brox, 305, and Knight, 335, go further in suggesting that the writer is motivating the readers to show kindness to people who are difficult to live with and to treat them with kindness; but this is perhaps to press the passage too strongly. If this connection of thought is present, it is soon swallowed up in the development of the more basic contrast between what the readers were and what they now are, or, rather, between their sinfulness (like the rest of humankind) and the saving kindness of God, as in Rom 5. 6, 8. The main point is accordingly that the readers are now able to live differently from previously and therefore ought to do so (cf. Barrett, 140). But this point does not emerge fully until the writer offers his comment on the 'trustworthy saying' in v. 8.

The dominant thought is that God has saved the readers who were once enslaved by sin; he has transformed them by the power of the Holy Spirit so that they are now in effect delivered from slavery to sin and empowered to live a new life. The passage thus functions rather differently from the corresponding doctrinal passage in 2.11–14. Whereas in ch. 2 the function of the passage was more to explain that the purpose of God's act of redemption was to create a people who would do good works, here the function is more to explain how the readers are capable of doing good works in that they have been saved by God. If the thought in ch. 2 was more salvation-historical in that it described God's saving intervention in the world and its purpose, here the thought is expressed more in terms of the individual experience of conversion and salvation through which people are enabled to live a new life. Nevertheless, the contrast between the two passages should not be over-pressed. The thought of individual redemption is integral to the earlier passage, and the conversion of individuals is seen as part of the total saving action of God in the later passage.

The statement is shaped in the form of a contrast between what the readers once were before their conversion and the saving action of God in Christ. For the use of such schemes contrasting the previous state of believers with their conversion or with the manifestation of Christ see Rom 6.17f.; 7.5f; 1 Cor 6.9–11; Gal 4.8–10; Eph 2.1–10, 11–22; 4.17f.; Col 1.21f.; 3.7f.; 1 Pet 1.14–21; 2 Clement 1.6–8 (cf. Tachau 1972). The description of the readers' old life is expressed in the form of a vice list which shows that once they too were living in a pagan manner very differently from the pattern that has just been put before them.

The list of characteristics here is a stereotyped one that is generally true of non-believers as a group but does not appear to fit, for example, Paul's pre-conversion life too well (cf. Holtzmann, 494; Quinn, 200f.).[19] This disparity may be due to assimilation to the first-person format of vv. 4–7, if it be the case that traditional material is being cited there (Dibelius-Conzelmann, 147). At the same time, the use of the first person acts as a rhetorical means of persuasion by developing the relationship between the writer and the readers (Quinn, 201). The pre-Christian situation is painted in similar colours to heresy in the church (Brox, 305; Oberlinner, 167). Cf. 2 Tim 3.13.

The passage then describes the way in which God saved them by grace and renewed them by the Spirit so that they should be justified and so become heirs of eternal life. This section is generally regarded as a 'hymn', with a 'reference' in v. 8. But the extent of the traditional material is debated:

(a) The debt to tradition is interpreted most generously by those who see all of vv. 3–7 as pre-formed soteriological material with Pauline interpretative glosses in prose by the author.[20]

(b). Most scholars exclude v. 3 and restrict the traditional elements to vv. 4–7.

(c) Others restrict the traditional material to some or all of vv. 5–7. Thus Lock, 155, favours possibly only v. 5 with 6–7 as an expansion by the author. By contrast Easton, 99f., 102, identifies vv. 5b-7 as the section centred on baptism; he argues that the theological language in 5a would be out of place in a hymn. Even more restricted is the limitation of tradition to vv. 5b-6 by Kelly, 254, who argues that vv. 3–4 should be excluded as too much in the idiom of the PE; 5a and 7 have 'a strongly Pauline tang'.

---

[19] For lists of vices see 1.5–9 note; McEleney 1974:215; Quinn, 208–10, discusses parallels at Qumran.

[20] Dibelius-Conzelmann, 28, 147; similarly Hanson, 44 (a liturgical fragment; see also 1968:78–96); Boismard 1961:15–56; Lips 1979:260.

In view of the way in which the author has framed the material in his own style it may be unwise to be too precise. In any case, vv. 4–7 consist of one sentence which (although some of the relationships are uncertain) can be laid out as follows:

(1) ὅτε δὲ ἡ χρηστότης καὶ ἡ φιλανθρωπία ἐπεφάνη   Time
         τοῦ σωτῆρος ἡμῶν θεοῦ

(2)   οὐκ ἐξ ἔργων τῶν ἐν δικαιοσύνῃ
         ἃ ἐποιήσαμεν ἡμεῖς   Basis
         ἀλλὰ κατὰ τὸ αὐτοῦ ἔλεος

(3) ἔσωσεν ἡμᾶς   Main Action

(4)   διὰ λουτροῦ   Means
         παλιγγενεσίας
         καὶ ἀνακαινώσεως πνεύματος ἁγίου
           οὗ ἐξέχεεν ἐφ᾽ ἡμᾶς πλουσίως
             διὰ Ἰησοῦ Χριστοῦ τοῦ σωτῆρος ἡμῶν

(5) ἵνα   Purpose/Result
         δικαιωθέντες τῇ ἐκείνου χάριτι
      κληρονόμοι γενηθῶμεν
         κατ᾽ ἐλπίδα ζωῆς αἰωνίου

We should be wary of describing the passage as a 'hymn', since poetic elements are entirely lacking (Fee, 203). It is clear that material from traditional schemata is being used, but we may ask whether the writer has so adapted it to his own purposes here that the task of identifying a traditional basis will be fruitless.

Similar ideas are found in 1 Cor 6.9–11; Col 3.7f.; Eph 2.4–9;[21] 4.17–24; 1 Pet 1.3–5, 14–21 (Merkel, 101). The language is largely traditional, but the use of 'kindness and love' instead of 'grace' (2.11) suggests a picking up of a familiar Hellenistic pairing, and the word 'rebirth' is also unusual. Boismard held that the passage is a 're-reading' of the more primitive baptismal hymn cited in 1 Pet 1.3–5, but this is highly speculative and has not been widely accepted.[22] Mounce*, 214–45, holds that there is insufficient evidence to show that the two passages reflect a common source. There is a closer parallel with Gal 4.3–7, although the content of this passage is developed rather differently (Lohfink 1988:174–7).

The statement is entirely concerned with soteriology. It describes what has happened in the new era which dawned with the revelation of God's kindness and love. These words give a strong contrast with the vices in 3.2 (Spicq, 651) and may have been deliberately chosen to give parallels to desired Christian

---

[21] Here also the stress on 'not by works' follows a description of pagan sins (cf. Holtzmann, 495).

[22] Boismard 1961:15–23; idem, *DBS* VII, 1422f.; cf. Hanson 1968:78–96.

virtues (Brox, 306). The reference is to the saving act of God as a whole, and not simply to the Christian message. God's saving action towards Christians was not the result of righteous deeds done by them as a ground for his rescuing them but was rather in accordance with his unmerited mercy. The 'means' of salvation was the washing away of sin associated with a new beginning and a spiritual renewal brought about by the Holy Spirit. And the gift of the Spirit in rich measure was God's gift through Christ. God's ultimate purpose was that his people who have been justified by his grace should become heirs, living in hope of their share in eternal life. Nothing is said for the moment about the ethical implications of this statement, and this may be an indication that the writer is using traditional material that was originally used more to stress the concept of *sola gratia* and to depict in glowing terms the blessings that believers enjoy through God's gracious act of salvation. The statement is almost trinitarian (cf. Spicq, 655; Fee 1994, ch.11; *contra* Hanson, 192).

TEXT

3. ἀνόητοι Add καί (D a b t vg^mss sy^p Lcf). The addition is secondary since the author can and does write unconnected lists (1 Tim 1.7; Elliott, 212).

5. ἃ ὧν (C² D² Ψ 1881 TR) is an Atticistic alteration (cf. 1 Tim 4.3, 6; Elliott, 63).

αὐτοῦ ἔλεος Inverted order (D* E F G); Elliott, 191, claims that this is more Semitic (Lk 1.50, 58; cf 1 Tim 5.25). He notes that αὐτοῦ never separates article and noun elsewhere in PE (cf. 1 Tim 5.18; 2 Tim 1.8; 2.19; 4.1, 8, 18; Tit 1.3).

πνεύματος ἁγίου Praem. διά (D* F G b vg ^mss Lcf). Elliott, 191, argues that the preposition is possibly original and was omitted for stylistic reasons because of frequency of word in vv. 5–6. Alternatively, and more probably, the word could have been inserted par. 3.6b or is epexegetical to clarify whether 'of the Spirit' is subjective or objective.

6. οὗ ὅ (D* 1739 326). According to Elliott, 191, the PE avoid attraction of relative, and the text is Atticistic correction. See 1 Tim 4.4 note.

7. γενηθῶμεν γενώμεθα (ℵ² D² Ψ TR). Although Elliott, 192, argues that scribes disliked the aorist middle and so altered it, he appears to adopt the aor. pass. (233).

κατ' κατά (D*); Elliott, 120, accepts the variant, as at 2 Tim 1.9, but the MS evidence is weak.

EXEGESIS

3. Ἦμεν γάρ ποτε καὶ ἡμεῖς For this use of the first person plural of believers in general cf. 3.5*, Gal 4.3; Eph 2.3 (cf. 2nd person in Col 3.7). The first person sing. is used of Paul in 1 Tim 1.13–16 in a similar once/now description, but there the reference is to him personally. γάρ introduces doctrinal motivation, as before. ποτε is used of believers' non-Christian past in Rom 7.9; 11.30; Gal 1.13, 23a, 23b; Eph 2.2, 3, 11; 5.8; Col 1.21; 3.7; Philem 11; 1 Pet 2.10 (3.20). This is a remarkably frequent and consistent usage, amounting to 14 out of 29 occurrences of the word in the NT. Here it probably functions with ὅτε δέ of v. 4 to form the transition formula 'formerly ... but now' (more typically ποτε ... νῦν[ι], Rom 6.20–22; 11.30–32; Gal 1.23; 4.8–9; Eph 2.1–22; 5.8; Col 1.21–22; 3.7–8; Philem 11; 1 Pet 2.10; but also with variations, Rom 5.8–9; 7.5; Gal 1.13; 1 Pet 2.25; cf. Tachau 1972:79–95). καί draws the analogy with those who are still not Christians. In this way their need of the gospel is implicitly underlined (cf. Oberlinner, 166f.).

Seven vices are listed here (corresponding to the seven virtues in 3.1f., according to Spicq, 649).[23] The first three belong together and have to do with human ignorance, folly and religious disobedience; the resultant state is one of bondage to human desires; the remaining three vices have to do with antisocial sins.

(a) Wandering in ignorance

ἀνόητοι, ἀπειθεῖς, πλανώμενοι The first three characteristics belong together as a description of people ignorant of God, disobedient and deluded. Although ἀνόητος[24] can be used of people who are merely uneducated and simple (Rom 1.14), it generally refers in the NT to those who are insensible and obtuse, especially to spiritual values. They lack the knowledge that brings salvation. Hence it is not clear whether the thought is simply of ignorance or of deliberate obtuseness. For the thought see Eph 4.17f.; Rom 1.21–32. The disobedience – echoing 1.16 (cf. note) – is clearly towards God or his agents. The list of vices does not stand in direct correspondence with the virtues in 3.1f., but a contrast with obedience to the authorities is likely. As a result of these two qualities they are easily deceived.

πλανάω[25] is used literally of leading people astray, namely from the right path, and hence refers to people who wander

---

[23] The attempt to detect a chiastic structure which emphasises the fourth item (Quinn, 201f.) is not persuasive.

[24] ἀνόητος is 'unintelligent, foolish'. Cl.; LXX (Prov 15.21; 17.28; Ecclus 21.19; 42.8; 4 Macc 8.17); Philo; Josephus. Of persons, Lk 24.25; Rom 1.14; Gal 3.1, 3; *CH* 1.23. Of things, 1 Tim 6.9***. noun, 2 Tim 3.9. Cf. Behm, J., *TDNT* IV, 961f.

[25] πλανάω act. 'to lead astray, mislead, deceive', 2 Tim 3.13a; Mt 24.4, 5, 11, 24; Mk 13.5, 6. Jn 7.12; 1 Jn 1.8; 2.26; 3.7; Rev 2.20; 12.9; 13.14; 18.23; 19.20; 20.3, 8, 10; *Didache* 6.1; Ignatius, *Mag.* 3.2; *Philad.* 7.1a. Mid. and pass. 'to wander, to be led astray', lit. Mt 18.12f.; Heb 11.38; metaph. 2 Tim 3.13b; Mt. 22.29; 24.24; Mk 12.24, 27; Lk 21.8; Jn 7.47; 1 Cor 6.9; 15.33; Jas 1.16; 5.19; 1 Pet 2.25; 2 Pet 2.15; Rev 18.23. Cf. 1 Clement 16.6; Cebes, *Tabula* 6.3; 24.2; Dio Chrysostom 4.115: πλανῶνται ... δεδουλωμέναι δὲ ἡδοναῖς. Cl.; LXX; Philo; Josephus. There is a double force of being deluded and being misled from the right path in the verb; cf. for the former 2 Tim 3.13; Lk 21.8; Jn 7.47; 1 Cor 6.9; 15.33; Jas 1.16; and for the latter Heb 11.38; 2 Pet 2.15; Jas 5.19; Heb 5.2 (Spicq, 650). See also πλάνη (Rom 1.27); πλάνος (1 Tim 4.1); ἀποπλανάω (1 Tim 6.10). Cf. Braun, H., *TDNT* VI, 228–53.

about and are lost. It also contains the element of deceiving people so that they are deluded. Quinn, 202–4, wants to link the motif here to the false prophecy current in first-century Palestine and reflected in Mt 24.10–12, 23f. (cf. Rev 2.20), but a more general reference to the delusions of paganism is likely, with perhaps a passing glance at the heresy which seems to produce a 'spirituality' marked by pagan characteristics. Such delusion may be both doctrinal and ethical. It is particularly associated with the last days when evil powers delude people in general and attempt to captivate believers. The force here may be that the unbelievers were deceived or that they were 'lost' and directionless.

(b) Slaves to pleasure

δουλεύοντες ἐπιθυμίαις καὶ ἡδοναῖς ποικίλαις Human beings prior to conversion are regarded as being held captive[26] by all kinds of[27] powers such as sin, lawlessness, uncleanness, false gods, the elements of this world, and even the law. Cf. Rom 6.16–21; 2 Pet 2.19. (It is possible for Christians to fall back into this situation.) The idea of slavery to evil was commonplace in the Graeco-Roman world (Menander, Koerte 568/541K, cited by Quinn, 204) and in Judaism (*T. Jud.* 18.6; *T. Jos.* 7.8; 4 Macc 3.2; 13.2). According to Spicq, 650, the Stoics regarded slavery to the passions[28] and pleasures[29] as the worst of all. It stands in strong contrast to loving God (2 Tim 3.4). Hort 1909:88

---

[26] δουλεύω 'to be a slave, to perform the duties of a slave, serve, obey', with dat. of person, lit. of slaves or slave-like service, 1 Tim 6.2**; Mt 6.24/Lk 16.13; Lk 15.29; Rom 9.12; Eph 6.7; metaph. of subjection to evil, false gods, Jn 8.33; Rom 6.6; Gal 4.8f.; of service to God, Rom 7.6, 25. Cf. Rom 6.12f.; 1 Cor 6.9–11. See also δουλόω (2.3); δοῦλος (1.1). Cf. Rengstorf, K. H., *TDNT* II, 261–80.

[27] ποίκιλος 'of various kinds, diversified, manifold' (also 'many-coloured'), almost equivalent to 'fickle, shifting', Simpson, 145 (cf. Vettius Valens 45, 47. Menander). Cl.; LXX; Philo; Josephus, 2 Tim 3.6** (also of desires); Jas 1.2 and 1 Pet 1.6 (temptations); Mk 1.34; Heb 2.4 *et al.* Cf. Seesemann, H., *TDNT* VI, 484f.

[28] ἐπιθυμία, 2.12 note; (cf. Rom 6.12). The link with ἡδονή (only one other time in the NT, Jas 4.1f.) is found in Stoicism along with grief and fear as the cardinal faults (Easton, 99, 187f.); cf. Dio Chrysostom 49.9; 4 Macc 5.23; Philo, *Agr.* 83, 84, *et al.*; Diognetus 9.1 But in fact it goes back to Plato, *Phaedo* 83B. Cf. Büchsel, F., *TDNT* III, 171 n. 36: 'when ἐπιθυμία is satisfied we have ἡδονή, and when ἡδονή is sought we have ἐπιθυμία'.

[29] ἡδονή 'pleasure, enjoyment', Lk 8.14; Jas 4.1, 3; 2 Pet 2.13*** (cf. φιλήδονος, 2 Tim 3.4***). Cl.; LXX; Philo (*Mos.* 1.28, 154, 295); Josephus, *Ap.* 2.189. According to Easton, 216f., the word is rare in the LXX ('taste', Num 11.8; Wis 16.20; 'sexual pleasure', Wis 7.2; 'happiness', Prov 17.1). Plato and Aristotle used the word of good and evil pleasures and made the former into a virtue; this idea is reflected in 4 Macc 9.31. Pleasure was regarded in a poor light by Stoics (as opposed to Cyrenaeans and Epicureans) who replaced it by χαρά, and it was seen as evil in itself by Philo. It can be almost personified,

distinguished between ἐπιθυμία as 'desire' and ἡδονή as 'indulgence of desire, indulged desire'. But the line between the longing for pleasure and the actual enjoyment of it is a thin one.

(c) Anti-social behaviour

ἐν κακίᾳ καὶ φθόνῳ διάγοντες, στυγητοί, μισοῦντες ἀλλήλους

The three remaining characteristics may probably be seen as the outworking of the anti-religious, selfish attitudes just described. A way of life[30] is described with its evil qualities. κακία is an evil of the mind, contrasted with πονηρία as its manifestation (Ellicott, 191).[31] Linked with φθόνος,[32] it is 'a force which destroys fellowship' (Grundmann, W., *TDNT* III, 484). Envy itself leads to hatred[33] of those who have what we desire, and is not surprisingly linked on occasion with ἔρις (Rom 1.29; Phil 1.15). Malicious and envious people are odious;[34] they cause other people to react with hatred, and they respond in kind. Community and society collapse.

---

as here, in the image of slavery (cf. the conflict in Jas and choking of seed in Lk 8). It is closely linked to pagans and false teachers (2 Tim 3.4; 2 Pet 2.13). The word is neutral in 2 Clement 15.5; evil (κακός) in Ignatius *Trall.* 6.2; *Philad.* 2.2. Cf. the very full treatment by Stählin, G., *TDNT* II, 909–26.

[30] διάγω (with or without βίον), 'to spend, pass one's life' (LN, 'to behave' is not quite right). Cl.; LXX; Josephus; (with βίον) 1 Tim 2.2***. With a prepositional phrase, as here, Plato, *Phaedr.* 259D; ἐν ἁμαρτίᾳ, *T. Abr.* 10.13.

[31] κακία** 'malice'. Cl.; LXX; Philo, *Mut.* 30; *Spec.* 2.11; *Opif.* 168); Josephus; It is used of wickedness in general (Acts 8.22; 1 Cor 5.8; 14.20; Jas 1.21; 1 Pet 2.16; 'evil, trouble', Mt 6.34), but also more particularly of malice and ill-will in lists of vices (Rom 1.29; Eph 4.31; Col 3.8; 1 Pet 2.1***; Barnabas 20.1; *Didache* 5.1). Holtzmann, 494f. prefers 'badness', arguing that 'malice' is too narrow (cf. Arichea-Hatton, 300). Cf. Grundmann, W., *TDNT* III, 482–4. Cf. κακός, 1.12.

[32] φθόνος, 'envy'. Cl.; LXX; Philo; Josephus; Mt 27.18/Mk 15.10; Phil 1.15; Jas 4.5. In lists of vices, 1 Tim 6.4**; Rom 1.29; Gal 5.21 (with κακία, as in *T. Benj.* 8.1); 1 Pet 2.1***. According to Spicq, 650 it signifies depreciation, denigration, malevolence, calumny. Cf. Josephus, *Vita* 80; Plutarch, Περὶ φθόνου καὶ μίσους (*Mor.* 536E); Thucydides 6.78. Cf. *TLNT* III, 434–6; Johnson, L. T., 'James 3:13–4:10 and the *Topos* ΠΕΡΙ ΦΘΟΝΟΥ', *NovT* 25 (1983), 327–47. The word is not discussed in *TDNT*.

[33] στυγητός***. The sense may be (1) passive: 'hated', hence the kind of people whose character makes them objects of hate, 'hateful, odious' (Aeschylus, *Prom.* 592; = μισητοί, Hesychius, acc. to Holtzmann, 495; Philo, *Decal.*131; Heliodorus, *Ethiop* 5.29.4 [Spicq, 650f.]; 1 Clement 35.6); so NRSV ('despicable'), NIV; GNB; REB; Dornier, 151. (2) active: 'hating, hostile' (P. Oxy. 433.28 [AD III]; 1 Clement 45.7), which Knight, 337, prefers. Cf. θεοστυγής (Rom 1.30) for the same problem of interpretation.

[34] μισέω** 'to hate'. Cl.; LXX; Philo; Josephus. Also used with ἀλλήλους** in Mt 24.10; of hatred within a congregation, 1 Jn 2.9, 11; 3.15; 4.20, but here the reference is to the hatred within a non-Christian society. Cf. Michel, O., *TDNT* IV, 683–94.

The statement in verses 4–7 falls into five parts:

(a) **4. ὅτε δὲ ἡ χρηστότης καὶ ἡ φιλανθρωπία ἐπεφάνη τοῦ σωτῆρος ἡμῶν θεοῦ** A loose contrast is drawn (δέ) between the sinful past state of the readers (ποτε) and the new era of salvation which ensued (ὅτε[35]) with the revelation of the kindness of God (cf. Eph 2.4). The temporal clause describes the event which inaugurated the saving activity of God. Although the ethical imperative to live the life that the event has made possible is less direct than in 2.11f. (with its ἵνα ... ζήσωμεν), the connection of vv. 3–7 with v. 2 suggests that the implication is present.

Hasler, 96, holds that the clause refers merely to the revelation[36] in the preaching and not to the historical salvation-event in Christ. See, however, Knight, 338–40, who rightly argues that this statement must be understood in the light of 2 Tim 1.9f., and concludes that the phrase encompasses both the historical appearing of Christ and his manifestation to the readers in their personal experience (cf. Towner 1989:66–71, 112f.; Oberlinner, 170).

Two nouns express the grace shown by God. χρηστότης is used of the 'kindness, goodness, generosity' of God (Rom 2.4; 11.22a, 22b, 22c; especially Eph 2.7; cf. adj. Lk 6.35; 1 Pet 2.3) and of people (Rom 3.12; 2 Cor 6.6; Gal 5.22; Col 3.12***).[37] φιλανθρωπία, 'love for mankind', occurs here only in the NT in this sense (also 'hospitality', Acts 28.2***).[38] It refers to a virtue found in the gods, but also in rulers in relation to their subjects (e.g. 2 Macc 14.9). Lock, 153, notes passages where it was linked with ransoming captives. It was highly regarded in later Stoicism.[39] It was seen as a divine virtue

---

[35] ὅτε, 2 Tim 4.3**; cf. Gal 1.15; 4.4 of the time when God acted to save. ὅτε δέ introduces the conclusion of the transition ('formerly/now') begun with ποτε (see v. 3 note).

[36] ἐπιφαίνω is used as in 2.11 of God's grace. Again revelation is personified and not hypostasised (Dibelius-Conzelmann, 148). For τοῦ σωτῆρος ἡμῶν θεοῦ cf. 1.3.

[37] The word can mean 'goodness, uprightness, honesty' (Rom 3.12 = Ps 13.3 LXX), then 'goodness' in the sense of 'kindness, friendliness, mildness', contrasted with ἀποτομία (Rom 11.22). It is frequent in the LXX and is used of God in Ps 30.20 (31.19); cf. Philo. *Mig.* 122; Josephus, *Ant.* 11.144; 20.90; *Ps. Sol.* 5.18; 1 Clement 9.1; 2 Clement 15.5; 19.1; Diognetus 9.1,2, 6; 10.4; Ignatius, *Mag.* 10.1; *Smyr.* 7.1. Quinn, 213, cites Demosthenes, 21.148, for its equivalence to χάρις; here it also stands in close relationship to συγγνώμη, 'pardon'. The concept is frequently linked with φιλανθρωπία (Plutarch, *Demetr.* 50.1; Philo, *Leg. Gai.* 73; [Spicq, 254 n. 1; 663 n. 2]; Josephus, *Ant.* 10.164; Diognetus 9.2; cf. Field 1899:222f.). Note how here the pair is followed by a singular verb. Cf. Weiss, K., *TDNT* IX, 489–91; Spicq*; Spicq, 252–4; *TLNT* III, 511–16.

[38] Cl.; LXX (Est 8.13 and non-canonical books only); Philo; Josephus.

[39] According to Easton, 99, the word had descended to mean 'sociability, conviviality' in popular speech and was avoided by moral writers. He gives no evidence for this assertion.

that ought to be practised by human beings, especially rulers
(Dibelius-Conzelmann, 144 n. 23; cf. φιλανθρώπως, Acts 27.3,
of the kindness of a centurion towards Paul. According to Spicq,
651f., it corresponds to *humanitas* ('kindness') and was defined
by the Stoics as 'a friendly disposition in human intercourse'.
This use is found in the LXX (3 Macc 3.15, 20; 2 Macc 9.27;
14.9; 4 Macc 5.12; cf. *Ep. Arist.* 208); it is a quality of the
righteous generally (Wis 12.19), and wisdom itself shows it
(φιλάνθρωπός, Wis 1.6; 7.23). Josephus, *Ant.* 1.24 uses it of
God. Philo, *Virt.* 51–174 discusses it at length. Justin, *Apol.* I.10
links it with sobriety and righteousness as divine attributes to be
shown by believers. The word is rarely used in the NT, but the
usage recurs in Justin, *Dial.* 47.5; Diognetus 9.2.[40]

The precise background of the language as it is used here is
uncertain. Luck states that 'the phraseology is influenced by
the worship of manifested gods as seen especially in emperor
worship' (*TDNT* IX, 111). Kelly, 251, holds that the writer is
deliberately using the language of the imperial cult so as to bring
out the claims of Christianity more powerfully (cf. Wendland
1904:335–53). Quinn, 213–15, thinks that here we have a Jewish-
Christian response to the common attacks on Jews as being
misanthropic, drawing attention to Philo's designation of God
as loving humanity. But the imperial cult background seems
more compelling.

There is also the question whether the description has an
implicit paraenetic function. Luck (*TDNT* IX, 111, n. 37) states
that the text is not thinking of a virtue shown by God which is
to be imitated by believers. This is rightly disputed by Brox, 306,
who further argues that it should not be seen especially as a
virtue of rulers towards their underlings. The contrast with the
description of the readers before their conversion in v. 3 suggests
that one of the implicit purposes of God in the eschatological
'appearance' of his 'kindness' is to equip his people to do the
same. Scott's view (174) that it is the natural sympathy which
man bears to his fellow men is too weak in this context. Rather,
the effect of vv. 5f. is to define the nature of God's kindness by
the way in which he acted to save us.

(b) **5. οὐκ ἐξ ἔργων τῶν ἐν δικαιοσύνῃ ἃ ἐποιήσαμεν ἡμεῖς
ἀλλὰ κατὰ τὸ αὐτοῦ ἔλεος** There is a lengthy qualification
before we reach the main verb ἔσωσεν in order to introduce as
emphatically as possible the works/mercy contrast (for which

---

[40] Cf. Luck, U., *TDNT* IX, 107–12; Le Déaut*; Spicq, 657–76 (detailed
excursus); *TLNT* III, 440–5; *New Docs.* I, 87f. §47; Quinn, 192).

cf. 2 Tim 1.9).[41] The intention is to rule out decisively the thought that people can be saved on the basis of (ἐξ) any kind of human works.[42] The phrase ἐξ ἔργων is Pauline (Rom 3.20; 28, 4.6; Rom 9.12; 11.6; Gal 2.16a, 16b, 16c; Eph 2.9) and is often clarified by the addition of νόμου. The verb ποιέω is likewise used to express doing what God requires (Rom 2.14; 10.5; Gal 3.10, 12; 5.3).[43]

But here the thought is widened out to exclude any kind of actions done 'in[44] righteousness'. Righteousness[45] is the quality required by God in human action and represents conformity to his norms, doing what the law requires. Hence it can refer to the general quality of life shown by people who act in this way or to the verdict which is passed upon them. It thus means conduct in accordance with God's requirements or laws. Cf. Acts 10.35; 13.10; 24.25; Phil 1.11; 1 Clement 5.7. The process of justification (cf. 3.7, δικαιόω) is the recognition by God of people as righteous, regardless of their past actions, on the basis of the work of Christ; it is the conferring of a status which must then be demonstrated in practice in righteous living (cf. adv. δικαίως, 2.12). The verb ποιέω is not used elsewhere with 'works' as its object. The phrase is added here to give the required contrast between 'what we (ἡμεῖς, emphatic) did' and 'what by his (αὐτοῦ emphatic[46]) mercy God did'.[47] ἔλεος is used by Paul of God showing favour to people who do not deserve it (Rom 9.23; 11.31; 15.9; Gal 6.6; Eph 2.4); for the OT background see Exod 34.6–7; Ps 85.15 LXX. In the present context it is equivalent to χάρις elsewhere and it sums up the reference to χρηστότης and φιλανθρωπία earlier in the sentence.[48]

---

[41] Oberlinner, 170, links the phrase with the preceding part of the sentence, but this seems very awkward.

[42] For ἔργον see 1.16 note. The anarthrous noun is followed by a qualification with the article.

[43] ποιέω, 'to do, make' (1 Tim 1.13; 2.1; 4.16; 5.21; 2 Tim 4.5**). Cf. Braun, H., *TDNT* VI, 458–84, espec. 482.

[44] The construction of ἐν to express sphere is regarded as unusual by Holtzmann, 496. Cf. 2 Tim 3.16; Eph 4.24; 5.9. However, phrases of this kind with ἐν are very common with verbs, and here we should probably supply a verb on the basis of the following ἐποιήσαμεν.

[45] δικαιοσύνη, 'righteousness' (1 Tim 6.11; 2 Tim 2.22; 3.16; 4.8; Tit 3.5**). Cf. Schrenk, G., *TDNT* II, 192–210; Kertelge, K., *EDNT* I, 325–30; Luz*; Friedrich*.

[46] BD § 284³; Holtzmann, 496; Spicq, 652. Cf. Rom 11.11; Heb 2.4.

[47] κατά has the sense 'in accordance with' (see 1.1 note). It is used of God's saving purpose in Rom 4.16; 8.28; 11.5; Eph 1.8, 9; *et al.* For the phrase here see the parallel in 1 Pet 1.3 (White, 198).

[48] For ἔλεος see 1 Tim 1.2; 2 Tim 1.2; 2 Tim 1.16, 18** (verb, 1 Tim 1.13, 16**). Cf. 2 Tim 1.9 for different wording of the same thought (Holtzmann, 495). Cf. Bultmann, R., *TDNT* II, 477–87; Staudinger, F., *EDNT* I, 429–31; *TLNT* I, 471–9.

The thought is paralleled in 1QM 11.3f.: 'You have also saved us many times by the hand of our kings because of your mercy and not according to our works by which we have done evil nor [according to] our sinful deeds', which in turn reflects Ezek 20.44: 'when I deal with you for my name's sake, not according to your evil ways, or corrupt deeds' (Spicq, 652).

The point of the contrast here is uncertain.

(a) The thought is Pauline, contrasting God's mercy with works done in obedience to the law and required of Gentiles in order that they may be saved. The echoes of Pauline language make this the most obvious interpretation (cf. Brox, 306f.).

(b) More probably, however, there is a widening out of Pauline thinking in the direction of opposing moral effort generally as a means of salvation (Scott, 174f.) However, this emphasis is already present in Paul (Rom 9.11f.; Eph 2.9; Kelly, 251). Trummer argues that the author has made Pauline teaching more radical: not just the value of works generally but even of 'works done in righteousness' is nullified (1978:187).[49]

(c) Rather than a generalisation of Pauline thinking, some scholars see here rather a misunderstanding of Paul (Hasler, 96; cf. Schlarb 1990:189; discussion in Löning*, 247–50), but it is hard to discover just how they think Paul has been misunderstood.

(d) Klöpper 1904:59 states that there is no polemic against Jewish works in the PE, and therefore the reference can only be to 'such ethical activities which were so valued from the darkness of Gnosticising circles (which prided themselves on possessing the light-kernels and consequently considered themselves to be excellent over against the psychic and hylic elements) that they regarded themselves in a special way as worthy of obtaining salvation'.

In Rom 9.30f. Paul comments on Gentiles who did not seek righteousness but gained it by faith; he is drawing a contrast between their past life of sin and ignorance and their new status as believers; however, the Jews who followed the 'law of righteousness' did not attain to it. Here in Tit the deeds are those done in observance of the righteousness required by the law (the phrase 'denotes the human attainment envisaged in Phil. 3:6,9', Schrenk, G., *TDNT* II, 202). Barrett suggests that Paul would have added τοῦ νόμου (cf. Wilson 1979:25; but Rom 9.12; Eph 2.9 might challenge the suggestion).

Two possibilities arise: (a) The author is thinking of Gentiles who were not saved by righteous deeds before their conversion because they had not in fact performed any (Parry, 83); or

[49] Cf. Marshall 1996b.

(b) he may be thinking of people (both Gentiles and Jews) who tried to do righteous deeds but who were saved by God not because of these deeds but by his mercy, because these deeds were irrelevant and could not win salvation (Käsemann*, 300). In either case, to the degree that this portion of the statement intends to inform the ethical response of believers (3.2), the emphasis is most likely to be generally one of mercy in dealings with others (cf. Knight, 340).

(c) ἔσωσεν ἡμᾶς διὰ λουτροῦ παλιγγενεσίας καὶ ἀνακαινώσεως πνεύματος ἁγίου The main clause describes how God effected salvation.[50] The reference is to personal experience of salvation[51] rather than to God's action at the cross.[52]

The use of the aorist ἔσωσεν, as in Eph 2.8, may be thought to form a sharp contrast with Paul's use of the future tense to express 'the definitive final deliverance of believers',[53] but salvation is in some sense a past and present experience in Paul (Rom 8.24). What is unusual is the description of the means. To be sure, the three concepts of regeneration, renewal and the Spirit that are associated here with baptism are familiar elsewhere in the NT.[54] It is the terminology and the way in which the concepts are linked which cause problems.

The syntax of the διά phrase[55] is debatable in two respects:

The first problem is the relation of the following two nouns in the gen. to λουτροῦ.

(a) They may both be dependent upon it ('Through a washing of rebirth and of renewal').[56]

---

[50] σῴζω, 'to deliver', comes to be a technical term, 'to bring Christian salvation', 1 Tim 1.15; 2.4, 15; 4.16; 2 Tim 1.9; 4.18**; see 1.3 note.

[51] ἡμᾶς refers to Christians generally, including the author and readers. Cf. Cranfield, C. E. B., 'Changes of Person and Number in Paul's Epistles', in Hooker, M. D., and Wilson, S. G., *Paul and Paulinism* (London: SPCK, 1982), 280–9.

[52] But see Holtzmann, 496, for a potential reference to latter.

[53] So Klöpper 1904:60f.; cf. Trummer 1978:174–91; Luz 1976:376–81; Hasler 1977:207f.

[54] For regeneration and new birth see Jn 3.3–8; 1 Pet 1.3, 23; 2.2; 1 Jn 3.9; 5.18; Justin, *Apol.* I.61.3, 10; 66.1; *Dial.* 138.2; Tatian, *Or.* 5.3 (Merkel 102f.). For renewal see Rom 6.4; 2 Cor 5.17; Gal 6.25; Jas 1.18; *et al.* For the association of the Spirit with baptism see 1 Cor 6.11; 12.13; 2 Cor 1.22; Gal 4.6; Eph 1.13 (Kelly, 253).

[55] διά 'by means of', expressing instrument and occasion. With σῴζω, 1 Cor 15.2 (gospel); Eph 2.7 (faith); cf. Rom 3.24; 5.10; *et al.*; 1 Tim 2.15.

[56] vg; RV t; GNB; Holtzmann, 497; Lock, 154f.; Parry, 83; Dibelius-Conzelmann, 147; Kelly, 251f.; Barrett, 142; Spicq, 653; Fee, 205; Quinn, 187; Oberlinner, 175; Büchsel, F., *TDNT* I, 688; Oepke, A., *TDNT* IV, 304; Schweizer, E., *TDNT* VI, 445 n. 776; Klöpper 1904:62f.; Flemington*, 101 n. 5; Beasley-Murray 1962:211; Dunn 1970:166; Towner 1989:115–17; and most scholars. This interpretation appears to be adopted in NIV; NJB; REB; NRSV; but their wording is not free from ambiguity.

(b) λουτροῦ and ἀνακαινώσεως may stand in parallel ('Through a washing of rebirth and [through] renewal').[57]
The second problem is the construction of πνεύματος ἁγίου. Here there are three possibilities:
(i) with ἀνακαίνωσις (only) as subj. gen., of 'renewal associated with[58] the Holy Spirit' (cf. 2 Th 2.13);[59]
(ii) with both παλιγγενεσία and ἀνακαίνωσις. (In this case construction (a) is required.);[60]
(iii) with λουτροῦ.[61]
Combining these possibilities we have four possible interpretations of the whole phrase:
(1) (a) + (i) Through a washing of rebirth and of renewal which is associated with the Holy Spirit.
(2) (a) + (ii) Through a washing of rebirth and of renewal which are associated with the Holy Spirit.
(3) (a) + (iii) Through a washing associated with the Holy Spirit which brings rebirth and renewal.
(4) (b) + (i) Through a washing of rebirth and through a renewal associated with the Holy Spirit.[62]
A decision between these fine distinctions is difficult, and it is very doubtful if there is any major difference in understanding whichever set of possibilities we adopt. We can assume without further ado that the author would have agreed that the Holy Spirit was associated with the ʼwhole process. Syntactically, the simplest understanding of the expression is (1). (3) is not an obvious rendering of the Greek. The difficulties with (4) are the lack of a second διά and the fact that the two dependent genitives (παλιγγενεσίας, πνεύματος ἁγίου) have different functions. Construction (2) is also awkward.
λουτρόν, 'washing',[63] has been taken in three ways. (a) We can safely put aside the novel view of Hanson, 190f., that it

[57] pesh; RV mg; older commentators; White, 199; Guthrie, 217f.; Knight, 343f., correcting his earlier view in Knight 1968:96f., 100. Cf. Mounce*, 185–91; Quesnel*, 171–4.
[58] For the moment we leave the nature of this 'association' undefined.
[59] Parry, 83; Spicq, 653; Knight, 344; Mounce*, 185–91.
[60] Klöpper 1904:63; Schweizer, E., TDNT VI, 445 n. 776.
[61] Dunn 1970:168; Fee, 205; Towner 1989:115.
[62] Fee, 204f., lists three possibilities. His first is (4) above. His second is (2) above. His third is (3) above. An even fuller list is given by Quinn, 218f.
[63] λουτρόν, 'washing', Eph 5.26*** Cl.; LXX; Josephus, Ant. 8.356; Philo. (1) 'bath, bathing place' (cf. RV mg. 'laver'; Ct 4.2; 6.6); Quinn, 220, thinks that the word evokes the public baths in Rome; (2) 'the water with which one is washed'; (3) 'act of washing' (Sir 34.30); Josephus, Ap. 1.282.
The word was used of ceremonial washings (see refs. in BA; Philo, Cher. 95; et al.); Philo, Mut. 124 (τοῖς φρονήσεως λουτροῖς χρησαμένη [ἡ ψυχή]); Justin, Apol. I.61.3; 66.1 (τὸ...εἰς ἀναγέννησιν λουτρόν); Oepke, A., TDNT IV, 295–307, espec. 304; TLNT II, 410–14.

refers to 'some sort of archetypal baptism.... Christ is regarded as having undergone an archetypal baptism on behalf of all Christians in the waters of death.' He appeals to Eph 5.25–27 as a parallel. But the passage contains no hint of such an intent (cf. 1 Tim 6.13); the author's thought here is of the individual application of salvation. (b) The majority of commentators assume that it refers primarily to baptism (cf. 1 Cor 6.11).[64] (c) But it may also be used metaphorically for spiritual cleansing (Simpson, 115; Towner 1989:116f.; Fee 1994:780f.; Mounce*, 195–202). Dunn 1970:168f. claims: 'of water-baptism as such there is here no mention'. The reference is to the 'washing of regeneration and renewal which the Spirit effects'.[65] The case for a metaphorical use would be strengthened if πνεύματος ἁγίου is syntactically linked to λουτροῦ (Towner). Even if this view of the syntax is not accepted, it still remains the case that a reference to an outward rite as the means of salvation is very unlikely in a context which is replete with references to divine action. Even if a reference to water-baptism is primary, the washing is at least symbolical of an inward process (see Holtzmann, 496f.). But it is more likely that the term refers primarily to that spiritual cleansing which is outwardly symbolised in baptism with water. 'Washing' implies the forgiveness and removal of the sins described in v. 3. Such a removal of sin is part of the new creation in which the saved individual already participates, and is associated with a renewal.

The washing is associated with regeneration and renewal effected by the Spirit. The precise significance of the connection expressed by the use of the gen. is debatable. The phrase has been taken to mean either (i) a washing that *conveys* new birth, in the sense of new life and moral renewal, or (ii) a washing characterised by new life and renewal (Fee 1994:782). However, it is hard to see how washing can convey new birth, and therefore the second possibility is to be preferred. It is, then, rather the new birth that leads to cleansing. In any case, whether we link πνεύματος ἁγίου directly with λουτροῦ or, more probably, indirectly through ἀνακαινώσεως, the washing is the work of the Spirit. The process is then equivalent to baptism in the Spirit.

---

[64] Holtzmann, 496; Dibelius-Conzelmann, 148; Beasley-Murray 1972:209; Trummer 1978:186; Lips 1979:92, 260–2; Schnackenburg*, 10–17; Luz 1976:376–7; Schlarb 1990:189.

[65] However, he allows that if the writer is not Paul, or Luke as amanuensis, then an interpretation closer to Jn 3.5 in terms of baptism is possible; even so it is not baptism which effects spiritual renewal.

The concept of 'regeneration' (παλιγγενεσία) is the most difficult in the passage.[66] It was a term in use in everyday language to refer to any kind of rebirth, regeneration or re-creation.[67] It can signify both a return to a former existence and renewal to a higher existence. It is used of life after death.[68] The concept was used by the Pythagoreans (Plutarch, *Mor.* 379F, 998C), and was developed in Stoicism to signify the renewal of the world after the conflagration.[69] It was also used in the Dionysiac mysteries and Osiric mysteries.[70] Here it refers to the renewal of individuals (cf. Heraclitus, *Ep.* 4.4). Similarly, it is used of the renewal of a race (*CH* 3.3); and of renewal into a higher form of existence by means of an incantation (*CH* 13.1, 3 *et al.*; cf. Plutarch, *Mor.* 998C for transmigration of souls). In the one other NT reference it expresses the renewal of the world in the time of Messiah (Mt 19.28; for the thought cf. Acts 3.21; 2 Pet 3.13; Rev 21.1).

The origin of the usage here is disputed.

(a) Derivation of the concept from the Mysteries is defended by Dibelius-Conzelmann, 148–50. They cite Philo, *Cher.* 114, and Apuleius, *Met.* 11.21 (*quodam modo renatos*); *CIL* VI, 510, 17ff., (*in aeternum renatus*); Mithras liturgy (Berger-Colpe, § 563); *CH* 13.3. However, they note that there are significant differences between the 'ecstasy "for a brief time"' and the 'new and lasting life in the spirit' which is available to all believers.

(b) Büchsel disputes that the usage rests on the Mysteries, since first-century usage cannot be demonstrated (cf. Mounce*, 62–120; Trummer, P., *EDNT* III, 8–9), but argues that behind it lies the Jewish form of the Stoic concept of renewal of the world (cf. Mt 19.28). One might then argue that baptism anticipates the renewal of the world and initiates the believer into the new age.

(c) More recent scholarship has stressed that the word and concept are widely used in the ancient world for 'renewal' in all

---

[66] On παλιγγενεσία (Mt 19.28***) see Dibelius-Conzelmann, 148–50; Büchsel, F., *TDNT* I, 686–9; Burnett*; Dey 1937; Mounce*. Ysebaert, 1962:87–154.

[67] E.g. restoration after exile (Cicero, *ad Att.* 6.6.4); of the recovery and 'rebirth' of their native land after the exile by the Jews (Josephus, *Ant.* 11.66); of the new life of an individual in another person (Philo, *Post.* 124); of relapse in health (Galen 13.83). Cf. Dey 1937:3–131; Spicq, 653; Mounce*.

[68] Philo, *Cher.* 114; *Leg. Gai.* 325. (Cf. use of πάλιν γένωμαι in Job 14.14 [LXX] and πάλιν γενέσθαι in Josephus, *Ap.* 2.218).

[69] Philo, *Aet.* 9, 47, 76, 107; *Mos.* 2.65 (applied to period after flood); cf. 1 Clement 9.4; cf. ἡ περιοδικὴ παλιγγενεσία τῶν ὅλων (sc. of the world, M. Antoninus 11.1).

[70] Plutarch, *Mor.* 364F; 389A; 996C (of gods coming to life again); 438D; *Mithras Liturgy* (*PGM* 4.718), πάλιν γενόμενος.

kinds of areas (Mounce*, 17–61). Brox, 307f., argues that the general use of the term in ordinary speech is found here.

(d) But it is more probable that the term reflects the concept of new birth which is already associated with baptism and conversion (cf. Oberlinner, 174; *pace* Mounce*, 192f., who thinks that the reference is to the cleansing aspect of conversion). Note, however, that etymologically the term is connected with γίνομαι and γένεσις, not with γεννάω.

The use of an unusual term raises the question whether there is any special significance in the choice of it.

(a) The use of a term that is elsewhere (Mt 19.28) cosmic and eschatological in scope may indicate that the reference is to 'the incorporation of the individual into the work of kindness and generosity which God is doing in the last days' (Barrett, 142).

(b) The allusion to the Pentecost experience in ἐκχέω (see v. 6 note) may suggest that the term refers not so much so the experience of the individual as to the ' "rebirth" of the Messianic community which was inaugurated at Pentecost' (Flemington*, 104, following Thornton, L. S., *The Common Life in the Body of Christ* [London: Dacre, 1941], 190f.).

(c) However, it is not necessary to regard these individual and corporate understandings as alternatives. The reference is to the Pentecost event as fulfilled in the lives of the readers: 'the counterpart in the individual's experience of the sending of the Spirit at Pentecost' (Beasley-Murray 1962:211).

(d) Quinn, 195f., 220f., goes a stage further in noting that the word was sometimes used of bodily resurrection: baptism brings believers 'into the mystery of the death and resurrection of Jesus and sets them on a course that culminates at last in the bodily resurrection of all human beings, with its accompanying judgment'. In any case, the connection of thoughts in Rom 6 (cf. Phil 3.10) would seem to suggest that the promise of bodily resurrection would have been closely related to the present experience of rebirth.

The word ἀνακαίνωσις[71] can refer to renewal as an event or as a process. It can be taken as passive (the renewal of the mind, Rom 12.2) or as active, with the genitive of the object which is renewed or of the subject which effects the renewal (cf. Holtzmann, 497). Easton, 100, comments that the thought is of a new creation (2 Cor 5.17), not of the renewal of former

---

[71] ἀνακαίνωσις, 'renewal' (Rom 12.2***), is a koine noun formation first found in Paul; Hermas, *Vis.* 3.8.9; cf. the noun καίνωσις, first found in Josephus, *Ant.* 18.230. The noun ἀνακαίνισις is found in early Christian writers. ἀνακαινίζω is found from Isocrates onwards (Heb 6.6) and ἀνακαινόω is attested first in Paul (2 Cor 4.16; Col 3.10). Cf. Behm, J., *TDNT* III, 453.

abilities. For the thought cf. Rom 6.4 with its link of baptism and newness of life and Eph 4.23.

The concept of renewal is closely related to regeneration. Nevertheless, some scholars have argued that two distinct acts are meant. A distinction between baptism and confirmation is made by some scholars (cf. Quesnel*, 171–4), or between conversion and a subsequent baptism in the Spirit by scholars in the Pentecostal/charismatic tradition. However, the two terms are nearly synonymous (Spicq, 653), and it is significant that only one preposition is used.[72] It is most likely, then, that the two phrases describe one and the same event from different angles. Knight, 343f., holds that the one event is seen 'from two different perspectives': cleansing seen as a new beginning or transformation and renewal brought about by the Holy Spirit. The nouns are arranged chiastically with the results in the centre.[73] Cleansing and renewal are distinguished in other passages (Ezek 36.25–27; 1 Cor 6.11). This view assumes that λουτροῦ and ἀνακαινώσεως stand in parallel, which we have already seen reason to doubt.

Spiritual renewal always has moral effects. It is difficult, therefore, to understand the way in which E. Schweizer, *TDNT* VI, 445, comments that the formula cited here associates the Spirit[74] with new birth but that 'the author himself, however, seems to have understood this ethically'; there is no tension present.

Consequently, through the allusion to washing (in which is a reference to baptism and the work of the Spirit depicted in the rite), v. 5b depicts the Holy Spirit as the source of the 'washing' which results in a transformation characterised here from the dual perspective of 'regeneration' and 'renewal'. The genitive is one of author or cause (Spicq, 654). The single preposition and the conceptual closeness of 'regeneration' and 'renewal' suggest unity. The one event of salvation is viewed specifically from the standpoint of the work of the Holy Spirit. While the rite of water

[72] Dunn 1970:165f.; Beasley-Murray 1962:210f.; Fee 1994:781f.

[73] According to Beasley-Murray 1962:210 this view goes back to Theodoret. It is not, however, visible in the latter's commentary on the passage (*PL* LXXXII, 867f.)

[74] πνεῦμα, 'spirit', 1 Tim 3.16; 4.1a, 1b (of deluding spirits); 2 Tim 1.7, 14; 4.22 (of the individual's spirit); here with ἅγιον (1 Tim 5.10 note), as in 2 Tim 1.14. Cf. Schweizer, E., *et al.*, *TDNT* VI, 332–455, especially 445.

For the anarthrous use of the phrase see Rom 5.5; 9.1; 14.17; 15.13, 16; *et al.* It is the more common use in the NT except in cases where: (a) The Spirit is represented as giving messages; (b) people act (e.g. blaspheme) against the Spirit; (c) 'Holy Spirit' is in the gen. case dependent on an arthrous noun. Where the Spirit is a power or gift conveyed to believers, both uses are found, but the anarthrous is the more common. For the type of action by the Holy Spirit (anarthrous) found here cf. Rom 5.5.

baptism may not be far from mind (as a symbolic expression depicting the work of the Spirit), it is that which it signifies – the individual's experience of the Spirit – that is the primary focal point, and this is probably linked with the paradigmatic experience of the church at Pentecost (v. 6, ἐκχέω). Nevertheless, while the rite of baptism might celebrate, illustrate or commemorate the work of the Spirit and therefore be immediately called to mind or alluded to by such a statement (here and throughout the NT; cf. Kelly, 252), this is not a prooftext for baptismal regeneration or sacramental salvation (*contra* Schlarb 1990:189).

Although the doctrine of the Spirit is not prominent in the PE, here the association of the Spirit with salvation, baptism (as spiritual cleansing) and regeneration (Jn 3.5) is thoroughly traditional. Elsewhere in the PE the Spirit is associated with prophecy (1 Tim 4.1a) and with the endowing of the believer with power, love and sobriety (2 Tim 1.7). It is the source of the spiritual gifts (1 Tim 4.14; 2 Tim 1.6) which are associated with the laying of hands on Timothy (Haykin 1985).

(d) **6.** οὗ ἐξέχεεν ἐφ' ἡμᾶς πλουσίως διὰ Ἰησοῦ Χριστοῦ τοῦ σωτῆρος ἡμῶν The fourth element is a development of the reference to the Spirit[75] which emphasises both the fulness of God's provision for his people and the fact that it is given through Jesus Christ. ἐξέχεεν in itself suggests profusion,[76] but even so is strengthened by πλουσίως.[77] The verb is used of the Spirit in Zech 12.10; Acts 2.17, 18 (=Joel 3.1, 2), 33; 10.45; 1 Clement 46.6; Barnabas 1.3 (cf. 1 Clement 6.2, ἔκχυσις); cf. Rom 5.5. The verbal link thus provided with Acts 2 suggest an allusion to the Pentecost event of the Spirit's outpouring upon God's people.[78] For the bestowing of the Spirit from above see Isa 44.3f; Ezek 36.26f.; 39.29 (MT). The clause comes to a

---

[75] οὗ is normal relative attraction for ὅ (BD 294), referring to the Spirit (detail in Knight, 344f.).

[76] ἐκχέω, 'to pour out', hence 'to shed (blood)', Rom 3.15 (LXX); Cl. (the Hellenistic form ἐκχύννω is used in Acts 10.45; Rom 5.5); LXX; Josephus; Philo. For figurative use cf. Aelian, *N. An.* 7.23; *Ps. Sol.* 2.24 (anger); Philo, *Spec* 1.37 (light); Josephus, *Ant.* 6.271 (murder). Used of whatever comes from above, like grace, Ps 44 (MT 45).3; mercy, Ecclus 18.11; Hos 5.10; Philo, *Aet.* 147; *Abr.* 76; *T. Levi* 18.5; of God pouring out wrath, Ezek 9.8; 39.29 (LXX wrath = MT 'Spirit'); Lam 2.4.

[77] πλουσίως, 'richly, generously' (1 Tim 6.17; Col 3.16; 2 Pet 1.11***; Barnabas 1.7; 9.7). The adjective is used of God (2 Cor 8.9; Eph 2.4; 1 Tim 6.17; 2 Pet 1.11; Rom 10.12; 1 Cor 1.5; Rev 3.18) and his generosity (Rom 2.4; 11.33; Eph 1.7, 18; 2.7; 3.8, 16; Phil 4.9; Col 1.27; 2.4; Rev 5.12). Cl.; Philo. Cf. Hauck, F., and Kasch, W., *TDNT* VI, 318–32 (who make the extraordinary comment [329] that the word is 'without theological significance'!).

[78] Dunn 1970:165–70; Fee 1994:755–95; Towner 1989:112–18; cf. Behm, J., *TDNT* II, 467–9.

climax with the full reference to Jesus Christ our Saviour[79] as the giver of the Spirit (Acts 2.33).[80]

(e) 7. ἵνα δικαιωθέντες τῇ ἐκείνου χάριτι κληρονόμοι γενηθῶμεν κατ' ἐλπίδα ζωῆς αἰωνίου Now comes the ultimate purpose, and, in effect, the result of God's act.[81] It is theological, not ethical!

The aorist participle δικαιωθέντες[82] is coincident in time with the main verb 'become heirs'. 'The saving purpose of God, which is that we might be justified and become heirs, is effected by baptism in the Spirit' (Dunn 1970:167; cf. Fee 1994, ch. 11). The relationship of the participle to what precedes is uncertain:

(a) Justification is coincident with the gift of the Spirit or baptism.

(b) Justification is the presupposition for receiving the Spirit (Holtzmann, 499).

(c) Justification is the intended result of receiving the Spirit. It is most probable that the participle sums up the previous statements. Justification is unlikely to be seen as the result of baptism; the participle is coincident with ἔσωσεν. In 1 Cor 6.11 justification and being washed are simultaneous. That justification is a past event in the life of believers is clear from Rom 5.1, 9; 8.30. Here the various events cannot be placed in a chronological series (Brox, 309).

Grace (1.3 note) is expressed, as in Rom 3.24, in God's act in Christ.[83] The understanding of justification is regarded as different from that of Paul by numerous scholars (cf. Oberlinner, 177f.). The possibility that grace is seen as a gift to enable us to live righteously rather than as acquittal is raised by Klöpper 1904:66f.; cf. 'given potentialities to achieve righteousness' (Easton, 100). Dibelius-Conzelmann, 150, ask whether 'the act

---

[79] For this full form cf. with variations 1.4; 2.13; 2 Tim 1.10.

[80] The force of the διά phrase is uncertain: (a) It simply refers to Jesus as the agent who bestows the Spirit (Holtzmann, 498; cf. Dunn 1970; Fee 1994:783f.). Cf. Acts 2.33; Jn 14.26. (b) It refers to Jesus as the redeemer through whose action we have been saved and made fit to receive the Spirit (Spicq, 654). The solemn language favours the latter interpretation.

[81] ἵνα may be dependent on: (a) ἔσωσεν; (b) ἐξέχεεν (Holtzmann, 498; Klöpper 1904:65); or (c) the whole of 3.4–6 (Spicq, 655). But a decision surely makes little difference to understanding (Brox, 309). The result of the gift of salvation is that we become heirs.

[82] The verb δικαιόω (1 Tim 3.16**) is here used of justification, in the Pauline sense. Cf. Schrenk, G., TDNT II, 211–19; Trummer 1978:187; Dunn 1970:167.

[83] ἐκείνου, placed emphatically, may refer to: (a) God (Spicq, 654; Quinn, 226; Oberlinner, 177); (b) Christ (Holtzmann, 498f.; Klöpper 1904:65f.; Brox, 309. Cf. 2 Cor 8.9. The same pronoun is used in 2 Tim 2.13); (c) the Holy Spirit. The grace associated with justification would normally be God's or Christ's, and a reference to the latter is most likely. However, the writer may not have had a clear identification in mind.

of justification itself is actually meant, or rather a life which is righteous by virtue of grace (as substantiation for the latter alternative see above on Tit 2:11–14)'. Similarly, in a manner which Hanson, 191, characterises as seeing the passage as 'a parody of Paul's doctrine', Houlden, 154, suggests the possible meaning 'so that having been made morally upright by his grace'; Similarly, the force is not forensic, but circumstantial, says Hasler, 97. These opinions have no visible support in the text and are rightly rejected by Schrenk, G., *TDNT* II, 217 n. 22.; Barrett, 143.

Some commentators claim that the non-mention of faith, except in 3.8, is significant (see Klöpper 1904:86–8). But there is no suggestion that it is excluded (so rightly Merkel, 103), much less that its absence indicates that baptism had acquired saving powers and is on the way to being considered as magical (*contra* Scott, 176f.; Schlarb, 1990:189). A number of similarly oriented passages in the Pauline corpus (in which the importance of faith would be assumed) omit an explicit reference to faith (e.g. Rom 6.1–11; 1 Cor 6.11; 12.13; 2 Cor 1.21f.; cf. Beasley-Murray 1972:213).

The consequence of being saved and justified is that believers become[84] heirs of God's promises;[85] cf. Gal 3.11–29 for the same link of justification and inheritance. The heir has a right to future possession and is already in a sense a partaker of it. For the relationship between inheritance and the Spirit see Rom 8.15–17; 1 Cor 6.9–11; Gal 3.14, 18; 4.6f.; Eph 1.13f. The thought of sonship is implied (Brox, 310; Spicq, 655).

In the slightly unusual phrase κατ' ἐλπίδα[86] the preposition modifies γενηθῶμεν thus providing the standard or pattern for the granting of heirship; in principle the inheritance and eternal life are equivalent; but here the promise/hope element provides the framework for understanding accession to the status of heir. The phrase is variously interpreted to mean that the readers are:

(a) 'heirs in accordance with the hope of eternal life' (Brox, 303);

(b) 'heirs of eternal life in accordance with hope' (Holtzmann, 499);

(c) 'heirs, as we hope for eternal life' (Dibelius-Conzelmann, 150: 'the text does not say "heirs of eternal life"');

---

[84] γενηθῶμεν is ingressive (Holtzmann, 499; Spicq, 655).

[85] κληρονόμος, 'heir' (Cl.; LXX; Josephus; Philo. cf. Mt 21.38 = Mk 12.7 = Lk 20.14; Gal 4.1), is used of Christ (Heb 1.2; of Abraham (Rom 4.13; Heb 11.7); by law (Rom 4.14); of Christians (Rom 8.17a, 17b; Gal 3.29; 4.7; Heb 6.17; Jas 2.5***). Cf. Foerster, W., and Herrmann, J., *TDNT* III, 767–85.

[86] The usual phrase is ἐπ' ἐλπίδι (1.2). For use of κατά cf. Phil 1.20.

(d) 'heirs of the life for which we hope' (Klöpper 1904:70f.; Jeremias, 74; Dey*, 135).

There is not much difference between these views, and the first is probably the best. Tit 1.2 suggests that ἐλπὶς ζωῆς αἰωνίου had already become a formula which is here joined loosely to κληρονόμοι with the preposition κατά. Hence the phrase ζωῆς αἰωνίου is dependent on ἐλπίδα (Brox, 309f.) rather than κληρονόμοι (Holtzmann, 499). The inheritance and the hope of eternal life are clearly related, and eternal life is undoubtedly assumed to be an important part of the content of the inheritance (and does not need to be expressed; Brox, 310). The present phrase, however, expresses a slightly different aspect of the relationship of the two things, with κατά ... explaining the promise-pattern that guides the gracious 'justification-to-heirs' transaction.

According to Spicq, 656, the eternal life is not fully realised, as some heretics hold (cf. 2 Tim 2.18), but is nevertheless certain. However, there is no hint in this letter that this particular heresy is being combatted, and there is nothing to suggest a polemical intent here.[87]

c. Recapitulation; how to deal with the recalcitrant (3.8–11)

Colson, F. H., '"Myths and Genealogies" – A note on the polemic of the Pastoral Epistles', *JTS* 19 (1918), 265–71; Deer, D. S., 'Still more about the imperatival *hina*', *BT* 148 (1979), 148; Kittel 1921; Sandmel, S., 'Myths, Genealogies and Jewish Myths and the Writing of the Gospels', *HUCA* 27 (1956), 201–11.

After the doctrinal backing for the ethical instructions which Titus is to give to the churches, the author returns to giving instructions to him, insisting, first, on the need to pass on the teaching to the church so that the believers will practise the good works commended in 3.1f., and, second, on the avoidance of futile arguments and the disciplining of those who persist in them. Thus the motif of heresy, which was very much in the background in 2.1–3.7, now returns to the foreground. The strong language used to condemn the opponents in ch. 1 is matched by the vigorous stress on the need for action to deal with them. Yet it should be noted that the writer's emphasis in this brief section is rather on the positive need to engage in doing good rather than in time-wasting disputes, and the directions regarding factious people are, if not an after-thought, at least

---

[87] Scott, 176, states that the thought is quite different from Paul: the reference is to 'the deliverance which we owe to God's goodness as displayed in the whole Christian message'. Nothing in the passage suggests such an interpretation.

secondary in importance to the thought of doing what is worthy and profitable.

TEXT

8. καλά Praem. τά (D² Ψ TR); Elliott, 193, rejects the article, stating that the adjs. must be in apposition to ταῦτα.
θεῷ Praem. τῷ (Kilpatrick).
9. γενεαλογίας: λογομαχίας (P61 F G g) is assimilation to 1 Tim 6.4, Elliott, 193.
ἔρεις ἔριν (ℵ* D F G Ψ *pc* Ambst; WH). Elliott, 92, argues that the original sing. was assimilated by a scribe to the surrounding plurals; the intermediate reading ἔριδας (241, 462; cf. 1 Cor 1.11 for this Hellenistic pl.) was then corrected by Atticist scribes to the Cl. pl. See further 1 Tim 6.4 note. But Metzger, 586, argues that, although a change of sing. to plural is more likely, there is strong external evidence for the plural, which is also required by the sense.
10. καί δευτέραν νουθεσίαν νουθεσίαν καὶ δευτέραν (D [D* δύο] Ψ 1505 1881 *pc* sy^h); νουθεσίαν (1739 b vg^ms Ir^lat Tert Cyp Ambst); νουθεσίαν ἢ δευτ. (F G). Elliott, 194, states that 1739 is prone to omissions (1 Tim 4.12; 5.19; 6.11), and argues for retention of the text.

EXEGESIS

8a. Πιστὸς ὁ λόγος The first part of the verse is generally taken to be a validation of the preceding doctrinal statement and the accompanying ethical instructions. These are meant to serve as a basis for the renewed exhortation to good works and the avoidance of futile discussions and speculations which follows. The phrase thus functions as a bridge between the two parts of the section.

πιστός (1.6) is used frequently of speech; see especially Rev 21.5; 22.6. λόγος (1.3) can refer to a saying, whether oral (e.g. Jn 4.37) or written (Rom 13.9; 1 Cor 15.54), dependent on the context.

EXCURSUS 9

The trustworthy sayings

Bover, J. M., 'Fidelis Sermo' [in Spanish], *Biblica* 19 (1938), 74–9; Brox, 112–14; Campbell, R. A., 'Identifying the Faithful Sayings in the Pastoral Epistles', *JSNT* 54 (June 1994), 73–86; Dibelius-Conzelmann, 28f.; Grant, R. M., 'Early Christianity and Greek Comic Poetry', *CP* 60 (1965), 161; Hanson, 63f.; Knight 1968; Moule, C. F. D., *The Birth of the New Testament* (London, Black, 1981³), 283f.; Nauck 1950:45–52; North 1995; Oberlinner, 181f.; Oldfather, W. A., and Daly, L. W., 'A Quotation from Menander in the Pastoral Epistles?' *Classical Philology* 38 (1943), 202–4; Quinn, 230–2; Roloff, 88–90; Schlarb 1990:206–14; Spicq, 277 n.2; *TLNT* I, 176f.; Swete, H. B., 'The Faithful Sayings', *JTS* 18 (1917), 1–7; Young 1994:56–9.

The phrase πιστὸς ὁ λόγος is found altogether five times in the PE (1 Tim 1.15; 3.1; 4.9; 2 Tim 2.11; Tit 3.8). A longer form with καὶ πάσης ἀποδοχῆς ἄξιος is found in 1 Tim 1.15 (see note there); 4.9. In 1 Tim 1.15 and 3.1 there is a textual variant with ἀνθρώπινος replacing πιστός. The repetition of the phrase indicates that it has become a stereotyped formula. It is peculiar to this author and is used by him to emphasise the truth of the statement which it accompanies. The expanded form is not significantly different in force. The addition simply reinforces the basic saying (Roloff, 89) and indicates that the saying is 'worthy of the fullest, most whole-hearted acceptance'; it is 'used when the response is not evident within the saying' itself (Knight 1968:29, 144).

1. The origin of the phrase

The same wording is found in Dionysius Halicarnassensis 3.23.17; 9.19.3; Dio Chrysostom 45.3 (cited in Knight, 1968, 5); *et al.*, where it is a perfectly natural part of a sentence affirming that a particular saying is credible.[88] The addition 'and worthy of fullest acceptance' uses a current Greek phrase (1 Tim 1.15 note).

There is also a possible usage behind Terence, *Adelphi*, 954 (*et dictum est vere et re ipsa fieri oportet*) if this phrase is translated back into Greek; this is a legitimate procedure since Terence's play was based on Menander (Oldfather and Daly*; cf. *TLNT* I, 177 n. 7: see Grant*).

A Jewish parallel has been seen in 1Q27 1.8, 'This word is certain to come to pass and this oracle is truth' (see Nauck 1950:50). However, the addition 'to come to pass' reduces the force of the parallel (cf. Hanson, 63).

Despite Quinn's synthesis of this material (Quinn, 230–2), the evidence is insufficient to show that the author was taking over an existing 'formula' from the Hellenistic world, perhaps one already appropriated by Hellenistic Judaism. As a formula, it appears for the first time in the PE. The most that can be said is that the author is using language that reflects turns of phrase current in Hellenistic Greek.

The view of Theodore of Mopsuestia (II, 97 Swete) that there is a similarity between the phrase and the 'Amen, I say' formula in the Gospels is hardly a basis for a theory about the origin of the phrase (Knight 1968:12f.; *pace* Schlatter, 61, and [cautiously] Quinn, 230f.).

The adjective is also applied to God, especially in the phrase πιστὸς ὁ θεός (e.g. 1 Cor 1.9; 10.13; 2 Cor 1.18; cf. 1 Th 5.24;

---

[88] Spicq, 277 n. 2, gives a succinct summary of the background material.

2 Th 3.3; Heb 10.23); Fee, 52, thinks that this usage may be the source of the language here. This hypothesis is over-simple. It is better to note with Knight that the words which are 'faithful and true' in Rev 21.5; 22.6 are the words of God. Further, in Tit 1.9 the overseer holds fast to the faithful word which is 'according to the teaching', and in 1 Tim 1.12 Paul is regarded as faithful in the service of the Lord. It would therefore appear that the sayings are faithful and reliable in that they are part of the teaching sanctioned by God himself.

2. The reference of the formula

There should be no dispute that the reference is forwards in 1 Tim 1.15 and 2 Tim 2.11, and that it is backwards in Tit 3.8. These examples show that the formula can be used both ways, and there is legitimate room for dispute over 1 Tim 3.1; 4.9. Campbell* argues for a forward reference in each case, but his argument that 1 Tim 3.16 is the saying to which reference is made in 3.1 is unconvincing. It has been suggested that in each case the reference is to a text that has to do with salvation (Lock, 33; Nauck 1950; Campbell*; Young 1994:56f.; Wagener 1994:71), but this result can be achieved only by some dubious identifications of the sayings. The actual extent of the sayings is disputed in several cases.

3. The significance of the formula

The question arises whether this is basically a formula (a) for introducing or concluding a citation and indicating that the words are a citation or (b) primarily for confirming the truth of what is said.

There is now general agreement that the stress lies on (b). Dibelius-Conzelmann, 28f., 150, claim that the contents of the clauses referred to tend to go beyond the needs of the context, and therefore it is likely that the author is quoting, although not all quotations in the letters are accompanied by this formula. Nevertheless, this does not show that the formula is strictly a 'quotation'-formula (cf. Lips 1979:40, n. 43) and it is better to see it as an affirmation of a statement that is the basis for application and exhortation (cf. Donelson 1986:150f.; Oberlinner, 181f.).[89] Roloff, 89, claims that a citation formula cannot follow a citation. Similarly, Trummer, 204, describes it as 'a formula of asseveration' (cf. Lips 1979:40, n. 43; Merkel,

---

[89] Simpson, 50, thought that the writer used the phrase to endorse propositions put up to him by those to whom he was writing.

105; Hanson, 64). Knight 1968:19f. argues that both senses are present in what he calls a 'quotation-commendation' formula, but with the stress on the latter. The formula emphasises the truth of what is said. It introduces a solemn note into the context, and it serves to underline the importance of the statement. An antiheretical stress may be present (cf. Schlarb 1990:214).

But does the formula relate to the truth of *traditional* teaching? For Brox* the reference is to traditional teaching about salvation and its realisation in the church. The author has in effect access to a reservoir of traditional teaching, and Brox sees significance in the way that 'official validation' is given to the formal character of the material as trustworthy tradition. Similarly, according to Spicq (277, n. 2) the formula refers to an article of faith or liturgical statement that is universally accepted; it stresses the importance of the statement and the need to adhere to it. Hanson, 63, questions whether this can apply to 1 Tim 3.1, and speaks vaguely of 'credal, cultic and church-order material'. His insights are developed by Roloff, 90, who states that the formula is used of different types of assertions – kerygmatic, hymnic and worshipping, and church ordering – and that it is used only when the statements allow for application; not all traditional material is accompanied by the formula. It is found only when thematic shifts are taking place or new ideas being introduced.

However, while it may be granted that the material is ultimately based on tradition, in general it has been given its formulation by the author himself, and therefore it can hardly be regarded as a *citation* of tradition. Consequently, Hanson's claim that its function is to link disparate materials into the author's composition is not justified. Rather, the formula has a definite purpose in commending teaching that the author wishes to emphasise. Its use is flexible, referring to teaching that is usually based on tradition and is related to salvation and to the consequent practical behaviour.

In the present case, Scott, 177f., and Campbell 1994:78f. appear to be alone in arguing for a reference forwards; but the following καί prevents this. Likewise, Hanson, 193, is alone in claiming that the formula need not be tied down in its application; for him it is simply a means of transition from one part of the author's source material to another. The view of most scholars is that here it refers backwards.[90] Barrett, 144, however, notes the difficulties that accompany this interpretation.

Likewise, the extent of the 'saying' is a matter of dispute (See Knight, 347–9; more fully in Knight 1968:81–6). For many

---

[90] E.g. Holtzmann, 499; Spicq, 656 (despite the erroneous report in Hanson, 193); Brox, 310f.; Knight, 347–9; Merkel, 105.

commentators a decision is related to the question of how far there is quoted tradition in 3:3–7 (see above). Most scholars opt for vv. 4–7; others prefer 3–7 (Dibelius-Conzelmann, 147; Ellis 1987:247; Schlarb 1990:213; Oberlinner, 181f.); 5b–7 (Easton, 99); 5b–6 (Kelly, 254). Knight argues that the other faithful sayings are single sentences.

According to Brox, 311, the effect here is to give formal validation of church teaching by the ostensible author to Titus and then through him as the official church teacher to the congregations (similarly, Oberlinner, 182). In Merkel's opinion, the formula underlines the significance of the preceding passage, while also forming the transition to the authoritative instruction 'to testify solemnly to this kerygma': 'only this form of the proclamation leads to "good works", i.e. to a Christian manner of life, which demonstrates goodness to fellow-men in a godless world and thereby extends the kindness of God' (105).

8b. καὶ περὶ τούτων βούλομαί σε διαβεβαιοῦσθαι, ἵνα φροντίζωσιν καλῶν ἔργων προΐστασθαι οἱ πεπιστευκότες θεῷ The first part of the instructions to Titus follows naturally. In view of the significance of all that has just been said in 3.1–7, the author now reiterates his strong desire, tantamount to a command, that Titus will stress these things positively in the church with the aim that believers will express their faith by concentrating their minds on zealously doing good (rather than wasting time in useless 'theological' discussions); thus the believers are to demonstrate that they do not belong with the opponents (Oberlinner, 183). The point is that the believers are not simply to be obedient to ethical commands but must develop a personal concern that arises out of their faith (Brox, 311). Such activities are good and profitable for everybody, a comment which recalls the goal of living in a way that influences all people laid down in 3.2.

The shift from the singular 'saying' to the plural περὶ τούτων probably indicates that more than simply the 'saying' is in mind. The reference is rather to what is contained in it. The scope may be limited to the teaching in 3.3–7.[91] More probably it includes all that is included in the previous section of the letter,[92] since the concern is with good deeds and not just with doctrine. Cf. the similar usage in 2.15 (and note). βούλομαι, 'to wish, will', can have the weaker sense 'to wish, desire' (1 Tim 6.9) but is also used with acc. and inf. to express a strong command

---

[91] Holtzmann, 499; Parry, 84; Easton, 101; Schlarb 1990:213.
[92] Guthrie, 219; Knight, 350; cf. Quinn, 241, who suggests that it refers to 1.5, τὰ λείποντα.

(1 Tim 2.8; 5.14 **).[93] In 1 Tim 2.8; 5.14 the verb is used to introduce apostolic commands directed to the church, but here the command is characteristically addressed to Titus himself who is to pass on the author's teaching to the church. διαβεβαιοῦσθαι is 'to give assurance, testify', hence 'to speak confidently, to insist'; it is used of the activity of false teachers in 1 Tim 1.7***.[94] ἵνα introduces purpose, rather than indirect command.[95] φροντίζω*** is 'to think of, be intent on'; it encompasses both intention and execution (Spicq, 656).[96] προΐστημι, used only intransitively in the NT, has a wide variety of meanings, but here it will mean either 'to devote oneself to' or 'to exercise [sc. a profession]'.[97] For καλὰ ἔργα see **Excursus 6**; 2.7 note. The phrase has its usual meaning throughout the PE of 'good deeds' (cf. Knight, 351). Hanson, 194, regards this as quite banal, and suggests that in the present context one may think of acts of social welfare, but this is an unjustified narrowing down. The older rendering 'honourable occupations' (RSV mg; NEB) arises

[93] This is a Hellenistic usage found in pap. and Josephus (e.g. *Ant.* 12.150). It is a stronger expression than a phrase like 'I want you to know' (Phil 1.12; Jude 5), since here action is demanded on the part of the recipient. It is the language of edicts (Wolter 1988:173f. and n. 60). The uncontested Pauline letters use παραγγέλλω (Holtzmann, 500). Cf. Schrenk, G., *TDNT* I, 629–33.

[94] The verb is found in Cl. and Hel. but not in the LXX.

[95] *Pace* Deer*, 148.

[96] The verb usually takes gen. of thing, but here has the inf. (cf. BA for parallels). Cf. *TLNT* III, 467–9.

[97] The verb has four possible meanings:
(a) 'to rule, direct, administer' (with gen.; Amos 6.10; 1 Macc 5.19; 1 Tim 3.4f., 12; 5.17; Hermas, *Vis.* 2.4.3; Josephus, *Ant.* 8.300; *Vita* 93, 168). In the NT this may also include the idea of caring for those under one's direction (cf. Rom 12.8; 1 Th 5.12). Hence possibly 'to take the lead in [doing good deeds]' (Spicq, 657, in his translation 'être les premiers dans les belles oeuvres'; Simpson, 117; Quinn, 234); 'to distinguish oneself [*sich darin hervortun*]' (Oberlinner, 183). See Lips 1979:126–32, who notes 2 Sam 13.17, of being in charge of a household.
(b) 'to care for, give aid'; used with reference to children (Ps-Plutarch, *Mor.* 875A; of God as caring like a father, Epictetus 3.24.3; so here Dibelius-Conzelmann, 151).
(c) 'to devote oneself to', here and in the parallel, 3.14. Cf. Sophocles, *El.* 980; Prov 26.17; Josephus, *Ant.* 5.90. Hence 'to practise virtue' (Lock, 156; Barrett, 144f.; Reicke, B., *TDNT* VI, 703; *EDNT* III, 156f.)
(d) 'to exercise a profession', i.e. here to 'profess honest occupations' (RV mg; cf. Plutarch, *Pericles* 24.3 [165] [of keeping a brothel]; Athenaeus 13.612A; Philostratus, *Ep. Apollonii* 53 [philosophy]. Literally 'to stand in front of', the verb was used of a tradesman standing before a shop to display his goods and hence of the activity of prostitutes. Field 1899:223f. provides the evidence but does not accept the rendering here, since καλὰ ἔργα must mean 'good deeds' rather than 'honourable occupations'. Holtzmann, 500, adopts this meaning but in a metaphorical sense, 'to make good works your business'; similarly, MM 541; Parry, 84; cf. Spicq, 656f.
The uncertainty reflected in Spicq's commentary shows that a decision is not easy between these possibilities. Views (a) and (b) are improbable, and the choice lies between (c) and (d). Cf. Reicke, B., *TDNT* VI, 700–3.

in the context from the use of the governing verb, but it rather narrows down the meaning (Fee, 209). The term describes acts of service (demonstrating God's kindness) resulting from faith throughout the PE.

οἱ πεπιστευκότες are 'those who have come to belief'. The use of the perfect of Christian believers is quite common.[98] When used with the dat., the verb generally signifies 'to give credence to',[99] but it is also used of the full act of religious faith in God or Christ.[100] Clearly *Christian* faith in God is meant here, as in Acts 16.34. It is the God whose grace has been portrayed in the preceding verses.

ταῦτά ἐστιν καλὰ καὶ ὠφέλιμα τοῖς ἀνθρώποις The reference of this comment is not clear.

(a) Some take the plural pronoun ταῦτα to refer to the 'good works' just mentioned (NEB text; Fee, 207f.). The problem is that if the pronoun refers to the good works, then tautology results – unless the phrase καλὰ ἔργα was so stereotyped that the repetition of καλός with a stronger meaning was acceptable.

(b) It may pick up περὶ τούτων, the things about which Titus is to give instruction (Parry, 84; Spicq, 657; cf. Brox, 311).

(c) Others refer it to the activities commended and expressed by either διαβεβαιοῦσθαι or φροντίζωσιν, i.e. the activities of teaching or taking thought which lead to good works (Holtzmann, 501; hence the translation 'these precepts are good in themselves and also useful to society' [REB]; Barrett, 144f.).

(d) Another proposal is that it may refer both to the teaching and to the 'good deeds', i.e. the content of 3.1–7.[101] But this is a very artificial combination and quite unlikely; more correctly the thought is of both the specific teachings and exhortations which Titus is to give, as described in 3.1–7.

The determining factor is the contrast to the foolish disputations in v. 9 (Knight wrongly regards v. 9 as referring to both teachings and deeds). The problems of understanding may arise from the fact that the act and the content of teaching

---

[98] 1 Cor 9.17; Gal 2.7; 2 Tim 1.12; 1 Jn 4.16; 5.10b; Acts 15.5; 16.34; 18.27; 19.18; 21.20, 25.

[99] Jn 5.24; Rom 4.3 [17]; Gal 3.6; Jas 2.23; 1 Jn 5.10b; 1 Clement 10.6 (=Gen 15.6).

[100] It is used of faith in God (a) with the article: Acts 16.34; 27.25; Rom 4.3; Gal 3.6; *Preaching of Peter* 4, p. 16.2; Barnabas 16.7; Hermas *Mand.* 12.6.2; *Sim.* 5.1.5; cf. *Mand.* 1.2; *Vis.* 4.2.6; *Sim.* 9.13.5; (b) without the article: Prov 30.1; 4 Macc 7.21. It is used of faith in Christ: 2 Tim 1.12; Jn 6.30; 8.31; Acts 5.14; 18.8a; Rom 10.14; Ignatius, *Trall.* 9.2.

[101] Fee, 207; Knight, 352; in order to avoid tautology, the latter then argues that it is the teachings which are 'good' and the good deeds which are 'beneficial', but this is over-ingenious.

cannot be separated: it is the activity of sound teaching which is being commended.

Such teaching is 'good', in that it gives rise to good deeds. It is also ὠφέλιμος, 'useful, beneficial, advantageous', i.e. profitable spiritually; a contrast with 3.9 is intended.[102] Cf. 1 Clem 56.2; 62.1.

τοῖς ἀνθρώποις (1.14 note; cf 1 Tim 6.9; 2 Tim 3.2) must refer to people in general (cf. 3.2), but commentators have attempted to be more precise and suggest that any of the following may be specially meant: (a) the people who do the good deeds; (b) the people to whom they are done or who witness them;[103] (c) generally of the church, in contrast to what follows which is bad for the church. The preceding reference to believers (οἱ πεπιστευκότες θεῷ) suggests that this reference is at least not limited to the church; however, neither is it automatically limited to unbelievers, since believers can do 'good deeds' for other believers.[104]

9. μωρὰς δὲ ζητήσεις καὶ γενεαλογίας καὶ ἔρεις καὶ μάχας νομικὰς περιΐστασο· εἰσὶν γὰρ ἀνωφελεῖς καὶ μάταιοι If v. 8 was concerned primarily with what Titus was to teach the church, vv. 9–11 describe how he himself is to act with regard to his opponents. He is to avoid both disputes and disputatious people. On the one hand, he is to avoid entering into their disputes, for these will lead nowhere and (by contrast with engaging in sound teaching and exhortation) are profitless. It is usually said that this means that debate with the opponents is forbidden, but Wolter 1988:137f., holds that the point is rather to maintain a sharp contrast between the behaviour of the church leaders and the foolish disputations characteristic of the opponents (cf. Thiessen 1995:322). On the other hand, if there is anybody who is αἱρετικός, he is to take disciplinary measures, which are justified because such people are self-evidently sinning.

For the content of this section cf. 1.10–16, with which it perhaps forms a chiasmus.[105] There are significant parallels with 2 Tim 2.23–26, which has much the same structure:

---

[102] Cl.; Philo; Josephus, *Ant.* 16.25, *et al.*; with dat. of person (Hermas, *Vis.* 3.6.7); with πρός τι of object (1 Tim 4.8a, 8b; 2 Tim 3.16***; Plato, *Rep.* 10, 607d). For the combination of the adjectives Spicq, 657, refers to Zeno in Stobaeus II.7.5D (II, 69): πάντα δὲ τἀγαθὰ ὠφέλιμα εἶναι καὶ εὔχρηστα καὶ συμφέροντα...; cf. Xenophon, *Mem.* 3.8.3–10; Cicero, *Orat.* III, 178–81 [45f.]; Philo, *Abr.* 18. Johnson, 90, notes that the term expressed 'one of the central criteria for authentic moral teaching in the hellenistic world'.

[103] Fee, 208, of outsiders to whom the gospel is commended; cf. Merkel, 105.

[104] Do the 'good deeds' here and the instruction to do them recall the instructions in vv. 1–2? If so, perhaps the reference to 'people' here is to be linked with (or explained by) 'all people' in v. 2.

[105] Fee, 210: A: 1.10–16; B: 2.1–14; B′: 3.1–8; A′: 3.9–11.

Titus 3.9–11	2 Timothy 2.23–26
⁹μωρὰς δὲ ζητήσεις ... περιΐστασο· εἰσὶν γὰρ ἀνωφελεῖς καὶ μάταιοι.	²³τὰς δὲ μωρὰς καὶ ἀπαιδεύτους ζητήσεις παραιτοῦ, εἰδὼς ὅτι
	γεννῶσιν μάχας· ... ²⁵ἐν πραΰτητι παιδεύοντα
¹⁰αἱρετικὸν ἄνθρωπον μετὰ μίαν καὶ δευτέραν νουθεσίαν παραιτοῦ, ¹¹εἰδὼς ὅτι ...	τοὺς ἀντιδιατιθεμένους, ... μήποτε ...

In each case there is a stress on positive teaching (3.8; 2 Tim 2.24) followed by a warning against useless debates and a command to discipline those who persist in opposition.

Four phrases describe what is to be avoided, and the language used (μωρός, ζήτησις, γενεαλογία, ἔρις, μάχη, νομικός, ἀνωφελής, μάταιος) belongs to the author's polemic, though it is not a disguise for an imaginary opponent.[106] Holtzmann, 501, interprets the first two phrases as causes of strife and the latter two as actual quarrels, but ζητήσεις are probably disputes. The disputes are 'pointless', rather than 'half-witted', but they are pointless precisely because they are inane. They do not contribute to godliness (Cf. the comment of Calvin: they are foolish *non quod primo adspectu tales appareant (quin saepe inani sapientiae ostentatione fallunt), sed quia nihil ad pietatem conducunt*, cited by Bertram, G., *TDNT* IV, 844). They are concerned in part at least with 'genealogies', idle speculations based on the genealogies and possibly other early material in Genesis. This understanding of them as basically Jewish and arising out of the Torah is confirmed by the reference to 'legal disputes' which is also best understood in terms of Judaism; it is hard to see what other kind of law might be meant. Titus is personally to avoid involvement in such disputes and the discord which they engender in the church. They achieve nothing positive, by contrast with the activities commended in v. 8, and they lead to no solid conclusions.

ζήτησις, 'enquiry, dispute', was used in Classical Greek for searching and enquiring, and hence for philosophical enquiries (so also in Philo; the word is not found in LXX). Greeven comments that it was not used for 'clash of opinions' or

---

[106] *Contra* Karris 1973:549–64; Trummer 1978:164–7; see esp. Schlarb 1990:63–73.

'disputation' in pre-Christian Greek. Holtzmann, 501, apparently adopts 'matters of dispute' in view of the link with γενεαλογίας, but the word appears to signify the action of discussing rather than the subject-matter. With μωρός it refers to mere bandying about of words rather than serious investigation.[107] μωρός means 'foolish, stupid'; in 2 Tim 2.23** it also describes ζητήσεις, and hence it probably applies only to that word here (Knight, 353; *pace* Spicq, 686). In the wisdom literature and in Philo folly is not only intellectual but also religious. [108]

γενεαλογία (cf. 1.14 note), 'genealogy', 'the tracing of a genealogy' (1 Tim 1.4***) is Cl.[109] The link with myths is traditional, being found in Plato, *Tim.* 22A; Polybius 9.2.1, with reference to stories of early times. The usual reference is to human family trees. According to Hort 1894:135–7, the term was used for the tales attached to the births of rulers and heroes and associated with their genealogies. Genealogies occupied an important place in Judaism, both in early history and in the family trees of living individuals; e.g. a priest's position depended on his having an appropriate genealogy that could be traced back. The word is not found in the LXX (but cf. γενεαλογεῖσθαι, 1 Chr 5.1), but Philo can refer to the parts of Genesis dealing with people (as opposed to the creation of the world) as τὸ γενεαλογικόν (*Mos.* 2.47), reflecting the use of βίβλος γενέσεως (Gen 5.1).[110] The reference here is disputed:

(a) Jewish speculations based on the genealogies and similar matter in the Scriptures, such as *Jub.*; 1QGenApoc; Ps-Philo.[111]

---

[107] In Josephus, *Ant.* 15.135; *Ap.* 1.11 it appears to mean 'dispute about a controversial matter' rather than, as BA suggests, 'controversial question, controversy'. In the NT it can mean (a) '(legal) investigation' (Acts 25.20); (b) 'discussion, debate' (1 Tim 6.4; 2 Tim 2.23; Jn 3.25: Acts 15.2, 7***). Cf. ἐκζήτησις (1 Tim 1.4*** and textual note). Cf. Greeven, H., *TDNT* II, 893f.

[108] Ecclus 22.12; cf. Bertram, G., *TDNT* IV, 832–47, espec. 833–7; Spicq, 686; *TLNT* II, 536–41).

μωρός can be used of persons (Mt 5.22; 7.26; 23.17; 25.2, 3, 8; 1 Cor 3.18; 4.10; cf. Deut 32.6.), and, as here, of things (1 Cor 1.25, 27***); cf. 1 Clement 39.1; *Sib. Orac.* 3.226; Hermas, *Vis.* 3.6.5; *Mand.* 5.2.2, 4; 11.11; 12.2.1; *Sim.* 8.7.4; 9.22.2, 4). Cf. μωραὶ διδαχαί (Hermas, *Sim.* 8.6.5); μωρολογία (Eph 5.4).

[109] Plato, *Crat.* 396C; the verb is used of drawing up pedigrees, Herodotus 2.146; cf. Heb 7.6.

[110] Colson's note (Loeb, VI, 606) states that this term was used in the grammatical schools of material that dealt with persons rather than places, dates and events. Cf. Spicq, 93–104; Dibelius-Conzelmann, 16f; Hort 1894:133–8; Büchsel, F., *TDNT* I, 663–5; Schlarb 1990:86–90.

[111] Spicq, 322f., 686; Schlarb 1990, 86–93; Hasler, V., *EDNT* I, 242; cf. Kittel 1921 and Quinn, 245f., who suggest that Christ's lineage was being disputed. Dibelius-Conzelmann, 16f., claim that Jewish genealogies would not be coupled with myths, and therefore something else must be meant.

(b) Gnostic speculations, whether interpretations of scriptural genealogies or about the aeons and their relationships.[112] However, there is no first-century evidence for such material and indeed no evidence that the term 'genealogies' was used for Gnostic systems of aeons or that the Gnostics equated names from biblical genealogies with those of aeons.[113] Further, there is no trace of speculation about the aeons in the PE, and the terminology points more clearly in a Jewish direction. The use of this term thus links the Cretan problems in some way with the Jewish teaching opposed in 1 Tim.

The two remaining items are quite general terms for strife[114] and quarrelling.[115] Such behaviour is characteristic of non-Christian society and makes the church no better than the society which it is seeking to change. The motif recurs in 1 Tim 6.4 (λογομαχία) and in the pattern for the church leaders in 1 Tim 3.2 (ἄμαχος). In 2 Tim 2.23 strife is the result of the foolish disputes condemned here.

The quarrelling here is concerned with the law. νομικός 'pertaining to the law (cf. 1 Tim 1.7) is found here only in the NT in this sense.[116] In Tit 3.13 and elsewhere in NT it means '[a person] knowing the law', hence 'lawyer'. Only the Jewish law is in mind; other systems of law are unlikely to have had theological significance for early Christians. But what kind of questions were arising? Gutbrod offers the two possibilities: (a) 'the validity of the Law as a norm of life for Christians' (cf. 1.10; 1 Tim 1.8f.); (b) 'theories which are to be proved from Scripture', and favours the latter. Another possibility is rules for asceticism (cf. Dibelius-Conzelmann, 151).

The mid. voice of περιΐστημι has the sense 'to go around so as to avoid, avoid, shun' (2 Tim 2.16***).[117] The thought here appears to be of personally avoiding involvement in

[112] Irenaeus, *AH* I Praef.; I.30.9; Tertullian, *De prae. haer.* 33; Easton, 112f.; Dibelius-Conzelmann, 16f.; Hanson, 194; Schmithals 1961:145; Haufe 1973:329; Rudolph 1977:321f.
[113] Irenaeus, *AH* 1.30.9 does not mean this.
[114] ἔρις is 'strife, discord, contention' (Philo, *Her.* 246; 1 Tim 6.4**; Rom 13.13; 1 Cor 1.11; 3.3; 2 Cor 12.20; Phil 1.15; in lists of vices, Rom 1.29; 2 Cor 12.20; Gal 5.20***). Cf. *TLNT* II, 69–72.
[115] μάχη is lit. 'battle, contest', hence 'fighting, quarrels, strife, disputes', including personal quarrels (2 Cor 7.5; Jas 4.1); 'verbal disputes' (2 Tim 2.23***; cf. Plato, *Tim.* 88A: μάχας ἐν λόγοις ποιεῖσθαι; Ct 1.6). Cf. Bauernfeind, O., *TDNT* IV, 527f., who emphasises that strife in all forms is always regarded negatively in the NT.
[116] Cf. Origen, *Cels.* II, 76.9 of the Pentateuch; Philostratus, *VS* 522, with ἀγῶνες. Cf. Gutbrod, W., *TDNT* IV, 1088.
[117] This use is Hellenistic: Philodemus, *Rhet.* 1.384 S (with τὰς ἁμαρτίας; cited by BA); Josephus, *Bel.* 2.135; *Ant.* 1.45; 4.151; 10.210. Cf. the use of παραιτέομαι (Tit 3.10; 1 Tim 4.7; 2 Tim 2.23) and ἐκτρέπομαι (1 Tim 6.20). The verb is also used act. 'to place around'; intrans. 'to stand around' (Acts 25.7; Jn 11.42).

such disputes, but elsewhere it is of suppressing them in the church (1.11f.). Perhaps both ideas are present.

The reason[118] for avoiding such discussions is because of their harmful effects and uselessness. ἀνωφελής can mean both 'useless' (Heb 7.18***) and 'harmful'.[119] The word creates a deliberate contrast with v. 8. μάταιος is 'vain, idle, empty, fruitless'; 'without result' (Holtzmann, 501) (Acts 14.15; 1 Cor 3.20 [LXX] 15.7; Jas 1.26; 1 Pet 1.18***).[120] The concept is also applied to speech in 1.10 (ματαιολόγος) and 1 Tim 1.6 (ματαιολογία).

10. αἱρετικὸν ἄνθρωπον μετὰ μίαν καὶ δευτέραν νουθεσίαν παραιτοῦ The problem of tackling opponents is discussed more fully in 2 Tim 2.23–26 (cf. Brox, 312). The αἱρετικός*** is a person who holds sectarian opinions and promotes them in the church, thereby causing dissension in the congregation.[121] The reference is to the kind of person described in Rom 16.17. Cf. Holtzmann, 502: 'Within Christianity a heresy is, as the etymology indicates, a form of thinking according to an egotistical choice and inclination, associated with a tendency to separation and party spirit.' Thus the elements of holding doctrines at variance from those of the congregation and of causing divisions over them are both present (Lock, 157).

Every effort is to be made to encourage such people to abandon the assertion of their views. Three stages are envisaged. The first and second consist in a formal warning. νουθεσία is 'admonition, instruction, warning' (1 Cor 10.11; Eph 6.4***).[122] The corresponding verb is used by Paul of the admonition given by

---

[118] εἰσὶν γάρ is used as in 1.10. Cf. 2 Tim 2.16 and similar constructions in 2 Tim 3.2; 4.3, 11; Tit 3.3.

[119] Plato, *Protag.* 334A; Prov 28.3; *Ps. Sol.* 16.8; Ignatius, *Mag.* 8.1 of myths.

[120] Cf. Bauernfeind, O., *TDNT* IV, 519–22 who comments: 'Speculation is still speculation even though it is pious speculation' (522).

[121] The word is found in Ps-Plato, *Def.* 412A, to mean 'one who can choose aright' (further refs. in BA). Here it has the sense 'factious, causing divisions' (so Barrett, 146; Fee, 211); perhaps 'the adherent of a heresy, heretical' (BA). For use in early church see *Didasc.* 33.31; 118.33; Irenaeus, *AH* 3.3.4; Clement, *Strom.* 1.95.4; Hippolytus, *El.* 4.47.5. Cf. Schlier, H., *TDNT* I, 184; Oberlinner, 187.
  Cf. the use of αἵρεσις (Ignatius, *Eph.* 6.22; *Trall.* 6.1; *Epil. Mosq.* 1), originally 'sect, party, school'; it was applied to groups in Judaism (Acts 5.17; 26.5) then to the early church by their Jewish opponents (Acts 24.5). Hence it can refer to groups in the church (1 Cor 11.19; Gal 5.20; 2 Pet 2.1). The term suggests separatists, with their own opinions (Spicq, 687).
  ἄνθρωπος (1.14) is here used pleonastically with the adjective (cf. 2 Tim 3.8; Jn 9.1, 16).

[122] Cf. Wis 16.6; Philo, *Det.* 3; *Cong.* 157, 160; Plutarch, *Alc.* 4.2 [193] [verb] (Spicq). The word is synonymous with νουθέτησις (1 Clement 56.2). Cf. Behm, J., *TDNT* IV, 1019–22; *TLNT* II, 548–51.

members of the church to one another and also by its leaders.[123] The word can be used of verbal criticism and physical punishment, Holtzmann, 502. Here, however, it is 'the attempt to make the heretic aware of the falsity of his position, a pastoral attempt to reclaim rather than a disciplinary measure' (Behm, J., *TDNT* IV, 1022; cf. Jeremias, 76; *pace* Hasler, 98, who thinks that pastoral care is absent). The procedure in Mt 18.15f. is in mind. This gave the person ample opportunity for restoration to the congregation. More than one opportunity was to be given.[124] But if repeated persuasion failed, the church leader must take strong action to silence the offender, presumably by some form of exclusion from the congregation (Oberlinner, 188). The force of παραιτέομαι is debatable. It means 'to reject, repudiate, decline', hence (with acc. of person; Josephus, *Ant.* 7.167) 'to reject, refuse somebody' (1 Tim 5.11; Heb 12.25a, 25b); here perhaps it has the stronger force 'to dismiss, drive out'.[125] It also means (with acc. of thing) 'to reject, avoid' (1 Tim 4.7; 2 Tim 2.23; Acts 25.11***; Diognetus 4.2; 6.10).[126]

Action here is apparently taken by the leader; contrast the congregational action in 1 Cor 5 (Hanson, 195). According to Spicq, 687, it is not as extreme as excommunication but is rather the refusal of fellowship, and the verb has the sense of keeping one's distance from the offender. Fee, 212, notes the parallel in thought at the end of Romans (Rom 16.17, ἐκκλίνω).

Rabbinic procedures at this time are not altogether clear. Later practice involved the imposition of a ban (*nidduy, shammata*) for a period of 30 days. If this failed to induce penitence, it was followed by a further, similar period. And if this in turn failed to be effective, the more severe *herem* was imposed. However, this practice is not attested for the first century, when the *nidduy* was imposed for an unlimited period of at least 30 days on religious leaders rather than ordinary people. A better parallel is to be found at Qumran where dissidents might be temporarily or permanently excluded from the community.[127] The general

---

[123] Rom 15.14; 1 Cor 4.14; Col 1.28; 3.16; 1 Th 5.12, 14; 2 Th 3.15; cf. Acts 20.31***.

[124] εἷς (1.6) here is equivalent to πρῶτος 'first'. The usage is found in Gk. authors (e.g. Herodotus 4.161; cf. BA) and is not necessarily Semitic. For examples of the link with δεύτερος** see BA.

[125] Cf. Diogenes Laertius 6.82; Plutarch, *Mor.* 206A.

[126] Elsewhere it means 'to ask for, request' (Mk 15.6; [with inf.] Heb 12.19); hence 'to beg off, request to be excused' (Lk 14.18a, 18b, 19). Cf. Stählin, G., *TDNT* I, 195.

[127] 1QS 6.24–7.25; CD 9.23; 20.3; cf. Hare, D. R. A., *The Theme of Jewish Persecution of Christians in the Gospel according to St Matthew* (Cambridge: Cambridge University Press, 1967), 48–56.

principle of two warnings followed by a penalty does not seem to be paralleled except in Mt 18.15–17.

It would seem, then, that the procedure here may depend on the tradition of Jesus' teaching. The question must also be raised whether it represents a milder approach than that in 1 Tim 1.20, but it is best to assume that that passage represents the last stage in the process with recalcitrant opponents. The spirit here is that of 2 Tim 2.24–26.

11. εἰδὼς ὅτι ἐξέστραπται ὁ τοιοῦτος καὶ ἁμαρτάνει ὢν αὐτοκατάκριτος Justification[128] for the severe action lies in the fact that the opponent[129] has proved to be recalcitrant. He is impervious to persuasion and is following a course that can only be described as sinful. The perf. ἐξέστραπται indicates a continuing, permanent state of perversion.[130] The culprit, therefore, persists in sinning. Spicq, 688, holds that ἁμαρτάνω (1 Tim 5.20**) here has its original sense 'to miss the mark, deceive oneself', hence 'commit a folly'.[131] In any case the force is 'and is [deliberately] sinning'. His sin is now witting and deliberate (cf. Lk 19.22; Jn 3.18; 8.9–11). The implication may be that he has been warned about his conduct.[132] He is without excuse and self-condemned, and therefore is to be disciplined.[133]

Parry, 85, notes that the sin is not the holding of false views but rather the breaking up of the congregation. When Brox, 312, suggests that the underlying message is in effect 'don't waste time on such people', this is true only when every reasonable effort to persuade the offender has failed. On the problem of the limits of pastoral care see further Oberlinner, 190–3.

---

[128] For εἰδὼς ὅτι cf. Philem 21.

[129] τοιοῦτος**, 'such a person', is used for evil people in 1 Cor 5.11; 2 Cor 2.6; 2 Th 3.12; et al.

[130] ἐκστρέφω*** is 'to turn inside out, alter completely'; hence 'to turn aside, pervert' (Hermas, Sim. 8.6.5); pass. 'to change completely' (Deut 32.20; Amos 6.12). Cf. διαστρέφω (Mt 17.17; Phil 2.15; et al.).

[131] For the noun ἁμαρτία see 1 Tim 5.22, 24; 2 Tim 3.6; for the noun ἁμαρτωλός see 1 Tim 1.9, 15. The word-group is used in the PE of the behaviour of non-believers and (as here) of persons within the congregation. Cf. Quell, G., Bertram, G., Stählin, G., and Grundmann, W., TDNT I, 267–316, and Rengstorf, K. H., TDNT I, 317–35.

[132] Büchsel, F., TDNT III, 952; pace EDNT I, 179.

[133] For the appending of a comment with the part. ὢν cf. 1.16. αὐτοκατάκριτος***, 'self-condemned', has been found elsewhere only in a fragment from Philo, cited by John of Damascus, Sacra Parallela (Mangey II, 652; text in Dibelius-Conzelmann, 151, and Büchsel, F., TDNT III, 952).

PERSONAL INSTRUCTIONS
(3.12–14)

The letter concludes with material of a more personal and occasional character. It is explained by advocates of pseudonymity as an attempt to demonstrate that Paul was concerned also for the 'third generation' of leadership, i.e. the period after Titus had completed his duties. The reference to Nicopolis is an indication that the scope of the letter is wider than simply Crete, and the mixture of names of known companions of Paul and fresh persons indicates the combination of continuity with the past and the appointment of new leaders (Oberlinner, 193–202). This seems very artificial.

There is the usual abrupt transition from the preceding 'body' material. The structure follows the typical pattern of a Pauline letter (Merkel, 106) with elements that can be broadly categorised as follows:

12–13	Travel plans	1 Cor 16.10–12	Rom 15.22–33
14	Personal instructions	1 Cor 16.13–18	Rom 16.17–20
	Recommendations	1 Cor 16.15–16	Rom 16.1–2
15a	Greetings	1 Cor 16.19–22	Rom 16.3–16, 21–23
15b	Grace	1 Cor 16.23–24	Rom 16.20

The structure is clearly flexible. It is also found in Heb 13.17–25, and therefore nothing about authorship can be deduced from it.

TEXT

13. Ἀπολλῶν The spelling varies: Ἀπολλῶν (א H* C*); Ἀπολλῶνα (F G); Ἀπολλῶ (the Attic form; C D* TR). Elliott, 195f., is undecided.

λείπῃ λίπῃ (א D* Ψ 1505 pc; T WH mg). Elliott, 196, prefers the aorist; cf. 1.5 note; 2 Tim 4.10 note.

14. ὦσιν ἄκαρποι Inverted order (F G Hier); Elliott, 196, accepts the variant on the basis that the PE have the order ἵνα – adj. – εἶναι in 1.9; 1 Tim 4.15; 5.7. But the external evidence is weak.

EXEGESIS

12. Ὅταν πέμψω Ἀρτεμᾶν πρὸς σὲ ἢ Τύχικον, σπούδασον ἐλθεῖν πρός με εἰς Νικόπολιν, ἐκεῖ γὰρ κέκρικα παραχειμάσαι The first of two personal instructions given to Titus concerns his own movements. Paul will send to him one of his colleagues,

340

and at this juncture Titus is to travel to the same destination as Paul where the latter (and presumably Titus also) will spend the winter season when travel tended to be avoided.

ὅταν, 'when, whenever' (1 Tim 5.11**), is used of an action that is conditional and possibly repeatable in the indefinite future; it does not necessarily imply uncertainty.[1] πέμπω**[2] is frequently used of Paul sending colleagues.[3] Ἀρτεμᾶς*** is a shortened form of Ἀρτεμίδορος (BD § 125[1]), 'gift of Artemis'.[4] Like Artemas, Τύχικος is also a Greek name ('Fortunate').[5] It doubtless refers to Paul's colleague who accompanied Paul on his last journey to Jerusalem, and was sent with Col and Eph (Acts 20.4; Eph 6.21; Col 4.7***). The listing of the two alternative possibilities (ἤ, 1.6) implies uncertainty in plans and sounds genuine – Paul had not yet made up his mind what to do (Kelly, 257). If a historical scenario lies behind the verse, then, since according to 2 Tim 4.12*** he was to be sent from Paul in his imprisonment in Rome to Ephesus to relieve Timothy, presumably it was in fact Artemas who was sent to replace Titus in Crete so that there would be a continuity in leadership there (Spicq, 689f.).

Once his replacement had arrived, Titus was to join up with Paul. The whole phrase σπούδασον ἐλθεῖν πρός με is paralleled in 2 Tim 4.9 (cf. 4.21). σπουδάζω can mean 'to hasten, hurry' (REB; 2 Tim 4.9, 21**; Ignatius, *Eph.* 1.2; *Mart. Poly.* 13.2) or 'to be zealous, eager' as a morally praiseworthy form of conduct (Gal 2.10; *et al.*). Clearly the former meaning (which is dominant in LXX usage; cf. Jdt 13.12) is required here (*pace* BA), but perhaps the command is 'to be taken with a pinch of salt' as 'epistolary style' (Spicq, 690; cf. Jude 3).[6]

There were at least nine known towns called Νικόπολις*** ('Victory town'; Spicq, 690). It is generally agreed that the reference here is to Actia Nicopolis which was the major city in Epirus, a Roman *colonia* founded in 31 BC by Augustus after

---

[1] For use in similar contexts cf. Acts 24.22; 1 Cor 16.2, 3, 5 12; Col 4.16.

[2] The form πέμψω could be fut. indic. or aor. subj. Spicq, 689, and Quinn, 254, say the form is fut. indic., but this is extremely rare in the rest of the NT.

[3] 1 Cor 4.17; 16.3; 2 Cor 9.3; Eph 6.26; Phil 2.19–28; Col 4.8; 1 Th 3.2, 5.

[4] For examples see Dittenberger, *Syll.* 851.17 (II BC) and other references in BA.

[5] It is attested in inscriptions from Magnesia and elsewhere. (It is accented on the last syllable in BAG, but on the first in BA.)

[6] For the adverb σπουδαίως see v. 13 below. Cf. Harder, G., *TDNT* VII, 559–68; *TLNT* III, 276–85 (espec. 278). Spicq objects that the verb cannot mean 'hurry' here, since Titus has to wait until his colleague arrives and Paul is not yet at Nicopolis. But the objection assumes that the reference is to hurrying immediately, whereas the point is rather that Titus is not to delay to join Paul once Artemas or Tychicus has arrived.

the defeat of Antony and Cleopatra at the battle of Actium; Herod the Great contributed to the building costs.[7] Epictetus had a school here (c. AD 90), had Arrian as a pupil and seems to have known a Christian community whom he refers to as 'Galileans' (Epictetus 4.7.6; Aulus Gellius 15.11). This identification fits in with 2 Tim 4.10 where Titus is in Dalmatia. In Rom 15.19 Paul states that he had preached the gospel as far [west] as Illyricum. Other possible locations are discussed and dismissed by Dibelius-Conzelmann, 152f.

The reason for the choice of meeting place lies in Paul's travel plans. The use of ἐκεῖ, 'there' (Rom 9.26 LXX; 15.24 in travel information), clearly implies that Paul had not yet arrived there (Holtzmann, 503). κρίνω is here 'to decide', and the perfect expresses 'a settled decision' (Knight, 357).[8] παραχειμάζω, 'to spend the winter', can be used of ships staying in port over the winter season (Acts 27.12; 28.11; 1 Cor 16.6***; noun, Acts 27.12), but equally of people. A date of writing in the autumn or late summer is indicated.

The uncertainty as to which of Paul's colleagues will actually come is admitted to be surprising by commentators like Hasler, 99, who think that the details are fictitious (cf. Trummer 1978:132–7; Donelson 1986:23f., 56, 58). Defenders of the authenticity of at least the personal notes hold that the motif is unlikely to have been invented.

The reason for the haste (cf. also v. 13) is not clear. The similar instruction in 2 Tim 4.9, 21 is motivated by the onset of winter and the imminence of Paul's trial. Commentators have asked whether it is consistent with the duties in 1.5f. (Hasler, 98; Merkel, 106; see above on 1.5) and with the fact that Paul is not yet at Nicopolis (Holtzmann, 503; Spicq, 690). Certainly the onset of winter is also implied here, which would be a reason for not delaying to travel. Ancient travellers did not travel in the winter, even in the Mediterranean.

Why was Paul going to Nicopolis? It is probable that he settled in major cities during the winters for an extended period of evangelism and church development. If the letter belongs to the last period in his life, he may have had his sights on Spain, in which case Nicopolis would have been a convenient location for

---

[7] Cassius Dio 50.12; 51.3; Strabo 7.7.5 [324]; 10.2.2 [250]; Tacitus, *Ann.* 2.53; 5.32; Suetonius, *Aug.* 18; Pausanias 5.23.3; Plutarch, *Ant.* 62; Josephus, *Ant.* 16.147.

[8] Usually κρίνω is 'to judge' (2 Tim 4.1**; Rom 2.1 and frequently). For the meaning here cf. 1 Cor 2.2; 5.3–5; 7.37; Acts 3.13; 16.4; 20.16; 25.25; 27.1. Cf. Büchsel, F., *et al.*, *TDNT* III, 921–41, especially 923.

missionary activity before leaving the Aegean area and travelling further west. But this must be speculative.

So the real problem is why Titus's presence is needed with Paul and why he is no longer needed in Crete. No reason is given why Titus should join Paul, nor is the period mentioned. It is not explicitly stated that he was to be replaced (permanently?) by one of the two people mentioned here (*pace* Hasler, 99), although this is a reasonable interpretation. We do not know how long it would take to appoint elders in the churches, but it may well have been possible in the time still at Titus's disposal. The ongoing instructions are more of a problem. Oberlinner, 194f., solves the problems by claiming that the intent is simply to indicate the widening of Titus's sphere of influence.

What does stand out is the fact that Paul is decisively in charge and can issue instructions to his colleagues. This picture agrees with that in the acknowledged letters where colleagues bustle to and fro at his direction.

13. Ζηνᾶν τὸν νομικὸν καὶ Ἀπολλῶν σπουδαίως πρόπεμψον, ἵνα μηδὲν αὐτοῖς λείπῃ The second personal instruction to Titus is about the arrival of two further members of Paul's missionary group, probably travelling together, who are to be given whatever resources they need for the continuation of their travels. It may be implied that they are Christian workers who trust the Lord (and hence his servants) to provide for their needs. For Oberlinner, 196, the author's purpose is to portray Paul as being concerned for the third-generation situation.

Ζηνᾶς*** is yet another Greek name reflecting pagan religion; it is a contraction for Ζηνοδωρός, 'gift of Zeus'. This is the only mention of Zenas in the NT, but the attached adjective has suggested that another person of the same name was known in the church (Spicq, 691); this is an unnecessary supposition, since Paul does the same thing in Rom 16.23; Col 4.14. νομικός (3.9) is here a noun, 'lawyer'. This sense of the term is well-attested in Hellenistic sources (4 Macc 5.4; cf. BA; Spicq, 691) and is common in Lk for Jewish experts in the law (Lk 7.30; cf. Mt 22.35). The word in itself does not indicate what kind of law is meant, whether Jewish, Greek or Roman law, but a Jewish lawyer is unlikely with such a pagan name (*pace* Lock). Some think that the mention of the detail has some connection with Paul's own trials, but nothing in the context supports this.[9]

---

[9] Against Hasler's (99) wild speculations here see the robust commonsense of Hanson, 196.

Ἀπολλῶς is a common Greek name,[10] found for a colleague of Paul in Acts 18.24; 1 Cor 1.12; *et al.* The same person is probably meant throughout.[11]

σπουδαίως has two nuances, corresponding to those of the verb (3.12 note), either 'with haste' (in the comparative form, Phil 2.28), or 'with diligence, zeal' (Lk 7.4; 2 Tim 1.17***). Here the latter force is more likely.[12] προπέμπω can mean 'to accompany, escort' (Acts 20.38; 21.5); Holtzmann, 503f., holds that this is also the meaning in all the remaining NT references except here and 3 Jn, but in fact it is more likely to mean 'to help on one's journey' (by providing food, money, companions, etc.).[13] The reference here is certainly to material provision in view of the next clause (Dibelius-Conzelmann, 152).[14] But there appears to be a contrast between what Titus himself is to do and what the members of the congregation are to do (v. 14).

The question arises whether these two missionaries are the bearers of the letter.[15] The principle of sending missionaries in pairs would then have been followed. If the information is fictitious, it was created to give concrete evidence of what is demanded in v. 14 and introduce the paraenesis there (Brox, 313); however, the fit between the duties in vv. 13 and 14 is not all that close. Merkel, 107, thinks it odd that two bearers of the letter, one of them a lawyer to boot, were necessary and holds that they were simply travelling evangelists; but nothing suggests that carrying a letter was their only reason for travel, and they were in fact going on elsewhere.

14. μανθανέτωσαν δὲ καὶ οἱ ἡμέτεροι καλῶν ἔργων προΐστασθαι εἰς τὰς ἀναγκαίας χρείας, ἵνα μὴ ὦσιν ἄκαρποι After the personal instructions comes a further implicit command to Titus regarding the instruction which he is to give the church in doing good and living fruitful lives. Although Brox, 314, notes that the instruction to do good works is rather stereotyped, in fact there may well be a fresh nuance here.

---

[10] It was used as an abbreviation for various names (Ἀπολλώνιος [Acts 18.24D], Ἀπολλόδωρος, Ἀπολλωνίδης; cf. BD § 125¹); it is replaced by Ἀπέλλης in Acts 18.24 and 19.1 ℵ.

[11] Spicq, 691; *pace* Merkel, 107, who queries whether Apollos was a colleague of Paul.

[12] Cf. Harder, G., *TDNT* VII, 559–68.

[13] 1 Macc 12.4; 1 Esdras 4.47; *Ep. Arist.* 172; Rom 15.24; 1 Cor 16.6, 11; 2 Cor 1.16; Acts 15.3; 3 Jn 6***; Polycarp 1.1. Spicq, 692, compares the duties people might have with regard to government travellers.

[14] ἵνα is clearly expressive of purpose or result; it can hardly be imperatival (*pace* Lock, 158). For λείπω (1.5**), intrans. 'to be lacking', cf. Lk 18.22; Josephus, *Bel.* 4.257.

[15] Spicq, 691, following Theod. Mops. II, 256 Swete; cf. Wieseler, cited by Holtzmann, 503; Jeremias, 77; Dibelius-Conzelmann, 153.

οἱ ἡμέτεροι (cf. 2 Tim 4.15**) is 'our people', i.e. in this context [Cretan] Christians (cf. Lips 1979:157). This usage to refer to one's own group is common parlance[16] and need not include any particular stress on the exclusion of other people such as heretics and non-Christians (*pace* Brox, 314), although a delimited group is in mind (Spicq, 692f., with further examples).[17]

μανθάνω can be used of learning by receiving instruction, in this case Christian instruction in the church given by a teacher.[18] Here, however, the force is more 'to learn through practice' and hence 'to begin to do something' rather than 'to receive instruction how to' (Heb 5.8; 1 Tim 5.4, 13**; Ignatius, *Mag.* 10.1; *Rom.* 4.3). Hence the remark of Rengstorf that 'members of his churches will always be fruitful in piety if they will accept and learn from the Gospel as the new Law' (*TDNT* IV, 410) is wide of the mark.[19]

The phrase καλῶν ἔργων προΐστασθαι repeats 3.8. The injunction is now applied specifically (cf. Lips 1979:179 n. 72) and may have a fresh nuance, depending on how the next phrase is understood. Lock, 156, thinks that 'to practise honourable occupations' may again be the sense here (but see note above).

χρεία is 'need, necessity', hence 'something that is lacking, necessary'. In the plural it can refer to the things needed for daily life (food, clothes and the like).[20] ἀναγκαῖος** is 'necessary';[21] hence it is used of 'close' friends (Acts 10.24), and here of 'pressing needs'. The addition of the adjective to χρεῖαι seems strictly unnecessary, but the combination was evidently a stock phrase.[22] Nevertheless, its force is disputed:

---

[16] Cf. Plato, *Menex* 248 (members of a family); Latin *nostri*; Josephus, *Ant.* 14.228; *Vita* 401, 406; *Mart. Poly.* 9.1; Irenaeus, *AH* 5.28.4.

[17] The force of the connective δὲ καί is disputed. (a) It may qualify the verb: 'Let our people also learn', *scil.* to provide for others as well as the missionaries. Or (b) it may qualify the subject: 'Let our people also', *scil.* (i) in addition to you personally and following your example (Spicq, 692); or (ii) in addition to the heathen (and as a witness to them) (Parry, 86; Lock, 158, tentatively).

[18] Rom 16.17; 1 Cor 14.31, 35; Eph 4.20 (cf. ἐδιδάχθητε in v. 21); Phil 4.9; Col 1.7; 1 Tim 2.11; 2 Tim 3.7, 14a, 14b.

[19] Cf. Rengstorf, K. H., *TDNT* IV, 390–413; Lips 1979:136.

[20] αἱ τοῦ βίου χρεῖαι, Geminus [c. 70 BC; cited in BA]. Cf. Philo, *Decal.* 99; Josephus, *Bel.* 6.390; *Ant.* 13.225; Polybius 1.52.7; *Ep. Arist.* 11, 258; Acts 20.34; 28.10; Rom 12.13; Papias 2.15.

[21] 1 Cor 12.22 of the indispensable parts of the body; Acts 13.46; 2 Cor 9.5; Phil 1.24; 2.25; Heb 8.3.

[22] It is attested in Diodorus Siculus 1.34.11; inscr. and pap. in MM 31; Philo, *Prob.* 76; *TLNT* I, 97–100; see Spicq, 693, for many examples. Easton's (105) claim that it was a Stoic technical term does not seem to be justified, although it was used in popular philosophy (Dibelius-Conzelmann, 152).

(a) 'To obtain[23] the things necessary for life' (sc. for themselves so as not to be a burden on others.[24] However, this interpretation depends on taking the previous part of the verse as a reference to engaging in honourable professions (and thereby earning wages); but we have already seen that this interpretation is unlikely in v. 8, and there is nothing else in the letter to suggest that this was a problem.

(b) 'So as to help cases of urgent need';[25]; specifically 'to help the needs of Christian travellers' (Holtz, 237; Hasler, 98), or more broadly 'in order to facilitate the Christian mission' (Barrett, 148). Cf. Rom 12.13; Eph 4.28.

(c) 'To help with problems in the community at large'. Spicq, 693f., notes that the language is unusual in the New Testament and suggests that Christians are here being summoned to generosity in dealing with disasters affecting the community at large, such as epidemics and famine, which were dealt with in the ancient world through the gifts of public-spirited citizens (similarly, Hanson, 196f.).[26]

There would seem to be some special reason for emphasising this point at the end of the letter. This makes view (c) attractive, although it does seem a big jump from caring for Christian missionaries to setting up disaster aid funds. View (b) certainly fits the context best. In any case, such action will ensure that Christians live useful lives.[27]

A closing instruction of this kind is found elsewhere in Paul.[28] It repeats and sums up a main point of the letter (3.8; cf. 1.16; 2.7, 14; 3.1; Spicq, 689; Fee, 215). The letter thus ends with a stress on fruitful Christian living, expressed in deeds that benefit others, rather than wasting time in fruitless speculations. The faith of believers must be translated into action that is beneficial to others. Their purpose must be evangelistic in contrast to the heretics who are set on personal gain (1 Tim 6.5, Spicq, 694). Lock, 159, cites the taunt of the Romans that Christians were '*infructuosi in negotiis*' (Tertullian, *Apol.* 42.1).

---

[23] εἰς has the force 'to help, with reference to'.
[24] Cf. 1 Th 4.12; 2 Th 3.6–16; NIV; Easton, 105.
[25] REB; NRSV; Simpson, 119; Fee, 215.
[26] Spicq claims that P. Oxy. 1068, 16 and P. Grenfell II, 14 c, 1 and 6, refer to such situations. However, the first reference is simply to problems caused by delay in a burial.
[27] μή ... ἄκαρποι is litotes. ἄκαρπος, literally 'lacking in fruit' (Jude 12), is metaphorical, 'fruitless, useless' (1 Cor 14.14; Eph 5.11; Mt 13.22; Mk 4.19; 2 Pet 1.8***; cf. Philostratus, *Gym.* 42 [cited in *TLNT* I, 56f. n. 4]). Cf. Hauck, F., *TDNT* III, 616; *TLNT* I, 56f..
[28] 1 Tim 6.20f.; Rom 16.17–20; 1 Cor 16.13f.; 2 Cor 13.11; Gal 6.11–16.

CLOSING GREETING
(3.15)

Weima, J. A. D., *Neglected Endings: The Significance of the Pauline Letter Closings* (Sheffield: JSNT Press, 1994; but he more or less neglects the PE).

TEXT

15. ἀσπάσαι ἀσπάσασθε (A b); not discussed by Elliott. Possibly assimilation to plural in v. 15b.

ἡ χάρις add τοῦ θεοῦ (F G 629 vg^{mss}); τοῦ κυρίου (D b vg^{mss}). These are natural additions to a brief benediction by scribes.

μετὰ πάντων ὑμῶν μετὰ τοῦ πνεύματός σου (33); add καὶ μετὰ τοῦ πνεύματός σου (81). Both are attempts to assimilate to 2 Tim (Elliott, 197), and the latter is a good example of conflation.

Add at end ἀμήν: (ℵ^2 D^1 F G H Ψ 0278 TR lat sy bo). Rejected by Elliott, 104; Metzger, 586f. Cf. 1 Tim 6.16.

EXEGESIS

15a. Ἀσπάζονταί σε οἱ μετ᾽ ἐμοῦ πάντες. ἄσπασαι τοὺς φιλοῦντας ἡμᾶς ἐν πίστει The letter closes in a conventional but nonetheless meaningful way with greetings from the writer and his immediate companions to Titus, a request to pass on greetings to the Christian community, and an actual greeting in the form of an implicit prayer for God's grace to be with them all. Oberlinner, 200, deduces that contacts between the churches are mediated through the leaders, but this impression arises simply because this letter is from one church leader to another.

In v. 15a ἀσπάζομαι is 'to express good wishes to, greet' (2 Tim 4.19, 21), but in v. 15b** it has the sense 'to convey one person's greetings to a third party'.[1] Although it is common at the ends of letters (cf. BA for examples), Windisch notes that the epistolary use is not unknown in the pre-Christian period but is certainly rare, and follows O. Roller in suggesting that Paul was the first to see great significance in it.[2] Greetings from the writer's companions are a normal feature in NT letters.[3] Here the senders of

---

[1] 2 Tim 4.19; Rom 16.3, 6, *et al.*; 1 Cor 16.20; 2 Cor 13.12; Phil 4.21; Col 4.15; 1 Th 5.26; Heb 13.24; 1 Pet 5.14; 3 Jn 15 (the only example not to use the aorist imperative).

[2] Windisch, H., *TDNT* I, 496–502.

[3] Rom 16.16b; 1 Cor 16.19f.; 2 Cor 13.12b; Phil 4.21f.; Col 4.10, 12, 14; Philem 23; Heb 13.24b; 1 Pet 5.13; 2 Jn 3; 3 Jn 15a.

347

the greetings are οἱ μετ' ἐμοῦ πάντες, i.e. the writer's companions; the more common terms 'saints' or 'brothers' are not used, but similar, rather vague phrases are found in Paul.[4]

The vagueness of the reference to Paul's companions may imply either that none of the writer's companions was known to the recipient or that he knew their names so well that there was no need to list them. One possibility is that the writer was on a journey with a few companions, none of them known to Titus (cf. the vagueness in Acts 20.34; Spicq, 694).

Titus is called to pass on greetings to Paul's friends and acquaintances who are with him. The phrase οἱ φιλοῦντες ἡμᾶς is attested in secular literature,[5] but it is Christianised by the following words. With the exception of the (traditional?) formula in 1 Cor 16.22 φιλέω** is not found in the Pauline corpus, nor are there references to fellow-Christians as φίλοι (as in 3 Jn 15).[6] Paul, however, does use ἀγαπητός of his friends and congregations (cf. 2 Tim 1.2). The switch from the singular 'me' to the plural 'us' is presumably to take account of the broad group of Paul and his colleagues mentioned in the immediate context.

Most scholars take the qualification ἐν πίστει to mean 'in the faith', so as to qualify 'those who love us' as Christians (cf. 1 Tim 1.2).[7] Another possibility is that it means 'faithfully'.[8] Either way the phrase refers to 'believers' or 'true believers'; Barrett, 148, finds the double sense that the readers are Christians and that they can be trusted.

This description of the wider circle around Titus may carry a note of exclusion directed against heretics. But this may be to press the force of ἐν πίστει too far, and it may simply be a way of characterising the people greeted as those who have a loving relationship to Paul within the community constituted by faith. If there is an exclusion in the phrase, it lies in 'those who love *us*', since it may be assumed that Titus's opponents were also opposed to Paul. To suggest that Titus is to make an appraisal of his congregation to decide who is to be greeted (Knight, 359f.) exaggerates the point, especially in view of the inclusiveness of the next phrase.

15b. ἡ χάρις μετὰ πάντων ὑμῶν This form of wording of the closing benediction (but without πάντων) is also found in

---

[4] οἱ σὺν ἐμοί (Gal 1.22; Phil 4.22); see also 1 Cor 16.20; 2 Cor 13.12; Gal 1.22; Phil 4.21, 22.
[5] The fullest list is in *TDNT* IX, 137 n. 214; e.g. Sb 7253.18.20 (AD 296): ἀσπάζομαι τοὺς φιλοῦντας ἡμᾶς κατ' ὄνομα (cited in BA); cf. *TLNT* III, 448–51.
[6] Cf. Stählin, G., *TDNT* IX, 113–46.
[7] Jude 1, cited by Stählin, 137, is hardly a parallel.
[8] Simpson, 199; Arichea-Hatton, 314; cf. Eph 6.24, ἀγαπῶντες ἐν ἀφθαρσίᾳ; 2 Jn 1; 3 Jn 1.

1 Tim 6.21; 2 Tim 4.22. The use of πάντων shows that it is a real plural referring to the church, corresponding to the 'all' in v. 15a. The phrase is probably a wish, and we should supply some such word as εἴη or πληθυνθείη. To ask for grace to be with people (μετά is common at the end of letters to express the presence of God/grace/love with believers; cf. BA) is to pray to God that he will act graciously towards them. The benedictions in the other Pauline letters (except Eph 6.24; Col 4.18) regularly include a reference to Christ as the source of grace. Hasler, 100f., thinks that this one is thus very formal; but the use of the same form in Col 4.18 and Heb 13.25 rather weakens the evidence for his assertion (cf. Oberlinner, 201, who suggests that χάρις itself signifies the totality of salvation).

THE FIRST LETTER TO
TIMOTHY

THE FIRST LETTER TO TIMOTHY

OPENING SALUTATION
(1.1–2)

See bibliography for Tit 1.1–4.

The letter opens with a salutation which follows the pattern familiar to us from Paul's letters with slight variations.[1] The wording draws attention to the position of Paul as an apostle by virtue of a command that issues both from God and from Christ and to the relationship in which Timothy, the recipient, stands to him, like a child to a parent, in their common faith. It characterises this faith as one which is in God as a Saviour and Christ as the basis of hope. Here the content of the gospel is expressed succinctly and powerfully.[2] The greeting itself is the normal Pauline one, but the addition of 'mercy' singles out a divine quality which is particularly important later in the chapter (1.13, 16).

Although 1 Tim is ostensibly addressed to Paul's younger colleague and he is described in warm tones, the total effect of the salutation may seem somewhat formal and official for a personal letter – although it is quite in harmony with Paul's style when addressing his congregations; it gives apostolic instructions for officebearers (Knoch, 19). This impression arises from the description of Paul himself. If the letter is in fact from Paul, the stress on his apostolic authority may well be with an eye to the congregations for which Timothy is responsible: the letter contains instructions regarding their life which they must carry out when they are passed on by Timothy. Thus the letter in effect gives backing to Timothy as a church leader (Calvin, 187). At the same time it must be remembered that we do not know how Paul as an older man would address a young man who was his junior colleague. He may well have preserved a certain formality with regard to his own position over against that of a junior colleague. If the letter is not directly from Paul, the effect is still to enhance the authority of what is taught and hence of any church leader who tries to lead his congregation according to

---

[1] See Tit 1.1–4 and notes.
[2] See the excellent exposition in Oberlinner, 7.

Pauline teaching. On the assumption of later authorship, however, it is hard to see why the letter needed to reinforce Timothy's authority as Paul's legitimate colleague and successor, since the figure of Timothy himself would belong to the fictional set-up of the letter. It would be necessary to assume that the church leaders who were really addressed in the letter claimed to stand in the succession of Timothy and hence ultimately of Paul.

TEXT

1. Χριστοῦ 'Ιησοῦ The order is inverted (as in 1 Pet 1.1; 2 Pet 1.1) in both occurrences in some MSS: (a) A K L I TR 33 6 1739 *et al.* vg sy^hl; (b) ℵ D² K L *et al.* co. In view of the superior attestation the order in the text should be adopted in both cases, as in Tit 1.1 (see note).

ἐπιταγήν ἐπαγγελίαν (ℵ only) is either an assimilation to 2 Tim 1.1. (Metzger, 571), or (less likely, in our view) an attempt to avoid a non-Attic word (Elliott, 15).

σωτῆρος Praem. τοῦ (D 104 81; some minn. have τοῦ σωτῆρος ἡμῶν θεοῦ). Elliott, 15, accepts the addition on stylistic grounds to gain balance and to conform to usage at Tit 1.4; 3.6. See, however, BD §268 and MHT III, 206. It is more likely that scribes assimilated to pattern elsewhere in view of the poor MS evidence.

2. πατρός Add ἡμῶν (ℵ² D² Ψ TR a vg^mss sy sa bo^mss; Kilpatrick). The variant is apparently an assimilation to normal Pauline usage, but it is accepted as original by Elliott, 16f., on the ground that it balances σωτῆρος ἡμῶν in 1.1 and was omitted on stylistic grounds because of the frequency of ἡμῶν elsewhere in the salutation.

EXEGESIS

1. Παῦλος ἀπόστολος Χριστοῦ 'Ιησοῦ 1 Tim begins, like all of the letters in the Pauline corpus, with the name which he regularly used, and shares with the majority of them in following this closely with a reference to his apostolic office (2 Cor; Eph; Col; 2 Tim are identical; cf. Rom; 1 Cor; Gal; Tit; see Tit 1.1 and notes). The mention of his position as apostle of Christ Jesus sounds a note of authority, but at the same time emphasises that he is a missionary of the gospel.

Roloff, 56, maintains that Paul is the only apostle for the PE. But the only real evidence offered in defence of this is the absence of any polemic related to competing claims to apostolic authority; otherwise, the connection of the apostolic office with the gospel and the mission to the Gentiles in the PE[3] is typically Pauline. The argument is thus dubious. In the PE there is no occasion to mention other apostles, and there is no indication that there were any others who were in opposition to Paul and his teaching.

[3] 1.11; 2.6f.; cf. 2 Tim 1.10f.; 2.8; Tit 1.3.

He is also the only writer of the letter (cf. Rom; Gal; Eph), which for some scholars is an indication that the real author is placing him on a pedestal.[4] But there is nothing remarkable in this, especially since it is Timothy who was Paul's most frequent co-author in 2 Cor; Phil; Col; Philem (cf. 1, 2 Th).

κατ' ἐπιταγήν See Tit 1.3 note. We have to supply some such word as 'appointed' with 'apostle' to provide the verbal component which is qualified adverbially by this phrase. Paul became an apostle in accordance with a command from God and Christ. He therefore passes on divine commands to the churches (1 Cor 7.25), and he and his colleagues can issue commands to the congregations.[5] If one can be an apostle only by the direct command of God, the appointment entitles the apostle to respect and obedience from people like Timothy and also from the congregation (See Fee, 35; Oberlinner, 2f.).

θεοῦ σωτῆρος ἡμῶν For σωτήρ in reference to θεός see Tit 1.3 note. This particular designation is used of both God and Christ, linking them each with the salvation that is the content of Christian experience and hope. The effect here is to indicate that the keynote of the letter is the salvific purpose of God who is the source of all blessings (cf. Hasler, 11, who, however, regards the salvation as future). The use of ἡμῶν emphasises the reality of the purpose of God as it is experienced by his people and is not meant in any kind of exclusive manner (2.4; 4.10; Tit 2.11). There may even be a polemical note against any opponents who denied the universality of God's saving purpose.

καὶ Χριστοῦ Ἰησοῦ τῆς ἐλπίδος ἡμῶν The collocation of God and Christ in phrases such as this (and in the actual greeting formula) indicates how natural it was for early Christians to place the two persons alongside one another without any sense of incongruity and demonstrates the way in which Christ was seen to belong on the divine side of reality (the inverted order in Gal 1.1 makes the point all the more strongly). It is natural to name God the Father first as the ultimate origin of salvation. The description of Jesus as ἡ ἐλπίς (Tit 1.2; 2.13; 3.7**) is a natural personification which can be used of ordinary people (e.g. Noah, Wis 14.6), but it may reflect the OT description of God as the hope of his people, especially in that he is their saviour.[6] Later the word became virtually a title for Christ.[7] The

[4] Houlden, 45f.; Oberlinner, 1f.; but see Prior 1989:37–59. See further discussion at Tit 1.1.
[5] Tit 2.15; cf. 1 Cor 7.6; 2 Cor 8.8; Delling, G., *TDNT* VIII, 36f.
[6] Ps 64 [MT 65].6; 70 [MT 71].5; Jer 14.8; 17.13; *Ps. Sol.* 5.13; 15.2; cf. Ecclus 34.13; cf. *1 Enoch* 48.4 of the Messiah. The description is also found in pagan religion. Ἴσις ἡ μεγάλη [ἐ]λπίς (*New Docs.* II, 77 § 30).
[7] Ignatius, *Eph.* 21.2; *Mag.* 11; *Trall.* Inscr.; 2.2; *Philad.* 11.2; cf. Polycarp 8.1.

expression may refer to the hope of future glory (Col 1.27) at the parousia or to Jesus as the source of eternal life (cf. Tit 1.2), but probably both aspects are included, especially since salvation has both present and future aspects in the Pastorals. The language is on the way to becoming stereotyped, but it still retains its living quality.

2a. Τιμοθέῳ γνησίῳ τέκνῳ ἐν πίστει The second part of the salutation is (as usual) briefer than the first; it is designed to express the Christian standing of the recipient and his relationship to Paul. The language is very close to that of Tit 1.4: Τίτῳ γνησίῳ τέκνῳ κατὰ κοινὴν πίστιν.

Τιμόθεος (1.18; 6.20; 2 Tim 1.2**) was associated with Paul in his mission[8] and in the writing of his letters (apart from Gal and Eph).[9] He is also mentioned in Acts 16.1; 17. 14f.; 18.5; 19.22; 20.4; and Heb 13.23***. The name was a very common one.[10]

τέκνον is used in a metaphorical sense (2 Tim 1.2; Tit 1.4; Philem 10).

(a) It may simply be a term of affection from an older person to a younger (cf. Lk 16.25 and the use of τέκνιον in 1 Jn 2.1 et al.); Jesus is represented as addressing other people in this way (Mk 2.5; 10.24).

(b) Paul, however, uses the metaphor for people whom he had brought to faith or nourished in the faith (1 Cor 4.15; Gal 4.19). It is not certain, however, whether Paul was directly responsible for Timothy's conversion.[11]

(c) The more likely thought, as in Tit 1.4, is that of the relationship between two people of different ages, expressed in terms of paternal love and filial obedience and faithfulness (1 Cor 4.15 of Timothy). Timothy's subordinate position vis-à-vis the apostle is probably implicit (cf. Houlden, 46), but it is the certainty of the close relationship and the authority with which Timothy is invested because of it that are stressed. Timothy may be expected to share the outlook of Paul in his care of the church (Phil 2.19–22) and in his commitment to the faith (thus he is γνήσιος ... ἐν πίστει). Hanson, 56, suggests that secondarily the author is depicting a paradigm of the warm relations that should exist among church leaders.[12]

---

[8] 1 Cor 4.17; 16.10; 2 Cor 1.19; Phil 2.19; 1 Th 3.2, 6.
[9] Rom 16.21; 2 Cor 1.1; Phil 1.1; Col 1.1; 1 Th 1.1; 2 Th 1.1; Philem 1.
[10] Cl.; Hel.; 1 Macc 5.6 et al.; 2 Macc 8.30 et al.; Josephus, Ant. 12.329–44.
[11] See Acts 16.1–3; Knight, 63–4; Fee, 36; Oberlinner, 5, n. 10, denies that there is any positive evidence for the supposition.
[12] Influence from usage in the mystery religions (e.g. CH 1; Dibelius-Conzelmann, 13) is unlikely.

Although the alternation with ἀγαπητός (2 Tim 1.2) might suggest that γνήσιος (see Tit 1.4 note) has the nuance of 'dear' here, it is more likely that, in the the metaphorical setting and in this context in which genuine belief in Christ is uppermost in mind (ἐν πίστει), the term denotes the apostolic authentication of Timothy as coworker.[13] As with Titus in Tit 1.4, the language here authenticates Timothy as the legitimate and authorised successor of Paul to the church.[14]

ἐν πίστει corresponds to κατὰ κοινὴν πίστιν in Tit 1.4 and verifies that the relationship in mind is metaphorical or rather spiritual. ἐν has the sense 'in the sphere of' (Roloff, 58; Fee, 36) and the phrase qualifies τέκνῳ. The sphere, which is the basis for the relationship between Paul and Timothy, is the shared commitment of trust (in Christ) rather than Christianity as 'the faith'; see **Excursus 4**.

2b. χάρις ἔλεος εἰρήνη ἀπὸ θεοῦ πατρὸς καὶ Χριστοῦ Ἰησοῦ τοῦ κυρίου ἡμῶν. The third part of the salutation is the actual content of the greeting. It is identical with that in Tit 1.4 (see notes), except for the addition of ἔλεος to the formula.[15]

ἔλεος (Tit 3.5 note) was often a translation of the Hebrew *hesed* which carried the connotation of God's lovingkindness by which he made and sustained the covenant with Israel. It is not found in Pauline salutations, but occurs in 2 Tim 1.2 (not in Tit 1.4); 2 Jn 3; Jude 2; Polycarp inscr.; *Mart. Poly.* inscr.; cf. Ignatius, *Smyr* 12.2. Paul uses the term in the benediction in Gal. 6.16, and it is found in Jewish usage in *2 Apoc. Bar.* 78.2; Tob 7.11א; cf. Wis 3.9 and 4.15 for the combination χάρις καὶ ἔλεος. The addition here can be explained:

(a) As the result of simple literary variation.

(b) Possibly under the influence of Judaism or contemporary practice in worship, which could tend to greater fulness (Spicq 318; cf. the use in AF); the formula could then be a combination of Jewish and Pauline forms (Dibelius, 12). Knight, 66, suggests this expansion of the typical Pauline salutation might correspond (1) to Timothy's Jewish background (over and against Titus's Gentile background), and (2) to his particular need in a time of struggle to be reminded of God's special care for him. This is rather speculative.

(c) It has also been suggested that it has been inserted (the unrhythmical σοι being dropped) to replace the usual ὑμῖν

---

[13] The suggestion that there may be a hint at the illegitimacy of his physical birth in Jewish eyes (since his father was non-Jewish; Stott, 40) is highly unlikely in view of the use of the same term with respect to Titus.

[14] Calvin, 187; cf. Brox, 99; Fee, 36; Oberlinner, 5.

[15] The listing of the three nouns without any linking word is also found in 2 Tim 1.3; 2 Jn 3; contrast Jude 2.

in the standard Pauline formula (Dibelius-Conzelmann, 14; Jeremias, 12; Kelly, 41); this explanation will not hold for the non-Pauline letters addressed to communities, and it is significant that there was felt to be no need for ἔλεος in Tit 1.4.

(d) It is possible that the inclusion of ἔλεος in the salutation reflects the influence of the theology of the PE which stress mercy (2 Tim 1.16, 18; Tit 3.5; in 1 Tim 1.13, 16 Paul is the proto-typical recipient of God's saving mercy [ἠλεήθην]; cf. Hasler, 12; Roloff, 55). The argument might be stronger, if it were also included in Tit 1.4.

(e) The suggestion that the benediction of Gal 6.16 (εἰρήνη ἐπ' αὐτοὺς καὶ ἔλεος καὶ ἐπὶ τὸν Ἰσραὴλ τοῦ θεοῦ) somehow stands behind the form of the salutation here (Roloff, 55) is also worth considering, though beyond showing that the connection of peace and mercy was known in the Pauline writings little more can be drawn from this observation.

On the whole, while the addition of ἔλεος to the salutation might be peculiar for Paul, the thought expressed by the threefold wish is clear enough. Paul wishes Timothy the blessing of labouring in the power and protection of God. The wish itself is an indication that the salvation of God, by which these things become accessible to his people, is very real and present for the writer (cf Lips 1979:92).

ἀπὸ θεοῦ πατρὸς καὶ Χριστοῦ Ἰησοῦ τοῦ κυρίου ἡμῶν is the usual expression of the source of Christian blessings. See Tit 1.4 note. The entire phrase with the same order Χριστὸς Ἰησοῦς ὁ κύριος ἡμῶν is also found in 2 Tim 1.2 (cf. Tit 1.4 which differs only in replacing replacing κύριος with σωτήρ);[16] the order here is similar to that in 1.1 and may have been influenced by it.

κύριος ('lord') is used of Jesus in 1.12, 14; 6.3, 14; 2 Tim 1.2; in 2 Tim 1.8, 16, 18a, 18b; 2.7, 14 v.l., 19a, 19b (in some of these cases the reference may be to God the Father). The language is stereotyped but preserves the sense that Jesus is the Lord acknowledged by Christians. On ἡμῶν see the note above on 1.1.

---

[16] It is not found in other epistolary salutations but does occur in Rom 6.23; 8.39; 1 Cor 15.31; Eph 3.11; (Ph 3.8 sing.); 1 Tim 1.12; cf. Rom 1.4; 7.25; 1 Cor 1.9; Jude 25 with the order Ἰησοῦς Χριστός.

BODY OF THE LETTER – A. TEACHERS AND CHURCH LEADERS
(1.3–3.16)

The body of the letter falls into parts, 1.3–3.16 and 4.1–6.21a. In the first part the author is concerned, as he is throughout the letter, largely (but not exclusively) with the question of heresy in the church and the antidote to it. The topic is important because it deals with a threat to the gospel which was summarised in the salutation, and it is not surprising that the basis of Paul's apostleship is developed in terms of his conversion and call which are paradigmatic of God's saving mercy.

The section is divided into four subsections. The first is a general instruction to Timothy to take action against people who promote false teaching in the church (1.3–20). This is followed by a section on the conduct of the church meeting which emphasises the need for prayer for all people, including the Gentiles, and for the avoidance of heretical teaching by the women in the church (2.1–15). Third, there is a statement on the choice of the right candidates for leadership in the church (3.1–13). Finally, there is a summarising statement which emphasises the character of the church as the bulwark of the truth about Jesus Christ (3.14–16).

What is the rationale of this major section? The function of the first subsection is evident. It reminds Timothy of his duty in this respect, stressing the fact of the problem, and reinforcing Timothy's calling by reference to Paul's own calling and to the task which he has passed on to Timothy.

In the second subsection a primary stress is laid on the need for prayer for all people, which is related both to the need of the church for peace and security and also to the proclamation of the gospel to all people. The roots of this may lie in an implicit narrowing of the scope of the gospel by the heretics. The topic slides over into a discussion of how prayer should be conducted, and this in turn leads into a restriction on the women in the church as regards teaching. The women are called to sobriety in dress and the practice of good works, to learning but not to teaching, and to the care of their families. This may suggest that the conduct of the women was associated with the heresy.

359

In the third subsection the qualities required in leaders are listed, and it is probable that this deals with weaknesses in the church that could be cured by more careful appointment of leaders.

In the concluding section the instructions are placed in the context of the reminder that church is God's foundation, intended to maintain the truth of the gospel. It is important, therefore, that the whole of what precedes is seen in the light of this concluding statement (Wagener 1994:70).

From this survey we see that the main theme is the preservation and teaching of the truth of the gospel which brings salvation to sinners and which stands under threat from the opponents who teach otherwise.

I. INSTRUCTION TO AVOID FALSE DOCTRINE (1.3–20)

Most of Paul's letters begin with a prayer-report in which Paul thanks God for the spiritual progress of his recipients and states how he prays for them in a way which anticipates themes to be discussed later in the letter. (A somewhat different pattern, but still related to prayer and thanksgiving is found in 2 Cor and Eph.) The prayer-report is omitted in Galatians, Titus and here. In Gal this omission reflects the urgency of the situation of heresy in the church and the strong emotional response of the author. In 1 Tim and Tit the writer plunges straight into ecclesiastical directions, demanded in part by the existence of false teaching in the church.

Yet the omission of a thanksgiving is also seen in Jas, 2 Pet and 2 Jn, where this consideration does not apply, and therefore it may be wrong to detect too much significance in the omission. The situation is of course different in 2 Tim which is a personal letter; Holtz, 33, therefore is right in finding the reason in the character of the letter as a set of official instructions. The opening is intended to to give an impression of authenticity and get down to the evils to be confronted without delay (Houlden, 51).

The detailed structure of the section is not easy to discover. Roloff divides it into three sub-sections (1.3–11, 12–17, 18–20), while Oberlinner produces four by separating 1.3–7 and 8–11. Any attempt to explain the structure must take into account three features. First, it opens and closes with instructions to Timothy (vv. 3–7, 18–20). Second, several contrasts are introduced: (a) the results of false teaching (3b–4, 6) and of Christian teaching (5); (b) the content of false teaching (4) and of the authorised message (11); (c) the description of the false teachers (6–7) and of Paul (12–16); (d) the persons for whom the law is not necessary and those for whom it is (9a, 9b–10). Third, there is 'head–tail' linkage between 1.7 and 8, 11 and 12, and 13 and 15f.[1]

The resulting structure is complicated, but essentially the denunciation of the false teachers and their message is carried out by means of contrast and by emphasising the apostolic authority of the message that they have rejected. This suggests the following analysis:

1.3–7 Timothy is to [continue to] warn people not to teach false doctrines which lead to speculations instead of the truth which leads to love. Rejection of it leads to false teaching about the law.

1.8–11 It is not that the law has no place. It is there to condemn the sinners, who offend against sound doctrine that is according to the gospel.

1.12–17 Paul is grateful to have been called to be a missionary despite his earlier sins of ignorance. He was saved by grace, in accordance with a traditional statement about Christ as Saviour, and in order to be an example for others who believe. This leads into an ascription of praise to God which acts as a caesura after the apparent digression.

1.18–20 Timothy, then, who has also been called, must obey Paul's instructions and himself hold to the faith and good conduct. Not all have been able to do so, and some have had to be disciplined. The situation is a serious one.

This gives the section a broad A B A' structure with 'inclusio' between the first and last subsections. It makes use of traditional elements, the trustworthy saying and the language of the doxology. But it is essentially the author's own composition.

a. Forbid opponents to promulgate false teachings (1.3–7)

Reumann, J., 'Oἰκονομία-Terms in Paul in comparison with Lucan *Heilsgeschichte*', *NTS* 13 (1967), 147–67.

The passage introduces three intermingled themes, which continue throughout the ch. (Roloff, 61):

(1) Timothy's previous commission and its renewal (1.3/5, 18);

(2) A contrast between the introspection of the false teachers and sound teaching (1.4, 6f./5, 10b, 11);

(3) The right use of the law and the gospel (1.6, 8–10/5, 11). The main purpose of the letter is thus expressed in terms of contrasts. Timothy is to continue to take action against opponents

---

[1] This raises the question whether the author works by accidental association of ideas, or whether the 'tails' are deliberately introduced to prepare for what follows. The latter appears to be the case.

of Paul whose teaching is subversive of God's purpose for his 'household' and leads to strife, and he is to promote the development of love in the congregation. The false teaching claims to be based on the law but is in fact pretentious nonsense. It diverts people into intellectual arguments away from the concern for the Christian living which is the matter of supreme importance.

TEXT

4. ἐκζητήσεις ζητήσεις (D F G Ψ 0285^vid 1739 1881 TR Iren), 'debates, disputes', is preferred by Elliott, 18, on the grounds that the word forms part of the author's vocabulary (6.4; 2 Tim 2.23; Tit 3.9; verb, 2 Tim 1.17) and has the appropriate meaning for the context, whereas ἐκζητήσεις should mean 'researches'. However, (a) Elliott admits that scribes frequently reduced compound to simple forms; (b) the author likes unusual words and new forms; (c) the word is previously unattested and the meaning could well involve an element of disputation; speculation forms a good contrast to οἰκονομία. In any case, futile disputes are in mind. Cf. Metzger, 571.
οἰκονομίαν οἰκοδομίαν (D^c 625); οἰκοδομήν (D* sy^p hl^mg goth Iren Epiph. cf. *aedificationem* g m vg). The difficulty of the term led to scribal emendations (Metzger, 571). However, Elliott, 19, argues that οἰκοδομήν is original and was objected to by Atticists. But although the word is frequent in Paul, it is not found in the PE, and the attached gen. θεοῦ is rather awkward. WH *Notes*, 132, hold that it arose by a conjectural adaptation of οἰκονομίαν to *aedificationem*. Lock, xxxvi, cites Tit 1.7 to show that PE use this idea.

EXEGESIS

3a. Καθὼς παρεκάλεσά σε προσμεῖναι ἐν Ἐφέσῳ πορευόμενος εἰς Μακεδονίαν The syntax is not clear. The sentence begins with a καθώς clause that has no apodosis.[2] The following ways of dealing with the syntax have been suggested:[3]
(a) V. 3 is to be attached to the main clause in 1.2b (Wohlenberg, 82f.).
(b) ἵνα is elliptical and introduces the main clause (Lock, 7).
(c) The missing words 'so I command you now' should be supplied at the end of v. 4 (Holtzmann, 284).[4]
(d) The apodosis does not come until 1.18 after a long digression (Bengel).
Views (a) and (b) are implausible. The most probable solution is that the author failed to conclude the sentence which he had begun owing to the piling up of fresh ideas; view (c) thus

---

[2] καθώς** is frequently used as a loose connective in Paul. It introduces a ground rather than a comparison (Roloff, 63; BD §453²).
[3] For similar anacoloutha at the beginning of letters see Ignatius, *Eph.* 1.3; *Rom.* 1.1.
[4] For a similar construction see P. Oxy. 1299.9 (AD IV, cited by MM 314); see also BA *s.v.* for a similar omission.

represents what he originally intended to do but failed to do, and view (d) indicates what he actually did do to retrieve the situation. Such lengthy digressions are not unknown in the Pauline corpus (Rom 5.12–18; Gal 2.4–6; Eph 3.2–13). Roloff, 62f., and Oberlinner, 11, suggest that the anacolouthon is deliberate, and is a means of indicating that the original command still remains in force; or the construction may have been deliberately intended to create a sense of urgency (Schlarb 1990:17; Holtz, 34). Wolter 1988:180f. has drawn attention to official documents which use the device of reminding the recipient of previous instructions in order to relate the present task to his overall responsibility.

παρακαλέω (Tit 1.9 note) here, as elsewhere, expresses a command in the form of a request. Timothy was already in Ephesus (Ἔφεσος, 2 Tim 1.18; 4.12**) when he was instructed to remain there (προσμένω, 5.5**; cf. Acts 11.23; 13.43).[5] Roloff, 63, holds that Timothy is portrayed as the resident teacher and not as a travelling evangelist, but it is doubtful whether so much is to be drawn from this one statement (cf. 2 Tim 4.5; and see Ollrog 1979:23). Paul's command came when he was on his way (πορεύομαι, 2 Tim 4.10**) to Macedonia (Μακεδονία**).

On the assumption of a historical scenario this can be taken in two ways. It might imply that Paul was leaving Ephesus but told Timothy to stay on (so, very strongly, Dibelius-Conzelmann, 15). Scholars taking this view tend to associate these movements of Paul with a release from prison (Fee, 39). Van Bruggen (1981) links them with Acts 19.21–22, where Paul left Ephesus to go to Macedonia; but on this occasion Timothy was sent on before him to Macedonia (cf. Merkel, 18). A second possibility is that Paul was elsewhere and sent word to Timothy not to go elsewhere (e.g. to join Paul on his way to Macedonia after his release from imprisonment in Rome; Schlatter, 27; cf. Simpson, 27).

For those who view the letters as pseudepigraphical, the information is a part of the fiction and serves purely to make a close link between Timothy and Paul, on which link Timothy's authority rests.[6] The choice of Ephesus serves to give a specific setting for the letter in the fictional scenario, but the situation is in fact quite typical and general and does not reflect anything peculiar to Ephesus (Oberlinner, 10).[7]

---

[5] Possibly the verb is to be given some stress and translated 'to persevere'; cf. Schlarb 1990:17.

[6] Hasler, 12; see further the discussion above and at Tit 1.1. Note also the element of appointment by a higher authority detected by Wolter 1988:183–5.

[7] See Thiessen 1995 for a thorough attempt to relate the PE historically to the post-Pauline situation in Ephesus.

1 Tim 1.3 (and Tit 1.5) plays an important role for some who regard the PE as reflecting a post-apostolic situation. Stenger 1974, for instance, suggests that the emphasis on leaving Timothy and Titus behind represents a modification of the Pauline parousia topos. The change from 'sending' co-workers to 'leaving behind' co-workers reveals the post-apostolic situation; originally, Paul represented his presence (when absent) through the sending of delegates, but the pseudepigraphical development finds 'presence' being expressed through the 'leaving behind' of co-workers (cf. Trummer 1978:124). Wolter (1988:180-4) has taken this further. The Pauline practice was characteristically first to establish a community, and then later, as needed, to send the co-workers to continue the work (1 Cor 4.17; 16.10; 2 Cor 2.4–7; *et al.*; cf. Ollrog 1979:127f.). Thus the 'leaving behind' of the addressees reflects the consciousness that Paul has passed from the scene and abandoned the churches in time (cf. Brox 1975:113).

The question that is asked only infrequently is whether in writing directly to co-workers (as 1 Tim and Tit purport to have been), Paul would not have used the language of 'leaving behind' (see Tit 1.5 note) to denote 'sent'. The time frame (writing after the fact) would have required the past tense, and if Paul was actually on the move, 'left behind', or in the case of 1 Tim 1.3, 'stay in place', would have conveyed the message to the co-workers to keep at the work. A church might benefit from a reminder of the co-worker's 'sending = apostolic authority' status; but only a later church would read into προσμεῖναι (or ἀπέλιπον in Tit 1.5) the implication suggested by Wolter and Stenger. The question therefore remains whether the assumption of church situations significantly later than the apostle has been proved. The language used here certainly does not require the later setting.

3b. ἵνα παραγγείλῃς τισὶν μὴ ἑτεροδιδασκαλεῖν The purpose (ἵνα) in commanding Timothy to remain in Ephesus is to carry out the task of a church leader, namely to resist heretical teaching. παραγγέλλω (4.11; 5.7; 6.13, 17**; noun 1.5, 18**) is a verb with a military flavour, 'to command'. It is one of several terms which describe authoritative speech in the PE (e.g. παρακαλέω, ἐλέγχω, διδάσκω), and it depicts the church leader as one having the authority (stressed by Knoch, 20) to command other people in the church, as Paul himself already did.[8]

---

[8] 1 Cor 7.10; 11.17; 1 Th 4.11; 2 Th 3.4, 6, 10, 12; cf. Brox, 103; Lips 1979:130f.; Roloff, 63; Radl, W., *EDNT* III, 16f. There is nothing to be made of the choice of this term over παρακαλέω (*pace* Holtz, 34); Paul uses both words when addressing Christians, and the heretics are probably viewed as erring church members who, if they accept it, are subject to the leader's authority.

The practice of not referring to opponents in the church by name but by using τις (1.6, 19; 4.1; 5.15, 24; 6.10, 21) or some other circumlocution is already to be found in Paul and continued in the church,[9] although on occasion specific people can be named (1.20; 2 Tim 2.17). In some cases the author may not know the actual names, or he may be writing in the spirit of 'if the cap fits, put it on'; but probably there is also a pejorative sense to the expression (cf. Roloff, 71). The allusion may be to certain elders (Fee, 40).

False teaching (ἑτεροδιδασκαλέω, 6.3***; Ignatius, *Poly.* 3.1) is teaching that differs from accepted teaching (cf. διδαχαὶ ξέναι, Heb 13.9).[10] As with διδασκαλία, ἑτεροδιδασκαλέω might view false teaching from the angle of content or activity (cf. Lips 1979:39 n. 39). While the activity or method of teaching is admittedly somewhat in view (speculation and use of the law), the main interest seems to be in the content of the teaching that results. The verb presupposes the existence of an accepted standard of teaching; this authorised standard is identified, as the contrast of the section unfolds, in 1.10[11] with the term ἡ ὑγιαίνουσα διδασκαλία and in 1.11 with the term τὸ εὐαγγέλιον.[12] It may seem surprising that the first and principal task of Timothy is to deal with false teaching, but this is clearly the result of a specific situation, and is in fact analogous to what happens in Galatians.

4a. μηδὲ προσέχειν μύθοις καὶ γενεαλογίαις ἀπεράντοις Behind the unacceptable teaching lies a specific interest which comes to expression in it and is leading to barren speculation and argument in the church instead of to spiritual and moral growth.[13]

The false teachers have become preoccupied (προσέχω, Tit 1.14** note) with a speculative approach to the Old Testament, seeing it as a source of μύθοι καὶ γενεαλογίαι. μύθος is the same language as is used in Titus (1.14; 3.9 see notes), though it is probably not necessary to argue that precisely the same false teaching is in view in each case. The connection in this passage with 'Jewish' ideas in νομοδιδάσκαλοι and the discussion of the law (vv. 7–10) suggests the OT source of the 'myths'. The plural 'myths' itself is pejorative, indicating the fallacious nature of the

---

[9] Rom 3.8; 1 Cor 4.18; 5.1; 2 Cor 3.1; 10.2; Gal 1.7; 2.12; Phil 1.15; Heb 10.25; Ignatius, *Eph.* 7.1; 9.1; *Mag.* 4.1; 8.1; *Trall.* 10.1; *Philad.* 7.1; 8.2; 1 Clement 1.1; 47.

[10] The word is formed on the analogy of other ἑτερο- compounds (1 Cor 14.21; 2 Cor 6.14) and of other compounds of -διδάσκαλος (νομοδιδάσκαλος, 1.7; καλοδιδάσκαλος, Tit 2.3; ψευδοδιδάσκαλος, 2 Pet 2.1); cf. ἑτεροδιδάσκαλος, Eusebius, *HE* 3.32.

[11] See also 6.3; cf. Tit 1.9 note.

[12] Cf. Lips 1979:48–51; Roloff, 63; Guthrie, 67.

[13] μηδέ (5.22; 6.17; 2 Tim 1.8; Tit 2.3 *v.l.***) is 'and not'.

teaching (more so than referring to any specific content – on which see below) and perhaps also making a statement about the behaviour associated with the teaching. The significance of the term here depends on the pairing with γενεαλογία.

γενεαλογία (Tit 3.9*** note) refers to the content of the teaching and takes the discussion into the realm of Jewish use of the OT accounts of the biblical characters (as Philo used the term) or speculation based on OT family trees. The futility of this line of exegesis begins to emerge in the description ἀπέραντος***. 'Endless' may be meant literally but can have the sense of 'leading nowhere', hence 'unintelligible' and 'useless', or 'exhausting, wearisome' (Fee, 42; they could 'be spun out for ever', Scott, 8).[14] From Tit 1.14; 3.9 and from vv. 7–10 below it is most likely that use of Jewish genealogies, or OT material that could be so categorised, is in mind here.

Thus 'myths and genealogies' describe (a) an untruthful teaching with an ethical dimension; it was probably aimed at authenticating questionable practices by (b) rooting them in the OT history (in much the same way as attempts by certain philosophers to ground their teaching in stories about the gods; see Tit 1.14 note); the latter term probably identifies the kinds of OT material exploited. The close link with the law, noted by Schlarb 1990:83–93, is significant. We are dealing with a form of Jewish teaching which was particularly concerned with the interpretation of the Pentateuch in ways that Pauline Christians found unacceptable.

Hence several interpretations are to be ruled out. There is no evidence to suggest either that the false teachers speculated on their own genealogies which would give them standing in Judaism (Schlatter, 34f.), or that the reference might be to Gnostic systems of aeons standing in genealogical relationship to one another, despite the fact that Irenaeus (*AH* praef. 1) applied this verse to Gnostics (see Tit 1.14; 3.9 and notes).[15]

4b. αἵτινες ἐκζητήσεις παρέχουσιν μᾶλλον ἢ οἰκονομίαν θεοῦ τὴν ἐν πίστει This clause completes the thought begun in v. 3 by supplying the reason that the false speculation is to be discouraged, namely, because its results undermine or interfere with responsible execution of the ministry given by God.

[14] The word was used of inconclusive arguments; see Philo, *Cong.* 53; cf. ἀπείριτος (Athenaeus 1.22d); ἀπεραντολογία (Cicero, *ad Att.* 12.9); Spicq, 323; *TLNT* I, 159.
[15] Yet the fascination with Gnosticism continues to animate commentators: 'a kind of judaising Gnosis without the need to presuppose Gnostic systems that are already firmly established' (Oberlinner, 14). But the fact that later Gnostics developed these rudimentary speculations in their own way hardly justifies using the term 'Gnosis' for what is happening here and is potentially misleading.

Preoccupation with the 'myths and genealogies'[16] promotes (παρέχω, 6.17; Tit 2.7**) 'useless speculations' (ἐκζήτησις***). This term is a part of the author's polemical arsenal designed to discredit the opposition.[17] In polemical fashion, the author contrasts this result[18] with the result of genuine Christian teaching. Christian teaching should promote (the same verb is in mind) οἰκονομίαν θεοῦ.

οἰκονομία** generally refers to the task or office of an οἰκονόμος (Lk 16.2–4) and is applied metaphorically to the work of Paul as an apostle (1 Cor 9.17; Eph 3.2; Col 1.25).[19] It can also mean a plan or arrangement made by somebody. The context in Eph 1.10; 3.9 would suggest that God's salvation plan is in mind; but in other contexts the usage may be more general (cf. Ignatius, *Eph.* 18.2; 20.1; Diognetus 4.5). The meaning here is uncertain:

(a) 'Training' in (or which leads to) salvation.[20] This meaning is found in later writings.[21]

(b) God's 'plan' of salvation.[22] However, οἰκονομία in this sense does not provide a very logical counterpart to ἐκζήτησις (useless speculation) with which it is contrasted (Roloff, 65).

(c) It is thus best to understand the term against the background of the οἶκος-οἰκονόμος-οἰκονομία concept which the PE employ to depict the church (οἶκος θεοῦ, 3.15; 2 Tim 2.20–21) and the stewardship of ministry (οἰκονόμος θεοῦ, Tit 1.7 [note]; 1 Tim 3.4–5). On this analogy οἰκονομία θεοῦ denotes 'the responsibility', and hence 'authority', laid on the leaders of his people by God; it is in effect the performance of the duties of an οἰκονόμος.[23] Knight, 75f., suggests that this view and the preceding one may be combined to give 'the outworking, administration or stewardship of God's plan of salvation through the gospel and its communication'.

---

[16] αἵτινες (3.15; 6.9; 2 Tim 1.5; 2.2, 18; Tit 1.11**) refers to the 'myths and genealogies'; it can have the sense 'of a kind which' (BD § 293²), hence 'inasmuch as they...'.

[17] Cf. Tit 3.9 (and note); 2 Tim 2.23; Schlarb 1990:59–73.

[18] μᾶλλον, 'rather than' (6.2; 2 Tim 3.4); Nauck 1950:26 suggests that μᾶλλον ἤ is a Hebraism giving the exclusive sense 'instead of'.

[19] Cf. for similar uses Ignatius, *Eph.* 6.1; Diognetus 7.1. Reumann* draws attention to the use in Isa 22.21 (LXX) where it renders *memshalah*, 'authority, ruling power'.

[20] BA; Dibelius-Conzelmann, 17f.; Easton, 109f.; Hanson, 57; Oberlinner, 14f.; Michel, O., *TDNT* V, 151–3; Reumann*, 156.

[21] Clement Alex., *Paed* 1.8.64.3; 70.1.

[22] NIV; Brox, 103; Kelly, 45; Dibelius-Conzelmann, 17f.; Fee, 42; Knoch, 20; Merkel, 19; Arichea-Hatton, 17; cf. the usage in Eph 1.10; 3.2, 9.

[23] Cf. 1 Cor 9.17; 4.1; Col 1.25; White, 93; Parry, 3; Scott, 9; Spicq, 323f.; Hasler, 13; Roloff, 66; Lips 1979:145–7.

The false teachers do not in fact carry out, or by teaching false doctrine fail to carry out, the kind of responsibility given to stewards in God's household. Their influence is disruptive and they constitute a liability to the welfare of the οἶκος θεοῦ (see esp. Lips 1979:145–7; Verner 1983). This corresponds well with the issues of what constitutes legitimate teachers and teaching addressed in this passage and throughout 1 Timothy (cf. Tit 1.7).

The emphatic phrase which closes the sentence, τὴν ἐν πίστει, creates still more distance between the activities of the false teachers and authentic Christian ministry.[24] The point is that such administration of the church is ἐν πίστει. The phrase has the appearance of being rather formal (cf. 2 Tim 1.13), but the force is by no means formal (pace Brox, 103): such administration takes place only through the faithfulness which genuine faith in Christ produces in the leader (i.e. a good steward; cf. Tit 1.7; see **Excursus 4**) and is completely unlike the kind of spirit which leads to disputes (cf. Lock, 10; Roloff, 66).[25]

5. τὸ δὲ τέλος τῆς παραγγελίας ἐστὶν ἀγάπη ἐκ καθαρᾶς καρδίας καὶ συνειδήσεως ἀγαθῆς καὶ πιστέως ἀνυποκρίτου With this verse the author changes his apparent direction of thought, and the intended sentence structure in 1.3–4 is lost as a new sentence begins. Over against the erroneous teaching of the opponents he wants to indicate what is the nature of proper instruction in the church and thereby to show how they went astray. In effect he is explaining the nature of the οἰκονομία committed to Timothy. The δέ is thus adversative and leads to a fresh thought.

In contrast to the results of the myths and genealogies, 'the command' achieves a very different goal (τέλος**). τέλος can be the factual result of an action or, as here, its purpose or goal.[26]

But to what 'command', does the author refer? παραγγελία (1.18**; Acts 5.28; 16.24; 1 Th 4.2***) has been taken in three ways. (a) It refers back to the command in 1.3, the specific instructions for ministry given to Timothy. The effect of forbidding the false teachers to give teaching which causes dissension will be to promote love in the church.[27] (b) It refers more

---

[24] It is not uncommon to find a qualification attached to a noun with the article as here, although the noun itself is anarthrous. According to BD § 269³ the article is necessary when a genitive intervenes. MHT III, 185f. comments that the combination noun-article-attribute is Hellenistic; cf. Lk 23.49; Jn 14.27; 2 Tim 1.13. See also Tit 1.1 note.

[25] It is possible that the anarthrous πίστει means 'the faith' (White, 93; cf. Oberlinner, 15f.: almost 'orthodoxy') rather than 'faith'.

[26] Delling, G., TDNT VIII, 49–56, espec. 54.

[27] Spicq, 324; Schlatter, 39; Hanson, 57; Schmitz, O., TDNT V, 761–5 (764 n. 33); Fee, 42.

generally to apostolic exhortation and defines the goal of preaching.[28] Brox, 103, insists on this meaning, though recognising that preaching may include discipline. (c) Roloff, 66, takes a third course, which combines the two ideas, thus taking the term as a reference to the binding instruction of the office of the church leader which issues in teaching and preaching; in v. 3 a specific, limited aspect of this broader function is emphasised, while the reference in v. 5 is general (cf. Oberlinner, 16).

The points made by Brox and Roloff are obviously correct enough as general principles, but the context favours (a) as the line of thought. To adopt (b) or (c) requires that the author has digressed from instructing Timothy to make a parenthetical comment about ministry in general, but v. 5 makes perfect sense as a continuation of the command to Timothy; it is also not clear that the word can be generalised to lose its specific sense of 'command'. There is also the question of the degree to which the author intends to present 'Timothy' here as a model of the church official, an aspect which both Brox and Roloff place high on the author's agenda. παραγγελία in 1.18 may refer to the commands or instructions of the whole letter, or be a summary reference back to the initial command of 1.3–4, but in either case specific instruction from the apostle is meant, and here the reference is to Paul's command to Timothy.

What follows is in effect a list of four qualities which define the 'goal' (cf. 1.19; 2.15; 4.12). Hasler, 13, suggests that the language of Christian piety here expresses itself in lists of virtues and vices, taken from the emancipated synagogue and from Stoic-Cynic wandering teachers. While this may explain the source of the language (and form), the theological understanding of the language as the author applies it must be noted.

ἀγάπη sums up the quality which should result from obeying Paul's command – or perhaps from obedience to the gospel message as a whole. It is thus to some extent a criterion of correct preaching (Schneider, G., *EDNT* I, 11). For a similar thought see Gal 5.6. It stands in contrast to the strife and consequent division in the church which results from false teaching (Hasler, 13). The active exercise of love is what is meant here (Dibelius-Conzelmann, 16). The context suggests that mutual love in the church, leading to a peaceful and harmonious atmosphere, is in mind. In its other nine appearances in the PE[29] ἀγάπη occurs as one of a list of qualities and (in all but 2 Tim 1.7) in close proximity to πίστις. 2 Tim 1.7 links this quality

[28] Dibelius-Conzelmann, 15; Knight, 76; Merkel 19; BA notes that the word almost means 'preaching'.
[29] 1.5, 14; 2.15; 4.12; 6.11; 2 Tim 1.7, 13; 2.22; 3.10; Tit 2.2**.

to the indwelling Spirit, and here its link is to conversion and the authentic Christian faith. For the relation of love to faith and the influence of a paraenetic tradition known by the earlier Paul, see Tit 2.2 note.

The source (ἐκ) of such love is in the inward personality, which is described by means of three expressions, the first of which is the 'cleansed heart'. The expression καθαρὰ καρδία occurs here and in 2 Tim 2.22 and represents the inward perspective of Christian existence in its totality. καρδία (2 Tim 2.22**) is the seat of personality, the 'self', the origin of desires and emotions, the seat of intentions.[30] It is particularly seen as the aspect of being which is directed to or away from God. Hence worship is done 'from the heart' (LXX Deut 4.29; 10.12; 11.13), and a 'pure' heart (καθαρός, Tit 1.15 note) is one which is not defiled by sin and self-seeking. It is 'cleansed from past sin and wholeheartedly directed to God' (Hauck, F., *TDNT* III, 425). See especially Ps 51.10; Gn 20.5f.; Ps 24.4; Mt 5.8. The language of cleansing is rooted in baptismal tradition (cf. Tit 2.14; Heb 10.22; 1 Pet 3.21; Roloff, 67f.).

καὶ συνειδήσεως ἀγάθης (1.19; Acts 23.1; 1 Pet 3.16, 21; cf. Heb 13.18) describes the second dimension of the inner person as depicted here (**Excursus 5**). Heart and conscience are almost synonymous terms (cf. 2 Tim 1.3 and 2.22). Here, however, they must be differentiated, and, if the heart is the origin of desires, the conscience functions to direct, evaluate and control behaviour along lines set by given norms. The qualification 'good' shows that the conscience is viewed from a theological perspective; that is, the interest is in the condition of the conscience which acceptance of the gospel determines. The connections suggest that ἀγάπη (love acted out in service done for others) results in part from the effective conscience, which makes morally good decisions leading to godly conduct and can do so because of one's commitment to the apostolic faith. For ἀγαθός see Tit 1.16 note.

From aspects of personality the author turns to the category of faith to complete the triad: καὶ πίστεως ἀνυποκρίτου (**Excursus 4**). Clearly it is the whole attitude of the Christian which is in mind here, and this attitude is seen as one determined by trust in God and commitment to him. This Christian faith-attitude is to be ἀνυπόκριτος (2 Tim 1.5; Rom 12.9; 2 Cor 6.6 [both times of love]; Jas 3.17; 1 Pet 1.22***), 'free from pretence', hence 'whole-hearted' in the sense that one does not believe in God (or profess to do so) and behave in an inconsistent manner,

---

[30] Baumgärtel, F., and Behm, J., *TDNT* III, 605–14; Sorg, T., *NIDNTT* II, 180–4; Jewett 1971:448; Lips 1979:65f.

and consequently 'authentic' (*TLNT* I, 134–6; III, 412f.). The word is found for the first time in the LXX (Wis 5.18; 18.15), and signifies the avoiding of deceit and dissembling. Wilckens, U., *TDNT* IX, 570f., argues that the word is used in connection with a concept of faith as orthodox belief: πίστις here denotes orthodoxy or fidelity to the tradition, so that the attribute ἀνυπόκριτος can be combined with it', and thus heresy is hypocrisy. This interpretation seems to be read into the PE, and it seems more likely that the reference is to a single-minded commitment to God. The phrase is nevertheless intended to be descriptive of the true believer in contrast to the false (cf. 4.2), and takes its place alongside 'good conscience' and 'cleansed heart' (Lips 1979:66–8). Dibelius-Conzelmann, 16, find in the inclusion of faith in a triad like this (other than the Pauline, faith, hope and love) the evidence that it is becoming one of the Christian virtues rather than the mainspring of the Christian life (cf. Oberlinner, 17f.). This is unlikely after the decisive references in 1.2 and 4. Faith is rather concerned with upright piety (Hasler, 13).

6. ὧν τινες ἀστοχήσαντες ἐξετράπησαν εἰς ματαιολογίαν Having stated positively the Christian qualities, the writer goes on to describe the people who have rejected them. There is clearly a polemical statement being made here, indirectly through Timothy. The contrast is drawn between responsible teaching and those (the derogatory τινες, see 1.3 and note) who have rejected these things (ὧν[31]). The process of apostasy is described, in terms which become characteristic in the PE, as following a pattern: (a) There is a rejection of the normative faith or aspects of it; (b) this leads to or causes deviation; and (c) it manifests itself in false teaching.

The verbs belong to the author's polemical repertoire. ἀστοχέω in each of its three occurrences in the PE (6.21; 2 Tim 2.18***) alludes to the heretics' mistakes regarding the true faith. Here with the gen. ὧν the thought is 'to depart from' (cf. Ecclus 7.19; 8.9; 2 Clement 17.7). The heretics ignore the means that could help them to the right goal of love (Spicq, 328). Instead they turn away from the right path. ἐκτρέπομαι in the PE is applied exclusively to the change in direction that adherence to the false teaching produces (5.15; 6.20; 2 Tim 4.4; cf. Heb 12.13***; for the thought cf. Jas 5.20; 2 Pet 2.15; cf. Simpson, 29). Synonymous terms describe the same process in 1.19; 4.1; 5.15; 2 Tim 4.4.

The result (εἰς) of such rejection of the faith is false teaching. ματαιολογία*** (Polycarp, *Phil.* 2.1) places the heretical

---

[31] For the use of the rel. pron. in this way as a link see cf. 1.19b, 20; 2.7; 6.4, 10; 2 Tim 2.17.

speculation into the category of things which are futile because they are pagan (see Tit 1.10 note; Hos 5.11; Isa 2.20; Jer 2.5). It belongs to the battery of terms used to denounce the false teaching as 'vain, empty talk'.[32] The attitude described in 1.4 is thus traced back to a rejection of basic Christian commitment. To the degree that a process is envisaged, 'empty talk' characterises false teaching generally. In Ephesus it is specifically the myths and genealogies, which the heretics regard as a way of salvation and edification, which are denounced as in fact contradictory to the gospel (Hasler, 14).

7. θέλοντες εἶναι νομοδιδάσκαλοι, μὴ νοοῦντες μήτε ἃ λέγουσιν μήτε περὶ τίνων διαβεβαιοῦνται The participial phrase closes this part of the caricature of the false teachers with an ironic jab (cf. Roloff, 71; Schlarb 1990:91). It is loosely attached. The motivation (θέλω, 2.4; 5.11; 2 Tim 3.12**) of the heretics is 'to be teachers of the law'. The force created by the following negatives is almost concessive: 'although they want to be teachers, they understand neither what they say nor the things about which they speak with confidence', and so it is not surprising that their efforts produce empty talk. Although Schlarb 1990:91 suggests that θέλοντες εἶναι νομοδιδάσκαλοι might indicate that the false teachers were not Jews or Jewish Christians (in contrast to the situation in Crete), the point of the irony is that what they claim (or desire) is denied by their actual behaviour and ignorance (Roloff, 71; cf. Tit 1.16).

According to Rengstorf, K. H., *TDNT* II, 159, νομοδιδάσκαλος is 'a Christian construction designed to mark off Jewish from Christian teachers at the decisive point, namely the absolutising of the νόμος'. The term is used of Jewish teachers in Lk 5.17; Acts 5.34***, and is found only in Christian writings.[33] It is possible, therefore, that from the perspective of the Christian community the term would be derogatory and polemical and may not have been a self-designation of the heretics (Roloff, 71). It indicates, nevertheless, that the OT law plays a special role in the false teaching. Whether they would use the term of themselves or not, these people want to have a role like that of Jewish teachers by teaching the law in the church.

---

[32] Cf. ματαιολόγος, Tit 1.10 and note; βέβηλος, 1 Tim 1.9; 4.7; 6.20; 2 Tim 2.16; κενοφωνία, 1 Tim 6.20; 2 Tim 2.16; μωροὶ ζητήσεις, 2 Tim 2.23; Tit 3.9; ἀνωφελής, μάταιος, Tit 3.9; ἀπαίδευτος, 2 Tim 2.23; γραώδης, 1 Tim 4.7; ἀντιθέσεις, 1 Tim 6.20; ἐντολαὶ ἀνθρώπων, Tit 1.14; the thought is found in Rom 1.21; see esp. Schlarb 1990:59–73; Roloff, 70; Brox, 104; Bauernfeind, O., *TDNT* IV, 519–24, esp. 524.

[33] Cf. νομοδιδάκτης, used by Plutarch, *Cat. Ma.* 20.4.

The emphasis lies on the participial phrase μὴ νοοῦντες..., which explains the lack of qualifications of the heretics.[34] Even if their aim of teaching the law was a good one, they are incapable of fulfilling it because of their lack of understanding, which may be the result of rejection of the faith and is therefore culpable (Tit 1.15 note).

The double negative, μήτε ... μήτε...** (only 2 Th 2.2 in the Pauline corpus), is for rhetorical effect and stresses the totality of the ignorance of the teachers; the progression from 'saying' to 'insistently professing' (διαβεβαιόομαι, Tit 3.8***) further strengthens the condemnation.[35] They do not even know the meaning of what they are saying, let alone teaching, as doctrine.[36]

b. The true purpose of the law (1.8–11)

Westerholm, S., 'The Law and the "Just Man" (1 Tim 1,3–11)', *ST* 36 (1982), 79–95.

Vv. 3–7 formed a rounded section complete in itself, but it raised a problem. The condemnation of those who wished to be teachers of the law (νομοδιδάσκαλοι) could be regarded as implying criticism of the law itself (νόμος). The writer, therefore, proceeds to comment that, however much the law is misunderstood by his opponents, it is basically good, provided that it is properly understood and used as a means of bringing into the open whatever is evil in human conduct. In fact, it is taken in under the umbrella of the gospel in that it stands alongside specifically Christian teaching as a statement of divine standards. When the writer states that the law is not for the righteous person, he means that it does not condemn believers who live godly lives and was not laid down to bind them; his comments are made particularly in the context of the misuse of the law by his opponents who were applying some aspects of the law, as they misunderstood it, to Christians, and they are not intended to give a full account of its positive use. In fact, the law plays

[34] For νοέω, 'to understand' cf. 2 Tim 2.7**; Behm, J., *TDNT* IV, 948–51. For the theme of ignorance cf. Tit 1.15 note; 1 Tim 6.4, 20; 2 Tim 2.23; Tit 3.9; cf. 2 Tim 3.7 (Fee, 44).

[35] Spicq, 330, cites Job 35.16; 36.2; Philo, *Det.* 18 as examples of people not knowing what they profess to know or teach. Hort (WH *Notes*, 167) argued that the form of the verb διαβεβαιόομαι here is really subjunctive, but MHT II, 200, argues that the indicative here gives just as good a sense.

[36] ἅ is the usual abbreviation for ταῦτα ἅ. Similarly ταῦτα should be supplied with περὶ τίνων, but Barrett, 42, suggests that the antecedent is masculine and the force of the relative clause is 'they talk about the Law, but apply it to the wrong persons'. τίνων is an example of the interrogative pronoun being used for the relative pronoun (MHT III, 49; cf. BD §298[4]). BD §293[5] notes that after a verb of knowing both interrogative and relative clauses are possible.

no part elsewhere in the PE (cf. Oberlinner, 22f.). Following Baur, Lütgert 1909:8–30 argued that the justification of the law given here is directed against antinomian opponents who claimed emancipation from the law; but if so, why are they categorised as 'teachers of the law'?

TEXT

8. αὐτῷ αὐτόν (P 1149 vg Aug). Elliott, 21, argues that the dat. is an Atticist correction (cf. 5.23). But the MS evidence for the variant is too weak, and the dat. is found without variants at 1 Cor 9.12, 15.

χρῆται χρήσηται (A P Cl). ἐάν is found with both the pres. (3.15; 2 Tim 2.5) and aor. subj. (2.15; 2 Tim 2.5, 21) in the PE. Elliott, 21, argues that the scribal tendency was to change from the pres. to the aor.

10. ἐπιόρκοις ἐφιόρκοις (D* P). Elliott, 24, notes that the variant is Hellenistic (MHT II, 314) and regards it as original. But the MS evidence is weak.

11. κατὰ τὸ εὐαγγέλιον Praem. τῇ (D* H 263; cf. *quae* d f g vg). Elliott, 16, argues that recapitulation of the article is characteristic of PE, and therefore adopts the variant. The MS evidence is weak.

EXEGESIS

8. οἴδαμεν δὲ ὅτι καλὸς ὁ νόμος The polemic against the opponents is indirect; neither the basis of the wrong estimation of the law, nor the reason that it is false is explained (Roloff, 72). This indirect argument is understandable in view of the *prima facie* recipient of the letter. The teaching given represents the church's understanding of the law, which, in keeping with the purpose of the letter, is expressed by citing two Pauline statements, and introduced as common teaching tradition, in each case, with the οἴδαμεν ὅτι (εἰδὼς [τοῦτο] ὅτι) formula (Roloff, 72).

An appeal to commonly accepted tradition, particularly when it is the authoritative apostolic tradition from which the heretics have departed, is one way to discredit the false teaching. οἴδαμεν ὅτι is a phrase found frequently in Paul.[37] The general force is

---

[37] The same form as here with δέ is found in Rom 2.2; 3.9; 8.28 (2 pl., Phil 4.15). The participial form εἰδότες [δὲ] ὅτι comes in Rom 5.3; 6.9; 1 Cor 15.58; 2 Cor 1.7; 4.14; 5.6; Gal 2.16; Eph 6.8, 9; Phil 1.16; Col 3.24; 4.1. It occurs with γάρ in Rom 7.14; 8.22 (sing., 15.29); 2 Cor 5.1; and it comes in the question form οὐκ οἴδατε ὅτι in Rom 6.16; 11.2 (without ὅτι); 1 Cor 3.16; 5.6; 6.2, 3, 9, · 15, 16, 19; 9.13, 24. Note also οἴδαμεν ὅτι, 1 Cor 8.1, 4; (sing., Phil 1.19, 25); οἴδατε δὲ ὅτι, 1 Cor 12.2; Gal 4.13; 1 Th 4.2; (with γάρ, 5.2). The participial form is used in the PE (εἰδὼς [τοῦτο] ὅτι, 1.9; 2 Tim 2.23; Tit 3.11; Philem 21; οἶδας τοῦτο ὅτι is also found in 2 Tim 1.15). The phrase is, however, not peculiar to Paul: see Jas 3.1; 4.4; 1 Pet 1.18; 2 Pet 1.14; 1 Jn 3.2, 5, 14, 15; 5.15, 18, 19, 20; 3 Jn 12.

The use of the first person plural is somewhat infrequent in the PE. It is used where the writer includes his readers in statements (1 Tim 1.1f.; 2.2f.; 4.10; 6.7f., 17; 2 Tim 1.2, 7–10, 14; 2.11–13; Tit 1.4; 2.11–14; 3.3–7, 14) and in Tit 3.15.

to indicate something that is known both to the writer and to the readers, although it may also be used as a means of teaching by giving them the benefit of the doubt. Perhaps it is similar to our English persuasive phrase: 'This is what you ought to do, don't you think?' It would be unwise, therefore, to deduce in all cases that the statement which is made represents knowledge already held or insight fully understood by the readers, but that such knowledge should be so embraced is implicit. The effect, in any case, is to introduce what is to some extent a concession (Holtzmann, 295; White, 94).

νόμος (1.9*) must surely refer in the context of the preceding verse primarily to the Jewish law as expressed in the OT (most commentators; Oberlinner, 24f.). Although v.9 possibly conceives of law in a general sense as the civil and moral law of the ruling State,[38] it is not necessary to generalise the meaning here.[39] The description employs a term used frequently in the PE: καλός (**Excursus 6**). Applied to the law, καλός indicates that it is useful and leads to good results (cf. Lock, 22f.), but in the light of usage elsewhere there may be the implication of its divine origin and status (1.18; 2.3; 2 Tim 4.7; *et al.*).

The statement καλὸς ὁ νόμος, which introduces the apostolic response to the heretical use of the OT law, affirms its moral usefulness, and does so in a way that the earlier Paul might have done. What is said here stands over against the subsequent denigration of the OT law by Marcion and Gnostics (cf. Oberlinner, 24). It could have fitted easily into the discussion of Rom 7.12–25. In Rom 7.16 the very similar statement (concerning function and purpose), σύμφημι τῷ νόμῳ ὅτι καλός, is made by Paul as a recognition that what the law commands is morally right. There the law is also called ἅγιος (v.12) and πνευματικός (v.14).

Hanson, 58–9, maintains that 1 Tim 1.8 intends an echo of such Pauline statements but that the author betrays his divergence from Paul in the qualification that follows (cf. Merkel, 19). Roloff, 73, claims that instead of the law being considered from the standpoint of its meaning in the light of the Christ-event, it is viewed in terms of its correct use; instead of corresponding to the Torah of Israel, the author has in view law as the category of norms which direct human life, of which the OT law is a special case. Understanding law in this broader sense, even if it is couched in the terms of Pauline theology, is a reflection of the line of thought the church would follow in its Hellenistic environment, where, under the influence of popular

[38] Cf. Roloff, 73; Knoch, 20; Merkel, 19.
[39] *Pace* Hasler, 14.

philosophy and without specific relation to the Jew/Gentile question, anything but a positive affirmation of the law would amount to the negation of creation. Apparently Roloff (and others) would have expected a genuine Pauline answer to would-be 'teachers of the law' to start from the same bases that Paul did in Romans or Galatians, where the notion of righteousness through the law was addressed on the basis of salvation history and from the perspective of the Christ-event (Rom 10.4; Gal 2.19–21; 3.19–25). But in those instances, and particularly in the Galatian church, the discussion centred on problems and 'judaising' misunderstandings of the law. In 1 Timothy the misuse of the law (vv. 4, 6) seems most unlike that addressed in Galatians and Romans. In view of the differences, it is arguable that the only aspect of the earlier arguments relevant to this discussion would have been those related to the law's proper function and purpose, and it is here that the argument of 1 Tim 1.8 is most Pauline.

ἐάν τις αὐτῷ νομίμως χρῆται ἐάν has almost the force of 'provided that'.[40] The clause reveals that it was the application of the law that was in mind in the previous statement. In this context χράομαι is, strictly speaking, raising the issue of the 'use' of the law (i.e. 'to apply' it in order to regulate the life of the community) rather than that of the 'observance' of law.[41] The adverb νομίμως (2 Tim 2.5***) further defines the issue as one of 'appropriate' use of the law. νομίμως can mean 'in accordance with the law';[42] But here where 'the law' is the object of χρῆται, 'appropriately' makes better sense.[43]

But what is the appropriate way? The author appears to suggest in v. 9 that it is inappropriate to use the law to regulate the life of the righteous but correct to use it to regulate the life of the unrighteous. More to the point, perhaps, is a concern to use it as law (i.e. as it is meant to be used) rather than as a source of speculative thinking which produces ascetic rules for spiritual living (cf. Fee, 10).

9a. εἰδώς τοῦτο, ὅτι δικαίῳ νόμος οὐ κεῖται The participial phrase εἰδώς τοῦτο[44] qualifies τις in v. 8 and introduces the definition of 'appropriate' use: the way to use the law correctly is by knowing that it is not for the righteous (the content of τοῦτο).

---

[40] The use of ἐάν with subj. rather than εἰ with indic. is probably not significant. τις means 'anybody', equivalent to our vague 'you' or French 'on'.
[41] Cf. Euripides, *Hipp.* 98; Josephus, *Ant.* 16.27; see Sand, A., *EDNT* III, 471f.
[42] As a description of how the Jews behave (Josephus, *Ap.* 2.152, 318; 4 Macc 6.18).
[43] Cf. Gutbrod, W., *TDNT* IV, 1088f.
[44] For εἰδώς cf. 2 Tim 2.23; 3.14; Tit 3.11; Paul uses it in Philem 21, and frequently in the pl.; for the use of τοῦτο cf. 2 Tim 1.15; Eph 5.5.

Viewed from the perspective of its condemnatory purpose, the law was not 'set up' to bind the righteous.[45] For the righteous person (δίκαιος, 2 Tim 4.8; Tit 1.8** and note) is the person who keeps the law and does not need to be told what to do; the concept of being justified by faith is not in view.[46] The principle here expressed could be true generally of any law-abiding citizen, but it may be used to describe true believers as they ideally are (see especially the theological orientation given to the concept in Tit 2.12). They keep God's law from the heart. The word can be used to refer to Christians (Heb 12.23; 1 Pet 3.12 ; 4.18, using OT language). Such is the view of Westerholm*, who holds that the heretics used the law as a basis for speculation and for asceticism. The author also holds the law in high regard (2 Tim 3.15f.), but he sees it as having a different purpose. It is for those who oppose the gospel. The sentiment is expressed in Hellenistic terms and has parallels in Greek thought, where the idea that the good man does not need the law is present. Commentators have drawn attention to the belief in a golden age when there was no law because none was needed, and the general idea was proverbial.[47]

Roloff, 73f., however, suggests that δικαίῳ νόμος οὐ κεῖται is an attempt to understand the situation through the lens of Pauline tradition, by means of a free adaptation of something like Rom 3.21, 29. Paul argued that righteousness was apart from the law, but the false teachers argued that the law, or rather their speculative understanding of it, was essential to the believer. Nevertheless, in applying the Pauline teaching, the salvation-historical understanding of the law is lost, resulting in the formulation of a static universal rule and a moralising of the gospel (Roloff, 74). But it is doubtful that the phrase is a conscious reflection back on Pauline statements (cf. Oberlinner, 31). Rather, in this context, there is a specific allusion to the false teachers' misunderstanding of the OT law (v. 8) followed by a universal reference to law in general (v. 9) so as to create the broadest possible denunciation of the opponents.

9b–10 consist of a so-called vice list (in actuality a list of sinners) inserted to describe the sort of people to whom the

---

[45] κεῖμαι as the passive of τίθημι has the sense 'to be enacted', or 'to be valid, have legal existence' (2 Macc 4.11; Philo, *Det.* 18; Büchsel, F., *TDNT* III, 654). The dat. δικαίῳ is thus one of interest.

[46] *Pace* Kelly, 49; Spicq, 332. For Lock, 11, the righteous person is one in whom the true love of God has been created. See also Merkel, 19.

[47] Tacitus, *Ann.* 3.26; Ovid, *Metam.* 1.89f.; Antiphanes, *Frg.* 288 (attributed by Simpson, 30, to Menander). Cf. Dibelius-Conzelmann, 22; Spicq, 332; Roloff, 74 n. 99; Oberlinner, 25.

law applies.[48] The law was established to forbid these kinds of activities and therefore is correctly applied to people inclined to them.

In form, the list includes four pairs of sinners, followed by a further series of six single items. It consists of types of sinners who would in general be condemned by Jews and pagans alike. It contains an inventory of persons guilty of severe and shocking crimes such as would be included in a criminal code, and is therefore certainly not to be specifically applied to the readers.

The function of the list may be twofold, given that the author's intention is both to instruct his readers and to denounce the opponents. On the one hand, the list supports the argument about the proper use of the law: the vices are so far removed from the readers' way of life as to demonstrate the irrelevance of the law for them (cf. Hasler, 15). On the other hand, the list may also have some polemical force. In this case, the vices are to be associated in some way with the heretics' teaching. Either it is applied for effect as a sort of 'poster' to create a strongly repulsive stereotype,[49] or it lays the blame for committing such crimes upon the false teachers who distort the law (McEleney 1974:210). In either case, the polemical application is made only at the end of the list where conformity to the 'sound teaching' is mentioned and the attack is not as direct as in 6.4f. The point intended is probably that the false teachers stand alongside such criminals and ironically are condemned by the law they seek to teach. Those who follow their teaching may finally end up in such evil deeds (Oberlinner, 27).

A broad correlation with the commandments in the decalogue (cf. *Didache* 2),[50] has been proposed, as follows:

Introductory (disobedient and insubordinate)

(1) godless (not honouring God)
(2) sinful (worshipping idols)
(3) impious (not respecting God's name)
(4) profane (not keeping the Sabbath holy)
(5) dishonourers of parents
(6) murderers
(7) adulterers, homosexuals[51]

---

[48] See Tit 1.5–9 note.

[49] Dibelius-Conzelmann, 23; Karris 1973:557; Haufe 1973:336.

[50] See especially Nauck 1950:8–16. A hint is given by Bengel and was taken up by nineteenth-century commentators (Ellicott, 11). The allusion is questioned by White, 95; Merkel, 20.

[51] The order of the sixth (murder) and seventh (adultery) commandments varies in the sources. The reverse order (adultery; murder) is found in some MSS of the LXX (Exod 20 20.13–15 B; Deut 5. 17f. B); Philo, *Decal.* 121, 132, 168–70; Lk 18.20; Rom 13.9; Jas 2.11.

(8) enslavers (stealing people)
(9) liars, perjurers
(10) (covetous – omitted)[52]

The correspondence is clearest for nos. 5–9 (Nauck 1950:8–16). The individual correlations suggested for nos. 1–4 are those proposed by Knight, 84, but they have not found supporters, and it is preferable simply to see a general correlation between the list here and the dishonouring of God in the first four commandments (Oberlinner, 27). But it is clear that the list has been developed considerably from the inspiration given by the decalogue. Dibelius-Conzelmann, 23, claim that the list as a whole represents a Christianisation of Hellenistic-Jewish paraenesis.[53]

ἀνόμοις δὲ καὶ ἀνυποτάκτοις The first pair depicts rebelliousness. ἄνομος is 'disobedient to the law' (used of criminals in Lk 22.37 = Isa 53.12), especially of disobedience to God's law (1 Cor 9.21; cf. 2 Th 2.8; Acts 2.23); it can even refer to people who do not keep the law because they are ignorant of it, but here the idea is of behaving as if there were no law or no concern for the law.[54] ἀνυπότακτος (see Tit 1.6 and note, 10; Heb 2.8***) means 'insubordinate', used of the person who refuses to be subject to a higher authority. Both words convey the idea of disobedience to God. For subordination as a feature commended in the PE see 2.11; 3.4; Tit 2.5, 9; 3.1. Thus this type of behaviour is that which is especially attacked in the PE because it leads to other vices (Oberlinner, 28).

ἀσεβέσι καὶ ἁμαρτωλοῖς ἀσεβής, 'godless, impious', is often linked with ἁμαρτωλός, 'sinful', to refer to people who flout God's authority, deny his existence, and thus are sinful.[55] For ἁμαρτωλός cf. 1.15; Tit 3.11** note.

ἀνοσίοις καὶ βεβήλοις ἀνόσιος (2 Tim 3.2***) is 'unholy, wicked', used especially of those who do not practise religious rites or appropriate conduct.[56] βέβηλος is 'accessible to everyone', hence 'profane' as opposed to sacred, and hence unhallowed, unholy in character, of things which are unholy (4.7; 6.20; 2 Tim 2.16) and here of people who despise God and blaspheme his name (Heb 12.16***).[57]

---

[52] Note how Paul omits the ninth commandment in Rom 13.9.
[53] The various vices can be paralleled in Hellenistic sources (Merkel, 20); Deissmann 1927:317 gives an interesting parallel from Plautus, *Pseudolus*, 357–68, where a pander is attacked abusively.
[54] See Gutbrod, W., *TDNT* IV, 1086f.
[55] Jude 15b; 1 Pet 4.18 = Prov 11.31 LXX. Cf. Rom 4.5; 2 Pet 2.5, 6 [?]; 3.7; Jude 4, 15a***; see further Tit 2.12 note; 2 Tim 2.16.
[56] Cf. Hauck, F., *TDNT* V, 492.
[57] See Hauck, F., *TDNT* I, 604f.; *TLNT* I, 284–6.

The whole description so far is given in general terms of people who flout God's authority and openly act against his holiness. Now the writer moves to specific types of sinner.

πατρολῴαις καὶ μητρολῴαις πατρολῴας*** and μητρολῴας*** are usually taken to refer to 'parricides' and 'matricides' respectively.[58] If so, this is the extreme form of disobedience to the fifth commandment. Some commentators pay attention to the etymological meaning of the nouns (from ἀλοάω, 'to smite') and hold that the dishonouring of parents is what is meant (Ellicott, 11; Bernard, 27; Simpson, 31; Knight, 85; *pace* White, 95).

ἀνδροφόνοις (10.) πόρνοις ἀρσενοκοίταις ἀνδραποδισταῖς ψεύσταις ἐπιόρκοις ἀνδροφόνος*** is 'murderer' or 'assassin' (2 Macc 9.28; Philo, *Spec.* 3.84 *et al.*).

πόρνος is a person guilty of sexual immorality, usually an adulterer or fornicator.[59] In Cl. Gk. it could mean a male prostitute, but this specialised reference is excluded here. ἀρσενοκοίτης (1 Cor 6.9***; Polycarp 5.3) is a rare word meaning 'homosexual'. Cf. Rom 1.27.[60]

ἀνδραποδιστής*** is 'slave dealer, kidnapper'. Philo distinguished the kidnapper as the worst of thieves: κλέπτης δέ τίς ἐστι καὶ ὁ ἀνδραποδιστής, ἀλλὰ τοῦ πάντων ἀρίστου, ὅσα ἐπὶ γῆς εἶναι συμβέβηκεν (*Spec.* 4.130). Rabbinic exegesis distinguished between theft of things and the kidnapping of people and understood the eighth commandment as applying to the latter.[61]

ψεύστης (Tit 1.12 and note), 'liar', and the more specific category of liar, ἐπίορκος***, 'perjurer' (a person who takes an oath and then breaks it), are categories with a traditional connection (cf. Lev 19.11f.) known in the Hellenistic-Jewish ethical lists.[62]

As in Rom 13.9 (Nauck 1950:13), there is nothing equivalent to the tenth commandment, which refers to conduct that is not usually susceptible to law. The omission of 'those who covet', in

---

[58] The words are also found in the forms πατραλοίας (Josephus, *Ant.* 16.356) and πατραλῴας and μητραλῴας or μητραλοίας respectively (BD § 26; § 35²; § 119²; MHT II, 68). For the pairing see Plato, *Phaed.* 114a; Lysias, 10.8.

[59] 1 Cor 5.9, 10, 11; 6.9; Eph 5.5; Heb 12.16; 13.4; Rev 21.8; 22.15. See Hauck, F., and Schulz, S., *TDNT* VI, 579–95.

[60] Wright, D. F., 'Homosexuals or Prostitutes: The Meaning of ΑΡΣΕΝΟΚΟΙΤΑΙ (1 Cor 6:9; 1 Tim 1:10)', *VC* 38 (1984), 125–53; Petersen, W. L., 'Can ΑΡΣΕΝΟΚΟΙΤΑΙ be translated by "Homosexuals"? (1 Cor 6:9; 1 Tim 1:10)', *VC* 40 (1986), 187–91; Wright, D. F., 'Translating ΑΡΣΕΝΟΚΟΙΤΑΙ (1 Cor. 6:9; 1 Tim 1:10)', *VC* 41 (1987), 396–8. The verb is attested in *Sib. Orac.* 2.73.

[61] *Mek. Exod.* 77b on Exod 20.15 (see SB I, 810–13; Jeremias, 14). Here the term does not mean 'procurer' (a possibility listed by BA).

[62] Wis 19.25; Philo, *Spec.* 1.235; cf. Roloff, 77.

the midst of a list setting out specific actions, might be due to the general nature of covetousness (Roloff, 77).

καὶ εἴ τι ἕτερον τῇ ὑγιαινούσῃ διδασκαλίᾳ ἀντίκειται The phrase καὶ εἴ τι ἕτερον ... is added loosely *ad sensum*. It provides a blanket 'catch-all' conclusion which parallels Rom 13.9 (καὶ εἴ τις ἑτέρα ἐντολή...), and thus appears to be a stock phrase.[63] The effect of the phrase, however, is to bring the thought back to the polemical contrast between the Pauline co-workers and their message and the teaching of the opponents. It also serves to link together the law and the gospel (Stott, 50).

This movement is carried out mainly by the reference to 'the sound teaching'. ὑγιαίνουσα διδασκαλία (Tit 1.9 note) is a technical term in the PE for the approved, apostolic doctrine. The dominant use of the sing. διδασκαλία in the PE (14 times) reflects an emphasis on the concept of a fixed body of Christian doctrine (already present elsewhere in the NT). In the plural (1 Tim 4.1), the term denotes the false teaching. The addition of the participle ὑγιαινούσα converts the term into a polemical reference to the true and reliable teaching of the apostle which is constructive and edifying for those who accept it. The false teaching is conversely unreliable and destructive to the faith of believers (2 Tim 2.17; 1 Tim 6.4). And the general phrase τι ἕτερον will have been intended to include the current false doctrine (vv. 4, 6) which stands in opposition[64] to the apostolic teaching (cf. Lips 1979:48).

11. κατὰ τὸ εὐαγγέλιον τῆς δόξης τοῦ μακαρίου θεοῦ At this point in the argument, the transition from 'the law' to 'the sound teaching' develops into an even sharper contrast as the apostle and his reception of the gospel are introduced (cf. Wolter 1988:27; Collins 1975:166). The κατά phrase may be loosely attached but it nevertheless grounds the corrective teaching just given on the authoritative Pauline gospel. It can be linked:

(a) to 'the sound teaching' (Knight, 89f.); in this case it defines what is meant by sound teaching, i.e. that which is in accordance with the gospel handed down via Paul in the church. The variant reading, which repeats τῇ for clarification (see above), suggests that some understood it this way.

(b) broadly to 1.8–10 (White, 96; Lock, 13; Brox, 108; Spicq, 336; Roloff, 79); in this case the meaning is that the whole understanding of the correct use of the law just expounded corresponds to the gospel entrusted to Paul.

(c) even more broadly to 1.3–10 (Karris, 54).

---

[63] ἕτερος is also used at 2 Tim 2.2**.
[64] For ἀντίκειμαι see 5.14; 1 Cor 16.9; Gal 5.17; Phil 1.28; 2 Th 2.4; Lk 13.17; 21.15***; *TLNT* I, 129f.

The question is really whether the author sought to validate the substance of the sound teaching or his interpretation of the appropriate use of the law. The second view is probably best. Within the argument that is developing, it would seem most crucial to validate the author's counter-view of the law and so denounce the heretical use of it. Furthermore, just as in 2 Tim 2.8 the phrase κατὰ τὸ εὐαγγέλιόν μου validates the kerygmatic material that precedes, so in this case the phrase functions similarly to provide the norm for the instruction about the law, vv. 8–10, which precedes. It is not so much a question of the position of the phrase in relation to its referent (Knight, 90) as it is the kind of material it validates. While not denying the normative value of 'the sound teaching', 'the gospel' stands somehow (perhaps in terms of salvation history, or in terms of its revelatory nature) prior to it (cf. Lips 1979:48).

By this time, εὐαγγέλιον 'good news, gospel', had become the stereotyped term for the Christian message in its broadest sense as the good news of salvation.[65] The thought is the same as in Rom 2.16 where Paul states a view that is 'according to my gospel', that is to say, in accordance with and derived from the statement of the gospel. Here too it is being claimed that the view of the law put forward here is fully in accordance with and stems from a proper understanding of the gospel. But how? Paul would have said that Christ delivers us from being under the law and places us under grace; therefore, it can be argued that the law is not needed for the person who does God's will through faith in Christ; nevertheless, Paul understood it to have a continuing function in relation to the conviction of sin (Rom 7.7–12) – it is needed when people are disobedient and their evil conduct needs to be shown up for what it is – and also as a moral guide that has not been abolished but is fulfilled by love (Rom 13.8–10). So here also, the writer has already shown in 1.5 that the gospel leads to love in association with purity of motive; it follows that Christians do not come under the condemnation of the law.

The gen. τῆς δόξης (Tit 2.13 note; 1.17; 3.16; 2 Tim 2.10; 4.18**), expresses the glorious character of God, originally his splendid shining appearance, and then all that makes him the transcendent God. This could be the reflection of his power and holiness, but in Christian usage the glory of God is increasingly seen as the wonder of his grace and love expressed in his saving act in Christ. Here, however, the way in which the double genitive phrase describes τὸ εὐαγγέλιον poses a problem:

---

[65] 2 Tim 1.8, 10; 2.8; cf. Rom 2.16; 16.25; see Roloff, 79f.; Friedrich, G., *TDNT* II, 707–37; Strecker, G., *EDNT* II, 70–4, especially 73; *TLNT* II, 82–92.

(a) τῆς δόξης might be equivalent to an adjective – 'the good news from the glorious and blessed God' (GNB; cf. Eph 1.17) or 'the glorious gospel of the blessed God' (NIV; NRSV). But the revelatory character of 'glory' (cf. Isa 35.2; 50.5; Ps 7.2) makes a gen. of content (or quality) more likely.

(b) The glory of God is what is manifested in those who believe the gospel as they are changed from one degree of glory to another (2 Cor 3.7–18). It is thus the content of salvation (White, 96; Lock, 13).

(c) Following a hint by Hort 1909:103, Lock also raised the possibility that Christ is implicitly identified as the glory of God.

(d) The reference is to the personal glory of God which is revealed in the gospel as through it God brings people to Christ and saves them.[66] A combination of (b) and (d) is best: the glory of God is his personal glory which is revealed in the gospel and conferred on believers.

God is described as 'blessed' (μακάριος; 6.15; cf. Tit 2.13** and note, of the Christian hope which lies in the divine sphere). The term is to be understood as a predicate of God which characterises him, in Hellenistic fashion,[67] in terms of happiness and immortality.[68] Spicq, 337f., notes how the term in its Latin translation *felix* (cf. the noun *felicitas*) was attached to rulers with the twin senses of their being fortunate in themselves and providing blessings for their subjects. He sees here a polemical note against the imperial cult which exalted Caesar to a divine position (*TLNT* II, 439). While the possibility of some sort of dialogue with the imperial cult exists, the viability of this thesis[69] depends on how far a similar trend can be perceived elsewhere in the PE or in other Christian documents of this date; the probable influence of Greek-speaking Judaism and of Hellenistic religious language upon the church in Asia Minor may provide an easier explanation of the language used here. Oberlinner, 30, stresses that the thought is not so much of the blessed state of God as of the obligation of people to give him praise and honour; he is '*seliggepriesen*' rather than '*glückselig*'.

ὃ ἐπιστεύθην ἐγώ The relative clause introduces the language of 'commissioning'. ὅ is a cognate accusative used with the passive verb. In the PE, the gospel (τὸ εὐαγγέλιον) is consistently

---

[66] 'The gospel which tells of the glory of the ever-blessed God' (REB; cf. NJB); cf. 2 Cor 4.4, 6; Col 1.27; Spicq 337; Dibelius-Conzelmann, 25; Kelly, 51; Fee, 47; Roloff, 79.
[67] Cf. Philo, *Spec.* 1.209; 2.53; 3.1; *Abr.* 202; *Deus* 26; Josephus, *Ant.* 10.278.
[68] Cf. 1.17; 6.16; Dibelius-Conzelmann, 25–6; Roloff, 80.
[69] It is rejected by Dibelius-Conzelmann, 31.

connected with discussion of Paul's relation to it,[70] which thereby distances it from the false teaching. πιστεύω (Tit 1.3 note; **Excursus 4**) is used in the passive in the sense 'to be entrusted with', alluding to the commission of Paul as a missionary (1 Cor 9.17; Gal 2.7; Lips 1979:42). Here the point seems to lie not in the missionary task of Paul but rather in his responsibility to preserve the content of the gospel faithfully in the face of error.

The effect of the clause is to introduce a personal reference to Paul,[71] and this serves as a bridge to the next section, the Pauline testimony (vv. 12–16), which shows how Paul became a trustworthy servant of God. In this polemical context, the clause stresses that the authentic gospel is to be found in its Pauline formulation; that is the criterion of truth over against the errors of the legalists. But whether this is seen as the reflection of a Paulinist's attempt to establish Paul as the guarantor of the message for the later church,[72] instead of as a device which the apostle himself or a close follower employed[73] will depend upon prior assumptions about the purpose of the PE (see discussion at Tit 1.1; 1 Tim 1.3). In any case, the thought that apostolicity assures the authenticity of the message is not immediately followed up.

c. The source of Paul's power and commission (1.12–17)

Oke, G. C., 'A Doxology not to God but to Christ', *ExpTim* 67 (1955–6), 367–8; Wanke 1977:176–81; Wolter 1988:27–64; Wolter, M., 'Paulus, der bekehrte Gottesfeind. Zum Verständnis von 1. Tim. 1:13', *NovT* 31 (1989), 48–66.

1.12–17 forms a unit clearly concluded with the doxology in 1.17. It expresses Paul's thanks that he was appointed to act as a steward of the gospel despite his previous opposition to the gospel. He was shown mercy because he had acted in ignorance. Grace was shown to him, leading to the growth of faith and love. Thus he is a proof of the general statement that Christ came to bring salvation for all sinners by reason of the fact that Paul could regard himself as the worst of sinners, the object of God's mercy so that he might act as a paradigm for future converts. The thought fills Paul with praise to God.[74] The

---

[70] 2 Tim 1.8, 10f.; 2.8f.; cf. Tit 1.3; Roloff, 80.
[71] Cf. 1.15; 2.7; 2 Tim 1.11; 2.8f.; Tit 1.3.
[72] Hasler, 15; Roloff, 80; Wolter 1988:27; Brox 108.
[73] Gal 2.7 (cf. 1.8); 1 Th 2.4; Rom 2.16; 1 Cor 9.16.
[74] Roloff, 84, finds 3 lines of thought: (a) mercy; (b) salvation through Christ; and (c) Paul as an example.

statement is characterised by superlatives – great grace, over-
flowing, shown to the worst of sinners, the first convert, infinite
mercy. God is described in superlative terms and in a Greek
style.

Oberlinner, 35, argues that this thanksgiving corresponds to
the opening thanksgivings in other letters in the Pauline corpus;
where they are concerned with the congregation addressed, here
the theme is Paul himself and his place in the mediation of the
gospel. The statement is intended to bring in the recipients of
the letter to share in the thanksgiving which culminates in the
closing doxology.

The passage has come to occupy a central role within the
debate about the presentation of Paul in the PE in relation to
the earlier Paul's self-testimony. Is the relation to such passages
as 1 Cor 15.8–11; Gal 1.13–16; 2 Cor 4.1–6; Phil 3.4–11; Rom
1.1–7 to be understood in terms of literary dependence (Trummer
1978:116–20) or tradition-historical redaction and development
(Roloff, 85–8; Wolter 1988:27–64)? Dibelius-Conzelmann, 23,
argue that the description of Paul here does not correspond to
the self-consciousness expressed in Phil 3.4–7; it is stylised and
very general and is based on current vice-catalogues. The picture
is not meant to be biographical but rather an edifying example
of the 'formerly/now' pattern. But the explanations of Roloff
and Wolter suggest a more complicated function within the
author's programme to establish the priority of the Pauline
apostolate, and there are indeed elements in the passage which
could be biographical.

The purpose of the statement must be ascertained in the light
of its role in relation to the charge to Timothy and its content
as a self-description of Paul, and is probably manifold. (a) It
may emphasise the authority of Paul, who occupies a unique
position as a convert. He is both example and steward of the
gospel. (b) It certainly stresses how God can save the worst of
sinners, because they acted in ignorance and unbelief. (c) Implicitly
it shows how salvation is effected independently of the law
through faith in Christ. Thus the traditional formulation of the
Christ-event, which Paul has experienced and which as apostle
he authenticates (the statement at the end of v. 11 leads into the
Pauline testimony), is used to form an exemplary statement of
the gospel which must be intended to contrast with false teaching.

The passage is highly significant for what follows in that it
demonstrates that the concern of 1 Tim (and of the PE generally)
is basically with the gospel and perversions of it rather than
purely or primarily with church order and bourgeois ethics. It is
the maintenance of the purity of the gospel which matters most
of all.

TEXT

12. χάριν ἔχω Praem. καί (D TR a b s; Kilpatrick). Elliott, 207, states that καί at the beginning of a sentence was unpopular with scribes, and that the PE do use it at 1 Tim 3.1; 2 Tim 2.2; he therefore adopts the addition here. However, he also cites 2 Tim 1.3 where it does not occur, and therefore the decision should be made on the basis of the MS evidence which favours the text.

ἐνδυναμώσαντι ἐνδυναμοῦντι (א* 33 330 451 g sa Epiph Theoph). The variant may be assimilation to Phil 4.13 (Metzger[1], 639) or a natural 'correction' to give a timeless relationship instead of a specific reference to a conversion experience. It is, however, preferred by Elliott, 24f., on the grounds that scribes tended to correct the pres. to the aor. in moods other than the indic. Since the paragraph is throughout concerned with the past event of Paul's conversion the aor. remains more likely (Roloff, 92; Fee, 55).

Χριστῷ Ἰησοῦ Praem. ἐν (D* 3 d g vg). Elliott, 25, argues that the phrase is awkward without 'in', and proposes that the participle refers to God who acts in Christ; ἐν was omitted on stylistic grounds by scribes who reduced the number of prepositions in the text. But the MS evidence is weak. Possibly the variant arose under the influence of Phil 4.13.

13. τὸ πρότερον τὸν πρότερον (D² Hᶜ TR (a r vgᵐˢˢ); Kilpatrick). Cf. Elliott, 26f. Scribes evidently took πρότερον as an adj. rather than an adv.

ὄντα βλάσφημον Insert με (A Ψ 81 pc). Elliott, 26, suggests confusion with the earlier use in the verse as a reason for the insertion.

ἀλλὰ ἠλεήθην Insert καί (635 1927 76 1923 Tert). Elliott, 207, lists the variant as doubtful. The MS evidence is very weak.

14. δὲ ἡ χάρις Insert καί (2401). Elliott, 207, lists as doubtful.

15. πιστός The variant ἀνθρώπινος/*humanus* occurs at 3.1 in both Greek and Latin sources; here it is found only in Latin sources. The evidence for it is given differently by the various editions. The most authoritative list is that of North 1995:51: b m r vgᴿ Ambrosiaster Augustine Ps-Augustine? Facundus MSS acc. to Jerome Ps-Hyginus Julian-Eclanum Mar-m Ps-Pelagius 1 Ps-Vigilius.[75]

Most commentators accept the text, and some do not even think the variant worthy of mention (Roloff; Oberlinner). The variant was adopted here by Lock, xxxvi, as 'possibly right' ('true to human needs'), Zahn, NEB, Moffatt, Elliott, 27f. North 1995:67, while accepting the variant in 3.1, argues that it is to be rejected here both because of the weak MS evidence and because it is inappropriate here. Its presence here is due to harmonisation to 3.1 (so WH, *Notes*, 132; Metzger, 571). Spicq, 302 follows Jerome who spoke of this *latinorum codicum vitiositatem*.

Χριστὸς Ἰησοῦς Inverted order (623 103 1518 2401 489 1319 syᵖ; Kilpatrick). Elliott, 198–205 argues that in the nom. and acc. the author uses the order Ἰησοῦς Χριστός. But the MSS hardly inspire confidence. Elliott assumes that the author would adopt this 'natural order' rather than the other, and this has not been proved. The fulness of the language suggests that a formula is being cited.

16. Χριστὸς Ἰησοῦς Inverted order (א D² H K L P 6 1911 88 TR sy eth bo arm vgᴰ Chrys Theod Euthal; AV RV RSV; del. Χριστός F G 1739 1881 pc; Ἰησοῦς ὁ Χριστός 614 pc). Spicq, 302, adopts the *v.l.*, holding that scribes would conform to the two preceding instances. Similarly Elliott, 202. But to accept this view does not imply that the author was stressing the humanity and compassion of *Jesus* Christ (Spicq, 345, wrongly citing Hendriksen).

ἅπασαν πᾶσαν (D K L P Ψ TR 1739 6 1912 Chrys Theodoret) is preferred by Elliott, 29, on the grounds that ἅπας is rare in the NT outside Lk-Acts and

---

[75] The reference to g in UBS³ appears to be an error and is deleted in UBS⁴.

there is usually a variant; it was a more literary word which scribes were inclined to introduce. This argument does not explain why it is introduced only here in the PE; on the other hand why should the author use it only once? The evidence for it tends to be Alexandrian.

μακροθυμίαν Add αὐτοῦ (D 1702 2587 d co syᵖ; praem. 1908). Elliott, 29, holds that the frequent use of unemphatic enclitic pronouns offended scribes who removed them. (MHT III, 38)

17. ἀφθάρτῳ ἀοράτῳ ἀθανάτῳ ἀοράτῳ (D*ᶜ Hᶜ lat syʰᵐᵍ Tert; ἀφθάρτῳ ἀοράτῳ ἀθανάτῳ (F G (a m r)). Elliott, 30, argues that ἀθάνατος was a favourite patristic adjective which found its way into the text here.

μόνῳ θεῷ Insert σόφῳ (ℵ² D¹ Hᶜ Ψ 1881 TR syʰ Epiph). Elliott, 30f., regards the insertion as uncertain in view of its omission by Latin witnesses (cf. the similar problem in Rom 16.27; Jude 25). Metzger, 572, regards it as a scribal gloss from Rom 16.27.

EXEGESIS

12. Χάριν ἔχω τῷ ἐνδυναμώσαντί με Χριστῷ Ἰησοῦ τῷ κυρίῳ ἡμῶν The last phrase in v. 11 with its emphatic ἐγώ forms the link to the exposition of Paul's calling to service. χάριν ἔχω (2 Tim 1.3; Lk 17.9; Heb 12.28) is a Cl. idiom for 'to give, express thanks' (*TLNT* III, 503–6). It is never used by Paul who prefers εὐχαριστέω.[76] It has been claimed that the verb conveys the idea of a lasting sentiment rather than a single act of gratitude (Parry, 6; Spicq, 340); if this suggestion is intended to create a contrast with the Pauline use of εὐχαριστέω, it seems far-fetched. On the contrary, it is possible that εὐχαριστέω is used for references to Paul's regular times of prayer which he reports in his letters, whereas the χάρις phrases are used for outbursts of thanksgiving at the actual time of writing the letter (Couser 1992:188). Oberlinner, II, 13f., argues that the change in vocabulary is partly due to the increasingly specialised use of εὐχαριστέω for the eucharist (but even in *Didache* 9; 10 the usage is fluid), and partly because this verb expresses more strongly the fellowship of the apostle with his readers, whereas here the thought is more of Paul's own relationship with God. But this does not in any way explain the change in the choice of verb.

The object is Christ rather than God, which is unusual for Paul but here is due to the interest in 'Christ who empowered me', and perhaps reflects a reference back to the Damascus event in which Christ revealed himself to Paul.[77]

---

[76] But Paul does use χάρις with dat. for 'thanks [be] to God' (Rom 6.17; 7.25; 1 Cor 15.57; 2 Cor 2.14; 8.16; 9.15; Fee, 50). It has been suggested that the use here is a Latinism (Simpson, 21; Roloff, 92).

[77] Cf. Fee, 50; in any case there is no pattern elsewhere in Paul for thanksgivings made in the context of discussions about his calling to ministry.

The participial phrase, τῷ ἐνδυναμώσαντί με, appears to be attributive, providing a further description of Christ.[78] However, Wolter 1988:29–49, notes that in a Jewish eulogy the participial construction typically provides the primary reason for thanksgiving (Deichgräber 1967:40–3). He therefore suggests that this phrase gives the reason for thanksgiving here rather than (as most commentators assume) the following ὅτι clause. The latter, then, will specify more nearly the scope and demonstration of the 'empowering'. The usefulness of this closer association of empowering and appointment to ministry comes in Wolter's argument for a new development in the conception of office in the PE (see note below). But taking the participial phrase as descriptive of Christ does not empty the participle of meaning.

The verb ἐνδυναμόω means 'to give strength, empower'; it is used of Christ's action (2 Tim 2.1; 4.17**; Eph 6.10; Phil 4.13); and of God's (Rom 4.20); in Acts 9.22 it is used of Paul's growth in confidence as a preacher immediately after his conversion. W. Grundmann (*TDNT* II, 284–317, espec. 313) stresses how the power arises out of the personal relationship between Christ and Paul. As a reflection back (aorist), the reference may be to the Damascus event (Roloff, 92; Wolter 1988:38, leaves the question open). Given the immediate context, which centres on the Pauline call to ministry, traditional connections are apparent:

(a) The power of God or Christ is closely associated with the calling and authority of the one called.[79] Moreover, the NT pattern has OT roots in the calling of the prophetic leaders of the people.[80] Those whom God calls, he strengthens for the task.

(b) In some cases the power of God is bestowed in a revelatory experience (Dan 10.1Θ), and is closely associated with the presence of God (Deut 31.6f.; Josh 1.9; 1 Chr 28.20; 2 Tim 4.17).

(c) God's power often manifests itself in the working of miracles (Acts 3.12; 4, 7–10; 2 Cor 6.7; 12.9; 13.4).

(d) The empowering is to be related implicitly to the Holy Spirit or the promised gift of the Spirit.[81] Here the immediate reference is to the Lord's empowering for service (διακονία) as an apostle (2 Tim 2.1; 4.17; cf. 2 Tim 1.7); but the implicit

---

[78] The form 'Christ Jesus our Lord' occurred in 1.2. Although the construction with a participle phrase inserted into the title may appear strange, it represents a familiar form of expression: see 2 Cor 13.3; Jas 1.5; 2 Pet 2.1; 3 Jn 9; cf. 2 Tim 2.6; Jn 8.16 and freq.

[79] Rom 15.19; 1 Cor 2.4f.; 2 Cor 4.7; 6.7; 12.9; Phil 4.13; Eph 3.7; Col 1.29; cf. Lk 4.14, 36; 5.17; 9.1; 24.29; Acts 1.8; 3.12; 4.7, 33; 10.38; Ignatius, *Smyr.* 1.1.

[80] Mic 3.8; Isa 41.10; 42.6; Exod 4.12f. [LXX]; cf. Josephus, *Ant.* 2.270–2; Wolter 1988:32–6.

[81] Isa 42.1, 6; Mic 3.8; Isa 11.2; Wis 5.23; 11.20; Lk 1.17, 35; Acts 1.8; 10.38; Rom 15.19; 1 Cor 2.4; Eph 3.16; 1 Th 1.5; 2 Tim 1.7.

biographical reference probably penetrates back to the experience
of calling and bestowal of the Holy Spirit which in Paul's case
is normally associated with the Damascus event (cf. Roloff, 92).[82]
    In the particular context of heresy, the implication of
'empowering' for the divine authentication of the recipient's
authority might also be intended. The claim made here contrasts
sharply with what is in the case of the opponents merely a desire
to be teachers of the law (v. 7).
    ὅτι πιστόν με ἡγήσατο θέμενος εἰς διακονίαν The primary
reason for the thanksgiving is the apostle's conversion (esp.
vv. 13–15) and calling to ministry. In the light of the three
accounts in Acts (Acts 9.1–22; 22.6–16; 26.12–20) and Paul's
own testimony (1 Cor 15.8; Gal 1.16), the point at which this
decisive event occurred is almost certainly to be understood
as the Damascus revelation of Christ to Saul. The participle
θέμενος[83] may be understood to introduce either an attendant
circumstance ('considered me faithful and appointed me to
ministry') or the demonstration of the assessment ('he considered
me faithful having appointed me to ministry'). In either case,
the language describes the apostolic appointment in terms of
divine initiative and necessity.[84] διακονία (2 Tim 4.5, 11**),
'service', is a fitting term for Paul's task. The word is used of all
kinds of commissions from God to serve him in the church,
including the task of an apostle.[85] Paul calls himself correspondingly a διάκονος in 1 Cor 3.5; 2 Cor 3.6; 6.4; 11.23; Eph 3.7;
Col 1.23, 25, and regards his work as a form of διακονία

---

[82] The significance of the Holy Spirit is played down by Wolter 1988:40–5,
who argues that in the PE it is not so much that the locus of the gift of the
Spirit is narrowed down from the congregation to the ministry in particular but
rather that its place is generally underemphasised. He claims that the pneumatic
element (reference to the Spirit and works done in the Spirit as proof of authority
from God) usually associated with 'empowering' in Paul is purposely altered in
this presentation. Here the apostle's receipt of authority has been interpreted in
ecclesiastical, 'unpneumatic' terms as the appointment to ministry (διακονία).
Behind this conception some scholars have detected a post-Pauline understanding
which links the Spirit with office and the author's/later church's concern to
inhibit enthusiastic elements within the church as it sought to consolidate its
place in the world (see also Dunn, J. D. G., *Jesus and the Spirit* [London: SCM
Press, 1975], 347–50; Lips 1979:213f.; Quinn 1979). This is a questionable
interpretation of the understanding of the role of the Spirit in the Christian life.
See further Tit 3.5; 2 Tim 1.6f. and notes; Haykin 1985; Fee 1994.
[83] 2.7 par 2 Tim 1.11**; 1 Cor 12.28; cf. Maurer, C., *TDNT* VIII, 152–8.
[84] Cf. 2 Tim 1.11; Acts 13.47; Isa 49.6; Jer 1.5; cf. 1 Cor 12.18, 28; 1 Th 5.9;
Heb 1.2.
[85] Cf. **Excursus 11**. In the second century the term tended to be used for
the lowest of the three levels of ministry (bishops, presbyters and deacons);
consequently, Bernard, 30, holds that the application here to apostleship is likely
to reflect an earlier date of composition.

(Rom 11.13; 15.31). The call to service comes directly from Christ, which again fits the Damascus allusion. The content of the task is clear from 1.11: it is the proclamation and preservation of the gospel (cf. Collins 1990:215).

πιστός (**Excursus 4**) is a characteristic word in the PE, here in the sense of 'faithful' rather than simply 'believing', i.e. as a designation for Christians (cf. Isa 8.2; Tob 5.3 א; 10.6 א). The term must be used proleptically of what God foresaw that Paul would be. Paul uses πιστός with particular reference to the need for faithfulness in church leaders (1 Cor 4.2; 7.25).[86] It is commonly argued that 1 Cor 7.25b (γνώμην δὲ δίδωμι ὡς ἠλεημένος ὑπὸ κυρίου πιστὸς εἶναι) was one of the traditions worked into the present Pauline testimony.[87] Although dependence cannot be proved, the parallel is nevertheless instructive. In the earlier setting, the thought of trustworthiness in teaching or with regard to the faith is obviously in view, while in the present context, the contrast with Paul's pre-Christian condition of ἀπιστία (v. 13) and with the unfaithfulness of false teachers suggests a similar meaning – trustworthiness is to be measured in relation to the true faith. The theme pervades the section (vv. 11, 12, 14, 15, 16, 19).

This assessment raises some unanswerable questions. The relationship between Christ's critical assessment of Paul's character (ἡγέομαι, 'to consider, regard', 6.1**; cf. Heb 11.11) and the appointment to ministry (θέμενος εἰς διακονίαν) leads inescapably to logical antinomies when one begins to think it out in detail. The meaning is not that Christ saw that Paul was a reliable person, despite his sin, and therefore appointed him an apostle. Rather, the language takes us into the mysterious realm of the effectiveness of God's/Christ's calling and his knowledge of the future (cf. Spicq, 340f.; Roloff, 92). The writer is thinking of God in human terms as one who can see the future potential of his servants; NT writers were comfortable with the concept of God knowing the future in detail and seem not to have been troubled with the logic of it.

13. τὸ πρότερον ὄντα βλάσφημον καὶ διώκτην καὶ ὑβριστήν As the ὅτι clause continues to spell out the reason for Paul's thanksgiving, the 'formerly/now' formula contrasts his previous way of life with his new life in Christ and heightens the sense of gratitude even more. The adverbial phrase τὸ πρότερον** ('formerly'; Jn 6.62; 9.8) introduces the schema; in its application to ethics[88] it draws attention to the central role of the

---

[86] For parallels see Wolter 1988:39.
[87] Dibelius-Conzelmann, 26; Roloff, 85; Merkel, 21; Trummer 1978:120.
[88] Cf. Tit 3.3f.; Tachau 1972:79–95, 113–15, 128f.; Towner 1989:63f.

Christ-event and the grace of God in producing the new life of
faith (cf. Roloff, 93; Knoch, 21). The concessive participle ὄντα
(2.2; 3.10; 2 Tim 2.19**) depends upon the preceding verbal
construction, ἡγήσατο θέμενος, preparing the way for the effusive
celebration of grace in v. 14. Within the developing transition
pattern (Eph 2.1, 5, 13; Col 1.21; 2.13), it points back to the
pre-conversion state, which is described with a brief vice list (cf.
Tit 3.3), containing terms found elsewhere in longer lists (Rom
1.30). It depicts Paul as a model of pre-conversion sinfulness
(Roloff, 93), but at least the first term is also characteristic of
the present conduct of the false teachers who are implicitly living
a life outside of Christ (1.20; 2 Tim 3.2; cf. the variant at Tit 1.11;
Oberlinner, 37). βλάσφημος[89] is used of denying the majesty of
God by speaking of him in a disrespectful way. For the Rabbis
it involved actually using the divine name 'Yahweh', which pious
Jews avoided, even when reading the Scripture. The NT usage
is broader and suggests that the Rabbinic is a later, tighter
definition. From a Christian point of view the term also refers,
as here, to abuse of Jesus as God's Son and Messiah, shown
actively in the persecution of his followers. Persecution of
Christians could thus be regarded as blasphemy (1 Pet 4.4), and
the term thus suits an allusion to the apostle's history as an
enemy of the church.

διώκτης***, 'persecutor',[90] goes directly back to the traditional
Pauline self-testimony (1 Cor 15.9; Gal 1.13, 23; Phil 3.6; Acts
9.4f.); it expresses the active form taken by the blasphemous
attitude.

ὑβριστής (Rom 1.30***) indicates the 'violent, insolent person'.
The description implies contemptuous, insulting behaviour,
stemming from pride and arrogance.[91] Paul himself was to know
these kinds of behaviour from the other side.[92]

The combination of these three terms, especially the first and
third, strongly suggests that Paul is cast here in the role of the
θεομάχος, the enemy of God, a category which is abundantly
documented in ancient literature from Pentheus in Euripides,
Bacchae, onwards; the distinctive element in the present depiction
is that, whereas God's enemies are normally destroyed, this one
received mercy because he acted in ignorance (Wolter* 1989).

---

[89] 2 Tim 3.2; Acts 6.11; 2 Pet 2.11***; βλασφημέω, 1.20; 6.1; Tit 2.5; 3.2**;
βλασφημία, 1 Tim 6.4**. Cf. Beyer, H. W., *TDNT* I, 621–5; Hofius, O.,
EDNT I, 221.

[90] Barnabas 20.2; Diognetus 5.2; cf. Oepke, A., *TDNT* II, 229f.

[91] Roloff, 93 n., says that the word is stronger in the LXX than in Hel. Gk.
Spicq, 341, characterises it as insane behaviour that goes beyond all bounds. Cf.
Bertram, G., *TDNT* VIII, 295–307.

[92] Rom 3.8; cf. 1 Cor 4.12; 10.30; 2 Cor 4.9; 12.10; Gal 5.11; 1 Th 2.2.

In strong contrast to this description Paul himself states that before his conversion he was 'blameless, as far as the law was concerned' (Phil 3.6). The contradiction between these self-testimonies has been emphasised by various scholars.[93] However, the different points of view must be taken into account. First, there Paul is assessing his conduct from the point of view of a non-Christian Jew who measures himself by the law, and his point is that by that standard he was blameless; indeed his zeal for the law was seen in his persecution of those who were opposed to the law. He makes this assessment as part of an *argumentum ad hominem* with anybody who thought that one could put confidence in the achievements of the flesh in obedience to the law; he is saying that nobody could have kept the law more fully than he, but even this perfect performance was worthless in the light of the revelation given in Christ. Second, as to the harshness of the testimony, it is quite clear from 1 Cor 15.9 and Gal 1.13 that he regarded his persecution of the church as sinful. Roloff maintains that it is uncharacteristic of Paul to cast himself as a model of sinners (as the vice list seems to do), but the application of the self-testimony in 1 Timothy 1 is different from previous applications, and the role of the apostle-as-model-of-salvation is also unparalleled. There is no contradiction here with what we find in the letters of Paul (cf. Fee, 55; Johnson, 122f.).

ἀλλὰ ἠλεήθην, ὅτι ἀγνοῶν ἐποίησα ἐν ἀπιστίᾳ Here in the flow of thought the 'now' of salvation history is reached. The eschatological salvation of God, and Paul's personal experience of it, comes clearly into focus with the second part of the formerly/now schema. ἀλλά begins the transition from the past (expressed in the participial phrase in v. 13a) to the present state of affairs, characterised by mercy, which will conclude with v. 14.

The thought of receiving divine mercy[94] is intrinsic to a Pauline understanding of salvation (1 Cor 7.25 and 2 Cor 4.1). The prerequisite to enrolment in divine service is the divine pardon of the sinner. The personal experience of being saved is viewed here from the perspective of enjoyment of undeserved mercy from the Lord. The passive indicates the fundamental place of God's initiative (Roloff, 94). Bultmann (*TDNT* II, 477–87) shows how in the Greek world ἔλεος signified an emotion caused by somebody else's affliction, and expressing itself in compassion. From an OT perspective, however, the connection of ἔλεος with *hesed* associates it with Yahweh's attitude of commitment to the covenant with Israel; there is an element of obligation in the showing of kindness. Hence the word tends

---

[93] Cf. Dibelius-Conzelmann, 27f.; Hanson, 60; Hasler, 16; Roloff, 93; Knoch, 22.
[94] ἐλεέω, 1.16**; for ἔλεος see 1.2; Tit 3.5 note.

to oscillate somewhat between the ideas of faithfulness and compassion. It is probably this latter sense of undeserved mercy which is present here.

Yet there is a kind of condition attached to God's mercy, namely, that Paul acted out of ignorance[95] of what he was doing (cf. Houlden, 52). The suggestion that the participle is equivalent to the legal phrase *per ignorantiam* ('without premeditation'; Schmithals, W., *EDNT* I, 21) does not capture the full force. Apparently, the thought is that in his zeal for the law, he did not perceive that his actions were sinful, and thus his actions fell into the category of 'unwitting sins'[96] as opposed to those 'committed with a high hand' (cf. Heb 9.7). The point expressed here creates tensions which have been resolved in two ways. First, one way to understand this 'reason' is literary. Brox (110) and Collins (1975:168) argue that the point amounts to an apologetic excuse, intended to expunge from the emerging Pauline hagiography an otherwise damaging piece of history. But if so, the hagiographer made an inexplicable error by including in 1.15 the Pauline admission ὧν πρῶτός εἰμι ἐγώ (cf. Roloff, 94). It is preferable, second, to adopt a theological perspective. Here there is a clear recognition that non-Christians commit sins as a result of ignorance, and that pagans are characterised by ignorance of God and his will.[97] One tradition insists that sins committed in ignorance are forgivable simply because they are committed unconsciously: 'Father, forgive them, for they do not know what they are doing.'[98] But there is another tradition which regards ignorance as a guilty condition (Wis 13.8f.). Roloff says that ignorance does not lessen guilt: all the heathen are ignorant, and grace is awarded to them all.[99]

The point to be observed again is that the model of Paul is being contrasted with the caricature of the false teacher (see Schlarb 1990:179). It is this distinction that calls forth the ὅτι-clause of explanation. The sinfulness of the pre-enlightened apostle's persecution of the church is not downplayed here in the least – on the contrary it serves to heighten the response of wonder and thankfulness at the experience of grace. Paul's actions (ἐποίησα, referring to the behaviour implied by the preceding adjectives; Tit 3.5) were done in unbelief (ἀπιστία**; see **Excursus 4**), i.e. as a Jew who did not accept Jesus as the

---

[95] ἀγνοέω**; cf. Rom 10.3; 2 Pet 2.12; cf. Bultmann, R., *TDNT* I, 115–21.

[96] Lev 22.14; Num 15.22–31; Acts 3.17; 13.27; 17.30.

[97] Eph 4.18; 1 Th 4.5; 1 Pet 1.14 – note the use of πρότερον here.

[98] Lk 23.34; cf. Wis 13.1–7; Acts 3.17; 13.27; 17.30; Rom 10.2; *T. Jud.* 19.3; SB II, 264.

[99] There is no need to find here an anthropology akin to that of Gnosticism, in which people are blind and ignorant before they are enlightened (*pace* Hasler, 16).

Messiah (Rom 3.3; 11.20, 23; cf. the thought of 1 Cor 2.6–8). The heretics, however, are depicted as having been enlightened and having chosen to reject the faith (1.19; 2 Tim 2.17f.), which may not put them beyond the reach of forgiveness, but which does place their sin into a different category from Paul's (cf. Heb 6.4–6; 2 Pet 2.15–22).

According to Oberlinner, 38–42, the verdict on Paul's pre-conversion life here is to be regarded as completely impossible for the historical Paul who was a zealous upholder of the law and in no way an unbeliever. Not only so, but there is a tension between vv. 12b–13a and 13b–c as the author combines his desires to emphasise both the normative function of Paul as the apostle specially called by divine grace and his paradigmatic function as the typical sinner who is converted.

This understanding of the passage is dubious. It overlooks the fact that for Paul faith is now to be understood as faith in Christ and an attitude to Jesus which is expressed in persecution of his followers is tantamount to blasphemy.

14. ὑπερεπλεόνασεν δὲ ἡ χάρις τοῦ κυρίου ἡμῶν μετὰ πίστεως καὶ ἀγάπης τῆς ἐν Χριστῷ Ἰησοῦ The experience of mercy is now spelled out more fully. The change of subject to 'the grace of our Lord' and the superlative verb help to emphasise the thought of the superiority of the power of grace to that of sin. That the eschatological and salvific outpouring of grace in the redemptive work of Christ[100] is in mind becomes absolutely clear in the tradition of v. 15 (cf. Tit 2.11, 14). The abundance of sin and super-abundance of grace may also pick up a theme associated with the messianic age.[101]

χάρις is understood soteriologically as God's saving power.[102] Its dramatic effect is described in Pauline fashion as 'super-abounding' (Rom 5.20; 6.1; 2 Cor 4.15). ὑπερπλεονάζω*** is 'to be present in great abundance' (*Ps. Sol.* 5.19). Since the simplex already has a strong sense, the compound expresses a comparative idea: grace abounded even more than sin (White, 97). The translation in Lock, 15, 'simply above its usual measure', is far too weak.[103]

At the existential and practical level, the result of salvation is to produce an entirely new life. This result is described here in a slightly unusual way with a prepositional phrase. The usage of μετά here and elsewhere in the PE seems somewhat loose and

---

[100] τοῦ κυρίου ἡμῶν is clearly Jesus; see Knight, 96f.; *pace* Arichea-Hatton, 31.
[101] Cf. Ps-Philo 39.6; Berger, K., *EDNT* III, 459.
[102] See Tit 1.4 note; 2.11 note; Rom 5.20f.; Easton, 115; Roloff, 94; and, (on the background), Nolland, J., 'Grace as power', *NovT* 28 (1986), 26–31.
[103] Paul is fond of ὑπερ- compounds; hence the use of this unusual word here is fully in accord with his style.

the connection is by no means precise.[104] Here the writer seems to mean that faith and love were abundant as well as grace. In any case, two things are clear enough: the role of grace is predominant (cf. Roloff, 95), and as the characteristic use of the two qualities together in the rest of the PE and Paul suggests, the experience of God's saving grace produces a life marked by faith and love 'in Christ' (cf. 2 Tim 1.13 for the same phrase).

πίστις (**Excursus 4**) and ἀγάπη together describe the authentic Christian life. Faith denotes both the human response to the gospel evoked by grace and the ongoing attitude or disposition of trust in God and belief in the gospel. It may be thought of as a gift bestowed by God, alongside grace. ἀγάπη is frequently linked with faith, whether as a pair or along with other Christian qualities (see Tit 2.2 note). It characterises the life of faith in terms of action done in behalf of others (cf. Gal 5.6). With the denunciation of the false teachers in mind, the Pauline conversion story intends to establish the traditional model of faith working itself out in active service and linking this to the apostolic gospel. That is, a genuine response to the saving grace of God proclaimed in the gospel (v. 11) will result in a life of faith and love. Hence it is not surprising that grace can be closely linked to the call to apostleship (cf. Wolter 1988:48).

The theme of πίστις runs through this passage (ἐπιστεύθην [v. 11], πιστός [v. 12], ἀπιστία [v. 13], πίστις [v. 14], πιστός [v. 15], πιστεύω [v. 16]). It creates a holistic framework for salvation in which the apostolic gospel and the faith rsponse to it are seen to be determinative for authentic Christianity. Competing 'gospels' and life-styles devoid of the fruit of salvation are thereby condemned (cf. Collins 1975:165).

Eschatology and soteriology converge in the concluding phrase, τῆς ἐν Χριστῷ Ἰησοῦ, and establish the context for a proper understanding of these qualities of faith and love. The article shows that the phrase qualifies the preceding noun (and by implication the earlier one of the pair as well; on the syntax see Tit 1.1 note. The phrase ἐν Χριστῷ Ἰησοῦ occurs nine times in the PE (1.14; 3.13; 2 Tim 1.1, 9, 13; 2.1, 10; 3.12, 15); other forms such as 'in the Lord' are not found.

Allan 1963 found differences from the Pauline usage of 'in Christ' on the basis that the latter (a) expresses a personal identification with Christ as the basis of salvation; (b) is associated with strong emotion; and (c) is associated with the idea of Christ as a corporate personality and inclusive representative. In the light of other studies it is dubious whether Paul's usage is correctly

---

[104] For μετά meaning 'along with' cf. 2.9, 15; 3.4; 4. 3, 4; 6.6; 2 Tim 2.10. In general μετά is used when referring to a quality that is present along with another one (cf. Eph 6.23; Holtzmann, 411).

characterised in this way,[105] and the alleged differences, especially (b) and (c), are illusory. More weight attaches to Allan's comment on the impoverishment of expression compared with Paul who certainly uses the phrase in a greater variety of ways. The PE have two uses with verbs, 'living a godly life in Christ Jesus', which is similar to expressions in Paul (Rom 16.12), and 'grace given to us in Christ Jesus', which is also similar to Pauline expressions (1 Cor 1.4).

The remaining seven uses refer to abstract qualities (faith, love, life, grace, and salvation) which are in Christ Jesus. When used in this way (e.g. 'faith and love which are in Christ', 2 Tim 1.14), the phrase expresses a sense of union with Christ (Guthrie, 146) and thus refers to qualities which arise from abiding in Christ (Parry, 52f.); the sense 'given by Christ', i.e. 'Christian' (Easton, 210f.) is much too weak. Paul speaks similarly of faith (Col 1.4), redemption (Rom 8.34), the love shown by God (Rom 8.39), his 'ways' (1 Cor 4.17), and the churches of Judaea (Gal 1.22). The redemption and love are God's action and active character effected in the death and resurrection of Christ. Paul's ways are the types of conduct which he commands others to do 'in Christ/the Lord'. There can accordingly be no doubt that the language and thought derive from that of Paul, while granting that the range is less than in Paul.

Here faith and love are those qualities which must be shown 'in Christ', i.e. in a way determined by the death and resurrection of Jesus. Faith is related to the saving event as faith in the crucified and risen Saviour, and love is determined by the pattern of self-giving love displayed in Christ. Wallis 1995:134–44 claims that faith and love are the outworkings of grace rather than responses to it, and they are characteristics of Christ which are conveyed to Christians by his enabling presence. They are not virtues but 'the visible expression of the Christian's living relationship with his Saviour' (Kelly, 53f.). Faith thus has 'Christ as its source, object and content'.

In the present context, the peculiar form of expression may well be determined by the need to contrast the Christian way of salvation and genuine Christian existence, with its basis in the authorised, apostolic gospel (vv. 11, 15), with competing claims to spirituality. Faith and love have already been established as the fundamental goal of the gospel ministry (1.5), and it is not accidental that the opponents are said to have departed from these things (1.6), nor that the apostle's paradigmatic conversion experience is thus described (cf. Fee, 52).

---

[105] Donfried, K. P., and Marshall, I. H., *The Theology of the Shorter Pauline Letters* [Cambridge: Cambridge University Press, 1993], 138–44.

15. πιστὸς ὁ λόγος καὶ πάσης ἀποδοχῆς ἄξιος The account of the theological rationale of Paul's conversion is confirmed by reference to a traditional saying which indicates that what has been said rests on a firm basis of church teaching and is in line with it; thus implicitly any other way of salvation – for example, by the law or by an arcane interpretation of it – is ruled out.

The theological statement is introduced by a formula, found here and in 4.9 in its full form (**Excursus 9**).[106] Only here is the formula used with ὅτι to introduce the following statement. The formula primarily emphasises the truth of what is said (not simply that it is a citation), and characterises it as 'received' tradition bearing official validation. As such, the teaching is to be acknowledged and an appropriate response is due (see below). Here and in 4.9 the formula is strengthened by the addition καὶ πάσης ἀποδοχῆς ἄξιος.[107] ἀποδοχή, literally a 'good welcome' (*Ep. Arist.* 257) and metaphorically 'acceptance, favourable reception',[108] may contain the nuance of consideration or high estimate, implying the need to make a rational decision (Spicq, 343). πᾶς is common with abstract nouns in the PE (Tit 2.10 note). Here it may be intensive, calling for the fullest acceptance (Knight 1968:25–9; Roloff, 95; Hanson, 61) or extensive, calling for universal acceptance (Bernard, 32; Spicq, 343); Lock, 15, suggests both senses are in mind. On the basis of the similar phrase in 1 Tim 6.1 (πάσης τιμῆς ἀξίους), an intensification of ἀποδοχῆς is to be understood.[109] The addition of the phrase stresses the need for the reader to respond by accepting the truth of the statement. This would have been implicit in each case, but possibly here and in 4.9 the traditional material itself did not make evident the need for response.

ὅτι Χριστὸς Ἰησοῦς ἦλθεν εἰς τὸν κόσμον ἁμαρτωλοὺς σῶσαι The ὅτι (*recitativum*) clause introduces the quotation which ends with σῶσαι. Salvation related to the historical Christ-event is thus the subject of this theological tradition. The saying reflects traditional motifs and wording. The use of ἦλθον in combination with σῶσαι is reminiscent of the similar statement in Lk 19.10, and this has been seen as its source.[110] However, the tradition

---

[106] See textual note above.

[107] The language is paralleled in Hellenistic sources with regard to both people and things. Cf. Philo, *Fug.*, 129; *Praem.* 13; Field 1899:203; MM 62; Knight 1968:24; *TLNT* I, 176f.

[108] 4.9***; Grundmann, W., *TDNT* II, 55f. The phrase is used of a respected public official in an inscr. from Ephesus (*New Docs.* IV, 74, 77 § 19 [AD II]).

[109] White, 98, compares the Latin use of *summus* with abstract nouns.

[110] Michel 1948:86; Brox, 111; Kelly, 54. Oberlinner, 43, regards Lk 19.10 as a Lucan formulation which does not tie redemption to the cross but to the whole Christ-event and takes the present verse to be an independent formulation of a Christian affirmation; neither point is convincing.

as the author knew it may have been influenced by the logion preserved in Mk 2.17 (cf. Mt 9.13) which connects ἦλθον with ἁμαρτωλοὺς (1.9**). εἰς τὸν κόσμον represents a further modification. The resemblance to Johannine phraseology should be noted,[111] but most commentators give it little weight,[112] and fewer still think it likely that the incarnation or pre-existence theology of the Fourth Gospel is present.[113]

Jesus' mission to save was traditionally described as a 'coming' and sometimes (especially in John) particularly as a coming 'into the world'.[114] The aorists ἦλθεν and σῶσαι (see Tit 1.3 note) describe the historical mission of Christ as the saving act of God in Christ. In both Johannine and Pauline thought the location of this mission (κόσμος; 3.16; 6.6**) is the world of mankind, regarded as sinful mankind, which becomes the sphere in which salvation is wrought (Sasse, H., *TDNT* III, 892–4). Thus the tradition clearly affirms the central point of the gospel – that God's salvation is the result of Christ's entrance into history.

What is less clear is the degree to which the concepts of pre-existence and incarnation are to be associated with the phraseology. Sasse maintains that 'coming into the world' expresses a Jewish idiom for becoming a human being or simply 'being born' (*TDNT* III, 888; Windisch 1935:222) and therefore contains no necessary incarnational overtones. But in John the language indicates pre-existence, i.e. that an existing divine being came from outside into this world, rather than that somebody simply says 'I was born'. In the PE the context is the author's epiphany Christology[115] within which pre-existence is a likely implication. It is also likely that the use here intends to focus on the salvation-historical moment rather than the means by which 'Christ came'. Elsewhere the author also clearly employs the category of incarnation (3.16), which again may suggest that the present brief saying implies a rather full Christology.[116]

But any such implications are incidental to the author's main purpose which has less to do with fine points of Christology and more to do with the fact of salvation and the linkage with the traditional gospel. Roloff, 90f., suggests that the allusion to Mk 2.17 (and par.), and thus to Jesus' debate with the Pharisees, woven here into a baptismal piece, underlines the 'global' accessibility to God's salvation in Christ through baptism. Elsewhere the

[111] Jn 1.9; 3.19; 11.27; 12.46; 16.28; 18.37; see Knight 1968:48f.; Spicq, 344.
[112] See the discussions in Windisch 1935:221f.; Roloff, 9f.
[113] Roloff, 90f.; Dibelius-Conzelmann, 29; Wolter 1988:49 n. 2.
[114] Cf. Schneider, J., *TDNT* II, 668–72; Balz, H., *EDNT* II, 311.
[115] **Excursus 8**; cf. Hasler 203; Oberlinner 1980:206f.
[116] Roloff, 95, says that the PE stress the incarnation more strongly than in Paul. Lock, 16, uses Jn 6.14; Rom 5.12 to demonstrate the opposite position.

universal scope of salvation (2.4, 6; cf. 4.10) is emphasised and the role of baptism is considered in some way (Tit 3.5f.), but here, while universal accessibility is implicit, the message is simpler.

Hasler, 16, argues that the theology has moved on from what Lk 19.10 enunciates.

> The linking of salvation to the Saviour of sinners who has come has become a linking to a proclamation of Christ, which represents itself as pauline and apostolic, which passes on the saving will of God revealed in the cross and resurrection to all men, and gives hope of redemption to eternal life.... It is not the saving work completed by Christ but the revelation of the merciful and patient will of the Redeemer in the appearing of Christ, the simultaneous incarnate promise of eternal life in Christ, which is the impregnable basis for the faith which is sure of future salvation.

Some of this is doubtful. On the one hand, the focus on the message as the continuation of the event simply represents the typical way in which the church attempted to work out the significance of the Jesus-tradition and the Christ-event for its life (cf. 1 Cor 1.21; Tit 1.3; 2 Tim 1.10). On the other hand, Hasler pays insufficient attention to the aorist infinitive and its connection to the main verb which seem to establish a historical location for the reference.

On the whole, the phrase is best regarded as a definite echo of Lk 19.10 (or a saying based on that tradition which had already undergone modification; see above). In the process of formulation of the trustworthy saying, it would have been natural for the church to drop the original phrase 'Son of man' and replace it with Χριστὸς Ἰησοῦς.[117] The pastoral imagery of 'seeking the lost' has also disappeared to make the statement more general, in keeping with the salvation-historical thrust. The statement is thus a christological/soteriological one based on a saying of Jesus (cf. 2.6; 5.18) which in the course of the whole argument links Paul to the mission of God and the gospel of Christ.

ὧν πρῶτός εἰμι ἐγώ A personal comment is added to make the specific application of the general principle to the pre-conversion life of Paul; it thus serves as the first part of a second application of the then/now schema to him with the second part in v. 16. It may be significant that the writer uses the present tense, εἰμί: the converted sinner remains conscious that he is a

---

[117] It is possible that the order of names has been assimilated to the phrase ἐν Χριστῷ Ἰησοῦ in v. 14.

sinner, saved by grace (cf. Roloff, 96). In describing the apostle as the πρῶτος (1.16; 2.13; 5.12; 2 Tim 4.16**) among sinners, the testimony probably picks up on the theme of 1 Cor 15.9; Eph 3.8. But the precise intention of the πρῶτος characterisation and its relation to the second πρῶτος of v. 16 must be considered.

(a) Some have understood πρῶτος in v. 15 as qualitative (or hyperbolic) and the second πρῶτος of v. 16 with its forward look (μέλλοντες πιστεύειν), as chronological in whatever sense is required to establish the 'pattern'.[118]

(b) Modern translations tend to translate both occurrences qualitatively.[119]

(c) More frequently, the temporal and qualitative possibilities of πρῶτος are combined to form an *a fortiori* argument: 'As "the first", Paul is the typical representative of those who have received mercy which the sinner can experience.'[120]

(d) In slightly different ways, Roloff and Wolter see the dual πρῶτος as a part of the priority-of-Paul theme. Roloff, 95f., suggests that the relative clause, which returns the reader to the theme of 'Paul', identifies the apostle as 'first' both in terms of the depth of his sin and in his position at the beginning of the gospel; the aspects of his order (among apostles) and temporal sequence come together, though in view of v. 16 the latter is dominant. He notes that the thought here is related like a mirror image to the argument of 1 Cor 15.9; Eph 3.9 (Paul, because of his sin, is least of the apostles). Wolter 1988:49–61[121] maintains that the temporal aspect is dominant in each πρῶτος. In each case it emphasises the priority of the Pauline experience of salvation in the thinking of the author: (a) the qualitative meaning ('chief') in the case of v. 15 is difficult and would not further the argument of the passage because of the present tense which would make 'Paul' claim that as the bearer of the gospel he is (still) the worst of sinners; (b) the syntax of v. 16, which links eternal life directly to the Pauline ὑποτύπωσιν (not to πιστεύειν! but see below) and thus makes Paul's conversion the normative and exclusive exemplar of God's saving grace: 'Paulus ist nicht nur ein prominentes Beispiel des sich allen Menschen zuwendenden göttlichen Heilswillens, sondern er und sein Geschick sind selbst Bestandteil des Heilshandelns Christi an den

---

[118] Cf. the shift in AV ('chief ... first'; cf. REB: 'among them I stand first ... the first occasion for displaying his inexhaustible patience'); Spicq, 345; Hanson, 61f.

[119] RV; NIV; GNB; NJB; NRSV; cf. Fee, 56; Arichea-Hatton, 33–6.

[120] Dibelius-Conzelmann, 30; see also Brox, 115; Collins 1975:168; Kelly, 54f.; Knight, 102f.

[121] Wolter gives the credit for this interpretation to Klein, G., *Die Zwölf Apostel* (Göttingen: Vandenhoeck und Ruprecht, 1961), 136–8.

Glaubenden' (59). So the passage is not meant to establish an
a fortiori argument from the case of Paul to that of other (lesser)
sinners. Rather, in contrast to the argument of 1 Cor 15.8–9,
which establishes the inferiority and posteriority of Paul, the
πρῶτος argument determines the priority and authority of the
Pauline gospel.

While there is no need to question that the authority of the
apostle Paul was under stress, it is not at all clear that the passage
utilises the testimony of Paul to establish him as the guarantor
of the gospel rather than to guarantee the effectiveness of the
gospel he has preached. These are two different things. Probably
the 'first' in v. 15 is qualitative, meaning 'I am foremost of
sinners' – the present tense need be nothing more than an allusion
to a continuing sense of unworthiness to have received God's
grace.[122] Salvation history is certainly in view, and the role of
Paul's conversion in the launching of the mission to the Gentiles
will not have been far from mind in v. 16 (v. 11). But what the
double πρῶτος emphasises is not the exclusive link of salvation
to Paul, but the superabundance of grace and mercy associated
with the authoritative message he preached.

16. ἀλλὰ διὰ τοῦτο ἠλεήθην The contrast with the preceding
clause completes the pattern which is repeated from v. 13. Thus
the general description of the apostle's experience of grace is
repeated here and connected specifically with the traditional
formulation of the gospel. The repetition of ἠλεήθην from v. 13
is now used to form the basis for a forward-looking statement
of God's reason and purpose in saving Paul (note the 'divine
passive'!), in contrast to the backward-looking statement about
his sinfulness there.

The ἵνα-clause that follows probably establishes the forward
reference of the prepositional phrase διὰ τοῦτο (2 Tim 2.10**):
'but I received mercy because of this, namely, that in me Christ
might show...'.[123]

**ἵνα ἐν ἐμοὶ πρώτῳ ἐνδείξηται Χριστὸς Ἰησοῦς τὴν ἅπασαν
μακροθυμίαν πρὸς ὑποτύπωσιν τῶν μελλόντων πιστεύειν ἐπ'
αὐτῷ εἰς ζωὴν αἰώνιον** God's purpose in showing mercy to Paul
was to demonstrate and set out as a pattern the full extent of
his patience towards sinners by means of Paul's conversion
experience.[124] The adj. πρώτῳ resumes the theme of v. 15c

---

[122] Cf. Barnabas 5.9. Bernard, 32f., notes the similar hyperbolical language of
Ignatius, *Eph.* 21.2; *Magn.* 14.
[123] Cf. the sequence in Rom 4.16; 9.17; 2 Cor 13.10; Eph 6.13; 2 Th 2.11;
Philem 15; cf. Rom 13.6.
[124] For ἐν ἐμοί in the sense of 'in my case' see Moule, 1953:77 (1 Cor 4.6;
9.15; Gal 1.16, 24).

and also establishes the temporal sequence necessary for the pattern. Elsewhere in the PE ἐνδείκνυμι (Tit 2.10 note) is used of demonstrating human qualities of character, but here it is used of a divine characteristic as in Rom 9.17, 22; Eph 2.7; cf. Rom 3.25, 26. Here the subject is Christ Jesus which may reflect the tendency in the PE to assign to Christ the attributes of God. ἅπας** is used intensively in the sense of 'immense' (cf. BD § 275⁷; cf. πᾶς, v. 15).[125] μακροθυμία (2 Tim 3.10; 4.2**) describes a quality of both God (Christ) and Christians. The testimony here draws on the OT theme of God's forbearing to unleash his wrath in order to allow people to repent and be saved.[126] This became a natural part of NT thought.[127] It is the attitude expressed in 'mercy', and it is the parallel of χρηστότης in the case of God and people.[128] This forbearing patience is thus also required as a quality in missionaries who must not despair of sinners but continue to seek to bring them to repentance and faith (2 Tim 4.2).

Within this discussion of Paul's conversion the purpose, but not the only purpose, given for this display of divine patience is so that the converted persecutor might be a pattern for future converts.[129] ὑποτύπωσις (2 Tim 1.13***) is capable of a range of meanings: '[preliminary] sketch'; 'pattern'; 'model'; 'prototype' ('Urbild'),[130] but here must have the sense of a general pattern. The use of the gen. for the persons/events that conform to the pattern is found in 2 Pet 2.6; cf. 1 Cor 10.6; 1 Tim 4.12. τῶν μελλόντων (cf. 4.8; 6.19; 2 Tim 4.1**) with the inf. is a periphrasis for the future participle. It might have the sense of 'those who are destined to believe', but the future seems rather to be entirely logical. πιστεύειν (see 1.11) here means 'to believe' in the sense of having saving faith. The construction with ἐπί with dat. is accepted NT usage.[131] The object of faith is of course Christ.

---

[125] NIV 'limitless' is probably too strong, however.

[126] Num 14.18; Joel 2.13; Ecclus 5.4; 4 Ezra 7.74; the LXX translates the Hebrew 'erek 'appayim 'the delay of wrath'; cf. Horst, F., TDNT IV, 374–87; Hollander, H. W., EDNT II, 380f.

[127] Rom 9.22; 1 Pet 3.20; 2 Pet 3.9, 15; cf. Ignatius, Eph. 11.1.

[128] For the former see Rom 2.4; Wis 15.1; cf. Rom 3.25, 26; for the latter see 2 Cor 6.6; Gal 5.22; Col 3.12; cf. 1 Cor 13.4.

[129] For πρὸς ὑποτύπωσιν expressing purpose cf. BD § 239⁷.

[130] The word can variously refer to a preliminary sketch in contrast to a complete picture (so MM 661), or to an outline as opposed to a fuller treatment, or to a model or pattern (cf. LSJ; Goppelt, L., TDNT VIII, 248, 250).

[131] With dat.: Lk 24.25; Rom 9.33 (= Isa 28.16 LXX = 1 Pet 2.6); 10.11. With acc.: Mt 27.42; Acts 9.42; 11.17; 16.31; 22.19; Rom 4.5, 24. Hence Spicq's suggestion (346; cf. Lock, 17) that it is like putting one's faith on a rock (Mt 7.25) is unnecessary and over-subtle.

εἰς ζωὴν αἰώνιον (Tit 1.2 note) is the goal of belief in Christ. For the connection between belief in Christ and eternal life, see Jn 3.15f.; 11.26; Acts 13.48. The phrase conforms to NT thinking elsewhere in depicting eschatological salvation in terms of the Christian hope in everlasting, spiritual life.[132] It may be thought of as already present (4.8a) or future (4.8b; 6.19), but the decision is not easy and most references are ambiguous.

The context suggests that Paul is presented as something more than a moral example to be followed or an edifying illustration (Roloff, 97; de Boer 1962:196–9; Wolter 1988:56f.). A temporal sequence is established in the development from ἐν ἐμοὶ πρώτῳ to τῶν μελλόντων πιστεύειν ἐπ᾽ αὐτῷ, and, as the recipient of saving grace, Paul is in some sense the pattern or prototype of the saved sinner. But in what sense? Those who see the author as a Pauline exclusivist (Roloff, 97; Wolter 1988:57; Donelson 1986; Collins 1975) understand the thought to be that Paul is not just an example of what the gospel can do but also in his person and experience becomes *the* embodiment of the gospel ('Paul's life creates the framework of the Christian experience which is filled in by those who follow him', Donelson 1986:103). He is thus the prototype of the saved sinner not simply in the sense that he is first or typical, but in the sense that the salvation of those coming after actually hangs on his experience and his gospel. He is the decisive prototype of God's action in saving sinners. His entire life is a representation of the power of the gospel and so he himself is part of the message. According to Roloff, Paul's whole life has thus been 'gospelised' (*Kerygmatisierung*) to establish the authentic contours of the gospel, which is in keeping with the way Paul is characterised in the PE.

Wolter 1988:58f. backs up this proposal by attempting to demonstrate that the prepositional phrase εἰς ζωὴν αἰώνιον is dependent upon ὑποτύπωσιν instead of πιστεύειν and therefore that eternal life is also linked definitively to the Pauline prototype. However, the parallels he offers (e.g. 2 Macc 6.28; 1 Cor 10.6; 2 Th 3.9), which do employ a synonym of 'model' or 'typos' language, use εἰς in an infinitive construction entirely unlike 1 Tim 1.16.

But it is certainly open to question that so much is intended in describing Paul as the 'prototype'. The relation between the verb ἐνδείξηται and the purpose of this action, πρὸς ὑποτύπωσιν..., should be observed closely. What Paul's experience seems to

---

[132] Mt 25.46; Lk 18.30; Jn 3.15f.; 4.14; 11.26; Acts 13.48; Rom 2.7; 5.21; 6.22; Gal 6.8; 1 Tim 6.19; Tit 3.7; 1 Jn 2.25; 5.20; Jude 21; 2 Clement 5.5; 8.4; 17.7; Ignatius, *Eph.* 18.1.

exemplify more than anything else is the magnitude of Christ's patience in choosing to save one who had opposed God so vehemently. Within the orbit of the Pauline mission and within the particular church addressed, the history of Paul and the logic used here would have pastoral significance; the gospel Paul has preached (vv. 11, 15) and experienced (vv. 13f., 16) will do for others what it did for him; heretics too, if they acknowledge their ignorance, may experience God's saving grace (cf. Donelson 1986:100–4). Paul is both witness and proof (Roloff, 98), and alongside the author's pastoral concern to reach the lost is the polemical goal to authenticate the gospel associated with the apostle (v. 11). In view of the heresy and its challenge to the gospel, to argue more than this by claiming that the author views the 'Pauline' gospel as the only or normative means of salvation is not substantiated by the text itself. Actually, the expression of 'the gospel's' content ends with σῶσαι in v. 15: what follows is offered, along with vv. 12–14, as a testimony to its truthfulness.

17. Τῷ δὲ βασιλεῖ τῶν αἰώνων, ἀφθάρτῳ ἀοράτῳ μόνῳ θεῷ, τιμὴ καὶ δόξα εἰς τοὺς αἰῶνας τῶν αἰώνων, ἀμήν The passage closes with a doxology which expresses thanks to God for the gift of eternal life to Paul and to people in general. It demonstrates that God lies behind all that happened in salvation history and in Paul's experience of it, and in this way it establishes the balance between God and Christ after the Christocentric Pauline testimony (cf. Roloff, 98; Merkel, 22). Its tone suggests that the wonder of God's grace and mercy and the hope in salvation, even in the case of the errorists, are more central to the thrust of the testimony than polemics. For such doxologies see 6.16; 2 Tim 4.18; Rom 11.36; 16.27; Gal 1.5; Eph 3.21; Phil 4.20; 1 Pet 4.11; 5.11. Their background is to be found in the Hellenistic synagogue (Tob 13.7, 11) and not in the language of the non-Jewish Graeco-Roman world.

It is addressed to God and not to Christ. This is made explicit in the doxology, and is in keeping with usual practice.[133] Spicq, 346, comments that the language is chosen in opposition to the laudatory epithets piled up to describe the emperors. While that kind of interest may well have influenced the early church in framing its doxologies, it is not certain that 1.17 was inserted for such a purpose (although if it is a pre-formed piece, it may originally have had this thrust). Nor is it anti-Gnostic in thrust (*contra* Holtz, 48f.; cf. Roloff, 98).

---

[133] For the view that it addresses Christ, see Oke*, who argues that the anarthrous θεῷ could refer to Christ and express his quality as divine. Oke admits, however, that 'king of the ages' is more likely to refer to God (cf. 6.15f.). See the criticism by Harris 1992:256 n. 1.

God is described with four terms. βασιλεύς τῶν αἰώνων is a Jewish title for God.[134] The pl. of αἰών, 'age' (Tit 2.12 note), may be adjectival ('the eternal king')[135] or intend a reference to the scope of God's rule, i.e. over the unending series of future ages, or possibly over the periods of salvation history (Knoch, 23) or over the worlds in existence during the various 'ages' (Heb 1.2; BA *s.v.* 3).

ἄφθαρτος, 'immortal' or 'incapable of perishing', is a term that was used by the Stoics and taken over into Judaism.[136] It represents a quality proper only to God, as the ἄφθαρτος θεός/φθαρτός ἄνθρωπος contrast in Rom 1.23*** suggests.[137] ἀόρατος (Col 1.15; Heb 11.27 of God; Rom 1.20; Col 1.16**), 'invisible', was a standing attribute of God, especially among the Jews in opposition to pagan idolatry which conceived of the gods as being present in images.[138]

The concluding description, μόνος (6.16**) θεός, occurs also in Rom 16.27, describing God the Father as the one and only God.[139] The motif of God's 'oneness' or unity was a traditional one in the early church's worship; sometimes it is merely a way of saying that he is 'supreme' (Spicq, 347f.). It can be traced back to the OT and intertestamental Jewish polemic against Gentile polytheism.[140]

There is no verb in the doxology. The indicative or the optative of εἰμί should be supplied. Only in 1 Pet 4.11 do we find a verb, and there it is indic. (cf. Rom 1.25 and other εὐλογητός statements which have the indic.). There is not much difference between saying in a tone of praise that God possesses honour and expressing the wish that he will have what one already knows that he has.

τιμή[141] and δόξα[142] are basically synonyms. δόξα in this usage goes back to the LXX translation of the Hebrew *kabod* in the

---

[134] Tob 13.6, 10; Jer 10.10 (MT); Rev 15.3 *v.l.*; 1 Clement 61.2 (cf. Ps 9.37 [MT 10.16]; Ecclus 36.22). βασιλεύς is used of human rulers (2.2) and of God (6.15*; Rev 15.3; Mt 5.35; parabolically for God in Mt 18.23; 22.2–13; It is used of Christ in Mt 21.5 = Lk 19.38; Rev 17.14; 19.16; parabolically in Mt 25.34, 40.

[135] Knight, 105; SB III, 320, 643; Sasse, H., *TDNT* I, 201; Holtz, T., *EDNT* I, 45.

[136] Wis 12.1; Philo, *Mos.* 2.171; *Deus* 26; *Sacr* 101.

[137] Cf. Holtz, T., *EDNT* III, 422f.

[138] Philo, *Cher.* 101; Spicq, 347; Kremer, J., *EDNT* II, 528. Cf. Jn 1.18; 5.37; 6.46; 1 Jn 4.20; 1 Tim 6.16.

[139] For the use of εἷς in the same sense see 2.5 (cf. Rom 3.29f.; Gal 3.20; 1 Cor 8.4–6; Eph 4.5f.).

[140] Deut 6.13; Ps 85 (MT 86).10; Isa 44.24 LXX; 2 Macc 7.37; *Sib. Orac.* 1.16f.; Josephus, *Ant.* 8.335; Jn 17.3; cf. Delling 1970:391–400; Dalbert 1954:124–30; see further 2.5 note.

[141] 6.16; cf. 5.17; 6.1; 2 Tim 2.20, 21. Cf. Schneider, J., *TDNT* VIII, 169–80.

[142] 1.11 note; 2 Tim 4.18; Tit 2.13 note.

sense of 'the weight of esteem and honour' due a person, a king or God (Hegermann, H., *EDNT* I, 345). The combination of terms here, which occurs in the LXX (Exod 28.2; Pss 8.6; 95 [MT 96].7), becomes a stereotypical acknowledgement of God's honour in the NT (e.g. Rev 4.9, 11; 5.13) and serves to form a superlative 'all honour' (cf. Hübner, H., *EDNT* III, 358).

The phrase εἰς τοὺς αἰῶνας τῶν αἰώνων (or the simpler εἰς τοὺς αἰῶνας) is the typical closing note in doxologies.[143] The pl. does not refer to specific epochs of time, and the gen. does not envisage the capturing of time by God's eternity.[144] The phrase is a Hebraism (Ps 83.5 [not MT]; 4 Macc 18.24) which functions as a superlative ('for ever and ever'): 'the structure as a whole raises the infinity of God's future to *eternity*' (Holtz, T., *EDNT* I, 45).

ἀμήν (6.16; 2 Tim 4.18) is the appropriate response to a doxology, inserted by the writer but probably intended to be uttered by the congregation listening to the reading. In accordance with OT and Jewish usage,[145] the term is a way of agreeing that what is said is true and joining in affirming it.[146]

d. Renewal of commission to Timothy (1.18–20)

Brox, N., 'Προφητεία im ersten Timotheusbrief', *BZ* 29 (1976), 229–32; Thornton, T. C. G., 'Satan – God's Agent for Punishing', *ExpTim* 83 (1971–2), 151–2.

The final paragraph in chapter 1 resumes the charge which the author began to give in 1.3f. before he diverged into a discussion of the heretics, the right use of the law and his own credentials to proclaim the gospel. It now does so, however, in the light of that intervening discussion: Timothy receives the gospel from Paul as Christ's representative and he is to take action against the opponents whose turning to heresy has caused them to lose their faith. Nevertheless, the purpose here is not to state the content of the charge but to emphasise the responsibility which lies upon Timothy to act as Paul's agent in executing it himself. So reference is made to the choice of Timothy for this task as

---

[143] 2 Tim 4.18; Rom 16.27; Gal 1.5; Phil 4.20; Heb 13.21; 1 Pet 4.11; 5.11 *v.l.*; Rev 1.6; 5.13; 7.12 *et al.* – not all the examples are textually certain; for the sing. form see Heb 1.8.

[144] Barr 1969:67–71.

[145] Hebrew: Num 5.22; Deut 27.15–26; Neh 8.6. LXX: 1 Chr 16.36; 1 Esdr 9.47; *et al.*

[146] For the usage specifically in doxologies see Hebrew examples in Ps 44.14 (MT 41.13); 71 (MT 72).19; 88 (MT 89).53; 105 (MT 106).48; Isa 25.1; and Greek examples in 3 Macc 7.23; 4 Macc 18.24; Odes 12.15; 14.28, 35; 2 Cor 1.20; Gal 1.5; Rom 16.27; cf. Schlier, H., *TDNT* I, 335–8; Wildberger, H., *THAT* I, 193–6; SB III, 456–61; Fee, 54.

seen in the prophecies associated with his appointment; to the need for him to act vigorously in the Lord's warfare and to preserve a good conscience; and to the danger of failing to do, as evidenced by the danger of heresy affecting teachers illustrated by two specific cases. Similar personal exhortations, often concluding sections of teaching, are found at 3.14; 4.6, 11; 5.21; 6.11–16; cf. 2 Tim 1.6–8; 2.1–7, 8, 14; Tit 2.15.

TEXT

18. ἐπὶ σέ εἰς σέ (H 256). Elliott, 32, adopts the variant, since scribes would have objected to it as a non-classical use of the preposition (Cl. = 'into') which is firmly attested in Rom 5.12; 2 Cor 10.14. The evidence is weak.

στρατεύῃ στρατεύσῃ (ℵ* D* Ψ 1175 *pc* Cl). The variant was accepted by Bernard, 20. Elliott, 21, defends the text on the grounds that the pres. subj. is needed to convey a present possibility rather than a future.

EXEGESIS

18. Ταύτην τὴν παραγγελίαν παρατίθεμαί σοι, τέκνον Τιμόθεε, κατὰ τὰς προαγούσας ἐπὶ σὲ προφητείας Timothy comes back into view with the second person sing. pronoun (σοι) and the affectionate epithet τέκνον Τιμόθεε. τέκνον (1.2 note; Tit 1.4 note), is here used as an address, as in 2 Tim 2.1, τέκνον μου, indicative of affection (Gal 4.19) or of the relationship of a son to a father who expects obedience from him (applied to a teacher and his pupil). The vocative Τιμόθεε (6.20**; cf. Gal 3.1; Phil 4.3) makes the instruction very direct and personal. For Oberlinner, 51f., however, its main function is to underline and legitimate the close relationship between Paul and his appointed successor for the sake of the congregation.

παρατίθημι is used for committing someone/something into the care of another.[147] The reference of παραγγελίαν (cf. 1.5), qualified as it is by ταυτὴν τήν, is not clear. A survey of the uses of οὗτος in the PE suggests that it refers backwards more often than forwards. A forward reference would make the content of τὴν παραγγελίαν the need to wage a good warfare. Since the passage opened similarly with Paul instructing Timothy about dealing with false teachers (1.3) and referred to that instruction in v. 5 as τῆς παραγγελίας (see note), a reference backwards is necessary in order to gain some kind of connection within the chapter.[148] Various nuances are possible: (a) The *task* committed by Paul to Timothy himself which involves stopping the heretical teachers from further activity, i.e. the παραγγελία of 1.5 which

[147] 2 Tim 2.2**; cf. Acts 14.23; 20.32; 1 Pet 4.19. Cf. Exod 21.1 of teaching; Maurer, C., *TDNT* VIII, 162f.
[148] Cf. Fee, 59, for the possibility of a reference both forwards and backwards.

is described in v. 3b.; (b) the actual *content* of the παραγγελία which Timothy was to give to the heretics; (c) the παραγγελία of 1.5, interpreted as the *apostolic message* generally (and, for Dibelius-Conzelmann, 32, thus a reference to the letter as a whole).

In support of (c) a connection may be made between the verb παρατίθημι and the related noun παραθήκη (1 Tim 6.20; 2 Tim 1.12, 14) which becomes an important concept in the development of the theme of 'tradition' in the PE.[149] There is general agreement that the content of the παραθήκη is the apostolic proclamation in some sense (see 6.20 note). But the verb is not restricted to discussions about transmitting the tradition. The interpretation of the content of the παραγγελία depends rather on the question whether the topic is still the response to the heresy or has slid over into the safeguarding of the gospel. Even if Dibelius-Conzelmann are correct that the subject of heresy was dropped in vv. 12–17, it was clearly resumed in vv. 18–20. This observation and the unlikelihood that the παραγγελία of 1.5 is to be taken as a broad reference to the apostolic proclamation (on which see 1.5 note) make interpretation (c) less likely.

Apart from 1.5 παραγγελία does not occur elsewhere in the PE. In 1 Th 4.2 the word refers to the individual commands that formed part of the ethical instruction in the church; a specific meaning is equally likely in the case of 1.5. Further, the context refers to 'fighting the good fight'; while this may possibly be a reference to ministry in general, ministry in this context is viewed from the angle of the responsibility to oppose heresy (see below; cf. 6.12; 2 Tim 4.7). It therefore seems most likely that the reference is a return to the original instruction to Timothy to stand up to the heretics: the flow of thought in v. 18 seems to increase the gravity of the original instruction (1.5 referring back to 1.3b–4) by first relating it to Timothy's commission and then raising the stakes by describing it more broadly in terms of warfare. Thus the whole phrase, ταύτην τὴν παραγγελίαν παρατίθεμαί σοι, refers back to the instruction or charge passed on from Paul to Timothy to oppose and correct the heretics.[150] It is concerned with the task rather than the actual teaching that Timothy was to give.

To strengthen his motivation, the prepositional phrase which follows recalls the event of Timothy's appointment. κατά indicates that in some sense the instructions given to Timothy are 'in accordance with' prophecies (προφητεία, 4.14**), i.e. so that

---

[149] Dibelius-Conzelmann, 32; Roloff, 101; Wolter 1988:118f.; Trummer, P., *EDNT* III, 22.

[150] For the thought cf. 6.20; 2 Tim 1.12, 14; 2.2.

those prophecies may be fulfilled. But the description of those prophecies as τὰς προαγούσας ἐπὶ σὲ προφητείας is problematic. The first question is whether ἐπὶ σὲ depends upon the preceding τὰς προαγούσας or upon προφητείας. If taken with the participle, the result is 'prophecies leading to or going on before you', i.e. προάγω is understood in a local sense (Scott, 16; Knight, 108). However, on the one hand, this would be the only instance in the NT of προάγω with ἐπί (εἰς is common; cf. 5.24), and on the other, the connection of 'prophecy/prophesy' with ἐπί is more natural.[151] The syntax here is best understood by the parallel in 4.14: τοῦ ἐν σοὶ χαρίσματος. In this case, the intransitive προάγων means 'going before in time', i.e. 'preceding, earlier'.[152] The reference is then to prophecies made 'concerning' Timothy at some point in the past. The further reference to prophecies in 4.14 strongly suggests that they were associated with Timothy's appointment. There are two possible references.

(a) Roloff, 102, understands 'prophecies' to be words of exhortation and orders spoken during the ordination ceremony by the elders prior to the laying on of hands; the content corresponds to 6.11f. (cf. Brox 1976:229–32). This interpretation presumes a development of 'ordination' beyond the concept of commissioning seen in Acts 13.1–3 (Roloff, 101; Lips 1979:232–40). It also places the term in a category of meaning that is more institutional and rigid than the texts (cf. 4.14) require.[153]

(b) On the analogy supplied by Acts 13.2 the prophecies are words originating with the Spirit spoken through those present at his appointment which confirm his choice by God (Fee 1994:758–61). This indicates the importance of prophecy (cf. 4.1), and the pl. is evidence for the existence of prophets in the church despite the lack of notice paid to them elsewhere in the PE (cf. Roloff, 101f.). However, if this is a reflection back on an earlier event (e.g. Acts 16.2 or some other event in Timothy's life; see Fee, 57f.; cf. Scott, 16), rather than to his appointment to office in Ephesus (Brox, 118), it is difficult to see what light this would shed on the understanding and role of prophecy in Ephesus. Apart from the line of interpretation which understands the Spirit and ministry to be linked solely to the offices (for which Timothy supplies the model), there is no reason to see in the reference to 'prophecies' in 1.18 much more than a setting apart

---

[151] There is ample precedent in the LXX; in addition to Ezek see e.g. Ezra 5.1; Amos 7.15, 16; Jer 33 (MT 26).12; see also Rev 10.11.

[152] BA s.v. 2.b; BD § 308; Lips 1979:173; Roloff, 101.

[153] The view that προφητεία is the equivalent of the Latin *praefatio* and thus a prayer accompanying the laying on of hands during ordination is dismissed by Lips 1979:243f.; Brox 1976; Roloff.

for a mission such as is described in Acts 13.2 (see further 4.14 note).[154] Oberlinner, 52f., rejects the idea that the prophecies are some form of advice and encouragement the memory of which will encourage Timothy; they are not from the side of the congregation but rather confirm to the congregation the fact of the leader's appointment and his dependence upon Paul who is regarded as the author of the actual prophecies. In any case, so far as Timothy is concerned, the description implies some local autonomy.[155] The context, however, strongly favours the view that the content of the prophecies was related to the content of the commission of which Timothy is here reminded (cf. NJB).

ἵνα στρατεύῃ ἐν αὐταῖς τὴν καλὴν στρατείαν One purpose of the charge given to Timothy is now developed. By fighting the good fight in obedience to it, he will fulfil the prophecies. Timothy is cast in the role of a soldier (στρατεύομαι, 2 Tim 2.4**)[156] who must display perseverance and courage, and ministry is viewed as warfare. στρατεία (2 Cor 10.4***; Pfitzner 1967:156–71) is probably used as a cognate accusative (BA; 6.12; cf. 4 Macc 9.23; et al.) purely in order to carry the qualifier καλή, 'good, noble'; it is the warfare of the faith (cf. 6.12) which is worth fighting, and which is more valuable than other kinds. In fighting this battle, remembrance of the above mentioned prophecies (ἐν αὐταῖς)[157] or the commissioning by God which they confirmed is intended to guide, motivate and inspire (cf. Spicq, 349–50). The charge to engage the heretics is related directly to Timothy's commission and call to ministry (Roloff, 104).

The military metaphor is a familiar one.[158] The charge is related to the similarly constructed Agon-motif which occurs in 6.12 and 2 Tim 4.7.[159] The use of these related motifs in the PE represents an extension of earlier Pauline use which might depict the personal conflict of faith (cf. Rom 13.10; Eph 6.10–17),

[154] Hasler, 17, comments that earlier prophets gave eschatological threats and promises, but now they give the church advice on its personal and common life. But can an accurate job description of prophets or of Timothy be derived from this passage?

[155] Timothy is an apostolic coworker rather than a diocesan bishop (cf. Ollrog 1979:23; Holmberg, B., *Paul and Power: The Structure of Authority in the Primitive Church as Reflected in the Pauline Epistles* [Lund: Gleerup, 1978], 58–69; Maehlum 1969; Towner 1989:228f.).

[156] For the metaphorical use cf. the inscr. from Nikaia (AD II/III) in *New Docs.* IV, 25, 28 §6.

[157] White, 101, paraphrases with 'as in defensive armour'; other translations include 'resting on them' (Spicq, 349f.); 'inspired by them' (RSV); 'by following them' (NIV).

[158] Cf. Bauernfeind, O., *TDNT* VII, 701–13, especially 711f. On the PE see Dibelius-Conzelmann, 32; Spicq, 350f. For the use of the metaphor to apply to life generally in ancient philosophers, see Epictetus 3.24.34 and Maximus of Tyre 13.4d (MM, 592; BA *s.v.* στρατεία); Lock, 18.

[159] Pfitzner 1967:177–80; Roloff, 103.

or his and his churches' struggle in the gospel ministry.[160] In this
case, ministry is in mind. The application here to the successor
of Paul is natural. In some of the earlier Pauline contexts the
language reflects ministry in the midst of severe opposition. Thus
here the charge to Timothy is to one called to ministry to engage
in conflict with false teachers (so rightly Roloff, 103f., who refers
to 'ordination language': 4.12–16; 6.11–16; 2 Tim 1.6).

19. ἔχων πίστιν καὶ ἀγαθὴν συνείδησιν The participial phrase
possibly continues the metaphor by describing the soldier's
equipment (so apparently Spicq, 351f.; *pace* White, 101). In any
case, it details two elements essential both to effective ministry
and authentic spiritual life. For ἔχων ('possessing', 'holding fast',
'maintaining') with faith as its object see Mt 17.20; 21.21; Acts
14.9; Rom 14.22; 1 Cor 13.2; Jas 2.18; with conscience as the
object see Acts 24.16; Heb 10.2; 13.18; 1 Pet 3.16.

πίστις and ἀγαθὴ συνείδησις combine, as in 1.5 (cf. 3.9), to
characterise authentic Christian existence. Faith denotes not just
belief but the whole attitude of the Christian which is determined
by trust in God (1.5 note; **Excursus 4**).[161] The conscience
functions to direct, and monitor conduct according to a set norm,
which would be understood to be not only the objective content
of 'the faith' but also the patterns of thought shaped by commitment to it. As we have seen, the PE present the conscience, as
good or bad, from a theological perspective; its condition is
related to one's disposition towards the gospel. At the same time,
the conscience is needed to safeguard the faith. As the following
description of apostasy shows, faith and a good conscience are
interdependent elements in the author's concept of Christian
existence (Roloff, 104). The concentration on these two factors,
especially in relation to the neglect of them by the opponents
(v. 20) explains the failure to repeat ἀγάπη from v. 5.

ἥν τινες ἀπωσάμενοι περὶ τὴν πίστιν ἐναυάγησαν The relative
pronoun followed by τινες is a favourite device of the author
for describing graphically the actions which lead to apostasy
(1.6; 6.21; 2 Tim 2.18). Here and in 1.6 the interjection introduces
a contrast between the true faith and the heresy, the faithful
minister and the heretic.

ἀπωθέομαι[162] conveys a picture of deliberate rejection of the
voice of the conscience, i.e. refusal to listen to it; ἥν must refer
only to συνείδησιν and not to πίστιν. The influence of the

---

[160] 1 Cor 9.7; 2 Cor 10.3–5 (cf. 6.7); Phil 2.25; 1 Th 5.8; cf. 2 Tim 2.3–4; cf.
the athletic δρόμος in Acts 20.24; 1 Cor 9.24–27; Gal 2.2; Phil 1.27–30; 2.16;
3.12–14; 1 Th 2.1–2; cf. Pfitzner 1967:157–65; Roloff, 103.
[161] Calvin, 201f., took faith to mean 'sound teaching' here, but this is to
narrow the meaning.
[162] Acts 7.27, 39; 13.46; Rom 11.1, 2***; cf. Jer 23.17.

conscience upon one's adherence and response to the faith is such that failure to heed it (i.e. failure to conduct oneself according to its norm or rejection of the norm altogether) will close off access to a right understanding of the faith (cf. Roloff, 104; Brox, 119). While this may indicate that the heresy involved the kind of behaviour that conscience would have rejected, the point to be observed from the connections made in vv. 18f. (and elsewhere) is not so much that moral lapse can threaten one's faith (Kelly, 58), although it certainly can, but that conduct and belief are viewed here as inseparable parts of a whole (Prov 15.32; Hos 4.6; *T. Ash.* 1). One of the tendencies of the false notions of spirituality may have been to emphasise the cognitive dimension of faith and ignore practical ethics (see Schlarb 1990:122–34; **Excursus 1**, Introduction). Where the morality of the opponents is criticised, the author tends to link it closely with their perversion of the faith (cf. Roloff, 104 n. 57). Rejection of the one must influence the other.

This rejection has devastating consequences. ναυαγέω (2 Cor 11.25***) means 'to suffer shipwreck'. The metaphor was well-known and signified total disaster.[163] But the reference in περὶ τὴν πίστιν is ambiguous. (a) The articular ἡ πίστις (**Excursus 4**) often refers to the objective content of the faith, which leads Fee, 58, to suggest that it is *the* faith which has suffered shipwreck, i.e. their teaching has brought the gospel itself to ruin. But the intransitive ναυαγέω, the fact that it is the opponents who suffer, and the preposition περί ('with respect to'; cf. 6.21; 2 Tim 2.18; 3.8; Tit 2.7**) all make the reference to τὴν πίστιν rather indirect. (b) Consequently, a reference either to the faith that has just been mentioned (that of the genuine believer) or to 'their faith' which used to be healthy (Lock, 19; Arichea-Hatton, 41f.) would seem better.

There is a close parallel to 6.21 which (along with the implications to be drawn from 1.3b–7) may suggest that it was by following a false 'knowledge' which they regarded as superior to conscience that the heretics went astray as regards their faith.

In this restatement of the charge to Timothy in light of his commissioning, an implicit warning not to go astray like some have is probably intended (Lips 1979:211; Hasler, 18).

20. ὧν ἐστιν Ὑμέναιος καὶ Ἀλέξανδρος The seriousness of the command and of the warning implicit in the statement just made is underlined by reference to a specific example of heretics falling away from the faith. The two mentioned are part of (ὧν ἐστιν 'among whom', 'including [for example]'; cf. 2 Tim

---

[163] See refs. in Dibelius-Conzelmann, 33, n. 12; and Spicq, 353; e.g. Cebes, *Tabula* 24.2; Philo, *Decal.* 14.

1.15; 2.17) a larger number (τινες). The use of the sing. verb in this construction is normal (cf. 2 Tim 2.17; BD § 135). The disciplinary measures described demonstrate that the danger is by no means imaginary or merely prospective, as well as that the apostle has already passed verdict on the heresy (Knoch, 23). Thus this verse is in no sense a digression.

Ὑμέναιος (2 Tim 2.18***) is a name found in legends (cf. *Acts of Paul and Thecla*; see BA *s.v.*). A person of the same name reappears in 2 Tim 2.17 as one who denies the resurrection and so upsets the faith of other Christians. There is no good reason to doubt the identity of the two characters. Since he is still active in the church in 2 Tim, Easton, 18, argues that the chronological order of the letters should be inverted. However, nothing in 2 Tim precludes the possibility that Hymenaeus was active from outside the church, or that the argument in 2 Tim 2 better suited an explanation of the false resurrection doctrine, which may have already been current when 1 Tim was written.[164]

Ἀλέξανδρος is a common name (Mk 15.21; Acts 4.6; 19.33). An Alexander appears in 2 Tim 4.14*** as a coppersmith who had done Paul much harm. Identification of the two men is possible; Fee, 296, holds that after the excommunication described here he left Ephesus and was in Troas (cf. van Bruggen: 1981:55f.) But the fact that the Alexander in 2 Tim has to be identified by his occupation may suggest that he is a different figure from the one here. Calvin, 203, identified him with Paul's opponent in Acts 19.33.

Some regard the characters as a part of the author's fiction. The claim is that his method was to invent persons to illustrate for the later church the emergence of heresy and in some sense authenticate procedures adopted by the church (such as 'excommunication') and link them to the historical Paul (Oberlinner, 56f.; cf. Trummer 1978:137–41). However, even from the standpoint of pseudepigraphy, it is much more likely that the author would begin with personalities known by the churches; indeed, the impression (especially from the twofold reference to Hymenaeus) is that this is a well-known figure, and there is no reason to doubt the historicity of the Alexanders, Philetus or Onesiphorus (see Roloff, 105; Dibelius-Conzelmann, 127f.; Barrett, 48; Brox, 120). The reference to these two heretics in the context of a discussion of Timothy's commission may indicate that they were elders (Roloff, 105; Fee, 59). Knoch, 23, thinks they are actual opponents of the writer, while Brox, 120, suggests that they were prominent leaders of heretical sects. Whatever the case, they were well known and probably still influential in the church. The apostle's verdict and the report of

---

[164] Schlarb 1990:179–82; Towner 1989:100–7, 30f.; Roloff, 231.

the disciplinary action which had been taken would be aimed to discredit them and limit what further damage they could do in the community.

οὓς παρέδωκα τῷ σατανᾷ The phraseology is identical with 1 Cor 5.5 παραδοῦναι ... τῷ Σατανᾷ ἵνα ... and reflects Job 2.6.[165] A disciplinary measure is clearly in view. Roloff, 105f., notes that whereas in 1 Corinthians Paul instructs the church to hand over the sinner, here Paul himself does it, which corresponds to the later author's emphasis on Paul's absolute authority (also Brox, 121). However, this may be straining the texts somewhat. For example, since the apostle commanded the Corinthian course of action, and it is clear that apostolic authority and 'presence' are required for the action to proceed, in another letter might not he have used the first person to describe the execution of the disciplinary measure? In this case, in the reference to a past action (παρέδωκα), can we be certain the church was not somehow involved? What seems to be present in each text is an emphasis on apostolic authority. Another difference is noted: in the later situation of the PE the discipline is said to lack the Pauline eschatological dimension; i.e. there is no consciousness of the need to be pure for salvation on the day of the Lord (Roloff, 106). But though the present text does not mention it, 2 Tim 2.25 suggests that repentance/salvation is the goal of discipline, and expectation of Christ's return is not absent from the letters (6.14; 2 Tim 1.12; 4.1; Tit 2.13). For handing over for punishment cf. Mt 18.34.

The disciplinary measure is a handing over to Satan. Σατανᾶς[166] appears here and elsewhere as an agent of God, carrying out punishment on especially recalcitrant sinners.[167] But the reference in the phrase is unclear. The language may have become a formal reference to excommunication from the church into the area 'outside' regarded as Satan's province (Fee, 59). Or it might refer to the infliction of physical suffering or even death as in Acts 5.1–11; 13.11; 1 Cor 11.30 (Lock, 20; Easton, 118f.). In these cases, however, God, not Satan, himself inflicts the disaster. Spicq, 354, cites as a parallel 4QFlorilegium 1.9 'delivering their soul to Belial', but this restoration of the fragmentary text is no longer accepted.[168]

---

[165] παραδίδωμι**; New Docs. IV, 165 §73, cites an epitaph which threatens that disturbers of tombs will be handed over to the infernal gods. Cf. MM 483; Büchsel, F., TDNT II, 169–72.

[166] 5.15**; Foerster, W., and Schäferdieck, K., TDNT VII, 151–65.

[167] He is also God's enemy; cf. Thornton 1971–2:151f.

[168] Spicq was dependent upon Allegro, J. M. 'Fragments of a Qumran Scroll of Eschatological Midrašim', JBL 77 (1958), 350f.; but see now Brooke, G. J., Exegesis at Qumran: 4QFlorilegium in its Jewish Context (Sheffield: Sheffield Academic Press, 1985), 109f.

Thus Satan is seen to be an agent to discipline sinners. In the biblical and Jewish tradition there is no absolute consistency in the way in which Satan is seen as God's enemy and as his agent.[169] Apparently, in the Pauline churches it was believed that in extreme cases of persistent sin God employed Satan as an agent, but nevertheless God himself remained firmly in control of the situation.

ἵνα παιδευθῶσιν μὴ βλασφημεῖν The action has a purpose. παιδεύω (Tit 2.12**; 2 Tim 2.25) in this context means to correct by discipline (Fee, 59). If taken literally, the action is seen as a remedial form of discipline to lead the heretics to repentance. The form of that discipline is apparently to exclude the offenders from the church, to put them outside of God's grace. In 1 Cor 5.5 the aim is that the sinner will be saved. The possibility that the word may be heavily ironical and refer simply to severe punishment (as in our English 'That will teach him' or 'That will learn him!') is unlikely in view of the redemptive goal linked to παιδεύοντα in 2 Tim 2.25 (see further Roloff, 106).

Their sin is now interpreted as blasphemy. βλασφημέω (1.13 note) implies that the behaviour of the heretics was insolent. But the issue here is not entirely clear. Since the fundamental sin (1.3b–4) is false teaching, 'blaspheme' is probably to be understood in the religious sense as slander or misrepresentation of the true and divine faith,[170] rather than malicious talk (cf. 6.4) or insults levelled against Paul and people (cf. Tit 2.2) associated with the heresy (but see Fee, 59).

II. INSTRUCTION ON PRAYER (2.1–15)

The opening section of the specific instructions addressed to Timothy forms a self-contained unit clearly marked off from what precedes and what follows. There is a single theme followed by a related digression. The theme is prayer in the church meeting (but private prayers may also be in mind, Knoch, 24). In vv. 1–7 the need for prayer is inculcated and stress is laid on its universal scope, embracing all kinds of people. Then follows an extended justification based on the implications of the gospel. A fresh start is made with a statement of the moral requirements for prayer, first in respect of men (v. 8) and then (v. 9) in respect of women; the two are treated as separate categories, which must reflect something about the relationships within the church.

---

[169] Cf. Job 2.6; references to the angel of death, Exod 12.23; *Jub.* 49.2 (all the powers of Mastema). See also Num 16.41–50; 4 Macc 7.11; Wis 18.25; 1 Cor 10.10; CD 8.2 and *1 Enoch* 53.3 with its reference to angels of punishment preparing the chains of Satan. Satan is the angel of death in BB 16a (SB I, 144–9).

[170] 6.1; 2 Pet 2.2; cf. 1 Cor 15.15; Lock, 20; Hasler, 18; Hofius, O., *EDNT* I, 220.

The mention of women at prayer leads to the digression. It is concerned with the fact that they should not teach but learn in silence and comments that they may still find spiritual salvation in the bearing and nurture of their children. Their demeanour at prayer is to be seen also in the teaching and learning situation.

Parallels have been seen between 1 Tim 2–3 and the order of discussion in Didache 8.2–10; 14; 15f. where similarly the treatment covers prayer, moral requirements and the appointment of overseers and deacons. But this seems to be purely a matter of coincidence. For the view that 2.1–3 and 1 Clement 59–61 are using a common source document see Hanson 1968:59–61.

It is not immediately clear whether the governing theme of the section is the conduct of the church meeting, or even the relation of the church to the secular authorities, or rather the role of the church in the propagation of the gospel (Parry, 11). In any case, the structure of the passage rules out the theory that the author's main interest lies in the subordination and silencing of women in the church meeting.[1] Most probably the main theme is the gospel; the association of prayer with the fulfilment of the task of mission is characteristic of the earlier Paul, and this appears to be the dominant connection of thought here.

a. Prayer for all people (2.1–7)

Bartsch 1965:27–46; Denk, F., 'Die Geschichte der Deutung von 1 Tim 2,5', Diss. Wien, 1954 (not accessible); Dibelius, M., ''Επίγνωσις ἀληθείας', in Dibelius 1956:1–13 (= *Neutestamentliche Studien für G. Heinrici* [Leipzig, 1914], 176–89); Le Fort, P., 'La responsibilité politique de l'église d'après les épîtres pastorales', *ETR* 49 (1974), 1–14; Légasse, S., 'La prière pour les chefs d'état: antécédents judaïques et témoins chrétiens du premier siècle', *NovT* 29 (1987), 236–53; Marshall 1989; Murphy-O'Connor, J., 'Community and Apostolate. Reflections on 1 Timothy 2:1–7', *BibTod* 67 (1973), 1260–6; Oberlinner, L., ''"Ein ruhiges und ungestörtes Leben führen". Ein Ideal für christliche Gemeinden?', *BK* 46 (1991), 98–106; Turmel, J., 'Histoire de l'interpretation de 1 Tim II.4', *Revue de l'histoire et de littérature religieuse* 5 (1900), 385–415 (not accessible); Wolter 1988:69–82.

Verses 1–7 form a compact section which bases the command to pray for all people in the universal saving will of the one and only God, evidenced in the coming and the self-giving of the one Mediator – as taught in the message of which Paul is a teacher to the Gentiles. The stress on the universality of the gospel (note the repetition of πᾶς) and on the place of Paul in what has been described as the first and longest discussion of prayer in the NT

---

[1] *Pace* Roloff, 132, who holds that the injunction to the men was inserted by the author merely in order to counterbalance the injunction to the women; originally the injunction would have been for the whole congregation, but it was then focused on the men only.

(Houlden, 65) is particularly striking. The emphasis on the latter – almost polemical in character – suggests that there was some opposition to the idea. It is plausible that the false teachers, who stressed Jewish myths and genealogies and apparently also the law, were not enthusiastic for the Gentile mission. Consequently, it was necessary to stress the significant place of Paul as the missionary to the Gentiles and the relation of his position to the central affirmation of the gospel.

But, while this may explain the rationale for the statement in vv. 3–7, it does not explain so easily the placing of prayer in such a prominent place ('first of all'!). That at least some prayer took place in the church is evident (5.5; grace at meals is also mentioned in 4.4f.), and the list of words for prayer in 2.1 suggests a broad range of modes. Read on their own, vv. 1–2 might suggest that prayer was being offered not for the salvation of mankind but simply for peaceable conditions for Christians! This topic must have been important, but it is not taken up in 1 Tim, although it is significant in 2 Tim where Paul himself is in the hands of the Roman authorities. Merkel, 24, argues that the mention of prayer for the authorities is a subordinate theme occasioned by the ever-present threat of persecution.

It appears, therefore, that prayer was not happening, and where it did it was disturbed by the wrong attitudes of those taking part. The writer took it for granted that prayer was essential for the life and witness of the church, and found it necessary to stress the need for it in a church where it was becoming impossible because of the splits and divisions within the congregation – a lack of human harmony and a love of dispute whose first victim was corporate prayer. The opposition to the gospel of Paul in the church was threatening not only the teaching but also and (first in importance) the effectiveness of the church's prayers.

TEXT

1. παρακαλῶ παρακάλει (D* F G b vg^{ms} Hil Ambst). The western variant would make the verse an instruction to Timothy to exhort the church, as in 5.1; 6.2; Tit 2.6 (Metzger, 572). Elliott, 33f., notes that no imperatives to Timothy appear before 4.6 and that it is less usual to place imperatives at the beginning of a sentence.

3. τοῦτο καλόν Insert γάρ (א² D F G H Ψ TR latt sy). Elliott, 35, notes that γάρ is often added to texts unnecessarily, as here where the demonstrative pronoun acts as a connective.

5. εἷς καί καὶ εἷς (51 547 876). Elliott, 36, favours the variant on the grounds that Semitic idiom puts καί first and that it could have been changed for greater emphasis. But this is also perfectly good Greek idiom. It is more likely that scribes removed the asyndeton.

Χριστὸς ᾿Ιησοῦς Inverted order (K 1836 460 216 223). Elliott, 199, 202, adopts the variant, as at 1.5, 16, but the MS evidence is very weak.

6. τὸ μαρτύριον καὶ μαρτύριον (ℵ*); omit (A); praem. οὗ (D* F G 104 *pc* a (m) vg⁵ Ambst) and add ἐδόθη (D* F G it vg^mss Ambst). The various changes and additions ease the construction (Elliott, 36f.).

7. εἰς ὃ ἐτέθην ὃ ἐπιστεύθην (A). Elliott, 37, suggests that the variant arose when the preposition was lost by homoioteleuton with the preceding ἰδίοις and then the verb was altered by assimilation to 1.11.

λέγω Add ἐν Χριστῷ (ℵ* D² H 33^vid TR a vg^mss). The variant is caused by assimilation to Rom 9.1 (Elliott, 38; Metzger, 572).

πίστει γνώσει (ℵ *pc*); πνεύματι (A). Both variants are secondary. See Elliott, 38.

EXEGESIS

1. Παρακαλῶ οὖν πρῶτον πάντων ποιεῖσθαι δεήσεις προσευχὰς ἐντεύξεις εὐχαριστίας ὑπὲρ πάντων ἀνθρώπων At first sight the connection with the preceding material intended by οὖν is not clear. Elsewhere οὖν is used (with verbs of exhortation) to make the transition to paraenesis after a digression (2.8; 3.2; 5.14; 2 Tim 1.8; 2.1), and that is the probable intention here; it picks up 1.18 after the digression in 1.19b–20 (Easton, 120). Prayer in the church is seen as a part of the means by which the church is to combat heresy. Encouraging the practice as it is laid out here is thus a part of the task ('the fight') Timothy is to carry out.

The tone of the instructions is personal and somewhat urgent. As in the earlier Paul (Rom 12.1; 1 Cor 1.10; 2 Cor 10.1; cf. 1 Pet 2.11), the verb παρακαλῶ (see 1.3; Tit 1.9 notes) expresses a command within the context of a mutual relationship and can mark the beginning of the instructional part of a letter. Although the instruction is really addressed to the churches, it is communicated via Timothy, who is responsible for the leadership (Dibelius-Conzelmann, 35).

The superlative πρῶτον[2] stresses either the priority (first in time or sequence) or the importance (first in degree) of the instruction. Here it may simply indicate that this is the first instruction to be given in the letter.[3] Or the meaning might be 'above all',[4] implying that this is the most important instruction and therefore the first thing that should happen in the church.[5] In many cases it is difficult to judge whether priority of degree or time is stressed (e.g. Mt 6.33; Rom 1.16; 2.9f.; Acts 3.26), but where the latter is meant the former may be implied. Thus, although this is the

[2] 3.10; 5.4; 2 Tim 1.5; 2.6**; with πάντων = 'first of all' (Mk 12.28; Hermas, *Mand.* 1.1; *Vis.* 5.5).
[3] Similar formulae are used to introduce the body of a Greek letter (Spicq, 356).
[4] 2 Cor 8.5; 2 Pet 1.20; 3.3; Josephus, *Ant.* 10.213.
[5] BA; Bernard, 37; Roloff, 113; Fee, 62.

first command in the letter intended for the church, the priority given to it probably also implies its importance for church life. The content of the instruction comes to expression in the complementary infinitive, ποιεῖσθαι. It may be understood as a passive with its four accusative subjects which are to be 'done' by the unnamed actor (the church),[6] or as a middle with the unexpressed acc. τοὺς ἀνθρώπους as 'subject'.[7]

The four terms which describe prayer characterise it in its totality and emphasise the scope of the responsibility which has 'all people' in view. Most scholars claim that a precise analysis of modes of prayer is not intended.[8]

δέησις (5.5; 2 Tim 1.3**) is a general term for a petition; placed at the head of the list it implies actively petitioning God to act on behalf of people.[9] προσευχή (5.5**) is a more general term for any kind of prayer or for prayer in general (e.g. Rom 1.10; 1 Th 1.2; Eph 1.16; Philem 4); intercession for various things is often in view as it is here (Rom 15.30; Philem 22).[10] The two words evidently formed a pair (Eph 6.18; Phil 4.6; 1 Tim 5.5). While in some contexts δέησις may mean a 'special request' (cf. BA *s.v.*; Rom 1.10; 1 Th 3.10; Eph 6.18), a rigid distinction between it and προσευχή as a 'general request' cannot always be maintained.[11] Oberlinner, 66, attempts to differentiate between the terms by holding that προσευχή is prayer by the congregation rather than the individual and that it is praise rather than petition. This is hard to substantiate.

ἔντευξις (4.5***) is a petition or request addressed to a superior, hence in this context a prayer.[12] εὐχαριστία (4.3, 4**), 'thanksgiving' (Acts 24.3) or the expression of thanks, is used of prayer in 1 Cor 14.16; 2 Cor 9.12; Rev 7.12. Thanksgiving was a normal part of prayer; the assumption is that, when praying, the congregation remembers with gratitude how former prayers have been answered, and therefore prays with all the

---

[6] Cf. BD § 392⁴.

[7] Cf. Lk 5.33; Phil 1.4; BA *s.v.* δέησις and ποιέω II; Holtzmann, 305; Bernard, 38.

[8] *Pace* Origen, *Orat.* 14.2 p. 331 Koetschau; Hendriksen, 91–3.

[9] Cf. Greeven, H., *TDNT* II, 40f.

[10] Cf. Herrmann, J., and Greeven, H., *TDNT* II, 775–808, espec. 807f.; Balz, H., *EDNT* III, 164–9.

[11] *Pace* Schoenborn, U., *EDNT* I, 287; cf. Phil 4.6 where the context in which requests (τὰ αἰτήματα) are made is ἐν παντὶ τῇ προσευχῇ καὶ τῇ δεήσει μετὰ εὐχαριστίας.

[12] Hermas, *Mand.* 5.1.6; 10.3.2f; 10.11.9; cf. the use of the verb ἐντυγχάνω (Acts 25.24; Rom 8.27; 11.2; Heb 7.25). Originally the word-group referred to appearing before somebody to speak with them (2 Macc 4.8), and hence it came to refer to expressing a request or prayer (Philo, *Det.* 92). The noun is frequent in pap. and inscr. for petitions (MM 218). Cf. Dibelius-Conzelmann, 36 nn. 7–8; Bauernfeind, O., *TDNT* VIII, 238–45; *TLNT* II, 6–10.

more confidence; in fact, 'in their request, they can already express their gratitude for the expected answer' (*TLNT* II, 9). The importance of this dimension of prayer can be seen in the place it occupies in paraenetic passages (Eph 5.4; Phil 4.6; Col 2.7; 4.2).[13]

The prayers are to be offered 'on behalf of' (or 'concerning') 'all human beings' (ὑπὲρ πάντων ἀνθρώπων).[14] The phrase is not confined to men only, nor is it dependent upon the last aspect of prayer ('thanksgiving'). What is said goes beyond Judaism in which prayer is said to have been offered only for neighbours and not for all people (see Dornier, 48; Roloff, 115). It is sometimes claimed that other NT documents have a limited horizon which does not extend beyond the bounds of the Christian community; this is emphatically not the case here (Johnson, 130f.). Prayer in its fullest sense is to be made for all human beings that they may be saved (see vv. 3–4). The use of πᾶς here and its repetition in vv. 2, 4 and 6 is thematic, establishing a universal emphasis which is probably polemical.[15] The instruction is a pointer to the church's world consciousness. This universalistic thrust is most probably a corrective response to an exclusive elitist understanding of salvation connected with the false teaching.[16]

2. ὑπὲρ βασιλέων καὶ πάντων τῶν ἐν ὑπεροχῇ ὄντων Verse 3 offers the logical continuation of v. 1 with its justification of universal prayer from the purpose of God the Saviour. Verse 2 seems to be a digression. It is concerned with prayer for a specific group of people and the purpose is that Christians may live a peaceful life. Its place here, however, is not unexpected when considered alongside the traditional emphasis in the NT household codes on the church's reponsibility towards the State. Elsewhere this responsibility is described with the customary verb (ὑποτάσσεσθαι; Rom 13.1–7; 1 Pet 2.13–17; Tit 3.1), and the duties and motives connected with 'submission' may vary (e.g. paying taxes in Rom 13.7; 'honouring' in 1 Pet 2.17 and 'obeying' in Tit 3.1 those in authority). Here prayer for those in authority may well be seen as the application of the traditional principle.

---

[13] A reference to a specifically eucharistic prayer (cf. Ignatius, *Eph.* 13.1; *Philad.* 4; *Smyrn.* 8.1) is unlikely here; see Roloff, 114.

[14] Spicq, 358, finds a priestly function here in which the church has a priestly role with application to the entire world. But there is no evidence for this in the PE.

[15] Note also the indefinite ἀνθρώπων in v. 5 (Towner 1989:202).

[16] Haufe 1973:332 and Schmithals 1983:117 find here a response to an alleged Gnostic disregard for the State (cf. v. 2). However, there is nothing in the PE that cannot be reasonably explained on the basis of the sort of spiritual enthusiasm that developed in Corinth (Towner 1989:33–42).

The explanation of the State's role that appears in Rom 13 and 1 Pet 2 (to execute justice and maintain an orderly society) is arguably present in the ἵνα clause that follows, although the dominant evangelistic focus of the passage requires a different expression of it (cf. Towner 1989:202f.). The motif that Christians will benefit by a right attitude to the State is clearly present in each occurrence of the tradition. The mission motive should also not be excluded, especially in the present passage.[17] In such a situation Christians will be able to live a life that will not bring reproach from outside (cf. Fee, 63; 1 Th 4.11f.; cf. van Unnik 1980:307–22).

βασιλεύς**, 'king', can be used for any ruler in the Hellenistic world (Spicq, 359). The term was applied to the Roman emperor in the Greek-speaking world, although the Romans themselves eschewed the use of *rex* in Latin to signify the emperor.[18] The plural form could refer to emperors, but hardly of the time when co-emperors existed (after AD 137) and more probably in a generalising sense; this would make good sense after AD 69, the year in which there were four emperors in swift succession. But a general reference to kings, including Roman client kings is possible (Polycarp 12.3; Justin, *Apol.* I.17.3). This would not be outside the horizon of Christians in Rome or Asia Minor.

The scope of this prayer is broader, however, and includes πάντων τῶν ἐν ὑπεροχῇ ὄντων. ὑπεροχή, 'excellence' (1 Cor 2.1***), was commonly used in phrases referring to people of high status.[19] Here it refers to the subordinate officials of the emperor at every level.[20] 'All' probably functions to generalise (rather than universalise) the prayer: Christians are to pray for whatever persons are in authority over them rather than for every single ruler.

Christian prayer for pagan rulers was probably based on the practice of the Diaspora Jewish synagogue. Prayers and the offerings of sacrifices for pagan authorities formed a well-attested Jewish practice.[21] Such prayer was meant to ensure the welfare of God's people under pagan rule (Jer 36 [29].7) and came to be regarded as a sign of loyalty; it avoided the necessity to pray

---

[17] It is not far from mind in 1 Pet 2 (cf. vv. 11f.); Rom 13 (cf. 12.20) and Tit 3.1; cf. 3.8 note; Goppelt 1993:155–62; Kamlah 1970:241.

[18] Josephus, *Bel.* 3.351; 4.596; 5.563; 1 Pet 2.13, 17; Rev 17.9; 1 Clement 37.3; Aristides, *Apol.* 1; Justin, *Apol.* I.14.4; Athenagoras, *Suppl.* 2.1. See further Dibelius-Conzelmann, 36 nn. 10, 11; *TLNT* I, 264f.

[19] 2 Macc 3.11; 6.23; cf. *Ep. Arist.* 175; Josephus, *Ant.* 9.3.

[20] Cf. the use of ὑπερέχω, Rom 13.1; 1 Pet 2.13; Delling, G., *TDNT* VIII, 523f.; MM 653f.

[21] 1 Esdr 6.9f.; Bar 1.10–13; Ezek 6.9f.; 1 Macc 7.33; *Ep. Arist.* 44f.; Josephus, *Bel.* 2.197, 409; Philo, *Flacc.* 49; *Leg. Gai.* 157, 317; ʼ*Abot* 3.2; cf. Nauck 1950:76; Bartsch 1965:34–9; Dibelius-Conzelmann, 37f.; Schürer II, 309–13; Légasse*.

to the rulers themselves or acknowledge them as worthy of divine honours (Johnson, 129). In the present context, the first instruction to pray 'for all people' takes us beyond the rationale of Diaspora Judaism (cf. Bartsch 1965:35f.). As it developed in the early church, the instruction to pray for the State, which was aimed at peaceful existence, occurred alongside specific prayer for deliverance of God's elect (cf. 1 Clement 59.4; 60f.) and prayer for all people (which implied salvation, Ignatius, *Eph.* 10; Polycarp, *Phil.* 12.2–3). It does not necessarily follow that in every case the prayer for the authorities is specifically for their conversion, although in the present passage this is surely implicit.[22] What this prayer shows is the church's awareness of civil government as an institution ordained by God (Rom 13.1–7. 1 Pet 2.13–17) as well as the need to live and minister in a way that observes this reponsibility. The explanation that this awareness is a reflection of 'the changeover from an eschatological world view to an ecclesiastical form of existence' which would allow more space for the church's long life in the world (Dibelius-Conzelmann, 37) is too simplistic.[23] The tension created as the earlier Paul tried to reconcile the church's eschatological existence with the mundane realities (Rom 13.1–10; 1 Th 4.11f.) is still felt here, as a comparison between 2 Tim 3.12 and the present verse clearly shows.[24]

ἵνα ἤρεμον καὶ ἡσύχιον βίον διάγωμεν ἐν πάσῃ εὐσεβείᾳ καὶ σεμνότητι ἵνα may express the purpose or the content (White, 103) or the result of the prayer; here probably the purpose or the intended result that should come from prayer for the authorities is in view. It need not necessarily be the sole purpose of the prayer (Roloff, 109f.). Certainly prayer for the authorities has the benefit of the church in view. It is meant to ensure that they will do whatever is necessary to foster and maintain a tranquil environment. The phrase used for this, ἤρεμον καὶ ἡσύχιον βίον, is Hellenistic and reflects the desires of people in general at the time.[25] ἤρεμος*** is 'quiet, tranquil'[26] and is

---

[22] So rightly Légasse*, 246. V. 4 can hardly be understood otherwise, *pace* Dibelius-Conzelmann, 38. See 1 Clement 59.4; Bartsch 1965:47.

[23] The use of the motif of 'Christian citizenship' to characterise the outlook of the PE goes back at least to Holtzmann, 307, who draws a contrast between Rev and the attitude here: 'Das bürgerliche Leben ist der Kreis, in welchem das innere christliche Leben sich äusserlich verwirklichen soll als weltliches Christenthum.'

[24] See further discussion in Towner 1989:201–5; Young 1994:40f.

[25] Note the close parallel, ἤρεμον καὶ γαληνὸν τὸν βίον διαγόντων (Dittenberger, *Or.* II, 519,10 [c. AD 245]; MM 281; Dibelius-Conzelmann, 38 n. 24); cf. Josephus, *Bel.* 1.201; Philo, *Mos.* 2.235; *Conf.* 43; *Div.* 285; Dibelius-Conzelmann, 38f.

[26] According to LSJ the word is a late form for ἠρεμαῖος (Plutarch, *Sol.* 31.2); Esther 13.2 (*v.l.* in A for ἤμερον); cf. Spicq, 361.

synonymous with ἡσύχιος (1 Pet 3.3***).[27] Together they depict the living out of one's life (βίος, [2 Tim 2.4**], 'physical existence') in a dignified way, without undue stress or trial. But the peaceful life is not an end in itself; what is envisaged in the use of the verb διάγω (Tit 3.3***) is the observable life (cf. Roloff, 116 and refs.), and the following description defines it as the life made possible by faith in Christ (see below). It is thus possible to place the instruction to pray for State authorities within the context of the prayer for salvation for all people; the effective leadership of the State will maintain an environment conducive to witness.

The prepositional phrase which closes the sentence, ἐν πάσῃ εὐσεβείᾳ καὶ σεμνότητι, uses current ethical language to describe the genuine life of faith and the manner (ἐν + dat.) in which the Christian is to pursue life. εὐσέβεια (**Excursus 1**) describes spiritual life from the interrelated perspectives of the knowledge of God and the life which that knowledge produces. Despite some development and correction in recent interpretations of εὐσέβεια, the tendencies (a) to rely exclusively on the use of the term in this passage, (b) to seek for a background more in Hellenistic ethics and ignore the usage of the term in Hellenistic Judaism for 'the fear of the Lord', and (c) to minimise the careful theological grounding given to the term elsewhere in the PE continue to lead to the conclusion that a rather static respectability is in view. Nevertheless, εὐσέβεια in the PE is not to be confused with the goals of Greek ethics; nor should the nature of εὐσέβεια as genuine Christian existence be confused with the environment which the author hopes that prayer for authorities might bring about.[28] The life so described must be lived out in any environment for Christianity to be genuine, and it normally leads to persecution (2 Tim 3.12). Oberlinner, 68, emphasises that the purpose is to set the church free for missionary service.

σεμνότης (**Excursus 3**) adds the idea of serious and worthy behaviour to the picture of genuine Christian existence. This is a quality especially expected in church leaders, but here required of the congregation generally. Although it has an inward dimension, there is also an outward orientation (cf. the ἵνα clause in Tit 2.8). The behaviour of believers should be such as to win respect from other people because they take life seriously and devoutly and do not trifle. Hence εὐσέβεια and σεμνότης together describe a life that is completely acceptable both to God and people.

[27] It is often used with πραΰς of persons. For its use with βίος see Dittenberger, *Syll.* 866.15; cf. ἡσυχάζω, 1 Th 4.11; *TLNT* II, 178–83.
[28] For this tendency see Dibelius-Conzelmann, 39–40; Foerster 1959:216; Trummer 1978:230.

From the prayer request it is clearly implied that rulers might provide the right conditions for such a life to flourish; yet the references to persecution (2 Tim 3.12) show that whatever help the environment might provide, it is not intrinsic to Christian piety. This fact alone casts doubt on Dibelius's idea that the ethics of the PE express a Christian bourgeois ideal. Yet it must be admitted that language that was typical in pagan thought was being used to describe the ideal context for, and the manner of, the Christian life. Fee, 63, suggests that εὐσέβεια may have been a term current in the heretics' vocabulary taken over by the author so that it might be redefined. This is possible, but in view of the background of the language it is more likely that here (and throughout the PE) it was aimed rather at communicating the gospel in a way that would ensure its relevance for the culture. In this case, the church's prayer for the authorities that they might create a stable society would commend the church to society. At the same time, however, it is conceivable that the present passage helps to make the statement that the high goals of secular ethics are realisable only in Christ.

3. τοῦτο καλὸν καὶ ἀπόδεκτον ἐνώπιον τοῦ σωτῆρος ἡμῶν θεοῦ At this point the author begins to give a basis for the instructions about prayer, and the foundational argument is concerned with God's own evaluation of the behaviour enjoined. τοῦτο must refer back to the universal prayer in v. 1 and not just to prayer for rulers, for the description of God as σωτήρ corresponds to the more general prayer for the salvation of all.[29]

The whole phrase is patterned after the formula τὸ καλὸν καὶ τὸ ἀρεστόν ἐναντίον κυρίου τοῦ θεοῦ σου (Deut 12.25, 28; 13.19; 21.9), which describes various kinds of behaviour as in keeping with the law and therefore as meeting God's standard. Its use here connects the church with the OT people of God to whom God gave instructions that their behaviour might be unique, unlike the nations around them. The phraseology here may reflect the cultic use of δεκτός to refer to sacrifices which are acceptable to God (Lev 1.3f.; *et al.*); in the NT the δεκτός word-group functions similarly (cf. Rom 15.16; Phil 4.18; 1 Pet 2.5). In this context it is the community's prayer which is evaluated as being καλόν (1.8; for the phrase cf. 1 Cor 7.26)

---

[29] Roloff, 119; Fee, 64; *pace* Link, H.-G., *NIDNTT* III, 746. Murphy-O'Connor*, 1262, wants to see the antecedent in the more immediate phrase, namely the living of a life characterised by godliness (and including prayer); such a life will commend the gospel to the non-believer and thus back up the preaching of the message (cf. Tit 2.9f.). However, the verbal link between v. 4 and v. 1 created by the use of πᾶς strongly supports the usual understanding.

and ἀπόδεκτος (5.4***; cf. 1.15 noun).[30] In the NT community of God prayer in the church replaces sacrifice.[31]

The next part of the traditional phrase, ἐνώπιον τοῦ σωτῆρος ἡμῶν θεοῦ, establishes that the behaviour is judged to be good and acceptable by God. In both the OT use and here the phrase may express the ideas of God's presence, or God's assessment, and the thought of accountability may be in view.[32] Each nuance would fit the worship setting of this instruction; but in any case it describes behaviour which is to typify the life of God's people.

The description of God in his character as Saviour, which is certainly more than titular (Roloff, 119), corresponds to the theme of salvation developed in this passage (σωθῆναι, v. 4). He is presented as the source of salvation, the architect of the salvation plan (Tit 1.3 note). As Saviour, he calls for the involvement of his people in and through their prayer for all. This concept of saviourhood is then explicated in the next verses.

4. ὃς πάντας ἀνθρώπους θέλει σωθῆναι καὶ εἰς ἐπίγνωσιν ἀληθείας ἐλθεῖν ὅς is used to append theological statements in 4.10; Tit 2.14 (Christ); cf. 1 Tim 3.16 where there is no antecedent. The effect is causal: 'because he wishes…' (Arichea-Hatton, 48). πάντας ἀνθρώπους continues the theme of 'all' in this passage. It expresses the extent of God's will: to save all humankind. The PE stress this universal aspect.[33] Two questions arise.

First, why is this emphasis present? As the polemical intention of ἐπίγνωσις ἀληθείας suggests (see below), the emphasis on 'all' is presumably directed at the false teaching in some way. There were various types of exclusivism in the environment of early Christianity which may underlie the attitude implicitly criticised here: (a) Jewish or Judaising ostracism of the uncircumcised led to the exclusion of Gentiles from the church in certain circles (cf. *T. Sanh.* 13.2). Paul addressed the Jew/Gentile debate in Galatians and Romans, and maintained that all had equal access to God. In such contexts an exclusive perception of salvation must have been entertained. (b) The Qumran community practised a separatist exclusivism, but this is surely rather distant from the PE. (c) A third explanation is that the heretics taught a Gnostic

---

[30] Cf. Grundmann, W., *TDNT* II, 58f.; see also *TLNT* II, 137f.

[31] Cf. Bartsch 1965:30f.; Link, H.-G., *NIDNTT* III, 744–6; cf. 1 Clement 7.3; 21.1; 35.5; 60.2.

[32] For ἐνώπιον cf. 5.4, 21; 6.13; 2 Tim 2.14; 4.1 with θεοῦ; 5.20; 6.12**; cf. Wikenhauser, A., 'Ἐνώπιος-ἐνώπιον-κατενώπιον', *BZ* 8 (1910), 263–70; Krämer, H., *EDNT* I, 462. See further 2 Cor 8.21; 1 Pet 3.4.

[33] 2.1, 4, 6; 4.10; Tit 2.11; cf. Rom 5.18; 2 Cor 5.19; and Ezek 18.23; 33.11; Wis 16.7; cf. the statement in Epictetus 3.24.2.

doctrine of salvation which limited it to a group of the 'elect'.[34] But Gnosticism in the strict sense of the word is unlikely to be present.

The decisive factor is surely the stress on the mission of Paul to the Gentiles in v. 7, and therefore it is most likely that explanation (a) is to be accepted. The tendency may have been strengthened by other factors. If there were realised eschatological elements in the false teaching (e.g. 2 Tim 2.18; 1 Tim 6.20), the tendency towards exclusivism is possibly to be understood as a combination of an enthusiastic belief that the church is 'not a part of this world' and the elitism that would naturally have been attached to claims to have a better gospel (cf. Towner 1987:112). Nor should it be forgotten that when a church turns aside to speculation and disputes, it quickly becomes introverted, and one of the first casualties is evangelism together with prayer for the world.

The second question concerns the scope of πάντας (cf. Marshall 1989). Four suggestions have been made:

(a) 'All people without exception'. This may be understood in two ways. One possibility is what is generally called 'universalism', namely that God's purpose, which he will accomplish, is to save all people regardless of their disposition towards the gospel.[35] In the context of the PE this understanding is impossible; the importance of faith for salvation is implicit in the next statement and is expressed clearly throughout the PE (cf. also 1 Tim 1.16; 3.16; 4.10; 2 Tim 1.5).[36] The other possibility is that the reference is to God's desire that all people should be saved, whether or not they actually respond to his gracious offer.[37] There can be little doubt that this is the right interpretation. Nevertheless, other possibilities have been suggested.

(b) 'All people, except the worst sinners'. This modification of view (a) is based on the kind of qualification expressed in Rabbinic Judaism (M. Sanh. 10). But in view of 1.15 this is untenable.

(c) 'All the elect, i.e. the people who have been predestined by God to be saved'.[38] This interpretation assumes that the PE presuppose a doctrine of rigid predestination and reads it into the text.

---

[34] Lütgert 1909:55; Schmithals 1961:145; Roloff, 119; Knoch, 25; Oberlinner, 72f.

[35] Hasler 1977:204–7.

[36] Dibelius-Conzelmann, 41 and n. 35.

[37] Cf. the distinction betwen God's general will and his subsequent will made by various church fathers (Kelly, 62f.).

[38] 'All the predestined because they include every kind of person' (Augustine, De Corr. et gr. 44; cited by Spicq, 364f.). See, however, Tit 1.1 note on the reference of the term ἐκλεκτοί.

(d) 'All kinds of people, not necessarily including all individuals'. This interpretation means that vv. 3f. provide justification for praying for the government authorities in 2.2. This interpretation (like the previous one) is followed by scholars who find a doctrine of particular election underlying the NT.[39] However, nothing in the context suggests such a limitation. Nor does this interpretation secure the desired result, since in the last analysis divisions between individuals and classes of humankind merge into one another.

The context shows that the inclusion of Gentiles alongside Jews in salvation is the primary issue here, and the best solution is to adopt (a) with the recognition that the point of stressing God's desire to save all people is to indicate that his desire includes Gentiles as well as Jews. The emphasis is thus on universal accessibility to God's salvation on the basis of a faith open to all and a gospel preached to all.

θέλω can have the strong sense 'to will' and the weaker sense 'to wish, desire'.[40] Some scholars try to find a weak sense in contrast with βούλομαι in the sense 'to order'.[41] However, this contrast is not well founded. The verb βούλομαι is rarely used of God. The noun θέλημα (2 Tim 1.1) can be used in both strong and weak senses. θέλω is used of purposes which are effected in Rom 9.18; 1 Cor 4.19; 12.18; 15.38; Col 1.27; see especially 1 Cor 12.18 alongside 12.11. There is accordingly no case for weakening θέλω to express a mere desire, behind which is concealed God's real purpose which is merely to save the [limited number of the] elect. There is no reason to think that God's 'real' will is other than what is expressed here (cf. 2 Tim 1.9, κατὰ ἰδίαν πρόθεσιν). Equally, however, there is no guarantee that this purpose will necessarily be fully accomplished, any more than other things which God wishes. The condition of belief in the gospel, the human responsibility in the process, places limits on the results which will be achieved.

σωθῆναι, immediately preceded by the reference to σωτήρ and followed by the traditional allusion to the death of Jesus, refers to salvation from sin (1.15 note; Tit 1.3 note).[42] The suggestion that the verb means here 'to be preserved, protected' can be confidently rejected.[43] The second infinitive phrase spells

---

[39] Hendriksen, 93f.; Knight, 119. The same interpretation is given by Calvin, 209f.; cf. *Inst.* 3.24.16: 'He assuredly means nothing more than that the way of salvation was not shut against any order of men.'
[40] Schrenk, G., *TDNT* III, 44–62; Limbeck, M., *EDNT* II, 137–9; Schrage 1961:163–73.
[41] Cf. 2.8; 5.14; Tit 3.8; Philo, *Her.* 112, 115; *Quaest. in Ex.* 2.51; Spicq, 365.
[42] For God's *will* to save cf. *Od. Sol.* 9.13.
[43] Simpson, 41f., holds that the verb may be used of the function of rulers (2.2!) in making places and people safe (cf. Plutarch, *Brut.* 31.2, 4; Mt. 14.30;

out the meaning of σωθῆναι with a hendiadys.[44] εἰς ἐπίγνωσιν
ἀληθείας ἐλθεῖν is a technical phrase in the PE for coming to
faith in Christ (Tit 1.1 note).[45] 'To come to a knowledge' views
conversion from the standpoint of the rational decision about
the divine message, 'truth', which it entails.[46] In the PE ἀλήθεια
(see Tit 1.1 note) refers to the authentic revelation of God
bringing salvation. The background is Jewish; truth, a quality of
God, is the criterion by which his saving message is determined
(Wolter 1988:70–7; see further Tit 1.1 note). Throughout the
PE its content and polemic thrust are evident as it contrasts
the apostolic message as God's message with that of the false
teachers.[47] Here the phrase implies the need to commit oneself
to the traditional gospel and reject competing messages.
Salvation is inextricably bound to the apostolic doctrine and a
right decision about it. For ἐλθεῖν cf. 2 Tim 3.7; 2 Macc 9.11;
Cebes, *Tabula* 12.3. The concept of 'coming' is common in the
NT, literally of coming to Jesus, and figuratively of 'coming' to
knowledge, salvation, etc.[48]

5. Εἷς γὰρ θεός Verses 5–6 may be a traditional formulation,
or, more probably, the author has combined materials that
were well known to provide the theological grounding (γάρ)[49] for
the statement that God is the Saviour who wishes all people to
be saved (Fee 64f.; Läger 1996:38–43). Although the εἷς θεός
formula provides evidence that God's salvific will is indeed
universal (see below), the movement of thought within the sentence
gets quickly to Christ's role as sole mediator of salvation. Its force
is: 'Just as there is [only] one God, so also there is [only] one
mediator between God and man, the man Christ Jesus who gave
himself as a ransom for all.' Thus the sentence brings out basically
the fact that there is one mediator, just as there is one God, and
his task is valid for all humankind. Beyond this the implication

---

Jn. 11.12; 12.27; Acts 27; Judg 3.9; Neh 9.27). The reference would then be to
the achievement of the peaceful conditions in which people can come to a
knowledge of the truth. This interpretation cannot evacuate the verse of God's
saving purpose which is in any case present in the second infinitive. But it is
more likely that the two infinitives form a hendiadys.

[44] καί is 'explicative' (cf. BA *s.v.* 3; BD §442[9]; Wolter 1988:71).

[45] White, 104, notes that 'to be saved' means 'to be in a state of being saved',
within which an increasing knowledge of the truth takes place. Hence the order
of the two phrases is not a *hysteron proteron*.

[46] See further Dibelius 1956:1–13; Lips 1979:32, 35–8; Sell 1982:3–7 *et passim*.

[47] 1 Tim 6.5; 2 Tim 4.4; Tit 1.14; 2 Tim 2.18; 2 Tim 3.8; cf. 2 Tim 2.15; 2.25; 3.7.

[48] See Hanson, 67, for the view that there is a Christian midrash on Isa 45.21f.,
seen by the Rabbis as prophetic of the salvation of the Gentiles.

[49] γάρ has the force 'indeed, to be sure'; it is explanatory rather than causal.
According to BA *s.v.* 4, late writers preferred δέ.

is that the one gospel that proclaims the Christ-event is that which Paul preaches.

Since there is only one God and not several, there can therefore only be one way of salvation. If there were many gods, there could be different ways of salvation for their worshippers, but since there is only one, the possibility is excluded (Stott, 66f.). εἷς θεός should be translated 'for God is one' or 'there is [only] one God'.[50] Its use in the NT is formulaic with an origin in pre-Christian Diaspora Judaism. As a crystallisation of the thought expressed in the Shema (Deut 6.4), it served a polemical purpose in addressing pagan polytheism.[51] The stress was on the singularity, not the unity of God; there are no other gods. Paul applies the formula in 1 Cor 8.6 in a polemical manner (Kramer 1966:55). However, its application in Rom 3.29f.; Gal 3.20; Eph 4.5f. serves the different purpose of establishing the open access which all people – Jews and Gentiles – have to God's grace.[52] Its use here resembles Rom 3.29f., where the affirmation of 'one God' for Jews *and* Gentiles demonstrated that the Gentiles have equal access to God. In neither passage is the polemic directed against many gods (or Gnostic emanations), but against Jewish exclusivism on the one hand and something akin to it on the other; here 'there is one God' substantiates the claim that God wills to save 'all', by declaring that there is one God for all people (cf. Roloff, 120; Fee, 65).

εἷς καὶ μεσίτης θεοῦ καὶ ἀνθρώπων The fact that there is only one mediator between God and man is grounded in the fact that there is only one God. εἷς, used now with reference to the mediator, continues the argument 'oneness = universality'; it is not simply a way of expressing majesty (*contra* Trummer 1978:196; cf. Roloff, 121). μεσίτης, 'mediator' (Gal 3.19f.; Heb 8.6; 9.15; 12.24***), is a Hellenistic term (from Polybius onwards) found in diplomatic, legal and commercial language. It has cosmological and soteriological applications in Philo,[53] as well as

---

[50] Dibelius-Conzelmann, 41 and n. 38; Oepke, A., *TDNT* IV, 623. See further Peterson 1926; Kramer 1966:95–8; Wengst 1973:138–43; Towner 1989:50f.

[51] For a possible use in the worship of the synagogue, see Peterson 1926:302; but cf. Kramer 1966:95f.

[52] See Meeks 1983:91f.; Kelly, 63; Spicq, 366. The use of the formula in Eph 4.4–6, which may rest on language used in church meetings, is similar to that in Rom and Gal, although the Jew/Gentile debate is less of a central issue (cf. Trummer 1978:121f.). For other non-Pauline uses of the formula, see Mt 23.8. 9, 10; Mk 12.29, 32; Jn 8.41; Jas 2.19; 4.12. For μόνος see 1 Tim 1.17; 6.15; Jn 17.3; Jude 25.

[53] *Vit. Mos.* 2.166; *Div.* 206; cf. Plutarch, *Mor.* 369 E. The view that εἷς μεσίτης is a response to the Gnostic doctrine of numerous emanations (for which see Wengst 1972:72; cf. Michel 1948:86) is improbable (see Roloff, 122).

in religious contexts.[54] The basic sense is of a person who facilitates a transaction of some sort between two parties. His relationship to the parties involved, their relationship to one another, and the nature of the transaction may vary. Thus he may be a neutral agent executing some legal transaction; he may represent one group to another; he may bring together parties in opposition, belonging to one side or both (see Roloff, 121 and refs.).[55] The use of the term elsewhere in the early church in connection with Christ's mediation of the new covenant (Heb 8.6; 9.15; 12.24) or the mediation of the law through Moses (Gal 3.19, 20) may suggest that the meaning here is covenantal: Christ the one mediator establishes the new covenant between God and people (not just Israel; cf. 2.7) on the basis of his death.[56] Heb 9.14f. links mediation of the covenant with the death of Christ, and despite the lack of other indications of covenant (e.g. the word διαθήκη) in the present passage, this nuance must be regarded as possible (*pace* Roloff, 122). In any case, the mediator here is the sort who is related, implicitly at least, to both parties and whose task is to bring about reconciliation between them (cf. Roloff, 122). As such his task may be better illustrated by *T. Dan*. 6.2, where the peace-making of the angelic mediator is done without explicit reference to the covenant (cf. Philo, *Mos.* 2.166; cited by Roloff, 121). It is because of this task of mediation that Jesus is not placed directly alongside the Father but rather between him and humankind.[57]

ἄνθρωπος Χριστὸς Ἰησοῦς This stress on the humanity of Jesus[58] requires clarification. Its intention here is best seen in its reference both backwards and forwards. First, it is as a human being that he 'mediates' between God and humanity.[59] Second, it is in his humanity that he carries out his redemptive mission which culminated in his self-offering. There is a strong link between the suffering and humanity of Christ in the early church,[60] and this link may be sufficient for an understanding of the phrase.

---

[54] *T. Dan* 6.2, where Michael is the angelic mediator between God and man; Job 9.32f. LXX. Hanson's suggestion of a deliberate allusion here to Job (1968:56–64; cf. Houlden, 68) has not been taken up by other scholars.

[55] Oepke, A., *TDNT* IV, 598–624, especially 619; Roloff, 121f.; *TLNT* II, 465–8.

[56] Dibelius-Conzelmann, 42; Brox, 128; Trummer 1978:196; Oepke, A., *TDNT* IV, 619.

[57] Oberlinner, 74, sees a move towards subordinationism away from 1 Cor 8.6; Eph 4.5f.

[58] Rom 5.15; 1 Cor 15.45, 47; Phil 2.7f.; Heb 2.11, 14, 16f.

[59] See Brox, 128; Kelly, 63; Windisch 1935:216f.

[60] Phil 2.7f.; Gal 4.4f.; Rom 8.3; Heb 2.14. Cf. Martin 1967:165–228; Dunn 1989:38–42.

Other explanations have been offered. Second-Adam Christology has been cited as the source and implied reference of the phrase.[61] Yet, although the thoughts of human representation and death are intrinsic to the Christ–Adam analogy,[62] the interplay between Adam as representative of fallen humankind and Christ as representative of redeemed humankind is missing here. It has also been suggested that ἄνθρωπος represents the graecising of the earlier, Semitic designation ὁ υἱὸς τοῦ ἀνθρώπου which introduces the Son of Man logion (Mk 10.45 par.) that bears some relation to 2.6a (Trummer 1978:197; Jeremias 1966:226–9). But the omission of the original intervening statement about servanthood and the addition of Χριστὸς Ἰησοῦς in this passage make this uncertain at best. Even less plausible is an anti-docetic thrust; elsewhere in the PE there is no evidence of this tendency which might corroborate such a reading here. On the dubious view that a Gnostic doctrine of mediators is here countered, see note on μεσίτης above. Any dependence upon the myth of the heavenly ἄνθρωπος-redeemer can probably also be safely rejected on the basis of the date of that character.[63] The point is rather that Jesus is one of the human race. Nothing is said here about his also being God (and therefore linked to both parties), but 3.16 surely indicates something to this effect.

6. ὁ δοὺς ἑαυτὸν ἀντίλυτρον ὑπὲρ πάντων The phrase is based on the saying of Jesus and expresses (in a way that may suggest some degree of further theological reflection) a doctrine of redemption which was still alive for the PE (cf. Tit 2.14 note). The formulation is a version of the saying in Mk 10.45 (δοῦναι τὴν ψυχὴν αὐτοῦ λύτρον ἀντὶ πολλῶν) in better Greek (Jeremias 1966:226–9; Roloff, 111f.). Some of the alterations may have been made to fit the new context. Thus the change to the aor. part. δούς is required because the statement in this context does not function to express purpose (as δοῦναι does in Mk 10.45) but rather to describe an event which has happened in the past, and also because the articular part. forms the relative connection necessary in this context with the preceding 'man Christ Jesus'. For δίδωμι used of Christ see Mk 10.45; Tit 2.14; Gal 1.4. ὑπὲρ πάντων is basically equivalent to ἀντὶ πολλῶν in Mk 10.45 (cf. Mt 12.15b diff. Mk 3.10) which corresponds to the Hebrew of Isa 53.12 (Roloff, 111). It expresses more clearly in Greek the

[61] Cf. τοῦ ἑνὸς ἀνθρώπου Ἰησοῦ Χριστοῦ, Rom 5.15; cf. 1 Cor 15.21f., 45; Kelly, 63; Fee, 65.
[62] Rom 5.18f.; cf. 1 Cor 15.3f., 12 and 21f., 45; see further Dunn 1989:107–13; Popkes, W., *Christus Traditus* (Zürich: Zwingli, 1967), 199f.
[63] *Contra* Dibelius-Conzelmann, 42; see the dating by Colpe, C., *Die religionsgeschichtliche Schule* (Göttingen: Vandenhoeck und Ruprecht, 1961) and Yamauchi, E., *Pre-Christian Gnosticism* (London: Tyndale Press, 1973), 163–9.

universal or inclusive idea latent in the more Semitic idiom of
the Jesus-tradition. Whoever was responsible for the change,
the 'all' of the traditional saying serves the theme developed
throughout the passage that God wishes all to be saved, and
that therefore prayer should be offered for all.

Better Greek also accounts for the choice of the reflexive
ἑαυτόν for the Semitic τὴν ψυχὴν αὐτοῦ of Mk 10.45 (Tit 2.14;
Büchsel, F., *TDNT* IV, 349). Similarly, ἀντίλυτρον*** replaces
the earlier λύτρον. ἀντίλυτρον is a variant of λύτρον with the
same basic meaning of ransom price.[64] The compound may
intensify the thought of substitution already contained in
λύτρον.[65] But the thought was already present in the ransom
concept of Mk 10.45, and ἀντίλυτρον may simply have been the
best Greek term to bring this out for the Greek-speaking
church.[66]

The change from ἀντί to ὑπέρ may be incidental.[67] But ὑπέρ
is the preposition which predominates in Pauline discussions of
Christ's self-offering, especially where a form of (παρα)δίδωμι is
employed.[68] The probable meaning is 'for' (cf. Patsch, H.,
EDNT III, 397) and it possibly expresses a note of representation
(Harris, M., *NIDNTT* III, 1197).

τὸ μαρτύριον καιροῖς ἰδίοις The remaining phrase is difficult.
It either concludes or was appended to the traditional material
to make the transition to the personal statement which follows.

μαρτύριον (2 Tim 1.8**) is 'witness', either the act of bearing
witness or the content, a piece of evidence, thus 'the Christian
message'. 'Testimony ... is ... not only a means of persuasion, ...
but it adds the seal of conviction.'[69] καιροῖς ἰδίοις functions here
in precisely the same way as it does in the similar discussion in
Tit 1.3, namely, to underline the fact that the time in view is the
time appropriate in God's plans for 'the testimony' (Gal 4.4).[70]

---

[64] It is a rare word not found in LXX (see BA for occurrences). The verb
ἀντιλυτρόω occurs in Aristotle, *EN* 9.2.4 (1164b. 35). For similar formations
see ἀντιμισθία (Rom 1.27; 2 Cor 6.13); ἀντίψυχον (4 Macc 6.29). ἀντί has the
force 'instead of' (Josephus, *Ant.* 14.107, λύτρον ἀντὶ πάντων, of offering a
plunderer a gold beam instead of the contents of the temple). See Büchsel, F.,
TDNT IV, 349 (cf. 340–56); *TLNT* II, 423–9, espec. 425 n. 10.

[65] Cf. Jeremias 1966:226; Büchsel, F., *TDNT* IV, 349; Roloff, 111; Hill, D.,
Greek Words and Hebrew Meanings (Cambridge, 1967), 76f.; Davies, R. E.,
'Christ in our Place – The Contribution of the Prepositions', *TynBul* 21 (1970),
74–81; Morris 1965:51f.; Kertelge, K., *EDNT* II, 366.

[66] For the Rabbinic development of the concept see SB III, 644.

[67] Morris 1965:62–4; Jeremias 1966:226; cf. MHT I, 105.

[68] Rom 8.32; Gal 1.4; 2.20; Tit 2.14; cf. Harris, M. J., *NIDNTT* III, 1197;
BD §231.

[69] Spicq, *TLNT* II, 450; cf. Strathmann, H., *TDNT* IV, 504; cf. Acts 4.33;
1 Cor 1.6; 2.1; 2 Th 1.10.

[70] Kelly, 64, mentions the possibility that the phrase means 'the testimony to
appointed times to come [sc. to the final redemptive event]', but rightly rejects it.

The plural both here and in Tit 1.3 need not envisage a continuing time of revelation (against Hasler, 86); its use in 1 Tim 6.15 in reference to a single point in time (the future epiphany of Christ) rules this out. It is an idiomatic use of the plural for the singular, and whether the apostolic ministry or the parousia is in view, the term καιροῖς ἰδίοις views it as a development in God's redemptive history.

The whole phrase can be related to its context in two ways. (a) It might be in apposition to the previous phrase, i.e. to vv. 5–6a, so that the emphasis is on the content of the witness, namely the Christian message. This gives the translation: 'who gave himself..., the testimony [to which is to be given] at the right time, sc. by Paul'.[71] (b) It might be in apposition to the verb (διδόναι) implied in ὁ δούς, so that Christ's self-offering is regarded actively as God's testimony to the world. This gives the rendering: 'who gave himself, [and this act of giving was] a [sc. God's or Christ's] testimony [given] at the right time'.[72]

The former of these views is preferable in the light of the probable force of μαρτύριον. This term corresponds to the apostolic proclamation in Acts 4.33; 2 Th 1.10 and 2 Tim 1.8 (rightly Roloff, 123). On the analogy of Tit 1.1–3, where Paul's apostolic calling is identified with the salvation-historical (καιροῖς ἰδίοις) manifestation of God's word (namely, in the apostolic proclamation, see note), it would seem that this phrase intends similarly to identify the message of the self-offering of Christ with the apostolic ministry to which (v. 7) Paul is called.

7. εἰς ὃ ἐτέθην ἐγὼ κῆρυξ καὶ ἀπόστολος The final statement in the section underlines (not necessarily for Timothy, Knoch, 25) the fact that the gospel has Paul as its appointed apostle, and that his mission is specifically to the Gentiles. This statement may be polemical against any attempt to confine the gospel to Jews or to require adherence to Jewish practices from Gentiles by referring to the historical mission of Paul which was universal in scope. The universality of the gospel is the central theme of this passage. Additionally, since the Ephesian church came within the orbit of this mission to Gentiles, such a statement might at the same time contribute to the overall assertion of Paul's apostolic authority in a situation in which it was being challenged (cf. 1.1; 1.11–16; 2 Tim 1.11; Tit 1.1–3).

---

[71] NRSV; Holtzmann, 309; Bernard, 42; Brox, 128; Lips 1979:42 n. 55; Beutler, J., *EDNT* II, 393; Wolter 1988:77f.

[72] REB; NIV; GNB; NJB; Delling, G., *TDNT* III, 461; Dibelius-Conzelmann, 43; Kelly, 64; Arichea-Hatton, 50f.; cf. Rom 12.1 'to present..., [the presentation of which is] your service'; cf. Holtz, 62, who takes the noun as tantamount to 'martyrdom'.

The verse has a close parallel in 2 Tim 1.11: τοῦ εὐαγγελίου, εἰς ὃ ἐτέθην ἐγὼ κῆρυξ καὶ ἀπόστολος καὶ διδάσκαλος (cf. Col 1.23, 25). In this case εἰς ὃ establishes the connection between Paul's appointment by God (ἐτέθην, see 1.12 note; 2 Tim 1.11) and τὸ μαρτύριον. In each case, the appointment is to the gospel ministry (cf. Lips 1979:42; see Eph 3.7 for a similar construction and link). ἐγώ is included for emphasis.

Although other uses of the word-stem occur frequently in relation to preaching, the noun κῆρυξ, 'herald', is used only rarely in the Christian sense of a preacher.[73] While the usage could be derived from the use of the noun for a herald, it is more likely that it is simply the noun corresponding to the verb κηρύσσω.[74] The term is equivalent to εὐαγγελιστής (see 2 Tim 4.5 note; cf. Roloff 1965:251f.). ἀπόστολος (Tit 1.1 note) is Paul's more usual self-designation. It is placed second to 'preacher'. Wanke 1977:172f. thinks that in the PE the concept of apostle is unimportant and not developed in any way. The present verse suggests rather that the importance of preaching is being stressed. Possibly the apostolic task is conceived as being concerned more broadly with the establishment of a church after the initial preaching.

ἀλήθειαν λέγω οὐ ψεύδομαι Before the next description of Paul there is a strong asseveration which is frequently regarded as dependent upon Rom 9.1 (Roloff, 112, Trummer 1978:120–3). The two clauses are also found separately in Paul (for ἀλήθειαν λέγω cf. 2 Cor 12.6; for οὐ ψεύδομαι see 2 Cor 11.31; Gal 1.20). The presence of the asseveration is variously explained: (a) It is a Pauline phrase awkwardly added to give liveliness and verisimilitude (Hanson, 70). (b) Doubts were being cast on Paul's appointment as an apostle (Dibelius-Conzelmann, 43). (c) It rounds out the argument initated in v. 1 concerning the universality of the gospel for the Gentiles [75] and therefore points forward to the next phrase.[76] This explanation is the most plausible. For Paul, apostleship and the gospel for the Gentiles belonged indissolubly together. The force of the comment indicates that the statement must have been a contested one.

---

[73] 2 Tim 1.11; 2 Pet 2.5***; cf. 1 Clement 5.6, of Paul.

[74] Friedrich, G., *TDNT* III, 683–96; Dibelius-Conzelmann, 43 nn. 54, 55; Roloff, 124 nn. 79, 80; Spicq, 369f.; Roloff 1965:241–4. It may well be that in the Greek world the noun already had too specialised a use of inviolable sacral messengers to be capable of undergoing Christian semantic change (*TDNT* III, 696; so Barrett, 52). See further Mounce, R. H., *The Essential Nature of New Testament Preaching* (Grand Rapids: Eerdmans, 1960).

[75] Interestingly the same asseveration in Rom 9.1 expresses Paul's concern for *Jews!*

[76] Roloff, 112; Trummer 1978:121; Jeremias, 15; Kelly, 65; Spicq, 370; Fee, 67.

διδάσκαλος ἐθνῶν ἐν πίστει καὶ ἀληθείᾳ While it is true that διδάσκαλος, 'teacher', as a designation of a Christian worker is used exclusively of Paul in the PE (2 Tim 1.11; but cf. 4.3; Rom 2.20), it is doubtful that the author/church views him as such and excludes others because it regards Paul alone as the source of the only binding and authoritative teaching which he delivered to the church (*pace* Roloff, 124; Wolter 1988:77f.). Rather he is Timothy's teacher and the source of the material to be used against the opponents (Schlarb 1990:283–7). Teaching was a mark of Pauline churches;[77] he himself and others taught in them.[78] In the PE, the activity (and presumably authority) of teaching is expected of those who are church leaders (3.2; 5.17; 2 Tim 4.2), and the ability or gift is not limited to office (2 Tim 2.2; cf. Tit 2.3). Preacher (κῆρυξ) and teacher (διδάσκαλος) sum up the task of the apostle; some distinction, perhaps in purpose or audience, and fluid rather than rigid, is probably implicit.[79] But in describing the Pauline apostolate, the stress lies on ἐθνῶν, 'Gentiles' (3.16; 2 Tim 4.17). Paul is the ἐθνῶν ἀπόστολος (Rom 11.13; cf. Gal 2.7f.), charged to communicate the gospel to this section of 'all people'.

For πίστει see **Excursus 4**. For ἀλήθεια see Tit 1.1 note (for the combination in this connection cf. Tit 1.1). The phrase seems vague and the varied use of the πίστις word-group in the PE makes two meanings possible here. The sense is either 'faithfully and truthfully' (Hanson, 70); or 'in the (sphere of) the faith and the truth'.[80] As Wolter 1988:70–82 points out, 'truth(fulness)' and 'faith(fulness)' are legitimating marks of the OT prophet sent by God. Just as they are qualities of God, they authenticate the sending and the authority of the one commissioned by God to bear his word to the people. There is an intentional connection with the description of salvation as ἐπίγνωσις ἀληθείας in 2.4, which (again on the basis of the background in the OT and Judaism) similarly legitimates the apostolic proclamation on the basis of the criteria of 'truth' and 'sending' by God (see above and Tit 1.1). Thus faithfulness and truthfulness here are not human characteristics but rather the marks of the one whose ministry and authority originate in God.

[77] 1 Cor 12.28f.; Eph 4.11; 4.21; Col 2.7; 2 Th 2.15; cf. Rom 6.17; 16.17; 1 Cor 14.6.

[78] For Paul see 1 Cor 4.17; Col 1. 28; for others see Rom 12.7; Col 3.16. Cf. Rengstorf, K. H., *TDNT* II, 158.

[79] Wegenast, K., *NIDNTT* III, 771; McDonald 1980:5, 135 n. 28; Rengstorf, K. H., *TDNT* II, 162. According to Holtzmann, 394, Paul himself distinguished between apostles and teachers and allotted himself to the former group.

[80] Lock, 29; Spicq, 370f.; Easton, 123; Fee, 67; see NIV 'of the true faith'.

b. Men and women at prayer and in the church meeting (2.8–15)

Baldwin, H. S., 'A Difficult Word: αὐθεντέω in 1 Timothy 2:12', in Köstenberger* 1995:65–80; idem, 'Appendix 2. αὐθεντέω in Ancient Greek Literature', in Köstenberger* 1995:269–305; Barnett, P. W., 'Wives and Women's Ministry (1 Timothy 2:11–15)', *EvQ* 61 (1989), 225–38; Bartsch 1965:47–59, 60–81; Baugh, S. M., 'A Foreign World: Ephesus in the First Century', in Köstenberger* 1995:13–52; Baumert, N., *Woman and Man in Paul. Overcoming a Misunderstanding* (Collegeville: Liturgical Press, 1996), 232–57 (= *Frau und Mann bei Paulus: Überwindung eines Mißverständnisses* [Würzburg: Echter, 1992], 209–30); Delling 1931:116–19, 130–2; Edwards 1989:67–9; Ellis, E. E., 'The Silenced Wives of Corinth (1 Cor. 14.34–35)', in Epp, E. J., and Fee, G. D., *New Testament Textual Criticism: Its Significance for Exegesis* (Oxford: Oxford University Press, 1981), 213–20; Ellis, E. E., *Pauline Theology: Ministry and Society* (Grand Rapids: Eerdmans, 1989), 71–8; Falconer, R., '1 Timothy 2, 14.15. Interpretative Notes', *JBL* 60 (1941), 375–9; Feuillet, A., 'La dignité et le rôle de la femme d'après quelques textes pauliniens', *NTS* 21 (1975), 157–91; Fiorenza 1983; Gritz, S. H., *Paul, Women Teachers and the Mother Goddess of Ephesus* (Lanham: University Press of America, 1991); Hugenberger, G. P., 'Women in Church Office: Hermeneutics or Exegesis? A Survey of Approaches to 1 Tim 2:8–15', *JETS* 35 (1992), 341–60; Huizenga, H., 'Women, Salvation and the Birth of Christ: A Re-examination of 1 Timothy 2:15', *SBTh* 12 (1982), 17–26; Hurley, J. B., *Man and Woman in Biblical Perspective* (Leicester: Inter-Varsity Press, 1981); Jebb, S., 'Suggested Interpretation of 1 Tim 2,15', *ExpTim* 81 (1969–70), 221f.; Jervell, J., *Imago Dei, Gen 1.26ff. im Spätjudentum, im der Gnosis und in den paulinischen Briefen* (Göttingen: Vandenhoeck und Ruprecht, 1960); Kähler, E., *Die Frau in den paulinischen Briefen. Unter besonderer Rücksichtigung des Begriffes der Unterordnung* (Zürich: Gotthelf, 1960); Kamlah 1970; Keener, C. S., *Paul, Women and Wives. Marriage and Women's Ministry in the Letters of Paul* (Peabody, MA: Hendrickson, 1992); Kimberley, D. R., '1 Tim 2:15: A Possible Understanding of a Difficult Text', *JETS* 35 (1992), 481–6; Knight, G. W., 'ΑΥΘΕΝΤΕΩ in Reference to Women in 1 Timothy 2.12', *NTS* 30 (1984), 143–57; Köstenberger, A. J., *et al.*, *Women in the Church. A Fresh Analysis of 1 Timothy 2:9–15* (Grand Rapids: Baker, 1995); idem, 'A Complex Sentence Structure in 1 Timothy 2:12', in ibid., 81–103; Köstenberger, A. J., 'Ascertaining Women's God-Ordained Roles: An Interpretation of 1 Timothy 2:15', *BBR* 7 (1997), 107–44; Kroeger, C. C., 'Ancient heresies and a strange Greek verb', *Reformed Journal* 29 (1979), 12–15; Kroeger, C. C., 'Women in the Church: A Classicist's View of 1 Tim 2.11–15', *Journal of Biblical Equality* 1 (1989), 3–31; Kroeger, R. C. and Kroeger, C. C., *I Suffer Not a Woman: Rethinking 1 Timothy 2:11–15 in Light of Ancient Evidence* (Grand Rapids: Baker, 1992); Küchler 1986:9–53; Malingrey, A.-M., 'Note sur l'exégèse de *I Tim 2,15*', *Studia Patristica* 12:1 (1968), 334–9; Mickelsen, A. B. (ed.), *Women, Authority and the Bible* (Downers Grove: InterVarsity Press, 1986); Moo, D. J., '1 Timothy 2:11–15: Meaning and Significance', *TrinJ* ns 1 (1980), 62–83; idem, 'The Interpretation of 1 Timothy 2:11–15: A Rejoinder', *TrinJ* 2 (1981), 198–222; Motyer, S., 'Expounding 1 Timothy 2:8–15', *Vox Evangelica* 24 (1994), 91–102; Osburn, C. D., 'ΑΥΘΕΝΤΕΩ (1 Timothy 2:12)', *ResQ* 25 (1982), 1–12; Padgett, A., 'Wealthy Women at Ephesus. 1 Timothy 2:8–15 in Social Context', *Int* 41 (1987), 19–31; Panning, A., 'ΑΥΘΕΝΤΕΙΝ – A Word Study', *Wisconsin Lutheran Quarterly* 78 (1981), 185–91; Payne, P. B., 'Libertarian Women in Ephesus: A Response to Douglas J. Moo's Article, "1 Timothy 2:11–15: Meaning and Significance"', *TrinJ* ns 2 (1981), 169–97; idem, 'The Interpretation of 1 Timothy 2:11–15: A Surrejoinder', in Liefeld, W. L., Moo, D. and Payne, P. B., *What does Scripture Teach about the Ordination of Women?* (Minneapolis: Evangelical Free Church of America, 1986), 96–115; idem, 'αὐθεντέω and 1 Tim 1:12', unpublished paper, 1995; idem, *Man & Woman, One in Christ* (Grand

Rapids: Zondervan, forthcoming);[81] Perriman, A. C., 'What Eve Did, What Women Shouldn't Do: The Meaning of AΥΘΕΝΤΕΩ in 1 Timothy 2:12', *TynBul* 44 (1993), 129–42; Piper, J., and Grudem. W. (eds.), *Recovering Biblical Manhood and Womanhood* (Wheaton: Crossway, 1991); Porter, S. E., 'What does it mean to be "saved by Childbirth" (1 Timothy 2.15)?', *JSNT* 49 (1993), 87–102; Scholer, D. M., 'Women's Adornment. Some Historical and Hermeneutical Observations on the New Testament Passages', *Daughters of Sarah* 6:1 (1980), 3–6; Schottroff, L., *Lydias ungeduldige Schwestern. Feministische Sozialgeschichte des frühen Christentums* (Gütersloh: Mohn, 1994); Schreiner, T. R., 'An Interpretation of 1 Timothy 2:9–15: A Dialogue with Scholarship', in Köstenberger* 1995:105–54; Spencer, A. D. B., 'Eve at Ephesus (Should women be ordained as pastors according to the First Letter to Timothy 2:11–15?)', *JETS* 17 (1974), 215–22; Towner, P. H., 'Feminist Approaches to the NT: 1 Tim 2:8–15 as a Test Case', *Jian Dao* 7 (1997), 91–111; Ulrichsen, J. H., 'Heil durch Kinderbären. Zu 1 Tim 2,15 und seiner syrischen Version', *SEÅ* 58 (1993), 99–104; van der Jagt, K., 'Women Are Saved Through Bearing Children (1 Timothy 2.11–15)', *BT* 39 (1988), 201–8; Wagener 1994:67–113; Wilshire, L. E., 'The TLG Computer and Further Reference to AΥΘΕΝΤΕΩ in 1 Timothy 2:12', *NTS* 34 (1988), 120–34; Witherington 1988; Zucker, F. 'αὐθεντής und Ableitungen', (Sitzungsberichte Sächs. Akad. d. Wiss. Leipzig, Phil.-hist. Kl. 107,4. Berlin, 1962).[82]

After giving the theological backing for prayer for all people on the basis of the universal character of the gospel in 2.3–7, the author returns to the theme announced in 2.1f., the need for prayer to be offered in the church meeting, and he proceeds to comment on how it is to be offered. Verses. 8–15 must reflect attitudes and problems that were actually present in the church. The author issues a command to the men in the congregation, with the stress being on the absence of the kind of dissension which characterises the false teaching (2.8). Then follows a section (2.9f.) which appears to deal with the deportment of the women at prayer and stresses the need for modesty and good deeds rather than expensive clothing. The nature of the two instructions makes it clear that the requirements apply to life in general and not just to behaviour in church. Finally (2.11–15), there is a command that the women are not to teach, supported by a reference to the sin of Eve who was deceived. At the same time it was necessary to emphasise the positive role of women over against the antipathy to the material creation and in particular to sexuality: women can still accomplish a spiritual aim in childbearing and a godly life. Again, some special circumstance must be at work to explain this change from the situation elsewhere in which women had a less restricted role.[83]

---

[81] I am grateful to Dr Payne for allowing me to use his unpublished paper 'αὐθεντέω and 1 Tim 1:12' which forms part of the preparation for his book.

[82] The literature on this topic is enormous, and especially here no attempt has been made at completeness.

[83] Oberlinner, 88f., argues that the growing freedom of women in Gnostic sects may have led to orthodox groups being regarded as infected by heresy if they allowed too active a role to women. Cf. Rudolph 1983:211f. However, the evidence cited is slight and belongs to a later period than the PE.

This final section appears to be a digression loosely related to the theme of the place of women in worship.[84] Nevertheless, there is an implicit link in that the extravagance in dress and hairstyles which is criticised in v. 9 was in all probability a status-symbol used by wealthy women to express their dominant position (Padgett*), and this may well have gone along with some kind of emancipatory tendencies expressed in the adoption of teaching roles and superiority over men.

The interpretation of 2.11–15 is especially liable to be influenced by the attitudes of commentators to the *Wirkungsgeschichte* of the passage. Contemporary interpretations tend to fall into three categories:

(a) Traditional interpretations regard the passage as a universally binding prohibition of women teaching or holding any authoritative office in the church, since this would be incompatible with their subordinate position over against men. The passage is then held to impose such a prohibition on the contemporary church. This view has been strongly defended by a group of conservative interpreters in recent years.[85]

(b) Strongly feminist interpreters have tended to adopt the same understanding of the passage as the traditionalists but, if anything, to affirm it all the more strongly. Thus, for Wagener 1994 the aim of the letter is to put women in their place by whatever means and to assert the superiority of men in a patriarchal system. The passage is then regarded as one of those parts of Scripture which are to be in effect rejected by a feminist hermeneutic.[86]

(c) Other interpreters who are sympathetic to the ministry of women in teaching and church leadership today claim that the passage does not give a blanket condemnation of these activities, and argue that it is dealing with an unusual ecclesiastical situation that required unusual measures and/or that the teaching reflects

---

[84] For women in the congregation see further 5:3–16; Tit 2.3–5; and the role of Timothy's relatives in 2 Tim 1.3–5.

[85] See especially Köstenberger* 1995 for the most mature, scholarly defence of this position. Other representative defenders include Hurley*; Knight, 130–49; Moo*.

[86] Thus Roloff (147) insists on rejecting the teaching of the passage as unacceptable by NT standards (quite apart from modern social considerations, he points to wrong exegesis of Gen 3). Fiorenza*, 260–6, 285–342, regards the teaching of the passage as a reversion from the Pauline ideal of coequal discipleship (Gal 3.28) to a post-Pauline patriarchal authority pattern which was regarded as a convenient way to protect the church's image in an increasingly critical and hostile world. For a rather more positive verdict see Oberlinner, 104–8.

a particular cultural situation and therefore should not be universalised.[87]

The prior question should be whether there can be an agreed exegesis of the passage, on whose significance for today people might agree to differ. However, the stances of the interpreters inevitably influence their exegesis no matter how objective they claim to be, and the present treatment will doubtless fare no better. Attempts to locate 1 Tim 2.11–15 within the development of Pauline tradition invariably relate the passage to 1 Cor 14.33b–35. The verbal and conceptual parallels are striking: silence (σιγάτωσαν, 1 Cor 14.34; ἡσυχία, 2.11, 12); prohibition of speaking/teaching (οὐ ... ἐπιτρέπεται ... λαλεῖν, 1 Cor 14.34, 35; διδάσκειν ... οὐκ ἐπιτρέπω, 2.12); learning (μαθεῖν, 1 Cor 14.35; μανθανέτω, 2.11); subjection of the woman (ὑποτασσέσθωσαν, 1 Cor 14.34; ἐν πάσῃ ὑποταγῇ, 2.11). The possibility of some form of literary relationship is frequently raised, and three main suggestions have been advanced.

(a) 1 Cor 14.34f. is an interpolation based on 1 Tim 2.11–15.[88] The case depends mainly on text-critical considerations, but also on the claim that silencing the women in the church is inconsistent with what is said earlier in the letter. The Western evidence, including some early witnesses (D F G), locates vv. 34f. following v. 40. It is argued that the hypothesis that vv. 34f. were originally a marginal gloss explains all the extant readings. Since no extant MSS omit the verses altogether, this gloss would have had to have led to the two interpolations before the beginning of the textual tradition. Most recently, Fee suggests that 1 Tim 2.9–15 may have played a part in the introduction of the marginal gloss (1994:281). This view can be challenged on various grounds; it can be argued that λαλεῖν has a specific meaning in 14.34–35 which does not contradict the permission enjoyed by all (including women) to engage in various kinds of speaking, and that no MSS actually omit the text.[89]

(b) 1 Cor 14.34 is Pauline and earlier, while the differences in 1 Tim 2.11–15 reveal it to be later *Paulustradition*.[90] The basic

---

[87] See, for example, Baumert*; Kroeger and Kroeger*; Payne*; Scholer*; Witherington*.

[88] Fee 1994:272–81; Oberlinner, 93f.

[89] See Feuillet*, 162–70; Trummer 1978:144–51; Ellis 1981:213–20; Hurley*, 185–94; Niccum, C., 'The Voice of the Manuscripts on the Silence of Women: The External Evidence for 1 Cor 14.34–5', *NTS* 43 (1997), 2.42–55.

[90] Trummer 1978:144–51; cf. Michel 1948:90–4; Witherington 1988:90–104. Roloff, 128, combines views (a) and (b), suggesting that the author of the PE knows 1 Cor 14 in its final interpolated form, and then develops its interpretation for the new situation. Wagener 1994:103f. holds that the material in 1 Tim is later but leaves it open whether it is based on 1 Cor 14.33b–6 or on a rule taken from tradition. She draws attention to the use of οἱ ἅγιοι in 1 Cor 14.33b as being closer to Paul than the language of the PE (Wagener 1994:92f.).

contention is that, since the text of 1 Cor 14.34 is more general, 1 Tim 2.11–15 is an attempt to interpret the earlier teaching.[91]

Evidence for this development is drawn from the move from the more general λαλεῖν (which Trummer understands to be the 'teaching dialogue'; cf. Michel 1948:91) to the more specific διδάσκειν. Thus, according to the later interpretation it was not 'speaking' as such that was prohibited in 1 Cor 14.34 but participation in the activity of teaching. Also, what was expressed as a desire ('if they wish to learn', 1 Cor 14.35) has become a command in 1 Tim 2.11. In each passage the subordination of women provides the foundation of the prohibition, but the basis of this, described only vaguely as 'the law' in 1 Cor 14.34, is specified more clearly in 1 Tim 2.13f. Finally, the change from the impersonal ἐπιτρέπεται to ἐπιτρέπω fits the pattern of the transition from authentic Pauline material to *Paulustradition*.

This suggested development from general to specific rests upon the assumption that λαλεῖν carries a general meaning in 1 Cor 14. But, whether it means speaking in tongues, or evaluating prophecy or even engaging in the teaching dialogue, it is still specific enough for the occasion, as long as the recipients of the letter understood it, which we must assume they did. Equally, Paul's apparently vague reference to ὁ νόμος as the ground for the injunction in 1 Cor 14.34 is not vague at all, if the reference is back to the same material (Gen 2.21–23) cited in 1 Cor 11, or if a simple reference to ὁ νόμος was sufficient to call to his readers' mind some specific OT material. The change from the impersonal ἐπιτρέπεται to ἐπιτρέπω cannot prove anything. If one passage influenced the other, there does not appear to be any way to determine the sequence.

(c) There is no literary relationship between 1 Cor 14.33–35 and 1 Tim 2.11–15 (Ellis* 1981:214f.). Rather, the similar features of the passages, alongside the differences, point to a tradition lying behind each of the passages which has been applied in different ways.

View (c) is probably the most defensible. View (a) depends on a delicate textual argument, and (b) seems to rest more on assumptions about the late production of the PE than on convincing evidence of later adaptation of an earlier paraenetic tradition.

The exegesis to be offered below will substantiate the view that in this passage the author allows women in the church to learn, provided that they do so quietly with deference (*sc.* to the teacher). This demand for 'quietness' is extended into a prohibition of their teaching and wielding authority over men.

---

[91] Trummer 1978:145; Roloff, 129f.

In the context it seems most likely that through their being 'deceived' there was a false content to their teaching and that this element included some kind of emancipatory tendency, especially by wealthy women (cf. 2.9f.), expressed in what was a socially unacceptable way in that time and culture. There may well have been a misreading of material in Genesis as part of the speculative use of 'myths and genealogies' practised by the writer's opponents; further, the tendency to abstain from certain foods and from marriage on the part of the opposition must have included a rejection of sexual relations and the bearing of children.

Over against this tendency the author makes three points. First, there is a specific prohibition of the women teaching in a way that involves the assertion of authority over men (including their husbands). Second, in what is syntactically something of a parenthesis the author rejects their claims to any superiority over men by insisting that Adam was created first and that it was not Adam who was the first to be deceived (and sin) but Eve. Third, although women might regard teaching as an appropriate, even necessary, accompaniment or means of salvation, he states that in their case childbearing fulfils this function, always provided that they persevere in the qualities of character which are expected in all believers. It is possible that teaching was seen as the alternative to a traditional, domestic pattern of life; in any case, the false teaching discouraged women from giving themselves to motherhood. Thus v. 15 affirms the natural order of marriage and motherhood as an appropriate life in which to actualise salvation.

If this interpretation is sound, it means that the 'silencing' of the women can and must be placed alongside the other references to the prohibition and refutation of false teaching by men (1.3; 4.7; 6.3f., 20; 2 Tim 2.16f., 23; Tit 1.11, 13; 3.10f.). It is probably to be understood, therefore, as mainly motivated by the author's opposition to heresy in the church.[92] The particular form that it took involved the women in activities that were socially unacceptable, involving some kind of domination or exercising authority over men on the basis of false teaching. Elsewhere in the PE women are encouraged to be good teachers, with the older women instructing the younger and mothers teaching their children. It would, therefore, follow that the prohibition here is related to the circumstances and is not absolute or for all time.

---

[92] Scholars who deny that the context here is heretical teaching by the women because only the women are prohibited from teaching (Schreiner*, 112) overlook the general silencing of false teachers in the PE. The focus on women here is because a form of false teaching specific to them is in mind.

Nevertheless, it has been so treated in the church. The principal argument for seeing a universal prohibition lies in the use of the Genesis story which has been thought to give a binding, scriptural principle. However, given the fact of heresy and the likelihood that it provides a part of the answer as to why women were prohibited from teaching, vv. 13–14 (and 15) must be understood as an argument against specific aspects of the heresy – even if precision is not possible. It is probable that the point here is to refute claims of female superiority to males by means of an interpretation that may have been meant expressly to refute the opponents on their own ground of drawing speculative rabbinic conclusions from the text. The text does not stand in the way of recognising the equality of men and women or of allowing teaching and other roles in a culture where these are no longer unacceptable.

A second argument for a universal prohibition is that the use of household material (*Haustafel*), such as may be reflected here, provided a corrective to tendencies towards greater emancipation in the ancient world and specifically in the church which might threaten the status quo (see discussion at Tit 2.1). In the NT, the household codes (Eph, Col, 1 Pet), other instructions belonging to this stream of teaching (1 Cor 14.33–35; Rom 13.1–7) and the further adaptation of this line of teaching to the whole church in the form of the *Gemeindeordnung* (Tit 2.1–10; Weiser 1989; Witherington 1988:118) may have been intended to settle disturbances of various sorts by reverting to conventional ethics of the household.

While such a trend may indicate sensitivity to wider social conventions (and may do so purposefully to create a respectable impression in the minds of outsiders), a strict return to patriarchal tendencies or household rule is far from evident.[93] The mistaken tendency to see in the PE (as well as in Eph, Col) a stage of development characterised by institutionalisation rather than the church's response to a specific situation colours the way in which the use of the household or community code is interpreted. What might appear to some as a reversion to a strict Hellenistic Jewish authority structure, must be seen rather from the perspective of the church's awareness of the sensibilities of secular society. Interests throughout the letters and the fact that the author shaped this teaching in the form of a household code suggest that awareness of and sensitivity to the outsider are not far from mind. The author of the PE continues to view the church's responsibility towards the world to be to make a redemptive impression in it (cf. 1 Th 4.11–12; 1 Tim 3.7; 6.1; Tit 2.5, 8, 10;

---

[93] *Contra* Roloff, 135–7; Fiorenza*, 279.

3.1–2, 8). If this is the case, then this sort of presentation of Christian ethics has the dimension, however implicit, of maintaining a dialogue with the world. Finally, if 1 Tim 2.8–15 attempts to solve one part of the confusion caused by a heresy-related emancipation movement that was bound to be misunderstood in a strongly patriarchal cultural situation, then there is no reason to conclude that the teaching is inferior or necessarily retrograde when compared with the earlier Paul (cf. 1 Cor 14.33–35). Authority that is abused is taken away. Misconceived emancipation movements connected with false teaching might require putting temporary restraints on freedom.

TEXT

8. διαλογισμοῦ διαλογισμῶν (א² F G H 33 81 104 365 630 1505 1739 1881 *al* g sy^phl bo Orig Eus Bas Hier; WH t). The word occurs elsewhere in the NT in the pl. (except Lk 9.46f.) with the sense of 'evil intentions' (Mt 15.19 = Mk 7.21). Elliott, 39, prefers the pl., which might have been altered to the sing. by assimilation to ὀργῆς. But alteration to the pl. form found elsewhere is also possible (cf. the use of sing. forms in ethical lists in Col 3.8; Eph 4.31f.).
9. |καὶ| γυναῖκας The καί (א² D* F G 6 365 1739 *pc* b vg Ambst Spec; καὶ τάς, D¹ Ψ 1881 TR; Kilpatrick) should perhaps be retained by analogy with the style of 5.25 (Elliott, 207f.), although the attestation is not strong, and the word is omitted by WH; Knight, 131f.; Wagener 1994:68 n. 11.
κοσμίῳ κοσμίως (א² D* F G H 33 365 1739 1881 *pc*; WH mg). The variant is possibly due to scribes who did not realise that the noun means 'clothing' rather than 'quiet demeanour', Elliott, 40. The effect of this and the previous variant together would be to tie the v. more closely to v. 8 (Roloff 132 n. 113).
καί ἤ (D² H Ψ TR lat sy^h Cl.; omit P 33 *pc*). A connective is needed, and ἤ was substituted as being more precise and as assimilation to what follows (Elliott, 41, 208).
χρυσίῳ χρυσῷ (א D Ψ TR Cl; WH mg). The variant is due to a dislike of diminutives (Elliott, 41).
10. ἀλλ᾽ ὅ ἄλλο (comm.) is listed by NA, but I have not found any other reference to it.
12. ἀλλ᾽ ἀλλά (A 33). Elliott, 26, accepts the variant on the ground that elision tends to be later. Similar problems arise at 1.13; 3.3; 5.23; 2 Tim 2.9, 24. However, in 2.10 and elsewhere the elided form occurs without variant.
14. ἐξαπατηθεῖσα (ἀπατήθεισα א² D² TR). The variant is due to scribes' dislike of compound verbs (Elliott, 44).
15. σωφροσύνης Add καὶ συνέσεως (1611 2015 1022 sy^h ^mg; before σωφροσύνης 1245). The variation in position raises suspicions of interpolation (Elliott, 45, 236).

EXEGESIS

8. Βούλομαι οὖν προσεύχεσθαι τοὺς ἄνδρας ἐν παντὶ τόπῳ The conjunction οὖν resumes the teaching on prayer in 2.1f. (see 2.1 note) after the theological grounding and link with the Pauline mission (v. 7). The tone in βούλομαι (which can have the weak force 'to wish', 6.9) is imperatival (5.14; Tit 3.8**), and, in view of v. 7, authoritative, expressing a strong command by the writer. This command 'to pray' (προσεύχεσθαι**; noun 2.1) repeats the earlier command of 2.1 with added directions related to the manner in which prayer is to be made.

In this household code pattern of teaching, men (ἀνήρ, 2.12; Tit 1.6 note) are addressed first (as opposed to the women in 2.9). It has been argued that the reference is specifically to husbands. Normally men and women would be married, and v. 15 certainly assumes so; elsewhere in the PE ἀνήρ has the sense of 'husband'. The passage as a whole has been thought to be concerned with the way husbands and wives relate to one another (Ellis* 1989:72–5; Hugenberger*, 350–60). The parallels with 1 Cor 14.34f.; 1 Pet 3.3–6 and Tit 2.5 are the strongest point in favour of this interpretation. The allusion to Adam and Eve in vv. 13f. has also been thought to support the narrower reference (Kähler*, 11; cf. Barrett, 55). However, in both Hebrew and Greek the words for man and woman are ambiguous and therefore often use a possessive pronoun or some other means of indicating husband or wife (cf. 1 Pet 3.1; Eph 5.22; Tit 2.5; Col 3.18). In the PE the contexts always make this delimitation clear (3.2, 12; 5.9; Tit 1.6; 2.5**). Nothing suggests that the instructions here are to be limited just to married men and married women; an unmarried man might pray, and an unmarried woman might dress ostentatiously and teach. For women to teach might have threatened their husbands' standing, but it is not clear how this would hold in the case of praying and dress. The instructions are accordingly directed to men and women in the church and not specifically to husbands and wives.[94] In any case, the practical difference may not be great since marriage was the normal situation for men and women.

ἐν παντὶ τόπῳ, 'everywhere', may continue the theme of the universal gospel (Brox, 131; Roloff, 130f.; Bartsch 1965:48). In the NT, the phrase is Pauline (1 Cor 1.2; 2 Cor 2.14; 1 Th 1.8), and usually associated with the gospel ministry or prayer. It was probably developed in some way from Mal 1.10f. which belongs to the prophetic stream of a promised blessing to the Gentiles,[95] and which was understood in the Targum as a reference to prayer.[96] This background requires something more than a simple local reference to prayer 'in all the house churches'.[97] A line back to Mal 1.11 would be in keeping with the unique Pauline consciousness of being one through whom the promise

---

[94] So rightly Schreiner*, 115–17.
[95] Cf. *Didache* 14.2f. for citation of this passage.
[96] Cf. Justin, *Dial.* 117.2; cf. Simpson, 45; see Gordon, R. P., 'Targumic Parallels to Acts XIII 18 and Didache XIV 3', *NovT* 16 (1974), 285–9.
[97] *Pace* Koester, H., *TDNT* VIII, 187–208, 203; Knight, 128; Fee, 71.

to the Gentiles was being fulfilled.[98] Such an allusion also ties in with the argument for the universality of the gospel in 2.1–6 and with the claim that the Pauline apostolate to the nations plays an instrumental part in God's salvation plan (v. 7). Although 2.1 already implicated the church in this ministry, v. 8 ties the effectiveness of the church's prayer for the mission to the behaviour and attitudes of men.

ἐπαίροντας ὁσίους χεῖρας χωρὶς ὀργῆς καὶ διαλογισμοῦ After the earlier command to pray has been taken up and summarised, the writer uses a participial phrase to make a fresh main point concerning the ethical condition for prayer (cf. Parry, 14). The effectiveness of prayer is linked to holiness and the avoidance of attitudes and behaviour which cause dissension. 'Raising' (ἐπαίρω**) the hands (Lk 24.50) in prayer was a common gesture in the early church.[99] It was a natural gesture, but its background here is doubtless in Judaism, where the practice was widespread in acts of prayer.[100] The need for hands (χείρ, 4.14; 5.22; 2 Tim 1.6**) to be pure or holy (ὅσιος; Tit 1.8**; not in Paul)[101] refers originally to the practice of washing them on entry to a sanctuary (Exod 30.19–21). But this outward cultic purity quickly came to symbolise an inward piety expressed by the outward act.[102] The purity is not merely moral but also spiritual (Oberlinner, 86). The implication is that prayer in the Christian meeting is the equivalent of worship in the OT and Judaism and elsewhere.

One aspect at least of the holiness expected is an absence (χωρίς, 5.21**) of anger and argument. Abstention from ὀργή**, 'anger' (cf. Tit 1.7), is equivalent to forgiving other people (Mk 11.25; Mt 5.23f.; 6.14f.; Col 3.8, 13; Eph 4.31f.) as the condition for prayer being heard. For similar conditions for prayer see 1 Pet 3.7; Jas 1.19f.; *Didache* 15.3f. διαλογισμός** can have a positive sense ('thought, reasoning', Rom 1.21), but

---

[98] Rom 9–11; 15.9–13; Gal 1.15–16; cf. Hengel, M., *Between Jesus and Paul* (London: SCM Press, 1983), 49–54; Kim, S., *The Origin of Paul's Gospel* (Grand Rapids: Eerdmans, 1981), 60, 91–9.

[99] Lk 18.13; Jas 4.8; 1 Clement 2.3; 29.1; Tertullian, *Apol.* 30.4.

[100] Exod 9.29; Ps 27 (MT 28).2; 62 (MT 63).5; 76 (MT 77).3; 134 (MT 133).2; 140 (MT 141).2; 142 (MT 143).6; Lam 3.41; 1 Kgs 8. 22, 54; Neh 8.6; Isa 1.15; 2 Macc 14.34; Philo, *Flacc* 121; *Virt.* 57; *Cont.* 66, 89; Josephus, *Ant.* 4.40; cf. Nauck 1950:78; Bartsch 1965:54–7; Spicq, 372f.

[101] The adj. has two endings (BD §59.2).

[102] Cf. Meyer, R. and Hauck, F., *TDNT* III, 421–6. See especially 1 Clement 29.1. The phrase ὅσιοι χεῖρες is Cl. (Aeschylus, *Cho.* 378; Sophocles, *OC* 470); for similar language see Exod 30.17–21; Ps 25 (MT 26).6; 72 (MT 73).13; Isa 1.15f.; *Ep. Arist.* 305; *Apos. Canons* 224, 241. Whereas καθαρός is used of ritual purity, ὅσιος tends to be used more of persons and expresses obedience to the will of God.

here alongside anger it has a negative sense, more probably 'dispute or argument',[103] rather than 'doubt'.[104]

The comment ties in with the other references to the dissension characteristic of the false teaching.[105] Although Roloff, 132, holds that this teaching to men is incidental and unrelated to the present situation, the link with the disruption caused by the heresy suggests that the author was addressing the involvement of men in the doctrinal disputes. The teaching to men is no less relevant than the teaching to women.

9. Ὡσαύτως καὶ γυναῖκας ἐν καταστολῇ κοσμίῳ μετὰ αἰδοῦς καὶ σωφροσύνης κοσμεῖν ἑαυτας ὡσαύτως, 'in the same way' (3.8, 11; 5.25; Tit 2.3, 6**), compares a fresh comment with a preceding one, as it here turns the discussion to women. It is peculiar to the PE and is used exclusively in lists of instructions; it functions similarly to ὁμοίως in the household code of 1 Pet 3.1, 7; 5.5.

This connection makes it clear that βούλομαι is to be supplied to complete the thought expressed with the accusative noun [καὶ] γυναῖκας and the infinitive κοσμεῖν (BA 1794). But how is the command to be understood?

(a) As the sentence stands, the command could be understood to be simply that women (rather than just 'wives') adorn themselves with godliness, and there is no reference to them praying (so all translations; Holtzmann, 312; Scott, 25; Knight, 132f.).[106] The infinitive κοσμεῖν with βούλομαι makes a complete thought, even though the content of the specific command differs from that given to men. If 'likewise' simply makes the transition necessary within the paraenetic (household code) form from one party or partner to another (like ὁμοίως in 1 Pet 3.1, 7), then there is no more reason to expect the content of the instruction to the men in v. 8 to carry over to the women than there is in the household code of 1 Peter to expect the instructions to slaves (2.18–25) to carry over to the women and then the instructions to the women to (3.1–6) to apply to

---

[103] Phil 2.14; Lk 24.38; Holtzmann, 311; Lock, 31; Jeremias, 20; most commentators.

[104] Lk 12.29; Rom 14.1; Jas 1.6; So Chrysostom, PG LXII, 540; Theodoret III, 650 Schulze; Theod. Mops. II, 91 Swete (both cited by Dibelius-Conzelmann, 45 n. 5); White, 107. Oberlinner, 86, holds that this interpretation fits in with a basic thought of the PE, and especially with the emphasis on truth in the preceding verses, but this argument is weaker than the one from the immediate context.

[105] 3.3, 8, 11; 5.13; 6.11; 2 Tim 2.24; Tit 1.7; 2.3; 3.2; cf. Mt 5.23–25, 6;12, 14; Mk 11.25; Spicq, 374.

[106] Cf. Wagener 1994:72–4, who holds that the context requires that the behaviour of women at prayer is in mind, but that προσεύχεσθαι is not to be supplied.

the men. The common factor is 'instruction' not the content of the instruction. In Tit 2.1–8, where very similar instructions are introduced for each of the groups addressed, it can be claimed that ὡσαύτως simply functions to make the transition to the next person addressed.

(b) The weakness of the previous view is that the introduction of the reference to women's adornment is an unmotivated digression if it is not related to prayer in some way or other; after an injunction to the men about how they are to worship, it would be strange if something parallel was not being said to the women. One possibility is that there is anacolouthon and that the whole thought of βούλομαι προσεύχεσθαι is to be added. In this case the sense would be 'I desire women also to pray being adorned [appropriately]'.[107]

(c) Alternatively, Parry, 14, suggests that the participle προσευχομένας is to be understood with γυναῖκας, so that the injunction is concerned with women when they are praying. This is probably the best way to understand the command. The peculiarity of the construction is due to the fact that the general behaviour of women (and not merely when they are at prayer) is in mind. Spicq, 374f., claims that Christian women here have the privilege of being called to pray in contrast to Talmudic Judaism (but not the OT!).

Even if view (a) is adopted, the fact that only the men are addressed with regard to prayer would not imply that women are not to pray (*pace* Holtzmann, 310). The whole preceding context is one of prayer, and the reference to the women is unmotivated if prayer is no longer in mind.[108] It can be safely assumed that women were free to pray in the absence of any explicit prohibition such as the author felt it necessary to make in respect of their teaching.[109] It is thus most probable that behaviour that poses a hindrance to prayer is in mind in each case, arguments and dissension on the one hand, ostentatious or seductive dress on the other. It is entirely conceivable that, with disruption in the assembly for worship as the motivation for the instruction, inappropriate adornment was seen as a disruptive

---

[107] Chrysostom, *PG* LXII, 540f.; Calvin, 215; Spicq, 375; Barrett, 55; Dibelius-Conzelmann, 45; Bartsch 1965:60; Witherington 1988:119, 263 n. 203.

[108] The question arises whether the instruction applies only to behaviour in church meetings or is to be applied more generally to home and public life. Cf. Oberlinner, 87f., who believes that an original cultic direction has been broadened in application here. The 'good works' in which the women are to clothe themselves are, in any case, part of their total life-style rather than what they do in a church meeting. They come to the meeting, as it were, 'clothed' in them.

[109] It is out of the question that the women were teaching and not praying, so that only teaching needed to be forbidden.

influence in the case of women, just as arguments were in the case of men.

The contrast between approved and prohibited kinds of adornment shows close correspondences to 1 Pet 3.3, 5, and this suggests the use of traditional teaching.[110] As in 1 Pet 3, the thought of external adornment is only the starting place for a discussion of a more thorough sense of adornment (μετά...) which, in the case of the godly woman, is to be guided by deeper spiritual realities. Thus the opening comment implies something about the actual outer adornment that is deemed to be fitting for Christian women but is not limited to it.

καταστολή*** can mean either 'adornment' or 'deportment, demeanour',[111] and perhaps even combine them at the same time.[112] κόσμιος (3.2***) expresses a range of meanings: 'respectable, honourable, modest, orderly, beautiful'. It was especially used by philosophers to convey the sense of orderliness, discipline and decorum, and is the opposite of licence. From this it has the sense of well-mannered and honourable. The impression is of a character which is tidy and neat, not slovenly nor showy (although the verb has the sense of adorning). With the sense of 'modest'[113] it described a traditional virtue used of honourable women.[114] The specific nuance 'free from sexual immorality' may be intended, but this may be too narrow a meaning.[115]

μετὰ αἰδοῦς καὶ σωφροσύνης carries the discussion from mere appearance to the place of attitudes determined by faith (cf. 1 Pet 3.4: ἀλλ' ὁ κρυπτὸς τῆς καρδίας ἄνθρωπος). For μετά of attendant circumstances, see discussion at 1.14.

αἰδώς***, 'modesty, respectful fear, discretion, propriety', is often linked with σωφροσύνη, which was one of the cardinal virtues (Cf. TLNT I, 41-4). According to Bultmann it has much the same sense as 'piety', being used for dread and fear before what is awful, and hence for fear before God and whatever is associated with him, for the institutions of society and for justice. It became used for individuals' attitude to themselves and thus

---

[110] κοσμεῖν, κόσμιος/κόσμος; ἱματισμός/ἱμάτιον; χρυσίον; πλέγμα/ἐμπλοκῆς τριχῶν; Goppelt 1993:217f.

[111] For clothing see Isa 61.3; Josephus, Bel. 2.126. For demeanour see Ep. Arist. 284; Epictetus 2.10.15; so Rengstorf, K. H., TDNT VII, 595f.; Dibelius-Conzelmann, 45f.

[112] Epictetus 2.21.11 is cited by BA for this use, but it is surely an example of 'deportment'.

[113] Sasse, H., TDNT III, 895f.

[114] See Dibelius-Conzelmann, 46 n. 13. See further New Docs. IV, 151f. §56 (AD II), for the adj. in a laudatory epitaph for a wife. The word is not found in the LXX but is used by Philo (e.g. Mut. 226).

[115] For the interlinking of this attribute with self-control see TLNT II, 330–5.

developed the idea of 'shame' or 'modesty'.[116] Here it refers to the modesty or decency with which women should behave. This includes the avoidance of clothing and adornment which might be both showy and extravagant as well as sexually enticing.[117] The target is probably rich women who are to behave modestly and exercise self-control and to adorn themselves rather with good works.

The σώφρων cluster is prominent in the PE, describing a life characterised by balance and self-control which is linked to the Christ-event and the change of life which faith in Christ produces (see **Excursus 3**). Applied specifically to women, σωφροσύνη might suggest chastity and sexual purity as a form of self-control.[118] It may be the traditional pairing that accounts for the appearance of αἰδώς here,[119] but in the context of the PE and alongside σωφροσύνη it is to be understood equally as a quality determined by faith in Christ. κοσμεῖν (Tit 2.10** note) can refer to the arrangement of clothing and jewelry so as to beautify (of women, 1 Pet 3.5; Rev 21.2) or be used in a metaphorical sense.[120]

μὴ ἐν πλέγμασιν καὶ χρυσίῳ ἢ μαργαρίταις ἢ ἱματισμῷ πολυτελεῖ. To describe the kind of adornment to be avoided, the author employs a disparaging caricature of wealthy women. Polemic against luxury in dress and ostentation in general was a common secular theme. Plutarch, *Mor.* 141E, cites Crates: κοσμεῖ δὲ τὸ κοσμιωτέραν τὴν γυναῖκα ποιοῦν. ποιεῖ δὲ τοιαύτην οὔτε χρυσὸς οὔτε σμάραγδος οὔτε κόκκος, ἀλλ' ὅσα σεμνότητος εὐταξίας αἰδοῦς ἔμφασιν περιτίθησιν.[121] The

---

[116] Hence it was used to refer to the sexual organs as those parts of the body which one covers up from sight (cf. αἰδοῖον in Ezek 23.20). It was scarcely used in the LXX (3 Macc 1.19; 4.5) but is frequent in Philo. Josephus, *Ant.* 2.52 uses it for the shameful feeling which one should have with regard to sexual sin and lack of self-control. See Bultmann, R., *TDNT* I, 169–71; *TLNT* I, 41–4.

[117] For the qualities praised in women in the secular world see *New Docs.* III §§ 8, 11, 13 with the discussion there.

[118] Spicq, 376. Cf. Philo, *Spec* 1.102; 3.51; Josephus, *Ant.* 18.66–80; Cicero, *de Fin.* 2 in Simpson, 46.

[119] Bultmann, R., *TDNT* I, 169–71, suggests that the term is rare in the NT because it represents a ἕξις, a skill acquired for one's own sake; since Christians are not to be primarily related to themselves but to God and their neighbours, pursuit of such a skill has little place; cf. Josephus, *Ant.* 2.52; *Bel.* 2.325; *T. Jud.* 14.7; *Sib. Orac.* 1.35. This explanation seems most implausible.

[120] *T. Jud.* 13.5; Josephus, *Bel.* 2.444; *Apoc. Pet.* 9.24.

[121] Epictetus, *Ench.* 40; Seneca, *Ben.* 7.9; Ps-Lucian, *Amores* 40–3. Spicq (*TLNT* II, 331 n. 8) cites a close parallel from Athenaeus 12.521b. See further the pseudo-Pythagorean letter of Melissa to Cleareta (Malherbe 1986:83 (§ 34), paraphrased in P. Haun. II.13 (*New Docs.* VI, 18–23 § 2)). Cf. Scholer* for further examples.

motif is taken over in Judaism;[122] it was based on romantic ideas of early Roman or Jewish women (1 Pet 3.6) and then Christianised (Roloff 127f.). Goppelt (1993:221) holds that the vivid negative contrast is meant to emphasise the positive description rather than to imply that women in the community actually were wealthy enough to attire themselves in this way. But in view of 1 Tim 6.17–19 a concrete corrective intention may well be present. The traditional concern was that such external adornment had seductive powers (Philo, *Virt.* 39f.; Seneca, *Ben.* 7.9). The phrase μετὰ αἰδοῦς καὶ σωφροσύνης thus expresses the discretion and decorum befitting a Christian woman which stands in contrast to the seductiveness and wealthy display of the worldly woman.[123]

πλέγμα***, 'anything that is twisted', can be used of embroidery (Philo, *Somn.* 1.204, 206) or, as here, of various types of plaited hairstyle.[124] These were often highly elaborate, incorporating jewelry. They were the marks of both wealth and beauty and were often criticised.[125] Similar comments are made on ἐμπλοκή in 1 Pet 3. χρυσίον, 'gold', refers to items of jewelry or ornaments, also typically and critically associated with wealthy women.[126] μαργαρίτη, 'pearl', is similarly a female decoration.[127]

ἱματισμός (Lk 7.25; 9.29; Jn 19.24; Acts 20.33***) πολυτελής means 'expensive clothing'. Here the description is a stock one for rich clothing.[128] The picture is of a flashy luxury that is out of place in sinners seeking the mercy of God (*TLNT* III, 134f.) In the contrast described in 1 Pet 3.4 πολυτελής is used for the effect of spiritual qualities in contrast to outward beauty (cf. Mk 14.3***).

It may seem puzzling that ostentation and seduction would be a concern when the heresy insisted on asceticism and celibacy (4.3), but the presence of wealthy women and motives of greed (6.3–10) and the concern for the perceptions of outsiders who would not appreciate fine points of doctrine are probably sufficient to make sense of the inclusion of the traditional

[122] Philo, *Virt.* 39f.; *Mig.* 97; *T. Reub.* 5.1–5; *1 Enoch* 8.1f. But see earlier Isa 3.16–26.

[123] Cf. Roloff, 132; for similar rules in the mysteries see 133 n. 116, citing Dittenberger, *Syll.* 736.15ff.

[124] Hurley*, 198f. The word is not found in the LXX; Isa 28.5 Aq, Theod.; Josephus, *Ant.* 2.220.

[125] Juvenal, *Sat.* 6.492; Petronius, *Sat.* 67; cf. Balsdon, J. P. V. D., *Roman Women* (Westport: Bodley Head, 1962), 252–8; Spicq, 377.

[126] 1 Pet 3.3; Rev 17.4; 18.16; Demosthenes 27.10, 13; Plutarch, *Tim.* 15.6.

[127] Rev 17.4; 18.12, 16; see also Mt 7.6; 13.45f; Rev 21.21a, 21b***; Petronius, *Sat.* 67; Spicq 377.

[128] Plutarch, *Mor.* 218E (Simpson, 46); Xenophon, *Anab.* 1.5.8; Philo, *Sacr.* 21; Josephus, *Bel.* 1.605.

paraenesis.[129] Oberlinner, 90, rightly observes that part of the author's purpose may be to guard against the development of social divisions between the rich and the poor in the congregation. In any case, the main point is that true adornment will be internal, expressing itself outwardly in Christian character, whereas an emphasis on the external suggests a desire to attract attention to oneself, perhaps to seduce (cf. Calvin, 216).

10. ἀλλ᾽ ὃ πρέπει γυναιξὶν ἐπαγγελλομέναις θεοσέβειαν, δι᾽ ἔργων ἀγαθῶν ἀλλ᾽ introduces the contrast to the kind of decoration rejected in v. 9. The construction is elliptical as there is no expressed antecedent to ὅ; we are to supply κοσμεῖν and read 'not with braided hairstyles ... but [adorn themselves with that] which befits..., namely by means of good deeds'.[130] The paraenesis applies the pressure of an accepted Christian norm of appropriateness (πρέπει, Tit 2.1 note). To acknowledge the norm is to accept the responsibility to act as it dictates.

The controlling factor in this case is the woman's profession of authentic faith. The phrase is similar to others which employ ἐπαγγέλλομαι in the sense of an individual's or group's strong claim to an identification that is determined by some notable quality.[131] In this case, the identifying characteristic is θεοσέβεια***, 'reverence for God'.[132] The adj. θεοσεβής was used of Jews (Deissmann 1927:451f.; Jn 9.31***) and of women. It was a self-description of people who claimed that theirs was the true religion.[133] The quality is equivalent to εὐσέβεια, which defines genuine Christian existence as the combination of the knowledge of God and the behaviour which grows out of that knowledge (see **Excursus 1**). Thus women are called to substantiate their claim to faith by exhibiting the appropriate adornment, which is nothing other than the Christian character and practice expected of all believers (Oberlinner, 91).

δι᾽ ἔργων ἀγαθῶν relates to the infinitive κοσμεῖν, in the same way as the ἐν phrases do in v. 9, to fill out the meaning of

---

[129] There are also the examples of contemporary sects which insist on various ascetic practices alongside licence permitted to the leaders.

[130] Cf. Ellicott, 34 (not discussed in BD or MHT). Holtzmann, 313f., prefers to translate 'but [to adorn themselves] with what is proper for women who profess godliness by means of good deeds', on the grounds that practising good deeds is hardly what one does in the church meeting.

[131] 6.21; Wis 2.13; Philo, *Cont.* 2; Ignatius, *Eph.* 14.2. See Wolter 1988:265f. The verb also means 'to promise' (Tit 1.2; Rom 4.21; Gal. 3.19).

[132] Xenophon, *Anab.* 2.6.26; Gen 20.11; Job 28.28; Ecclus 1.25; Bar 5.4; Philo, *Opif.* 154 (cf. *Mig.* 97; *Fug.* 150); 2 Clement 20.4; Diognetus 1; 3.3; 4.5, 6; 6.4; see further refs. in Roloff, 133 n. 119; cf. Bertram, G., *TDNT* III, 123–8; *TLNT* II, 196–9.

[133] Murphy-O'Connor, J., 'Lots of God-Fearers? *Theosebeis* in the Aphrodisias Inscription', *RB* 99 (1992), 418–24.

'adorn'. The use is thus instrumental (cf. 4.5). In this phrase the internal and external combine as the adornment befitting godliness is described in terms of service (ἔργα ἀγαθά; Tit 1.16 note and **Excursus 6**) done for the benefit of others which genuine faith produces. Roloff's insistence (134) that the plural formulation, 'good works', reflects a post-Pauline development is dubious (cf. 2 Cor 9.8; 2 Th 2.17; Col 1.10); but in any case the connection between 'good works' and salvation in the PE is clear from Tit 2.14 (cf. Eph 2.10).

11. Γυνὴ ἐν ἡσυχίᾳ μανθανέτω ἐν πάσῃ ὑποταγῇ A new topic, which extends through to v. 15, is introduced with asyndeton (cf. BD §459–63) and a switch to the third-person imperative. At this point, the main issue becomes that of the inappropriateness of women teaching men in the worship setting and the appropriate alternative(s). Verses 11–12 contain the specific instructions, while vv. 13–14 substantiate in some way the author's decision to prohibit women from teaching. Verse 15 then expresses an alternative understanding of the salvation and the domestic role of a woman.

The first injunction sets out the appropriate role of women in the congregational meeting as that of quiet learners. This may be intended as a positive assertion of the women's role over against the prohibition on teaching which follows. The keynote is ἡσυχία which is to characterise both the woman's learning and then her forgoing of teaching. The shift to the generic singular γυνή is natural; it generalises the instruction. Although the married state is taken as normal (2.15), the term must refer to woman in general and is not limited to wives.

The verb μανθάνω (Tit 3.14**) envisages Christian instruction given by a teacher (cf. Rom 16.17; 1 Cor 14.31, 35; Eph 4.20; Phil 4.9; Col 1.7). The situation of the Christian meeting is in view (1 Cor 12.7–11, 28–30; 14.1–33); an integral part of it was instruction, and all believers in attendance, except the one teaching, would be in the position of learners. It is sometimes said that the use of the term 'learn' distinguishes the Christian situation from that of Judaism where women merely listened, but there does not appear to be any strong early evidence for this view.[134] Certainly in the church it would not be regarded as

---

[134] Statements about the low opinion which some men had of women can easily be provided. The inferior position of women in Judaism is reflected in their exclusion from certain parts of the temple (cf. Josephus, *Ant.* 15.418f.; *Bel.* 5.199). But women had to fulfil certain aspects of the Torah and must have been taught it to some extent. See *m. Sota.* 3.4 (where the saying of R. Eliezer should not be misunderstood as a prohibition of teaching women the law; see Edwards 1989:29); *m. Ned.* 4.3; *b. Pesah* 62b; *j. Sota* 3.4 (19a); *b. Qidd.* 29b, 34a; *b. Sanh.* 94b; cf. Witherington, B., *Women in the Ministry of Jesus* (Cambridge: Cambridge University Press, 1984), 6–10.

unusual for women to be instructed 'to learn' along with the men. The emphasis in the imperative μανθανέτω is, therefore, to be found not so much in 'learning' as such but rather in the manner in which women are to learn, namely 'in quietness and subjection', as the next verse with its closing return to the thought of quietness shows.

Wagener 1994:96f. holds that the heretics and the women valued learning in the sense of intellectual discovery, which the author wished to discredit in favour of their simply assenting to the truths that they were taught by 'orthodox' teachers; learning was to be merely passive rather than active. This opinion appears to rest on a somewhat anachronistic understanding of the situation and is speculative. There is more to be said for Keener*, 107f., who holds that many women would have been less educated than the men and therefore needed to learn and to do so as novices rather than to teach. But this cannot be the whole story.

ἡσυχία (2.12**)[135] can be understood as meaning either absolute 'silence', or silence in the sense of not teaching,[136] or 'quietness'.[137] Any of these are possible meanings,[138] but the more normal sense is of being at peace, enjoying solitude and tranquillity (2 Th 3.12; cf. ἡσύχιος, 1 Tim 2.2), or of keeping silent while somebody is speaking (Acts 22.3; cf. Philo, *Somn.* 2.263) and thereby showing deference to teachers, but not necessarily excluding the interchange which is appropriate to the teaching event (cf. 1 Cor 14.35). In the present context listening quietly with deference and attentiveness to the one teaching is indicated. Other forms of utterance (praying, singing, prophesying, encouraging) are not ruled out; the limited reference here is to speaking out of turn and thereby interrupting the lesson. Wagener 1994:97–9 finds the background in the view that those who are ruled should be receptive of what they are told to do or taught by those over them and not engage in strife; the thought is not so much of silence as of acceptance without demurring.[139]

---

[135] Acts 22.2; 2 Th 3.12***; cf ἡσυχάζω, 'to be at rest, silent' (Lk 14.3; 23.56; Acts 11.18; 21.14; 1 Th 4.11***); ἡσύχιος, 2.2 and note; 1 Pet 3.4 (of women)***.

[136] Cf. GNB; Hurley*, 200; Kelly, 68; Dibelius-Conzelmann, 47; Grudem, W., *The Gift of Prophecy in 1 Corinthians* (Washington: University of America, 1982), 244.

[137] Payne*, 1981:169f.; Witherington 1988:120.

[138] Cf. BA *s.v;* LSJ 657; Harris, M. J., *NIDNTT* III, 111f.

[139] The view that women should be silent was not uncommon in the ancient world: Sophocles, *Ajax* 293, γύναι, γυναιξὶ κόσμον ἡ σιγὴ φέρει. Cf. Democritus, frg. 110, γυνὴ μὴ ἀσκείτω λόγον· δεινὸν γάρ; Aelius Aristides, 45, p. 41D, ὁ ἀνὴρ λεγέτω, γυνὴ δὲ οἷς ἂν ἀκούσῃ χαιρέτω; Prov 11.12; Philo, *Her.* 14; Josephus, *Ant.* 3.67 Ignatius, *Eph.* 15.2. It is clear that men have always thought that women talk too much or at least more than they themselves do!

The activity of learning is further described in terms of submission. Role relationships within the household and, as here, in the church are typically described with ὑποτάσσομαι (see Tit 2.5 note). Here the noun ὑποταγή (3.4; 2 Cor 9.13; Gal 2.5***) serves the same purpose and reflects contact with the tradition. The superlative sense with πᾶς calls for complete subjection. In the case of women, the relationship normally in view is that of wives to husbands.[140] But in this passage the subjection is not to husbands but to teachers (unless the teacher was her husband, but the subjection appears to be to any teacher) and is part of that subjection that accompanies confession of the gospel (2 Cor 9.13). Those who understand the author to be reverting to a traditional household ethic argue that the pattern of a male-dominant authority structure is simply taken as the pattern for life in the church. Goppelt 1982:168 argued that the emphasis in the term was on the root, τάσσεσθαι = 'to be ordered', rather than on the prefixed ὑπό = 'under'. Thus it is possible that the nature of the particular relationship, the issues involved, and perhaps even cultural expectations will have determined what 'submission' entailed. The term may in fact mean anything from allowing others to take the lead[141] to willingly practising Christian humility.[142] It carries different shades of meaning in different contexts. Submission here is descriptive of the attitude or posture appropriate to learning; it implies acceptance of the teaching and of the authority of the teacher. Presumably men who were not teaching would also be expected to learn in quietness and in submission to the leaders (1 Cor 16.16; cf. Gal 6.6), just as women who pray must do so like the men by lifting holy hands without anger and dispute.

12. διδάσκειν δὲ γυναικὶ οὐκ ἐπιτρέπω οὐδὲ αὐθεντεῖν ἀνδρός, ἀλλ' εἶναι ἐν ἡσυχίᾳ The positive imperative is now followed by a prohibition. It is signalled with the present tense οὐκ ἐπιτρέπω, 'I am not permitting'. Nothing can be determined from the aspect or from the verb itself as to the length of tⁱme that the injunction would be in effect,[143] and nothing in ἐπιτρέπω itself binds it to use

---

[140] 1 Cor 14.34 (if this is not an exception); Eph 5.22; Col 3.18; Tit 2.5; 1 Pet 3.1, 5; 1 Clement 1.3. For children to parents cf. 1 Tim 3.4. For congregation to leaders Ignatius, *Eph.* 2.2; 1 Clement 1.2; 37.5.

[141] Delling., G. *TDNT* VIII, 39–48, espec. 46f.

[142] Kamlah 1970:241–3; see further Barth, M., *Ephesians* (New York, 1974), II, 708–15.

[143] The present tense of other verbs can obviously be used of universal commands (1 Cor 7.10; 1 Th 4.1, 10; 5.14 *et al*), but it is contextual reasons which are decisive.

in situations which are somehow restricted.[144] The form of the prohibition here is thus to be distinguished from the impersonal third-person singular in 1 Cor 14.34.[145] What we have is apparently a fresh injunction rather than one that carries the weight of church tradition (Witherington 1988:120). It does, however, carry the same authority implied in βούλομαι above (Schlarb 1990:276 n. 3).

In the context of the PE with their opposition to heretical teaching it is likely that, just as the noun διδασκαλία refers to the received (apostolic) teachings, so the verb διδάσκειν here connotes the task of conveying authoritative instruction in a congregational setting.[146] In itself the term says nothing as to the acceptability or otherwise of the teaching as such (contrast ἑτεροδιδασκάλειν, 1.3), but the context makes it clear that the prohibition is stated because there was something wrong with the teaching given by the women.[147] Although, then, the prohibition may appear to be universally applicable to women, it is in fact meant for a specific group of women among the recipients of the letter.

Although the task of teaching is denied to women here, by contrast older women must be καλοδιδάσκαλοι (Tit 2.3); women teach in Acts 18.26 (cf. 1 Cor 14.26) and prophesy in Acts 21.9; 1 Cor 11.5, and the exercise of various forms of ministry by women is recognised in the PE themselves (1 Tim 3.11; 5.9f.). The harmonistic distinction sometimes drawn between 'private' teaching (permitted) and 'public' teaching (forbidden) is surely anachronistic and in any case would be impossible to maintain consistently. Hence what we have here is a shift from earlier practice.

There must, then, be special reasons for the prohibition here (2 Tim 3.6f.; cf. Rev 2.20). It is probable that the women were being influenced in some way by the heresy (cf. 5.14f.). If the contrast is not simply between women and men, but between women and the legitimate (male) teachers, as Wagener 1994:101–3, argues, then it follows that the same contrast is implicit between the men in general in the congregation and the legitimate teachers. However, there is clearly something specific to women in the prohibition here, as the next phrase shows.

---

[144] *Pace* J. Toews, as cited by Kroeger and Kroeger*, 82f. Against the evidence cited there from the LXX see Heb 6.3; Ignatius, *Eph.* 10.3; 1 Clement. 1.3; Josephus, *Ant.* 20.267.

[145] This is possibly a Rabbinic formula; Aalen, S., 'A Rabbinic Formula in 1 Cor. 14,34', *SE* II (1964), 513–25.

[146] *Pace* Witherington 1988:121; see Tit 1.9 note; Schlarb 1990:274–313.

[147] However, the claim that the following phrase αὐθεντεῖν ἀνδρός expresses the content of the false teaching (Kroeger and Kroeger*, 79–86) is unjustified.

The meaning of αὐθεντέω is much disputed. Most Eng. translations have 'to have authority over' (NIV; GNB; NJB; NRSV; cf. 'to have dominion over', RV); one or two have 'to domineer over' (NEB; revised in REB to: 'to dictate to'; cf. 'to tell a man what to do', JB). BAG gives: 'to have authority, domineer over someone'; similarly LN § 37.21 defines: 'to control in a domineering manner'.

Earlier authorities gave only scant references to the word and its cognates,[148] but more recent research, especially thanks to the *TLG*, has produced over 300 uses of the word-group, including 82 uses of the verb itself.[149] Baldwin analyses the usage as follows:

(1) To rule, to reign sovereignly
(2) To control, to dominate
    (a) to compel, to influence someone/thing
    (b) (mid.) to be in effect, have legal standing
    (c) (hyperbolically) to domineer/play the trant
    (d) to grant authorisation
(3) To act independently
    (a) to assume authority over
    (b) to exercise one's own jurisdiction
    (c) to flout the authority of
(4) To be primarily responsible for or to instigate something
(5) (late) To commit a murder[150]

This analysis is broadly convincing, although there may be doubts whether Baldwin always assigns examples to the correct categories. He himself allows that any of the meanings (2), (2a), (3a) and (3c) are possible here, depending upon the context.

Basically three interpretations of the meaning of the verb in its present context have been offered.

(a) Baldwin*, 65–80, holds that the essential motif that unites the various uses of the verb is the exercise of authority. Knight*, 143–57, has identified certain cases in which the term is used in

---

[148] LSJ *s.v.* gave only four references (including this passage) and offered the two meanings 'to have full power *or* authority over' and 'to commit a murder'. The list is extended somewhat in BA.

[149] The most accessible listing with texts and translations is given by Baldwin*, 269–305, but unfortunately there are numerous misprints and errors in translation. A very full discussion is given by Payne* 1995. For earlier discussions see Deissmann 1927:88f.; MM 91; *PGL*, 262; Knight* 143–57; Wilshire*, 120–34 (his discussion is flawed by his failure to distinguish the various members of the word-group from one another and to assume that what is true for the meaning of the noun will also be true for the verb); Kroeger and Kroeger*; Kroeger* 1979:12–15; Kroeger* 1986:225–44; Osburn*, 1–12; Panning; Witherington 1988:121; Zucker 1962 (surprisingly ignored by many subsequent writers, but much the best treatment of the noun αὐθέντης; he takes the verb to mean 'aus eigener Machtvollkommenheit handeln', 'herrschen über', [18]).

[150] Baldwin*, 73.

a purely neutral sense 'to have authority over'. However, the conclusion that this is the basic meaning or normal sense has been rightly questioned (see Wilshire*, 120–34; Witherington 1988:121; Payne* 1995).

(b) In the course of three attempts to adduce the term's meaning, Kroeger* has depended upon the word-group's associations in some cases with violence, murder and erotic seductive power, and attempted to see in it a reference to practices associated with the heresy, possibly showing the influence of the Artemis cult. This led her first to the conclusion that the term means 'to engage in fertility cults' (1979; see the criticisms in Panning* and Osburn*) and finally to the meaning 'to proclaim oneself the author or originator of another' (Kroeger and Kroeger*, 87–104). Though ideas of 'authorship' and 'origination' can be linked to the word-group (cf. 2 Clement 14.3), it is hard to see how the verb can be understood to mean 'to *proclaim oneself...*'.

(c) Ideas such as autocratic or domineering abuses of power and authority appear to be more naturally linked with the verb in view of the meanings of the cognate nouns αὐθέντης and αὐθεντία, and there is one clear instance of this.[151]

The noun αὐθέντης means (1) 'murderer';[152] (2) 'author, perpetrator'; perhaps as opposed to an accomplice (cf. Bernard, 48);[153] (3) 'master'.[154] It is sometimes suggested that we have a case of homonymity, with the two main meanings representing two different etymologies.[155] αὐθεντία means 'absolute authority' (*CH* 1.2). αὐθεντικός means 'warranted, authentic', of legal documents and the like, and 'original', as opposed to a copy (2 Clement 14.3).

[151] Witherington 1988:121 notes that Chrysostom, *Homily 10 on Colossians* (*PG* LXII, 366; cf. *PGL* 262) uses the verb in this sense. Cf. Wagener 1994:100: 'the word need not have a pejorative tone in itself, but the context requires a negative meaning here.' The boundaries between exercising legitimate authority, doing so in a domineering manner, and exercising unlawful authority are manifestly fluid, and it is not surprising that scholars differ in their estimates of the effect of the context on the meaning. A case in point is *BGU* 1208.3 where Knight* 1984:154 and Payne* 1995 differ over whether any nuance of domineering or compulsion is evident. In my opinion Payne has the better of the argument that compulsion is implied by the context.

[152] Herodotus 1.117; Thucydides 3.58; Euripides, *Her. Fur.* 1359; Clement, *Strom.* 2.38.3 (cf. Turner, C. H., *JTS* 28 (1927), 272); Wilshire*, 125f. Surprisingly, the verb is not attested in this sense until the tenth century AD.

[153] Polybius 22.14.2; Diodorus Siculus 16.61.1; Josephus, *Bel.* 2.240; cf. MM 91: 'master, autocrat'.

[154] Euripides, *Supp.* 442; Hermas, *Sim.* 9.5.6; cf. Phrynichus 96. In P. Fam. Tebt. 15 (AD 114–15) the noun is used of the keepers of archives. See Jobes, K. H., 'αὐθεντέω and Cognate Forms in the Documentary Papyri', unpublished paper, 1996.

[155] Parry, 15; Kretschmar, P., argues that the sense 'murderer' comes from αὐτοθέντης (the original longer form) which is connected with θείνω, 'to slay', while the sense 'master' comes from αὐτ-ἕντης, derived from ἀνύω, 'to accomplish' (as reported by MM; Köstenberger 1996:77 n. 31).

Against view (c) Baldwin argues that, while the strong meanings of these nouns are attested for the earlier period, this is not true of the verb itself, although he has to admit one (as he says, the only one!) case of the strong meaning in Chrysostom. Further, Köstenberger argues on syntactical grounds that if the teaching is regarded as something positive which is prohibited to the women, so too is the exercise of authority to be seen as something positive (see below on οὐδέ).

Nevertheless, the fact that so unusual a word (only four known references before the Christian era) is used here is surely significant and suggests that there is a nuance not conveyed by more common words. There appears to be a tendency on the part of Knight and others to play down the nuance of exercising autocratic power which is present in several examples. This meaning fits best into the context, which is characterised by argumentation and dogmatic intimidation (Schlarb 1990:277).

Köstenberger* 1995:81–103, has argued convincingly on the basis of a wide range of Gk. usage that the construction employed in this verse is one in which the writer expresses the same attitude (whether positive or negative) to both of the items joined together by οὐδέ. It follows that if 'teaching' is regarded positively, so also is 'having authority', and that if 'teaching' is regarded negatively, so also is 'having authority'. Since, in Köstenberger's view, 'teaching' is a positive activity, it follows that 'having authority' is also a positive activity, and therefore the writer is denying two positive activities to women. This means that the verb must have the positive sense 'to have authority' rather than the negative sense 'to domineer'.

The matter, however, is not quite so simple. In the context the fact that Eve was deceived is cited as a parallel, and this strongly suggests the conclusion that behind the present prohibition lies some particular false teaching by some women.[156] Otherwise, the reference to Eve's being deceived and sinning is pointless. The activity of teaching here is thus judged negatively; it follows that the attitude expressed in it towards the men is also something of which the writer disapproves.[157]

---

[156] Strictly speaking, the text does not say that Eve gave false teaching to Adam, but the implication of her being deceived is obviously that she held a false opinion and then sinned by acting on it.

[157] Köstenberger does not appreciate the point that, if the second unit is seen pejoratively, then this will also be the case with the first unit; he frames his argument solely in terms of the writer's attitude to the first unit from which he draws conclusions to the second. His comment that, if the writer had meant to refer to false teaching by the women, he would have used ἑτεροδιδασκαλεῖν rather than διδάσκειν overlooks the fact that to say 'But I do not permit women to give false teaching' (!) in this context would imply 'But I do allow men to do so'; in short, ἑτεροδιδασκαλεῖν would be an inappropriate choice of word.

There was probably an associated trend towards emancipation behind the women's aspirations to teach. Such an understanding is appealing because it is the exercise of overbearing authority over men that seems to be in view.[158] Although perhaps not widespread, there is some evidence to suggest the development of emancipation tendencies among women in Graeco-Roman society.[159] In the Pauline churches the way towards greater freedom for women had already been paved (Gal 3.28). But abuses could occur and, as Schlarb argues (1990:93–131; cf. Towner 1987), a case can be made to show that in both Corinth and Ephesus the behaviour of women was influenced by an over-realised eschatology as indicated by the belief that the resurrection of believers has already occurred (1 Cor 15; 2 Tim 2.18); one possibility is that such a belief could encourage the women to assume roles apparently denied them by the curse on Eve (καὶ πρὸς τὸν ἄνδρα σου ἡ ἀποστροφή σου, καὶ αὐτός σου κυριεύσει, Gen 3.16), perhaps with the encouragement of false teachers. Within such a reconstruction αὐθεντέω is understandable as a reference to the exuberant and excessive flaunting of freedom in the face of men.

Kroeger and Kroeger*, 84–113, claim that the verb in question actually refers to the specific doctrine of Eve as the originator of Adam upon which the women were (erroneously) basing their right to teach. With regard to the present context, they maintain that Ephesus was the centre of a feminist emancipation movement in which allegedly Gnostic traditions extolled the feminine Sophia or Zoe; as a result the idea that Eve was the originator of Adam developed, and this notion lay behind the aspirations of women to the role of teacher in the community. This reconstruction of the Ephesian background is highly conjectural.

The issue seems rather to be the way in which one exercises the authority involved in teaching, the danger being that the women were acting in a way that threatened the men. This understanding presents a more logical contrast to the following ἀλλ᾽ εἶναι ἐν ἡσυχίᾳ. Whether or not the verb αὐθεντέω in itself is pejorative, it is the exercise of authority *over men* which is the problem, so that the whole phrase is pejorative.

It has been assumed in the foregoing discussion that the teaching and the exercise of authority are closely related. The relationship between διδάσκειν and αὐθεντεῖν depends upon how οὐκ ... οὐδέ, 'neither ... nor', (6.7, 16**) is understood. οὐδέ could introduce either a separate item (so Moo*, 1980:68

[158] Ἀνδρός of course will include husbands.
[159] Cf. Meeks, W. A., 'The Image of the Androgyne: Some Uses of a Symbol in earliest Christianity', *HR* 13 (1974), 165–208, espec. 172–4.

n. 41; Köstenberger* 1995:90f.) or a closer definition of the previous one (Hurley*, 201; Wagener 1994:75f.). In the first case, the two infinitives would probably envisage teaching and exercising the authority of leadership (in general); in the second case, the exercise of authority would take place in the act of teaching. In both cases, the action may have been 'neutral' but could have been perceived as belittling the traditional role of men, or it may have been carried out in a domineering fashion or been perceived as such; the boundary between acting in an autocratic manner and being perceived to do so is manifestly a fluid one. Although the parallelism is not exact, the relation between vv. 11 and 12 suggest that 'learning' and 'teaching' form the main point of contrast: learning can be done quietly and in full submission, but the teaching in which women were engaged was characterised by an overbearing attitude. In other words, the quiet demeanour and recognition of authority which are to characterise the learner are contrasted with teaching in a manner which is heavy-handed and abuses authority. αὐθεντεῖν as a reference to 'authority' (leadership) unrelated to teaching would exceed the scope of the discussion initiated at v. 11. It is, therefore, more likely that the verb characterises the nature of the teaching rather than the role of the women in church leadership in general.

The specific focus on learning/teaching is further confirmed by the repetition of the contrast in the phrase ἀλλ᾽ εἶναι ἐν ἡσυχίᾳ.[160] In v. 11 ἐν ἡσυχίᾳ describes the demeanour appropriate for learning; it does the same here. Nevertheless, it has to be recognised that the effect of the prohibition would probably have been to encourage subordination in women's life generally (cf. Oberlinner, 92, 96f.).

13. Ἀδὰμ γὰρ πρῶτος ἐπλάσθη, εἶτα Εὔα γάρ gives a reason or explanation in the form of an illustration for the prohibition (Payne*, 1981:176; Witherington 1988:122).

The precise function of vv. 13f. in the argument is disputed.

(a) Küchler*, 13, claims that vv. 13f. ground all of vv. 9–12 and not just vv. 11f. He analyses the passage as a chiasmus:

A Prohibition of adornment: linked to sexual seduction (vv. 9–10)
    B Command regarding role: learning, not teaching (vv. 11–12)
    B′ Grounds for role: created second (v. 13)
A′ Grounds for prohibition of adornment: deceived first (v. 14)

---

[160] Normally one would supply the governing verb from the first part of the sentence, but here we have a case of zeugma in that ἐπιτρέπω needs to be replaced by a stronger verb giving a positive command.

On this view there is correspondence between vv. 9–10 and v. 14 and between v. 11 and v. 12; if so, v. 14b responds to the seductive dress of the women by taking up the tradition of the serpent's sexual seduction of Eve and is erotic in tone.

This interpretation is unconvincing. The issue of adornment seems to conclude with the positive alternative in v. 10 (cf. Roloff, 139 n. 148). Küchler's argument that vv. 9f. need an exegetical grounding is weak (none is provided for v. 8), since the case is self-evident. The likelihood that sexual connotations are contained in v. 14 is fairly remote (see below). In any case, the author does nothing to capitalise on them, and the relationship between deception and false teaching seems much more obvious.[161]

(b) A second suggestion is that vv. 13f. provide a negative illustration and then v. 15 a positive alternative to reinforce what women ought to do. Again, on this view, v. 13 has little to do with the argument. The weight falls on v. 14 which constructs an analogy between the deception of Eve and those consequences and the deception of some women in Ephesus; the point is to urge women not to follow in Eve's footsteps, but rather to follow v. 15 (Payne*, 1981:176; Witherington 1986:122f.).

This approach makes good enough sense of vv. 14f. in view of the local situation, but v. 13 would seem to be more central to the argument than this view allows.

(c) It remains most probable that vv. 13f. belong closely together, making two points that reinforce the prohibition in v. 12.

Clearly the allusion is to the Genesis story of the creation of Adam and Eve. Ἀδάμ[162] and Εὕα[163] are introduced into the discussion here according to the temporal sequence of their creation.

πρῶτος ... εἶτα ... is common (Mk 4.28; cf. 1 Cor 15.46; 1 Th 4.16). πρῶτος (1.15) designates Adam as the first created person (cf. Hermas, *Vis.* 3.4.1; *Sim.* 5.5.3). εἶτα, 'then', establishes Eve's secondary status within the sequence (3.10**). It should be needless to observe that her creation by God is taken for granted.[164]

---

[161] Fee, 73–5, also suggests that the order of creation (v. 13) is somehow linked to proper adornment and cites similar thinking in 1 Cor 11.8f. However, the main reason for citing the Genesis material is v. 14; Eve is the negative model for women who are being deceived by false teachers.

[162] 2.14; Lk 3.28; Rom 5.14a, 14b; 1 Cor 15.22, 45a, 45b; Jude 14. Cf. Jeremias, J., *TDNT* I, 141–3.

[163] 2 Cor 11.3***; Gen 4.1; Tob 8.6; Philo, *L.A.* 2.81; Josephus, *Ant.* 1.49; *Sib. Orac.* 1.29. Not treated in *TDNT*.

[164] There may be the suggestion that woman should obey man because she was formed out of him, but it is at best only implicit.

The verb πλάσσω (Rom 9.20***; Philo, *Opif.* 137; *Sib. Orac.* 3.24) connects this statement with the story in Gen 2.7–8, 15 (LXX) of God's forming of the man. Eve is not so described in Gen 2, but use of the verb for the creation of man and woman is common in later reflections back on the event (2 Macc 7.23; Josephus, *Ant.* 1.32; 1 Clement 33.4). There is no explicit reference here to the fact that the woman is derived from him (1 Cor 11.8f.).

The statement provides a justification for vv. 11f. by an application of the rabbinic argument for the superiority of the man on the basis of being first created.[165] The development of this line of thought in Judaism has been carefully and thoroughly documented by Küchler*, 17–32.[166] He argues that the logic of the argument draws its force from both the literary sequence (the order in which events are narrated) and the actual historical sequence (the order in which events occur). Thus the intended conclusion, 'the first is best', seems unmistakable.[167] P. B. Payne (private communication) suggests that the text alludes to the creation of Eve from Adam, in consequence of which she owed respect to him as her source.

The motive for adducing this argument is variously understood.

First, the author may simply be applying a general principle which he accepted. One possibility is that this approach to over-enthusiastic women (cf. 1 Cor 14:33–35; Roloff, 128–30; Fiorenza*), reflects a post-Pauline divergence from the Pauline ideal of equality stated in Gal 3.28. Various pressures and a changed outlook could have led to the application of a logic more typical of the synagogue. Another possibility is that the logic is that of the earlier Paul (1 Cor 11:3–16), who, unaffected by rabbinic speculation on the Genesis creation story, simply applies the creation rule to explain why women are to be submissive and not teach.[168] Either way the conclusion is the same; 'the first is best'.

Second, the author's reference to the order of creation may be in some sense *ad hominem* (or should we say *ad mulierem*?). It is a reply to some specific aspect of the false teaching which has

[165] For this temporal type of argument see Plato, *Rep.* 412c; *Leg.* 11, 917a (of older and younger people). Cf. Dibelius-Conzelmann, 47; Roloff, 136–8; Oberlinner, 97–9.
[166] Cf. *Sipre Deut.* 11, 10 §37 (76a) (SB III, 256f.; cf. 626, 645); Jervell*, 71–121. However, we also find the inverse argument that what comes later is superior in *Gen. Rab.* 19 (12d) (SB III, 249); see Nauck 1950:95–7.
[167] One can poke fun at the argument by remarking that the animals were created before man and are therefore superior to him. The principle evidently was applied only within the limits of a pericope; cf. Küchler, 31.
[168] E.g. Knight, 142f.; Hurley*, 195–220; Moo*, 1980:68.

influenced women to behave in the church meeting in a way that
threatens the dignity of men. Kroeger and Kroeger* thus explain
v. 13 as an answer to the false notion that the woman is the
originator of man, which was in their opinion a Gnostic tenet,
associated with the Artemis cult in Ephesus, that had somehow
crept into the church, possibly by way of the false teaching.
However, this explanation cannot be substantiated (except from
later Gnostic writings).[169]

More plausibly, Schlarb 1990:123f. suggests that the false
teaching included or influenced a new interpretation of women's
roles and perhaps sought to understand Christian existence in
terms of a pattern of life based on speculation on the 'myths
and genealogies' in the early chapters of Genesis (celibacy and
vegetarianism, 1 Tim 4.3); this may have been associated with a
claim to be living a resurrected life in which the new order included
a position of equality or even domination for women. What the
writer is doing here is to refute it by reference to the actual
wording of the text of Genesis.

**14. καὶ Ἀδὰμ οὐκ ἠπατήθη, ἡ δὲ γυνὴ ἐξαπατηθεῖσα ἐν
παραβάσει γέγονεν** The attention now shifts from Adam's
priority in creation to the woman's priority in being deceived
and subsequently falling into sin (Gen 3.6, 13). The main
questions are to what degree this is a statement about women in
general, which (if any) of the traditional developments of this
motif are in mind, and how this statement is to be understood
in relation to women teaching and the situation of heresy in the
community.

In the statement that Adam was not deceived, the verb
ἀπατάω[170] makes the connection to Gen 3.13, where the verb is
used of the serpent deceiving Eve (cf. Küchler*, 33–5). By itself,
the verb can be used of sexual deceit,[171] but it and the noun
ἀπάτη can also refer to other kinds of deception (related to
wealth and philosophy). Here the point is simply either that
Adam was not deceived by the serpent, as Eve was, or that
Adam was not [the first to be] deceived, but Eve was [and
therefore by the argument of temporal priority he is superior to

---

[169] Another possibility is that the women claimed that they came 'before' men
on the basis of the kind of point made in 1 Cor 11.12b, where Paul places
women on the same level as men since men are born from women. It is more
probable that there was some bizarre interpretation of the Genesis account,
perhaps using Gen 3.20 where Eve is described as 'the mother of all living'.

[170] Eph 5.6; Jas 1.26***; cf. Josephus, *Ant.* 12.20. Cf. Oepke, A., *TDNT* I,
385f.; Kretzer, A., *EDNT* I, 117.

[171] Josephus, *Ap.* 2.245; Küchler*, 36–9; but the references are usually to
deceit by the woman, whereas the issue here is deceit by a [male] serpent.

her].[172] The statement cannot mean that Adam was not deceived by Eve, since this would be an obvious contradiction of what the Genesis account clearly implies. However, it has been argued that Eve was deceived and transgressed, whereas Adam simply obeyed Eve (without knowing from which tree the fruit came!) and so transgressed.[173] The suggestion that the thought is of Eve's sexual seduction of Adam[174] is also improbable. If the reference is directly to the discussion of women teaching, the meaning of deceit in a general sense is sufficient.

The shift from Εὕα to ἡ δὲ γυνή ('the woman' or 'his wife') may be intended to make the connection back to the women of vv. 9–12 and also to prepare for the generalising reference to women in v. 15. Here, the participle of ἐξαπατάω[175] may intensify the meaning ('Adam was not deceived, but the woman was completely deceived', cf. Spicq, 381) or be simply a stylistic variation with the same force as the simplex form (White, 109; Kretzer, A., EDNT I, 117). It serves to underline the contrast between Adam and Eve. It identifies the cause of the woman's difficulty, described here as ἐν παραβάσει γέγονεν. παράβασις, 'transgression',[176] views the woman's state from the perspective of breaking the law or command of God (Wolter, M., EDNT III, 14). The term is not used in Gen 3, but see Wis 5.14. ἐν with γέγονεν is a slightly odd expression;[177] it suggests entry into a state or situation: the woman became (and remained) a transgressor. The reflection here does not go beyond consideration of the woman's sin (cf. Ecclus 25.24), which suggests it is her own susceptibility to deception and sin that is under discussion.

Attempts to explain the rationale of the argument have explored several strands of speculation about Eve and the fall into sin.

(a) Ecclus 25.24 (ἀπὸ γυναικὸς ἀρχὴ ἁμαρτίας, καὶ δι᾽ αὐτὴν ἀποθνήσκομεν πάντες) simply identifies 'woman' as the source of sin and death (cf. Nauck 1950:96–8).

---

[172] For this second possibility see Jeremias, J., TDNT I, 141; Barnett*, 234. Cf. Philo, Quaest. in Gen. 1.37; Theodoret III, 651 = PG LXXXII, 801 (cf. Küchler, 34 n. 68).

[173] Delling 1931:118 cites Pirqe R. Eliezer 13 (SB I, 137f.) as evidence for this interpretation, but this source is not earlier than the eighth century; cf. Küchler*, 33–5.

[174] Dibelius-Conzelmann, 48; Kretzer, A., EDNT I, 117; Küchler*, 36–8; Wagener 1994:104–6. Wagener seems to confuse the two different points of sexual 'deceit' of the man by the woman and doctrinal deceit. See further below on Küchler.

[175] Rom 7.11; 16.18; 1 Cor 3.18; 2 Cor 11.3; 2 Th 2.3***; Ignatius, Eph. 8.1; Ignatius, Rom. 6.2.

[176] Rom 2.23; 4.15; 5.14; Gal 3.19; Heb 2.2; 9.15***. Cf. Schneider, J., TDNT V, 736–44; Wolter, M., EDNT III, 14f.

[177] See, however, Lk 22.44; Acts 22.17; 2 Cor 3.7; Phil 2.7.

(b) The thought may be that the woman's greater weakness makes her more susceptible to sin (Philo, *Quaest. in Gen.* 1.33, 46; *Pirqe R. El.* 13 [SB I, 137f.]). Therefore, she is more likely to teach error.

(c) Judaism also developed the teaching that Eve's temptation and sin were sexual in nature.[178] Eve is seduced by the serpent and then in turn seduces Adam. It has been claimed that this sexual development also lies behind the use of the motif in 2 Cor 11.3.[179] Paul's intention there, however, is more likely to illustrate the dangers of false teaching by referring to the effect of Satan's lies on Eve (Ellis 1957:63; Trummer 1978:148f.). This gives a close parallel to the present passage with some striking points of contact: Eve; the deception (ἐξαπατάω); and the common interest in false teachers. However, in 2 Cor 11 there is no interest in Eve's tempting of Adam.

(d) Gnostics made use of the Eve story and developed the view that the woman is superior to the man. Much of this is found only in later sources (see Rudolph 1983:211f., 215f., 270–2). But Kroeger speculates that something similar may have been current in earlier Ephesus in connection with the Artemis cult (Kroeger and Kroeger*, 105–25).

Against these possible backgrounds several suggestions have been made to explain how vv. 13 and 14 serve to ground the instructions to women.

(a) The connection of thought may be that it was Eve who was the source of Adam's sin in that he listened to what she said (= taught; Gen 3.17),[180] and therefore men in general ought not to listen to what women or their wives say (so Küchler, 35); but this is to go well beyond what the text actually says.

(b) The fact that Eve sinned first may suggest a greater liability of women to error and sin. But a deduction from the story to the greater propensity of women in general to be deceived and yield to temptation is unlikely in view of the positive estimate of women as teachers elsewhere in the PE.

(c) Verses 13f. are intended to reinforce the prohibition of women teaching by giving a universally applicable basis for the subordination of the woman to the man. V. 13 redresses an unbalanced, enthusiastic view of women's rights; it draws on Gen 2 to substantiate male dominance from the order of creation, and v. 14 illustrates from Gen 3 the dire consequences resulting

---

[178] *2 Enoch* 31.6; 4 Macc 18.6–8; *Yebam.* 103b; *Gen. Rab.* 18.6; *Prot. Jas.* 13.1; *b. Sota* 9b; cf. Barnabas 12.5; Diognetus 12.8; Küchler*, 44–50; Nauck 1950:96–8; Hanson 1968:65–77; Dibelius-Conzelmann, 47f.; Jervell*, 304f.

[179] Jervell*, 304; Hanson 1968:74; Nauck 1950:156 n. 30.

[180] Schreiner*, 141, is thus mistaken when he says that Genesis does not suggest that Eve taught Adam.

from disturbing that order (see also Moo*, 1980; Hurley*, 195–220). Traditional Jewish logic is being applied to re-establish the place of men in the community (on the model of the household). Teaching by the woman reflects an unacceptable role reversal (Roloff, 138f.; Knight, 142–4).

However, a strict application of Jewish chauvinism is unlikely, and some of the other Jewish elaborations are missing. Since women taught and prophesied[181] elsewhere in the early church (Acts 18.26; 1 Cor 14.26), and since the role of women in teaching other women and children is clearly recognised elsewhere in the PE, it can be taken as certain that what is being opposed here is the teaching of false doctrine and/or their teaching of men in a particular manner. The likelihood is that a drastic measure is being taken to counteract the effects of false teaching. Some modern conservative interpreters seek to establish some difference in roles between men and women which has the effect of disqualifying women from authoritative teaching. Schreiner*, 145f., argues that:

> Generally speaking, women are more relational and nurturing and men are more given to rational analysis and objectivity. Women are less prone than men to see the importance of doctrinal formulations, especially when it comes to the issue of identifying heresy and making a stand for the truth.... What concerns [Paul] are the consequences of allowing women in the authoritative teaching office, for their gentler and kinder nature inhibits them from excluding people for doctrinal error.

However one may evaluate this judgement, there is no evidence that such a thought was in the author's mind, and therefore it must be pronounced totally irrelevant to the exegesis of the passage.

(d) The most promising hypothesis is that specific aspects of false doctrine are being countered by vv. 13–15. If Kroeger has exceeded the evidence in reconstructing the Ephesian situation and Artemis cult on the basis of doctrines only found in later Gnosticism, there remain nonetheless strong indications that (1) women were involved in the heresy (and therefore teaching falsely); (2) that certain aspects of the traditional role of the woman (marriage, childbearing) were being challenged. Later Gnosticism is not necessary as a basis for this in view of the

---

[181] If the early church generally had prohibited women from teaching, the ban would surely also have been extended to their prophesying. Since 'spiritual' activity, such as prophecy, could be the work of spirits that were not from God in the view of the early church (1 Jn 4.1–6), one could understand that prophecy by women could have been prohibited, on the grounds that women were more likely to be misled by evil spirits.

foundation that a realised resurrection doctrine might provide (see Schlarb 1990). If it is teaching in a way that misuses authority and domineers and if women were forcing their way into the teaching rota on the basis of an enthusiastic understanding of the reversal of fortunes connected with the Eschaton, then v. 13 merely calls for balance and a respect for their first-created male counterparts (cf. Witherington 1986:123). If a claim to the women's right to teach was being defended by appeal to the Adam–sinner representative model (Rom 5), then v. 14 counters with an effective illustration of longstanding precedent that parallels the Ephesian women with their present state of deception at the hands of false teachers.

The conclusion to be drawn is that two closely related things were happening. The women were associated with the heretical teaching of the opponents and they were exercising their role as teachers in a way that was not acceptable and that appears to have been based on the heretical teaching with a bizarre interpretation of Gen 1–3. The author responds to them by insisting that Gen 1–3 does not support their claim to have authority over men.

15. σωθήσεται δὲ διὰ τῆς τεκνογονίας The possibility that this verse is a gloss (or an expression from an aged Paul) is raised by Spicq, 382, because he cannot reconcile it with Pauline teaching on salvation (cf. Roloff, 140). Its meaning is a puzzle, and a number of interpretations have been offered. The four main questions are the meaning of σωθήσεται, the meaning of τεκνογονία, the relation between them implied by διά, and the consequent relationship of the statement to the preceding verses.

σῴζω[182] consistently refers to salvation from sin in the PE.[183] The subject is clearly no longer Eve; after the parenthesis of vv. 13f. the implied subject of the verb is the γυναικί in v. 12.[184] Its possible senses are: (a) 'She will be "converted"'; (b) 'She will be saved [from divine wrath at the judgement]';[185] (c) 'She will be delivered [sc. from the devil/serpent and his temptations]';[186] (d) 'She will persevere towards [final] salvation';[187] or (e) (if the non-soteriological sense is allowed) with the curse of Gen 3 in

[182] Here fut. pass.; cf. Rom 5.9f.; 1 Cor 3.15.
[183] Tit 1.3 note; see espec. 2.3–6; Marshall 1984:206. The spiritual sense is found almost invariably throughout the NT epistles (exceptions: Heb 5.7; Jas 5.15; Jude 5).
[184] *Pace* Padgett*, 27, who claims that the reference is both to Eve and to the believing woman. See the detailed discussion of the possibilities in Porter*, 90–3.
[185] As in Rom 5.9f.; 1 Cor 3.15; Foerster, W., *TDNT* VII, 995.
[186] Köstenberger 1997:128–33.
[187] Hurley*, 221–3; Moo* 71–3, Knight, 144–9; cf. 1 Tim 4.16 note; for the idea cf. 1 Cor 9.27; Phil 2.12.

view, 'she will be brought safely through [childbirth]' (Moule 1953:56).

διά with gen. (τῆς τεκνογονίας) might make 'childbearing' the means of obtaining or ensuring salvation (Oepke, A., *TDNT* II, 67); in 1 Cor 15.2 it certainly comes very close to stating the 'means' of salvation (see Rom 5.9 for agency). The possibility of this construction is denied by some scholars but not convincingly.[188] They understand the construction as an expression of the (accompanying) circumstances or conditions under which salvation must be executed.[189] In fact, these two interpretations appear to represent different points on a spectrum between instrument and accompaniment, and it may be best to say that the construction expresses a somewhat loose and ambiguous relationship (Harris, M. J., *NIDNTT* III, 1177).

τεκνογονία*** is a medical term whose basic meaning has to do with giving birth. It therefore connotes strictly the physical act of 'bearing children'.[190] If the thought here is of being brought safely through the experience of childbirth, the word may imply the physical pain associated with it (Bernard, 49). It is more probable that the term here is meant to encompass the whole process of bearing and raising children;[191] but it certainly cannot refer merely to the latter.[192]

In the light of these possibilities the following interpretations of the clause have been proposed:[193]

---

[188] Both Roloff, 142 n. 167 and Spicq, 383, appeal to Moule 1953:56[c], but he allows that the construction is possible here. Spicq's point is that διά with gen. never expresses the complement or instrument of a pass. verb. But this is surely not correct: see the list given by Moule and especially Acts 15.11.

[189] So BA *s.v.* διά, A.III.1.c; cf. Xenophon, *Cyr.* 4.6.6; Josephus, *Bel.* 4.105; Rom 2.27; 4.11; 8.25; 14.20; 1 Cor 3.15; 2 Cor 2.4; 1 Pet 3.20.

[190] The term is found in Aristotle (with the variant τεκνοποιία) and medical writers. Fee, 75, holds that the term always has to do with the activity of bearing children and does not mean 'the birth of a child', and this is confirmed by the *TLG* search reported in Porter*, 96 n. 28. Cf. τεκνογονέω (verb: 5.14; Diognetus 5.6); τεκνοτροφέω, 5.10. Cf. Köstenberger 1997:140–2 who adds a reference from Chrysippus, *Frg. Mor.* 611, which may justify a broadening of the term to include the subsequent rearing of the child.

[191] Calvin, 219; Brox, 101; Dibelius-Conzelmann, 48; Oberlinner, 101. Porter*, 96, resists this extension of the term, but his argument that the author uses τεκνοτροφέω (5.10) for this activity is weakened by the fact that there the allusion is probably to bringing up other people's children.

[192] *Pace* Chrysostom, *PG* LXII, 545, who interprets it as παιδοτροφία and thus opens up salvation to women who cannot bear children; see Holtzmann, 316.

[193] One or two unusual interpretations can be safely dismissed: 'She will be saved from lording it over her husband by being a model wife and mother and caring for children' (Jebb*, 221f.). Or 'she will be saved from error by fulfilling her domestic role' (Hurley*, 222). In both cases this is a very unusual use of the verb in the NT context, and the suggested meaning is too subtle to have been obvious to the reader.

(a) Salvation by the birth of Jesus: 'She will be saved by the bearing (of the Messiah by Mary).'[194] This picks up on the promise of Gen 3.15 and stresses the presence of the article τῆς. But, as noted above, the word τεκνογονία refers to the bearing of children and not to the actual birth of one specific child, and an allusion to the birth of Jesus would be highly cryptic. Despite its popularity, this view can safely be rejected.

(b) Salvation despite having to bear children: 'She will be saved despite bearing children with pain.'[195] Childbearing is the accompaniment or route to salvation, not the means. This is a rather negative, concessive statement which is hardly relevant to the preceding argument.

(c) Physical safety during childbirth: 'She will be brought safely through childbirth.'[196] Verse 14 can then be understood to have implied the curse of Gen 3.16, to which this promise of physical protection is added (cf. Nauck 1950:100). Against this interpretation is the fact that elsewhere in the PE σῴζω is used for spiritual salvation and a different verb, ῥύομαι, is used for physical deliverance in 2 Tim 3.11; 4.18; but this in itself is not a decisive objection (cf. διασῴζω in 1 Pet 3.20). More decisive is the fact that a reference to safety in childbirth is entirely unmotivated in the context.

(d) Salvation by means of bearing children: 'She will be saved by (the physical pain of) childbirth.' In favour of this interpretation it is argued that this was the Jewish view: enduring the pains of childbirth overcomes the curse pronounced in Gen 3.16.[197] However, nothing in the present context suggests that the pain of childbirth is specifically in mind. The point is rather the contrast between teaching and bearing children.

(e) Deliverance from the temptations of Satan by keeping to their proper role: 'She will be delivered from Satan by [not transgressing into the role of teacher and] restricting herself to family responsibilities.'[198] Despite the plausibility of the motif of deliverance from Satan in the context of the PE as a whole (3.6f.; 5.15; 2 Tim 2.26), there is no explicit mention of Satan in this

---

[194] Lock, 32f.; Guthrie, 89f.; Knight, 146f.; Spencer*; Baumert*, 255; Payne* 1981. Various scholars comment that it was popular in the early church (cf. Porter*, 90 n. 8). However, the references offered do not seem to bear this out. Ignatius, *Eph.* 19 is hardly an allusion to the present passage. Justin, *Dial.* 100; Irenaeus, *AH* 3.22.4; 5.19.1 all draw a contrast between Eve and Mary without any signs of dependence on this passage. Cf. Tertullian, *De carne* 17.

[195] Scott, 28; Holtz, 70f.; Roloff, 141; for the construction cf. Acts 14.22; Rev 21.24.

[196] Moffatt; GNB mg; Bernard, 49; Simpson, 48; Barrett, 56f.; Moule 1953:56; Keener*, 118–20; Oepke, A., *TDNT* II,

[197] *EDNT* III, 340 (unsigned); Falconer*; Nauck 1950:99.

[198] Köstenberger 1997.

passage and the context favours a reference to salvation in the broader sense.

(f) Perseverance in (and towards final) salvation in the proper role of women: 'She will be (finally) saved by fulfilling her domestic role (the bearing and nurture of children).'[199] Here the stress is not on the pain of childbirth but rather on the fulfilment of the role of mother. The added condition requires also the practice of true Christianity as described with the following virtues.[200]

This condition has been sometimes interpreted as expressing the need for good works in order to be saved.[201] Wägener 1994:107–9, argues that salvation by works is found elsewhere in the PE (4.16; 5.8). However, it is unlikely that the διά phrase should be pressed to express instrumentality; it expresses circumstances rather than instrument. The point is probably directed against a belief that women should abstain from childbirth, just as they should abstain from marriage (cf. Kimberley*, who reads the text against a later Gnostic background.[202] Though they may not teach, women will still be saved by fulfilling their Christian duty in motherhood.[203]

This understanding does not rule out some allusion back to Gen 3.16 with which there are in fact some strong points of contact.[204] But rather than focusing on the pain of childbirth, the writer argues for the normativity of childbearing as an answer to those who (on whatever basis) deny it (4.3).

ἐὰν μείνωσιν ἐν πίστει καὶ ἀγάπῃ καὶ ἁγιασμῷ μετὰ σωφροσύνης. ἐάν introduces the condition that links the successful outworking of salvation to the continued practice of specifically Christian behaviour. The shift to the plural subject

---

[199] The dutiful and faithful wife and mother was praised in Judaism; however, b. Ber 17a., which is cited in this connection, refers to the mother letting her children be educated rather than doing it herself (Holtz, 71).

[200] Spicq, 382; Easton, 125; Kelly, 69; Fee, 75; Bauer, G., NIDNTT I, 187; Porter* (but restricting the reference to childbearing without any allusion to child-rearing).

[201] Clearly it cannot mean that all women must bear children in order to be saved.

[202] For Gnostic prohibition of sexuality and procreation Kimberley cites: G.Thomas, 114; 2 Clement. 2.12; Hippolytus, Ref. 5.7.39; G.Egyptians; similarly Merkel, 28, G.Philip 73.

[203] It is an excessive literalism which would deny this understanding of the verse on the grounds that not all women are capable of fulfilling the condition of childbearing in order to be saved. Schreiner*, 151, argues that what the author is doing is to select the most notable example of 'the divinely intended difference in role between men and women' which is the experience of most women.

[204] πλάσσω links Gen 2.7 to 1 Tim 2.13; ἀπατάω links Gen 3.13 to 1 Tim 2.14 (ἐξαπατάω); τεκνογονία suggests a link between Gen 3.16 (τέξῃ τέκνα) and 1 Tim 2.15. Cf. Küchler*, 16.

in the verb μείνωσιν ('they remain') is problematic. (a) It might represent a loose shift of number which expresses the general application of the singular (vv. 11–12, 14a) to all women;[205] (b) It could refer to the woman and her husband;[206] (c) It may refer to the children, who then are to be raised in the faith (cf. 3.4; Tit 1.6);[207] (d) It may include both the mother and her children.[208]

The reference must surely include the woman, and there is no mention of husbands in the context. Despite the common interpretation in the early church, the use of μείνωσιν seems quite inappropriate as a reference to children since they are surely to be brought to faith rather than to continue in it. The use of σωφροσυνή forms a link with the description of godly women in v. 9 and confirms that the woman/mother continues to be the subject.

The description of the Christian life to be pursued contains typical elements. For the pairing of πίστις and ἀγάπη as fundamental Christian qualities, cf. notes at 1.14 and Tit 2.2. ἁγιασμός** is 'holiness, consecration, sanctification'. Its use elsewhere makes it the antithesis of sin and uncleanness, as well as the will and goal of God for believers.[209] There may be a particular application to chastity here. There is no reason to suppose that the traditional triad of 'faith, hope and love' has been revised to produce the present one.

σωφροσύνη (2.9; see **Excursus 3**) is listed separately as the key virtue that must accompany the others.[210] As in v. 9, the emphasis will be on self-control which in the case of women must be expressed in behaviour that is chaste.

III. QUALIFICATIONS FOR OVERSEERS AND DEACONS (3.1–13)

This section is composed of two closely connected but self-contained sub-sections with clear boundaries which deal

[205] Calvin, 219f.; Holtzmann, 316f.; Roloff, 142; cf. Trummer 1978:149, who describes the shift as stylistic; Wagener 1994:107f.

[206] White, 110; Spicq, 384.

[207] Jeremias, 22; Witherington 1986:124. The actual birth of children would generally be regarded as the mother's responsibility, and sometimes the Christian nurture of the children is so described (5.16, Tit 2.4f.). Elsewhere, the father shares or oversees the responsibility (3.4; Tit 1.6). Malingrey* shows that early interpreters, with the exception of Augustine, uniformly interpreted the verb as referring to the children, so that the verse in effect stresses the duty of the mother to bring them up in the faith.

[208] Hasler, 25.

[209] Rom 6.19, 22; 1 Cor 1.30; 1 Th 4.3, 4, 7; 2 Th 2.13; Heb 12.14; 1 Pet 1.2***; cf. Balz, H., EDNT I, 17f.

[210] For the use of μετά to add a final item to a list Almquist 1946:124 compares Plutarch, Mor. 468B.

respectively with the qualities required in overseers and deacons (3.1–7, 8–13). Nothing is said about the duties of these two types of leader, although something may be read between the lines.[1] The author's concern is with the kind of people to be appointed rather than with a job-description, and therefore the latter is not required.

Whereas in Tit the similar instruction is related to Titus's task of appointing leaders, here there is no mention of appointment. It can, therefore, be argued that, although the material is presented as if it were instruction for Timothy, here, if anywhere, it is meant for the congregation; the section is really indirect ethical admonition to church leaders rather than an instruction for Timothy himself. However, the analogy of Tit and the comments on the desirability of people seeking to lead suggest that the appointment of leaders is the context, and the situation of Timothy in relation to supervision of the church indicates that he will have played a role in appointment (cf. 5.22). The chapter accordingly offers guidance to whoever is responsible for the appointment of leaders as well as setting up norms for those who wish to be appointed and (by implication) for those who are already acting as leaders.

Nothing is said here about the manner of appointment; the situation envisaged is one in which Timothy himself is responsible, presumably in concert with the local congregation or its existing leaders (cf. 4.14 of Timothy's own appointment); if 'Timothy' is a fictitious character, the question arises as to whether in the next generation there were persons fulfilling similar supervisory roles over groups of churches.

On the whole, the qualities[2] required are the same for both overseers and deacons and are also such as would be required in any member of the Christian congregation (Dibelius-Conzelmann, 50); there is no 'higher standard' for church leaders, but it is expected that they will actually show the qualities which are desirable for all believers. The characteristics are those of observable behaviour for the most part, but a sharp distinction cannot be made between inward and outward qualities. The spiritual and ethical stress and the emphasis on holding to the faith indicate that the leaders to be chosen stand over against the heretical teachers and opponents. The concern is thus largely with Christian character rather than with specific qualities or skills appropriate to the task in mind. Nevertheless, there is

[1] Lock, 35, deduces from the qualities that the tasks of the leader included: presiding and exercising discipline; teaching; control of finance; representing the congregation to other Christians and to the world.
[2] The term 'duties' (Ger. *Pflichten*) used by some commentators is less appropriate. 'Virtues' (Ger. *Tugenden*) is nearer the mark.

reference to hospitableness, ability to teach and to lead, and the attainment of Christian maturity and a good reputation, all of which are specific to leadership.

The listing of qualities in this way is found in secular lists which also describe the requirements for particular professions in ethical terms (so-called *Pflichtenlehre*; cf. Dibelius-Conzelmann, 50f.). The omission of discussion of the duties of the profession is thus in no way remarkable.

The fact that many of the qualities are such as are found in secular lists, which are equally general in content, suggests that part, at least, of the aim is to have leaders who will not bring the church into disrepute, which may have been happening through the activity of the opponents (Fee, 78f.). Johnson, 155f., suggests that there was in fact a 'leadership crisis', seen in the problems caused by leaders with dubious morals (5.20–25) and the competition for leadership roles (1.7); in particular, scrupulosity in administration of the congregations' funds was essential.

A contrast with Paul's ecclesiology is drawn by Houlden, 74, who asks whether Paul would have approved of these qualities and the implied task of maintaining a peaceful congregation, and comments on the lack of mention of evangelism or preaching! This comment does not take adequate note of the fact that the concern is here for oversight in a local congregation, rather than for the work of itinerant missionaries, and that the context is the pressing need to deal with opposition and false teaching in the church.

a. Qualifications for overseers (3.1–7)

Bartsch 1965:82–111; Bover, J. M., 'Fidelis Sermo (1 Tim. 3.1)', *Bib* 19 (1938), 74–9; Ellingworth, P., 'The "True Saying" in 1 Timothy 3,1', *BT* 31 (1980), 443–5; Holzmeister, U., '"Si quis episcopatum desiderat, bonum opus desiderat" (1 Tim 3.1)', *Bib* 12 (1931), 41–69; 'S. L.', 'Si quis episcopatum desiderat, quid tandem desiderat?', *VD* 11 (1931), 106–9; North 1995; Spicq, C., 'Si quis episcopatum desiderat', *RSPT* 29 (1940), 316–25; see also bibliography for Tit 1.5–9.

The section at first sight has no connection with what has just preceded. However, the author is dealing throughout the letter with the problem of heresy and heretical teachers in the church. He has just dealt with the undesirability of women teaching, very probably because of their association with the heresy, and he now passes to the right kind of church leaders who will promote sound teaching rather than heresy. The list of qualities required, therefore, is to some extent a contrast with the vices of the heretics.

One may speculate whether the author is following some kind of church manual which dealt first with the conduct of the church meeting and then with the appointment of the church leaders. A similar pattern is to be seen in *Didache* 7–10/11–13 and 14/15. The actual content is similar to that of Tit 1.5–9; see comments there. However, the actual wording shows a considerable amount of variation which is perhaps more consistent with literary variation by a single author than with reproduction of an existing source.

TEXT

1. πιστός ἀνθρώπινος (D* b d g [*humanus vel fidelis*] mon Ambst Ps-Augustine ?Facundus Ps-Jerome Sedulius-Scottus; cf. North 1995:51). Although the vast majority of authorities have πιστός, and it is accepted by most modern scholars, the variant is adopted by Zahn;[3] cf. Wohlenberg, 122; Moffatt; Lock, 35; Easton, 133; Elliott, 27f., NEB (but not REB). ἀνθρώπινος is 'human' (1 Cor 10.13; Rom 6.19; Jas 3.7; Acts 17.25; 1 Cor 2.13; 4.3; 1 Pet 2.13***). Here it could mean 'commonly accepted, popular' (BA); 'true to human needs' (Lock, xxxvi). The force could be 'to seek to be an overseer is a purely human ambition'. North 1995 argues strongly for ἀνθρώπινος: the author thus challenges a view (that of Timothy?) 'that desire for office is good'; although he must nevertheless concede that such leaders are necessary, he 'immediately hedges it [the ambition for office] about with ethical, sanitising prescriptions, to show that ἐπισκοπή is more than the exercise of naked power' (66). The variant πιστός entered once the office of ἐπισκοπή had come to be regarded as God-given and teaching such as 1 Tim 3.1–7 became the normative scriptural definition of the office (66). Metzger, 572f., suggests that πιστός was altered by scribes in view of the non-theological content of what follows. Fee, 86. North's argument perhaps attributes rather more subtlety to the author than seems likely; since the πιστός formula was already known, the form with ἀνθρώπινος would surely have been seen as a parody on it and therefore intensely scornful of the following statement; the view that the author then, as it were, retrieves the situation by nevertheless drawing a picture of the high ideals for the overseer seems rather artificial.

2. νηφάλιον For the spelling in the MSS see Elliott, 48, who adopts νηφάλεον with Dᶜ K 1908 223 1960 2401 *et al.* as the less Attic spelling; cf. 3.11; Tit 2.2 for the same problem..

3. μὴ πλήκτην The addition μὴ αἰσχροκερδή (326 365 614 630 *pm*) is due to assimilation to Tit 1.7 (Elliott, 48f.; Metzger, 573).

7. The whole verse is omitted by G* 205 g as a result of homoioteleuton with the preceding verse (Elliott, 51).

δεῖ δέ Add αὐτόν (D 1739ᵐᵍ TR, Kilpatrick). Elliott, 51 and 236, adopts the variant with hesitation. It gives the sense correctly.

καλὴν ἔχειν Inverted order (ℵ A H K L P *minn* vgʷ). The placing of καλός in relation to its noun varies in PE. Possibly it was moved nearer the noun here (Elliott, 51).

παγίδα Praem. εἰς (D* d g m vgᵐˢˢ PelᴮJerome). Elliott, 51, argues that the repetition is Semitic and scribes would remove it. But the prep. could easily have been repeated by accident, especially since the phrase does not follow directly after the previous one.

³ *Introduction to the New Testament* (Edinburgh: T. and T. Clark, 1909), II, 124 (German original cited in North 1995:54f.).

EXEGESIS

1. πιστὸς ὁ λόγος The section opens with a brief statement, 'trustworthy is the saying', similar to that in 1.15. But scholars are divided as to whether the λόγος consists of material which precedes or follows.

(a) Defenders of a backwards reference point to the theological nature of the statement in 2.15 compared with that in 3.1b. More specifically, it has been claimed that all the occurrences of the formula have to do with salvation.[4]

(b) The aphoristic character of the next phrase favours a reference forwards.[5] If the formula identifies the wording as a citation, then a reference forward is demanded, but it is more probable that it is simply an affirmation of the truth of a statement.[6] Further, the textual variant ἀνθρώπινος presumes that the formula points forwards.

The arguments are finely balanced, but the second view seems more probable, since nothing that can really be called a λόγος precedes. The formula stresses the need for readers to accept the truthfulness of the λόγος (see **Excursus 9**). The full formula with the addition 'worthy of all acceptation' is not used here because this saying is not relevant to everybody.

Εἴ τις ἐπισκοπῆς ὀρέγεται, καλοῦ ἔργου ἐπιθυμεῖ The section begins with a statement about the desirability of seeking the task of oversight, while the following section on deacons closes with a statement that has a similar function (3.13). The statement must surely imply that some people thought it undesirable. This could be because the office was thought to be tainted by the wrong people being appointed; or because the upholders of orthodoxy were unwilling to come forward; or again because other forms of ministry were more attractive (cf. *TLNT* II, 592 n. 5; Oberlinner, 115).

The frequent construction εἴ τις ... introduces a general condition either to be fulfilled (3.1, 5; 5.4, 16; Tit 1.6) or to be avoided (5.8; 6.3; cf. 1.10).[7] It may reflect use of a source, a church order with 'cases' in it. Although the language used here (εἴ τις, ὀρέγομαι, καλὸν ἔργον) belongs to the vocabulary of

---

[4] Cf. NA²⁷; Chrysostom *PG* LXII, 546; White, 110; Lock, 33; Parry, 15; Knight, 152f.; Bover*; Nauck 1950; Metzger, 572f.; Dibelius-Conzelmann, 51 (note that the reference to 3.16 towards the end of their comment is a printing error for 3.1b.); Houlden, 76f. (but the variant reading would of course point forwards); Schlarb, 208–10 (all of 2.11–15); Wagener, 70f.

[5] Cf. Eng. versions; Theodoret III, 651 Schulze = *PG* LXXXII, 804 (cited in Dibelius-Conzelmann, 51); Theod Mops. II, 97 Swete; Calvin, 221; Holtzmann, 317; Scott, 29; Jeremias, 23; Spicq, 427f.; Simpson, 50; Easton, 129f.; Brox, 139; Roloff, 148; Fee, 79.; Oberlinner, 112; Ellingworth*, 443.

[6] Campbell, 1994, holds that the reference is to 3.16.

[7] It is not found in 2 Tim.

the PE, the degree to which the author has reshaped a saying with his own language or, alternatively, the degree to which the materials he uses have influenced his vocabulary cannot be determined.

ἐπισκοπή is used here of the task or position of an overseer.[8] The reference is evidently to a task of leadership in a local church (or area) probably carried out by a plurality of πρεσβύτεροι/ ἐπίσκοποι (for full discussion see **Excursus 3**). The concept of a diocesan bishop is not present and would be anachronistic.[9] The expression suggests that there was a function or office in the church to which a person might be appointed. There probably never was a situation in which people functioned as leaders purely on a charismatic basis.

The task is described positively as the object of one's aspirations and striving; the point is not so much to commend people who aspire to hold the office as to commend the office itself as a worthy activity (Fee, 79). The link of ὀρέγομαι[10] to ἐπιθυμέω (cf. Lk 22.15) in the following phrase (cf. *Ep. Arist.* 211) does not necessitate a reference to a wrongful ambition (Field 1899:204) or a leadership contest (cf. Fee, 79). The two verbs are roughly synonymous here (cf. Hübner, H., *EDNT* II, 28) and to be taken in a neutral sense (Holtzmann, 318). The positive tone, however, is confirmed by the further definition of the task as a καλόν ἔργον (see **Excursus 6**). Spicq (*TLNT* II, 591f.) suggests that people may have valued the gifts of teaching and power and were less interested in administration and (we may add) pastoral care and discipline. Although throughout the PE the plural form 'good works' depicts the observable life of faith as a life of service and has become something of a formula, the sing. used here may be less formulaic. Lips (1979:74 n. 163) understands ἔργον to refer to the activity of the preacher (e.g. 2 Tim 4.5) and takes καλόν simply as an approving attribute (e.g. 1 Tim 4.6). The sense is probably 'an excellent occupation' (Moffatt; Spicq, 440 n. 6) or 'work of ministry'.

It has been suggested that the author grants (reluctantly) the truth of the saying but insists that what is more vital is that the

---

[8] Num 4.16. The noun is used of the position of Judas as an apostle in Acts 1.20 = Ps 108 (MT 109).8; cf. the sense of 'divine visitation' (Lk 19.44; 1 Pet 2.12***; cf. Lucian, *Dial. Deorum* 6, the only earlier secular example, acc. to Simpson, 50). It is used of the office of an overseer in 1 Clement 44.1, 4 and in an inscr. (AD IV; cf. BA *s.v.*). Beyer H. W., *TDNT* II, 606–8, holds that in effect the use of the term here is based on the word ἐπίσκοπος rather than any previous background.

[9] Holzmeister* (in Latin) demonstrates that the text cannot be understood of a bishop in the modern sense.

[10] Mid. 'to aspire to, strive for, desire'; with gen., as here, 6.10; Heb 11.16***; see BD § 171[1]. Cf. Heidland, H. W., *TDNT* V, 447f.; *TLNT* II, 591f.

right people hold office.[11] But, in the light of the qualifications that follow, the force is rather to stress that church leadership, which is indeed a worthy task as the saying testifies, should be done well, and therefore (οὖν) it requires people of the highest moral and spiritual character with the appropriate qualities.

2. δεῖ οὖν τὸν ἐπίσκοπον ἀνεπίλημπτον εἶναι The parallel statement in Tit 1.7 suggests that this general requirement is the beginning of what may be a set form (see notes on Tit 1.6 and 7). The requirement itself corresponds to the high calling to leadership (οὖν). δεῖ (Tit 1.7 and note) in effect controls the syntax right through to v. 11; the verb can indicate what is necessary, compulsory for various reasons (divine destiny, requirements of duty, law, custom; inner necessity), or, less strongly, what is fitting, in this case for church officials. The tradition employed refers generically (with the sing. τὸν ἐπίσκοπον) to overseers in general; consequently, the number holding this office in the church cannot be determined from the instructions.

The structure of the sentence suggests that ἀνεπίλημπτος is a general requirement, which is then followed by a set of detailed qualifications which give shape to it (cf. the similar structure in Tit 1.7). In Tit 1.6–9 the list is related to the appointment of presbyters (= overseers) and appears to be for the guidance of Titus in appointing them. Here the introduction suggests that the concern is more to tell aspiring overseers what is required of them and to remind actual overseers of the ideal that they should be embodying.

ἀνεπίλημπτος, 'irreproachable' (5.7; 6.14***),[12] represents the general basic requirement to be fulfilled by the overseer, for which the remaining qualifications in the list will provide concrete definition. Its function is precisely the same as ἀνέγκλητος in the parallel statement in Tit 1.7 (cf. 1 Tim 3.10 of the deacon).[13] The qualifications which follow reveal that this broad requirement is holistic, calling for a life that is both outwardly and inwardly beyond reproach[14] – the opponent or critic is very much in view (cf. 3.7).

μιᾶς γυναικὸς ἄνδρα, νηφάλιον σώφρονα κόσμιον φιλόξενον διδακτικόν The phrase 'one-woman man' occurs in discussions of qualifications for leadership in 3.12; Tit 1.6 (for the female

[11] Swete 1917:2f.; Dibelius-Conzelmann, 51; see also discussion above on the variant reading ἀνθρώπινος.

[12] Cl., but not found in the LXX; it is used of a dancer in Lucian, *de Salt.* 81 (cited in Dibelius-Conzelmann, 160) and of one's βίος in Dionysius Halicarnassensis 2.63.3.

[13] See Tit 1.6 note; Schwarz 1983:46; Roloff, 154.

[14] Cf. Philo, *Opif.* 142; *Spec.* 3.135; Schwarz 1983:45f.

equivalent see 5.9). It is positive in tone and stresses faithfulness in marriage, rather than prohibiting some specific unsanctioned form of marriage. It is unlikely that the phrase specifically means 'a married man as opposed to an unmarried man', but nevertheless the assumption in the phrase that the man is married may be intended polemically against the opponents (4.3). (See full discussion at Tit 1.6.)

νηφάλιος (3.11; Tit 2.2*** note; verb, 2 Tim 4.5) is 'temperate (in the use of wine)', 'sober'. The word may have the same literal reference to avoidance of drunkenness as in the following phrase (μὴ πάροινον, v. 3), since ethical lists showed a tendency towards repetition (so White, 112; Dibelius-Conzelmann, 52f.). However, most commentators hold that the word has the broader metaphorical sense of sober-mindedness or sound judgement.[15]

σώφρων calls for a balanced comportment marked by prudent, thoughtful, self-controlled behaviour. Although this represents a stock virtue in ethical discussions,[16] in the PE it is a characteristic of the life made possible by faith in Christ.[17]

For κόσμιος see 2.9 note; here the meaning is 'well-behaved' and 'disciplined' (cf. Schwarz, 1983:51). Oberlinner, 116, comments that these three qualities are hardly distinguishable from one another. σώφρων and κόσμιος are often linked (Spicq, 432; TLNT II, 332).

For φιλόξενος see Tit 1.8 note. 'Hospitableness' is required of all Christians; the church leader, who normally would take up this responsibility, is therefore to be a model of this quality.

διδακτικός in this context (and in 2 Tim 2.24***) must mean 'skilful in teaching'.[18] The thought is developed more fully in the discussion of the practical situation in Tit 1.9. Thus to some degree the ability to teach is associated with the task of the overseer (5.17), though apparently not exclusively so (2 Tim 2.2). It must be presumed that the person was already engaged in teaching before becoming an overseer.

3. μὴ πάροινον μὴ πλήκτην, ἀλλὰ ἐπιεικῆ ἄμαχον ἀφιλάργυρον The list of qualifications continues, adding four items which are very much concerned with public behaviour towards other people. The first two are prohibitions. First, μὴ πάροινον

---

[15] Cf. νήπτης in Onasander, *De imper. off.* 1.4; Schwarz 1983:48f. The idea of cultic abstinence, on the model of the high priest (e.g. Philo, *Spec.* 1.100; Josephus, *Ant.* 3.279), is not in view.

[16] Cf. Onasander, *De imper. off.* 1.1.2; *Jos. et As.* 44.8.

[17] For discussion see **Excursus 3**.

[18] Cf. Rom 12.7; Brox, 144; Dibelius-Conzelmann, 53; Rengstorf, K. H., *TDNT* II, 165; Schwarz, 1983:52f. The sense 'teachable' is less likely, but is regarded as possible by Spicq, 433. Cf. Philodemus, *Rhet.* II, p. 22, 10; Philo, *Praem.* 27; *Mut.* 83, 88; *Cong.* 35.

prohibits drunkenness or an addiction to wine (see Tit 1.7 note). Pugnacious and bullying behaviour (πλήκτης, see Tit 1.7*** note), which was often linked to drunkenness, is also prohibited.[19]

Two positive qualities are to take the place of the hostile attitude just prohibited. ἐπιεικής (see Tit 3.2 note; Phil 4.5; Jas 3.17; 1 Pet 2.18***) calls for an attitude which is conciliatory, meek, yielding, gentle and kind (cf. the ἐπιείκεια of Christ in 2 Cor 10.1). The occurrence of this quality in a traditional format does not diminish its eschatological basis in the author's thought (see Tit 3.2 note). There may be an intended contrast with the heretics, 6.3–5; 2 Tim 2.22–26; Tit 3.9. ἄμαχος (see Tit 3.2*** note; Schwarz 1983:57) means 'peaceable', 'not quarrelsome'.

ἀφιλάργυρος (Heb 13.5***) means 'not greedy', or, positively, generous (cf. *TLNT* I, 245f.). The qualification here correponds to μὴ αἰσχροκερδῆ (3.8; Tit 1.7 and note; cf. 1 Pet 5.2; Acts 20.33) and sets the church's leaders off from the false teachers (cf. 6.5–10). This was a quality held in high regard (just as greed was soundly denounced) in the Graeco-Roman and Hellenistic Jewish cultures.[20]

4. τοῦ ἰδίου οἴκου καλῶς προϊστάμενον At this point, the focus changes from qualities of the overseer's personal behaviour to his performance as a leader in the household. The phrase τοῦ ἰδίου οἴκου (3.5, 12; 5.4) effects the change, referring to his own household as opposed to the church. Manifestly οἶκος is to be understood as 'household' (Tit 1.11 note) rather than as a building (for which cf. οἰκία, 5.13); it refers to the people who constitute a family, including children and slaves.[21] Here the stage is set for the introduction of idea of the church as οἶκος θεοῦ in 3.15**. It is assumed that householders are appointed to the task of ἐπίσκοπος (cf. Verner 1983:128), and it may be that in the strongly patriarchal culture the concept of the authority of the church overseer would run parallel to concepts of the

[19] Although the list of qualities in general stands over against the vices of the writer's opponents, the latter are less likely to have been guilty of this failing in view of their asceticism.

[20] For the Greek background see BA *s.v.*; Onasander, *De imper. off.* 1.1, 8. For the Jewish background see Prov 11.25–8; 15.16; 16.8; 28.27; Eccles 1.3; 5.9–11; Wis 5.1; Ecclus 29.10f. For the theme in Paul see 1 Cor 16.1–4; 2 Cor 8.9. Heb 13.5 reveals that it was expected of all believers. See further *Didache* 15.1; Polycarp 5.2; Spicq, 218; *TLNT* I, 245f.; Schwarz 1983:57–8.

[21] For details of the Greco-Roman background, structure and status of the household and householder, see Meeks 1983; Strobel, A., 'Der Begriff des "Hauses" im griechischen und römischen Privatrecht', *ZNW* 56 (1965), 91–100; Verner 1983.

authority of the male householder.[22] The conceptual link between church and household is clear in v. 5; the church/household analogy is not in itself an innovation (Eph 2.19–22; cf. Towner, *DPL* 417–19), but some new ground is broken in developing the implications of the analogy into a concept of leadership.

The qualification is that the overseer direct the affairs of the household well (καλῶς, 3.12, 13; 5.17**). προΐσταμαι (Tit 3.8 note) can be used of administration: 'to be at the head (of), rule, direct' (3.12; 5.17; Rom 12.8; 1 Th 5.12); or of attention: 'to be concerned for', 'to apply oneself to' (Tit 3.8, 14**).[23] Where the main idea, as here, is of direction and management, the nuance of 'care for' is also present to some degree (*EDNT* III, 156; Fee, 82).[24]

τέκνα ἔχοντα ἐν ὑποταγῇ, μετὰ πάσης σεμνότητος The preceding rather broad qualification is now narrowed in scope, as the oversight of his children becomes the main area of the householder's task (cf. Tit 1.6 and note). The fatherly role rather than any other (e.g. that of husband) is decisive (Lips 1979:138–40).

In view of the disturbance caused by false teachers in the community (Tit 1.10), the sense of ἐν ὑποταγῇ (cf. 2.11) probably extends beyond just general obedience to acceptance of the faith confessed by the householder (cf. Tit 1.6 note). The disposition of one's own children towards the apostolic faith reveals something about one's suitability to lead the church. But the responsibility to keep them in this faith and obedience rests with the householder (ἔχοντα is active; Oberlinner, 123).

The attached phrase μετὰ πάσης σεμνότητος may refer to the father (NA[27]; REB) or (less probably) to the children (NIV; GNB; NJB; NRSV). If the former, it is to be understood as a comment on the bearing of dignity and worthiness of respect that should characterise the father's exercise of authority over his children (see **Excursus 3**). If the latter, it is to be understood as the Christian quality of seriousness and dignified bearing, i.e. as one of the marks of the faith which believing children would display (cf. 2.2 where it is the ideal for all believers; cf. Fee, 82).

5. εἰ δὲ τις τοῦ ἰδίου οἴκου προστῆναι οὐκ οἶδεν, πῶς ἐκκλησίας θεοῦ ἐπιμελήσεται The rhetorical conditional question

---

[22] Cf. Lips 1979:126–43; Schwarz 1983:58f.; Roloff, 159f. This consideration must be weighed against arguments that inclusive rather than male language should be used in translating this passage. Clearly the writer is thinking of men as overseers; it is not clear that he would have opposed the appointment of a woman who was a householder.

[23] On the force of the term see Lips 1979:130f.

[24] For use with the behaviour of children in mind, see Ps-Plutarch, *Mor.* 875A (Simpson, 52).

is a parenthesis to justify v. 4.[25] There is an analogy between caring for an ordinary household and caring for the household of God, which makes a working knowledge of the former a condition for success at the latter, and implies that the same qualities are required in both spheres. The thought expressed here – that performance in the private sphere bears on suitability to hold a position of wider responsibility – is paralleled in secular Greek ethics.[26]

οἶδα is used with the infinitive in the sense of 'to know how to'.[27] By means of the conditional argument, oversight or direction (προΐσταμαι) is translated into 'care for' (ἐπιμελέομαι[28]) the church. The conjunction of the two verbs brings together the concepts of authority and concern to describe the overseer's responsibility in the church (Oberlinner, 126). This is language drawn from the household ethos which describes the responsibility of the father.[29]

The description of the church itself as the ἐκκλησία (3.15; 5.16**) θεοῦ resembles the Pauline term ἐκκλησία τοῦ θεοῦ.[30] Although in 3.15 and in some instances in the earlier Paulines the term may refer to the church in a universal sense, here the reference is to a local congregation.[31]

This qualification implies a 'patriarchal' rule of the church by persons who act like heads of households. The reference must be to a larger group/congregation, comprised of people drawn from several households, over which it would be most likely to appoint a person or persons of 'householder' status to lead other householders who might be members.

6. μὴ νεόφυτον, ἵνα μὴ τυφωθεὶς εἰς κρίμα ἐμπέσῃ τοῦ διαβόλου The list is resumed with another quality and a purpose statement to justify the requirement. At this point, the content of the qualifications has become Christian, which may reflect the modification of a secular duty code (so Dibelius-Conzelmann, 53).

---

[25] For πῶς and the form of the argument, cf. 1 Cor 14.7, 9, 16.

[26] Cf. Sophocles, *Ant.*, 661f.; Plutarch, *Mor.* 70C (Almquist 1946:280); Lips 1979:127; Klauck 1981:66; refs. in Dibelius-Conzelmann, 53 and notes; Roloff, 159f.; Spicq, 436. See also Polycarp 11.2.

[27] Cl.; Mt 7.11/Lk 11.13; 12.56; Phil 4.12; 1 Th 4.4; Jas 4.17; 2 Pet 2.9; cf. Horstmann, A., *EDNT* II, 494. For the use of οὐ in a 'real' conditional clause see BD §428¹.

[28] Lk 10.34f.***; Gen 44.21; Ecclus 30.25; Plato, *Gorg.* 520A; Josephus, *Ant.* 1.53; 8.297; *CH* 10.22b. Cf. *TLNT* II, 47–53.

[29] Philo, *Ebr.* 91; cf. *Jos.* 37; cf. Aristotle, *Pol.* 4.15.1299a.

[30] 1 Cor 1.2; 10.32; 11.16, 22; 15.9; 2 Cor 1.1; Gal 1.13; 1 Th 2.14; 2 Th 1.4; Acts 20.28***; EXCURSUS I: ἐκκλησία τοῦ θεοῦ in Paul', in Thrall, M. E., *2 Corinthians* (Edinburgh: T. and T. Clark, 1994), I:89–93; Schmidt, K. L., *TDNT* III, 501–36; Roloff, J., *EDNT* I, 410–15.

[31] Oberlinner, 124; Lips 1979:95f.; Roloff 1985:232f.

The term νεόφυτος*** is found only in the literal sense of 'newly planted' in secular sources.[32] In the LXX (Ps 127 [MT 128].3; 143 [MT 144].12; Isa 5.7) it is applied to an infant in the family. The figurative meaning of 'newly converted' developed in Christian literature.[33] This requirement presupposes that the church has been in existence for a few years; Titus depicts the churches in Crete at a much earlier stage. In any case, such age qualifications in the case of leaders are found elsewhere (cf. Onasander, De imper. off. 1).

The purpose (ἵνα) behind this qualification is that two related dangers might be avoided. First, the participle τυφωθείς indicates a condition of the mind to which, in this case, the immature person thrust into leadership might be particularly prone. The pass. of τυφόω means either (a) 'to be blinded' in the fig. sense of being deluded or dazzled, or (b) 'to be puffed up, conceited'.[34] Either weakness is reasonably associated with youth, but the connection of this flaw with the false teachers elsewhere (6.4; 2 Tim 3.4**) suggests infatuation and bedazzlement with the authority and power related to office and perhaps the function of teaching, rather than simply foolishness or conceit.[35]

Second, related to this is the danger described as εἰς κρίμα ἐμπέσῃ τοῦ διαβόλου. κρίμα here has the sense of a judicial verdict (5.12; for the phrase cf. 1 Cor 11.34), with the accompanying condemnation and subsequent punishment.[36] Together with ἐμπίπτω (fig. 'to fall into'),[37] the idea expressed is that of coming under condemnation.

Elsewhere in the PE διάβολος is an adjective meaning 'slanderous' (3.11; Tit 2.3 note) or is a designation for the devil (3.7; 2 Tim 2.26).[38] The force of the gen. is uncertain:

(a) Subj. gen.: 'into the condemnation pronounced by a slanderer', i.e. the reference is to malicious attacks made on an overseer by other people, whether justified or not (cf. 5.14).[39] But the sense is probably determined by v.7 and 2 Tim 2.26 where the reference is clearly to the devil.

---

[32] Dibelius-Conzelmann, 53 n. 27; see Deissmann 1901:220f.; Schwarz 1983:59; Job 14.9.

[33] The imagery of planting used to depict church growth in 1 Cor 3.6-9 may in some sense prepare the way for νεόφυτος here, and Roloff, 160, assumes the term was already in use, but this is guesswork; cf. Oberlinner, 127 n. 57.

[34] TLNT III, 388f.

[35] Schwarz 1983:60; Spicq, 437; Roloff, 161; Oberlinner, 127.

[36] Cf. Büchsel, F., TDNT III, 942; Rissi, M., EDNT II, 317f.

[37] Cf. 3.7; 6.9; Prov 12.13; 17.20; 1 Macc 6.8; Ecclus 9.3; Tob 14.10. Lit. in Mt 12.11; Lk 6.39; 10.36. Cf. TLNT II, 1f.

[38] Cf. Eph 4.27; 6.11; Heb 2.14; Jas 4.7; 1 Pet 5.8; et al.

[39] RSV mg.; Bernard, 56; MacDonald 1988:167.

(b) Obj. gen.: 'into the condemnation reserved for the devil', i.e. because of his pride.[40]

(c) Subj. gen.: 'into the condemnation pronounced/wrought by the devil'. This has been understood in various ways: (1) as the punishment inflicted by devil as God's agent (cf. 1.20);[41] (2) as the punishment which the devil, as 'the accuser' (Rev 12.10; cf. Job 1.9–11), requires God to carry out (cf. 5.14; 3.7);[42] (3) as the 'doom which the devil has contrived for him by tempting him to be proud'.[43] The parallelism between this phrase and παγίδα τοῦ διαβόλου in v. 7 supports this interpretation.

In combination with v. 7, where 'the devil's snare' refers to his capturing of people to use them for his own ends (see below and note 2 Tim 2.26), the two references to the devil bring together the complementary ideas of coming under his sway and sharing in his condemnation (Mt 25.41; cf. also Oberlinner, 127).

7. δεῖ δὲ καὶ μαρτυρίαν καλὴν ἔχειν ἀπὸ τῶν ἔξωθεν The culminating requirement in the list is introduced by δεῖ δὲ καί. The emphatic conjunction and the repetition of δεῖ from 3.2 is meant to underline the importance of this particular requirement: in addition to the qualities already described, which are concerned with the person's character and abilities displayed within the church setting, it is important that he also has a good reputation in the world at large. The requirement corresponds to the initial qualification of being ἀνεπίλημπτος, but here is situated on a broader stage. μαρτυρία (Tit 1.13** note) here means 'testimony', in the sense of a judgement, usually positive, passed by one person on another.[44] In this case, the adjective καλή (**Excursus 6**) underlines the positive meaning of good reputation or recommendation.

Those delivering the judgement are unbelievers (οἱ ἔξωθεν**, 'those outside').[45] The concern expressed for the reputation of

---

[40] Cf. Mt 25.41; NIV; GNB; NJB; Moffatt; Calvin, 227; White, 114; Simpson, 53; Guthrie, 94; Knight, 164; Fee, 83; Oberlinner, 127; Johnson, 144. For the early church's interpretation cf. Theod. Mops. II, 113 Swete: *vane vero extollens se propter inpositam magisterii speciem, nihil differre videbitur diabolo, qui minister Dei creatus quae magna de se sapere est adnisus, Dei sibi adsciscens et nomen et honorem.*

[41] Kelly, 79; Spicq, 437.

[42] Foerster, W., *TDNT* II, 81; Jeremias, 25; Roloff, 161.

[43] Scott, 33; Hanson, 76.

[44] Josephus, *Ant.* 6.346; cf. 1 Jn 5.9a; 3 Jn 12; Tit 1.13; 1 Clement 30.7; Barnabas 1.6.

[45] E.g. Herodotus 9.5; Josephus, *Bel.* 4.179; *Ant.* 15.316; cf. οἱ ἔξω Mk 4.11; 1 Cor 5.12f.; Col 4.5; 1 Th 4.12; Plutarch, *Mor.* 220D (of people outside the family).

the church and individual believers among non-Christians is not confined to the PE.[46]

ἵνα μὴ εἰς ὀνειδισμὸν ἐμπέσῃ καὶ παγίδα τοῦ διαβόλου The immediate purpose (ἵνα ... ἐμπέσῃ..., parallel to 3.6) of the good witness is viewed from two perspectives. 'Falling into disgrace' (ὀνειδισμός, Rom 15.3; Heb 10.33; 11.26; 13.13***)[47] is generally understood in terms of reproach from people outside the congregation,[48] but the reference could also be to the accusation brought by the devil (cf. Rev 12.10). This is not the unjust abuse by insults which Christ experienced and his followers must be prepared to undergo. Rather, it is the complete loss of credibility that comes when unacceptable behaviour leads to the damage of one's reputation.

The immediate motivation of this concern for outsiders may appear to be simply 'defensive' (see Lippert 1968:32f.) However, in view of the dominant interest in the church's role in God's salvation plan (2.1–6; 4.9f.) and the concern to safeguard the gospel sounded throughout 1 Timothy, it seems unlikely that the leader's 'good testimony' with those outside could be unrelated to the effectiveness of the church's mission: the health (good witness) of the church and its leaders impinge on the acceptance of the gospel by those outside (cf. Roloff, 161f.).

Another danger that must be avoided is described with the traditional combination ἐμπίπτειν εἰς παγίδα (Prov 12.13; Ecclus 9.3; Tob 14.10b).[49] The sense of the whole phrase is determined by the gen. τοῦ διαβόλου. It is hard to see how, in connection with disgrace, the 'trap' or 'snare' could refer to the devil's sin (sc. pride). As in 2 Tim 2.26, the reference here is to the trap laid by the devil.[50]

It is the summarising function of 3.7, which returns to the thought of 3.2a, that determines the relationship between disgrace and the devil's trap. The 'good witness/reputation' (μαρτυρία καλή = ἀνεπίλημπτος) is measured on the basis of the kinds of individual qualities listed in 3.2b–6. For the leader to fail in one or more of the qualifications, opens him up to disgrace (ὀνειδισμός) and is either evidence of, or will lead to, coming under the devil's influence. If the author thinks in terms

---

[46] In addition to 1 Tim 5.14; 6.1; Tit 2.5, 8, 10; 3.2, 8; see 1 Cor 10.32; 1 Th 4.12; Col 4.5; 1 Pet 2.13, 15; 3.1; 16; Ignatius, *Eph.* 10.1; cf. van Unnik 1980:307–22; Lippert 1968.

[47] Ezek 34.29; Ps 68 (MT 69).10; *T. Reub* 4.3, 7; *T. Jud.* 23.3; *1 Enoch* 103.4; Josephus, *Ant.* 19.319; Schneider, J., *TDNT* V, 241f.; *TLNT* II, 585–7.

[48] So the Eng. tr.

[49] παγίς is a 'snare', lit. Lk. 21.35; cf. 1QS 2.11f, 17; CDC 4.15; fig. Rom 11.9; (Ps 68 [MT 69].23); 1 Tim 6.9; 2 Tim 2.26**.

[50] As in v. 6 the reference might be to a slanderer (Bernard, 56f.), but this is unlikely here (Kelly, 80). Yet cf. Ecclus 51.2.

of disgrace brought on the overseer and the church by association with the false teaching, then the first thought is viewed as a concrete illustration or proof of the second (cf. Roloff, 162). Viewed positively, the overseer who maintains the good witness guards himself and the church from the disgrace which association with the divisive and disruptive heretical movement would bring (cf. Oberlinner, 129).

b. *Qualifications for deacons (3.8–13)*

Blackburn, B. L., 'The Identity of the "Women" in 1 Tim. 3.11', in Osburn, C. D. (ed.), *Essays on Women in Earliest Christianity* (Joplin: College Press, 1993), I, 303–19; Lewis, R. M., 'The "Women" of 1 Timothy 3.11', *BS* 136/542 (1979), 167–75; Lohfink, G., 'Weibliche Diakone im Neuen Testament', *Diakonia* 11 (1980), 385–400; Nauck, W., 'Probleme des frühchristlichen Amstverständnisses', *ZNW* 48 (1957), 200–20 (=Kertelge 1977:442–69); Stiefel, J. H., 'Women Deacons in 1 Timothy: A Linguistic and Literary Look at "Women Likewise..." (1 Tim 3.11)', *NTS* 41 (1995), 442–57; Ysebaert 1994:124–50.

This is a further self-contained unit which is concerned in the same way with the qualities required in deacons (and 'women') and indeed demands much the same kind of qualities as in overseers. The structure is somewhat complicated. Verses 8f. continue the construction (with δεῖ implied) from the previous section (3.2, 7). There is a shift to the third-person imperative in v. 10 which is demanded by the subject-matter. The same construction is continued in v. 12 with a final comment in v. 13. But the description is broken by the inclusion of a set of requirements for 'women' in v. 11, also couched in the acc. after an implied δεῖ.

The qualities are appropriate (Kelly, 81) and fit those working in house-church situations (cf. Hasler, 28). One surprising feature is the inclusion of the condition in v. 9 which is absent from the requirements for overseers. The surprise is more in the absence from the earlier section than in its inclusion here. The implication must be that the deacons also had some share in the teaching and instruction of the congregation. It is also noteworthy that it is said that deacons are to be tested in some way before appointment, whereas this is not said about overseers. A possible implication is that the period of the diaconate is in effect 'probation' for the overseership, but this assumes that it is taken for granted that overseers will be appointed from the deacons, an assumption which was either so obvious to the readers that it did not need to be stated or was not in fact the case. Alternatively, the construction in v. 10 (καὶ οὗτοι δέ...) implies that overseers were examined before appointment as a matter of course and that this requirement must also be extended to potential deacons.

EXCURSUS 10

Deacons and their relation to overseers

Beyer, H. W., *TDNT* II, 81–93; Brox, 151f.; Campbell 1994a:132–5, 199–200; Collins 1990; Gnilka, J., *Der Philipperbrief* (Freiburg: Herder, 1987⁴), 32–9; Lips 1979:116–18; Oberlinner, *Titusbrief*, 93–6; Weiser, A., *EDNT* I, 302–4; Young 1994a:111–14.

Although the ἐπίσκοπος/ἐπισκοπή/ἐπισκοπέω nomenclature appears to have no specifically Christian bearings before being pressed into use to describe a church office (see **Excursus 2**), the word-group διάκονος/διακονία/διακονέω is used widely in reference to Christian ministry of various kinds (as well as in the general sense of service and servant; e.g. Lk 10.40; Mt 20.26; 22.13; *et al.*).[51] It figures prominently in the Jesus-tradition (Mk 10.43–45 par.), and Paul uses it of Christian work of all kinds[52] and workers.[53] The whole word-group figures prominently in 2 Cor 3.3–8 in description of the ministry entrusted to Paul.[54]

The older view that the word-group connotes primarily humble service of other people[55] has been decisively criticised by Collins*, who argues that the term refers rather to holding a commission or assignment from some higher authority to serve them. He plays down the significance of the usage of the terminology for service at table and emphasises rather the notion of being a messenger or representative of somebody. The word διάκονος accordingly means 'agent', and it may convey a status of authority inasmuch as the agent carries the master's authority.

Nevertheless, the associations of the term are often with the kind of tasks done by slaves, and the statements made about

[51] διακονία (1 Tim 1.12; 2 Tim 4.5, 11**); διάκονος (1 Tim 3.8, 12; 4.6**); διακονέω (1 Tim 3.10, 13; 2 Tim 1.18**).

[52] διακονία is used of the work of the gospel in general (2 Cor 3.7–9; 5.18) and hence of Paul's own work (Rom 11.13; 2 Cor 4.1; 6.3; 11.8; διακονέω, Rom 15.25; 2 Cor 3.3); of charitable aid (Rom 15.31; 2 Cor 8.4; 9.1, 12, 13; cf. διακονέω, 2 Cor 8.19f.); of tasks of ministry in the congregation (Rom 12.7; 1 Cor 12.5); of the tasks of church leaders (1 Cor 16.15; Eph 4.12; Col 4.17) and missionaries (διακονέω, Philem 13).

[53] Of Paul and his fellow missionaries (1 Cor 3.5; 2 Cor 3.6; 6.4; 11.15a, 15b [by analogy, of Satan's servants], 23; Eph 3.7; 6.21; Col 1.7, 23, 25; 4.7); of Phoebe as a servant of the church (Rom 16.1).

[54] For usage in the early fathers see 1 Clement 42.4f.; Ignatius, *Eph.* 2.1; *Mag.* 2.1; 6.1; 13.1; *Trall.* 2.3; 3.1; 7.2; *Philad.* Inscr; 4.1; 7.1; 10.1f.; 11.1; *Smyr.* 8.1; 10.1; 12.2; *Poly.* 6.1; Polycarp 5.2f.; *Didache* 15.1; Hermas, *Vis.* 3.5.1; *Sim.* 9.15.4; 9.26.2.

[55] 'διακονεῖν is now much more than a comprehensive term for any loving assistance rendered to the neighbour. It is understood as full and perfect sacrifice, as the offering of life which is the very essence of service, of being for others...' (Beyer, *TDNT* II, 86).

service by Jesus indicate that, although 'humble service of others' is not innate to the term, it may well have come to be associated with it.

The noun διάκονος can carry various nuances from that of being a servant/representative of a master (God) to being a worker of any kind in a church setting to exercising a specific role that came to be known by this term. Thus in 1 Tim 4.6 it is applied in a very general way to Timothy as a servant of Jesus Christ, acting on his behalf in the congregation. But in 1 Tim 3.8, 12 it clearly refers to people with a specific function in the church alongside the overseers, and the verb in 1 Tim 3.10, 13 has the specialised meaning 'to serve as a διάκονος'.

This specialised task appears only twice in the NT (Phil 1.1[56] and 1 Tim 3.8–13), and its history of development is unknown. Its beginnings have often been seen in Acts 6.1–6, but the term διάκονος is not used there; there is no evidence of the continuance of this practice/office; and the use of διακονέω in reference to practical service (v. 2) cannot be understood in a technical sense in view of the use of διακονία in reference to the apostles' ministry (v. 4) which follows. All that we know is that a specific group came later to be designated 'deacons' and that, presumably, a certain function or functions within the church's ministry and life came to be associated with the office (Schwarz 1983:39). It may be, of course, that the division of labour which Luke describes in Acts 6 corresponds to a distinction between the work of two groups of church leaders in his own day, but that Luke has carefully avoided any anachronistic use of titles; if so, then it is possible that Luke knew of a distinction between the work of preaching and teaching and the work of practical care for the needy.

As with the lists of qualities desirable in overseers, descriptions of function are absent from the deacon code in 1 Tim 3. The lists are mainly concerned with character, and the word-group is used in the NT of practically every sort of ministry. Consequently, the claim that the omission of any reference to teaching or authority in the list of the deacons' qualifications (cf. 3.2; 5.17; Tit 1.7) implies that they were restricted to tasks pertaining to practical needs (Beyer, *TDNT* II, 90; Brox, 151f.) lacks any foundation. In fact, v. 9 strongly implies some responsibility

---

[56] Collange, J.-F., *The Epistle of Saint Paul to the Philippians* (London: Epworth, 1979), 37–41, has revived the view of Chrysostom that 'overseers and deacons' constitute a single group of people (sc. elders) who are so called to indicate that their function was both oversight and service (similarly, Hawthorne, G. F., *Philippians* [Waco: Word, 1983], 10). Schenk, W., *Die Philipperbriefe des Paulus* (Stuttgart: Kohlhammer, 1984), 78–82, argues that the phrase is a post-Pauline gloss.

within the gospel ministry (cf. Gnilka*, 35).[57] It is striking that this quality is not mentioned in the description of the overseer, although there is an equivalent in Tit 1.9. Moreover, the requirement that deacons should be effective leaders in their households implies that like the overseers they exercised reponsibility in the church.

The deacon's relation to the overseer is unclear, but the order of mention in both passages and the comparative brevity of the description may well suggest a subordinate appointment. The question then arises whether they are thought of as the servants or assistants of the overseers rather than directly of God/Jesus Christ (Brox, 151). Beyer, *TDNT* II, 91, cites the analogy of the synagogue where the head of the synagogue (*rōsh hakkeneseth*) was accompanied by the servant of the synagogue (*hazzan hakkeneseth*). Campbell 1994:199f. adopts this view and makes the further suggestion that in fact they were those leaders of house churches who assisted the overseer (i.e. the person set over a group of house churches) by caring for their own house churches.[58] Similarly, Oberlinner, 93f., holds that they were the overseers' assistants in the author's conception although probably not in historical reality.

It will be argued below that the 'women' in 1 Tim 3.11 are more probably female deacons than the wives of deacons. There is no mention of deacons in Titus, which might mean that the emergence (and/or necessity) of the office was related to the size and complexity of the church, larger and older churches perhaps requiring delegation of duties (cf. Acts 6.1–6).

TEXT

8. σεμνούς Omit (‭ℵ‬* pc). The omission is due to homoioteleuton or carelessness in ‭ℵ‬ (Elliott, 52).

10. οὗτοι αὐτοί (H 442). The variant is accepted by Elliott, 53, as more Semitic than οὗτοι (cf. Acts 10.6 *v.l.*; Lk 8.41 *v.l.*). But the MS evidence is extremely weak.

11. νηφαλίους See 3.2 note.

EXEGESIS

8. Διακόνους ὡσαύτως σεμνούς, μὴ διλόγους, μὴ οἴνῳ πολλῷ προσέχοντας, μὴ αἰσχροκερδεῖς The qualifications for deacons (see **Excursus 10**) are presented in the same format as those for

---

[57] It is even more baseless speculation to deduce from the deacon code a reference to administering the Lord's supper (as does Holtz, 82–8).

[58] Since, as Campbell admits, the evidence of Ignatius shows that this view did not 'catch on', this suggestion is rather speculative.

overseers and in continuity with them.[59] Although the lists for men and women are designed to determine blamelessness (v. 10), as in the overseer codes (v. 2; cf. Tit 1.6), they begin by requiring positively that they be σεμνόι, moving next to things to be avoided, followed by the requirement of faithfulness.[60] The succeeding negative traits may be intended to define in practical terms what is meant by σεμνός.

σεμνός (**Excursus 3**) calls for dignified and serious behaviour that elicits respect from others. It is an inner quality with an outward expression which the author understands to have a theological origin.

The next three items are prohibitions probably intended to enlarge on the meaning of respectability. First, δίλογος*** (lit. 'double-tongued') means 'insincere' in reference to speech and therefore 'devious'.[61] It is the equivalent of δίγλωσσος ('double-tongued', 'deceitful'; cf. Spicq, 457; Schwarz 1983:63), a characteristic which is condemned in the Wisdom literature and elsewhere.[62] Thus what is to be avoided is saying one thing and meaning another, or the habit of saying one thing to one person, another to another.[63]

Second, μὴ οἴνῳ πολλῷ προσέχοντας condemns excessive use of wine leading to drunkenness. This qualification is closest in form to Tit 2.3 (μὴ οἴνῳ πολλῷ δεδουλωμένας) and parallel to the prohibition μὴ πάροινον in 3.3 and Tit 1.7 (see notes).[64]

Third, μὴ αἰσχροκερδεῖς (see Tit 1.7, 11), 'not fond of dishonest gain', parallels the qualification, 'not greedy' (ἀφιλάργυρον) in the case of the overseer (3.3) and may pick up on one of the tendencies of the false teachers.[65] A particular failing may be

---

[59] The use of ὡσαύτως (2.9 note) indicates that δεῖ εἶναι (v. 2) must be supplied to complete the thought here and in 3.11 (cf. Fee, 88).

[60] Oberlinner, 135, is mistaken to equate ἀνεπίλημπτος and σεμνός; in fact it is possible that ὡσαύτως calls for the entire phrase, δεῖ ἀνεπίλημπτον εἶναι, to be supplied from 3.2. σεμνός may in effect summarise and replace νηφάλιον σώφρονα κόσμιον φιλόξενον in 3.2.

[61] It is also used of deacons in Polycarp 5.2, which may be dependent on this verse (Holtzmann, 320).

[62] Prov 11.13; Ecclus 5.9, 14f.; 28.13; Philo, *Sacr.* 32; *Didache* 2.4; Barnabas 19.7; cf. *T. Benj.* 6. Simpson, 55, notes that δίγλωσσος means 'bilingual' in Cl. Gk., and holds that the author of the PE coined δίλογος to avoid perpetuating the misuse of the term to mean 'deceitful' found in the LXX. However, Philo and the AF both use the former word in this sense. The word is rare and is not attested in the papyri.

[63] Spicq, 457, alluding to Chrysostom (*PG* LXII, 553) and Theodoret (III, 656 Schulze = *PG* LXXXII, 808) respectively; but Chrysostom merely paraphrases as 'deceitful'.

[64] For προσέχω (1.4 and note) in the sense of 'devotion to' (which here like δεδουλωμένας in Tit 2.3 indicates addiction) in this connection, cf. Polyaenus, *Strateg.* 8.56 (τρυφῇ καὶ μέθῃ; cited in BA *s.v.*).

[65] 6.5–10; cf. Tit 1.11; cf. Schlarb 1990:325f.; Oberlinner, 135f. and n. 13.

envisaged, such as financial motives for ministry (cf. 1 Pet 5.2), or participation in dishonest trades. Or more generally the prohibition may underline the need for faithfulness and honesty in handling financial matters (Roloff, 162f. and n. 273). The phrase is broad enough to cover the range of nuances.

9. ἔχοντας τὸ μυστήριον τῆς πίστεως ἐν καθαρᾷ συνειδήσει To the requirement of respectable conduct as outlined with the three prohibitions is added a Christian responsibility: namely, to 'hold fast to or preserve'[66] the faith. ἡ πίστις (**Excursus 4**) is the content of what is believed rather than the act or disposition characterised by faith (yet so Holtzmann, 321). The relation to τὸ μυστήριον (3.16**) intended by the gen. may be apposition: 'the mystery which is the faith' (cf. BD §167; Dibelius-Conzelmann, 58) or possession: 'the mystery which is accepted/believed by faith'.

μυστήριον, 'secret, mystery', was used in Cl. Gk. to apply to the so-called 'mystery religions' and their esoteric teachings. However, its use in the NT is generally held to reflect the Aram. רָז (Dan 2.18 et al.) and to refer to the secret plans of God which he reveals to his servants. It is used in this sense in Mk 4.11 and par. τὸ μυστήριον in the earlier Paul is related to God (1 Cor 2.7; 4.1; 13.2; 14.2; 15.51f.; Col 2.2) and spoken of as having been revealed (Col 1.26; 2.2; 4.3; Eph 1.9; 3.4), but the content of the mystery is the Christ who is proclaimed. The thought is of God's secret plan which is not accessible to reason but which has been revealed in the church and is the content of faith.[67]

The phrase τὸ μυστήριον τῆς πίστεως may reflect a new nuance or application of a Pauline concept. If the form of the phrase here is 'developed' from the earlier Pauline usage, the development is perfectly natural in a setting in which the faith, the gospel, has come under attack by false teachers who promulgate false doctrines (cf. Oberlinner, 137). To rule that the phrase is conventional[68] is entirely arbitrary, when the variety evident in earlier Pauline usage[69] is considered. In view of the explanation of τὸ μυστήριον in 3.16 as the revelation of Christ (cf. Roloff, 163), the probability is that 'the faith' is envisaged here as 'the faith whose content is the message about the manifested Christ'. But we have to wait until the full explanation is given in 3.14–16 (cf. Bockmuehl 1990:211). Thus the phrase characterises the

---

[66] For ἔχω, see 3.4 note; cf. Oberlinner, 137.

[67] Bornkamm, G., TDNT V, 802–28; Krämer, H., EDNT II, 446–9; Bockmuehl 1990:129–210.

[68] Cf. Bornkamm, TDNT IV, 822; Dibelius-Conzelmann, 58; Houlden, 80.

[69] Sometimes with reference to the content of faith (1 Cor 2.7; Eph 3.4; 6.19; pace Roloff, 163; cf. Spicq, 99; Bockmuehl 1990:212).

apostolic, accepted expression of the Christian faith, in contrast to the perversions of it introduced by the heresy.

ἐν καθαρᾷ συνειδήσει links the deacons' cleansed conscience to 'holding to' the faith. The conscience, which functions to control and direct behaviour according to a given norm, is regarded here from a theological perspective as 'clean'. In 1.5, 19 faith is linked to a 'good conscience'. If there is a difference between the two adjectives, it is that the clean conscience is one that has been purified by the action of God and is not conscious of having done wrong, whereas the 'good' conscience is more one that works effectively. This condition of the conscience is closely related to adherence to the apostolic faith (**Excursus 5**).

The relationship implied by the preposition ἐν is problematic. Roloff, 163 (cf. Dibelius-Conzelmann, 58), maintains that the 'clean/pure conscience' is the main point of emphasis: the deacon must be fully aware and constantly affirm that it is the gospel which provides the norm for Christian living. But more probably the thoughts of holding to the faith and having a clean conscience form a loosely connected whole. For the author of the PE, the function of the conscience is to guide behaviour, while the condition of the conscience is determined by one's disposition (of commitment) to the faith. Belief determines the conscience which, according to the norm supplied by the content of belief, determines conduct. Thus to require adhererence to the faith and a clean conscience is to require belief and praxis which are equally untainted by the false teaching.[70]

The connection between conscience and hypocrisy found here has been shown to be a more widespread idea by Lips 1979:59f., who draws attention to Philo, *Leg. Gai.* 165; *Prob.* 99; *Spec.* 1.203; Josephus, *Bel.* 1.453. He finds the same motif further in 1 Th 2.1–7. Where conscience is not at work, there is a sharp discrepancy between belief and teaching, so that the latter can be characterised as hypocritical.

10. καὶ οὗτοι δὲ δοκιμαζέσθωσαν πρῶτον, εἶτα διακονείτωσαν ἀνέγκλητοι ὄντες A further requirement is expressed in different style (third-person imper.). Deacons[71] also[72] are to be examined

---

[70] Cf. Lips 1978:67f.; Oberlinner, 137; Schlarb 1990:325 n. 45.

[71] For οὗτοι with a backward reference see BD §277, §290. Holtzmann, 321f., notes that the whole phrase καὶ οὗτοι δέ can be translated 'but these also', contrasting the deacons with the overseers, or simply 'and in addition' (for which cf. 2 Tim 3.12).

[72] The connecting words καὶ ... δέ ('and also, but also'; 2 Tim 3.12; BA *s.v.* δέ 4b) link the phrase either to vv. 8f. or, more probably, to the requirements for overseers ('as well as bishops', NEB, Fee, 87; Oberlinner, 138; cf. Schwarz 1983:64f., citing *Apost. Const.* II.3.1).

or tested in some way.[73] Although the precise nature of the test and who is to carry it out are uncertain, the πρῶτον/εἶτα sequence indicates that the examination may not be waived and that procedure must be followed. The requirement may stipulate that candidates serve first as probationers (e.g. Brox, 153; Jeremias, 26). But the wording suggests rather that deacons 'first' pass some kind of test (cf. πρῶτον in 5.4 for the same sense) before they serve (Roloff, 164; cf. Lips 1979:173f.). In view of the determining general criterion, ἀνέγκλητος (see Tit 1.6 note), which parallels the broad requirement of ἀνεπίλημπτος in 3.2, the test covers the whole record of the candidate's conduct and faith.[74] This can be examined by the congregation by applying the code, vv. 8–12, as in the case of aspiring overseers.[75] Thus the sense of the requirement is to underline the need to apply the code to would-be deacons as well as to overseers. The impersonal passive form of the verb (δοκιμαζέσθωσαν) may suggest the whole community is in mind (Roloff, 164; Acts 6.3); but it is possible that leaders would bear the primary responsibility (cf. Lippert 1968:33).

Only after passing the test[76] may the candidates serve. διακονέω (3.13; 2 Tim 1.18**) often means 'to serve' in a general sense or is used as non-technical term for ministry in general (Rom 15.25; 2 Cor 3.3; 8.19f.; Philem 13; Heb 6.10; 1 Pet 1.12; 4.10f.), but in this context refers to carrying out the tasks of a deacon.[77]

11. **Γυναῖκας ὡσαύτως σεμνάς, μὴ διαβόλους, νηφαλίους, πιστὰς ἐν πᾶσιν** The description of qualifications for male deacons is interrupted by a discussion of 'women'.[78] Four interpretations of this vague reference have been suggested, two of which can be safely rejected. We may exclude a reference to women in the church in general as being altogether unlikely in the middle of a discussion of deacons; we can also reject the suggestion that a group of female deaconesses (as distinct from female deacons) are meant.[79] Two possibilities demand serious consideration.

---

[73] δοκιμάζω**, 'to put to the test, examine' (LXX; *Ep. Arist.* 276; Josephus, *Ant.* 1.233; 3.15; *T. Ash.* 5.4), is used of testing candidates for office; in this context it acquires the force 'to approve after testing' (Lysias 16.3; Plato, *Leg.* 6, 765c). See also CD 13.11; 1QS 6.14–21; Josephus, *Bel.* 2.137f.; 1 Clement 42.4; 44.2; Cf. Grundmann, W., *TDNT* II, 255–60; Schunak, G., *EDNT* I, 343; *TLNT* I, 353–61, espec. 357 n. 22.

[74] Lippert 1968:33; Schwarz 1983:64–65; Roloff, 164.

[75] Cf. Acts 16.1f.; 1 Cor 16.3; Dibelius-Conzelmann, 58.

[76] ἀνέγκλητοι ὄντες is conditional in sense.

[77] Weiser, A., *EDNT* 1:302–4.

[78] The literal translation is adopted by RV; NJB; NRSV (with the two main interpretations in fn.)

[79] For the view that 'women' refers to female assistants of deacons, see Lewis*.

(a) The wives of deacons.[80] The sense here is that, if the prospective deacon has a wife, she too must be approved.

In favour of this view it is argued:[81]

(1) The fact that the qualifications concerning 'women' are placed in the midst of the deacon code, instead of on their own, and the cursory nature of the qualifications and the lack of detail do not suggest that something so important as church office is in mind.

(2) A reference to 'wives' fits in with the immediately succeeding reference to deacons' being married (3.12).

(3) γυνή is too general a term to designate an office, but is a common reference for a 'wife'.

(4) Prohibitions against women teaching and ruling in 1 Tim 2.11–15 make a reference here to women workers unlikely; widows (5.9f.) are an exceptional case where certain competent women may engage in limited aspects of ministry.

(b) Female deacons.[82] In favour of this view it can be argued:

(1) Just as in v. 8, the use of ὡσαύτως in v. 11 suggests that a distinct, though similar, group is now under consideration; furthermore, δεῖ εἶναι must be understood from 3.2, as with διακόνους ὡσαύτως in v. 8, and this suggests that the section is parallel to the two preceding sections (Oberlinner, 141).

(2) If 'wives' were meant, it would be normal to indicate this with a possessive pronoun or the definite article.[83]

(3) No feminine form of διάκονος existed to serve as a technical designation; in lieu of this, a generic reference to 'women' in the context of a discussion of deacons would be sufficient to indicate female deacons.

(4) The conspicuous lack of a reference to the wives of overseers makes it unlikely that the reference here is to the wives of deacons. Why should the wives of deacons, as opposed to overseers, need special qualifications?[84]

---

[80] NIV t; NEB (altered in REB); GNB t; Ambst; Moffatt; Jeremias, 26; Easton, 132–4; Houlden, 80; Hanson, 80f.; Knight, 170–2; Lips 1979:117f.

[81] Some of the arguments offered are palpably weak, such as that the practical nature of the deacons' work (unlike that of overseers) might have required their wives to work alongside them, or that the wives of deacons would be young and need rules (cf. Tit 2.3).

[82] Theodoret III, 656 Schulze = PG LXXXII, 809; Theod. Mops. II, 128 Swete; NIV mg; GNB mg; REB 'women in this office'; Holtzmann, 322; Bernard, 58f.; White, 115; Lock, 40; Scott, 36f.; Simpson, 56f.; Dornier, 173; Barrett, 61f.; Brox, 154; Kelly, 83; Spicq, 460f.; Karris, 75f. Roloff, 164–5; Merkel, 31–2; Oberlinner, 139–43; Arichea-Hatton, 75f.; Johnson, 153; Lohfink*, 395f.; Blackburn*; Young 1994:113.

[83] Blackburn*, 308f. tabulates the evidence.

[84] The positioning makes it impossible that the wives of both overseers and deacons are in mind, pace Calvin, 229.

(5) Rom 16.1 (Φοίβην ... διάκονον) is a clear example of a female deacon (cf. Pliny, *Ep.* 10.96; *Didasc.* 3.9–12).

(6) In this context, the virtues required are similar to those required of deacons and are thus those of church workers.

On the whole, a reference to 'wives' seems less likely than a reference to women deacons.[85] The strongest argument in favour of taking the women as wives is the peculiar position of the discussion of the women. However, it is probable that the writer made his main points about male deacons in vv. 8–10, then discussed female deacons, and then returned to a point which had been temporarily forgotten (v. 12) before reaching his general conclusion on the topic (v. 13). On this view v. 12 reverts to qualifications applicable only to men after discussing what is in effect common to both sexes (cf. Roloff, 164f.), and v. 13 can apply to both men and women.

Another argument advanced in favour of 'deacons' is the author's attitude to women teaching and exercising authority over men. Oberlinner, 141–3, holds that the deacons were active in preaching and raises the question of the activity of female deacons in this respect (2.11f. is clear evidence that they were so active!). He claims that the author could not overlook the existence of female deacons in the church, but he could and did give them the briefest of treatments, hedged in between two sections about the male deacons, so that they are relativised. This would be a highly sophisticated and subtle form of demotion and it does not seem very likely. It is more probable that the author simply forbade women deacons from doing all that the men did.

The list of qualifications for the female deacons corresponds closely to that for the male deacons in v. 8. The first item is the same, a dignified, respectable bearing (σεμνός), which was equally fitting in women.[86] Again, as in the case of the male deacons in v. 8, the next qualifications may be regarded as an explanation of the primary one. Truthfulness of speech is in mind in the prohibition of slander (μὴ διαβόλους; Tit 2.3 note); it parallels μὴ διλόγους in 3.8 (cf. Roloff, 165). νηφάλιος (3.2 note, of overseers) probably includes literal sobriety instead of drunkenness in relation to strong drink, as the parallel in 3.8 suggests (cf. Tit 2.3). In the closing phrase πιστὰς ἐν πᾶσιν, the emphasis could be either on 'faithfulness' on or 'belief' (see **Excursus 4**). The qualifying phrase ἐν πᾶσιν (2 Tim 2.7; 4.5; Tit 2.9; 2.10b; 2 Cor 11.6) supports the former meaning, giving the sense 'absolutely trustworthy' (cf. Schwarz 1983:66f.). However,

---

[85] It may well have been, of course, that the women deacons were drawn in part from the wives of deacons (Holtzmann, 322).

[86] For the use of the word with respect to women see especially *TLNT* III, 247f.

the parallel with 3.9 might suggest that the thought is of the faithfulness (the adjective πιστός) in all aspects of life which grows out of one's commitment to Christ (πίστις; so Roloff, 165f.).

12. διάκονοι ἔστωσαν μιᾶς γυναικὸς ἄνδρες, τέκνων καλῶς προϊστάμενοι καὶ τῶν ἰδίων οἴκων The instruction now reverts to the male deacons, employing the style of v. 10.[87] The reference to faithfulness in marriage (μιᾶς γυναικὸς ἄνδρες, see Tit 1.6 note) and to effective leadership in the household (cf. v. 4) may appear unmotivated at this point (cf. Roloff, 166), but only if it is assumed that the deacons had no authority or responsibility for leadership in the congregation, perhaps as leaders of house churches. The requirement concerning effective exercise of leadership of children and more generally of the household (see 3.4f.; Tit 1.6 and notes) abbreviates that in 3.4 of overseers. The placing of τῶν ἰδίων οἴκων after τέκνων implies that the reference is to servants/slaves and suggests that the prospective church leaders are people of some standing. Slaves are not envisaged as church leaders!

13. οἱ γὰρ καλῶς διακονήσαντες βαθμὸν ἑαυτοῖς καλὸν περιποιοῦνται καὶ πολλὴν παρρησίαν The code closes with what appears to be an encouragement to good service or a promise. γάρ gives the wider ground rather than the reason for the instructions; it may serve the same purpose as 3.1 (cf. Roloff, 166). There are two benefits for the deacon (οἱ διακονήσαντες; cf. 3.10 note) who has served well (καλῶς; cf. 5.17). Each presents problems for interpretation.

The first reward is a βαθμὸς καλός. βαθμός may be a 'step' in a staircase[88] and has the figurative meaning of 'grade' or 'rank'.[89] Use of the term to describe spiritual advancement (steps or stages) is possible in Gnostic sects (Clement, *Strom* II, 45, 4 Stählin) and in connection with the mystery religions (see *CH* 13.9); but it could also be used of the different ranks in the army or the levels of precedence in the Qumran sect with its hierarchical arrangement.[90] The meaning here depends partly on whether the deacon's first reward is in relation to God (Scott, 37f.) or to the community. With the former possibility, the term might indicate spiritual advancement in understanding of salvation (Holtz, 86). But this would run counter to the author's

---

[87] ἔστωσαν is the 3rd pers. imper. of εἰμί, as in Lk. 12.35***.
[88] 1 Sam 5.5; Ecclus 6.36; Acts 12.10D; Josephus, *Ant.* 8.140.
[89] Josephus, *Bel.* 4.171; *TLNT* I, 250f.
[90] 1QS 2.20; cf. 2.23; 5.23f; 1QSa 1.17f. Cf. Nauck* 1957; Braun 1966:I, 237f. notes that at Qumran there was an annual examination that affected the ranking of all members of the community.

emphasis on salvation for all and his desire to discourage this kind of elitist enthusiasm (cf. Roloff, 166f.; Oberlinner, 144). In view of the second part of the reward, which may envisage the deacon's faith, the first part is probably to be understood in relation to the community.

Within this context there are two possibilities. The reward for faithful service could be advancement (a step of promotion) to higher office.[91] However, the logic of the context requires encouragement to faithful service *as* a deacon (Scott, 37). To call the βαθμός 'good' (καλός) in reference to the office of overseer, might imply that the diaconate was less good (Knight, 174; cf. Oberlinner, 144). Holtzmann, 323, holds that the diaconate itself is the good rank. Spicq thinks that encouragement to occupy a lowly position with its duties is in mind (*TLNT* I, 250f.). The best explanation is that faithful service leads to a good standing or esteem in the eyes of the community and of God.[92] This link between the ideas of 'greatness' or recognition and 'service' (διακονέω) in the community has a parallel in the Jesus tradition.[93]

In the case of the deacon, as with the overseer (see 3.4 note), personal responsibility for behaviour and service is indicated. The reflexive pronoun and middle voice construction (ἑαυτοῖς περιποιοῦνται) put the responsibility for 'obtaining' the reward at least partly on the deacon.[94]

There is also a second reward for good service. παρρησία** is capable of expressing a number of ideas depending upon its context, such as outspokenness, frankness, plainness of speech, openness to the public, courage, confidence, boldness, fearlessness.[95] While the thought of boldness in speech might fit the task of deacons in exhortation,[96] the prepositional phrase, ἐν πίστει τῇ ἐν Χριστῷ Ἰησοῦ, has changed the orientation toward Christ. Thus the more likely sense here is that of 'confidence' or 'assurance'.[97] The sphere of this sense of confidence is the deacon's faith which is ἐν Χριστῷ Ἰησοῦ. With the activity of

---

[91] Chrysostom, *PG* LXII, 554; White, 116; Bartsch 1965:91, 107; Nauck 1957:216f.; Spicq, 462; Knoch, 30; Merkel, 32 (but secondary to a good reputation in the congregation); so especially Hitchcock 1928:64 who draws an analogy with the Roman *primus gradus honorum*; cf. Roloff, 167: 'fraglich'.

[92] Calvin, 229; Simpson, 57f.; Dibelius-Conzelmann, 59; Brox, 155; Kelly, 85; cf. Merkel, 32; cf. 1 Clement 54.3; Hermas, *Mand.* 4.4.2.

[93] Mk 10:43f.; Lk 22:26f.; cf. Dibelius-Conzelmann, 59; Roloff, 167.

[94] See espec. 1 Clement 54.3; Hermas, *Mand.* 3.5; 4.4.2; *Sim.* 6.5.7; 9.26.2; Xenophon, *Anab.* 5.6.17; Demosthenes 19.240; Oberlinner, 144; *TLNT* III, 100–2.

[95] Cf. Balz, H., *EDNT* III, 45–7; *TLNT* III, 56–62.

[96] Philem 8: πολλὴν ἐν Χριστῷ παρρησίαν ἔχων ἐπιτάσσειν σοι; cf. 2 Cor 3.12; Phil 1.20; Lock, 41; Arichea-Hatton, 77.

[97] See the discussion in Fee, 89f.; Kelly, 85, thinks that the word here encompasses both boldness in preaching and confidence in approaching God.

belief having been mentioned, the second ἐν phrase indicates that Christ Jesus is the object of faith (cf. Moule 1953:81). The thought is of the relationship with Christ which is characterised by faith.[98] This of course is a many-faceted concept, which includes assurance of salvation, trust in God and belief in the gospel whose content is Christ Jesus; the point of the promise is that faithful service brings a greater[99] sense of confidence in God and assurance of salvation.

IV. THE CHURCH AND THE MYSTERY OF THE FAITH (3.14–16)

Betz, O., 'Felsenmann und Felsengemeinde. (Eine Parallel zu Mt 16.17–19 in den Qumranpsalmen', *ZNW* 48 (1957), 49–77; Blair, H. A., *A Creed before the Creeds (1 Tim 3,16)* (London, 1955)[1]; Bockmuehl, M., 'Das Verb φανερόω im Neuen Testament', *BZ* 32 (1988), 87–99; Bockmuehl 1990:210–14; Deichgräber 1967:133–7; Dunn, J. D. G., 'Jesus – Flesh and Spirit: an Exposition of Romans 1.3–4', *JTS* ns 24 (1973), 40–68; Fowl 1990:155–94; Gundry, R. H., 'The Form, Meaning and Background of the Hymn Quoted in 1 Timothy 3:16', in Gasque, W. W., and Martin, R. P., *Apostolic History and the Gospel*, (Exeter: Paternoster, 1970), 203–22; Hofius, O., *Der Christushymnus Philipper 2,6–11* (Tübingen: Mohr, 1976); Jaubert, A., 'L'image de la colonne (1 Timothée 3,15)', in *Studiorum Paulinorum Congressus Internationalis Catholicus 1961* (AnBib 17–18. Rome, 1963), II, 101–8; Klöpper, A., 1902:339–61; Lau 1996:91–114; Lewis, A. S., '1 Timothy 3,16', *JTS* 19 (1917), 80; Lohmeyer, E., *Kyrios Christos* (Heidelberg: Winter, 1928, 1961); Löning. K., '"Säule und Fundament der Wahrheit" (1 Tim 3,15). Zur Ekklesiologie der Pastoralbriefe', in Kampling, R., and Söding, T. (ed.), *Ekklesiologie des Neuen Testaments. FS K. Kertelge* (Freiburg: Herder, 1996), 409–30; Massinger, M. O., 'The Mystery of Godliness', *BS* 96 (1939), 479–89; Metzger, W., *Der Christushymnus 1 Tim. 3.16*, 1979; Murphy-O'Connor, J., 'Redactional Angels in 1 Tim 3:16', *RB* 91 (1984), 178–87; Roloff 1985:229–47; 1993:250–67; Sanders, J. T., *The New Testament Christological Hymns: Their Historical Religious Background* (Cambridge: Cambridge University Press, 1971), 81–96; Schweizer, E., *Lordship and Discipleship* (London: SCM Press, 1960), 64–6; 'Two New Testament Creeds Compared *I Corinthians 15.3–5 and I Timothy 3.16*', in Klassen, W., and Snyder, G. F. *Current Issues in New Testament Interpretation: Essays in Honor of Otto A. Piper* (London: SCM Press, 1962), 166–77; Seeberg 1966 [1903], 113–25; Slater, W. F., '1 Timothy 3,15', *ExpTim* 5 (1893–4), 64–6; Stenger, W., *Der Christushymnus 1 Tim 3,16. Ein strukturanalytische Untersuchung* (Regensburg, 1977); Stenger, W., 'Der Christushymnus in 1 Tim 3,16. Aufbau – Christologie – Sitz im Leben', *TTZ* 78 (1969), 33–48; idem, 'Textkritik als Schicksal', *BZ* 19 (1975), 204–7; idem, 'Der Gottesbezeichnung "lebendiger Gott" im Neuen Testament', *TrThZ* 87 (1978), 61–9; Strange, J. F., 'A Critical and Exegetical Study of 1 Tim 3:16. An Essay in Traditionsgeschichte', Diss. Madison, 1970 (not accessible); Weiser 1991:107–113; Wengst 1973:156–60.

This section stands out as a unit on its own, quite different from anything else in the letter. It appears to offer a context for what

[98] 1.14 note; **Excursus 4**; cf. Gal 3.26; Col 1.4; Eph 1.15; 2 Tim 3.15; 1 Clement 22.1.
[99] πολλήν, 'much, great'; cf. 2 Cor 3.12; 7.4a; Wis 5.1.
[1] Despite its title, this is a somewhat discursive study of the early church that sheds regrettably little light on the present text.

has been written in the letter so far (ταῦτα), specifically for the instructions to Timothy in 2.1–3.13 which are intended to guide Timothy until Paul's possible visit with the implication of fuller, oral instruction at that point. Moreover, the exposition of 'the mystery of piety' in v. 16 is probably a development of the reference to 'the mystery of faith' in v. 9. Nevertheless, ταῦτα may well refer to all of the letter in process of composition, so that the section is related to the letter as a whole and acts as a kind of pivot joining the two main sections of instruction. It provides the theological perspective for the instructions with its emphasis on the nature of the church and the content of the gospel.[2]

The theology of the church given in 3.15 is central to the instruction of the letter (e.g. Roloff, 189f.; See **Excursus 11**). In connection with vv. 14 and 16, it indicates that what has been said in the letter is in effect instruction about behaviour in the house of God. Verses 14–15a indicate both the importance and the urgency of what is said here. If the letter is not by Paul, then the impending visit is part of the picture painted to convey the same point: Paul's teaching is vital for the welfare of the church. The motif is, of course, found in other Pauline letters where the letter announces a hoped-for visit but nevertheless teaching at some length is given (e.g. Phil 2.12–18). Roloff, 197f., claims that in the second case the readers would know that Paul did not in fact pay the visit; in that case the letters take their place as his teaching. But on the hypothesis of deceptive pseudonymity, the readers would not know this! They could, however, think that, since Paul had not come to *them*, the letter provided his abiding instructions to them. Roloff's theory is in fact closer to the situation of non-deceptive post-Pauline authorship.

The importance of right behaviour in the house of God is underlined by the stress on its character as the church of the living God, the pillar and foundation of the truth. If the church is founded on truth, the manner of life of its leaders and other members must be appropriate; equally, if the church upholds the truth, it cannot do so if it is not in sound condition.

The importance of the instructions is emphasised further by the solemn statement of the 'mystery', the divine revelation of the saving event which is the foundation of true religion. In its present context this 'hymn' is manifestly intended to be significant in relation to the teaching in the letter. 3.14 tells us that the instructions in the letter describe conduct appropriate to God's household. The conduct so described may also be called εὐσέβεια (2.2; 3.16), i.e. that life consisting of knowledge of God/Christ

---

[2] Lau 1996:107–14 discusses how the section prepares for what is to follow in ch. 4.

and the appropriate response. Prayer for the universal mission, responsible behaviour on the part of men and women, and unimpeachable character on the part of leaders – these all come under the category of conduct appropriate to God's household. The hymn, which explicates 'the mystery of εὐσέβεια', thus offers a theological and salvation-historical explanation of the life introduced in part through the instructions. It is this wonderful (μέγα!) secret which must be safeguarded by the church, since its content is the divinely attested revelation of Jesus Christ who is to be the Saviour and Lord of the entire cosmos. The author's aim is accordingly to establish the intrinsic link between the Christ-event and Christian existence. The implicit reference to mission in lines 4–5 corresponds to the theme stressed in 2.1–8, so that the hymn provides additional theological grounds for the prayer enjoined at that point by demonstrating the salvation-historical necessity of the worldwide mission (Stott, 108).

It is less certain whether the hymn is intended to correct specific aspects of the opponents' errant theology. Most of the doctrinal texts in the PE can indeed be understood as succinct statements of the apostolic gospel, but 'mirror-reading' them for clues to false doctrine is a speculative task. But by placing Christ at the centre this text may well be calling attention back from the profitless 'myths and genealogies' and other speculations which were diverting people's attention from the Saviour.

This statement is manifestly a structured piece. In itself this categorisation does not settle the question whether it has been taken over or composed by the author. In terms of form, it is generally classified as a confession or hymn[3] or (less probably) a hymn fragment;[4] 'hymn' is to be understood 'in the very general sense of poetic accounts of the nature and/or activity of a divine figure'.[5] How such a poetic piece would have been used in a church meeting, and whether its function or effect would have differed from that of a corporate confession of a creed are questions that cannot be answered. What is clear is that this piece is a celebration of Christ in six balanced lines each

---

[3] To characterise it in this way does not necessarily mean that it is a piece of tradition used by the author rather than his own composition. The view that it is a pre-formed tradition is held almost universally (cf. Stenger*, 11–13), but Hasler, 30, has revived the view of Klöpper*, 360, that the hymn was composed by the writer of the letter. The similarities to the theology expressed elsewhere in the PE are so strong that this possibility is preferable. Other structured material in the PE may well also be the author's composition.

[4] Brox, 160; Kelly, 89; Deichgräber 1967:134 n. 1, insists that the text is too self-contained to be merely a fragment; cf. Wengst 1973:157.

[5] See Fowl 1990:31–45 (citation from 45). On the development of research into NT hymns, see Deichgräber 1967:11–21.

consisting of an aorist passive verb followed by an adverbial phrase (ἐν + dat., except in line 3 where there is a simple dat.).[6] Its structure has been explained in several ways.

(a) The hymn consists simply of six lines arranged chronologically which describe in order: the historical manifestation of Jesus; his vindication by the Spirit (whether in his mighty works or the resurrection); the association of angels with his ascension; the church's preaching to the world; the response to the preaching; the parousia.[7] The merit of this scheme is its simplicity. Its weakness is in understanding the last line as a reference to the parousia, since the verb used points rather strongly to the ascension. This is a difficulty which may be overcome if the line can be interpreted to refer rather to the final enthronement of Christ alongside the Father after the completion of his work (cf. 1 Cor 15.25; Phil 2.9–11).[8]

(b) The hymn consists of two sets of three lines.[9]

	ὅς
I.a.	ἐφανερώθη ἐν σαρκί,
I.b.	ἐδικαιώθη ἐν πνεύματι,
I.c.	ὤφθη ἀγγέλοις,
II.a.	ἐκηρύχθη ἐν ἔθνεσιν,
II.b.	ἐπιστεύθη ἐν κόσμῳ,
II.c.	ἀνελήμφθη ἐν δόξῃ.

The general rationale of this arrangement is that the first triplet refers to the life of the incarnate Jesus on earth, while the second refers to the exalted Lord. It has further been suggested that the

---

[6] *Odes Sol.* 19.8–11 has been cited as a parallel to the structure, but it is hardly close. Diognetus 11.3 is probably based on the passage (ἀπέστειλε Λόγον, ἵνα κόσμῳ φανῇ, ὃς ὑπὸ λαοῦ ἀτιμασθείς, διὰ ἀποστόλων κηρυχθείς, ὑπὸ ἐθνῶν ἐπιστεύθη).

[7] Schlatter, 114f.; Metzger*, 131f.; Barrett, 66, but with hesitation.

[8] An unusual view is taken by Murphy-O'Connor* who argues that the idiosyncratic form of line 3 ('he appeared to angels'; mid. form of verb; absence of ἐν) suggests that it is an interpolation by a redactor. When it is removed, we have five lines which deal with the earthly career of Jesus, and provide a pattern for Timothy to follow as the agent of the church in its witness to the truth, as well as a statement of the historical foundation of Christianity over against the myths of the opponents; the redactional addition refers to his appearing before human messengers. However, the problems which Murphy-O'Connor has with line 3 are insufficient to justify rejecting the more usual interpretation and resorting to the rather desperate theory of interpolation (by whom and when and for what purpose?).

[9] It is so arranged in UBS; cf. Seeberg*; Lock, 45; Fee, 93–6; cf. *idem* 1994:767f. The view that the first line is a relative clause providing the subject for the remaining five verbs ('He who was manifested in the flesh was justified in the spirit...'), or that the first three lines together form the subject for the last three, is no longer seriously entertained.

first two lines of each triplet form a couplet and the third line adds a refrain.[10] Justice is thereby done to the obvious parallelism between lines 4 and 5, which the three-strophe view (see below) must play down. The hymn is thus an expression of salvation history:

I. earthly life and vindication (followed by present exaltation)
II. ongoing vindication in the world (followed by present exaltation).

Against this scheme it is claimed that the parallelism between lines 4 and 5 is no stronger or structurally more significant than the other parallels.

The two strophes are interpreted rather differently by Lohmeyer*, 63. In the first we have the historical existence of Christ; his victory over the shame of death, and his return to the Father. In the second we have the effects of this career, presented not historically but as a completed eschatological fact. In line 4 the reference is not a historical one to the missionary preaching of the church but to a completed eschatological fact, reflecting the myth of his completion of a divine work affecting all peoples. In line 5 is depicted the confession of the universe, i.e. the whole world believes (not just the spasmodic effects of mission), which is again not a historical but an eschatological fact. Finally, in line 6 there is the final transfer of his Kurios-dignity; the reference is accordingly not to the ascension and thus the statement is correctly placed chronologically (cf. Rev 5). It is hard to see how this interpretation emerges from the actual wording.

(c) The hymn consists of three sets of couplets. The rationale behind this arrangement can be understood in various ways. Much the most widely accepted analysis finds three contrasting couplets with a chiastic arrangement of statements giving an alternation between earth and heaven.[11] The pattern is:

I.a.	(Earth)	ἐφανερώθη ἐν σαρκί,
I.b.	(Heaven)	ἐδικαιώθη ἐν πνεύματι,
II.b.	(Heaven)	ὤφθη ἀγγέλοις,
II.a.	(Earth)	ἐκηρύχθη ἐν ἔθνεσιν,
III.a.	(Earth)	ἐπιστεύθη ἐν κόσμῳ,
III.b.	(Heaven)	ἀνελήμφθη ἐν δόξῃ.

---

[10] Scott, 42; Easton, 136.

[11] Dibelius-Conzelmann, 60–3; Kelly, 92; Brox, 160; Knoch, 31; Gundry*; Deichgräber 1967:133–7; Schweizer, E., *TDNT* VI, 416f. Martin 1967:236, 238; Roloff, 192f.; Lau 1996:91.

This explanation of the structure is attractive but not finally compelling.[12] The proposed pattern of contrasts is certainly odd and no convincing rationale for it has really been offered (cf. Fee, 96).

The most detailed analysis of the structure is made by Stenger*, 37–70, who shows how various patterns of parallelism and contrast (synonymous and synthetic parallelism) can be seen between different combinations of lines. He apparently wants to link together lines 3 and 6 expressing the heavenly acceptance of Christ with lines 4 and 5 expressing the simultaneous earthly acceptance of him; thus the vindication of the one who was incarnate in the flesh (lines 1 and 2) is expressed in greater detail (cf. Stenger*, 232–4; Johnson, 157).

The difficulties attending all of these hypotheses suggest that the text may not be amenable to such analysis. In any case, it celebrates the fact of the manifestation and vindication of Jesus, both in earth and in heaven, and the way in which that manifestation has been confirmed. It therefore begins with his manifestation on earth; Diognetus 11.3 recognises the 'hidden' character of this manifestation in that he was dishonoured by the [Jewish] people; hence we have the immediate contrast that he was vindicated 'in the Spirit', sc. by being resurrected. Then we have the immediately following manifestation in both the heavenly sphere to the angels and in the earthly sphere by the preaching of the gospel. The seal is set on this manifestation both in the world by the belief of the people and in heaven by his glorification.[13]

The problems of arranging the statements in some kind of convincing order may be met by the hypothesis that the 'hymn' has gone through two stages of composition; the first stage consisted of lines 1, 2, 3 and 6, and they celebrated the heavenly vindication of the One who was revealed on earth; at a later, second stage, the author included lines 4 and 5 which affirm the proclamation and vindication of the Saviour on earth, but with the result that the smooth progress from line 3 to line 6 was interrupted. The contrast between 'angels' and 'nations' is thus accidental, and is not to be pressed as part of the structure of the hymn. What this hypothesis suggests is that a more traditional understanding of Christ being vindicated by resurrection and exaltation has been enlarged by a specific reference to the mission of the church as an essential part of the process of vindication.

[12] Merkel, 33, finds a pattern of proclamation (lines 1, 3 and 4) and acceptance (lines 2, 5 and 6), giving the pattern: x y, x x, y y. But can one really call this arrangement a 'pattern'?

[13] Cf. how Roloff, 194, finds elements of increasing effect as the text progresses.

The reference to mission which earlier scholars have detected in the hymn thus turns out to be an essential and emphatic theme.

The interpretation of the hymn is also disputed. Clearly it celebrates the Christ-event, elsewhere understood as the epiphany of divine grace, emphasises his revelation to angels (cf. 1 Pet 1.11) and to humankind, and stresses that he was revealed to the Gentiles and accepted in faith by them. Schweizer* 1962:113–25 argues that the point is that earth and heaven are reunited in the Christ-event, so that people facing the problem of imprisonment and loneliness in a world that seems to be completely separated from God now know that Christ has entered the world and is now lord in both heaven and earth: 'the important point is only that heaven and earth have become one again' (Schweizer* 1960:66; similarly, Roloff, 195). Similarly, Fowl 1990:180 argues that the opponents' separation of the Creator from his creation with its ascetic consequences (1 Tim 4.1–5) was answered by the text: 'If God vindicated Christ's appearance in the realm of the flesh, then by analogy followers of Christ should be able to take part in the material world with the confidence that the same God will also vindicate them.' Thus Jesus' experience is seen as being in some sense paradigmatic and foundational for Christian εὐσέβεια, and so the text may have been intended to re-establish the readers' centre of gravity in thinking about spiritual completion and resurrection in the present age (cf. 2 Tim 2:18). While this may possibly be a secondary motif, it is open to the criticism that it lays the accent on the secondary features (the adverbial phrases) at the expense of the central affirmations which are about the person of Jesus.

Rather, the text is an exposition of the 'mystery', i.e. of what was secret but has been revealed; this secret is now seen to be the Saviour himself, and the church is the body to whom the secret has been revealed that he has been revealed in flesh in the world and then vindicated and exalted as proof of his position. Admittedly, even the vindication is hidden: these statements are statements of faith about what has happened in heaven.[14]

All this is affirmed, however, in the context of an unmistakable missionary motif, to which Jeremias drew attention.[15] It is the universal significance of Jesus which is portrayed.[16] And the

---

[14] There is no reference to the future (cf. Houlden, 85), but throughout the PE the emphasis is on salvation as a historical fact which determines the present, not on its future consummation.

[15] Jeremias, J., *Jesu Verheissung für die Völker* (Stuttgart: Kohlhammer, 1956), 32f.

[16] So rightly also Strecker, G., *Theologie des Neuen Testaments* (Berlin: De Gruyter, 1996), 612.

church's missionary task is to proclaim this Jesus so that he is vindicated visibly also in this world.

The question of the background of the text finally arises.[17] An influential interpretation traces the pattern in the text to an Egyptian enthronement rite which took place in three stages: exaltation (conferment of divine status); proclamation of the exaltation (to the gods); ascent to the throne. This pattern has also been traced in Phil 2.9–11; Heb 1.5–14; Mt 28.18–20; 1 Pet 3.18–22.[18] On this view the pattern here is:

I. *Elevation*: vindication by resurrection of him who was manifested on earth.

II. *Proclamation*: announcement to heaven and earth of exaltation.

III. *Enthronement*: assumption of kingdom on earth and in heaven.

Accidentally or not, the hymn does contain elements of the coronation formula but not the precise structure. It would seem, rather, that a broad pattern of thought, reflected in the Egyptian material, was current among early Christians and has affected the formation of this and other texts. Merkel, 34f., disputes the existence of this pattern and its application to this passage.[19] He favours rather the motif found in 3 Enoch where Enoch is exalted to heaven and a herald announces his installation. Läger 1996:49f. is also sceptical of the use of an existing scheme but suggests that the threefold structure of the hymn is nevertheless to be seen as: Appearance; Proclamation; Recognition. Schweizer's interpretation would appear to rest on an assumption that a Gnostic world view is being opposed, which we have seen reason to doubt. Gundry*, 216–22, pleads strongly for a basically Jewish background, and this is corroborated by Stenger*, 235–40.

The hymn, however, has closer relationships with the scheme found elsewhere in the NT which contrasts the 'once hidden' nature of God's saving plan with its 'now revealed' character in the concrete events of the coming of Christ and the proclamation of the gospel.[20]

---

[17] For an attempt to reconstruct an Aramaic original see Barnes, W. E., in Badcock 1937:134.

[18] See especially Jeremias, 28f. Cf. Spicq, 471; Wengst 1972:159f.; Deichgräber*, 134; somewhat cautiously, Schweizer* 1960:64–6 (cf. *TDNT* VI, 416f.); see further Hofius, O., *Der Christushymnus Philipper 2,6–11* (Tübingen, 1976), 29–34. The comparison, however, goes back to Norden, E., *Die Geburt des Kindes: Geschichte einer religiösen Idee* (Darmstadt, 1958 [originally 1924]).

[19] See more fully Stenger*, 177–81.

[20] Cf. Tit 1.1–3 note; 2 Tim 1.9f.; Roloff, 195f., notes the close relationship to 1 Pet 1.20f.

TEXT

14. πρὸς σέ Omit (F G 6 1739 1881 *pc* vg^mss sa; [WH]); the phrase is placed elsewhere in other MSS. The phrase was possibly omitted to reduce the number of prepositional phrases; Elliott, 56, 236, retains it with hesitation (and notes similar problems in 2 Tim 4.9; Tit 3.12).

ἐν τάχει: τάχιον (א (D²) F G 1739 1881 TR; NA²⁵). The variant is a late form of θᾶσσον. Elliott, 56, argues that it is original and was altered by Atticists, but Roloff, 197 n. 435, states that it is a secondary accommodation to colloquial style.

16. ὁμολογουμένως ὁμολογοῦμεν ὡς (D* 1175 *pc*) is the classic case of a simplification arising out of wrong word division (Elliott, 57f.).

Ὅς ὅ (D* (061) lat Latin fathers) is a development from ὅς to get the gender right; the late reading θεός (א² Aᶜ C² D² Ψ 1739 1881 TR vg^mss; cf. ὁ θεός [88 *pc*]) is impossible in the context but attempts to solve the problem of the lack of an antecedent.[21] It is not found in any church father before the late fourth century (Metzger, 573f.). Elliott, 58f., states that there is no antecedent to the relative pronoun because the quotation is out of context: = '[he] who was...'. See the full discussion in Stenger* 1975.

EXEGESIS

14. Ταῦτά σοι γράφω ἐλπίζων ἐλθεῖν πρὸς σὲ ἐν τάχει Two things happen at this point of the letter. First, vv. 14–15 return to the direct address to Timothy (σοι, σε), last used at 1.18. Second, the purpose for giving the teaching (ταῦτα) is laid down with a ἵνα clause. The backdrop for this turn in the instruction is the reason given for employing the 'letter' mode of instruction at all – the apostle's absence.

The phrase ταῦτα γράφω ... ἵνα is a typical device of ancient letters (cf. Stenger* 1974:255–7). The present tense of γράφω lends vividness but usually refers to what has been written (cf. 2 Cor 13.10; 1 Jn 1.4; 2.1; 5.13). The precise reference of ταῦτα is uncertain. The demonstrative pronoun is usually anaphoric in the PE, pointing backwards to what has just been said and summarising or concluding sections of teaching (Tit 2.15 note; Roloff, 197). The function here is to reach back and summarise the connected instructions about church life in 2.1–3.13, just as in 1.18 ταύτην τὴν παραγγελίαν refers back to 1.3–17 (see note). Yet, in view of the striking character of what follows, especially the hymn in v. 16, it is tempting to understand ταῦτα and the explanation following as a comment on the whole letter, both what has been already said and what remains to be said. Even if the reference is purely backwards, it is of course true that any additional teaching in the letter related to church life would share the same purpose.

---

[21] In his day Calvin, 233, could state that all the Greek MSS agreed on this reading.

ἐλπίζων ἐλθεῖν πρὸς σὲ ἐν τάχει announces the author's intention to visit Ephesus and with some urgency; cf. Phil 2.23–24 for a parallel. For ἐλπίζω in the sense of future expectation and in reference to future travel to recipients, see Rom 15.24; 1 Cor 16.7; Phil 2.19, 23; Philem 22. ἐν τάχει establishes the imminent time frame.[22] At the same time, the concessive participial phrase introduces the theme of apostolic absence and 'parousia'. The letter makes up for the writer's absence (cf. 2 Cor 11.10; Trummer 1978:124). To call this statement a cliché (Stenger* 1974:256) is an entirely arbitrary judgement which is based on the assumption that such personal notes are all part of a literary fiction (see also Trummer 1978:123–5; Wolter 1988:132).

15. ἐὰν δὲ βραδύνω, ἵνα εἰδῇς πῶς δεῖ ἐν οἴκῳ θεοῦ ἀναστρέφεσθαι The syntax is not particularly smooth. It would appear that the author intended to write something like Ταῦτα σοι γράφω ἵνα εἰδῇς ... He then introduced a qualification by adding the comment that he hoped to pay a visit soon; then he qualified this by the comment that he could be delayed, but indicated this by a conditional clause with no main clause following; probably we should understand that γράφω is repeated. However, it has been argued that there is no ellipsis, and that the translation should be: 'I am writing to you in the hope of coming to you soon, but if I am delayed, to remind you how...'.[23] The clumsiness of the construction appears to make the purpose clause apply only if the writer is delayed in coming, whereas it must be intended to apply whether or not he comes. Thus this teaching is valid for a short or somewhat longer period (or if Paul never came at all). Paul gives it even though he hopes to come soon. When/if he comes, there will presumably be more to be said. What is said in the letter is important because it is concerned with conduct in the house of God.

Whether remote or likely, the possibility (ἐάν) is of delay (rather than hesitation or slowness to act).[24] It heightens the sense of the writer's absence and the importance of the instructions.

The following ἵνα clause expresses the purpose in writing the instructions (or possibly the whole letter, but see above). It is to make known to Timothy what constitutes fitting behaviour in God's house. Both the apostle's personal address and the link to God's house underline the normativity of the instruction

---

[22] Cf. Rom 16.20; Lk 18.8; Acts 12.7; 22.18; 25.4; Rev 1.1; 22.6***. The variant τάχιον *may* have the force 'as quickly as possible' (cf. BD §244[1]). However, Simpson, 58, says that it has much the same meaning as ταχύ.

[23] *New Docs.* VI, 68 n. 82.

[24] For βραδύνω, 2 Pet 3.9***; cf. Gen 43.10; Deut 7.10; Josephus, *Bel.* 5.566; *Vita* 89; Hermas, *Sim.* 9.19.2; *M. Poly* 11.2.

thus grounded. εἰδῇς πῶς δεῖ is a formulaic phrase for citing something that is (or must be) accepted.[25] It tends to be assumed that the implied subject is people in general addressed indirectly through Timothy as intermediary (Kelly, 87). But since the letter is addressed to Timothy, it is perhaps more likely that he is the implied subject (Reed 1993:111–14; Gibson 1996).

ἀναστρέφομαι (cf. 4.12**) is used of conduct in a general sense, often with prepositional phrase or adverb.[26] While the context (2.1–3.13) reveals that this conduct includes a spiritual dimension, it goes more widely to encompass all aspects of normal life within the life-style proper to God's people.

ἐν οἴκῳ θεοῦ introduces a metaphor which has determined to a great extent the manner in which the ecclesiastical and ethical teaching has been presented.[27] There is some question as to its intended significance and its relation to Pauline theology. The following clause states that the house(hold) of God is the church, but the elevated language and the wider context suggest that a reference merely to a place of assembly is unlikely. A reference to the people of God gathered together is more likely (see Dibelius-Conzelmann, 60), but this does not explain completely the οἶκος imagery.

(a) The house of God as the temple.[28] Temple imagery in Paul is sometimes thought to be decisive for interpreting the house imagery. As Paul applies it, the temple imagery is woven into a concept of God's people *as* the new temple, the new dwelling place of the Spirit of God (1 Cor 3.16; 6.19; 2 Cor 6.16; Eph 2.21–22). God's people are thus a spiritual building. Although in Paul it is the term ναός that consistently appears, in two cases outside of Paul οἶκος is employed in discussions about spiritual houses (Heb 3.6; 1 Pet 2.5).[29] In NT thought the church had become the dwelling place of God and so succeeded the temple in Jerusalem. Moreover, a similar pattern of succession is evident in Qumran which may in some sense have influenced

[25] Col 4.6; 2 Th 3.7; cf. Spicq, 465; Roloff, 198.

[26] 2 Cor 1.12; Eph 2.3; Heb 10.33; 1 Pet 1.17; 2 Pet 2.18. For the noun ἀναστροφή; 1 Pet 1.15; *et al.*; Josephus, *Ant.* 15.190. The verb (Deissmann 1901:88, 194; 1927:311f. may be equiv. to *halakh* (1 Kgs 6.12; Prov 20.7; 1QS 1.8f., 25; 3.9f.; 6.2; CD 2.17; 7.4f., 7f.; 12.21); cf. *T. Ash.* 6.3; Bertram, G., *TDNT* V, 941–3. Paul uses περιπατέω similarly of ethical or spiritual conduct. Cf. Baumgarten, J., *EDNT* I, 93; *TLNT* I, 111–14.

[27] Cf. Roloff 1985:229–67; Knoch, 31; Verner 1983. For the use of the metaphor in the NT cf. Heb 10.21; 1 Pet 4.17; Mk 2.26 par.; 11.17 par (of temple); Jn 2.16, 17.

[28] Weigandt, P., *EDNT* II, 501–2; Gärtner 1965:66–71; Michel, O., *TDNT* V, 129; Hendriksen, 136.

[29] Cf. Vielhauer, P., *Oikodome, Aufsätze zum Neuen Testament. Band 2* (ed. G. Klein. München: Kaiser, 1979), 136–42; Michel, O., *TDNT* V, 126. For οἶκος as a term for temples in Hellenism see MM 443.

the development of NT thought (see Gärtner 1965:49–71). Thus the imagery employed here is probably capable of expressing such 'new temple' ideas, but the shape of ethical thought in 1 Tim speaks against it as the dominant thought.

(b) The house of God as God's household.[30] In view of the concepts employed in 1.4 (οἰκονομία θεοῦ) and 3.4–5 (οἶκος), it is far more likely that the model of the secular 'household' is adopted in this description of the church (cf. 2 Tim 2.20f.). This has been seen as a post-Pauline development, since Paul prefers οἰκοδομή, and the church as household is thought to conform to a later development in which the church becomes the great religious institution (Roloff, 211–17; Brox, 157–8; Trummer 1978:224f.). However, if Paul did not think in terms of the church as household, he clearly laid the groundwork for such thinking with his use of household language.[31] Eph 2.19 clearly combines household and temple imagery (Gärtner 1965:60–6). Gentiles are told that faith in Christ has made them οἰκεῖοι τοῦ θεοῦ, members of God's household. Against the use of this imagery here it has been claimed that the central point in the NT temple imagery (when ναός is present) is that of God's dwelling place, and that this is lacking in the description of the church in 3.15 (cf. Schnackenburg 1974:96). But the reference to God here as the 'living' God may be intended to allude precisely to this fact, and to emphasise that right conduct is needed in the church because of God's presence. On the whole, then, the language here primarily reflects the concept of the church as a household, but the thought of the church as temple is secondarily present.[32]

It has also been argued that in the PE there is no identification of the actual people of God with the οἶκος θεοῦ; it is an existing entity in which they live (Trummer 1978:224f.; Lips 1979:96f.), but this is surely to split hairs. The main point here is to emphasise conduct (ἀναστρέφεσθαι), and the οἶκος θεοῦ provides the framework for understanding conduct in terms of mutual responsibilities and stewardship, in a way that corresponds to the interest in the household and its relationships throughout the PE (cf. 3.4, 5, 12; 2 Tim 1.16; 2.20f.; Tit 1.11). The feature which some commentators find problematic is that the household imagery is more conducive to a patriarchal understanding of relationships within the church as compared with the mutuality

---

[30] Roloff, 198f. (but with temple symbolism present in the context); Brox, 157–9; Weiser*, 107–11; Lips 1979:143–5.

[31] Cf. Paul's use of οἰκοδομή (1 Cor 3.9); οἰκονόμος (1 Cor 4.1); οἰκονομία (1 Cor 9.17); τοὺς οἰκείους τῆς πιστέως (Gal 6.10; cf. Michel, O., *TDNT* V, 134, 150–2).

[32] See further Towner, *DPL* 417–19; Towner 1995.

envisaged by Paul in the body metaphor. Yet even in the context of the body metaphor there is a certain priority accorded to some people (1 Cor 12.28) and there are rules for relationships and procedure laid down by divine commandment mediated by Paul (1 Cor 14).

ἥτις ἐστὶν ἐκκλησία θεοῦ ζῶντος ἥτις[33] functions as a relative to expand on or clarify the immediately preceding term οἶκος θεοῦ. ἐκκλησία θεοῦ (see 3.5 note; 5.16) provides the basic identification tag. There is some question whether, in view of the reference to the local community in 3.5, it means the local church (Lock, 43; Kelly, 87; cf. Lips 1979:96), or the universal church (Roloff, 198, n. 440). On the whole, the 'fundamental' tone of the language surrounding the phrase and the concepts themselves suggest that here 'church of God' is to be understood in a theological and therefore universal sense. 3.5 and 5.16 each envisage the local manifestation of God's larger work in the world, and the use of the same language for both universal and local ideas is undoubtedly intentional (cf. Roloff 1985:232f.).

It is difficult to tell if θεοῦ ζῶντος bears any special force here. The phrase occurs in quotations of OT material (Rom 9.26 [Hos 2.1]), and can be used to emphasise God's presence with his people (Num 14.28; Josh 3.10); in many cases it serves as an identification of the true God of Israel or the church where apologetic or polemical purpose is not certain.[34] It can refer to him as the originator and sustainer of life,[35] or as the living and true God in contrast to idols.[36] But there does not seem to be any indication of a polemic here against pagan gods, and it is thus more likely that 'living God' simply emphasises God's presence with his people (cf. Oberlinner, 157).[37] On the basis of the presence of temple imagery in the next phrase (στῦλος καὶ ἑδραίωμα τῆς ἀληθείας), it is possible that the author is working from 2 Cor 6.16 (ἡμεῖς γὰρ ναὸς θεοῦ ἐσμεν ζῶντος; Roloff, 198 and n. 441; cf. Merkel, 34). The absence of both the term ναός and the thought of the identification of the people with the temple or church may be thought to counterbalance this possibility (see Towner 1995:308f.).

This means that the church is God's dwelling and household. Ethical and theological implications come together in these images. On the one hand, within God's household there is a

---

[33] 'which is, inasmuch as it is'; see 1.4 note. The rel. pron. is attracted to the gender of the following noun (BA *s.v.* I.4.c).

[34] E.g. Heb 3.12; 9.14; 10.31; 12.22; Mt 16.16.

[35] E.g. 4.10; Deut 5.26; Ecclus 18.1; Tob 13.2.

[36] E.g. 1 Sam 17.26, 36; 2 Kgs 19.4, 16; Isa 37.4; Acts 14.15; 1 Th 1.9; cf. Ps 83 (MT 84).3.

[37] See further Kreuzer, S., *Der lebendige Gott* (Stuttgart, 1983); Goodwin 1996.

standard of behaviour and responsibilities which must be acknowledged. On the other hand, where God dwells there is salvation.

στῦλος καὶ ἑδραίωμα τῆς ἀληθείας A final phrase, in apposition to ἐκκλησία, fills out the description of the church in terms of its responsibility and function.[38] στῦλος in its literal sense is an architectural term, meaning a pillar which supports (1 Kgs 7.3; Josephus, *Ant.* 8.77) but it can also refer to that which looks like a pillar (Exod 13.21–22; 14.24; Ecclus 24.4; Rev 10.1). It is figuratively applied to people who are leaders (Gal 2.9) or who are given a place of importance (Rev 3.12).[39] The question here is whether in relation to τῆς ἀληθείας, i.e. the true gospel,[40] it expresses the idea of a visible or lofty sign, such as the pillar of cloud in the OT (Hanson, 82f.), or the idea of support, help (cf. Ecclus 36.24) and strength.[41] ἑδραίωμα*** means 'foundation', or perhaps 'mainstay, fortress',[42] and carries the ideas of firmness and steadfastness.[43] Together the two terms (perhaps as a hendiadys; Lips 1979:98) express the ideas of visible support (pillar)[44] and solidity (foundation) (cf. 2 Tim 2.19).

The church, which these ideas describe, performs these related functions with regard to 'the truth'.[45] Attention has been drawn to a parallel description of the Qumran community as סוד אמת

---

[38] Holtzmann, 326f., raises the possibility that the phrase is descriptive of God, despite the change of case. Jaubert* discusses the early church understanding of it as referring to Timothy himself (cf. the application to Attalus in the Letter of the Churches in Vienne and Lyons [Eusebius, *HE* 6.41.14]). But the syntax surely forbids this interpretation. Johnson, 152, suggests that it is a delayed appositional phrase which goes with πῶς δεῖ ... ἀναστρέφεσθαι and thus expresses what individual members of the church should be (Gal 2.9; 1 Cor 15.58). But there is no noun with which the phrase could stand in apposition. In any case, to say that the church must uphold the truth is to say that its individual members, and especially its leaders, must fulfil this task since the church is its members.

[39] *Exod. Rab.* 2.69a (SB III, 537); cf. Wilckens, U., *TDNT* VII, 732–6.

[40] Tit 1.1 note; Brox, 157; Oberlinner, 159.

[41] Lips 1979:99; Oberlinner, 159; *pace* Roloff, 201.

[42] BA; cf. 'bulwark', Moffatt; Hasler, 29. Guthrie, 100, notes that the church is a bulwark rather than the foundation of spiritual truth.

[43] Stauffer, E., *TDNT* II, 363–64; Betz*, 52; Lips 1979:98f.; cf. the adj. 'firm, steadfast' in 1 Cor 15.58. The use of ἑδρασμα in the problematic LXX text 1 Kgs 8.53 (MT 13), which translates מְכוֹן, may confirm the thought of 'foundation' (cf. Roloff, 200; Spicq, 467), but any conscious reflection here of 1 Kgs 8.13 and the temple of Solomon (Hanson, 1968:5; Roloff, 200 'möglich') is uncertain in view of the use of οἶκος in the sense of household.

[44] Weiser 1991:111; Stott, 105.

[45] The gen. τῆς ἀληθείας may be objective (cf. Brox, 157), or *auctoris* (Oberlinner, 160); a gen. of quality (Roloff, 200) is unlikely, since 'the truth' is almost certainly a reference to the apostolic gospel.

(1 QS 5.5f.).[46] In each case, the language links the believing community to 'the truth' in an exclusive way, but at this the similarities end (cf. Schnackenburg 1974:97). Thus although the concepts in Qumran thought and here bear some kind of relationship, it is not possible to go beyond the analogical to the genealogical. It is dubious whether these architectural pieces can be assembled into a precise description (e.g. Knoch – the church on pillars which rest on the foundation of truth). Rather, the church is to be understood as that which exists to maintain and protect the truth (Scott, 39f.; Easton, 136) because it is itself founded on the basis of that truth (cf. Roloff, 200).

This picture of the church as the foundation of the truth differs from the pictures in 1 Cor 3.11 and Eph 2.20 which also speak of foundations ($\theta\epsilon\mu\epsilon\lambda\iota\varsigma$). In the first case, Christ (i.e. the gospel about him) is the foundation of the church. In the second, the foundation is said to be the apostles and prophets (i.e. the message which they proclaim).[47] In this setting the relationship between the church and the truth is depicted differently. The building metaphor is not employed in reference to the church's source or cause, as in 1 Cor 3 and Eph 2, but rather, in a way that resembles the Qumran self-understanding noted above, in reference to the church's responsibility and mission. The church is thus depicted as being entrusted with the task of supporting, carrying and serving the truth. This is undoubtedly a point stressed in light of the threat to the truth presented by the heresy. But the implications drawn from this church–truth relationship in the present context have mainly to do with conduct: that is, it is the church's relationship to the truth that demands a certain kind of behaviour from its members (cf. Roloff, 201).

Does this picture of the church in its relationship of service to the truth reveal 'an essential shift' (Lips 1979:99; Roloff, 200f.; cf. Brox, 157)? The consensus is that here we have a novel thought which goes beyond the concerns of the earlier Pauline letters: the church, as the immovable historical fixture, repository and representative of the truth in the world, has assumed proportions in relation to the gospel ministry and authority formerly limited to the apostles. But this is to underestimate the implications of the earlier Paulines (i.e. 1 Th 1; cf. Eph 4); for Paul the church is something more than the happy result of apostolic ministry. This interpretation also exaggerates the picture in the PE which stresses the fundamental importance of

[46] Cf. 1QS 8.5–9; 9.3; 1QH 6.26; 4QpPs37 3.16; Gärtner 1965:68f.; see also Betz*, 53, 59f., 63–5; Schnackenburg 1974:97; Braun 1966:I, 238 comments that the language is not peculiar to Qumran.
[47] '*Columna autem et firmamentum ecclesiae est evangelium*' (Irenaeus, *AH* 3.11.8).

the church, but does not necessarily characterise it as a *feste Grösse* in the world. A later Paul or one of his followers, in the kind of situation depicted by 1 Tim, might have conceived of the church's responsibility to 'the truth' in this way. Rather, the passage emphasises that the church is fundamental to the gospel ministry, a point that would need to have been stressed quite soon after (if not before) the apostle's departure (cf. Towner 1995).

EXCURSUS 11

The church in the Pastoral Epistles

Brox, 157–9; Brox 1963; Brox 1969a; Brox 1969b; Fung, R. Y. K., 'Charismatic versus Organized Ministry? An Examination of an Alleged Antithesis', *EvQ* 52 (1980), 195–214; Käsemann 1964:63–94; Kertelge 1972:140–51; Lohfink 1977; Oberlinner [1996], 74–101; Rogers 1979; Roloff, 211–17; Roloff 1985; Roloff, J., *Die Kirche im Neuen Testament* (Göttingen: Vandenhoeck und Ruprecht, 1993), 250–67; Sand 1976; Schlier 1977 (orig. 1948); Schnackenburg 1974:94–102; Schweizer 1961:77–88 [6]; Towner 1989:129–38.

1. The development of the 'Early Catholic' interpretation

Discussion of the concept of the church in the PE has tended to be dominated by German-speaking scholars and especially by Roman Catholics. The current agenda was set in Schlier's seminal essay on the ordering of the church according to the PE. He began by recognising that God's saving work includes both the sacrificial death of Jesus and the revelation of his word through which people are actually saved. The task of making the gospel known belonged in the first instance to the apostles. The PE picture the gospel as belonging to the apostle (i.e. Paul) who has a number of functions. These can be summed up as teaching (i.e. the normative expression of the gospel and its proclamation), criticism of error, the authority to regulate what happens in the church, the power of directing other people and of discipline over individuals (including excommunication), and the authority to ordain his representatives. These same functions can also be seen in his disciples, Timothy and Titus, who each have rule over a number of churches. Their teaching, however, is simply the unfolding of what Paul has taught. They exercise their authority only with the office-bearers, not with the congregation or any charismatics. They are not called directly by Christ but indirectly by the apostles. There are also local officials, the most important being the presbyers or bishops who stand in an apostolic succession, and who teach, exhort and refute. Thus the ordering of the church rests on 'office'. The principle of 'office' is dominant. It is passed on by apostolic succession, and there is a pyramidical structure. The congregation and charismatic individuals retreat into the background.

From the Protestant side Käsemann*, 85–9 (in a paper originally given in 1949) regarded the PE (and Acts) as offering the antithesis to Paul's concept of the church (which he assumed to be strongly charismatic). The church is on the defensive and was using the weapons of popular philosophy to fight Gnostic heresy. Presbyteries suddenly appear; they represent a Jewish Christian closed form of government and practise a Jewish form of ordination. The office now becomes the real bearer of the Spirit instead of 'every Christian'. The PE are in reality directed to 'monarchical bishops' who are being addressed under the guise of Timothy and Titus, and an apostolic succession has developed.[48]

Brox admittedly warns that Schlier's use of later concepts can lead to misunderstanding, but nevertheless he remains fairly close to him. What is said about the church is determined by the fact of heresy and the need to preserve unity by teaching and discipline. The theology is now static, something to be taught rather than proclaimed. Everything depends on the authority of Paul (no other apostles come into view). There is a strong sense of continuity with Paul. Paul is expounded for a later situation. The theology is correspondingly static, formulae to remind the readers of accepted truths. There is no originality, only an arsenal of advice for a practical Christianity.

The church is an institution which stands over against believers to proclaim the truth to them and to guard them from heresy. But this does not happen in any peaceful, undisturbed kind of way. On the contrary, there is a battle raging, and there is a hierarchy of office to preserve the truth. People are appointed to the various tasks in a carefully regulated and orderly manner. Nothing happens in the church apart from the officials who do

---

[48] Less extremely Schweizer 1961:77–88 observes that the church now has an extended history that stretches into the future. The OT and Israel play no part in the concept. The church is now established and static. Yet OT phraseology like 'a people of his own' (Tit 2.14) is found. The church is a house or household, but it is no longer in process of construction but is rather an established entity. It has become a sociological entity determined by its origin, i.e. by tradition. It is not significantly determined by the Holy Spirit. Yet the church is open to new converts and is conscious of mission. It is also characterised by discipline and the need to keep faithful to the message of Paul.

We have reached the outermost point in the New Testament. This one-sidedness was necessary in the fight against *gnosis*; but it is clear that there are other dangers too, and that the development from the New Testament would take a wrong course if the other side, the witness of the Lord who lives today and of the freedom of the Spirit, were not also allowed to take shape clearly. (Schweizer 1961:88 [6k]).

everything. Everything in the church depends on the quality and zeal of the leaders. The congregation merely prays and listens. There is no other charisma but that of the church official, received by the laying on of hands.

Thus the earlier charismatic and dynamic element has given way to the principle of office, and the latter has reached an advanced stage of development. The church is dominated by 'office'.[49] The picture, says Brox, may be one-sided, but it is a fully valid witness to the Spirit-led church and not a testimony to degeneracy.

It is doubtful whether this interpretation in its full-blooded form is widely held any longer. The stress on the dominance of 'office' has not prevailed under subsequent criticism. Lohfink 1977 notes that at one time it was common ground between Catholic interpreters who saw in it the basis for their understanding of the church and Protestant interpreters (such as Käsemann) who condemned it as 'early catholicism'. He disputes the exegesis that lies behind this interpretation, and questions whether everything in the PE is to be regarded as normative for the church. Two things are normative and of key importance. The one is the concept of the 'deposit', which is none other than the gospel, the most precious thing that the church of the PE possessed in its conflict with Gnosis. The other thing is the 'teaching' which is the totality of what is guaranteed by the apostolic authority of Paul.

The question is then whether the church order in the PE is part of this authoritative teaching. Lohfink denies that this is so. The teaching is about the requirements laid down for holders of office and these are concerned solely with their spiritual and ethical conduct. Virtually nothing is said about the duties of overseers and deacons. The PE are not interested in a detailed church order. Certainly the thought of succession is present, but the purpose of ordination is not primarily the handing on of official authority but the safe transmission of the tradition which has been entrusted to the official. It is a succession in teaching, not in official authority. In short what dominates the PE is not the 'principle of office' but the 'principle of tradition'. These points are developed more pointedly in Lohfink's later (1980) very positive discussion of the role of women as deacons in the early church.[50]

---

[49] Kertelge 1972:141f. comments that the overseer/bishop is taking over from the 'servant' conception.

[50] Similarly, Sand 1976 sees in the PE the beginnings of a co-ordination of different types of church order, but he emphasises the flexible and indeterminate nature of the church structures; it is merely the beginning of the process and nothing more.

2. *The current consensus*

The two leading commentators on the PE from Protestant and Roman Catholic positions take very similar positions.[51]

Roloff 1985 (cf. Roloff, 211–17) begins with the points of agreement with Paul. The local congregation is the concrete realisation of the church, although the latter is a worldwide entity. But the salvation-historical/eschatological horizon is weakened. There is little sense of continuity with the OT people of God. The church is the fruit of the proclamation of the gospel, but there is a new stress on teaching and on the apostolic tradition, the 'deposit'. The most significant mark is the emphasis on church offices, with Timothy and Titus functioning as ideal bishops and Paul himself as the pattern.

But equally important is the new element compared with Paul. The church is the household of God with a definite structure, by contrast with the Pauline body of Christ with no authority-structure (cf. Verner 1983). The overseer/bishop is the householder. The patriarchal structure of a household is carried over to the church. The roots of the concept lie in the church as the temple, built on a foundation. But the temple idea is now virtually absent. There is no concept of growth, but the church is a given entity, in short an institution, which is to be understood in terms of the social order.

Two central statements give a more nuanced picture. In 1 Tim 3.15f. the church is a household with a firm foundation. The term foundation comes from temple terminology (cf. 1 Kgs 8.13) and the language has parallels in Qumran. The church is a secure foundation because it is determined by the truth (gen. of quality). It cannot be moved. The term pillar means a towering sign rather than a support: it expresses the visibility of the church as the sign of God's saving purpose. The truth is nothing other than the 'mystery' of Christ himself so that the church is the place where Christ is encountered in worship. Hence Christ and his present work make up for the lack of the concept of the Holy Spirit.

In 2 Tim 2.19–21 the foundation is again the church which is God's and therefore cannot be destroyed by heresy. The seal is the mark of ownership and Roloff identifies it with baptism, and the two OT texts fit in with this. The Lord knows his own people who are baptised. Those who are baptised must cease from evil. The vessels which are unclean must be cleansed so that they can serve God. Repentance is possible! So the church is not simply to be a *corpus permixtum*, and it is not simply a minority or remnant which constitute it. Since every individual believer belongs to God, so also does the church.

---

[51] Surprisingly Davies 1996 in her survey of the thought of the PE does not even thematise the church!

Thus for Roloff: (1) The church is an institution in which the gospel is manifested. (2) It is centrally determined by the present work of Christ experienced in worship and baptism. (3) What makes the church is not tradition or the structures but baptism. The church is not so much before as alongside the believers (cf. Brox above). (4) Hence in a certain sense it is the dispenser of salvation.

The second major contribution is that of Oberlinner. For him the church in the PE is conditioned by its place as the divinely instituted mediator of salvation and as an institution engaged in the struggle with heresy. It acts defensively against heresy but also maintains a witness in the non-believing world. Timothy and Titus function as links with Paul but are presented in a rather flexible way. The church is supremely the household of God, an idea reflecting both the household ideal in the ancient world and the actual reality of the early congregations. But the metaphor is now used to emphasise stability; believers are no longer the temple but live in the household and have their set places in it. It follows that super- and sub-ordination are characteristic of relationships. Obedience and subjection are thus an indication of a right faith. But the congregations themselves are not directly addressed but only through the leaders. The problem with understanding the leadership is that the letters are not a description of a state of affairs but an attempt to encourage certain developments which are motivated by the need to deal with the opposition.

To summarise: it can be said that the general consensus is that the PE represent the development of an early catholic view of the church which was occasioned by the rise of heresy and the consequent need to preserve apostolic teaching by an appeal to the 'deposit' handed down from Paul, by the development of structures to ensure that teaching was in the hands of trustworthy leaders, and by the development of a discipline to restrain the opponents. The motif of the household provided a framework within which a hierarchical structure was appropriate. The result was an understanding of the church which tended to be pragmatic and which had lost the sense of continuity with Israel which was so important at an earlier stage. It also placed the emphasis on teaching and on 'office' in a way that reduced the congregation to mere 'hearers and doers' of the word.

3. Beyond the consensus

While there is much in this consensus that commands assent, it does need some qualification. In particular, it is easy to exaggerate the differences between the understanding of the church in the PE and in earlier NT writings. Four points are relevant.

First, we must avoid making the mistake of assuming that, because the PE are written to church leaders, the congregations themselves no longer matter or are no longer active. The contrast made between Paul writing to congregations and the Pastor writing to leaders may be a false one. Letters continued to be written to congregations (cf. 1 Clement; Ignatius; Polycarp). The simple fact is that we do not know whether Paul himself wrote to his colleagues in mission, although he could certainly address himself to Philemon as a local church leader. Moreover, it is significant that the PE are not written to local church leaders but to persons identified as Paul's colleagues in mission. The antithesis between the congregations and their (local) leaders is not there. Writing to leaders inevitably alters the perspective compared with writing to congregations.[52] It is natural to deal with their duties and responsibilities.

Second, there is the danger of anachronism. Commentators who live in the environment of the highly organised, hierarchical churches of today inevitably have difficulty in visualising the problems of the first century on their own terms. To be sure, Käsemann*, 93, regrets that Protestantism has never been able to implement the Pauline church order 'but has left this to the sects'. But otherwise commentators find it difficult not to read back their own church setting – hierarchy, ordination, office, liturgy, sacraments, bishops, and the like – into the picture. The result is a tendency to see elaborate order and formal structures of organisation and worship where there may have been none or merely rudiments. The laying on of hands is easily assumed to be the same thing as ordination to a lifelong office. There is no actual term corresponding to 'office' in the PE, and one must beware of making the concept too concrete.

Third, concern for the gospel lies at the heart of the letters, and the gospel is presented in new formulations. Nevertheless, it is in essence the same gospel as we know from Paul. Above all, although the immediate occasion of the PE is the reality of opposition and heresy, it is nonetheless clear that the ultimate concern of the author is a missionary one, for the preaching of the gospel by evangelists to gain a believing response among all the nations. The stress on the place of Paul as missionary to the Gentiles is so powerfully affirmed (1 Tim 2.7) that a polemical stress against a lack of missionary fervour in the congregations must be presumed. A missionary theology pervades the PE, and

---

[52] The force of this point is not blunted by the fact that the PE are evidently intended to be read by the local church leaders and congregations.

there is a deliberate recasting of Christian teaching in ways that will be intelligible in the Hellenistic world.[53] The implicit claim of the letters to be inspired by Paul and his teaching is fully justified.

However, fourth, the gospel is threatened by a heresy which downplays the importance of prayer and mission to the Gentiles and which introduces errors that cloud over the gospel. The PE are primarily concerned with this situation and with the steps that must be taken to remedy it, rather than with giving a balanced picture of the church for all times and places. Consequently, the emphasis is on the need to proclaim the truth and to refute error. But this raises the questions of where the truth is to be found and how it is to be preserved. It is not surprising, then, that the church is called back to the deposit handed down by Paul. Whether the PE depend upon Paul's own teaching or are the work of a later follower, they are intended to prepare people in his mission area for the time when he is not there to instruct them. Equally, there must be people who will faithfully teach it and pass it on. They are in effect servants of the Word, and the Word remains supreme over the church and is not subordinated to it in any way.[54]

4. *Some characteristics of the church in the PE*

In the light of these considerations we can appreciate better what is happening in the letters.

First, there is a stronger emphasis on teaching than in earlier letters. This leads inevitably to a greater stress than in Paul on the place of teachers in the church, but there is no fundamental change brought about by this. The need to teach the truth as well as to proclaim the gospel is not surprising in the context of opposition. The antithesis between proclamation and teaching is a false one.[55]

Second, the understanding of the church is closer to Paul than is sometimes suggested. The concept of the church as God's household is already found in Paul (Gal 6.10; Eph 2.19), but it has become more central and is developed in fresh ways. It has

---

[53] Nauck 1950:104f. argues that what is going on in the PE is not the Hellenising of Christianity into a *bürgerliche Lebensgestaltung* but rather the solving of the hermeneutical problem of making Jewish thoughts clear to Hellenistic readers.

[54] Hence the church of the PE cannot be said to be 'early catholic' if by this term we understand a situation where the gospel and teaching are subordinated to the institution.

[55] Compare how in the NT generally a hard-and-fast line cannot be drawn between the activities described by the verbs κηρύσσω and διδάσκω.

been claimed that the church in the PE is more of a solidly founded and finished edifice than in Paul, where there is more emphasis on growth. Nevertheless, the element of struggle and warfare is very much present. The church contains both true and false believers, and one should separate oneself from the latter (cf. 2 Cor 6.14). The church has to contend against error, and, while the victory of God may be certain to believers, they have a hard fight, with tribulation and persecution, ahead of them. The idea of the church of the PE as being a static, completed institution is onesided and misleading.

One important aspect of this metaphor has been noted by Young 1994:79–84. She observes that the ancient household functioned as a school where education was practised and links this function to the strong element of teaching in the PE.

Third, it has been claimed that in the PE 'there is a perceptible shift in the principal way Christians were identifying themselves socially – from "God's household" to "God's people"' (Young 1994:108). Unfortunately, Young does not pursue and ground this line of thought any further. Earlier, however, Towner 1989:129–31 had observed that the phrase 'church of God' identifies the church as the people of God and has OT echoes. It is God's possession (Tit 2.14) and he 'knows' his people (2 Tim 2.19). The concept of the new Israel is latent. There is continuity between the old and the new Israel (2 Tim 1.3). Scripture – the Jewish Scripture – contains the wisdom that leads to salvation and is valuable for every aspect of the church's teaching.

Fourth, any claim that the Holy Spirit is not integral to the life of the church must be resisted. In the Pauline churches there is a delicate balance between ministry and leadership, both of which are empowered by the Spirit. In the PE there is admittedly a shift to a stress on leaders who minister, but they continue to do so under the guidance of the Spirit. The experience of individual believers is determined by the rich outpouring of the Holy Spirit. The suggestion that the role of the Spirit in the congregation has been played down because of the 'enthusiasm' of the opponents seems most dubious. The evidence that the Spirit played a more significant role in the experience and teaching of the opponents (and that therefore the author played it down) is simply not forthcoming.

Fifth, the impression of a rigidly organised church is mistaken. The author is not over-concerned with what the leaders do. The details of their functions and duties are not defined. There is uncertainty about the precise roles of Timothy and Titus. No official position is named for them (except possibly 'evangelist'). They certainly cannot be held to be local church leaders, even if they are models for them.[56] The main concern is that the right people occupy the leadership. Virtually nothing is said about any specific duties associated with their roles. There is no rigid fixing of the terminology for leaders. In Titus the need is to appoint elders who act as overseers and there is no specific mention of deacons; this does not exclude the possibility that they existed, but evidently there were churches which did not have them. In 1 Tim the emergence of elders who take a leading role and are active in preaching and teaching is under way. It is reasonable to assume that these are the same as the overseers, but in ch. 5 no attempt is made to give them a specific designation. Consequently Sand is right to insist that we are only at the beginning of a 'co-ordination' of roles, just as Lohfink correctly insists that there is a flexibility about the church order.

Sixth, the importance of right teaching is stressed, but in the one passage where the need to pass on the deposit received from Paul is mentioned, the language is very general: the teachers are simply 'faithful people' who will be able to instruct others also. Nothing in this passage requires that we assume the existence of an 'office'. Commentators have been misled by this emphasis on 'office', a concept that the PE do not know. What they do know is the development of a leadership that is recognised by the congregation with a certain amount of formality. The people chosen for it already have the gift of the Spirit, and they display the appropriate qualities. They have the potential for teaching. It is important that people are not chosen who are sinners whose way of life calls in question the value of their teaching.

It is also the case that women were involved in teaching; otherwise, the prohibition makes no sense. But if women were doing this without any apparent appointment to positions of leadership, it would follow *a fortiori* that there were men also who did the same. It should hardly be necesssary to remind members of the more hierarchically ordered churches of today that there are plenty of modern congregations which may have appointed elders or even a pastor who do the bulk of the teaching, but it by no means follows that other people in the congregation are prevented from doing so.

Seventh, the same flexibility can be seen in the conduct of church meetings. There is no 'liturgy' in the sense of specific rules for the conduct of church meetings. Nothing is said about who is responsible for presiding at church meetings, there is no

---

[56] Brox 1969b:87–9 gets round this by insisting that they do not correspond to any real office in the church at any time. They merely represent the guarantors of the tradition. At times they stand for the local leaders who are really the people addressed.

mention of the Lord's Supper, and baptism is mentioned only indirectly in the language of conversion.

The author particularly stresses the importance of prayer; there is nothing to suggest that different individuals could not utter prayers in the church meeting, as was evidently the case at Corinth. The implication of 1 Cor 14.14–19 is that several people prayed and that they did so both intelligibly and in tongues, and the types of prayer included thanksgiving. The reference to different kinds of prayer in 1 Tim 2.1 probably indicates that different people took part, and from what follows we can be sure that both men and women took part.

Eighth, it is certainly true that there are some 'rules' being introduced. Action is to be taken against opponents who are to be silenced. Again this implies that teaching was not necessarily carried out only by appointed elders. In particular, the women are excluded from teaching in 1 Tim *en masse*, although this is not inconsistent with older women teaching younger women and with the teaching of the children. This may suggest that the ban in 1 Tim 2 is not as total as is generally maintained and was particularly linked to the heresy and to something about the form of the teaching which infringed unacceptably upon the social position of men.

There was also discipline for what were probably moral lapses rather than errors in teaching. The wording of 1 Tim 5.19 indicates that discipline could be invoked against any member of the congregation, but that great caution was needed in bringing charges against leaders. But discipline already was practised in the Pauline churches and was nothing new.

When these points are assembled, it is evident that the structures in the PE are much looser and less 'official' than the consensus might lead us to suppose. Over against the dangers of heresy the church is closely associated with the gospel and is the guardian of the true message which leads to salvation. This message is contained in the teaching handed down from Paul and ultimately resting on Scripture. It requires that there be faithful people in the congregation who will teach it and take action against those who pervert it. The Spirit continues to be active in the congregations and it is clear that the activities in church meetings were far from following a formal pattern administered only by a few appointed leaders. The stress on 'office' and 'order' which is often thought to be determinative, must be seen in its context, and when this is done, the ecclesiology of the PE emerges as being more akin to that of Paul.

16. καὶ ὁμολογουμένως μέγα ἐστὶν τὸ τῆς εὐσεβείας μυστήριον
The writer now develops the thought of the ἀλήθεια which has

just been mentioned, by making use of a compact statement of its wonderful content.

The hymn-like character of this statement has suggested to some that the introductory phrase is framed to be the prelude to a confession used in church meetings (Michel, O., *TDNT* V, 213). This may well be true, regardless of how we interpret the adv. ὁμολογουμένως***, which is a formation from the pres. pass. part. of ὁμολογέω, 'to confess'.[57] Spicq's analysis of ancient usage indicates that it may have either of two nuances.[58] The first is rhetorical, with reference to something that is uncontested and indubitable, i.e. 'incontestably' and hence 'obviously' (vg. *manifeste*).[59] The second is legal, with reference to what should be affirmed, and has the force of 'that which must be affirmed, confessed', 'as everybody agrees'.[60] Although several commentators uphold the latter interpretation here,[61] it is hard to see any real difference between these nuances since the basis of the universal affirmation is the incontestable nature of the proposition. Certainly, there is no trace of a polemical tone here; the phrase is designed to elicit from the readers a corporate acknowledgement that what is about to be said is accepted truth. Following on from 2.1–7, the idea of a Christian confession would not seem to be out of place.[62] But whether through an act of corporate worship or acknowledgement, the readers are forced to consider the connection between what has just been taught about behaviour and what will next be said about the Christ-event.

The adjective μέγας expresses the idea of being 'great' in the sense of wondrous, sublime, or important.[63] It is used here to

---

[57] Simpson, 60, compares such forms as φειδομένως (2 Cor 9.6), and notes the verbal parallels in Isocrates, *Evag.* 68; Plutarch, *Ages.* 10.5 ('beyond question').

[58] The Stoic use to refer to what is in agreement with nature (Epictetus 3.1.25) is obviously not relevant here.

[59] This nuance is found in the current Eng. tr. 'without any doubt' (NJB; NRSV), 'no one can deny' (GNB); 'beyond all question' (NIV; REB). In 4 Macc the word is used to affirm polemically the undeniability of ὁ εὐσεβής λογισμός over human emotions (6.31; 7.16; 16.1; cf. Philo, *Det.* 18; *Deus.* 71). For the rendering 'demonstrably' here see Hanson 1968:21f.; Hanson, 83f.

[60] In Josephus it emphasises the universal acceptance of an idea (*Ant.* 1.180; 2.229; 19.206; cf. Thucydides 6.90.3; Xenophon, *Anab.* 2.6.1. Cf. *TLNT* II, 583f.; Michel, O., *TDNT* V, 213.

[61] Holtzmann, 328; Easton, 134; Spicq, 468 (cf. *TLNT* II, 584 n. 8); Roloff, 202, n. 463.; cf. Fowl 1990:182f.; Hofius, O., *EDNT* II, 516f. Spicq wishes to understand the initial καί not as a conjunction but as an emphatic adverb, 'really, truly, certainly'.

[62] The connection between the adverb and the Christian act of confession is hard to avoid.

[63] Cf. Eph 5.32; Acts 19.28, 34; Philo, *L.A.* 3.100; *et al.* The adjective appears to express the greatness of the degree to which the thing or person is what it is; a 'great mystery' is especially mysterious.

stress the sublimity of the 'mystery of piety/godliness'. μυστήριον
(3.9) is another way of referring to the 'truth' (v. 15); it is the
secret, revealed by God, which forms the basis or ground for the
life described as εὐσέβεια.[64] The language picks up the thought
adumbrated in v. 9, where church leaders are to be people who
hold to the mystery of the faith with a clear conscience. In effect,
the nature of this mystery is now delineated, and the shift from
τῆς πίστεως to τῆς εὐσεβείας need not imply that a different
mystery with a different content is in mind. εὐσέβεια (see
Excursus 1) stands for the whole of Christian existence, viewed
from the perspective of a life which is lived in response to
the knowledge of God. In this position, between the previous
reference to conduct (v. 15) and the succeeding citation of
theology, the connection between life and faith is emphasised.
There is a further connection implicit in the phrase τὸ τῆς
εὐσεβείας μυστήριον between Christian piety (in the full sense
of the author) and Christology (the sending of the Son; see
Bockmuehl 1990:211-12).

(a) ὃς ἐφανερώθη ἐν σαρκί The first line of the hymn characterises the divine event of Jesus' salvation-historical manifestation.
The abrupt beginning with the masc. rel. pron. ὅς leads most
scholars to assume that a citation of tradition commences here
since there is no masc. antecedent. Wengst 1973:157 cites Phil
2.6 as a parallel, although there there is an antecedent. However,
there is the possibility of a *constructio ad sensum* with the relative
pronoun,[65] and this is what has happened here; the μυστήριον
is Christ, and the change of gender is essential in the pronoun.[66]
The author elsewhere appears to identify a quality or gift of God
with Christ (Tit 2.11; 3.4, where the grace or goodness of God
is effectively revealed in Christ). It is not, therefore, necessary to
assume that he has created a grammatical tension here by making
a citation. Rather, the mystery is at one and the same time the
message about Christ and the Christ-event.

φανερόω (Tit 1.3 note; 2 Tim 1.10**) occurs elsewhere
in relation to Jesus.[67] The connection here with 'the mystery'
establishes that the author intends to interpret God's saving activity
as taking place in the historical appearance of Christ.[68] The
passive form of the verb suggests that God is the initiator of the

---

[64] Cf. Roloff, 201; the gen. is one of aim or direction. Cf. τὸ δὲ τῆς ἰδίας
αὐτῶν θεοσεβείας μυστήριον (Diognetus 4.6).
[65] Mk 3.28; Jn 6.9; Acts 15.36; Gal 4.19; Phil 2.15; 2 Pet 3.1; BD §296.
[66] Cf. Massinger*.
[67] Jn 1.31; Heb 9.26; 1 Pet 1.20; 1 Jn 1.2; 3.5, 8; Barnabas 5.6; 6.7–9, 14;
12.10; Ignatius, *Eph.* 19.3; Windisch 1935:222, 224. For use with reference to the
parousia see Rom 16.26; Col 1.26; 3.4; 1 Pet 5.4; 1 Jn 2.28; 3.2.
[68] Cf. Bockmuehl* 1990:211f.

event (Knoch, 31). σάρξ is used with reference to Christ by Paul and other writers.[69]

It is unlikely that the statement is a reference to Jesus' post-resurrection appearances[70] or a response to a docetic epiphany Christology (contra Hasler, 31). It refers rather to the incarnation (Gundry*, 209f.; Stenger*, 119–47; and most commentators). The 'once hidden/now revealed' pattern of thought found elsewhere in the PE is probably echoed here also. It seems probable that pre-existence is implied; this would tie in with the Christology of the PE generally, but does not appear to be a point of emphasis.[71] Rather, the point is that the Saviour has been made manifest in the world; a positive soteriological emphasis is thus intended (Lau*, 92–5).

Attempts to detect more delicate nuances in this reflection on the incarnation place undue weight on the reference to 'flesh' and the preposition ἐν. There does not appear to be any hint at the weakness or humiliation of Christ (so rightly Roloff, 204). Mainly on the basis of the use of σάρξ in texts such as Rom 8.3; Col 1.22 and Eph 2.14 it has been suggested that the accent is on the crucifixion.[72] Yet the statement is clearly expressed in general terms with a wide scope (contrast the more specific intention of 1 Pet 3:18). There is considerable uncertainty whether the prepositional phrase ἐν σαρκί is intended to express the *mode* of Jesus' manifestation, i.e. as a human being,[73] or the *sphere* of his manifestation, i.e. either the world as the place where salvation-historical events occur (Roloff, 203) or the sphere of human existence in which Jesus participates (Gundry*, 210; Kelly, 90). The most that can be said is that the historical event of the incarnation is in mind; the stress is similar to that in 1 Tim 2.5, and the thought of Jesus' participation in human experience is therefore probably uppermost in mind.[74] The

---

[69] Rom 1.3; 8.3; 9.5; Eph 2.14; Col 1.22; cf. Jn 1.14; 6.63; Heb 2.14; 5.7; 10.20; 1 Pet 3.18; 4.1; 1 Jn 4.2; 1 Clement 32.2; Ignatius, *Eph.* 20.2; Barnabas 5.6; 6.7; 9.14; 12.10; Hermas, *Sim.* 5.6.5–7. Schweizer, E., *et al.*, *TDNT* VII, 98–151; Sand, A., *EDNT* III, 230–3; *TLNT* III, 231–41.

[70] *Contra* Schneider, B., '"Kata Pneuma Hagiōsynēs" (Romans 1,4)', *Bib* 48 (1967) 367, 384–5; Dupont, J., Σὺν Χριστῷ *L'union avec le Christ suivant Saint Paul* (Bruges: Nauwelaerts, 1952), 108–10, who cite Acts 10:40; Lk 24:39 in support.

[71] Cf. Holtzmann, 329; Kelly, 90; Deichgräber 1967:133f.; Wengst 1973:158; *contra* Dunn 1989:237.

[72] Stenger* 1977:90; cf. Martin, R. P., *Reconciliation* (London: Marshall, 1981), 184, who notes that the idea of identification with human sin is inherent in the thought of Christ's 'flesh'. See Gundry*, 209–10, for the view that the reference extends beyond the death of Jesus 'right up to the ascension' (209).

[73] Dunn 1972:62–4.

[74] The view that the emphasis is on *appearing in the world* (Roloff, 204f.) corresponds more closely to the tradition cited in 1:15.

statement is sufficiently general to be capable of suggesting a number of concepts by which Jesus' redemptive participation among people was interpreted, including his suffering and death for sin which the early church understood to be the climax and goal of the incarnation (Rom 8.3; Phil 2.7f.).[75]

(b) ἐδικαιώθη ἐν πνεύματι What Jesus experienced in his identification with humanity, is immediately followed by the declaration of vindication. A number of attempts to explain δικαιόω on the basis of other religious concepts have found little support.[76] Here clearly the thought is not of forgiveness but of vindication on the OT model.[77] In the early church's tradition this is associated with Jesus' entry into the heavenly sphere by his resurrection from the dead (Dibelius-Conzelmann, 62; Klöpper*, 347–53). However, the essential point is not his entry into the heavenly sphere but rather his vindication by God (Hofius*, 14 n. 48). By his resurrection Jesus is confirmed to be what he gave himself out to be despite his purely human appearance (Holtzmann, 331).[78]

ἐν πνεύματι (4.1), which is clearly intended to form a contrast or complement to ἐν σαρκί in previous line and thus establishes a couplet, is problematic. Taking clues from 1 Pet 3.18f., in which he finds the tradition of Christ's pre-resurrection preaching mission and a 'vivification distinct from and prior to resurrection and exaltation', Gundry*, 211–14, suggests that 'in spirit' refers to Christ's pre-resurrection spirit which is vindicated during the descensus. But the interpretation is unlikely: apart from uncertain conclusions drawn from 1 Pet, he seeks much more precision than the general description can provide.[79] The phrase may refer to the means or agent of vindication, i.e. the Holy Spirit (NIV; GNB t), if vindication and resurrection are identical.[80] However, the frequent antithesis of flesh and spirit in the NT with its OT background,[81] suggests that the contrast is between the human mode (or sphere) and the supernatural mode of

[75] See Jeremias, 24; Hofius*, 14f., argues convincingly that the next phrase in the hymn is concerned with the vindication of the One who was crucified.

[76] E.g. the Hellenistic 'divinisation' (Wengst 1972:158; cf. Stenger* 1977:92); see Deichgräber 1967:134.

[77] Cf. Rom 3.4 = Ps 50 (MT 51).6 (= 1 Clement 18.4); *Pss. Sol.* 2.16; 3.5; 4.9; 8.7 (of men/righteous); *Odes Sol.* 17.2; 25.12; 29.5.

[78] Calvin, 233, took the reference to be to the way in which the Spirit led to the declaration of Christ to be Son of God in his earthly life and to his recognition by some people (Mt 11.19 = Lk 7.35; Lk 7.29).

[79] See criticism in Towner 1989:91; Fowl 1990:161f. For the view that 'in Spirit' refers to Jesus' earthly ministry see Metzger*, 82–90.

[80] Cf. Rom 8.11; so Jeremias, 29; Hasler, 31; Barrett, 65f.

[81] Mt 26.41; Mk 14.38; Jn 3.6; 6.63; Rom 1.4; 8.4, 5, 6, 9, 13; 1 Cor 5.5; 2 Cor 7.1; Gal 3.3; 4.29; 5.16, 17[2x], 19; 6.8; Col 2.5; Heb 12.9; 1 Pet 3.18.

Jesus' two-stage existence as characterised by the activity of the Holy Spirit.[82] However, adoption of this view is in no way to imply that the Holy Spirit was not active in the life of Jesus while he was 'in the flesh'.[83]

The occasion of the vindication is amply indicated in the testimony of the early church.[84] According to this testimony, the basis or proof of Jesus' vindication before hostile powers (human or angelic) was his resurrection from the dead and exaltation to the right hand of God (cf. Marshall 1977:103f.); resurrection allowed access to this realm in which the operative agent is the Holy Spirit.[85]

Thus Jesus' human experience (which culminated in his suffering in human weakness) is followed by his return to power and vindication in the Spirit. In the Christ-event humanity and weakness give way to Spirit and power, and yet the two stages of Christ's complete existence are not so much contradictory as they are complementary (cf. Fowl 1990:162).

(c) ὤφθη ἀγγέλοις Line 3 may extend the thought just introduced. The passive verb ὤφθη often expresses the idea of 'becoming visible' or of 'self-exhibition',[86] and it is preferable to take this as an appearing of Christ to 'angels', rather than as a reference to 'angels' observing Christ. But who are these 'angels'? The term ἄγγελος (5.21**) may have either of two possible meanings.

The first is a reference to human messengers, namely, the disciples of Christ who witnessed his resurrection.[87] In support appeal is made to the alleged chronological awkwardness of a reference to angels at this point in the sequence and to a so-called 'technical' use of ὤφθη to describe these resurrection appearances.[88] But it is straining to call the term 'technical', for it is not limited

---

[82] Cf. Rom 1.4; Schweizer, E., *TDNT* VI, 416–17; *TDNT* VII, 126–8; Dalton, W. J., *Christ's Proclamation to the Spirits* (Rome: Pontifical Biblical Institute, 1965, 127–32); Roloff, 204f.; Oberlinner, 165f.; Fowl 1990:159–62; Fee 1994:765f.

[83] Some hold that the reference is therefore to the way in which the Spirit vindicated Jesus to his followers during his lifetime by enabling them to see through the 'veil of flesh' (cf. Simpson, 61, for this as one possibility).

[84] Rom 1.4; 1 Cor 2.1–9; Phil 2.5–11; Col 2.8–15; Eph 1.20f.; Acts 2.22–36; 3.11–15; 4.10–2; 10.34–43; 1 Pet 3.21f.; cf. Oberlinner, 167.

[85] Lohfink 1971:81–95.

[86] Gen 12.7; 17.1; Exod 3.2; Judg 6.12; Lk 1.11; 22.43; Acts 7.2, 30, 35; Mt 17.3/Mk 9.4/Lk 9.31; of the risen Christ Lk 24.34; Acts 9.17; 13.31; 26.16a; 1 Cor 15.5–8; of the parousia Heb 9.28; cf. Michaelis, W., *TDNT* V, 358; Selwyn, E. G., *1 Peter* (London: Macmillan, 1946), 325f.

[87] For earlier supporters of this view, see Micou, R. W., 'On ὤφθη ἀγγέλοις, 1 Tim iii.16', *JBL* 11 (1892), 201–5; Holtzmann, 333; Seeberg*, 119f.; Metzger*, 97–100; see also the discussion in Bockmuehl 1990:211 n. 105.

[88] Lk 24.34; Acts 1.2; 9.17; 13.31; 26.16; 1 Cor 15:5–8.

to description of the resurrection appearances (see above), and such appearances are described with other terms. Furthermore, only a handful of occurrences of ἄγγελος in the NT have people in mind (Mk 1.2 and pars; Lk 7.24; 9.52; Jas 5.21; cf. Rev 2–3 possibly).

The second, generally accepted, interpretation is that the reference is to angelic beings.[89] But to which angels and when? The reference is possibly to the appearance of the triumphant Christ to the fallen angelic powers, which Gundry locates during the descensus.[90] But it is more likely that the allusion is to the better known tradition of Christ's exaltation and appearance to the heavenly hosts in the spiritual realm, which is sometimes associated with the thought of their subjection and worship.[91] The 'disarming' of specifically hostile powers (Col 2.15) is only infrequently mentioned. Christ is implicitly superior to the angels (cf. Broer, I., *EDNT* I, 14), but in keeping with the general aims of the hymn, neither subjection nor worship is mentioned (but may well be implicit); the emphasis is on Christ's manifestation (communication) as Lord to them,[92] just as the next line refers to proclamation of him in the earthly sphere.

(d) ἐκηρύχθη ἐν ἔθνεσιν Especially for a church in the Pauline tradition, the advance of the evangelistic mission to the world was central to the belief that the OT promises of God were in the process of being fulfilled. The next two lines underscore the place of the missionary task in an understanding of salvation history. κηρύσσω (2 Tim 4.2**), here in the passive,[93] conveys the sense 'to preach, proclaim'. The implied subject, ὅς, Jesus Christ, is the content of the proclamation, and lines 1–2 of the hymn have already provided a rough summary of the gospel (cf. Roloff, 207). As the author has already stressed, the nations/Gentiles have a central place in God's salvation plan. At this point the hymn echoes that thought by characterising the summary of the preaching of the gospel in terms of its penetration into a Gentile or universal context.[94] The clause is clearly

[89] Kittel, G., *TDNT* I, 83.
[90] Cf. 1 Cor 2.8; Eph 2.6f.; 3.9ff.; Gal 4.3, 9; Col 2.8, 15, 20; Easton, 136f.; Nauck 1950:82; Gundry*, 219.
[91] Cf. Phil 2.9–11; Eph 1.21; Heb 1.3f.; 1 Pet 3.22; Rev 5.8–14; cf. *Asc. Is.* 11.23. In Ignatius, *Trall.* 9.1, however, it is the crucifixion which is observed by spiritual powers. Other possibilities include the activity of angels at the resurrection of Jesus or at different stages during his life (cf. Arichea-Hatton, 85f.; Feuillet 1978:199 draws attention to Lk 2.13).
[92] Stenger*, 185–90.
[93] Cf. 1 Cor 15.12; 2 Cor 1.19; Hermas, *Sim.* 8.3.2; 9.17.1; Diognetus 11.3.
[94] ἐν = 'among'; 2 Cor 1.9; Gal 2.2; Col 1.23; cf. Roloff, 208. If the hymn is related to ancient enthronement language, it is significant that the proclamation is not made to the demonic powers but, as in the OT, to the nations (Hofius*, 32).

written from the church's post-resurrection perspective; the aorist ἐκηρύχθη sums up an ongoing process which in principle has already decisively taken place. Through the apostle's ministry, the Gentiles have been reached (cf. 2.1–7; cf. Gal 2.2), but the scope is doubtless wider. ἔθνη (2.7; 2 Tim 4.17), which does not necessarily exclude Jews, regards the gospel ministry in its universal scope.[95]

This earthly proclamation to all people must take place after the resurrection. It creates a contrast with a heavenly revelation to angels. Positive results are not guaranteed, but as the hymn continues, it becomes evident that preaching *and* believing are included in the saving event (cf. Dibelius-Conzelmann, 63).

(e) ἐπιστεύθη ἐν κόσμῳ Line 5 is also concerned with the missionary task.[96] It states the successful effect of the preaching, and confirms that the gospel ministry is conceived of as worldwide in scope (cf. Oberlinner, 169). Therefore this line is linked to the previous one, and 'nations' is parallel to 'world' (cf. Fowl 1990:168). The theatre in which the salvation drama unfolds, ἐν κόσμῳ, is the world of humanity into which Christ came (1.15 note). Roloff, 209, points out rightly that the response of belief in the salvation message is a human possibility, and that thus the human perspective is central (cf. Stenger* 1977:206). The hymn's record of the progress of salvation history has moved from Christ's identification with humanity to exaltation in the spiritual realm and back to the effects of that event in the earthly realm. It is significant that the object of belief is not the gospel but the actual person to whom it testifies.[97] Such belief implies the success of the salvation plan, but not necessarily a universal turning to Christ (*contra* Brox, 160).

(f) ἀνελήμφθη ἐν δόξῃ The hymn closes with a rather enigmatic phrase. ἀναλαμβάνω (2 Tim 4.11**), when used elsewhere of Christ, refers to his ascension.[98] If the ascension of Christ is in view (cf. Gundry*, 204; Spicq, 474), a straight chronological understanding of the piece comes to grief. Nevertheless, despite the clear connection with the ascension tradition (so Roloff, 210; Oberlinner, 169; Lohfink 1971:89), the emphasis is rather on the installation or exaltation of Christ to the realm of glory, for which the event of the ascension stood as

---

[95] *Pace* Barrett, 65; see 2.4 note; cf. Fee, 55; Oberlinner, 168f.; Stenger*, 190–8; Läger 1996:52f.

[96] πιστεύω is the language of mission (Barth, G., *EDNT* III, 93).

[97] ἐπιστεύθη, 1.11, 16 note, is here 'to be believed on'; cf. BD 312.

[98] Mk 16.19; Lk 24.51; Acts 1.2, 11, 22; cf. Lk 11.51; Lohfink 1971:213; Delling, G., *TDNT* IV, 8. See also 2 Kgs 2.10f.; 1 Macc 2.58; Philo, *Mos.* 2.291.

a symbol. The phrase ἐν δόξῃ (1.11, 17*) is to be understood either as a local reference to the glorious sphere of heaven,[99] or as a reference to his glorification or exalted status (attendant circumstances), but in any case as the proof and reward of his triumph.[100] In either case, the thought of the victorious exaltation/ascension of Christ concludes the piece.

---

[99] Roloff, 210; Stenger* 1977:216; Kelly, 92. The preposition εἰς would more typically express the destination of a verb of motion, ἐν has local force in the hymn; cf. Fowl 1990:169f.

[100] Gundry*, 216; Kittel, G., *TDNT* II, 237, 247–9.

BODY OF THE LETTER – B. THE ATTITUDE OF THE CHURCH LEADER TO THE CHURCH AND THE GROUPS IN IT
(4.1–6.21a)

The second main part of the letter is concerned with the same broad kind of topics as the first part. Again the opening theme is the problem of the false teaching in the church, characterised as apostasy from the faith, and Timothy is given instructions about his personal bearing in relation to it. The letter then moves on to give instructions regarding specific groups in the church. The instruction in 1:3f. is thus developed in some detail (Knoch, 32). In contrast to the earlier part of the letter, the teaching is expressed more in the form of instruction to Timothy regarding his own life-style and what he is to put before the church (4.6, 11, 16; 6.2, 17), but there is still material which is in effect directly addressed to particular groups. The instruction can be subdivided into three sections. In the first (4.1–16) Timothy is reminded of his duties as a Christian teacher in a situation of growing heresy. In the second (5.1–6.2a) he is given instruction as to how he is to treat different groups in the church. Finally, he is given further personal exhortation which is set in a context of avoiding the temptation to seek after material advancement (6.2b–21).

I. TIMOTHY'S DUTIES AS A TEACHER IN THE FACE OF HERESY
(4.1–16)

This section breaks up into three sub-sections, with the transitions marked by the imperatives in vv. 6 and 11. The first sub-section (4.1–5) describes the teaching and practice of the opponents more fully and specifically, but swiftly passes over into a reasoned refutation of their position. The second sub-section (4.6–10) reiterates the need for sound teaching by the church leader which will promote godliness. The third sub-section (4.11–16) is concerned with the personal behaviour of Timothy through teaching and example which will promote his own salvation and that of the church.

a. The rise of heresy and the need for sound doctrine (4.1–5)

Fee 1994:768–70; Ford, J. M., 'A Note on Proto-Montanism in the Pastoral Epistles', *NTS* 17 (1970–1), 338–46; Lane, W. L., '1 Tim. 4.1–3: an early instance of over-realised eschatology', *NTS* 11 (1964–5), 164–7; Schlarb 1990:91–3, 132f.

The theme of this section is related to what has gone before in that the opening section of the letter was concerned with heresy (1.3–7, 19f.), and the task of the church in upholding and maintaining the truth was stressed in 3.15 (cf. Hasler, 33; Oberlinner, 171). In ch. 1 we found that the opponents were concerned to be teachers of the law and laid stress on genealogies, which the author characterised as mythical; as a result they promoted what the author regarded as empty speculations. We now learn more about the teachings (and hence the practices) of the opponents,[1] and this serves to reinforce the need for the instruction which follows. Whereas 2 Tim also is concerned with the rise of heresy (2 Tim 3.1–9) but deals more with the moral and spiritual decline associated with the heresy, here the concern is directly with the teaching of the heretics and characterises it as part of the moral and spiritual deterioration that is prophesied for the last days.

Dibelius-Conzelmann, 51, and Brox, 166, observe that this is the only section in 1 Tim that is concerned systematically with the heresy, but in fact the section is rather more concerned with Timothy's personal bearing in the situation than with detail about the heresy, although 4.4f. is in fact a reasoned response to one aspect of it.

The teaching contains some elements that may be associated with the 'form' of a farewell discourse, the fact of impending moral decline and the need for the recipient to strive after godliness;[2] vv. 1–5 correspond roughly to 2 Tim 3.1–9, 13; 4.3; and vv. 6–11 correspond with 2 Tim 3.14–4.5.[3]

The presence of heresy is described in the form of a prophetic statement by the Spirit which describes from Paul's point of view what will happen 'in later [*or* the last] times' (cf. 2 Pet 3.3; Jude 18). The prophetic form of statement is used to show the inevitability of what is happening, but it also indicates that it is not beyond God's knowledge, and therefore his control (Knoch, 32). Further, what is prophesied is in fact already happening (*pace* Simpson, 64), so that current events are identified as signs of the last days. It is not clear where the prophecy ends and whether the writer is quoting or paraphrasing an existing form

---

[1] Jeremias, 29f., states that ch. 1 is concerned with the beliefs of the opponents and ch. 4 with their practices.

[2] Cf. Wolter 1988:228–30.

[3] Note how the section is structured with pairs (spirits and teachings; liars and branded; to marry and to abstain from foods; believers and people who have come to know the truth; good and not to be rejected; word of God and prayer).

of words and/or making his own comments on it (Couser 1992:109). The awkward syntax may be due to incorporating material.

For the content of the warning cf. Mk 13.5f., 21–23; 2 Th 2.3, 9–11; Acts 20.29–31. It will be a time of apostasy affecting the church. The source of the apostasy is identified in two ways. On the one hand, it is seen as demonic in origin. On the other hand, it is the work of teachers who tell lies but pretend to be speaking the truth or to be righteous people. But their consciences do not prevent them from acting falsely in this way, either because they have ceased to operate effectively or because they have been perverted. Their teaching is summed up in two practical prohibitions directed against entering into marriage and eating [certain] foods.

The author begins to respond to this teaching with a relative clause which ignores the question of marriage and takes up the issue of foods. The foods in question were created by God for human consumption, more particularly for consumption by believers who have come to know the truth revealed in the gospel and who can give thanks to God for them. There are thus two elements in the author's response, and these are developed in vv. 4 and 5 in a way reminiscent of Paul's response in 1 Cor 10:30f. If God has created foods, they are good (like the rest of creation) and are not to be rejected; on the contrary, they can be received with thanksgiving, because they are sanctified by the word of God and prayer.

It is important to notice that the passage continues through to the end of v. 10. Already in v. 3 it is clear that the antidote to the false teaching lies in the Christian gospel (the 'truth') accepted by believers. That gospel promises life both now and in the hereafter and centres on God the Saviour. Hence it is arguable that it is not only the doctrine of God as Creator but also of God as Saviour which forms the basis for the argument (Couser 1992:109–17).

The nature of the false teaching demands attention. What exactly was being taught, and what, if any, was the rationale behind it? Some possibilities can be rejected either because the evidence is inadequate that both celibacy and abstinence from certain foods were practised, or because the author's arguments against them here do not seem to fit the rationale for their abstention. It is widely held that a basic view of (certain aspects of) the creation as evil is the underlying issue. Thiessen 1995:326 questions this assumption on the basis that the argument against the false teaching appeals to creation as a fact acknowledged on both sides, but it remains possible that an inconsistent attitude to creation lay at the root of the trouble.[4] It is significant that the false views are attributed to demonic inspiration. The implication is that the opponents claimed the authority of prophetic inspiration for their views. A variety of background influences may have been at work.

(a) The opponents were simply Jews or Jewish Christians for whom certain types of ritual abstinence were normal.[5] However, rejection of marriage was not characteristically Jewish.

(b) Some Essenes were celibate[6] and would not eat 'other men's food' (hence they lived on grass when they were expelled from the community; Josephus, *Bel.* 2.143f.). Philo, *Cont.* 34–7 refers to the asceticism (but not abstinence from marriage) of the Therapeutae. At Qumran there is evidence that some were celibate while others were not (CD 7.6f.), but, apart from their general frugality and abstemiousness, nothing is said about restrictions on diet (which certainly included bread and wine), and animal bones have been discovered at Qumran.[7] Apart, then, from the restriction on marriage we do not have a full parallel here.

(c) Spicq, 497f., suggests a broad background in the general mentality that surfaces from time to time in the ancient world; desires for purity were expressed in abstinence from sexual activity and from certain foods. Such a general rejection of aspects of the created order may have influenced a Jewish-Christian group in the church, but it hardly seems an adequate background on its own.

(d) Celibacy for the sake of the kingdom of God was recognised by Jesus (Mt 19.12) and Paul himself remained celibate and encouraged it in certain circumstances (1 Cor 7). Whether Rev 14.4 is to be taken literally is debatable. But in all these cases the abstention from marriage has to do with the needs of the mission and not with the basic asceticism and possible hostility to aspects of the created order that is evident here.[8] Nor is there any teaching of Jesus that would forbid

[4] The fact that such rejection would have been inconsistent, in that people still had to eat and reproduction still had to take place somehow, is not an argument against the possibility of people who felt that they must reject the world as much as possible.

[5] Jeremias, 30f., who thinks that Jewish ritual observances lie behind the abstention from foods, has to allow that the rejection of marriage stems from another background, such as taking Paul's own attitudes to extreme lengths.

[6] Josephus, *Ant.* 18.21; *Bel.* 2.120f.; Philo, *Hyp.* 11.14–17; for other Essenes who did marry see Josephus, *Bel.* 2.160f.

[7] Beall, T. S., *Josephus' description of the Essenes illustrated by the Dead Sea Scrolls* (Cambridge, 1988), 38–42.

[8] Consequently, the present passage cannot be used to rule out the possibility of voluntary celibacy for the sake of the kingdom of God, even though a requirement of celibacy for certain orders of Christian ministry has no biblical basis.

certain kinds of food or that might be twisted in that direction; if anything, he discouraged Jewish ideas of unclean foods. However, the teaching of Jesus about the absence of marriage in the life to come apparently influenced later Encratites.[9]

(e) The possibility of a connection with the (Jewish-Christian) apostolic decree which forbade foods sacrificed to idols and sexual immorality (which could be stretched to include marriage, as it was at Corinth) should at least be mentioned. The cult of Jezebel in Rev 2 was characterised by precisely the opposite attitudes and would appear to represent a reaction to the decree. However, a connection is not likely since abstinence from marriage is hardly to be read out of a prohibition of sexual immorality which is usually intended to safeguard marriage.

(f) An over-realised eschatology, with no marriage in the 'heavenly state' (Lane*; Spicq, 498) is another possibility. Lane suggests that the example of the risen Jesus who ate (only) fish and honeycomb (and possibly bread?) could have been used to defend the prohibition on meat, and also Rom 14.17 with its denial that the Kingdom of God is meat and drink may have played a part. He further argues that the distinction between this life and that to come, which is made here, is directed against those who thought that the former age had now passed away. But the appeal to Jesus can only be seen as a rationalisation of some existing practice and not as the origin of it.

Schlarb 1990:132f. notes the author's *ad hominem* use of the Genesis material in 1 Tim 2.13f. and suggests that the prohibition of marriage (or, positively, the encouragement of celibacy) reflects the attempt to return to a pre-Fall pattern of life – since awareness of sexual distinctions and commencement of sexual relations occur after the Fall. Likewise food asceticism, which he understands as prohibition of eating meat, can be linked to the vegetarian pattern of life in the Garden.[10] This 'return to Eden' motif can be incorporated in this over-realised eschatology: the heavenly existence is to be similar to that of the original paradise.

(g) The apocryphal Acts bear witness to a development of such attitudes among groups of Christian ascetics and attribute them to Paul.[11] Irenaeus refers to so-called Encratites led by Tatian who proclaimed celibacy and 'introduced abstinence from eating what they call "animate" food, ungrateful to the God

---

[9] Aune, D. E., 'Luke 20:34–6: A "Gnosticized" Logion of Jesus', in Lichtenberger, H., (ed.), *Geschichte – Tradition – Reflexion. Festschrift für Martin Hengel zum 70. Geburtstag* (Tübingen: Mohr, 1996), 187–202.

[10] However, the prohibition of marriage contradicts Gen 1.27f., which would indicate inconsistency on the part of the teachers!

[11] Cf. *Acts of Paul and Thecla* 12; *Ps-Titus, passim.*

who made all' (Irenaeus, *AH* 1.28); cf. the attitude reflected in *Didasc.* 24 (*Apost. Const.* 6.11). They held that the world was so evil that they should not procreate more people to share in its misery (Clement, *Strom.* 3.45.1; Hasler 34). Some believed that they were now risen and the ways of the old world were inappropriate.[12] But the Encratites described by Irenaeus are to be placed in the later second century. At a later date the *Apostolic Canons* (*Apost. Const.* 8.47.51, 53) commanded clergy to marry and also to partake of flesh and wine on festival days.

(h) Some second-century Gnostics practised asceticism. The followers of Saturninus regarded marriage and generation as from Satan and abstained from animal flesh (Irenaeus, *AH* 1.24.2). Brox, 168, goes a step further in holding that the opponents must have distinguished between the God who created the world and the God who saves; but there is no indication in the text of belief in a separate creator. Further, there is no reason to believe that such attitudes were peculiar to Gnostics, and therefore it is sensible to look for earlier possible sources.

(i) These prohibitions may have been due to drawing wrong conclusions from the creation story (Knoch, 33), or, more probably, they were defended by appeal to it. Rejection of marriage could have been deduced from the curse on Adam and Eve (or on the prohibition of nakedness and seeing in it an implicit taboo on sexual behaviour) and abstinence from foods from the command not to eat of the two trees in the garden.

Several of these postulated backgrounds are manifestly unconvincing, whether singly or in combination. There is probably a combination of influences at work here. We need to distinguish between the origins of the asceticism and the justification that was actually proffered for it. Problems about food and drink arose in Corinth and also in Colossae. It appears that some people rejected marriage in Corinth. A belief that it was 'spiritual' to be ascetic is not at all surprising. It could have been defended on the grounds that people were already living in the resurrection era and that the conditions of paradise were restored (cf. Towner 1989:33–42; Towner, 103f.). More probably, there may have been people who felt that, if this was how it was to be in the restored paradise, then they should anticipate it here and now. The closest links are thus with a tendentious reading of Genesis and with the tendencies to vegetarianism and abstinence from marriage that are reflected at Corinth and Colossae and that blossomed in the communities reflected in the apocryphal Acts.

---

[12] Clement, *Strom.* 3.48.1; 63.1f; 64.1; contrast Mk 12.25; similarly, Roloff, 224; cf. Wolter 1988:258f.

TEXT

1. τῆς πίστεως Praem. ἀπό (206 1149 1799); cf. 1 Tim 6.10. Elliott, 61, argues that the prep. is needed after this verb (cf. Lk 4.13; 13.27; Acts 5.38; *et al.*). But Hellenistic usage (see exegetical note below) supports the text.

πλάνοις πλάνης (P Ψ 104, 614 630 945 *al* lat). The variant is said to be a Semiticism avoided by scribes (Bartlet, J. V., *JTS* 18 [1917], 309), and therefore to be adopted (Elliott, 61f.). But the gen. could be due to assimilation to the next phrase or to 1 Jn 4.6 (Holtzmann, 335) or to itacism (NA).

2. κεκαυστηριασμένων (ℵ A L *al* b m*; Elliott, 62): καὶ καυ[σ]τηριασμένων (F 0241^vid *al* lat sy^p); κεκαυτηριασμένων (C D G I Ψ 33 1739 1881 TR Cl Did Epiph). According to Simpson, 65, from καυτήριον, 'branding iron', comes the verb καυτηριάζω (found in *Corpus Hippiatricorum Graecorum* 1,28 according to BA) = 'to brand with a red hot iron'; and from καυστήρ, 'cauterising apparatus', comes καυστηριάζω (*v.l.* in Strabo 5.1.9;). However, both nouns can be spelled with or without the sigma. The σ in καυστήριον is vulgar (LSJ), and MHT III, 342, 405 brackets it. The textual variants are thus spelling variants rather than separate words with different meanings.

4. λαμβανόμενον μεταλαμβανόμενον (81 2005). Elliott, 64, adopts the variant on the ground that simplex verbs were seen as better style. But the MSS evidence is too weak.

EXEGESIS

1. Τὸ δὲ πνεῦμα ῥητῶς λέγει ὅτι ἐν ὑστέροις καιροῖς ἀποστήσονταί τινες τῆς πίστεως προσέχοντες πνεύμασιν πλάνοις καὶ διδασκαλίαις δαιμονίων The new section begins with an implicit contrast between the apostasy about to be described and what has just preceded, the statement of the true gospel (Holtzmann, 335); but δέ is a weak link before a new topic, and on the whole a fresh start seems to be indicated. The basis for the instruction is a prophetic forecast attributed to the Spirit and standing in sharp contrast to the view of the opponents which are attributed to false spirits. It is debated whether the message is regarded as having come through Christ himself or through a Spirit-inspired prophet (perhaps Paul himself), but the latter is more likely, since elsewhere Christ's teaching is attributed to him personally as 'the Lord'. Nevertheless, in broad terms the message is similar to his teaching (cf. Mt 24.10; Mk 4.17; 13.21f.).

This is the only reference in 1 Tim to the present activity of τὸ πνεῦμα.[13] It functions as the source of prophecy (cf. 2 Sam 23.2; Acts 21.11; 2 Th 2.2; Justin, *Apol.* I.63.10). Roloff, 220, however, claims that even here the reference is to a *past* activity of the Spirit: the Spirit is no longer active in prophets in the congregation or even in individual members. But this claim is too sweeping; it ignores Tit 3.5 and the activity of prophets in 4.14 which is not to be regarded as now defunct.

[13] 1 Tim 3.16; 2 Tim 1.7, 14; Tit 3.5 (note) of Holy Spirit; 1 Tim 4.1b of deceptive spirits; 2 Tim 4.22** of human spirit.

There are, however, various possible ways of envisaging the mode of prophecy attributed to the Spirit. (a) Through Christ, according to his teaching handed down (Knight, 188). But this is improbable here, since elsewhere his teaching is attributed to him personally as the Lord. (b) Through Christian prophets.[14] (c) Specifically through a private revelation to Paul, whether in reality or as part of a pseudepigraphical fiction.[15] In this case Paul may be (or is envisaged as) setting down exactly the contents of a revelation that he is receiving (Acts 20.29f. is a possible instance of this). A decision between (b) and (c) is not easy.

λέγει (pres. tense) introduces a statement which remains valid though spoken in the past.[16] There is, therefore, no need for the explanation that the author means that the Spirit is speaking to him even as he is writing, but equally there is no implication that the activity of the Spirit belongs to the past and no longer takes place.

The usage of ῥητῶς*** is ambiguous. It may mean: (a) 'in these words' (= 'totidem verbis'). It then serves to introduce a verbally accurate statement.[17] (b) 'expressly, explicitly' ('mit klaren Worten', BA).[18] Both possibilities have linguistic support, but the absence of any indications that there is a precise citation favours the second one.

The prophecy relates to the last days.[19] For καιροί in the pl. cf. 2.6; 2 Tim 3.1; Ignatius, *Eph.* 11.1. ὕστερος, 'last', 'later' (Mt 21.31 *v.l.****; cf. adv. ὕστερον), is a comparative adj. = 'second of two'; but here it can have superlative force = 'last' (cf. BD §62). Bernard, 65, takes it comparatively of a period future to the speaker, i.e. the post-Pauline period. Spicq (*TLNT* III, 427–31 [431]) holds that it means not 'in the last days' but rather 'in days to follow, later times, the future'.[20] But it can be used absolutely for the last times (*Acta Carpi* 5, cited by Lane*, 164), and the parallel in 2 Tim 3.1 (ἐν ἐσχάταις ἡμέραις) strongly favours this option.[21] The rendering 'prior to the last times' (White, 120) is impossible.

---

[14] See Rev 2.7; 14.13; 22.17; *EDNT* III, 211; Fee 1994:769.

[15] For the latter cf. Holtzmann, 335 (who also suggests that the author may have had access to a written prophecy); Hasler, 33f.

[16] 1 Tim 5.18; Rom 4.3, 6; 9.15; *et al.*; Heb 1.6f.; 3.7; 5.6; *et al.*

[17] Justin, *Apol.* I.35.10; 63.10, also with reference to the content of prophecies. Cf. Philo, *L.A.* 1.60; Plutarch, *Mor.* 1041A; (so Lock, 47).

[18] Josephus, *Ant.* 1.24; *Ap.* 1.83 [of one word having a particular equivalent in another language]; Philo, *L.A.* 1.60; Dittenberger, *Syll.* 685.76, 83 (II BC); Polybius 3.23.5; Plutarch, *Brut.* 29.4; Diogenes Laertius 8.71; so Parry, 24; Simpson, 64; Knight, 188; Roloff, 219 n. 6.

[19] For the thought see 1QpHab 2.5f.; Acts 20.29; 2 Th 2.1–12; 1 Jn 2.18; Rev 13.

[20] Cf. Plato, *Leg.* 9.865A: ἐν ὑστέροις χρόνοις = 'at a later time'.

[21] Cf. Wilckens, U., *TDNT* VIII, 592–601. cf. ἔσται ἡμέρα ὅτε … (2 Tim 4.3).

The kind of danger prophesied is regarded as present in 2 Tim 3.6. In both passages fut. verbs (ἀποστήσονται, 1 Tim 4:1; ἐνστήσονται ... ἔσονται, 2 Tim 3:1–2) give way to a discussion that clearly relates to the present of the writer and the readers/hearers (Towner 1989:65). Hence it is generally agreed that here also the present period is understood as belonging to the last days before the End (but not necessarily the very last era, though the distinction is probably not to be pressed). The use of the prophetic form emphasises both the inevitability of what is happening and the fact that it should not take people by surprise. It brings out the need to take the rise of heresy seriously as part of the disasters associated with the last days: what was prophesied as a fearsome future evil is now taking place.

Hence if the letter is post-Pauline the force is: 'The Spirit prophesied in the past (through Paul) that in the last days there would be apostates – and the prophecy is already being fulfilled: we are living in the last days, and we can see the signs around us!' If the letter is genuine, we have to understand Paul as saying implicitly that the last days are here, or that the kind of conduct characteristic of them is already beginning to show itself. If the implied author is quoting a prophecy made in the past (e.g. a saying of Jesus) then the tense is future from the point of view of the prophet but the prophecy is now being fulfilled in the present time of writer (cf. Knight, 188f.).

The prophecy begins with a very general statement concerning people departing from the faith. ἀφίστημι is used intrans. 'to go away, withdraw', hence 'to desert, fall away, become apostate'.[22] The word was used of apostatising, i.e. of giving up the faith or denying it. τινές (1.3 note) refers vaguely to the heretics, or more probably to those deceived by them (Calvin, 236; Holtzmann, 335; Fee, 97). The gen. τῆς πίστεως has the force either (a) 'from *the* faith' (Simpson, 64; Roloff, 220), or (less probably) (b) 'from believing the gospel'.

The general statement is particularised by describing what leads people astray. They are deceived by paying attention to teaching that is ultimately of demonic origin, and this is mediated by people who teach what is false and pay no heed to conscience. Thus a distinction is made between the people who go astray and those whose influence leads them astray. The demonic background means that discussion and argument is fruitless (Roloff, 220f.).

For προσέχω cf. 1.4; Tit 1.14 note. πνεύματα here are evil spirits. For the thought of demonic influence behind the

[22] Deut 32.15; Jer 3.14; Dan 9.9Θ; 1 Macc 11.43; *1 Enoch* 5.4; Lk 8:13; Hermas, *Sim.* 8.8.2; with ἀπό Heb 3.12; with gen. as here Polybius 14.12.3; Wis 3.10; Josephus, *Vita* 158; Justin, *Dial.* 8.2; 20.1; 111.2; Hermas, *Vis.* 3.7.2. Cf. Schlier, H., *TDNT* I, 512f. (For the sense 'to keep away' see 2 Tim 2.19**).

heresy cf. 2.14; 3.6 of deceit by devil.[23] πλάνος is 'leading astray, deceitful'.[24] Deceit is frequently associated with apostasy and heresy and the influence of Satan.[25]

διδασκαλίαι (1.10) are pieces of teaching. The use of the plural is possibly traditional.[26] It may have a derogatory sense by comparison with the singularity of the truth of the gospel (Holtz, 100). δαιμόνιον**, 'demon', originally meant 'deity, divinity'.[27] The gen. is one of origin – 'taught by demons' (White, 120).

2. ἐν ὑποκρίσει ψευδολόγων, κεκαυστηριασμένων τὴν ἰδίαν συνείδησιν The deceitful teaching ultimately emanates from demonic powers and is mediated through the deceitful teaching of liars with seared consciences who forbid marriage, and so on. Cf. 2 Tim 2.16–18; 3.13; 4.3f. for related descriptions of apostasy from the faith.

The force of ἐν may be instrumental ('through the hypocrisy of...') or more general ('in association with' cf. 2 Tim 1.13). The phrase is to be linked with ἀποστήσονται (or with προσέχοντες) indicating the instrument that leads people into apostasy – 'through the hypocritical behaviour of liars...'. Another possibility is that the phrase is dependent on the following word, giving 'paying attention to ... the teachings [emanating] from demons who hypocritically speak lies' (Simpson, 64; Fee 1994:768 n. 59),[28] but it falls foul of the following participle which must surely apply to human beings, not demons.

ὑπόκρισις is 'pretence, hypocrisy, outward show' (Mt 23.28; Mk 12.15; Lk 12.1; Gal 2.13; Jas 5.12 v.l.; 1 Pet 2.1***). In Cl. Gk. the word meant 'answer' and then the 'delivery' of a speech'; the corresponding verb was used of acting on the stage. In Hellenistic Judaism the word-group took on a bad sense. The LXX uses it to refer to people who are godless and evil (but not

---

[23] Cf. 1 Jn 4.6; for the link with demons cf. Rev 16.14; 18.2; Jas 3.15 (δαιμονιώδης). More generally, cf. 2 Cor 4.4; 11.3, 13f.; 1QS 3.18–22; T. Ash. 6.2 (Skarsaune 1994:12).

[24] It is used as a noun in Mt 27.63; 2 Cor 6.8; 2 Jn 7b***. Cf. Menander, Frg 288; Theocritus 21.43; Josephus, Bel. 2.259. Cf. πλανάω, 2 Tim 3.13; Tit 3.3 (note). Cf. Braun, H., TDNT VI, 228–53, especially 249f.

[25] Mt 24.5; 1 Jn 4.1–3, 6; 1 Cor 10.20f.; 12.3; 2 Cor 4.4; 11.3, 13f.; 2 Th 2.3; 2 Pet 2.1–3; 3.3; Jas 3.15; Rev 16.14; Ass. Moses 7.3–10.

[26] Mt 15.9/Mk 7.7 = Isa 29.13; Col 2.22; the sing. with πᾶς in Eph 4.14 is similar.

[27] Cf. Rev 16.14; the word is found in Paul only in 1 Cor 10.20f.; Foerster, W., TDNT II, 1–20.

[28] According to Simpson this is how Chrysostom took it. But this does not seem to be borne out by the text (PG LXII, 557f.): the opponents 'do not utter these falsehoods through ignorance and unknowingly, but as acting a part, knowing the truth indeed, but "having their conscience seared", that is, being men of evil lives'.

in the sense of being two-faced or 'hypocritical' in the modern sense). However, the word-group came to refer to deception; it is associated with lying and contrasted with truth.[29] The word-group figures prominently in the castigation by Jesus of people who appeared to be or pretended to be pious but were really evil. The force of the word here, then, is to express the fact that what was said appeared to be true but was in fact in contradiction of the truth (4.3). Cf. 6.5; 2 Tim 3.8; 4.4; Tit 1.14 for such opposition to the truth.[30] Such conduct is the opposite of what is expected in believers (1 Tim 1.5; 2 Tim 1.5).

How they practised their hypocrisy is debatable:

(a) They may have deliberately pretended to be Christian teachers and to be speaking the truth in order to deceive people.

(b) They may have put up a show of asceticism which was regarded as an indication of good character (Kelly, 94; Fee, 98). But the phrase is concerned with what they said rather than what they did.

(c) They may have been self-deceived in claiming to be Christian teachers.

The implication of the next phrase is probably that they did not respond to their consciences but sinned deliberately and consciously. They deliberately turned their backs on the truth and silenced their consciences, so that they themselves were by no means innocent victims of deception (Roloff, 221). So active deceit (a) is meant.

From this point the description is of the heretics themselves. They are characterised as liars. ψευδολόγος***, 'speaking falsely, lying' (Cl.), can be used as an adj. or a noun.[31] Cf. ψεύστης (1.10). According to Fee, 98, the heretics were not necessarily being deliberately deceitful but did not know any better. But in view of the previous word this is not very likely.

συνείδησιν (cf. 1.5; Tit 1.15 note) is acc. of respect with passive verb (6.5). καυστηριάζω*** (see textual note) is a word that was used of branding animals with a red hot iron and cauterising wounds using a καυ(σ)τήρ. Its force here is disputed:

(a) 'to sear, render callous, anaesthetise'.[32] For the thought cf. Eph 4.19.

---

[29] Philo, Jos. 67f.; Her. 43; Josephus, Bel. 1.628; Ant. 16.206; T. Benj. 6.5.

[30] See further 1 Clement 15.1; Ignatius, Mag. 3.2; Polycarp 6.3; Barnabas 19.2; 20.1; Didache 4.12; 5.1; Hermas, Vis. 3.6.1; Mand. 2.5; 8.3; Sim. 8.6.2; 9.27.2. Cf. Wilckens, U., TDNT VIII, 559–71; TLNT III, 406–13.

[31] In Cl. it is a pejorative word (Aristophanes, Ranae 1521, cited in TLNT III, 517). Josephus, Ant. 8.410 and Philo, Virt. 182 both have the noun ψευδολογία.

[32] Chrysostom PG LXII, 558; Theodoret III, 659 Schulze = PG LXXXII, 812; NIV; NRSV; GNB; BA; LN; Parry, 24f.; Simpson, 65; Guthrie, 104; Spicq, 496f.; Hanson, 86f.; Elliott, 62; Knight, 189; Arichea-Hatton, 90f.; Johnson, 161f.

(b) 'to brand' (REB) (like a prisoner of war or slave), either with the mark of the devil's ownership,[33] or as a penalty.[34] Oberlinner, 177 n. 19, comments that a distinction between branding as a mark of ownership (to prevent a slave running away) and as a dishonourable stigma should not be made; the two functions belong together.

Roloff, 221f., defends the second possibility – a shameful mark, in this case, on people who are guilty of rejecting conscience; the mark is not necessarily visible to any except themselves. The author is not interested in the subjective reasons for their attitude. However, the absence of any reference to who carries out the branding and the oddity of a mark that cannot be seen combine to make this view unlikely. The former view is to be preferred, since it makes the point that it is the conscience which is affected and is not working (cf. 1.19b; Tit 1.15). Consequently, their consciences did not forbid them to act deceitfully, or they paid no attention to them. The point is that their conscience was no longer effective in condemning what was morally unacceptable.

3a. κωλυόντων γαμεῖν, ἀπέχεσθαι βρωμάτων Two examples of their false teaching are given, the forbidding of marriage and asceticism in regard to food. The former presumably implies abstinence from sexual activity (within or outside of marriage), and the latter must refer to abstinence from some foods rather than others (Arichea-Hatton, 91, thinks of general abstinence from foods, 'eating as little food as possible'). The reference may be specifically to meat (Knight, 190), and possibly to abstinence from alcohol (cf. 5.23) or food regarded as unclean by Jews (Tit 1.10–16; Kelly, 95). Abstinence from sexual relationships was the issue in Corinth (1 Cor 7) and abstinence from certain foods emerges as an issue in Rom 14.15, 20; 1 Cor 8.8, 13, where it is a question of not eating foods that caused problems for other people in the church; in Col 2.16, 21–23 Paul is concerned with ascetic rules which he strongly rejects. The similarities with the situation at Colossae should be noted. The problem, however, was a continuing one. The creed in *Didasc.* 24 (6.12) includes the statement 'and that you make use of all his creatures with thanksgiving; and that men should marry'.[35]

Roloff, 223f., detects a sharpening of Paul's attitude (1 Cor 10.30); whereas Paul made eating or non-eating a matter of indifference, provided one acted out of thankfulness to God and concern for other Christians, here eating or non-eating has become a matter of orthodoxy and heresy and has become linked

---

[33] Lock, 48; Dornier, 73f.; Kelly, 94f.; Fee, 98f.
[34] Bernard, 65; Scott, 45; Easton, 139; Dibelius-Conzelmann, 64.
[35] Cited by Skarsaune 1994:13.

to a basic theology of creation. However, the shift in argument is due to the shift in the gravity of the situation; in Corinth Paul was not dealing with people who reckoned the material world to be evil in itself.

The part. κωλυόντων**, 'to forbid',[36] is either parallel to or explanatory of the preceding participle. γαμέω, 'to marry', can be used of man or woman.[37] The sentence continues with a construction in which the infinitive is apparently dependent on the participle 'forbidding', but this would give the opposite sense to what must be intended. The simplest proposal is to supply κελευόντων from κωλυόντων by zeugma.[38] This is quite possible and emendation is unnecessary.[39] ἀπέχομαι** is 'to keep away from, abstain'.[40] βρῶμα**, 'food', refers especially to solids as opposed to liquids (1 Cor 3.2).

3b. ἃ ὁ θεὸς ἔκτισεν εἰς μετάλημψιν μετὰ εὐχαριστίας τοῖς πιστοῖς καὶ ἐπεγνωκόσι τὴν ἀλήθειαν The rel. pron. ἃ manifestly has βρώματα as its antecedent.[41] An extension of the reference to cover both foods and marriage is very difficult, if not impossible, syntactically.[42] The writer thus does not pause to refute the former prohibition here. He has done so implicitly in ch. 2 (especially 2.15) and ch. 3 (Holtzmann, 337; Knight, 190), and in ch. 5 he will encourage marriage for younger widows. He can thus move straight on to a refutation of the second prohibition.[43]

The doctrine that God is Creator is based on the narrative in Genesis, and there may be a deliberate use of this passage from the law to refute opponents who appealed to the law. The author implicitly draws on the fact that food was created for human nourishment (Gen 1.29; 2.9, 16; 3.2; 9.3; Deut 26.11). It can,

---

[36] Rom 1.13; 1 Cor 14.39; 1 Th 2.16; Légasse, S., *EDNT* II, 332f.

[37] 5.11, 14**; 1 Cor 7.9, *et al.* Cf. Stauffer, E., *TDNT* I, 648–57; Niederwimmer, K., *EDNT* I, 235–8.

[38] BD §479²; Holtzmann, 337, but his alleged parallel in 1 Cor 14.34 is hardly close; Bernard, 65, supplies a closer parallel from Lucian, *Charon* 2: κωλύσει ἐνεργεῖν ... καὶ ... [sc. ποιήσει] ζημιοῦν, but according to BD the passage is corrupt.

[39] Nevertheless amendments to the text have been suggested: the suggestion that κελευόντων has fallen out of the text was made by Bentley (cf. WH *Notes*, 134) and Toup (cf. NA²⁷); WH suggest a primitive corruption of ἢ ἅπτεσθαι or καὶ γεύεσθαι (cf. Col 2.21) to ἀπέχεσθαι.

[40] With gen., as in Acts 15.20, 29; 1 Pet 2.11; with ἀπό 1 Th 4.3; 5.22; the active form = 'to be distant', 'to receive'; cf. *TLNT* I, 162–8. For the phrase here cf. ἀπέχεσθαι σιτίων (Plutarch, *Mor.* 157D, cited by Horstmann A., *EDNT* I, 120f.).

[41] For the lack of attraction to the gen. cf. Tit 1.2; BA *s.v.* I.4e.

[42] Fowl 1990:185 n. 3; Couser 1992:113f.; Knight, 190. The alleged parallel in Col 2.22 is not a true parallel.

[43] Roloff's claim, 223, that the author had no Pauline teaching to appeal to in respect of marriage is hardly persuasive.

therefore, be received and eaten gladly with due expression of thanks to the Creator by Christians. The form of expression is not meant to restrict eating to believers, but to emphasise that their status as believers does not prevent them eating; the truth of the gospel includes the truth of God as Creator and provider and not the false assertions put out by the opponents. There may also be the implication that the asceticism of the false teachers is a form of unbelief.

The writer summarises the account of creation[44] and draws attention to the Creator's purpose (εἰς) that people should partake of the foods which he provided.[45] The fact that they can express thanks (εὐχαριστία, 4.4; 2.1) to God for them indicates that he wishes them to have them. The reference here may be to thankfulness as a general feeling or emotion, but more like to 'a [prayer of] thanksgiving'. A specific reference to the eucharist is hardly likely (*pace* Holtz, 102). For grace at meals see Rom 14.6; 1 Cor 10.16, 30 (cf. Phil 4.6). In view of Jewish practice[46] and its specific exemplification in the practice of Jesus (cf. also Eph 5.20) this is doubtless what is meant. Those who take the view that the author is here dealing with both marriage and food restrictions have to understand the phrase as referring to prayers of thanksgiving in general (cf. Phil 4.6).

The construction of τοῖς πίστοις, 'believers' (4.10, 12), i.e. those who have come to faith, is debatable. It is either (a) dat. of advantage with ἔκτισεν (White, 122; cf. Tit 1.15); or (b) dat. of agent after the pass. verb implicit in μετάλημψιν (Holtzmann, 337; cf. Lk 23.15).

The phrase is defined more precisely by stressing that those who have come to faith acquire a true knowledge of God and of his purpose in creation (cf. Tit 1.1). The whole phrase, τοῖς πιστοῖς καὶ ἐπεγνωκόσι τὴν ἀλήθειαν, which refers to believers who have come through the process (note the perfect tense!), is an adaptation of the phrase which describes the process involved in coming to faith in 1 Tim 2.4 (... σωθῆναι καὶ εἰς ἐπίγνωσιν ἀληθείας ἐλθεῖν). Those who have come to know the gospel should know also that foods were created to be received with thanksgiving. The perf. of ἐπιγινώσκω**, 'to come to know', expresses a state of acquired knowledge of the truth contained in the gospel; elsewhere the phrase ἐπίγνωσις τῆς ἀληθείας is

---

[44] κτίζω, Rom 1.25; 1 Cor 11.9; Eph 2.10, 15; 3.9; 4.24; Col 1.16a, 16b; 3.10; Rev 4.11a, 11b; 10.6; Mt 19.4. Mk 13.19***; cf. κτίσμα, 4.4; cf. Foerster, W., *TDNT* III, 1000–35; Petzke, G., *EDNT* II, 325f.

[45] μετάλημψις*** (TR μετάληψις), 'sharing, taking, receiving'; Cl. (verb, 2 Tim 2.6; Acts 2.46). Cf. Delling, G., *TDNT* IV, 10f.

[46] 1QS 6.4f.; 10.14f.; 1Q28a 2.17–22; *Ber.* 6–8; *Ber.* 35a.

used.[47] Yet believers may be ignorant and weak and lack such knowledge (1 Cor 8.7). Oberlinner, 181, holds that the identification of believers as people who know the truth is polemical against Gnostic opponents who claimed that *they* had knowledge.

4. ὅτι πᾶν κτίσμα θεοῦ καλὸν καὶ οὐδὲν ἀπόβλητον μετὰ εὐχαριστίας λαμβανόμενον The writer expands and explains the basic objection to the heretics already given in v. 3b.[48] The explanation falls into two parts. The first part takes it for granted that the various foods were all created by God: in the light of OT teaching whatever God created is good. The reply may be an attack on Jewish food laws or on Gnostic dualism. Cf. Mk 7.15; Rom 14.14; Tit 1.14f. for Jewish food restrictions and Paul's answer in 1 Cor 10.26 using Ps 24.1. In Acts 10 the sheet let down from heaven by its four corners may symbolise the world with its four corners, everything within which is declared to be clean (Jeremias, 31).

κτίσμα is 'that which is created (sc. by God)'.[49] Paul uses κτίσις (but more of the act of creation [Rom 1.20] and of creation as a whole [Rom 8.19–22] as well as of individual created things [Rom 8.39]). Here it refers to created things as opposed to human beings (Wis 9.2; Holtzmann, 337). θεοῦ is subj. gen., '[created by] God'. καλόν (1.8; Tit 2.7 note) probably echoes Gen 1.31. Thus scriptural backing is implicitly given for the statement; again the use of the Pentateuch could be a deliberate *arg. ad hominem*.

The second part states that in view of their creation by God no foods should be rejected but should be accepted with thanksgiving to him for his provision. Oberlinner, 182f., suggests that this is stated in an extreme fashion and must be understood in its context. In other words, a distinction between the goodness and the fallenness of creation needs to be made and carried through.

It should be noted that καί introduces a separate clause with οὐδέν ('and none [of them]') as a fresh subject.[50] ἀπόβλητος*** may mean 'rejected' [sc. by God] and hence to be regarded as 'unclean'. But it may simply = ἀποβολῆς ἄξιος, 'worthy to be thrown away'.[51] There could be a distant reminiscence of the proverbial saying from Homer (*Il.* 3.65 οὔ τοι ἀπόβλητ᾽ ἐστι

---

[47] 2.4 note; Tit 1.1 note; see further 1 Clement 32.1; Hermas, *Sim.* 8.6.3; 8.11.2.

[48] The ὅτι clause is usually taken as explanatory; it could also be a noun clause, expressing the content of τὴν ἀλήθειαν (cf. Johnson, 159). The difference in meaning is minimal.

[49] Jas 1.18; Rev 5.13; 8.9***; cf. Wis 9.2; 13.5; 14.11; Ecclus 39.16, 25–7, 33–4; 3 Macc 5.11; *Ep. Arist.* 17; verb in 4.3 (note).

[50] Hence the verse is not a true parallel in form to 2 Tim 3.16; see note there.

[51] Cf. LSJ; Cl.; Philo, *Spec.* 2.169; *CH* 6.1.

θεῶν ἐρικύδεα δῶρα) which is echoed in several authors (Field 1899:208; Spicq, 499).

λαμβάνω (2 Tim 1.5**) can mean simply 'to take, receive'; but here it may have the force 'to take food [sc. into the hand and consume it]'.[52] The whole phrase creates a slightly awkward asyndeton which can be interpreted in various ways:

(a) 'Nothing is to be rejected but is to be received with thanksgiving.'

(b) 'Nothing that is received with thanksgiving is to be rejected.'

(c) 'Nothing is to be rejected if it can be received with thanksgiving.' This last is possibly the best elucidation.

5. ἁγιάζεται γὰρ διὰ λόγου θεοῦ καὶ ἐντεύξεως A further reason is added, apparently to explain the significance of 'receiving with thanksgiving'. It now becomes clear that the foods rejected by the heretics were regarded as unclean and therefore inedible. No such taint applies to foods for which Christians can give thanks.

ἁγιάζω is 'to set things aside or make them suitable for ritual purposes'.[53] The cleansing of foods rejected under Jewish food laws is probably not in mind (Roloff, 225). In the early church a distinction was drawn between foods on sale in the market place and those consumed in pagan temples. Paul remained opposed to the eating of εἰδωλόθυτα, i.e. food sacrificed to an idol and actually consumed in the temple precincts as part of a pagan religious rite.[54] Some believers may have rejected even the former on the basis of Acts 15.20, 29 (see Rom 14.5f.). But believers can claim as holy anything for which they can properly give thanks to God. This would apply, for example, to foods sacrificed to idols and available in the market which were regarded as unclean by some Christians. To be sure, for Paul nothing was unclean of itself but only to people who thought it was unclean (Rom 14.14), and therefore food cannot be really 'cleansed', but the person who thinks it unclean can purify it by prayer to God.[55] In fact, all foods are made 'holy' and therefore 'edible' by the Word of God and by prayer. It is easy to understand Christians who were worried as to whether the food was

---

[52] Bel 37 Θ; Mk 15.23; Jn 19.30; Acts 9.19; cf. BA *s.v.* For the usage with μετά cf. Libanius, *Or.* 63, p. 392.3F, μετὰ ψόγου λαμβάνειν (cited by BA).

[53] 2 Tim 2.21**; of profane things, Mt 23.19; *Act. Thom.* 71; cf. Procksch, O., *TDNT* I, 111f.

[54] Witherington III, B., 'Not so idle thoughts about *eidolothuton*', *TynBul* 44:2 (1993), 237–54.

[55] Calvin, 241, however, maintains that 'the use of all God's gifts is unclean unless it is accompanied by true knowledge and supplication of God's name.'

really edible praying that it might be made so; they were in effect praying for God to give them assurance about his good gifts.[56]

The phrase διὰ λόγου θεοῦ (cf. 2 Tim 2.9; Tit 2.5) has given rise to very varied interpretations. λόγου is anarthrous, possibly because the writer means 'a divine oracle [out of a choice of several possible ones]'. The word may be something quoted in the prayer before the meal or a separate saying. The reference may then be to:

(a) Gen 1.31 as the divine oracle by which God created the world and which once for all declares all food edible.[57] Against the objection that an OT text would not be referred to in this way, see Mt 15.6 = Mk 7.13; cf. Jn 17.14, 17 (=what God says); Rom 9.6; anarthrous, 1 Th 2.13; 1 Pet 1.23; arthrous, 2 Tim 2.9; Tit 2.5. The fact that elsewhere in the PE the phrase refers to the gospel message does not necessarily demand that reference here.

(b) A saying of Jesus, either his statement that his disciples are clean because of his word (Jn 15.3) or his promise that prayers will be heard (Jn 16.23) (Spicq, 500). But neither of these possibilities really fits the present context.

(c) A more general use of Scripture (including possibly the text in (a) above) or of scriptural language in grace before meals (cf. the use of the pres. tense, which is admittedly not decisive).[58] That the practice existed in the later church is clear from *Apost. Const.* 7.49 (cited by Bernard, 67f.).

(d) The saying of a blessing in the name of God and Christ on the food (Knoch, 33).

(e) The consecration of the elements at the eucharist (i.e. 'Do this' or 'Take, eat') understood as sanctifying the bread and wine.[59] Hasler, 35, holds that the sacramental elements stand for daily food, which is thus regarded as 'clean'.

(f) The gospel as the message that promises salvation (Hasler, 35; Roloff, 227).[60] On this view the message proclaimed by the church would include teaching about God's gift of food.

(g) The incarnate Word who blessed food for his followers' use (mentioned as a possibility by Lock, 48f.).

Views (a) and (c) are probably best. The parallelism with v. 4 and the context of refuting Jewish ideas make a reference to OT teaching most likely. The word of God is Scripture used as the

---

[56] The thought that some kind of 'extra' sanctification is conveyed (Dornier, 77f.) is rejected by Kelly, 97.

[57] Easton, 143; Houlden, 88; cf. *Didache* 10; *PK* 2.

[58] BA *s.v.* 1.b.; Holtzmann, 338; Bernard, 67f. and 74–6; Dibelius-Conzelmann, 64; Scott, 46f.; Lock, 48f.; Guthrie, 105; Jeremias, 32; Kelly, 97; Brox, 169; Spicq, 500.

[59] Cf. *Didache* 10.2f.; Justin, *Apol.* I.66.2; Hanson, 88f.; Hanson 1968:97–109.

[60] Cf. 2 Tim 2.19; Tit 1.3; 2.5; cf. 1 Tim 5.17; 2 Tim 2.15; 4.2.

basis for the prayer which specifically applies it to the food in question (cf. Kittel, G., *TDNT* IV, 118). Roloff, 227f., explores the implications for the blessing and dedication of material objects.

However we understand the preceding noun, ἔντευξις (2.1) is clearly the prayer at mealtime. But, whereas the prayer was characterised as thanksgiving in v. 4, here a word meaning 'request' is used, since the prayer could well include a request to God to cleanse or consecrate what had been 'defiled' by idolatry. 'Grace before meat disinfects even what has been offered to idols' (Chrysostom, cited by Simpson, 66). Thus Christian food is holy (1 Cor 10.30).

b. The need for instruction that leads to godliness (4.6–10)

Baugh, S. M., '"Savior of all people": 1 Tim 4:10 in context', *WTJ* 54 (1992), 331–40; Goodwin 1996; Spicq, C., 'Gymnastique et morale d'après 1 Tim 4:7–8', *RB* 54 (1947), 229–42.

Verse 6 clearly brings the previous sub-section to a conclusion and provides a transition to the next one which is at first sight concerned with the quality of Timothy as a church leader – or rather as a servant of Christ. Faithful teaching will be the evidence that he himself is nourished on good learning from Paul. By not engaging in fruitless discussions he will make space in his own life for progress in godliness. The metaphor is developed to indicate the surpassing worth of such training in godliness, and it is backed up by a trustworthy saying which states that the effort involved in such spiritual gymnastics is worthwhile because Christian hope is rooted in God who saves all who believe. What is said here is put in terms of Timothy's own spiritual progress, but it is universally applicable, especially since vv. 16f. will show that he is an example to others concerned with their salvation as well as his own. The passage could almost be a closing and summarising section. It sums up the contrast between sound teaching and godliness and the folly of the opponents.

TEXT

6. ἐντρεφόμενος ἐκτρεφόμενος (919 876 1518 242). Cf. Eph 5.29; 6.4 and LXX. Elliott, 65, 237, prefers the variant, but the MS evidence is weak and it could be assimilation to usage elsewhere in NT.

ᾗ ἧς (A 365 *pc*) is relative attraction. Cf. BA *s.v.* I.4.b. Elliott, 63, follows the text. Cf. BD § 294.

παρηκολούθηκας παρηκολούθησας (C F G *pc* WH mg); Elliott, 65, prefers the variant since the perfect is rare in PE – which proves nothing. It is the form used in 2 Tim 3.10.

10. κοπιῶμεν Praem. καί (F G 1881 TR; Kilpatrick); Elliott, 208, notes that the author likes the καί ... καί ... construction (cf. 4.16) – but this can hardly stand against the poor MS evidence.

ἀγωνιζόμεθα ὀνειδιζόμεθα (א² D 0241^vid 1739 1881 TR latt sy co WH mg; UBS mg); Holtzmann, 340; Easton, 148. Metzger, 574, says choice is not easy. But the context favours the text. (Elliott, 68, prefers in view of 2 Tim 4.7.)

ἠλπίκαμεν ἠλπίσαμεν (D* 33 WH mg). The variant is adopted by Elliott, 66. (see 3.14 and note).

EXEGESIS

6. Ταῦτα ὑποτιθέμενος τοῖς ἀδελφοῖς καλὸς ἔσῃ διάκονος Χριστοῦ 'Ιησοῦ There is a sharp change of theme. After gathering together what has been said, the author moves to a discussion of the character of the Christian leader. Such personal instruction has already been given in 1.3, 18f., but will figure again in 6.2b, 11–14, 17, 20; 2 Tim 1.6; 2.1, 4–8, 14f., 22, 3.10f.; 4.1–5; Tit 2.1, 15; 3.8. Although Timothy is addressed, he is meant to be an example to the church readers (Knoch, 33).

ταῦτα (Tit 2.15 note) must refer to what has just been said and cannot refer forwards (Holtzmann, 338). Some think that the scope includes 2.1–4.5 (Parry, 26; Fee, 110); but others hold that only the prophecy is meant (i.e. 4.1–5, Oberlinner, 188). More probably, 4:3b–5 is specifically in mind: Timothy is to share with the congregation the refutation of the opponents (cf. Wolter 1988:146). ὑποτίθημι[61] is used in the mid. to mean 'to suggest, point out something to somebody, recommend'; 'to enjoin, order'; 'to make known, teach'.[62] It has been claimed that the thought is more of suggestion;[63] there is an element of discussion and brotherly exhortation towards the faithful contrasted with the more authoritative attitude to the heretics (cf. Roloff, 241). Nevertheless, Oberlinner, 188f., argues that the thought is of conveying authoritative teaching, based on what Paul has said.[64] Hanson, 89f., thinks that only the 'ordained ministers' may teach, in contrast to the situation in Paul's time; the text hardly requires this interpretation.

ἀδελφός, 'brother' (literal, 5.1), is common for members of the same group, especially religious group (6:2; 2 Tim 4.21**).[65] Easton, 180, comments that its use is 'scanty' in the PE, but it is equally rare in Eph (twice). The religious usage is ambiguous:

---

[61] Act. 'to lay down', hence 'to risk' (Rom 16.4***; cf. 1 Clement 63.1).

[62] When Scott, 47f., suggests that the word 'carries with it the idea of putting something beneath their feet' and regards the preceding precepts as being 'like stepping-stones', he is plainly committing the etymological fallacy.

[63] So Chrysostom, PG LXII, 559, cited by Kelly, 98. Philo, Mos. 2.51 contrasts it with κελεύω.

[64] Cf. Philo, Post. 12; Josephus, Bel. 2.137; Ant. 1.76.

[65] Cf. Soden, H. von, TDNT I, 144–6; Beutler, J., EDNT I, 28–30.

are the brothers the members of the church (see Fee, 102) or the leaders (cf. 2 Tim 4.21)? Although Ellis 1978:13–22, developed a case that 'brothers' could signify 'co-workers', he did not apparently apply his hypothesis to this verse. It is so understood by Schlarb 1990:282, 289, who argues that the passage then becomes evidence for the passing on of the apostolic teaching to Timothy's successors. But nothing requires this limitation of reference here. The reference must surely be to the members of the church who are threatened by the heresy.[66] The use of the term means that Timothy is a brother to the members of the congregation, but is not inconsistent with his holding a position of authority (Oberlinner, 189).

ἔσῃ is a logical future. καλός, when used of a teacher, implies that he does the job well (in God's sight). διάκονος (3.8 and note) here has the broader sense of a servant of Christ.[67]

ἐντρεφόμενος τοῖς λόγοις τῆς πίστεως καὶ τῆς καλῆς διδασκαλίας ᾗ παρηκολούθηκας Language used in Stoic references to education is here adapted to Christian nurture (Hanson, 89). ἐντρέφω*** is 'to bring up, rear, train in',[68] hence 'to nourish on' (Epictetus 4.4.48). If the form is mid., it will mean 'deepening in, nourishing yourself on', if pass., 'educated in'. The reference (present participle!) is not simply to Timothy's past upbringing (as NIV) but primarily to his continuing nourishment (Holtzmann, 338; Fee, 103), and the expression indicates that the effects of the teaching are not narrowly intellectual.

The force of the participle may be: (a) 'provided that you are nourished...'; or (b) 'if you give them this [sound] teaching, it shows that you yourself are a good servant of Christ Jesus, [and that you are] nourished by...'. View (b) fits the logic of the passage better.

τοῖς λόγοις τῆς πίστεως, 'the words of the faith' is not equivalent to 'faithful words' (Tit 1.9), but to other phrases that sum up the truth expressed in the gospel. It is almost synonymous with the next phrase: καὶ τῆς καλῆς διδασκαλίας 'and [the words] of the good teaching'. This wording is not paralleled; it gives a contrast with the teachings of demons (4.1) and is close to the 'good deposit' in 2 Tim 1.14. The 'goodness' of the teacher depends on the 'goodness' of what he himself has learned and now imparts. ᾗ is the correct case with the verb παρακολουθέω (Lk 1.3; [Mk 16.17]; 2 Tim 3.10***). The verb means lit. 'to follow, accompany, attend' ([Mk 16.17] Papias 2.4, 15);

---

[66] It is unlikely that the word excludes the women members of the churches!

[67] Col 1.7; 2 Cor 11.23; used of servants of God, 2 Cor 6.4 and Rom 13.4a, 4b (of magistrates).

[68] Plato, Leg. 7, 798A; Philo, Spec. 1.314; Leg. Gai. 195 (of instruction in τοῖς ἱεροῖς γράμμασιν); Josephus, Bel. 6.102, of law; Ap. 1.269.

fig. 'to follow with the mind, understand, make one's own';[69] hence 'to follow faithfully, as a rule'.[70] The sense is that Timothy has become familiar with the teaching over a period of time and follows it. The thought is developed more fully in 2 Tim 3.10–16.

7. τοὺς δὲ βεβήλους καὶ γραώδεις μύθους παραιτοῦ The thought proceeds by a double contrast. The positive exhortation in v. 6 is followed by a negative prohibition of the kind of teaching characteristic of the opponents. But then this in turn is followed by a further positive exhortation.

The prohibition is expressed rather forcefully (Spicq, 503). The kind of teaching to be avoided is that associated with the opponents and already characterised as μύθοι (1.4 note; Tit 1.14 note). Out of the possible references of the word the most likely is to any kind of superstitious nonsense based on OT material. Could it possibly refer to stories of what will happen to people if they eat the forbidden foods? In any case, such teaching is βέβηλος (1.9 and note), 'profane, defiling', and so devoid of 'any Divine or sacred character' (Hort 1894:138). It is further denigrated by the use of the adj. γραώδης***, 'characteristic of old women'. This derogatory expression (cf. Eng. 'old wives' tales') was quite common in philosophical circles.[71] Finally, we have the strong verb παραιτέομαι, here with acc. of thing, 'to reject, avoid'.[72] It could mean that Timothy himself is to avoid teaching such stuff, or that he is not to enter into debate with opponents who teach it, or that he is to reject such teaching when it is given by others and prevent them teaching it, or a combination of all these. The contrast that follows strongly suggests that Timothy himself is not to waste his time with myths or with those who teach them. He is not to get involved in it so as to leave himself free for better things, rather than that he is to prevent others from teaching it (for which cf. 1.3).

Γύμναζε δὲ σεαυτὸν πρὸς εὐσέβειαν A different kind of activity (δέ) is recommended. Alongside the metaphor of being nourished by spiritual food (v. 6) we now have an application of the

---

[69] Polybius 3.32.2; Epictetus 1.7.33; Vettius Valens 276, 23.

[70] Dittenberger, *Syll.* 718.9 (c. I BC); 885.32 (III BC) P. Tebt. 124.4 (I BC); 2 Macc 9.27 *v.l.*; 'following a teaching which has been grasped' (Kittel, G., *TDNT* I, 215f.; cf. MM 485f.). The meaning of the term in Lk 1.3 has been much debated; it may refer to the author's investigation of his subject-matter or to his personal involvement with what had happened.

[71] Plato, *Rep.* 1, 350E: γραῦσι ταῖς τοὺς μύθους λεγούσαις; *Gorg.* 527a: μύθοι ὥσπερ γραός; Strabo 1.2.3: γρ. μυθολογία; Cleomedes 2.1, p. 162.14 H Ziegler: μυθαρίῳ γραώδει πιστεύσας; Galen XI 792 K; εἰς μύθους γραῶν ἐξετράπετο; Lucian, *Philops.* 9; γραῶν μύθοι; Epictetus 2.16.39; *TLNT* I, 285 n. 5.

[72] Cl.; Epictetus 2.16.42; *Ep. Arist.* 184; Philo *Post.* 2; Josephus, *Ant.* 3.212; 5.233; Diognetus 4.2; 6.10; so 2 Tim 2.23; Acts 25.11; Tit 3.10 note.

metaphor of exercise to what we would call Christian growth.
Bodily exercise and competitive sport were highly esteemed in
Greece and became metaphors for mental and spiritual striving
for perfection. The idea of competition faded away in this
connection, and concentration on bodily exercise alone was
regarded as inadequate. Similar ideas developed in Hellenistic
Judaism, but were linked to the development of godliness.[73]

γυμνάζω, 'to exercise the (often naked) body, train' (2 Macc
10.15; Josephus, *Ant.* 6.185), is used fig. of mental and spiritual
powers (Heb 5.14; 12.11; 2 Pet 2.14***).[74] πρός means 'in
relation to'; i.e. Timothy is to carry out the kind of exercise which
promotes godly behaviour (εὐσέβεια; see **Excursus 1**) or a godly
character as opposed to a fit body (cf. Spicq, 505 on syntax).
The thought is of the spiritual discipline which helps a person
to become godly. In practice this will refer to the fulfilment of
the requirements in the household rules and virtue lists and
readiness to suffer for the gospel. Some scholars take it to be a
contrast to the effort required to maintain an ascetic outlook
(Brox, 172f.; Roloff, 245f.).

8. ἡ γὰρ σωματικὴ γυμνασία πρὸς ὀλίγον ἐστὶν ὠφέλιμος The
value and necessity of spiritual exercise is explained (γάρ).
Possibly a secular proverb, originally referring to philosophy, has
been Judaised or Christianised (Merkel, 37); if so, this explains
how the writer can talk of pious exercises, since elsewhere he
emphasises that salvation is a gift.

The point is made by a contrast with bodily exercise which
was current in the ancient world.[75] γυμνασία***, 'training',
usually refers to bodily exercise (Dittenberger, *Syll.* 1673.19),
but can also be used figuratively.[76] Here the reference is fixed by
the adj. σωματικός, 'bodily, corporeal', i.e. 'being, consisting of
a body' (Lk 3.22***), or, as here, 'pertaining, referring to the
body'. Its value (ὠφέλιμος, Tit 3.8 note) is relativised. πρὸς
ὀλίγον may mean 'for a short time' (cf. Jas 4.4); but this is
excluded by the contrasting πρὸς πάντα; hence the meaning
must be 'for a little' (BA). However, the rendering 'of no profit'
(Easton, 145; cf. Col 2.20–23) surely goes too far; a limited value

[73] See Wis 10.12; 4 Macc 9.23; 11.20; 17.11–16; *T. Job* 27; *T. Ash.* 6.2; 4 Ezra
7.88, 92 (see the excellent summary in Roloff, 243–5).
[74] This is a Stoic usage, not found in the LXX (cf. Epictetus 1.26.3; *et al.*;
Philo, *Mos.* 1.48; Josephus, *Ant.* 3.15. Cf. γυμνασία (4.8); Oepke, A., *TDNT* I,
775f. For the construction with σεαυτόν cf. Ps-Isocrates, *Ad Demonicum* 21:
γύμναζε σεαυτὸν πόνοις ἑκουσίοις (cited by BA).
[75] Josephus, *Ap.* 2.217f. cf. further Seneca, *Ep. Mor.* 15.2, 5; 80.2, cited by
Lightfoot, J. B., *Philippians* (London: Macmillan, 1890), 290.
[76] Plato, *Leg.* 648c; Polybius 1.1; Plato, *Theaet.* 169c, of philosophical disputes
(cf. Philo, *Prob.* 88); 4 Macc 11.20 of martyrdom.

is allotted. Towner, 107, cites the *Epistles of Crates* 3; 'Take care of your soul, but take care of the body only to the degree that necessity requires.'[77]

But with what exactly is the writer comparing godliness? Two different possibilities have been suggested:

(a) Physical training (e.g. running, jumping). We would then have the same kind of contrast as Paul draws in 1 Cor 9.24–27 (Holtzmann, 339), where he is thinking of the effort to curb sinful, bodily passions. A reference to the limited value of bodily exercise seems perfectly possible in the context.

(b) Ascetic restrictions (e.g. abstinence from food) to restrain sinful passions, as practised by the opponents, seem more likely to many commentators.[78] Kelly, 100, takes 'bodily training' as a 'caricature description of the exclusively physical self-discipline practised by the sectaries' rather than 'metaphorically as referring to ascetic self-mortification'. But it is hard to see any real distinction between the two. Similarly, Oepke, A., *TDNT* I, 775f., states that there is 'no attack on Hellenic development of the body, as lexical association might seem to demand (cf. v. 7), but rather a rejection of narrow encratitic strivings (cf. 4:3; 5:23; Tt. 1:15)'. This interpretation would allow a limited value to asceticism, unless Easton, 145, is right in saying that the author means 'really of "no value at all"'. But there is no evidence that γυμνασία can have this meaning. It is not attested.[79]

It seems much more likely that, having used γυμνάζω metaphorically in v. 7, the writer dwells on the idea and develops it by means of a contrast with the literal sense (Holtzmann, 339; Dornier, 80). The asceticism in 4.3 is so thoroughly rejected that even a limited approbation of it here is very unlikely (Simpson, 68). Roloff, 246, recognises that a Hellenistic-Jewish maxim is being quoted which originally referred to bodily exercise, but holds that the author has re-applied it to ascetic practices, which he cannot wholly reject since Paul himself practised them. But there is a clear distinction between what Paul practised, namely the restraint of sinful passions and the willingness to suffer for the sake of the gospel, and the kind of asceticism mentioned here, even if the opponents may have claimed his authority for their practices.

Roloff, 244f., also attacks the view that vv. 7–10 are concerned with all believers and their goal of spiritual perfection: for them

---

[77] Cf. the Essene attitude in Philo, *Hyp.* 11.7 (Dornier, 79).

[78] Cf. 4.1–5; so Calvin, 243; Easton, 145; Brox, 173; Towner, 107; Lea-Griffin, 134f.; Pfitzner 1967:171–7; cf. *EDNT* III, 511f.

[79] Note that the word ἄσκησις was used for the physical training of athletes, doubtless including dieting.

bodily exercise is of limited value and must be integrated into the moral and spiritual conflict. Against this view he argues that the passage is concerned with missionaries and their striving in the work of the gospel:

(a) The context is concerned with the asceticism of the opponents, and the picture of bodily exercise could easily be applied to this. Then v. 8 is concerned to reject the wrong kind of exercise, as in the Hellenistic Jewish tradition (Philo, *Spec.* 2.91; of different kinds of physical training; Josephus, *Ap.* 2.217f.).

(b) In the context 8b is not the central statement but rather v. 10 which brings the theological interpretation of the picture.

(c) Verse 10 shows that the struggle is for the gospel and the particular task of the apostle; 'we' signifies the apostle and his co-workers.

But against this view it can be urged: (a) If adopted, it would give some value to the kind of asceticism practised by the opponents. (b) The gospel is the concern of all believers and not just of church leaders. (c) The reference of v. 11 becomes vague. Why is Timothy to teach these things to people who are not required to follow them? (d) The application in v. 9 is unambiguously universal.

ἡ δὲ εὐσέβεια πρὸς πάντα ὠφέλιμός ἐστιν ἐπαγγελίαν ἔχουσα ζωῆς τῆς νῦν καὶ τῆς μελλούσης εὐσέβεια is regarded in effect as 'spiritual exercise'[80] which needs to be 'practised'. Such exercise is worth practice since it carries (ἔχουσα) the promise of eternal life. ἐπαγγελία, Cl. 'announcement', is here (with gen. of source, content) 'promise, pledge, offer' (2 Tim 1.1**; also found as a *v.l.* in 1 Tim 1.1 [א]).[81] The thought is similar to Eph 6.2, where keeping the commandment carries with it the promise of divine reward. However, it would be mistaken to contrast this emphasis on reward for keeping commandments with that on faith found elsewhere in the NT. As the expression of faith and obedience towards God, godliness is the path to receiving what he promises (Tit 1.2). The reference to two kinds of life might suggest that eternal life is purely a thing of the world to come, but the writer can hardly mean that godliness leads to a good existence on a purely worldly level as well. 'Life' must cover both the present and the future dimensions of salvation. μέλλουσα (1.16 note) obviously refers to future, eternal life.[82] Qualified by νῦν used adjectivally (6.17; Tit 2.12 note), ζωή may refer to:

---

[80] The word is used by brachylogy for ἡ πρὸς εὐσέβειαν γυμνασία (Parry, 26).

[81] Josephus, *Ant.* 3.77; Heb 9.15; 2 Pet 3.4; for the verb ἐπαγγέλλομαι see 2.10; Tit 1.2 note. Cf. Friedrich, G., and Schniewind, J., *TDNT* II, 576–86.

[82] Cf. the usage with αἰών Mt 12.32; Eph 1.21; 2 Clement 6.3; Polycarp 5.2; cf. Heb 6.5; with καιρός Barnabas 4.1; and also 2 Clement 20.2; 5.5; Heb 2.5; 13.14; *et al.*

(a) Physical life as such. This view assumes that there is a contrast between (present) physical life and (future) spiritual life, but it is unlikely that godliness contains the promise of the former. Therefore one kind of life in its two temporal stages must be meant.[83] Hence the second reference is to be preferred.

(b) Spiritual blessings now. Cf. Ps 90.16 for promise of long life and salvation. The saying of Jesus in Mt 19.29 = Mk 10.30 = Lk 18.30 may be echoed (Kelly, 101). For the combination cf. also *'Abot* 6.4, 7.

9. πιστὸς ὁ λόγος καὶ πάσης ἀποδοχῆς ἄξιος The verse gives the 'faithful saying' rubric in its full form; it is identical to 1.15 with no textual variants. But to what saying does it refer?[84]

(a) All of the preceding sentence (4.8a, b, which sounds proverbial);[85]

(b) 4.8b only (Kelly, 101; Fee, 104f.);

(c) The following sentence (4.10a,b).[86] Roloff, 240, holds that v. 10 is the climax of the section rather than v. 8, and that it is a paraphrase of Col 1.29 and therefore in effect a piece of tradition;

(d) 4.10b only;[87]

(e) Yet another possibility is that in effect the rubric refers to the whole saying in vv. 8 and 10 taken together as a recommendation of godliness and then a fuller description of it (Oberlinner, 196).

A backward reference is clearly required. Verse 10 is a personal statement rather than a doctrinal statement and is unlikely (at least in itself) to be the 'saying'.[88] Fee argues that v. 10 is simply a reflection on v. 8b; only 8b has the form of a saying, whereas 8a is constructed for the sake of the contrast. Schlarb 1990:210 appears to maintain that v. 10 really takes up v. 7. Verse 8 and v. 10 both offer comments on v. 7, v. 8 defining godliness and v. 10 explaining the need for spiritual exertion in a doxological statement. The only question then is whether the saying is simply v. 8 (or part thereof) and v. 10 is a backup comment on it, or whether v. 10 is in effect part of the saying. Whichever view be adopted (the former is preferable), the effect of the rubric is to underline the importance of godliness for all believers.

---

[83] The double use of the article may be due to the two different constructions that are being employed rather than to a distinction between two objects.

[84] We can ignore the view that it is merely a solemn connective with no real reference (Hanson, 91).

[85] Lock, 51; Dornier, 80; Barrett, 70; Spicq, 508; Brox, 177; Knight, 198; Arichea-Hatton, 100; Stott, 117f.; Couser 1992:104f.

[86] Cf. use of γάρ as in 2 Tim 2.11; REB; Guthrie, 107; Easton, 146; Hasler, 37.

[87] So apparently NIV which punctuates v. 10a very awkwardly as a parenthesis.

[88] The use of γάρ in v. 10 may further appear to rule out that verse as the saying, but cf. 2 Tim 2.11.

10. εἰς τοῦτο γὰρ κοπιῶμεν καὶ ἀγωνιζόμεθα, ὅτι ἠλπίκαμεν ἐπὶ θεῷ ζῶντι, ὅς ἐστιν σωτὴρ πάντων ἀνθρώπων μάλιστα πιστῶν The final verse in the sub-section has the effect of backing up what has been said but at the same time brings in fresh material. The truth of what has been said and the need for all believers to accept is confirmed by the fact that (γάρ) Christian 'exercise' expressed in hard toil for the gospel has as its end in view the fulfilment of their hope in God to grant salvation to all believers. The thought is akin to that in Col 1.29, which may be echoed (see especially Roloff, 247). The language, however, is not so close and shows clear signs of the author's own style.

εἰς τοῦτο probably links backwards and means (a) 'for this reason', i.e. because godliness leads to life (v. 8) (Dibelius-Conzelmann, 68f.); or (b) 'with this aim'. γάρ is hardly 'and' (as in NIV, which awkwardly takes it with v. 10a as a parenthesis). κοπιάω can mean either (a) 'to become weary, tired'; or (b) 'to work hard, toil, struggle, strive' (2 Tim 2.6). Here it is used in the latter sense of missionary work (5.17, of elders) – possibly regarded as Christian exercise.[89] ἀγωνίζομαι, 'to struggle' (6.12; 2 Tim 4.7**) can express two metaphors: (a) 'to engage in an athletic contest' (1 Cor 9.25); (b) 'to fight, struggle'.[90] The ἀγών word-group was used in Hellenism for the moral struggle against the passions. It entered Hellenistic Judaism as a metaphor for life according to the law (Wis 4.2; 10.12; Philo, *Agr.* 113), including the need to suffer for it (4 Macc 9.23f.; 17.11–16) and for battling against Satan and the evil impulse (*T. Ash.* 6.2; 4 Ezra 7.88, 127). It was used by Paul for the hardship and risky life of the Christian believer surrounded by opponents (Phil 1.30) and especially of the missionary working for the gospel and the care of the congregations (1 Th 2.2; Col 1.29), and praying zealously (Rom 15.30; Col 4.12). The link here with κοπιάω (cf. Col 1.29) may suggest that missionary work is particularly (but not exclusively) in mind, and that this is therefore a missionary slogan which backs up the exhortation to the congregation and at the same time encourages Timothy and other Christian leaders to the hard work of mission because their hope is fixed on a God who wishes to save all people (and needs missionaries to carry out his purpose). The word appears here to pick up the

---

[89] Cf. 1 Cor 15.10; Col 1.29; Phil 2.16; *et al.*; cf. Hauck, F., *TDNT* III, 827–30; *TLNT* II, 322–9.

[90] Jn 18.36; fig. Col 1.29; 4.12; Lk 13.24***; 1 Clement 35.4; Barnabas 4.5. See MM 8; Stauffer, E., *TDNT* I, 135–40; Dautzenberg, G., *EDNT* I, 25–7; Pfitzner 1967. (The *v.l.* ὀνειδιζόμεθα ['to be reproached', Rom 15.3; 1 Pet 4.14; Mt 5.11; 11.20; Lk 6.22; Mk 15.32; 16.14] brings in a combination of toil and persecution which seems less appropriate in this context; cf. Schneider, J., *TDNT* V, 239f.).

earlier reference to spiritual exercise, thus continuing the athletic metaphor (Fee, 105).[91]

The basis for striving follows.[92] This clause is seen as a paraphrase of Col 1.28 by Roloff, 247. The strife is not for personal fulfilment and perfection but for the sake of the gospel. But this would be true for all believers and not just for apostles and other leaders.

The perf. of ἐλπίζω (3.14; cf. Tit 1.1 note) conveys the thought of having fixed one's hopes on somebody.[93] God is the living God (3.15 and note; 1 Th 1.9) inasmuch as he gives the promise of life (4.8). The force of σωτήρ (1.1; Tit 1.3b note) is disputed: (a) 'Preserver, sustainer';[94] (b) 'Saviour, who offers salvation to all people'.[95] Those who take the former view are almost compelled to allow that the word has a double sense; thus Barrett, 70, has God preserving all people in life but also preserving the faithful through this life until they attain the life of the world to come. The latter view is therefore to be preferred, and the problems in the phrase are to be solved by a correct interpretation of the genitive phrase which follows.

The universal scope of salvation is expressed by πάντων (cf. 2.3f. for the same stress). The whole phrase is paralleled in Hellenistic Greek.[96] Adoption of the traditional translation of μάλιστα (Tit 1.10 note) as 'especially' (so most scholars) leads to some strained exegesis. The usual solution is to distinguish between the 'all' to whom salvation is offered and the believers who accept the offer (Dornier, 81). Kelly, 102f., distinguishes between believers who have assurance of salvation and others who may obtain salvation. Easton, 146, is forced to regard the phrase as addition to original formula (like Phil 2.8b in the opinion of some scholars). These problems disappear if we accept the other possible translation, 'to be precise, namely, I mean' (Skeat:1979, 173–7). 'All' is thus limited here to believers'

[91] Cf. Pfitzner 1967:175–7, who emphasises that the struggle is not for the cultivation of moral virtue, as in Cynic-Stoic philosophy. This view, he argues, rests on a misunderstanding of εὐσέβεια as a moral virtue, and he suggests that Spicq* tended to fall into this error.

[92] ὅτι must mean 'because', not 'that' (NIV); poss. 'in that'.

[93] Cf. 5.5; 6.17; Jn 5.45; 2 Cor 1.10; 1 Cor 15.19; cf. McKay 1985:223; for the use with ἐπί and dat. cf. 6.17; Rom 15.12 (Isa 11.10); Barnabas 12.2f; See further 1 Jn 3.3; Ps 7.2; 15 (MT 16).1.

[94] Calvin, 245; Guthrie, 108; Barrett, 70; Simpson, 69 (citing Ps 35 [MT 36].7, but then claiming that the word has a double significance!); Baugh 1992:331–40 argues for 'benefactor'.

[95] Easton, 146; Kelly, 102; Knight, 203, in view of parallel with 2.3f.

[96] Cf. P.Petr. III.20 I.15 (246 BC) πάντων σωτῆρα. Heracles is τῆς γῆς καὶ τῶν ἀνθρώπων σωτήρ (Dio Chrysostom 1.84). Aelius Aristides 45.20K (8, p. 90D) of Serapis: κηδεμόνα καὶ σωτῆρα πάντων ἀνθρώπων αὐτάρκη θεόν (cited by BA).

(Knight, 203; cf. Ger. *erst recht*, Jeremias, 32; Holtz, 98),[97] but the universal emphasis remains: all people are potentially believers.

According to Dibelius-Conzelmann, 69, the contrast between men and believers is indicative of the position of a later generation. 'For Paul all men are, theoretically, capable of becoming believers. The Pastorals are reconciled to the fact that the faithful represent only a portion of humanity. Thus the church is not just a preliminary form of the kingdom but already its substitute.' This judgement is both vague and misguided. The issue is rightly grasped by Roloff, 248: because God is potentially the Saviour of all but only those who believe are saved, there arises the necessity for the spiritual battle to which the apostle and his co-workers are committed. Thus it is the context of this battle which leads to the apparently unusual phraseology here. Brox, 178, correctly notes that it is not said that one can also be saved without faith.

c. Timothy as a teacher (4.11–16)

Brox, N., 'Προφητεία im ersten Timotheusbrief', *BZ* 29 (1976), 229–32; Daube, D., *The New Testament and Rabbinic Judaism* (London: Athlone, 1956), 244–6; Dekkers, E., 'Προφητεία-praefatio', in *Mélanges offerts à Mademoiselle Chr. Mohrmann* (Utrecht-Antwerpen, 1963), 190–5; Ehrhardt, A., *The Framework of the New Testament Stories* (Manchester: Manchester University Press, 1964); Fee 1994:771–6; Ferguson, E., 'Laying on of Hands: Its Significance in Ordination', *JTS* ns 26 (1975), 1–12; Hofius, O., 'Zur Auslegungsgeschichte von πρεσβυτέριον 1 Tim 4,14', *ZNW* 62 (1971), 128f.; Jeremias, J., 'ΠΡΕΣΒΥΤΕΡΙΟΝ ausserchristlich bezeugt', *ZNW* 48 (1957), 127–32; idem, 'Zur Datierung der Pastoralbriefe', *ZNW* 52 (1961), 101–4 (reprinted in Jeremias 1966:314–16); Katz, P., 'Appendix: Πρεσβυτέριον in 1 Tim 4,14 and Susanna 50', *ZNW* 51 (1960), 27–30; Lips 1979:160–6, 183–265; Mantel, H., 'Ordination and Appointment in the Period of the Temple', *HTR* 57 (1964), 325–46; Roloff, 263–81; Skeat 1979; Spicq, 722–30; Warkentin 1982:136–52; Ysebaert 1994:151–64.

This sub-section, which forms a bridge between more specific units of church instruction, constitutes a personal appeal to Timothy to be courageous, active and diligent in the task of teaching, ignoring his disadvantage of youth and relying on the power of the Spirit. The concentration of imperatives (ten!) is remarkable.[98] There is a significant stress on his being an example to others, which indicates that the qualities expected in a church leader are to be encouraged in the members of the church generally – including the ability to speak. There is a twofold

---

[97] It is less likely that Gal 6.10 is an example of this meaning in view of the use of δέ.

[98] Cf. Ps-Pythagoras, *Carmen Aureum*, 45f., cited by Dibelius-Conzelmann, 72.

emphasis on the hard work which Timothy must put in to his
Christian life and service and on the spiritual resources which
he needs if he is to be able boldly to uphold the truths in 4.6–10
and to refute the heretics (4.7). The personal life and the work
of the church leader are closely related and cannot be separated
from one another. Roloff, 250, argues that the theme is rather
the relationship of Timothy to the congregation, but it is evident
that the concern is more with duties than with relationships and
especially with his example to the congregation.

Some commentators take this section as the beginning of the
set of instructions about how to deal with specific problems and
people in the church (Roloff, 250; NA²⁷ has a major break here).
A general instruction about how to behave as a church leader
is then followed by more specific pieces of instruction. Roloff
includes 5.1f. in this section, although it surely forms a section
on its own, comparable with the much longer section that follows
on widows. The boundaries between the various sections are
narrow, and it seems probable that 4.11–16 is tied more closely
to 4.6–10 than to what follows.

TEXT

12. ἐν ἀγάπῃ Add ἐν πνεύματι (K L P 69 2344 TR sy Thdt); Praem. (257).
Elliott, 70, accepts the addition on the ground that items were easily omitted
from lists, with the confusion that could be caused by the repetition of ἐν. But
Metzger, 574, rejects it on the basis of the best Alexandrian and Western evidence.
Fee 1994:770f. notes that none of the textual evidence is earlier than the ninth
century and that the variant was unknown to Chrysostom.

14. πρεσβυτερίου πρεσβυτέρου (ℵ* 69* 1881ᶜ); Elliott, 71f., rejects the variant
as an accidental slip.

πᾶσιν Praem. ἐν (D¹ Ψ 1881 TR vgᵐˢˢ). Cf. 2 Tim 1.7; 4.5; Tit 2.9. Elliott, 72,
regards the omission as a stylistic improvement.

16. ἔπεχε πρόσεχε (6 33 88 206 424** 436 1799). Elliott, 72, says that the
variant fits in with PE usage and ἔπεχε is an Atticistic improvement. But the
MS evidence is too weak.

EXEGESIS

11. Παράγγελλε ταῦτα καὶ δίδασκε The opening phrase is
paralleled in general structure by 6.2b and Tit 2.15, and has the
same function as 4.6. In each case there is a verb expressing
teaching and a verb expressing command or exhortation.

1 Tim 4.11	παράγγελλε ταῦτα		καὶ	δίδασκε
6.2		ταῦτα δίδασκε	καὶ	παρακάλει
1 Tit 2.15		ταῦτα λάλει	καὶ	παρακάλει

Timothy is commanded to provide authoritative directions and
instruction for the church. παραγγέλλω is used of authoritative

instruction and commands by a church leader.[99] ταῦτα must refer generally backwards;[100] it cannot refer forwards. For διδάσκω see 2.12 and note. The order of command followed by instruction is mildly surprising (contrast the parallels above); but the stress in the preceding passage was on heretical practices and the need for practical piety. The command refers to what has been said already and makes it the object of transmission to the church, but it does so in a rather general sort of way.[101] Rather than referring specifically to what has just been written, it refers to what may be taken out of it as exhortation and instruction for the church. Hence there is some doubt as to whether the formula closes the preceding section (Roloff, 248; Oberlinner, 199; Schlarb 1990:280f.) or introduces the new one by acting as a bridge. Holtzmann's view, 340f., that it simply repeats v. 6 and closes the section is improbable. Hanson, 92, sees it as purely a formula of transition to the specific instruction to Timothy. Most probably it takes up what has just been said and makes instruction in it part of what Timothy is to do in the church.

12. Μηδείς σου τῆς νεότητος καταφρονείτω Timothy has been told to give authoritative instruction to the church. But his position of comparative youth may make him reluctant to do so. The situation envisaged is one in which a younger person is to have authority in relation to older people, which would be against the custom of the time. Two points are made. On the one hand, he is not to be despised because of his youth. This should be understood as primarily an encouragement to Timothy not to be intimidated by other people, and secondarily as a word to the congregation not to show disdain towards him.[102] On the other hand, he is to act in such a way as to be an example of godly living, with the implication that this will win him the respect of the other people who may be measuring him by human standards.

The command in the first part of the verse is paralleled in an identical context in Tit 2.15 (see note), where there is the same danger that the authority of the church leader will be challenged, and there is an echo of 1 Cor 16.11.

In contrast to Tit 2.15, which has περιφρονείτω, here we have καταφρονέω, 'to look down on, despise, scorn, treat

---

[99] 1.3 and note; with acc. as in 5.7; Philo, *Spec.* 3.80; 2 Th 3.4.
[100] Either to 4.1–10, Spicq, 511, or 4.7–10, if Lips 1979:95 n. 4 is correct; cf 3.14; Tit 2.15 and notes.
[101] Cf. 5.7; 6.2b; 2 Tim 2.2, 14; Tit 2.15; 3.8.
[102] Cf. Tit 2.15 and note; Brox, 178f; Roloff, 251; *pace* Oberlinner, 202, who holds that, since the office is the significant thing and the personality of the holder is secondary, the directive must be concerned with correcting church attitudes.

with contempt' (6.2 of slaves with reference to their believing masters).[103] σου may be construed either with the verb, as in Tit 2.15, or with νεότητος;[104] the meaning is scarcely affected. Elsewhere in the NT νεότης, 'youth', is always found in the stereotyped phrase ἐκ νεότητος (Mk 10.20; Lk 18.21; Acts 26.4***).

For age groups at this time see Tit 2.2 note. In Acts 7.58 Paul is young. Jeremias, 34, says Timothy was called in AD 49, so would now be in his 30s. Bernard, 70, estimates his age at 30, Simpson, 69, at 35–40; but Easton, 146, thinks that he is envisaged here as not much more than 25. He would probably have to be less than 40 years old to be accounted 'young' at this point, and there is evidence that in some circles 50 was the minimum age for official positions (Spicq, 512). But the term may be simply relative compared with Paul or with the members of the church (cf. Hasler, 37). The significant point is the way in which the church leader is young compared with the other members and hence his position needs to be asserted.

The subordination of youth and reverence for the old were a standard part of ancient culture.[105] The appointment of younger people as missionaries and leaders led to friction in the early church (1 Cor 16.11). Ignatius, *Mag.* 3.1 similarly tells the church not to despise its youthful bishop, but to reverence him as the presbyters are doing (Brox 1976). Cf. *Apost. Const.* 2.1. Hence for some commentators the author is using a fictitious epistolary situation (based on the picture of Timothy as a young man in 1 Cor 16.10f.) to deal with a widespread problem in the developing churches at a time when the elder system' was being replaced by an episcopal system and authority based on age was being replaced by authority based on appointment and position (Roloff, 251). Oberlinner, 203f., wishes to generalise the problem to cover any kind of perceived lack or weakness in the officebearers and to regard the statement as being based on a legitimation of the offices in terms of the authority which arises from their apostolic appointment. Here we would then have the roots of apostolic succession! This is to over-interpret the text.

ἀλλὰ τύπος γίνου τῶν πιστῶν ἐν λόγῳ, ἐν ἀναστροφῇ, ἐν ἀγάπῃ, ἐν πίστει, ἐν ἁγνείᾳ Positively Timothy is urged to use

---

[103] Mt 6.24; 18.10; Lk 16.13; Rom 2.4; 1 Cor 11.22; Heb 12.2; 2 Pet 2.10***; the verb is used in pap. of defenceless people who have been wronged (MM 334f.); cf. Schneider, C., *TDNT* III, 631f.; *TLNT* II, 280–4. There is a verbal parallel to the present passage in Diodorus Siculus 17.7.1: καταφρόνησας τῆς Ἀλεξάνδρου νεότητος; cf. P. Genève. 6.13 in BA 855.

[104] For the former see Parry, 28; for the latter see BA 1085; Field 1899:209; Holtzmann, 341.

[105] E.g. Plato, *Rep.* 3.412C; *Tim.* 34c; Ecclus 32.7–9; detail in Spicq, 511f.

his position as a leader to present[106] an example (τύπος; Tit 2.7 and note) to the believers of how to live. The gen. τῶν πίστων (cf. 4.3; 5.16) has the force 'to believers' (1 Pet 5.3; 1 Cor 10.6) rather than 'what believers should be' (cf. Tit 2.7).[107]

The same qualities of life should characterise both the leaders and the congregation.[108] Spicq, 513, notes that the type is not just an example but the normative mould or 'determinative example' which shapes the product. Appointment to leadership must be accompanied by a moral life which will act as a refutation of heretical leaders (Hasler, 37). Timothy can be a 'type' to others because he himself is moulded by the gospel (Goppelt, L., TDNT VIII, 249f.; Roloff, 252).

Five areas are listed covering both spheres of conduct and types of character. The first two cover the speech and conduct of the leader, while the latter three cover the qualities that he must show. To call the latter group 'inward' is misleading as they are expressed outwardly and meant to be seen and imitated by the congregation.

λόγος may refer either (a) to 'speaking, conversation' (cf. Col 3.8; 4.5f.; most commentators; Spicq, 513) or (b) to 'preaching the word' (Roloff, 253). In 5.17 word and teaching are linked as activities of the elders, and Tit 1.9 refers to the 'faithful word according to the teaching'. This suggests that spiritual talk is meant, 'counselling' in the broadest sense rather than just ordinary conversation. However, the word stands on its own in association with other terms expressive of personal behaviour, and this may suggest that conversation is meant, especially since this is a topic of moral exhortation elsewhere in the NT. But the term may be wide enough to cover both simultaneously, since the line between what a leader says formally and informally is hard to discern.

ἀναστροφή** is 'way of life, conduct, behaviour';[109] Roloff, 253, holds that it is the way of life appropriate to the word of the gospel. For ἀγάπη see 1.5; Tit 2.2 note, and for πίστις see 1.2; Tit 1.1 note. Growth in basic Christian trust is meant, rather than trustworthiness (Kelly, 104; Roloff, 253) or any special

[106] γίνου, imper. sing., as in Rev 2.10; 3.2.

[107] Lock, 52; Holtz, 109; Wolter 1988:191; *contra* Roloff, 252 n. 151; Oberlinner, 205 n. 13.

[108] For the thought cf. Tit 2.7; 1 Cor 4.6; 11.1; Phil 3.17; 2 Th 1.6, 7; 3.9; 2 Th 3.7; 1 Pet 5.3; Ignatius, *Mag.* 6.2. For the motif of imitating leaders and older people in Hellenistic ethics see Roloff, 252 n. 155, with Dittenberger, *Or* I, 383 (cited in Dibelius-Conzelmann, 70).

[109] Gal 1.13; Eph 4.22; Heb 13.7; Jas 3.13; 1 Pet 1.15, 18; 2.12; 3.1, 2, 16; 2 Pet 2.7; 3.11***; cf. Tob 4.14; 2 Macc 6.23; *Ep. Arist.* 130, 206; for the verb cf. 3.15 and note. Cf. the synonym ἀγωγή (2 Tim 3.10). Cf. Bertram, G., TDNT VII, 715–17; TLNT I, 111–14.

type of faith. Finally, ἀγνεία[110] is 'purity, chastity, propriety' (5.2***).[111] Although it is used of cultic purity in the LXX (Num 6.2, 21; 2 Chr 30.19; 1 Macc 14.36), here it is used of character. It may refer specifically to chastity (Josephus, *Ap.* 2.198; Holtzmann, 341; Hanson, 92), but it is more likely to refer to purity and integrity of motive (for this usage in laudatory inscriptions see Spicq, 513).

13. ἕως ἔρχομαι πρόσεχε τῇ ἀναγνώσει, τῇ παρακλήσει, τῇ διδασκαλίᾳ The exhortation to Timothy moves on to what actually happens in church, whether carried out by him personally or organised by him. The instruction to do these things until Paul comes may be meant to imply that these are the things that he himself would have done if he had been present.

ἕως** can mean 'while' or (as here) 'until', with pres. indic. equivalent to fut.[112] Although MHT III, 344, argues that ἕως clauses follow the clause to which they refer, Mt 5.18 and 2 Cor 3.15 indicate the contrary (Knight, 207). The motif of Paul's coming and possible delay has already figured in 3.14f. The clause here leaves the time of Paul's coming uncertain, but not the fact that he will come. His continuing authority, despite his absence, is implied. The function of the clause is ambiguous. It could be a latent threat (cf. Philem 21f.) Or does it imply that Timothy's task is temporary until Paul arrives? Or perhaps it simply reinforces the point that what Timothy is to do is what Paul himself would do (Roloff, 254), and therefore his teaching carries the authority of Paul whose representative he is (Oberlinner, 208). For the view that the 'apostolic parousia' alluded to here is a literary device by a pseudepigrapher, see 3:14 note. It remains a curious comment in a pseudepigraph in a situation where Paul was known to be dead and is better explained as a fragment from a genuine letter incorporated in a later revision.

Three items are mentioned for Timothy's attention (προσέχω, 1.4; Tit 1.14 and note).[113] The use of the article with each of the three following nouns indicates that these are familiar, recognised activities in the congregational meeting (Spicq, 514; Roloff, 254).

---

[110] Spelled ἀγνία in WH.

[111] For the adjective see 5.22; Tit 2.5 note; the noun is linked to ἀναστροφή in 1 Pet 3.2. Cf. also ἀγνότης (2 Cor 6.6). The word-group is frequent in AF: 1 Clement 64; Ignatius, *Eph.* 10.3; Polycarp 4.2; Hermas, *Sim.* 9.16.7; 5.6.5; 9.15.2; *Mand.* 6.2.3; *et al.* See further Westcott, B. F., *The Epistles of St John* (London: Macmillan, 1892³), 101; Hauck, F., *TDNT* I, 123.

[112] BD § 323; § 383¹; cf. Jn 21.22f. Hermas, *Sim.* 5.2.2; 9.10.5f; cf. 9.11.1; it is often used with aor. subj. Cf. Kretzer, A., *EDNT* II, 96f.

[113] MM 547f. cite an interesting parallel where a father tells his son to devote himself to his books (P. Oxy. 3.531.11).

However, they are by no means all that would be done in a meeting. Rather they are the activities based on the use of Scripture.

This makes it less significant that the list of Timothy's duties contains no reference to the sacraments. Nevertheless, this may be an indication of the early date of the letter (Kelly, 104f.). Merkel, 38, opines that the Lord's Supper was celebrated on a household basis, but this is precisely the setting in which Timothy and others like him would be working.

The reading aloud of Scripture and other appropriate material thus occupies a central place. ἀνάγνωσις is 'reading, public reading' (2 Cor 3.14; Acts 13.15***).[114] The reference is not to private study[115] but to public reading to the believers (Neh 8.8). The reference may be to the reading of the law and prophets, as in the synagogue.[116] It is the earliest reference to the reading of the OT in the Christian church (Jeremias, 34). However, there is good reason to believe that the reading of specifically Christian material was also practised. Paul's letters were read in church meetings (1 Th 5.27; Col 4.16; cf. Rev 1.3).[117] The reference is probably not so much to the need for skill in performance (perhaps in the right choice of passages or in clear enunciation) as to the need to do the task regularly.

The reading of Scripture forms the basis for the second item, the 'exhortation' or sermon. παράκλησις**, 'exhortation',[118] is clearly the activity expressed by the verb παρακαλέω (1.3; Tit 1.9 and note). It is probably the exposition of Scripture (cf. 1 Macc 12.9; 2 Macc 15.9–11), leading to commands or encouragements. Roloff, 254, refers to it as 'preaching' (cf. Acts 13.15; Heb 13.22).

Thirdly, there is 'teaching' which may also have been based on what was read, but may also be more independent instruction (so Kelly, 105). Elsewhere in the PE διδασκαλία (4.16; 1.10 and note) means 'doctrine, teaching', but here it refers to the activity of teaching and doctrinal discussion (Rom 12.7). It is also linked with παράκλησις in Rom 12.7. It may be that in the present context 'exhortation' has more to do with life-style whereas 'teaching' has to do with expounding the true faith over against the opponents (Oberlinner, 207).

---

[114] Also of the actual passage read (Hermas, Vis. 1.4.2). The meaning 'knowledge, recognition' (1 Esdr 9.48) is not found in the NT. Cf. Bultmann, R., TDNT I, 343f.; TLNT I, 101f.

[115] Ecclus. Prol. 10, 17; Ep. Arist. 127, 283, 305.

[116] Cf. the synagogue inscription συναγωγὴν εἰς ἀνάγνωσιν νόμου (BA s.v.); Acts 13.15; 2 Cor 3.14.

[117] So especially Oberlinner, 207, who holds that in the post-Pauline situation the reading of a collection of Pauline letters is probable.

[118] Rom 12.8; 15.4; 1 Cor 14.3; 1 Th 2.3; Heb 12.5; 13.22 et al.

14. μὴ ἀμέλει τοῦ ἐν σοὶ χαρίσματος The tasks just listed are 'charismatic' activities, as in Rom 12.6–8. It follows that Timothy needs the aid of the Spirit to do them. It is generally held that, since in this case the charisma was conveyed by the laying on of hands, it is restricted in principle to office-bearers or leaders and not available to all believers (so, e.g. Roloff, 256; Knoch, 35). However, 'the fact that the Pastorals do not speak in a general fashion about the charismata of the baptized does not allow us, given the nature of the genre (among other things, personal addressees), to draw any reliable conclusions' (Berger, K., *EDNT* III, 461). Since the instruction is concerned with Timothy's own responsibilities, it may not be significant that there is no mention of what the members of the congregation do. One purpose of the instruction may be to remind the congregation that Timothy possesses authority to teach in virtue of his charismatic endowment (Fee 1994:772). However, the specific concern is worry that Timothy may not utilise the spiritual gifts with which he is endowed. To neglect the duties in the preceding verse would be to neglect the charisma which he has received and the obligations which possession of it lays on him (Roloff, 255).

χάρισμα, 'gift, favour bestowed', is rare in pre-Christian literature.[119] It is used with broader and narrower reference in the NT: (a) Of the gifts of God, including the Spirit, in a general sense;[120] (b) Of special, varied gifts to individual Christians.[121]

Commentators differ as to whether the gift is the Spirit himself or a particular quality associated with the Spirit (cf. Arichea-Hatton, 105). It has been claimed that, whereas in 1 Cor 12 the Spirit is the source of varied such gifts, here the Spirit himself is the gift (2 Tim 1.6f.). But the distinction is artificial. At least in the PE the Spirit himself is the charisma, whose influence can then be sub-divided into different spiritual qualities. Although nothing is said explicitly, the charisma is manifestly the gift of the Holy Spirit who empowers people for the functions of ministry.

For some scholars the charisma is the *Amtsauftrag* and the authority which Timothy has received, i.e. the task of his office (Roloff, 255; Oberlinner, 208, 211); it is this task which he is not to neglect. It is further argued that in the PE charisma refers exclusively to this. This is an improbable shift and produces an impossible meaning (Fee 1994:772f.); what is surely meant is the

[119] Ecclus 7.33 *v.l.*; 38.30 *v.l.*; Ps 30 (MT 31).22 Θ; Philo, *L.A.* 3.78 *bis*; *Sib. Orac.* 2.54; Alciphron 3.17.4; other late secondary references in BA. Cf. Conzelmann, H., *TDNT* IX, 402–6; Lips 1979:206–23; Berger, K., *EDNT*.III, 460f.; Roloff, 255–7.

[120] Rom 1.11; 5.15f.; 6.23; 11.29; 1 Cor 1.7; 2 Cor 1.11; Ignatius, *Smyr.* Inscr.; *Poly.* 2.2; *Eph.* 17.2; *Rom.* 6.23; *Didache* 1.5.

[121] Rom 12.6; 1 Cor 7.7; 12.4, 9, 28, 30, 31; 2 Tim 1.6; 1 Pet 4.10***; 1 Clement 38.1.

spiritual gift to enable Timothy to perform his specific task in the church, just as prophets and others received the appropriate gifts for their task in 1 Cor 12. But the language cannot mean that a Christian believer who did not possess the Spirit was later given the Spirit, since for the PE the Spirit is given to all believers (Tit 3.5). Therefore, a general equipping of Timothy for ministry is meant. The Spirit who is already at work in him grants him further gifts for his ministry.

The use of ἐν σοί in connection with charismata is unusual: usually one 'has' a gift.[122] But if the Spirit 'indwells' believers (2 Tim 1.14), so do his gifts.

ἀμελέω is 'to neglect, be unconcerned about' (with gen.).[123] Spicq (*TLNT* I, 87–91), comments that neglect is the 'typical offense of a proxy or of one responsible for carrying out a function, but who shirks his obligations', and hence the command is typically given by a superior (see Wolter 1988:185–9). The danger faced by Timothy is that of not making use of the spiritual power and authority which he has received; the injunction is similar to that in 2 Tim 1.6 where the responsibility lies on him to fan into flame the gift of God. The command may be in effect a litotes, 'see that you cultivate' (cf. v. 15; Roloff, 255). The solemn responsibility to do so is underlined by a reminder of the circumstances in which Timothy received his charisma.

ὃ ἐδόθη σοι διὰ προφητείας μετὰ ἐπιθέσεως τῶν χειρῶν τοῦ πρεσβυτερίου The gift is one which was bestowed in connection with an act of prophecy and the laying on of hands. The thought of conveying of authority in the congregation is not stressed in this connection, although the position is one that carries a certain authority with it. Nor is the thought of transmission of the truth of the gospel in a formal setting present (2 Tim 2.1f.). The emphasis here is much more on the spiritual strengthening to carry out specific tasks and to develop a Christian character.

The key problem is how the gift is conceived to have been given (ἐδόθη). Similar language is used of the Spirit in 2 Tim 1.7 and of the qualities given by means of the Spirit in 1 Cor 12.7, 8 (cf. 2 Cor 12.7 of Paul's thorn in the flesh). The giving is associated with a particular public occasion characterised by two activities.

The first of these is prophecy (see 1.18 and note). But its role is not clear. Since προφητείας may be acc. pl. or gen. sing., the construction with διά is ambiguous: (a) with the acc. pl. it

---

[122] Cf. 2 Tim 1.6, 14 and notes; for the position of the phrase cf. 1 Cor 6.19.
[123] Mt 22.5; Heb 2.3; 8.9***; Cl.; Hellenistic examples in Roloff, 255 n. 170; cf. Polycarp 6.1; Ignatius, *Poly.* 4.1; AP 15.30; Lips 1979:207f.

means 'on account of prophecies'[124] or possibly 'with accompanying prophecies'; or (b) with gen. sing. it means 'by means of prophecy' or 'to the accompaniment of prophecy'.[125] Roloff, 257 n. 181, supports the latter construction on the grounds that when the following noun is anarthrous διά is found c. 120 times with the gen. and only 16 times with the acc., and that the article would have been included to avoid ambiguity if the acc. pl. had been intended. Such an argument can, of course, only establish a statistical probability.

The sense with the former construction is that, because prophecy pointed (beforehand) to Timothy, therefore people laid hands on him and so he received the charisma.[126] The sense with the latter construction is that the gift of the Spirit was conveyed to him by means of, or accompanied by, a 'prophetic' word. This has been taken as a word of encouragement, 'a proclamatory, encouraging and exhortatory address in which the official duty was transmitted to him' or as a prayer spoken by the elders.[127] On this view, the appointment of the leader did not necessarily take place in response to prophecies marking him out as the person of God's choice, and there is no need to assume that prophets were active in the congregation; there is, it is alleged, no room for prophets in the situation, and 'prophetic words' did not need prophets to give them.[128] This interpretation is very dubious. It is better to interpret the passage in the light of 1.18 and Acts 13.1f. The objection that the prophetic choice of leaders is hard to harmonise with the 'seeking' for authority in 3.1 is irrelevant since the two situations are different; here we are concerned with the historical appointment of Timothy, and it is mistaken to see in the passage a reflection of the appointment of local leaders in the post-Pauline situation.

The second associated activity is the laying on of hands. The phrase with μετά has the force 'accompanied by'; it may qualify ἐδόθη or διά προφητείας. Although it expresses accompanying circumstances rather than instrument (*pace* NEB 'through'),

---

[124] Cf. 1.18; Acts 13.1–3; Moule 1953:57; Knight, 208.

[125] 'Through prophecy' (NRSV); cf. RV; NIV; 'under the guidance of prophecy' (REB); 'when the prophets spoke' (GNB); MG; Holtzmann, 342; Bernard, 72; Fee 1994:773 n. 86; Lips 1979:250–3. See the discussion at 1 Tim 2.15 for the width of usage of διά with gen.

[126] It is going too far to say that prophecy is here reduced to merely confirming the choice of candidate (Knoch, 36).

[127] For the former view see Roloff, 258; Lips 1979:246; anticipated tentatively by Bernard, 72; for the latter, Oberlinner, 211. The view that 'prophecy' here refers to the prayer of consecration at ordination (so also in 1 Tim 1.18) was argued on the basis of later usage by Dekkers*, but is adequately refuted by Brox*.

[128] Lips 1979:245f.; Roloff, 257 and n. 183; Oberlinner, 210f.

it presumably expresses much the same as διά in 2 Tim 1.6 (Lips 1979:250–3).[129]

ἐπίθεσις – always with (τῶν) χειρῶν in the NT[130] – is an action with varying significance (including violent action against a person). It may be part of an invocation of God's blessing on a person (including acts of healing) or of the conveying of the Spirit (Acts 8.16–18; 9.17; 19.6). In the OT and Judaism appointment to some task or office is indicated or the act is associated with healing and prayer for divine blessing. In Hebrew there is a distinction between the laying on of hands as conveying authority (סמך) and as a means of blessing or healing (שׂית). The former use of the rite is said to be peculiar to Judaism and Christianity, while the latter is widely attested.[131] A distinction needs to be drawn between the communication of something possessed by the donor and a request to God to pass something on directly to the recipient.

There are parallels for appointments being made in this way in Judaism. In Num 27.18–23 the action is of giving authority to a person who already has the Spirit, but in Deut 34.9 the same person is said to have the spirit of wisdom because Moses had laid his hands on him. Presumably the 'fulness' of the gift was due to the commissioning. But the preposition μετά, like διά, may well imply accompaniment rather than means. The physical action is to be seen as the outward occasion or symbol of an inward action by God.

πρεσβυτέριον is used elsewhere in the NT to mean a 'council of elders', namely the Sanhedrin (Lk 22.64; Acts 22.5***), and then it came to refer to a Christian group of elders.[132] The vast majority of scholars assume that this is the meaning here: a group of elders laid their hands on Timothy. The word is not found at all in pre-Christian literature. Jeremias* 1957 drew attention to a *v.l.* to Sus 50 Θ, where he took the term to mean 'the rank of an elder'.[133] His reading of the evidence was disputed by Katz* who argued that the reading was simply a scribal error,

---

[129] NIV 'when' wrongly subordinates the act (Fee, 108). REB subordinates the preceding phrase: 'when, under the guidance of prophecy, the elders laid their hands on you'. NRSV gets the balance right: 'through prophecy with the laying on of hands'.

[130] 2 Tim 1.6; Acts 8.18; Heb 6.2***; cf. Philo, *L.A.* 3.90; *Spec.* 1.203.

[131] See Dibelius-Conzelmann, 70f.; Maurer, C., *TDNT* VIII, 159–61; Lohse, E., *TDNT* IX, 433f.; Lips 1979:224–40. On ordination see also the excursus in Roloff, 263–81; Merkel, 39f.

[132] Ignatius, *Eph.* 2.2; 4.1; 20.2; *Magn.* 2; 13.1; *Philad.* 4; 5.1; 7.1; *Smyrn.* 8.1; 12.2; *Trall.* 2.2; 7.2; 13.2. Cf. Bornkamm, G., *TDNT* VI, 651–80; Rohde, J., *EDNT* III, 148.

[133] In his later article (1961) Jeremias also cited Josephus, *Ap.* 2.206 *v.l.*

probably due to a Christian reviser. Nevertheless, this sense of the word is attested in later Christian writings (Jeremias* 1961).

Whereas here the elders lay hands on Timothy, in 2 Tim 1.6 Paul himself is said to lay hands on Timothy. Further, in 1 Tim 5.22 Timothy himself is to lay hands on elders; however, this passage need not imply that other people were not involved in the act. But how are the present passage and 2 Tim 1.6 related?

(a) The simplest, and perfectly satisfactory, explanation is that Paul and the elders shared together in the rite; in 1 Tim, which is more of a church order, reference to the elders is appropriate whereas in 2 Tim, which is a more personal letter, reference to Paul himself is appropriate.[134] Roloff, 259, suggests that here the point is to lay down what congregations with elders should proceed to do, namely to ordain those of their number who are capable of the tasks in v. 13. More likely, however, in the context may be the necessity to remind the elders that they authorised Timothy for his role and therefore they must respect the authority which they entrusted to him (cf. Johnson, 170).

(b) The reference may be to two different occasions for separate acts of service, e.g. general ordination for ministry in 2 Tim and installation as church leader at Ephesus in 1 Tim (cf. the earlier editions of Jeremias). Fee 1994:785–9, develops the view that the reference in 2 Tim is to Timothy's original reception of the Spirit, whereas here it is to his recognition by the congregation and to his specific gift for ministry stemming from the Spirit.

(c) It is argued that the practice here is that of the church in the writer's time, whereas the reference to Paul alone in 2 Tim 1.6 is either what happened historically to Timothy (Hanson, 121) or the author's fiction (Oberlinner, 210), intended to give a basis for the apostolic authorisation of the office (cf. Brox, 42–6).

(d) Daube* proposed a fresh translation of the phrase as an equivalent to the Rabbinic formula *semikhath zeqenim* ('the leaning on of elders', i.e. 'appointment to the eldership'); the whole phrase signifies 'appointment to the rank of presbyter' (with τοῦ πρεσβυτερίου as a gen. of purpose), and the appointment was carried out by Paul alone. This proposal was taken up by Jeremias* 1957 who claimed that the Greek word had this meaning in Sus 50 Θ *v.l.*[135] The Peshitta understands the text in this way.

[134] Lohse, E., *TDNT* IX, 433f.; Lips 1979:241–3; similarly, Roloff, 258f.; Merkel, 39.

[135] Cf. NEB mg. (omitted in REB); Jeremias, 35; Holtz, 111; Barrett, 72; Kelly, 107f.; the proposal was in effect anticipated by J. Calvin, *Institutio* 4.3.16 (Hofius*), but surprisingly in his commentary (247) he prefers the traditional understanding. The rabbinic formula was also understood in this way by SB II, 653f. in a comment on *Sanh.* 13b, but no application was made to the phrase here.

Various points have been made against this suggestion.[136] (1) The Rabbinic practice is an obscure rite, and the technical term would not have been comprehensible to non-Jewish readers, whereas Ignatius uses the word quite clearly to mean a body of elders; (2) The Jewish commissioning of rabbis was not the same thing as ordination. This is a weak objection, because 'ordination' at this time may still have been comparatively informal. It is true that the Jewish parallels lack any reference to the Spirit, which was not associated with Jewish commissioning. (3) Nowhere else is Timothy called an elder, and in view of his age he may not have been one (cf. Fee, 111). However, if 'elder' was a general term for the senior leaders of the church, it is perfectly possible that younger people may have been appointed to this group. On balance, the majority view of the passage is probably right, but the Daube-Jeremias view is not impossible.

It is important not to interpret the passage anachronistically in the light of later concepts of ordination. What we find in the NT is the acknowledgement by the church of a person's appointment to some task of ministry and hence the recognition of, or the conferring of, the appropriate authority for the task. It may be accompanied by prayer to God to enable the person in the task and to give the appropriate gift of the Spirit. The best parallels are those in Acts where people are appointed to particular duties (in Acts 13 to a temporary mission) and this is related to their possession and/or the guidance of the Spirit who assists them in their subsequent tasks.[137]

In any case, if the passage is to be applied to later times, it supports presbyterian rather than episcopal ordination.[138] It may appoint Timothy to a different position from that of a presbyter in a local setting. The implication is that he was made into a kind of 'superintendent' in the Pauline mission field with the approval of the congregations themselves. It may be assumed that appointments of elders and other leaders took place in a similar fashion, but the passage is primarily concerned with Timothy himself.[139]

---

[136] Bornkamm, G., *TDNT* VI, 666 n. 92; Fee, 111; Roloff, 258f.; Meier 1973:340–2.

[137] Roloff, 257 n. 183, denies the force of the parallel precisely because he sees no connection between what he calls 'ordination' here and the sending out of missionaries there.

[138] Unless Daube's proposal that the laying on of hands was carried out by Paul alone is correct. Bernard's view, 72f., that the laying on of hands by the presbyters merely attested the authoritative χειροθεσία of the apostle, has no basis in the text.

[139] Note how in what follows it is how *Timothy* is to treat older men not how *elders* are to treat older men.

15. ταῦτα μελέτα, ἐν τούτοις ἴσθι, ἵνα σου ἡ προκοπὴ φανερὰ ᾖ πᾶσιν ταῦτα is somewhat vague, but must refer to the various things that must be done according to vv. 12–13. The reference of ἐν τούτοις will be the same. The writer thus returns to the qualities and activities required from Timothy. The injunction in v. 14 is in effect repeated in a different form, this time in terms of the actual tasks to be performed and the qualities to be developed. Total commitment to the work is required.

μελετάω (Acts 4.25***) has various possible shades of meaning, here probably 'to practise'.[140] ἴσθι here has the sense 'to devote oneself to'.[141] It implies complete commitment.

Timothy's progress is intended to be seen by the congregation (v. 12). προκοπή is 'progress, advancement, furtherance' (Phil 1.12, 25***).[142] The word-group belongs more to Hellenism and is found in the LXX only in Ecclus 51.17 and 2 Macc 8.8.[143] It was used in Stoic philosophy for human ethical and spiritual development, and from there it found its way to Philo who makes considerable use of it (cf. Epictetus 1.4.12f.).[144] Stählin, 714, notes that the effects of true spiritual progress are visible, and that, while there is stress here on human effort, progress is ultimately the gift of God (cf. Philo, *Agr.* 168; *Post.* 154). Here the reference is to Timothy's development (the σου is emphatically placed) in Christian character and effective ministry. However, the verb can be used to indicate the development of evil (*T. Jud.* 21.8) as well as of good. The implication drawn from 2 Tim 3.9, that it was a term used positively by the opponents, which the author turns sarcastically against them (Stählin, 716; Fee, 109; Schenk, 158), is without any real support.

---

[140] The verb can mean: (a) 'to take care, endeavour' (Barnabas 19.10); (b) 'to think about, meditate on, plan' (Job 27.4; Prov 15.28; *Ep. Arist.* 160; Josephus, *Ant.* 4.183; Mk 13.11 TR; Acts 4.25 (=Ps 2.1); Barnabas 10.11; Bernard, 73); (c) 'to practise, cultivate, take pains with' (Philo; Josephus, *Bel.* 6.306; Barnabas 4.11; 11:5; 21.7; Ignatius, *Eph.* 19.3). Epictetus, 1.1.25, links it with γυμνάζω, in a way which suggests synonymity (Parry, 28f.; cf. Hesychius: 'to exercise'). It is so understood here and in Acts by MM 395; cf. Field 1899:209; BA; *EDNT* II, 403; Fee, 109.

[141] Prov 23.17; cf. Xenophon, *Hel.* 4.8.7 ἐν τοιούτοις ὄντες; Josephus, *Ant.* 2.346, cited by BA *s.v.* III.4; cf. *Ant.* 5.109; but Lk 2.49 is probably to be interpreted as being in a place. Cf. MHT I, 184; III, 265. The phrase here can be compared with similar Latin phrases, *Omnis in hoc sum* (Horace, *Ep.* 1.1.11; cf. *totus in illis*, Horace, *Sat.* 1.9.2).

[142] For the verb see 2 Tim 2.16; 3.9, 13; cf. Stählin, G., *TDNT* VI, 703–19; Schenk, W., *EDNT* III, 157f.; Lips 1979:163–5; *New Docs.* II, 95f. §71; IV, 36 §10 gives useful information.

[143] Cf. *Ep. Arist.* 242; Josephus, *Ant.* 10.189.

[144] However, *TLNT* III, 185–8, claims that it was in general use and was not specifically Stoic. The noun is Cl. For the importance of progress in virtue in contemporary teaching see Plutarch, *Mor.* 75B–86A; Epictetus, 3.6; *Ench.* 12f. (Johnson, 166).

φανερός* is 'visible, clear, plainly to be seen' (Phil 1.13), here
with dat. pers. For the thought cf. 1 Jn 3.10.[145] ἐν πᾶσιν may be
neut., 'in every respect' (Calvin, 248), but all recent translations
take it as masc., 'to everybody'. The point is that by his position
Timothy is more visible and his influence has greater effect. But
the suggestion that the leader is to live on a higher Christian
level (Hasler, 38) is misleading.

16. ἔπεχε σεαυτῷ καὶ τῇ διδασκαλίᾳ, ἐπίμενε αὐτοῖς The final
command is a reiteration of the need to attend closely to his
own spiritual progress and to the character of his leadership,
here summed up in terms of teaching.

ἐπέχω can mean: (a) 'to hold fast' (Phil 2.16); (b). intrans.
'to fix one's attention on', hence 'to pay attention to', with dat.
(Lk 14.7; Acts 3.5); (c) 'to stop, stay' (Acts 19.22***). Here it
is used in sense (b) with the force 'to take pains with yourself'.
It is not clear whether καὶ τῇ διδασκαλίᾳ refers to Timothy's
attention to doctrine in order to forward his own personal spiritual
progress or to his teaching of others. Probably the latter is
intended in view of vv. 13 and 16b. The command is reinforced
by a second imperative: ἐπιμένω, lit. 'to stay, remain' in a place,
here is used fig. 'to persist, continue in something' (cf. Rom 6.1;
11.22f.; Col 1.23; Josephus, *Ant.* 8.190); αὐτοῖς refers back
loosely to the activities designated as ταῦτα in v. 15 (Kelly, 109).

τοῦτο γὰρ ποιῶν καὶ σεαυτὸν σώσεις καὶ τοὺς ἀκούοντάς σου
Finally, the command is backed up by the salutary reminder that
the leader needs to persevere in doing this (τοῦτο ποιῶν) lest
he himself should fail to be saved; by full commitment to his
tasks he will bring both himself and his congregation to final
salvation.[146]

Despite comments to the contrary (Easton, 150; Merkel, 40),
the language and thought is Pauline. For the use of the verb 'to
save' with a human subject see Rom 11.14; 1 Cor 7.16a, 16b; 9.22.
The use of 'to hear' with reference to the gospel and Christian
instruction, which is characteristic of 2 Tim (1.13; 2.2, 14; 4.17**),
is Pauline (Rom 10.14; 15.21; Eph 1.13; Col 1.6, 9, 23) and
indeed common to the NT (e.g. Acts 4.4; Heb 2.1; 1 Jn 2.7).
Paul himself feared the possibility of not being saved by the
gospel which he preached to other people (1 Cor 9.27).

---

[145] According to Dibelius-Conzelmann, 72, the formula is found in commendatory
inscriptions. Cf. Bultmann, R., and Lührmann, D., *TDNT* IX, 2f.; Müller, P.-G.,
EDNT III, 412f.

[146] For this sense of σῴζω cf. 2.15; Phil 2.12; Jas 5.20; for the thought cf. Ezek
33.9. For the combination of oneself and others cf. 2 Clement 15.1; 19.1; *Deut.
Rab.* 11 (206d) (SB III, 652).

II. THE TREATMENT OF VARIOUS GROUPS IN THE CHURCH (5.1–6.2a)

More detailed instructions about how Timothy is to treat various groups of people in the church follow the general instructions about his demeanour and bearing as a church leader. The types of instructions about the different groups are rather varied. 5.1–2 deals with Timothy's own attitudes to young and old in the church. 5.3–16 is about the treatment of widows; however, after the initial imperative setting the leader's attitude to them, it is framed more as a code of conduct for the church in its treatment of them coupled with a pattern of life to be followed by the people concerned. 5.17–25 deals with the church's attitude to elders (largely in the form of directives to Timothy) but appears to range more widely. Finally, 6.1–2 is a brief set of instructions directed to slaves, but again expressed in the third person. There is thus a combination of (1) directives to Timothy personally about his own conduct as a church leader; (2) rules for how certain groups of people are to be treated in and by the church and its leaders; (3) rules for the way of life of certain groups of people, expressed as teaching to be passed on to them by Timothy.

a. How to deal with the old and the young (5.1–2)

This brief section is about the appropriate style of leadership to be adopted in dealing with both old and young, and is couched as instruction to Timothy, although it is of general application. Opinion varies as to whether it is the conclusion of the preceding section (Roloff, 250, links it closely to 4.12–16) or the first of a set of instructions structured around different groups in the church. Fee, 112, suggests that in form it belongs with what precedes (use of imperatives), but that in content it goes with what follows. It is certainly closely tied to what precedes in that it offers a more particular comment on how the 'young' leader' is to carry out the duties previously outlined with reference to the different age groups in the church. His authority does not entitle him to harshness. But the categorisation by groups in the church links it equally clearly to what follows.

The instruction about different age-groups is not part of an existing 'household table'. Rather it reflects a pattern of behaviour found in popular moral philosophy. People of different ages are to be treated as one would the corresponding members of a family. A close parallel is cited by Deissmann 1927:309f. in an inscription from Olbia on the Black Sea: τοῖς μὲν ἡλικιώταις προσφερόμενος ὡς ἀδελφός, τοῖς δὲ πρεσβυτέροις ὡς υἱός, τοῖς δὲ παισὶν ὡς πατήρ, πάσῃ ἀρετῇ κεκοσμημένος.[1] In Plato, *Rep.* 5, 463C, the guardians are depicted as people who treat everybody as if they were members of their family. Within this pattern respect for the elderly is standard teaching,[2] and is incorported in the Jewish legal system in Lev 19.32 (cf. Lam 5.12; Ecclus 8.6).

The type of relationship which is to be developed in the church is not patriarchal but rather brotherly (cf. Mt 23.9). One can understand that the younger leader must show respect to the older men, but what is important is treating other people of similar age (and younger!) as brothers and sisters (Knoch, 37).

EXEGESIS

1. **Πρεσβυτέρῳ μὴ ἐπιπλήξῃς ἀλλὰ παρακάλει ὡς πατέρα** πρεσβύτερος (Tit 1.5 note) is here clearly an older person in contrast to a younger.[3] Elsewhere πρεσβύτης is used (cf. Tit 2.2; Philem 9; Lk 1.18; and fem. Tit 2.3). πρεσβύτερος also means 'elder' (5.17, 19; Tit 1.5**), but we can safely assume that the two uses of the word were so familiar that the readers would have no difficulty with the switch between 5.1f. and 17.[4]

ἐπιπλήσσω*** is 'to strike at, rebuke, reprove';[5] it suggests the use of very severe censure. The prohibition thus reflects the requirement that the church leader should not be a πλήκτης (3.3; Tit 1.7). The need to treat the elderly in particular with respect is inculcated by Hierocles: one should treat aged parents with παρακλῆσις and not with rebuke as one would with lesser or equal people.[6] However, the injunction here should be taken as referring implicitly to the treatment of all four groups of people listed here.

For παρακαλέω see 1.3; 2.1; the sense here may be 'to try to console, conciliate, speak in a friendly manner'.[7] For the noun

---

[1] See also the honorific inscriptions cited by Dibelius-Conzelmann, 72; Polybius 6.4.4; Spicq, 522.

[2] Plato, *Leg.* 9.879C; cf. Cicero, *De Off.* 1.34; Aulus Gellius 2.15.

[3] So REB, correcting NEB; cf. Jn 8.9; Acts 2.17; 1 Pet 5.5 (but here possibly of elders); Lk 15.25 (='older'); 1 Clement 1.3; cf. 3.3; 21.6; Hermas, *Vis.* 3.1.8. Fem. form in 5.2; Gen 19.31.

[4] Jeremias, 41f., holds that Paul means 'old man' throughout the PE. See, however, Meier 1973:343f.

[5] Usually + dat. or acc.; Cl.; Philo, *L.A.* 2.46; Josephus, *Ant.* 1.246; 19.346.

[6] Hierocles, p. 58, 20–4 (van der Horst 1975:159; Eng. tr. in Malherbe 1986:90–3).

[7] BA *s.v.* 5, cites as possible cases: 2 Macc 13.13; Lk 15.28; Acts 16.39; 1 Cor 4.13; 1 Th 2.12.

see 4.13. The object αὐτόν is easily supplied from the preceding noun.[8]

ὡς πατέρα expresses the thought 'with the respect appropriate to a father'. Contrast how Paul (an older man) in 1 Th 2.11f. exhorts the congregation in general like a father to his children! But here the concern is with a younger person who needs to give instruction/commands to older people. For ὡς see Tit 1.5 note. πατήρ (1.2) is used here only in the PE of earthly fathers (cf. the use in 1 Jn. 2.13, 14 for older members of church). In view of what we have seen to be the ancient climate of opinion the assumption is that people would treat earthly fathers with respect and deference (Fee, 112). Knight, 215, however, notes that other sources refer only to *respect* for the elderly, whereas here Timothy is to give them instruction and exhortation.

νεωτέρους ὡς ἀδελφούς νεώτερος 'young' (5.2 [fem.], 11, 14; Tit 2.6**; 1 Pet 5.5) is a comparative of νέος, but with little comparative force (cf. Acts 5.6; Polycarp 5.3); it is often found as the antonym to πρεσβύτερος. This and the succeeding nouns in the acc. are all dependent on παρακάλει.

ἀδελφός (4.6 note) here refers to a member of the same family, but can also be used of people in the same group. It is often used in the vocative with παρακαλέω.[9] Paul addresses his readers generally as brothers (fellow-believers) but describes them as (his) children when expressing affection and fatherly concern.

2. πρεσβυτέρας ὡς μητέρας, νεωτέρας ὡς ἀδελφὰς ἐν πάσῃ ἁγνείᾳ The fem. form πρεσβυτέρα occurs here only in the NT of older women. μητήρ is used literally (2 Tim 1.5**) to express the respect due to parents (for the metaphorical usage, expressive of the attitude encouraged here, see Rom 16.13). νεώτερος (5.1) is fem. as in 5.11, 14; Tit 2.4 has νέος in the same sense. ἐν [πάσῃ] ἁγνείᾳ (cf. 4.12) refers in this context to sexual purity and expresses the need to act with the utmost propriety to avoid any needless suspicion. Explicit mention of the need for this attitude suggests that there may have been a problem in the church for a young leader (cf. 5.11; 2 Tim 3.6f.; Fee, 112).

b. Instructions about widows (5.3–16)

Bangerter, O., 'Les veuves des épîtres pastorales. Modèle d'un ministère féminin dans l'église ancienne', *Foi et Vie* 83 (1984), 27–45; Bartsch 1965:112–43; Bassler, J. M., 'The Widow's Tale: A Fresh Look at 1 Tim 5:3–16', *JBL* 103 (1984), 23–41; Brox, 185–7; Campbell, R. A., 'Καὶ μάλιστα οἰκείων – A New Look at 1 Timothy 5.8', *NTS* 41 (1995), 157–60; Edwards, R. B., 'The

---

[8] Note the combination of aorist and present in this sentence with apparently similar force.

[9] Rom 12.1; 15.30; 16.17; 1 Cor 1.10; 16.15; 1 Th 3.7; 4.10; 5.14.

Christological Basis of the Johannine Footwashing', in Green and Turner 1994:367–83; Ernst, J., 'Die Witwenregel des ersten Timotheusbriefes – ein Hinweis auf die biblischen Ursprünge des weiblichen Ordenswesens?', *TGl* 59 (1969), 434–45; Fiorenza 1983:309–15; Harrison, J. R., *New Docs.* VII, 106–167; Lightman, M., and Zeisel, W., 'Univira: An Example of Continuity and Change in Roman Society', *CH* 46 (1977), 19–32; Müller-Bardorff, J., 'Zur Exegese von 1 Tim 5:3–16', *Gott und die Götter: Festschr. E. Fascher*, Berlin, 1958, 113–33; Rapske, 1987:183–227; Sand, A., 'Witwenstand und Ämterstrukturen in der urchristlichen Gemeinden', *BibLeb* 12 (1971) 186–97; Stählin, G., *TDNT* IX, 440–65, espec. 453–8; Synge, F. C., 'Studies in Texts: 1 Timothy 5, 3–16', *Theology* 68, 1965, 200f.; Thurston, B. B., *The Widows: A Women's Ministry in the Early Church* (Minneapolis: Fortress, 1989), 36–55; Trummer, P., 'Einehe nach den Pastoralbriefen', *Bib* 51, 1970, 471–84; Verner 1983:161–6; Wagener 1994:115–233; Winter, B., 'Providentia for the widows of 1 Timothy 5:3–16', *TynBul* 39 (1988), 83–99 (=idem, *Seek the Welfare of the City* [Carlisle: Paternoster, 1994], 61–78).

The remaining set of instructions (5.3–6.2a) appears to be loosely linked together by the catchword τιμή/τιμάω (5.3, 17; 6.1) which is used with varying senses. The opening sentence in this subsection seems about to begin a passage simply on treating widows with honour and respect, but in fact it develops into one of the longest sustained sections in the letter, evidently dealing with a matter of considerable importance or, rather, of great difficulty.

There are two main approaches to the interpretation of the passage.

(a) *The 'order' of widows.* The first approach takes the passage to be primarily concerned with the existence of an 'order' of widows who had various duties (possibly including functions in the church meeting) to perform in return for which they were supported or even 'paid' (Dibelius-Conzelmann, 73f.; Thurston*). Admission to the list involved the taking of a vow not to (re)marry (Bartsch 1965). The characteristics of the group thus included celibacy for the future and a life of prayer (Roloff, 285f.; cf. Ernst*).[10]

Wagener develops this theory in connection with an attempt to distinguish between a tradition which was ascetically orientated and the writer's own reworking which was orientated to marriage and the family. Within his conception of the patriarchal 'household' of the church there was no room for an active role in ministry by women, and they were to be confined to the domestic scene. The tradition is to be detected in vv. 3, 5, 9, 11f.[11] The passage is·then claimed to be the oldest evidence for a special 'order of widows' in the church along with Ignatius,

---

[10] Some scholars have argued for the existence of two types of widows, those who are to be supported by the church because of their destitution ('genuine widows', vv. 3–8) and a sub-group of those who are to form an active group or 'order' of workers (vv. 9–10; Bernard, 80f.; Verner 1983:161–6).

[11] For details see Wagener 1994:125–7, 165–9, 221–3, 223–6.

Smyr. 13.1 ('I greet the houses of my brothers with their wives and children and [I greet] the virgins who are called widows'); *Poly.* 4.1; Polycarp 4.3; Hermas, *Vis.* 2.4.3; *Didasc.* 14f. (*Apost. Const.* 3.1–15); Lucian, *De Morte Peregrini* 12 (hardly an order!); Tertullian, *De virg. vel.* (cf. Bartsch 1965). That widows formed a recognised group in the church is clear from Polycarp 4.3, where they are said to be 'God's altar' and are people of blameless lives engaged in intercession.

Bassler*, 36, suggests that the appeal of such a group lay not just in the financial support which it provided nor in the esteem in which widows were held, but rather in that it provided a structure which gave some release from patriarchalism and provided equality and freedom. It can then be suggested that the author was primarily attempting to curb the place of widows in the church by insisting that, as far as possible, they devote themselves to domestic duties (so especially Wagener 1994). The passage then takes its place as evidence that a primary concern of the author of 1 Tim was to reassert the domination of male leaders in the church.

(b) *The care of needy widows.* The second interpretation of the passage is that it is concerned with the situation of widows in the church and its responsibilities towards them. In the ancient world widows were in a difficult position both socially and financially. They might well be left without support if their husbands' property passed to the children and no provision had been made in a will for their maintenance. Many women were widowed early in life (cf. Rapske 1987).

Particular problems arose over the question of dowries. There was a legal requirement in the Graeco-Roman world to pay a dowry on marriage. The husband as holder of the dowry was legally responsible for the maintenance of his wife. If he died she could (a) stay in her husband's home under a new κύριος, usually the son; (b) return to her parents with her dowry and be maintained there. Remarriage was expected and normal – cf. *Lex Papia Poppaea* (AD 9). Where a woman was left without provision *providentia* was provided by city or State.[12]

Widows are depicted (along with orphans) as the special objects of God's concern in the Old Testament. Since they might otherwise have been ignored, care for them was commended in the OT and practised in Judaism, and it is reflected in accounts of the earliest Palestinian church (Acts 9.39, 41; Jas 1.27; cf. Lk 7.12f.). Clearly, the primary responsibility lay on the families concerned to display *providentia* (cf. προνοέω, v. 8!). The church

---

[12] The legislation appears to assume that there was no shortage of men for widows to marry – contrary to the usual situation in the modern world.

saw itself responsible for widows who 'slipped through the net' and could not care for themselves financially. Following the precedent of the synagogue, the Jerusalem church cared for widows (Acts 6.1).[13]

From the present passage we can see that there was already provision by private individuals for widows (v. 16) and by their families (vv. 4, 8 – but see below on the disputed interpretation of these verses). Further, there was some kind of system of church provision which involved the placing of widows on a list. 5.3, therefore, is not urging congregations which did not honour widows to do so, but rather to confine their attention to 'real' widows. Two main problems had arisen:

(1) The number of widows being supported by the church was a strain on the available resources, and it seems fairly certain that cases of genuine need were not receiving adequate support while people who could be cared for in other ways were draining away the available funds.

(2) Younger widows were being maintained, and problems arose with them wanting to marry and/or making a nuisance of themselves by misusing their subsidised leisure.

The writer's concern is that the church should not expend care on those who did not need or deserve it, and he attempts to solve the problem by restricting church care to 'real widows' and defining those who came into this category. He therefore insists that where family provision can be made, it should be provided. Help is to be given only to those who are genuinely indigent and live godly lives. Church provision is to be confined to those over sixty who have demonstrated their practical piety. Younger widows are not to be included on a church list but rather encouraged to marry (cf. Sand*).

The passage can thus be interpreted in terms of restricting the development of a female 'order' within the church or in terms of concern to ensure that charitable care is properly directed. It is apparent that both aims could be present side by side. Nevertheless, there can be little doubt that the second interpretation is the correct one. A strong argument in favour of it is found in v. 16, which Wagener is compelled to regard as a later gloss because it conflicts with her interpretation of the rest of the passage. Further, the first view ignores the manifest concern of the author to balance limited resources against increasing need to provide relief for the poor (Johnson, 178–80).

Specific points at issue which influence the interpretation of the passage as a whole are:

---

[13] For later evidence of concern regarding widows see *Didascalia* 14 (*Apost. Const.* 3:1–15); *New Docs* II, § 108 (AD V).

(a) *The scope of the term 'widow'.* In addition to widows strictly so called (i.e. persons whose husbands have died), there have been suggestions that the category may also include: (1) the abandoned wives of polygamists (Simpson, 74); (2) women who left their families to join/serve the church (Synge*, 200f.); (3) celibate women, including virgins and divorcees (Bassler*, 34f.; Wagener 1994:132).

It is certainly possible that 'widows' might include elderly women who had never married (cf. the German custom of referring to older single women as 'Frau' rather than 'Fräulein'). It is much less probable that young women who remained celibate were called 'widows', especially since the word 'virgin' was available for use. Ignatius, *Smyr.* 13.1 is an isolated early reference to 'virgins who are called widows',[14] but it may represent a later development when unmarried women were admitted to the group supported by the church.[15]

(b) *The situation of widows on the church list.* The first interpretation assumes the existence of an 'order' with specific duties. But the case that they constituted an 'order' at this time is weak (Sand*). Ignatius, *Poly.* 4.1 is evidence only of church care for widows. Lucian speaks of widows and orphans in the same breath. This leaves only Ignatius, *Smyr.* 13.1, where greetings are sent to the church leaders, the congregation as a whole, 'the households of my brothers with their wives and children', 'and the virgins who are called widows'; but nothing is said about their functions. In *Didasc* . 14f. there is an order of widows aged 50 and upwards who care for the poor. How widows were related to deacon(esses) is problematic. In any case, it is dangerous to read back the ascetic tendencies of later times into the first century.

In favour of the view that a list of 'working widows' is being drawn up it is argued that the qualifications for being placed on the list are too high merely for the recipients of charitable care in the church. However, it is probable that the description is somewhat idealistic. It must also be noted, as is admitted by advocates of the theory, that nothing is said about the duties of the widows; the interest of the passage is purely in limiting the numbers to be cared for (cf. Hasler, 40). We must also ask how realistic it would be to place a set of duties on women of this age in the ancient world. If it is argued that their role was rather

---

[14] The interpretation of this passage is not clear: is the word παρθένος used only of those who had never had sexual relationships, or could it be used of those who renounced them for the future? For a clear reference to a young unmarried woman being enrolled among the widows we have to wait until Tertullian, *De Virg. Vel.* 9.

[15] Cf. Schoedel 1985:252.

to pray and intercede (cf. v. 5), it must be said that there is no clear indication of this. The point of v. 10 is much more the rewarding of faithful service in the past.

(c) *The widows in relation to their families.* In vv. 4–8 widows with families are in effect being excluded from those eligible for church support, but the passage has been interpreted in two different ways.

(1) It may state that children who have widowed parents should care for them as a priority. True widows worthy of enrolment are those who are genuinely on their own with no support and therefore dependent upon God, by contrast with those who live it up. This instruction to the children is so that they may not gain a bad reputation, for failure to look after one's (sc. elderly) relatives is to act worse than unbelievers. There is strong condemnation for those not living up to secular standards of care, particularly if the holders of dowries were not maintaining widows (Winter*).

(2) It may state that widows who have families should first and foremost devote themselves to care for them rather than seeking admission to a church list. Widows who are to be 'enrolled' are those who are genuinely on their own and dependent upon God. For others, who have families, to fail to look after them is to act worse than non-believers and to bring blame upon themselves. On this view, the number of widows to be enrolled is cut down by insisting that widows with families look after them (Roloff, 287–9).

In both interpretations the passage indicates that 'genuine widows' are those who are bereft of family and have cast themselves upon God to supply their needs in response to their prayers. And the aim is to remove such widows with families from the category of people supported by the congregation.

(d) *The younger widows.* Apart from those already excluded because they have families, the list is to be restricted to women aged 60+ who have lived commendable lives. Younger widows are excluded because they may wish to marry and give up their 'faith' and because they misuse their subsidised leisure. They should be encouraged to remarry and engage in domestic pursuits.[16]

The simple interpretation is that these were women widowed early in life who had the opportunity of support by the church. The author hesitates to enrol them (whether for support or

---

[16] According to Fee, 114f., the real concern of the passage is with the younger widows, and the mention of the older ones is a foil to them. However, this appears to be special pleading to justify the view that the letter is motivated at each point by opposition to heresy.

service) because they misuse their leisure. More importantly, he knows that some have already 'gone after Satan' and turned against Christ, wishing to marry. It is not clear what is meant by this: (1). The reference can hardly be to widows not yet on the list who simply wanted to marry (this explanation is surely excluded by v. 14). (2) The widows may have turned aside into heresy (Bassler*, 37) or apostasy.[17] (3) They were marrying non-believers (Hasler, 41f.; Fee, 121f.). This last possibility is not stated in so many words, but, since a wife normally adopted the religion of her husband, the reference to giving up the faith in v. 12 could imply this. Clearly, when the writer speaks about remarriage in v. 14 he is thinking of marriage to fellow-believers. (4) Much the most popular solution is that they were enrolled on the list and now wished to break the vow of celibacy which, it is claimed, was part of the requirements for enrolment. It is not, then, simply the desire to marry which is the cause of concern, but the desire to break a vow of celibacy which the writer takes seriously. But it is hard to see why such a distinction would be made in the church, and the language used (their *first* pledge) is very odd.

We should not overlook v. 14b with its reference to verbal abuse. This is most plausibly interpreted of non-believers who pour scorn on believers who 'go after Satan' and cannot keep up the requirements of the faith (just as modern journalists go for clergy who commit marital offences, even though their own standards of morals may fall short of Christian standards). It could be that the 'judgement' in v. 12 is also passed by the outsiders. The judgement of 'blamelessness' in v. 7 may also be in terms of one's public reputation.

With this in mind, solution (3) above becomes more plausible. In any case, a reference to abandoning the faith seems most likely.

The structure of the passage is loose but nevertheless unified. A general instruction is given in v. 3 and then developed in detail. Verses 4 and 8 belong together with their instruction regarding widows and their families; vv. 5 and 6 are in effect a parenthesis which defines the 'real' widow and places the dissipated widow as a foil over against her. In vv. 9f. the qualifications for enrolment in the church's list are given. Verses 11–13 and 14f. are concerned with the danger of enrolling younger women as widows and with the recommendation that they should marry. Finally, v. 16 reinforces the need to free the church to care for

---

[17] The desire to (re)marry (v. 11) may seem to be incompatible with the heresy reflected in 4.3, but, human nature being what it is, it would not be surprising if adherents to other aspects of the heresy eventually found the sexual urge too strong for them.

'real' widows. Three groups of people are mentioned and recur in what follows. In effect, the writer goes over the same territory three times

(1)	The families of widows	4	7–8	16a
(2)	pious widows	5	9–10	16b
(3)	impious/young widows	6	11–13	14–15

First, the families of widows are instructed to care for them, destitute widows are urged to cast their needs on the Lord, and those who live voluptuously are condemned. Second, those who do not care for their families are condemned, the church is told who should be given care, and younger widows are excluded. Then, third, younger widows are encouraged to remarry, families are reminded to care for their widows, and the church is encouraged to care for genuine widows.

TEXT

4. ἔκγονα ἔγγονα (D* Ψ *pc*; = 'grandsons', LS), is said to be more appropriate here (Elliott, 74). However, both spellings of the word occur (Mayser I.228), and the MS evidence for the variant is weak.

μανθανέτωσαν μανθανέτω (945 pc d f m vg^cl Ambst Pel Spec). The variant is unlikely because of its weak attestation; it is an attempt to clarify an ambiguous sentence. See exegetical note and Elliott, 74.

ἀπόδεκτον Praem. καλὸν καί (323; 365; 945 *pc* sa^mss bo). The variant is due to assimilation to 1 Tim 2.3 (Elliott, 75).

5. ἤλπικεν ἤλπισεν (88). The variant is adopted by Elliott, 66, but the evidence is far too weak (cf. 4.6 note).

θεόν (C F G Ψ 048 *pc*) θεόν (א² A D² 1739 1881 TR lat sy co; WH); τὸν κύριον (D* 81 *pc*); κύριον (א* WH mg.) The text (without the article) should be accepted, as in 4.10; 6.17. The variants are stylistic (Elliott, 75, 202–4).

8. οἰκείων Praem. τῶν (C D¹ 1881 TR). Elliott, 76, argues that the article is original and was omitted by scribes to avoid repetition. The evidence is weak.

προνοεῖ προνοεῖται (א* D* F G I K 104 1881 *pc*; WH mg Kilpatrick); Elliott, 76, argues that the mid. was preferred by Atticists and is therefore not original.

10. καλοῖς ἀγαθοῖς (P). Elliott, 77, 237, accepts the variant with hesitation on grounds that the text shows an unusual word order for the PE. But there could be influence from the phrase later in verse, and one MS is hardly an adequate basis for the text.

12. τὴν πρώτην πίστιν τὴν πίστιν τὴν πρώτην (440). Elliott, 78, thinks that scribes altered the ungreek word order in the variant (cf. 5.25 note). But the MS evidence for the variant is too weak.

16. πιστή (א A C F G P 048 33 81 1175 1739 1881 *pc* m vg co Ath) πιστὸς ἢ πιστή (D Ψ TR a b vg^mss sy Ambst; Kilpatrick; adopted by Moffatt; Easton, 157f.; NEB); πιστός (g Eth (Arm) Theod Mops (lat) Aug Amb; 'a patristic peculiarity' [Elliott, 80]). Elliott, 80, says that it is unlikely that the charge was laid purely on women and (following Von Soden) argues for loss by homoioteleuton (similarly, Easton, 157f.). Metzger, 574f., argues that the short text is better attested and was altered to avoid unfair restriction of task to women. Or scribes may have thought that a woman would not be head of a household (Johnson, 172). Cf. Rapske 1987:183 n.172. The longer text is unlikely, since εἴ τις alone would have conveyed the meaning; v.4 has a similar construction.

ἐπαρκείτω ἐπαρκείσθω (א A F G 33 2344 1175 pc; WHmg). The variant is rejected by Elliott, 54; it is possibly due to confusion with the next verb; and all examples of the verb in LS are in Active.

βαρείσθω ἐπιβαρείσθω (81 181 917 1836 1898) is preferred by Elliott, 80, on grounds that scribes tended to reduce number of compounds. But the MS evidence for the variant is weak, and it could be due to assimilation to 1 Th 2.9; 2 Th 3.8.

EXEGESIS

3. Χήρας τίμα τὰς ὄντως χήρας χήρα, 'widow', is the fem. form of χῆρος 'bereft (of one's spouse)'.[18] In the LXX particularly the references often stress the needs of widows and link them with orphans.[19] Care for widows appears in Acts 6.1; 9.36–42; and early Christian literature.[20]

τιμάω** 'to honour, set a price on, estimate, value, honour, revere', is variously interpreted here: (a) simply 'to respect';[21] (b) 'to show respect and give material support';[22] (c) to 'make payment for services rendered'.[23] It should be taken broadly of respect which finds appropriate expression; here this will include (among other things) some material provision, since vv. 4–8 are clearly concerned primarily with this aspect and especially since ὄντως is pointless on any other interpretation. It would not make sense to restrict 'respect' simply to one class of widows, since all widows were surely regarded as worthy of respect; therefore the restriction must be related to the particular expression of honour in terms of material support. However, that the verb means 'to pay' in the sense of giving a reward or wage for services rendered is impossible; the interpretation rests on the parallel with 5.17 where this sense is also improbable (Verner 1983:162f.). The use of the verb may echo Deut 5.16 = Exod 20.12.[24] In the context of the congregation as a family believers are to treat widows like other parents. Note, however, that the instruction is addressed in the first instance to Timothy himself, i.e. to a church leader, and the decisions about widows are apparently made by him.

[18] 5.4, 5, 9, 11, 16; 1 Cor 7.8; Jas 1.27; Acts 6.1; 9.39, 41; Rev 18.7; Mk 12. 40, 42; Lk 2.37; 4.25, 26; 7.12; 18.3–5; 20.47; 21.2, 3***; Cl. Cf. Stählin, G., *TDNT* IX, 440–65.

[19] E.g. Exod 22.22; Deut 10.18; 14:29; 16.11, 14; 24.17, 19–21; 26:12f.; Job 29.13; Ps 67 (MT 68).6; 145 (MT 146).9; Isa 1.17; 2 Macc 3.10; 8.28.

[20] 1 Clement 8.4; Barnabas 20.2; Ignatius, *Poly.* 4;1; Polycarp 6.1; Hermas, *Man.* 8.10; *Sim.* 1.8; 5.3, 7; 9.26.2; 9.27.2.

[21] Holtzmann, 344; Dibelius-Conzelmann, 73 ('probably'); Brox, 187; Hanson, 96; Oberlinner, 223f.; Sand*, 194.

[22] Cf. 5:17 note; Acts 28.10; Lock, 57; Jeremias, 37; Kelly, 113; Spicq, 525; Fee, 115; Dornier, 88; cf. Schneider, J., *TDNT* VIII, 169–80, espec. 179.

[23] So especially Wagener 1994:144–9. Cf. Müller-Bardorff*, 115; Bartsch 1965:112, 120.

[24] Cf. Mk 7.10; Mt 15.4, 6; Eph 6.1. Holtz, 115; Kelly 112; Jeremias, 37.

But an important condition is attached. The widows to be given this tangible honour must be ὄντως χῆραι, 'genuine widows'. It is not necessary to take χῆραι as an adj. so that the phrase means 'those who are really desolate, destitute'. It is likely that the author is using 'genuine' as a way of redefining the category of those whom the church should support, and the following remarks indicate how he restricts the term for this purpose. ὄντως means 'really, certainly, in truth'.[25] The whole phrase here and in the parallel phrases in 5.6 and 16 describes those who are genuinely destitute, with no relatives and beyond marriageable age, people who 'have lost husband *and* support' (Scott, 57).

4. The exposition proceeds by listing two exceptions who do not count as real widows, but the first exception is expressed in terms of the duties that exist between relatives and constitutes an implicit command to them to care for the needy members of their family. The point is reiterated in 5.16 (where the conditional clause is stated inversely).

εἰ δέ τις χῆρα τέκνα ἢ ἔκγονα ἔχει The reversed order of noun and indef. pronoun (τις χῆρα) is odd.[26] The τέκνα (1.2; 3.4) are presumably adult and able to undertake the prescribed duties. The adjective ἔκγονος*** is usually masc. or fem. in the sing., but here the neuter pl. expresses 'descendants' or more specifically 'grandchildren'.[27]

μανθανέτωσαν πρῶτον τὸν ἴδιον οἶκον εὐσεβεῖν The interpretation of the sentence hangs on the identification of the subject of μανθανέτωσαν (2.11; cf. Tit 3.14 and note). If we may set aside the possibility, mentioned by Stählin, that all the members of the family, including the widows, are meant, two possibilities arise:

(a) The most natural view of the pl. form is that the children/ descendants of the widow are meant.[28] The point is then that such widows do not need church care.

(b) Alternatively, the subject is the widow(s).[29] If so, there is a shift from the generalising sing. to the plural (cf. the same

---

[25] 5.6, 16; 6.19**; Lk 23.47; 24.34; Jn 8.36; 1 Cor 14.25; Gal 3.21; Mk. 11.32; the attributive use of the adverb as equivalent to an adj. is Cl. usage (BA).

[26] Cf. 5.16; 1 Cor 9.12; BD §473[1] is about a different phenomenon.

[27] Hesychius; Dittenberger, *Or.* 740 (I BC); Dio Chrysostom 38.21; Chariton, 2.9.2; *CH* 10.14b; vg and pesh take it in the specific sense; cf. the textual note for the variant spelling ἔγγονα.

[28] Rengstorf, K. H., *TDNT* IV, 410; Dibelius-Conzelmann, 74; Jeremias, 36f.; Holtz, 115; Lock, 58; Scott, 58; Brox, 188; Kelly, 113; Guthrie, 101; Hanson, 96; Dornier, 88f.; Oberlinner, 225.

[29] Chrysostom *PG* LXII, 566f.; Holtzmann, 344f.; Stählin, *TDNT* IX, 453f.; Roloff, 287f. prefers; Wagener 1994:149–54 presents the most powerful case for this interpretation.

problem in 2.15).[30] On this view the widows are to show
respect to *their* forebears by caring for their own children, just
as their parents did for them. Calvin, 251, adopted this view but
took τὸν οἶκον as an acc. of respect: the widows are to show
piety, namely to God in respect of their duties to their own
families. The point is then that such widows should concentrate
on their duties at home (πρῶτον) rather than undertake church
duties.

In favour of the second view it is argued: (1) It gives a unity
to the section. Verse 4 requires widows who have dependants to
care for them. Whereas the 'real' widow spends her life in prayer,
the widow who lives expensively is as good as dead. So widows
must be taught this. Widows who do not care for their dependants
are worse than unbelievers. (2) Verses 4 and 8 are parallel and
make the combined point: if persons have relatives, they must
care for them, and if they do not, they are worse than unbelievers
(Wagener 1994:122). Since there is no change of subject in the
two clauses in v. 8, it is argued that the same must be the case
in v. 4 (Wagener 1994:150). (3) The use of ἴδιος and πρῶτον
most aptly refers to the widows' primary duty to their household
over against the church. (4) The 'recompense' to the (deceased)
ancestors can be made by care for the next generation in their
turn. (5) The use of προνοέω (v. 8) refers to the householder's
role taken over by the widow, and the omission of any specific
reference to the older members of the family as the objects of
care means that there is in fact no reference to them.

Against the second understanding of the passage it can be
argued: (1) On this view the shift from the sing. to the pl. in v. 4
is unmotivated and unlikely in view of the fact that v. 8 maintains
the sing. throughout, as does v. 16.[31] (2) The use of εὐσεβέω =
τιμάω is more likely to refer to duty towards the older rather
than the younger members of the family; v. 4 could equally well
refer to families which gave their resources to the church rather
than to their aging relatives (cf. Mk 7.11f.). (3) The reference
to recompensing the ancestors is unmotivated in the context.
(4) The role described in v. 8 can be that of a son who is now
head of the household. (5) The resulting line of argument is too
subtle (Scott, 58) and impairs the artistic structure and thrust of
the section (Lock, 58). (6) The contrast in v. 5 is with a widow
who has been left without relatives and therefore has to put her

---

[30] This understanding of the passage is given apparent support by the weakly
attested variant μανθανέτω, which could be interpreted of the widow (so vg;
Stählin). Alternatively, the singular verb could refer to the children (neuter
plural subject with singular verb), or perhaps be used in an individualising way,
but this would be very harsh.

[31] Though note the problem in 2.15.

trust in God instead, it is implied, of having human *support*; this
fits ill with v. 4 interpreted of widows who have families whom
they must look after. (7) The closing 'summary' in v. 16 must
not be overlooked. This sentence is unambiguously about the
care of widows and the need to avoid burdening the church with
them and furnishes a parallel in the light of which the present
verses must be interpreted. The first interpretation is accordingly
to be preferred.

The force of πρῶτον will vary according to which interpretation
is accepted. (a) If the subject is the relatives, care of the widow
is their first priority, before other forms of Christian service
(Lock, 73). (b) If the subject is the widow, she must show her
worth by caring for her relatives before being accepted on the
church list.

τὸν ἴδιον οἶκον (cf. 3.5) is quite general, but the author uses
this general obligation to their household as a basis for the care
of an elderly mother/grandmother.[32] εὐσεβέω (Acts 17.23***) is
'to be reverent, respectful, devout' (+Acc.), both towards gods
(Acts 17.23 Josephus, *Ap.* 2.125; MM 265), and towards people;
hence it expresses the showing of filial devotion as a religious
attitude.[33] There may be the implicit criticism that people were
showing their piety (financially or in terms of devoting time and
attention) towards the church instead of towards their family.
Roloff, 288, holds that on view (a) there is nothing religious
about the expression of respect for the family, but on view (b)
the reference is to a duty arising out of one's faith.

For the duty of care by children to parents in the non-Christian
world see Spicq, 526f. Hierocles (cited above in 5.1 note) likens
children's care for parents to being priests serving deities in a
temple (Spicq, 527).

καὶ ἀμοιβὰς ἀποδιδόναι τοῖς προγόνοις The conjunction καί
has the force 'and thus'. ἀπόδιδωμι is 'to make a return',[34] here
in the sense of giving something in return for what has already
been received from parents. ἀμοιβή*** 'return, recompense' is
common in laudatory inscr. where people show thanks to their
fatherland.[35] πρόγονος (2 Tim 1.3***) lit. 'born earlier', is

---

[32] Stählin holds that the adjective has a stronger force in relation to the widows
rather than to the children.
[33] Philo, *Decal.* 23 (116f.; cf. 112); for such respect see Aristotle, *EN* 9.2
(1164b–65a); Euripides, *Iph Aul.* 1230; Plato, *Leg.* 4.717C; Dittenberger, *Or.* 383,
212ff. (quoted in Dibelius-Conzelmann, 70), which cites the care of offspring for
ancestors as an example of piety; see **Excursus 1**.
[34] Also 'to give away, award', 2 Tim 4.8; 'to reward', 2 Tim 4.14**.
[35] *TLNT* I, 95f. For the link with ἀποδίδωμι see MM 27; BA *s.v.*; Josephus,
Ant. 5.13; Ignatius, *Smyr.* 9.2.

'parent, forbear, ancestor'.[36] Holtzmann, 345, states that the word always refers to those who are already dead. It would then be a very generalised reference to repaying to former generations what is owed to them for their care of their children. However, Plato, *Leg.* 11.931D, uses the word for living parents, and the vg translates with *parentibus* (similarly, pesh). Fee, 116, states that the widowed mothers/grandmothers are clearly meant here, but more probably the author is arguing from the general to the particular. Perhaps the choice of word here is to give a contrast with ἔκγονα in the earlier part of the sentence. (a) If the reference is to children (see above), they they must repay the care shown by their mother/grandmother. (b) If it is to the widows, they must do for the next generation what the previous one did for them; but is this the natural way to express this thought? The thought is of a *quid pro quo* which is not quite the same thing as showing respect for ancestors. The whole concept is part of the motif of reciprocity which was of fundamental importance in Greek ethics (Harrison*, 113–16).

τοῦτο γάρ ἐστιν ἀπόδεκτον ἐνώπιον τοῦ θεοῦ is parallel to 2.3 with γάρ ἐστιν added. The reason why such conduct is pleasing to God is probably because it fulfils the fifth commandment, echoed in v. 3. (This specific motivation disappears if the verse refers to the duty of widows.)

5. Now comes as a contrast a positive description of the real widow. She is a person who in her destitute state and lack of human support has placed her trust in God and is shown to do so by her continual prayer. The author's thought proceeds by a double contrast between the widow who is not destitute and the widow who is destitute and pious, and then between the latter and the self-indulgent widow. The pattern is thus:

v. 4. the widow who is provided for
v. 5. the widow who is destitute and pious
v. 6. the widow who is   impious

According to Knoch, 38, the author now reaches the real point of the section which is to indicate who should be placed on the 'order' with its duties of prayer and good works. This interpretation is unlikely. The thrust of the section in 5.3 is the honouring of genuine widows, and we are now told who they are.

ἡ δὲ ὄντως χήρα καὶ μεμονωμένη δέ draws the contrast with the implied provided-for widow in 5.4. μεμονωμένη must be taken as an added description to clarify the preceding phrase,

---

[36] Cl.; LXX; *Ep. Arist.* 19; Philo, *Deus* 150 and freq.; Josephus, *Ant.* 12.150; *Ap.* 2.157.

'namely (καί), the one who is on her own'. μονόω*** is 'to make
solitary'; pass. 'to be left alone' (Cl.). The word is generally
understood to mean that the widow is socially needy. Wagener
1994:135–43, 165–9, has a lengthy discussion intended to show
that in this context the word need not imply material need;[37] it
can apply to rich widows who are truly religious by contrast
with those who are not (v. 6). Hence the passage is not concerned
with poor widows but only with rich widows who are either
living piously or are ignoring their household duties or acting in
other unacceptable ways in the eyes of the writer. It is more
probable that both poor and rich (cf. v. 6) are in mind.

ἤλπικεν ἐπὶ θεὸν The perfect of ἐλπίζω (4.10; 6.17; cf. 2 Cor
1.9f.) expresses the settled religious attitude that looks to God
to supply needs. For the ideal applied to women in general cf.
1 Pet 3.5. Stählin, *TDNT* IX, 456, takes this to mean that she has
determined not to look to human helpers, i.e. not to remarry. But
this is to read something into the passage. More probably the
widow's need is so desperate that she turns to God for help.[38]

καὶ προσμένει ταῖς δεήσεσιν καὶ ταῖς προσευχαῖς νυκτὸς καὶ
ἡμέρας The practical expression of her hope in God is prayer.
προσμένω (1.3) means 'to continue in' with dat. of thing (cf.
Acts 13.43). δέησις and προσευχή (both in 2.1) with the article
might mean 'the appointed prayers', whether in church or in
private devotion (Lock, 58; Kelly, 114), but not necessarily so
(Phil 4.6; Col 4.12). νυκτὸς καὶ ἡμέρας (2 Tim 1.3)[39] is gen. of
time within which. For the phrase in this order with reference to
prayer cf. 1 Th 3.10; 4 Ezra 9.44 of a barren woman who prayed
for 30 years for a child; it is also used with reference to serving
God more generally (Jth 11.17; Rev 4.8; 7.15) and of other
activities (Mk 5.5; Acts 9.24; 1 Th 2.9; 3.10; 2 Th 3.8).[40] The
specific example of a widow engaged in this manner is Anna.
The virtue of persevering in prayer is, however, to be cultivated
by all believers (Eph 6.18) and not just by one particular group.
The point is that the widow who deserves help from the church
is characterised by this quality which demonstrates her lack of

[37] Cf. the pictures of Esther and Aseneth (Add. Esth 14.3; *Jos. et As.* 11.3, 16;
12.5, 13f.; 13.2).
[38] ἐπί is used here with the acc. (1 Chr 5.20; 2 Chr 13.18; *et al.*; 1 Pet 1.13;
with dat. 4.10; 6.17). Holtzmann, 345, states that the acc. expresses the
object of hope, whereas the dat. expresses the ground or basis of hope, but
this may be too precise a differentiation.
[39] νύξ (2 Tim 1.3**); ἡμέρα (1.12, 18; 4.8; 3.1** of last day[s]).
[40] The acc. of duration of time is used in much the same way (Lk 2.37 [Anna
praying in the temple]; of serving and worshipping God, Acts 26.7; Rev 4.8;
7.15; of other activities, Mk 4.27). The phrase is also found in reverse order,
of prayer and serving God (Lk 18.7; Acts 26.7; Rev 4.8; 7.15); of Christian pastoral
care (Acts 20.31); of other activities (Acts 12.10; 14.11; 20.10).

earthly helpers. No doubt it can be assumed that, if she is enrolled by the church on its list, she will continue in prayer. But in the context the prayers would appear to be an expression of her dependence upon God rather than intercessions for the church (*pace* Brox, 189). Consequently, it is unlikely that she is engaged in an activity for which she should be rewarded by the church.

6. A second type of widow who does not qualify as a 'real widow' is introduced by contrast with the piety of the widow who is destitute. Although the term 'widow' came to be associated with destitution, this was certainly not true of all widows (Rev 18.7!). This type of woman lives voluptuously, which suggests that she is not only lacking in piety but also has the means to live a life of luxury. She is probably to be found among the rich women described in 2.9b. Roloff, 291, argues that the 'rule' here is only for women contemplating entering the church's 'order' and does not apply generally.

σπαταλάω is 'to live luxuriously, be self-indulgent' (Jas 5.5***).[41] But commentators differ whether it refers (a) to living well (and therefore not being destitute),[42] or (b) to indulgence in sexual immorality.[43] The former option is the right one.[44] There is nothing in the context to suggest sexual immorality. The condemnation is, of course, not because the widows are rich but because they misuse their wealth, 'living for pleasure' (NIV); in the general context of the letter an allusion to ignoring the needs of the poor (cf. Ezek 16.49; Jas 5.5) is probable.[45] The widow's spiritual condition is expressed in a vigorous oxymoron (MHT IV, 102). Although she is alive (ζῶσα), she is [spiritually] dead (τέθνηκε; 3.15).[46] The implication is that such a person has no claims on the church. The question of well-off widows who are free from any accusation of misusing wealth or the like is not raised.

---

[41] Wagener 1994:155–61 discusses in detail the 11 occurrences of the word up to the second century AD: Polybius 36.17.7; IG 14.2002.6; Ps-Pythagoras, *Ep.* 4.4; Ps-Diogenes, *Ep.* 28.7; Ezek 16.49; Ecclus 21.15; Barnabas 10.3; of sheep, Hermas, *Sim.* 6.1.6; 6.2.6; Clement, *Strom.* 3.59.1. Cf. κατασπαταλάω, Prov 29.21; Amos 6.4.

[42] Barrett, 74f.; Kelly, 114.

[43] Easton, 152; Hanson, 97; Dornier, 89.

[44] So rightly Wagener. Cf. Stählin, *TDNT* IX, 454 and n. 131 for ancient materials on 'flighty widows'.

[45] Roloff, 291 n. 341, *pace* Wagener 1994:161.

[46] For the paradox of being simultaneously alive and dead cf. Rev 3.1; Hermas, *Sim.* 6.2.3; Aelius Aristides 52.2K (28, p. 551 D); Philo, *Fug.* 55 ζῶντες ἔνιοι τεθνήκασι καὶ τεθνηκότες ζῶσι; *Det.* 49; *Praem.* 70; Timocles, *Com* (IV BC) 35; Sextus 7b, 175 (cited by Dibelius-Conzelmann, 74 n. 11); SB I, 489. White, 129, cites Stobaeus 238: πένης ἀποθανὼν φροντίδων ἀπηλλάγη, ζῶν γὰρ τέθνηκε.

7. καὶ ταῦτα παράγγελλε, ἵνα ἀνεπίλημπτοι ὦσιν. The initial καὶ ... παράγγελλε echoes 4.11. The further teaching in this section is also to be passed on to the church. Whereas Hanson dismisses the verse as a feeble connecting sentence, others rightly see in it a strong and sharp apostolic command.[47] But the reference of ταῦτα is disputed. A reference backwards, whether to 5.3–6; or 5.4–6; or 5.4 (Knight, 220); or 5.5f. (Fee, 117; Rapske) is more likely than a reference forwards or a reference to the whole of 5.3–8 (Spicq, 530).

The ἵνα clause gives the purpose of the exhortation rather than its content. Attention to the exhortation will ensure that 'they' are 'blameless'. But to whom is the reference? Some commentators single out the widows (and indeed regard it as self-evident and needing no proof), and others the children.[48] We are not helped by the fact that ἀνεπίλημπτος (3.2) is an adjective of two terminations and could, therefore, refer to females, i.e. the widows (Bernard, 80; cf. Spicq, 530: 'elles'); it is interpreted as feminine in the Syriac. The decisive point is that v. 8 takes up the command of v. 4 in a negative fashion, so that the focus rests on the families of the widows. The blamelessness is probably in the eyes of other people rather than of God at the last judgement (*pace* Stählin, *TDNT* IX, 454).

Thus, v. 7 strengthens the command in v. 4, passing over vv. 5f. as a parenthesis. Then v. 8 deals with relatives not obeying this command, and vv. 9–16 deal further with the church's responsibility.

8. We now have a repetition of 5.4 in more forcible terms, this time not stating what should be done, but condemning if it is not done. Roloff, 292, curiously compares it with the requirement that the candidate for church leadership should keep his household in order (3.5), but here the point is rather different: on Roloff's view the widow must look after her household (if she has one) rather than be enrolled on the church list. This view assumes that the direction is about widows looking after their families (cf. Wagener). But the more usual interpretation is that it is about families looking after their widowed relatives rather than passing them over to the church's care. (Naturally, this interpretation can include an application to widows with families for whom they are responsible.)

εἰ δέ τις τῶν ἰδίων καὶ μάλιστα οἰκείων οὐ προνοεῖ τὶς is used specifically of householders who have a responsibility for other members of their household, but the reference is obviously

---

[47] Schmitz, O., *TDNT* V, 765; Kelly, 114; Holtz, 117; Rapske 1987:199.
[48] For the former: Roloff, 288; cf. Jeremias, 36f.; Brox, 190; Fee, 117; for the latter: Karris, 93; Knight, 220.

somewhat general. In accordance with his general interpretation of the passage, Holtzmann, 346, applies it to the widows and their care for members of their family (so also Roloff, 292; cf. Oberlinner, 230).

τῶν ἰδίων are the members of the family in a broad sense.[49] The meaning is made precise in the author's manner with the phrase καὶ μάλιστα, usually translated 'and especially', but more correctly 'namely' (4.10 note). The reference is in fact to the members of the household (οἰκεῖος, Eph 2.19; Gal 6.10***; Lev 21.2); the word refers to those relatives who actually lived in the household.[50] προνοέω is 'to think of beforehand, take care, provide for' (Rom 12.17; 2 Cor 8.21***).[51] The noun πρόνοια (Acts 24.3; Rom 13.14), 'forethought', is equivalent to *providentia* in Latin with its sense of provision for people's needs. The virtue was one associated with rulers and with persons in superior positions generally (Harrison*, 109–13). Here it is used with respect to family relationships.

τὴν πίστιν ἤρνηται καὶ ἔστιν ἀπίστου χείρων The condemnation of the uncaring person could not be stronger. τὴν πίστιν is taken by Simpson to mean 'fidelity, respect for obligations', but it is more likely, in view of the article and the next part of the verse, to mean 'the faith' (cf. Rev 2.13; 3.8). Clearly the reference must be to Christian faith and the subjective and objective aspects can hardly be separated from one another. The verb ἀρνέομαι, 'to

---

[49] Cf. Verner 1983:138. The adj. can be used of comrades in battle, compatriots; of fellow-Christians (Acts 4.23; 24.23; cf. Jn. 13.1); and of relatives (Ecclus 11.34; Pap.; Vettius Valens 70.5: ὑπὸ ἰδίων καὶ φίλων [cited by BA]; cf. Jn 1.11b [metaphorical]; *CH* 1.31 of worshippers of a god).

[50] Josephus, *Vita* 183; *M. Poly.* 6.1; Barnabas 3.3 (Isa 58.7); Dittenberger, *Syll.* 317, 38; 560, 21; 591, 59 φίλοι καὶ οἰκεῖοι; *T. Reub.* 3.5 γένος καὶ οἰκεῖοι. Cf. Michel, O., *TDNT* V, 134f. Scholars who take καὶ μάλιστα to mean 'and especially' have to offer a meaningful explanation of the difference between ἴδιοι and οἰκεῖοι. Suggestions offered are: (a) a broader group including slaves and freedpersons of the household/blood relatives (Spicq, 531; however in *TLNT* I, 385, he recognises that the terms are often equivalent); (b) relatives in general/members of the immediate family (Kelly, 114; Verner 1983:138); (c) the family including those living away from home/those living at home (Winter*, 90–3); (d) members of God's household, i.e. fellow Christians (Campbell*, 157–60). View (d) is in agreement with the Syriac which interprets the phrase as 'members of the household of faith', but it is open to the strong objection that elsewhere the word is qualified in some way (as in pesh) when it refers to Christians (Gal 6.10; Eph 2.19). View (c) widens the scope of the directive to include widows resident away from the family as well as especially those at home; however, it is likely that the reference is to the family in general. View (a) is in effect the same as the one adopted above.

[51] The usage is Cl. Maximus of Tyre (AD II) 5.4c (of God's providential care); Wis 13.16; Philo, *Virt.* 216. Horapollo (AD IV) 2, 108 ὑπὸ τῶν οἰκείων προνοούμενος and προνοούμενος ἑαυτοῦ (cited by BA). Cf. Behm, J., *TDNT* IV, 1009–11; Radl, W., *EDNT* III, 158f.

deny, repudiate' (Tit 1.16 and note),[52] expresses here not formal apostasy but practical denial (cf. Spicq, 531). Cf. Mt 10.33 for a possible echo (Müller-Bardorf*, 113⁵). ἄπιστος, 'faithless, unbelieving' (Tit 1.15), is used here of non-Christians who are regarded as having a higher family morality than Christians in that they maintain their reciprocal obligations.[53] χείρων, 'worse' (2 Tim 3.13**), is used in a moral sense (cf. Hermas, *Sim.* 9.17.5; 9.18.1). The thought may be that a believer who denies the faith is worse than a person who has never believed and therefore is not breaking a religious commitment. Unbelievers might well act better out of obedience to the laws.

9. Verses 9–10 describe the type of widow who is to be 'enrolled'; there are three qualifications in terms of age, sexual morality and attested good works; the last qualification is developed by listing five examples and is intended to be the crucial factor in the choice of widows to be 'enrolled'. Some commentators regard the new beginning here as indicating that a new category of widows is now being discussed (Spicq, 532; cf. Stott, 129). This is faulty logic, since the purpose of the preceding paragraph was to stress the need for families to care for their own widowed relatives and there was in fact no discussion of a 'category' of widows eligible for some kind of positive honour from the church in it. Again, Roloff, 293, comments on the absence of a qualification in terms of need and thinks that this argues for an 'order' in the church; this overlooks the point that the preceding verses have clearly implied that neediness is the qualification for 'honour' by the church.

Χήρα καταλεγέσθω In the light of vv. 4–6 it can be assumed that the generic χήρα here by implication excludes those who have a family to look after them or are morally unworthy and is now tantamount to 'genuine widow'. But not all destitute widows are included, and a 'role model' is now given. This is the first, and only, reference to 'enrolment'. καταλέγω*** can mean 'to choose, reckon as', but here has the stronger sense 'to select, enlist, enrol'.[54] There is a thin line between the nuances 'to be selected' and 'to be enrolled' (with the implication of being

---

[52] Cf. 2 Tim 2.12, 13; 3.5; Rev 2.13; 3.8; Hermas, *Sim.* 8.3.7; 4 Macc 8.7; 10.15. The verb is used here with an impersonal object, as in Cl. Gk. (contrast the personal acc., Tit 1.16; Simpson, 73).

[53] Anaximander, in Stobaeus 79.37, as cited by Bernard, 80. Cf. Hierocles, Περὶ καθηκόντων (Stobaeus 3.52); Iamblichus, *Vita Pyth.* 38, cited by Harrison*, 114f.

[54] According to BA it was used especially of soldiers, members of the senate (Plutarch, *Pomp.* 13.7) and religious bodies (P. Oxy. 416.4 [AD III–IV]). The active verb can be used with a double acc. ('to regard x as y', Plato, *Leg.* 5, 742E), but here the pass. is used.

entered on some kind of official list; cf. Müller-Bardorff*, 118 n. 11). Within a small, intimate group such as a first-century congregation the difference should not be pressed. χήρα is used predicatively: 'let a woman be enrolled as a widow'.

The reference to enrolment is introduced in a way which indicates that the practice was already known and being practised: nothing is said to clarify the procedure, as would be necessary if something new was being introduced. What is going on here is a regulation of existing practice which is entrusted to Timothy. The real problem is the purpose of the enrolment. Solutions fall into three categories:

(a) To receive help. Since the theme of the previous paragraph is care for widows by their families and widows who are truly destitute, and there is reference to church provision in v. 16, this is much the most likely purpose (Oepke, A., *TDNT* I, 788).

(b) To render service. The description of the kind of person to be enrolled indicates that they were distinguished by service in the church. It is then arguable that they were enrolled to continue this function in an 'official' role.

(c) To receive help and to render service.

Since the passage is concerned with those who are destitute of family help, we can safely exclude possibility (b) on its own. The question is then whether there is some kind of official recognition of a group of 'working' widows within the larger group of those receiving assistance (Guthrie, 114). Since, however, nothing is said about what is to be done for this 'wider' group, the idea of two groups should be dismissed. The list of qualifications is pointedly in the past tense and refers to the establishment of the good character of candidates for church aid rather than to on-going good works (though doubtless they could continue doing them). The comment of White, 130, is commonsensical: 'It is difficult to suppose that St. Paul, or any other practically minded administrator, would contemplate a presbyteral order of widows, the members of which would enter on their duties at the age of 60, an age relatively more advanced in the East and in the first century than in the West and in our own time.' We should, therefore, accept the first view, while recognising that this does not exclude the possibility of some service by the widows.

μὴ ἔλαττον ἐτῶν ἐξήκοντα γεγονυῖα The usual construction for an expression of age is εἶναι/γίνεσθαι + gen.;[55] it is here complicated by the use of ἔλαττον***[56] with gen. of

[55] Cl.; Mk 5.42; Lk 3.1; 8.42; Acts 4.22; Josephus, *Ant.* 10.50.
[56] Adverb from the adj. ἐλάττων 'smaller, less' (Rom 9.12; Jn 2.10; Heb 7.7); *TLNT* I, 468–70.

comparison.[57] ἔτος** is here 'year' of age (Jn 8.57); the perfect γεγονυῖα signifies 'having reached the age of'.[58] For the significance of 60+ as 'old age' cf. Tit 2.2 note.[59] 'Real' old age is meant, presumably beyond the age at which a person might reasonably be thought able in general to provide for their own needs.[60] For some commentators there is significance in the fact that remarriage was less likely at this age. The point may be in fact to move the age of acceptability upwards to curtail the numbers seeking assistance (Knoch, 38). The same age-limit is found in later church documents (but is reduced to 50 in *Didasc.* 14, from which Roloff, 293, suggests that the PE may be deliberately raising the age). There is perhaps a problem in that there is a gap in the support provision between the widows aged 60+ and the younger widows who were still of child-bearing age (v. 14; cf. Johnson, 183), but it must be remembered that these instructions are probably more in the nature of ideals than precise regulations.

ἑνὸς ἀνδρὸς γυνή The second condition prescribed is the female equivalent of 3.2. As in that case, the sense is disputed. The possibilities are basically a woman who has been married only once ((a) – (c) below; so GNB text; NRSV) or a woman of impeccable morality ((d) below; NIV):

(a) A woman who is not in a state of remarriage after the death or divorce of a previous husband. But this is surely so obvious a qualification as not to need to be stated.

(b) A widow who has been married only once, and has not remarried after the death of her husband and subsequently been widowed for a second time. (On this view it is taken for granted that remarriage after divorce is also excluded.)[61]

In favour of this interpretation of the phrase commentators cite the ideal depicted by Anna (Lk 2.36); the later tradition and interpretation of the church; the evidence of inscriptions praising μονανδρία; the analogy of the overseers and deacons in ch. 3; the exclusion of women who might wish to remarry (vv. 11–13). In Roman society the ideal of one marriage for women was upheld (Brox, 19), whereas in Greek society remarriage was common for practical and material reasons. Further, the ideal of not remarrying after taking a 'vow' of widowhood would point in the same direction; but the existence of this 'vow' is

---

[57] Cf. Acts 4.22; Plato, *Leg.* 6, 755A: μὴ ἔλαττον ἢ πεντήκοντα γεγονὼς ἐτῶν; *Ep.* 2, 314B: οὐκ ἐλάττω τριάκοντα ἐτῶν; BD § 185[4].

[58] A verbal parallel to the age limit is offered by *Kyr. Inschr.* 1.16: μηδένα νεώτερον πέντε κ. εἴκοσι (cited by BA).

[59] However, *'Abot* 5.21 distinguishes between being an elder (60) and having grey hair (70).

[60] Cf. Lock, 59; Dornier, 90; Kelly, 115, Jeremias, 38; Holtz, 118.

[61] Kelly, 116; Scott, 60; Spicq, 533; Fee, 119; Roloff, 293f.; Rapske 1987:204f.

questionable (see below). Rapske further argues that the context strongly indicates only single marriage; a woman twice married would have lots of relatives.

But the argument that younger widows were excluded in any case (Fee, 119) surely means that there could be substantial numbers of women who were twice widowed, and this makes the exclusion very unlikely. The recognised legality of marriage after widowhood, especially in the light of recommending it for younger widows, sufficiently excludes this view. No obvious reason why the author should have made this particular exclusion can be seen. Roloff, 294, has to admit that the author does not seem entirely to have shared this view.

(c) A woman who has remarried after divorce and then subsequently been widowed (possibly more than once). The objection would then be to polyandry (Oepke, A., *TDNT* I, 788; Jeremias, 38). Since remarriage of younger widows is permitted, this interpretation is more plausible than (b).

(d) A woman who has been faithful to her husband and is not guilty of any sexual immorality (Lock, 60; Dibelius-Conzelmann, 75; Oberlinner, 231–3; Winter*, 95). This was the interpretation of Theodore of Mopsuestia: 'If she has lived in chastity with her husband, no matter whether she has had only one, or whether she was married a second time' (*si pudice cum suo vixerit viro, sive unum tantum habuerit, sive et secundo fuerit nupta*; Theod. Mops. II, 161 Swete, cited by Dibelius-Conzelmann, 75).

In line with the interpretation which we have adopted of the similar phrase used of men (d) remains the most likely interpretation (see Tit 1.6 note).

10. The third requirement is a good reputation on the basis of what the widow has done. The specific qualifications are expressed in the past tense, and are thus indications of Christian character attested by service rendered in the past rather than a list of duties to be performed for the future. It is not specified whether these are things that she has done since being widowed or throughout her adult life; either or both can be meant. Some commentators see these as an indication of fitness for continued service (Knoch, 38). It can be assumed that these duties would continue while the woman was able to do them. However, there is nothing in the list which suggests some kind of special service in the church which would justify talking of an 'order' of ministry.

ἐν ἔργοις καλοῖς μαρτυρουμένη The plural ἔργα καλά (5.25; 6.18; Tit 2.7, 14; 3.8, 14) is equivalent to ἔργα ἀγαθά (2.10; cf. the use of the sing. form as a virtual pl. later in the verse). μαρτυρουμένη (6.13* cf. μαρτυρία, 3.7) is from μαρτυρέω, 'to bear witness'; hence eventually 'to be a martyr' (see 6.13 note); the pass. has the sense 'to be witnessed', hence 'to be well spoken of, to be approved'.[62] The verb is used with ἐν, 'in the sphere of, by reason of' (Heb 11.2). The motif that God's people must have a good reputation, whether in the church or in society, is widespread.[63]

A list of four typical examples of good deeds and one general description follows. These are simply examples of the kind of good deeds that may have been practised, and not a check-list for scoring 'brownie points'. Nevertheless, they all appear in a sixth-century epitaph for the deacon Maria which is confessedly paraphrasing this verse (*New Docs.* II, 193–5 § 109).

(a) εἰ ἐτεκνοτρόφησεν This use of εἰ clauses to express a set of possible conditions seems to be unparalleled. The verb τεκνοτροφέω***, 'to bring up children',[64] could refer simply to the bringing up of her own family[65] or to care for other people's children, including orphans.[66] While some commentators think primarily of the former, the latter is the more likely (but not necessarily exclusively so), since by definition the widow has no children or grandchildren to look after her, and the other qualities are all concerned with service to other people.

(b) εἰ ἐξενοδόχησεν ξενοδοχέω***, 'to show hospitality', is a later form for ξενοδοκέω and was rejected by Atticists.[67] For the virtue in general see Mt 25.35; Rom 12.13; Heb 13.2. The necessity and importance of showing hospitality to travelling Christians has already been mentioned in 3.2; it was not to be confined to church leaders.

(c) εἰ ἁγίων πόδας ἔνιψεν ἅγιος (2 Tim 1.9; 2 Tim 1.14 and Tit 3.5 of the Holy Spirit) is used freqently in the pl. of Christians in general.[68] There is no justification for the view that a special group is meant (*pace* Wagener 1994:188f.).[69] It appears rather to be a name that became traditional in the church, following

[62] Acts 6.3; 10.22; 16.2; 22.12; 3 Jn 12; 1 Clement 17.1; 18.1; 19.1 *et al.*; Ignatius, *Philad.* 11.1; cf. also Lk 4.22; Acts 13.22; Heb 11.4, 5, 39. For the use of the terminology in secular inscriptions see Spicq, 533.

[63] Cf. Strathmann, H., *TDNT* IV, 474–508, espec. 496f.

[64] Cl.; Epictetus 1.23.3.

[65] Spicq, 534; Arichea-Hatton, 118; Stählin, G., *TDNT* IX, 456 n. 153.

[66] Lock, 60; Dibelius-Conzelmann, 75; Jeremias, 38; Kelly, 116f.; Hanson, 98; Rapske 1987:207.

[67] *TLNT* II, 55–60, espec. 59.

[68] Acts 9.13, 32; Rom 8.27; 12.13; 15.25; 2 Cor 1.1; *et al.* Cf. Procksch, O., *TDNT* I, 88–115; Balz, H., *EDNT* I, 16–20; and especially Dunn, J. D. G., *Romans* (Waco: Word, 1988), I, 19f.

[69] She argues correctly that a traditional phrase is used, which Paul uses on occasion in the context of being served. (Similarly, Easton, 209, is correct in talking of a formula-phrase.) But she then claims that washing the feet of all the congregation cannot be meant.

OT and Jewish usage;[70] but, whereas in the OT and Judaism the adjective is often predicative (Isa 4.3; *Ps. Sol.* 17.36) or qualified (e.g. 'the holy ones of the Most High', Dan 7.18, 21, 25, 27), in the NT the simple phrase οἱ ἅγιοι is used.[71] It is significant that the term is used in Rom 12.13 in the context of menial service in the congregation.

The washing of feet (πούς**)[72] is widely attested.[73] νίπτω is Hellenistic for νίζω, used of washing a part of the body rather than the whole.[74] The references show that it was a menial act performed by slaves (cf. SB I, 427f.), but also by women (SB II, 557; III, 653) and was thus a symbol of humble service. It may have had sexual associations but also expressed the service of a wife to her husband (1 Sam 25.41; *Jos. et As.* 13.15); it is not attested as an act of a man to a woman (Wagener 1994:189–91).

The problem is why it is mentioned here, and why it is the feet of the saints in particular which are washed. The fact that it is not described as a mutual action (as Jn 13 might be held to require) may indicate that it was not a cultic or symbolic act (*pace* Holtz, 118); this may have been practised in the Johannine community, but there is no certain evidence for it elsewhere before the time of Augustine and Ambrose.[75]

Wagener 1994:187–99 disputes whether foot-washing was associated with hospitality. She argues that in Lk women are dissociated from preaching and are given the task of ministering to the male preachers (Lk 8.1–3); the story of the sinful woman who anointed Jesus' feet may have helped to develop a church practice of foot-washing by women as a token of loving service. The foot-washing in Jn is interpreted as a preparation of the (male) disciples for service, and although in Jn it was a sign of inversion of position between the leader and his followers, this significance did not affect the relationship between the sexes. It was a complementary activity to preaching, which confirmed the male preachers in their role and was assigned to the women.

A manifest weakness in this speculation is that there is no evidence that ἅγιοι refers to the men or church leaders in their

---

[70] Ps 15 (MT 16).3; 33 (MT 34).10; 82 (MT 83).4; Tob 8.15.

[71] Cf. Dan 7.21f.; Wis 18.9; *T. Levi* 18.11, 14; *T. Iss.* 5.4; *T. Dan.* 5.12; cf. *1 Enoch* 38.44f.; 43.4; *et al.*; cf. 'the men of holiness' in 1QS 5.13; *et al.*

[72] For omission of the article with πόδας cf. BD §259³; it is not an example of Hebrew idiom (status constructus) but assimilation of the noun to the anarthrous gen. ἁγίων.

[73] Gen 18.4; 19.2; 43.24; 1 Sam 25.41; Josephus, *Ant.* 6.308; Herodotus 6.19; Plutarch, *Pomp.* 73.7; Jn 13.5f., 8–10, 12, 14; cf. Lk 7.44 (anointing and kissing feet). Cf. Weiss, K., *TDNT* V, 624–31.

[74] Of the hands, Mt 15.2; Mk 7.3; the face, Mt 6.17; cf. Jn 9.7, 11, 15; the feet, Jn 13.5–14. Cf. Hauck, F., *TDNT* IV, 946f.

[75] Fee, 125; Edwards*, 379 n. 32.

role as preachers. Further, the position of the reference, which is sandwiched in between references to necessary acts of care for the needy, makes such an interpretation out of context. Rather, the washing of feet was a necessary service which may have stood out by its meniality as a particular example of willingness to serve. There is the further possibility that the language is metaphorical for 'being prepared to do even the most menial of tasks in the church'.[76] If part of the problem arose from the attitudes of rich widows, then willingness to undertake the most humble of tasks in service of the needy could have been especially important; foot-washing was especially symbolical of this. In any case, it is not an activity especially ascribed to widows, since the verse deals with their life before being enrolled as widows (and therefore possibly while their husbands were still alive).

(d) εἰ θλιβομένοις ἐπήρκεσεν The passive participle of θλίβω, 'to press upon, oppress, afflict',[77] may refer to people suffering from (a) ordinary human afflictions – bereavement, destitution (so possibly Schlier), etc.; (b) persecution (cf. Lucian, *De Morte Per.* 12 for the care of widows and orphans for him in prison); or (c) both (Holtz, 118). Since persecution was a constant possibility in the early church (2 Tim 1.8; 2.3), it may be included in this very general reference, even though it does not figure elsewhere in 1 Tim and when it does occur in 2 Tim it affects Paul and Timothy rather than the congregations. The verb ἐπαρκέω, 'to help, aid',[78] has equally a very general meaning, but its use for giving help to widows in 5.16 strongly suggests that help to the destitute is also in mind here. The requirement corresponds with the injunctions to the rich generally in 6.18.

(e) εἰ παντὶ ἔργῳ ἀγαθῷ ἐπηκολούθησεν The phrase πάντι ἔργῳ ἀγαθῷ has a verbal parallel in Col 1.10. Good works are characteristic of godly women in 2.10, and of believers in general (2 Tim 2.21; 3.17; Tit 1.16; 3.1; cf. **Excursus 6**). The reference is very broad, to whatever kind of good works the widow could find to do; for good works by widows see Hermas, *Vis.* 2.4.3. In Acts 8.36 Dorcas, who helped widows, may have been one herself (but she is not so called and she is hardly evidence for some kind of organised 'order'). ἐπακολουθέω means lit. 'to follow, come after' (5.24) and fig. (as here) 'to follow after, devote oneself to'.[79] The word implies that the widow has been zealous

[76] Edwards*, 371 n. 12; cf. Scott, 61; Holtz, 118.
[77] 2 Cor 1.6; 4.8; 7.5; 1 Th 3.4; 2 Th 1.6, 7; Heb 11.37; for use as a noun see Ignatius, *Smyr.* 6.2; Barnabas 20.2; Diognetus 5.2; cf. Schlier, H., *TDNT* III, 139–48.
[78] 5.16a, 16b***; Cl.; 1 Macc 8.26; 11.35; Josephus, *Ant.* 1.247; 8.113; 15.119; *et al.*
[79] Lit.: Mk 16.20; 1 Pet 2.21***; Ignatius, *Smyr.* 10.1; 1 Clement 43.1; fig.: Josh 14.14; Plato, *Rep.* 2, 370C; Josephus, *Ap.* 1.6.

in finding opportunities for doing good and following them through. In a Jewish context these are works of love, as distinct from alms (Jeremias, 40).

Especially in view of its presence in v. 5 a noteworthy absentee from the list is prayer. There is consequently not the slightest indication that an order of women devoting themselves especially or exclusively to prayer is in mind.

11. Verses 11–15 deal with younger widows. First, reasons are given for not including them in the list of women who are to be given aid. These reasons are concerned with their loyalty to Christ and their nuisance value if they are unoccupied and causing mischief. Second, positive instruction is given that they should marry and occupy themselves in domestic duties rather than cause opprobrium for the church. The implication is that the enrolment of younger widows had been practised already, but is now to be discontinued because of its unfortunate results.

νεωτέρας δὲ χήρας παραιτοῦ δέ draws a contrast with v. 9: 'but as for younger widows [don't enrol them but] reject (4.7) them'. However, the alternative translation 'but as for younger women [don't enrol them but] reject them as widows' has been proposed on the grounds that this gives a closer parallel to v. 9 (Wagener 1994:123 with n. 44); but it is not clear that the writer construes this verb with a double acc. νεωτέρας (5.1) clearly means at least below the age of 60 (5.9). But it could be confined to people much younger than this in view of the possibility of their bearing children. Wagener 1994:200f., thinks that it refers to a distinct age group (like νεώτεροι) rather than being used comparatively. However, if we take v. 14 as referring to different possible occupations, then the wording could easily include widows beyond child-bearing age who nevertheless could bring up the existing children and/or take care of their husband's household. But the general tone of the remarks suggests that the focus is on a younger age-group.[80]

ὅταν γὰρ καταστρηνιάσωσιν τοῦ Χριστοῦ, γαμεῖν θέλουσιν ὅταν, 'when, whenever' (Tit 3.12**) introduces an action that is conditional and possibly repeatable. καταστρηνιάω***, 'to become wanton against', is a hapax legomenon unattested elsewhere.[81] The simplex verb is found in Rev 18.7, 9 in the context of a woman declaring that she is not a widow and can therefore do as she pleases (Holtzmann, 348). The sense is that they

---

[80] The view that the word means 'newly baptised' (Elliott, J. H., 'Ministry and Church Order in the New Testament: A Traditio-Historical Analysis (1 Pt 5,1–5 & plls.)', *CBQ* 32 [1970], 367–91) is unlikely when a reference to age is plainly demanded.

[81] The statement in Schneider, C., *TDNT* III, 631, that it occurs in the LXX is incorrect.

'feel sensuous impulses that alienate them from Christ' (BA), i.e. that their sexual impulses form a temptation that lead them away from devotion to Christ. The form τοῦ Χριστοῦ (i.e. article + Χριστός) is found only here in the PE. The present tense suggests that cases are already happening, as v. 15 confirms. This might mean that they fall into sexual sin which is inconsistent with Christian ethics. But this is apparently excluded by the fact that they wish to marry (γαμέω, 4.3; 5.14), unless the sin is entering into marriage with a non-believer (cf. Rapske 1987:210) or possibly cohabiting before marriage. Possibly the thought is that they rebel 'against Christian service' (Scott, 61; *pace* Rapske), having made some kind of vow to serve Christ. The syntax leaves it open whether the wish to marry follows the rebellion against Christ, or is the cause, or is simultaneous. Rapske 1987:210 suggests that a widow's inclusion on the church list for support makes her desire for remarriage wrong.

12. ἔχουσαι κρίμα ὅτι τὴν πρώτην πίστιν ἠθέτησαν ἔχουσαι has the force 'and so they incur' condemnation (κρίμα, 3.6).[82] The condemnation is presumably that of God, and Calvin, 258, took it to be to eternal death. ἀθετέω** is 'to declare invalid, nullify, set aside' and may include the nuance of perfidy.[83] πρῶτος (1.15) is 'first', i.e. 'chief' or 'former' (cf. Rev 2.4: 'you have lost your first love, *sc.* the love you used to have for Christ'). It need not imply that there is a 'second' πίστις: the contrast is with ἀπιστία.[84]

πίστις here can be taken in various ways, depending on whether it is understood as 'vow' or 'faith'. The meaning of a 'solemn promise' or 'oath' (= συνθήκη, Dibelius-Conzelmann, 75 n. 17, citing patristic evidence) is well-attested.[85]

(a) The oath could have been understood to be to their first husbands to whom they are somehow unfaithful by remarrying.[86] This would fit in with a stress in Judaism on the virtue of not remarrying, presumably out of loyalty to the deceased partner.[87] But this consideration is not explicit in the context, and the

[82] The phrase in 1 Cor 6.7 obviously has a different sense. The verb λαμβάνω is more common for incurring condemnation (Mk 12.40; *et al.*).

[83] For use with πίστις, 'pledge', see Polybius 11.29.3; for other uses cf. Mk 7.9; Lk 7.30; 1 Cor 1.19; Gal 2.21; 3.15; Heb 10.28; The verb has the meaning 'to reject, not recognise [a person]' in Mk 6.26; Lk 10.16; Jn 12.48; 1 Th 4.8; Jude 8***; Cf. Maurer, C., *TDNT* VIII, 158f.; *TLNT* I, 39f.

[84] Michaelis, W., *TDNT* VI, 866; cf. BA *s.v.* 1.a.

[85] Cf. BA *s.v.* 1.b. (Xenophon, *Hel.* 1.3.12; 3 Macc 3.10; Josephus, *Ant.* 12.382).

[86] *TLNT* III, 112 n. 8 cites more fully the inscription quoted in BA *s.v.* 1.b about the punishment of a woman because she πρώτη ἠθέτησεν τὴν πίστιν to her husband.

[87] Jth 8.4; 16.22; Lk 2.36–38; 1 Tim 5.9 (if so interpreted).

permission to younger widows to remarry rather goes against it. Moreover, the use of πρώτην is very odd.

(b) Some kind of vow not to remarry and so be at the disposal of the church for Christian service is defended by many commentators.[88] Such a vow, it is assumed, would have been a public part of the process of enrolment on the church's list.

(c) Some go further and understand the vow not to remarry as a kind of betrothal to Christ.[89] This would make the breaking of it all the more serious and liable to judgement. However, the concept of an individual relationship to Christ of this kind is unparalleled in the NT and developed much later. There is no OT warrant for this, but Philo, *Som.* 2.273, speaks allegorically of those 'who are as orphans and widows to creation, and have adopted God as the lawful husband and father of the servant-soul' (Stählin, G., *TDNT* IX, 448); this is hardly evidence that widows thought of themselves as married to God (for the phrase 'widow of God' in a Christian inscription see Winter*, 99). A promise not to re-marry is more defensible, but 'the first vow' is a strange way to refer to it. But in any case such a vow at the age of 60 is unlikely, and such negative vows are said to be unknown (Sand*, 196f.)

(d) In view of these difficulties it is more likely that πίστις has its more common meaning of 'faith', i.e. they apostatise from the faith. This is strong language, but the author may have felt it to be justified if the issue was wanting to marry non-believers and presumably then adopting the religious position of their husbands (cf. Hasler, 42; Fee, 121). The objection that in v. 13 the widows appear to be still active in the Christian community does not hold because this verse is about their activities while they are still widows and refers to dubious activities short of apostasy. The parallel in v. 8 strongly favours this interpretation of πίστις. The writer is concerned throughout with conduct which is in effect a denial of the faith that they previously held. Here the language is stronger because an actual falling away from devotion to Christ is envisaged rather than simply conduct which is inconsistent with faith.

A bigger problem is that marriage is precisely what is encouraged in v. 14. Clearly there is some difference between the two types of marriage, that which is implicitly forbidden in v. 11 and that which is commended in v. 14. As we have seen, one explanation is that v. 11 is concerned with people who have taken a vow of

---

[88] Holtzmann, 349; Bernard, 83; Barrett, 76; Spicq, 535f. (cf. *TLNT* I, 40; III, 112); Knight, 222, 226f.

[89] Stählin, G., *TDNT* IX, 454f.; Easton, 154; Jeremias, 39; Holtz, 119; Spicq, 535; Kelly, 117; Hanson, 98; Roloff, 296f.; Ernst*; Wagener 1994:202–4. The line between this and the previous interpretation is a fine one.

celibacy whereas v. 14 is about people who have not done so and are therefore free to marry. Wagener apparently suggests that to tie 'widowhood' to celibacy/virginity is to include what is in effect a marriage to Christ, the breaking of which comes under severe judgement. Therefore, it is highly dangerous for people to take such a vow because of the possibility of breaking it; it is, therefore, wiser not to enter into it, and people who may be tempted subsequently to break it should marry (v. 14) rather than take it. Behind this interpretation is the claim that the term 'widow' can include unmarried virgins. To 'marry' Christ as one's 'first vow' excludes a previous marriage.

Against this interpretation it can be argued that the logic of v. 11b is the wrong way round for it: it speaks of turning against Christ and wanting to marry, whereas the expected order would be that they want to marry and so turn against Christ. Further, it is unwarranted to visualise unmarried young women being accepted as 'widows' and for binding vows of this nature to be taken.

In view of all the difficulties inherent in this explanation, it is more likely that the distinction is between marriage to unbelievers and believers respectively. What the writer is contemplating is the ultimate danger if young widows are enrolled and cared for by the church. However, there are less serious, but nevertheless real dangers short of this final step, and to them he now turns.

13. ἅμα δὲ καὶ ἀργαὶ μανθάνουσιν περιερχόμεναι τὰς οἰκίας, οὐ μόνον δὲ ἀργαὶ ἀλλὰ καὶ φλύαροι καὶ περίεργοι, λαλοῦσαι τὰ μὴ δέοντα This verse must refer to something distinguishable from what is happening in vv. 11b–12. It is an additional argument against enrolling younger widows, in that they have the subsidised leisure to become nuisances. Therefore the writer counsels marriage instead. It is not directed against those who want to get married, but against those who are happy with subsidised leisure and misuse it.

The adverb ἅμα, 'at the same time, together', is used of things happening simultaneously.[90] The force appears to be 'At the same time as some are wanting to marry, others are learning to be lazy'. The difficulty arises because the fact that two groups of people or types of behaviour are being described is not clearly expressed. What is being described here is what the young widows

---

[90] Acts 27.40. When it is linked to καί, as here, it stresses the idea of something also happening at the same time (Acts 24.26; Col 4.3; with δέ: Philem 22; Josephus, *Ant.* 18.246); other uses are in the sense of 'together' (Rom 3.12); and as a preposition with dat. (Mt 13.29). It is used pleonastically in 1 Th 4.17; 5.10; cf. Mt 20.1.

may do while they are still being cared for by the church and before they have begun to grow uneasy with their situation.

ἀργός has here the sense of 'idle, having no work to do' or 'lazy, not wanting to work' (Tit 1.12** and note). The positioning of this word and its repetition in 13b indicate that this is the key thought in the first part of the verse (Dibelius-Conzelmann, 75). The implied reason for their idleness is that they have no children or household to occupy their time.

μανθάνω (2.11; Tit 3.14 note) is here used as effectively the passive of διδάσκω. But the construction is puzzling in that the verb is followed not by an inf. (as e.g. Phil 4.11) but by an adj. (ἀργαί). The simplest solution is to assume that εἶναι is to be supplied, and parallels can be cited to support this interpretation.[91] Nevertheless, it is regarded as difficult by many, and has led to the unlikely conjecture λανθάνουσιν (Mangey; followed by Moffatt; Jeremias, 39). Wagener 1994:204–6 adopts a different approach by taking the verb absolutely of the desire of the women to learn (so also Holtz, 114) and the adj. is then understood predicatively to mean 'useless, without fruit' (cf. Jas 1.20; 2 Pet 1.8). The verse then discredits and condemns women learning because it produces no good works. In support of this interpretation 2 Tim 3.7 is cited as a parallel. But the use of ἀργαί predicatively is extremely harsh, and the meaning of the word is more likely to be the same as in Tit 1.12.

The idle women wander around people's houses. περιέρχομαι is 'to go around';[92] in the present context it probably has a bad sense, 'to gad about'.[93] Some scholars think that the reference is to a misuse of pastoral visitation.[94] This is unlikely because the point is not that they were misusing the role of visitors but that they were using their spare time to do visiting that they would not otherwise have done (Oepke, A., *TDNT* I, 788; Verner, 164f.; Rapske 1987:216f.). They were not meant to be visitors but to work in their own homes (Fee, 122; cf. Roloff, 297).

---

[91] See Field 1899:210; MHT I, 229. Plato, *Euthyd.* 276B: Οἱ ἀμαθεῖς ἄρα σοφοί [sc. εἶναι] μανθάνουσιν is cited as a parallel, but it should be noted that σοφοί is missing in some MSS and is omitted in Burnett's text. The idiom can be used of learning a profession. Cf. Dio Chrysostom VII p. 699A; IX p. 259B: εἰ ἰατρὸς μέλλοις μανθάνειν (cited by Field). Cf. BD §416².

[92] Acts 28.13, of circling round the coast. It also can mean 'to go from place to place' (Acts 19.13; Heb 11.37; so P. Oxy. 1033, 12 περιερχόμενοι τὴν πόλιν [AD IV]; Job 2:9 *v.l.*: οἰκίαν ἐξ οἰκίας περιερχομένη).

[93] Cf. the effect of περί in περίεργος (v. 13b) and περιεργάζομαι (2 Th 3.11). SB III, 653, cite some Rabbinic remarks about widows who were always gadding about and gaining a bad reputation.

[94] Scott, 62; Dibelius-Conzelmann, 75; Dornier, 91; Kelly, 118; Hanson, 99; Knight, 227.

The phrase οὐ μόνον δέ ... ἀλλὰ καί ... ('and not only ... but
also...') introduces a worse aspect of the situation.[95] φλύαρος***
is 'given to gossiping', 'talking nonsense', 'foolish', i.e. 'talking too
much and saying nothing worth saying' (Wagener 1994:208).[96]
Here the context shows that talking nonsense rather than
gossiping about other people is the problem (Fee, 122).
περίεργος describes somebody who pays attention to things that
do not concern them, 'curious', hence 'busybody'.[97] In Acts
19.19*** the word refers to things belonging to magic. Some
find this sense here,[98] but nothing in the context supports it, and
the link with φλύαρος speaks against it (so rightly Roloff, 297
n. 382). Fee, 63, 125f., holds that the reference is to idle busybodies
(cf. περιεργάζομαι, 2 Th 3.11***, 'to do useless things') who
bring the church into disrepute with outsiders, as in the situation
reflected in 1 Th 4.11f. (cf. Dornier 92). Wagener 1994:208–11,
goes back to the basic meaning of the word and holds that it
could refer to women interfering in men's affairs instead of
sticking to their household duties (Philo, *Spec.* 3.169–71) or to
curiosity about other people's households (Plutarch, *Mor.*
515–23 [Περὶ πολυπραγμοσύνης]). The context shows that the
latter is in mind. λαλέω here probably refers to talking (Rapske
1987:217) rather than teaching in a formal sense.[99] τὰ μὴ δέοντα
(δεῖ, 3.2; Tit 1.7 note) are 'things which ought not [to be said]'.[100]
The reference may be to: (a) indecent language (Easton, 151);
(b) the betrayal of confidences (Bernard, 83; Guthrie, 116;
Rapske 1987:218); (c) magic spells (Hanson, 99); (d) general
gossip; or (e) heretical teaching; the similar reference in Tit 1.11
with reference to teaching by opponents is probably decisive for
the meaning here. Their conversation is promoting false teaching
in a less formal, but equally destructive manner.

14. Βούλομαι οὖν νεωτέρας γαμεῖν, τεκνογονεῖν, οἰκοδεσποτεῖν
In view of all the dangers attendant on enrolling younger widows
(οὖν), the author recommends that they should remarry and
occupy themselves with the resulting duties. They are to emulate
the virtues of the older widows but in the context of marriage
(Fee, 123). This course of action will have the added advantage

---

[95] Cf. 2 Tim 2.20; 4.8; Acts 19.27; 2 Cor 7.7; *et al.*
[96] Cl.; 4 Macc 5.10; Josephus, *Vita* 150; cf. φλυαρέω, 3 Jn. 10; φλυαρία, Prov
23.29 *v.l.*; the word is 'used in polemic to denounce the inaneness of an argument
or accusation' (*TLNT* III, 466).
[97] Cl.; Josephus, *Ap.* 1.16; *T. Iss.* 3.3; Hermas, *Vis.* 4.3.1. περιεργάζομαι is
used similarly (2 Th 3.11).
[98] So possibly Jeremias, 39; Spicq, 537; Kelly, 118; Hanson, 99; Holtz, 120.
[99] For the latter possibility see Tit 2.1, 15; Wagener 1994:206f.
[100] For the use of μή for Cl. οὐ cf. Rom 1.28; 4.17; 1 Cor 1.28; 2 Cor 4.18a,
18b; 5.21; Heb 12.27; Philo, *Op.* 81; 3 Macc 4.16; BD §430.

of warding off the criticism of the church by outsiders which the way of life of the widows might otherwise invite. The motive is the same as in Tit 2.8.

βούλομαι is used as in 2.8 (cf. Tit 3.8) to issue a strong directive. νεωτέρας must refer in this context to the young widows, but it could refer to young women in general who are counselled to marry rather than become 'widows' (Lock, 61). γαμεῖν must also refer to remarriage unless the 'young' are virgins. Rapske 1987:219f. regards this as a special case consistent with the instructions in 1 Cor 7 and now easier if the sense of crisis/ imminence of the parousia had weakened. Dibelius-Conzelmann, 75f., notes that the motive is no longer eschatological, as in 1 Cor 7, but is the need for 'good order'. The command to marry is seen sometimes as a contradiction to 1 Cor 7.8, 40, where Paul does not recommend remarriage; but Paul does say that people should marry rather than 'burn' in 1 Cor 7.9, and v. 39 equally explicitly allows that a widow may remarry. There is no need for elaborate attempts to find a tension or ways of resolving it.

τεκνογονέω*** is 'to bear, beget children'[101] and οἰκοδεσποτέω*** is 'to manage one's household, keep house'.[102] The women are thus expected to spend their time in family life and domestic pursuits. There was, of course, no diffficulty about a woman being in charge of what went on in the home.

μηδεμίαν ἀφορμὴν διδόναι τῷ ἀντικειμένῳ λοιδορίας χάριν ἀφορμή is a 'starting point, opportunity', hence an 'occasion' or 'pretext' for doing something.[103] λοιδορία is verbal abuse which injures and damages people, always by human beings (βλασφημία is used of the devil in Jude 9).[104] For χάριν see Tit 1.5 note. The whole phrase is then generally construed as 'giving no occasion for abuse to the adversary'; i.e. people are to give opponents no occasion for criticism because of the abuse which this might produce (rather than to give no opportunity to the opponents to indulge in abuse). The construction is awkward, and therefore Wagener 1994:213f. adopts the older suggestion that we should translate 'giving no occasion to the adversary because of abuse'.[105] On this view, the point is that people should not live lives which give occasion for criticism by outsiders and

---

[101] Not Cl.; it is used of animals as well as human beings; Diognetus 5.6; cf. τεκνογονία, 2.15.

[102] Not Cl.; Plutarch, *Mor.* 908C.

[103] Lk 11.54 *v.l.*; Rom 7.8, 11; 2 Cor 5.12; 11.12; Gal 5.13***; cf. Bertram, G., *TDNT* V, 472–4. For the combination with διδόναι cf. 2 Cor 5.12; Prov 9.9; Polybius 28.6.7; P. Oxy. 3057.19 (*New Docs.* VI, 169f. §25).

[104] 1 Pet 3.9a, 9b; Cl.; cf. λοιδορέω, Jn 9.28; Acts 23.4; 1 Cor 4.12; 1 Pet 2.23; ἀντιλοιδορέω, 1 Pet 2.23; λοίδορος, 1 Cor 5.11; 6.10; cf. Hanse, H., *TDNT* IV, 293f.; *TLNT* II, 407–9.

[105] Wohlenberg, 184.

therefore place them open to accusation by the devil (cf. 1 Tim 3.7). The ἀντικείμενος, 'adversary',[106] may be understood as (a) a human adversary of the gospel (cf. references above);[107] (b) a collective sing. for the hostile world (G. Stählin, *TDNT* IX, 455 n. 142); (c) the devil as 'the accuser of the brothers' (Rev 12.10).[108] Most scholars adopt view (a), but on Wagener's view the third interpretation is clearly demanded. It may be a difficulty for this interpretation that the devil figures in the next verse as the tempter, but there is nothing really problematic about his being the tempter who often accuses those who yield to his temptation.

In any case, the concern is for the outsider's criticism as in 1 Tim 3.7; 6.1; Tit 2.5, 8; 1 Pet 2.13; 3.16. Disturbance of the social framework by any group which is in a position of subordination (including young men, Tit 2.8) is seen as a cause of criticism from outside the church.[109]

15. ἤδη γάρ τινες ἐξετράπησαν ὀπίσω τοῦ σατανᾶ The instruction is made all the more urgent by the fact that some people have already (ἤδη; 2 Tim 2.18, 4.6**) yielded to temptation and fallen; the description of what can happen in 5.11b is based on experience.[110] τινές is the usual Pauline indefinite way of referring to such people (1.3 note). For ἐκτρέπομαι see 1.6 note; 6.20; ὀπίσω**, 'after', is frequently used as prep. with gen., e.g. with reference to following good or bad leaders (Mk 1.17; Acts 20.30; Rev 13.3); for Σατανᾶς see 1.20** (cf. 2 Tim 2.26). Following Satan is the reverse side of turning away from Christ (v. 11) and therefore refers to turning away from the faith and yielding to the attendant temptations, i.e. apostasy (cf. Winter*, 97). The similarity of the language to 1.6 and the probable allusion to spreading false teaching in v. 13 reinforce this interpretation. Some scholars think more specifically of turning to immoral living (Hanson, 99) or to

---

[106] Lk 13.17; 21.15; 1 Cor 16.9; Phil 1.28; 2 Th 2.4; Exod 23.22; Est 9.2; 2 Macc 10.26; *Ep. Arist.* 266; cf. 1.10 note.
[107] Holtzmann, 350; Simpson, 76; Easton, 151; Scott, 62f.; Bertram, G., *TDNT* V, 473.
[108] So in Ps 37.21 Σ (MT 38.20); cf. 2 Tim 2.4; 1 Clement 51.1; *Mart. Poly.* 17.1; Dornier, 93; Kelly, 119; Holtz, 121; Spicq, 538; Hasler, 41; Hanson, 99; Fee, 123; Rapske 1987:221.
[109] Wagener 1994:215-18 argues that the motive for acceptable behaviour is no longer a missionary one, but is purely defensive in a situation of persecution; the outside world is determining what is acceptable in the church and the criterion of salvation has become the reaction of the non-Christians. The denial of a missionary concern in the PE is hardly justified in the light of the evidence of the PE as a whole.
[110] Wagener 1994:218, notes (following Berger) that the formulation ἤδη γάρ ... is used in Hellenistic letters to reinforce polemic.

false doctrine (Bartsch 1965:134). The abuse, therefore, was presumably aimed at their inability to live up to their faith and their apostasy from it which gave the church a bad name for not being able to maintain the loyalty of its members.

16. The passage is concluded with a reiteration of the need for people who can do so to provide for widows in their family, so that the church may be able to concentrate its resources on those who are truly destitute.[111] Roloff, 301, finds this sudden attention to 'economic' issues surprising, but only because he has ruled out the 'economic' motif in the earlier part of the section. Less strongly, White, 133f., suggests that the comment is an after-thought. Rather, it is a concluding summary which reinforces the interpretation of the passage as being primarily concerned with relieving the church of an impossible burden.

εἴ τις πιστὴ ἔχει χήρας The conditional form (εἴ τις) is the same as in v. 4, but whereas there it was couched in terms of widows with families, here there is inversion and we have believers who have widows in their family. Such people, it must be assumed, have sufficient means to care for them (Hasler, 42; Kelly, 121; Verner, 139). If πιστή is the correct text, then the responsibility for widows is laid on women alone, presumably as the members of a family who would make the arrangements (Knight, 229). If the variant πιστὸς ἢ πιστή is accepted, the responsibility lies on any believers, men or women, who have family responsibilities (cf. Lock, 61). ἔχει is used, as in v. 4, of 'having' relatives (cf. Winter*, 93f.). The plural χήρας is surprising, but may simply refer to the parents of a husband and wife. (Might the point then implicitly be that a wife must look after her mother-in-law as well as her own mother?) Alternatively, the verse refers to rich Christian women who took ('had') widows into their homes (Meinertz, cited by Easton, 157; Kelly, 121; Hasler, 40; Roloff, 301). If so, one suggestion is that she was providing a home for them but expected the church to provide for their upkeep. Hasler, 42, takes the suggestion further in speculating that in this case it was women who had been twice widowed and were therefore not eligible for church support who were being provided for privately. But this refinement is not in the text. More generally, it is difficult to envisage people 'having', i.e. providing homes for the church's widows, but not otherwise caring for them and demanding church assistance for their board. More likely is Roloff's suggestion that the women were considering handing over their charges to the church, and the

---

[111] If vv. 9–16 refer to a separate class of widows serving the church, then this v. could refer to family care for them in particular, so that the church is able to devote its resources to other serving widows (Parry, 33).

instruction is that they should continue to look after them and not let them be a burden on the church. Nor is it necessary to suppose that the 'believing woman' is herself a widow. Some suggest that the reference is to a widow who was not doing church duties and could help the church by looking after other widows (note the plural!), and so she should continue to do so. The case of Dorcas is cited as an example by Verner, 139, but he goes beyond the evidence in suggesting that she had taken poor widows under her protection.

ἐπαρκείτω αὐταῖς καὶ μὴ βαρείσθω ἡ ἐκκλησία, ἵνα ταῖς ὄντως χήραις ἐπαρκέσῃ For ἐπαρκέω see v. 10. βαρέω is 'to weigh down, burden',[112] here of one person being a burden to another, whether generally (Ignatius, *Philad.* 6.3) or more specifically financially.[113] The congregation's resources would be limited. Some kind of 'benevolent fund' must have been set up.[114]

Wagener 1994:223–7 finds it puzzling that the instruction here is not directed to the widows (as in vv. 4 and 8 on her interpretation) and that the question of church finance is introduced. Further, the definition of 'widow' has shifted from 'a member of a church order' to 'a person in need of support'. She also questions whether the strategy in v. 16 is sensible in relation to vv. 11–15. She is therefore led to conclude that v. 16 is a gloss, based on misinterpretation of vv. 4 and 8 and the practice attested in Acts 9.39 and Hermas, *Vis.* 2.4.3. Elsewhere in the early church the ascetic and needy aspects of widowhood are mixed. To have to regard an otherwise entirely unobjectionable text as a gloss is generally a weakness in a hypothesis, and the effect is rather to show that there are substantial difficulties in Wagener's view of the passage.

c. Instructions about elders (5.17–25)

Adler, N. 'Die Handauflegung im NT bereits ein Bussritus?', in Blinzler, J. (ed.), *Neutestamentliche Aufsätze (Festschrift J. Schmid)* (Regensburg: Pustet, 1963), 1–6; Fuller, J. W., 'Of Elders and Triads in 1 Timothy 5.19–25', *NTS* 29 (1983), 258–63; Galtier, P., 'La réconciliation des pécheurs dans la première Épître à Timothée', *RSR* 39 (1951), 317–20; 'La reconciliation des pécheurs dans saint Paul', *RSR* 3 (1912), 448–60; Goldhahn-Müller, I., *Die Grenze der Gemeinde. Studien zum Problem der Zweiten Busse im Neuen Testament unter Berücksichtigung der Entwicklung im 2. Jh. bis Tertullian* (Göttingen: Vandenhoeck und Ruprecht, 1989); Haraguchi, T., 'Das Unterhaltsrecht des frühchristlichen Verkündigers.

[112] Cl.; Mt 26.43; Lk 9.32; 21.34; of misfortune 2 Cor 1.8; 5.4***.
[113] Dittenberger, *Or.* 595, 15 (AD 174) ἵνα μὴ τὴν πόλιν βαρῶμεν (quoted by BA); other examples in Schrenk, G., *TDNT* I, 558–61. Cf. ἐπιβαρέω, 1 Th 2.9; 2 Th 3.8.
[114] Knoch, 39, comments that the passage does not deal with the 'desolate' widow of under 60. Not all widows would be able to get married. But these points ignore the fact that this is an ideal description and not necessarily a set of rigid rules.

Eine Untersuchung zur Bezeichnung ἐργάτης im Neuen Testament', *ZNW* 84 (1993), 178–95; Harvey, A. E., ' "The Workman is Worthy of His Hire": Fortunes of a Proverb in the Early Church', *NovT* 24.3 (1982), 209–21; Kilpatrick, G. D. '1 Tim. v. 22 and Tertullian, *De Baptismo* xviii.1', *JTS* ns 16 (1965), 127–8; Kirk, J. A., 'Did "Officials" in the New Testament Church receive a Salary?' *ExpTim* 84 (1972–3), 105–8; MacArthur, J. S., 'On the Significance of ἡ γραφή in 1 Tim. 5.18', *ExpTim* 53 (1941–2), 37; Meier 1973:323–45; Schöllgen, G., 'Die διπλῆ τιμή von 1 Tim 5,17', *ZNW* 80 (1989), 232–9; see also Bibliography to **Excursus 2.**

This section commences as another item in the 'honour' series, but then moves into other, related topics (for the structure cf. 2.1–10/11–15). While some scholars think that a set of somewhat unrelated sayings have been strung together, a clear, unified theme is visible.[115]

The text falls into five parts, four instructions (17–18, 19–21, 22, 23) followed by a general comment (24f.).[116] The first section (vv. 17f.), connected with what precedes by the theme of 'honour' contains instruction about the material recognition to be given to active elders, backed up by scriptural teaching. The second section (vv. 19–21) deals with the discipline that applies to elders. Their position is not to be prejudiced by ill-based charges against them; these are not to be given a hearing. Nevertheless, if elders do sin, they are to be openly disciplined so that the others will not follow their example. This instruction is so important that it is strongly reinforced with an admonition in which the need for strict impartiality is laid down. The third section (v. 22) concerns the need for care in appointing people to tasks in the church, lest they turn out to be sinners and those who appoint them stand in danger of being held to share in their actions. Fourth, and somewhat marginally (v. 23), a personal comment is added to Timothy that such avoidance of sin need not be misunderstood as requiring a continuing total abstinence from wine, even when it could be helpful healthwise. Finally (vv. 24f.), there is a general comment that people's sins may be obvious or hidden, like their good deeds, but all will be revealed at the last judgement. Thus the instructions are placed in an 'eschatological'

---

[115] Oberlinner, 260f., regards vv. 23–25 as a separate section of interjections which have no real connection with what precedes or follows (cf. Brox, 203). They bridge the gap between the sections on elders and on slaves. This is hardly a satisfying explanation of a passage in a letter which otherwise appears to hang together reasonably well.

[116] Meier*, 336, finds a chiastic arrangement:

A		17–18		Honour elders
	B		19–22	Elders who sin
		C	23	Digression
	B'		24	Unworthy candidates for office
	A'	25		Worthy candidates for office.

setting (Roloff, 316f.), with the implication that even if church leaders make mistakes and are deceived about the choice of leaders, God will judge all people fairly and take account of their deeds, both evil and good.

The passage is closely connected with the preceding one in that in both cases we have instructions for dealing with a group in the church where respect and some kind of tangible recognition are due – the widows and the elders. In both cases the 'real' thing is to be honoured, and a group is to receive some kind of support from the congregation. Also in both cases there is the danger of unworthy people being involved. It would then follow that 5.1f. is an appropriate introduction to this section, since in both cases we are dealing with older members of the congregation.[117]

TEXT

18. λέγει γάρ Omit γάρ (226* 1960). Elliott claims that the variant is original and the conjunction was possibly added to remove asyndeton (Elliott, 43, 237). But the MSS evidence is too weak.

βοῦν ἀλοῶντα οὐ φιμώσεις (ℵ F G D² 1739 1881 TR it vg^mss) (1) οὐ φιμώσεις βοῦν ἀλοῶντα (A C I P Ψ 048 33 81 104 365 1175 pc (lat) Or Ambst; Kilpatrick); (2) βοῦν ἀλοῶντα οὐ κημώσεις (D*). Deut 25.4 has οὐ φιμώσεις βοῦν ἀλοῶντα. Similar variations are found in 1 Cor 9.9 (οὐ κημώσεις [B* D* F G 1739]; οὐ φιμώσεις [P46 ℵ A B² C D¹ Ψ TR Or Epiph]). Elliott, 82, prefers the text that differs from LXX and 1 Cor, and therefore rejects variant (1); he prefers variant (2) with κημόω (a non-Attic word which is used by Xenophon, *Eq.* 5.3).[118] It seems more likely that D has assimilated the text to 1 Cor 9, and that the text, which differs from the word order in the LXX, should be adopted.

τοῦ μισθοῦ τῆς τροφῆς (ℵ* (vid) (a*) (Clement)). The variant is assimilation to Mt 10.10 (Elliott, 82f.; Metzger, 575).

19. ἐκτὸς εἰ μή ... μαρτύρων is omitted by b Pel^A Ps-Hier^codd Hier^codd, and 'perhaps also from the copies used by Cyprian and Ambrosiaster who quote no further than παραδέχου' (Metzger, 575). Elliott, 83f., offers various possible reasons for the omission, such as mechanical oversight or deliberate attempt to rule out accusations under any circumstances. See WH *Notes*, 134.

ἢ τριῶν καὶ τριῶν (1022 1739 1245 2005 vg^codd Aug Cass Eucherius). The variant is accepted by Elliott, 83f., arguing that καί (as in Deut. 19.15) was thought to be too loose and was altered and ἤ may be assimiliation to Heb 10.28 or Deut 17.6. But the MS evidence is too weak. See Elliott, 83f., for other variants including the omission of the quotation in b Cyp Ambst Pel.

20. τοὺς ἁμαρτάνοντας Insert δέ (A D* (F G) 1175 pc it vg^mss Ambst; [WH]). The variant is rejected by Elliott, 214, as an addition to remove asyndeton.

21. Χριστοῦ Ἰησοῦ (ℵ A D* G 33 81 104 365 629 pc latt co Cl) (1) κυρίου Ἰησοῦ Χριστοῦ (D² K L P TR 69 1908 et al. sy^p hl goth arm eth Chrys); (2) Ἰησοῦ Χριστοῦ (F Ψ 630 1175 1739 1881 pc bo^ms). See Elliott, 201, 204, who supports the text and rejects both variants as not typical of the style of the PE.

[117] It is just possible that 6.1f. fits in with this, in that, where slaves had Christian masters, these on the whole would have been older men or elders.

[118] Elliott's claim that Philo has this word in a citation of Deut 25.4 seems to be mistaken (Philo, *Virt.* 145).

ἀγγέλων (1) αὐτοῦ ἀγγέλων (88 436 327 Bas Hier); (2) ἀγγέλων αὐτοῦ (33 syᵖ bo Patricius). Elliott 85, 237 accepts the second variant with hesitation (cf. 2 Tim 4.1 for similar phrases). Neither variant has early attestation.

πρόσκλισιν πρόσκλησιν (A D Ψ 33 1739 TR). The variant is purely orthographical (MHT II, 51; Elliott, 85).

23. οἴνῳ ὀλίγῳ οἶνον ὀλίγον (P 1311); Elliott, 21, holds that the text is an Atticistic correction. But the MS evidence strongly supports the text.

τὸν στόμαχον Add σου (D² F G TR a vg sy Clement; Kilpatrick); Elliott, 86, adopts the variant on the grounds that personal pronouns were often used with parts of body (Mt 3.12; Lk 6.6; for scribes dropping the pronoun cf. 1 Tim 4.16 א). The textual evidence is weak.

τάς ... ἀσθενείας Praem. διά (F G g syᵖ). Elliott, 86, holds that the preposition was removed to improve the style. The MS evidence for the text is superior.

25. ὡσαύτως Add δέ (A F G 81 pc a mᶜ vgᵐˢˢ). Elliott, 214, rejects the addition as possibly assimilation to Rom 8.26.

πρόδηλα (א A 1739 424**) πρόδηλα ἐστίν (K L TR 104 69 1908 Chrys); πρόδηλα εἰσίν (D F G P 33 424* 8 88 it vg Or). The clause could be elliptical as at 4.8 (note). Elliott, 87, holds that the plural verb is original and was altered to the singular by Atticistic scribes. The ellipse of εἶναι is not as common in Hellenistic as in Attic. But the verb could have been added by assimilation to 5.24. The MS evidence is finely balanced.

δύνανται δύναται (א F G L 6 326 1241 1505 1739 pm). Elliott, 87f., argues that scribes were more likely to correct a plural verb with a neuter plural subject to the singular form than vice-versa (cf. 2 Tim 3.11; 4.17).

EXEGESIS

17. Οἱ καλῶς προεστῶτες πρεσβύτεροι The verse refers somewhat ambiguously to a number of groups of 'elders'. Within (a) the group of πρεσβύτεροι it appears to distinguish (b) a smaller group who 'serve well' (presumably by contrast with those who do not 'serve well') and (c) a group 'who speak and teach', but it is not immediately apparent whether it identifies (c) as a sub-group within (b) or equates (c) with (b).[119] The latter is the preferable view (see below). In any case, it would appear that this group (or groups) is distinguished from the 'elders' in general.

The wider term πρεσβύτεροι (5.1; Tit 1.5; **Excursus 2**) may refer here to (1) the elders in the congregation (most commentators); (2) both the overseers and the deacons who were still collectively known as 'elders';[120] or (3) the older men in the congregation (Jeremias, 41f.; Barrett, 78f.).

---

[119] Merkel, 44, thinks of apparently separate groups of those who lead well and those who teach and regards them as people who assisted the bishop in larger congregations. Yet another possibility is that there are four groups: presbyters in general, presbyters who lead, presbyters who lead well, and presbyters who lead well especially by preaching and teaching; Meier*, 326, raises this possibility only to reject it on the grounds that it is improbable that there were any presbyters who did not lead, since this is the defining characteristic of presbyters.

[120] So expressly Chrysostom on Phil 1.1 (PG LXII, 183) quoted in Simpson, 55; Fee, 128.

Jeremias argues that, if the word means 'elders' here, there would be two levels of elders, and therefore it is preferable to think of older men, some of whom have taken on church leadership; the former group will receive the same support as the widows, while the latter receive double this amount (especially if they take part in teaching). Bernard, 85, however, asserts that there were not two classes of elders, those who ruled and those who did not rule: the verse is concerned to encourage all elders to fulfil their role well. But it is much more probable that the passage is distinguishing a sub-group of elders who had fuller duties than the others.

Roloff, 305–9, explains the wording by arguing that the author found an existing set-up of elders in the churches and regulates it here to bring it into line with his own concept of the church leader as a teacher. By establishing an 'office' to which an emolument is given he took the church along the road to the idea of a 'profession' or 'vocation' of principal church leaders fully supported by the church. Similarly, Oberlinner, 249f., holds that the author has integrated presbyters with his own preferred structure of overseers and deacons by having the presbyters participate in the ordination of a overseer as the leader of the congregation; but his interpretation of 4.14 rests on the dubious assumption that there 'Timothy' functions as a local church overseer.

However the wider term be understood, it is immediately qualified to indicate that the author's concern is with those of them who actually serve the church. προΐστημι (3.4 note) is a general term used by Paul for the exercise of leadership functions (1 Th 5.12; Rom 12.8);[121] it can include both care of other people and having an authoritative role.[122] Barrett, 79, surmises that it would involve general superintendency of the congregation's affairs, including discipline, pastoral oversight and presiding at meetings.[123] Some take this reference to be to a narrower group who are overseers/bishops.[124]

καλῶς is also used of performing duties in the congregation in 3.13 (cf. 3.4, 12). It may be used here:

(a) of outstanding service;

(b) simply of carrying out duties properly, without neglect or failure. Thus it could apply to all elders (Schöllgen*, 239 n. 32;

---

[121] The use of the perf. suggests that the elders have already acquitted themselves well and are continuing to do so.

[122] The 'compatibility of the two notions of benevolent actions and structured authority' is illustrated in an inscription in honour of Artemis, discussed in *New Docs.* IV, 82 § 19 (Ephesus, AD II).

[123] By the time of Justin (*Apol.* I.67) there is a single 'president' at the Lord's Supper (Hanson, 100f.).

[124] Brox, 198; Roloff, 307; Knoch, 40.

Knight, 232); it would then be a case of formal language that could be invoked if necessary;

(c) of carrying out a fuller range of duties, i.e. the teaching (Dibelius-Conzelmann, 78; Bornkamm, G., *TDNT* VI, 667);

(d) possibly as a paraphrase for 'full-time service' (Kelly, 124).

The analogy with 3.13 may suggest that (a) or (b) is correct, but (c) gives the best sense in view of the following phrase.

μάλιστα οἱ κοπιῶντες ἐν λόγῳ καὶ διδασκαλίᾳ μάλιστα (Tit 1.10) is capable of two meanings. It could mean 'especially'. However, this interpretation does not give an intelligible, unambiguous meaning: are those who do not labour in teaching to get the double honour or not? The other possibility is that it means 'namely', identifying those who lead well with those who teach. This interpretation gives better sense. A threefold division into elders/older men; those who rule well; and those who teach (Meier 1973:326f.) is complex and hard to envisage in practice. With the author's stress on the importance of teaching, he is likely to have regarded the outstanding elders as those who performed this duty (Roloff, 307).

κοπιάω (4.10) is especially used of church work. The implication is that teaching is demanding work (Roloff, 307). For λόγος see 1 Tim 1.15 and note (cf. 4.12; Tit 1.9) and for διδασκαλία see 1.10 and note. The two words may form a hendiadys or possibly refer to two different types of teaching. See 6.3; Tit 1.9. 'Preaching' and 'instruction' are two broadly separable but not altogether distinguishable activities, possibly evangelistic and edificatory respectively (Jeremias, 42).

διπλῆς τιμῆς ἀξιούσθωσαν The language is still that of worthiness; those who are served in the gospel must appreciate those who serve and give them due recognition (Gal 6.6). The verb ἀξιόω, 'to consider worthy, deserving',[125] is doubtless chosen in anticipation of the use of the saying of Jesus in v. 18b. The injunction is implicitly addressed to the congregation as a whole rather than just to Timothy.

The force of τιμή (1.17 *et al.*) is disputed:

(a) Some take it to refer purely to 'respect'.[126] In favour of this interpretation is adduced the fact that the church leaders in 3.4, 12 are householders who presumably have adequate means.

---

[125] With gen. of thing; Cl.; Lk 7.7; 2 Th 1.11; pass. Heb 3.3; 10.29; Josephus, *Ant.* 2.258; also 'to desire, request', Acts 15.38; 28.22***; cf. Foerster, W., *TDNT* I, 380.

[126] W. Michaelis, cited by Schneider, J., *TDNT* VIII, 177 n.43; cf. Aelius Aristides 32.3K (12, p. 134 D): διπλῇ τιμῇ τιμῆσαι (cited by BA *s.v.* τιμή 2.e.). This appears to be the interpretation favoured by Oberlinner, 252–4, who regards the preceding discussion about honouring widows as decisive for the understanding of the verse. For the whole phrase cf. διπλασίας τιμῆς ἄξιοι (Plato, *Leg.* 230; Simpson, 77).

But it makes the false assumption that the alternative is a salary or support by the church rather than some more modest form of tangible recognition.

(b) The suggestion that a salary is meant (Lips 1979:109f.)[127] fails since τιμή is attested only of a once-for-all payment rather than an ongoing salary (Schöllgen*, 234 n. 14), and nothing suggests that a salary in the sense of an adequate income to live on is in mind. Consequently, a broader reference to an 'honorarium' is more likely (Kirk*; Roloff, 308).

(c) It is better, therefore, to think simply of honour expressed in some tangible form.[128] That some form of gift was made to those who served is clear from 5.18; 1 Cor 9.7–14; 2 Cor 11.8f.; Gal 6.6; 1 Th 2.7; Didache 13; Apost. Const. 2:28. The backing provided in v. 18 surely implies that the thought is of material honour rather than simply of respect. Moreover, the fact that some people expected to make money out of godliness, i.e. out of teaching godliness (6.5), indicates that some kind of material return was expected (Holtzmann, 352).

The nature of the material honour is not clear, and is complicated by the fact that it is to be 'double'. διπλοῦς, 'double' (Cl.; Mt 23.15) is used of payments in Rev 18.6a, 6b.[129] A wide variety of interpretations have been offered:

(a) The elders are to be honoured on two accounts, their age and their service both being honoured (Michel 1948:98 n. 46).

(b) The elders are to receive both honour and remuneration (Brox, 199; Fee, 129; Arichea-Hatton, 126; Stott, 137).

(c) The word may be taken in a broad sense, so that the whole phrase refers simply to great, or perhaps additional honour compared with the other elders.[130] Roloff, 308, argues that a broad meaning is not possible in a document with a legal style to it. The phrase is to be taken literally of a double material reward.

(d) The elders receive double the amount given to the widows.[131] This is unlikely because the two passages may rest on separate traditions. It would also imply that the elders were

---

[127] Haraguchi*, 185f., assumes that a financial payment is meant by analogy with 5.3.

[128] Jeremias, 42; Bornkamm, G., *TDNT* VI, 667; Meier*, 327; Sand 1976:226 n. 18; Schneider, J., *TDNT* VIII, 176f. For parallels cf. the physician's honorarium in Ecclus 38.1; so probably Acts 28.10; cf. Diogenes Laertius 5.72 (a will).

[129] For the combination with τιμή see the pap. cited in BA *s.v.* διπλοῦς, e. g. διπλᾶ ὀψώνια (*PGM* 4, 2454).

[130] Holtzmann, 352; Bernard, 85; Easton, 159; Hasler, 43; Brox, 199.

[131] Cf. *Didasc.* 9 (*Apost. Const.* 2.28), where the deacons receive twice as much as the widows and the elders twice as much as the deacons; cf. Lock, 62; Calvin, 261f.; Jeremias, 42; Barrett, 79; Lips 1979:109f., who sees a parallel between 'elders who rule well' and 'real' widows.

fully supported by the congregations like the widows. Further, other evidence for a paid 'clergy' is not found before the end of the second century (Schöllgen*, 235). Above all, it is difficult to envisage small congregations being able to give financial support to members on such a scale, especially if the care of widows was being burdensome. There is no obvious rationale why elders should receive a wage for services rendered at a level of twice the support given to indigent widows.[132] Oberlinner, 253f., holds that the author is playing down the place of the widows and the honour due to them and insisting that the elders are worthy of more honour (not payment) than them. 'Double' is not to be taken too literally. But this proposal is hardly likely, especially since the preceding section is concerned more with the care of needy widows.

(e) The elders in question receive double what the [widows and the] other old men receive (Jeremias, 42). But nothing has been said about old men in general receiving anything. The same objections as to view (d) also apply here.

(f) The elders in question receive a double material reward compared with what other elders with lesser duties receive (Dibelius-Conzelmann, 78; Roloff, 308f.; Meier*, 327). This is regarded by Schöllgen* as impracticable in view of the limited resources possessed by a congregation.[133]

(g) The elders are honoured by being given portions double in size to what the rest of the congregation receive at the church meal (Schöllgen*, 239 n. 320; Merkel, 45). In Gen 43.34 Benjamin's portion is five times that of his brothers! The practice is attested for later times by Tertullian,[134] and there are abundant secular parallels for the practice in Graeco-Roman collegia (Schöllgen*, 236–8). The parallels are compelling, however culturally odd it may appear to us. If this interpretation is correct, it follows that this is not the first stage in the development of a paid clergy, although later readers may have misinterpreted it in this way.

Schöllgen's solution is attractive, but not entirely free from problems. He admits that the word 'honour' is not attested in this connection, but claims that this is not a serious objection, since the word can mean 'gift in honour of somebody' (Schöllgen*,

---

[132] The analogy with modern pensions (equal to about half a person's previous salary) is anachronistic.

[133] Consequently, no weight should be placed on the analogy with elite soldiers who received a double salary (Spicq, 542).

[134] Tertullian *Ieiun.* 17,4: *'Ad elogium gulae tuae pertinet, quod duplex apud te praesentibus honor binis partibus deputatur, cum apostolus duplicem honorem dederit ut et fratribus et praepositis'*, cited by Schöllgen*, 235f. The practice is further attested in *Didasc.* 9 (*Apost. Const.* 2.28).

239 n. 33). A further difficulty is that v. 18 may seem to imply that something more than simply an honorific portion of food is in mind. Nevertheless, of the various proposals that have been made this one is perhaps the best.

18. λέγει γὰρ ἡ γραφή A proof text is added to justify payment/material provision for elders.

For the expression cf. Jn 7.38, 42; 19.37; Rom 4.3; 9.17; 10.11; 11.2; Gal 4.30; Jas 2.22; 4.5; 2 Clement 14.2. ἡ γραφή (2 Tim 3.16) is used in the specific sense of '*the* writing', namely 'Scripture'. It is commonly held that the word can refer either to a specific passage or to Scripture as a whole (BA). But these two senses should probably be combined: 'The Scripture says in this particular verse.' Although many commentators think that the reference is purely to Deut 25.4 with v. 18b added as a kind of afterthought or backup from another source,[135] it is quite possible that both quotations are envisaged as coming from 'Scripture'.[136] If so, this is early evidence for the conferral of scriptural status on a collection of sayings of Jesus. The arguments for taking the two quotations closely together in this way are so strong that Michaelis 1930:62 was forced to regard 5.18b as a gloss since he did not think that Paul could have referred to a saying of Jesus as 'Scripture'. The commentators are divided over the issue. Fee, 134, alleges that 'Scripture' meant only the OT for Christians right up to the end of the second century, but Roloff, 309, argues for a looser understanding of 'Scripture' and notes that the citing of sayings of Jesus as 'Scripture' is found in Barnabas 4.14 and 2 Clement 2.4; the reference is to written texts used in worship and teaching. Holtz, 126f., thinks that it is simply an inexact expression, and Harvey*, 212, claims that the author committed the 'pardonable error' of thinking that the citation came from the OT. Oberlinner, 255f., strongly opposes the suggestion that there was any kind of Christian Scripture at this time and holds that only the first citation is regarded as Scripture. In any case, for the author the second citation had equal authority with the OT (Scott, 65).

βοῦν ἀλοῶντα οὐ φιμώσεις The citation is from Deut 25.4 = 1 Cor 9.9; cf. Philo, *Virt.* 145; Josephus, *Ant.* 4.233. βοῦς is 'head of cattle, ox, cow'. ἀλοάω is 'to thresh' (Cl.; 1 Cor 9.9 [=Deut 25.4], 10***); the allusion is to the practice of driving oxen over a threshing floor to trample the corn with their hooves, separating the wheat from the chaff. The law laid down that the farmer must not prevent the animal from taking its share of the

---

[135] Brox, 199f.; Dibelius-Conzelmann, 79; Kelly, 126; Fee, 134.
[136] Simpson, 77f.; Roloff, 309; Merkel, 45; Wolfe 1990:74–82.

harvest. φιμόω is 'to tie shut, muzzle'.[137] The fut. indic. conveys a prohibition. The parallel with 1 Cor 9.9 raises the question whether the author of 1 Tim knew 1 Cor.[138] The implication of the command is obvious and therefore not explicitly expressed: just as the ox is entitled to eat while threshing, so (a fortiori) the church worker is entitled to provision for his needs. Knoch, 40, notes that 1 Tim follows the Jewish interpretation of the verse. The point is thus backed up with Scripture and then by appeal to Jesus.

καί· ἄξιος ὁ ἐργάτης τοῦ μισθοῦ αὐτοῦ καί can be used to join two quotations (cf. 2 Tim 2.19).[139] For ἄξιος cf. 1.15 and note; 4.9; and especially 6.1.[140] ἐργάτης is a 'workman, labourer, especially agricultural'.[141] μίσθος is 'pay, wages for work done'.[142] The citation is in verbal agreement with the saying attributed to Jesus in Lk 10.7/Mt 10.10: ἄξιος γὰρ ὁ ἐργάτης τοῦ μισθοῦ [Mt τῆς τροφῆς] αὐτοῦ.

But where did the author get it from? Here opinions vary considerably:

(a) An apocryphal book (Dibelius-Conzelmann, 79; Kelly, 126);

(b) A secular proverbial saying (Bernard, 86; Brox, 199f.).[143] In both this and the previous case it may then have been taken over also by Jesus or ascribed to him in the tradition;

(c) A collection of sayings of Jesus, such as Q (Roloff, 310);

(d) Luke (or a hypothetical proto-Luke). Spicq, 543f., notes the personal contact between Paul (the author of the letter) and Luke (2 Tim 4.11). Easton, 161, holds that the author knew Luke-Acts. Cf. Knight, 233f.;

(e) The citation is a late gloss (Michaelis 1930:62);

(f) Oral tradition (Oberlinner, 254f.).

A written source is surely required, and one that would have been authoritative. The knowledge may of course be indirect, but it is unlikely that the saying was not known to be attributed

---

[137] Literal, as in Deut 25.4 = Philo, Virt. 145; 1 Cor 9.9 v.l. Also figurative: 'to silence', Mt 22.12, 34; Mk 1.25; 4.39; Lk 4.35; 1 Pet 2.15.

[138] Cf. also 2 Tim 2.6; so Hanson, 102; Roloff, 305f.; Oberlinner, 254; but see Wolfe 1990:22–6.

[139] Cf. Heb 1.10. Paul uses καὶ πάλιν, Rom 15.10–12; cf. Heb 1.5; 2.13a, 13b; 10.30.

[140] It takes the gen., as in Mt 10.10; Lk 10.7; Acts 13.46; Didache 13.1f.

[141] Mt 9.37f. par. Lk 10.2; Mt 20.1f, 8; Acts 19.25; Jas 5.4; Mt 10.10 par Lk 10.7, also cited in Didache 13.2), metaphorical of doing evil (Lk 13.27; Phil 3.2) and good (2 Tim 2.15), then a term applied to church workers (2 Cor 11.13***).

[142] Literal, as here; also of divine recompense, Mt 5.12; et al.; Preisker, H., and Wurthwein, E., TDNT IV, 695–728, espec. 698, 723f.

[143] Cf. Euripides, Rhesus 161f.: πονοῦντα δ' ἄξιον μισθὸν φέρεσθαι; Phocylides, Frg. 17: μισθὸν μοχθήσαντι δίδου.

to Jesus; otherwise it would not have had authority. The basic principle, which could have been equally accepted in the secular world (cf. 2 Tim 2.6), is applied to work done in the church.[144]

19. The next section deals with the double danger of false accusation and failure to deal with elders publicly (cf. Brox, 200). The first danger carries the risk that trials cause harm even if the verdict is 'not guilty'. It is implied that Timothy had regional authority to deal with problems of church discipline, just as Titus has authority to appoint elders (Knoch, 40). Or the real addressee is somebody within the congregations with episcopal authority to discipline the elders (Roloff, 310). Then the danger of misuse of authority by such a leader to discipline (or refrain from disciplining) others is being forestalled.[145] But whether there was some specific reason for protecting elders against false accusations of this kind cannot be determined. Nothing in the context indicates whether any particular kinds of sin are in mind, but it seems probable that moral misdemeanours, possibly involving misuse of money (cf. Polycarp 6.1; Johnson, 188f.), rather than the holding of heretical opinions are envisaged.

κατὰ πρεσβυτέρου κατηγορίαν μὴ παραδέχου κατηγορία, 'accusation' (Tit 1.6 note), is constructed, as is normal, with κατά (cf. John 18.29), which is regularly used of accusations and other actions against people (Lk 23.14; Rom 8.33 *et al.*). παραδέχομαι is 'to accept, acknowledge [as correct]' (4.20; Acts 16.21; 22.18; of a person Acts 15.4; Heb 12.6***).[146]

ἐκτὸς εἰ μὴ ἐπὶ δύο ἢ τριῶν μαρτύρων ἐκτός, 'outside, except' (Mt 23.26; Acts 26.22; 1 Cor 6.18; 15.27), is used in the post-Cl. phrase ἐκτὸς εἰ μή, 'unless, except' (1 Cor 14.5; 15.2***; BD §376). ἐπί + gen. is 'in the presence of' and is used of appearing before judges in lawsuits (6.13** 1 Cor 6.1),[147] but here it must signify rather 'on the basis of [witnesses]'.[148] The principle of multiple witnesses is found in Deut 17.6 (ἐπὶ δυσὶν μάρτυσιν ἢ ἐπὶ τρισὶν μάρτυσιν) and 19.15 (ἐπὶ στόματος δύο μαρτύρων καὶ ἐπὶ στόματος τριῶν μαρτύρων). The phrase here, ἐπὶ δύο ἢ τριῶν μαρτύρων, is a mixture of wording from both passages. Deut 19.15 is cited in 2 Cor 13.1 (ἐπὶ στόματος δύο μαρτύρων

---

[144] For the principle in the OT see Num 18.30f.

[145] Bartsch 1965:106 suggests that originally the underlying church order said 'no charges against elders' but 1 Tim modifies this.

[146] For a verbal parallel cf. Sextus 259: διαβολὰς κατὰ φιλοσόφου μὴ παραδέχου (cited by BA).

[147] So Holtzmann, 354: 'do not listen to a charge except there are witnesses present with you to hear it'.

[148] BD §234[5]; *EDNT* II, 22; cf. Heb 7.11; Xenophon, *Hel.* 6.5.41; Bernard, 86; Spicq, 545; Knight, 235.

καὶ τριῶν) and also in Mt 18.6 but with ἤ for καί. Heb 10.28 (ἐπὶ δυσὶν ἢ τρισὶν μάρτυσιν) is based on Deut 17.6. Cf. Josephus, *Vita* 256; *Sanh.* 5.4 for the principle.

μάρτυς, 'witness' (6.12; 2 Tim 2.2**), is used in its legal sense.[149] The general principle of Deut 19.15, applied particularly to capital charges in Deut 17.6, is that trials cannot be conducted on the basis of a single unsubstantiated testimony. This avoids malicious slanders.[150] The instruction is addressed to Timothy and the implication is that he has authority to 'hold court'; if he is in charge of a group of churches, presumably he was the 'higher authority' to whom accusations and appeals would be made. There must have been some reason for including such an instruction, and it will lie in the problem of heresy affecting the congregations with the inevitable accusations not only of false teaching but also of a sinful life-style that could be made by both sides.

20. Τοὺς ἁμαρτάνοντας ἐνώπιον πάντων ἔλεγχε Τοὺς ἁμαρτάνοντας (Tit 3.11**) in this context refers to sinners within the church, and it must refer to the elders rather than to members of the church in general,[151] although the principle was presumably extended to the rest of the congregation. The participle may be simply a general designation of elders who sin, but in view of the procedure described it is more likely that it refers to persistent sinners who did not respond to the private exhortation that was the first stage in church discipline. The implication is that sin was still going on in the church (Fee, 131). The public discipline corresponds to the procedure before the ἐκκλησία in Mt 19.17; 1 Cor 5. It is not stated who carries out the rebuke; Timothy is being addressed, but in effect the instruction is given to the elders as a group. ἐνώπιον (2.3; *et al.*) is used of a congregational meeting (3 Jn 6; Acts 6.5); most commentators assume that πάντων indicates the whole church.[152] For ἐλέγχω see Tit 1.9 note; Roloff, 311 n.433. It can simply mean 'to reprove, correct' or 'refute', but also 'to punish, discipline' (Heb 12.5; Rev 3.19). The reproof in itself can be a punishment. Roloff, 311, thinks that a comparatively mild reproof is meant without a public rebuke or the threat of excommunication. This

---

[149] Strathmann, H., *TDNT* IV, 474–508, espec. 489f.

[150] For the danger of envy in the church see 1 Clement 5.2.

[151] Brox, 200; Hanson, 102f.; Oberlinner, 250. Roloff, 310 n.432, states that the participle is attributive and applies to the aforementioned elders. Cf. Meier*, 330–2, who lists the use of the participle rather than the noun, the lack of evidence for a group of 'penitents' at this date, and the series of three participles which must all apply to the same group despite the sing. noun in v. 19.

[152] Cf. the OT principle in Deut 13.11; 17.13. Holtzmann, 354, and Bernard, 87, limit the reference to all the elders.

does not fit in too well with the extremely solemn character of v. 21.[153]

ἵνα καὶ οἱ λοιποὶ φόβον ἔχωσιν The purpose of the discipline is expressed in language that continues to echo the OT background, Deut 19.20 (Fuller*, 260). For the use of φόβος**, 'fear', with ἔχω cf. Hermas, *Man.* 7.2c; 12.4, 7a; *Sim.* 1.10. Clearly this clause expresses only one aspect of the purpose of the action. However, the καί indicates that those disciplined are also to feel fear which may encourage them not to persist in sin. οἱ λοιποί (adv. λοιπόν, 2 Tim 4.8**) is vague. It must include the rest of the elders, since vv. 19 and 20 belong together,[154] but one can hardly exclude the rest of the church.[155] Roloff, 311, however, thinks of a procedure that took place within the circle of the elders and was not necessarily brought before the congregation as a whole.

21. Διαμαρτύρομαι ἐνώπιον τοῦ θεοῦ καὶ Χριστοῦ Ἰησοῦ καὶ τῶν ἐκλεκτῶν ἀγγέλων The instructions regarding discipline are followed by a surprisingly strong injunction to impartiality. The verse is clearly linked backwards by ταῦτα (Holtzmann, 354).

διαμαρτύρομαι has the strong sense 'to charge, warn, adjure' (2 Tim 2.14; 4.1**; Lk 16.28; cf. 1 Th 4.6; also 'to testify, bear witness') and is followed by a ἵνα clause expressing content (as in Lk 16.28).[156] ἐνώπιον (5.20) functions to put the charge into the context of a heavenly court. The solemnity is indicated by reference to three witnesses, which Fuller*, 261f., interprets as a parallel to the triad in Deut 19.15. There is nothing surprising about the mention of τοῦ θεοῦ (as in 6.13; 2 Tim 2.14; 4.1) and Χριστοῦ Ἰησοῦ (also as in 6.13 and 2 Tim 4.10) but καὶ τῶν ἀγγέλων (3.16**) adds a novel third element. When God acts as judge, he is surrounded by heavenly beings (Ps 81 [MT 82].1; Dan 7.9f.). The association of angels with parousia and judgement is well-attested (Lk 9.26 = Mk 8.38 = Mt 16.27; cf. Lk 12.9; Mt 24.31; 2 Th 1.7; *et al.*), and this may be sufficient to explain their presence here.[157] ἐκλεκτός, 'chosen, select' refers to human beings in Tit 1.1 (note) and 2 Tim 2.10. For its application to angels see *1 Enoch* 39.1; cf. *Odes Sol.* 4.8 (elect archangels; *OTP* II, 736). Although the wording may simply be 'liturgical' (Dibelius-Conzelmann, 80), i.e. traditional and therefore not

---

[153] For the practical problems in applying the rule see Augustine in Brox, 201.
[154] Dibelius-Conzelmann, 79; Spicq, 545; Brox, 200; most commentators.
[155] Holtzmann, 354; Knight, 237; von Campenhausen 1969:147.
[156] Cf. Strathmann, H., *TDNT* IV, 510–12. Paul uses the simple μαρτύρομαι in this sense (Gal 5.3; Eph 4.17; 1 Th 2.12; Acts 20.26).
[157] Angels function as witnesses in *T. Levi* 19.3; Dittenberger, *Syll.* 1181,10 (AD II, Jewish or Christian; cf. Deissmann 1927:413–24; MM 3); Josephus, *Bel.* 2.401; 4 Ezra 16.68.

especially significant, it is more likely that the choice is deliberate. The language is solemn (cf. holy angels, Rev 14.10), and may indicate that the angels are the chosen instruments of judgement (Bernard, 87).[158] Roloff, 312f., finds traces of a primitive Christology which linked Christ closely to certain angels, namely the 'seven spirits before the throne' or 'angels of the presence'.[159]

ἵνα ταῦτα φυλάξῃς χωρὶς προκρίματος, μηδὲν ποιῶν κατὰ πρόσκλισιν ταῦτα must refer to the preceding instructions (*pace* Dibelius-Conzelmann, 80), since otherwise the references to impartiality lose their force. φυλάσσω, 'to watch, guard, defend' (6.20; 2 Tim 1.12, 14; 4.15**), has the sense 'to keep a law, etc., from being broken', hence 'to observe, follow' (cf. Mt 19.20; Lk 18.21; Gal 6.13; *et al.*). For χωρίς cf. 2.8**. πρόκριμα*** is 'prejudgement, discrimination', whether good or bad. It is found as a legal technical term and is said to be a Latinism = Lat. *praeiudicium* (cf. *absque praeiudicio*, χωρὶς προκρίματος in Pap.). For μηδὲν ποιῶν cf. Phil 2.14; Col 3.17. πρόσκλισις***, lit. 'leaning against', hence fig. 'inclination, predilection', can be used neutrally, but also in an unfavourable sense, 'partiality' (1 Clement 21.7; 47.3f; 50.2). The language appears repetitious, but in fact the first phrase says that one is not to come with pre-formed opinions, the second that one is not to be ruled by partiality to one party or the other (cf. Knight, 239).

22. χεῖρας ταχέως μηδενὶ ἐπιτίθει ἐπιτίθημι**, 'to lay, put upon', is frequently constructed with χεῖρας (2.8) followed by ἐπί or dat. of the person to refer to an action intended to convey divine blessing (Mk 10.16) leading to healing (e.g. Mk 5.23; 6.5) or to bestow authority in some kind of commissioning (e.g. Acts 6.6; 13.3). The action may be used to convey the gift of the Spirit (Acts 8.17–19; 19.6; cf. Maurer, C., *TDNT*, VIII, 159–61). ταχέως, 'quickly, at once, without delay' (2 Tim 4.9**), can have the nuance 'too quickly, hastily'.[160]

The interpretation of the action here is disputed, and there are two main possibilities.[161]

(a) *The appointment of church leaders*, for which Timothy (like Titus, Tit 1.5) would be responsible in the congregations under

---

[158] A contrast between angels chosen for salvation and fallen angels seems less likely, *pace* Holtzmann, 355; Kelly, 127; Fee, 131.

[159] Rev 1.4f.; 14.6–20, where the Son of man is linked with six angels; cf. Col 2.18; Ignatius, *Trall* 5.2; *Smyr.* 6.1.

[160] Prov 25.8; Wis 14.28; Gal 1.6; 2 Th 2.2; Polycarp 6.1.

[161] The suggestion (which I have been unable to trace) that the reference is to the reception of catechumens into the church has nothing in its favour.

his care.[162] Most commentators assume that in the context it is the appointment of elders which is envisaged. If the imposition of discipline led to the removal of some from office, comment on the appointment of worthy replacements would be appropriate at this point (e.g. Fee, 127; Merkel, 45).[163] In favour of this view it can be argued:

(1) Laying on of hands as a ritual of appointment was a known practice in the early church, and it is already mentioned in this sense in this letter (4.14; cf. 2 Tim 1.6; Acts 13.1f.).

(2) This is the interpretation of all the Greek fathers.[164]

(3) The PE are particularly concerned with the appointment of leaders (3.1–7, 8–13; Tit 1.6–9).

Against this view the objection that Timothy could not have taken this action on his own (Hanson, 103) is without force, since there is nothing to indicate that he was to act unilaterally.

(b) *The forgiveness and restoration of a penitent person who has been disciplined*, specifically, the elder in v. 20.[165] In favour of this view it can be argued:

(1) It is favoured by the context. Verse 21 can be seen as the beginning of a bridging section which leads to the statement about sin in v. 24.

(2) The restoration of penitent sinners was part of church practice (Jas 5.15; 2 Cor 2.6–11) and the practice of doing so by laying on of hands is well attested for a later period.[166]

(3) The passage was interpreted in this way by later writers, including Tertullian, *De pudicitia* 18.9; and Nicholas of Lyra (Spicq, 548) and also probably by the Synod of Carthage, AD 256 (Roloff, 313).

---

[162] Calvin, 266; Bernard, 87f.; Parry, 36; Michaelis, 1930:77f.; Jeremias, 42f.; Scott, 67f.; Simpson, 79f.; Guthrie, 119f.; Dornier, 97; Brox, 201f.; Kelly, 127f.; Barrett, 81; Spicq, 546f.; Karris, 96f.; Roloff, 313; Knoch, 41; Knight, 239; Oberlinner, 259f.; Adler*; Schlier 1958:143; Lips 1979:174–7; Maurer, C., *TDNT* VIII, 161; Radl, W., *EDNT* III, 462f.; Meier*, 333f.; Fuller*, 261. For the arguments in favour of this view see especially Lips. Lohse, E., *TDNT* IX, 434, is undecided, though earlier he favoured this view.

[163] Roloff, 314, however, argues that appointment was to specific duties of leadership and teaching, and therefore of persons who were already elders to the duties outlined in v. 17. This presupposes a separation within the eldership which is not clearly made in the PE. Cf. Oberlinner, 260.

[164] Spicq, 547; cf. Roloff, 314 n. 447.

[165] Ellicott, 81; Holtzmann, 355f.; White, 137; Lock, 64; Easton, 160; Dibelius-Conzelmann, 80; Holtz, 129; Hasler, 43; Hanson, 103; Hort 1897:214; Galtier* 1912; Galtier* 1951; Schweizer 1961:207 n. 804; Bartsch 1965:101f.; von Campenhausen 1969:147f.; Bornkamm, G., *TDNT* VI, 666 n. 93; in Marshall 1995:132 I originally adopted this view tentatively, but in later editions left it simply as a possibility.

[166] For the practice of laying on of hands see Cyprian, *Ep.* 74.12; Eusebius, *HE* 7.2; *Didasc.* 10 (*Apost. Const.* 2.41); cf. Bernard, 88; Spicq, 548; Kelly, 128.

Against this view it is argued:

(1) In the case of taking back a penitent, it is necessary only to be sure that his repentance is genuine; a long period of testing ('not hastily') was not imposed.

(2) The link with the teaching about sins in v. 24 is also maintained if the reference is to the possible appointment of sinful elders to office.

(3) It is the past sins of penitents that matter rather than the future ones with which the person restoring them would be associated (cf. below).

(4) The practice of laying on of hands as the method of readmitting penitents is clearly attested only at a much later date.

It is clear that the first view is much the more strongly supported.

μηδὲ κοινώνει ἁμαρτίαις ἀλλοτρίαις The conjunction μηδέ (1.4) closely links the clause with what precedes, suggesting that it is explicative of it; to lay hands on somebody hastily would entail sharing in their sins. κοινωνέω, 'to share, have a share in',[167] can be used of sharing in gifts and experiences (Rom 15.27; 1 Pet 4.13), or in actions (2 Jn 11); it may also be used for giving a share in something to somebody (Rom 12.13; Gal 6.6; Phil 4.15). Here the thought is clearly that by showing some kind of positive attitude to a sinner one is approving of the person and thereby sharing in that person's sins in the sense of sharing in the responsibility and hence the guilt for them.[168] For ἁμαρτία, 'sin', cf. 5.24; 2 Tim 3.6**; see Tit 3.11 note. ἀλλότριος** is 'belonging to another' (Rom 15.20; 2 Cor 10.15f; Heb 9.25; *et al.*)

Which sins are in mind? Roloff, 314f., notes that it could be the sins already committed by the person or those that will be committed in the future when in office, and suggests that, while the emphasis lies on the future sins, the two categories cannot be distinguished too sharply. The person who appoints is responsible for what the person appointed does while holding office.

σεαυτὸν ἁγνὸν τήρει The warning is emphasised by repetition in a positive form. τηρέω, 'to keep watch over, guard', has the force 'to keep unharmed' (6.14); 'to avoid losing' (2 Tim 4.7**); it is used with the acc. and a predicative adj. to express a condition that is to be preserved (with a reflexive pronoun, as here, 2 Cor 11.9; Jas 1.27).[169] Timothy is to keep himself (σεαυτόν, 4.7, 16a, 16b*) pure (ἁγνός, here in the sense of

---

[167] Cf. Hauck, F., *TDNT* III, 797–809, espec. 804.

[168] 2 Jn 11; cf. Prov 28.24; Isa 1.23; and the verbal parallel in Artemidorus 3.51: κ. τῶν ἁμαρτημάτων ἐκείνῳ (BA). See Fee, 132.

[169] Cf. Jude 21; Wis 10.5; Riesenfeld, H., *TDNT* VIII, 140–6.

'guiltless, blameless'; cf. Jas 1.27; 2 Clement 8.4, 6; Tit 2.5**),
both for his own sake and presumably also so that he is in a
position to discipline other people (so Balz, H., *EDNT* I, 22f.).

**23. Μηκέτι ὑδροπότει, ἀλλὰ οἴνῳ ὀλίγῳ χρῶ διὰ τὸν
στόμαχον καὶ τὰς πυκνάς σου ἀσθενείας** Timothy is understood
to drink [only] water, i.e. to abstain from alcohol. The motivation
for his doing so must have been religious. He is counselled that
the moderate use of wine for health reasons is permissible and
is not in conflict with his religious attitude.[170]

The maxim is perfectly intelligible as a detached saying. The
problem is its sudden appearance in this context, where it appears
to be a digression from the theme that is resumed in 5.24. In a
modern document it would be a footnote or in parentheses. The
possibility that it has no connection whatever with the context
can be dismissed.

The specific basis for Timothy's abstinence and the rationale
for the permission given here are variously understood:

(a) The injunction may function as a qualification of v. 22b.
The purity enjoined there may have been interpreted as strict
abstinence under all circumstances. One may compare the
practices of the Nazirites who sought ἄγνεια.[171]

(b) If the heretics practised abstinence, Timothy may have
followed their example in this respect. He is advised to avoid
being like his ascetic opponents. The advice is then anti-gnostic
(Dibelius-Conzelmann, 80f.; Roloff, 315). But it is not at all
clear why Timothy would have copied the opponents in this
respect (whether historically or in a fictitious scenario), and the
advice is clearly concerned with his health rather than with the
exercise of an anti-legalistic standpoint. As a riposte to Gnostics
the statement is rather weak.

(c) Oberlinner, 261f., develops the previous suggestion more
cogently by arguing that the command has nothing to do with
the figure of Timothy himself, but is meant to develop the true
meaning of ἁγνός by attacking a Gnostic ascetic practice which
was based on a false understanding of the created order.

(d) The sins of the elders may have included drunkenness
(3.3, 8; Tit 1.7), and reaction against this may have encouraged
Timothy to practise complete abstinence. He is therefore
encouraged not to abstain completely but to take what is necessary
for health (Bernard, 88).

---

[170] Commentators differ widely on whether the verse reflects the historical
situation of Timothy. On the one side see Spicq, 549; Hanson, 104; on the other,
Roloff, 316, who insists that all the information of this kind is meant to be
exemplary; Oberlinner, 261f.

[171] Num 6.1–21; cf. Dan 1.12; Jer 42 [35].5f; *'Abot* 6.4 for abstinence; cf.
Spicq, 549; Simpson, 80.

(e) There could be a reaction against the use of wine in pagan cults and festivals (Roloff, 316).

A convincing solution must take into account the likely link with the direction to purity in v. 22. Drunkenness would have been regarded as incompatible with spiritual purity (and self-control). A combination of suggestions (a), (d) and (e) is probable. Nothing in the letters indicates that the opponents practised abstinence from alcohol.

The point which is being made is that limited use of wine is not incompatible with the basic attitude taken by Timothy. In no way is the injunction a licence for indulgence: οὐ πρὸς τρυφήν (Chrysostom; *PG* LXII, 587f.). Even to say that the moderate use of alcohol is *recommended* (Brox, 203) goes rather beyond the *permission* to use it for health reasons. Nothing is said that criticises Timothy's fundamental attitude. The claim that the recommendation is part of the 'bourgeois' ethic of the author which is concerned with what is practicable and withdraws from any kind of heroic asceticism (Brox, 203) completely misses the point.

μηκέτι**, 'no longer, from now on', is used with an imperative (Lk 8.49; Jn 5.14; 8.11; Eph 4.28; Hermas, *Vis.* 3.3.2) to urge somebody to stop what he or she is already doing. ὑδροποτέω***, 'to drink [only] water', seems to be used always as the opposite to drinking wine.[172] Hence the command is not to stop drinking water (!) but not to drink only water. One can only speculate whether there was danger of contaminated water causing danger to health or whether Timothy needed wine for other, medicinal reasons.[173] στόμαχος***, originally 'throat' (Homer), has here its usual sense, 'stomach'.[174] πυκνός is 'frequent, numerous' (Lk 5.33; Acts 24.26***; Cl.) and ἀσθένεια is 'weakness' (2 Cor 12.5, 9f.), hence 'illness' (Mt 8.17; Acts 28.9; *et al.*).[175]

24. Τινῶν ἀνθρώπων αἱ ἁμαρτίαι πρόδηλοί εἰσιν προάγουσαι εἰς κρίσιν The author resumes the topic of sins with some proverbial-sounding comments whose relevance is not immediately apparent. τινῶν is normally enclitic, but is placed first here because of contrast with following τισίν (see especially Horstmann, A., *EDNT* III, 362f.). ἀνθρώπων refers to people in

---

[172] οἴνῳ διαχρῆσθαι, Herodotus 1.71; Xenophon, *Cyr.* 6.2.26; Plato, *Rep.* 8, 561c; Epictetus 3.13.21; Dan 1.12; cf. '*Abot* 6.4.

[173] The moderate (ὀλίγῳ) use of οἶνος (3.8 and note) is mentioned or commended in various ancient authors (Theognis 509f.; Plutarch, *Mor.* 132B–F; Mor. 353B – χρῶνται μὲν ὀλίγῳ δέ, cited in BA) For the medicinal use of wine see further *Ber.* 51a; *B. Bat. 58b*; Hippocrates, *De Med. Antiq.* 13; and the texts in *New Docs.* VI, 190f. §28; *TLNT* III, 298f.

[174] *T. Naph.* 2.8; *TLNT* III, 296–9.

[175] Cf. ἀσθενέω, 2 Tim 4.20; Stählin, G., *TDNT* I, 490–3.

general (Brox, 204), but it may refer specifically in this context to elders or potential elders (Kelly, 129; Hasler, 44; Meier 1973:334f.). αἱ ἁμαρτίαι gives a catchword connection to v. 22. πρόδηλος is 'clear, evident, known to all' (not 'known beforehand'; so rightly Parry, 37).[176] The sins are said to go before (προάγω, 1.18) [the sinners] to judgement (κρίσις**);[177]. the judgement is surely that of God rather than of men.[178] The point appears to be that some deeds of these people are clearly visible here and now in their character as sins of such enormity that they are certainly going to judgement and dragging their perpetrators after them. Is the picture that the sins are hypostatised (Heiligenthal, R., *EDNT* II, 50) and depicted as going on ahead of the perpetrators to the court so that when they arrive the odds are already stacked against them? Here a decision as to whether spatial or temporal precedence is meant (cf. Schmidt, K. L., *TDNT* I, 130f.) is pointless. For the thought of a good reputation preceding people cf. Isa 58.8; Barnabas 4.12.

τισὶν δὲ καὶ ἐπακολουθοῦσιν By contrast the sins of other people (τισὶν δέ) are not so obvious. They 'follow' (ἐπακολουθέω, 5.10) their perpetrators and only come out into the open at the judgement when the secrets of people's hearts and their hidden deeds are revealed and judged (Cf. Rev 14.13; Kittel, G., *TDNT* I, 215). The force of the καί is dubious: does this give a contrast or does it mean 'but with other people they [both precede] and follow'?[179]

But what does the phrase signify? (a) The fact that the sins of some people are seen only later is perhaps meant to comfort Timothy if he makes mistakes in judgement and appoints people to office who later turn out to be sinners (cf. GNB; Fee, 133). Or (b) it may be an incentive to wait before acting or not to act on the basis of outward appearances, so as to give time for people's real character to emerge (Knight, 241; Merkel, 46); but this is difficult if the reference is to things that emerge only at the final judgement. (c) Roloff, 316f., denies this view on the grounds that the perspective here is not human but divine judgement. The point is that all sins, overt and secret, will be judged by God. This is a conclusion to the whole of 5.3–22 to remind Timothy – and everybody else – that in the last analysis

---

[176] 5.25; Heb 7.14***; Cl.; LXX; *Ep. Arist.* 133; Philo, *Gig.* 39; Josephus, *Vita* 22, 212; *Sib. Orac.* 5.37; 1 Clement 11.1; 12.7; 40.1; 51.3. MM 538f.

[177] Cf. Isa 58.8; Barnabas 4.12; Rev 14.13b (ἀκολουθέω); Dibelius-Conzelmann, 81. Cf. Oenomaus in Eusebius, *Praep. Evang.* 5.24.1: εἰς τὴν κρίσιν προάγειν (BA). White, 139, takes the verb transitively: they lead them to judgement (cf. Acts 11.1; 17.5; 25.26).

[178] *Pace* White, 138f.; Parry, 37; Lock, 64; Knight, 241.

[179] The collocation of preceding and following in Polycarp 3.3 is purely rhetorical.

everything they do stands under divine judgement. Roloff's interpretation is correct, but it does not rule out view (a) as part of the significance.[180]

25. ὡσαύτως καὶ τὰ ἔργα τὰ καλὰ πρόδηλα, καὶ τὰ ἄλλως ἔχοντα κρυβῆναι οὐ δύνανται The same point now appears to be repeated with regard to good deeds. ὡσαύτως (2.9) draws a comparison; 'in the same way'. τὰ ἔργα τὰ καλά are good deeds (cf. 3.1; 5.10, but this particular form is unique in PE). The statement is presumably true in general: good deeds [usually] cannot be hidden. But the comparison is not precise, because only some evil deeds were manifest.

Those which are[181] 'otherwise, in another way' (ἄλλως***) are either (a) those which are otherwise than good, i.e. bad, or (b) those which are otherwise than evident, i.e. presently hidden. They cannot be kept concealed (κρύπτω**), whether from God (Scott, 69) or from other people. The force of the whole statement is thus either: (a) 'Some good works are obvious; those which are otherwise (namely, not good) cannot be finally hidden from God and so remain unjudged' (Simpson, 81; Johnson, 186); or (b) 'Some good works are obvious; others which are not obvious cannot be [finally] concealed' (Knight, 241f.). The second possibility gives direct parallelism with v. 24. The first possibility leads to repetition of v. 24b, and is less likely.

The loosely added clause is meant as encouragement or reassurance (cf. Mt 10.26; Lk 8.17; 12.2; Knoch, 42). Knight takes it also as giving a basis for waiting to see if people demonstrate good deeds before appointing them to office. Or it may encourage the appointment of people 'who at first sight do not seem to possess the qualities demanded' (Kelly, 130).

d. Instructions about slaves (6.1–2a)

Bartsch 1965:144–59; Kidd 1990:140–54; Towner, P. H., 'Can Slaves be Their Masters' Benefactors?', *Current Trends in Scripture Translation* 182/183 (1997), 39–52; Verner 1983:140–5.

The fourth area of church life to be addressed is the status of slaves. The inclusion of the section is doubtless due to the fact that this was an actual problem in some of the congregations. Problems would arise in church between people who were of equal spiritual status but of unequal or inferior social status; they could also arise in the secular world between Christian

---

[180] Brox, 204, rejects all attempts to link the statements to v. 22 and claims that there is simply a loose collection of independent sayings; but he can offer no good reason why the author follows this practice at this point.

[181] ἔχω can be used intrans. with an adverb or adverbial phrase (BA).

slaves and non-Christian masters. There is nothing to indicate
that the tensions were due to the false teaching attacked elsewhere
in the PE. Rather it is probable that orthodox teaching about
Christian freedom and oneness in Christ (Gal 3.28) was causing
some slaves to move faster than the Christian or secular societies
could cope with. Also there was always the possibility that slaves
might develop a disdain for their masters that was inconsistent
with regarding them as brothers in the faith. The problem would
have been exacerbated if some elders were slaves and some
masters were not elders; this remains probable whether or not
we accept the view that the passage is particularly addressed to
slaves who were elders.[182]

It is motivated in two ways, by the aim of avoiding people
speaking ill of the Christian faith and because, in the case of
Christian masters, there is a bond of fellowship in the faith and
love. The former motive would apply particularly in the case of
slaves with non-Christian masters, but also more generally if
outsiders commented unfavourably on how slaves behaved in
Christian households. There is a similar approach in 1 Clement,
laying the stress on loyalty to the State and society in order to
give no cause for persecution (Knoch, 43). Here, however, as in
Tit 2.10, the aim is more missionary (Barrett, 82; MacDonald
1988:168)

In both cases the practical point is that masters must be
appropriately honoured by the giving of faithful and devoted
service. The section thus continues the theme of 'honour' (cf.
Brox, 204f.; Rapske 1987:318f.). Nevertheless, whereas the previous
sections are about the honour to be displayed by the church and
its leaders, this section is about slaves honouring their masters.
It is thus rather different in character from what precedes.

Teaching about the roles of slaves is common in early Christian
literature, especially in the context of household tables. Other
passages dealing with the same theme are Eph 6.5–9; Col 3.21 –
4.1; 1 Pet 2.18–25; *Didache* 4.10f.; Ignatius, *Poly.* 4.3; Barnabas
19.7. Common sources or traditions are reflected (Bartsch 1965;
Weidinger 1928:71f.). Teaching about the duties of slaves to be
in subjection and to please their masters is also found in Tit 2.9f.
In both cases, although the material is of a kind found in a
household table (see Weidinger 1928:72f.), the context is not
instruction to the different groups in a household but is concerned
more with slaves as a class in the church.

As in Tit 2.9f., the passage deals exclusively with the duties of
slaves to their masters; nothing is said to masters (or about the
parent/child relationship), although the existence of Christian

[182] Parry, 37; Barrett, 82; Hasler, 46; but see Hanson, 106.

masters is clearly stated (6.2). The passage could be said to be written from the angle of masters and to reflect a desire to maintain the status quo (Oberlinner, 266). The Christian status of the masters is made a ground for better service by the slaves, and no change in the attitude of the masters is called for. It goes without saying that no change in the social system is envisaged (Hasler, 45).

These comments ignore the fact that what we have here is not part of a household table dealing with mutual duties, but rather instructions for life in the church, dealing with the particular problem of the tendency of slaves to disregard their position (Roloff, 319). Oberlinner, 264, also notes that reciprocal instructions are not possible where non-Christian masters are concerned (v. 1).

The 'form' of the passage is again indirect exhortation: this is instruction to the church leader about how people in the church ought to behave, which he is to pass on in his teaching (6.2b). There are two parallel injunctions, one to slaves in general (6.1) and the other to those with Christian masters (6.2a). In both cases the injunction is to give them appropriate honour. In the former case the motivation provided is so that the gospel should not be made the object of slander because of the behaviour of Christians; this could apply to recalcitrance towards Christian masters being the object of comment by non-Christian neighbours as well as to disrespect to non-Christian masters. In the latter case, the lack of honour may have been based on the fact that the masters were seen as 'brothers'; this status, however, should entitle them to greater respect. The masters are in fact described as 'believers and beloved', and this description is in effect an indirect injunction to them to live out their faith.

TEXT

1. θεοῦ κυρίου (D* 33 330 2400 d f g m r vg goth Ambst). Elliott, 88f., prefers the variant, as being NT usage (cf. 2 Tim 2.19), which was altered because it was ambiguous. But the MS evidence for the variant is weak; the phrase in the text is less usual, and assimilation to NT usage elsewhere is likely.

EXEGESIS

1. Ὅσοι εἰσὶν ὑπὸ ζυγὸν δοῦλοι ὅσος (2 Tim 1.18**) is originally a correlative expressing the force 'as much/many as'; the plural is frequently construed with πάντες giving 'all, as many as...', i.e. 'all who...'. Frequently, as here, the antecedent is not expressed (supply οὗτοι) and the pronoun simply means

'all who' (Rom 2.12; Gal 3.10). In the present context there might possibly be a link with what precedes, giving the sense 'all elders who are slaves' (Parry, 37; Barrett, 82), but the instruction is quite general and would fit all Christian slaves.

ὑπό with acc.** is used of being under somebody's power or rule.[183] ζυγός (masc. in Koine Gk. for Attic ζυγόν), is a 'beam', hence a 'beam-balance, scales' (Rev 6.5) or a 'yoke' for pulling a burden. In this latter sense it is always fig. in the NT. The phrase is a stock one for being under a tyrant or in a condition of slavery and brings out its burdensome character.[184] Slavery is recognised as a situation of low standing on a social level in which the slave was subject to the will of the master and had no innate personal freedom. δοῦλοι (Tit 2.9 [literal]; 2 Tim 2.24; Tit 1.1** [spiritual]) stands in apposition to the adjectival phrase ὑπὸ ζυγόν, 'under the yoke, as slaves'.

The force of the double description is problematic: (a) It may be intended to indicate that people in general are under some kind of bondage, of which slavery is an example (Scott, 70f.); (b) It may signify 'under the yoke of Christ' (Bartsch 1965:150; cf. Mt 11.29; 1 Clement 16.17). (c) It may be with reference to being under non-Christian masters (White, 140; Lock, 65; Hanson, 105; Knight, 244); (d) Most probably it is intended to remind slaves that in the eyes of the world they remain slaves with no choice but to obey their masters ('total dependence', Holtz, 131). It is probably better to take the verse to indicate all slaves (with v. 2 as a sub-class having Christian masters; Roloff, 321 n. 481); another possibility is to make a distinction between slaves with pagan masters (v. 1) and slaves with Christian masters (v. 2; Simpson, 81; Hasler, 45; Holtz, 131f.).

τοὺς ἰδίους δεσπότας πάσης τιμῆς ἀξίους ἡγείσθωσαν The implication is that slaves are not required to be obedient to masters other than their own (and so perhaps to constitute an inferior social class in the church; cf. Roloff, 322).[185] In the context the reference is primarily but not exclusively to non-Christian masters, since unseemly conduct in Christian households would be the object of gossip outside. πᾶς functions as a

---

[183] BA s.v. 2.a.β categorise the present expression as a local one, answering the question 'where?', but it is surely a metaphorical usage expressing rule (s.v. 2.b).

[184] Cf. Sophocles, Ajax 944; Herodotus 7.8.3; Plato, Leg. 6, 770E; Ep. 8, 354D; Demosthenes 18.289; Ecclus 33.27; 1 Macc 8.17f., 31; 13.41; Gen 27.40; Gal 5.1; cf. Mt 11.29f.; Acts 15.10***; cf. Bertram, G., and Rengstorf, K. H., TDNT II, 896–901.

[185] For ἴδιος meaning 'respective' (Prov 22.7) and for δεσπότης see Tit 2.9 note.

superlative (Tit 2.10). For τιμή, 'respect', see 1.17; and 5.17 note; for ἄξιος see 1.15; 5.17; and for ἡγέομαι see 1.12**. The implication is that even bad masters should be treated as persons (Knight, 245). The absence of reference to obedience may not be significant (cf. Rapske, 320).

ἵνα μὴ τὸ ὄνομα τοῦ θεοῦ καὶ ἡ διδασκαλία βλασφημῆται Cf. Tit 2.5. The name[186] of God (cf. Rev 3.12) is his reputation in the world. Here it is significantly linked to ἡ διδασκαλία (cf. Tit 2.10), i.e. the Christian teaching which might be thought responsible for the wrong social attitudes developing (a) if social relationships were upset in church; (b) if slaves refused to obey their non-Christian masters. For the thought cf. 3.7. But the comments that would arise are characterised as slanders (βλασφημέω, 1.20) since they are untrue: Christian teaching does not, or rather should not, lead to anti-social behaviour.

Behind the phrase we can detect an echo of Isa 52.5: τὸ ὄνομά μου βλασφημεῖται ἐν τοῖς ἔθνεσιν (cf. Ezek 36.20). This phrase was probably a commonplace by this time and therefore we do not necessarily have a conscious quotation (cf. CD 12.7f.; Rom 2.24; 2 Clement 13.2; Polycarp 10.3; et al.). The conduct of slaves should in fact have the opposite result (cf. Tit 2.10). The possibility that non-Christian masters might be converted through the quality of life and the witness of the slaves is not explicitly raised (Rapske 1987:323; Roloff, 323), but it is implicit in the light of the general missionary motivation in the PE (Knoch, 42; Towner 1989:177f.).

2a. οἱ δὲ πιστοὺς ἔχοντες δεσπότας μὴ καταφρονείτωσαν The weak conjunction δέ draws a contrast with a different class of slaves from those in 6.1 who have pagan masters, or has the force 'and in particular'. The danger is that Christian slaves may show lack of respect (καταφρονέω; 4.12**) to Christian masters; πιστός here simply means 'believing, Christian' (1.12 note). They may not give them the consideration due to their position (Spicq, 554; Roloff, 323 n. 490), or possibly even disdain them because they regard them as equal to themselves in the church. Therefore they must be all the more made aware of their position!

ὅτι ἀδελφοί εἰσιν The clause is ambiguous at every point. The subject of the clause is presumably the masters (Holtzmann, 359). They are brothers (4.6), a word used of people in the slave/master relationship in Philem 16, but this time primarily from the angle of the slaves being brothers to the master rather than the master to the slaves. However, since the word 'brothers' has

---

[186] ὄνομα, 2 Tim 2.19**; cf. Bietenhard, H., *TDNT* V, 242–83.

a reciprocal sense, the clause could mean 'on the ground that they are [all] brothers [of one another]'. ὅτι has the force 'on the ground that' (NRSV), but the relation to the preceding clause is uncertain. (a) Nearly all translations and commentators take the connection to be: 'slaves should not show less respect to their masters on the grounds that they are [merely] brothers [and so not superior to them]' (NIV; REB; NRSV; Arichea-Hatton, 138; Verner 1983:142; Lock, 65, cites Prov 23.22 as a good parallel). (b) But the thought could be: 'the reason why slaves should respect their masters is because they are brothers [and therefore to be treated with love]' (cf. GNB; Fee, 139). The former view gives the sense that the slaves think that their masters need not be placed on a higher plane than themselves because they are brothers. The latter view gives the sense that the slaves are to honour their masters because they are brothers and in fact to give them all the better service because of what is implied in this title. A decision between the two views hangs on whether it is more likely that regarding people as brothers leads to lesser or greater respect. On the whole, the former interpretation seems more probable, but even when taken this way the sentence may well imply the corollary that if the masters are brothers (with all that this description implies), this should rather be a basis for even better service. Brothers should at least be respected as equals, and if the master is a believer this makes him all the more worthy of loving service.

ἀλλὰ μᾶλλον δουλευέτωσαν δουλεύω is 'to be a slave', 'to perform the duties of a slave, serve, obey' (Tit 3.3 note; cf. Mt 6.24; Lk 16.13; 15.29; Eph 6.7). According to BA, μᾶλλον (1.4) can have three nuances: (a) 'to a greater degree' (Phil 1.9, 12; so BA *s.v.* δουλεύω, for this passage), i.e. 'let them serve all the better'; (b) 'for a better reason', i.e. 'rather, sooner' (so BA *s.v.* μᾶλλον, for this passage); (c) 'instead of something else' (1 Tim 1.4; 2 Tim 3.4). Usage elsewhere in the PE suggests that nuance (c) is appropriate here: let them serve rather than despise their masters! The passages listed by BA under (b) are better understood under categories (a) and (c).

ὅτι πιστοί εἰσιν καὶ ἀγαπητοὶ οἱ τῆς εὐεργεσίας ἀντιλαμβανόμενοι The clause is about certain persons who are believers and *therefore* beloved (ἀγαπητοί, 2 Tim 1.2**). This word can refer to people who are actually the objects of love or who are 'worthy of love'.[187] The reference in this context is not to a human, emotional relationship but to a Christian one (which does not exclude human feelings). The word is frequent in the NT for

---

[187] Cf. Xenophon, *Mem.* 3.10.5.

being loved by God (e.g. Mk 1.11; Rom 1.7; 11.28). It then expresses, by implication, worthiness of being loved by human beings, i.e. the relationship that should exist between fellow-believers. It is understood purely in the sense of being loved by God here by Dibelius-Conzelmann, 82, who argue that slaves cannot be enjoined to fulfil the duty of service out of love for their masters, and therefore take the description to be purely of the Christian standing of the masters;[188] but people can and do need to be reminded of the duties that spring from a relationship of love. Roloff, 324 n. 494, stresses that, where ἀγαπητός is used for being loved by God, the context always makes this clear and therefore takes the broader sense here. The passage says that Christian masters should be loved by their slaves. It is striking that Onesimus is to be 'beloved' by Philemon (Philem 16); nevertheless, the idea that slaves should be loved by their masters is not explicitly expressed here.

The next phrase is ambiguous. εὐεργεσία is 'the doing of good', 'kindness', hence 'a good deed, service' (Acts 4.9***).[189] ἀντιλαμβάνομαι (in the mid. voice) can mean: (a) 'to lay hold of, lay claim to' (lit. and fig.); (b) 'to help, come to the aid of';[190] (c) 'to take part in, devote oneself to, practise';[191] (d) 'to grasp with the mind, perceive, notice';[192] (e) 'to enjoy, benefit from'.[193] The resulting phrase has been interpreted in various ways:

(a) 'Those who benefit by their service', of the masters receiving service from the slaves.[194] If this interpretation is adopted, the effect is to offer a new evaluation of what slaves do, to transform the obedience of servitude into the giving of a noble benefit (Spicq). 'The slave is raised from a chattel to a spiritual equal in grace' (Simpson, 82). The thought would not be peculiarly Christian. Seneca, *De Benef.* 3.18, 21: *an beneficium dare servus domino possit? ... quidquid est quod servilis officii formulam excedit, quod non ex imperio sed ex voluntate praestatur, beneficium est* (Bernard, 92). Attractive though the consequences of this

---

[188] Holtzmann, 359; Schneider, G., *EDNT* I, 8–12, espec. 12.
[189] Cf. Bertram, G., *TDNT* II, 654f.; *TLNT* II, 107–13.
[190] Pap. in MM 47f.; LXX; Lk 1.54; Acts 20.35.
[191] Xenophon, *Cyr.* 2.3.6; Pap. in BA; Dittenberger, *Or.* I, 51.9f.; 339.32f. quoted by Dibelius-Conzelmann, 82; Isa 26.3; Baruch 3.21; Josephus, *Ant.* 5.194; 19.238. Cf. Delling, G., *TDNT* I, 375f.
[192] Ps-Plato, *Axioch.* 370A; *M. Polycarp* 15.2; Philo, *L.A.* 3.56; *Det.* 101.
[193] Field 1899:210 explains this as an extension of the previous sense; it is supported by the vg and pesh, but he can provide no Gk. parallels.
[194] NIV; NRSV; NEB; NJB; Field 1899:210; Bernard, 92; Parry, 37; Scott, 71; Spicq, 554f.; Dornier, 100; Simpson, 82; Kelly, 132; Fee, 139; Knight, 247; Arichea-Hatton, 139; Danker 1982:324; Towner*.

translation are, it has been objected that this meaning for the verb is in fact unattested, and also that εὐεργεσία signifies a service done by a superior to an inferior. But then the point may be precisely to subvert the normal understanding of the slave–master relationship (cf. Johnson, 186f.).

(b) The punctuation in WH mg suggests the interpretation 'But rather let [the slaves] who receive the benefits serve [the masters] because they are faithful and beloved'. But the order of words hardly favours this view, and it also faces the same basic objection as view (a).

(c) 'Those who devote themselves to their welfare [or to good works]', of the masters who care for the slaves.[195]

(d) '[The masters], who share [with the slaves] in Christian service' (Hanson, 105f.; cf. Lea-Griffin, 164f.). But can the verb have this force?

If view (c) is correct, it implies that masters must care for the welfare of the slaves, and it is assumed that this takes place in the case of Christian masters. The presence of this implication would greatly lessen the force of the criticism that there is no corresponding mention of the need for masters to treat slaves as persons (Eph 6.9; Col 4.1; Philem 15–20; 1 Cor 7.20–24). Nevertheless, it is hard to grasp the logic of describing the masters in this way – 'because they are believers and beloved – I mean, the people who care for you'. Why is this qualification tagged on at the end? With view (a), however, the thought flows smoothly and τῆς εὐεργεσίας functions to explain more clearly what is meant by μᾶλλον in this context.

III. TRUE AND FALSE TEACHERS CONTRASTED (6.2b–21a)

Thurén, J., 'Die Struktur der Schlussparänese 1 Tim 6,3–21', *TZ* 26 (1970), 241–53.

The closing section of the letter is at first sight a set of miscellaneous instructions and injunctions. Dibelius-Conzelmann, 83–91, found a lack of coherence in the section, but their verdict is rightly rejected by subsequent commentators (cf. Thurén*). The section falls fairly clearly into defined sections.

---

[195] Holtzmann, 359f.; Dibelius-Conzelmann, 82; Brox, 204; Hasler, 45; Holtz, 132; Knoch, 42f.; Roloff, 324f.; Oberlinner, 267; Bertram, G., *TDNT* II, 655; Verner 1983:143f.; Towner 1989:179 (but cf. n. 194); Kidd 1990:140–56. According to Towner this was the view of Chrysostom, Theodoret, Pelagius and Estius.

Verse 2b is transitional, summing up the previous material and stressing the need to teach it. At the same time, it provides the positive statement to which the activity of the opponents forms a contrast.

Verses 3–5 then describe opponents who disagree with this teaching and characterises them as ignorant and covetous. The line of thought is that if any people do not share Timothy's sound teaching, they are arrogant and ignorant and infected with ideas about making money out of religion.

Verses 6–10 give a general reflection on wealth and the desire for it, stressing its dangers and temptations. While religion does lead to true 'gain', those who desire to get rich plunge themselves into spiritual destruction. This section is therefore still concerned with false teachers in the church, and warns them against the danger of spiritual destruction.

A clear break at v. 11 signals the beginning of a section addressed to Timothy personally concerning his own conduct. It stresses the need for positive Christian virtues and perseverance in holding to the truth, and it indicates the solemn character of this calling.

Following the brief doxology in v. 16b there is a fresh start at v. 17 where Timothy is instructed on what to say to rich people in the congregation so that they will overcome the temptations of wealth and use it properly. This section deals in a matter-of-fact way with the fact that the congregation does include people who are well-off materially, and for whom there is perhaps less spiritual danger than for those who desire to be wealthy.

Finally, vv. 20f. give a last injunction to Timothy to guard the truth and to resist the advances of the kind of [false] teaching which leads to apostasy and loss of faith.

From this summary we see that vv. 5b–10 and 17–19 deal with the danger of wealth and the proper attitude to it, although the style varies between the two sections, descriptive comments in vv. 5b–10 and teaching to be transmitted to the wealthy in vv. 20f. The intervening section is concerned with Timothy's own personal behaviour in the midst of these temptations and is a call to personal faithfulness. The final injunction may be seen as a reinforcement of this injunction, but it may perhaps better be seen as a conclusion to the whole letter, forming an *inclusio* with the teaching in ch. 1 (cf. especially Roloff, 327; Oberlinner, 270).

Nevertheless, despite the prominence of the theme of wealth, the main theme is false teaching and false teachers and the contrasting way of life of godly people and Timothy in particular. The topic of wealth is introduced because it is one important aspect of the general topic. The passage as a whole represents a further treatment of the opening theme of the letter, Timothy's own conduct and example. Thus the basic structure is:

2b	Timothy's own task of faithful teaching.	
3–5		The character of the false teachers, culminating in their desire for wealth.
6–8	Comment on the right attitude to wealth,	
9–10		contrasted with the disastrous results of greed.
11–12	The way of life that the man of God should follow,	
13–16	reinforced by a powerful adjuration.	
17–19		What the faithful teacher should say to wealthy believers.
20–21a	Final injunction to Timothy to be faithful and to beware of false teaching.	

The pattern is not a simple one, but the line of thought is transparent and logical.

The section contains several motifs with Hellenistic parallels, which leads some commentators to find a particularly close relationship to the popular philosophy of the day. But the ideas are equally at home in Judaism and the teaching develops naturally from that of Jesus (Kelly, 138). The warnings against riches and the stress on being content with a little have been thought to be in tension with the 'world-friendly, anti-ascetic' outlook elsewhere in the letter (Roloff, 339f.), but the problem is imaginary.

a. Teachers with false doctrines and false motives (6.2b–10)

Byington, S. F., '1 Timothy 6, 10', *ExpTim* 56 (1944–5), 54; Dschulnigg, P., 'Warnung vor Reichtum und Ermahnung der Reicher. 1 Tim 6,6–10,17–19 im Rahmen des Schlussteils 6,3–21', *BZ* 37 (1993), 60–77; Menken, M. J. J., '*hoti en* 1 Tim 6, 7', *Bib.* 58 (1977), 532–51; Zeilinger, F. 'Die Bewertung der irdischen Güter im lukanischen Doppelwerk und in den Pastoralbriefen', *BLit* 58 (1985), 75–80.

The sub-section begins with a transitional statement that introduces the main theme of the larger section, namely the personal responsibility and way of life of Timothy (vv. 2b, 11–16, 20f.). Over against Timothy's own activity of faithful teaching is placed the activity of opponents, mentioned here for the third time (1.3–7; 4.1–3), who teach other doctrines and reject his teaching. Any who do this are characterised as swollen-headed, despite their ignorance, and their diseased longing for debates leads into strife and dispute. In particular, they are further characterised as people whose minds are corrupted, and they think that religion can be a source of wealth.

At this point the emphasis shifts from false teaching to the desire for wealth. Its dangers are taken up in a series of comments. Two points are placed side by side: (a) Godliness accompanied by a sufficiency of what we need and contentment with that is a source of great wealth. The adjective 'great' almost carries the sense of 'real' and serves to redefine wealth in spiritual terms. This principle is backed up by the statements that, if we have food and clothing, we shall have sufficient for what we need for life in this world; after all, we should remember that we cannot take anything with us into the next world. (b) The desire for wealth is the source of all kinds of evils and leads people into temptations which cause spiritual destruction, as various erstwhile believers have experienced.

Verses 6–10 in particular have numerous parallels in the popular philosophical teaching of the day, and there is an absence of strictly theological considerations. This leads many scholars to conclude that the writer is here particularly indebted to Hellenistic philosophy and is less in touch with the biblical tradition or the teaching of Jesus, despite the possible allusion to the teaching of Jesus in v. 3. In fact, there are significant parallels in the Gospels and Hellenistic Judaism, and we appear to have yet another case where the thought of the PE is couched in terms that would speak to a Hellenistic audience, while still remaining faithful to the biblical, Christian tradition.

TEXT

3. μή οὐ (Ψ). Elliott, 90, holds that οὐ is original and μή is Atticising – a Cl. usage untypical of NT. εἰ takes οὐ if the condition is real (cf. 3.5; 5.8). But one MS is insufficient as a basis for altering the text. BD §428 suggest there is a remnant of Cl. usage here (cf. 1 Cor 15.2; 2 Cor 13.5; Gal 1.7). Cf. MH III, 281, 283.

προσέρχεται προσέχεται (ℵ* *pc* lat Cyp; cj. Bentley). Elliott, 90, accepts the variant on the grounds that the author likes this verb (1.4 *et al.*) and that it gives a Hellenistic turn of phrase; the variant was rejected as not found elsewhere in NT or as an orthographic slip. He further argues that the point is not that the heretic 'does not come to' sound teaching, and that the verb cannot mean 'consent to'. But the verb is fully acceptable here (see exegetical note below), and the variant could be assimilation to 1.4. Metzger, 575, thinks that later scribes found the text difficult and altered it. (There is a similar variant at Acts 13.44 between ἔρχομαι and ἔχω.)

4. γίνεται γεννῶνται (D*ᶜ lat). The singular verb is correct with a list where the first item is singular. The plural is possibly due to the variant φθόνοι or to a desire to get a stronger verb. See Elliott, 91f.

φθόνος Plural (D* *pc* latt bo). The variant is probably assimilation to the other plurals in the list, Elliott, 92.

ἔρις ἔρεις (D F G L Ψ 6 81 365 629 1175 *al* latt syʰ saᵐˢ bo). The variant is simply an alternative spelling for sing., the normal plural being ἔριδες (1 Cor 1.11) (Elliott, 92).

5. ἀπεστερημένων ἀπεστραμμένων ἀπό (D*); ἀπερριμένων (365; a singular variant). The variant is not suitable in the context (Elliott, 93).

εὐσεβείαν Add ἀφίστασο ἀπὸ τῶν τοιούτων (D² Ψ TR a b m vgᵐˢˢ sy Iren Cyp Lcf Ambst). Cf. 2 Tim 3.5 for the thought. Elliott, 94, says that the language fits the PE (cf. 1 Tim 4.1; Tit 3.11; 1 Tim 6.11), and argues that a line was carelessly omitted (note how 4.9f. may have a similar clause breaking the sense). See, however, Fee, 146, who states that the PE do not use this verb to express the idea, and that the addition breaks the link to 6.4. Metzger, 575f., states that though the variant is ancient, the best Alexandrian and Western authorities omit it; there is no reason for omission if it is original.

7. ὅτι (ℵ* A F G 048 33 81 1739 1881 *pc* r Did) (a) ἀληθὲς ὅτι (D* a b vgᵐˢˢ Ambst Spec); (b) δῆλον ὅτι (ℵ² D² Ψ TR (f m vg) sy Poly; Kilpatrick); (c) Omit (co Hier Aug Cyril). Most scholars would agree with Metzger, 576, that the simple ὅτι is original; it was difficult and scribes tried to improve the sense.

Nevertheless, variant (b) is accepted as original by Simpson, 85 (cf. 1 Cor 15.27; Gal. 3.11); it was altered by homoioteleuton.

Variant (c), which omits the connective, is a 'rhetorical expedient when quoting a difficult text' (Metzger; similarly, Elliott, 95, 237).

Another possibility is that there was a primitive corruption, with variant (c) representing a correct emendation of the dittography ΚΟΣΜΟΝΟΤΙ for an original ΚΟΣΜΟΝ (WH *Notes*, 134; Hanson, 107f.; cf. Easton, 167). Certainly this gives the easiest sense.

Parry, 39, emended the text to οὐδ' ὅτι (i.e. 'not to speak of being able to carry anything out').

8. διατροφάς (ℵ A Ψ 33 1739ᵐᵍ ᵛⁱᵈ 1881 TR f vg syh): διατροφήν (D F G K P 048ᵛⁱᵈ 1739* ᶜ *al* a b r vgᵐˢˢ syᵖ co Cyp Ambst; WH mg). Reicke (*ConNT* 11 [1947], 196–206) and Elliott, 96, hold that the plural is assimilation to the next noun. The MS evidence is evenly balanced, and the variant should possibly be accepted.

9. παγίδα Add τοῦ διαβόλου (D* F G [629] *pc* ar b d f g o vgᶜˡ Spec). The addition is assimilation to 3.7 (Elliott, 96; Metzger, 576). But it is a correct interpretation (Knight, 255f.).

πολλάς Add καί (547). Elliott, 209, says that the addition after πολύς is Cl. and hence Atticistic. His later adoption of the variant (230) appears to be a slip.

ἀνοήτους ἀνονήτους ('useless'; 629 *pc* lat). The variant is rejected by Elliott, 97.

10. πολλαῖς ποικίλαις (ℵ* H). The variant was introduced on stylistic grounds to cut down the number of occurrences of πολύς (cf. 6.9, 12, Elliott, 98).

EXEGESIS

2b. ταῦτα δίδασκε καὶ παρακάλει The transitional formula has the same structure as 4.11 (παράγγελλε ταῦτα καὶ δίδασκε) but is verbally different. Despite the minority opinion that it refers forwards (Scott, 72f.), ταῦτα must refer backwards, either to the teaching in the Epistle so far,[1] or possibly just to 5.3–6.2 (but hardly to 6.1–2a only). 6.3 will then refer to those who disagree with what has been said in the Epistle. The clause thus concludes the teaching given so far before writer reaches the final exhortation (Knoch, 43). For διδάσκω see 2.12 note, and for παρακαλέω see 1.3 note.

3. εἴ τις ἑτεροδιδασκαλεῖ καὶ μὴ προσέρχεται ὑγιαίνουσιν λόγοις τοῖς τοῦ κυρίου ἡμῶν Ἰησοῦ Χριστοῦ καὶ τῇ κατ' εὐσέβειαν διδασκαλίᾳ Whereas the parallel instruction in 4.11 led on to further, detailed exhortation to Timothy about his own way of life, here the command is followed by a discussion of the people who disagree with the teaching in the letter.

εἴ τις introduces a factual premise, relating to any false teacher with such views (Fee, 140).[2] The use of ἑτεροδιδασκαλέω (1.3) is a deliberate contrast with δίδασκε in the previous verse, and the word may have been chosen to strengthen the *inclusio* with ch. 1. It indicates that the teaching of the opponents is not merely false but actually contrary to apostolic teaching. This gives support to the view that a major theme of the epistle is the need for right teaching as the antidote to false teaching.

The force and construction of προσέρχομαι are disputed. The whole phrase could mean 'to come [to you] with sound words', but this option has not been adopted by any authority. The literal meaning is 'to come to, approach'. The figurative sense 'to come to, approach [a deity]' (Heb 7.25; 1 Pet 2.3) is just possibly present, with the thought that the sacred teaching is the object of something like religious devotion (Holtz, 133; Roloff, 330f.). A number of references support the meaning 'to turn to, occupy oneself with'.[3] This would give the sense 'to devote oneself to' (REB; Schneider, J., *TDNT* II, 683f.) or 'to agree with' sound words' (GNB, NIV, NRSV).

The phrase ὑγιαίνουσιν λόγοις (cf. 1.10 note) recurs in 2 Tim 1.13. Here the addition τοῖς τοῦ κυρίου ... forces the question of reference on us. The possibilities are:

(a) The sayings of Jesus.[4] Despite the strong criticisms by Kelly, 133f., this interpretation has been taken up by Roloff,

---

[1] Cf. 3.14; 4.6, 11, 15; 5.2, 21; see 1.18 note; Knight, 247; Fee, 140; Arichea-Hatton, 140f.

[2] εἴ τις is used with the indic., as in 3.1, but with the Cl. negative μή (Moule 1953:148; BD §428[1]; cf. Lk 6.4D).

[3] Diodorus Siculus 1.95 (τοῖς νόμοις). Plutarch, *Cat. Mi.* 12.2 πολίτεια); Epictetus 4.11.24 (φιλοσοφία); Ecclus 4.15 *v.l.*; 6.19, 26 (σοφία); Philo, *Agr.* 123 (good deeds); *Mig.* 86 (ἀρέτη); *Didache* 4.14 + ἐπὶ προσευχήν; cf. 1 Clement 33.8 πρ. τῷ θελήματι αὐτοῦ [sc. θεοῦ]; Field 1899:211; Palzkill, E., *EDNT* III, 163f. Simpson, 83, compares the use of προσήλυτος, *accedere* (Silver Latin).

[4] Lock, 68; Schlatter, 160; Jeremias, 44; Holtz, 134; Spicq, 557; Wolfe 1990:82–6.

331, who notes that where λόγος is used in the broader sense of 'teaching' in the PE it is always in the sing. form, and that teaching of Jesus has already been cited at 5.18. On this view the sayings of Jesus are to be distinguished from 'the teaching which is in accord with godliness'. Against Roloff it should be noted that the plural is found in 2 Tim 1.13 (cf. Oberlinner, 273). Nevertheless, this interpretation is attractive.

(b) Teaching coming from Christ, where he is seen as the authority behind it.[5]

(c) Teaching about Christ.[6] This could include sayings of Jesus (Knoch, 43). The phrase is equivalent to διδασκαλία or λόγος τοῦ κυρίου (1 Th 1.8).

It is hairsplitting to distinguish between views (b) and (c). While (c) corresponds to usage elsewhere, (b) is more appropriate in the context which is to place the authority of teaching emanating from Jesus over against heresy. The solemn fulness of ὁ κύριος ἡμῶν Ἰησοῦς Χριστός (repeated in 6.14) is intended to make the source and character of sound teaching more precise.

There is a similar combination of λόγος and διδασκαλία in 5.17 (but note the shift from the singular form there). Again the problem of whether these are seen as two distinct entities arises.

The teaching is κατ᾿ εὐσέβειαν, like the 'truth' in Tit 1.1. As in Tit 1.1 the thought is of teaching that promotes godliness (and therefore is in accordance with it). See further **Excursus 1**.

4a. τετύφωται, μηδὲν ἐπιστάμενος, ἀλλὰ νοσῶν περὶ ζητήσεις καὶ λογομαχίας The character of the person who does not teach the truth is now depicted in a comprehensive way. The heretics are described in the manner used by Jews of Gentiles (Dibelius-Conzelmann, 83). What is stated as fact is probably to be regarded as the totally evil state that may develop (just as the factual description of the widows to be helped by the church really represents an ideal to be sought after). There are three basic evil qualities, empty pride, ignorance and disputatiousness. From these (or from the third of them) develop further evil characteristics, which (v. 5) are then said to be found in people who are corrupted in their minds, and finally their corrupt thinking is specifically identified as thinking that religion leads to material gain (and presumably using it for that purpose). The characteristics which are implicitly condemned are those which should not be found in believers and especially in their leaders, or which should be replaced by the corresponding virtues.

---

[5] Parry, 38; Easton, 164; Fee, 141; Oberlinner, 273.
[6] Holtzmann, 360; Dibelius-Conzelmann, 83 (but *Didache* 11.8 is hardly an analogous phrase); Guthrie, 123; Kelly, 134.

Thus the first characteristic listed is one that should be avoided by overseers (3.6). See note there on whether τετύφωται should be understood as (a) 'puffed up, conceited';[7] or (b) 'blinded, foolish'.[8] Either sense is possible here with what follows. The person who knows nothing but disputes idly may be filled with empty pride or is simply foolish. The REB translation, 'a pompous ignoramus', captures both nuances neatly. Cf. Polycarp 7.1f. for the uselessness of false teaching. The sheer foolishness of people, confident in their knowledge, who affirm nonsense has already been mentioned in 1.7, and is repeated here emphatically. Cf. 2 Tim 3.4 for conceit as a vice of the last days. ἐπίσταμαι** is frequently 'to know, be acquainted with a person, thing', but here 'to understand something'.[9]

The author pursues the metaphor inherent in 'healthy words' as he describes the sickness of the false teachers. νοσέω***, 'to be sick, ailing', can be used literally and figuratively.[10] Here it has the specific force 'to have a morbid craving for'.[11] For ζήτησις see 1.4 v.l. (for ἐκζήτησις); Tit 3.9 note. Here it has the sense 'discussion, debate', in parallel with λογομαχία. The Hellenistic noun λογομαχία***, 'word-battle', 'dispute about words', is not found elsewhere in the NT (except as a v.l. in Tit 3.9 G), but the verb is found in 2 Tim 2.14.[12]

4b. ἐξ ὧν γίνεται φθόνος ἔρις βλασφημίαι, ὑπόνοιαι πονηραί The clause has the form of a catalogue of vices, and the specific form is that of a *Filiationsreihe* where vices are related to their origin (ἐξ ὧν; Roloff, 329). ἐξ ὧν is a fairly loose connective, used here only in the PE. It is followed by a catalogue of the vices which develop (γίνεται) from ignorant controversies; these results of strife are characteristic of the community as well as individuals (Vögtle 1936:12, 220). The description is psychologically appropriate and based on concrete relationships in church (Vögtle, 35). One sin leads to others (Vögtle, 69, 70, 122). For the form cf. *Didache* 3.

---

[7] Versions; Kelly, 134; Knight, 251.

[8] Bernard, 93; Brox, 207f.; Oberlinner, 274. (Roloff, 332, is unclear. At 3.6 he translates with *hochmütig*, but in his comment he rejects the meaning *aufgeblasen werden* in favour of *verblendet werden*, which he says is found in 6.4 and 2 Tim 3.4; on the present verse he says that the word combines *Eitelkeit* and *Dummheit* and is equivalent to *borniert sein* [narrow-minded] and rejects the meaning *verblendet, töricht werden*.)

[9] Xenophon, *Symp.* 3.6; Wis 8.8; Mk. 14.68. According to Bouwmann, G., *EDNT* II, 36f., the language 'is derived from a rhetorical background'.

[10] For the latter see Xenophon, *Mem.* 3.5.18; Wis 17.8; Philo, *L.A.* 3.211 Josephus, *Ant.* 16.244; 18.25.

[11] Sophocles, *Trach.* 435; Plutarch, *Mor.* 546F: v. περὶ δόξαν, 'to have an unhealthy ambition'. Cf. Oepke, A., *TDNT* IV, 1091–8, especially 1095.

[12] Cf. Kittel, G., *TDNT* IV, 143.

The list contains five items which can all be regarded as aspects of strife, bitterness and mutual suspicion which break down fellowship. The piling up of the language indicates that the internal bickering in the congregation is an especial problem. The first two items are in the sing. and form a stereotyped pair (Rom 1.29; Roloff, 332 n. 27), while the others are in the pl.

(a) φθόνος, 'envy' (Tit 3.3 note; cf. Plutarch, *Mor.* 468B, 556B), is found in ethical lists in Rom 1.29; Gal 5.21; 1 Pet 2.1. It is associated with ἔρις in Rom 1.29; Phil 1.15.

(b) ἔρις, 'strife' (Tit 3.9**), is found in ethical lists in Rom 1.29; 2 Cor 12.20; Gal 5.20. It is readily understandable that these two results issue from disputes in the church. They are characteristic of non-Christian society (Tit 3.3).

(c) βλασφημία**, 'defamation' (Tit 2.5 note), refers to abusive speech which can be defamatory and may be true or false ('slander'). With reference to God and what is closely associated with him it has the narrower sense of 'blasphemy'. It is found in lists of vices in Mark 7.22; Eph 4.31; Col 3.8; cf. Hermas, *Mand.* 8.3; *et al.* Probably the broad meaning is correct here in a list of typical results of argument and controversy, although the author would probably have regarded what was said as derogatory to God and Christ. See further the use of βλασφημέω (1.20; 6.1) and βλάσφημος (1.13; and the list in 2 Tim 3.2).

(d) ὑπόνοια***, 'suspicion', possibly 'innuendo' (Simpson, 83),[13] is neutral in itself (cf. ὑπονοέω, Acts 13.25). It is also linked with πονηρός in Ecclus 3.24. For πονηρός, 'wicked, evil', cf. 2 Tim 3.13; 4.18**; the noun πονηρία is not used in the PE but is found in an ethical list in Rom 1.29.

5a. διαπαρατριβαὶ διεφθαρμένων ἀνθρώπων τὸν νοῦν καὶ ἀπεστερημένων τῆς ἀληθείας

(e) διαπαρατριβή***, 'mutual, constant irritation', is a stronger form of παρατριβή, 'irritation, friction'.[14] At this point the sentence takes a decisive twist and is developed by a genitive construction. The effect is to make the last item in the list particularly significant and to suggest that it is in apposition to the preceding items.

The word order with the participle preceding the noun (ἀνθρώπων) is odd (cf. 2 Tim 1.13). διαφθείρω, 'to spoil, destroy'

---

[13] Orig. 'secret [inward] opinion', hence 'conjecture, suspicion'; Cl.; *Ep. Arist.* 316; Philo, *Leg. Gai.* 35; Josephus, *Bel.* 1.227, 631; for a link with the previous item see Clement, *Paed.* 3.81.3, cited by Behm, J., *TDNT* IV, 1017–19.

[14] παρατριβή is listed as a variant in Elliott, 93; cf. also παραδιατριβαί (216 2344 d f m; Lcf.; TR); Vögtle 1936:222 comments on the use of word-creation in ethical lists, but this seems inappropriate in view of the attestation of the word elsewhere (Polybius 2.36.5 *et al.*).

(lit. 2 Cor 4.16; Lk 12.33; Rev 8.9; 11.18a), has the fig. sense 'to corrupt, ruin'.[15] νοῦς is the 'mind' as the faculty of thinking (Tit 1.15); the word is, of course, morally neutral, but is used, as here, of corrupted minds in 2 Tim 3.8 (with καταφθείρω, passive); Tit 1.15**.[16] ἀποστερέω is 'to steal, rob, defraud' (1 Cor 6.7, 8; 7.5; Mk 10.19***). The passive participle means 'deprived' (here with gen.; cf. Ecclus 29.6; Josephus, Ant. 2.303). There is an echo of Tit 1.14 (ἀποστρεφομένων τὴν ἀλήθειαν) which refers to those who deprive others of the truth by spreading false teaching which drives out the true.

The reference in ἀλήθεια is to the gospel (2.4). For other references to loss of the truth see 2 Tim 2.18; 3.7, 8; 4.6; Tit 1.14. The implication is that, if people lose hold on the truth of the gospel, they become corrupt in mind and turn to quarrels that engender strife.

5b. νομιζόντων πορισμὸν εἶναι τὴν εὐσέβειαν After godliness has been mentioned positively in v. 3 we now have an allusion to misunderstanding of it by the deceived people who think that it is a source of gain. This may be an expression of the nature of their corrupt thinking or a further characteristic of people when they lose their hold on the truth of the gospel and develop a warped understanding of it. The participle of νομίζω**, 'to think, suppose' (with acc. and inf. cf. 1 Cor 7.26, 36), has the force 'in that they think that ...'. Schenk, W., EDNT II, 470, notes that the verb is often used for false assumptions. πορισμός 6.6*** means 'gain'[17] or, as here, 'means of gain'.[18]

The precise force of the statement is debated:

(a) The false teachers (v. 3!) thought that being religious would make them rich; cf. Seneca, Ep. 108: *qui philosophiam velut aliquod artificium venale didicerunt* (Bernard, 94), and/or they promised their followers that their new teaching would help them to become rich – an ancient parallel to the contemporary 'prosperity gospel' (Knoch, 44).

---

[15] Diodorus Siculus 16.54.4; Dio Chrysostom 43.10; Josephus, Ap. 2.264; Rev 11.18b***; Ignatius, Rom. 7.1; Hermas, Sim. 4.7 et al.; passive with acc. of respect, as here, Plato, Leg. 10.888A; Josephus, Ant. 9.222; cf. Aeschylus, Agam. 932; Dionysius Halicarnassensis 5.21. Cf. καταφθείρω in the same context, 2 Tim 3.8; and also φθείρω, 2 Cor 11.3. Cf. Harder, G., TDNT IX, 93–106.

[16] See also Rom 1.28; Eph 4.17; Col 2.18. Cf. the similar use of νοήματα, 2 Cor 11.3.

[17] Wis 13.19; 14.2; Ep. Arist. 111; Philo, Op. 128.

[18] Josephus, Bel. 2.603; Plutarch, Cat. Mai. 25.1 δυσὶ μόνοις πορισμοῖς, γεωργίᾳ καὶ φειδοῖ ('farming and thrift'); T. Iss. 4.5 si vera lectio.

The noun is literary Hellenistic (Philodemus, Oec. 44, Simpson, 84). However, it is found in an inscr. from Ephesus (AD I), cited in New Docs. IV, 169 § 79.

(b) The false teachers were cashing in on the piety of other people by charging for esoteric teaching – i.e. hoping to get rewards from offering novel teaching (Kelly, 135; Knoch, 43; cf. Lips 1979:81–3).

(c) The false teachers were pretending to be pious themselves in order to deceive others to pay them for their teaching (Scott, 74). This seems the most likely interpretation.

(d) Kidd 1990:96–100, sees the flow of the argument here thus: Timothy is faced with an opposition which has emerged from the church's wealthy members; wealth is regarded as the prerequisite to leadership in the church since it has come somehow to be associated with 'piety'; it allows the enthusiasts to pursue the kinds of behaviour that bring honour in the community (false εὐσέβεια); in contrast the author connects true 'piety' with αὐταρκεια which is characterised by the kind of qualities outlined in v. 11. Love of money and financial standing are thus placed in contrast to true qualifications for leadership and true godliness.

In any case, the accusation that philosophers practised for sordid, venial motives was common, and Paul defends himself against it in 1 Th 2.5. Cf. Roloff, 333f. Nevertheless, Oberlinner, 276f., holds that the accusation is a stock one with no concrete basis, since it appears that orthodox church leaders also were remunerated in some way for their work (5.17). This objection underestimates the significance of vv. 9f. which would hardly be so forceful if a real danger was not present.

6. **Ἔστιν δὲ πορισμὸς μέγας ἡ εὐσέβεια μετὰ αὐταρκείας** The mention of gain leads into a discussion of the problems of wealth (vv. 6–10). It is doubtless directed at people in the congregation who were tempted to greed and saw in godliness a way of becoming wealthy – contrast the 'double honour' above! The teaching is evaluated rather negatively by some commentators on the grounds that it is a loose collection of comments and maxims to which parallels can be found in the secular world, especially in Stoic and Cynic philosophy (cf. Dibelius-Conzelmann, 84), and that it smacks of being worldly-wise (Easton, 167, contrasts its appeal to worldly prudence with Col 3.5). For a different view see Kelly, 138.

In fact the passage is carefully constructed. There is a careful balance between vv. 6–8 and vv. 9–10. Verses 6–8 make the points: (a) godliness is in fact a source of great gain (cf. 4.8); (b) We neither brought anything into the world nor can we take anything out – therefore material wealth is irrelevant in the long term; (c) We should be content to have merely what we need in this world (because longing for more will lead to long-term spiritual destruction).[19] By contrast, in vv. 9–10 there is a warning that the desire for wealth in this world leads to temptations yielding to which destroys people. Verse 10 is reinforcement of v. 9 which appeals to what has actually been happening in the church.

The author attaches his comment to what has preceded by a repetition of the thought of the false teachers in the form of a direct statement introduced by ἐστίν.[20] He goes beyond the previous statement, however, in two ways, first by qualifying the πορισμός which results from godliness as μέγας, 'great' (the adjective functions like a superlative; cf. 3.16); and, second, by qualifying the nature of εὐσέβεια. The effect is that by the end of the clause the reader should recognise that he has shifted the reference of πορισμός from 'material' to 'spiritual gain', both in this world and the next. There is a similar line of thought in 4.7f. where material and spiritual 'usefulness' are compared. εὐσέβεια (see **Excursus 1**) is the [true] practice of the Christian religion.

The key word in the sentence is αὐτάρκεια (2 Cor 9.8***; Hermas, *Man.* 6.2.3). This word (and its cognates) can be used concretely of what is sufficient or adequate for a purpose;[21] hence it signifies a 'sufficiency, competence', i.e. the income or property of a person who supports himself without help from others.[22] Spicq, 561, takes the word in this sense here: 'la piété avec [la] suffisance [de ce qu'on a]' (cf. Calvin, 274, for this possibility).

It can also mean the situation or the state of mind of the person who has a 'sufficiency' and is able so to live.[23] This can be taken in two ways:

(a) It can mean 'self-sufficiency', the quality of the person who relies on his or her own inner resources without outside assistance. This was the essence of virtue in Stoic philosophy, to have no needs and to acquiesce in one's situation in independence. It was opposed to having excess, living in luxury and being greedy for wealth.[24] Diogenes Laertius describes Socrates as αὐτάρκης ... καὶ σεμνός (2.24). It was also a virtue in Epicureanism, where it was understood, not as always using only a little but rather as

[19] This line of thought is continued in vv. 17–19 which say that God provides richly for us; if we do good and use our wealth to help others, we shall gain eternal life for ourselves.

[20] It corresponds to εἶναι in v. 5 and is the only example of εἰμί as first word in clause in the PE.

[21] E.g. water for flocks (Josephus, *Ant.* 2.259); cf. αὐτάρκης (Ecclus 34.28a). See Deut 32.10 (αὐταρκέω) for God giving the Israelites sustenance in the desert.

[22] Pap. in BA; Philo, *L.A.* 3.165 – τὰ αὐτάρκη; Hermas, *Sim.* 1.6; 2 Cor 9.8.

[23] Plato, *Rep.* 2.369B; Aristotle, *Pol.* 7.5 (1326b, 29f.).

[24] BA *s.v.*; Kittel, G., *TDNT* I, 466f.; Wilpert, P., *RAC* I, 1039–50.

being content if one only has a little (Diogenes Laertius 10.130f.).
Not surprisingly it was also regarded as a virtue by Cynics
(Diogenes Laertius 6.104). Hence, on this interpretation the
present passage is in effect based on the Stoic/Cynic philosophical
tradition.[25]

(b) It can also signify the virtue of 'contentment', the quality
of the person who has enough and is not longing for more
(Arichea-Hatton, 146). αὐτάρκης is found in Prov 24.30 LXX;
Ecclus 5.1; 11.24; 34 (31).28 for what is sufficient.[26] These
references all suggest people receiving what they need, rather
than less or more. The philosophical notion of self-sufficiency is
absent. The adjective αὐτάρκης (Phil 4.11) means 'self-sufficient'
and hence 'content' with what one has. Here the quality is related
to the new resources given in Christ who strengthens the believer.

Nothing is said here in 1 Tim about the source of self-
sufficiency, which could give some support to the view that a
secular virtue has been incorporated into Christianity, but in fact
the quality is associated with and accompanies godliness; the
implication is that godliness provides all that one needs, and the
temptation is to long for material wealth in addition instead of
being content with God's provision. Hence Barrett, 84, is fully
justified in concluding that 'our author is thinking of a man
whose resources are in God', and noting that the next verse
indicates that we have no resources in ourselves. Knight, 253,
suggests that εὐσέβεια is the source and αὐτάρκεια the inward
result. Not self-sufficency but 'Christ-sufficiency' is what is meant
(Fee, 143; similarly, Roloff, 334f.).

7. οὐδὲν γὰρ εἰσηνέγκαμεν εἰς τὸν κόσμον The statement is
supported by a proverbial-sounding couplet. It reappears in
Polycarp 4.1.[27] Hasler, 47, stresses the use of the first person
plural here to include Timothy as a church leader who may be
tempted by his position to enrich himself.

The logic (γάρ) is not entirely clear. The general thought is
along the lines: we brought[28] no material possessions (οὐδέν)
into the world and can take nothing from it. We brought nothing
into the world because we cannot take anything with us when

---

[25] NEB; Dibelius-Conzelmann, 84–6; Hanson, 107; Brox, 209f.; Oberlinner,
278f.
[26] Cf. 4 Macc 9.9, where it seems to mean 'appropriate'. Similarly in *Ps. Sol.*
5.16. the noun means 'sufficiency' (*pace GELS*). Cf. Ps-Phocylides 5f. (*OTP* II,
574). See also Simpson, 84f.
[27] Barrett 1973–4:238. The argument of Dibelius-Conzelmann, 85, that the
thought is so common that we cannot prove the dependency of Polycarp on the
PE is severely weakened by the fact that 1 Tim 6.10 is also reflected in the verse.
[28] εἰσφέρω**, 'to bring in, carry in'; Lk 5.18f.; cf. Mt 6.13; Lk 11.4; Acts
17.20; Heb 13.11***; cf. Weiss, K., *TDNT* IX, 64f.

we leave it; and similarly there is no point in accumulating goods while we are here because we cannot take them with us either. Therefore we need little while we are in the world.

But the fact that we cannot bring things into or out of this world does not by itself prove that we only need a little while we are in it. Spicq, 562, suggests that the first and final states define the intermediate state, so that whatever we have then does not really belong to us. This does not altogether deal with the difficulty. Perhaps rather than understanding this as a statement that is logically precise and comprehensive in its application, we should be satisfied to see that it says something fairly general about temporality versus eternality and the relative values of each.

The thought is well-paralleled in the ancient world, both in Judaism and in Hellenism. Note, however, that two motifs tend to be associated and confused. One is the impossibility of taking one's possessions with one into the next world (Lk 12.16–21), and the other is the fact that only the soul survives this life, and the body is left behind. Only the former is in focus here, and the various parallels that can be cited[29] all emphasise the impossibility of taking anything with us who brought nothing into the world (Menken*, 535f.)

ὅτι οὐδὲ ἐξενεγκεῖν τι δυνάμεθα Corresponding to the fact that we brought nothing into the world is the fact that we cannot even (οὐδέ, 2.12) take anything out.[30] However the connection between the two clauses, expressed by ὅτι is problematic, as is reflected in the textual variants (see above). Assuming that the text is correct, the following possibilities have been proposed:

(a) ὅτι expresses cause, 'because'. This gives the sense: 'We brought nothing into this world, because we cannot even take anything out.' This is paraphrased by Barrett, 84: 'There was no point in bringing anything into the world with us, because we shall not be able to take anything out.'

(b) ὅτι is loosely used to mean 'just as' or even 'and': 'We brought nothing into the world, just as we cannot even take anything out.'[31] This is the sense adopted by Spicq, 561–3: 'En

---

[29] See Job 1.21; Ps 49.17; Eccles 5.15; Philo, *Spec.* 1.294f.: σὲ τί ποιεῖν ἁρμόττει πρὸς ἀνθρώπους ... τὸν μηδὲν εἰς τὸν κόσμον ἀλλὰ μηδὲ σεαυτὸν εἰσενηνοχότα. γυμνὸς μὲν γὰρ, θαυμάσιε, ἦλθες, γυμνὸς δὲ πάλιν ἄπεις; Ps-Phocylides, 110f. (*OTP* II, 578): 'It is impossible to take riches and money (with you) into Hades. All alike are corpses, but God rules over the souls'; *Anth. Pal.* 10.58 (*The Greek Anthology*, IV, 33): γῆς ἐπέβην γυμνὸς γυμνὸς θ' ὑπὸ γαῖαν ἄπειμι; Seneca, *Ep.* 102.25: *Non licet plus efferre quam intuleris;* '*Aboth* 6.9 (SB III, 655); *b. Yoma* 86b; Lk 12.16–21; Hermas, *Sim.* 1.6; see Dibelius-Conzelmann, 84f.; Menken*, 535f.

[30] ἐκφέρω**, 'to carry, bring out'; Polycarp 4.1; not in Paul.

[31] Cf. Dibelius-Conzelmann, 85 n. 14; Dornier, 102f.; Kelly, 136f.

effet, nous n'avons rien apporté dans le monde, aussi bien nous n'en pouvons rien emporter.' There is an element of result here.

(c) A similar sense is gained by supposing that there is an ellipsis (cf. the scribal emendations): 'For, nothing did we bring into the world, [just as it is evident] that neither are we able to carry anything out of it' (Hendriksen, 198f.; similarly, Knight, 254). Jn 6.46 is cited as a parallel, but the construction there is different. Field 1899:212 cites the second use of ὅτι in 1 Jn 3.20 as a parallel, but it is unlikely that this is an instance of ellipsis.

(d) ὅτι is resumptive: 'We brought nothing into the world; [I say] that neither can we carry anything out' (Bernard, 95). But this is hardly feasible.

(e) The clause is a quotation of a well-known proverb, introduced by a citation formula (cf. Gal 6.7f.; a possibility suggested by Spicq, 561f.).

(f) ὅτι is not the conjunction but the neuter form of ὅστις = 'wherefore' (cf. the use of ὅ in Euripides, *Hec.* 13; Hillard, cited by Lock, 69). But the alleged parallel is without force.

(g) A number of scholars argue that there is evidence that ὅτι can mean 'so that', expressing result.[32] At first sight, the idiom appears to be well-attested (cf. MHT III, 318), but it is striking that all of these alleged parallels are in interrogative sentences. The syntax is better explained otherwise.

(h) The ὅτι clause may give the basis of knowledge for affirming the other clause. A good parallel is Lk 7.47: 'On the grounds that she loved much, I tell you that her sins are forgiven.' The examples cited under (g). are better explained as falling into this category with an ellipse of the verb of affirmation. Thus Mk 4.41 has the sense 'Who then is this? [We ask the question] because the winds and the sea obey him.'

(i) Somewhat similarly Menken* translates: 'For we have brought nothing into the world, [and I say this] because we cannot take anything out of it.' On this view the second line does not give the reason why the content of the first line is known, but rather the reason why the author puts it forward. But then he claims that the thought is inverted: the fact that we have brought nothing into the world somehow becomes a reason for the fact that we cannot take anything out. We must abandon our possessions at death, and a reason for this fact is our birth without any possessions: we have no right to possessions because we are born without them. The rationale for this inversion eludes me, and Menken's original proposal seems better syntactically.

[32] BA; Holtz, 137; Lea-Griffin, 168 n. 156; Oberlinner, 280. Parallels cited include Mk 4.41; Lk 4.36; Jn 7.35; 14.22; Heb 2.6 = Ps 8.5. See Gen 20.9; Judg 14.3; 1 Sam 20.1; 1 Kgs 18.9. Cf. Plato, *Euthyph.* 2A (cited by Taylor, V., *Mark* [London: Macmillan, 1952], 277).

COMMENTARY ON 1 TIMOTHY

No solution is wholly satisfying.[33] Although the assumption of a primitive corruption that led to the wrong insertion of ὅτι is attractive, the best explanation is the first possibility (a).

A clear line of thought emerges if, unlike the majority of scholars, we take v. 7 closely with v. 8. The resulting line of thought in vv. 6–8 is something like: 'Godliness with [only] a sufficiency of material goods is a great gain; to put it otherwise and justify it: we brought nothing into the world [and there was no point in our doing so] because we shall not be able to take anything out of it as well, but if [while we are here] we have food and clothing, we can be content with these things. [Therefore, we should not seek more than we need.]' The force of the verse is then to emphasise the folly of accumulating goods additional to what we brought into the world; we can and should be content with the things that we need for our passage through it.

8. ἔχοντες δὲ διατροφὰς καὶ σκεπάσματα, τούτοις ἀρκεσθησό-μεθα The participle ἔχοντες is conditional – 'if we have...'. διατροφή*** is 'support, sustenance', i.e. food, and can be used in the sing. or the plural.[34] σκέπασμα***, 'covering', can refer to (a) 'clothing'[35] or (b) 'house'.[36] ἀρκέω can be used intrans. act., 'to be enough, sufficient', and pass. of persons, 'to be satisfied, contented with'.[37] For the thought cf. Heb 13.5; 1 Clement 2.1. The future indic. possibly functions as an imperative.[38]

Basic food and clothing are the irreducible necessities of life (cf. Gen 28.20; Ecclus 29.21). The belief that people can be content with these bare necessities is found both in Christian and in Hellenistic sources. For Hellenistic teaching see above on αὐτάρκεια and also Plutarch, *Mor.* 155D (Almquist 1946:281); Epictetus, *Enchir.* 33.7; Musonius Rufus 94–109 Hense; Dibelius-Conzelmann, 85; Fee, 144. Some interpreters hold that the author

---

[33] Roloff, 335f., argues that the second clause of the saying gives the actual reason for 'the statement', the grounds for knowing which are given in the first clause. He paraphrases: 'We brought nothing into the world, in order to be led to see that we can also take nothing out'. But this analysis does not convince, because the 'statement' to which he refers does not exist. Surely the second clause gives the reason for affirming the first.

[34] See BA for examples: sing. 1 Macc 6.49; Josephus, *Ant.* 2.88; 4.231; pl. Epictetus, *Enchir.* 12.1.

[35] Aristotle, *Pol.* 7.17 (1336a, 17); Philo, *Det.* 19; Josephus, *Bel.* 2.129.

[36] Aristotle, *Metaph.* 7 (1043a, 32): οἰκία σκέπασμα ἐκ πλίνθων κ. λίθων.

[37] With dat., as here; Lk 3.14; Heb 13.5; cf. 3 Jn 10; cf. Kittel, G., *TDNT* I, 464–6.

[38] Mt 5.48; Kelly, 137; White; Roloff, 336. Cf. the similar use of the imperfect in Hebrew.

is here dependent on Hellenistic philosophy rather than the teaching of Jesus (Oberlinner, 281). However, Fee, 147, stresses that the key words are not those used by philosophers in this context, and that the Gospel parallels (Lk 12.22 = Mt 6.25) are closer. Roloff, 336f., holds that the thought is more radical than Heb 13.5 but not as radical as that of Jesus whose teaching was more dictated by eschatological considerations (cf. Oberlinner, 281); the radicality goes beyond the rest of the PE and is to be explained as applying to the church leaders who are contrasted with the opponents who want to be leaders and teachers. This restriction is unnecessary, and the contrast seen with teaching elsewhere in the PE is illusory. What is being commended is not destitution but a simple life-style (Stott, 153).

9. The thought develops by the typical method of contrast, contrasting the attitude of the godly (v. 8) with that of those who seek to be rich. The contrast is between two ways of life and their results.

οἱ δὲ βουλόμενοι πλουτεῖν The statement is concerned with those who are seeking to be rich rather than more narrowly with those who are rich (v. 17). However, the force could be 'to stay rich', and nothing is implied about the present economic state of the recipients, although they are probably 'on the way up'. The focus may be the opponents, but the warning is quite general.

Verner 1983:174f. argues that v. 9 and v. 17 indicate two distinct groups (the would-be rich and the already rich), whereas Kidd 1990:95–7 argues on the basis of both grammar and context that one group (the already rich) is in mind, since the 'love of money [v. 10] ... is preeminently a vice of those who have money to love'. But this statement is patently false.

For βούλομαι see 2.8; 5.14. πλουτέω is 'to be rich', but the aorist has the force 'to become rich' and the perfect 'to have become rich'.[39]

ἐμπίπτουσιν εἰς πειρασμὸν καὶ παγίδα καὶ ἐπιθυμίας πολλὰς ἀνοήτους καὶ βλαβεράς The fatal results of seeking after riches are indicated in a series of three nouns, the last of which is expanded into a lengthy phrase (cf. 6.4f.) and presumably carries the main emphasis. ἐμπίπτω is used in the same way as in 3.6 (cf. Tob 14.10b; Prov 12.13; Ecclus 9.3). The thought is that the desire for riches leads people into other actions, whether to acquire wealth or to use it, which are evil in character. πειρασμός can mean 'test, trial' (a meaning which is rare outside the Bible) or 'temptation, enticement to sin'. It can be used actively of the

[39] Literal: Lk 1.53; 2 Clement 20.1; Diognetus 10.5; Hermas, *Vis.* 3.6.7; *AP* 15.30. Figurative: 6.18**; Hermas, *Vis.* 3.6.6; with ἐν, 2 Cor 8.9; Rev 3.18***; cf. πλοῦτος, 6.17; πλούσιος, 6.17; Tit 3.6 note.

action of tempting (Lk 4.13) or passively of the state of being tempted (cf. Jas 1.12), here the latter.[40] It is a common idiom that one goes 'into' temptation (Mt 26.41; Mk 14.38; Lk 22.40; Mt 6.13; Lk 11.4). παγίς (3.7 note; 2 Tim 2.26) is employed as a further description of temptation to bring out its character, either as a trap which takes one unawares or as a snare from which one cannot escape once caught. For a broad parallel cf. Seneca, *Ep.* 87 (Bernard, 96).

Both of these nouns are more formal and indicate the results of seeking riches in terms of situations that tempt people to evil acts and catch them unawares. The third item states more explicitly the actual nature of the results. The longing to be rich engenders a whole range of desires which are foolish and positively harmful. For ἐπιθυμία see Tit 2.12 note (Tit 3.3; 2 Tim 2.22; 3.6; 4.3**); there it was noted that the context often indicates that the desires are evil. πολλάς has the sense 'many, many kinds of'. ἀνόητος is 'unintelligent, foolish' (Tit 3.3 note), whether of persons or (as here) of things.[41] βλαβερός*** signifies 'harmful'.[42]

αἵτινες βυθίζουσιν τοὺς ἀνθρώπους εἰς ὄλεθρον καὶ ἀπώλειαν A relative clause is added which indicates how the desires are harmful (cf. Ecclus 21.4). αἵτινες has the force 'of a kind which, inasmuch as they...' (1.4 note). βυθίζω is used trans. 'to sink', i.e. to plunge something into water or deluge it, 'to swamp'.[43] τοὺς ἀνθρώπους are people in general: this is what can happen to anybody, including members of a Christian congregation.

Two words describe their fate. ὄλεθρος is 'destruction, ruin, death',[44] and ἀπώλεια is another word for 'destruction'.[45] Commentators dispute whether the two nouns have distinct forces (cf. the similar problem in 1 Cor 5.5): (a) (Present) material disaster and (future) spiritual destruction respectively;[46] (b) Both refer to spiritual destruction and the repetition is for emphasis (Oberlinner, 282). Since both words were in common use for

---

[40] Cf. Seesemann, H., *TDNT* VI, 23–36; *TLNT* III, 80–90.

[41] Sophocles, *Ajax* 162 (γνῶμαι); Plato, *Phileb.* 12D (δόξαι); *CH* 6.3b.

[42] Xenophon, *Mem.* 1.3.11 (ἡδοναί); Prov 10.26; Hermas, *Vis.* 3.9.4; *Sim.* 6.5.5–7; *Man.* 6.1.3. It can be used of major disasters and minor inconveniences (*TLNT* I, 292).

[43] Simpson, 86; 2 Macc 12.4. Pass. of a boat. being swept beneath the waves, Lk 5.7***. For the active voice used fig., as here, cf. Alciphron 1.16.1, cited by BA; cf. καταβυθίζω of a city submerged in wars, Dittenberger, *Syll.* 730.7 (I BC).

[44] Cl.; 1 Th 5.3; 2 Th 1.9; 1 Cor 5.5***; Ignatius, *Eph.* 13.1; 1 Clement 57.4; cf. Schneider, J., *TDNT* V, 168f.

[45] Act.: Mk 14.4; cf. Mt 26.8. Pass.: Mt 7.13; Jn 17.12; Acts 8.20; Rom 9.22; Phil 1.28; 3.19; 2 Th 2.3; Heb 10.39; 2 Pet 2.1, 3; 3.7, 16; Rev 17.8, 11***; cf. Oepke, A., *TDNT* I, 396f.

[46] Dornier, 103; Kelly, 137; Knight, 256f.

the effects of final judgement, this interpretation is perhaps preferable. Nothing in the text suggests that a neat division between present and future loss can be made on the basis of the two terms. The thought is of the present effects which last into the next life.

10. ῥίζα γὰρ πάντων τῶν κακῶν ἐστιν ἡ φιλαργυρία The verse contains a proverbial-sounding statement which explains or clarifies why the desire for wealth is so destructive.[47] This is followed by a factual statement which shows that the desire for wealth has led to apostasy and consequent self-destruction in the church.

ῥίζα, 'root' (lit. Mt 3.10; 13.6; Mk 4.6; 11.20; Lk 3.9), is used symbolically in parables and parabolic sayings (Mt 13.21; Lk 8.13; Rom 11.16–18) for the beginning from which something grows (Heb 12.15; it can also be used for the shoot that comes from a root, Rom 15.12; Rev 5.5; 22.16***). The usage here is found in proverbial sayings with reference to results both evil and good.[48] As the predicate preceding the verb ἐστιν, ῥίζα is anarthrous, and therefore there is ambiguity whether it signifies (a) 'a root'[49] or (b) 'the root'.[50] The forcefulness of the statement and the emphatic position support the second possibility. This does not necessarily mean that the desire for wealth is literally the source of *every* evil.[51] More probably we simply have a hyperbolical statement. κακός, 'bad, evil', can have more than one nuance. It can refer to things which are 'morally wrong' (Rom 1.30; 1 Cor 10.6; Jas 1.13), or to things which are 'injurious, pernicious', whether to other people or to the perpetrators (Tit 1.12; 2 Tim 4.14**).[52] Both nuances may be present here. φιλαργυρία*** is 'love of money, avarice, miserliness'.[53] It occurs in vice lists in 2 Clement 6.4; Polycarp 2.2; 4.3; 6.1.

---

[47] Byington* suggested that it has been drawn from a comic author.

[48] See BA s.v. and Maurer, C., *TDNT* VI, 985–91 (985) for the following: Euripides, *Frg.* 912.11: ἀρχὴ καὶ ῥίζα παντὸς ἀγάθου; Epicurus, *Frg.* 409 in Athenaeus 7, p. 280A: ἀρχὴ καὶ ῥίζα παντὸς ἀγαθοῦ ἡ τῆς γαστρὸς ἡδονή; Plutarch, *Mor.* 4B; Constantin. Manasseh 2.9H: φθονὸς ἡ ῥίζα τῶν κακῶν; Himerius, *Ecl.* 32,5 W (AD IV): παίδεια ἡ ῥίζα τῶν ἀγαθῶν. Cf. Ecclus 1.6, 20; Wis 15.3; Polycarp 1.2.

[49] RV; NIV; GNB; NRSV; Holtzmann, 363; Easton, 165; Kelly, 138; Knight, 257; Stott, 152.

[50] REB; NJB; Field 1899:212f.; Simpson, 86; Fee, 147.

[51] Escaping from the problem by recognising that πάντων can mean 'all kinds of' (Knight, 258, citing 2.1, 4, 6; 4.10 as parallels) comes to grief on the use of the article.

[52] Cf. Grundmann, W., *TDNT* III, 469–87.

[53] Cl.; 4 Macc 1.26; 2.15; Philo, *Spec.* 4.65 (see below); *T. Jud.* 18.2; 19.1; cf. φιλάργυρος, 2 Tim 3.2. *TLNT* III, 446f.

The sentiment is a familiar one (Plato, *Leg.* 9.870A) and the saying has abundant parallels in ancient literature.[54] It is ascribed, with varying wording, to several philosophers.[55] For the thought cf. 3.3; 2 Tim 3.2. The word corresponds to Paul's πλεονεξία (reckoned as the greatest of evils in Dio Chrysostom, 17.7, 9).[56] In Judaism greed is linked with sexual immorality and idolatry.[57]

ἧς τινες ὀρεγόμενοι ἀπεπλανήθησαν ἀπὸ τῆς πίστεως καὶ ἑαυτοὺς περιέπειραν ὀδύναις πολλαῖς The writer continues with a comment which ties the secular proverb to apostasy in the church. ἧς refers strictly to 'love of money' but clearly must mean simply 'money' in a condensed expression (BA). τινές is the usual vague reference to the opposition group in the church. For ὀρέγομαι see 3.1; any negative sense in the word is derived from the context.

Two results follow from straining after wealth. The first is apostasy. ἀποπλανάω (Mk 13.22***; cf. πλανάω, Tit 3.3 note) is (act.) 'to mislead', (pass.) 'to wander away from' (Ecclus 4.19; 13.8; 2 Macc 2.2).[58] It became a term for apostatising (Polycarp 6.1; Hermas, *Sim.* 6.3.3; 9.20.2; *Man.* 10.1.5). ἀπὸ τῆς πίστεως is in effect 'from believing what is to be believed'. Cf. Ahiqar 137 (*OTP* II, 504): '[Do not amass] wealth, lest you pervert your heart.'

---

[54] But not in Dio Chrysostom 3.17 (cited by one commentator) where κολακεία is not said to be the root of all sins, but rather the most shameful.

[55] The following citations have been culled from: BA Sp. 1473; Dibelius-Conzelmann, 85f.; *TLNT* I, 45 n. 5; III, 446f.

Hippocrates, *Ep.* 17.43 (V–IV BC): τούτων ἁπάντων αἰτίη ἡ φιλαργυρίη.

Democritus in *De Gnomologio Vaticano inedito*, 265 (c. 400 BC): Δημόκριτος τὴν φιλαργυρίαν ἔλεγε μητρόπολιν πάσης κακίας.

Bion the Sophist in Stobaeus, *Eclog.* 10.36–7 (II BC): τὴν φιλαργυρίαν μητρόπολιν ... πάσης κακίας εἶναι.

Diogenes (IV BC), in Diogenes Laertius 6.50: τὴν φιλαργυρίαν εἶπε μητρόπολιν πάντων τῶν κακῶν.

Apollodorus Comicus 4 (Vol III p. 280 Kock. III BC): ἀλλὰ σχεδόν τι τὸ κεφάλαιον τῶν κακῶν εἴρηκας· ἐν φιλαργυρίᾳ γὰρ πάντ' ἔνι.

Diodorus Siculus 21.1 (I BC): πλεονεξίαν ... μεγίστων κακῶν αἰτία ... μητρόπολις οὖσα τῶν ἀδικημάτων.

Plutarch, *Mor.* 108A–B, regards greed as the cause of wars.

Sib. Orac. 2.111 [*OTP* I, 348] (=Ps-Phocylides 42 [*OTP* II, 575]): ἡ φιλοχρημοσύνη μήτηρ κακότητος ἁπάσης; 3.235: φιλοχρημοσύνην ἥτις κακὰ μύρια τίκτει; cf. 3.642; 8.17 [*OTP* I, 367, 376, 418].

Philo, *Spec.* 4.65: φιλοχρήματον, ὅπερ ὁρμητήριον τῶν μεγίστων παρανοημάτων ἐστι.

Polycarp 4.1: ἀρχὴ δὲ πάντων χαλεπῶν ἡ φιλαργυρία.

Ammianus Marcellinus, 31.4: *aviditas materia omnium malorum.*

[56] Or would he have cast pride in this role (as Hanson, 108, suggests)?

[57] *T. Dan* 5.5–7; *T. Jud.* 19.1; Philo, *Spec.* 1.23–5; CD 4.17f.; cf. 1 Th 4.3–6; Roloff, 338f.

[58] Cf. Dionysius Halicarnassensis, *Comp. Verb.* 4: ἀπ. ἀπὸ τ. ἀληθείας.

The second result is that people cause themselves (ἑαυτούς, 2.6; *et al.*) great harm. περιπείρω*** is 'to pierce through, impale',[59] and ὀδύνη is 'pain, woe'.[60] The pain is that of unfulfilled desires for wealth rather than the pangs caused by conscience (Hauck, F., *TDNT* V, 116).

b. Instructions on true teaching (6.11–16)

Baldensperger, G., 'Il a rendu témoignage devant Ponce Pilate', *RHPR* 2 (1922), 1–25, 95–117; Käsemann, E., 'Das Formular eine neutestamentlichen Ordinationsparänese', in Käsemann 1960:101–8; Lips 1979:177–80; Seeberg 1966 [1903]:97–112; Turner, C. H., '1 Tim vi. 12, 13: ἐπὶ Ποντίου Πειλάτου', *JTS* 28 (1927), 270–3.

Following the warning against the danger of seeking riches, the author might have gone straight on to give positive advice regarding riches. He will do so in vv. 17–19, but, formally at any rate, this section is not the original continuation of vv. 3–10, since it is couched in the form of instruction to be given by Timothy. Instead the author reverts again to instruction to Timothy (and so to the church in general). But it is not immediately clear what is the thrust of the section, and it may well be that there is a variety of themes. (a) Negatively, there is the need to avoid the desire for wealth and the evils to which it gives rise (v. 11a). (b) Timothy is to strive to develop various positive Christian qualities (v. 11b). (c) He is to persevere in the faith and to seek after eternal life. This may refer to personal perseverance or to his work in preserving the faith in the congregation (v. 12). (d) He is to be perfect and blameless in keeping the 'commandment' until the epiphany of Jesus which will come when the sovereign God determines (vv. 13–16).

There is a break between vv. 12 and 13. Verses 11–12 can be regarded as following on directly from what precedes, in that they counsel the man of God to set his aim on things other than getting rich, to cultivate godliness and not to be diverted from seeking the eternal life to which he was called by God and which he publicly professed to be his aim. The φεῦγε – δίωκε pattern is repeated in 2 Tim 2.22, and a similar thought is expressed in Tit 2.12.

Verses 13–16 are linked to what precedes by the concept of the 'good confession'. Timothy is given a solemn admonition which is strengthened by the references to God and to Christ who also made a 'good confession' and thus provides a pattern

---

[59] Fig.: Philo, *Flacc.* 1 ἀθρόους ἀνηκέστοις περιέπειρε κακοῖς; the compound has an intensive sense (White, 144).

[60] Cl.; Philo, *Op.* 161; Josephus, *Ant.* 15.62; Rom 9.2***.

to follow. He is to live blamelessly until the epiphany of Jesus. The appeal closes with a remarkable description of God in his majesty and sovereignty which may be intended simply to impart solemnity to the appeal, but which may also stress the significance of the epiphany of Jesus through whom the invisible, unapproachable God may be seen and approached.

The reference to the confession which Timothy made suggests that a particular occasion is in mind, and that associated language or tradition is being used. The occasion may be baptism, ordination, or some specific occasion of persecution. Correspondingly the material is thought to reflect tradition associated with such an occasion, and some scholars think that it fits awkwardly into the flow of the letter (Dibelius-Conzelmann, 87; Brox, 212). Various possible occasions have been suggested:

(a) teaching given at baptism;[61]

(b) an ordination discourse which includes some material (vv. 11f.) based on baptismal instruction;[62]

(c) a personal confession made by the individual Christian (Thurén*);

(d) a forensic situation during persecution.[63]

Käsemann and Brox in particular argue that the whole of vv. 11–16 is material that has been taken over as a unit by the author and that it represents the formal instruction given at an ordination. However, the material is not necessarily all from the same source; there is a clear break between vv. 11f. and 13–15. Knoch, 45, argues that two originally independent exhortations have been run together: 11–12 are baptismal instruction to all Christians; 13–16 is ordination instruction to office-bearers. There are differences in style: note the short imperatives in 11f. and the use of παραγγέλλω with infinitive in vv. 13f. Similarly, Roloff holds that traditional material from the charge by the bishop (!) at an ordination service is cited word for word in 13–16.

Roloff claims that there is a series of references to Timothy's ordination in the PE (1.18; 4.14; 2 Tim 1.6; 2.2); this passage deals with the life-style of the leader, and it is because this is exemplary for all believers that the ambiguity of the instructions arises. He also argues that the *agon* motif is specific to church leaders.

---

[61] Bernard, 98; Lock, 71; Easton, 165; Kelly, 142; Spicq, 569; Merkel, 50; Windisch 1935:219.

[62] Jeremias, 46; Simpson, 88; Dibelius-Conzelmann, 87; Brox, 212; Barrett, 86; Holtz, 141; Hasler, 50; Hanson, 110; Roloff, 340–5; Knight, 264f.; cf. Holtzmann, 364; Michel, O., *TDNT* V, 216; Käsemann*.

[63] Cullmann, O., *The Earliest Christian Confessions* (London: Lutterworth, 1949).

There is in fact nothing which is specific to ordination in either section, although the material could be fittingly applied to a church leader. It is best, therefore, to assume that the writer has used material based on traditional baptismal instruction, and there is no need to postulate an intermediate stage at which it was used for ordination (cf. Lips 1979:177–80; Oberlinner, 288). Merkel, 49, rightly notes that the style throughout is that of the author, and comments that a confession is appropriate at baptism but is unattested at ordination. Läger 1996:58–63 notes that there is a wide-reaching parallelism between the beginning and end of the letter, which would suggest that the author himself is responsible for the formulation.

This leaves the question whether a confessional statement of some kind lies beneath the text. Wengst 1973:124f. (followed by Roloff, 344) identified the formula:

(πιστεύω καὶ ὁμολογῶ)
τὸν θεὸν ζῳογονοῦντα τὰ πάντα
καὶ Χριστὸν Ἰησοῦν τὸν μαρτυρήσαντα ἐπὶ Ποντίου Πιλάτου.

This is said to be a comparatively late formulation, as attested by the Hellenistic language; it refers to God as Creator and to Jesus as giving a verbal testimony in the presence of Pilate. For Jesus as witness cf. Rev 1.5. But such a two-member confession is improbable, since it fulfils no obvious function. The doubts of Oberlinner, 287, are justified.

TEXT

11. θεοῦ Praem. τοῦ (א² D F G H Ψ TR). Elliott, 203, adopts the text.

ἀγάπην Add εἰρήνην (1836 181). The variant could be original or assimilation to 2 Tim 2.22; Elliott, 99 and 237, is doubtful about accepting it. But in any case the MS evidence for the variant is very weak.

πραϋπαθίαν πραύτητα (א² D) and πραότητα (K L TR) represent glosses on a rare word with one that was part of the vocabulary of the PE (2 Tim 2.25; Tit 3.2; cf. Elliott, 99f.).

12. ἐκλήθης Praem. καί (81 *pc* sy^h** TR; Kilpatrick). Cf. Col 3.15. Elliott, 209, holds that the variant fits the author's style (4.10; 4.16) and was omitted as otiose. The MS evidence is poor.

13. [σοι] (א² A D H TR lat sy sa^ms bo Tert; WH; Kilpatrick): Omit (א* F G Ψ 6 33 1739 *pc* m sa^mss; Spicq, 568; Roloff, 350 n. 103). Elliott, 100, argues that it was omitted by scribes to make epistle more general (cf. 4.10; 5.23; 6.14).

ζῳογονοῦντος ζῳοποιοῦντος (א TR; Elliott, 101; Simpson, 88). In Cl. ζῳοποιέω has the same meaning as ζῳογονέω; in the LXX it is used of God 'giving life', i.e. creating (2 Kgs 5.7; 2 Esdr 19.6.; Job 36.6; Ps 70.20; cf. Rom 4.17). Elliott argues that ζῳοποιοῦντος is original here, and the change in the majority of MSS may be due to Atticising. Simpson, 88, also prefers the variant, which is used elsewhere by Paul, and says that the other reading, which means 'to preserve alive', gives a feeble sense. However, since the MS evidence for the text is strong, and since the required meaning ('to give life') is attested in 1 Sam 2.6, it should be accepted; as Hanson, 111, says, the variant is a gloss which gives the correct interpretation.

Χριστοῦ Ἰησοῦ (A D Ψ TR lat sy^h): Inverted order (ℵ F G 326 *pc* sy^p Tert; WH mg.). Elliott, 201, argues that the text represents the usage in the PE.

Πιλάτου Πειλάτου (A D* WH). MHT I, 35, 47, and Elliott, 101, 237, are doubtful about the original spelling. See WH *Notes*, 155.

16. φῶς Praem. καί (D* 629 a b m vg^cl Tert Ambst). Elliott, 209, argues that the variant is original and the conjunction was removed because it seemed superfluous. The MS evidence is weak.

EXEGESIS

11. Σὺ δέ, ὦ ἄνθρωπε θεοῦ, ταῦτα φεῦγε This is the only place in 1 Tim where the author uses this device (σὺ δέ) for turning from heretics and opponents to the recipient himself and so applying what is said in a very personal way (Tit 2.1 note; 2 Tim 2.1; *et al.*). The use of ὦ (6.20**) in the NT includes direct address to a person (but never to God) in the vocative, as here (Cl.), or in the nom.; it is often, but not necessarily, expressive of emotion.[64] According to Holtzmann, 364, it is used in adjurations (as here) or expressions of blame.

The simple ἄνθρωπε (voc.) is found in Rom 9.20, but here it is part of the stereotyped phrase ἄνθρωπος θεοῦ (2 Tim 3.17***; 2 Pet 1.21 TR). The phrase derives from the LXX where it is used of a variety of figures, mostly leaders and prophets.[65] It is used of all Jews as worshippers of God (*Ep. Arist.* 140). Philo, *Gig.* 61, refers to three classes of men, the third of which are 'those born of God', namely priests and prophets who turn their backs on the world; he takes up the description of Moses and applies it to those who seek to be perfect (*Mut.* 24f., 125–8); he also applies the phrase to the Logos (*Conf.* 41). Thus for Philo the phrase has become a description of those who are truly the people of God.[66]

There are two main ways in which the designation can be taken in the present passage. First, it is simplest to align Timothy as God's representative and a Christian leader with the OT prophets and similar people who were called to be prophets (Roloff, 345f.). But the designation is not just functional and unrelated to character (*pace* Hasler 49); dedication to God's service with its consequent obligations is included. It would be correct to say that the language is applied to Timothy because

---

[64] E.g. Mt 15.28; Lk 24.25; Rom 2.1, 3; 9.20; Gal 3.1; Jas 2.20; contrast Acts 1.1; 18.14; 27.21.

[65] Moses (Deut 33.1; Josh 14.6; 1 Chr 23.14; 2 Chr 30.16; Ezra 3.2; Ps 89 [MT 89].1); David (2 Chr 8.14); various prophets (1 Kgs 13.1; 2 Kgs 23.17; 1 Sam 2.27), including Samuel (1 Sam 9.6); Shemaiah (1 Kgs 12.22); Elijah (1 Kgs 17, 18, 24; 2 Kgs 1.9–13; cf. Philo, *Deus*, 138f., where it is said to allude to their inspiration); Elisha (2 Kgs 4.1, 9, 16); Job (*T. Job* 53); an angel (Judg 13.6).

[66] See further Sextus 2; 3; *CH* 1.32; 13.2; Jeremias, J., *TDNT* I, 364f.

he falls into this class; it is not a designation confined to him. Some scholars then generalise the reference to include any 'ordained' church leaders like Timothy; no doubt the reference can be generalised to include any such people, but we should be careful not to link it anachronistically to formal ordination. Another view is that the term specifically describes certain people as being Spirit-inspired or charismatic persons exercising a ministry in the congregation (Brox, 212f.; Holtz, 139; cf. Knoch, 45). But the claim that this is the force of the term in Hellenistic Judaism seems to be unsubstantiated, and Roloff argues that church leaders are not thought of as 'pneumatics' in the PE.[67]

Second, the term may refer to any Christian (Karris, 35; Merkel, 49f.). This is the force in 2 Tim 3.17, since here Timothy is being addressed as a typical believer (2 Tim 3.12) rather than as a church leader (*pace* Roloff, 345f.; so rightly Sand, A., *EDNT* I, 103, but he thinks that in the present verse it is 'a title associated with his office'). Since the context is baptismal, it is tempting to see here a phrase addressed to the newly-baptised although confirmatory evidence is lacking. In any case Timothy is addressed as a leader whose way of life is to be an example to all believers, and what is said to him can be applied to them all (Knight, 260; Oberlinner, 289).

The following instructions, therefore, are to be followed by all of God's people and therefore especially by their leaders. They are summoned to turn their backs on the sinful desires of the world and to cultivate spiritual qualities which will have practical expressions. The flee/pursue antithesis is repeated in 2 Tim 2.22 (cf. Rom 12.9 for a similar antithesis) and was found in Hellenistic moral instruction (Epictetus 4.5.30 in Spicq, 567). ταῦτα is in effect 'all these things' (cf. NIV) and refers back very broadly to the desire for wealth and the attendant temptations, but also to the vices in 6.4f. (Simpson, 87). φεύγω (2 Tim 2.22**), lit. 'to flee, escape', has the figurative sense 'to avoid, shun' and is common in ethical exhortation.[68]

δίωκε δὲ δικαιοσύνην εὐσέβειαν πίστιν, ἀγάπην ὑπομονὴν πραϋπαθίαν The positive side of the injunction consists of three imperatival phrases. The first of these is a command to aim to achieve a combination of six basic Christian qualities of character. The verb διώκω has a variety of meanings in the NT,[69] including

---

[67] Nor should we postulate 'mystical overtones' along the lines of Philo's usage (cf. Dibelius-Conzelmann, 87f.; *contra* Kelly, 139f.).

[68] With acc., as here, or ἀπό; cf. Epictetus 1.7.25; Ecclus 21.2; 4 Macc 8.19; *T. Reub.* 5.5; 1 Cor 6.18; 10.14; 1 Clement 30.1; 2 Clement 10.1; Ignatius, *Trall.* 11.1; *Philad.* 2.1; 6.2; 7.2; *Poly.* 5.1; Barnabas 4.1, 10; *Didache* 3.1.

[69] 'To pursue' (Lk 17.23); 'to press forward' (Phil 3.12, 14); 'to persecute' (2 Tim 3.12; cf. Rom 12.14; 1 Cor 15.9); cf. LN *s.v.*

(as here) 'to strive toward' some quality or activity (2 Tim 2.22).[70] There may be a hint of the metaphor of pressing on towards the goal in a race to gain the prize that awaits the winner; this would tie in nicely with the second command in the series. What is demanded is steadfastness in aiming at what is good in situations of conflict. It has been suggested that the thought is not Pauline, for Paul thinks of righteousness and godliness as God's gifts; moreover, it is held, these are moral virtues and not theological ones, such as Paul commends (cf. Gealy, 452). This verdict is unjustified. 1 Cor 14.1 is adequate to demonstrate that Paul calls for effort to gain the quality of love, and the preceding chapter shows that it is an eminently practical, moral virtue that is envisaged. Moral effort is also called for in Col 3.12–17.

Despite the suggestion that the list is quite general (Easton, 165), it is in fact appropriate to the context (Hasler, 48). It has been suggested that some of the qualities would be especially appropriate in dealing with the false teachers (Knoch, 46), but actually they are basic qualities for all Christians. All of them, except the last, figure prominently elsewhere in the PE, notably in ethical lists (2 Tim 2.22–25; 3.10). They also appear in different combinations (and with some synonyms) in other NT lists, both in Paul and elsewhere (2 Cor 6.6f.; Gal 5.22f.; Col 3.12–14; 2 Pet 1.5–7). Some commentators group them in pairs (Bernard, 97; Knight, 262). Three of them (righteousness, faith, love) reappear in 2 Tim 2.22, and gentleness here corresponds to peace (i.e. peaceableness) there. But we can also trace the influence of the traditional triad, faith, love and patience (where patience replaces 'hope'), as in Tit 2.2; 1 Th 1.3. The concept of patient forbearance is filled out by the addition of 'gentleness' to make the meaning clear. The qualities are a combination of spiritual and ethical virtues, but it is false to draw a line between the more spiritually and the more ethically oriented nuances of the vocabulary.[71]

The first two qualities are those which sum up comprehensively the ethical and spiritual outlook of the PE. For δικαιοσύνη see Tit 3.5 note; cf. 2 Tim 2.22; 3.17; 4.8** and the use of δικαίως (Tit 2.12). For εὐσέβεια see 2.2 and **Excursus 1**. For πίστις see 1.2; Tit 1.1 note. In the wider context of the section the thought of faithfulness in holding fast to truth is attractive, but this is less likely in the narrower context of this list. For ἀγάπη see 1.5; Tit 2.2 note; it is not elevated to the primary position,

---

[70] Cf. Rom 9.30f.; 12.13; 14.19; 1 Cor 14.1; 1 Th 5.15; Heb 12.14; 1 Pet 3.11; 2 Clement 10.1; cf. Ps 33 (MT 34).15; Prov 15.9; Hos 6.3; Ecclus 31.5; Philo, *Somn.* 1.199; Josephus, *Ant.* 6.263. See Oepke, A., *TDNT* II, 229f.

[71] Cf. Kertelge, K., *EDNT* I, 325–30, who holds that a Greek ethically-oriented usage prevails in passages like the present one.

as in Paul (1 Cor 14.1; Col 3.14). For ὑπομονή, 'patience, endurance', see Tit 2.2 note; 2 Tim 3.10**; it is more appropriate here than ἐλπίς on account of the conflict setting, and therefore its presence should not be explained as due to a replacement of hope by perseverance as a result of the development of early catholicism.[72]

The final item is peculiar to this list: πραϋπαθία***, 'gentleness', is a rare word, found in Philo, *Abr.* 213; Ignatius, *Trall.* 8; it is the equivalent of πραΰτης (2 Tim 2.25; Tit 3.2; 1 Cor 4.21; *et al.*) and some scribes substituted the more common word (see above).[73] It may well be added here as an appropriate virtue in dealing with opponents in the church.

12. ἀγωνίζου τὸν καλὸν ἀγῶνα τῆς πίστεως The second positive command is possibly a continuation of the metaphor in the first (see above). But there has been some dispute as to what metaphor is being employed here. For the verb ἀγωνίζομαι see 4.10 note; 2 Tim 4.7. The background may be sought in (a) athletics;[74] or (b) warfare;[75] the same problem arises in 2 Tim 4.7. The same ambiguity is present in the cognate noun used here as an internal acc., ἀγών; it can refer to an 'athletic contest'[76] or to a 'struggle, fight'.[77] On the whole the athletic metaphor seems to be required (cf. 2 Tim 2.5; 1 Cor 9.24–27; Phil 3.12–14) in view of the allusion to the prize (v. 12b), but there are military overtones (Simpson, 87). This is one of those cases where the two areas tend to merge with each other, and the thought is simply of a desperate struggle to win. There is not much difference in practice between two gladiators in the stadium and two warriors on the battlefield. For the application of the metaphor to the Christian life cf. ὁ τῆς ἀφθαρσίας ἀγών (2 Clement 7.5). τῆς πίστεως will then refer to faith as the characteristic quality of the Christian life that must be maintained to the end, rather than to 'the faith' as an object to be defended (which is not the immediate issue in this context); the gen. is one of apposition (Pfitzner 1967:179). It follows that the metaphor is being used, not as in 1 Cor 9 (cf. Col 1.29) for the work of the missionary, but as in Phil 3 for the personal life of the believer. The injunction

---

[72] So rightly Denton, D. R., 'Hope and Perseverance', *SJT* 34 (1981), 317 n. 26 (313–20).
[73] According to BA, Hesychius defines it in terms of ἡσυχία and πραΰτης. The accent and spelling are uncertain. BA has πραϋπάθεια. Cf. WH *Notes*, 154. For πραϋπαθής cf. Philo, *Spec.* 4.93; *Leg. Gai.* 335; and for πραοπαθέω cf. Philo, *Fug.* 6. See *TLNT* III, 171.
[74] 1 Cor 9.25; Pfitzner 1967:179 n. 1; Fee, 149f.; Roloff, 348.
[75] Cf. Jn 18.36; see 1 Tim 1.18; 2 Tim 2.4.
[76] Cl. refs. in BA; Heb 12.1; cf. 1 Clement 7.1.
[77] Phil 1.30; 1 Th 2.2; 2 Tim 4.7.; 2 Clement 7.1, 3, 5.

is necessary, for even church leaders can fall away. For the use of καλός in this context see 1.18 note; the same idea of life as 'noble contest' is found in Philo, *L.A.* 2.108; 3.48, but the language is traditional military language.[78] The repetition of the adjective with reference to the confession in vv. 12b, 13b is significant. It serves to single out the contest and confession as the ones of supreme worth because they are required by God.

ἐπιλαβοῦ τῆς αἰωνίου ζωῆς The third element in the injunction is a command to grasp hold of eternal life. ἐπιλαμβάνομαι (6.19**; always mid. in the NT) is 'to take hold of, grasp, catch', literally (Mk 8.23; Acts 23.19) or figuratively (Lk 20.20, 26); hence 'to take hold of, in order to makes one's own' (BA; Prov 4.13). ζωὴ αἰώνιος was stated to be the result of belief in Christ in 1.16 (cf. Tit 1.2 note). Here it is used with the article because of the following relative clause. It is tempting to interpret the command in terms of seeking to gain the prize offered in a contest. However, no parallel for the use of the verb with respect to gaining a prize in a competition has been found. Moreover, the word means 'to take hold of' rather than 'to reach after' (Parry, 41). This consideration should settle the dispute whether the injunction is (a) to enjoy the blessings of eternal life now and for ever (Pfitzner 1967:179f.); or (b) to be sure not to lose the life of the world to come. Eternal life is thus a goal to be achieved here and now in this world (Stott, 157) and not just at the end of the contest. Hasler's interpretation (49) of the appeal as one to the church leader to pursue a higher level of personal holiness so that by his good works he may guarantee his otherwise uncertain hope of final salvation is far wide of the mark.

εἰς ἣν ἐκλήθης Eternal life is described as the goal to which Timothy was called. καλέω is regularly used of God's invitation to (εἰς) salvation and its associated blessings (2 Tim 1.9**);[79] the origins of the concept lie in the OT.[80] The reference, then, is to conversion (Lock, 71) and can apply to any Christians, not simply leaders.

καὶ ὡμολόγησας τὴν καλὴν ὁμολογίαν ἐνώπιον πολλῶν μαρτύρων The second half of the clause is very loosely connected (cf. Tit 1.3) with καί; translate 'when you confessed...'. ὁμολογέω (Tit 1.16**) takes the internal acc. ὁμολογίαν. ὁμολογία is the 'action of confessing' (2 Cor 9.13) or the actual 'confession, acknowledgment' that people make (1 Tim 6.13).[81] The confession

---

[78] Cf. Euripides, *Alc.* 648; Thucydides 7.68.3 (καλὸς ὁ ἀγών).

[79] Rom 8.30 and frequently; with εἰς, 1 Cor 1.9; Col 3.15; 2 Th 2.14; 1 Pet 2.9; 5.10; 1 Clement 59.2.

[80] Isa 41.9; 42.6; 48.12; 50.2; see Schmidt, K. L., *TDNT* III, 487–91; Eckert, J., *EDNT* II, 240–4.

[81] Heb 3.1; 4.14; 10.23***; cf. Michel, O., *TDNT* V, 210f.

is of Jesus (Rom 10.9f.). The whole phrase can mean 'to make a promise'[82] or 'to bear testimony to a conviction'.[83] NT usage and the connection with μαρτυρέω (v. 13) indicate that the latter nuance is primary here.

Although the maintenance of the confession is a continuing attitude (Heb 13.15; 1 Jn 2.23; 4.2f., 15; 2 Jn 7), the aorist suggests a reference to a specific occasion, such as being on trial in situations of persecution. More probably the specific situation in mind is the initial act of Christian commitment and initiation in view of the link with God's calling. Other possibilities have been suggested. Many commentators favour ordination (see above; Hasler, 48, cf. 50, writes of a vow taken at ordination). This suggestion faces the difficulties that the context of the wording here, taken on its own, favours baptism and that there are no known contemporary parallels for a confession at ordination. Oberlinner, 293, avoids the difficulty by observing that a reference to a baptismal confession is here being used to strengthen the commissioning which is being reaffirmed to Timothy here and now in the letter. The parallel with Jesus in v. 13 has been thought to favour a trial context, but Windisch 1935:219 rightly observes that the parallel is only in the content that Jesus is the Christ. Calvin, 277, suggested that the reference was to ongoing confession throughout Timothy's ministry made by action rather than just by words, but the tense (aor.) hardly fits this proposal. The confession is καλός (cf. 6.12a), as is that of Jesus himself in v. 13; this must mean that it is approved by God in that it is a Christian confession. The solemnity and binding nature of the confession is underlined by the reference to the presence (ἐνώπιον, 2.3 et al.; 5.20) of witnesses (μαρτύς, 5.19; 2 Tim 2.2). The repeated references to witnesses suggest that the Christian congregation, or perhaps its leaders, constitute a particularly significant body.

The content of the confession is not explained; the point is its binding character and the obligation of Timothy to remain faithful to it. There is no indication that it was anything more than a confession of Jesus Christ as Lord (cf. Roloff, 349).

13. παραγγέλλω [σοι] ἐνώπιον τοῦ θεοῦ τοῦ ζῳογονοῦντος τὰ πάντα The language of the previous command is now taken up into a fresh, solemn injunction which uses the specific language of command (παραγγέλλω, 1.3 et al.) to underline the importance of what is said; the repetition of ideas from 1.18 may indicate that there is an *inclusio* so that this injunction rounds off the whole content of the letter as solemn instruction to Timothy.

---

[82] Plato, *Crito* 52A; Jer 51 [45].25.
[83] Philo, *Mut.* 57; *Abr.* 203.

Nevertheless, the facts that further teaching for the rich is found in vv. 17–19 and that there is a final injunction to Timothy in vv. 20f. are probably sufficient to rule out this possibility. As throughout the letter, it is the authority of Paul which lies behind the command (Roloff, 350). The solemnity and binding force of the command is further strengthened by the references to God and to Jesus. The double phrase ἐνώπιον τοῦ θεοῦ ... καὶ Χριστοῦ Ἰησοῦ is paralleled in 5.21 and 2 Tim 4.1, but in each case the basic formula is expanded in different ways. The form here elaborates both of the references to God and to Christ, and the question that arises is whether the language is merely stereotyped or has a specific relevance to the context. God is defined as the one who gives life to all or preserves them in life. In Cl. ζῳογονέω means 'to give life to', and this meaning is found in 1 Sam 2.6; elsewhere in the LXX it normally means 'to spare alive' (i.e. 'to preserve from death'; Cl. ζωγρέω; so in Lk 17.33; Acts 7.19***).[84] Fee, 151, thinks that a reference to God preserving life is more appropriate in the context of possible martyrdom. In view of the object τὰ πάντα (the universe, Eph 1.11, 23; et al.) the sense 'to give life' seems more appropriate rather than the thought that God preserves the life of his people, and the expression is a way of stating God's omnipotence. The present participle is consistent with the idea of God's continuous activity in the universe rather than merely the initial act of creation. The thought of God as the giver of the eternal life in v. 12b may well be included, but does not seem to be stressed.

καὶ Χριστοῦ Ἰησοῦ τοῦ μαρτυρήσαντος ἐπὶ Ποντίου Πιλάτου τὴν καλὴν ὁμολογίαν The second person in the pair of heavenly witnesses is inevitably Jesus, as in 5.21. He is especially qualified to be a witness in that he has borne his own 'good confession'. Instead of the cognate verb the writer here uses μαρτυρέω (5.10**). For Dibelius-Conzelmann, 88, originally Christ simply 'witnessed' (absolute use of verb with no object); i.e. not his conduct but his fate (as a martyr) was described,[85] but to get a parallel with Timothy ὁμολογία was added by the author – hence the reference to the witness by word. This explanation breaks down in view of the close relation between the two word-groups exemplified in Jn 1.9f. where the μαρτυρία of John is expressed by the verb ὡμολόγησεν. Further the usage in 1 Clement 5.4, 7 of Peter and Paul probably refers to a court appearance preceding execution rather than to execution itself. It is the faithfulness of Jesus to the end that is especially in mind. The sense is presumably that Jesus made 'the good confession' in that he held

---

[84] See Bultmann, R., *TDNT* II, 873f.; *TLNT* II, 164f.; Turner*. The attempt to find an echo of Lk 17.33 (Brown, 1963:39) is futile.

[85] Cf. Turner*, 271–3.

fast to his self-testimony as Messiah and Son of man despite the risk entailed (cf. Michel, O., *TDNT* IV, 499); to be sure, if we are to think of a testimony 'before Pontius Pilate', then it is the acknowledgement by Jesus that he was 'the king of the Jews' (Mk 15.2; Seeberg*, 100). It is not clear whether the translation 'testify to the good confession' (BA) is meant to convey a different sense. Another possibility is that the witness of Jesus to the truth (Jn 18.33–37) is in mind.[86] In any case, it is the faithfulness of Jesus which is stressed rather than the precise content of what he said.

The force of ἐπί with gen. here is disputed. It probably means 'in the presence of' (*coram*);[87] but many commentators prefer 'in the time of' (*sub*, as in the Apostles' Creed).[88] However, the court context is so strong that the former interpretation must be correct, and the force of a purely temporal reference is not obvious. The phrase draws a parallel between Jesus appearing before a hostile ruler and Timothy (and Paul) bearing witness before hostile people inside and outside the church. References to the Roman governor naturally became a stock part of the description of Jesus' passion and were used to date it historically (Ignatius, *Mag.* 11.1; *Trall.* 9.1; *Smyr.* 1.2). For Πιλᾶτος[89] (a Roman *cognomen*) cf. Acts 3.13; 4.27; 13.28. His *nomen*, Πόντιος, is rarely used in the NT (Lk 3.1; Acts 4.27; Mt 27.2 *v.l.****).[90]

14. τηρῆσαί σε τὴν ἐντολὴν ἄσπιλον ἀνεπίλημπτον μέχρι τῆς ἐπιφανείας τοῦ κυρίου ἡμῶν Ἰησοῦ Χριστοῦ After the lengthy and solemn adjuration we now come to the actual command which is the object of such emphasis. It is a call to personal faithfulness in 'keeping the commandment'. The vocabulary is typical of the PE. τηρῆσαι (5.22 note) is dependent on παραγγέλλω (v. 13) and takes a double acc.[91] The construction here is slightly complicated by the inclusion of σε, which is strictly unnecessary, but perhaps re-emphasises Timothy's own role which could have been forgotten during the lengthy preamble. In this kind

---

[86] Hasler, 50; but his further suggestion that the author sees no saving and atoning significance in his death is baseless.

[87] Cf. Mk 13.9; Acts 23.30; BA; Lock, 72; Knight, 265; Roloff, 351; Baldensperger*, 97.

[88] Cf. Lk 3.2; Acts 11.28; Bernard, 99; Dornier, 106; Brox, 216; Kelly, 143f.; Spicq, 570f.; Oberlinner, 295; Turner*, 271.

[89] For the spelling see BA *s.v.*

[90] Cf. Sherwin-White, A. N., *Roman Society and Roman Law in the New Testament* (Oxford: Oxford University Press, 1963), 159–62. It was the name of a Roman, originally Samnite *gens* (BA *s.v.*) and is occasionally found as a *nomen* (Dittenberger, *Syll.* 797, 2 [AD 37]).

[91] Cf. 2 Clement 6.9; 8.4, 6; Ignatius, *Philad.* 7.2; Hermas, *Sim.* 8.6.3; cf. the reflexive use in 2 Cor 11.9; Jas 1.27; passive, 1 Th 5.23. See Riesenfeld, H., *TDNT* VIII, 144.

of context the verb usually has the sense 'to keep/obey the commandment',[92] and this is confirmed by the phrase in 1 Cor 7.19. An alternative possibility is that it means 'to preserve the commandment', *sc.* from being corrupted or misunderstood. The double acc., however, complicates the construction. If the adjectives qualify the commandment, then the injunction is to keep the commandment in its pure form and free from being wrongly criticised. But one would normally expect the adjectives to describe a person.[93] Probably the best solution is that we have a case of transferred epithet (see below).

Difficulties also surround the reference of ἐντολή (Tit 1.14** note) with commentators offering a wide range of possibilities:

(a) 'the whole Christian religion thought of as a commandment or new law' (BA), hence 'Christian instruction based on Jesus' commandments' (cf. Mt 28.20);[94]

(b) the baptismal charge (cf. 2 Clement 8.6);[95]

(c) the undertaking to believe as a Christian (cf. Fee, 151f., a command to Timothy to persevere);

(d) the commission to the newly ordained;[96]

(e) the command in 6.11f.;[97]

(f) the letter as a whole, i.e. everything that was commanded to Timothy;

(g) everything that Timothy himself is to do (whether recorded in 1 Tim or not).[98]

Knight's comprehensive discussion (266–8) shows that many of these options are variants of a basic understanding of the commandment as comprising everything that Timothy is charged to do as a Christian, i.e. view (a). But it is more likely that the 'commandment' is what Timothy is specifically told to do. Roloff,

---

[92] Mt 19.17; Jn 14.15 and frequently; 1 Jn 2.3 and frequently; Acts 15.5; Jas 2.10; Rev 1.3; 12.17; 14.12.

[93] Two suggestions have been offered to solve the difficulty. The first is to translate 'to keep yourself (σε!) pure with respect to the commandment [and] blameless' (Calvin, 278). The difficulties with this view are (a) that the reflexive pronoun would be expected (as in 5.22; cf. 4.7, 16), and (b) that the word order is very awkward. The second is to suppose that the adjectives are added asyndetically to describe what Timothy ought to be ('I charge you ... that you keep the commandment, [and that you be] spotless [and] blameless'; so apparently Parry, 42); but this is equally difficult.

[94] Kratz, R., *EDNT* III, 355. Cf. 2 Pet 2.21; 3.2; Ignatius, *Trall.* 13.2; Lock, 72; Kelly, 144; Spicq, 571.

[95] Bernard, 99; Parry, 42; Dornier, 107.

[96] Barrett, 87; Brox, 217; Hasler, 50; Hanson, 112; Roloff, 352; Käsemann*, 106; Limbeck, M., *EDNT* I, 460. Note that Roloff has abandoned his earlier proposal that it is tantamount to the charisma given at ordination (Roloff, 1965:262), and now states that the command and the charisma are complementary.

[97] Easton, 166; cf. Guthrie, 127f.

[98] Calvin, 278; Dibelius-Conzelmann, 89.

352, notes that the word can mean a 'commission' as well as a 'command', and holds that it refers broadly to the ordination commission given to Timothy rather than to a specific form of words or list of instructions to be fulfilled. Oberlinner, 295f., combines the two ideas, the doctrine and teaching which Timothy is to give and the authoritative 'official' position which he fulfils in doing so. Probably the reference is to what Timothy is commissioned to do, including the specific instructions given to him, especially in view of the way in which this chapter tends to repeat the themes of ch. 1.

ἄσπιλος, 'spotless, flawless, without blemish', is a word rarely attested outside Christian literature that is used here in a moral sense.[99] In 2 Clement 8.6 we have τηρήσατε τὴν σάρκα ἁγνὴν καὶ τὴν σφραγῖδα ἄσπιλον, ἵνα τὴν ζωὴν ἀπολάβωμεν, where the 'seal' is the gift of the Spirit at baptism (2 Clement 6.9); this gives a good parallel to the present phrase, in that in both cases we have in effect a transferred epithet (or hypallage) that really applies to the people who do not let their subsequent life be out of harmony with the seal of the Spirit or the commandment. For ἀνεπίλημπτος see 3.2; 5.7***. As with the previous adjective, it really refers to Timothy. It is possible that it means that the commandment must be kept pure in the sense of not being spotted by people's disobedience (Dibelius-Conzelmann, 89, with linguistic parallels). For Brox, 217, the purity and truth of the message must be guaranteed by the blameless life of the church leader.

There follows an expression which apparently gives the time-span during which Timothy is to continue to maintain the commandment. It provides the broader context within which the somewhat different perspective in 3.14f.; 4.13 is to be understood. μέχρι (2 Tim 2.9**) is 'until, as far as' with gen. of space, time, degree, or measure. For ἐπιφάνεια see **Excursus 9**. Here, as in 2 Tim 4.1, 8; 2 Th 2.8, it refers to the parousia of τοῦ κυρίου ἡμῶν Ἰησοῦ Χριστοῦ (par. 6.3). However, the expression is probably meant to spur the reader on with hope of the reward associated with the parousia and with fear of the judgement (2 Tim 4.1). The parousia is linked with morality in this kind of way in 1 Th 3.13; 5.23; 1 Cor 1.8; Phil 2.15f. Contrary to the assertion of many commentators (e.g. Hasler, 50; Roloff, 352) the parousia is considered to be a possibility within the lifetime of Timothy. Although Timothy is to be prepared for martyrdom, like Paul, it is always possible that the epiphany may intervene.

[99] Cf. Job 15.15; of believers, 2 Pet 3.14; Jas 1.27; Hermas, *Vis.* 4.3.5; cf. Hermas, *Sim.* 5.6.7 (flesh). It can be also be used in a ritual sense of animals (including sacrificial victims, 1 Pet 1.19***). Cf. Oepke, A., *TDNT* I, 502.

15. ἣν καιροῖς ἰδίοις δείξει But the time of the epiphany (ἥν) is in the hands of God and cannot be calculated or foretold. The phrase καιροῖς ἰδίοις, 'at his/its appointed time', is repeated from 2.6 (see Tit 1.3 note). Dibelius-Conzelmann, 89, say that the effect is to lose the sense of imminence, but the belief that the apocalyptic calendar is known to God alone is too commonplace to allow this deduction. δείκνυμι**, 'to point out, show, make known', can be used of divine acts of revelation (cf. Jn 5.20), including apocalyptic visions (Zech 3.1; Rev 1.4; *et al.*). But the use here is strange, and Schlier states that it has the meaning 'to bring to pass': God will effect the epiphany 'in such a way as to make Christ visible'.[100]

Nevertheless, one has the impression that the clause was created not to stress that the timing of the epiphany is in the hands of God but rather to provide an occasion for the remarkable description of God which now follows. The seven phrases which compose it have been said to be 'as far from Paul's style and thought as anything in the Pastoral Epistles' (Hanson, 113). The sentiments are, however, well-attested in Hellenistic Judaism and firmly based in OT ideas. The language may well be drawn from the synagogue. Fee, 154, suggests that the doxology is a polemic against the claims of pagan religion. Four of the principal attributes of God, that he is the supreme and only God, eternal and invisible, have already been used in the doxology in 1.17.

(a) **ὁ μακάριος καὶ μόνος δυνάστης** The two adjectives have already been used for God in 1.11 and 1.17 respectively (see notes). New is the noun δυνάστης, meaning 'ruler, sovereign'. The noun was used for human rulers (Lk 1.52; Acts 8.27***) but also for God.[101] God as supreme ruler is 'blessed' in the sense that he is to be pronounced fortunate by his worshippers in his exalted state; he alone occupies this status over against all possible rivals.

(b) **ὁ βασιλεὺς τῶν βασιλευόντων** Again earlier terminology (1.17) is repeated. The combination with τῶν βασιλευόντων** is found in 3 Macc 5.35 (see also BA *s.v.*); the similar phrase βασιλεὺς βασιλέων is used of Christ (Rev 17.14; 19.16).[102] The OT also knows such combinations as 'God of gods' and 'Lord of lords' (Deut 10.17; Ps 135 [MT 136].2f.).[103] There is thus nothing particularly Hellenistic about this phrase nor the next

[100] Schlier, H., *TDNT* II, 25–30, here 26; similarly, Schneider, G., *EDNT* I, 280; Roloff, 355.

[101] Sophocles, *Ant.* 608; Ecclus 46.5; 2 Macc 3.24 (linked with epiphany!); 12.15; 3 Macc 2.3; *Sib. Orac.* 3.719; Grundmann, W., *TDNT* II, 286.

[102] Cf. Dan 4.37 LXX; 2 Macc 13.4; Philo, *Decal.* 41.

[103] See further 1QM 14.16; *'Aboth* 3.1; 4.22; SB III, 656. Beale, G. K., 'The Origin of the Title "King of Kings and Lord of Lords" in Revelation 17.14', *NTS* 31 (1985), 618–20.

one, even though their roots lie in oriental court style (Ezra 7.12; Ezek 26.7; Dan 2.37) and they are found in pagan religion (of Zeus, Dio Chrysostom 2.75 [c. AD 100]). Stereotyped language used in worship may be reflected.

(c) **καὶ κύριος τῶν κυριευόντων** This is the only use of κύριος (1.2, of Christ) for God in 1 Tim. κυριεύω, 'to be lord, master, rule, lord it over, control', is used of human rulers (Lk 22.25), church leaders (2 Cor 1.24) and of various powerful forces (Rom 6.9, 14; 7.1), and also of Christ (Rom 14.9).[104] The phrase resembles κύριος κυρίων (Rev 17.14; 19.16; cf. 1 Enoch 9.4) used of Christ. Here its reference is probably quite unlimited: whatever forces there are in the universe are subject to God.

16. (d) **ὁ μόνος ἔχων ἀθανασίαν** From the unique sovereignty of God the writer turns to his unique possession of immortality; the emperor does not have it; nor does the human soul. ἀθανασία (1 Cor 15.53f.***) is 'immortality'.[105] It 'implies not so much persistence of life after death, as freedom from death' (Parry, 43). This is a Hellenistic way of stating that God alone has and can confer life. It corresponds to the description of him as ἄφθαρτος in 1.17, and it rejects claims made for other divine beings and heroes. It is not a description of God that is found in Hellenistic Judaism and has therefore been taken over from the language used of gods and emperors (Roloff, 356).

(e) **φῶς οἰκῶν ἀπρόσιτον** The fifth phrase emphasises the unapproachableness and glory of God in his heavenly dwelling. οἰκέω is used intrans. 'to live' in the sense of dwelling in a place,[106] or trans. 'to inhabit' with acc. of the place dwelt in.[107] God's dwelling place is envisaged as brilliant light (φῶς**). Light is regarded as the element or sphere of divine. According to Plutarch, *Per.* 39.2, the gods dwell in τὸν τόπον ἀσάλευτον φωτὶ καθαρωτάτω περιλαμπόμενον. But the idea is already there in the OT with its ideas of divine glory (Exod 33.17–23) and light as God's clothing (Ps 103 [MT 104].2); a vision of flaming fire is developed in *1 Enoch* 14.8–25.[108] No lamps are needed in the heavenly city because of the brightness of God himself (Rev 2 2.5). God is described as light itself (1 Jn 1.7). Theophanies and epiphanies are not surprisingly accompanied by bright light and similar phenomena, and the language of light is used to

---

[104] *TLNT* II, 351f.
[105] Cl.; Wis 3.4; 4.1; 8.13, 17; 15.3; 4 Macc 14.5; 16.13; Philo, *Deus.* 26; Josephus, *Ant.* 7.348; 17.354 Sib. Orac. 2.41, 150; 1 Clement 35.2; Ignatius, *Eph.* 20.2; *Didache* 10.2. Cf. Bultmann, R., *TDNT* III, 22–5.
[106] Cl.; Rom 7.18, 20; 8.9, 11; 1 Cor 3.16; 7.12f.***.
[107] Pap.; Gen 24.13; Philo, *Conf.* 106; Josephus, *Ant.* 14.88; *Ap.* 1.9; Diognetus 9.5; Michel, O., *TDNT* V, 135f.
[108] Cf. *Tg. Ezek* 8.2, in SB III, 656.

depict the new existence of God's people in a world which is correspondingly characterised by darkness.[109] The idea that the light is so bright that people cannot gaze at it or so intense that it burns them up is a natural complement, expressed here in the description of it as ἀπρόσιτος***, 'unapproachable'.[110]

(f) ὃν εἶδεν οὐδεὶς ἀνθρώπων οὐδὲ ἰδεῖν δύναται The next phrase, loosely linked by ὅν, reinforces the previous one by spelling out its point in the simplest terms. Nobody[111] has ever seen God who is ἀόρατος (1.17) or presently can.[112] The thought is biblical (Exod 33.20; Jn 1.18), and there is no need to seek a Gnostic origin for the vocabulary (*pace* Brox, 218).

(g) ᾧ τιμὴ καὶ κράτος αἰώνιον, ἀμήν The solemn description is fitly concluded with a doxology, introduced in typical NT fashion by ᾧ.[113] Two characteristic attributes are credited to God. Knight, 271, correlates them chiastically with the descriptions of God in vv. 16 and 15 respectively. τιμή was already used in the doxology in 1.17; κράτος**, 'power, might', is frequently ascribed to God in both pagan and Jewish writings.[114] The adjective αἰώνιος (1.16) has the same function as εἰς τοὺς αἰῶνας in other doxologies (1.17; 2 Tim 4.18); For ἀμήν cf. 1.17; 2 Tim 4.18.

c. What to teach to the rich (6.17–19)

This section has been regarded by some commentators as a digression. Spicq, 575, suggests that a pause in dictation may account for the lack of connection with the preceding material. It has even been regarded as a later addition at a time when there were wealthy Christians in the church (Easton, 170). However, the appearance of a break is due to the use of the doxology, and doxologies do not mark the ends of letters (*contra* Roloff, 365; cf. 1.17; Rom 1.25; 11.36; *et al.*; Kelly, 147). Above all, the presence of the rich is taken for granted in the letter, and there are other signs of their presence (Knoch, 47). Social stratification

---

[109] See Conzelmann, H., *TDNT* IX, 310–58, espec. 347 n. 299; *TLNT* III, 470–91.

[110] The adj. is Hel.; cf. BA; Philo, *Mos.* 2.70, of the physical inaccessibility of the mountain where God appeared to Moses; Josephus, *Ant.* 3.76, of the same mountain regarded as unapproachable also because of God's presence on it. The phrase is taken up in Clement, *Exc. ex Theod.* 12.3.

[111] οὐδείς, 4.4 *et al.*; with ἀνθρώπων, Mk 11.2; cf. Lk 14.24.

[112] For ὁράω (6.16b; 2 Tim 1.4**) used of seeing God in visions cf. Rev 4.1f.; *T. Levi* 5.1.

[113] Rom 16.27; Gal 1.5; 2 Tim 4.18; Heb 13.21; 1 Pet 4.11.

[114] Cl.; 2 Macc 3.34; 7.17; 11.4; Philo, *Spec.* 1.307; Josephus, *Ant.* 10.263. For its use in doxologies see 1 Pet 4.11; 5.11; Jude 25; Rev 1.6; 5.13; 1 Clement 64; 65.2; *M. Polycarp* 20.2. See further Eph 1.19; 6.10; Col 1.11; Heb 2.14 (of the devil); 1 Clement 27.5; 33.3; 61.1; 2 Clement 17.5. See Michaelis, W., *TDNT* III, 905–10.

was a common problem in early Christian congregations. The passage is best seen as forming an *inclusio* with 6.3–10. As such, it acts as a final summing up of the writer's instructions for the congregation, and has a similar function to Gal 6.11–16 and Rom 16.17–20, where important material receives a final emphasis. If there is a digression anywhere, it lies in the preceding doxology (Kelly, 147).

Its function is to offer help and guidance to those in the church who already *are* rich (cf. Eccles 5.18–20) and therefore may be tempted to act in ways inconsistent with their faith, but note that it is preceded by warnings in vv. 10–17 (Fee, 156). It does so by explaining to them what εὐσέβεια μετὰ αὐταρκείας means in their case (Kidd 1990:100). For the thought cf. Lk 12.16–21. The motif of complete renunciation of riches is not present, and some have found here a tension or even contradiction with the teaching of Jesus. Roloff, 366, holds that it is intended to guard against an ascetic interpretation of the earlier criticism of seeking after wealth in vv. 6–10.

The section takes the familiar form of an injunction to Timothy as to what he is to instruct people to do. Two negative commands against pride and trusting in their riches are followed by a series of positive commands; first, they are to recognise that it is God who provides for their needs and indeed their enjoyment and to put their trust in him; and, second, they are to do good, to display their wealth in the performing of good deeds, to be generous and share their possessions. In so doing they will lay a good foundation for their ultimate future and so attain to the 'real' life of heaven.

Distinctive of the teaching is the recognition that there are rich people in the world and in the church, in the sense that they have been well-endowed by God. Their danger is to become proud of their riches and to think that the riches are the basis of their security in this life (and possibly in the next). Instead they are to recognise that God is the provider of what they enjoy and he provides lavishly. Moreover, they are to use their wealth properly, and the series of instructions sharpens up to the focus of giving generously. By giving away they will gain for themselves a future treasure, here described as a foundation or basis, and thus gain real life.

Roloff, 366, suggests that the brevity of the instructions indicates that already familiar teaching is being summed up. The general tenor shows similarities to Lucan teaching, especially to Lk 12.16–21; 16.1–14.

The problem of why some people are poor and others are rich is not raised here. The concern is with the ethics and salvation of the rich. It is natural that in the conditions of ancient society, where the lots of the rich and the poor were generally unchangeable, there should be no discussion as to how the mass of poor might become rich. (It has to be remembered that, on the whole, simply redistributing the existing wealth will not make for a vast change in the lives of the poor; the solution generally lies in increased productivity and ensuring that the poor get their fair share of the proceeds.) Nevertheless, the need for giving freely is recognised as part of God's will.

TEXT

17. ὑψηλοφρονεῖν ὑψηλὰ φρονεῖν (א I Or WH mg). Elliott, 105f., notes that the compound verb appears only in Rom 11.20 (with a *v.l.*, as here) and that compounds with ὑψηλός are rare. He argues that the variant is original and scribes altered it through misunderstanding.

ἠλπικέναι ἐλπίζειν (F G John of Damasc.). Elliott, 66, argues that the perf. inf. is rare (Acts 14.19; 2 Tim 2.14; Tit 1.16), and that the pres. inf. fits in with the other pres. tenses in the context. This is not a strong enough argument to upset the MS evidence.

ἐπὶ θεῷ (א D* F G arm Origen^gr) (a) ἐπὶ τῷ θεῷ (A I P Ψ 075 0150 6 33 81 104 256 263 365 424^c 459 1175 1739 1881 2127 *pc* (f) g vg^ww Basil Didymus; WH mg); ἐν τῷ θεῷ (D² K L TR). Elliott, 106, 203, rightly adopts ἐπί in view of the author's usage elsewhere (4.10; cf. 5.5) and the parallelism with v. 17a. He also includes the article on the grounds that an arthrous participle follows and in this situation the preceding article gives Semitic word order and idiom. However, the PE often have an arthrous phrase follow an anarthrous noun (Tit 1.1 note).

(b) Add τῷ (-D*) ζῶντι (D 424* 436 1241 1573 1185² 1912 1962 2200 TR ar b d mon o vg^cl sy bo^ms Ambst Spec). The addition is probably assimilation to 4.10 (Elliott, 106; Metzger, 576f.).

πάντα πλουσίως τὰ πάντα πλουσίως (A I H 33 81 1739 Basil Chrys); τὰ πλουσίως πάντα (1836 TR); πλουσίως (F G 81* g). Elliott, 107, notes that an object is needed for παρέχοντι; he retains the article in accordance with usage elsewhere (Col 1.16; 1 Tim 6.13; Heb 2.8, 10; Acts 17.25; 20.18; Mk 4.11; 1 Cor 15.28; Rev 4.11); the order of words (object – adverb) is as in Tit 3.6; Col 3.16. The problem is, then, whether or not to include the article with quite respectable support. A verdict is difficult, but it may be relevant that 'everything' here means 'everything we individually need' rather than the sum total of all things; the article should be omitted.

19. θεμέλιον καλόν The oddity of the noun as the object of ἀποθησαυρίζοντας has led to conjectures: (a) Emend to θέμα/θῆμα λίαν καλόν, 'a right good treasure' (Bos Moff.).[115] This is impossible Greek, according to Scott, 81; (b) emend to κειμήλιον καλόν, 'good treasure' (Cl.) (so P. Junius in NA²⁷).

ὄντως αἰωνίου (D² 1881 TR vg^mss bo^mss Chrys); ὄντως αἰωνίου (1175 *pc*). The variants are rejected by Elliott, 108f.; Metzger, 577. The text is well-attested and agrees with usage in the PE.

EXEGESIS

17. Τοῖς πλουσίοις ἐν τῷ νῦν αἰῶνι παράγγελλε The use of the same verb 'instruct' as in v. 13 (cf. 4.11; 5.7) suggests that

---

[115] θέμα, 'deposit, prize' (Hel.; Lev 24.6; *et al.*), is found in Ignatius, *Poly.* 2.3. The conjecture was possibly inspired by Tob 4.9.

Timothy has the same authority in teaching other people as
Paul has towards him (cf. Oberlinner, 303). The objects of his
instruction are characterised as 'wealthy' (πλούσιος** 'rich,
wealthy'; cf. 6.9 note; Tit 3.6 note). The word is used in the pl.
for the class (Lk 6.24; 21.1; Jas 2.6; 5.1; Rev 6.15; 13.16;
1 Clement 16.10; *et al.*). It indicates in effect people with large
resources.[116] The qualification ἐν τῷ νῦν αἰῶνι (= Tit 2.12 [see
note]) is surprising. The reference is clearly to the present world
or age, i.e. this world, as long as it lasts. It may imply that they
are rich only by this world's standards and hence that they may
be poor in respect of the next world (whose existence is clearly
implied). They are rich only until the parousia, and so their
riches are uncertain and temporary (Knoch, 46). The dangers
against which the rich are warned thus stem from the recognition
that this world is transitory and that they must live as those who
already belong to the world to come. Warnings against pride in
one's wealth and concerning the uncertainty of wealth are
commonplace.[117]

μὴ ὑψηλοφρονεῖν μηδὲ ἠλπικέναι ἐπὶ πλούτου ἀδηλότητι
ὑψηλοφρονεῖν is a late and rare word with the sense 'to be
proud, haughty' (cf. BA; BD § 119⁵*). Elsewhere in the NT it is
found only as a *v.l.* in Rom 11.20 TR for ὑψηλὰ φρονεῖν (Rom
12.16). It is derived, however, from Cl. ὑψηλόφρων. According
to Spicq, 576, it is not so much to be proud as to be scornful of
others who have not managed to gain a social position on the
basis of their possessions. The sin is thus one of condemning
other people who have less wealth and creating social divisions
(Oberlinner, 305).

The switch of aspect to the perfect ἠλπικέναι (4.10; 5.5) is
appropriate with this verb: 'to hold great hopes' (McKay
1985:223). The term πλοῦτος, 'riches', is always used pejoratively
of human wealth in the NT.[118] ἀδηλότης*** is 'uncertainty',
and the whole phrase means 'riches that are not to be depended
on' (cf. BD § 165); the construction emphasises the thought of
insecurity. Earthly wealth belongs entirely to this world and
therefore is no basis for security in the world to come. Dibelius-
Conzelmann, 91, note the irony of people who put their hope in
uncertainty. It is implicit that this attitude, which stands in

---

[116] Furfey, P. H.,'ΠΛΟΥΣΙΟΣ and cognates in the New Testament', *CBQ* 5
(1943), 241–63, however, holds that the term refers to people such as rich
farmers, financiers and merchants who had large incomes rather than simply
people who possessed wealth.
[117] Prov 23.4f; Jer 9.23; Ps-Phocylides, 62 (*OTP* II, 576).
[118] Mt 13.22 = Mk 4.19 = Lk 8.14; Jas 5.2; Rev 18.16; cf. Heb 11.26; see Tit
3.6 note.

contrast to trust in God, is sinful as well as foolish. The point is put graphically in the parable in Lk 12.16–21.

ἀλλ' ἐπὶ θεῷ τῷ παρέχοντι ἡμῖν πάντα πλουσίως εἰς ἀπόλαυσιν Rather hope is to be put in One who is not only dependable but lavish in his provision (cf. Ps 52.7). The plentiful provision of good things is not meant to be a basis for self-security but is a pointer to the goodness of God who supplies them (Roloff, 368). παρέχω** (1.4; Tit 2.7), 'to give, supply', is also used elsewhere of God (Diognetus 3.4; 8.11; Acts 17.31). πάντα is used in the limited sense of 'everything we get' or perhaps 'everything we need'. For πλουσίως, 'richly, abundantly', see Tit 3.6 and note; Col 3.16***; Barnabas 1.7; 9.7. God's gifts go beyond our needs; they are given generously for our enjoyment (ἀπόλαυσις).[119] The positive attitude of 4.3f. is echoed; the implication is that the letter has to deal with two opposing tendencies, the asceticism which forbade enjoyment of the good gifts of God[120] and the self-sufficiency which was based on greed for possessions. These two tendencies can coexist in the same people.

18. ἀγαθοεργεῖν, πλουτεῖν ἐν ἔργοις καλοῖς, εὐμεταδότους εἶναι, κοινωνικούς God thus appoints that riches are to be enjoyed, but also shared generously. They are not for self-indulgence but for thankful acceptance and helping other people. ἀγαθοεργέω is a rare form, 'to do good'; the contracted form ἀγαθουργέω is used for God's action in Acts 14.17***. It expresses 'a demand for good action consisting in the demonstration of love to others'.[121] The same thought is expressed elsewhere in the letters in terms of the next phrase with its injunction to do good works (2.10; 5.10; et al.). Contrast the use of πλουτεῖν in 6.9, where it means 'to become rich' rather than 'to abound in'. Behind the phrase may lie an echo of Lk 12.21 (Roloff, 369 n. 194). εὐμετάδοτος*** is Hellenistic for 'generous' (BA s.v.). κοινωνικός is 'giving or sharing what is one's own, liberal, generous', again a mainly Hellenistic term.[122] The two words are close in meaning. Attempts to distinguish between them include such contrasts as: (a) giving to others in charity and readiness to share with one's

---

[119] Heb 11.25***; Cl.; 3 Macc 7.16; Philo, Mos. 1.70; Josephus, Ant. 2.52, 174; 2 Clement 10.3f; Didache 10.3; 1 Clement 20.10 has πρὸς ἀπόλαυσιν, a Hellenistic expression like the one here. Cf. TLNT I, 181f.

[120] Thiessen 1995:325f. traces this attitude to wandering ascetic missionaries.

[121] Grundmann, W., TDNT I, 17; cf. the synonym ἀγαθοποιέω (Lk 6.33; 1 Pet 2.15; et al.). Although the verb itself is late, ἀγαθουργός and ἀγαθουργίη are found in Herodotus (BA s.v.).

[122] BA; TLNT II, 121f.; Roloff, 369 n.196. Cf. Josephus, Bel. 2.122 of the Essenes; Philo, Prob. 13. Against the possible translation 'ready to sympathise' (RV mg), see Field 1899:213f. Cf. the use of μεταδίδωμι (Rom 1.11; 12.8; 1 Th 2.8).

friends; (b) visible action and inner disposition; (c) generosity and motivation by a social consciousness ('d'être largement donnant, d'avoir le sens social', Spicq, 577–9; cf. Lock, 74f.); (d) generosity in giving and sharing one's possessions with others (Roloff, 369). The virtues in this verse are expected of the rich by Aristotle.[123] The conclusion of Hanson, 114, and Hasler, 52, that there is no emphasis on the rich sharing with others in the community is astonishing (Towner 1989:190; Kidd 1990:100).

19. ἀποθησαυρίζοντας ἑαυτοῖς θεμέλιον καλὸν εἰς τὸ μέλλον The final participial phrase gives an interpretation of what the rich believers effect by their trust in God and their generosity. To live in this way is to create a future for themselves. To give away one's goods in this world is paradoxically to 'create wealth' for the future, i.e. for their eternal existence in the presence of God. The thought echoes teaching of Jesus about laying up treasure in heaven.[124] The thought is of what the rich gain for themselves. Roloff, 368f., finds here an individualistic ethic which is not motivated so much by the thought of duty towards the community as by one's personal good. This is somewhat unfair, since in the context the thought is of the personal spiritual dangers of wealth and the right use of it that brings the appropriate reward.

ἀποθησαυρίζω***, 'to store up, lay up', here used fig., is Hel.;[125] it takes ἑαυτοῖς as a dat. of advantage. The metaphor is mixed, with the curious idea of storing up a foundation; θεμέλιον, 'foundation', is used metaphorically in 2 Tim 2.19; see note.[126] Here, according to BA, it is 'about equal to "treasury, reserve"', but, although the parallels adduced (Philo, *Sacr.* 81; *L.A.* III.113) do not support this meaning (so rightly Parry, 44), it would seem to be the required sense. For the attempts of scholars to emend the text see above. καλός has the sense of 'good' as opposed to perishing, worthless, material. The phrase εἰς τὸ μέλλον (for the verb see 1.16) means 'for the future' (cf. Lk 13.9; in each case the context determines the range envisaged).

ἵνα ἐπιλάβωνται τῆς ὄντως ζωῆς The purpose clause might almost be thought to suggest that people can lay up a treasury of credit for their generous deeds which will win reward in the next life (for the motif see Tobit 4.9); but 2 Tim 1.9 forbids this idea (Kelly, 149). Rather, we have the normal NT teaching that lack of the expression of faith in good works is an indication of

---

[123] *EN* 4.1f. (1119b–1123a) (Spicq, 577). Cf. also Menander, *Dysc.* 797–819.
[124] Mt 6.19–21 par Lk 12.33f.; Mk 10.21 par. Mt 19.21; par. Lk 18.22. Cf. Brown 1963–4:35.
[125] BA; Ecclus 3.4; Josephus, *Bel.* 7.299 *et al.*
[126] Rom 15.20; 1 Cor 3.10, 12; Heb 6.1; Schmidt, K. L., *TDNT*, III, 63f.

the lack of faith itself, and conversely. For the whole phrase cf. 6.12, but corresponding to ἡ αἰώνιος ζωή there is ἡ ὄντως (cf. 5.3) ζωή here; cf. the contrast between τὸ ἀληθῶς ἐν οὐράνῳ ζῆν and ὁ ὄντως θάνατος in Diognetus 10.7. Clearly heavenly life is meant, but the phrase includes spiritual life here and now (cf. 6.12).

d. Final warning to Timothy, summing up earlier themes (6.20–21a)

Lau 1996:26–39, 61–3; Médebielle, A., 'Dépôt de la foi (1 Tim 6,20; 2 Tim 1,12; 1,14)', *DBS* II (1932), 371–95; Schlarb, E., 'Miszelle zu 1 Tim 6.20', *ZNW* 77 (1986), 276–81; Spicq, C., 'Saint Paul et la loi des dépôts', *RB* 40 (1931), 481–502; Wolter 1988:114–30.

While some defenders of Pauline authorship think that this may be a final message in the writer's own hand (Lock, 75), Easton (170) thinks that this section (like vv. 17–19) may be a late addition. The sentence has three parts. The main command lays positive stress on the need to preserve inviolate the tradition which has been entrusted to Timothy; the thought of handing it on to others in an apostolic succession (2 Tim 2.2) is at most implicit (cf. Dibelius-Conzelmann, 92 n. 31). But the tradition can only be preserved by action against the opposition, here regarded as laying claim to being 'knowledge'; in reality it is falsely so-called and gives rise to controversies and to assertions which are contrary to the truth. Adherence to this 'knowledge' is full of danger, to which some people have already succumbed and thereby fallen away from the Christian faith. The position of this injunction and its content strongly reinforce the view that it sums up the positive and negative thrusts of the letter. But it is important to note that the positive point is the main one; heresy is a danger precisely because it threatens the truth of the gospel which is to be maintained.

TEXT

20. κενοφωνίας καινοφωνίας (F G lat [*novitates*] Ir^lat). The variant is rejected by Elliott, 109f., as a dictation or orthographical error.

EXEGESIS

20. ῏Ω Τιμόθεε, τὴν παραθήκην φύλαξον The transition to the final part of the letter is marked by the same direct address (with ὦ) as in 6.11 to reinforce powerfully the appeal which the author is making to Timothy. The use of the personal name echoes 1.18, where the same crucial theme was first developed. Thus the letter begins and ends with significant emphasis on the task and message entrusted to Timothy. The injunction also serves in the canon as a transition to 2 Tim, where the same injunction is repeated in 1.14.

παραθήκη (2 Tim 1.12, 14***) is a 'deposit, property entrusted to another' for safekeeping and for return when required;[127] hence the elements of trustworthiness and faithfulness on the part of the recipient were important associations of the term.[128] It was used as a legal technical term. Oberlinner 1995:46f., notes the important point that the deposit could be passed on to a third party but of course still remained the property of the owner.[129] The vocabulary can be used figuratively of passing on teaching.[130] Here it is clearly the gospel which is meant, i.e. the whole of the apostolic teaching, or 'the Gospel enshrined in the traditional confession and disputed by the false teachers' (Maurer, 163f.); it is not the charge to Timothy expressed in 1.18 but rather that which Timothy is charged to preserve. For Fee, 161, it is the task which has been entrusted to him rather than the gospel itself; for Calvin, 283, it was the grace given for the discharge of the office. It may be significant that the word παράδοσις = 'human tradition' is not used for what is God's truth (Barrett, 89). For Oberlinner, 309, the ground for the new terminology lies in the fact that whereas in Paul 'tradition' is based on the authority of the gospel itself, here the authority is that of Paul himself.[131] More probably the difference is due to the fact that for Paul the main interest was in accepting and maintaining the growing body of apostolic tradition, whereas here the language suggests a primary interest in protecting the deposit and safely transmitting it to future believers (Towner 1995:306f.)

φυλάσσω (5.21) is used in the same way in 2 Tim 1.12, 14. Spicq, 580f., emphasises the legal background to the responsibility of keeping the deposit intact. But (*pace* Merkel, 53) the wording does not suggest that the deposit cannot be expounded and interpreted for new situations.

[127] Herodotus 9.45; Sextus 21 = 'soul'.

[128] For Attic παρακαταθήκη (TR of 6.20 and 2 Tim 1.14; cf. Elliott 109 note). See Brox, 235f.; Spicq*, with later references in Spicq, 580–2; cf. *TLNT* III, 24–7; Maurer, C., *TDNT* VIII, 162–4; Hellebrand, W., in PW 36 (1949), 1186–1202; Ranft, J., in *RAC* III, 778–84; Lips 1979:266–70; Wegenast 1962:144–50; Roloff 1965:245–7; *New Docs.* II, 85 §48.

[129] For the use of the word in the LXX see Lev 6.2, 4 (MT 5.21, 23); Tob 10.13; 2 Macc 3.15; cf. παρακαταθήκη, Exod 22.8, 11 (MT 22.7, 10); Tob 10.13 *v.l.*; 2 Macc 3.10, 15 *v.l.*; 4 Macc 4.7.

[130] Ps-Isocrates, *ad Demon.* 22; Philo, *Det.* 65; cited by Dibelius-Conzelmann, 92. For an extension of the metaphor to pastoral care in the church see the story in Clement, *Quis Div.* 42.

[131] An extreme position is taken by Donelson 1986:163f., for whom the deposit is the author's fictitious creation.

Roloff, 372f., raises two issues. First, is the 'depositor' God who has entrusted the deposit to Paul (who then passes it on to Timothy) or is it Paul himself as the author of the deposit? The former view is that of Brox, 234, and Roloff himself in his earlier work, but he now adopts the latter (along with Wegenast 1962:140; Wolter 1988:116–19). In favour of the latter view are the two considerations that it is called 'my deposit' in 2 Tim 1.12 (cf. Marshall 1995:247 n. 21) and that the contextual metaphor is that of a testament handed down by the author. Note how in 1.18 the author uses the corresponding verb παρατίθεμαι. Neither of these arguments is decisive here; there is no personal pronoun in this passage to identify the deposit as Paul's, and nothing prevents a person passing on what he has received from somebody else.

The second question is the content of the deposit. Roloff lists three possibilities: the gospel; the Pauline letters; the content of the PE.[132] He argues for the sense of the Pauline gospel as handed down by 'Paul', and therefore inclusive of whatever Paul taught and wrote.[133]

There is no doubt that the reference is to the gospel in this broad sense, which has been the centre of attention in the letter; it is to be preserved by Timothy in his present situation over against the attacks of heretics. Since the horizon of the PE is exclusively Pauline, the question of the relation of the Pauline gospel to other forms is simply not raised.

ἐκτρεπόμενος τὰς βεβήλους κενοφωνίας καὶ ἀντιθέσεις τῆς ψευδωνύμου γνώσεως The negative side of the commission is concerned with the rejection of the heretical teaching which threatens the gospel. ἐκτρέπω (1.6 note) here is 'to turn away from, avoid'.[134] This seems to refer to Timothy's own attitude to such teachings: he is to avoid being enticed by them (in contrast to those who have fallen away because of them, v. 21a), but it may also imply that he is to turn those who embrace such foolishness away and keep them out of the church. Even debate with the heretics can be a waste of time in view of the nonsensical and irreligious character of their teachings (2 Tim 2.14). βέβηλος was used in 1.9 of people who act in godless ways and in 4.7 of old wives' tales; appropriately here it describes teaching that is opposed to the gospel. κενοφωνία by its form clearly refers to teaching that is devoid of sense and thus futile (2 Tim 2.16***);

---

[132] Spicq (TLNT III, 27) rightly notes that the pastoral office itself is not in view.
[133] See 1.18 where he identifies the reference of ταύτην τὴν παραγγελίαν as being to the specifically Pauline tradition which has been passed on to Tim.
[134] Josephus, Ant. 4.290. For the use of the verb with reference to teaching see BA s.v.

it is the sort of language that was used in philosophical polemic.[135]

ἀντίθεσις*** is 'opposition, objection, contradiction'.[136] The term could conjure up the character of rabbinic discussions (Hort 1894:139f.). A number of scholars have asked whether there is an allusion to Marcion's book, Ἀντιθέσεις,[137] but this is unlikely (Hort, 1894:138f.; and most commentators). Later Marcionites accepted the PE, and Marcion himself was not a Gnostic, was not Jewish and made no claims to Gnosis. Many commentators hold, however, that some form of Gnosticism is in mind (see also Schmithals, W., EDNT I, 250). Schlarb* argues that in characterising the teaching of the opponents the author uses three devices: (a) the same words as for true teaching but with negative indicators (cf. the use of ἀπό; ἀντί; ἀ-); (b) a special use of τίθημι in compounds (2 Tim 2.25; contrast 1 Tim 4.6; 1.18; 2 Tim 2.2; and παραθήκη); (c) the use of the pl. to describe false teachings – in contrast to the sing. for true teaching; they are variform and confusing. Hence the phrase here bears the marks of composition by the author and is not derived from the title of Marcion's book but is rather a negative description of the opponents' teachings. What is not clear is whether it refers to teaching that is opposed to the true teaching, and perhaps expressed in polemical statements, or to false teachings that are mutually contradictory. Thiessen 1995:336f. argues that it is more likely to be a rhetorical term used by the opponents themselves, perhaps referring to the setting up of scriptural texts over against one another.

ψευδώνυμος*** is 'falsely bearing a name, falsely called'.[138] γνῶσις**, 'knowledge', is a term of wide application and need not point to the 'gnosis' of Gnosticism (pace Wolter 1988:265f.). It can be used of knowledge derived from the Jewish law.[139] For the view that Jewish lore is meant see especially Hort, 1894:140–3. In any case, it can be assumed to be a term used positively by the opposition themselves.

---

[135] The word is Hel. BA offer only one contemporary reference which comes from AD I (Dioscurides); according to Hesychius and Suidas it is synonymous with ματαιολογία (1.6). Simpson's reference to Plutarch, Mor. 1069, is actually to κενολογία.
[136] Cl.; Plutarch, Mor. 953B; Lucian, Dial. Mort. 10.10; CH 10.10; Philo, Ebr. 187. See especially Spicq, 113 n. 1.
[137] Bauer 1972:226; von Campenhausen 1963:205f.; Knox, J., Marcion and the New Testament (Chicago: University of Chicago Press, 1942), 73–6; See Rist, M., 'Pseudepigraphic Refutations of Marcionitism', JRel 22 (1942), 39–62.
[138] Cl.; Plutarch, Mor. 479E; Philo, Mos. 2.171.
[139] Hos 4.6; Mal 2.7; 4 Macc 1.16f.; cf. Lk 11.52; Rom 2.20f.

21a. ἥν τινες ἐπαγγελλόμενοι περὶ τὴν πίστιν ἠστόχησαν The final clause warns against the dangers – actual and not merely potential – of following the teaching of the opponents, and does so in a form and language strongly reminiscent of 1.19b (ἥν τινες – participle – περὶ τὴν πίστιν – main verb); note, however, that here the relative pronoun refers to the teaching of the opposition, whereas in 1.19 it refers to the activity of conscience which is rejected. ἐπαγγέλλομαι is 'to profess' (2.10) and ἀστοχέω (1.6) 'to miss the mark'.[140] Whereas in 1.6 this is a stage on the way to folly, here it is the result of embracing folly in the form of the false teaching. It is not necessarily the final stage in apostasy, but may leave open the possibility of return to the truth (Roloff, 375).

---

[140] With περί, as in Plutarch, *Mor.* 46A.

CLOSING GREETING
(6:21b)

The greeting, which is in the pl. form, is almost identical with that in Tit (with πάντων omitted); 2 Tim has the identical wording, but preceded by a prior greeting addressed to Timothy himself. The same very brief wording is also found in Col 4.18, but elsewhere longer forms are found.

The closing of the letter is surprisingly brief and lacking in any personal messages or greetings to and from named persons, such as are found in all the other Pauline letters except Galatians. Defenders of pseudonymity are surprised that the author did not use the opportunity to imitate Pauline characteristics here, but then assume that this was unnecessary in a letter which is part of a trilogy which has adequate 'circumstantial details' elsewhere (Roloff, 370f.).

TEXT

21b. μεθ᾽ ὑμῶν (ℵ* A F G 33 81 g bo^mss): μετά σου (D [K L] Ψ 048 1739 1881 TR lat sy bo^mss). Elliott, 110f., argues that the sing. form, which is consistent with the rest of the Epistle (cf. especially 6.20), was generalised by scribes; Metzger, 577, however, states that the pl. is adequately supported and was changed to fit the rest of letter.

At the end of the letter: add ἀμήν (ℵ² D¹ Ψ 1739^c TR f vg^cl ww sy bo Ambst). The addition is rejected by Elliott, 104; Metzger, 577 (cf. Tit 3.15).

EXEGESIS

21b. Ἡ χάρις μεθ᾽ ὑμῶν As elsewhere, the phrase is a wish grammatically, but in effect a prayer with which the letter is sent on its way. The analogy with Tit 3.15 indicates that the pl. form ὑμῶν is a real plural, referring to the recipient's companions, and not a case of the mixing of the pl. and sing., as is sometimes found in the pap.[1] Roloff, 375, however, thinks that it is due simply

---

[1] Moulton, J. H., 'Notes from the Papyri II', *Expositor* VI.7 (1903), 107 (104–21).

to taking over the normal greeting used in a congregational meeting. It is true that in Tit and 2 Tim the greeting is preceded by references to other named persons who are with the addressee, whereas there are no such references here, but throughout 1 Tim there is constant reference to the members of the congregation to whom the letter would have been read.

THE SECOND LETTER TO TIMOTHY

THE SECOND LETTER TO TIMOTHY

SALUTATION
(1.1–2)

See bibliographies for Tit 1.1–4; 1 Tim 1.1–2.

The salutation has the usual three-part structure, and resembles that in 1 Tim fairly closely.

1 Tim	2 Tim
Παῦλος ἀπόστολος Χριστοῦ Ἰησοῦ	Παῦλος ἀπόστολος Χριστοῦ Ἰησοῦ
κατ᾽ ἐπιταγὴν θεοῦ σωτῆρος ἡμῶν	διὰ θελήματος θεοῦ
καὶ Χριστοῦ Ἰησοῦ τῆς ἐλπίδος ἡμῶν	κατ᾽ ἐπαγγελίαν ζωῆς τῆς ἐν
	Χριστῷ Ἰησοῦ
Τιμοθέῳ γνησίῳ τέκνῳ ἐν πίστει,	Τιμοθέῳ ἀγαπητῷ τέκνῳ,
χάρις ἔλεος εἰρήνη	χάρις ἔλεος εἰρήνη
ἀπὸ θεοῦ πατρὸς	ἀπὸ θεοῦ πατρὸς
καὶ Χριστοῦ Ἰησοῦ τοῦ κυρίου ἡμῶν.	καὶ Χριστοῦ Ἰησοῦ τοῦ κυρίου ἡμῶν.

(a) The name of the sender is given in identical form with his status as an apostle. In both cases the apostleship is traced back to the one who appointed him, namely God, but the phraseology is different, 1 Tim referring to God's command in his purpose as saviour, and 2 Tim simply referring to the will of God. 1 Tim further traces this command back to 'Christ Jesus our *hope*' alongside God, but 2 Tim states that it is in accordance with the *promise of life* which is in Christ Jesus. There is thus an allusion to salvation as a gift of God in both salutations.

(b) The name of the recipient is given in similar terms, but the child who is 'genuine in faith' has now become 'beloved'.

(c) The actual greeting is given in identical language, and differs from the characteristic Pauline greeting through the addition of 'mercy'.

The differences that have been noted indicate that the author exercised flexibility in expression while sending greetings which are essentially identical in their theological and factual content. What was said, therefore, about the character of the greeting in 1 Tim applies here also. 2 Tim is generally more 'personal' in character than 1 Tim, especially in its extended epistolary conclusion, but it is significant that the personal character of the salutation here is already found in 1 Tim. Commentators who assume the pseudonymity of the letter hold that the purpose of the stress on Paul's apostleship and the close relationship of Timothy to him is to stress the apostolic commission of Timothy himself. The reference to the promise of life points up the relevance of apostleship to the church (Oberlinner, 10). But neither of these points requires a post-Pauline setting, and the implication that the letter is really meant for the church does not fit its essentially personal character. There is more to be said for the possibility that the letter is intended for church leaders who have received their commission from Timothy, i.e. the faithful men of 2.2. It is for their benefit that the letter is handed on.[1]

TEXT

2. Χριστοῦ Ἰησοῦ inverted order (629 1739 1881 *pc* vg^mss); κυρίου Ἰησοῦ Χριστοῦ (ℵ* 33 *pc* [sy^p]). The text should be retained (Elliott, 201).

EXEGESIS

1. Παῦλος ἀπόστολος Χριστοῦ Ἰησοῦ is parallel to 1 Tim 1.1. In what appears to be much more of a personal letter than 1 Tim the inclusion of Paul's official status may seem odd (Holtzmann, 370). In terms of an attempt to maintain verisimilitude (if the letter is not authentic), or if the letter is authentically personal various possibilities arise:

(a) The letter is meant for the church which Timothy leads as well as for him personally (Spicq, 697). It serves to legitimise his position as a church leader (Hasler, 55). Therefore the legitimator (real or fictitious) stresses his own authority in virtue of which he confers authority on Timothy (Parry, 47; Oberlinner, 10). But see below on v. 2.

(b) As the older man Paul is conscious of his position and status over against a younger man for whom he has affection but who is still his junior colleague. A sense of personal status can accompany warm feelings of affection for a colleague. And Paul took his status seriously.

(c) The letter is an appeal to Timothy for loyalty to Paul and his gospel, and therefore the authoritarian stress is appropriate (Knight, 363; Fee, 219).

(d) Paul is thinking of his own situation rather than reminding Timothy of it.

A combination of reasons is likely. (i) Paul is (or is presented as being) conscious of his position as the older man; (ii) he holds a special position in the church as an apostle; (iii) he is giving

[1] The salutation is briefer than that in Tit, but all the features found here are included in the longer form (with the exception of the use of 'mercy').

instructions that are authoritative both for his junior colleague and for the congregations under his care. Even a communication to a colleague is more than a personal letter, since the gospel is at stake.

διὰ θελήματος θεοῦ The phrase qualifies ἀπόστολος and is paralleled in 1 Cor 1.1; 2 Cor 1.1; Eph 1.1; Col 1.1. It corresponds to κατ' ἐπιταγὴν θεοῦ in 1 Tim 1.1.[2] Paul owes his position in the church to specific appointment by God.

Wolter 1988:149–52 argues that there is a clear difference in nuance between the two phrases. The phrase used here anchors Paul's apostolate in the divine will which is his eternal purpose of bringing salvation. But the phrase in 1 Tim 1.1 and Tit 1.3 refers to an act of communication in which a specific commission is given to somebody, and legitimates not so much the person as the task. Hence it is claimed that here the concern is with the person of Paul whose call to apostleship is part of God's plan, whereas in 1 Tim and Tit the concern is with the specific commission given to Paul which includes the content of the letters themselves. This difference is then related to the different literary characters of the letters, which are in effect more personal (in the case of 2 Tim) and more community-directed (1 Tim and Tit).

κατ' ἐπαγγελίαν ζωῆς τῆς ἐν Χριστῷ Ἰησοῦ For κατ' ἐπαγγελίαν cf. Gal 3.29; Acts 13.23.[3] For ἐπαγγελία 'promise' see 1 Tim 4.8**, and for ζωή see 1.10*; 1 Tim 1.16; 4.8; Tit 1.2 note; the same phrase (ἐπαγγελία ζωῆς) appears in 1 Tim 4.8. Jeremias, 48, argues that the mention of life is partly motivated by Paul's impending martyrdom (cf. Holtz, 152f.). In any case, the phrase sums up the content of Paul's gospel (Brox, 223).

The qualification ἐν Χριστῷ Ἰησοῦ makes clear that spiritual life is meant (Rom 8.2; cf. Gal 2.20); this is confirmed by the parallel usage of ἐπ' ἐλπίδι ζωῆς αἰωνίου in Tit 1.2. But it is not confined to future life (cf. Holtzmann, 372), as the parallel in 1 Tim 4.8 proves. The promise is one which God made in the past and which is now realised in the gift of life 'in Christ' (cf. Jn 1.4). The use of ἐν Χριστῷ Ἰησοῦ is Pauline (cf. Rom 3.24; 8.39 for the attachment to an abstract noun). It may be taken in a 'mystical' sense of what is given to believers through their union with Christ (Kelly, 154) or in a more instrumental sense of Christ as the one through whom God's saving plan is brought to effect. See further on 1.13; 1 Tim 1.14.

The whole phrase forms a second qualification of the description of Paul as an apostle, but its force is disputed:

[2] Hasler, 11, suggests that the usage is post-Pauline, evidently assuming that 2 Cor 1.1 is the work of an editor and overlooking 1 Cor 1.1.
[3] *New Docs.* IV, 147 § 51.

(a) 'In conformity with the [whole divine scheme which comprises God's] promise of life'.[4] It is appropriate and necessary that God who promised eternal life should also raise up his agent to make it known. Paul's apostleship is thus a result of God's promise;

(b) 'To announce God's promise of life';[5]

(c) 'In order to fulfil the promise of life', expressing the object and intention of Paul's calling.[6]

Paul's apostleship is 'in accordance with God's promise', in the sense that it springs from that promise and is intended to bring that promise to fruition by proclaiming it. Apostleship is tied to the service of God's saving purpose (Oberlinner, 8).

2. Τιμοθέῳ ἀγαπητῷ τέκνῳ The description of the recipient differs from that in 1 Tim 1.2 and Tit 1.4 in the use of ἀγαπητός instead of γνήσιος. ἀγαπητός (1 Tim 6.2) is also used of Timothy in 1 Cor 4.17. There may not be any great significance in the variation in the use of semi-conventional terms (White, 152). The adjective may be used here:

(a) As an expression of affection. It may reflect the attitude of an older to a younger man (cf. especially Phil 2.22 of Timothy as Paul's junior colleague), or the fact that Timothy became a Christian through Paul. Similar language is used of Onesimus (Philem 10), who was presumably younger than Timothy, however. This note of love and affection runs through the letter (1.4; cf. 4.9, 21; Jeremias, 49).

(b) As a description indicating that Timothy is Paul's 'first-born' son and hence his heir (Spicq, 698f., citing Gen 22.1, 13, 16; Jer 6.26; Amos 8.10; Zech 12.10).

(c) As part of the total portrait of the 'typical', 'ideal' relationship between the apostle and his colleague (Brox, 223). According to Hasler, 55, it functions as part of the process of 'legitimising' Timothy as a leader authorised and commended by Paul. This is comprehensible if the letter is authentic. But it is not clear how this works on the assumption of inauthenticity. One possibility is that the letter is part of an attempt to legitimise the historical Timothy after the death of Paul as his successor; this would require a date soon after the death of Paul. The other possibility is that the letter is intended to legitimise the existing leaders of the church who can claim authorisation along a line that extends down from Paul through Timothy (cf. 2.2). Neither

---

[4] Holtzmann, 371; Parry, 47; Kelly, 153 (the aim and purpose of Paul's apostleship); Hanson, 118f.; Spicq, 697, combines this and the next interpretation.
[5] Dibelius-Conzelmann, 97, following Theodoret III, 676 Schulze = *PG* LXXXII, 832; cf. Calvin, 289; Jeremias, 48; Kelly, 153; Dornier, 180; Houlden, 108; Knoch, 51; Oberlinner, 7; Arichea-Hatton, 167.
[6] White, 152; Holtz, 151; Knight, 364.

of these scenarios is possible if 'Timothy' is a purely fictitious character. In any case, there is little if anything in this letter to suggest that it is really addressed to a congregation, rather than to Timothy himself or to church leaders. Hence the view that legitimisation to the church is present here is dubious (so rightly Fee, 220). View (a) is accordingly to be preferred.

χάρις ἔλεος εἰρήνη ἀπὸ θεοῦ πατρὸς καὶ Χριστοῦ Ἰησοῦ τοῦ κυρίου ἡμῶν The salutation is identical with 1 Tim 1.2. The concepts mentioned in it all figure later in the letter: χάρις, 1.(3), 9; 2.1; 4.32*; ἔλεος, 1.16, 18*; εἰρήνη, 2.22*.

BODY OF THE LETTER – TIMOTHY AS A CHURCH LEADER (1.3–4.8)

I. THE NEED FOR TIMOTHY TO SHOW COURAGE AND TO HOLD FAST TO THE GOSPEL (1.3–18)

a. Thanksgiving for Timothy's faith (1.3–5)

Spicq, C., 'Loïs, ta grandmaman (II Tim, 1, 5)', *RB* 84 (1977), 362–4; Wolter 1988:203–14.

2 Tim is the only one of the Pastorals to begin conventionally with thanksgiving, and this corresponds with the fact that it is more personal in character than the others. Although it might seem to be a literary convention, in fact it anticipates themes developed later: Paul's longing to see Timothy, springing out of his loneliness and his affection for him and expressed in frequent prayer; the character of Timothy's faith, 'inherited' from his family, and forming the basis of the appeals that follow. It has been argued that Paul is presented typically here as a man of prayer and as an apostolic martyr, in contrast to 1 Tim and Tit where the gospel is more prominent (Hasler, 56; cf., less extremely, Brox, 224f.). For the thought cf. Rom 1.8–11 and Phil 1.3. Close similarities in structure, language and thought between the larger section 1.3–12 and Rom 1.8–17 have been detected by Lohfink 1988:172–4.[1]

As in other NT letters, there are several typical features of the epistolary style of the time, shaped in a Christian fashion; these can be characteristic both of authentic and of pseudonymous letters. In 2 Tim these features are those characteristic of the literary motif of a letter of friendship (Brox, 225f.; Wolter 1988:203–14) – the prayer-report, which serves partly as a *captatio benevolentiae*, the personal concern of the writer for the addressee and the longing to see him again, and the development of the idea of fellowship that emerges especially in vv. 7f.

The thanksgiving is a single sentence whose structure is loose and ambiguous. It may be analysed as follows:

---

[1] Cf. Barnett 1941:263; Oberlinner, 11.

Χάριν ἔχω τῷ θεῷ,

   (ᾧ λατρεύω ἀπὸ προγόνων ἐν καθαρᾷ συνειδήσει),

  ὡς ἀδιάλειπτον ἔχω τὴν περὶ σοῦ μνείαν

      ἐν ταῖς δεήσεσίν μου νυκτὸς καὶ ἡμέρας,

  ἐπιποθῶν σε ἰδεῖν,

      μεμνημένος σου τῶν δακρύων,

      ἵνα χαρᾶς πληρωθῶ,

ὑπόμνησιν λαβὼν τῆς ἐν σοὶ ἀνυποκρίτου πίστεως,

    (ἥτις ἐνῴκησεν πρῶτον ἐν τῇ μάμμῃ σου Λωΐδι

        καὶ τῇ μητρί σου Εὐνίκῃ,

    πέπεισμαι δὲ ὅτι καὶ ἐν σοί).

We can bracket off the two relative clauses, whose syntactical function is clear enough. The two key problems are: (a) whether Paul expresses the reason(s) for his thanksgiving: is the ὡς clause the object of the thanks or is it adverbial?; (b) the relationship of the three participial phrases. It seems most likely that ἐπιποθῶν is dependent on ἔχω ... μνείαν. μεμνημένος is subordinated to it, and the ἵνα clause will then be dependent on it. The third participial phrase then is probably dependent on χάριν ἔχω and in effect gives the reason for the thanksgiving, namely Timothy's faith, which is then described more fully.[2] It is in the light of this last clause that the introduction of the previous one, which parallels Timothy with Paul, is inserted. The thrust is then: Paul expresses thanks to God for the faith of Timothy which he shared with his mother and grandmother (just as more broadly Paul served God in the same way as his ancestors). This thought comes to his mind in his unceasing prayers which are accompanied by his strong desire to see Timothy again (especially because the latter sorrowed at being separated from him) so that he might have the joy of a reunion.

The purpose of a thanksgiving in the Pauline correspondence is not to offer an actual prayer to God but rather to *report* what Paul says in his prayers as a means of encouragement and exhortation to the readers. Here the intent of the 'prayer-report' is not simply to give news of Paul's concern for him to Timothy but rather to give him strong encouragement through the knowledge of the fact that Paul remembers him ceaselessly in prayer and that Paul is convinced of the reality of his faith. This will then form the basis for the appeal to him that will follow. The connections of thought are intricate, but no more so than, say, in the opening of Phil.

---

[2] Bernard, 107; White, 153; but see Holtzmann, 381f., for a detailed discussion which identifies the ὡς clause as the object of the thanks.

TEXT

5. λαβών λαμβάνων (ℵ² D (365) TR syʰ; Kilpatrick); Elliott, 114, adopts the variant, stating that scribes tended to alter present forms to aorist. But Holtzmann, 381, regards the variant as assimilation to other pres. participles in the context.

καὶ τῇ μητρί insert ἐν (2625 *et al.*). Elliott, 115, defends the repetition as Semitic idiom and claims that scribes removed the preposition because of the frequent usage in the sentence. The external evidence, however, is very weak.

EXEGESIS

3. Χάριν ἔχω τῷ θεῷ For χάριν ἔχω see 1 Tim 1.12. The reason for thanksgiving can be expressed by a participle (Heb 12.28) or by a ὅτι clause (1 Tim 1.12; Lk 17.9) or by a prepositional phrase. Neither of the last two possibilities arises here. The options are: (a) 'for you' is to be understood; (b) the participle phrase in 1.5 gives the reason; (c) the ὡς clause is equivalent to a ὅτι clause.[3] The second option is clearly right, despite the distance from the verb. Although the form is that of a prayer-report expressing what Paul does whenever he prays, this naturally does not rule out the possibility that Paul is praying even as he writes or dictates these words (Couser 1990:188).

ᾧ λατρεύω ἀπὸ προγόνων ἐν καθαρᾷ συνειδήσει λατρεύω** is used of religious service: (a) of cultic duties by priests and others (e.g. Acts 7.7, 42; Rom 1.25; Heb 8.5); (b) of offering prayer and praise and worship (Mt 4.10 = Lk 4.8; Lk 2.37); (c) of the whole of life as service to God (Lk 1.74; cf. Strathmann, H., *TDNT* IV, 58–65). Paul uses it of his apostolic service in Rom 1.9.[4] The nuance of taking part in the worship offered by Israel is expressed here and elsewhere. The Gk. pres. tense is best rendered by the Eng. perf.: 'whom I have served and continue to serve'. The importance attached to inheriting and practising the virtues of one's forebears is amply attested in the Hellenistic world (Spicq, 701f.).[5]

πρόγονοι, 'parents, forebears, ancestors' (1 Tim 5.4***)[6], could refer either to Paul's Jewish ancestors in the broad sense (for which Paul uses πατέρες), or specifically to his parents. The latter reference would give a direct parallel to Timothy with his godly upbringing, but the former is on the whole more likely.

---

[3] Oberlinner, 14, thinks that Paul (also) gives thanks that he can look back on his own service to him. This is pushing the text rather far.

[4] Cf. Rom 12.1 (noun); Phil 3.3; Acts 27.23; Heb 9.14; 12.28.

[5] The use of ἀπό may appear unusual, but the formula is attested with the force 'in the same way as [his] forebears' (Dittenberger, *Syll.* 730.27; 854; 1228.5; further refs. in BA and Dibelius-Conzelmann, 98 n. 3).

[6] According to BA it is always used in pl. in 'our lit.'.

For συνείδησις see 1 Tim 1.5 and for the combination with καθαρός see 1 Tim 3.9 (with ἐκ).

The statement implies that Paul's ancestors also served God with a clear conscience (Parry, 48), and thus a line of continuity is drawn between the faithful service of Israel and the service of Christians. It may also suggest that Paul has served God all his life and has done so with a clear conscience. These implications, particularly the second one, have been thought to run counter to Paul's consciousness of a definite break in his life at his Christian conversion and especially to what is said in 1 Tim 1.13, 15 about his sinfulness. However, when similar statements are made in Acts 23.1 and 24.14–16, the latter at least must refer to his life as a Christian, and it is probable that this is true here also. The reference is to Paul's service as an apostle, and it ties in with the usage in Rom 1.9. Moreover, to establish continuity between the worshipful service of pre-Christian Israel and that of Christians does not deny that there can be lapses and failures in both periods. The statement here compares Paul's present service with the ideal past of Israel and says nothing that contradicts or is in disharmony with the consciousness of sin that is attributed to him in 1 Tim 1.

The function of this self-reference in the present context is probably multiple: (a) The establishment of a line of continuity between the service of Israel and Christian service may be important in reassuring the congregations associated with Timothy that they stand in the true line of succession from Israel over against any claims made by Jewish opponents. It may perhaps suggest that they have the true interpretation of the Old Testament over against their opponents. The reference to a clear conscience may possibly be a reply to any suggestions that Paul's imprisonment on a criminal charge impugned his loyalty to his ancestral religion (Kelly, 155). It has the effect of placing Paul alongside the godly church leaders desiderated in 1 Tim 3.9 and contrasting him with the opponents (Couser 1992:190 n. 640). (b) In Rom 1.9 Paul refers to his service of God in the context of his prayers for the Christians in Rome and his longing to minister to them. The point here may similarly be that his prayers for Timothy arise out of and form part of his service of God. But this does not explain the emphasis on his conscience. (c) Above all, Paul may be trying to establish an encouraging parallel between himself and Timothy, whose *Christian* faith can also be traced back to his forebears. Expressions of Paul's 'uprightness' are found elsewhere (1 Cor 4.4; 2 Cor 1.12; 1 Th 2.10) and suggest that he felt it necessary to vindicate himself on occasion. It may be right to see the need to defend Paul against accusations made by his opponents to Timothy. In any case, Brox's view (227) that the writer (unlike Paul) sees no problems in regarding Christianity as a development from Judaism and in emphasising the solid foundation of faith in past generations does not do justice to the text.

ὡς ἀδιάλειπτον ἔχω τὴν περὶ σοῦ μνείαν ἐν ταῖς δεήσεσίν μου νυκτὸς καὶ ἡμέρας ὡς (1 Tim 5.1; *et al.*) is used here only in the PE as a conjunction. The force must be: 'I give thanks when/as often as I remember you.' It cannot be linked to the following adjective and translated 'how unceasingly I remember you'. Holtzmann, 377f., insisted that it must give the content of the thanksgiving with the force 'that in such a way'; he attributed the roughness of expression to an attempt to imitate Rom 1.8–11 which has not been entirely successful. The proposal is unnecessary and wrong, since the content of the thanksgiving is given in v. 5.[7]

ἀδιάλειπτος is 'unceasing, continual' (Rom 9.2***; cf. the adv. in Rom 1.9; 1 Th 1.3; 2.13; 5.17, always with reference to prayer[8]). It was evidently a traditional characteristic associated with deep piety, and Spicq (*TLNT* I, 32–4) argues that it expresses the idea of a heart that is continually oriented towards God, even if it is not always engaged in conscious prayer. μνεία, 'memory, mention', belongs to the language of prayer-reports (Phil 1.3); the phrase μνείαν ποιοῦμαι means 'I mention'.[9] The use of περὶ σοῦ with μνεία is unpauline (Holtzmann, 378f.). For δέησις see 1 Tim 2.1; it always occurs in the pl. in the PE (cf. Lk 2.37; 5.33; Heb 5.7), whereas Paul uses the sing. (cf. Phil 1.4), but this is hardly significant.

The construction of the phrase νυκτὸς καὶ ἡμέρας (1 Tim 5.5) is disputed: (a) It may be linked with the preceding phrase.[10] Cf. 1 Tim 5.5 for a link with prayers. (b) It may be linked forwards with v. 4 as in 1 Th 3.10.[11] The former construal is correct. The language is hyperbolical but natural; Spicq, 703, cites a parallel from a letter from a wife to her husband.

4. ἐπιποθῶν σε ἰδεῖν The sentence proceeds with a loosely attached participle which expresses the circumstances of Paul as he gives thanks and prays. ἐπιποθέω, 'to long for intensely', often

---

[7] ὡς does mean 'how' in Rom 1.9, but there the construction is different.

[8] Cf. 1 Macc 12.11; 2 Macc 13.12; 3 Macc 6.33; *Ep. Arist.* 92 (of priestly service). For non-religious uses see 2 Macc 3.26; 9.4; 13.12.

[9] For μνείαν ποιοῦμαι see Rom 1.9; Eph 1.16; 1 Th 1.2; Philem 4***; for the phrase ἔχω [τὴν] μνείαν, 'I remember', cf. 1 Th 3.6. Cf. Michel, O., *TDNT* IV, 678f.; *TLNT* I, 32 n. 5; II, 496.

[10] NA; NEB; NIV; NJB; NRSV; GNB; Holtzmann, 379; Kelly, 156; so also Spicq, 703, apparently.

[11] RV; RSV; Bernard, 107; Lock, 83; Easton, 37; Barrett, 92.

expresses the hope of seeing an absent person or group.[12] The thought of the writer's longing to see Timothy recurs strongly in 4.9, 21, so that the letter as a whole is bracketed by this strong emotional tie. Such expressions may be conventional in correspondence, but they do not always have to be!

μεμνημένος σου τῶν δακρύων A second participle follows, qualifying the previous one. The intense longing is due, at least in part, to Paul's memory of Timothy's sorrow at their separation. μεμνημένος**, the perfect participle of μιμνήσκομαι, has present force (1 Cor 11.2); the verb may carry undertones of emotion and concern.[13] Timothy's tears (δάκρυον**, always plural or virtual plural in the NT) were presumably shed at their last parting.[14] There is no other reference to this episode, unless we accept the bizarre hypothesis that the allusion here is based on the scene depicted in Acts 20.37 (κλαυθμός), at which Timothy is assumed to have been present and then left behind in Ephesus by Paul (Holtzmann, 380).

ἵνα χαρᾶς πληρωθῶ The following purpose clause is clearly dependent on ἐπιποθῶν. For πληρόω**, 'to fill', cf. Delling, G., *TDNT* VI, 286–98. χαρά**, 'joy', is here the natural human emotion rather than the Christian quality, but the two are hardly to be distinguished in the NT (cf. Conzelmann, H., *TDNT* IX, 359–72). The metaphor of being filled with joy is well-attested.[15] Spicq (*TLNT* III, 498f.) observes that the word is rare in the pagan papyri,[16] and claims that this reflects the general pessimism of contemporary paganism.

5. ὑπόμνησιν λαβὼν τῆς ἐν σοὶ ἀνυποκρίτου πίστεως The third participle phrase functions to express the circumstances in which Paul gives thanks (v. 3) and thus in effect gives the grounds for thanksgiving. Alternatively, the participle may be linked with the immediately preceding phrase: seeing Timothy again would remind Paul of his faith and give cause for joy (Parry, 48); but this is less likely. ὑπόμνησις may be used actively of the act of remembering (2 Pet 1.13; 3.1***); it is 'substantially identical with ἀνάμνησις in the active sense' (Behm, J., *TDNT* I, 348f.). It can also be used passively, as here, of what is remembered (cf. ὑπομιμνήσκω, 2.14; Tit 3.1). However, it is not clear whether the phrase here employing λαβὼν is simply a case of the idiom

---

[12] Rom 1.11; 1 Th 3.6; Phil 2.26; cf. Phil 1.8 (without ἰδεῖν); *TLNT* II, 58–60.
[13] Cf. Heb 13.3; so Leivestad, R., *EDNT* II, 430f.; cf. *TLNT* II, 489–96.
[14] Proponents of inauthenticity find it unnecessary to look for a historical occasion that may lie behind this statement.
[15] Josephus, *Ant.* 15.421; Philo, *Abr.* 108; Acts 13.52; Rom 15.32; Phil 2.2; Diognetus 10.3.
[16] There is an example in *New Docs.* III, 10–12 §2 (AD II).

'to call to mind'[17] or means 'to receive a reminder', i.e. by news being brought to him.[18] Since no specific incident is mentioned, the former is preferable. The recollection is of Timothy's faith,[19] the quality which expresses the essential aspect of Christian character, but which here may tend to faithfulness (Fee, 223). The description of it as being 'in' Timothy (ἐν σοί) is Pauline (Rom 1.12; also Eph 1.15; contrast 2 Cor 13.5). Its special quality is that it is 'sincere' (ἀνυπόκριτος), as in 1 Tim 1.5 (see note there). The stress is presumably made to give a contrast with the false teachers whose motives are regarded as suspect. Possibly it is made with an eye to the church to confirm Paul's trust in his coworker.

ἥτις ἐνῴκησεν πρῶτον ἐν τῇ μάμμῃ σου Λωΐδι καὶ τῇ μητρί σου Εὐνίκῃ, πέπεισμαι δὲ ὅτι καὶ ἐν σοί ἥτις may have the sense 'of a kind which' (Tit 1.11). ἐνοικέω, 'to dwell in' (1.14**), is used with reference to the presence of sin, the Holy Spirit, God and the word of Christ in people by Paul;[20] the aorist is inceptive, 'took up its abode' (Parry, 48). Faith is thus seen as a divine gift rather than a human quality or work (Jeremias, 49), although it would be wrong to press the expression too far. The succession stretched back to Timothy's grandmother, presumably his mother's mother.[21] Her name, Λωΐς***, is otherwise unattested except for one occurrence in an AD III document.[22] Holtzmann, 383, holds that, despite Acts 16.1, she was a Greek, became a proselyte and brought up her daughter as a Jew.[23] Εὐνίκη*** is an uncommon but well-attested Greek name.[24] πέπεισμαι, perf. pass. of πείθω, has the force 'I am convinced, certain'.[25]

The description raises problems. What kind of faith is envisaged on the part of Timothy's family? It is disputed whether

[17] Cf. BA for parallels and the similar idiom in 2 Pet 1.9.
[18] Bengel; Holtzmann, 381; Bernard, 108; Simpson, 122; Spicq, 704, is undecided.
[19] πίστις, 1.13; 2.18, 22; 3.8, 10, 15; 4.7*; Tit 1.1 note.
[20] Rom 7.17; 8.11; 2 Cor 6.16; Col 3.16; not discussed in TDNT; see Dabelstein, R., EDNT I, 456.
[21] μάμμη***, originally 'mother', in Hel. Gk. it came to mean 'grandmother' (Attic τήθη); 4 Macc 16.9. Philo, Spec. 3.14; Josephus, Ant. 10.237. Cf. Spicq*, 362f., for this word and also for the conjunction in ancient sources of mother and grandmother; he refers to Plutarch, Agis 4.1, for a close literary parallel to Timothy's upbringing.
[22] Spicq*, 363f. (P.Cair.inv.n. 10585 line 4).
[23] See further Cohen 1986.
[24] Cf. BA; for the spelling Εὐνείκη found in TR and 7 minn. see MHT II, 76; Elliott, 115, 237. There is nothing unusual in a Jewess, as Timothy's mother was (Acts 16.1), having a Gk. name, since the use of Gk. names by Jews was common enough.
[25] Heb 6.9; Lk 20.6. With ὅτι, Rom 8.38; 14.14; 15.14; 2 Tim 1.12**; Polycarp 9.2; Bultmann, R., TDNT VI, 1–9; TLNT III, 66–77.

the reference is to (a) Christian faith;[26] (b) Jewish piety;[27] or (c) both, but primarily Christian faith (Fee, 223). The first possibility is the most likely. Presumably they were first converted (πρῶτον) and then brought up Timothy as a Christian (*pace* Holtzmann, 383). The question then arises as to how this account relates to that in Acts (would a pious Jewess have married a non-Jew?) and to the description of Timothy as Paul's 'child' if this indicates that Paul had led him to the faith. But there is no good reason to argue that the picture here is fictitious (*pace* Brox, 226f.). The lack of mention of Timothy's father here suggests that he was not a Christian and possibly dead. Consequently, the theory that the whole description is a fiction intended to give an ideal picture of how Christian influence spread over the generations (Houlden, 107) is weakened. What may be significant is the stress on the implied role of *women* in bringing up Timothy as a believer. Clearly this point could be used paradigmatically to encourage Christian women among readers of the letter, but this is not the reason for the reference. The hypothesis that Timothy is described as a third-generation believer because this reflects the situation of the actual readers of the letter and encourages them to hold fast to the faith which they have inherited (Oberlinner, 22f.) is speculative.

b. *Appeal to Timothy to stir up the gift of the Spirit and not to be fearful (1.6–7)*

The thanksgiving served the purpose of encouraging Timothy, but the expression 'I am convinced' does in fact paradoxically suggest an element of doubt in the writer's mind that Timothy's faith is giving him some concern (Johnson, 48), and it is on this basis that Paul now gives him what is in effect a command. The key thought appears to be that witness to the gospel involves suffering, and therefore there is a strong temptation to 'be ashamed' of it; Timothy, therefore, needs to be encouraged to depend on the gift of the Spirit which has been imparted to him and which takes away fear.

The section comprises two sentences. The first reminds Timothy that he has received the spiritual gift which he needs for ministry and encourages him to let it have its full force. The second explains that the Spirit conveys the qualities which are needed, but uses a figure of speech which indicates that those who possess this gift should not suffer from fear.

---

[26] Kelly, 157; Spicq, 706; Hanson, 120.
[27] Holtzmann, 376, 383: 'Christian faith in its pre-existence as Jewish faith'; Scott, 89.

The significance of Paul as the one through whom Timothy received the Spirit is matched by the stress on him in the following verses (1.8, 11, 12, 13), and it can be argued that the effect here (as is also claimed for elsewhere in the PE) is to accentuate the exclusive position of Paul as the source and pattern of the gospel, and as the authority on whom subsequent leaders are dependent. Those who take this view admit that a similar accent can be found in the authentic letters of Paul, but claim that it has developed here into a greater and more exclusive stress and combined with the idea of an 'apostolic succession' (e.g. Oberlinner, 26f.). But this stronger emphasis on the thought of faithful succession would not be surprising in the envisaged situation of Paul at the end of his life.

TEXT

6. ἀναμιμνήσκω ὑπομιμνήσκω (D Ψ 365 1505 *pc*). Elliott, 116, holds that the variant (2 Tim 2.14; Tit 3.1**) is original and was accidentally altered because of preceding or following use of αν.

θεοῦ Χριστοῦ (A). Elliott, 116, rejects the variant, since apart from 1 Tim 5.11 Χριστός is not used on its own in PE.

EXEGESIS

6. Δι᾽ ἣν αἰτίαν ἀναμιμνήσκω σε ἀναζωπυρεῖν τὸ χάρισμα τοῦ θεοῦ The instruction is linked to what precedes by the phrase δι᾽ ἣν αἰτίαν, 'because of this' (1.12; Tit 1.13 note). The reason in question is doubtless the fact that Timothy is a genuine believer.[28] ἀναμιμνήσκω is 'to remind',[29] here as a means of admonition; it is sheer coincidence that the same verb is used in 1 Cor 4.17 of Timothy reminding the Corinthian church of Paul's ways. ἀναζωπυρέω*** is 'to rekindle, kindle, inflame'.[30] The ἀνα- is perfectivising (MHT I, 111f.), giving the sense 'to fan fully into flame'. There is agreement among commentators that the implication is not that the fire is extinguished or nearly so, but that it must be kept brightly burning.[31] For the same imagery with respect to the Spirit cf. 1 Th 5.19. Thereby the gift of the Spirit is clearly to be understood as something dynamic and not static (so rightly and powerfully Oberlinner, 30f.)

[28] A broader link to the whole of 1.3–5 is found by some commentators.

[29] 1 Cor 4.17; pass. 'to remember' (2 Cor 7.15; Heb 10.32; Mk 11.21; 14.72***); cf. Patsch, H., *EDNT* I, 86.

[30] The verb is found in Cl. and the LXX (Gen 45.27; 1 Macc 13.7) in a metaphorical sense, as here (cf. Josephus, *Bel.* 1.444 [love]; *Ant.* 8.234; it is also used intrans. in 1 Clement 27.3 [faith]; Ignatius, *Eph.* 1.1; cf. Lips 1979:208–10).

[31] Cf. M. Antoninus 7.2 (quoted in Parry, 49). Arichea-Hatton, 167, say that the significance of the metaphor is uncertain.

The χάρισμα (1 Tim 4.14 note) which comes from God (as in Rom 6.23; 11.29; cf. 1 Cor 7.7) is here the spiritual equipment for ministry, and the next verse identifies it as the Spirit who is given by God.

ὅ ἐστιν ἐν σοὶ διὰ τῆς ἐπιθέσεως τῶν χειρῶν μου ὅ ἐστιν must obviously have the force 'which is', and is not equivalent to *id est*. It is 'in' the recipient, like faith (1.5; similarly 1 Tim 4.14; 1 Cor 12.6; Phil 2.13; Eph 2.2). The gift is accordingly an inward grace which affects the personality and manifests itself in outward actions. The conferral of it on Timothy is associated with the laying on of hands, as in 1 Tim 4.14. There are, however, two differences from the phrase there.

The first is that here the preposition is διά which can express accompaniment (attendant circumstances) or instrumentality (Harris, M. J., *NIDNTT* III, 1182f.). Lips 1979:251 correctly notes that μετά, which was appropriate with ἐδόθη in 1 Tim 4.14, would not be possible with ἐστιν. The former possibility (accompaniment) is less likely since it leaves the mention of the laying on of hands unmotivated and does not explain what the point of it was. Nevertheless, the phrase does not mean that it was the act of laying on of hands which conveyed the Spirit possessed by Paul to Timothy,[32] nor does it imply that Timothy did not already possess the Spirit. The force is that the charisma for ministry, one of the specific charismata associated with the Spirit, was conveyed to Timothy by God as the necessary accompaniment to the laying on of hands which conveyed Paul's authority to him (cf. Num 27.18–23).

The second difference from 1 Tim 4.14 is that here μου is added (cf. Num 27.18 LXX), stressing Paul's own part in the ceremony, whereas in 1 Tim it was the act of the elders. Brox, 228f., explains the difference by regarding the present reference as fictitious (like the other one), created to stress the close link between Paul and Timothy. Oberlinner, 29f., holds that the two passages are to be taken together: ordination at the time of the PE takes place through the elders but is dependent on the authorisation which can be traced back to Paul, so that the leaders have their legitimation ultimately from him. Wolter 1988:218–22 draws attention to the literary antecedent in the commissioning of Joshua by Moses as his successor, and deduces that in 2 Tim Timothy is regarded as Paul's successor with the authority to commission others. This explains why the laying on of hands is here seen as the act of Paul rather than of the elders.[33]

---

[32] Similarly, the Spirit was not conveyed by the instrumentality of prophecy in 1 Tim 4.14.

[33] Strictly speaking, the present passage is not focused on ordination to an office but on the reception of the Spirit to enable witness to the gospel.

Warkentin 1982:136–52 likewise develops the Moses/Joshua pattern, but emphasises that nothing is said about Joshua laying hands on his successors.

Fee, 226, appears to accept this explanation, but in a later work (Fee 1994:785–9) he inclines to the view that two separate incidents are meant (cf. White, 155). Further, whereas the gift in 1 Tim 4.14 is the giftedness for ministry, here it is more the source of ministry, the Spirit. Since the Spirit is given to all believers, the way opens up to claim that the reference here is to the indwelling of the Spirit in believers as such and not just in leaders. The laying on of hands may then be associated with conversion and initiation rather than ordination (cf. Acts 19.6).

This explanation seems less likely than the view that one incident is referred to in both passages, but Fee is correct in maintaining that a hard-and-fast line should not be drawn between the gift of the Spirit to all believers and to persons involved in ministry, as v. 7 will illustrate.

7. οὐ γὰρ ἔδωκεν ἡμῖν ὁ θεὸς πνεῦμα δειλίας ἀλλὰ δυνάμεως καὶ ἀγάπης καὶ σωφρονισμοῦ The construction is similar to Rom 8.15 and there is a certain parallel in the thought: οὐ γάρ ... verb (give/receive) ... πνεῦμα + genitive (slavery leading to fear/cowardice) ... ἀλλά ... [Spirit] + genitive (sonship/power, etc):

οὐ γὰρ ἐλάβετε
    πνεῦμα δουλείας πάλιν εἰς φόβον
ἀλλὰ ἐλάβετε πνεῦμα
    υἱοθεσίας
ἐν ᾧ κράζομεν· ἀββα ὁ πατήρ.

οὐ γὰρ ἔδωκεν ἡμῖν ὁ θεὸς
    πνεῦμα δειλίας
ἀλλὰ
    δυνάμεως καὶ ἀγάπης καὶ
    σωφρονισμοῦ

God's giving of the Spirit is often expressed by forms of δίδωμι.[34] The question as to when the gift was conferred is bound up with the question as to the recipients, and this is turn is tied up with the nature of the gift. It is unlikely that πνεῦμα here refers to 'the human spirit as endowed by the Holy Spirit with the qualities proper for service' (Bernard, 109; Parry, 49), still less the human spirit alone (White, 155) or simply a human disposition (NRSV).[35]

There are two possibilities: (a) The Spirit is regarded as God's gift to all believers (ἡμῖν in a general sense).[36] In this case the gift may be regarded as gifted to the church at Pentecost (White,

[34] Lk 11.13; Acts 5.32; 8.18 (11.17); 15.8; Rom 5.5 (11.8); 1 Cor 1.22; 5.5; Eph 1.17; 1 Th 4.8; (1 Tim 4.14).

[35] The compromise in NJB ('God did not give us a spirit of timidity, but the Spirit of power...') is unlikely. See Arichea-Hatton, 173f.

[36] Cf. 1.9f.; Dibelius-Conzelmann, 98; Barrett, 93f.; Knight, 371.

155) or conferred on individual believers at conversion. (b) The
Spirit is regarded as God's gift to leaders (ἡμῖν referring to Paul
and Timothy but also broadening out to include other leaders);[37]
in this case the reference is probably not to conversion but to
an event which includes commissioning to ministry, and the gift
has the character of *Amtsgnade*.[38]

The determining factor is that the qualities here associated
with the Spirit are in no way peculiar to leaders, although they
are applied here especially to the ability of the leader to speak
the gospel without fear. One should also bring v. 14 into the
discussion where again nothing indicates that the indwelling of
the Holy Spirit is confined to leaders. Rather, the gift of the
Spirit given to all believers equips each for their particular needs,
including the particular needs of leaders. Admittedly, the gift is
more probably associated with commissioning rather than with
conversion-initiation in v. 6. But commissioning consists in
praying for the Spirit who is already present to give the new gifts
required for ministry.

The Spirit is frequently described in terms of particular qualities
by the gen.[39] δειλία*** means 'timidity, fear', or, more strongly
'cowardice'.[40] It is the opposite of faith (Spicq, 709) and the
weakness most to be avoided in time of war (*TLNT* I, 300–2).
The writer conceives of an inward power or disposition that
makes people timid – as if there was such a gift of the Spirit
(Rom 11.8 is irrelevant to the issue)! The fear is that of public
witness due to a sense of shame or fear of suffering (cf. Heb
10.32–39). The liability of the historical Timothy to be fearful is
clearly implied in 1 Cor 16.10. It is therefore appropriate to
reassure him that the Spirit does not produce fear, a thought
already expressed powerfully in Rom 8.15, although there the
fear is directed towards God rather than other people.

Instead the Spirit conveys three positive qualities. The first
and most relevant to the present context is δύναμις, 'power,
strength'.[41] The power in question is not so much the ability to
do mighty deeds or miraculous signs but rather something akin
to courage, the quality needed most by people who are timid.
The association of the Spirit and power is familiar in the NT;[42]
it is particularly associated with Christian witness. The second
quality is ἀγάπη,[43] which elsewhere is characterised as driving out

[37] Bernard, 109; Parry, 49; Lock, 85f.; Kelly, 159; Hasler, 57; Oberlinner, 31f.
[38] Brox, 229; *contra* Luck, U., *TDNT* VII, 1104, n. 1.
[39] Rom 1.4; 8.15; 11.8; 1 Cor 4.21; Gal 6.1; 2 Cor 4.13; Eph 1.17 (cf. 1.13).
[40] Fee, 227; Cl.; *M. Poly.* 3; Hermas, *Sim.* 9.21.3; for the verb see Jn 14.27;
for the adj. see Mk 4.40 = Mt 8.26; Rev 21.8.
[41] 1.8, 12; 2.1**; for the verb ἐνδυναμόω see 1 Tim 1.12; 2 Tim 2.1; 4.17.
[42] Lk 4.14; Acts 1.8; 10.38; Rom 15.19; 1 Cor 2.4; Eph 3.16; 1 Th 1.5.
[43] 1.13; 2.22; 3.10; 1 Tim 1.5 note.

fear (1 Jn 4.18). The third quality is σωφρονισμός***. This word can convey the idea of 'making to understand, making wise' (so pesh; similarly, Holtzmann, 387; cf. tentatively Johnson, 50), but this is not appropriate here. It is to be understood in the light of the use of the word-group in the PE to signify 'moderation, self-discipline, prudence' (see **Excursus 3**). The basic thought is of self-control, hardly of the capability to discipline and control others (*pace* Bernard, 109). It is a quality to be expressed in all believers and in church leaders. What Timothy is encouraged to do is to give free course to the Spirit which will enable him to manifest those outward qualities which enable him to fulfil his Christian witness (see Luck, U., *TDNT* VII, 1104).

c. The need to hold firmly to the gospel which Paul preaches and for which he suffers (1.8–12)

Barclay, W., 'Our Security in God – 2 Tim i.12', *ExpTim* 69 (1957–8), 324–7; Barrett, C. K., 'I am not ashamed of the gospel', in *Foi et Salut selon St. Paul*, AnBib 42 (1970), 19–41; Bover, J. M., '"Illuminavit vitam" (2 Tim. 1,10)' (in Spanish), *Bib* 28 (1947), 136–46; Hall, D. R., 'Fellow-workers with the Gospel', *ExpTim* 85 (1974), 119f.

The next section goes closely with what precedes in that, on the basis of his possession of the Spirit who gives power, Timothy is encouraged not be ashamed of the gospel or of Paul but to take his share of suffering for the gospel. The letter thus becomes an appeal for readiness to suffer in the course of Christian witness, and 1.8 could be regarded as summing up the letter (Läger 1996:66). The gospel and its teacher, Paul, are closely tied together, so that to be ashamed of one is to be ashamed of the other. The problem is whether the situation in which Timothy would feel ashamed is (a) persecution by people outside the church who know of Paul's imprisonment and/or (b) attacks by Paul's opponents in the church who could equally make capital out of his imprisonment as a means of discrediting him and his message. It may not be possible to distinguish the two sharply, since in any case Paul's imprisonment was due to the secular powers. The references in the letter to opponents of Paul within the church strongly suggests that (b) must be included as a factor in the situation. At the same time it should not be forgotten that in the context of the letter as a whole Timothy is being summoned to Rome where he would share the dangers to which Paul himself was exposed (Jeremias, 50).

The passage then opens out into a statement of the gospel. It has a balanced rhythmical form and could be part of a hymn (Holtz, 157–60; *pace* Fee, 234) or other existing form of words; cf. 2.8. But, as elsewhere in the PE, the language is that of the

author; it is not introduced with any formula, and the content
is appropriate to the context (cf. Läger 1996:67). It is couched
in the form of a description of God's action which then develops
into a sort of chain statement. The structure is as follows:

[θεοῦ]
τοῦ σώσαντος ἡμᾶς
καὶ καλέσαντος κλήσει ἁγίᾳ,
        οὐ κατὰ τὰ ἔργα ἡμῶν
        ἀλλὰ κατὰ ἰδίαν πρόθεσιν καὶ χάριν,
           τὴν δοθεῖσαν ἡμῖν
               (A) ἐν Χριστῷ Ἰησοῦ
               (B) πρὸ χρόνων αἰωνίων,
        φανερωθεῖσαν δὲ
               (B′) νῦν
               (A′) διὰ τῆς ἐπιφανείας
                   τοῦ σωτῆρος ἡμῶν Χριστοῦ Ἰησοῦ,
                   καταργήσαντος μὲν τὸν θάνατον
                   φωτίσαντος δὲ ζωὴν καὶ ἀφθαρσίαν
                   διὰ τοῦ εὐαγγελίου

The structure is intricate. Parallelism and head–tail links are
decisive. The main structure is given by three sets of balancing
participles, each attached to the preceding 'tail'. God is described
by two participles in synonymous parallelism. The second of
these is qualified by two prepositional phrases in antithetic
parallelism. The latter of these then becomes the bearer of a
second set of parallel participial phrases which are not so much
synonymous or antithetical but rather 'additive', describing two
phrases in the history of salvation. Within this contrast between
the giving and the revealing of grace we have a further parallel
structure with two sets of phrases arranged chiastically giving the
time of the action and the christological locus of it. Finally, the
mention of Christ Jesus provides the bearer for a description of
what he has done, again expressed by two contrasting participial
phrases which describe the negative and positive effects of his
appearing. With a final mention of the gospel, the link is provided
for a reference to Paul's own place in its proclamation; he has
to suffer but he is not ashamed of it because of his firm trust in
God/Christ.

The whole of this extended statement is an expression of the
kerygma, and some scholars think that it contains material that
is unnecessary in the context (Dibelius-Conzelmann, 99). It is
thoroughly Pauline in content, with close contacts with Eph 2.8f.
(Brox, 230). Its significant ingredients are:

(a) It identifies God as Saviour and stresses that salvation is by grace and not by works.

(b) It stresses the centrality of Christ Jesus as the one through whom God acted, and it further stresses that salvation has its beginnings before time and its manifestation 'now'.

(c) It identifies the content of salvation as the destruction of the power of death and the revealing of immortal life.

It is not clear whether there is a polemical note in all this. The accents are in fact characteristic of the PE (Tit 3.4–7) and probably represent a restatement of the gospel over against distorted views within the church and possibly with an emphasis on the final vindication of the people of God despite the possibility of suffering and death at the hands of opponents.

TEXT

9. καλέσαντος add ἡμᾶς (618 *pc*); cf. Gal 1.6 for the phrase. Elliott, 119, regards the variant as probably original and omitted to avoid repetition. But the evidence for it is too weak, and it probably arose through assimilation to biblical diction.

κατά² The full form should be retained, especially if the article follows, rather than the *v.l.* κατ' or καθ' (Elliott, 119). A few authorities insert τήν (436 and 4 minn. Athanasius), which is usually added with ἴδιος (1 Tim 3.4, 5, 12; 4.2; 5.4; 6.1; Tit 2.5; Elliott, 120). But the evidence is weak, and the unabbreviated κατά does not need to be followed by τήν.

Χριστοῦ Ἰησοῦ For the inverted order (ℵ² C D² F G Ψ 33 1739 1881 TR; lat sy Or) see Elliott, 201. The possibility that θεοῦ is read by I is noted in NA²⁷.

10. καταργήσαντος praem. τοῦ (D Severian). For the use of the article before the participle cf. 1.9, 14; 4.1. Elliott, 121, argues that it was omitted by scribes on stylistic grounds. But the evidence is too weak.

11. καὶ διδάσκαλος (a) καὶ διάκονος (33); (b) καὶ διδάσκαλος ἐθνῶν (ℵ^c C D F G Ψ 1739 1881 TR it vg sy^{ph} sa bo; [καί omitted by C P *pc*]). Variant (a) is probably due to assimilation to Col 1.23; Bernard, 106, adopts Variant (b), but it is rejected as assimilation to 1 Tim 2.7 by Metzger, 579; Elliott, 121.

12. καί Omit (ℵ* Ψ 1175 *pc* vg^{mss} sy^p); Elliott, 209, retains.

EXEGESIS

8. μὴ οὖν ἐπαισχυνθῇς τὸ μαρτύριον τοῦ κυρίου ἡμῶν μηδὲ ἐμὲ τὸν δέσμιον αὐτοῦ The imperative which follows is grounded (οὖν; 2.1, 21; 1 Tim 2.1 *et al.*) in the preceding statement. Since Timothy has received the Spirit and the accompanying power, it is both his duty and within his ability to fulfil the command. He is not to be ashamed of bearing witness. ἐπαισχύνομαι, 'to be ashamed, embarrassed', takes the acc. of the person or thing.[44]

---

[44] 1.12, 16; Mk 8.38a, 38b = Luke 9.26a, 26b; Rom 1.16; 6.21; Heb 2.11; 11.16***; Hermas, *Sim.* 8.6.4; 9.21.3; Ignatius, *Smyr.* 10.2; cf. Bultmann, R., *TDNT* I, 189–91.

Shame is a feeling which leads to action which hides witness. The implication is that witness may well lead to humiliating situations, but nevertheless it is to be carried out bravely. The shame arises because the gospel is considered shameful; a person is humiliated by being associated with it and its bearer, the imprisoned apostle. There may be an echo of the thought in Rom 1.16 (cf. Barrett*), and many commentators think that the writer is here dependent on that passage.

The verb has two objects. The first is 'witness' (μαρτύριον, 1 Tim 2.6**) followed by what must be an obj. gen., 'about our Lord'. It is unlikely that the word here has the technical sense of 'martyrdom', i.e. dying as part of one's witness for Christ (rightly Oberlinner, 34f.; *pace* Holtz, 156). Throughout 2 Tim κύριος is used frequently on its own for Jesus;[45] only here and in 1 Tim 1.14 do we have the simple form 'our Lord'.[46] The reference may be either to the gospel message or to the activity of proclaiming it, and probably the latter is chiefly in mind here (Trites 1977:210).

The second object is Paul himself who is described as a 'prisoner' (δέσμιος**; Eph 3.1; 4.1; Philem 1, 9). The word usually refers to prisoners in jail. The qualification 'his prisoner', namely, of the Lord (cf. Staudinger, F., *EDNT* I, 289f.), which is found also in Eph and Philem, might suggest a metaphorical sense (like 'servant of the Lord'), but here it is clearly literal, and αὐτοῦ has the sense 'for his sake'. It is true that Paul is not expressly described as a prisoner elsewhere in the letter, but this is the natural interpretation of the references in 1.16 and 4.6–22. The significance of the reference is that it is the gospel, as attested by Paul, which must be the content of Timothy's witness.

ἀλλὰ συγκακοπάθησον τῷ εὐαγγελίῳ κατὰ δύναμιν θεοῦ Instead of being ashamed of the gospel Timothy is instructed not merely to proclaim it but to submit to what proclamation may well involve. He is to be prepared for his share in suffering. συγκακοπαθέω (2.3***) is 'to share in suffering'. The simplex form is found in 2 Tim 2.9; 4.5, but the compound appears to be a new creation by the author for the occasion.[47] It is probable that τῷ εὐαγγελίῳ (1.10; 2.8*; 1 Tim 1.11) is dat. of advantage, 'take your share of suffering for the sake of the gospel' (not 'with the gospel', *pace* Easton, 40; Hall*). Then it is likely that we

---

[45] 1.16, 18; 2.7, 14, 19a, 19b, 22, 24; 3.11; 4.8, 14, 17, 18, 22; cf. 1 Tim 1.14; not used in Titus.

[46] Cf. Heb 7.14; 2 Pet 3.15; Rev 11.15; cf. Jn 20.13, 28.

[47] It is found elsewhere only in Schol. Euripides, *Hecuba*, 203 (cf. Michaelis, W., *TDNT* V, 936–8). On the spelling see Elliott, 129, who states that συγκ- is found without variant in all MSS (so Kilpatrick). Cf. MHT II, 104; BD § 19.

should supply 'with me' to indicate Timothy's companion in suffering, specially in view of v. 12;[48] the issue is left open in REB; GNB. In this way suffering for the sake of the gospel is introduced as a major theme of the letter.[49] κατὰ δύναμιν θεοῦ, 'in accordance with the power of God' (cf. 1.7), signifies 'as God strengthens you to do so', with the implication that his strength will be sufficient to enable Timothy to bear it.[50] The reference is clearly to the Spirit who gives power (v. 7; Fee 1994:789f.)

9. τοῦ σώσαντος ἡμᾶς καὶ καλέσαντος κλήσει ἁγίᾳ The statement which now follows begins as a characterisation of the God whose power enables his servants to endure suffering for the sake of the gospel, but is in fact a declaration of the gospel expressed in terms of what this God does to save his people. The first part is a confession of the action of God in saving people on the basis of his own grace rather than their works. The declaration is elaborately structured with careful balance throughout.

Two participles set in parallel express the action of God. For σώζω see 4.18; 1 Tim 1.15 note. The aorist expresses God's saving of us as a complete act in the past (Tit 3.5; Eph 2.5, 8). It sums up all that is involved in a process which culminated in the actual numbering of individuals in the people of God. The basic act is then unpacked in terms of divine calling, sc. to eternal life (1 Tim 6.12**), using a familiar Pauline term (1 Cor 1.9; Gal 1.6; Rom 8.28).[51] The verb is accompanied by a cognate noun (κλῆσις**).[52] The effect of this is that the qualification 'holy'[53] can be added by means of an adjective. But the force of the addition is ambiguous (Spicq, 714f.). The dat. may be (a) a dat. of means: 'he called us through a holy (sc. as coming from God) calling';[54] or (b) a dat. of interest: 'he called us to [lead] a holy [life]';[55] or (c) a dat. of association (functioning like an internal acc. to give a quality to the action of the verb: 'he

---

[48] NIV; NJB; NRSV; Holtzmann, 388; and most commentators.

[49] 1.12; 2.3–13; 3.10–12; 4.5–8, 16–18; cf. 1 Th 1.6; 2.14; 3.4; 2 Cor 4.7–15; Rom 8.17; Phil 1.12, 29; Col 1.24.

[50] Cf. 2 Cor 8.3; Eph 3.7, 20; Heb 7.16; see further Col 1.11, 29; 2 Th 2.9; Heb 7.16.

[51] Trummer, 185f., and Oberlinner, 38, find a shift in accent from Paul in that for him the verb is used of his gracious election, whereas in the PE it is concretised in the act of baptism. But this is an unwarranted use of Tit 3.5 to read into this verse what is not there. Calling is prior to baptism and not part of it.

[52] For the construction cf. Mt 2.1; Mk 4.41; 5.42; Lk 22.15; Acts 5.18.

[53] ἅγιος, 1.14 and Tit 3.5 of the Holy Spirit; 1 Tim 5.10 of saints; cf. verb 2.21.

[54] RSV; cf. NRSV 'with'; Holtzmann, 390; Knight, 374.

[55] Cf. NIV; GNB; NJB; REB; Parry, 50f.; Jeremias, 50; Dibelius-Conzelmann, 99; cf. 1 Cor 7.15 with ἐν for εἰς.

called us in a holy manner'.[56] Decision between these possibilities
is not made any easier by the possible parallels, both of which
involve the relative pronoun. In 1 Cor 7.20 the force is probably
'let each person remain in the [circumstances of the] calling in
which [s/he was when] s/he was called' (cf. v. 24). More to the
point is Eph 4.1: 'live in a way which is worthy of the calling
[by] which you were called.' It is most likely that the author is
thinking of a call from a holy God which should lead to a holy
way of life (Tit 2.12, 14), but this purpose would naturally arise
out of a calling by a holy God.[57] In view of the rarity of
construction (c), we should probably adopt (a).

οὐ κατὰ τὰ ἔργα ἡμῶν The author now spells out the fact that
God's initiative in saving us was not on the basis of anything
that we had done. The positive form of the phrase ('according
to works') is used by Paul to express the basis of God's judgement
on the wicked (Rom 2.6; 2 Cor 11.15; 2 Tim 4.14; cf. 1 Pet 1.17).
The force then is that, although God judges on the basis of
deeds, he does not save on that basis. Paul equally stresses the
same point using the phrase ἐξ ἔργων.[58] We need not doubt that
the Jewish stress on works of the law lies at the bottom of the
phrase, but here it is generalised to cover any kind of deeds (cf.
Tit 3.5 note). It must be insisted that this is not a *difference* from
Paul's teaching or 'a new soteriological conception' (Oberlinner,
39) but rather a widening out of what is already present there
(Marshall 1996). Equally, the claim that the absence of a contrast
with faith indicates that for the PE faith is a result of God's
saving revelation (Oberlinner, 39) is mistaken. Houlden's comment (112) that the phrase appears only here and in Tit 3.5 in
the PE (and is therefore unimportant for the author) is to be
countered with the observation that it appears only in Rom; Gal
and Eph of the acknowledged Pauline letters.

ἀλλὰ κατὰ ἰδίαν πρόθεσιν καὶ χάριν The balancing contrast
is not with faith but with grace, just as in Tit 3.5 where mercy
is the key term. The two terms which are used here might be
understood as forming a hendiadys, 'his own gracious purpose',
but the continuation of the sentence demonstrates clearly that
the thought is rather 'according to his purpose and [according
to his] grace'. πρόθεσις, 'purpose, plan', is used for human plans
(3.10**; Acts 11.23; 27.13) and also for God's (Rom 8.28; 9.11;
Eph 1.11; 3.11); in the latter case the thought is of a primal
purpose that goes back to the beginning of time or beyond. The

---

[56] The use of the dat. with an adjective is rare compared with the acc., but cf.
1 Macc 14.29; Mk 5.42; Hermas, *Sim.* 9.18.3; BD § 198⁶; MHT III, 241f.
[57] For the possible nuances of 'holy' here see Arichea-Hatton, 178.
[58] Tit 3.5; Rom 3.20; 4.2; 9.11, 32; 11.6; Gal 2.16a, 16b, 16c; 3.2, 5, 10; Eph
2.9; Jas 2.21, 22, 24, 25; for a different usage see 1 Pet 2.12.

language is intended to stress that salvation depends on God's choice (Rom 9.11), not our human works – or merit![59] God's will to save depends on his own willingness to act in grace to save us irrespective of what we have done (or of what he might foreknow us as doing).

τὴν δοθεῖσαν ἡμῖν ἐν Χριστῷ ᾿Ιησοῦ πρὸ χρόνων αἰωνίων The thought is extended in a new direction by a participial phrase which goes most naturally with 'grace', but not with 'purpose'. The participles which are used go much more naturally with 'grace' and are inappropriate with 'purpose'. The grace of God is said to be 'given',[60] in the sense that God shows favour to his people and grants them salvation. Two qualifications are added. The first is that grace is given ἐν Χριστῷ. He is the 'channel' through which God effects his purpose.[61] The second is that this donation took place πρὸ χρόνων αἰωνίων. Literally 'before eternal times', the phrase is a Semitism for 'before the ages' (Tit 1.2; Eph 3.11; 1 Pet 1.20). This is hardly a reference to a promise in historical time, such as Gen 3.15, but to an act of God prior to creation. In the similar passage in Tit 1.2f. God promised eternal life before eternal ages and then revealed his word at the right time.

It is not easy to find a form of words to express the paradoxical statement that is made here, namely that grace was given to us in Christ Jesus by God long before we were born. Holtzmann, 391, compares Jn 17.24. The divine gift was thus contained in the pre-existent Christ before the world was created, and it was given to us in that it was given to Christ (Lock, 87). It follows that, although grace was given in eternity, the effect of the gift is in time. 'Die Vermittlung "in Christus Jesus" gehört bereits zur präexistenten Gewährung der Gnade hinzu' (Brox, 230; cf. Cajetan in Spicq, 715). This is a more forceful understanding of the matter than is suggested by Bernard, 110: 'That which was unfalteringly promised is described as actually given' (cf. Holtzmann, 391); here the bold expression has been weakened by assimilation to the promise and fulfilment language of Tit 1.2. Rather, 'the thought is wholly of the original purpose of God as actualised, so to speak, in ... the Son contemplated already

---

[59] Maurer, C., *TDNT* VIII, 164–7 (167) makes the curious statement: 'Yet there also threatens in this text the danger of severing the fixed decision from the person of God along the lines of a *decretum absolutum* when it is said of this gracious foreordination that it was granted before all ages in Christ and manifested in the present, v. 9.' This judgement has no basis in the text, particularly since the purpose is explained in terms of χάρις (1.2).

[60] δίδωμι, Acts 7.10 (favour); Rom 12.3, 6; 15. 15.15; 1 Cor 1.4; 3.10; Gal 2.9; Eph 3.8; 4.7.

[61] There is a close parallel in 1 Cor 1.4; see also 2 Cor 5.19; Eph 1.3, 10, 20; 2.6f.; 3.11; 4.32.

as incarnate. The grace ... is described by a bold hyperbole, as already given to us though there can be no question of our then existence' (Parry, 51). The statement implies some kind of pre-existence for Christ Jesus.

10. φανερωθεῖσαν δὲ νῦν διὰ τῆς ἐπιφανείας τοῦ σωτῆρος ἡμῶν Χριστοῦ Ἰησοῦ With the second phrase that qualifies the concept of grace and balances the first one we move from what happened secretly in the mind of God to the open revelation of his grace. The plan is revealed in being brought to fruition. For φανερόω see Tit 1.3 (and note); Rom 16.26; Col 1.26; 1 Pet 1.20, where it occurs in a similar contrast. νῦν (1 Tim 4.8) refers to what we may call the Christian era. The adverb is used here with the aor. participle to refer to a new situation which has begun in the present time.[62] The means of revelation of divine grace is the ἐπιφάνεια of Jesus (4.1, 8; Tit 2.13 and **Excursus 8**; 1 Tim 6.14; 2 Th 2.8). This is the only use of the word in the PE for the first appearance of Christ. The reference is to the whole 'Christ-event' and is hardly confined to the resurrection and exaltation of Christ; the gospel and its proclamation form part of it. The writer has in mind the fact that this present era is now characterised by the revelation of the Saviour, so that in a sense the revelation is continuously present. A reference purely to the parousia is manifestly impossible. The language may possibly be polemical, directed against the claims of the emperor (Easton, 41). That the manifestation is indeed one of grace is underlined by the title applied to Christ, 'our Saviour' (σωτήρ, 1 Tim 1.1 note).

καταργήσαντος μὲν τὸν θάνατον The description of Christ as Saviour is substantiated by the third set of balancing phrases which are added on as a qualification, following the author's tail plus description pattern of composition. The two phrases express negatively and positively the saving work of Christ. On the one hand, he has rendered powerless that which people fear most and from which they long to be saved. καταργέω** is 'to destroy', or 'to render ineffective', and is used with reference to death, as here (1 Cor 15.26; Barnabas 5.6), the devil (who has power over death, Heb 2.14), and antichrist (2 Th 2.8).[63] Death, θάνατος**, is here regarded as an alien power (Cf. Bultmann, R., *TDNT* III, 7–21). It connotes spiritual as well as physical destruction.

---

[62] Cf. BA; Jn 13.31; Rom 5.11; 11.31; Eph 3.5, 10; 1 Pet 1.12; cf. Rom 5.9; 16.26; 1 Pet 2.10b; 25.

[63] The verb is rare but found in Cl. and Pap.; Simpson, 125f.; cf. Delling, G., *TDNT* I, 452–4.

φωτίσαντος δὲ ζωὴν καὶ ἀφθαρσίαν διὰ τοῦ εὐαγγελίου On the other hand, Christ has revealed the counterpart to death which causes human beings to perish. ζωή (1.1; Tit 1.2 and note) is a thematic word for salvation in the PE. The thought here is primarily of eternal life, but this does not exclude the present experience of it. ἀφθαρσία** is 'incorruptibility', hence 'immortality',[64] and is a characteristic of God himself (ἄφθαρτος, 1 Tim 1.17) which is shared with believers. The two terms form a hendiadys, 'immortal life', contrasting with ὄλεθρος καὶ ἀπώλεια (1 Tim 6.9). This life is not created by Christ. Rather, it already exists in the divine sphere, and what Christ does is to reveal its existence and the possibility of sharing in it. Hence the use of the verb φωτίζω**, 'to bring to light, reveal', both literally and meta-phorically (Eph 3.9; cf. 1 Cor 4.5; BA; for φῶς see 1 Tim 6.16).[65] The conceptualising of sin as darkness over against salvation as light is present, but there is no need to detect especially the language of Gnosticism or the mysteries (pace Conzelmann, H., TDNT IX, 349). The means of illumination is naturally διὰ τοῦ εὐαγγελίου, through the good news contained in the Christian message which took its beginning from Christ. No wonder that it is vital that the gospel be faithfully preserved in order to be powerfully effective in bringing salvation (Oberlinner, 44).

11. εἰς ὃ ἐτέθην ἐγὼ κῆρυξ καὶ ἀπόστολος καὶ διδάσκαλος The formal statement of the content of the gospel is followed by a personal statement regarding Paul's position as a proclaimer of it. The wording is paralleled in the fuller statement in 1 Tim 2.7: εἰς ὃ ἐτέθην ἐγὼ κῆρυξ καὶ ἀπόστολος, ἀλήθειαν λέγω οὐ ψεύδομαι, διδάσκαλος ἐθνῶν ἐν πίστει καὶ ἀληθείᾳ. The differences consist in omission of the words underlined. The stress on Paul's mission to the Gentiles is not needed in the present context. As a result the emphasis here falls more directly on the three nouns which sum up his role. Nevertheless, the effect is to focus on the gospel of which Paul is a servant and on the importance of proclaiming it (Fee, 231, 234) and the thought moves on quickly to the suffering which is inherent in the role. There is no indication that Paul was the only person to whom the gospel was committed; the article is conspicuously missing from the list of roles. And the tasks of proclamation and teaching

---

[64] Tit 2.7 TR; Rom 2.7; 1 Cor 15. 42, 50, 53, 54; Eph 6.24. The word belongs to higher Koine. Cf. BA; Wis 2.23; 6.19; 4 Macc 9.22; 17.12; Philo, Aet. 27; CH 12.14. It is frequent in the Apostolic Fathers, where the contrast between corruptibility and the incorruptibility brought by the gospel is common. Cf. Harder, G., TDNT IX, 93–106.

[65] The rendering 'showed us what immortal life really is' (Arichea-Hatton, 180) is too weak.

are shared with others. The stress is therefore less on the authority of the apostle and more on the importance of proclamation (cf. Oberlinner, 44f.).

12. δι' ἣν αἰτίαν καὶ ταῦτα πάσχω Although NA²⁷ punctuate this clause as a continuation of the previous sentence, it may be better to begin a fresh one, since this is not an appended thought but the goal towards which the passage has been moving.[66] It is because of his role as a preacher of this gospel that Paul is undergoing suffering. ταῦτα refers loosely to Paul's imprisonment, alluded to in 1.8, and the attendant hardships. πάσχω** can simply mean 'to undergo' in a neutral sense but here must mean 'to suffer, endure [a painful experience]'; it provides a verbal echo of συγκακο-πάθησον in 1.8. It is especially used of the sufferings of Christ (but not by Paul) and of the sufferings of believers especially through opposition and persecution, but the boundary between the sufferings of believers *qua* believers and the normal pains of life is quite vague.[67] No distinction is made between the sufferings of believers in general and proclaimers of the gospel in particular. Both situations inevitably entail the possibility of suffering, but here the writer is thinking especially of the latter.[68]

ἀλλ' οὐκ ἐπαισχύνομαι, οἶδα γὰρ ᾧ πεπίστευκα καὶ πέπεισμαι ὅτι δυνατός ἐστιν τὴν παραθήκην μου φυλάξαι εἰς ἐκείνην τὴν ἡμέραν The accent lies on this strong statement which in turn is eclipsed by the powerful affirmation of faith which is used to explain and buttress it. Despite his sufferings and imprisonment, Paul is 'not ashamed';[69] deliberately he puts himself forward as an example of the attitude which he commended to Timothy (1.8). The statement echoes Rom 1.16 and Phil 1.20 (αἰσχύνομαι). Whereas in v. 8 the thought was more of feeling shame because of the effects of proclaiming the gospel, here the thought may shift slightly to include the conviction that Paul does not feel that his work is in vain or that he has been let down by Christ. The language is not far in spirit from that of 2 Cor 4.8f.

---

[66] For δι' ἣν αἰτίαν starting a fresh sentence see 1.6.

[67] 1 Cor 12.26; 2 Cor 1.6; Gal 3.4; Phil 1.29; 1 Th 2.14; 2 Th 1.5. Cf. Michaelis, W., *TDNT* V, 904–24, especially 919–21.

[68] The function of καί perplexes the commentators: (a) It simply means 'correspondingly' and is used here as in the phrase διὸ καί (Holtzmann, 394). (b) It may qualify ταῦτα, i.e. these present sufferings (but not necessarily drawing a contrast with other, previous ones; Bernard, 111). (c) It qualifies πάσχω, giving the force that suffering is *also* part of his vocation (Alford and Ridderbos, cited by Knight, 378; so apparently Spicq, 718f.). (d) 'The καί, particularly as it goes with οὐκ ἐπαισχύνομαι, shows how necessary and almost natural suffering is' (W. Michaelis, ibid., 920). The last of these suggestions is too opaque to be helpful. Views (a) and (c) come to much the same thing.

[69] The verb can be used absolutely as here (BA).

This conviction is developed in the next statement. The object of the verb οἶδα[70] must be supplied from the pronoun ᾧ, which is used by relative attraction for αὐτὸν ᾧ (BA, 1182 [I.2.b.β]). The antecedent may be either God (cf. Tit 3.8; so here on grounds of the context Knight, 379) or, perhaps more probably, Christ (cf. 4.18; 1 Tim 1.16); maybe we should not attempt to make a choice, since it seems often that God the Father and Christ were so closely conjoined in Christian thought that the writers themselves were not consciously referring to one rather than the other. The verb is most commonly used for knowing facts, and thus could mean that Paul knows [about] the character of the One in whom he trusts; but it can also be used of personal acquaintance and of knowing or not knowing God.[71] Here the thought must be of a knowledge which conveys the fact that God is trustworthy, and a line between personal experience of God and knowledge about him would be hard to draw. Either way, the knowledge leads to a conviction about what God will do in the future for Paul.

Paul's relationship to God is therefore explained by the use of πεπίστευκα (Tit 3.8, also with dat. of God). The perfect expresses an abiding relationship with lasting consequences. The verb may be understood in two ways. (a) It may be used in its common New Testament sense: 'I have put my personal trust in him, namely, for my own salvation.' Or (b) it may anticipate the metaphor developed in the next clause; 'I have entrusted [my deposit] to him.' Again, a choice may be unnecessary; the writer is thinking of God's dependability for both himself and his work.

The main clause is continued with a repetition of πέπεισμαι (1.5), expressing a strongly felt conviction, as in Rom 8.28, of the ability of God to do what he promises; the thought and language (δυνατός ἐστιν) are paralleled in Rom 4.21; 11.23. The metaphor of the παραθήκη has already been used in 1 Tim 6.20 (see note) and is further used in 1.14*** (cf. the verb in 2.2; 1 Tim 1.18). The word signifies something deposited with a person to be kept undamaged and unused and returned to the owner, usually while he is absent on a journey. The reference here is disputed. 'My deposit' may mean:

(a) 'What God entrusted to me, Paul, namely, the gospel', which I have to preserve and proclaim.[72] Here the emphasis lies on the gospel itself.

[70] 1.15; 2.23; 3.14, 15; 1 Tim 1.8; *et al.*
[71] Tit 1.16; Gal 4.8; 1 Th 4.5; 2 Th 1.8.
[72] Bernard, 111; Easton, 45; Dibelius-Conzelmann, 105; Jeremias, 51; Barrett, 96f.; Kelly, 165f.; Spicq, 719f. (possibly also (b)); Brox, 234–6; Holtz, 160; Merkel, 60; C. Maurer, *TDNT* VIII, 162–4.

(b) 'What God entrusted to me, Paul', namely, the task of proclaiming the gospel, his 'office' as an apostle which he 'gives back' to the donor when he has completed it.[73]

(c) 'What God entrusted to me, Paul', namely the grace given for the task for ministry (a possibility suggested but not accepted by Barrett, 97).

(d) 'What I, Paul, have entrusted to God', i.e. primarily himself and all that is associated with him.[74] For this sense cf. Philo, *Her.* 129; Hermas, *Mand.* 3.2.

(e) 'What I, Paul, am entrusting to my successors'; what is elsewhere called 'my gospel' cf. Rom 2.16; 16.25; 2 Tim 2.8 (Marshall 1995:247 n. 21), or, as in (b), the task of preserving and proclaiming the gospel. The thought is then that, whatever happens to Paul personally, God will continue to guard the gospel which he hands over to Timothy. In view of the way in which it is called 'the good deposit' in v. 14, the reference must be to the gospel rather than to the task of proclaiming it (cf. Fee, 233).

We can exclude possibilities (a) (b) and (c) if the argument advanced by Wolter 1988:116–18, is sound, namely that in this phrase the gen. μου must indicate the depositor.[75] The fact that God is to do the guarding makes it certain that the deposit is made by Paul (Fee, 232). Possibility (d) reflects the common idea of committing oneself to God's care and keeping, especially *in extremis*,[76] and thus fits the broad context of the letter well. It also fits in with the reference to the 'day' of judgement. Nevertheless, possibility (e) fits in better with the thought in the immediate context (1.14; 2.2; cf. 1 Tim 6.20), and a shift in the use of the metaphor is unlikely. Hence Paul's statement provides a foundation for his injunction to Timothy: the God who has preserved the gospel during his own ministry will continue to do so for the future.

Most commentators take it that the deposit is the gospel (cf. 1.10), but it has also been claimed that it is more specifically the totality of Paul's teaching (Wegenast 1962:150–3; Wolter 1988:118–20; Schlarb 1990:230–9; Oberlinner, 47–50). These two interpretations, however, are scarcely distinguishable.

---

[73] RSV; GNB; NEB; Holtzmann, 397f.; Parry, 51f.; Guthrie, 144 (or (a)). Cf. Johnson, 55f., who wants to expand the term to cover Paul's whole way of life.

[74] NIV; NJB; NRSV t; Bengel, Lock, 88; White, 158; Simpson, 127; Fee, 232; Knight, 379f.; Arichea-Hatton, 182f.; Barclay*; Lau 1996:31–5.

[75] See Wolter, 117, for references, including Exod 22.7, 10, 2 Macc 3.10; Philo, *Spec.* 4.32; Josephus, *Bel.* 1.276; 3.372; Plutarch, *Antony* 21.3; *Lysander* 18.2. Cf. Schlarb 1990:230f.

[76] Ps 30 (MT 31).5; Wis 15.8; Lk 23.46; Acts 7.59; 1 Pet 4.19.

εἰς ἐκείνην τὴν ἡμέραν is clearly a reference to the parousia and day of judgement, and not to the day of Paul's death.[77] The phraseology reflects OT usage (Hos 1.5; Amos 2.16; 8.3, 9; *et al.*).

d. Injunction to hold fast to the gospel (1.13–14)

After the lengthy exposition of the gospel and Paul's relationship to it, the mood reverts to the imperative. But, whereas in vv. 6–8 the need was for Timothy to be bold and courageous in his witness to the gospel, here the demand is for holding fast to the truth. Thus the command takes up the theme of the 'deposit' which Paul is passing on to him and which was adumbrated in v. 12. There are two parallel commands. The first is to hold on to the pattern expressed in the 'healthy words' taught by Paul. This appears to refer specifically to Timothy's own way of life as a believer, especially since the command is accompanied by a reference to faith and love. The second command is to maintain the 'deposit', i.e. to prevent it being lost or altered, and for this purpose Timothy is reminded of the help of the Holy Spirit who is in believers. This combination of godly living and faithful preservation of the message is characteristic of the PE. The call to guard the gospel is appropriate in a letter in which the writer appears to be aware that he is at the end of his active ministry.

EXEGESIS

13. Ὑποτύπωσιν ἔχε ὑγιαινόντων λόγων ὧν παρ᾽ ἐμοῦ ἤκουσας ἐν πίστει καὶ ἀγάπῃ τῇ ἐν Χριστῷ Ἰησοῦ The word ὑποτύπωσις has already been used in 1 Tim 1.16***, where the merciful action of Christ towards Paul himself was said to act as a 'model' for subsequent believers. Most commentators take the word in the same sense here, that Paul's proclamation is to be a 'model' or 'standard' of sound preaching.[78] A suggested alternative is that the word means an 'outline', in the sense of a pattern or epitome that can be filled out in various ways,[79] but this is less likely in the context which stresses the maintenance of the gospel. The concept of 'healthy' teaching and speech is also familiar in the PE.[80] Here the reference is to the Christian teaching of Paul which Timothy has frequently heard directly

---

[77] Cf. 1.18; 4.8; 2 Th 1.10; Mt 7.22 24.19; pl. Mt 24.22, 29; 24.36; 26.29.

[78] Goppelt, L., *TDNT* VIII, 250. Cf. de Boer 1962:199f.

[79] REB; MM 661; Parry, xcviii; Simpson, 127; Guthrie, 145; Kelly, 166; Spicq, 721; Hanson, 124f.

[80] διδασκαλία, 4.3; Tit 1.9 and note; 2.1; 1 Tim 1.10; λόγοι, 1 Tim 6.3; λόγος, Tit 2.8.

from him.[81] He is to hold it, probably in the sense of holding fast to it.

The understanding of the sentence is complicated by two questions.

The first is whether the anarthrous ὑποτύπωσιν is used predicatively or is the object of the verb.

(a) The first alternative, taking the noun predicatively gives: 'Hold, as a pattern of sound words, in faith and love, what you heard from me.'[82] Despite its popularity, this interpretation seems to face an insurmountable obstacle in that the object is not expressed and must be supplied from the relative pronoun. ὧν must then stand for [αὐτοὺς] οὕς which is surely an impossible form of relative attraction. It can be taken as certain that ὧν is attraction of an original οὕς to the case of the antecedent. Holtzmann, 398, gets round the difficulty by seeing a case of brachylogy: the phrase τὴν ὑποτύπωσιν τῶν λόγων should be supplied to give the antecedent for the relative pronoun.[83]

Parry, xcvii–c, 52, in effect accepts this view but argues that ὑποτύπωσιν ἔχε is equivalent to the imperative ὑποτύπου with the force 'Keep representing [the] wholesome utterances heard from me by faith and love'. Timothy is constantly to represent or summarise in his life of faith and love the gospel teaching which he has received from Paul. On this view ὑποτύπωσις is not a pattern to be followed but 'a first sketch or outline, requiring to be filled up'. This gives an unlikely sense to the word, in view of the use in 1 Tim 1.16.

(b) The second possibility, taking the noun as the object of the verb, gives: 'Hold the pattern of sound words which you heard from me in faith and love.'[84] The absence of the article is awkward on this interpretation. It is also argued that the order of words and the use of ἔχε rather than κάτεχε (cf. 1 Cor 11.2; 15.2; 1 Th 5.21) prevent this interpretation.

---

[81] παρ' ἐμοῦ, repeated in 2.2; cf. 3.14; παρά curiously occurs only in 2 Tim of the PE: 1.18; 2.2; 3.14; 4.18*.

[82] REB mg; NIV; NJB; WH; Lock, 89; Easton, 44; Guthrie, 145; Dibelius-Conzelmann, 105; Spicq, 721; Lea-Griffin, 195. Some uncertainty is expressed by Barrett, 97; cf. Kelly, 166.

[83] Faced by what seemed to be insurmountable difficulties Hort (WH, *Notes*, 135) suggested a primitive corruption of the text with ὧν as an error for an original ὅν referring to an implied λόγον. This proposal is as difficult as the problem which it claims to solve.

[84] NRSV; GNB; REB t; Bernard, 112. The difference between this and the previous possibility is 'whether Paul was urging Timothy to keep what he had heard from Paul as a pattern of sound teaching (NIV) or to keep an outline of the sound teaching he had heard from Paul ... Was Timothy to make an outline of Paul's sound teaching, or was he to keep Paul's sound teaching as a pattern?' (Lea-Griffin, 195 n. 25).

Despite its awkwardness, the greater difficulties of the alternatives force us to accept the second interpretation. The absence of the article is tolerable, especially since the PE are notoriously free as regards its presence and absence. As regards the use of ἔχε, we have a similar usage in 1 Tim 3.9 and BA cite Diodorus Siculus 17.93.1, τὴν βασιλείαν ἔχειν, as a parallel. In any case the force of the command is scarcely affected.

The second question concerns the relationship of the final phrase ἐν πίστει καὶ ἀγάπῃ to the rest of the sentence. Three possibilities have been suggested:

(a) The phrase qualifies ἔχε, despite the lengthy separation of the words (Arichea-Hatton, 184).

(b) The phrase qualifies ἤκουσας as the nearest verb. But this seems weak.

(c) Punctuate with a full stop after ἤκουσας, so that the phrase goes with what follows: 'In faith and love ... guard the good deposit.' The suggestion achieved mention in the apparatus to UBS³, but it is hardly a natural order of words.

Despite the difficulty mentioned, view (a) is clearly right. The command is that Timothy's maintenance of orthodox teaching must be accompanied and backed up by a genuine Christian way of life involving faith in God and love to others. These qualities are given 'in Christ', i.e. arise from abiding in him (1 Tim 1.14 note).[85]

14. τὴν καλὴν παραθήκην φύλαξον διὰ πνεύματος ἁγίου τοῦ ἐνοικοῦντος ἐν ἡμῖν The second command to Timothy takes up the reference to Paul's 'deposit' from v. 12, but now characterises it as τὴν καλὴν παραθήκην. The language is paralleled in Philo, *Det.* 19 (ἐπιστήμης καλὴν παρακαταθήκην), but it should be seen rather in the context of the PE where καλός has the distinct sense of what is good because it is approved by God and has special reference to the gospel and whatever is associated with it (4.7; 1 Tim 1.18; 2.3; *et al.*). In the context the reference can hardly be to anything other than the content of the gospel which Paul has committed to Timothy and which he is to pass on faithfully to other teachers (2.2). It is unlikely that the reference is to the grace given to Timothy for the exercise of his ministry (a possibility discussed by Barrett, 98), still less to his own soul. The command to 'guard' the deposit is repeated from 1 Tim 6.20, where the parallel need to turn aside from error helps to explain the force. Already in v. 12 we had an expression of Paul's conviction that God himself would guard the deposit. Timothy, then, is to act as his agent and is therefore told to do what is

---

[85] Despite the sing. article, the sense requires that the phrase goes with both qualities.

needed so that God's purpose will be accomplished. What he is to do will in fact be done through the power of God given to him.[86] διὰ πνεύματος is a Pauline phrase (Rom 5.5; 8.11; 2 Cor 6.16. Cf. Jas 4.5), as is the use of ἐνοικέω (1.5*) for the presence of the Spirit in God's people (Rom 8.11; 2 Cor 6.16; Col 3.16; of sin Rom 7.17***). With or without this verb the preposition ἐν is used to express the relationship of the Spirit to Christians (Rom 8.9, 11; 1 Cor 3.16; cf. 2 Tim 1.6 of charisma). Elsewhere ἡμῖν in a statement of this kind would certainly apply to all believers (cf. Tit 3.5f.; Barrett, 98), but many commentators would want to restrict the reference here to Paul and Timothy as ministers who need the Spirit for a specific task.[87] It is best to conclude that the universal thought is present here, but that the thought is of the specific working of the Spirit to help Paul and Timothy in whatever they are particularly called to do.[88] According to Donelson 1986:143f., the effect of the statement is that the Spirit does not provide guidance on theology and ethics but only power to maintain the deposit and to live ethically. This is surely an unjustified argument from silence.

e. Paul's foes and friends (1.15–18)

Cabaniss, A., 'The Song of Songs in the New Testament', *Studies in English* 8 (1967), 53–6; Elliott, J. K., 'DIDOMI in 2 Timothy', *JTS* ns 19 (1968), 621–3; Gineste, B., '*Genomenos in rhômè (2Tm 1,17)*: Onésiphore a-t-il "été à Rome"?', *RevThom* 96 (1996), 67–106; Wilhelm-Hooijberg, A. E., 'In 2 Tim. 1:17 the Greek and Latin Texts may have a Different Meaning', in Livingstone, E. A., *Studia Biblica 1978* (Sheffield, 1980), III, 435–8; Willcock, J., 'St Matt. xxv.36; 2 Tim i.16–18', *ExpTim* 34 (1922–3), 43.

The exhortation to Timothy continues with a reminder of the way in which Paul has been abandoned by erstwhile supporters whose treachery stands out by comparison with the faithfulness of his friend Onesiphorus and his household. The first sentence is a straightforward statement that Paul has been abandoned by everybody in Asia, with two specific names mentioned. Then reference is made to the contrasting action and loyalty of Onesiphorus. Surprisingly, this is made initially in the form of a wish for the Lord to show mercy to his household because of what he has done. This is followed by a second wish for the Lord to show him mercy at the last day, and then comes what appears at first sight to be an appended comment about his service in Ephesus, of which Timothy is well aware. It seems

---

[86] Wolter 1988:43 draws attention to Ezek 36.27 for the connection between the gift of the Spirit and the keeping of God's commands.
[87] Holtzmann, 400; Scott, 97f.; Kelly, 167f.; Hanson, 125.
[88] Bernard, 112; Oberlinner, 52; Lips 1979:213f.; Fee 1994:790–2.

more likely, however, that it is the second wish (v. 18a) which is inserted as an aside, and that v. 18b is meant to be the direct continuation of v. 17.

The function of the section is partly clear and partly puzzling. It has the effect of corroborating and adding realism to the picture of Paul's suffering. However, it is not the suffering of persecution or physical pain which is the primary issue. Rather, it is implied, the fact of people who are ashamed of Paul and of the gospel makes Timothy's loyalty all the more necessary. By contrast Onesiphorus is an example of attitude to be emulated, and implicitly his example is intended to encourage Timothy to act likewise. The function is thus implicitly paradigmatic. The puzzling aspect is the double use of the wish that God will show mercy. It is so unusual that we need to ask why the wish needed to be uttered. The majority view is that it must be assumed that Timothy is aware that Onesiphorus has subsequently died, and therefore natural feelings for the welfare of his household are expressed. While this hypothesis may be possible if the letter is authentic, it is asking a lot of readers of a post-Pauline document to make this deduction. Rather, in an aside the author picks up the language of Onesiphorus finding Paul and plays on the word with reference to his finding mercy from the Lord. Although the closing reference to Onesiphorus' activity in Ephesus (v. 18b) may be explained as the sort of loose addition that is typical of epistolary composition, it is better to regard v. 18a as a parenthesis that interrupts the account of Onesiphorus's activities.

TEXT

15. Φύγελος The alternative spelling Φύγελλος is found in A TR *pc.* According to MHT II, 101, the spelling with -λ- is supported by inscriptions. According to Elliott, 124, the MSS tend both to double and reduce doublets (cf. 4.17); he accepts the alternative with hesitation, but it is difficult to see why it is the preferable option.

17. σπουδαίως σπουδαιότερον (D¹ Ψ TR syʰ); σπουδαιοτέρως (A 365 *pc*). Elliott, 125f., notes that σπουδαιότερον is the Attic form for the comparative adverb, whose non-Attic form σπουδαιοτέρως is found in Phil 2.28. He claims that the non-Attic form is original and was changed by scribes to either the simplex or the Attic form.

18. διηκόνησεν: add μοι (104 365 (inverted 629) *pc* it vgᶜˡ sy). Cf. Philem 13. Elliott, 127, omits the pronoun as unnecessary.

EXEGESIS

15. Οἶδας τοῦτο, ὅτι ἀπεστράφησάν με πάντες οἱ ἐν τῇ Ἀσίᾳ, ὧν ἐστιν Φύγελος καὶ Ἑρμογένης The phrase οἶδας τοῦτο (cf. 1 Tim 1.9 [participle] Eph 5.5 [pl.]) may be a literary device for conveying new information, since what is doubtless 'news' to Timothy follows; or it may introduce a mixture of old and new information. ἀποστρέφω (4.4; Tit 1.14) is used negatively of turning away from the truth of the gospel and, as here, of its representatives. οἱ ἐν τῇ Ἀσίᾳ most naturally refers to people in the Roman province of that name (cf. 2 Cor 1.8), but Bernard, 113, and Spicq, 732, wish to interpret it to refer to people from Asia in Rome, the latter arguing that ἐκ is a Hebraism for ἐν; but no parallel is adduced for this idiom. πάντες has been aptly described as 'the sweeping assertion of depression' (White, 159); it is no more part of a 'heroic picture' (*pace* Houlden, 114) than Phil 2.20f. It refers to all to whom he might have appealed for help at the time (Parry, 53). Presumably the desertion took place at the time of his arrest in Asia (Simpson, 129), and it may be that the two persons named later expressed solidarity with the opponents of Paul. με indicates that the defection was from Paul personally, not necessarily from the faith (Parry, 53; Dibelius-Conzelmann, 106; cf. 4.10), but in the light of the preceding verses it may well have included a rejection of Paul's version of Christian teaching.

For ὧν ἐστιν, 'including [for example]', see 2.17; 1 Tim 1.20 (where there is also a general reference to opponents followed by two specific names); cf. 1 Tim 1.15. Φύγελος is a name attested (only) in W. Asia.[89] The name Ἑρμογένης is more widely attested (BA; Josephus, *Ap.* 1.216). He is a character in the *Acts of Paul and Thecla* (*NTA* II, 353, 356f.) and the later *History of Abdias*). As with other named persons in the PE the question of their historicity arises. Three possibilities arise here:

(a) They are historical associates of Paul, whether in a genuine Pauline letter, or in a Pauline fragment contained in a later composition (Barrett, 98; Harrison), or known from oral tradition to the writer (Hanson, 126). Bernard, 113, and Spicq, 732, think they had been in Rome, turned away from Paul and returned to Asia.

(b) They are entirely fictitious (cf. Hasler, 60, who finds symbolical meaning in 'Phygelus', the cunning person who runs away from danger), whether as inventions by the author (Oberlinner, 55f.) or as accretions in oral tradition.

(c) The names are those of actual opponents of the pseudonymous author (cf. Merkel, 61). On the assumption of pseudonymity, this is unlikely, since it would split the fictional setting wide open.

Since there is no point in inventing names of opponents, the first possibility is much the most likely.

16. δῴη ἔλεος ὁ κύριος τῷ Ὀνησιφόρου οἴκῳ The second sentence is in effect a contrast to the first in that it describes the

---

[89] *CIG* II. 3027; Dittenberger, *Syll.* 599 n. 16; BD §42.3; MHT II, 101.

activity of one of Paul's supporters over against those who deserted him. It is couched in the form of a wish, for which Cl. Gk. used the optative mood.[90] The actual phrase διδόναι ἔλεος is a Hebraism,[91] although the LXX prefers ποιεῖν ἔλεος.

ἔλεος (1.2) recurs in the parallel statement in v. 18 where it is associated with the last day. But mercy is also something that God may grant to people here and now, and the content varies with the circumstances. In the salutation to the letter (1.2) mercy is a present blessing from God. God showed mercy to Paul at the time of his conversion (1 Tim 1.13, 16).[92] In the present context it may simply mean 'to do good' (Staudinger, F., *EDNT* I, 430). The wish here is a natural expression for care and protection by God for the household which has been bereft of its master. For the reference of ὁ κύριος (Christ) see 1.18. Ὀνησίφορος (4.19***) is a name which is attested in inscriptions[93] and recurs in *Acts of Paul and Thecla* (*NTA* II, 353–60, 364), where he is resident in Iconium. His οἶκος is his 'household', including his family and servants; greetings are addressed to them in 4.19. It may seem curious that in both places it is the household which is mentioned rather than simply Onesiphorus himself, and that in 4.19 the form of words might be held to exclude him (contrast 1 Cor 16.19; Col 4.15).[94] Possible reasons advanced are:

(a) Onesiphorus was now dead (Holtzmann, 401; and most subsequent commentators). The description, including the extra detail in v. 18b, may be thought to read rather like an obituary.

(b) He had left home whether to visit Paul in Rome or for some other reason (Simpson, 129; Dibelius-Conzelmann, 106; Guthrie, 148f.; Knight, 386).

---

[90] The opt. form δῴη is read here by NA[27]; it is also found in 1.18 (but is not the true text in 2.7; 4.14, where it is a weakly supported variant); Rom 15.5; 2 Th 3.16. The PE also use the subj. form δῷη, with which the opt. is easily confused (2.25). Elliott, 166f., argues for reading δῷη here, as a rare example of the jussive subj. This proposal is unnecessary and unlikely. Paul undoubtedly uses the opt. for wishes (Rom 15.13) and the PE certainly have the opt. in a wish (2 Tim 4.16); MHT III, 129 conclude that the verb here 'cannot be anything else than the optative'. According to MHT III, 94, the 2nd and 3rd person jussive subj. was not acceptable in Attic. There are some examples in inscriptions (V–III BC) and in post-Christian Greek (Ignatius, *Poly.* 8.3; Barnabas 19.1), but they are all aorists and could be confused with the fut. There was confusion in Attic poetry between the subj. and opt. for wishes, and this prepared the way for the use of the jussive subj. in Koine.

[91] Deut 13.17 (MT 18); Josh 11.20; Isa 47.6; Jer 16.13; 49 [42].12; Mic 7.20; cf. Dan 1.9Θ.

[92] See further Mk 5.19; Phil 2.27; Hermas, *Vis.* 1.3.2.

[93] *New Docs.* IV, 181f. §97.

[94] There are contextual reasons for the separation of the householder(s) and the household in Rom 16.3–5; Philem 1f.

From 1 Cor 1.16; 16.15–18 it is clear that the phrase 'the household of Stephanas' could be used while Stephanas was alive and probably means 'Stephanas and his family'. That Onesiphorus was still alive is assumed in Ps-Ignatius, *ad Hero* 9 (AD IV) who uses this prayer for praying for the living (Bernard, 114). The fact that the rest of the household supported him (and Paul) and may have been involved in some sacrifice for Paul's sake is ample reason for the width of the reference (cf. Oberlinner, 59f.).

ὅτι πολλάκις με ἀνέψυξεν καὶ τὴν ἅλυσίν μου οὐκ ἐπαισχύνθη
Onesiphorus is commended for three things. He had frequently (πολλάκις*) given Paul refreshment. ἀναψύχω*** ('to revive, refresh') is used of giving food and similar help.[95] Also he was not ashamed to be loyal to Paul (1.8, 12)[96] when the latter was a prisoner wearing a hand-fetter (ἅλυσις).[97] His loyalty to Paul and his gospel was thus apparent (cf. Oberlinner, 59).

17. ἀλλὰ γενόμενος ἐν ῾Ρώμῃ σπουδαίως ἐζήτησέν με καὶ εὗρεν
Finally, he had visited Paul, presumably in prison. γενόμενος has the force 'when he was in'.[98] The fact that Onesiphorus sought Paul in ῾Ρώμῃ[99] indicates beyond all doubt that he believed (rightly or wrongly) that Paul was there; it is therefore impossible to set the (real or dramatic) date of this episode before Paul's visit to Rome, unless we envisage a time shortly before when Paul was known or believed to be on his way there.[100] For the literal sense of ζητέω, 'to seek for' (without necessarily knowing where the object is to be found), cf. Jn 18.4, 7, 8; Acts 10.19, 21. Onesiphorus' zeal (σπουδαίως, Tit 3.13) emphasises that it was necessary to search hard in order to find Paul (εὑρίσκω 1.18**) and that he continued until he was successful;[101] his whereabouts were not a matter of common knowledge.[102] If the comparative is read (see textual note), the

[95] Cl.; LXX; Josephus, *Ant.* 15.54; Ignatius, *Eph.* 2.1; *Trall.* 12.2; intrans., Rom 15.32 *v.l.*; cf. ἀνάψυξις, Col 4.11; *TLNT* I, 120f.
[96] The absence of the augment with ἐπαισχύνθη is Ionic.
[97] Eph 6.20; Acts 28.20; Mk 5.3f; Lk 8.29; Acts 12.6f.; 21.33; Rev 20.1***.
[98] This is a common use (Mt 26.6; Mk 9.33; Acts 7.38; 13.5; Rev 1.9). Cf. BA, *s.v.* II.4; Spicq, 734. Wilhelm-Hooijberg* claims that the participle refers to a point in time before the action of the main verb, i.e. that after he had been in Rome, Onesiphorus searched for Paul elsewhere, namely in Caesarea. But, if so, why was Rome mentioned?
[99] Acts 18.2; 19.21; 23.11; 28.14, 16; Rom 1.7, 15***.
[100] On the possibilities of travel at this time note the inscription concerning Flavius Xeuxis of Hierapolis who visited Italy 72 times in the course of his business (Holtz, 162).
[101] A deliberate allusion to Ct 3.1 is detected by Cabaniss*.
[102] This would suggest that a different condition of imprisonment is envisaged from that in Acts 28.30f., where it was common knowledge where Paul was; cf. Kelly, 170.

force is 'very eagerly'. Robinson 1976:76 wishes to interpret the
sentence to mean something like: 'he did not find me in Rome,
but carried on elsewhere until he did.' It is difficult to extract
this sense, even if one is allowed to assume that the recipient of
the letter knew more about the presumed situation than we do.

18. δῴη αὐτῷ ὁ κύριος εὑρεῖν ἔλεος παρὰ κυρίου ἐν ἐκείνῃ
τῇ ἡμέρᾳ The wording of the wish in v. 16 is now repeated with
some changes. The meaning of the verb δῴη shifts naturally
from 'give' to 'grant' with the inclusion of the infinitive. The
resulting phrase εὑρεῖν ἔλεος, 'to find mercy', is common in
the LXX.[103] But the most important change is the addition
of ἐν ἐκείνῃ τῇ ἡμέρᾳ (cf. 1.12 [εἰς]) which must refer to the
day of judgement. The duplication of the reference to the Lord
by the addition of the phrase παρὰ κυρίου is curious but has a
precedent (Gen 19.24). Here it is most probably due to a mixture
of constructions: (a) 'The Lord grant him to find mercy'; and
(b) 'May he find mercy from the Lord' (Jeremias, 52f.). In
view of the NT usage of κύριος for both God and Christ the
reference of the two nouns is disputed. Out of the four possible
permutations commentators are fairly unanimous in adopting
the view that ὁ κύριος is Christ and κυρίου is God.[104] Nauck
1950:29f. notes that in the Tg. the phrase 'from the Lord' is
taken to mean 'from heaven'.

On the assumption that Onesiphorus was already dead, this
wish has been regarded as a prayer for the dead (So Parry, 54;
Bernard, 114; and many commentators; cf. 2 Macc 12.43–45;
early Christian inscriptions mentioned by Bernard). But this is by
no means the right interpretation.[105] It is true that some wishes
are equivalent to prayers (e.g. Rom 15.13 ; 1 Th 3.11–13; 5.23).
Here, however, the wish is simply the expression of what has
been called 'only a natural feeling' (Scott, 99) with no theological
significance (cf. Fee, 237). The explanation that Onesiphorus
was simply absent from home for a protracted period is also
possible, in which case the wish is that in due course the promise

---

[103] Gen 19.19; Dan 3.38 Θ; Dan 9.3 LXX; cf. Gen 6.8 (grace); 18.3; 30.27;
32.5; 33.8, 10, 15; 34.11; 39.4; 47.25, 29; 50.4.
[104] Holtzmann, 374–5, claims that in general anarthrous κύριος is God,
and arthrous κύριος is Christ.
[105] See especially Oberlinner, 64, who argues rightly that there is no proof that
Onesiphorus is regarded as dead, and that the question lies outside the horizon
of the PE. Nevertheless, he maintains that since confidence in God for the hope
of eternal life is a certainty of faith that extends beyond death, to exclude prayer
for the dead would be a contradiction of the teaching of the PE. On the contrary,
it is precisely because believers 'die safely' that there is no need to pray for their
salvation after they have died; if they are numbered among 'the dead in Christ',
Christians know that 'they will rise first' and have no need to pray for this to
happen; rather they can confidently thank God that it will happen.

in Mt 25.36 will be fulfilled for him. In any case it is notable that essentially the same wish is expressed in respect of living persons in v. 16, where there is no reason to suppose that the action and attitude of Onesiphorus, which were presumably shared by the household, are a basis for ultimate acceptance by God at the judgement. We thus have a two-stage reference to mercy, corresponding to the contrast between life now and life to come in 1 Tim 4.8. An allusion to the motif in Mt 5.7; 25.36 is unavoidable. But the hope of divine blessing rests on God's mercy, not on good works! 'Neither Onesiphorus nor Paul can evoke the mercy of God. God grants mercy because he is merciful' (Barrett, 100).

But why is the wish expressed at all? Maybe the best answer is that there is a play on words with εὑρεν in the preceding verse (Bengel), which led the writer to repeat the wish in v. 17 with an appropriate change in wording. V. 18b then becomes in effect parenthetic.

καὶ ὅσα ἐν Ἐφέσῳ διηκόνησεν, βέλτιον σὺ γινώσκεις καί introduces what is generally regarded as an afterthought. But, if what was said above is correct, it is a continuation of the sentence begun in v. 17 after a parenthetical wish. ὅσα with the antecedent omitted has the force 'and all [the things] that' (1 Tim 6.1**). The implication is that Onesiphorus was a native of Ἔφεσος (4.12; 1 Tim 1.30), where he had been active in the church (διακονέω, 1 Tim 3.10, 13**; cf. διακονία, 4.5, 11). The likelihood is that this refers to service in general, or to fulfilling the task of a deacon, rather than to helping Paul personally. The point is that Timothy already knows his reputation through being on the spot.[106]

II. EXHORTATION TO BE STRONG AND TO ENDURE SUFFERING
(2.1–13)

The structure of this part of the letter is determined by a series of imperatives: vv. 1f., 3, 7, 8. These are followed by material that backs them up (vv. [2b], 4–6, 9f., 11–13).

The passage begins with a general call to be strong. This is directly linked to a much more concrete command to commit Paul's message to trustworthy people who will act as teachers. For this combination of the general and the particular cf. Tit 1.5. Then there is a repetition of the command to take a share in suffering (1.8), like a soldier. This is immediately backed up by

---

[106] βέλτιον** is elative, conveying the sense 'very well' (Acts 10.28D; Acts 4.16D; cf. Acts 24.22; 25.10; Jn 13.27; BD §244²; MHT III, 30); it might just possibly be comparative: 'better [than I know]'; cf. Dibelius-Conzelmann, 106).

a general remark on military service requiring single-mindedness. Two further metaphorical comments based on athletics and farming follow; these appear to make quite different points, but they are linked by the common themes of single-mindedness and devotion to duty and the assurance of ultimate reward. It is perhaps not surprising that Timothy is then told to think carefully about what is being said.

All this is backed up by a further command to remember the resurrection of Jesus, which is the guarantee that God will vindicate his cause, but this leads into a more important statement about the sufferings of Paul and the purpose which motivates them; this has a paradigmatic function (Donelson 1986:104). A 'trustworthy statement' about the need for faithfulness culminates with a powerful expression of the faithfulness of God and backs up the instruction. Thus the appeal to Timothy is buttressed by the use of general principles, by appeal to the example of Christ[1] and to the sufferings of Paul himself, and by a trustworthy saying about the need for union with Christ in suffering. The motif of readiness for suffering and the consequent need for perseverance thus runs through the section and dominates it.

a. Be strong and single-minded (2.1–7)

Harris, R., 'Pindar and St. Paul', *ExpTim* 33 (1921–2), 456f.

The surface structure is clear enough. (a) The opening sentence (vv. 1–2) contains two separate commands to be strong and to pass on Paul's message to a wider group of teachers. (b) Timothy is encouraged to share in Paul's sufferings like a soldier enduring hardship (v. 3).[2] (c) This command is backed up by a general remark about the single-minded obedience demanded of soldiers (v. 4). (d) Two further metaphorical remarks are added about the need for athletes to keep the rules in order to win a prize, and for farmers to work hard to get the first share of the harvest (vv. 5, 6). (e) Timothy is urged to think about the significance of this, with the assurance that the Lord will enable him to understand it (v. 7).

The development of the theme is apparently broken by v. 2 which picks up the 'deposit' theme from 1.11–14 but stands apart from the rest of the section. The explanation of this is that

---

[1] While there is a strong emphasis on Christ in this passage, the general heading 'Christ Jesus as the model for Timothy's conduct' (Arichea-Hatton, 189) is misleading.

[2] Oberlinner, 65, observes that the three imperatives in vv. 1–3 correspond to activities of Paul himself.

vv. 1–2 are to be regarded as recapitulating and concluding what was said in 1.6–14 after the 'digression' in 1.15–18. The call is to loyalty to Paul and his gospel both in Timothy's own life and through gathering a team of faithful workers for the future to whom Paul's deposit can be passed. It follows that the main emphasis is on Timothy himself and his own loyalty to Paul and his gospel, and that the injunction to pass on the teaching to other faithful people is of secondary importance (Johnson, 61–3). With v. 3 the theme of readiness for the hardships and trials of the ministry is then resumed. Thus the two themes of 1.6–14, courageous bearing of witness and faithful maintenance of the message which has been handed down to Timothy, are brought together. There is, accordingly, a case for making the division at 2.2/3 rather than 1.18/2.1, but it is less likely that we should do so, since 2.1f. has more the appearance of a new start with a summing up or conclusion of the previous instruction before the introduction of new material.

TEXT

3. συγκακοπάθησον κακοπάθησον (1175 lat); σὺ οὖν κακοπάθησον (C³ D¹ Hᶜ Ψ 1881ᶜ TR syʰ; possibly a corruption of συν-). Elliott, 128f., states that scribes altered the text because of the rarity of the word and dislike of compounds. Metzger, 579, explains the TR reading as being influenced by v. 1 and the lack of any indication as to what the prefix referred to. On the spelling see 1.8 note.

4. στρατευόμενος Add τῷ θεῷ (F G it vgᶜˡ· ʷʷ Cyp Ambst); cf. 1 Tim 1.18. The variant is an interpretative addition to avoid misinterpretation (Elliott, 129).

πραγματείαις πραγματίαις (‏ℵ‎ D F G K Ψ 1739 al.; Kilpatrick). Elliott, 130, argues that the text is the Cl. form and is therefore secondary Atticising. But see MHT II, 339, who argue that the variant is due to itacising.

ἀρέσῃ ἀρέσκῃ (69* Origen). Despite very weak evidence, the variant is accepted by Elliott, 130, on the grounds that the scribal tendency was to alter presents to aorists.

6. πρῶτον πρότερον (‏ℵ‎*). The variant is sheer error, evident from study of the MS where the scribe started to write correctly (Elliott, 130).

7. ὅ ἅ (‏ℵ‎² D H Ψ 1881 TR lat syʰ). Cf. 1 Tim 1.7; probably the sing. is original (Elliott, 131).

δώσει δωη (C³ H Ψ 181 TR). Elliott, 167, understands the variant as δώῃ, an unusual subj. form which could be misread as an opt.; the text is to be explained as a correction. But surely the indic. is required here, especially in view of the following γάρ.

EXEGESIS

1. Σὺ οὖν, τέκνον μου, ἐνδυναμοῦ ἐν τῇ χάριτι τῇ ἐν Χριστῷ ᾿Ιησοῦ The emphatic σὺ οὖν draws a conclusion from what has just preceded. In effect it links back to 1.13f. after the digression in 1.15–18, but it does so in such a way that these verses are taken into account; thus 2.1 draws a lesson from the good and bad examples in 1.15–18 and 2.2 picks up 1.13f. (cf. Arichea-Hatton, 190). Timothy himself is encouraged to draw on divine strength to sustain him in the difficult situation where 'everybody' has deserted Paul and in order to emulate the good example on Onesiphorus. The motif is linked by Wolter 1988:215–18 to the concept of grace and strength being given to a person who is being installed as a successor, like Joshua to Moses.[3]

For the use of emphatic σύ in exhortation see 3.10; 1 Tim 6.11. The intimate address τέκνον μου picks up on the description of Timothy in 1.2 and adds force to the command. The life and service of the Christian believer should be characterised by the strength and power to do what God requires, by contrast with that of apostates who profess religion but lack the spiritual force that should be associated with it (3.5).

The form ἐνδυναμοῦ could be mid. (Lock, 93) or pass. The verb is used in the act. in 4.17 and 1 Tim 1.12 (see note); hence the force here is probably passive 'let yourself be strengthened by' (Bernard, 116).[4] The command expresses the thought of 1.6f. in different language: there the thought was of the Holy Spirit as the source of spiritual power, but here the source is divine grace. ἐν τῇ χάριτι is to be understood instrumentally as in Eph 6.10,[5] rather than locatively (Rom 4.20; Fee, 239f.). Grace (1.2; Tit 1.4 note) is here thought of as a powerful influence,[6] rather than simply as unmerited favour (pace Guthrie, 149). The thought is quite general; a special gift of grace to church leaders is not in mind; a limited reference to grace mediated at ordination (Oberlinner, 66) is too static. In the qualifying phrase τῇ ἐν Χριστῷ Ἰησοῦ the repetition of the article after a noun with adverbial phrase is correct style. The force of the phrase is, as usual, difficult to define (1 Tim 1.14 note). It may mean: (a) 'the grace which is to be found in Christ'; (b) 'the grace which is displayed in Christ'; (c) 'the grace which is obtained through fellowship with Christ' (Kelly, 172). The first of these possibilities is probably correct with the third linked with it: grace is given by God in Christ Jesus and is therefore received by being united to him through faith.

2. καὶ ἃ ἤκουσας παρ' ἐμοῦ διὰ πολλῶν μαρτύρων, ταῦτα παράθου πιστοῖς ἀνθρώποις, οἵτινες ἱκανοὶ ἔσονται καὶ ἑτέρους διδάξαι The second part of the command takes up 1.13f. The rel. pron. ἃ anticipates the following ταῦτα. The reference is a

---

[3] Deut 3.28; 31.7; Josh 1.6, 7, 18; Philo, *Virt.* 66–71; *Ass. Moses* 10.15; cf. also 1 Macc 2.64 for the same motif.

[4] Nauck 1950:22 claims that the imper. functions as an opt., i.e. it is effectively a wish by Paul for Timothy.

[5] GNB; Spicq, 737; cf. διὰ τῆς χάριτος, 1 Clement 55.3.

[6] Holtzmann, 403; cf. Nolland, J., 'Grace as power', *NovT* 28 (1986), 26–31.

general one to Paul's teaching, which is regarded as in effect a tradition to be handed on (cf. 1 Th 2.13; 1 Cor 11.2). The phrase ἤκουσας παρ' ἐμοῦ is repeated from 1.13. It indicates incidentally that the form of Christian instruction was oral rather than written at this point, but the main thrust is that it is what Timothy has heard from Paul that is to be passed on. 1.13f. was concerned with Timothy's own hearing and preaching; here the reference is to passing on this same message for others to hear and then teach.

The phrase διὰ πολλῶν μαρτύρων (cf. ἐνώπιον κτλ., 1 Tim 6.12) must qualify Timothy's hearing of Paul's words. The usual sense of διά with gen. of person is 'through the agency of'. Taking διά as instrumental in this way we get 'through the intervention of many witnesses', i.e. persons who could testify to what Paul had said and supplement Timothy's own knowledge (Bernard, 116; Guthrie, 150f.). Easton, 48f., interprets on the basis that the letter presumes that Paul is dead; the real recipients, 'various "Timothys" hear what he had said through intermediaries' (similarly, Merkel, 62f.). On either of these views the phrase παρ' ἐμοῦ is odd. Other explanations of the phrase, such as 'on the authority of many witnesses' to facts of the gospel 'outside Paul's own experience' (Parry, 54), or 'with the citation of many authorities' (Scripture, prophets, etc.) or 'with many forms of instruction' are unnecessary and unlikely. According to BA 361 the mediation can become actual presence, giving the sense 'in the presence of (supported by) many witnesses'.[7] The phrase is thus equivalent to the more common ἐπὶ μαρτύρων. The significance is that there are *many* people who could give their attestation as to what Paul had actually said. This would be at once a warning against any attempt to falsify what Paul had said, a reminder that any lapses of memory could be remedied by appeal to such witnesses, but also an encouragement to Timothy that what he preaches as the gospel received from Paul is backed up by many other people. The reference to witnesses is taken by most commentators to imply a formal occasion, e.g. Timothy's baptism or, more probably, commissioning[8] and the transfer of tradition in a formulated manner (Dibelius-Conzelmann, 108; Brox, 240). But nothing in the text demands such an interpretation, and a reference to what Timothy (and others) had heard on numerous occasions is perhaps more probable (cf. Guthrie, 149; Oberlinner, 68f.).

[7] Cf. Philo, *Leg. Gai.* 187: τὸ διὰ μαρτύρων κλαίειν; Plutarch, *Mor.* 338F: διὰ θεῶν μαρτύρων; Chrysostom, *PG* LXII, 619 (Field 1899:215); White, 160; Lock, 93; Simpson, 130; Moule 1953:57; Trites, 210; Oepke, A., *TDNT* II, 66.

[8] Holtzmann, 403; Dibelius-Conzelmann, 108; Spicq, 738; Brox, 240; Simpson, 130; Lips 1979:181f.

There is no need to define more closely who are meant by the witnesses, e.g. that they are the elders of 1 Tim 4.14 (Holtzmann, 403; Lock, 93) or Christian preachers in general (Hasler, 61f.) or Timothy's relatives. They are more probably the many people who have also heard Paul's message, 'the church at large' (Barrett, 101).

The statement naturally implies the continuing authority and validity of Paul's teaching. It also indicates that the tradition is open, well known and not esoteric (Barrett, 101). The need for passing it on arises because of the presence of opponents. But nothing suggests that Paul is the only channel of true tradition in the church as a whole; the horizon is simply the churches founded by Paul and for which he is the apostle. The suspicions of Hasler, 61, about rivalry with Peter and John are without a basis in the text. Moreover, what is important here is the message, and the 'reliable men' are important only in that they preserve and teach it and not because of any office that they hold (cf. Fee, 240). By contrast the important section in 1 Clement 42 is concerned purely with the appointment of overseers and deacons by the apostles and shows less interest in the preservation of the message (cf. Hasler, 62).

The verb παράθου is repeated from 1 Tim 1.18 (note), where Paul committed the 'charge' to Timothy. Now it is Timothy's task to commit the παραθήκη to others. The true teaching is preserved and spread by passing it to responsible people who will preserve it unchanged. The choice of appropriate people is important. They must obviously be πιστοί in the sense of 'reliable, trustworthy' (1 Tim 1.12 note; cf. Isa 8.2). The stress is on trustworthiness, not on ordination! Although ἄνθρωποι could be inclusive, probably only males are in mind (Knight, 391). οἵτινες is 'of a kind who' (1.5; 2.18), and ἱκανός** here means 'competent, able'.[9] The future ἔσονται is used because their activity lies in the future after they have been taught what to say. The implication found by some commentators that Timothy alone is the teacher at this time, but he is to prepare a plurality of teachers for the future after he is no longer active is dubious. The thought is rather that Timothy is to develop the ministry of teaching in the local congregations by preparing more people to give sound teaching. The activity of teaching is the same as that of Paul himself (1.11) and is an integral part of church leadership (1 Tim 3.2). Both the spread and the continuation of the work are in mind. Thus the expansion of the mission and witness is spatial (extending the scope here and now) as well as

---

[9] *TLNT* II, 217–22; for the combination with a verb to speak, cf. Josephus, *Ant.* 3.49.

temporal (preparing for the future). καὶ ἑτέρους (cf. 1 Tim 1.10) is a widening circle of 'others also' in addition to themselves. The horizon does not extend further than this. Yet, although it is not stated that these 'others' will also go on to teach in their turn, nothing excludes this possibility. The main point is that the people taught by Timothy must be both reliable and capable of teaching.

Some commentators find here the beginnings of a doctrine of 'apostolic succession',[10] or, more precisely 'Pauline succession' (Brox, 241). The *prima facie* historical situation is that Timothy is leaving Ephesus to be with Paul in Rome and providing for the needs of the church during his own absence (Fee, 240). If the letter is pseudonymous, the picture may be of Paul providing for people in the future to reproduce his teaching faithfully. The context implies that Timothy might act several times rather than on one single occasion despite the use of the aor. imper. (cf. 2.3; 4.2; McKay 1985:208). There is dispute whether the text envisages Timothy appointing people to be teachers and leaders (Lips 1979:181f.; Oberlinner, 67f.) or simply instructing people who will teach others (Wolter 1988:234); certainly the passing on of the teaching is in the foreground.

3. Συγκακοπάθησον ὡς καλὸς στρατιώτης Χριστοῦ Ἰησοῦ After concluding the topic of Paul's deposit to Timothy, the author returns to the theme of being prepared for suffering personally. Houlden, 116, claims to detect an artificial heroism. There is in his view a less paradoxical view of suffering than one finds in Paul; it does not arise out of mystical union with Christ, and there is no mention of Christ's suffering. This assertion is surely disproved by the presence of 2.11 in the context.

The use of συγκακοπάθησον recalls 1.8 (see note); the theme recurs with the use of the simplex, κακοπαθέω in 2.9; 4.5. Timothy is called to suffer (not simply 'endure hardship', as NIV) with Paul and other Christians. According to Heb 13.23 he did suffer imprisonment (and subsequent release). Nevertheless, the thought is not necessarily of martyrdom but of the self-denial and privation that may have to be endured, just as a soldier is not free to please himself (Oberlinner, 69f.). The basis and character of the hardships to be endured is developed by the metaphor of military service (cf. Bauernfeind, O., *TDNT* VII, 711f.). ὡς has the sense 'as befits [what you really are]'. Elsewhere in the NT στρατιώτης** is always used literally, but the term συνστρατιώτης is used metaphorically for Christian workers (Phil 2.25; Philem 2). The word generally refers to professional soldiers, not conscripts, and to NCOs rather than officers (Spicq,

---

[10] Scott, 100f.; *contra* Kelly, 174; Hasler, 62. See 1 Clement 42; 44.2.

740). καλός here has the role of expressing the quality of the service required rather than of indicating its Christian character (as, for example, in 4.7). The addition of Χριστοῦ Ἰησοῦ brings Christ into the metaphor in the role of military commander. This thought is then developed in the next verse.

4. **οὐδεὶς στρατευόμενος ἐμπλέκεται ταῖς τοῦ βίου πραγματείαις, ἵνα τῷ στρατολογήσαντι ἀρέσῃ** We now have a further development of the military metaphor, which forms the first of a series of three, proverbial-sounding statements. The themes are in fact those of the diatribe genre of literature (Dibelius-Conzelmann, 108) and are typical illustrations in Hellenistic moral teaching.[11] They echo metaphors already used in 1 Cor 9 – the soldier, 9.7a (cf. 1 Th 5.8); the athlete, 9.24–27; and the farmer, 9.7b (vineyard and flock) – but they are used in a different manner. The first of the three illustrations goes beyond the original point of the military metaphor in v. 3 to make a fresh application, and all three appear at first sight to have different applications from one another. We seem to have an example of the collection of loosely associated sayings found in works like Prov. Nevertheless, there is a certain coherence about the illustrations in that all of them indicate the need for commitment and the readiness for acceptance of a demanding way of life by the Christian leader. In the case of the soldier the point is the need to avoid other commitments which would prevent single-mindedness in serving Christ. It is a call to readiness for the stiff regime that characterises military life.

The metaphor of Christian leadership as military service has already been used in 1 Tim 1.18 and is common in Paul with various applications.[12] στρατευόμενος (1 Tim 1.18) probably conveys the sense of being actively engaged on military service (Spicq, 740f.) rather than simply being a soldier by profession (White, 161). ἐμπλέκω is 'to entangle', lit. of sheep caught in thorns (Hermas, *Sim.* 6.2.6f.), here metaphorically (2 Pet 2.20***).[13] πραγματεία*** is 'activity, occupation',[14] and βίος is everyday life (1 Tim 2.2). The whole phrase is well paralleled in Philo, *Spec.* 2.65: αἱ περὶ βίον πραγματείαι. Here the thought is of the affairs of civilian life according to the general principle affirmed in the *Codex Theodosianus* (Wetstein): *Militares viros civiles curas arripere prohibemus* (cf. Plutarch, *Aem.* 12); money-making

---

[11] Cf. Epictetus 3.15, 24; 4.8; Johnson, 62.

[12] Rom 6.13; 7.23; 1 Cor 9.7; 2 Cor 6.7; Eph 6.11–18. See also Ignatius, *Poly.* 6.2.

[13] Cl.; cf. Epictetus 3.22.69; Polybius 24.11.3: τοῖς Ἑλληνικοῖς πράγμασιν ἐμπλεκόμενος.

[14] Cl.; *TLNT* III, 149–51. Cf. Maurer, C., *TDNT* VI, 640f., who denies the restriction to 'business as a means of livelihood', *pace* Jeremias, 53.

and gaining a livelihood are meant.[15] The things forbidden are not necessarily wrong in themselves, but they are a distraction to a soldier (Easton, 51).

The purpose of the self-restraint is to give undivided attention to carrying out the commander's orders. στρατολογέω*** is originally 'to gather an army, enlist soldiers',[16] and hence, by implication, to be the commander. It is unlikely that the term is intended to arouse thoughts of divine calling/election. ἀρέσκω**, 'to please' (with dat.), is freq. in Paul. especially of pleasing God;[17] there is no particular significance in the use of the aor.[18] The language is echoed in Ignatius, Poly. 6.2: ἀρέσκετε ᾧ στρατεύεσθε, where the military metaphor is developed at length.

The application of the metaphor is essentially a call to single-minded service, a warning not to be preoccupied with the things of the world and the rewards that they bring.[19] Some have seen a specific command not to engage in commerce. Others, even more specifically, think that Timothy is being told not to follow Paul's own example of working to maintain himself if thereby the gospel suffers (Holtzmann, 405; Spicq, 742; Hanson, 129). Those who are supported by the church should be content with what the church gives them. It is very doubtful whether the application is so specific.

5. ἐὰν δὲ καὶ ἀθλῇ τις, οὐ στεφανοῦται ἐὰν μὴ νομίμως ἀθλήσῃ ἐὰν δὲ καί, 'but even if, but also if' (1 Cor 7.11, 28), introduces a fresh point here. Not only military service but also other occupations confirm the lesson that is being drawn. Nevertheless, the point comes across somewhat differently. ἀθλέω*** is 'to compete in a contest' (Cl.; 1 Clement 5.2; 2 Clement 20.2), and the combination with νομίμως is traditional.[20] The reference is to professionals, not to amateurs (Spicq, 742f.). No significance should be attached to the fact that, whereas the aim of the soldier should be to please the commander, here the athlete's aim is to win the prize for himself. στεφανόω is 'to wreathe, crown'.[21] For νομίμως see 1 Tim 1.8.

[15] Cf. Philo, Mos. 2.211, 219, of activities forbidden on the Sabbath.
[16] Hel.; Josephus, Bel. 5.380; TLNT III, 300.
[17] Rom 8.8; 1 Cor 7.32; 1 Th 2.15; 4.1; cf. Foerster, W., TDNT I, 455f.
[18] For the stress placed on obedience in a military context, as here, Spicq, 741, cites Aeneas Tacticus, Polyor. 165.; Epictetus 3.24.32–6.
[19] Cf. 1 Cor 7.26–34 (White, 161) and the warning to the rich in Hermas, Vis. 3.6 (Guthrie, 152; Kelly, 175; Fee, 242; Merkel, 63).
[20] Galen, ad Hippocr. Aphor. 18: οἱ γυμνασταὶ καὶ οἱ νομίμως ἀθλοῦντες (Wetstein); Epictetus 3.10.8: ὁ θεός σοι λέγει; δός μοι ἀπόδειξιν εἰ νομίμως ἤθλησας (cited by Parry, 55). Cf. MM 429.
[21] 2.9; Heb 2.7 (= Ps 8.6)***; 2 Clement 7.1, cf. 2f.; Hermas, Sim. 8.3.6; 8.4.6; Man. 12.2.5; M. Poly. 17.1. cf. στέφανος, 2 Tim 4.8.

The literal reference may be to the rules of a particular contest (Arichea-Hatton, 194) or to the general rules for athletes, which required, for example, ten months of prior training. On the latter view the reference is not so much to keeping the rules as to the element of self-discipline which was entailed (Kelly, 175f.). The application will be in terms of following the commands of Christ. A reference to specific rules for leaders[22] is unlikely. The call is thus again for self-denying service under a strict regime.

6. τὸν κοπιῶντα γεωργὸν δεῖ πρῶτον τῶν καρπῶν μεταλαμβάνειν The third illustration is drawn from the work of the farmer; γεωργός** (Mk 12.1–9 par.; Jn 15.1; Jas 5.7) signifies here a peasant farmer living off his land. The hard work required of him is proverbial (Prov 20.4). For κοπιάω see 1 Tim 4.10; 5.17. Moule 1953:95, 104, notes that the part. is used adjectivally, 'the hard-working farmer'. Whereas lack of effort leads to the ruin of the land and lack of crops (Prov. 20.4), the hard worker can normally expect a crop (Deut 20.6; Prov 27.18). In fact, his work entitles him to have first call on the produce (cf. 1 Cor 9.7).[23] δεῖ (1 Tim 3.2) expresses 'the compulsion of what is fitting'.[24] μεταλαμβάνω is 'to receive one's share of something', but does not necessarily involve sharing with others;[25] καρπός** is used broadly for the produce of the land.

The force of πρῶτον is vague. Most commentators assume that it is the worker who is entitled to the first share of the harvest, i.e. before other people get a share. Spicq, 744, suggests that he is entitled to his share even before the owner of the land, while Bernard, 118, holds that he is the first to get a harvest before the other, lazier farmers. The application is also disputed, as to whether the reference is to heavenly reward (Hasler, 63), or primarily to material support from the church (Hanson, 130), or to both material support and spiritual joy at the fruits of the mission (Spicq, 745; cf. Kelly, 176), and also as to whether the πρῶτον carries over into the church situation. See Knight, 395, for a discussion of the possibilities and the conclusion that it is merely part of the imagery. Holtzmann, 406f., thinks of the teacher being the first to get nourishment from what he teaches. But maybe no specific identification of the reward is in mind, and the stress is much more on the need for devoted service and hard work.

---

[22] Hasler, 63; Houlden, 117; cf. Holtzmann, 406: Mt 10.10 par. Lk 10.8.

[23] Arichea-Hatton, 195, mention the possibility that πρῶτον is an adj. and means specifically the designated 'first portion' of the harvest.

[24] BA s.v. 6; cf. 2.24; 2 Macc 6.20; 4 Macc 7.8.

[25] Heb 6.7; 12.10; cf. Acts 2.46; 24.25; 27.33f.***, of eating together; μετάλημψις, 1 Tim 4.3.

7. νόει ὃ λέγω· δώσει γάρ σοι ὁ κύριος σύνεσιν ἐν πᾶσιν This verse is a call to pay attention to what is being said by the author. νοέω (1 Tim 1.7) has the sense 'to think over and so come to a right understanding.[26] The rel. ὅ has no antecedent expressed. Since λέγω can be used of writing as well as speaking (cf. BA *s.v.* I.), the expression can and should be taken of what is written in the letter. But the reference is not clear. Most commentators assume a reference backwards: ponder the metaphorical statements and work out their application (Brox, 241; Hasler, 64); Harris* goes further in suggesting that it is a hint to the church to pay the pastor (similarly, Lock, 94), but this is highly unlikely in view of the sing. form (unless Timothy himself is being urged to claim it for himself!). But a reference forwards to the significance of Jesus for the suffering believer is also possible, though less likely in view of the fresh imper. μνημόνευε. A general reference to whatever is said in the letter is even less likely. The phrase is a cliché, already found in Plato, *Ep.* 8.352C: νοήσατε ἃ λέγω (Harris*).

The γάρ clause implies that the thinking will be fruitful because the Lord will give understanding (σύνεσις).[27] That understanding is a divine gift is frequently stated.[28] Hence some commentators identify ὁ κύριος here with God the Father (cf. Prov 2.6; Knight, 396). However, in accordance with the principle mentioned in the note on 1.18 arthrous κύριος should refer to Jesus. The fact that Jesus is referred to with different nomenclature in the next verse is not an obstacle to this interpretation, since there is a break between paragraphs and v. 8 may be based on traditional material. Oberlinner, 71–4, notes that this reference to personal insight based on direct guidance from God modifies the possible impression that everything is based on what is explicitly handed down from Paul.

b. *Motivation for endurance (2.8–13)*

Bassler, J. M., '"He remains faithful" (2 Tim 2:13a)', in Lovering Jr., E. H., and Sumney, J. L., *Theology and Ethics in Paul and his Interpreters* (Nashville: Abingdon, 1996), 173–83; Seeberg 1966 [1903]:70–6; Thompson, G. H. P., 'Ephesians III.13 and II Timothy II.10 in the Light of Colossians I.24', *ExpTim* 71 (1960), 187–9.

The continuing theme is undoubtedly that of readiness for suffering and the need for steadfastness. This comes out especially

---

[26] Mt 24.15 = Mk 13.13; 1 Clement 19.3; Barnabas 4.14; 8.2.
[27] Mk 12.33; Lk 2.47; 1 Cor 1.19; Eph 3.4 (with ἐν of sphere, as here); Col 1.9; 2.2***; cf. Conzelmann, H., *TDNT* VII, 888–96.
[28] 1 Kgs 3.9; Dan 2.21; *T. Reub.* 6.4; *T. Levi* 18.7; Col 1.9; Jas 1.5; Hermas, *Mand.* 4.2.2a.

clearly in v. 9a and 10a, and in the 'faithful saying' in vv. 11b–13.
The section falls into three parts. The first (vv. 8f.) is a call to
remember that Jesus has been raised from the dead in accordance
with Paul's gospel. To this is added the comment that although
Paul may suffer, the word of God is not bound and helpless.
The point must be that the power of God is at work and therefore
the gospel will make its way. Second (v. 10), Paul states the
motivation for his willingness to suffer; it lies in the aim of
enabling the people of God to attain to final salvation. His
witness and suffering – and those of other believers – are thus
part of the divine plan of salvation (Oberlinner, 88). Third
(vv. 11–13), a faithful saying expresses promises regarding future
reward for those who suffer together with a warning against
apostasy.

Oberlinner, 75, opposes the common view that the theme of
the section is suffering and that this links it to the preceding
section. He holds that in the present section it is Paul alone who
suffers, and that the content and weight of the suffering varies
between v. 3 and v. 9. Where the previous section was dominated
by paraenesis, this one is dominated by confession. However,
the attempt to distinguish too sharply between the character of
the sections is misguided. It is true that the intensity of the
suffering is greater in this section; in the former section it is
more the privations of self-sacrificing service, but here it is the
possibility of persecution and martyrdom. Both, however, are
facets of the basic theme introduced in 1.8.

Many commentators regard vv. 11–13 (or parts thereof) as an
existing hymn composed in Pauline circles and in one opinion
'more Pauline than the Pastorals' (Hanson, 132). Since in his
opinion the style is Semitic (e.g. the omission of the article with
ἐκ σπέρματος Δαυίδ) and there is an echo of Rom 6.8, Jeremias,
55, thinks that Paul himself may have been the author (similarly,
Spicq, 748).[29] Bernard, 123, held that it was composed in Rome
on the basis of phrases from Romans and then picked up by
Paul when he was imprisoned in the city (cf. Knight, 407f.).
Parry, 56, notes its close relationship to the context and suggests
that it is less likely to be a definite quotation and more probably
simply influenced by traditional language. Lohfink 1988:177–80
holds that the material is derived from a variety of traditions
(and therefore literary dependence on Rom is unlikely). This
view is probably right: Pauline language about dying and rising
with Christ is being used, together with the saying of Jesus about
denying him (Mt 10.33), but the material is adapted to the needs

---

[29] For an attempt to reconstruct an Aramaic original see Barnes, W. E., in
Badcock 1937:134.

of the author (Läger 1996:79–81). Thus the saying provides an additional motive for the endurance in v. 10 and it may give a reason for the initial reference to the resurrection of Jesus (v. 8) in that those who die with Christ will share his resurrection life (v. 11). The warning against being ashamed of Christ (1.8) also receives backing here (vv. 12f.).

The structure of the saying appears to be fairly simple, but is more complicated than may be apparent at first sight. There are two sets of two lines, the second followed by a comment. Each line is a real conditional clause. In the first couplet two things that believers should do that involve faithful endurance are rewarded by two expressions describing the future life that they will experience with Christ. In the second couplet two things that believers should not do, involving apostate behaviour, are followed by two statements describing the attitude that Christ will show, and the fifth line explains more fully what his attitude is. But, whereas in the third line there is a negative attitude to the apostate, in the fourth (and fifth) there is an ambiguous statement and the content falls out of the pattern. Holtzmann, 413, solves the problem by regarding v. 13 as an addition to the 'hymn' by the author;[30] but this leaves the unsolved problem of why the addition was made by the author. Rather, we should beware of attempting to fit the material into a neat scheme in which the couplets each follow the same internal pattern.

The structure is in effect:

+ Past If we died with him   + Fut. also we shall live with him
+ Pres. If we endure   + Fut. also we shall reign with
− Fut. If we shall deny him   − Fut. also *he* will deny us
− Pres. If we are faithless   + Pres.   *he* remains faithful
        Pres. For *he* cannot deny himself

TEXT

8. Δαυίδ The spelling varies in the MSS wherever it is found: Δαβιδ is found only later in cursive MSS, but there is earlier authority for Δαυειδ (א C D*; Kilpatrick). See WH *Notes*, 153; MHT II, 110; Elliott, 132, 237.

11. πιστὸς ὁ λόγος The phrase 'and worthy of all acceptation' is added in a few minn. Elliott, 133, rightly rejects the variant.

συζήσομεν συνζήσομεν WH *Notes*, 149, and Kilpatrick retain the -ν-. BD §19² note that the lack of assimilation is more common. LS usually has συζ-. Cf. Elliott, 133f. Some MSS have the subj., but this may be simply an orthographical variant.

12. συμβασιλεύσομεν συνβασιλεύσομεν (א A F G P John-Dam; WH; cf. 1 Cor 4.8 *v.l.*); the spelling is discussed by MHT II, 104f. Kilpatrick and Elliott, 134, adopt the etymological form.

[30] Similarly, Lohfink 1988:177f.; Oberlinner, 83; Easton, 52, goes further and omits vv. 12b–13.

ἀρνησόμεθα ἀρνούμεθα (‭א‬² D 1739 1881 TR Cyp Ambst; Kilpatrick). Elliott, 134, adopts the variant. MHT III, 115, states that the fut. indic. is almost causal, but here the thought is hypothetical. BD § 372²ᵃ says that the indic. is used for disjunctive deductions or other kinds of logical reasoning. Hence the pres. is to be preferred. But assimilation to other verbs in the hymn is more likely.

13. γάρ Omit (‭א‬² Ψ TR lat syʰ boᵐˢˢ Tert; Kilpatrick). The variant is adopted by Elliott, 43, on the ground that the conjunction was added to avoid asyndeton. This is possible.

EXEGESIS

8. Μνημόνευε Ἰησοῦν Χριστὸν ἐγηγερμένον ἐκ νεκρῶν, ἐκ σπέρματος Δαυίδ, κατὰ τὸ εὐαγγέλιόν μου Jesus is apparently presented as an example to inspire readiness to bear hardship (Johnson, 65). The way is prepared for 2.11–13. The verb μνημονεύω** can mean 'to remember, recollect' (Mk 8.13), or 'to think about, keep one's attention on' (cf. Acts 20.35); the verb is usually followed by gen. (Heb 13.7) or περί, but here by acc. The command is to think back to something that might be forgotten otherwise, to ponder its significance, and to act on it. What follows is a brief formula about Ἰησοῦς Χριστός. The order 'Jesus Christ' is unusual in the PE (Tit 1.1 note) and suggests use of an existing form of words. The two statements about him occur in a surprising order with his resurrection placed before his descent from David. Although the content shows similarities to Rom 1.3f. and is sometimes thought to be literarily dependent on it, it is unlikely that the author is here dependent on Rom.[31] The construction is that of acc. with part. equivalent to a noun clause: 'Remember that Jesus was raised from the dead, [that he was] from the seed of David.'

The verb ἐγείρω* is used frequently in the NT of God raising Jesus. The perf. indicative is used in 1 Cor 15.4; et al., but the use of the perf. participle is unprecedented. The force may be that he has been raised and therefore is now alive and exalted. Houlden, 118, thinks that it is a mere slogan and no use is made of the idea (cf. Hasler, 64). The phrase ἐκ νεκρῶν is stereotyped in this connection (cf. Rom 4.24 and frequently; for νεκρός see 4.1**).

ἐκ σπέρματος Δαυίδ is a stereotyped phrase found in Rom 1.3; Jn 7.42.[32] σπέρμα**, 'seed', is used collectively for 'descendants', both in Cl. and in LXX, notably with reference to David's offspring in Ps 88 (MT 89).5; cf. 2 Sam 7.12.[33] The phrase thus indicates the earthly descent of Jesus from Δαυίδ**

---

[31] Lohse 1986:273 n. 10; Marshall 1988:165–7; Läger 1996:73f.; *pace* Oberlinner, 76.
[32] Cf. Acts 13.23; Rom 15.12; Ignatius, *Eph.* 18.2; *Rom.* 7.3; *Trall.* 9; *Smyr.* 1.1.
[33] Quell, G., and Schulz, S., *TDNT* VII, 536–47.

and must refer to his messianic status. The view that it refers purely to his humanity (Hasler, 65; Oberlinner, 76) breaks down on the mention of David.

Commentators are generally puzzled by the fact that a reference to the resurrection of Jesus precedes the reference to his Davidic descent. However, U. Kellermann (*EDNT* III, 263f.) comments that the latter phrase 'confesses faith in the resurrected Jesus as the Messiah promised in Nathan's prophecy'. In other words, it is the combination of the two facts – resurrection and descent – that qualify Jesus as the Messiah, and there is no indication that the two descriptions are to be separated in order to suggest two stages in the development of the status of Jesus. Lindars 1961:200 speaks of 'two equally valid messianic proofs'. It follows, then, that the order is immaterial. The One who was resurrected is the descendant of David and this confirms that the latter is the Messiah. The hypothesis adopted by most commentators, namely that the phraseology used here reflected a two-stage Christology, should be abandoned. Nor is it evident that a Gnostic tendency to docetism is being implicitly attacked here; following Towner 1989:102, Oberlinner, 77f., finds an anticipation of 2.18, but a reference to the *past* resurrection of Jesus is hardly a way of answering the heretics in that verse!

It may well be, however, that the unique order here is intended to stress the fact of the resurrection and the implicit divine vindication of Jesus. To say 'resurrected' naturally implies 'crucified' (cf. Kelly, 177), and the point is that God did raise Jesus and vindicate him. This can then be the basis for affirming that God will vindicate his word and his servants, even though, like Jesus, they may suffer martyrdom (*pace* Merkel, 64, who claims that the PE do not use the passion of Jesus as a pattern for believers).[34]

The qualifying phrase κατὰ τὸ εὐαγγέλιόν μου indicates that the statement just made is part of the gospel preached by Paul. The phrase already occurs in Rom 2.16; 16.25. cf 2 Cor 4.3; 1 Th 1.5; 2 Th 2.14; it is equivalent to the fuller phrase in 1 Tim 1.11; the gen. μου is subj. of Paul as preacher. The phrase could mean 'according to my preaching', with no sharp line between the activity and the message. However, Paul uses the phrase not of an idiosyncratic version of the gospel but of common belief. A specific reason for emphasising Paul's gospel is not apparent,

---

[34] Similarly, Oberlinner, 77, holds that the statement is purely confessional and is not meant to be paraenetic. There is no implicit reference to the suffering and death of Jesus (Oberlinner, 80). The emphasis on the triumph of Christ over death, however, signifies that persecution cannot prevent his messengers from achieving their aim (Oberlinner, 88). This interpretation appears to take insufficient note of v. 11.

and it seems that the phrase is there to form a peg for the next statement: the gospel is about Jesus who [suffered and was] raised, and those who proclaim that gospel are also liable to suffer.

9. ἐν ᾧ κακοπαθῶ μέχρι δεσμῶν ὡς κακοῦργος, ἀλλὰ ὁ λόγος τοῦ θεοῦ οὐ δέδεται In terms of syntax the next phrase is added on loosely to the preceding phrase by a rel. pron., but it should probably be regarded as a main affirmation. The rel. construction is used, as frequently, as a link and not as a means of subordination. The reference of the pron. is disputed. A reference to Christ (Simpson, 133; Holtz, 166), giving a mystical sense, is unlikely because of the distance. The pron. must refer to the gospel, but the construction ἐν ᾧ is variously understood to signify: (a) 'for which';[35] or, perhaps better, (b) 'in which sphere of action'.[36] The simplex form κακοπαθέω[37] is naturally used here, but the verb picks up the use of συγκακοπαθέω in 2.3. The verb has the sense not simply 'to suffer misfortune, hardship',[38] but also 'to bear hardship patiently' (4.5). It is used of suffering due to activity[39] rather than to passive affliction. Cebes, *Tabula* 9.2f., contrasts it with self-indulgence (ἡδυπάθεια) and Philo, *Spec.* 2.60, with ῥαθυμία.[40]

μέχρι (temporal, 1 Tim 6.14**) is used of degree, measure.[41] The extent of Paul's hardships stretches as far as imprisonment, expressed in terms of being fettered (δεσμός**).[42] ὡς here will mean 'like' from Paul's point of view rather than 'as' from the Roman point of view. κακοῦργος (Lk 23.32, 33, 39**) is a 'common criminal, malefactor', 'one who commits gross misdeeds and serious crimes' and who therefore is associated with extreme penalties, such as crucifixion (BA; *TLNT* II, 241–3).

Over against Paul's own situation is set the ringing, contrasting affirmation. ὁ λόγος τοῦ θεοῦ (1 Tim 1.15; Tit 2.5; cf. the anarthrous form, 1 Tim 4.5) is almost personified, as in 2 Th 3.1; cf. 1 Th 2.13. The metaphor of fettering the word of God is

---

[35] Namely, as the basis of the charges against Paul or as the reason for his suffering; so most translations; Knight, 398; cf. 1.12.

[36] Rom 1.9; 2 Cor 10.14; White, 162; cf. Easton, 52; NEB (unfortunately changed in REB): 'in whose service'.

[37] 4.5; Jas 5.13**; 2 Clement 19.3; *TLNT* II, 238–40.

[38] Jon 4.10; *Ep. Arist.* 241; Josephus, *Ant.* 12.336; *Ap.* 2.203; Philo, *Somn.* 2.181.

[39] Arrian, *Anab.* 6.29.5; Plutarch, *Luc.* 28.3; *Alex.* 40.3; *Num.* 3.5.

[40] Cf. Josephus *Ap.* 1.135; *Ant.* 6.172 (holding out on military service); Philodemus, *Rhet.* 2.205 (the toil of the orator); Vettius Valens 294 (acquiring knowledge). Sallust comments on the hardships endured by the soldier: *hiemem et aestatem iuxta pati, eodem tempore inopiam et laborem tolerare* (*Bellum Jug.* 85.33).

[41] Cf. Phil 2.8, 20; Heb 12.4; 1 Clement 4.9; 2 Macc 13.14; Josephus, *Ant.* 11.81.

[42] Cf. Phil 1.7, 13f., 17; Col 4.18; Philem 10, 13; Ignatius, *Smyr.* 11.1; *Poly.* 1.1.

found here only in NT (δέω**; cf. Büchsel, F., *TDNT* II, 60f.),
and is obviously developed from the previous part of the verse.
Brox, 243, observes that the point is not that other preachers
are free to speak while Paul is in prison but that the word of
God operates freely precisely in the suffering and bondage of
its agents.

**10. διὰ τοῦτο πάντα ὑπομένω διὰ τοὺς ἐκλεκτούς, ἵνα καὶ αὐτοὶ
σωτηρίας τύχωσιν τῆς ἐν Χριστῷ Ἰησοῦ μετὰ δόξης αἰωνίου**
The second statement gives Paul's motive for his readiness to
suffer in terms of what he can achieve for God's people. The
opening διὰ τοῦτο (1 Tim 1.16) may be prospective. It will then
either mean 'because of the elect' (REB; Knight, 398f.) or be
anticipatory of the ἵνα clause (as in 1 Tim 1.16). This gives a
rather redundant expression. It may be better, therefore to take
it retrospectively. It will then mean 'on account of Christ and
the gospel', or 'because of the power and freedom of the Word'
(which ensure that God will accomplish his purpose), or 'because
the full course of the Gospel is promoted by the sufferings of
the preachers' (Parry, 56). The second of these possibilities is
perhaps best.

ὑπομένω (2.12**), 'to remain, stay one's ground', developed
the sense 'to hold out, endure'.[43] πάντα in this context signifies 'whatever may happen' (cf. 1 Cor 13.7), and 3.11 lists what
might be included. διὰ shifts in nuance from 'because of' to 'for
the sake of'. For ἐκλεκτός see Tit 1.1** and note. There, as
here, three possible meanings arise. (a) The first is that the
reference is to people who are at present non-believers but who
are destined by God to believe and belong to the kingdom
(Holtzmann, 410f.; Knight, 399). In addition to the points made
in the note on Tit 1.1 against this interpretation is the further
fact that the reference to salvation here appears to be to future
salvation. Moreover, to categorise unbelievers as 'the elect'
curiously excludes those who are already believers. (b) This
difficulty is overcome if a combination of the two groups (Lock,
95; Spicq, 747) is meant; but there remains the difficulty that
elsewhere 'the elect' is not a term used for those destined to be
saved but for those who belong to the actual people of God.
(c) The third possibility is preferable, namely that the allusion
here is to people who are already believers who must be helped
to persevere to the end. White, 163, expands the idea: 'those who
are selected for spiritual privileges with a view directly to the
salvation of others, as well as of themselves', but this idea of
selection for service is hardly central here.

[43] With acc., 1 Cor 13.7; Heb 10.32; 12.2f.; Jas 1.12; see also Ignatius, *Smyr.*
4.2; 9.2; *Poly.* 3.1; Polycarp 8.1; *et al.*; Diognetus 2.9; cf. ὑπομονή, 1 Tim 6.11.

The force of καί is not certain. Most probably it qualifies αὐτοί in the sense that 'the elect also' (in addition to Paul and Timothy) will gain salvation (Knight, 399), or, if non-believers are in mind, in addition to the existing body of believers; but to refer only to the set of unbelievers as 'the elect' over against existing believers who are surely also 'elect' would be very odd. Alternatively καί qualifies (future) salvation as another blessing for the elect in addition to what they already enjoy. In any case σωτηρία (3.15**) appears to refer to future salvation here rather than present (*pace* Knight, 400).

τυγχάνω** ('to meet, attain, gain, find, experience') tends to be used of what people cannot achieve but may be given, of what is beyond their control and yet not due to mere chance. It is used of gaining future salvation (Lk 20.35; Heb 11.35; cf. Bauernfeind, O., *TDNT* VIII, 238–42). The qualification τῆς ἐν Χριστῷ 'Ιησοῦ is used, as in 1.13, to signify the person in whom God's gifts are present and available. μετά indicates what accompanies salvation (Bar 4.24; 1 Tim 1.14 note). δόξα generally refers to God's glory (1 Tim 1.11 *et al.*), but here, as in Paul, believers will receive a share in it.[44] The glory is eternal (αἰώνιος).[45]

Jeremias, 54, develops the view that this verse reflects the idea of a fixed quantity of suffering to be fulfilled by the community before the End, with Paul taking as large a share as he can to spare others.[46] Against this view see Hanson, 131, who adopts the more likely theory that the thought of Phil 1.12–28 is closer to the passage (cf. also Brox, 243). Oberlinner, 81f., also resists the view that Paul's suffering is in any way substitutionary but emphasises that it is essential for missionary work and that where the willingness to persevere and suffer is absent, the legitimacy of the church leader is severely called into question.

The point is taken to its limit by Läger 1996:75f. *et passim*. She argues that Timothy's suffering here is motivated more by Paul's example than by reference to the death of Jesus. Paul is in effect given a soteriological role here and elsewhere in the PE and, as in 1 Tim 1.16, becomes a part of the message. This seems to be an exaggeration of the situation. Christ remains supreme in this passage, with references to him bracketing the reference to Paul himself. What the author is doing here is encouraging Timothy to be ready for the same experience as Paul in his calling to be a missionary; there is no implication that Paul's sufferings (or Timothy's) have become part of the gospel message.

---

[44] 1 Th 2.12; 2 Th 2.13f.; Rom 5.1f; 8.18–30; 2 Cor 4.17; *et al.*
[45] Cf. Wis 10.14; Josephus, *Ant.* 15.376; *Sib. Orac.* 8.410; 2 Cor 4.17.
[46] Cf. Col 1.24; Thompson*; similarly Kelly, 178; Holtz, 167.

11. πιστὸς ὁ λόγος· εἰ γὰρ συναπεθάνομεν, καὶ συζήσομεν
Since the preceding verse is a personal statement by Paul
rather than a doctrinal statement or command, the formula
πιστὸς ὁ λόγος (**Excursus 9**) must refer forwards (Knight, 400f.).
It is however taken as referring backwards by Lock, 96 (with
hesitation), and White, 163, because of the introductory γάρ
with the following statement; but a reference back to v. 8 is surely
impossible.[47] The formula is used to emphasise the authority of
what is being said. It does not necessarily imply that it is a piece
of tradition, but in the present case where the material is used
to back up what has been said previously by the author it seems
most likely that it gains its authority through being a summary
of traditional, received statements. Despite the opinion of many
commentators, it is unlikely that its presence indicates that part
of a putative hymn has been omitted. Rather it introduces statements that provide some basis and motivation for the attitudes
expressed in v. 10a. It has been suggested that vv. 8–10 contain
an anticipatory paraphrase of the hymn (Knight, 401).

The compound verb συναποθνήσκω occurs in the NT only
in 2 Cor 7.3; Mk 14.31***. In Cl. it means literally 'to die with
somebody' and is the antonym to συζάω;[48] cf. Jn 11.16 for the
thought. In secular usage it expressed the thought of loyalty in
military circles or between friends and lovers (Spicq, 748). Here
the reference could be to spiritual identification with Christ in
baptism and the Christian life, i.e. to dying to sin or to self and
safety.[49] Or the reference here (whatever it was in the putative
hymn) may be martyrological, especially in a letter which is looking
to Paul's own death.[50] However, the past tense is inappropriate
for this idea (especially when followed by a pres. in the next
line), and there would be something of an anticlimax with the
less strenuous requirement in the next line. It is more likely,
therefore, that the reference is to a past death to self which may
involve readiness even for martyrdom.[51] The statement, therefore,
is not simply confessional but has an implicit exhortatory force
for the reader.

---

[47] Johnson, 65, suggests that the use here is not formulaic, but refers back to
the word of God in v. 9, and hence developed its formulaic use elsewhere in
the PE.

[48] Cf. Nicolaus of Damascus 90 frg. 80, Jac. (BA; cited by Spicq, 748f. from
Athenaeus 6.249b); Grundmann, W., *TDNT* VII, 786; *TLNT* III, 330f.

[49] The language and thought are very similar to those of Rom 6.8 (cf. Läger
1996:78); cf. Rom 8.17; 2 Cor 4.10f.; Col 2.20.

[50] Holtzmann, 412; Bernard, 121; Jeremias, 55; Brox, 244; Hasler, 65f.; cf.
EDNT III, 298.

[51] Towner 1989:104f.; Barrett, 104; Fee, 249f.; Grundmann, W., *TDNT* VII,
793f.

The καί in the apodosis emphasises the certainty that the promise in the verb will be fulfilled; it is almost equivalent to 'certainly'. συζάω, 'to live with',[52] refers to future life with Christ in glory, but the thought of present life in union with Christ is also implied.[53]

12. εἰ ὑπομένομεν, καὶ συμβασιλεύσομεν The second line is almost exactly parallel in structure to the first. The differences are that the verb ὑπομένομεν, which gives a significant catchword connection with v. 10 (cf. 1 Tim 6.11), is in the pres. tense, and the simplex form does not express the idea of enduring 'with [Christ]' (the hypothetical form *συνυπομένω does not exist). Nevertheless, the idea of sharing in Christ's endurance may be faintly present in view of the surrounding context of συν- verbs. The present tense is appropriate for the continuing current experience of believers. συμβασιλεύω (1 Cor 4.8***) is to share rule as king with somebody (cf. Polycarp 5.2 for a close parallel). The thought of sharing Christ's role as king and judge with a share in the accompanying glory is widespread in the NT.[54] Its basis is Mt 19.28 par. Lk 22.30, a saying which may lie behind the present statement.[55]

εἰ ἀρνησόμεθα, κἀκεῖνος ἀρνήσεται ἡμᾶς The second pair of statements explores the consequences of unwillingness to die with Christ and to endure hardship with him and for his sake. The opposite attitude to identification with him is denial;[56] no object is supplied but the reference is obvious. The use of εἰ with fut. indic. is quite rare;[57] whether this tense expresses 'a mere contingency, improbable in itself' (Bernard, 121; Spicq, 750) seems dubious. One possibility is that denial at the judgement may be meant (so possibly Houlden, 119, but he may simply mean that God's action will take place then). This is an attractive interpretation, in that it explains the fut. tense well and gives a better explanation for the apparently opposite attitude in the next verse: deliberate rejection at the last judgement is fatal, but present lapses in faithfulness do not cancel out Christ's faithfulness to us; however, it remains unlikely since the passage is concerned with present attitudes. In the apodosis κἀκεῖνος* is an example of a frequent crasis. The reference in the emphatic pronoun is to Jesus (see 2.26 note).[58] The fut. ἀρνήσεται is

[52] Rom 6.8; 2 Cor 7.3***; cf. 2 Cor 4.10f.; Grundmann, W., *TDNT* VII, 787.
[53] Cf. 1 Tim 4.8; Parry, 57; Knight, 400; Oberlinner, 84f.
[54] Rom 5.17; 1 Cor 4.8; 6.2; Rev 5.10; 20.4, 6; 22.5.
[55] Schürmann, H., *Jesu Abschiedsrede* (Münster: Aschendorf, 1957), 38.
[56] For ἀρνέομαι see 2.12b; 2.13; 3.5; 1 Tim 5.8; Tit 1.16 note.
[57] Mt 26.33; Mk 14.29; 1 Pet 2.20; Lk 11.8.
[58] Cf. Mt 27.19, 63; Jn 1.18; 2.21; 3.28, 30; 5.11; 7.11; 9.12, 28, 37; 19.21; 2 Cor 8.9; 2 Pet 1.16; 1 Jn 2.6; 3.3, 5, 7, 16; 4.17.

usually taken to refer to Christ's action at the judgement. Nevertheless, Schenk, W., *EDNT* I, 154, holds that Christ's response is not definitive but rather 'punctiliar, preliminary and repeatable'. The use of the same verb to express the human action and the divine response places the saying in the category of 'sentences of holy law' identified by Käsemann,[59] and is clearly based on the saying of Jesus in Mt 10.33 = Lk 12.9 (in aor. subj.). The saying is meant to constitute a powerful warning.

13. εἰ ἀπιστοῦμεν, ἐκεῖνος πιστὸς μένει, ἀρνήσασθαι γὰρ ἑαυτὸν οὐ δύναται In the second line of the couplet the tense reverts to the present and the thought is of the opposite of endurance, apostasy. ἀπιστέω[60] can mean 'to disbelieve, refuse to believe' or 'to be unfaithful'.[61] The former meaning is hardly possible in the context which is concerned with loyalty, but Barth, G., *EDNT* I, 121–3, finds echoes of it 'for otherwise a distinction between being faithless (v. 13) and the denial of Christ spoken of in the previous line (v. 12b) would hardly be possible and the two lines would merely contradict each other'. The verb expresses acts of unfaithfulness, possibly even of apostasy, and is meant to serve as a warning to believers of a temptation to which they are exposed. It is not as strong as 'deny' and is more like 'if we fail to live up to our profession' (Spicq, 750; Kelly, 180).

Whereas in the previous line the choice of verb for the action of believers allowed a corresponding response on the part of Christ, the choice of verb here does not allow for this possibility. There is no way that Christ can be said to be ἄπιστος; on the contrary, like God the Father, he is supremely πιστός.[62]

The faithfulness of God is explained in the following clause. ἀρνήσασθαι with ἑαυτόν has the force 'to be untrue to oneself' (BA), i.e. to his faithful nature. This clause is widely regarded as the author's comment and not part of the hymn (Hanson, 133), but it is more likely that it belongs closely with the preceding line (Scott, 106).

Hence the fourth line falls out of the pattern that has been established in the preceding three lines which describe a divinely bestowed reward/judgement on believers. What is its force?

(a) The statement is widely taken to imply that Christ is faithful to the faithless. Despite their lapses, he does not finally

[59] Käsemann, E., *New Testament Questions of Today* (London: SCM Press, 1969), 66–81, curiously does not mention this passage.

[60] Mk 16.11, 16; Lk 24.11, 41; Acts 28.24; Rom 3.3; 1 Pet 2.7***; noun, 1 Tim 1.13; adj., 1 Tim 5.8.

[61] Rom 3.3; Num 23.19f.; cf. Xenophon, *Anab.* 2.6.19 of disloyal soldiers.

[62] 1 Tim 1.12; cf. 1 Cor 1.9; 10.13; 1 Th 5.24; 2 Th 3.3; for μένω (1 Tim 2.15) with an adj. see 1 Cor 7.11; Acts 27.41; Jn 12.24.

reject them and judge them; he leaves open the possibility of repentance and salvation (2.21, 24–26; Bassler*). 'The logic breaks down on the love of the Saviour' (Jeremias, 55). A distinction is made in effect between denial and unfaithfulness. The verse then becomes in the words of Jeremias 'ein Trost für erschrockene Gewissen'.[63]

(b) In sharp contrast others hold that precisely because Christ is faithful, he will act in accordance with his warnings and therefore in judgement against the faithless (Lock, 96; Oberlinner, 88); 'God's faithfulness makes it impossible for Him to acknowledge those who deny Him' (Horton, 153; cf. Calvin, 311). Although this view has logic on its side and brings the passage to a strong climax, it reads a lot into the word 'faithful'.

(c) The statement is about Christ's faithfulness in general terms. Divine faithfulness stands in contrast to the unfaithfulness of the opponents and functions as a model for true believers to follow (Bassler*). Despite the apostasy and faithlessness of some Christians (whom he will judge), Christ remains faithful to his cause and so to the church as a whole because he cannot be untrue to his own nature and his purpose of salvation.[64] Understood thus, the statement may simply be intended to show that unfaithfulness is inconsistent with the character of believers who are to be like Christ and God. More probably, it is intended to be an encouragement to believers suffering hardship by assuring them that the Lord whom they serve is faithful to the gospel (2 Tim 1.12) and to them; the thought is close to 1 Cor 10.13.

III.   THE CHURCH LEADER AND HIS OPPONENTS (2.14–26)

Arndt, W. M., '"ἔγνω" 2 Tim 2.19', CTM 21 (1950), 299–302; Brown, E. F., 'Note on 2 Tim. II.15', JTS 24 (1923), 317; Bunn, L. H., '2 Timothy 2, 23–26', ExpTim 41 (1929–30), 235–7; Capes, D. B., OT Yahweh Texts in Paul's Christology (Tübingen: Mohr, 1992), 145–9; Hanson 1968:29–41; Hitchcock, F. M., 'Miscellanea – New Light on a Passage in the Pastorals', Theology 34 (1937), 108–12; Lane, W. L., '1 Tim. iv. 1–3. An Early Instance of Over-realized Eschatology', NTS 11 (1964–5), 164–7; Larson, T. G., 'Prescriptions for Blasphemy. A Study of "Naming the Name" in 2 Tim. 2:19d as an Echo of Cursing God in Lev 24:16', unpublished MTh. thesis, Gordon-Conwell Theological Seminary, 1997; Metzger, W.,'Die neōterikai epithymiai in 2 Tim 2,22', TZ 33 (1977), 129–36; Penna, A., '"In magna autem domo..." (2 Tim 2.20 sq.)' (in Italian), AnBib 17–18 (Vol. II, 1963), 101–8; Roloff 1985; Rudolph 1983:189–94;

[63] Similarly, Bernard, 121; Scott, 106; Spicq, 750f.; Kelly, 181; Hanson, 132; Brox, 245; Barrett, 104; Holtz, 169; Knight, 407; Michel, O., TDNT V, 216; Läger 1996:79.

[64] Rom 3.3f.; Holtzmann, 413f.; Dibelius-Conzelmann, 109; Fee, 251. There is some similarity to the thought of v. 9 where the servants of the gospel may be bound but the gospel itself cannot be bound. Whatever happens to the Lord's servants, his purpose of salvation for the world will not be thwarted.

Schenke, H. M., 'Auferstehungsglaube und Gnosis', *ZNW* 59 (1968), 123–6; Sellin, G., '"Die Auferstehung ist schon geschehen". Zur Spiritualisierung apokalyptischer Terminologie im Neuen Testament', *NovT* 25 (1983), 220–37; Skiles, J. W. D., 'II Tim 2:15 and Sophocles Antigone 1195', *Classical Philology* 38 (1943), 204f.; Wedderburn, A. J. M., 'Hellenistic Christian Traditions in Romans 6?', *NTS* 29 (1983), 337–55 (350). Wilson, J. P., 'The Translation of 2 Timothy II, 26', *ExpTim* 49 (1937–8), 45f.

At first sight this section contains a number of separate admonitions which flow from one another without clear breaks. The structure is determined, as in 2.1–13, by a set of imperatives (vv. 14–16a, 22f.) each of which is followed by supporting matter (vv. 16b–21, 24–26). But the supporting matter also contains implicit commands (vv. 21, 24–25a). The writer uses the pattern of a prohibition or negative command followed by a contrasting positive command, which in turn is followed by a further negative command which takes the initial thought further (vv. 14/15/16a, 22a/22b/23). The intervening material is a mixture of warrants for the imperatives and further implicit commands. Smith 1981:62–80 analyses the section into a 'head' (2.14f.) followed by three 'specifics' (2.16–19, 20–22, 23–26); but these divisions do not seem to align with the natural breaks in the passage. We can analyse the main thrust of the passage as follows:

14a	*Tell* others to avoid disputes
14b	for they cause ruin to the hearers
15	Positively *be* an unashamed workman in God's sight
16a	*Avoid* disputes
16b–17a	**for** people will get worse,
17b	as typified by Hymenaeus and Philetus
18	who are upsetting people's faith
19	But (they will not succeed for) God's foundation is firm ...
20	There are different kinds of vessels,
21	so *purify* yourself to be a good one.
22a	Therefore *avoid* youthful desires
22b	and *seek* after Christian qualities
23a	and *avoid* disputes,
	because they cause fights
24a	The Lord's servant *must* not fight
24b	but *treat* opponents with gentleness,
25a	he *must* teach them gently
25b	**for** God may grant them repentance
26a	and they may escape the devil's snare
26b	after being taken captive to do his bidding.

From this summary it emerges that the constantly repeated theme is that of how to deal with opposition in the church. The presence of opposition and heresy is already implicit in the stress on guarding the deposit and in the mention of those who have forsaken Paul in ch. 1. The opposition is characterised by empty disputes over words, but it is dangerous. The command to avoid disputes is emphasised by its fourfold repetition. Most of the opposition are to be treated gently, but there are some who have gone so far that they can be seen not to belong to the Lord. (Excommunication is not mentioned [contrast 1 Tim 1.20], but may be implied.) Throughout the section the author keeps presenting the positive side of how Timothy himself and other Christian leaders and members of the congregations are to behave and teach by contrast (vv. 15, 21, 22, 24). The author sees a danger that Timothy may be infected by the very disease which he is to purge from the church; it is very tempting to use the enemy's own weapons to defeat them. But if 'the medium is the message', then false media must be avoided.

The theme and content of the whole section 2.14–4.5 are closer to those of 1 Tim than is true of the rest of 2 Tim. This leads Holtz, 170, to the hypothesis that 2 Tim is a combination of two separate letters. This view ignores the presence of material in the middle section which is of a piece with the rest of the letter, and of the presence of material in ch. 1 which is similar to teaching in 1 Tim. Nevertheless, the teaching in this particular section about heresy and the antidote to it is particularly reminiscent of 1 Tim (Fee, 253).

TEXT

14. θεοῦ κυρίου (A D Ψ 048 1739 1881 TR b vg sy sa^mss bo^pt; WH mg; Kilpatrick; RSV; NRSV mg; Holtzmann, 415); Χριστοῦ (206 *pc*). Elliott, 136f., adopts the text as giving an expression typical of the PE; the main variant may be due to the influence of 2 Cor 8.21. Similarly, Metzger, 579.

λογομαχεῖν λογομάχει (A C* 048 1175 *pc* latt). Dibelius-Conzelmann, 110f., note that the variant produces a clumsy asyndeton. Elliott, 137, holds that the variant is due to scribes who thought that this was a further direct command to Timothy himself and corrected what they took to be an imperatival infinitive.

ἐπ’ οὐδέν (a) εἰς οὐδέν (ℵ² D Ψ 1739 1881 TR) is a stylistic change (Elliott, 137f.); (b) ἐπ’ οὐδένι (F G 330 2400 g). The variant is accepted by Elliott, 137f., who claims that the use of the acc. here is Cl. and the dat. is Hellenistic. But the external evidence for the change is very weak.

16. κενοφωνίας καινοφωνίας (F G b d Lcf Spec); Elliott, 109f., regards the variant as phonetic and accepts the text; cf. 1 Tim 6.20 note.

18. |τὴν| ἀνάστασιν Omit article (ℵ F G 048 33 *pc* (eth) geo Cyril); for anarthrous use of noun cf. Mk 12.18; Lk 20.37; Polycarp 7.1; *Acts of Paul and Thecla* 14. Metzger, 579f., speaks of 'nearly overwhelming textual support' for retention of the article. Elliott, 139f., retains the article since the reference is to a definite event, the resurrection of believers.

τήν τινων πίστιν τὴν πίστιν τινῶν (ℵ^c F G 33 g). In the text the gen. is positioned unusually; it follows that the variant is original and scribes altered it to avoid a Semitism (Elliott, 140). But the MS evidence is too weak for the variant.

19. Part of this verse is preserved in P. Eger. 3 (c. AD 200–250), lines 130–133:[1]

τοῦ [...Παῦλος] δὲ ἐν
τῇ [β´ πρὸς Τιμόθε]ον λέγε[ι]
ἔγν[ω ὁ Κ(ύριο)ς τοὺς ὄν]τα[ς] αὐτοῦ α[ ]μερο[.]

τοὺς ὄντας αὐτοῦ Praem. πάντας (‭א‬*; Elliott, 140f., mistakenly gives the reading as πάντως). The variant is too weakly supported to be original.

21. εὔχρηστον Praem. καί (‭א‬² C* D² Ψ 1739 1881 TR lat syʰ Or; Kilpatrick). Elliott, 210, accepts the variant, arguing that scribes tended to omit καὶ to produce asyndeton. Perhaps addition to avoid asyndeton is just as likely!

22. τῶν ἐπικαλουμένων Praem. πάντων (C [- τῶν, F G] I 048ᵛⁱᵈ 33 81 104 326 *pc* syʰ sa? boᵖᵗ; WH mg); πάντων τῶν ἀγαπώντων (A – an error). Elliott, 144, accepts the addition on the ground that scribes tended to omit. But it could be equally well an addition due to the influence of Eph 6.24 (Metzger 1971:648).

24. ἤπιον νήπιον (D* F G) is a scribal error (Elliott, 144).

25. πραΰτητι πραότητι (Ψ Dᶜ minn. Basil Chrys). The variant is an Atticistic form (Elliott, 100). Cf. Tit 3.2 note.

δώῃ (WHᵐᵍ; NA²⁷; UBS³; subj.): δῷ (‭א‬² D² 33 1739 1881 TR; Kilpatrick; BD § 370³); δώῃ (NA²⁶; optative). See 1.16 note, 18; 2.7 textual note. The form expected here is subj., as in v. 26. Therefore, the form δωῃ should be read as subj., although elsewhere in this epistle it is to be read as an opt. (cf. MHT III, 129; Elliott, 167, proposes to read the other examples in 2 Tim as jussive subjs. See further BD § 95²; 369¹; 370³; MHT I, 55, 193f.; cf. Eph 1.17; 3.16; Jn 15.16 *v.l.*; δοῖ, Mk 8.37.

EXEGESIS

14. Ταῦτα ὑπομίμνησκε διαμαρτυρόμενος ἐνώπιον τοῦ θεοῦ μὴ λογομαχεῖν, ἐπ᾽ οὐδὲν χρήσιμον, ἐπὶ καταστροφῇ τῶν ἀκουόντων The section begins with a direction as to what Timothy is to teach the church, which is almost unique in this letter, concerned as it is more with Timothy's own behaviour. The command, however, is incidental to the main thrust of the verse which is concerned with the manner of the teaching (the participle thus carries the weight of the sentence). ὑπομιμνήσκω (Tit 3.1) is here used of reminding people of the teaching they already know which needs constant repetition. The content (ταῦτα) may be particularly the preceding teaching, whether generally or specifically vv. 11–13 (Holtzmann, 414; White, 164; Fee, 254) or, more generally, the apostolic teaching (cf. 2.2; Parry, 57) or both (Lock, 98; Spicq, 753). The first possibility is the most likely, but is not without problems in view of the link with the instructions in the rest of the verse.

The difficulty centres on the identity of the person(s) who need to be reminded. Three possibilities arise: (a) The congregation as a whole (the 'elect' of v. 10), 'your people' (GNB; similarly,

---

[1] Bell, H. I., and Skeat, T. C., *Fragments of an Unknown Gospel and Other Early Christian Papyri* (London: British Museum, 1935), 48.

REB; other translations have a vague 'them'). (b) The teachers in 2.2 (Lock, 98; Knight, 409f.). (c) Timothy himself (Prior, 158–60). This interpretation gives the sense: 'Do not ever let these things out of your mind, Timothy, as you bear witness in the presence of God.' Thus Timothy is encouraged to avoid empty chatterings. In the absence of a double acc. with the verb this view is attractive, but it is hard to defend in view of the parallel in Tit 3.1. The content of the injunction is especially applicable to church leaders, but since it could apply to any member of a congregation who was tempted to enter into disputes, view (a) should be accepted; in any case, Timothy himself is to take to heart the instruction which he gives to others. If so, the interpretation of ταῦτα as the immediately preceding instruction (vv. 8–13) is confirmed.

For διαμαρτύρομαι (4.1) see 1 Tim 5.21**, where the strong adjuration ἐνώπιον θεοῦ also occurs. With a following inf. the verb has the sense of giving a strong command. The point is then that Timothy and his colleagues are to remember the nature of their task and not to engage in futile arguments about contrary views and opinions. λογομαχέω*** is 'to dispute about words', i.e. 'to engage in verbal quibbling', rather than 'to bandy arguments' (Moffatt). The word is said not to be found elsewhere except for a Christian writer[2] who is presumably dependent on this passage. But the noun is used in 1 Tim 6.4 (Tit 3.9 v.l.), and the idea is present in 2 Tim 2.23; 1 Tim 1.4; Tit 3.9. The reference is to public debate with heretics or to getting involved in verbal theological discussion; it is not that discussion with the opponents is forbidden, but descending to their level of futile debate is (Wolter 1988:138 n. 31).

The syntax of the following phrase, ἐπ' οὐδὲν χρήσιμον, is obscure, but it must refer to the uselessness of verbal disputes.[3] The construction of χρήσιμος***, 'useful, beneficial, advantageous', with ἐπί is Cl.[4] It is, therefore, unlikely that we should understand the phrase as 'to no useful result' with χρήσιμον agreeing with οὐδέν (pace Lock, 98). For an excellent illustration of what is being condemned see the contrast between verbal arguments and the fruits of character in Athenagoras, Leg. 11, cited by Karris, 27.

---

[2] Eustathius, Opusc. p. 47, 96 (AD XII); see BA.

[3] (a) The best favoured solution is that the phrase stands in apposition with the inf., 'a practice that is in no way profitable' (Dibelius-Conzelmann, 110). (b) Or it may constitute an independent clause inserted parenthetically: '– it is in no way profitable –' (Simpson, 136). (c) The suggestion that it belongs to the preceding inf. ('not to dispute over what is not profitable') is impossible in view of the harshness of the two negatives and the switch to οὐδέν.

[4] For similar phrases to ἐπ' οὐδέν, cf. 3.9, 13; BA s.v. III.3.

A second independent phrase follows expressing the result of
the disputes somewhat ironically. ἐπί with dat. has the force 'with
the result of'.[5] καταστροφή (2 Pet 2.6***) is 'ruin, destruction';[6]
Simpson, 136, suggests that 'subversion' is the force (cf.
Philodemus, *Rhet.* 255). τῶν ἀκούοντων will be the congregation
as the hearers of the disputes with the heretical leaders.[7]

15 σπούδασον σεαυτὸν δόκιμον παραστῆσαι τῷ θεῷ Having
issued a warning against the wrong kind of conduct, the author
turns, as frequently, to a balancing positive instruction (which
will then be followed by a further negative prohibition in v. 16a).
Timothy is to be a model of correct use of Scripture and so
pleasing to God. The implication may be that his life-style is
thus to be an example to other people, but more probably he is
to give teaching which will be profitable by contrast with the
negative effect of controversy. The suggestion that instead of
offering a better theory than the heretics Timothy is simply to
live a better life (Hasler, 67) does not do justice to the accent
on teaching. The basic command is expanded by two explanatory
phrases. Elsewhere in the PE σπουδάζω means 'to hasten' (4.9,
21; Tit 3.12), but here it has its other common meaning: 'to be
zealous, eager, take pains, make every effort'. δόκιμος** is
'approved (by testing)' (cf. δοκιμάζω, 1 Tim 3.10), hence 'tried
and true', 'genuine', whether in the eyes of people (Rom 14.18b)
or of God (Rom 16.10; 1 Cor 11.19; 2 Cor 10.18; 13.7; Jas
1.12**). Simpson, 136, wishes to link it with ἐργάτην, '*a sterling
workman*, above reproach', but the word order hardly favours
this. παρίστημι (intrans. 4.17**) is used trans. 'to present
somebody to somebody', hence 'to make, render' (BA); it is used
with an adj., as here, in Eph 5.27; Col 1.22, 28 of making people
acceptable to God. The word can be used of in the context of
court ceremonial and royal service; it can also refer to the offering
of sacrifices (Rom 12.1), but its usage is so varied that there is
no good reason to read in this nuance here. Another suggestion
is that the ultimate origin of the figurative usage here may be the
ritual of presenting somebody to God to give evidence of cultic
cleanness.[8] For the thought see Rom 6.13; 14.18; cf. 1 Cor 8.8.

[5] Cl.; e.g. Xenophon, *Mem.* 2.3.19: ἐπὶ βλάβῃ; Herodotus 1.68: ἐπὶ κακῷ
ἀνθρώπου; see BA *s.v.* II.1.b.ε.
[6] Cf. the use of the verb, 1 Clement 6.4; Hermas, *Mand.* 5.2.1; Bertram, G.,
TDNT VII, 716 n. 6.
[7] The frequent comment that this instruction to avoid disputes is in direct
contradiction to the practice of Paul fails to take adequate account of the
persistent description of the opponents' arguments as sheer nonsense with which
it is impossible to argue. There *are* deviant forms of Christian belief which are
sheer nonsense!
[8] So Bertram, G., and Reicke, B., *TDNT* V, 837–41.

ἐργάτην ἀνεπαίσχυντον For ἐργάτης see 1 Tim 5.18 note; the word had taken on the sense of 'missionary, church worker' in Christian circles (2 Cor 11.13; Phil 3.2). ἀνεπαίσχυντος***, 'not needing to be ashamed', is a rare word found elsewhere only in Josephus, *Ant.* 18.243, and later Christian writers. If the description is detached from its context of appearing before God, the adjective might refer to not being ashamed of the task of proclaiming the gospel before other people, in line with the thematic command in 1.8 (so apparently, Brox, 247). The suggestion that Timothy is not to be ashamed to put his hand to anything (Chrysostom *PG* LXII, 626, cited by White, 165) is unlikely. In the context of being δόκιμος the application is primarily to not feeling ashamed in the presence of God for failing to do one's duty: the workman must produce an object of which he has no need to be ashamed because it is shoddy or ill made. Brown* claims that in Josephus the word has a passive sense 'not [something] to be ashamed of' and argues that the sense is that Timothy is not to be the kind of workman of whom God or Christ would be ashamed (cf. Mk 8.38). Either way, the application to Timothy must surely be that he must not fail to proclaim the truth clearly and faithfully, without fear of the opposition.

ὀρθοτομοῦντα τὸν λόγον τῆς ἀληθείας The meaning and application of the verb ὀρθοτομέω are far from clear. According to BA it is found previously only in Prov 3.6; 11.5 where it appears to mean 'to cut a path in a straight direction', e.g. by clearing difficult land to make a road.[9] The phrase τέμνειν ὁδόν is the basis of the metaphor in Plato, *Leg.* 7, 810E: τὴν νῦν ἐκ τῶν παρόντων λόγων τετμημένην ὁδὸν τῆς νομοθεσίας πορεύεσθαι ('to proceed along the way of legislation which has been cleared by our present discourse'). In the two instances in the LXX the verb means 'to open a way' (= יָשַׁר, Piel). The metaphorical concept of a straight road which is opened up by God and along which people should travel occurs in 1 Sam 12.23; Ps 106.7; Prov 20.11; Jer 38 [31].9; Prov 16.25; cf. κατευθύνω, Prov 9.15; κατορθοῦντες, Prov 2.7. The thought of a *straight*, i.e. correct, road is thus characteristic of Heb. Wisdom and explains the unusual choice of word here.[10] Similar phrases are applied to ploughing and reaping (Simpson, 137), and Spicq, 754, thinks that this is the image evoked by the word, but this

[9] The procedure is well-attested by Herodotus 4.136; Thucydides 2.100.2; Josephus, *Ap.* 1.309.
[10] For the later use of the idea see *T. Jud.* 26.1; *T. Sim.* 5.2; 1QS 4.2; 1QH 12.34; Hermas, *Vis.* 2.2.6. In general, see Köster, H., *TDNT* VIII, 111f.; *TLNT* II, 595. The suggestion by Skiles* that the writer was inspired by a phrase in Sophocles, *Ant.* 1195, is quite improbable.

is less likely than the proposal above. The analogy of similar word-formations strongly suggests that the metaphor in -τομέω may well have been lost and the force is simply to act correctly (MM, 456f.; Dibelius-Conzelmann, 111 n. 5; Hanson, 134). In the present passage it is not God but Timothy who is to act, and the object is ὁ λόγος τῆς ἀληθείας, i.e. the orthodox Christian message (Eph 1.13 = Col 1.5; cf. Jas 1.18). Various interpretations have been offered:

(a) The word is rendered vaguely as 'rightly handle' in various translations.[11] The implication appears to be that Timothy is to teach the gospel correctly (NRSV: 'rightly explaining').[12]

(b) An older view interprets the phrase as to 'cut' the word of truth according to the right norm, which is given in the gospel.[13] Behind this rendering may lie the metaphor of quarrying or cutting building stones (Parry, 57f.), but this is not supported by linguistic usage.

(c) In the context of disputes the thought may be 'to guide the word of truth along a straight path without being turned aside by wordy debates or impious talk'.[14] The stress is more on directness of speech than on faithfulness to the truth, although clearly these cannot be separated.

(d) The phrase may have more to do with conduct than with teaching. The metaphor has been lost and the Wisdom tradition suggests right conduct; the phrase is close to Gal 2.14: ὀρθοποδοῦσιν πρὸς τὴν ἀλήθειαν τοῦ εὐαγγελίου and Hermas, Vis. 3.5.3: κατωρθώσαντο τὰς ἐντολὰς αὐτοῦ. The point is not teaching but rather Timothy's own conduct which is to be in accord with the gospel. Hence the phrase means 'to do what is right with reference to the word of truth' and has to do with way of life rather than teaching.[15]

The broad choice thus lies between right teaching and right living. Since the surrounding context is wholly concerned with the content and manner of teaching rather than with Timothy's own way of life, it is preferable to understand the phrase of teaching, and view (c) has most to commend it. A contrast with the twisting of the truth by the heretics is intended (Guthrie, 160). There is a similar motif in 2 Cor 2.17; 4.2; 2 Pet 3.16.[16]

---

[11] Recte tractantem, vg; RV; RSV; Hanson, 134.

[12] REB: 'keep strictly to'; 'dispense', TLNT II, 595; EDNT II, 531, has 'correctly administer', which is meaningless.

[13] RV mg 2: 'rightly dividing the word of truth'; Bernard, 122.

[14] BA; Kelly, 183; Fee, 255; cf. Oberlinner, 95 – to bear witness to the gospel without any deletion or qualification.

[15] Köster, ibid.; Hasler, 67; contra Hanson, 134.

[16] Later writers developed the idea of ἀποστολικὴ ὀρθοτομία, 'apostolic orthodoxy', a quality ascribed to Quadratus by Eusebius, HE 4.3.1. (Hanson, 134, mistakenly attributes the phrase to Quadratus [c. AD 124] himself.)

16. τὰς δὲ βεβήλους κενοφωνίας περιΐστασο The danger of turning aside from the truth is developed further by what is in effect a repetition of the injunction in v. 14 to avoid strife, but the motive for the repetition is to introduce the reason for doing so. Allowing doctrinal debates will simply encourage the opponents to go further and say things which can upset faith, as evidenced by the actual cases of Hymenaeus and Philetus. For περιΐστημι, 'to avoid, shun', see Tit 3.9***; it is equivalent to παραιτέομαι (2.23) and ἐκτρέπομαι (1 Tim 6.20).[17] For βέβηλος see 1 Tim 1.9 note; 4.7; and 6.20 where it is used, as here, with κενοφωνία, to characterise heretical arguments as profane and futile. The point is not simply that Timothy is not to get involved personally in such disputes but probably also that he is to prohibit them in the congregation.

ἐπὶ πλεῖον γὰρ προκόψουσιν ἀσεβείας The reason for the prohibition now becomes the main theme in the form of a description of what can happen, and has already happened, when free rein is given to the opponents. Two effects are described. They will make progress, but it will be in the wrong direction. The term προκόπτω is used ironically and may reflect the claims of the opponents (cf. 2 Jn 9); it is normally used intrans., 'to go forward, make progress, prosper', generally in good contexts,[18] but also in a bad sense (3.9, 13***).[19] The construction with ἐπὶ πλεῖον recurs in 3.9 (cf. 3.13 ἐπὶ χεῖρον). For ἐπὶ πλεῖον, 'to a greater degree', see Acts 4.17; 20.9; 24.4. Here with the gen. the force is 'will reach an ever greater measure of godlessness' (cf. BA); for ἀσέβεια see Tit 2.12** and note. False teaching leads to godless behaviour.

17a. καὶ ὁ λόγος αὐτῶν ὡς γάγγραινα νομὴν ἕξει The second effect of allowing uncontrolled debate is the spread of the false teaching with poisonous effects. ὁ λόγος αὐτῶν is 'their teaching', sc. that of the opponents; it stands in sharp contrast to the word of truth (v. 15). It is compared to γάγγραινα***, 'gangrene', a medical term for a spreading disease; despite the similarity in its rapid spread, it should not be confused with cancer or ulcers (cf. Spicq, 756, citing Calvin, 314). The same comparison is used for the spread of slanders.[20] But the metaphor here also maintains the

---

[17] Cf. Lucian, *Hermot.* 86 (White, 165).

[18] Lk 2.52; Rom 13.12; Gal 1.14; cf. προκοπή, 1 Tim 4.15 and note.

[19] A problem is caused by the absence of a subject for the verb. GNB, NJB and NRSV assume that it is the godless disputes in the previous clause and therefore takes the verb as trans. This is unlikely in view of the following αὐτῶν and the parallels in 3.9, 13; the verb is intrans. and the subject to be supplied is 'people, especially the false teachers'.

[20] Plutarch, *Mor.* 65D, cited in Dibelius-Conzelmann, 111 n. 8; other parallels in Spicq, 756.

motif of unhealthy teaching in contrast to healthy (Tit 1.9 note).
It is continued in the main statement. νομή is originally 'pasture'
(i.e. the place and the fodder it provides; Jn 10.9***), but the
word was used fig. in phrases that describe the 'spread' of an
ulcer (Josephus, *Bel.* 6.164). According to Galen the term was
derived from the verb νέμομαι, 'to graze, feed', because of the
way in which the disease spreads like the way in which animals
move across the land as they seek food.[21] νομὴν ποιεῖται ἕλκος
(cited by BA). The fut. ἕξει describes the possible effect if the
false teaching is not stopped. Although Dibelius-Conzelmann,
111, suggest that the disease spreads in the individual human
soul (cf. 3.13), it is more likely that the congregation is in mind.
There is a superficial contradiction with 3.9.

**17b–18. ὧν ἐστιν Ὑμέναιος καὶ Φίλητος, οἵτινες περὶ τὴν
ἀλήθειαν ἠστόχησαν** There is no break in the sentence as a relative
clause is loosely added to give an example as an illustration and
warning; the danger is real, not just a possibility![22] For the
connective ὧν ἐστιν with the force 'including [for example]' see
1.15; 1 Tim 1.20. The teaching of Ὑμέναιος is described as
blasphemous in 1 Tim 1.20*** note; there he was paired with
Ἀλέξανδρος, but here with the otherwise unknown Φίλητος***.[23]
It has to be presumed that, despite his delivery to Satan in 1 Tim,
Hymenaeus was still able to influence the church (whether in
historical reality or in the author's scenario). For οἵτινες see Tit
1.11 note; it probably has the force 'inasmuch as they'. The
whole phrase echoes περὶ τὴν ἀλήθειαν ἠστόχησαν (1 Tim
6.21).

λέγοντες [τὴν] ἀνάστασιν ἤδη γεγονέναι The precise area where
the opponents have gone astray is specified. λέγοντες (here with
acc. and inf.) has the force 'teaching' (1 Tim 1.7). But what did
they mean by saying that the resurrection (ἀνάστασις**)[24]
had already taken place and in effect denying the statement
in vv. 11f.? If the article is omitted, then the statement might
simply mean that a resurrection of some kind has already
happened. The inclusion of the article (see textual note) implies
that *the* resurrection has taken place; this can only be the future

---

[21] *De Simpl.* 9: καλεῖν … νομὰς ἀπὸ τοῦ νέμεσθαι τὴν σηπεδόνα πρὸς τὰ
πλησιάσαντα μόρια (cited by Dibelius-Conzelmann, 111 n. 10); cf. Polybius
1.81.6:
[22] The verse division at 17/18 awkwardly divides up the remainder of the
sentence; it would have been more appropriate at 17a/17b.
[23] The name is rarely attested; cf. P. Oxy. 72.17 (AD I; cited by BA) and the
AD III/IV inscr. in *New Docs.* IV, 32f. §8.
[24] Rom 6.5; Mk 12.18, 23; Jn 11.24; Acts 17.18. It is often qualified by the
addition τῶν νεκρῶν (Rom 1.4; 1 Cor 15.12f., 21, 42). The word is only rarely
used of resurrection in Cl.; Oepke, A., *TDNT* I, 371f.

resurrection of the body, and the implication is that there is no other resurrection still to come.

Possibly related statements are found elsewhere. Some of them are apparently simple denials of a future resurrection,[25] while others are more explicit that in some sense it has already taken place. In the Pauline literature we have 1 Cor 15.12 with its reference to people who say that there is *no* resurrection. The outcome of a considerable discussion is that these people believed that in some way they had already entered upon a spiritual life and believed that the body would simply die and be destroyed. This would fit in nicely with the belief that they were 'already reigning' (1 Cor 4.8) and perhaps with the belief that the day of the Lord had arrived (2 Th 2.2).

Similar views persisted in the early church, especially among Gnostics, and were condemned by 'orthodox' writers.[26]

As regards the present statement, the possibilities are:

---

[25] The denial of a resurrection by the Sadducees falls into this category (Mk 12.18; Acts 23.8).

[26] Several texts refer to denial of the resurrection: 'The person who says that there is neither resurrection nor judgement is the firstborn of Satan' (Polycarp 7.1); 'Let none of you say that the flesh is not judged nor resurrected' (2 Clement 9.1); 'There are people who say that there is no resurrection of the dead, but at the time when they die their souls are taken up to heaven' (Justin, *Dial.* 80). Cf. Tertullian, *De carn. res.* 19.

Others refer to the belief that people have already been resurrected. Non-Christians alleged of Christians in general: 'You would think, to listen to them, that they were already resurrected' (Minucius Felix, *Octavian,* 11.2). Menander's 'disciples received resurrection through baptism into him, and they can no longer die, but remain without growing old and immortal' (Irenaeus, *AH* 1.23.5); Menander 'alleged to his disciples that they would not die. And even now there are some of them who affirm this' (Justin, *Apol.* I.26.4; cf. Eusebius, *HE* 3.26.3). Tertullian, *De praesc. haer.* 33, held that Paul was attacking the Valentinians. See also Clement, *Strom.* 3.48.1; Valentinus in Clement, *Strom.* 4.89, 91.

This type of belief is found in original Gnostic sources: 'Then indeed, as the Apostle said, we suffered with him, and we arose with him, and we went to heaven with him' (*Epistle to Rheginus* [*NHL,* 50–53] 45.23–28; 'Already you have the resurrection' (ibid. 49.15f.); 'Those who say they will die first and then rise are in error. If they do not first receive the resurrection while they live, when they die they will receive nothing' (*Gospel of Philip* [*NHL,* 131–51] 73.1–4); 'If one does not first attain the resurrection will he not die?' (ibid. 56.19).

An unusual view is found in *Acts of Paul and Thecla* 14 (*NTA* II, 357): The opinion of Demas and Hermogenes 'concerning the resurrection which he says is to come' is 'that it has already taken place in the children whom we have, and that we are risen again in that we have come to know the true God'.

Sometimes knowledge is identified with resurrection. Thus Irenaeus, *AH* 2.31.2 comments on Simon and the Carpocratians: '*esse autem resurrectionem a mortuis agnitionem eius quae ab eis dicitur veritatis*'. (cf. Ps-Clement, *Hom.* 2.22.5); cf. '*agnitio sacramenti* (= ἡ τοῦ μυστηρίου γνῶσις) *resurrectio est*' (Tertullian, *De carn. res.* 25). Note that *agnitio* means 'knowledge' (cf. *agnosco,* 'to recognise'), and should not be confused with Eng. words (like 'agnostic') derived from Greek words with α-privative.

(a) The opponents may have held the Greek view that the soul is immortal and therefore there is no need for a physical resurrection. Spicq, 757f., notes that the opponents may have been trying to get rid of an item of Christian faith that was unacceptable in a Greek environment.

(b) The usual understanding of the position of the opponents is that they held that the only resurrection to be experienced by believers was the mystical resurrection to new life which took place at baptism (cf. Rom 6.1–11; Eph 2.6; 5.14; Col 2.12; 3.1), and that therefore there was no future resurrection of the body (Lock, 99; Brown, 71; Spicq, 757; cf. Scott. 111).[27] It was to deal with this heresy that later creeds insisted on the future resurrection of flesh. For the use of resurrection language in connection with conversion see Lk 15.24, 32; Jn 5.25–29; Eph 2.4–6; 5.14; Rev 3.1–3 (Thiessen 1995:330–4).[28]

(c) Lane* proposes that the heretics believed that 'by virtue of the resurrection of Jesus Christ the Christian community had been projected into the Age to come, and that the conditions of life in that age were now in force'. It follows that people should not marry (Mk 12.25) or eat meat (only fish and honeycomb, like the risen Jesus; cf. Rom 14.17). Further, once people die, there is no further resurrection, no hope of future life (cf. 1 Tim 4.8). On this view, the heresy was not based on confusion between the future resurrection and the mystical resurrection but between the future resurrection and the new era inaugurated by the resurrection of Jesus. The implication could be that those who did not follow the heretics had missed out on this new life (Arichea-Hatton, 209).

This view seems less likely than that there was a reinterpretation of Paul's teaching on rising with Christ (correctly, Hanson, 136). The future hope of physical resurrection in Paul was spiritualised in later writers and combined with the idea of a resurrection at baptism.

For some advocates of this view, Paul himself in Rom 6 could not speak of a present resurrection experience of believers, but by the time of Col 2.11–13 and Eph 2.5f. the resurrection had come to be regarded as both spiritual (at baptism) and physical (in the future), and later still 'the tension between present and future may have been dissolved entirely in favour of the present,

---

[27] This was the view of Menander and Nicolas of Antioch (Hippolytus, *Phil.* 7.36; Tertullian, *de Anim.* 50; cf. Lane*, 165). Nicolas believed 'that the resurrection had already happened, meaning that we believe in Christ and received the washing, but he denied the resurrection of the flesh' (Hippolytus, *De Res.* Frg. 1 [GCS 1:2, 251], cited by Brox, 36).

[28] Thiessen also refers to 2 Macc 7.22f.; *Jos. et As.* 8.10f.; 20.7; *Apost. Const.* 7.39.4; Philo, *Mig.* 122f. for similar language.

a dissolution which the author of 2 Timothy roundly condemns' (Wedderburn*, 350). This is essentially the view adopted by Sellin* who links the error condemned in 2 Tim with that condemned in 2 Th. In both cases the Pauline author 'reapocalypticises' the concept and emphasises the importance of the future resurrection with which is linked the day of judgement.

Various scholars hold that this particular belief of the writer's opponents is essentially Gnostic. Oberlinner, 98, claims that the singularity of this statement concerning the actual content of the heresy indicates that this was a central issue, and that it is clearly Gnostic. The resurrection was spiritualised as 'the reception of the Gnosis, i.e. the rediscovery of one's divine self' at baptism (Kremer, J., *EDNT* I, 91; similarly, Brox, 246). 'The enlightened gnostic Christian is already removed from the influence of the material through his spiritual soul and has entered the area of the divine spirit' (Knoch, 58; cf. Rudolph 1983: 189–94). This interpretation, with its language about the 'divine self', reads considerably more into the text than is to be found there and makes the dubious assumption that later ideas were already fully formed by the end of the first century.

Most commentators assume that the implication of the heresy was that there was to be no future resurrection (Barrett, 106) because it was unnecessary. However, Hasler, 68, thinks that it is unlikely that the author would have passed in silence over an actual denial of the future resurrection; the problem may rather have been that because they claimed to be resurrected already, they did not need to do good works in order to attain future salvation. This is unlikely, since it is not easy on this view to see why the heresy was upsetting the faith of other believers.

The force of the statement may have been not so much in a denial of future resurrection as in a positive statement concerning the present age as one of eschatological fulfilment leading to an 'enthusiastic' Christianity (Oberlinner, 100). The heretics may also have understood baptism as a sacramental reception of the Spirit which led to a real change of nature. But the present passage is entirely silent on this issue, and it is hard to see any evidence for such 'enthusiasm' among the opposition, and certainly not for a special possession of the Spirit.

καὶ ἀνατρέπουσιν τήν τινων πίστιν. A concluding clause expresses the results of the false teaching. καί will have the force 'and so, in this way'; some of the Christian community (τινων) find that their faith is jeopardised[29] by the denial of what to them was an integral element of it, the hope of future resurrection.

---

[29] For ἀνατρέπω see Tit 1.11. For the use with τὴν πίστιν see Diodorus Siculus 1.77.2, but there the reference is to a pledge.

19. ὁ μέντοι στερεὸς θεμέλιος τοῦ θεοῦ ἕστηκεν, ἔχων τὴν σφραγῖδα ταύτην Despite the false teaching of the opponents and over against the threat that some people may be tempted to give up their faith, God's truth stands firm (cf. 2.9). It is solid and it will not shift. The church, if it is the solid foundation, is sealed by the Lord with an inscription containing two texts. Negatively, their effect is to say that he knows who are his people who maintain his truth, and therefore he does not recognise the heretics; there is also the command to depart from iniquity, which is implicitly a condemnation both of false doctrine and of the evil behaviour which is assumed to accompany it. Positively, there is the assurance that the Lord knows his people – and will preserve them – but they for their part must resist all iniquity. The passage is related to the somewhat similar description of the church in 1 Tim 3.15f., although there there is less stress on the invulnerability of the church.

Over against the activity of the opponents and their apparent success in upsetting faith there is placed the strong contrast of the firm, immovable work of God. μέντοι is an emphatic 'nevertheless.'[30] θεμέλιος is lit. a 'foundation', whether a single stone (Rev 21.14, 19a, 19b) or the foundation of a building (Lk 6.49; 14.2; 6.48; Heb 11.10), and hence by metonymy can represent a building or institution.[31] Metaphorically, it refers to the elementary beginnings of something (Rom 15.20; 1 Cor 3.10, 12; Heb 6.1). It is used of the divinely laid foundation of the church (1 Cor 3.11; Eph 2.20); for the unusual use in 1 Tim 6.19 (? 'treasury, reserve') see note there. Behind the application here to the foundation laid by God see especially Isa 28.16 (Gärtner 1965:71). The innate immovability of the foundation is expressed by the attrib. adj. στερεός, 'firm, hard, solid'.[32] Because it is established so firmly by God it remains standing.[33]

(a) With most scholars we assume that the reference is to the church.[34] The use of similar language in 1 Tim 3.15 is surely decisive. Other suggested possibilities are:

---

[30] Jn 4.27; 7.13; 12.42; 20.5; 21.4; Jas 2.8; Jude 8***; Cl.; the rendering 'though, to be sure, indeed' (BA) hardly does justice to the element of contrast and affirmation.

[31] Vettius Valens 82.24 (pl. LSJ say it = 'building site'); cf. Simpson, 138; Spicq, 759.

[32] Of a rock, Homer, *Od.* 19.494 (LSJ); LXX; *1 Enoch* 26.5; Barnabas 5.14; 6.3 = Isa 50.7. Cf. Bertram, G., *TDNT* VII, 609–14.

[33] For this sense of ἕστηκα** cf. the phrase μηδὲν ἑστηκὸς καὶ ἀκίνητον (Procopius Sophista, *Ep.* 47, cited by BA).

[34] Cf. 1QS 8.4–8; Hermas, *Sim.* 9.4.2; 9.15.4; Holtzmann, 419; Dibelius-Conzelmann, 112; Spicq, 759; Brox, 249; Hasler, 69; Oberlinner, 101; Grundmann, W., *TDNT* VII, 636–53, espec. 651.

(b) the Ephesian church in particular, or the group of genuine Christians in it (Scott, 112; Kelly, 186);

(c) God himself who both lays and is the foundation; 'the foundation stone ... is the constancy and faithfulness with which God calls His community afresh each day, and the individual within it, and holds them fast to Jesus Christ, the Crucified and Risen Lord. In this way he is the firm foundation of faith';[35]

(d) Christ himself, on the basis that Isa 28.16 was interpreted as referring to him; he will not fail despite the threats of heresy (Rom 9.33; Eph 2.20f.; Hanson, 136f.);

(e) Christ and his apostles (Lock, 100);

(f) 'the truth revealed in Christ, guarded by the community of those who live by it' (Gärtner 1965:71; cf. Parry, 59);

(g) there is no specific reference (Fee, 257 – but this is a counsel of despair).

The point is that the true church, characterised by its possession of the truth and as represented by the faithful believers in Ephesus, is certain to stand firm despite the activities of the opponents.

However, the added qualification defines the reason for the firmness of the building. Pursuing the metaphor, the author states that the building has (ἔχων), i.e. bears, a seal.[36] Since one cannot put a mark on stone by means of a seal, the reference must be metaphorical to the engraving of an inscription with the same function as the impression of a seal. The seal can have various purposes and functions; it can indicate ownership or attestation (Rom 4.11; 1 Cor 9.2). In 2 Cor 1.22 and Eph 1.13 the gift of the Spirit is God's seal on individual believers; they are his and are under his protection and bear the mark that proves it. Here the thought is that God marks out the foundation as being laid by himself and therefore being his property and under his protection. The reference is to the church as a whole, rather than to each individual member of it (*pace* White, 167). Nevertheless, some scholars see a baptismal reference (Roloff 1985:244f.; Oberlinner, 102; Holtz, 173;[37]) or attempt to combine the sealing of individuals in baptism with the inscribing of foundation stones (Hasler, 69). But surely we are not forced to see a reference to baptism every time a word that is sometimes associated with it is used.

---

[35] Bertram, G., *TDNT* VII, 612f.; cf. Calvin, 316 – 'God's election'.

[36] σφραγίς is used both of the stamp and of the impression or inscription caused by the stamp. Cf. Rev 5.1 and freq.; Fitzer, G., *TDNT* VII, 939–53; Schramm, T., *EDNT* III, 316f.

[37] How Hanson, 137, can say that the foundation is Christ and the seal is baptism, I cannot understand.

The actual content of the inscription is of great significance (cf. Rev 21.14). It is used to make a solemn proclamation which combines assurance and command.

ἔγνω κύριος τοὺς ὄντας αὐτοῦ Two citations are given, both based on LXX phraseology; they may possibly reflect forms of words current in the church, but there is nothing particularly 'poetic' about them.[38] The first citation is from Num 16.5 LXX with the substitution of κύριος (= MT יהוה) for ὁ θεός. It comes from the statement of Moses at the time of the revolt by Korah[39] that God was able to discriminate between the true and the false; he would show who was authorised to approach him in priestly service and who was not authorised. Thus the statement is used primarily in a negative fashion to show that the Lord will exclude those whom he does not recognise as his people.[40] Implicitly it asserts that he knows and protects those who are truly his people. Hence people should not judge who are the Lord's people by outward appearance and human considerations, such as the imposing claims made by heretics. The absence of the article with κύριος fits in with the practice elsewhere in the PE, where anarthrous κύριος refers to God (cf. 1.18 note; 2.19b, 24), but also reflects the influence of the usage elsewhere in Num 16.3, 7, 9, 15, et al.; it is plausible that a variant form of the text is being cited. Capes* holds that the reference is to Christ rather than to God.[41] γινώσκω expresses here, as elsewhere, the thought of God's personal knowledge and choice of his people (Jn 10.14f.). The language is not Gnostic (CH 10.15) but Hebraic.[42] For the idiom in τοὺς ὄντας αὐτοῦ, 'the people who belong to him', see BA s.v. IV.1. The tense in ἔγνω is strange. A timeless expression would be appropriate, but the past tense may be simply due to taking over a quotation unchanged or possibly to the clumsy translation of a Semitic perfective (McKay 1981:308f.). Arndt*, however, argues that the aor. is used of God's past act of electing his people (cf. ἐξελέξατο, Num 16.5b); 'knew' is equivalent to 'came to know', i.e. 'chose'.

καί· ἀποστήτω ἀπὸ ἀδικίας πᾶς ὁ ὀνομάζων τὸ ὄνομα κυρίου A second quotation is added with καί (cf. 1 Tim 5.18; Heb 1.10). ἀδικία**, 'iniquity, unjust action', is frequently used for what is

---

[38] Pace Dibelius-Conzelmann, 112; for detailed discussion see Wolfe 1990:26–38.

[39] Cf. Jude 11 for further attestation that the story was known and used in the early church.

[40] Cf. the negative form in Mt 7.23 par. Lk 13.27; Mt 25.12.

[41] Capes bases his argument on: (a) The identification of the 'foundation' as Christ (but see above); (b) the identification of 'the name of the Lord' in the second quotation as 'the name of Christ' (cf. Rom 15.20; Phil 2.9–11). Neither point is compelling.

[42] Bultmann, R., TDNT I, 706; Schmithals, W., EDNT I, 249; cf. Od. Sol. 8.15f.

sinful and wrong in God's sight but is not prominent in the vocabulary of the PE; it is used here, as elsewhere, in contrast to truth rather than to righteousness.[43] For ἀφίστημι see 1 Tim 4.1**, and for the construction here see Ecclus 35.5 (32.3); *T. Dan* 6.10. ὀνομάζω** is lit. 'to give a name to', 'to call by name'. The idiom ὀνομάζειν τὸ ὄνομα is found in the LXX;[44] the usual force is 'to call upon God [in prayer]'. Hence the phrase may be simply a way of referring to Christians or a reference to the actual practice of prayer. Most scholars hold that the phrase is modelled on Isa 26.13. The whole clause is then a summons to believers to refrain from evil. However, in Lev 24.16 the phrase refers to using the name of God blasphemously (as in Lev 24.11 and Ecclus 23.10). Larson* has argued cogently that this is the usage here.[45] The clause refers then rather to the opponents whose teaching is regarded as a form of blasphemy and urges them to mend their ways.

None of the OT passages where the idiom occurs contains the first part of the clause. Here, therefore, there is a combination of phrases.[46] The key word ἀποστήτω has led to the attachment of the statement to the preceding citation from Num 16.5. The predicate stands closest to Ps 6.9 in the form in which it is cited by Lk.[47] In any case, a connection with the thought in Lk 13.27 is possible, since here the οὐκ οἶδα πόθεν ἐστέ gives a sharp contrast with ἔγνω κύριος τοὺς ὄντας αὐτοῦ (Holtzmann, 419). Note, however, that the citation in Lk 13.27 is about evil-doers departing from the Lord, not about evil-doers abandoning their evil ways.

The effect of the two quotations is to give reassurance to God's people that he will preserve his church despite the threats caused by heretics; at the same time (on the traditional interpretation) those who call themselves believers are urged to depart from the evil practices (perhaps including the holding of false beliefs as

[43] Cf. Jn 7.18; Rom 1.18; 2.8; 1 Cor 13.6; 2 Th 2.10–12; Schrenk, G., *TDNT* I, 153–7, especially 156.

[44] Ὀνομάζων δὲ τὸ ὄνομα κυρίου θανάτῳ θανατούσθω (Lev 24.16); τὰ ὀνόματα τῶν θεῶν αὐτῶν οὐκ ὀνομασθήσεται ἐν ὑμῖν (Jos 23.7); τὸ ὄνομά σου ὀνομάζομεν (Isa 26.13); καὶ εἶπα Οὐ μὴ ὀνομάσω τὸ ὄνομα Κυρίου (Jer 20.9). Cf. καὶ ἐπονομάσας ... τὸ ὄνομα κατηράσατο (Lev 24.11).

[45] It is not clear whether the author interpreted κυρίου as referring to God, as in the first quotation, or to Christ (as in the usual NT usage of the phrase; so Larson*, 95).

[46] Parallels to the wording here are: καὶ ἀπέστησαν ἀπὸ τῆς σκηνῆς Κόρε (Num 16.26f.); ἀπόστητε ἀπ' ἐμοῦ πάντες οἱ ἐργαζόμενοι τὴν ἀνομίαν (Ps 6.9); ἔκκλινον ἀπὸ κακοῦ (Ps 33.15 [MT 34.14]); ἔκκλινε ἀπὸ παντὸς κακοῦ (Prov 3.7); ἀπόστητε ... οἱ φεροῦντες τὰ σκεύη κυρίου (Isa 52.11); ἀπόστρεφε ἀπὸ ἀδικίας (Ecclus 17.26). Cf. the citation of Ps 6.9 in Mt 7.23 (ἀποχωρεῖτε ἀπ' ἐμοῦ οἱ ἐργαζόμενοι τὴν ἀνομίαν) par. Lk 13.27 (ἀπόστητε ἀπ' ἐμοῦ πάντες ἐργάται ἀδικίας).

[47] The closeness of the language to Ecclus 17.26 is noted by Kowalski 1994:53.

well as impious conduct) which are associated with heresy; or (on Larson's view) there is a way back even for the heretics and those influenced by them, but people risk being shut out from God's saving power if they do not seek to live in a godly manner.

20. Ἐν μεγάλη δὲ οἰκίᾳ οὐκ ἔστιν μόνον σκεύη χρυσᾶ καὶ ἀργυρᾶ ἀλλὰ καὶ ξύλινα καὶ ὀστράκινα, καὶ ἃ μὲν εἰς τιμὴν ἃ δὲ εἰς ἀτιμίαν Verses 20–21 belong together, giving a metaphorical statement and its application. The statement in v. 20 serves as an explanation of the split in the church in v. 19 (Dibelius-Conzelmann, 113), but should not be taken as a justification of the existence of the opponents in a mixed church. V. 21 is in effect an elaboration of the command in v. 19b and a preparation for vv. 22–26 (Fee, 261). The literal situation and the metaphorical application are not clear. Scott, 114, calls the statement 'clumsy and confused'.

The argument begins with a statement that at first sight poses no problems on the literal level, although it is obviously intended to be metaphorical. The picture of a house (οἰκία, lit., 3.6; 1 Tim 5.13; cf. οἶκος, 1.16 *et al.*) is doubtless inspired by the preceding imagery of the foundation. The thought is of a building inhabited by a household and is a picture of the church.[48] A magnificent house is envisaged, belonging to wealthy people, the kind who alone would be able to afford costly vessels as well as ordinary ones. The reference to the size and implied grandeur may be partly inspired by the fact that the house is a metaphor for the church (Oberlinner, 104), but in fact it is needed to give a setting for the costly vessels. For the construction οὐκ ... μόνον ... ἀλλὰ καί ... cf. 4.8; 1 Tim 5.13. σκεῦος (2.21**) is a general word that embraces any kind of household vessel or utensil.[49] Four kinds are mentioned, as in Plutarch, *Caes.* 48.4 (730F). The first two adorn the rich person's table; they are expensive dishes, made of, or adorned with, gold[50] and silver.[51] The two metals are frequently linked together in ancient literature (cf. Gen 24.53). The second two types are ordinary vessels for kitchen use, made of wood[52] and earthenware;[53] the latter adj. elsewhere

[48] Spicq, 759f., appears to favour the view that the house is a temple, but while the term can be applied to a temple, nothing favours this narrower reference here.

[49] Lk 8.16; Jn 19.29; Rom 9.21; Rev 2.27; Maurer, C., *TDNT* VII, 358–67, espec. 364.

[50] χρυσοῦς; Heb 9.4a, 4b; Rev 1.12; *et al.*; cf. χρυσίον, 1 Tim 2.9; 1 Cor 3.12 in metaphorical use. The contracted forms of this and the next adj. are Cl.

[51] ἀργυροῦς (Acts 19.24; Rev 9.20***).

[52] ξύλινος (Rev 9.20*** of wooden vessels, Dittenberger, *Syll.* 962.44, 316; Lev 15.12; Num 31.20; 35.18).

[53] ὀστράκινος (2 Cor 4.7 ***; Lev 6.21; 11.33; the word is rare in Hel.; cf. Epictetus 3.9.18).

conveys the nuance of being breakable and fragile. Both types of vessel are good and necessary in their place – and this might lead to the readers' expectation that the metaphor would be developed, as in 1 Cor 12.21–26, in terms of the equal necessity and value of all the parts of the body. But at this point a fresh thought is added.

The καί may be explicative, indicating that 'evaluation by material is the same as that by purpose' (Maurer, C., *TDNT* VII, 364 n. 42). The pair of rels. ἃ μέν ... ἃ δέ ... are ambiguous.[54] There are two possibilities:

(a) The sense may be simply 'some ... others...', in which case the reference could be to distinctions among the vessels as a whole group or to a distinction among the ordinary vessels.[55]

(b) More precisely, some commentators interpret the sense to be specifically 'the former ... the latter...', referring respectively to the ordinary and the costly vessels.[56] However, it should be noted that in this kind of construction μέν ... δέ ... generally refers to 'the latter ... the former...' (2 Cor 2.15f.; Phil 1.15f.).

A decision between these two possibilities depends on the interpretation of the two categories of use. Vessels for honour (τιμή, 1 Tim 1.17) are those for honourable purposes; they acquire honour by the use to which they are put, and they are valued (BA; cf. Rom 9.21). This thought is taken up in 2.21.[57] Correspondingly, a vessel for dishonour[58] is dishonoured by the use to which it is put (e.g. as a rubbish bin).

Thus some vessels are for honourable purposes, such as serving food daintily on the table, and they are treated with respect and honour. Others are for dishonourable purposes, such as containing garbage and dirt, and they are kept out of sight. People would not use one type of vessel for the other type of purpose.

Returning to the question of syntax and interpretation, we now have two possibilities:

(a) There are household vessels of costly and ordinary materials, and some (of either kind) are for honour and others for dishonour.

(b) Some household vessels are of costly and some of ordinary materials, the former being for honourable purposes and the latter for dishonourable.

---

[54] The phrase was equivalent in Koine Gk. to τὰ μέν ... τὰ δέ ... used demonstratively (BD § 250; MHT III, 36; Simpson, 139).

[55] BA *s.v.* μέν 1c; NIV; GNB; NRSV; cf. how the sing. form can be used for 'the one ... the other...' (Mt 13.8, 23).

[56] NJB; REB; Simpson, 140; Kelly, 187; Knight, 418.

[57] Field 1899:215 cites Diodorus Siculus 17.66.3–7, where a table is used as a footstool, and instead of being 'honoured' it is 'dishonoured'.

[58] ἀτιμία (Rom 9.21; cf. 1.26; 1 Cor 11.14; 15.43; 2 Cor 6.8; 11.21***; cf. Philo, *Cont.* 7.

In favour of view (a) is the fact that a simple equation between gold and silver dishes for honourable purposes and wooden and earthenware ones for dishonourable cannot be carried through consistently; earthenware dishes can be used for either (e.g. cooking or garbage; rightly, Holtzmann, 420), and there can doubtless be gold-plated refuse bins in wealthy houses. However, there is no certainty that these more subtle considerations were in the author's mind; a broad contrast between the two types may be all that is intended. It is, therefore, difficult to be sure what he meant, but on balance view (b) is perhaps more probable, with the proviso that the author was making a rough distinction.

Although in the picture the 'dishonourable' uses are necessary and good (vessels for the disposal of garbage are essential), this again is probably not part of the metaphorical application. The positive value of the 'vessels for dishonourable purposes' in the house is not carried over. The implied point is surely rather that the normal practice is that the vessels which are used only for dishonourable purposes will eventually be treated with dishonour (Rom 9.21f.) and thrown out (like a black polythene bag thrown out with the waste it contains, even though theoretically it could be washed out and used again).

Consequently, the metaphorical application of the picture to the church appears to be simply in terms of people who hold to the truth and to godliness and are therefore useful and destined for honour in contrast to those who hold to error and ungodly conduct and therefore are useless and destined for judgement. The necessity or otherwise of the different kinds of people in the church as opposed to the vessels in the house is not in mind. The idea that the picture justifies the presence of heretics in the church (cf. Brox, 249f.) is dubious; at most there is the recognition that their presence is unfortunately 'normal'.

21. ἐὰν οὖν τις ἐκκαθάρῃ ἑαυτὸν ἀπὸ τούτων, ἔσται σκεῦος εἰς τιμήν, ἡγιασμένον, εὔχρηστον τῷ δεσπότῃ, εἰς πᾶν ἔργον ἀγαθὸν ἡτοιμασμένον οὖν is used loosely to draw a conclusion that is implied in the metaphor, but not actually stated. It goes beyond what is said in it. The point appears to be that a vessel which is used for so-called dishonourable uses (like storing garbage) can be thoroughly cleaned and would then be fit for a honourable purpose (such as cooking or even serving a meal). At this point the question of what the vessel is made of seems to have disappeared from sight, and equally questions of the suitability of the vessel for one purpose or another (in terms of its size and shape) are irrelevant. τις, 'anybody', is quite vague. Some commentators appear to take the reference to be to the church, which is to be purged of the opponents (NEB mg, not retained in REB), but this is an impossible interpretation; clearly the pronoun refers to 'any member of the congregation', and further specification (e.g. the false teachers or those influenced by them, orthodox believers, or even a delicate reference to Timothy himself) is unnecessary. All members of the church are called on to cleanse themselves from anything that would defile them. For ἐκκαθαίρω see 1 Cor 5.7***, where it is used metaphorically of purging out old leaven from the church; the verb is constructed with the acc. of what is removed or what is cleansed.[59] The phrase ἀπὸ τούτων has no obvious antecedent. (a) The empty disputes with the opponents (v. 16) are too far away, and do not give the right sense. (b) The nearest possibility is the vessels in v. 20 (cf. NIV: 'from the latter', presumably the 'some [articles] for ignoble purposes'). These, however, represent the false teachers in the church (vv. 17–18) from whom Timothy is to separate himself.[60] However, this interpretation is illogical in that what is envisaged is a vessel used for one type of service being transformed to be suitable for another type, not the separation of one kind of vessel from another in order to become clean. (c) The reference must accordingly be somewhat loosely to the activities of the opponents, including their false teaching and the associated evil way of life.[61]

Such persons will become (ἔσται) honoured vessels, used for good purposes. Whether likely or not in the literal sense, the metaphorical vessel can undergo a change of use and with it a change of status. Cleansed from evil, the 'vessel' is now 'pure' (ἁγιάζω, 1 Tim 4.5**) and capable of being used. For εὔχρηστος see 4.11; Philem 11***;[62] there is possibly a contrast with ἐπ' οὐδὲν χρήσιμον in v. 14. δεσπότης (1 Tim 6.1, 2; Tit 2.9) is equivalent to οἰκοδεσπότης, the owner of a house and its contents. With εἰς πᾶν ἔργον ἀγαθόν we return to a characteristic phrase and motif of the PE;[63] ἡτοιμασμένον[64] is a variant for ἕτοιμος (Tit 3.1) and ἐξηρτισμένος (2 Tim 3.17).

Behind this development of the metaphor lies the practice of the potter described in Wis 15.7 (NRSV): 'A potter kneads the soft earth and laboriously moulds each vessel for our service, fashioning out of the same clay both the vessels that serve clean

---

[59] For the fig. use cf. Plutarch, *Mor.* 64F; Epictetus 2.23.40; Vettius Valens 242.15.

[60] Holtzmann, 421; Knight, 418; Kelly, 188; Lane, W. L., *NIDNTT* III, 915.

[61] NJB is typical: 'from these faults I speak of'; Parry, 60; Spicq, 763; Fee, 262; Maurer, C., *TDNT* VII, 364 n. 43; cf. ἀδικία, v. 19b.

[62] The word is very freq. in Hermas; *Inscr. Rom.* IV. 818.23 (an honorific inscription for a public official): εἰς χρίας κυριακὰς εὔχρηστον γενόμενον (cited by MM 268; BA).

[63] 3.17 (πρός); Tit 1.16; 3.1; 2 Cor 9.8.

[64] ἑτοιμάζω** (Eph 2.10; 3 Macc 6.31; cf. Rev 9.7).

uses and those for contrary uses, making all alike; but which shall be the use of each of them the worker in clay decides.' Here the point, which is incidental to the main theme, is the authority of the potter to decide to what different uses the same clay will be put. The same point is developed by Paul in Rom 9.21, where there are also vessels for honour and dishonour which are the objects of wrath and mercy respectively. But the point here is different and has nothing to do with predestination, although the thought of the ultimate destruction of the vessels εἰς ἀτιμίαν is implicit. It is in the power of the individual to seek cleansing from evil and become fit for good use (Oberlinner, 106); again, the possibility that the heretics may return to the truth is allowed. Other points, such as that there will be good and bad alike in the church until the judgement (Mt 13.24) or that the church should excommunicate such people, are foreign to the context, whether or not it is legitimate to see them as implications.

The passage as a whole is difficult for three reasons: the shift from the initial description of materials, which in the end is not especially relevant, to that of functions; the stress on the value assigned to the vessels regardless of the fact that even dishonourable functions are necessary functions; and the loose reference of the phrase ἀπὸ τούτων. When allowance is made for these points, the basic lesson is fundamentally clear.

22. Τὰς δὲ νεωτερικὰς ἐπιθυμίας φεῦγε, δίωκε δὲ δικαιοσύνην πίστιν ἀγάπην εἰρήνην μετὰ τῶν ἐπικαλουμένων τὸν κύριον ἐκ καθαρᾶς καρδίας From the general, metaphorical direction to any members of the congregation to free themselves from the sins associated with the opponents, the writer turns directly again to Timothy with literal injunctions. The exhortation in vv. 22f. could, it is true, provide an example of what following the advice in v. 21 entails, but it is more probable that the writer is thinking here specifically of how the leader is to behave when faced with opponents. The appeal to him to act peaceably towards them is stressed again. Three points are made in vv. 22f. followed by a justification in vv. 24–26. (a) He is to avoid youthful desires. (b) He is to be a general example of good character. (c) He is to avoid disputes – a thought developed in detail in 24–26 with emphasis on how to deal with those who are dead set against the truth. The structure of the first two commands (φεῦγε/διώκε) is identical with that in 1 Tim 6.11.

First, there is the command to avoid what is evil. δέ is a loose connective, contrastive rather than adversative; over against preparedness for 'good works' stands the complementary command to avoid what are in effect 'bad works'. For ἐπιθυμία see

1 Tim 6.11. νεωτερικός*** is 'youthful',[65] but the reference is disputed. 'Youthful desires' have been generally understood as sensual desires,[66] but nothing in the immediate context favours this understanding. There is more to be said for a reference to the headstrong enthusiasm of youth which leads into impatience, immature conduct and eagerness for dispute;[67] admittedly these are not 'desires' but defects of character. Metzger* argues that desire for novelty is at least part of the picture; the pl. makes it unlikely that it is the whole story. Since the reference hardly fits in with the general picture of Timothy's timidity and lack of boldness in dealing with opponents (1.7f.), it is probable that the reference is to tendencies in the church that Timothy is to combat rather than to his own conduct. In *T. Reub.* 2 νεωτερισμός is associated with the seven spirits of error. Oberlinner, 111f., attempts to generalise as much as possible and to find the kind of enthusiastic, thoughtless, endeavours to deal with the heretics which would lead to disaster, but his playing down of the 'youthful' element does not convince.

Second, there is the positive command to aim at the qualities of Christian character. There is a brief list with four components, three of which also occur in the ethical list in 1 Tim 6.11 (δικαιοσύνη, πίστις, ἀγάπη); the fourth item, εἰρήνη (1.2; Tit 1.4 and note), is not in 1 Tim 6.11, which has ὑπομονή and πραϋπαθία, which might be regarded as equivalents. For Fee, 263f., this last term is the key one, standing in contrast to μάχη in 2.23.

The prep. phrase with μετά can be taken in two ways. It may go with the verb δίωκε: 'Join with other Christians in seeking...'.[68] Or it may go with εἰρήνην: 'Seek to be at peace with other Christians.'[69] It is curious that the translations are virtually unanimous in adopting the first interpretation, whereas the commentators are fairly unanimous in adopting the second. Since the passage is concerned with being peaceable towards all people, especially opponents (vv. 24f.), a restriction to being at peace merely with other people who are 'pure in heart' is less likely here, and so the former interpretation is more likely.

ἐπικαλέω** with τὸν κύριον or τὸ ὄνομα κυρίου is a phrase which was taken over from the OT (cf. 1 Sam 12.17f; 2 Sam

---

[65] Hel.; Ignatius, *Mag.* 3.1; cf. νεωτερικὰ ἁμαρτήματα (Vettius Valens, 118.3).
[66] So Hasler, 71, with reference to the young women in the church (3.6; 1 Tim 5.11).
[67] Kelly, 189: 'partiality, intolerance, quickness of temper, self-assertion, and the like'.
[68] So apparently most translations; Fee, 266 (with unconvincing parallels); Oberlinner, 113; Arichea-Hatton, 216; Foerster, W., *TDNT* II, 416f.
[69] NEB is ambiguous; BA *s.v.*; Holtzmann, 422; Bernard, 126; Kelly, 189; Knight, 421; cf. Heb 12.14; Rom 12.18.

22.7) and then became virtually a designation for 'Christians'.[70] τὸν κύριον is, of course, Jesus (Rom 10.12). The reference, however, might be specifically to the activity of prayer (cf. v. 19; Hasler, 71). Here the phrase is rescued from possible formality by the addition ἐκ καθαρᾶς καρδίας (par. 1 Tim 1.5), which is how one would express 'a pure conscience' in a language like Hebrew which lacked the word (Jeremias, 58; cf. SB III, 658).

23. τὰς δὲ μωρὰς καὶ ἀπαιδεύτους ζητήσεις παραιτοῦ, εἰδὼς ὅτι γεννῶσιν μάχας The author again follows his pattern of negative/positive/negative with the third element in the series of commands (Tit 3.9 and note). There is a renewed appeal not to get involved in debates (ζήτησις, 1 Tim 6.4; Tit 3.9**) with the opponents. These are presumably the discussions about the law, myths and genealogies. Such activities are regarded as both foolish or pointless (μωρός, Tit 3.9**) and stupid.[71] For παραιτέομαι, 'to turn away from, avoid', see 1 Tim 4.7; Tit 3.10 note.[72] The reason for not indulging in disputes is something that should already be evident (cf. 1 Tim 1.4; Tit 3.9). For this use of εἰδώς cf. 3.14; 1 Tim 1.9; Tit 3.11. γεννάω** is used fig. 'to bring forth, produce, cause';[73] for μάχη see Tit 3.9; 2 Cor 7.5; Jas 4.1***, and the requirement in Tit 3.2.[74]

24. δοῦλον δὲ κυρίου οὐ δεῖ μάχεσθαι ἀλλὰ ἤπιον εἶναι πρὸς πάντας, διδακτικόν, ἀνεξίκακον The prohibition is in effect repeated, and then developed positively by means of a δεῖ construction (2.6) and a catchword connection μάχη/μάχομαι.[75] δοῦλος is Paul's self-designation in Tit 1.1 (see note), but can be used of any Christian leader; the combination with κυρίου is found only here (but is implicit in 1 Cor 7.22). The phrase may give an allusion to the character of the Servant of Yahweh who does not strive.[76] It also indicates the leader's position both as a servant and also as one endowed with authority by the Lord (Oberlinner, 115).

---

[70] Acts 2.21 (Joel 3.5); 9.14, 21; 22.16; Rom 10.12–14; 1 Cor 1.2; cf. 1 Pet 1.17; Acts 15.17; Jas 2.7; 1 Clement 52.3; 60.4; cf. Schmidt, K. L., *TDNT* III, 496–500; *TLNT* II, 41–6.

[71] ἀπαίδευτος***, Cl.; LXX; used of people who are 'uninstructed, uneducated, illiterate' and hence 'stupid'; and then applied to their opinions: e.g. Plato, *Phdr.* 269B (ῥῆμα).

[72] Cf. the citation from Stobaeus in BA: τὰς πρὸς τοὺς πολλοὺς ὁμιλίας παραιτοῦ. Cf. 1 Tim 6.20 for the thought.

[73] Cl.; Philo, *Jos.* 254; Josephus, *Ant.* 6.144; Ignatius, *Trall.* 11.1.

[74] The metaphorical use for battles of words is Cl. (Plato, *Tim.* 88A: μάχας ἐν λόγοις ποιουμένη).

[75] The verb, used metaphorically here, is lit. in Acts 7.26 and fig. in John 6.52; Jas 4.2***.

[76] Isa 42.2; 50.6; 53.7; *pace* Oberlinner, 115.

The stronger conj. ἀλλά is followed by a list of the contrasting qualities that the church leader must show. It resembles the list of qualities of an overseer, but is adapted to the immediate context. Four qualities are indicated. First, the servant of the Lord must be ἤπιος, 'gentle', to all, allies and opponents alike; although this was a quality that would be expected of parents towards children and of private individuals, it was also associated with the gods and rulers.[77] Second, he must be adept at positively teaching the truth (διδακτικός, 1 Tim 3.2*** note). Third, he is to be ἀνεξίκακος***, 'bearing evil without resentment, patient'.[78]

25. ἐν πραΰτητι παιδεύοντα τοὺς ἀντιδιατιθεμένους The fourth quality is developed at greater length. The emphatic position of ἐν πραΰτητι[79] indicates its importance. Gentleness is to be shown to all people (Tit 3.2** and note) and especially to opponents who may be snatched away from Satan as a result (cf. 1 Pet 3.16). Although argument with opponents is forbidden, Timothy is positively encouraged to teach them (παιδεύω).[80] Although the verb can mean 'to discipline', even 'to inflict corporal punishment' (so Bunn*, 236), here the sense is 'to correct, give guidance'.[81] 'Not penal correction with words ... but the exercising of an educative influence which, if God permits, will bring about conversion...' (Bertram, 625). The assumption is that the opponents are in error and Timothy possesses the truth. The opponents are described by the rare verb ἀντιδιατίθημι***.[82] The form here could be mid., 'to be opposed to'.[83] A number of scholars understand the form as pass., 'to be adversely affected' (Field 1899:215f.; Bernard, 126f.). In that case, the reference might be to those who are misled by the opponents, seen as agents of the devil, rather than the opponents themselves (cf. Hasler, 72; Fee, 267). However, the preponderance of references to opposition in the PE supports Spicq's view that it is synonymous with ἀντιλέγω here (*TLNT* I, 128 n. 2).

μήποτε δῴη αὐτοῖς ὁ θεὸς μετάνοιαν εἰς ἐπίγνωσιν ἀληθείας The reason for treating the opponents with gentleness is now

---

[77] 1 Th 2.7 *v.l.****; Cl.; not in LXX; Philo, *Mos* 1.72.; *TLNT* II, 174–7.

[78] Formed from ἀνέχομαι + κακός; Hel.; for the noun, ἀνεξικακία, see Wis 2.19; Josephus, *Bel.* 1.624; Epictetus, *Enchiridion* 10.

[79] For the phrase cf. Ecclus 3.17; 4.8.

[80] 1 Tim 1.20; Tit 2.12** and note; cf. παιδεία, 2 Tim 3.16.

[81] BA; Simpson, 142; Kelly, 190;. cf. Hermas, *Vis.* 2.3.1; 3.9.10; 1 Clement 59.3; 1 Clement 21.6 = Polycarp 4.2. Cf. Bertram, G., *TDNT* V, 596–625.

[82] The verb is restricted to the 'Higher Koine' (BA), being absent from the Pap. (*TLNT* I, 128). In the act. it means 'to retaliate upon' (Philo, *Spec.* 4.103; Diodorus Siculus 34.12).

[83] LSJ; Simpson, 141; cf. Longinus, 17.1 πρὸς τὴν πειθὼ τῶν λόγων πάντως ἀντιδιατίθεται ('he sets himself totally against the persuasiveness of the speech').

expressed; there is some hope of a positive result, although it is expressed rather tentatively. μήποτε**[84] is equivalent to *num quando*, 'seeing whether God may perhaps...'.[85] δίδωμι has its common sense 'to grant'; the form δώη is subj. (see textual note above). This is the only reference to μετάνοια**, 'repentance', in the PE.[86] It is here regarded as a gift of God.[87] Repentance leads the person to recognise and accept the the truth, i.e. the gospel which brings salvation. Some scholars distinguish between God granting repentance itself or simply the opportunity for people to repent.

26. καὶ ἀνανήψωσιν ἐκ τῆς τοῦ διαβόλου παγίδος, ἐζωγρημένοι ὑπ᾿ αὐτοῦ εἰς τὸ ἐκείνου θέλημα The same point (καί is explicative) can be put in terms of recovering sobriety and sound sense (ἀνανήφω***, 'to become sober').[88] Interestingly Philo equates the verb with repenting.[89] The effect of sobering up is that one realises that one is a captive and so makes efforts to escape from bondage. The verb is thus used in a pregnant sense ('to come to one's senses again [and so escape] from...');[90] for παγὶς τοῦ διαβόλου see 1 Tim 3.7 (cf. 6.9), where even the church leader is not free from the danger.

A final phrase fills out the concept of the trap. ζωγρέω is used of taking captives alive.[91] The implication is perhaps that the devil (ὑπ᾿ αὐτοῦ cannot refer to anybody else, but see below) has gained them as converts. The final phrase εἰς τὸ ἐκείνου θέλημα is problematic in two respects. First, there is some dispute whether it is to be linked with ἀνανήψωσιν or with ἐζωγρημένοι. Second, and related to this problem, is the reference of ἐκείνου. There are three possibilities:

(a) The phrase refers to those captured by the devil to do *his* will (τὸ ἐκείνου θέλημα).[92] This view satisfies the argument that the participle needs a qualification. The difficulty is the change from αὐτοῦ to ἐκείνου with reference to the same person

---

[84] WH spells as two words.

[85] BA *s.v.*; cf. BD § 370³; Moule 1953:157 describes the issue as 'problematic'.

[86] Cf. Behm, J., and Wurthwein, E., *TDNT* IV, 975–1008.

[87] See Wis 12.10, 19f.; *Sib. Orac.* 4.168f.; Acts 5.31; 11.18; 1 Clement 7.4; Polycarp 11.4; Barnabas 16.9; Hermas *Vis.* 4.1.3; *Sim.* 8.6; 8.11.1; cf. 1QS 3.1; Philo, *L.A.* 3.106; χρόνον εἰς μετάνοιαν.

[88] Cl.; the metaphorical use is well-attested (e.g. Josephus, *Ant.* 6.241; Ignatius, *Smyr.* 9.1); not discussed in *TDNT s.v.* νήφω. The conjectural emendation ἀνανεύσωσιν proposed by Hitchcock* is unnecessary.

[89] Philo, *L.A.* 2.60: ἀνανήφει τοῦτο δ᾿ ἐστὶ μετανοεῖ.

[90] BA *s.v.*; cf. ἐκνήφω (1 Cor 15.31).

[91] Hence the application of the fishing metaphor in Lk 5.10***; *TLNT* II, 161–3. The positive sense 'to spare', defended by Bunn*, 236, is improbable.

[92] AV; NIV; GNB; NJB; REB t; NRSV t; BA; Parry, 61; Easton, 61; Dibelius-Conzelmann, 114; Brox, 252; Holtz, 177; Kelly, 191f.; Spicq, 769f.; Hasler, 72; Hanson, 142f.; Fee, 267; Knight, 426f.; Oberlinner, 110.

(contrast the use of the pl. in 3.9). As Field 1899:216f., notes, if αὐτοῦ followed ἐκείνου, both could refer to the same person, but the reverse order suggests that the second pronoun refers to somebody else; nevertheless, there are sufficient examples to show that even with the reverse order the same person may be referred to.[93] The force of the pronoun ἐκεῖνος was increasingly lost in Hel. Gk.[94] Its use here may be to give a slight emphasis (the devil's will, not God's, or 'that dreaded devil's will' [Arichea-Hatton, 219]).

(b) The phrase refers to those who were taken captive by the devil so as to do *God*'s will (so apparently Simpson, 142), or to those who, having been taken captive by the devil, escape [so as] to do God's will.[95] The latter of these two views is unlikely in view of the distance between the verb and the phrase, and the former is unlikely because there is nothing in the context to favour the idea.

(c) Some consideration should be given to the view that αὐτοῦ refers to *God himself* or to *the Lord's servant*, giving the interpretation that those who were in the devil's snare may be 'taken alive' (sc. as converts) by God or his servant to do *God*'s will.[96]

However, with either this or the previous view the phrase εἰς τὸ ἐκείνου θέλημα seems a very shorthand way of saying 'in order *to do* his will'. Moreover, the use of the perfect is awkward, and the shift to action by the Lord's servant is odd in a clause which is primarily about God's action. Finally, if the phrase refers to God's action, it comes very late in the sentence, and it is more likely that it is an explanation of the effects of being caught in the devil's παγίς and thus that this metaphor still controls the imagery. View (a) thus remains preferable.

IV. UNGODLINESS AND THE CONSEQUENT NEED FOR FAITHFULNESS AND TRUTH (3.1–4.8)

a. Prophecy of increasing ungodliness in the church (3.1–9)

Grabbe, L. L., 'The Jannes/Jambres Tradition in Targum Pseudo-Jonathan and its Date', *JBL* 98 (1979), 393–401; McNamara, M. *The New Testament and the Palestinian Targum to the Pentateuch* (Rome: Biblical Institute Press, 1978), 82–96; Pietersma, A. and Lutz, R. T., 'Jannes and Jambres', *OTP* II, 427–42;

---

[93] Thucydides 1.32.5; 4.29.3; Xenophon, *Cyr.* 4.5.20; Lysias 14.28 (cited by BA); Lucian, *Zeux.* 8 (noted by Simpson, 142 n.); Wis 1.16; Jn 19.35.

[94] BD § 291[6]; cf. Plato, *Phaedo* 106B; *Protag.* 310D; Josephus, *Ant.* 17.227.

[95] RV mg; REB mg; NRSV mg; Bernard, 127f.; White, 169; Scott, 117; Guthrie, 167f.; Barrett, 109f.

[96] RV t; Bengel; Holtzmann, 425f.; Lock, 102f.; Elliott, 146; Brown, 73f.

Sparks, H. F. D., 'On the Form Mambres in the Latin Versions of 2 Timothy III.8', *JTS* 40 (1939), 257f.; Thackeray, H. St J., *The Relation of St Paul to Contemporary Jewish Thought* (London: Macmillan, 1900), 215–22.

Already Timothy has been made aware of the fact of desertion of Paul by 'everybody in Asia' (1.15) and the danger of opponents in the churches, from whose influence he needs to protect himself (2.16–18, 23, 25f.). But now the extent of the danger becomes a theme in itself and is expressed in detail. Verses 1–5 are couched as a general prophecy of what will happen in the last days, using the form of a list of vices or rather of evil-doers, leading to the climax in v. 5a. Verse 5b concludes the list with a warning. Then the description is taken up again (vv. 6–9) but this time in the present tense with much more specific reference to the effects of the opponents on women who are led astray by them. The false teachers are thus identified in two ways. First, they are seen as part of the final upsurge in evil and evil-doers prophesied for the last days, and, second, they are compared typologically with the opponents of Moses in their opposition to the truth and their incorrigibility, but the same illustration indicates that they will not be finally successful. Thus the reader should not be surprised by an occurrence which was foreknown by the Spirit and revealed to Paul and which is sure to come to nothing in the end.

The section is similar in style and content to 1 Tim 4.1–5, which is also put in the form of prophecy (cf. also vv. 12f. below), but is briefer and does not have the pattern of a catalogue of evil-doers. In both passages the use of a prophetic style, explicit in 1 Tim 4 and implicit here in the use of the fut. tense, is meant to show that the occurrence of evil and apostasy is already known to God and therefore should not take the church by surprise or be regarded as something that is not under God's ultimate control. Again, in both passages the assumption is that heresy and sin go hand in hand, although the accent is more on heresy in 1 Tim 4 and more on immorality here (Holtzmann, 427). Although it is often argued that attacks on heresy employ the blackening of the opponents' character as a stock weapon and therefore are not to be taken as based on fact (Karris 1973), the biblical writers genuinely believed that apostasy led to a falling away in conduct. The view that wickedness would increase on a massive scale towards the end of the world was characteristic of apocalyptic writings (Mk 13; Rev 18; 1QpHab 2.5f.). Even professing Christians will show the signs of paganism (Bernard, 129). Oberlinner, 119–22, warns against assuming that the writer thought that he was living in the last days; the use of the future tense is to be taken seriously, although the activity of the heretics in the church is to be seen as part of the general deterioration in morality.

Prophecy about future evils of this kind is also characteristic of the farewell or testament genre (e.g *T. Dan* 5.4; Wolter 1988:228–30), although the passage in 1 Tim 4 hardly falls into this category.

TEXT

2. **γίνωσκε** γινώσκετε (A F G 33 *pc*); γινωσκέτω (1175 Ambst Spec; not discussed by Elliott). The plural form is a scribal attempt to universalise the command (Elliott, 146f.); the 3rd person sing. imper. is probably a slip.

ἔσονται γάρ Omit γάρ (1836 d m dem); καὶ ἔσονται (f vg). The citing of the evidence by Elliott, 43, 210, is not altogether consistent. He holds that Latin *et* = καί (a Semitic idiom) is original, though completely lost from the Greek MSS. Once it was removed scribes inserted γάρ to avoid asyndeton. But there can be few, if any, cases where the original reading is totally lost from the Greek MSS.

ἀχάριστοι ἀχρηστοι (C* K *pc*). For the variant cf. Philem 11. The text is more appropriate in the context (Elliott, 147).

ἄστοργοι ἄσπονδοι Reverse order (D 365 1175 *pc* (a) g m vgᵐˢˢ Ambst); omit ἄσπονδοι (ℵ); omit both words (431 syᵖ). The omissions are due to homoioteleuton. Elliott, 148, thinks that the original order is uncertain, but the MS evidence is strongly for the text.

6. **ἐνδύνοντες** ἐνδύοντες (P 226ᶜ 35 241 1960); εἰσδύνοντες (330 2400); Elliott, 148, 237, rejects the second variant as a word not used elsewhere in NT; he accepts the first variant with hesitation.

αἰχμαλωτίζοντες αἰχμαλωτεύοντες (D² TR). Cf. Eph 4.8. Elliott, 148f., refers to the creation of -ίζω verbs in Hellenistic Gk. (cf. BD § 108) and thinks that the text is more likely than the variant.

γυναικάρια Praem. τά (2 *pc* TR). Elliott, 149, holds that the generic use of the article could be original. The MS evidence, however, is poor.

ἁμαρτίαις Add πόλλαις (1022 syʰ); Elliott, 149, 237, comments that the adjectival phrase would have no parallel in the NT, but it would give balance to the following 'all kinds of desires'. However, the evidence is distinctly weak.

ἐπιθυμίαις Add καὶ ἡδόναις (A 1505 *pc* syʰ). The variant is rejected by Elliott, 149, as assimilation to Tit 3.3.

8. **Ἰάννης** Ἰωάννης (C* Euthaliusᵐˢ*); Ἰάμνης (m dem vg Origen). WH *Notes*, 135, state that the first variant agrees with some of the Jewish authorities for the story, but is probably coincidental. Elliott, 150, 237, accepts the variant with considerable doubt.

Ἰαμβρῆς Μαμβρῆς (F G d g vgᶜˡ ʷʷ goth Cyp Hipp Lcf Ambst Aug Ps-Aug). The variant is probably a learned correction based on a parallel form of the name in Jewish tradition (Elliott, 150; Metzger, 580).

οὗτοι αὐτοί (F). Elliott, 151, compares 2.10 and 1 Tim 3.10 (*v.l.*) for parallels to the 'strong Semitism' which is present in F and argues that it may be original despite the unreliability of F in orthography. This seems to be an exceedingly weak argument.

9. **ἄνοια** διάνοια (A 330 2400). The variant is a sheer error (Elliott, 151).

EXEGESIS

1. **Τοῦτο δὲ γίνωσκε, ὅτι ἐν ἐσχάταις ἡμέραις ἐνστήσονται καιροὶ χαλεποί** τοῦτο here refers forwards and anticipates the noun clause; for the whole phrase cf. Rom 6.6. The imperative γίνωσκε may have the force 'be receptive to this information'

(McKay 1985:210). For the omission of the article in the phrase ἐν ἐσχάταις ἡμέραις cf. Jas 5.3.[1] ἔσχατος** is used here either of the end-time conceived as an extended period, or of the days that lead up to the end. Despite the future tense, the shift to the present tense in 3.6 shows that the period has already begun.[2] The writer gives the impression of quoting prophecy, but it is surely a natural enough device to say that we believe that in the last days certain things will happen, and indeed they already are! It is difficult to see why many commentators think that this is a sign of the mask falling as a second-century writer tries to pre-serve the fiction of Paul prophesying what would happen after his death and then cannot sustain the picture and so slips into the present tense. Thus, for example, Brox, 253, argues that the writer wishes to identify the heretics who are presently at work in the church as the sinners *par excellence* of the Endtime, although he does not say that the Endtime has arrived. The verb ἐνίστημι** normally means 'to happen', and it is used frequently in the perf. with the sense 'to have come, be present, have set in' (2 Th 2.2; Heb 9.9; Gal 1.4; Rom 8.38; 1 Cor 3.22; Barnabas 17.2).[3] The pl. καιροί (1 Tim 2.6 and note) means a lasting period of time (cf. Acts 3.19). χαλεπός is 'hard, difficult' ('hard to deal with violent, dangerous', Mt 8.28***), in the sense of 'hard to bear'.[4]

2. ἔσονται γὰρ οἱ ἄνθρωποι φίλαυτοι φιλάργυροι ἀλαζόνες ὑπερήφανοι βλάσφημοι, γονεῦσιν ἀπειθεῖς, ἀχάριστοι ἀνόσιοι Although the sentence is added on as an explanation of the previous assertion (γάρ), it carries the main weight of the prophecy. The future ἔσονται continues the asseverative language of prophecy, expressing certainty about what will happen. Although οἱ ἄνθρωποι is vague and could refer to people in general, it must refer to nominal Christians in view of the description in

---

[1] Deut 32.20 uses ἐπί with Gen.; an inscr. dated to 116 BC has εἰς ἐσχάτην ἡμέραν = 'for ever' (BA); for the full phrase see Isa 2.2; Acts 2.17; *Didache* 16.3; Barnabas 4.9 (for other variations see Heb 1.2; 2 Pet 3.3); 1 Tim 4.1 has ἐν ὑστέροις καιροῖς; cf. ἐν καιρῷ ἐσχάτῳ (1 Pet 1.5).

[2] Hence Arichea-Hatton, 221, would translate 'in *these* last days'.

[3] The verb is perhaps equivalent to Lat. *instare* (Simpson, 143). Some scholars find the meaning 'to impend, be imminent' in 1 Cor 7.26 and elsewhere. This has been suggested as a possibility for this passage by BAG, but not by BA. But it does not make sense to say 'in the last days hard times will be imminent'; the force must surely be 'in the last days there will be hard times' (Oepke, A., *TDNT* II, 543f.).

[4] Like an 'ugly' wound (Plutarch, *Mor.* 131B), or disease (Josephus, *Ant.* 13.422); Simpson, 143, argues for 'menacing', citing Vettius Valens 236 of an astronomical conjunction, and *TLNT* III, 494f., suggests 'dangerous, perilous' (cf. 2 Macc 4.6).

v. 5. The list is basically descriptive of godlessness in general, but is applied to the heretics (Vögtle, 29). The problem described is apostasy in the church.

The list which follows is the second longest vice list in the NT with its nineteen items. It contains seventeen single adjectives, followed by two items in which comparisons are drawn (a) between what people are and ought to be and (b) between what they seem to be and what they really are. The content is general rather than specific (Dibelius-Conzelmann, 115). There are points of contact with the list in Rom 1.29–31, and Hanson, 144, holds that it is based on it (with adaptations based on the author's knowledge of Philo; similarly, Oberlinner, 123), but the resemblances are more probably due to the use of similar traditions. Attempts to find a pattern, such as Knight's 'somewhat chiastic arrangement' (429f.), have not been too successful. The list makes use of wordplays and jingles, but otherwise no order is apparent. There is a stress on self-centredness, especially in the first five characteristics, but the rest are generally descriptive of the unnatural and immoral tendencies that result (Holtzmann, 427). It begins and ends with misdirected love (Knight, 430). The qualities are the opposite of those expected in Christians and their leaders (Houlden, 125). Vögtle, 8, thinks that it may be Greek and non-Jewish in origin. Most of the vocabulary can in fact be paralleled from Hellenistic sources, both Greek and Jewish, and it is especially close to Philo and to 1QS 4.9–11. The qualities are thus those which would universally be regarded as evil and there is nothing peculiarly Christian in the description, although the list differs from that in Rom 1.29-32 in that these are all sins that could spread in the church (Jeremias, 59).

(a) It is reasonable to assume that the first item in the list sets the tone for what follows, and that the closing one(s) will wrap it up. On this assumption the dominant motif is that people will be self-centred rather than God-centred,[5] and this affects their relationships with other people so that they think only of their own interests and behave violently to gain their own ends. φίλαυτος***, 'loving oneself, selfish', originally referred to 'the self-respect which a good man has for himself' (Bernard, 129), but acquired a bad sense.[6] The Pauline contrast is found in 1 Cor 13.5 (White, 170).

(b) φιλαργυρία was singled out as the cause of all evils in 1 Tim 6.10. The adjective φιλάργυρος, 'fond of money,

---

[5] φίλαυτος καὶ ἄθεος (Philo, L.A. 1.49); cf. Fug. 81: φίλαυτοι δὴ μᾶλλον ἢ φιλόθεοι.

[6] It is found in Cl. and Hel. moralists (BA; see especially the references to Philo in Spicq, 773; cf. Hierocles p. 59, 21f., cited in van der Horst 1975:159).

avaricious', is found elsewhere in the NT only of the Pharisees in Lk 16.14***.[7]

(c) The next two vices can be grouped together as different expressions for pride and arrogance. ἀλάζων, 'boaster, braggart' (Rom 1.30***), is used in Cl. of boasting of things that are not in fact there, and in Judaism it is linked to the self-sufficiency which takes no account of God.[8]

(d) ὑπερήφανος, 'arrogant, haughty, proud', generally has a pejorative meaning with reference to having an exaggerated opinion of oneself and scorning others, including the gods (Cl.). It became prominent in the LXX and Judaism, and is associated with ἀλάζων in Josephus, Bel. 6.172; Wis 5.8; 1 Clement 16.2 (nouns). It refers more to opinions while ἀλάζων refers more to speech (Bernard, 130).[9]

(e) For βλάσφημος, 'blasphemer', 'slanderer', see 1 Tim 1.13 and note. The word could have either meaning here. Since the following words have to do with antisocial behaviour, the broader thought of slander may be uppermost.[10] But the presence of διάβολοι later in the list and the possible linking of the previous attitudes to antigodlessness may tend to favour the motif of blasphemy against God here (AV; cf. possibly Barrett, 110).

(f) Next comes a row (broken only by διάβολοι) of eight compounds with α-privative, as is not surprising in a list of vices. Several of them are part of the vocabulary of the PE elsewhere. They all have to do with attitudes to other people. For ἀπειθής see Tit 1.16; 3.3*** where it is used of disobedience to God. The combination here with γονεῦσιν** (used in the NT only in the pl. of parents) is already found in Rom 1.30 (cf. Deut 21.18).

(g) ἀχάριστος is 'ungrateful';[11] nothing suggests that only ingratitude to God is in mind (contrast 1 Tim 4.4).

(h) For ἀνόσιος, 'unholy, wicked', see 1 Tim 1.9*** note. This is the one 'religious' word in the list at this point.

[7] Cf. 4 Macc 2.8; Philo, Post. 116; Cong. 53, 127; Gig. 37, 39; T. Levi 17.11; Didache 3.5. Cl.; Hel.; TLNT III, 446f.

[8] Cf. Job 28.8; see especially Philo, Mos. 2.240. For the adj. with things see 1 Clement 57.2 et al. For the noun ἀλαζόνεια see Jas 4.16; 1 Jn 2.16***; and for the verb ἀλαζονεύομαι see 1 Clement 2.1; 38.2; Diognetus 4.4. Cf. Delling, G., TDNT I, 226f.; TLNT I, 63–5.

[9] It is found in a vice list in T. Levi 17.11; it is opposed to ταπεινός (Prov 3.34); the adj. is not used by Philo (but cf. ὑπερηφανία, Virt. 171, where it is linked with ἀλαζόνεια). Paul uses the word in the vice list in Rom 1.30; cf. Lk 1.51; Jas 4.6; 1 Pet 5.5***; Didache 2.6 et al. Cf. the noun ὑπερηφανία (Mk 7.22***, in a vice list) and the verb ὑπερηφανέω (Ignatius, Eph. 5.3; Poly. 4.3; Smyr. 10.2). Cf. Bertram, G., TDNT VIII, 525–9; TLNT III, 390–5.

[10] RV and most translations; Bernard, 130; Spicq, 775; Knight, 431.

[11] Lk 6.35***; Cl.; Wis 16.29; Ecclus 29.16; 4 Macc 9.10; Philo, Jos. 99; Josephus, Ant. 13.388; Vita 172.

3. ἄστοργοι ἄσπονδοι διάβολοι ἀκρατεῖς ἀνήμεροι ἀφιλάγαθοι

(i) The list includes the basic defects in character that give rise to antisocial behaviour. Thus ἄστοργος, 'unloving', suggests a lack of natural affection and feeling for other people. The word appears in the list in Rom 1.31*** (Cl.; Hel.).

(j) ἄσπονδος is 'implacable, irreconcilable' (Rom 1.31 v.l.***).[12]

(k) For διάβολος in the sense of 'slanderer' see 1 Tim 3.11; Tit 2.3 (but 'devil' in 1 Tim 3.6).

(l) ἀκρατής*** is 'without self-control, dissolute', not necessarily of sexual vice.[13] Such people are not deliberately profligate but find temptation too strong (Bernard, 130). 'It is not so much that they lead a dissolute life, but rather that they cannot control themselves, and so they no longer act as human beings – they are amoral beings' (*TLNT* I, 62). It stands in contrast to ἐγκρατής, a characteristic of the church leader in Tit 1.8** (cf. Philo, *Virt.* 180; *Praem.* 116).

(m) ἀνήμερος*** 'savage, brutal', like an animal which has not been tamed.[14]

(n) The adjective ἀφιλάγαθος***, 'not loving the good', is a hapax, not found previous to this list, but it is an obvious formation from φιλάγαθος (Tit 1.8***);[15] thus again we have a vice that is the opposite of the virtue demanded in church leaders. Grundmann, W., *TDNT* I, 18, suggests that it differs from φίλαυτος in that those who love/know only themselves have no knowledge of love or pity.

4. προδόται προπετεῖς τετυφωμένοι, φιλήδονοι μᾶλλον ἢ φιλόθεοι

(o) προδότης is 'traitor, betrayer'. It is associated with murder in Acts 7.52; cf. Lk 6.16*** (Judas!); Hermas, *Sim.* 9.19.3b *et al.*[16] It is thus the opposite of πιστός.

(p) προπετής is 'rash, reckless, thoughtless' (Acts 19.36).[17] The word is used of people who talk without thinking, but also generally of people who are impulsive and thoughtless in action, and who may act violently and unjustly.

[12] Cl.; Philo, *Virt.* 131, of parents committing infanticide; *Mos.* 1.242; Josephus, *Ant.* 4.264.

[13] Cl.; Hel.; Prov 27.20a; *Ep. Arist.* 277; Josephus, *Ant.* 16.399 ('intemperate in speech'). The noun ἀκρασία is associated with greed in Mt 23.25, and with inability to control one's sexual impulses in 1 Cor 7.5***. Cf. Grundmann, W., *TDNT* II, 339–42; *TLNT* I, 60–2.

[14] Cl.; Hel.; Epictetus 1.3.7; Dio Chrysostom 12.51; *Ep. Arist.* 289; Philo, *L.A.* 3.11; cf. Tit 1.12; Jude 10.

[15] BA cite the occurrence of ἀφιλοκαγαθία in P. Oxy. 33.II.13 (AD II).

[16] Cl.; Hel.; *Ep. Arist.* 270; Philo, *L.A.* 2.10; *et al.*; Josephus, *Bel.* 3.354; *Vita* 133.

[17] Cl.; Hel.; Prov 10.14; 13.3; Ecclus 9.18; Philo, *Spec.* 3.175; Josephus, *Ant.* 5.106; *Vita* 170; 1 Clement 1.1; *et al.*; cf. *TLNT* III, 189f.

(q) For τετυφωμένοι see 1 Tim 3.6; 6.4***, where it is a danger to be avoided in a candidate for church leadership, a characteristic of a false teacher.

(r) The list comes to a climax with two compound statements. φιλήδονος*** is 'loving pleasure, given over to pleasure'.[18] The motif recurs in Tit 3.3 with its reference to people who are slaves to ἡδοναί. μᾶλλον ἤ is used here in its exclusive sense, 'lovers of pleasure instead of lovers of God' (cf. 1 Tim 1.4 and note). Here particularly the description does not suggest that the asceticism of 1 Tim 4 is in mind (cf. Holtzmann, 428). φιλόθεος*** is 'loving God, devout' (Cl.; Hel.). The same or similar plays on words are found elsewhere: ἀδύνατον τὸν αὐτὸν φιλόθεόν τε εἶναι καὶ φιλήδονον (Porphyry, *ad Marcellam* 14 p. 283; 20f N).[19]

5. ἔχοντες μόρφωσιν εὐσεβείας τὴν δὲ δύναμιν αὐτῆς ἠρνημένοι· καὶ τούτους ἀποτρέπου

(s) The previous word gives the lead in for this climactic phrase. The pungent contrast is paralleled by Josephus, *Ant.* 13.409: τὸ ... ὄνομα τῆς βασιλείας εἶχεν αὐτή, τὴν δὲ δύναμιν οἱ Φαρισαῖοι. The description explains more fully the way in which people who do not know God behave. They claim to know God but do not do so. For ἔχοντες of having a particular disposition cf. 1 Tim 1.19 *et al.* The whole phrase is paralleled verbally in Rom 2.20, where we have the only other NT occurrence of μόρφωσις. This word can mean 'embodiment, formulation' (Rom 2.20***); along these lines Pöhlmann, W., *EDNT* II, 443f., interprets the present passage to mean that the people have received the embodiment of godliness in the training that they have received and rejects the generally accepted interpretation in terms of 'outward form, appearance', with the implication that it is only an appearance rather than reality. Nevertheless, this is how the passage was understood in vg: *habentes speciem quidem pietatis*, and this interpretation is buttressed by Philo, *Plant.* 70: εἰσί τινες τῶν ἐπιμορφαζόντων εὐσέβειαν.[20] For εὐσέβεια as the practice of religion see Tit 1.1 *et al.* δύναμις (1.7, 8*) is the vital power for Christian living, given by the Holy Spirit to believers. There may also be a reference to the power which comes from the truth, and Oberlinner, 125, detects polemic against Gnostic heretics who denied that people who lacked their special 'knowledge' were truly redeemed.

---

[18] Cl.; Hel.; cf. Stählin, G., *TDNT* II, 918, 925f.

[19] Epictetus in Stobaeus 46 p. 474 Schenkl (III.170) contrasts the φιλήδονος with the φιλάνθρωπος. Philo, *Agr.* 88, describes the soul which is φιλήδονον καὶ φιλοπαθῆ μᾶλλον ἤ φιλάρετον καὶ φιλόθεον. For attestation in inscr. see *New Docs.* II, 99 § 79.

[20] Behm, J., *TDNT* IV, 754f.

αὐτῆς is a gen. of association, 'the power that is exercised by godliness or stems from it'. For ἀρνέομαι see 2.12, 13; Tit 1.16; 2.12; 1 Tim 5.8**; cf. 2 Pet 2.1 for the thought. The perfect expresses a past decision already taken: they have long since lost the spiritual power.

καὶ τούτους may mean 'these also' – presumably in addition to the people in 2.23; perhaps it is simply emphatic. In any case, it implies that they are already active in the church (Dibelius-Conzelmann, 116). But perhaps it is the beginning of a new section, closely linked with v. 6 which explains why such people are so dangerous that they must be avoided. ἀποτρέπομαι***, mid. is 'to turn away from, cease from';[21] the verb may simply mean that one should avoid contact with such people, but the force is surely stronger: they must be kept out of the congregation where they can exercise a bad influence on the others. Some kind of excommunication may be in mind. Indeed, it is difficult to see what else can be meant other than exclusion from fellowship (despite the hesitation of Oberlinner, 125).

6. ἐκ τούτων γάρ εἰσιν οἱ ἐνδύνοντες εἰς τὰς οἰκίας καὶ αἰχμαλωτίζοντες γυναικάρια σεσωρευμένα ἁμαρτίαις, ἀγόμενα ἐπιθυμίαις ποικίλαις The linking ἐκ τούτων ... εἰσιν ('to this group belong...') comes here only in the PE; it is equivalent to ὧν ἐστιν (2.17), but this phrase would be less suitable here in a fresh sentence that gives the reason (γάρ) for avoiding/throwing them out. The verb ἐνδύνω***, 'to go in, enter, creep in', implies the stealthy infiltration practised in house to house visitation.[22] While it is possible that the homes are pagan (Spicq, 777; Hasler, 73), it is more likely that they are Christian (Hanson, 145), and presumably wealthy. For seeking out female audiences and their susceptibility to persuasion see Lucian, *Alex.* 6 (cited in Fee, 273f.); Irenaeus *AH* 1.13.3, 6 of Marcus (cited in Dibelius-Conzelmann, 116 n. 10). For women being duped see the well-known story of Paulina and Mundus in Josephus, *Ant.* 18.65–86; cf. the way in which her family think that Thecla is being duped by Paul in *Acts of Paul and Thecla*, but here the emphasis is on asceticism rather than licence.[23] Asceticism may of course be in mind here as a way of avoiding guilt feelings associated with sexual behaviour (Johnson, 85). Lütgert 1909:38–40 suggests that the asceticism of the opponents (1 Tim 4.3) unconsciously led them to this substitute religious activity with women.

---

[21] Cl.; Josephus, *Bel.* 3.500; *Ant.* 18.283; the sense 'to avoid' with acc. is unusual (4 Macc 1.33; Parry, 62f.).

[22] Barnabas 4.10. The form is an Ionic poetic one found alongside ἐνδύω. Cf. παρεισδύνω, Jude 4 (Hanson, 146f., catalogues a number of resemblances between 2 Tim and Jude at this point; see also Gal 2.4).

[23] See also *Tanchuma* ויקרא 134.9 (SB III, 659).

αἰχμαλωτίζω is lit. 'to capture (in war)', hence simply 'to mislead, deceive'.[24] The objects of the exercise are described somewhat derogatorily with the diminutive γυναικάριον***, lit. 'little woman', hence 'silly, idle woman' (Cl.; see BA). Nevertheless, to see a general devaluation of women here (Hasler, 73) is mistaken in view of the positive references elsewhere (1.5; cf. 3.14 by implication). The writer's attitude is justified (at least in his eyes) by reference to the sinfulness and folly of this particular group. σωρεύω is 'to heap, pile up',[25] 'to fill with'; hence, pass. 'to be overwhelmed with'. The perf. expresses a continued condition. The women are genuinely overwhelmed in their consciences with sins (ἁμαρτία, 1 Tim 5.22, 24**) and so ready to clutch at any remedy. They are lacking in the dignity and self-restraint that is commended elsewhere in the PE. Sexual guilt may be part of the problem, but there is no proof one way or the other.

The pass. of ἄγω (4.11**), 'to be led, allow oneself to be led' (1 Cor 12.2), can be used of impulses both good and bad (e.g. the Holy Spirit; Rom 8.14; Gal 5.18; Lk 4.1, 9).[26] The same thought is expressed in Tit 3.3 in terms of enslavement to ἐπιθυμίαι (2.22; on the word see Tit 2.12 note). For ποίκιλος, 'of various kinds', see Tit 3.3**.

7. πάντοτε μανθάνοντα καὶ μηδέποτε εἰς ἐπίγνωσιν ἀληθείας ἐλθεῖν δυνάμενα The writer sums up the inability of these women to change their sinful ways in a memorable epigram. For μανθάνω cf. 3.14, 14 b; Tit 3.14. It is also used specifically of women in 1 Tim 2.11; cf. 5.4, 13**.[27] μηδέποτε*** is 'never'.[28] The whole phrase εἰς ἐπίγνωσιν τῆς ἀληθείας ἐλθεῖν is paralleled in 1 Tim 2.4 where it is a description of conversion; here it may be meant more broadly. There is perhaps a suggestion of people receiving an endless series of lessons, perhaps for a fee? By contrast 3.15 indicates that study of the Scriptures can lead to saving knowledge.

The language used to describe the women is taken by some scholars to be a massive example of misogyny. Here not only the heretics but those influenced by them are subject to strong

---

[24] For the former meaning see Lk 21.24; fig. Rom 7.23; 2 Cor 10.5; Ignatius, *Eph.* 17.1; for the latter see Jth 16.9; *T. Reub.* 5.3; Ignatius, *Philad.* 2.2; Irenaeus, *A.H.* I Praef. 1.

[25] Rom 12.20*** = Prov 25.22; cf. ἐπισωρεύω, 4.3; Barnabas 4.6.

[26] See BA *s.v.* for references to being led by ἐπιθυμία (Aristotle, *EN* 7.3.10 (1147a, 35); anger (Euripides, *Medea* 310); pleasures (Plato, *Protag.* 355A); and words (Demosthenes 18.9).

[27] Cf. Epictetus 1.29.35: ἤθελον ἔτι μανθάνειν = 'I would fain go on learning (rather than face up to a crisis)'.

[28] Cl. but the usage here with the part. is Hel. for οὐδέποτε.

condemnation (Wagener 1994:96f.; Oberlinner, 133–5). Although the writer's vigour is due to his concern for the truth of the gospel, which he sees as threatened, there is a feeling that he has a fundamentally negative view of women and describes them in stereotyped ways that owe more to polemical fashions than to reality. This criticism does not take sufficient note of the facts that the condemnation of the heretical men in the same context is equally strong, and that there are women (just as there also are men) who are foolish enough to listen to plausible rogues (see especially Johnson, 84f.).

8. ὃν τρόπον δὲ Ἰάννης καὶ Ἰαμβρῆς ἀντέστησαν Μωϋσεῖ, οὕτως καὶ οὗτοι ἀνθίστανται τῇ ἀληθείᾳ, ἄνθρωποι κατεφθαρμένοι τὸν νοῦν, ἀδόκιμοι περὶ τὴν πίστιν The mention of the duped women is incidental to the writer's interest in the false teachers themselves. Their example has merely served to indicate the depths of depravity to which they sink and the danger of their influence. He now sums them up in terms of their opposition to the truth, but he draws on a historical example to illustrate their antagonism. The example is in fact a 'type', similar to other uses of the Exodus motif in the NT, and it serves to show that the problems faced by the church are of the same kind as those faced by Moses, and that, just as the attacks against him failed to succeed, so too the church will not be overcome by its opponents. ὃν τρόπον (originally καθ' ὃν τρόπον) had become an idiomatic phrase with the sense 'in the manner in which, just as'.[29] The parallel is taken quite literally by Spicq, 104–10, who holds that magical practices are implied (*contra* Karris 1973:560f.).

The names Ἰάννης*** and Ἰαμβρῆς*** are those of the two Egyptian sorcerers who opposed Moses before Pharaoh. Ἰάννης is said to be Johana Graecised, possibly from the verb *'anah*, to contradict (Thackeray*, 221). In place of Ἰαμβρῆς some of the Latin versions have *Mambres*, which appears in some Gk. MSS as Μαμβρῆς. The Latin form may be equivalent to Mamrey, from *marah*, to rebel (Thackeray*, 220), and thus be the correct representation of the original Semitic form.

The names do not occur in the story in Exod 7.8–13, which refers simply to 'the Egyptian magicians' who turned their staffs into snakes, but developed in Jewish tradition. The oldest known reference is CD 5.17–19: 'For formerly Moses and Aaron arose by the hand of the Prince of Lights; but Belial raised up Jannes and his brother, in his cunning, when Israel was saved for the first time.' Both names are found in the Palestinian Targum of

---

[29] Cl.; LXX; Mt 23.37; Lk 13.34; Acts 7.28 (Exod 2.14) [15.11; 27.25]). For the combination with οὕτως** as its correlate see Dittenberger, *Syll.* 685. 51ff.; Jos 10.1; 11.15; Isa 10.11; 62.5; Ezek 12.11 *et al.*; Acts 1.11; 2 Clement 8.2; 12.4.

Exod 7.11f.: 'And Pharaoh also called the wise men and sorcerers, and they also, Jannes and Jambres, the sorcerers who were in Egypt, did likewise with their magical charms. And every man threw his staff and they became basilisks, and immediately they were changed to become as they were at first, and the staff of Aaron swallowed up their staffs.' Thereafter there are numerous references to them in Jewish, Christian and pagan sources. A story about an Egyptian scribe predicting the birth of Moses but not giving his name is found in Josephus, *Ant.* 2.205, and reappears in the Palestinian Targum on Exod 1.15 with Jannes and Jambres replacing the unnamed scribe.[30] It is thus evident that the author, like other NT writers, knew and used Jewish embellishments of the story of Moses and legends that were circulating in his day;[31] Spicq, 779, thinks that Paul gained his knowledge from the Targum.[32]

The key word to describe the activity of the magicians and of the author's contemporaries is ἀνθίστημι (3.8b; 4.15**), act. 'to set against', mid. 'to resist, oppose'.[33] Μωϋσῆς** is seen as the representative of God in his day and the appropriate antitype to the truth of the gospel. The pleonastic καὶ qualifying οὗτοι[34] lays stress on the fact that the action of these people also is just as bad as that of Moses' opponents. ἀλήθεια is the gospel, as in v. 7. Implicitly the writer may be indicating that it is bad not to come to know the truth and worse to oppose it. Two parallel phrases spell out the depravity of people who behave like this. In the first phrase the use of ἄνθρωποι is hardly necessary, but quite normal (3.13; Tit 1.14; 3.10). καταφθείρω, 'to destroy', hence 'to ruin, corrupt', is used as in Cl. with acc. of respect.[35] διαφθείρω is used in the same sense in 1 Tim 6.5 with νοῦς (Tit 1.15 and note); their mind is regarded as not functioning properly as the guide to correct belief and moral

---

[30] Late Rabbinic texts give different names and different stories about them. An apocryphal work entitled *Iannes et Mambres Liber* is mentioned by Origen (*Comm. in Mt.* 23.37; 27.9). The Gelasian decree condemned a work called *Poenitentia Iamne et Mambre*. Fragments of the book have been discovered (*OTP* II, 427–42). For non-Christian references see Pliny the Elder, *NH* 30.1.11: *factio a Mose et Ianne et Iotape*; Apuleius, *Apologia* 90 (Iannes); Numenius (cited by Eusebius, *Praep. Evang.* 9.8.1: Iannes and Iambres). For further citations see Dibelius-Conzelmann, 117. See further McNamara*; Sparks*; SB III, 660–4; Schürer III:2, 781–3; Odeberg, H., *TDNT* III, 192f.; and especially Pietersma, A., *ABD* III, 638–40.

[31] Cf. Acts 7.22, 23, 53; 1 Cor 10.2, 4; Gal 3.19; Heb 2.2; Jude 9; Jeremias, 60.

[32] A link with Wis 15.18 – 16.1 (Hanson 1968:25–8) is unlikely.

[33] Usually with dat., as here (Acts 13.8 [Elymas!]; Rom 9.13; 13.2; Gal 2.11; Eph 6.13 *et al.*). For the spelling see Elliott, 150, 237.

[34] Cf. Rom 5.15, 18 *et al.*; BA *s.v.* καί II.3.

[35] Cf. Menander, *Epitr.* 461: καταφθαρεὶς ... τὸν βίον, cited by BA; cf. *TLNT* II, 278f.

principles. In the second phrase the heretics are characterised as
people who are would fail to pass the test and hence are rejected
by God (ἀδόκιμος; Tit 1.16** and note) with reference to faith
(cf. 1 Tim 1.19 where heretics are similarly said to have made
shipwreck with regard to faith). Since the people in question
claimed to be believers, some translate with such phrases as
'people of ... counterfeit faith' (NRSV; cf. NJB). 'Faith' here is
their personal faith (Parry, 63) rather than 'what is believed'
(Easton, 63).

**9. ἀλλ' οὐ προκόψουσιν ἐπὶ πλεῖον· ἡ γὰρ ἄνοια αὐτῶν ἔκδηλος
ἔσται πᾶσιν, ὡς καὶ ἡ ἐκείνων ἐγένετο** Although the threat
posed is real enough, nevertheless the situation is not completely
desperate. The opponents will not make the progress they hope
for. For προκόπτω see 3.13, and for the combination with ἐπὶ
πλεῖον see 2.16. The statement is ambiguous, depending on
whether ἐπὶ πλεῖον means 'any more' or 'even more' (1 Clement
18.3; Ps 50.4 [51.2]): either 'they will not get any further' (Kelly,
197), or 'they will not get far'. In both cases there is an obvious
tension between the positive statement in 2.16 and the negative
one here. However, two different things are being discussed,
here the ultimate end of the opponents, which is a source of
encouragement, but there a warning of the real danger to the
church if nothing is done about them.[36]
The writer's confidence is based on the belief that once the
folly of these people is evident, as it will be, all reasonable
believers will turn away from them. ἄνοια is generally used of
human ignorance and linked with πονηρία.[37] ἔκδηλος***
is 'evident, plain'.[38] The fut. ἔσται expresses certainty. ἡ ἐκείνων
(sc. ἄνοια) is that of Jannes and Jambres who also failed to keep
up their deceptions.[39]

b. Paul's example and teaching, and the importance of Scripture
(3.10–17)

Austin, M. R., 'How Biblical is "The Inspiration of Scripture"?', *ExpTim* 93
(1981), 75–9; Burkhardt, H., *Die Inspiration heiliger Schriften bei Philo von
Alexandrien* (Giessen/Basel: Brunnen, 1988); Piñero, A., 'Sobre el sentido de
ΘΕΟΠΝΕΥΣΤΟΣ: 2 Tim 3,16', *Filologia Neotestamentaria* 1 (1988), 143–53;
Riesner, R., 'Konservativ und dynamisch. Unser Umgang mit der Heiligen Scrift.
Bibelauslegung zu 2 Timotheus 3, 14–17', *Porta* 33 (1983), 2–6; Roberts, J. W.,

---

[36] *Pace* Brox, 256, the tension is natural in the circumstances and not an
indication that the whole account is both generalising and fictitious.
[37] Josephus, *Ant.* 8.318; 2 Clement 13.1; in Lk 6.11*** it means anger; cf.
Behm, J., *TDNT* IV, 962f.
[38] Cl.; 3 Macc 3.19; 6.5; *Ep. 'Arist.* 85.
[39] Exod 7.12; 8.18; 9.11; cf. the legendary development in *Jannes and Jambres*,
OTP II, 427–42.

'Every Scripture Inspired by God', *ResQ* 5 (1961), 33–7; Roberts; J. W., 'Note on the Adjective after *pas* in 2 Timothy 3,16', *ExpTim* 76 (1964–5), 359; Schlarb 1990:255–61; Sheriffs, R. J. A., 'A Note on a Verse in the New English Bible', *EvQ* 34 (1962), 91–5; Spence, R. M., '2 Timothy 3, 15–16', *ExpTim* 8 (1896–7), 563–5; Warfield, B. B., *The Inspiration and Authority of the Bible* (London: Marshall, Morgan & Scott, 1951); Wolfe 1990:106–56.

After the description of the character and activities of the opponents, which serves to emphasise the urgency of right living and teaching in the church, it is natural that there is a renewed appeal to Timothy to live in the right way. He is first reminded that he has witnessed the teaching, character and patiently borne sufferings of Paul from which God delivered him. This leads to a further reminder that godly people (implicitly including Timothy) will be persecuted while evil people flourish. All this forms the background to an appeal to Timothy to remain steadfast in the teaching and responsibility committed to him. He is reminded that the Scriptures form the basis of his commission, and their nature and role is stated in detail. Not only do the Scriptures lead to salvation for believers in Christ; their God-inspired character means that they are also able to provide such positive teaching and correctives to evil that the man of God will be prepared for every good task. It is not clear whether the point is that the Scriptures exercise this effect on the man of God to prepare him for his own good works or whether they provide him with the armoury that he needs for his teaching and admonition of other people. Both interpretations would be valid, but the balance perhaps favours the former.

The passage stresses the example of Paul, and the mixture of characteristics and experiences is reminiscent of 2 Cor 6.3–10. At the same time stress is laid on the family upbringing of Timothy, so that Paul is not presented as his only example and teacher. And both Paul and Timothy find the basis for their faith in the Scriptures. We have here the most explicit and positive statement of the value of the Scriptures, which may be partly polemical against the misuse of the opponents.

The section is structured in the ABA′ form, with vv. 10–12 describing the pattern that Timothy is implicitly to follow, v. 13 placing in contrast the activity of wicked people, and vv. 14–17 again calling Timothy, this time explicitly, to remain faithful to what he has been taught.

Some commentators see in vv. 10–13 a picture of Timothy as the ideal church leader, following closely the example of Paul, and regard this as a contradiction to the picture elsewhere in the letter, where Timothy is presented as fearful and diffident and in need of much encouragement. They argue that this confirms the unhistorical character of the presentation. Here an unhistorical image of Timothy is created, which really stands for a later generation of church leaders, presenting them with the ideal that they should follow (Brox, 257f.; Merkel, 73f.). This interpretation places undue emphasis on Timothy despite the clear focus of the passage on Paul's example. It also involves him more actively in suffering along with Paul than is justified either by other evidence or by the picture in the PE which is more one of preparing him for possible future sufferings.

TEXT

10. παρηκολούθησας παρηκολούθηκας (D Ψ 1739 1881 TR; WH mg). Cf. 1 Tim 4.6 note. Elliott, 151f., follows the text, since the perfect is rare in PE.

τῇ προθέσει Add τῇ πράξει (v. Wyss cj.). This proposal, recorded by NA, does not seem to have merited discussion by any recent commentator.

τῇ ἀγάπῃ Omit (A pc). The omission is due to homoioteleuton (Elliott, 152).

11. ἐγένετο ἐγένοντο (A K 81 614 629 1881 pc). Elliott, 152, holds that the plural is original and was altered to the Cl. sing. after a neuter subject (cf. the variants at 4.17 and 1 Tim 5.25).

ἐν Ἀντιοχείᾳ Add ἃ διὰ τὴν Θέκλαν ἔπαθεν (181^mg (sy^hmg). A clear gloss. There is an even longer addition in K^mg. Cf. 4.19.

12. εὐσεβῶς ζῆν Inverted order (ℵ A P 33 104 365 1505 1739 pc; WH; Kilpatrick). The normal order in the PE is that of the text, i.e. adverb followed by verb (Elliott, 153f.).

14. τίνων τίνος (C³ D Ψ TR lat). The sing. is a correction intended to give a reference to Paul only (Elliott, 20).

15. καὶ ὅτι Omit καί (206* vg^mss sy^p). Elliott, 210, 237, accepts the variant with hesitation, despite the very poor attestation.

[τὰ] ἱερὰ γράμματα (A C* D¹ Ψ 1739 1881 TR) Omit τά (ℵ C²vid D* F G 33 1175 pc co Clem; WH; BA 330; Dibelius-Conzelmann, 120 n. 7; Fee, 281). The text is accepted by Elliott, 155; Kilpatrick. Both forms of the phrase are attested elsewhere; see exegetical note. Since the PE often have an anarthrous noun followed by an attribute (1 Tim 1.14 et al.), there is a good case for omission of the article, and it is easier in any case to explain its addition than its omission.

διὰ πίστεως Insert τῆς (33, 69). Elliott, 155, 237, accepts the insertion as doubtful, possibly giving a reference to 'the faith'. The MS evidence is far too weak, and the pattern of anarthrous noun followed by an attribute is typical of the PE (see previous textual note and especially 2 Tim 1.13; contrast, however, 2.1 for the arthrous noun followed by attribute).

16. καὶ ὠφέλιμος Omit καί (it vg^cl sy^p bo Origen^lat Hil Ambst Prim). The conjunction was omitted because it 'seems to disturb the construction' (Metzger, 580; not discussed by Elliott).

ὠφέλιμος Add ἐστιν (483 it^mss vg^mss sy^h Theod Mops Latin fathers). Elliott, 156, 237, accepts the addition (as in the undisputed text of 1 Tim 4.8) with hesitation on the ground that Atticism tended to ellipse. The textual evidence for the insertion is too weak.

ἔλεγμον ἔλεγχον (D Ψ TR Clem) Elliott, 156, says that the variant (='reproof, censure, conviction', Heb 11.1) is acceptable, but in the end rejects it. (Cf. Pss. Sol. 10.1 v.l.)

17. ἄρτιος (a) τέλειος (D*); (b) ὑγιὴς τέλειος (104^mg). NA suggests that variant (a) is from the Latin (perfectus), and (b) is a marginal gloss. Elliott, 156, suggests that (a) is assimilation to Jas 3.2.

EXEGESIS

10. Σὺ δὲ παρηκολούθησάς μου τῇ διδασκαλίᾳ, τῇ ἀγωγῇ, τῇ προθέσει, τῇ πίστει, τῇ μακροθυμίᾳ, τῇ ἀγάπῃ, τῇ ὑπομονῇ The section commences with the familiar switch from the opponents and their evil characteristics to the reader and the positive qualities which he should show by means of σὺ δέ.[40] For παρακολουθέω see 1 Tim 4.6, where it is also linked to διδασκαλία. Here the sense of the verb is broad enough for it to govern the items in the following list which includes Paul's teaching, his way of life and qualities and his experiences. The verb may simply mean 'to be cognisant of, familiar with, observe' (Simpson, 147). A stronger meaning is given by Easton, 66, who suggests 'watch, note and imitate'.[41] Brox, 257f., takes the verb to mean that Timothy has imitated the example of Paul and shared in his experiences, which is true enough (Barrett, 112; Kelly, 198), but when he goes on to assert that here Timothy is presented as an ideal leader, possessing the qualities that he is elsewhere urged to acquire, he is misreading the text. Rather, the writer is simply laying the basis for the appeal which will follow in 4.1–5. Oberlinner, 137f., sees a shift from the teaching of Paul who did not present himself absolutely as an example but linked imitation to the figure of Christ; but the use of παρακολουθέω rather than ἀκολουθέω here somewhat weakens the element of imitation.

What follows is a virtue list, closely related to the specific question of truth and holding fast to it despite opposition. It is unusual in the PE in that it is a description of Paul himself (μου). Although some commentators find this reference gives an egotistical impression (Easton, 67), it can be understood as part of the picture of the past created by somebody approaching the end of life. It is of a piece with Paul's assertion of his authority and example in such passages as 1 Cor 11.1; 2 Cor 6.3–10; 10–13. The purpose of the list is to point to the authentic teaching and life-style for Timothy and to indicate where it is to be found in contrast to the false teaching and conduct of the opponents. 'Conscious integrity can affirm itself without self-assumption' (Simpson, 147; he must mean 'self-assertion').

The list has nine elements with the typical fuller development of the last item (in this case effectively the last two items). It moves from teaching to way of life and the characteristics especially required in a missionary facing attack, concluding with the actual painful experiences themselves.

---

[40] 3.14; 4.5; Tit 2.1 and note; contrast σὺ οὖν, 2.1.
[41] Similarly, 'to let one's way of life be determined by' (Holtzmann, 430f.); 'to follow' (NJB; GNB; Arichea-Hatton, 228f.).

(a) For διδασκαλία see 3.16; 4.3; 1 Tim 1.10 note.

(b) ἀγωγή*** is 'way of life, conduct', often in imitation of a model.[42] The word can have the sense of 'education' or its result (Plutarch, *Mor.* 1A: Περὶ παίδων ἀγωγῆς); it can hardly have both senses simultaneously (*pace* Simpson, 147). For the thought cf. 1 Cor 4.17.

(c) πρόθεσις was used in 1.9 for God's will, but here for a human characteristic. The thought is of the sense of the purpose and firm resolve that determined Paul's actions (Acts 11.23; 27.13; 1 Clement 45.7).[43]

(d) For πίστις as one Christian quality among others see 2.22; 1 Tim 6.11; Gal 5.22. The thought of faith as a quality conveying steadfast determination to attain a goal is probably present.

(e) μακροθυμία was a quality of Christ in 1 Tim 1.16 but of the believer here and in 4.2, where it is especially associated with the teacher.

(f) For ἀγάπη see 1.7, 13; 2.22, and for (g) ὑπομονή see Tit 2.2 and note; 1 Tim 6.11.

11. τοῖς διωγμοῖς, τοῖς παθήμασιν, οἷά μοι ἐγένετο ἐν Ἀντιοχείᾳ, ἐν Ἰκονίῳ, ἐν Λύστροις

(h) διωγμός (3.11b**; cf. διώκτης, 1 Tim 1.13) always refers to persecution for religious reasons in the NT.[44]

(i) πάθημα** is a more general word for 'suffering, misfortune', usually pl.[45]

The relative pron. οἷος (3.11b) means 'of what a kind'; the correlative has often to be supplied from the context. Tr. 'such as, for example, happened'. Three places are given as examples. Ἀντιόχεια was the name of many cities, but here refers to 'Pisidian Antioch', the seat of government of S. Galatia.[46] Here Paul was forced to leave the city (Acts 13.50). Ἰκόνιον[47] was the scene of an attempted stoning of the missionaries (Acts 14.5f.), and Λύστρα[48] was where Paul was actually stoned.

---

[42] Cl.; Esth 2.20; 10.3; 2 Macc 4.16; 6.8; 11.24; 3 Macc 4.10; *Ep. Arist.* Philo, *Det.* 16; Josephus, *Ant.* 14.195; 1 Clement 47.6; 48.1, of the Christian way of life; cf. Schmidt, K. L., *TDNT* I, 128f.; *TLNT* I, 29–31.

[43] It could also mean 'way of thinking' (Polybius 4.73.2).

[44] Cl.; sing. Mt 13.21; Mk 4.17; Acts 8.1; 13.50; Rom 8.35; 1 Clement 3.2; pl. of individual occasions Mk 10.30; 2 Cor 12.10; 2 Th 1.4; not discussed in *TDNT*.

[45] Cl.; not LXX; Rom 8.18; 2 Cor 1.5–7; Phil 3.10; Col 1.24; Heb 2.9f.; 10.32; 1 Pet 1.11; 4.13; 5.1, 9; 1 Clement 2.1; Ignatius, *Smyr.* 5.1; 'passion, impulse', Rom 7.5; Gal 5.24; Michaelis, W., *TDNT* V, 930–5.

[46] Acts 13.14; 14.19, 21***; Strabo 12.8.14; Pliny, *NH* 5.94.

[47] Acts 13.51; 14.1, 19, 21; 16.2***; Xenophon, *Anab.* 1.2.19; Pliny, *NH* 5.41; Strabo 12.6.1.

[48] Fem. sing. or neut pl.; BD § 57; MHT I, 48; II, 147; Acts 14.6, 8, 21; 16.1, 2; 27.5 *v.l.*****

Paul always looks back to the first missionary campaign in terms of suffering (Gal 4.13f.; 2 Cor 11.25). Here he goes back to the earliest days of Timothy's association with him: 'such sufferings were visible to him right from the moment he became a Christian' (Fee). However, Dibelius-Conzelmann, 119, asks why there is no reference to the sufferings in Acts 16–17 when Timothy was in company with Paul. If Timothy was converted on Paul's second campaign rather than the first, he could still be aware of them. Within the limited circle of the church, remembrance of the early days would be a matter of common knowledge (cf. Bernard, 134). Such reminiscence is natural, rather than references to the immediate past and present (*pace* Holtzmann, 431f.). Some scholars hold that Acts is dependent on the tradition used in 2 Tim (Haenchen, E., *Die Apostelgeschichte* [Göttingen: Vandenhoeck und Ruprecht, 1959], 374) or on 2 Tim itself (Houlden, 127), others that 2 Tim is dependent on Acts (Hanson, 148f.). Others hold that the traditions about Paul and Timothy known to the author were related to those used by Acts and it was natural to use these in a context of linking Timothy to Paul (Oberlinner, 139).

οἵους διωγμοὺς ὑπήνεγκα καὶ ἐκ πάντων με ἐρρύσατο ὁ κύριος The second use of οἵους is syntactically unclear. It could continue the existing construction, 'the persecutions which I endured, and yet...'; or it may introduce a separate exclamation: 'what persecutions I endured!' (so BD §304; BA). The inclusion of διωγμούς in the clause strongly favours the second possibility. ὑποφέρω can mean simply 'to undergo' but also 'to bear (up *or* under), submit to, endure'.[49] καί introduces the contrast: 'and yet'. At this point (ἐκ πάντων...) the language begins to echo Ps 33.18 (MT 34.19): καὶ ἐκ πασῶν τῶν θλίψεων αὐτῶν ἐρύσατο αὐτούς. Hence Paul interprets his suffering in the light of the Psalms of the righteous sufferer who is preserved by God (cf. 4.17f.), although paradoxically he also knows that death will come (on the usual interpretation of 4.6–8). This application of OT material that was understood to refer prophetically to Jesus to his followers also is already found in Paul's application of material about the righteous sufferer and the Servant of Yahweh to himself and the church's mission (Rom 8.36; cf. 10.16; Acts 13.47). ῥύομαι is 'to rescue, save, deliver', i.e. 'to bring safely through' (4.17, 18**).[50] The reminiscence has ἐκ, but ἀπό is also used. Although ὁ κύριος refers to God in the Psalm, here the reference is probably to Christ.

[49] Cl.; 1 Cor 10.13; 1 Pet 2.19***; cf. 1 Clement 5.4; Hermas, *Mand.* 10.2.6; *Sim.* 7.4–6.
[50] For the spelling (WH has one ρ) see BD §11[1]; 101; MHT II, 101f., 193. Elliott, 153, comments that the double ρρ is usual at all periods.

12. καὶ πάντες δὲ οἱ θέλοντες εὐσεβῶς ζῆν ἐν Χριστῷ Ἰησοῦ διωχθήσονται What happened to Paul is typical of what can happen to all the Lord's people. For the use of καί ... δέ ... see 1 Tim 3.10; the construction emphasises the intervening word, πάντες; the scope is thus widened to include all Christians and not just leaders (cf. Acts 14.21f.; 1 Th 3.4). The reason for the broadening of the application may be to emphasise that the congregation generally stands over against the opponents and the apostates and can expect the same difficulties as the leaders. The use of θέλω (1 Tim 1.7) to express determination to live as Christians is perhaps unusual (but cf. Phil 2.13). For εὐσεβῶς ζῆν see Tit 2.12*** and **Excursus 1**, and for ἐν Χριστῷ Ἰησοῦ see 1.1. The phrase is used here in a characteristically Pauline manner.[51] διωχθήσονται (1 Tim 6.11* note) picks up on the noun in v. 11.

13. πονηροὶ δὲ ἄνθρωποι καὶ γόητες προκόψουσιν ἐπὶ τὸ χεῖρον πλανῶντες καὶ πλανώμενοι The thought of the present affliction of the people of God is balanced by a reminder of the present triumph of the godless (cf. 3.1–9). It is important to emphasise that the horizon here is the present time and the immediate future; the long-term horizon gives a different perspective (4.1, 8, 14). Nevertheless, there is something of a contrast with v. 9, which is equally written within the short-term horizon. There, however, the thought was not that the activity of evil would be diminished but rather that it would not totally mislead the people of God.

πονηρός functions here as an adjective, 'wicked, evil, bad, base, worthless, vicious, degenerate'; Bengel, followed by Lock, 108, suggests 'malignant'.[52] The reference is quite general but is probably focused on apostate people in the church. Evil in general is linked with the activity of γόητες***. This word can refer specifically to a person who is a 'sorcerer, juggler', or more generally to a 'swindler, cheat'.[53] Delling compares Euripides, *Bac.* 234, where Dionysus 'entices to impious action by apparently pious words'. Probably this broader sense is present here, and the reference is to false teachers who deceive Christians (Karris 1973:552, 560f.). Yet the use of magic in imitation of Christian miracles (cf. Philo, *Mig.* 83) could well be part of the picture (Holtzmann, 433; so also with hesitation Bernard, 135; cf. Spicq, 104–10, 783).

---

[51] Kelly, 200; *pace* Hasler, 74; Oberlinner, 141. See Rom 6.11.

[52] Cl.; Mt 12.35a; Lk 6.45a; 2 Th 3.2; Mt 18.32; 25.26; Lk 19.22; Acts 17.5; *et al.*; it is also used as a noun (Deut 21.21; Esth 7.6; Mt 5.39; 1 Cor 5.13); pl. (Mt 5.45; 22.10; 13.49; Lk 6.35; *et al.*); Harder, G., *TDNT* VI, 546–62.

[53] Cl.; Philo, *Spec.* 1.315; *Her.* 302; Josephus, *Bel.* 4.85; *Ant.* 20.97; Diognetus 8.4; Delling, G., *TDNT* I, 737f.

The linking of persecution from outside the church with false teaching within it seems to be characteristic of the PE. But the reference may include the flourishing of false religions and sects which practised magic in the outside world (e.g. Acts 8.9; Mt 24.24). προκόπτω (3.9) is again used ironically of progress in the wrong direction, indicated by the qualification ἐπὶ τὸ χεῖρον (1 Tim 5.8***).[54] The activities of the deceivers are neatly encapsulated in the phrase πλανῶντες καὶ πλανώμενοι (Tit 3.3), which is also found in *CH* 16.16: ὁ πλανώμενος καὶ πλανῶν.[55] The two participles apply to the one group of people who deceive others without realising that they themselves have been misled. Being deceived religiously is characteristic of the last days (Mt 24.4, 5, 11, 24; Mk 13.5, 6. Jn 7.12; 1 Jn 2.26; 3.7; Rev 2.20 *et al.*; cf. Ignatius, *Mag.* 3.2; *Philad.* 7.1).

14. Σὺ δὲ μένε ἐν οἷς ἔμαθες καὶ ἐπιστώθης The instruction proceeds with the familiar reversion to exhortation to the reader with σὺ δέ (3.10) which contrasts him with the ungodly. Whereas the previous verses were descriptive of the patterns of conduct that he should implicitly follow and eschew, the exhortation now becomes direct. Appeals addressed to believers often contain the element of continuing in an already established pattern or relationship. The key word is μένω, 'to remain, continue' (2.13 of Christ; 1 Tim 2.15 of believing women), which is characteristic of Johannine exhortation.[56] Here the locus is expressed by ἐν οἷς,[57] referring to the items of teaching which constitute the παραθηκή committed to Timothy and which are based on Scripture. This doubtless includes baptismal teaching (Holtz, 186) but goes beyond it to include the teaching given by one Christian leader to another. It has not only been taught to Timothy. It has also been committed to him as a sacred trust,[58] so that he can then pass it on unchanged to others (2.2). But is this the point expressed here? The verb is not ἐπιστεύθης, which would require this sense, but ἐπιστώθης. The force of πιστόω*** is not clear. In the act. it means 'to make [somebody] trustworthy', e.g. to bind a person by a pledge so that he may be relied upon, or 'to make somebody into one who trusts' (Bultmann, R., *TDNT* VI, 178f.); in pass. 'to be made trustworthy, to give a

---

[54] For the whole phrase cf. Josephus, *Ant.* 4.59; 18.340; *T. Jud.* 21.18 *v.l.*

[55] Cf. Philo, *Mig.* 83; other examples of the wordplay in Lock, 109; Dibelius-Conzelmann, 119.

[56] Of remaining faithful to teaching (Jn 8.31; 2 Jn 9a, 9b); letting the divine word continue to take up its abode in believers (Jn 5.38; 15.7b; 1 Jn 2.14, 24, 27; 2 Jn 2).

[57] Relative attraction for ἐν τούτοις ἅ.

[58] '*Et tibi credita sunt*' (vg); '*quae tibi concredita sunt*' (Luther, cited by Holtzmann, 434).

pledge' or 'to be persuaded that' (3 Macc 4.20); in the mid. 'to give pledges of fidelity', 'to confirm, prove' (cf. LSJ). In the LXX it means 'to show oneself faithful' (Ps 77 [MT 78].37 = 1 Clement 15.4). For the present passage the sense 'to feel confident, be convinced' with an implied acc. of respect has been suggested.[59] However, in view of the root meaning of the word another possibility deserves to be explored. The force is 'you learned and you showed yourself faithful in respect of what you learned' or 'you have been bound to be trustworthy in respect of what you have learned'.

εἰδὼς παρὰ τίνων ἔμαθες What appears to be a motive for being faithful in the tradition is now grounded in knowledge of two things. The first is the character of the people from whom Timothy learned it. The integrity of the message is related to that of the teachers (cf. 1.5; 2.2).[60] In the context of v. 15 the plural τίνων includes all who taught Timothy, his mother and grandmother and Paul himself. The scribal alteration to τίνος is eloquent of later stress on an orderly succession of clerical teaching, entirely foreign to the PE. Brox, 259f., rejects the historical reference without adequate grounds and holds that here Timothy stands for later officebearers in the church who have learned the faith from various sources but always as part of an orderly succession (2.2); there is thus a tension in the PE between the 'historical' and 'typical' roles of 'Timothy'. But the point is rather that the value and truth of information in the ancient world is related to the identity and trustworthiness of the agents who transmit it. There may also be a warning against the newfangled ideas of the opponents.

15. καὶ ὅτι ἀπὸ βρέφους [τὰ] ἱερὰ γράμματα οἶδας, τὰ δυνάμενά σε σοφίσαι εἰς σωτηρίαν διὰ πίστεως τῆς ἐν Χριστῷ Ἰησοῦ The second part of the motivation is that to abandon the faith would mean abandoning that which Timothy has been taught from his earliest days. καὶ ὅτι introduces a second clause dependent on εἰδώς involving change of construction. The pres. form οἶδας is used for an action started in the past (Moule 1953:8). βρέφος is 'unborn child' or 'infant' (Cl.), and ἀπὸ βρέφους is a stock phrase, strictly 'from infancy' but here simply 'from childhood'.[61]

---

[59] BA; Simpson, 149; cf. Philo, *Leg. Gai.* 311; so Homer, *Od.* 21.208; Sophocles, *OC* 1039; cf. *Ep. Arist.* 91; 1 Clement 42.3). Suggested renderings are: 'to be made certain, believing' (Bultmann, R., *TDNT* VI, 204); 'what you ... acquired in faith' (*EDNT* III, 98); 'firmly believe' (NRSV and similarly other translations; Theophylact, cited by Holtzmann, 434).

[60] The use of μανθάνω with παρά is normal (Xenophon, *Cyr.* 2.2.6; Sextus 353; Philo, *Deus* 4).

[61] Philo, *Spec* 2.33; but ἐκ βρέφους is more common, Philo, *Somn.* 1.192; cf. BA; *New Docs.* IV, 40 § 12.

The implication is that Timothy was taught from the Scriptures prior to the conversion of his family, as would have been normal for a Jewish boy from the age of five years onwards ('*Abot* 5.21; SB III, 664–6). Questions have been raised as to whether this agrees with the account in Acts, where Timothy's father is a Gentile and Timothy himself was not circumcised at birth (Easton, 67f.). But the marriage of his mother to a non-Jew need not imply that she failed to bring up her child in the traditional manner. We are simply ignorant of all the facts.[62] It is also implied, of course, that Jewish instruction in the Scriptures could lead to salvation through Jesus. The alternative is that the writer is ignorant of the picture in Acts and portrays Timothy as the third generation child with a grandmother and mother who were converted before he was born.

ἱερός, 'holy', is rare in both the LXX and the NT (Josh 6.8; Dan 1.2; 1 Cor 9.13), but common enough in Hel. Judaism (Schrenk, G., *TDNT* III, 221–30). It is used of Scripture here only in the NT (cf. ἅγιος, Rom 1.2).[63] γράμμα is originally 'letter [of the alphabet]', then (usually pl.) 'document, writing'.[64] [τὰ] ἱερὰ γράμματα is found as a set phrase for the Scriptures.[65] There is, therefore, nothing unusual about the phrase, although in the present context it may perhaps stress that the OT is a textbook to be read by a child spelling out the letters. The reference is purely to the OT Scriptures, although later this and similar phrases were used for the Bible as a whole.

Now follows a further reason for holding fast to the Scriptures in the form of an extended attribute attached in the normal way to the preceding noun by the article. The use of δυνάμενα may provide an implicit contrast with v. 7. σοφίζω occurs rarely in the act. with the sense 'to make wise, instruct'.[66] The view taken

---

[62] There are plenty of mothers today who have married husbands who do not share their religion but nevertheless bring up their children according to their own faith.

[63] However, it occurs in the phrase αἱ ἱεραὶ γραφαί in Josephus, *Ap.* 2.45; Philo, *Fug.* 4; *Spec.* 1.214; *Her.* 106 and 159 (anarthrous); *et al.*; 1 Clement 53.1 (1 Clement also has αἱ ἱεραὶ βίβλοι [43.1]; cf. αἱ γραφαὶ αἱ ἀληθεῖς, 45.2); Mk 16 (shorter ending), of the κήρυγμα; Schrenk, G., *TDNT* I, 751.

[64] Of a letter (Acts 28.21); promissory note (Lk 16.6f.); book (the Pentateuch; Jn 5.47); of imperial letters and decrees (Deissmann 1927:375f.; *New Docs.* III, 64 §29); Schrenk, G., *TDNT* I, 761–9.

[65] It occurs with the article in (for example) Philo, *Mos.* 2.290, 292; *Leg. Gai.* 195; Josephus, *Ant.* 1.13; 10.210; and without the article in Philo, *Her.* 106, 159; Rom 1.2; 16.26; 2 Pet 1.20. Similar expressions are found in Philo, *Post.* 158; *Praem.* 79 (Cf. Schrenk, G., *TDNT* I, 763f., and especially Burkhardt*, 75–9).

[66] Cl.; Ps 18 (MT 19).8; 104 (MT 105).22; Ignatius, *Smyr.* 1.1; Barnabas 5.3; pass. Ecclus 38.31; mid. 'to devise craftily', 2 Pet 1.16***; cf. Wilckens, U., *TDNT* VII, 527f.

of the function of the Law in the Pss is here reaffirmed: Christians agree that the law, no doubt as expounded by Christian teachers, continues to lead people to salvation. Oberlinner, 145, suggests that the stress on the value of the OT may be in response to the negative attitude of some Gnostics to it. More probably, there may have been some reaction by orthodox Christians to the misuse of the OT by the opponents. In any case, the rejection of their 'myths and genealogies' does not entail a rejection of the OT properly understood.

The phrase εἰς σωτηρίαν expresses the goal of instruction and of Christian effort generally.[67] Most commentators bind διὰ πίστεως closely with it ('salvation [obtained] through faith'; Rom 3.22), but some attach it to the verb ('to instruct by means of faith ... in salvation'; Kelly, 202). Probably the phrase is to be taken broadly with what precedes: the whole process of coming to salvation is through faith. Properly understood, the OT instructs in the Christian way of salvation through faith, but (it is implied) without knowledge of Christ and faith in him the OT will be misunderstood. Accordingly, Christian interpretation is needed (Jeremias, 62; Kelly, 202). Such faith is described as τῆς ἐν Χριστῷ. The construction is similar to that in Rom 8.39 with reference to the love of God which is in Christ Jesus. But the phrase is ambiguous: does the writer mean faith which is directed to Christ as its object (Knight, 444; Harris, M. J., NIDNTT III, 1212) or faith which is 'given to us in Christ (or in union with Christ)'? The use of the phrase in the immediate context in v. 12 favours the second possibility.[68]

16. πᾶσα γραφὴ θεόπνευστος καὶ ὠφέλιμος πρὸς διδασκαλίαν, πρὸς ἐλεγμόν, πρὸς ἐπανόρθωσιν, πρὸς παιδείαν τὴν ἐν δικαιοσύνῃ
The statement about Scripture is backed up by a fuller explanation of its nature and purpose. The emphasis is on its value and usefulness for different purposes, so that it can provide whatever the servant of God needs for doing good. What is stated in Rom 15.4 about the value of the Scriptures for teaching is here affirmed in a broader and more inclusive manner. Ignatius, *Philad.* 8.2 is much less close.

The first part of the verse poses a number of exegetical problems: (a) the reference of the term γραφή; (b) the syntax of the adjective πᾶσα; (c) the syntax of the verbless clause; (d) the significance of θεόπνευστος.

---

[67] Cf. Rom 1.16; Acts 13.47; Rom 10.1, 10; 2 Cor 7.10; Phil 1.19; Heb 9.28; 11.7; 1 Pet 1.5; cf. Jn 5.39.
[68] The reinterpretation of 'faith' here as 'ecclesiastical piety' (Hasler, 75) is unwarranted.

(a) *The reference of the term* γραφή. The term γραφή can refer to what is written or to the art of writing. In the sing. it can refer to:

(1) A specific passage.[69] The whole collection of such passages is 'the Scriptures', and the pl. is used in this sense to refer to the whole or parts (cf. 2 Pet 3.16, where the pl. refers to 'various passages').

(2) Although the plural means 'the Scriptures', the sing. never occurs with the meaning 'a book of Scripture'; phrases involving βίβλος are used instead (Josephus, *Ap.* 2.45). In Acts 8.32 ἡ περιοχὴ τῆς γραφῆς could mean 'the passage of Scripture', i.e. 'the specific text in the book of Isaiah', but it could also mean 'the content of the passage'.

(3) There is dispute whether the sing. is used for the collection of Scriptures as a whole, equivalent to αἱ γραφαί, a sense which undoubtedly occurs at a later stage.[70] None of the background references listed in BA[71] absolutely require this sense except for *Ep. Arist.* 168; see, however, *T. Zeb.* 9.5; Philo, *Spec.* 1.1. Warfield*, 237–9, lists some 20 broader references in the NT where he claims that there is a wide reference to Scripture as a whole.[72] But some of these verses are better interpreted as references to specific passages (e.g. Jn 2.22), or to 'whatever is written about a specific topic in an unidentified passage or passages'. Just possibly some refer to 'whatever is in writing [sc. in the acknowledged collection of writings]', and one can see that it would be easy to slide from this sense to 'the writings as a whole collection'. In Rom 4.3 the sense of 'what does the Scripture say?' is surely not 'what does the OT as a whole say?' but rather 'what is said in the passage that I am about to quote?' Schrenk, G., *TDNT* I, 749–61, especially 754f., develops a case for γραφή signifying 'the unified totality of Scripture'; he observes that Scripture is personified as a unity in Gal 3.8, 22, and then claims that the passages in Jn listed by Warfield refer to 'the fulfilment of all Scripture, including its individual utterances' (cf. 1 Pet 2.6; 2 Pet 1.20). None of this evidence is fully compelling. He has not made out his case that the phrase is used to mean the OT as a single document; the cases in question seem to mean 'the [relevant] material that has been written' rather than 'the whole of the collection of Scriptures'.[73]

[69] Cf. 4 Macc 18.14; Philo, *Her.* 266; *T. Naph.* 5.8 (a non-biblical oracle).
[70] Warfield*; Brox, 261; Hübner, H., *EDNT* I, 260–4.
[71] Philo, *Mos.* 2.84; *Ep. Arist.* 155, 168; cf. 1 Chr 15.15; 2 Chr 30.5, 18.
[72] Jn 2.22; 7.38, 42; 10.35; 17.12; 19.28; 20.9; Acts 8.32; Rom 4.3; 9.17; 10.11; 11.2; Gal 3.8, 22; 4.30; 1 Tim 5.18; Jas 4.5; 1 Pet 2.6; 2 Pet 1.20; it is not clear whether he intended to include 2 Tim 3.16 in this list (cf. *ibid.* 134).
[73] See further, Burton, E. de W., *Galatians* (Edinburgh: T. and T. Clark, 1921), 160, 196; Burkhardt*, 79–81.

It is best to conclude that the word here refers to an individual 'Scripture', i.e. 'a passage in the collection identified as the Scriptures' (Oberlinner, 147).

(b) *The syntax of the adjective* πᾶσα. With an anarthrous sing. noun πᾶς means either 'every' or 'all the, the whole'.[74] In most cases the context makes it clear which interpretation is to be followed. Both senses can occur side by side (Acts 17.26a, b). The sense 'every kind of' is also found.[75] The following meanings have been suggested for the phrase here: (1) 'All of the Scripture', i.e. the whole of the OT;[76] (2) 'Every passage of Scripture';[77] (3) 'Every kind of inspired writing' – not confined to Scripture (Spence*).

The phrase is not paralleled in the NT; the nearest equivalent is in 2 Pet 1.20 which must mean 'every prophecy in [lit. of] Scripture'. We can safely rule out view (3) which does not agree with the universal NT usage of γραφή. The choice between (1) and (2) really depends on whether γραφή means 'Scripture as a whole' or 'an individual text of Scripture'. To say 'All of the Scripture' is in effect to say 'every passage of Scripture', and therefore in the end of the day a decision is not important. The objection that what is said about its fourfold usefulness does not apply to every individual passage (Wolfe 1990:129f.; cf. Houlden, 128; Knight, 445) is pedantic.

A further question is the reference of the phrase. The vast majority of scholars assume that the Jewish Scriptures are in mind. For the possibility that the reference has been expanded from v. 15 to the OT together with accounts of the gospel and even Paul's own letters see Spicq, 787f.; Hendricksen, 300–2; Knight, 447f.[78]

(c) *The syntax of the verbless clause.* The problem here is the syntax of the two adjectives following πᾶσα γραφή without a verb being expressed: the second must be predicative, but is this also true of the first? There are two possibilities: (1) 'Every/all Scripture which is inspired is also profitable for...';[79]

[74] 'Every': Jn 1.9; Eph 3.15; Heb 9.19; 2 Pet 1.20; 'all': Mt 3.15; 28.18; Acts 1.21; 2.36; 7.22; Rom 11.26; Eph 2.21; Col 4.12; in all of these cases the phrase could signify 'every part of'.

[75] Mt 4.23; Acts 10;12; Tit 1.16. Cf. BD §275; Moule 1953:93–5; MHT III, 199.

[76] AV; NIV; GNB; NJB; REB; NRSV t; Simpson, 150f.; Houlden, 128; Knight, 445; Moule 1953:95 – 'the whole of Scripture [is] inspired'.

[77] RV; NRSV mg; BA; Warfield*, 134; Schrenk, G., *TDNT* I, 754; Holtzmann, 440; Bernard, 137; Parry, 65; Kelly, 202; Holtz, 188; Hanson, 151f.; cf. Acts 8.35.

[78] A bizarre explanation is offered by Hasler, 75, who argues that in v. 15 the reference is to the OT understood allegorically, and in v. 16 to the apostolic writings, including 2 Tim itself.

[79] Pesh; RV t; REB; TNT text; Bernard, 137; White, 175; Parry, 65; Spicq, 793–5; Brox, 261; Dibelius-Conzelmann, 118; Barrett, 114; Hasler, 74; Schweizer, E., *TDNT* VI, 454; Sheriffs*; cf. Theod. Mops. II, 222 Swete.

(2) 'Every/all Scripture is inspired and profitable for...'.[80] Both translations are theoretically possible.

In favour of the first possibility it can be noted that phrases of the form 'every inspired Scripture' are common enough (cf. v. 17; 4.18). More weight attaches to the argument that the stress in the sentence is on the usefulness of Scripture and there is no apparent need to insist on its inspiration. Further, it is claimed that the word γραφή needs an attribute (corresponding to ἱερός in v. 15); in view of the clear usage of the word elsewhere in the NT, this is a weak argument.

Against this view stands the strong objection that nobody who wished to express this sense would have phrased the clause in this awkward manner. The use of καί is also hard to explain on this interpretation: what is the point of saying 'every inspired Scripture is *also* profitable'? Why mention inspiration at all? Finally, this interpretation might imply that some Scripture was not inspired, which is unlikely to have been a view held by either the author or his opponents.[81] It is more likely that the reference to inspiration is part of what the author wants to affirm about Scripture in order to defend its universal usefulness (Oberlinner, 148f.).

There has been much effort to find parallels to the form of the sentence in which a noun qualified by πᾶς is followed predicatively by two adjectives without a verb. 1 Tim 4.4 is often cited, but it is not a real parallel in view of the inclusion of a second subject (οὐδέν); for what it is worth, however, it supports the view that the first adjective is predicative. The closest parallel is 3 Macc 3.29: πᾶς δὲ τόπος, οὗ ἐὰν φωραθῇ τὸ σύνολον σκεπαζόμενος Ἰουδαῖος, ἄβατος καὶ πυριφλεγὴς γινέσθω.[82] Here both adjs. must be predicative. (The parallel, to be sure, is not exact, since there is a parenthetical relative clause in it.)

There is thus no barrier to accepting the second interpretation, and the first interpretation should be rejected as unnatural.

(d) *The significance of* θεόπνευστος*** *(vg. divinitus inspirata).* The form is passive and has the sense 'God-breathed'.[83] This is

---

[80] AV; RV mg; NRSV; NIV; GNB; NJB; Holtzmann, 440; Lock, 110; Easton, 65; Jeremias, 61; Simpson, 150; Dornier, 233f.; Guthrie, 175f.; Kelly, 203; Holtz, 188f.; Hanson, 152; Fee, 279; Knight, 445; Houlden, 128; Oberlinner, 148f.

[81] Admittedly, later Gnostics may have denied the inspiration of parts of the OT.

[82] I am grateful for this reference to an unpublished article by D. B. Wallace.

[83] See Warfield*, 245–96, who refutes the view of H. Cremer that it has an active sense; Schweizer, E., *TDNT* VI, 453–5; *TLNT* II, 193–5; Piñero*, 143–53.

The form is analogous to θεόπνοος. Cf. *CH* 1.30, θεόπνους γενόμενος τῆς ἀληθείας ἦλθον, of an ecstatic. Cf. Porphyry, *De antr. nymph*, 10 (AD III, of water); *Epigr Graec.* 1016 (AD III, of the face of the sphinx animated by the breath of God).

the earliest known occurrence, and it is possible that the writer coined it.[84] Similar language was beginning to be used elsewhere of God's activity in inspiring Scripture.[85]

E. Schweizer associates the concept with Hellenistic 'inspiration manticism', in which the spirit is inspirer of poets and prophets but not of writings, and this is also seen as the background to the present passage by Piñaro.[86] In the OT, although some material is dictated or actually written by God, the idea of inspiration is also known (Num 24.2; cf. Hos 9.7). This concept developed in Rabbinic Judaism where, according to Schweizer, the law was written or dictated by God, but the prophets and writings were inspired by God.[87] In Hel. Judaism the idea of inspiration was dominant.[88]

Later Christian writers developed Platonic ideas when they conceived of the Spirit as being like a flow of air causing a flute to sound or similar metaphors.[89] It has been claimed that these ideas are present in Philo, but this theory is convincingly refuted by Burkhardt* who demonstrates that Philo did not regard the biblical authors (especially Moses) as being inspired by God in such a way that they were not the real authors of what they wrote. Both Philo and 2 Tim hold rather to a view of inspiration which does fuller justice to the human authorship of Scripture.

The point of the adjective here is surely to emphasise the authority of the Scriptures as coming from God and to indicate that they have a divinely-intended purpose related to his plan of

[84] Otherwise the word occurs in Ps-Phocylides, 129: τῆς θεοπνεύστου σοφίας λόγος ἐστὶν ἄριστος (In the translation by van der Horst, P. W., in *OTP* II, 579, the line is regarded as inauthentic; Warfield*, 252, thought that it was Christian.); Ps-Plutarch, *de Plac. Phil.* 904F, distinguishes dreams inspired by God from natural dreams: τῶν ὀνείρων τοὺς μὲν θεοπνεύστους κατ᾽ ἀνάγκην γίνεσθαι; Vettius Valens, 9.1 uses it of the θεῖον δημιούργημα, i.e. human beings; *Sib. Orac.* 5.308: 'foolish Kyme, with her divinely inspired streams'; 406f: 'the great God, begetter of all who have God-given breath'; *Test. Abr.* A 20: angels tend the body of Abraham with μυρίσμασι θεοπνεύστοις (cf. Sanders, E. P., *OTP* I, 895; c. AD 100).
Later Christian use includes descriptions of Scripture (Maximus Conf. *MPG* 4.52A); an archbishop (*Epigr. Graec.* 1062); anchorites (Cyril of Scythopolis, *Vitae Sabae*, 16 in *TU* 49.2 (1939), 100.3; see Schweizer, E., *TDNT* VI, 454).
[85] Philo uses ἐπιπνέω (*Decal.* 35) and καταπνέω (*Conf.* 44; *Mos.* 1.175, 201; 2.69, 291; cf. *Plant.* 23), and Josephus, *Ap.* 1.37 has ἐπίπνοια. Cf. how the θεῖα ἐπίπνοια inspires people in Dittenberger, *Syll.*[2] 552.12 (II BC; see MM 287).
[86] Cf. the aretalogy of Isis in which the author claims that the writing is by a human but also by a divine mind (*New Docs.* I, 10, 15 § 2; see further III, 29f. § 6).
[87] See further Sjöberg, E., *TDNT* VI, 382f.
[88] Cf. 4 Ezra 14.22; Philo, *Spec.* 1.65; 4.49; *Her.* 259–66 See Burkhardt*.
[89] Josephus. *Ap.* 1.31ff. 2 Pet 1.21; Justin, *Apol.* I.36; and Theophilus, *ad Autolyc.* 2.9 do not develop the metaphor in this way, being content to refer to divine inspiration like a breath or wind that animates the writers. It is found in Athenagoras, *Suppl.* 7, 9.

salvation. They are therefore to be interpreted in line with this purpose and not in the fanciful ways favoured by the opponents.

The main thrust of the sentence lies in the second adjective. The writer declares that the Scriptures are inspired, as a datum with which his readers would agree,[90] and uses this as a basis for the point that he wants to stress: whatever is divinely inspired is therefore useful.[91]

The usefulness of Scripture is expressed by four phrases; the attempt has been made to group these in two pairs relating to belief (positive and negative) and action (negative and positive) (cf. Guthrie, 176; Knight, 449f.). This arrangement is artificial. Rather, there is a chiasmus with terms for teaching/education and conviction/correction. There would also seem to be a sequence in which the general term 'teaching' is followed by a sequence of three describing the steps in the conversion of sinners (cf. Preisker, H., *TDNT* V, 451).

The value of Scripture for teaching (διδασκαλία; 3.10; 1 Tim 1.10 and note) is obvious.[92]

ἔλεγμος*** is the 'conviction' of a sinner, i.e. getting a person to realise that they have done wrong (Num 5.18–22).[93] It is not obvious that this is necessarily doctrinal; conviction with regard to evil behaviour is equally possible.

ἐπανόρθωσις*** is 'correction, restoration, improvement'.[94] BA cite a passage from Epictetus 3.21.15 which gives a similar pattern of thought to the present passage: οὕτως ὠφέλιμα γίνεται τὰ μυστήρια ... ὅτι ἐπὶ παιδείᾳ καὶ ἐπανορθώσει τοῦ βίου κατεστάθη πάντα ... From conviction of sin there is a natural progression to the recovery of the sinner to a better life.

Finally, the Scriptures offer the basis for παιδεία, 'instruction, education', with a strong element of discipline and correction.[95] Here the sense of education is dominant (Bertram, G.,

---

[90] Unless perhaps he is making a point against opponents who held that only some of the Scriptures were inspired; cf. Hanson, 152.

[91] For ὠφέλιμος see Tit 3.8 and note; 1 Tim 4.8; for the use with πρός see Plato, *Rep.* 10, 607D.

[92] Cf Rom 15.4, which Hanson, 151, finds to be the basis of this passage.

[93] It can also mean 'reproof' (Ecclus 21.6; 32.17; 48.7; Josephus, *Ant.* 8.252); 'punishment' (2 Kgs 19.3.; Jth 2.10; 1 Macc 2.49; cf. ἔλεγξις, 2 Pet 2.16***; cf. Büchsel, F., *TDNT* II, 476).

[94] 1 Esdr 8.52; 1 Macc 14.34; *Ep. Arist.* 130; Philo, *Decal.* 174. Cf. Preisker, H., *TDNT* V, 450f.; *TLNT* II, 30f.; *New Docs.* II, 84 §46. Cf. the use of ἐπιδιορθόω (Tit 1.5).

[95] Ps 49.17; cf. Prov 5.12; Bar 4.13; Eph 6.4; Heb 12.5 (Prov. 3.11), 7, 8, 11***; 1 Clement 16.5 (= Isa 53.5); 21.6 (par. Polycarp 4.2); 21.8; 35.8; 56.2, 16; 62.3; Hermas, *Vis.* 2.3.1; 3.9.10; *Sim.* 6.3.6; cf. παιδεύω, 2.25; 1 Tim 1.20; Tit 2.12 and note.

TDNT V, 624 n. 184). δικαιοσύνη is clearly righteous behaviour (cf. Eph 4.24).

17. ἵνα ἄρτιος ᾖ ὁ τοῦ θεοῦ ἄνθρωπος, πρὸς πᾶν ἔργον ἀγαθὸν ἐξηρτισμένος The way in which the final clause is linked with the rest of the sentence is disputed. (a) It may express the purpose, or perhaps the result, of the activities in v. 16b; on this view the 'man of God' is any Christian (and especially leaders) who is instructed and so helped to become fitted for good deeds.[96] (b) It may express the purpose or effect of Scripture whose 'usefulness' is such that it equips the church leader to carry out the tasks of instruction, reproof, etc.[97] Since the broad concern of the passage is with the Scriptures as the source of divine wisdom that leads to salvation, the application here is probably to believers in general.

ὁ τοῦ θεοῦ ἄνθρωπος (1 Tim 6.11 note), is a phrase that can be used of any believer, although the thought here may be especially of Christian leaders. The accusation of 'clericalism' (Houlden, 129) is wide of the mark, since the point in any case is the training of Christian leaders for their tasks in the church. ἄρτιος*** is 'complete, capable, proficient', 'qualified' (LN), i.e. 'able to meet all demands', 'having all that is necessary to meet whatever demands are put upon him'; hence possibly 'sound, entire'.[98] The participle ἐξηρτισμένος has much the same sense; ἐξαρτίζω is 'to finish, complete', 'to put something into full working order' (cf. Acts 21.5***).[99]

For πρὸς πᾶν ἔργον ἀγαθόν cf. Tit 1.16; 3.1; and (with εἰς) 2 Tim 2.21; 2 Cor 9.8. If we follow interpretation (b) of the clause, the reference is to the way in which the Christian leader is equipped by the Scriptures for the tasks of leadership (Barrett, 115). However, 'any good work' sounds rather more general than this ('charitable works', Kelly 204), and favours view (a).

c. Closing charge to Timothy (4.1–8)

Barton, J. M. T., '"Bonum certamen certavi ... fidem servavi" 2 Tim 4,7', *Bib* 40 (1959), 878–84; Campbell, A., '"Do the Work of an Evangelist"', *EQ* 64 (1992), 117–29; Cook, D., '2 Timothy 4:6–8 and the Epistle to the Philippians', *JTS* ns 33 (1982), 168–71; Dieterich, A., 'εὐαγγελίστης', *ZNW* 1 (1900), 336–8; Malherbe, A., '"In Season and out of Season" 2 Timothy 4:2', *JBL* 103 (1984),

---

[96] Holtzmann, 441f.; Bernard, 137f.; Lock, 111; Spicq, 789; Holtz, 189; Hanson, 153; Arichea-Hatton, 237.

[97] Guthrie, 177; Barrett, 115; Kelly, 204; Fee, 280.

[98] So Simpson, 150, citing Lucian's description of Hephaestus: οὐκ ἄρτιος τὼ πόδε. Delling, G., *TDNT* I, 475f., prefers the sense 'right, faultless, normal'. The word is Cl., corr. to Latin *integer*. For the use with εἰς τι BA cite *IG* XIV 889.7; cf. *TLNT* II, 18. (The adj. also means 'even' of numbers.)

[99] The word is Hel.; cf. καταρτίζω (-ισμος, -ισις), Lk 6.40; Eph 4.12; 2 Cor 13.9; Heb 13.10; *et al.*; cf. *TLNT* II, 18–20.

235–43; Pfister, F., 'Zur Wendung ἀπόκειταί μοι ὁ τῆς δικαιοσύνης στέφανος', ZNW 15 (1914), 94–6; Whitaker, G. H., 'In Season, out of Season', *ExpTim* 34 (1922–3), 332f.

A further, final exhortation forms the climax of the instructions and tends to recapitulate them. It imparts a sense of urgency to all that has been said already.

The passage falls into four parts. A solemn adjuration introduces an exhortation to faithful teaching (vv. 1f.). The need for this is emphasised by a recapitulation of the prophecy of apostasy in the church with the implied temptation to teachers to give people what they want to hear instead of the truth (vv. 3f.). Over against such temptations Timothy is to carry out his commission, aware of temptation and ready to endure hardship (v. 5). Finally, Paul refers to the fact that his work is now complete; he has been faithful and can confidently await his reward, along with all who look forward to the appearing of the Lord (vv. 6–8): the implied appeal to Timothy to carry on his task needs no further words.

Prior 1989:154–63 argues that this along with other passages suggests that Paul was concerned about Timothy's stability, both as a believer and as an evangelist (cf. 1.7f.). But it seems more likely that it is motivated by the pressing needs of the times.

This part of the letter especially has the characteristics of a 'last will and testament'. But the material is also assignable to other genres. Thus vv. 1–5 could be used as a kind of 'ordination charge' and some of its material may have been used in such situations, although there is no reason to find a formal charge underlying it.

The tone of vv. 6–8 has posed problems for some commentators. Can a person actually speak like this of himself, or is this a later description of Paul from a historical distance at which he is a figure to be reverenced (Oberlinner, 161–3)? Against the view that Paul is here put on a pedestal it is important to observe that what is said about his future hope is something that is shared by him with all who love the Lord. Later Christians have felt no hesitation in taking over the sentiments expressed here and making them their own.

TEXT

1. διαμαρτύρομαι Add οὖν (Ψ 1505 *pc*); add ἐγώ (326*); add οὖν ἐγώ (D¹ TR). For the inclusion of οὖν cf. 1 Tim 5.14. Elliott, 156f., follows the text (cf. 1 Tim 5.21) and notes that the MSS which add words here also amplify the title of Christ Jesus with τοῦ κυρίου later in the sentence.

κρίνειν κρῖναι (F G 6 33 81 1881 *pc*; WH mg). This is an example of the scribal tendency to alter verbs to aorist (Elliott, 157).

καὶ τὴν ἐπιφάνειαν κατὰ τὴν ἐπιφάνειαν (‭א‬² D² Ψ 1881 TR vg^cl (sy) sa). The text has the more difficult construction, and scribes simplified (Metzger, 580f.; similarly, Elliott, 157f.).

2. ἐπιτίμησον παρακάλεσον Invert order (‭א‬* F G 1739 1881 *pc* latt co; WH mg). Elliott, 158, concludes that there is no contextual way to settle order.

3. κατά πρός (D P d f vg Lcf Ambst Aug). Elliott, 159, prefers the variant as the more difficult reading and thinks the text is assimilation to the phrase in Jude 16, 18; 2 Pet 3.3. But the MS evidence is weak.

τὰς ἰδίας ἐπιθυμίας τὰς ἐπιθυμίας τὰς ἰδίας (K L TR; Kilpatrick). Elliott, 159, holds that the variant is in a style with Semitic word order that copyists would dislike, but which is found in 4.7 (*v.l.*) and 1 Tim 5.25. But the MS evidence is late.

5. κακοπάθησον Omit (‭א‬* vg^ms). Elliott, 160, accepts the text. The addition ὡς καλὸς στρατιώτης Χριστοῦ Ἰησοῦ (A) is clearly assimilation to 2.3 (Elliott, 160).

6. ἀναλύσεώς μου ἐμῆς ἀναλύσεως (D Ψ TR a f t vg^st ww). The text is Semitic in style; the PE do not use possessive adjectives (Elliott, 160).

7. τὸν καλὸν ἀγῶνα τὸν ἀγῶνα τὸν καλόν (D Ψ 1739 1881 TR Origen; Kilpatrick). Cf. 4.3 note. Elliott, 160, adopts the variant as representing Semitic word order. On the analogy of 2 Tim 1.14; 1 Tim 1.18; 4.6; 6.12b, 13 and especially 6.12a, the text should be preferred.

8. πᾶσιν Omit (D* 6 424^c 1739* 1881 *pc* lat sy^p Ambst). The adjective is well attested, and could have been omitted by homoioteleuton (Metzger, 581). Elliott, 161, notes that the word order here is Semitic, and therefore retains the text. πᾶς is frequently omitted by scribes (cf. Elliott, J. K., 'The United Bible Societies Textual Commentary Evaluated', *NovT* 17 [1975], 148).

EXEGESIS

1. Διαμαρτύρομαι ἐνώπιον τοῦ θεοῦ καὶ Χριστοῦ Ἰησοῦ τοῦ μέλλοντος κρίνειν ζῶντας καὶ νεκρούς The section begins with a remarkably solemn adjuration in which Timothy is made aware of his obligations in the context of the coming judgement. Spicq, 798, comments that in Greece such adjurations were especially associated with legal acts of succession. The opening phrase of the adjuration, διαμαρτύρομαι ... Ἰησοῦ, echoes the language of 2.14 and is par. to 1 Tim 5.21, but does not go on to include the reference to the angels which may there be evocative of judgement, a theme expressed here more directly. The omission has the effect of linking God and Jesus Christ all the more closely together as co-actors in judgement, just as they are in salvation (as in 1.2 and similar formulae). μέλλω (1 Tim 1.16), used as a sort of auxiliary fut., occurs in the context of judgement in Acts 17.31; Jas 2.12 (pass.); Barnabas 7.2 (cf. 1 Pet 4.5); it may convey the thought of purpose and certain fulfilment more strongly than a plain fut. κρίνω (Tit 3.12** = to decide) is used here of final, divine judgement by Christ.[100] Traditional language (associated by some commentators with a form of words used at baptism)[101] is used to emphasise the universality of judgement.

---

[100] Similarly, Acts 17.31; Rom 2.16; for the noun see 2 Tim 4.8; Acts 10.42 (also in the context of διαμαρτύρομαι).
[101] Cf. Seeberg 1966 [1903]:96f.

It applies both to the living, i.e. those who will be physically alive when the end of the world comes, and also to the dead, i.e. those who have died but will be raised from the dead to face the judgement.[102]

καὶ τὴν ἐπιφάνειαν αὐτοῦ καὶ τὴν βασιλείαν αὐτοῦ The construction then shifts abruptly from ἐνώπιον with the gen. to a plain acc.[103] Elsewhere the acc. can be used in this way of witnesses who are summoned against a person (Deut 4.26; Jth 7.28). This seems to be the background to the construction here (cf. Mk 5.7; Acts 19.13; 1 Th 5.27; Jas 5.12). The fact that Christ will come and rule adds weight to the admonition. ἐπιφάνεια here refers clearly to the future parousia of Christ (1 Tim 6.14 note; see Pax 1955:236–8). βασιλεία (4.18**) is then the Lord's heavenly kingdom, the full manifestation of which is associated with the parousia.[104] The thought may be threatening (so one-sidedly Hasler, 76f.), but in view of v. 8 it is more likely to be positive: Timothy is being urged to do his work in a way that will lead to recognition and reward at the final judgement when Christ visibly rules. As Oberlinner 1980:200f., comments, the implication is that the future epiphany of Jesus for judgement is already determinative of present life and to that extent it has a contemporary character.[105]

2. κήρυξον τὸν λόγον, ἐπίστηθι εὐκαίρως ἀκαίρως, ἔλεγξον, ἐπιτίμησον, παρακάλεσον, ἐν πάσῃ μακροθυμίᾳ καὶ διδαχῇ The task is summed up in a series of five imperatives with accompanying qualifications; a further four will follow in v. 5. If v. 5 is concerned more with Timothy's own faithfulness to his task, here the point is rather the faithful presentation of the Christian message to the church with the accompanying discipline that is needed for people who are tempted not to listen or to heed it. There is a fairly close parallel in Tit 2.15 where authoritative teaching and discipline are linked. All five verbs are surprisingly in the aor. imper. (complexive aorist, BD § 337²). For the asyndeton cf. 1 Pet 5.10.

(a) κηρύσσω (1 Tim 3.16**) is found only here in the PE of ordinary Christian proclamation as a duty (but cf. the use of

---

[102] For this combination see Acts 10.42; 1 Pet 4.5; Rom 14.9; 2 Clement 1.1; Barnabas 7.2.

[103] Holtzmann, 443, claims that there is a co-ordinating καί ... καί ... construction. This is possible, but the distance of the phrase from the verb makes it difficult.

[104] *Pace* Luz, U., *EDNT* I, 205, who states that it is first manifest at this point in contrast to 2 Pet 1.11; see Eph 5.5; Col 1.13; 2 Th 1.5; see also *1 Enoch* 103.1 for mention of it in an oath.

[105] See further Läger 1996:83–6, who wishes to go further and in effect make no distinction between the future and the past epiphanies as different aspects of only one epiphany.

κῆρυξ, 1.11). There is an implied imperative in Rom 10.14, but elsewhere it is just assumed that preaching happens. The content of the proclamation is expressed with the acc. (Rom 10.8; Gal 2.2); ὁ λόγος (1 Tim 1.15 note) by itself is 'the Christian message'; it is usually qualified in some way as 'the word of God', 'the word of truth', etc. (2.9, 15; 1 Th 1.6; Gal 6.6; Acts 8.4; 10.36–44; 14.25; 16.6 *et al.*), but by this point in the letter no fuller description is needed. Oberlinner, 155, holds that the horizon here is the congregation itself: there is no missionary goal. The description of Timothy as an evangelist in 4.5 suggests a different verdict, although it is true that the immediate focus is the proclamation of the truth and the refutation of heresy.

(b) ἐφίστημι is 'to stand by or near, approach, appear' (perf. 4.6**). Here the force is 'to be ready, on hand',[106] i.e. to be always on the alert: 'be instant' (RV; NIV; cf. Jer 26 [46].14). The idea is that the teacher is always there to grasp opportunities that offer themselves. If an object is to be supplied, it will be the hearers rather than the teaching.[107] This sense of the verb is more likely than 'press it home'.[108] εὐκαιρῶς means when the time is convenient or appropriate for something;[109] ἀκαιρῶς*** manifestly denotes the opposite situation, when it is not convenient.[110] The convenience/inconvenience is not that of Timothy (*pace* Whitaker*) but of the hearers. Malherbe* has shown that the importance of recognising the right time for speech was a commonplace among rhetoricians. Polemic against the Cynics accused them of being indiscriminate in their propaganda. Speakers should choose the time which will be most favourable from the point of view of the people whom they hope to persuade. The sharp oxymoron calls Timothy to ignore this normal type of behaviour. According to Malherbe* the opponents are regarded as so evil and incurable that it does not matter when the teaching takes place. The writer is here thinking, not of people who are open to persuasion and pastoral counsel, but of those who are beyond a cure. On this interpretation, the proper time for preaching depends not on the readiness or otherwise of the heretics to respond but on the decision of God. The persuasiveness of this explanation is somewhat weakened by the fact that the immediately following phrases would seem to suggest a process that may be effective. It is perhaps more

[106] Cf. Euripides, *Andr.* 547; Demosthenes 18.60.
[107] Holtzmann, 444; the verb does not mean 'to pay heed'.
[108] REB; cf. GNB; NJB; Barrett, 116; 'be persistent', NRSV; cf. Arichea-Hatton, 240.
[109] Cl.; Ecclus 18.22; Philo, *Somn* 2.252; Josephus, *Ant.* 14.323; Mk 14.11; Mk 6.31 *v.l.***; cf. εὔκαιρος, Mk 6.21; Heb 4.16***; *TLNT* II, 118–20.
[110] Cl.; Ecclus 20.19; 32.4; Philo, *Mos.* 2.206; Josephus, *Ant.* 6.137; cf. *Exod. Rab.* 15 (76a), in SB I, 745.

likely that the unexpected advice is meant to bring home the stringency of the situation and the need to act before things become so bad that appeal to the hearers will be in vain; moreover, the audience includes not only the false teachers but also those who are succumbing or may succumb to their influence.

(c) From presentation of the message the thought moves to the task of getting people to realise that they are sinners. ἐλέγχω occurs in this sense in 1 Tim 5.20, and picks up on the use of the noun in 2 Tim 3.16.

(d) Those who have committed sin are to be made aware not only that they have done so, but also that they stand under reproof.[111] The thought appears to be of a public process,[112] but personal dealings with individuals are not in fact excluded by the language.

(e) The final element in the list is positive. παρακαλέω (1 Tim 1.3; cf. 5.1; 6.2; Tit 1.9; 2.6, 15) sums up the nature of teaching as persuasion and encouragement. The concluding phrase appears to be linked to the last imperative and lists the two qualities that must accompany the act of exhortation (ἐν = 'with'), but it may be intended to go with all five imperatives (White, 176). Patience (μακροθυμία) is frequently singled out as essential for Christian leadership (3.10.).[113] It may seem odd that a noun indicating the manner of exhortation is accompanied by one that expresses more the content (διδαχή); whereas in Tit 1.9** it refers more to content, here the stress is on manner, perhaps 'with every kind of instruction' (BA; cf. 1 Cor 14.6; Mk 4.2; 12.38). The point is that Christian exhortation is to be seen to have its basis in sound teaching of the gospel.

3. Ἔσται γὰρ καιρὸς ὅτε τῆς ὑγιαινούσης διδασκαλίας οὐκ ἀνέξονται The need for vigorous teaching is now developed in terms of the unwillingness of some people to listen to it. Proclamation of the truth is all the more necessary when it is being rejected and the temptation is to fall in with the prevailing mood. 'In 3.6 depraved teachers corrupt their pupils but here, as the world grows worse, men already corrupted seek out teachers who will encourage them in evil' (Easton, 69). Four clauses describe the character of the apostasy, the first and third expressing the negative attitude towards the truth, and the second and fourth the positive attitude towards error. The fut. ἔσται, as in 3.2, need not exclude the present time, but is used to lay

---

[111] ἐπιτιμάω**; Cl.; here abs. as in Lk 4.41; cf. ἐπιτιμία, 2 Cor 2.6; cf. Stauffer, E., *TDNT* II, 623–7.

[112] Malherbe*, 241f., comments on the absence of mention of any kind of private counselling or instruction.

[113] With πᾶς, 1 Tim 1.16; cf. Col 1.11; see further 2 Cor 6.6; Rom 9.22.

stress on the certainty and to warn against surprise (Knight, 455). It may also be used to indicate what will happen if the advice in v. 2 is not followed. καιρός (sing.) simply means a point of time (v. 6); elsewhere the author prefers the pl. of extended periods (3.1; 1 Tim 4.1). The conjunction ὅτε (Tit 3.4**) functions as a substitute for the relative pronoun after a noun denoting time (BA *s.v.*).[114] The phrase ὑγιαίνουσα διδασκαλία is repeated from 1 Tim 1.10; Tit 1.9; 2.1; cf. 2 Tim 1.13. ἀνέχομαι is 'to endure, put up with', hence 'to hear, listen to willingly'.[115] The contrast with the next clause suggests that 'healthy doctrine' is by metonymy for 'teachers of healthy doctrine' who are rejected in favour of heretical teachers.

ἀλλὰ κατὰ τὰς ἰδίας ἐπιθυμίας ἑαυτοῖς ἐπισωρεύσουσιν διδασκάλους κνηθόμενοι τὴν ἀκοήν Instead of being guided by the desire for objective truth the audience is governed by its own subjective desires. The phrase κατὰ τὰς ἐπιθυμίας is also used elsewhere of the determinative factor in the lives of sinners who are on the way to self-destruction (Eph 4.22), and the implication, of course, is that the desires are evil and selfish (2.22; 1 Tim 6.9 note).[116] They choose their own teachers (Knight, 455). ἐπισωρεύω*** is a late word, lit. 'to heap up', here in the sense of gathering together a large number.[117] διδάσκαλος (1.11) is used only here of the writer's opponents (but cf. 1 Tim 1.7).

The choice of teachers is explained by a participial phrase. The audience is said to have 'itching ears'. κνήθω*** is 'to scratch', literally or metaphorically.[118] τὴν ἀκοήν is acc. of respect with a passive verb; ἀκοή (4.4**; Hel., not Attic) is 'sense of hearing', 'ear', but also 'what is heard, account, report'.[119] There are two different interpretations of the present metaphor. (a) The people have painfully itching ears which they long to soothe with false teaching, a curiosity which is relieved by spicy bits of information (RSV 'what they are itching to hear').[120] (b) The people have ears which are pleasantly tickled

---

[114] For the use here followed by the fut. cf. Lk 17.22; Jn 4.21, 23; 5.25; 16.25; Rom 2.16 *v.l.* (with pres., Jn 9.4; Rom 2.16).

[115] With gen.; cf. Philo, *Prob.* 36; Josephus, *Ap.* 2.126; 2 Cor 11.4; Heb 13.22; of people, Mk 9.19 and par.; Acts 18.14; 2 Cor 11.1, 19; Eph 4.2; Col 3.13; of experiences, 1 Cor 4.12; 2 Cor 11.20; 2 Th 1.4; Schlier, H., *TDNT* I, 359f.

[116] For the use of ἴδιος cf. Polycarp 7.1.

[117] Hel.; not in LXX, but in Job 14.17 Σ; Ct 2.4 Σ; Barnabas 4.6, of repeated sinning; cf. σωρεύω, 3. 6; cf. Lang, F., *TDNT* VII, 1094–6. Simpson, 153, suggests that it is an imitation of Lat. *accumulare*.

[118] It is a later form for κνάω (BA).

[119] For the former meaning cf. 1 Cor 12.17; Mk 7.35; Acts 17.20; Lk 7.1; Heb 5.11; for the latter cf. Mt 4.24; Rom 10.16; *et al.* Lucian, *bis accus.* 1, comments proverbially on a person not having enough time to scratch his ear (BA).

[120] GNB; RV; NIV; NJB; NRSV; Dibelius-Conzelmann, 118, 120; Brox, 264; Knight, 456.

by the teaching which they receive.[121] The linguistic evidence supports the second possibility.[122] Either way, the thought is of insatiable curiosity, such as is depicted in Acts 17.21.

4. καὶ ἀπὸ μὲν τῆς ἀληθείας τὴν ἀκοὴν ἀποστρέψουσιν The third clause is a repetition of the thought in the first clause. It continues the thought of listening in the previous clause. For the use of ἀποστρέφω cf. 1.15 and especially Tit 1.14, where the verb is used in the different sense (mid. and pass.) of turning away from or rejecting a person or the truth. Here it signifies turning away one's attention (lit. 'one's ears') from the truth. ἀλήθεια (2.15) is singled out as the object which people turn away from or lack (1 Tim 6.5; 2 Tim 2.18; 3.7, 8; Tit 1.14). The close connection with the fourth clause is indicated by the μὲν ... δέ construction (1.10; 2.20**).

ἐπὶ δὲ τοὺς μύθους ἐκτραπήσονται Earlier language is repeated. For μῦθος see 1 Tim 1.4; Tit 1.4, and for ἐκτρέπω see 1 Tim 1.6 note.[123] Nothing is said about the content of the teaching; it is stigmatised as being incredible.

5. Σὺ δὲ νῆφε ἐν πᾶσιν, κακοπάθησον, ἔργον ποίησον εὐαγγελιστοῦ, τὴν διακονίαν σου πληροφόρησον The writer turns back to exhortation to Timothy in the light of this situation of apostasy and issues a renewed appeal for alert, dedicated fulfilment of his task as a church leader. Four imperatives conclude the list of instructions begun in v. 2. They are concerned more with Timothy's own dedication to the task. The contrast with the activity of heretics is again introduced by σὺ δέ (3.10, 14).

(a) The first command is to sobriety. νήφω** is common in NT exhortation, both in a lit. sense of not being intoxicated (which is hardly to be excluded from the NT usage) and a fig. sense of being sober, well-balanced, controlled, and wakeful.[124] ἐν πᾶσιν is 'in all respects', a favourite phrase of the author (2.7; 1 Tim 3.11; Tit 2.9, 10b**). Spicq, 802, notes that sobriety

[121] This alternative possibility is suggested by BA; *EDNT* II, 301; 'to tickle his fancy', REB; Holtzmann, 446; Parry, 66; Lock, 113; Simpson, 153.
[122] Plutarch, *Mor.* 167B, refers to a κνῆσις ὤτων which takes place τρυφῆς ἕνεκα. Clement, *Strom.* 1.22.5, describes the sophists as κνήθοντες καὶ γαργαλίζοντες οὐκ ἀνδρικῶς ἐμοὶ δοκεῖν, τὰς ἀκοὰς τῶν κνήσασθαι γλιχομένων (cited but mistranslated by Dibelius-Conzelmann, 120, as if it supported view (a)). Cf. also Philo, *Det.* 72: ἀποκναίουσι γοῦν [οἱ σοφισταί] ἡμῶν τὰ ὦτα; Seneca, *Ep.* 9.43 *aures demulcere* or *scabere*.
[123] The phrase is paralleled in Galen XI. 792K, εἰς μύθους γραῶν ἐξετράπετο (cf. 1 Tim 4.7).
[124] 1 Th 5.6, 8; 1 Pet 1.13; 4.7; 5.8***; Ignatius, *Poly.* 2.3; Polycarp 11.4; cf. νηφάλιος 1 Tim 3.2, 11; Tit 2.2; ἀνανήφω, 2.26; Bauernfeind, O., *TDNT* IV, 936–9.

is a quality of the orator who is in control of what he wants to say.

(b) For κακοπαθέω see 2.9 (cf. 2.3 for the compound form). It clearly means 'endure suffering', not simply 'to bear the difficulties of one's task, to work assiduously' (*pace* Spicq, 802). Hardship and opposition are taken for granted as part of the task in these circumstances.

(c) Timothy is to do the task of an evangelist. ἔργον can be used of the work assigned to a church leader (1 Tim 3.1). The word εὐαγγελιστής is rare both in the secular world[125] and in the NT (Eph 4.11; Acts 21.8***). Opinions are divided whether the term refers here to a particular type of church leader, occupying a position in time in between the apostles and the later bishops,[126] or is simply a characterisation of one of the tasks assigned to a church leader.[127] Older commentators suggested a kind of intermediate office between the apostles and local church leaders (Bernard, 141f.; Simpson, 154). G. Strecker's comment (*EDNT* II, 70) that the evangelists 'are not primarily missionaries, but instead serve the Church through the proclamation of the gospel' must surely rest on a failure to realise that missionaries are church-planters. What is important is that the work of the evangelist is closely related to teaching and leadership in the local church (Campbell*). 'It may be assumed that all ministers, whatever other designation they may bear, are evangelists' (Barrett, 117); would that it were indeed so.

(d) The final clause is a summary of the task. Timothy has been given what is in effect a commission (διακονία, 1 Tim 1.12 of Paul's work; 2 Tim 4.11 of Mark's); by faithful teaching he will prove to be a good διάκονος (1 Tim 4.6). But here his responsibility is to fulfil whatever requirements are associated with his role as a servant in the church. πληροφορέω is 'to fulfil, accomplish'.[128] The verb occurs in the pap. to signify paying back a debt fully, i.e. meeting an obligation in full.[129] Hence the sense is: 'discharge all the duties of your ministry' (NIV) or 'make good [one's task]'.[130] Paul uses πληρόω in the same sense in Col 4.17; cf. Acts 12.25; and also Acts 14.26; Rom 15.19; Col 1.25.

---

[125] Indeed, it is doubtful whether it existed before its Christian use. It occurs in *IG* XII 1.675.6 (cited in MM 259) where it has been thought to be a title of pagan priests who proclaim oracles. This is disputable, according to Spicq (*TLNT* II, 91f.; cf. Dieterich*); cf. Friedrich, G., *TDNT* II, 736f.

[126] Cf. Eusebius, *HE* 5.10.2; Goppelt 1962:130f.; cf. Holtzmann, 446–8.

[127] Brox, 264; Kelly, 207; Hanson, 154f.; Oberlinner, 158; Campbell*.

[128] Hel.; LXX; 4.17; Lk 1.1; Col 4.12; also, pass., 'to be firmly convinced' (Rom 4.21; 14.5***; Ignatius, *Mag.* 8.2; 11; *et al.*); cf. Delling, G., *TDNT* VI, 309f.

[129] Deissmann 1927:86f.; *TLNT* III, 120–3.

[130] Cf. Lat. *officium, munia sua, implere* (Simpson, 154).

6. Ἐγὼ γὰρ ἤδη σπένδομαι The exhortation to Timothy is rounded off by a passage in which Paul is presented as being at the end of a lifetime of faithful service after which he can expect his heavenly reward. The purpose is threefold: to put an example before Timothy which he is to follow; to indicate that he (and others) must take the place now being vacated by Paul; and to hold out the promise of reward for faithful service. It is, however, the second of these three purposes which basically structures the passage. The effect is to give urgency to what precedes. The function is thus somewhat similar to 2.8–13, and the passage repeats motifs about Paul's ministry found throughout the PE (1 Tim 1.12–17; 2.7; 2 Tim 1.3, 11f.).

Opinions on the origin of the material vary greatly. It has been said to be based on Phil 2.12–30 (Hanson, 155) and to be so similar in style to the rest of 2 Tim that it cannot be a genuine fragment in an otherwise pseudonymous letter (Cook*). The style of presentation is held to be unpauline: 'he praises himself and his work, proclaims himself as a victor, displays himself as the best example, and has not the slightest doubt of his success, his perseverance and the corresponding imminent reward. This is how one talks about a saint' (Brox, 265; cf. 266f.; Dibelius-Conzelmann, 121). This sarcastic characterisation ignores the realities of how people can and do look back on a life with which they can rightly be satisfied. Hanson, 156, who does not think that this is how Paul would have expressed himself, nevertheless claims that there is nothing exaggerated or sentimental about the language. Contrast also the verdict of Barrett, 118, on 4.6–18: 'There is nothing here that Paul could not have written, and much that could scarcely have been invented.'

The introductory ἐγώ is deliberate to give a contrast with σύ in v. 5. ἤδη is 'now' in the sense of 'already' (2.18; 1 Tim 5.15**); the need is thus immediate, although the rest of the letter implies that Paul is not facing imminent death. σπένδομαι is the pass. of a verb which means 'to offer a libation, drink-offering'; the reference is to the pouring out of a liquid as a sacrifice or accompaniment to a sacrifice.[131] Philo, *L.A.* 2.56, uses it metaphorically of pouring out one's blood as a sacrifice.

Prior 1989:93f. argues that the metaphor is not being used here of a sacrificial death, but rather of Paul's apostolic activity. He claims (correctly) that the word in itself used literally does not refer to sacrificial death but to the accompaniment to a sacrifice. Thus in Tacitus, *Ann.* 15.64; 16.35 a libation is made

[131] Cl.; e.g. Homer, *Il.* 11.775; *Od.* 18.51; Exod 29.40f.; Lev 23.13; 2 Sam 23.16; Hos 9.4; Philo, *Her.* 183; *Mos.* 2.150; *Spec.* 1.205; Josephus, *Ant.* 6.22; *Sib. Orac.* 7.81; Philo, *Ebr.* 152, uses the metaphor of total dedication to God. Hence it can be used for the making of a treaty (Philo, *Flacc.* 18).

at the moment of death, but the verb is never used of bloody sacrifice. In the other NT usage (Phil 2.17***) the reference is to something Paul does that accompanies the sacrifice and service of the faith of the church. Prior further argues that death is excluded by what is said in 2 Tim 1.

This argument is not convincing. In Phil 2.17 the 'even if' construction suggests that some extreme action is being contemplated, and the metaphor of 'being poured out' could refer to exhausting one's strength or possibly dying. Prior's discussion is in danger of confusing the literal meaning of the verb with its possible metaphorical application. He is right to argue that only the context can decide whether a reference to death is present. This is the case in Ignatius, *Rom.* 2.2; cf. Plutarch, *Mor.* 494D, of an animal (σπένδεσθαι περὶ τῶν τέκνων).

The pres. expresses the certainty that the process has already begun (Parry, 66; Simpson, 154); the present experience of imprisonment and the trial that has already taken place are part of the process that leads to the end. Hence Paul can feel that the time of his departure is not far distant. His life blood will be poured out as a sacrifice for the sake of the gospel. Moffatt vividly translates 'the last drops of my own sacrifice are falling'.[132]

καὶ ὁ καιρὸς τῆς ἀναλύσεώς μου ἐφέστηκεν For ἐφίστημι see v. 2 note; the perf. indicates that the time, once distant, has now drawn near and is imminent (Josephus, *Vita* 137). The sense is not that it is now present.[133] ἀνάλυσις*** is lit. 'loosing' (of mooring ropes and the like), hence 'departure';[134] fig. it refers to death.[135] Holtz, 193, holds that release from bonds in order to be executed is in mind. The figurative meaning is generally assumed for this passage, but it is questioned by Prior, 98–103.[136] He notes that the wider context in 4.9–21 assumes Paul's continued activity for some time. He further observes that the relation between vv. 6–8 and 9–21 is difficult if it is assumed that the former refers to impending death. Rather, he says, 'Paul is referring to the resolution of his case, which he is confident

---

[132] There is nothing to suggest that Paul's death is to be seen as vicarious or atoning (Jeremias, 64, comes close to this suggestion: 'sein Tod ist Opfertod, weil er als Märtyrer Gott zu Ehre stirbt und weil sein Leiden den Brüdern zugute kommt'); cf. 2.10 note.

[133] As in Acts 22.20; 28.2 (*pace* Bernard, 143); contrast the use of ἐνίστημι, 3.1.

[134] Cl.; e.g. of the end of a banquet (Josephus, *Ant.* 19.239).

[135] τελευταία ἀνάλυσις, Philo, *Flacc.* 115, 187; 1 Clement 44.5; cf. ἀναλύω, Phil 1.23; further refs. in BA and Büchsel, F., *TDNT* IV, 337.

[136] Prior offers three linguistic arguments, apparently aimed at showing that the noun does not necessarily refer to death (which is not in doubt). Where the noun refers to death in Secundus, *Sententiae* 19, it is qualified as ἀνάλυσις σώματος/μέλων.

will bring him release' (109). But Prior does nothing to defend this interpretation and explain how it fits the argument better. Moreover, the corresponding verb ἀναλύω certainly has the sense 'to die', and in Phil 1.23 the idea of departing to be with Christ is expressed.

7. τὸν καλὸν ἀγῶνα ἠγώνισμαι Three parallel clauses sum up Paul's career. Each is metaphorical. Although Simpson, 155, argues for three metaphors, drawn from war, athletics and stewardship, it is preferable to see the same athletic metaphor in all three clauses, especially in view of the reference to the winner's crown in v. 8. Most commentators think that the reference throughout is to athletics in general and running in particular (Pfitzner 1967:183), but it may be that the first clause refers to wrestling, the second to running (Barrett, 118; Kelly, 208). The first statement repeats phraseology already used in the concluding appeal to Timothy in 1 Tim 6.12 (see also 1 Tim 4.10) but there as a command. See the note there where it is concluded that the metaphor is athletic but with military overtones,[137] and that its application is to Timothy's personal life rather than more narrowly to his work as a missionary; the two are surely inseparable. The perf. expresses completion of the contest.

τὸν δρόμον τετέλεκα The second metaphor is again drawn from athletics and refers to the completion of the course. τελέω** is 'to finish, complete'.[138] δρόμος[139] is a 'course' or 'race', used of horse or foot races, also of the courses of heavenly bodies (1 Clement 20.2); the word is then applied metaphorically (Philo, *L.A.* 3.48) to the course of a person's life (Acts 13.25; 20.24***; Ignatius, *Poly.* 1.2; of martyrs, 1 Clement 6.2). The metaphor is an obvious and well-known one.[140] Bauernfeind, O., *TDNT* VIII, 233f., however, argues that in the NT references the thought is not simply of the biological course of life but rather of the specific vocation given by God. For other uses of the race metaphor see Phil 2.16; 3.13f. The point is not the winning of the race but the completion of the course.

τὴν πίστιν τετήρηκα The third picture refers to the keeping of the faith (cf. Tit 2.10 note), i.e. of a pledge. For the verb τηρέω cf. 1 Tim 5.22; 6.14. The phrase is a standard one for keeping faith with somebody. The metaphor may be drawn from (a) the athlete's promise to keep the rules of the contest (cf. 2.5; Easton, 70); (b) the soldier's oath of fidelity (Spicq, 805f.); (c) the

---

[137] A military metaphor is found by MM 8; Barton*, 880f.

[138] It is used with δρόμος in Homer, *Il.* 23.373, 768; Sophocles, *El.* 726 (cf. Delling, G., *TDNT* VIII, 57–61).

[139] The noun is derived from the defective verb δραμεῖν, found only to supply the missing parts of τρέχω.

[140] Cf. Virgil, *Aen.* 4.653 (of Dido): '*Vixi et quam dederat cursum fortuna peregi*'.

steward's keeping of a deposit (Simpson, 156; Guthrie, 181). The context strongly favours the first of these possibilities. But the Christian use of πίστις has inevitably affected the statement, and the idea of keeping the rules has given way to a more literal use of language.

Possible applications are: (a) 'I have kept on believing' (cf. Rev 2.13; 14.12), i.e. 'I have kept my trust, remained faithful';[141] (b) 'I have preserved the faith intact'.[142] Knight, 460, regards the first of these as primary and the second as secondary. Since v. 8 is general in application and not confined to church leaders, this broad sense is probably right. But trust in Christ can hardly be separated from perseverance and right belief. The question is rather whether the issue is Paul's own perseverance or the safekeeping of the message, and here it is probably the former.

8. λοιπὸν ἀπόκειταί μοι ὁ τῆς δικαιοσύνης στέφανος, ὃν ἀποδώσει μοι ὁ κύριος ἐν ἐκείνῃ τῇ ἡμέρᾳ, ὁ δίκαιος κριτής, οὐ μόνον δὲ ἐμοὶ ἀλλὰ καὶ πᾶσι τοῖς ἠγαπηκόσι τὴν ἐπιφάνειαν αὐτοῦ The metaphor of athletics is continued with the picture of the reward for the winner. Now that the contest is over there remains nothing but the award of the prize.[143] Dibelius-Conzelmann, 121, cite appropriately *British Museum Inscriptions*, III, 604. 7ff.: ἠγωνίσατο ἀγῶνας τρεῖς, ἐστέφθη δύω. λοιπόν is the neut. of λοιπός (1 Tim 5.20**) used as an adv., 'remaining', giving the meaning 'as for what remains (sc. for the future)'.[144] ἀπόκειμαι is 'to be put away, stored up' (Cl.; Lk 19.20; Col 1.5; Heb 9.27***). The verb is used of rewards in the games and metaphorically for civic and heavenly honours.[145] The award is a heavenly one.[146] It is qualified as 'the crown (στέφανος) of righteousness' (cf. Wis 5.18; Bar 5.2). This can be understood in two ways. (a) a crown consisting of righteousness;[147] it is 'the crown which will bring final justification';[148]

[141] Josephus, *Bel.* 2.121; *Ant.* 15.134; BA; Brox, 266; Kelly, 209; Spicq, 805; Fee, 289; Pfitzner 1967:183; *TLNT* III, 112f.

[142] Holtzmann, 449; Bernard, 143; Hanson, 155; Oberlinner, 162.

[143] 1 Cor 9.25; Phil 4.1; 1 Th 2.19; *et al.*; cf. στεφανόω, 2.5; Spicq (1931:501), however, wants to see it as a crown for keeping his deposit.

[144] Mt 26.45; Mk 14.41; 1 Cor 7.29; Heb 10.13; Diognetus 9.2; cf. BD § 160.

[145] Demophilus, *Similitudines* 22 gives the nice parallel: τοῖς μὲν σταδιοδρομοῦσιν ἐπὶ τῷ τέρματι τὸ βραβεῖον τῆς νίκης ... ἀπόκειται, cited by Dibelius-Conzelmann, 121 n. 20 with other parallels. A (possibly Jewish) epitaph for a midwife in *New Docs.* IV, 23f. § 5, uses the verb of a heavenly reward: ὅπου μοι τόπος εὐσεβίης ἀπέκειτο.

[146] For heavenly rewards see 2 Macc 12.45; cf. Philo, *L.A.* 2.108; Josephus, *Ant.* 6.368; cf. Pfister*; Büchsel, F., *TDNT* III, 655.

[147] Cf. Jas 1.12; Rev 2.10, 3.11; 1 Pet 5.4; Jer 13.18; Lam 2.15; *Ep. Arist.* 280; *T. Levi* 8.2; *M. Poly.* 17.1; 19.2; Holtzmann, 450; Fee, 290; Knight, 461.

[148] 'The victory prize of being put right with God' (GNB). Cf. Grundmann, W., *TDNT* VII, 629.

(b) a crown which is appropriate for a righteous person,[149] or is, more specifically, a reward for righteousness,[150] an idea which is regarded as quite incompatible with Paul (Hanson, 156). Probably both ideas should be combined, with (a) being primary. The crown connotes righteousness but is granted to those who are righteous. The discussion has been beclouded by drawing false contrasts with Pauline teaching. Thus the statement that ' "righteousness" in this context should not be understood in the Pauline fashion, since it refers here to the reward one can legitimately claim for a certain accomplishment, and not to righteousness effected and bequeathed by God' (Kraft, H., *EDNT* III, 274), is mistaken because it assumes too narrow a view for Paul. The NT holds out a motivation to believers that they will be rewarded 'not *propter opera sed secundum opera*' (Goodwin, cited by Simpson, 157).

In fact, the idea of a return or recognition for service rendered cannot be removed from the passage. The verb ἀποδίδωμι (4.14; 1 Tim 5.4**) expresses the idea of making some kind of recompense. The reward is bestowed by ὁ κύριος, who in accordance with the usage of the PE elsewhere is Christ. ἐν ἐκείνῃ τῇ ἡμέρᾳ refers to the day of judgement (1.12). Christ (not God, *pace* Büchsel, F., *TDNT* III, 942f.) is described as the κριτής**, a word not used by Paul; elsewhere it is applied to God[151] and to Christ (Acts 10.42; Polycarp 2.1; Jas 5.9).[152] The metaphor of the athletics contest probably still continues, but the use of δίκαιος may suggest a contrast with human judges, such as Nero (cf. possibly 1 Tim 6.15). δίκαιος is frequently used of God in the OT.[153] There is no implication that one person, and one person only, wins the prize; it is promised not only to Paul but also to all who look forward eagerly to the Lord's coming.[154] With this final comment Paul's backward look on his life and his forward look to heavenly reward are shown to be in no way egotistical or reflective of ideas of merit (so rightly Pfitzner 1967:184f.). ἀγαπάω (4.10**) in the perf. conveys the sense of setting one's love upon, longing for something or somebody (cf. Jas 1.12; Ps 39 [MT 40].17; Spicq, 808). The suggestion that the thought is unpauline in that for Paul salvation is conferred

---

[149] Bernard, 143; 'the crowning of the state of righteousness', Schrenk, G., *TDNT* II, 210.

[150] Wis 5.16; 2 *Apoc. Bar.* 15.7f.; BA; Parry, 67; Lock, 115; Kelly, 209f.; Hanson, 156.

[151] LXX; Heb 12.23; Jas 4.12; Hermas, *Sim.* 6.3.6; 2 Clement 1.1.

[152] For Christ as judge see also Jn 5.22, 27; Acts 17.31; Rom 2.16; 1 Cor 4.5; 2 Cor 5.10.

[153] E.g. Ps 7.12 (MT 10); cf. 1 Clement 27.1; 60.1; 56.5 (Ps 140 [MT 141].5); Jn 17.25; Rom 3.26; Rev 16.5.

[154] For οὐ μόνον ... ἀλλὰ καί ... see 2.20; 1 Tim 5.13**.

because God/Christ has loved us, whereas here it is dependent on the Christian's love for Christ (Oberlinner, 164), fails to recognise that much the same kind of longing is expressed in Phil 3.20 (cf. Rom 8.23–25). ἐπιφάνεια must here refer to the parousia, which becomes the basis for the appeal, rather than the incarnation of Christ.[155]

---

[155] Cf. 1.10; 4.1; see the detailed discussion in Holtzmann, 450; *pace* Oberlinner, 164.

APPEAL TO VISIT PAUL SOON – CLOSING INSTRUCTIONS
(4.9–18)

Bojorge, H., 'El poncho de san Pablo. Una posible alusión a la sucesión apostólica en II Timoteo 4,13', *RB* 42 (1980), 209–24; Davies, T. W. L., 'Pauline Readjustments', *Expositor* 50 (1924), 446–56; Erbes, K., 'Zeit und Ziel der Grüsse Röm 16, 3–15, und der Mitteilungen 2 Tim 4,9–21', *ZNW* 10 (1909), 128–47, 195–218; Lee, G. M., 'The Books and the parchments: Studies in Texts: II Tim. 4:13', *Theology* 74 (1971), 168f.; Meinertz, M., 'Worauf bezieht sich die πρώτη ἀπολογία (2 Tim 4,16)?', *Bib* 4 (1923), 390–4; Moffatt, J., 'Philippians II.26 and II Tim IV.13', *JTS* (1917), 311f.; Prior 1989; Ryrie, C. C., 'Especially the Parchments', *BSac* 117 (1960), 242–8; Schnider and Stenger 1987:113–18; Skeat 1979; Spicq, C., 'Pélerine et vêtements (A Propos de II Tim IV.13 et Act. XX.33)', *Mélanges E. Tisseront I* (Civitas Vaticana, 1964), 389–417; Stevenson, J. S., '2 Tim. IV.13 and the Question of St Paul's Second Captivity', *ExpTim* 34 (1922–3), 524f.; Trummer, P., 'Mantel und Schriften (II Tim 4,13). Zur Interpretation einer persönlichen Notiz in den Pastoralbriefen', *BZ* 18 (1974), 193–207.

Like Tit (3.12–15), but unlike 1 Tim, the letter closes with personal material, conveying instructions and news to Timothy together with greetings to and from various colleagues. The different items are arranged rather haphazardly with some repetition, but there is some logic and order.

(a) Verses 9–15 form a unit. It is an appeal to Timothy to visit Paul, who is alone, three colleagues having left him for various motives, bad and good; he is on his own, apart from Luke. Timothy is to bring Mark with him. Three isolated comments follow. First, apparently as an afterthought, the mission of Tychicus is mentioned; but the logic may be that Mark is to replace him (Holtzmann, 453). Next, comes a request regarding what Timothy is to bring with him. And finally, there is a reference to the ill-deeds of Alexander, of whom Timothy is warned to beware. It is less easy to see the relevance of this remark, but modern letter-writers can be equally given to adding fresh items of news with no apparent order.

(b) Verses 16–18 form a second unit. Having spoken about the disloyalty of Alexander, Paul goes on to comment about the lack of human support at his trial, to contrast it with the way in which the Lord enabled him to turn the occasion to good account, and to express his trust in him for the future.

Spicq, 809, claims that in 4.9–22 as a whole there is a fourfold pattern shared with other letters: (a) personal information and instructions (vv. 9–18a); (b) doxology (v. 18b); (c) greetings and other personal information (vv. 19–21); (d) double benediction (v. 22). But this precise pattern is not paralleled elsewhere.

Lock, 116, notes a number of echoes of Ps 21 LXX, particularly in vv. 16–18 which are in fact sufficient to suggest that the author was steeped in its language and thought (Spicq, 810; Hanson, 162; Munck 1959:331–3).

Of all the material in the PE it is this section (with the remainder of the ch.) which has made the strongest impression of coming from an authentic Pauline letter or letters. But these verses are not without problems (Holtzmann, 450f.; Easton, 75–8), and to some scholars they appear highly stylised and artificial (Dibelius-Conzelmann, 122). (a) It has been asked how the appeal to Timothy to visit Paul ties in with the detailed instructions earlier in the letter for his long-term leadership of the church. (b) There is said to be internal inconsistency between the description of Paul being alone (v. 11) and the list of friends with him who send their greetings (v. 21). (c) Personal details of this kind were invented as part of the apparatus of pseudonymity, and some of them belong to stock categories of literary material used in this way. (d) The effect of the material is to heighten the picture of Paul as the lonely martyr, an example to inspire later church leaders. (e) Houlden, 131, 135, suggests that the names of Paul's companions are drawn from Col.

The claim, then, is that the writer has exercised his own creative abilities, making free use of tradition, whether historical or legendary. The section is essentially an invention to give vivid colour to an edifying picture. Hasler, 78f., goes further in seeing an attempt to develop the idea of a succession between Paul and his followers, expressed in the presence of Timothy with the dying Paul and thus taking over the 'deposit' from him. The geographical range of the area to which Paul sends his colleagues is significant.

Most of the arguments employed on one side or the other are inconclusive. (a) There is nothing really strange about Paul giving written instructions, intended for the church as well as for Timothy, even if he hoped that Timothy would soon visit him; after all, there was no certainty either that he would survive to see him or that Timothy would be able to come. Moreover, nothing indicates that the putative visit to Paul by Timothy was intended to remove him permanently from Ephesus. We are to see already in 1.4 the hope that Timothy will visit him. (b) The people whose absence Paul refers to are on the whole members of his missionary group with whom he had worked for some time, and it is the absence of these old friends that he feels most; those who send greetings are all new names, doubtless from the local church. (c) Naturally the details could all be invented, and some of them are possibly 'stock remarks', but the possibility is in no way an argument that this must be the case. Such things as requests for clothing are found in genuine letters of the period. (d) Again, the picture is certainly that of the apostle deserted by some of his former colleagues, but who can deny that this is a perfectly possible historical scenario? (e) The recurrence of names found in Col is precisely what one would expect if the letters are authentic. (f) Perhaps the crucial question is whether the material gives the impression of being intentionally composed to give a stylised picture of the holy apostle facing martyrdom, alone and yet still concerned for the work of mission, facing bitter opposition and yet ready to forgive those who cannot stand the heat.[1] It is not at all obvious that this must be the case. How would the historical Paul have expressed himself differently in these circumstances?.

Where there is no compelling case against the authenticity of the material, it should be accepted for what it is. It is probable that genuine Pauline material is here incorporated in a composition which is intended to reflect the last known letter of Paul to Timothy, although the language and style have been conformed to that of the rest of the composition.

TEXT

9. ταχέως (a) τάχιον (I 33); (b) ἐν τάχει (442 *pc*). Elliott, 161f., adopts variant (a) as the non-Cl. word. The text is said to be more 'literary' (cf. BD § 102²). Variant (b) is said to be another effort by scribes to avoid the non-Cl. word. However, 1 Tim 5.22 (with no variant) reading supports the text, and the MS evidence is strongly in its favour.

10. ἐγκατέλιπεν (‏ℵ‎ I^vid Ψ 1739 TR; WH mg) (a) ἐγκατέλειπεν (A C D² F G L P 33 81 1175 1881 *al*; Kilpatrick); (b) κατέλιπεν (D*). Variant (b) is not part of the vocabulary of the PE. Elliott, 162f., prefers the aorist, since the imperfect is not used in the context. The variation is due to itacism. For the variant spelling ἐγκ- and ἐνκ- see Elliott, 163, who prefers the etymological form.

Κρήσκης: Κρίσκης (K minn.); Latin MSS have *Crescens* or *Cresces*. The variant may be due to itacism, Elliott, 163f. According to BA Κρίσπος is found as a *v.l.* here in sy goth, but I have not been able to check this. (It is not true of the British and Foreign Bible Society edition of sy^P.)

Γαλατίαν (a) Γαλλίαν (‏ℵ‎ C 81 104 326 *pc* vg^{st ww} sa bo^pt Eus Epiph); (b) Γαλιλαίαν (bo^pt arm). Variant (b) is simply carelessness. Variant (a) is possibly a deliberate correction by a scribe who knew that Γαλατία could refer to Asiatic

---

[1] A different interpretation is given by Prior 1989 who argues that Paul is expressing the hope of further ministry rather than facing death.

Galatia or to Gaul (e.g. Josephus, *Ant.* 17.344) and made a reference to Gaul unambiguous. But Elliott, 164, thinks that it is simply an orthographical slip. Metzger, 581, is undecided between these two explanations.

11. ἄγε ἄγαγε (A 104 365 (1881*) *pc*). My copy of Elliott lacks p. 165, but he apparently accepts the text. Elsewhere he suggests that scribes tended to alter presents to aorists.

12. δέ Omit (33 431 103 2412 1867 2143 vg^D Theod Mops). Elliott, 215, states that the author prefers short asyndetic sentences in such a context, and accepts the omission. But the evidence is too weak.

13. ἀπέλιπον (WH mg) ἀπέλειπον (A C F G L P 33 104 326 1175 1881^c *al*; Kilpatrick). Elliott, 162f., retains the aorist.

μάλιστα Add δέ (D* *pc* lat Ambst); add καί (1175). Elliott, 215, argues that the conjunction was added by scribes to stress the contrast.

14. ἀποδώσει ἀποδώῃ (D^2 Ψ TR b vg$^{st\,ww}$ Ambst). The variant is accepted by Elliott, 166f., who takes it as subj. expressing a wish, but it could be opt.; if so, did scribes alter to the future to avoid the imprecation? See 2.7 note; 2.25. The MSS evidence favours the fut. indic.

15. ἀντέστη ἀνθέστηκεν (ℵ^2 D^2 Ψ 1739 1881 TR a g vg^{mss}). The variant is Atticistic (Elliott, 168).

16. παρεγένετο συμπαρεγένετο (ℵ^2 D Ψ 1739^c 1881 TR; Kilpatrick). Elliott, 168, favours the variant (cf. Lk 23.48) on the ground that scribes tended to reduce compound verbs to simpler forms. Double compounds are found in various readings in 1 Tim 6.5, 20; 2 Tim 1.12, 14; 4.8, 10.

ἐγκατέλιπον (WH mg): ἐγκατέλειπον (A C D^1 F G L P 33 104 326 1175 *al*; Kilpatrick). Metzger 1971:649f., notes that the UBS committee was equally divided over this reading; there are similar problems in 4.10, 13, 20. Elliott, 162, retains the text; cf. 4.10.

17. ἀκούσωσιν ἀκούσῃ (TR). The variant is Atticising (Elliott, 169).

18. ῥύσεται Praem. καί (D^1 F G Ψ TR sy; Kilpatrick). Elliott, 210, holds that the word-order in the variant is Semitic and original, and was disliked by scribes.

EXEGESIS

9. Σπούδασον ἐλθεῖν πρός με ταχέως The first request is verbally identical with that in Tit 3.12, but is strengthened by the addition of ταχέως (1 Tim 5.22).[2] Commentators differ here, as there, whether σπουδάζω means 'to hasten' or 'to make an effort' (so most translations; cf. 2.15; Knight, 463), but the effort is surely in order that he may set off as soon as possible, and the added adverb conveys the urgency and need for haste. The phraseology may be conventional (Spicq, 810), but it is none the less earnest. Prior 1989:143–6 rightly disputes the view that this is just an epistolary cliché, not to be taken too seriously. It is a major concern of the letter, especially in view of the repetition. Paul wants Timothy both to share in the ongoing mission and also possibly to give support in the court room. Further, the possibility that Paul might die or be put to death at some unspecified date could well lead to the desire that Timothy should visit him before it was too late.

---

[2] Cf. 1 Tim 3.14; with verbs of motion, 1 Cor 4.19; Phil 2.24.

The sudden reference may be to a journey already agreed in principle, or, more probably, comes in the context of fuller, oral communication from the messenger. The problem arises whether the scenario is historical or fictitious, although in the latter case the author may not have thought too seriously about the envisaged circumstances. On the latter assumption, Oberlinner, 168, claims that the previous part of the letter leads one to expect that Timothy must remain at his post of duty. Hasler, 78f., links the motif of the journey to the need for maintaining continuity in the message between Paul and Timothy.

10. Δημᾶς γάρ με ἐγκατέλιπεν ἀγαπήσας τὸν νῦν αἰῶνα καὶ ἐπορεύθη εἰς Θεσσαλονίκην The appeal to Timothy to visit Paul is backed up by reference to the fact that three former colleagues are no longer with him. The first is Δημᾶς, who appears as a member of Paul's circle in Philem 24; Col 4.14. It can be safely assumed that one and the same person is meant in the three NT references.[3]

ἐγκαταλείπω implies not simply that Demas has departed and left Paul but that he has forsaken and deserted him.[4] The part. ἀγάπησας has ingressive force, 'having fallen in love with', and implies that the action still continues; 'it is the inception of the act only which precedes the action of the principal verb' (Burton, § 137, cited by Knight, 464). Whether by design or simply by the repetition of a word already in the author's mind, there is a contrast with v. 8. Longing for the Lord's appearing stands over against love for the present age (ὁ νῦν αἰών, par. 1 Tim 6.17); contrast the attitude of the martyrs in Polycarp 9.2. The point may then be that Demas was not prepared to face the possibility of martyrdom; he preferred life in this world (Holtz, 195). ἐπορεύθη (1 Tim 1.3) conveys the sense of going on a journey. The destination is Θεσσαλονίκη (Acts 17.1, 11, 13; Phil 4.16***). There was, to be sure, a Christian community here.[5] Demas was not a Jew (Col 4.10–14), and Chrysostom assumed that his home was at Thessalonica (*PG* 62.655); he is mentioned along with Aristarchus, a Thessalonian, in Philem 24. Although he had deserted Paul and chosen a more comfortable

---

[3] The name is possibly an abbreviation of Δημήτριος (BD § 125[1]) or of Δημάρατος (cf. BA), and is attested in inscr. and pap. (BA). Cf. Δαμᾶς (Ignatius, *Mag.* 2). Chapman, J., 'The Historical Setting of the Second and Third Epistles of St John', *JTS* 5 (1904), 357–68, 517–34, identified Demas with Demetrius in 3 Jn 12.

[4] 4.16; Cl.; the word is surprisingly frequent in the LXX (187 times; e.g. Mal 2.10–16); Josephus, *Vita* 205; Mt 27.46; Mk 15.34; Acts 2.27, 31; Rom 9.29; 2 Cor 4.9; Heb 10.25; 13.5; cf. *TLNT* I, 400–3.

[5] To find an implied criticism of that church here (Bauer, W., *Orthodoxy and Heresy in Earliest Christianity*, Philadelphia, 1971, 78f.; cf. Holtz, 195) is fanciful.

life, it remains possible that he continued actively as a Christian, even as a missionary (Spicq, 810f.; so possibly Barrett, 120; Kelly, 212f.).

Κρήσκης εἰς Γαλατίαν Although the next two of Paul's colleagues are mentioned in the same breath, nothing suggests that they have also deserted Paul; rather they have gone on missionary work. Κρήσκης*** is a familiar Latin name (*Crescens*), but is rare in Greek (Polycarp 14).[6] Γαλατία was a name used both for the Roman province in Asia and also for Gaul (*Monumentum Ancyranum*, cited by Dibelius-Conzelmann, 122 n. 3). Here it presumably refers to the former; even if the letter comes from Rome, it is less likely that the reference is to the province of Gaul (*Gallia*). Nevertheless, this interpretation is strongly defended by Spicq, 811–13.[7] One can see why it would appeal to a French commentator! This identification was made by some later scribes (see textual note), and it is reflected in the later legends that Crescens was a bishop in Gaul; admittedly this might be possible if the letter was written by Paul after a visit to Spain (White, 179), but all the other geographical references here are to the east.

Τίτος εἰς Δαλματίαν Τίτος (Tit 1.4) is said to have gone to Δαλματία***. This is the name of the Roman province in the southern part of Illyricum which was separated off after the Illyrian–Pannonian revolt in AD 6–9 and apparently known by this name from the Flavian period onwards (Josephus, *Bel.* 2.369).[8] No details are given which would help to fit this statement into the scenario implied by the letter to Titus. If 2 Tim is later than Tit, it may be presumed that Titus had gone there after his period in Crete, and that he did indeed go to the town of Nicopolis in that province (Tit 3.12). Since Paul himself worked in this area (Rom 15.19), the detail is credible (Brox, 269).

11. Λουκᾶς ἐστιν μόνος μετ᾽ ἐμοῦ The picture of complete loneliness is relieved by the continuing presence of Λουκᾶς (Philem 24; Col 4.14***).[9] The adj. μόνος (1 Tim 1.17) is emphatic; for μετά with a person see 4.11b; 2.22; Tit 3.15. The person meant is doubtless the companion of Paul mentioned in

---

[6] See *New Docs.* III, 91 §78 for the evidence.

[7] Earlier it was held by Lightfoot, J. B., *Biblical Essays* (London: Macmillan, 1893), 432; cf. MM 120; Kelly, 213; Holtz, 195; Hasler, 79f.

[8] Cf. *OCD*, 426f.; for the variant spelling Δελματία cf. BD §41[1].

[9] The name is equivalent to *Lucanus* (MHT II, 88) or, more probably, is an affectionate or pet name for Latin *Lucius* (BD §125[2]; cf. two inscr. from Antioch where the second refers to a Λούκιος who is the Λουκᾶς of the first one, Deissmann 1927:435–8). For Λούκιος see Acts 13.1; Rom 16.21***.

Col and Philem who was understood to be the author of Luke-Acts. As the only companion of Paul mentioned here he is a candidate for the authorship or co-authorship of the letter, a suggestion which would probably require that he acted in the same role for 1 Tim and Tit in view of the common style; but the literary style is not that of the author of Luke-Acts. On the assumption of pseudonymity and in an effort to find a motive for his mention here, it has been suggested that the author is attempting to claim Luke (and Mark, as the representative of Petrine Christianity) for the Pauline tradition (Hasler, 80).

The claim that Luke alone is with Paul stands in tension to 4.21 where other friends are mentioned. It has been claimed that the picture is stylised, but at the cost of contradiction with v. 21; we have the same pattern as 'everybody has deserted me, but Onesiphorus remained loyal' (1.15f.; Brox, 271); similarly, there is the stylised picture in vv. 16f. where nobody stands by Paul, except the Lord. More probably in the present context, Luke is the only one of Paul's intimate circle of missionary colleagues. The others have gone on mission or left him in the lurch. A less likely view is that he is the only member of the Asian churches (Hasler, 79).

Μᾶρκον ἀναλαβὼν ἄγε μετὰ σεαυτοῦ, ἔστιν γάρ μοι εὔχρηστος εἰς διακονίαν The lack of missionary colleagues motivates the request that Timothy should bring Mark with him. Μᾶρκος (Latin *Marcus*) is a very common name and refers to a colleague of both Peter and Paul in Acts 12.12, 25; 15.32, 39; Col 4.10; Philem 24; 1 Pet 5.13; Papias 2.15. ἀναλαμβάνω here means 'to take along', with reference to a travel companion.[10] ἄγω (3.6**) is here 'to bring' (Acts 11.26; 17, 15, 19; 21.16). For εὔχρηστος see 2.21; the same description is applied to Onesimus (Philem 11). Oberlinner, 170f., comments that the two other NT uses of the adjective refer to people who changed for the better, and wonders whether a deliberate rehabilitation of Mark after the debacle in Acts 13–14 is intended. εἰς διακονίαν is used for the service of Christ in 1 Tim 1.12 (cf. Acts 11.29; 1 Cor 16.15; Heb 1.14). Commentators differ whether the thought is primarily of personal help to Paul (Spicq, 814; Kelly, 214) or of church and mission work. But one does not summon an experienced missionary simply to be a valet (Holtz, 195f.); Prior 1989:146–9 also notes that Paul envisages further mission work and that Pauline usage of the phrase elsewhere is decisive (similarly, Oberlinner, 171; Collins 1990:224). Despite his own sense of having finished his course, Paul was still concerned for the work of mission.

---

[10] Cl.; 2 Macc 12.38; Josephus, *Bel.* 2.551; *Ant.* 4.85; Acts 23.31; cf. 20.13f.; also 'to take up', 1 Tim 3.16**.

It is not said where Mark is at the time of writing. In Col and Philem both he and Luke are with Paul in Rome. The implication is that he is either with Timothy or in a place that Timothy would pass through on his way to Paul.

12. Τύχικον δὲ ἀπέστειλα εἰς Ἔφεσον Τύχικος (Tit 3.12 and note) accompanied Paul to Jerusalem on his last journey in Acts and was the messenger who took Col and Eph; he or Artemas was to be sent to Titus in Crete. ἀπέστειλα may be an epistolary aorist (Jeremias, 65); if so, Tychicus would be the bearer of 2 Tim and intended to replace Timothy at Ephesus during his absence. But it is puzzling that the information is conveyed almost as an afterthought, and it is odd to phrase the reference in this way if Timothy is still in Ephesus (1 Tim 1.3) at this point. If it is a remark meant for the church to indicate the formal appointment of Tychicus, then it is rather casual. Oberlinner, 171, attributes the comment to sheer forgetfulness on the part of a pseudonymous writer that Timothy is at Ephesus or simply to lack of thought on the part of the author. The problems would disappear if Timothy was not in Ephesus at this time; but the next request demands that he be still in Asia. It is perhaps more probable that the aor. is not epistolary and that Tychicus has been despatched on a journey that will take him longer than the bearer of the letter to reach Ephesus.

13. τὸν φαιλόνην ὃν ἀπέλιπον ἐν Τρῳάδι παρὰ Κάρπῳ ἐρχόμενος φέρε, καὶ τὰ βιβλία μάλιστα τὰς μεμβράνας In the midst of these comments about people comes a sudden request for personal belongings. φαιλόνη*** is a masc. noun (BD § 25).[11] It is a Latin loan-word, *paenula*, originally transliterated as φαινόλας, φαινόλης or φαινόλιον, and itself originally a loan-word from Gk.[12] The later form developed by metathesis.[13] The garment was a heavy circular cloak, formed of a round piece of material with a hole for the head, like a modern poncho or an old-fashioned cycling cape.[14] There are numerous references in the pap., especially in requests for cloaks to be sent to the writers.[15]

---

[11] It is spelt φελόνης (P. Fay. 347 [ad II]) in Uncials (so Kilpatrick).

[12] It is also found as a loan-word in Rabbinic Hebrew (SB III, 666).

[13] BD § 32[2]; MHT I, 81, 106, 155. There is also a diminutive spelled in various ways, φαιλόνιον (-ώνιον), φαινόλιον.

[14] Cf. MM 665f. Cf. Aelius Lampridius *Alex. Severo: paenulis frigoris causa ut senes uterentur permisit*, cited by Wetstein. The older view, no longer accepted, is that it was a valise, book case (sy; Calvin, 340f.); Lock, 118, prefers this view; cf. Chrysostom (*PG* 62.656) who mentions but does not accept this interpretation (see Field 1899:217f.).

[15] In one of the oldest known preserved Greek letters (*IG* III. III; IV BC; Deissmann 1927:150-2) we have the request 'please send me some clothes'. P. Oxy. 1489 [AD III]: τὸ κιθώνιν {χιτώνιον} ἐπιλέλισμε παρὰ Τεκοῦσαν εἰς

For ἀπολείπω, 'to leave behind', cf. 4.20; Tit 1.5**. Τρῳάς is the town in the NW of Asia Minor which Paul passed through more than once.[16] Dibelius-Conzelmann, 123, connect the incident with Acts 20.13, in the sense that the author created the material on that basis. παρά with dat. means 'at, by, beside, near', usually of a person, hence 'in the house of [someone]'. Κάρπος*** is otherwise unknown, but was presumably Paul's host in Troas (for attestation see BA). ἐρχόμενος is temporal: 'when you come'.

Along with the clothing Paul mentions books. βιβλίον**, 'book, [papyrus] roll', is used of books of the OT.[17] μάλιστα can mean 'especially', or, as in 1 Tim 4.10 'I mean' (see note there). μεμβράνα*** is a Latin loan-word, *membrana*, 'parchment' used for making books (BD § 5[1]; see BA). The native Gk. term is εἰλητά or περγαμηνά.

In form the books may have been scrolls[18] or codices. Small codices made of papyrus or parchment ('notebooks') were in use at this time, and these are probably what is envisaged, at least under the parchments.[19] Speculation about their contents is affected by whether we envisage two sets of material, papyrus scrolls and parchments,[20] or one type, rolls, namely parchments.

Scholars who accept that two different kinds of material are listed identify them as copies of the Scriptures and 'Christian writings' respectively, the latter possibly including Paul's own personal notes[21] or letters to him from the churches (Jeremias, 65). Brox, 273f., claims that parchment was more expensive than papyrus and therefore would not have been used for notes; he proposes that the βιβλία are books in general and the μεμβράναι are the Scriptures. However, the reverse was the case, papyrus

τὸν πυλῶνα; πέμψον μοι. P. Oxy. 3057. 4f. is a letter of thanks for a gift including cloaks (AD I/II; text in *New Docs.* VI, 169–77 § 25; see also Judge, E. A., *Rank and Status in the World of the Caesars and St Paul* (University of Canterbury (NZ) Publications No. 29, 1982, 20–3); cf. *TLNT* III, 432f. Cf. Moffatt*.

[16] Acts 16.8, 11; 20.5f.; 2 Cor 2.12***. See Hemer, C. J., 'Alexandra Troas', *TynBul* 26 (1975), 79–112.

[17] Deut 28.58; Josh 1.8; Lk 4.17; Gal 3.10; Heb 9.19; Josephus uses the pl. of the OT; cf. Schrenk, G., *TDNT* I, 617–20, espec. 617 n. 9.

[18] Cf. Theodoret III, 695 Schulze = *PG* LXXXII, 853 (cited in Dibelius-Conzelmann, 123 n. 10); cf. Balz, H., *EDNT* I, 217.

[19] Cf. Martial, *Ep.* 14.7,184 *pugillares membranei.* cf. *Ep.* 14.186, 188, 190, 192; James, M. R., in Sandys, J. E., *A Companion to Latin Studies* (Cambridge: Cambridge University Press, 1913), 237f.; Skeat, T. C., 'Early Christian Book Production', in *Cambridge History of the Bible* II, 66; Roberts, C. H., and Skeat, T. C., *The Birth of the Codex* (Oxford: Oxford University Press, 1983); Richards, E. R., *The Secretary in the Letters of Paul* (Tübingen: Mohr-Siebeck, 1991); *New Docs.* VII, 249–56 § 12. Skeat notes that if the writer had wanted to specify rolls, he could have used διφθέραι.

[20] Lee* speculates that the reference is to the LXX and the Gospel of Mark.

[21] Cf. REB; Kelly, 216; Houlden, 135; Skeat*; *New Docs.* VII, 255.

being the more expensive material and parchment being used quite commonly as the cheaper material.[22] Some scholars have seen in the combination the beginnings of a canon (cf. Hasler, 80, who thinks that this is the transfer of the Christian canon to Rome!).

If there is one group of materials, then copies of the Scriptures and possibly Christian writings are most likely (Simpson, 159; Spicq, 815f.). It should be remembered, however, that copies of books of the OT would be quite bulky! It may be better, therefore, simply to think of notebooks and not to speculate about their contents (cf. Skeat*). Oberlinner, 173f., argues that the terms used say nothing about the contents and argues from the context that the writer is most likely to have been emphasising the importance of the (Old Testament) Scriptures and that he is concerned to continue the Pauline tradition in his own writings rather than to canonise the Pauline corpus.

The whole verse has raised historical questions.

(a) It is claimed that the reference is a literary cliché. This is sufficient to make sceptical scholars detect a mark of inauthenticity (Brox, 271–4). Further, it is claimed that the motif does not fit into the picture of the condemned prisoner who knows that he has only a very short time to live; it could be months before the cloak and the books arrived (Holtzmann, 453). But the motif is well-attested in genuine letters and therefore it is perfectly possible that it is a real request. Similar requests were made in similar circumstances by William Tyndale and Dietrich Bonhoeffer.[23]

(b) Somewhat similarly, it is claimed that the cloak is a symbol of an apostle, perhaps to be handed over to Timothy as Paul's successor (Hasler, 80), or that the reference serves to make Paul an example of apostolic self-sufficiency and a practitioner of frugality (Trummer*). The real purpose of the reference is thus paraenetic.

(c) If the letter is composed of fragments, this verse could have originated in an earlier period in Paul's mission. But we have no means of establishing or disproving this hypothesis.

(c) The most likely explanation is that the reference is historical. The cloak was required for winter in a Roman prison;

---

[22] See James, ibid.; Kelly, 215f.
[23] Mozley, J. F., *William Tyndale* (London: SPCK, 1937), 334f., gives the famous letter in which Tyndale asks for warm clothing and his Hebrew Bible and other books. D. Bonhoeffer's *Letters and Papers from Prison* (London: SCM Press, 1967³) are filled with requests for food, other necessities of life, books and writing paper.

the books may be Scriptures and the parchments are personal documents (Stevenson*).[24]

The implication that may be drawn (if the books are copies of the Scriptures) is that Paul is an example to be followed in his commitment to the Scriptures (Trummer, 1978:84–6; Oberlinner, 167); but, as frequently in the NT, the fact that the passage can be applied in this way does not require that it was composed purely with this aim in view.

14. Ἀλέξανδρος ὁ χαλκεὺς πολλά μοι κακὰ ἐνεδείξατο· ἀποδώσει αὐτῷ ὁ κύριος κατὰ τὰ ἔργα αὐτοῦ A fresh motif appears, or rather, a continuation of the motif of disloyalty from v. 10 but now in a stronger form; there is also the difference that this case of disloyalty may affect Timothy personally. An Ἀλέξανδρος appeared in 1 Tim 1.20, an opponent of Paul linked with Hymenaeus, who with him had been 'handed over to Satan'. He is presumably the same person.[25] Opinions differ whether he is located in Ephesus (one of the opponents in 1 Cor 16.8; cf. Brox, 274), Rome or elsewhere. If he lived in Troas, this would explain the association of ideas (Easton, 73). He is described as a χαλκεύς***, 'coppersmith', hence generally 'blacksmith, metalworker'.[26] The suggestion that the description is given to distinguish him from the other Alexander of 1 Tim 1.20 falls down on the fact that this is a different literary context. There was a guild of coppersmiths at Troas,[27] and the suggestion has been made that Alexander was a member of it; this would tie in with the sudden reference to him after the mention of Troas in the previous verse.

Against the identification of him with the Alexander of 1 Tim 1.20 it has been objected that, although he was excommunicated there, he is here carrying on his activities unhindered. Such an objection is anachronistic. We do not know enough about how far 'handing over a person to Satan' was effective in discouraging their activities in the church.

---

[24] Prior 1989:149–54, disputes that the request for the cloak implies that Paul was poor and had nothing else to wear. He hazards various explanations, e.g. that the thought is of preparedness for mission, or that it represents a gesture 'reminiscent of Elisha's reception of the prophetic mantle from Elijah'. He prefers the explanation that the items were needed for the forthcoming trial as proof of citizenship – did Paul want to be suitably dressed for the court, and did the documents include his *diploma civitatis Romanae*? All this is highly speculative and fails to carry conviction.

[25] Brox, 274; but Spicq, 816, is hesitant to make the identification as the name was so common.

[26] Cl.; Gen 4.22; 2 Chr 24.12; Hermas, *Vis.* 1.3.2; Diognetus 2.3; *TLNT* III, 496f.

[27] Quinn 1978:295f., referring to *CIG* II 3639 and p. 1130.

For ἐνδείκνυμι see Tit 2.10 and note. From the basic meaning 'to show, demonstrate' the possibilities here are 'to do something to somebody' (Gen 50.17; 2 Macc 13.9) or, specifically, 'to inform against',[28] i.e. 'he made many evil accusations against me'. But the general sense 'he did me much evil' is safer in view of our ignorance of the circumstances envisaged. It is certainly not impossible that he was responsible for the arrest of Paul which then led to his transfer to Rome (Simpson, 160). The evil done was sufficient to lead to a statement that he would be judged by the Lord, i.e. Christ or God (for the latter cf. Rom 2.6; Jeremias, 66). ἀποδώσει (4.8) is fut. indic., expressing certainty.[29] Although the anathema was used in the early church (1 Cor 16.22; Gal 1.8f.), vengeance is here left to the Lord.[30]

15. ὃν καὶ σὺ φυλάσσου, λίαν γὰρ ἀντέστη τοῖς ἡμετέροις λόγοις The real reason for mentioning Alexander is because he constitutes a continuing danger to Paul's associates. ὅν is an example of the relative used as a connective and an imperative. καὶ σύ means 'you, Timothy, as well as me, Paul'. If Alexander is at Troas, the implication is that he could be a danger to Timothy when he visits the church there. On the hypothesis of pseudonymity, he is presumably a person who is a danger to church leaders generally, but since we are told nothing of where he is, this is highly unlikely. φυλάσσου is an example of the mid., 'to be on one's guard against, look out for, avoid'.[31]

λίαν**, 'very, exceedingly', hence 'vehemently', can be used with verbs.[32] For ἀνθίστημι see 3.8 bis. (cf. Jth 8.28). ἡμέτεροι λόγοι has been thought to refer to 'our message', understood by some as an institutionalised set form of words used in church (Hasler, 81), or 'our defence in court' (Bernard, 148; Spicq, 817). Neither interpretation is compelling, and the reference is simply to whatever Paul and his colleagues said in the church setting. Alexander thus emerges as the leader of an anti-Pauline faction, hardly as a non-Christian attacker of the church.

16. Ἐν τῇ πρώτῃ μου ἀπολογίᾳ οὐδείς μοι παρεγένετο, ἀλλὰ πάντες με ἐγκατέλιπον· μὴ αὐτοῖς λογισθείη The theme of opposition to Paul is continued, but the focus shifts from unfaithful individuals to the larger question of his own trial.

---

[28] Dan 3.44; pap. in Spicq, 816f.; Hanson, 160; Fee, 295f.

[29] If the opt. or subj. is read (see textual note), it would be an imprecation; cf. 2 Sam 3.39; Ps 61.13 (MT 62.12); cf. 27 (MT 28).4.

[30] Rom 12.19; Jeremias, 66; Brox, 274; pace Hasler, 80f., who claims that God is being called to act on Paul's prior decision.

[31] Cl.; Ignatius, Eph. 7.1; Trall. 7.1; cf. Lk 12.15; Acts 21.25; 2 Pet 3.17; for the act. see 1 Tim 5.21.

[32] Ep. Arist. 312; Josephus, Vita 404; Didache 6.3; Mt 2.16; 27.14; Lk 23.8; et al.; not used by Paul, who has ὑπερλίαν (2 Cor 11.5; 12.11).

These three verses deal with Paul's 'first defence' and his hopes for the future. The background to their interpretation is manifestly the actual situation of Paul (if this section of the letter is in any sense 'authentic') or that situation as conceived by a later writer.

Paul's reference is to his first ἀπολογία. This word can refer to a speech in one's own defence in a court,[33] or, more generally, to the court action itself (Josephus, *Bel.* 1.621). πρώτη gives a reference back to a previous occasion compared with a second actual or envisaged occasion; as in Acts 1.1 there need be no more than two occasions in the series. The possible references in the phrase are to:

(a) Paul's earlier trial, embracing the events in Jerusalem and Caesarea (Acts 23–26; cf. 23.11).[34] Against this view is the fact that 4.17 appears to envisage a more cosmopolitan scene.

(b) If we adopt the scenario that 2 Tim was written during a second Roman imprisonment, then this could be an allusion to his first Roman trial before his release and subsequent re-arrest.[35] Then the 'lion' is a reference to Nero. The problem here is the distance in time from the present events, although the defence is spoken of as if it were something quite recent.

(c) The so-called *prima actio*, the first hearing in a two-part trial, the preliminary investigation of the case. Then the verdict could be *Non liquet* or *Amplius*.[36] This remains the most likely interpretation.

παραγίνομαι** is 'to come, arrive, be present', here with the narrower meaning 'to stand by, come to the aid of';[37] Simpson, 160, upholds 'to second', whether as advocate or friend. Paul was thus left on his own to make his own defence; everybody else deserted him. The strong expression ἐγκατέλιπον (4.10 note) implies fault, whether lack of courage or lack of concern for Paul. Nevertheless, he regards the failure as forgivable, and therefore instead of the statement that God will render to them accordingly (v. 14), there is a prayer that they will be forgiven.

[33] Cl.; Acts 22.1; 25.16; fig., 1 Cor 9.3; 2 Cor 7.11; Phil 1.7, 16; 1 Pet 3.15; cf. ἀπολογέομαι, Lk 12.11; 21.14.

[34] This suggestion was developed by Erbes* and Binder 1967 on the assumption that this fragment of the letter is written from Caesarea and the reference is to the Jerusalem hearing; cf. Introduction VII.A.3.

[35] Eusebius, *HE* 2.22.2f; Theodoret III, 696 Schulze = *PG* LXXXII, 856; Parry, 69f.; Lock, 119; Meinertz*; Quinn 1978:296f.

[36] Bernard, 148; Dibelius-Conzelmann, 124; and most recent commentators. See Mommsen, T., *Le droit pénal romain* (Paris, 1907), I, 283 *s.v.* It is a matter of regret that the problem was not discussed by Sherwin-White, A. N., *Roman Society and Roman Law in the New Testament* (Oxford: Clarendon Press, 1963).

[37] This meaning is required in view of the use of the dat. with the verb (MM, 481).

μή with opt. expresses a wish (BD §427⁴). λογίζομαι** is 'to count something against someone', hence 'to punish'.³⁸ For this attitude cf. Acts 7.60; 1 Cor 13.5. Brox's comment (275) that this wish 'completes the picture of the dying apostle who is raised above weakness and suffering' is not fair. According to Hasler, 81, there is no contradiction to the rest of the chapter: rather the point is that Paul needs only God's help.

17. ὁ δὲ κύριός μοι παρέστη καὶ ἐνεδυνάμωσέν με, ἵνα δι᾽ ἐμοῦ τὸ κήρυγμα πληροφορηθῇ καὶ ἀκούσωσιν πάντα τὰ ἔθνη, καὶ ἐρρύσθην ἐκ στόματος λέοντος The lack of human help is contrasted with the presence of divine help. ὁ κύριος (here and in v. 18) is Jesus rather than God, whose promise of help to Paul is given in Acts 23.11. παρίστημι (2.15) is here intrans., 'to come to the aid of, help'.³⁹ For ἐνδυναμόω see 2.1; the strength that Timothy is there urged to avail himself of is here the actual experience of Paul. The promise of Jesus that the Spirit will help his followers in such situations is fulfilled (Mk 13.11; Lk 21.15). ἵνα can express purpose or result, i.e. the fulfilment of a purpose. God's purpose is the proclamation of the gospel which took place δι᾽ ἐμοῦ, i.e. through Paul as his instrument. For κήρυγμα, the action of proclamation, preaching, see Tit 1.3** (cf. 1 Cor 1.21). ἐπληροφορήθη (4.5) indicates that Paul took full advantage of the opportunity to set forth the gospel. A situation like those in Acts 7; 22; 25; 26 is envisaged, with a full-scale defence that turns into a gospel sermon. ἀκούσωσιν means what it says; it does not necessarily indicate a positive acceptance. The point is that an opportunity to hear the gospel was given to a wide audience. πάντα τὰ ἔθνη may mean 'all the nations [including the Jews]' (Prior 1989:115–24 on assumption of Pauline authorship) or 'all the Gentiles' (Knight, 471).

The assumption in the above explanation is that the reference is to what Paul said in court. 'All the nations' is then obviously not literal but rather expresses the representative, cosmopolitan character of the audience (cf. Rom 1.5; 16.26; Kelly, 219). Or the reference may be metaphorical, to the effects of his pleading his case in the Emperor's court in Rome (cf. Mt 10.17–33).

Parry, 69f., and Prior 1989:125–39 argue that the reference is to a period of evangelism after his first trial in Rome; an appearance in a Roman court was hardly making the gospel known to all nations, and Paul has in mind his mission, which included going as far as Spain. This seems less probable. The objection, however, that the historical Paul could not have been referring to this

---

³⁸ Cf. Job 27.5; *T. Zeb.* 9.7; 2 Cor 5.19; Rom 4.8; pass., as here, Lev 17.4.

³⁹ Rom 16.2; cf. P. Hermopol. 125B, 8 (AD III): θεὸς παρίσταταί σοι, cited in BA; Josephus, *Ant.* 1.341; Philo, *Gig.* 55 (cited by Wolter 1988:46 n. 88).

because Timothy would already have known about it (Brox, 276), is invalid because people do as a matter of fact refer to things already known to their correspondents, especially when they are placing an interpretation on them.

A different type of explanation is that the clause refers to Paul's hope of future release after his impending trial and of a future ministry (Scott, 141f.). Following a hint by Holtz, 198, Oberlinner, 178f., appears to suggest that the work of the gospel will go on successfully through the activity of Paul's successors; but this suggestion rather weakens the force of δι' ἐμοῦ.

The relatively successful outcome of the trial is expressed with a well-known metaphor. For ῥύομαι see 3.11. στόμα** expresses metaphorically the ferocious and deadly power of wild animals.[40] The lion (λέων; Heb 11.4.7 et al.) is used metaphorically, as in Ps 21 (MT 22).22. The Psalm was understood to apply to Christ, but it is applied to Christians here and in Rom 5.5 (cf. Lindars 1961:93); however, there may be nothing more than use of OT phraseology here.[41] Attempts to see more than a metaphor for death here,[42] and to identify the lion as standing for being thrown to the lions, or for the emperor[43] or for Satan are dubious (so rightly Bernard, 148f.).

18. ῥύσεταί με ὁ κύριος ἀπὸ παντὸς ἔργου πονηροῦ καὶ σώσει εἰς τὴν βασιλείαν αὐτοῦ τὴν ἐπουράνιον The verb ῥύσεται deliberately picks up from the previous clause. Christ will continue to deliver Paul from every kind of evil deed.[44] The reference is to any kind of evil attack by other people. ἔργα πονηρά may be a deliberate contrast to καλὰ ἔργα, the result of hypocrisy and heresy (Hasler, 81). The language may possibly echo that of the Lord's Prayer; if so, τοῦ πονηροῦ there would have been interpreted as neuter (Mt 6.13; cf. 1 Pet 3.13; Jeremias, 66; *pace* Holtzmann, 459, who thinks that this is inconsistent with the clear expectation of martyrdom).

The negative motif of rescue from danger is complemented by the positive motif of entry into the kingdom of Christ. σῴζω (1.9) is generally understood to refer to being saved spiritually, in the sense of being successfully preserved from any threats to

---

[40] Heb 11.33; cf. Weiss, K., *TDNT* VII, 692–701.

[41] Cf. Ps 7.3; 34 [MT 35].17; 90 (MT 91].13; Dan 6.20, 27 Θ; *Ps. Sol.* 13.3; 1 Macc 2.60. Ignatius, *Rom.* 5.1 refers similarly to leopards. See Michaelis, W., *TDNT* IV, 251–3, who asserts that the OT models are primary, *pace* Dibelius-Conzelmann, 124.

[42] *New Docs.* III, 50f. § 16, shows that the symbolism expressed 'the ravening power of death'.

[43] Cf. Josephus, *Ant.* 18.228, τέθνηκεν ὁ λέων, with reference to Tiberius.

[44] For ἔργον with πονηρόν, normally in the pl. see Jn 3.19; 7.7; Col 1.21; 1 Jn 3.12b; 2 Jn 11; Hermas, *Vis.* 3.7.6; 3.8.4 *et al.*; sing. Hermas, *Vis.* 1.22.4b.

faith and being brought safely to eternal life.[45] The deliverance is from 'the power of evil to destroy him finally' (Knight, 472; Fee, 298). This makes it unlikely that the writer is thinking of literal deliverance from the opposition, so that Paul is able to continue his life and work (either for a further period until his death or until the parousia). Rather the hope is of spiritual deliverance, so that nothing prevents him from attaining his heavenly reward; he will be preserved from falling into apostasy under the pressure of persecution. Another, less likely, possibility is that Paul is expressing the hope that he will be preserved alive until the parousia and the coming of the kingdom (Barrett, 124). βασιλεία refers to the kingdom of Christ, as in 4.1. The description of it as ἐπουράνιος[46] indicates that it is thought of as future, or as presently existing in heaven and to be revealed openly at the parousia. For similar descriptions see Diognetus 10.2; *M. Poly.* 22.4 (cf. *Epil. Mosq.* 4)

ᾧ ἡ δόξα εἰς τοὺς αἰῶνας τῶν αἰώνων, ἀμήν The sentence – and the body of the letter – concludes with a doxology, expressive of thankfulness and praise to the Lord for his gifts. ᾧ is regularly used to link doxologies to what precedes (Rom 16.27; Gal 1.5; Heb 13.21; 1 Pet 4.11). The verb to be supplied is generally taken to be ἐστιν (1 Tim 1.17 note). The antecedent is ὁ κύριος, and therefore the doxology should be to Christ (so most commentators),[47] unless there is some looseness of construction and the writer is now thinking of God (so Kelly, 220; Oberlinner, 181). For εἰς τοὺς αἰῶνας τῶν αἰώνων and ἀμήν see 1 Tim 1.17.

---

[45] εἰς is used in a pregnant construction – 'will save me [and bring me] to' (BA *s.v.* 7; 4 Macc 15.3; cf. διασώζω, Gen 19.19; 1 Pet 3.20).

[46] 1 Cor 15.48, 49; Heb 12.22; 2 Clement 20.5; cf. Heb 3.1; 6.4; Traub, H., *TDNT* V, 538–42.

[47] On this interpretation, the verse has significant implications for the author's Christology.

GREETINGS, REPETITION OF APPEAL TO COME, AND FINAL BLESSING (4.19–22)

Verses 19–22 are structured by a framework of people to greet and people who send greetings. Sandwiched in between is further comment about two colleagues who are not with Paul, together with a further appeal to Timothy to come to him. A double benediction rounds the letter off.

The mention of faithful companions in v. 21 is often seen to be in contradiction with the picture of solitariness and even desertion (v. 16) in the immediately preceding verses; the writer, it is argued, is concerned at different points to bring out different facets of the ideal picture of Paul, his isolation as a martyr and his support by faithful colleagues (e.g. Oberlinner, 187). But would a pseudonymous author be so negligent? We simply do not know enough about the circumstances, real or fictitious, to come to such a conclusion. The desertion in v. 16 was on an earlier occasion, after which circumstances could have changed. The reference in vv. 9–15 is probably to members of Paul's missionary group, whereas v. 21 refers to local Christians.

TEXT

19. There is an extensive gloss in 181 and 460 giving the names of the wife and children of Onesiphorus from *Acts of Paul and Thecla* but attaching them to Aquila (Metzger, 581). Cf. 3.11 note.

20. ἀπέλιπον (WH mg): ἀπέλειπον (C L P 33 104 323 326 365 1175 1241 *al*; Kilpatrick). See 4.10 note.

Μιλήτῳ For the spelling see Elliott, 171. Beza's conjecture of Μελίτῃ has not found any subsequent support.

21. οἱ ἀδελφοὶ πάντες Omit πάντες (ℵ* 33 1739 1881 *pc*). Elliott, 172, rejects the variant on the grounds that scribes tended to remove the word rather than add it.

22. ὁ κύριος Add Ἰησοῦς (A 104 614 *pc* vg^st; WH mg); Add Ἰησοῦς Χριστός (ℵ² C D Ψ TR a b f vg^clww sy bo Ambst). These additions reflect compound forms typical of later church usage but not used in the PE (Elliott, 172; cf. Metzger, 582).

ἡ χάρις μεθ' ὑμῶν (ℵ* A C G 33 81 1881): (a) ἡ χάρις μεθ' ἡμῶν (460 614 *pc* vg^st bo^ms); (b) ἡ χάρις μετά σου (sy^p sa^ms bo^ms); (c) ἔρρωσο(ο) ἐν εἰρήνῃ (D*f a b (Ambst)); (d) Omit phrase (sa^mss). Metzger, 582f., holds that variant (a) is orthographical, since the two pronouns were pronounced very alike. The use of the sing. in (b) was through conformity to the rest of the epistle; cf. 1 Tim

6.21 *v.l.* Variant (c) is Western. Elliott, 172, however, argues that the sing. form is original, and the plural is an attempt to generalise the letter. However, the text has superior attestation.

Add ἀμήν (ℵ² D Ψ 1739ᶜ TR lat sy boᵖᵗ). Elliott, 104, rejects the addition, as in 1 Tim 6.21. Deliberate omission of it would be very unlikely (Metzger, 582f.).

EXEGESIS

19. **Ἄσπασαι Πρίσκαν καὶ Ἀκύλαν καὶ τὸν Ὀνησιφόρου οἶκον** Sending greetings to the writer's friends who are with the addressee is normal in Pauline and other letters; cf. Tit 3.15b and note. Whereas in Tit no specific names are listed, here three names are given. Πρίσκα[1] is also found in its diminutive form Πρίσκιλλα (Acts 18.2, 18, 26).[2] Ἀκύλας is the Gk. form of the common Latin name *Aquila*.[3] He was a Jew who came from Pontus, and Prisca was his wife (Acts 18.2). She is named before her husband except in Acts 18.2; 1 Cor 16.19. This may be because of her higher social rank (Ramsay, cited in BA) or her more active personality. Or it may be merely courtesy to a woman (Knight, 475). The couple had been in Ephesus and previously in Rome (Acts 18.2); if Rom 16 was addressed to Rome, it indicates that they had returned to Rome. Hasler, 82, thinks that the PE ignore Rom 16 and assume she is still in Ephesus. The current trend is to assume that no biographical information can be drawn from the present passage.[4]

For Ὀνησίφορος see 1.16 and note. Greetings are sent to a household (οἶκος) in Col 4.15. The phrase could (a) include the householder with his household; (b) exclude the householder because he was absent from home; or (c) exclude the householder because he was dead. The third possibility is unlikely, if only because there would be a new head of the house whose name would be known. In *Acts of Paul and Thecla* 2 (*NTA* II, 353–64) Onesiphorus is located at Iconium.

20. **Ἔραστος ἔμεινεν ἐν Κορίνθῳ, Τρόφιμον δὲ ἀπέλιπον ἐν Μιλήτῳ ἀσθενοῦντα** The list of greetings is broken by mention of two further colleagues who are not with Paul at the time of writing. Ἔραστος is a common name found in literary sources and inscr.[5] The name is found elsewhere in the NT as that of a Christian at Corinth who was ὁ οἰκονόμος τῆς πόλεως (Rom 16.23) and also of a companion of Paul who is mentioned alongside Timothy (Acts 19.22***; see Winter 1994:179–97).

---

[1] Or Πρῖσκα, BD §41³; MHT II, 155; Rom 16.3; 1 Cor 16.19.
[2] For other occurrences of the name see BA.
[3] E.g. Josephus, *Ant.* 19.110, 283.
[4] Weiser, A., *EDNT* I, 55f.
[5] For an inscr. at Ephesus see Dittenberger, *Syll.* 838.6.

Several commentators think that this latter person is to be identified with the Erastus here, whether historically (e.g. Lock, 120) or as the choice of a suitable name to mention in a fictional passage (Holtzmann, 460; Brox, 277). The fact that the Erastus mentioned here remained (μένω, 2.13) at Corinth (Κόρινθος, Acts 18.1; 19.1; 1 Cor 1.2; 2 Cor 1.1, 23***) also makes identification with the Corinthian Christian highly likely, and the probability is that we should identify all three persons.

Τρόφιμος appears in Acts 20.4; 21.29***; he came from Ephesus and was a companion of Paul on the way to Jerusalem.[6] In the scenario here he had been a travelling companion of Paul, but had fallen sick[7] at Μίλητος, a town on the W coast of Asia visited by Paul on his journey to Jerusalem (Acts 20.15, 17***). A reference here to the journey in Acts 20 is unlikely, both because of the timegap and because in Acts Trophimus continues with Paul to Jerusalem (Acts 21.29); the second difficulty remains even if the present verse is thought to be a fragment from an earlier letter. We have then to suppose that the reference is to a more recent journey, and that the time gap between Paul's arrival in Rome and the present letter is comparatively short, so that this information will be news to Timothy, even though he was geographically much nearer to Miletus. The proposal that the point of the allusion is to show that Paul is still in charge in Asia (Hasler, 82) suggests an unlikely degree of sophistication in a pseudonymous writer. It is not surprising, perhaps, that Beza emended the text to give a reference to Μελίτη, 'Malta', visited by Paul on his journey to Rome. This would create a fresh set of problems. Johnson, 101, holds that the clause could mean 'I left him to work there', apparently taking the verb to refer to the making of an appointment rather than to an actual physical leave-taking; elsewhere, however, the verb appears to refer to actually leaving somebody behind in a location with delegated authority.

21. Σπούδασον πρὸ χειμῶνος ἐλθεῖν There is a closing repetition of the request σπούδασον ἐλθεῖν from 4.9. This is entirely natural. The new element is the addition of the time span πρὸ χειμῶνος. χειμών is both 'rainy, stormy weather' and the season of such weather, 'winter'.[8] During the ancient Mediterranean winter navigation was impossible and travel was

---

[6] For the name in inscr. and pap. see BA; detailed discussion in *New Docs.* III, 91–3 §80.

[7] ἀσθενέω**, 'to be weak, ill'; Lk 4.40 *et al.*; Phil 2.26, 27; Jas 5.14; cf. ἀσθένεια, 1 Tim 5.23.

[8] For the former: Mt 16.3; Acts 27.20; for the latter: Jn 10.22; Mt 24.20; Mk 13.18***. Cf. *TLNT* II, 97f.

avoided if at all possible. Paul needed his cloak before then; hence the urgency. This suggests a date for the letter in the later part of the year, probably in autumn (AD 63 – Jeremias, 67).

Ἀσπάζεταί σε Εὔβουλος καὶ Πούδης καὶ Λίνος καὶ Κλαυδία καὶ οἱ ἀδελφοὶ πάντες Finally, in this section, greetings are sent from Paul's companions to Timothy. See Tit 3.15a, where the reference is general. Four individuals are named, followed by a general reference. Εὔβουλος*** is a name found frequently in inscr. and pap.,[9] but not found elsewhere in early Christian sources. Πούδης*** is for Latin Pudens.[10] It was a name used in upper class families.[11]

Λίνος*** was, according to Irenaeus, AH 3.3.3; Eusebius, HE 3.2, 13, the name of the first bishop of Rome, but according to Tertullian, De prae. haer. 32, it was Clement who succeeded Peter.

Κλαυδία*** was a common Roman name, not found elsewhere in early Christian sources.

οἱ ἀδελφοὶ πάντες is found in similar greetings in 1 Cor 16.20; 1 Th 5.26 (for ἀδελφοὶ cf. 1 Tim 4.6). The phrase creates difficulties in that this fairly wide circle contrasts with the lack of companions in 4.11 and with the sad reference to lack of support in 4.16. The former difficulty may be met by the hypothesis that the earlier reference is to members of Paul's missionary group, whereas these are local Christians; as for the latter, it is possible that there were no people prepared to appear in court and put themselves at risk.

22. Ὁ κύριος μετὰ τοῦ πνεύματός σου. ἡ χάρις μεθ' ὑμῶν The final benediction is twofold. The second part is identical with 1 Tim 6.21 and similar to Tit 3.15c. The first part is unusual. Phrases of this kind with ὁ κύριος are not found in the epistles, but the greeting 'The Lord be with you' is found in Lk 1.28.[12] Usually Paul uses a grace formula at the conclusion of a letter. However, the phrase μετὰ τοῦ πνεύματος is used in Pauline

---

[9] For all of these four names see the entries in BA.

[10] The ν was lost, as in Latin inscriptions, before the ς; it became nasalised; BD §41²; 54; MHT II, 134.

[11] Cf. BGU 455.4 (AD I); Pap.; Josephus, Bel. 6.172. For conjectured identifications with people mentioned elsewhere, namely the husband of the Claudia in CIL VI, 15066 and a person mentioned by Martial, see the discussion in Lightfoot, J. B., The Apostolic Fathers: Clement (London: Macmillan, 1890), I, 76–9; Edmundson, G., The Church in Rome in the First Century (London: Longmans Green, 1913), 244–9. Bernard, 151f., is rightly sceptical of all these possibilities. See further Thiede, C. P., s.v. 'Linus', 'Pudens', in Das Grosse Bibellexicon (Wuppertal: Brockhaus, 1988).

[12] Van Unnik, W. C., 'Dominus vobiscum: The background of a Liturgical Formula', in Sparsa Collecta III (Leiden: Brill, 1983), 362–91 (originally in Higgins, A. J. B., New Testament Essays: Studies in Memory of T. W. Manson [Manchester: Manchester University Press, 1959], 270–305).

benedictions.[13] Its force here may be to assure Timothy that the Lord will strengthen him in the area of his charisma for ministry. Hasler, 83, speculates that the wish is in fact a promise of apostolic office for Timothy, but this is fanciful. Since there has been reference to a wider group of people with Timothy in v. 19, the expansion of the greeting in the second clause is natural, just as in Tit 3.15.

[13] Gal 6.18; Phil 4.23; Philem 25; cf. Barnabas 21.9; all with pl. pronoun.

INDEXES

INDEX OF GREEK WORDS

This concordance of the Greek words used in the Pastoral Epistles will also serve as an index to where they are discussed, usually at their earliest occurrence in the order of treatment of the letters in the Commentary. Words not found elsewhere in the Pauline corpus are marked here with *; words not found in Luke-Acts are marked with †; words not found elsewhere in the New Testament are marked with **. Statistics of frequently occurring words are taken from R. Morgenthaler, *Statistik des neutestamentlichen Wortschatzes* (Zürich: Gotthelf-Verlag, 1958; *Beiheft*, 1982).

	1 Timothy	2 Timothy	Titus
**ἀγαθοεργέω	6.18		
ἀγαθός	1.5, 19; 2.10; 5.10	2.21; 3.17	1.16; 2.5, 10; 3.1
ἀγαπάω		4.8, 10	
ἀγάπη	1.5, 14; 2.15; 4.12; 6.4	1.7, 13; 2.22; 3.10	2.2
ἀγαπητός	6.2	1.2	
ἄγγελος	3.16; 5.21		
ἁγιάζω	4.5	2.21	
†ἁγιασμός	2.15		
ἅγιος	5.10	1.9, 14	3.5
**ἁγνεία	4.12; 5.2		
ἀγνοέω	1.13		
†ἁγνός	5.22		2.5
ἄγω		3.6; 4.11	
**ἀγωγή		3.10	
†ἀγών	6.12	4.7	
ἀγωνίζομαι	4.10; 6.12	4.7	
Ἀδάμ	2.13, 14		
ἀδελφή	5.2		
ἀδελφός	4.6; 5.1; 6.2	4.21	
**ἀδηλότης	6.17		
†ἀδιάλειπτος		1.3	
ἀδικία		2.19	
†ἀδόκιμος		3.8	1.16
ἀεί			1.12
†ἀθανασία	6.16		
ἀθετέω	5.12		
**ἀθλέω		2.5, 5	
**αἰδώς	2.9		
**αἱρετικός			3.10
**αἰσχροκερδής	3.8		1.7
†αἰσχρός			1.11
αἰτία		1.6, 12	1.13
αἰχμαλωτίζω		3.6	

835

	1 Timothy	2 Timothy	Titus
ἀιών	1.17, 17, 17; 6.17	4.10, 18, 18	2.12
αἰώνιος	1.16; 6.12, 16	1.9; 2.10	1.2, 2; 3.7
**ἀκαίρως		4.2	
†ἄκαρπος			3.14
**ἀκατάγνωστος			2.8
ἀκοή		4.3, 4	
ἀκούω	4.16	1.13; 2.2, 14; 4.17	
**ἀκρατής		3.3	
Ἀκύλας		4.19	
†ἀλαζών		3.2	
Ἀλέξανδρος	1.20	4.14	
ἀλήθεια	2.4, 7, 7; 3.15; 4.3; 6.5	2.15, 18, 25; 3.7, 8; 4.4	1.1, 14
ἀληθής			1.13
ἀλλά	(12)	(12)	1.8, 15; 2.10; 3.5
ἀλλήλων			3.3
ἀλλότριος	5.22		
**ἄλλως	5.25		
†ἀλοάω	5.18		
ἅλυσις		1.16	
ἅμα	5.13		
ἁμαρτάνω	5.20		3.11
ἁμαρτία	5.22, 24	3.6	
ἁμαρτωλός	1.9, 15		
**ἄμαχος	3.3		3.2
†ἀμελέω	4.14		
ἀμήν	1.17; 6.16	4.18	
**ἀμοιβή	5.4		
**ἀναγκαῖος			3.14
ἀνάγνωσις	4.13		
**ἀναζωπυρέω		1.6	
†ἀνακαίνωσις			3.5
ἀναλαμβάνω	3.16	4.11	
**ἀνάλυσις		4.6	
†ἀναμιμνήσκω		1.6	
**ἀνανήφω		2.26	
ἀνάστασις		2.18	
ἀναστρέφω	3.15		
†ἀναστροφή	4.12		
†*ἀνατρέπω		2.18	1.11
**ἀναψύχω		1.16	
**ἀνδραποδιστής	1.10		
**ἀνδροφόνος	1.9		
†ἀνέγκλητος	3.10		1.6, 7
**ἀνεξίκακος		2.24	
**ἀνεπαίσχυντος		2.15	
**ἀνεπίλημπτος	3.2; 5.7; 6.14		
ἀνέχομαι		4.3	
**ἀνήμερος		3.3	

	1 Timothy	2 Timothy	Titus
ἀποστρέφω		1.15; 4.4	1.14
†ἀποτόμως			1.13
**ἀποτρέπω		3.5	
**ἀπρόσιτος	6.16		
ἀπωθέω	1.19		
ἀπώλεια	6.9		
*†ἀργός	5.13, 13		1.12
*ἀργυροῦς		2.20	
ἀρέσκω		2.4	
ἀρκέω	6.8		
*ἀρνέομαι	5.8	2.12, 13; 3.5	1.16; 2.12
†ἀρσενοκοίτης	1.10		
**Ἀρτεμᾶς			3.12
**ἄρτιος		3.17	
ἀρχή			3.1
†ἀσέβεια		2.16	2.12
†ἀσεβής	1.9		
ἀσθένεια	5.23		
ἀσθενέω		4.20	
Ἀσία		1.15	
ἀσπάζομαι		4.19, 21	3.15, 15
*†ἄσπιλος	6.14		
*†ἄσπονδος		3.3	
†ἄστοργος		3.3	
**ἀστοχέω	1.6; 6.21	2.18	
†ἀσωτία			1.6
†ἀτιμία		2.20	
*†αὐθάδης			1.7
**αὐθεντέω	2.12		
†αὐτάρκεια	6,6		
**αὐτοκατάκριτος			3.11
αὐτός	1.8, 16, 18; 4.16; 5.16, 18	(16)	1.3, 12, 12, 13, 15; 3.1, 5, 13
†ἀφθαρσία		1.10	
†ἄφθαρτος	1.17		
**ἀφθορία			2.7
**ἀφιλάγαθος		3.3	
*†ἀφιλάργυρος	3.3		
ἀφίστημι	4.1	2.19	
†ἀφορμή	5.14		
*ἀχάριστος		3.2	
**ἀψευδής			1.2
**βαθμός	3.13		
βαρέομαι	5.16		
βασιλεία		4.1, 18	
βασιλεύς	1.17; 2.2; 6.15		
βασιλεύω	6.15		
**βδελυκτός			1.16

	1 Timothy	2 Timothy	Titus
δέσμιος		1.8	
δεσμός		2.9	
*δεσπότης	6.1, 2	2.21	2.9
δεύτερος			3.10
δέω		2.9	
†Δημᾶς		4.10	
διά	1.16; 2.10, 15; 4.5, 14; 5.23	1.1, 6, 6, 10, 10, 12, 14; 2.2, 10, 10; 3.15; 4.17	1.13; 3.5, 6
**διαβεβαιόομαι	1.7		3.8
διάβολος	3.6, 7, 11	2.26; 3.3	2.3
**διάγω	2.2		3.3
διακονέω	3.10, 13	1.18	
διακονία	1.12	4.5, 11	
†διάκονος	3.8, 12; 4.6		
διαλογισμός	2.8		
διαμαρτύρομαι	5.21	2.14; 4.1	
**διαπαρατριβή	6.5		
διατάσσω			1.5
**διατροφή	6.8		
διαφθείρω	6.5		
**διδακτικός	3.2	2.24	
†διδασκαλία	1.10; 4.1, 6, 13, 16; 5.17; 6.1, 3	3.10, 16; 4.3	1.9; 2.1, 7, 10
διδάσκαλος	2.7	1.11; 4.3	
διδάσκω	2.12; 4.11; 6.2	2.2	1.11
διδαχή		4.2	1.9
δίδωμι	2.6; 4.14; 5.14	1.7, 9, 16, 18; 2.7, 25	2.14
δίκαιος	1.9	4.8	1.8
δικαιοσύνη	6.11	2.22; 3.16; 4.8	3.5
δικαιόω	3.16		3.7
δικαιῶς			2.12
**δίλογος	3.8		
*†διπλοῦς	5.17		
διωγμός		3.11, 11	
**διώκτης	1.13		
διώκω	6.11	2.22; 3.12	
δοκιμάζω	3.10		
†δόκιμος		2.15	
δόξα	1.11, 17; 3.16	2.10; 4.18	2.13
δουλεύω	6.2		3.3
δοῦλος	6.1	2.24	1.1; 2.9
δουλόω			2.3
*δρόμος		4.7	
δύναμαι	5.25; 6.7, 16	2.13; 3.7, 15	
δύναμις		1.7, 8; 3.5	
*δυνάστης	6.15		

	1 Timothy	2 Timothy	Titus
ἐναντίος			2.8
†ἐνδείκνυμι	1.16	4.14	2.10; 3.2
ἐνδυναμόω	1.12	2.1; 4.17	
**ἐνδύνω		3.6	
†ἐνίστημι		3.1	
†ἐνοικέω		1.5, 14	
**ἔντευξις	2.1; 4.5		
ἐντολή	6.14		1.14
ἐντρέπω			2.8
**ἐντρέφομαι	4.6		
ἐνώπιον	2.3; 5.4, 20, 21; 6.12, 13	2.14; 4.1	
†ἐξαπατάω	2.14		
*ἐξαρτίζω		3.17	
*ἐξήκοντα	5.9		
ἐξουσία			3.1
ἔξωθεν	3.7		
ἐπαγγελία	4.8	1.1	
ἐπαγγέλλομαι	2.10; 6.21		1.2
ἐπαίρω	2.8		
ἐπαισχύνομαι		1.8, 12, 16	
*†ἐπακολουθέω	5.10, 24		
**ἐπανόρθωσις		3.16	
**ἐπαρκέω	5.10, 16, 16		
ἐπέχω	4.16		
ἐπί	1.16, 18; 4.10; 5.5, 19; 6.13, 17, 17	2.14, 14, 16; 3.9, 13; 4.4	1.2; 3.6
ἐπιγινώσκω	4.3		
†ἐπίγνωσις	2.4	2.25; 3.7	1.1
**ἐπιδιορθόω			1.5
†ἐπιεικής	3.3		3.2
*ἐπίθεσις	4.14	1.6	
ἐπιθυμέω	3.1		
ἐπιθυμία	6.9	2.22; 3.6; 4.3	2.12; 3.3
ἐπικαλέω		2.22	
*ἐπιλαμβάνομαι	6.12, 19		
*ἐπιμελέομαι	3.5		
ἐπιμένω	4.16		
**ἐπίορκος	1.10		
**ἐπιπλήσσω	5.1		
†ἐπιποθέω		1.4	
*ἐπισκοπή	3.1		
ἐπίσκοπος	3.2		1.7
*ἐπίσταμαι	6.4		
**ἐπιστομίζω			1.11
**ἐπισωρεύω		4.3	
†ἐπιταγή	1.1		1.3; 2.15
*ἐπιτίθημι	5.22		
ἐπιτιμάω		4.2	

	1 Timothy	2 Timothy	Titus
ἐπιτρέπω	2.12		
*ἐπιφαίνω			2.11; 3.4
†ἐπιφάνεια	6.14	1.10; 4.1, 8	2.13
†ἐπουράνιος		4.18	
Ἔραστος		4.20	
ἐργάτης	5.18	2.15	
ἔργον	2.10; 3.1; 5.10, 10, 25; 6.18	1.9; 2.21; 3.17; 4.5, 14, 18	1.16, 16; 2.7, 14; 3.1, 5, 8, 14
†ἔρις	6.4		3.9
**Ἑρμογένης		1.15	
ἔρχομαι	1.15; 2.4; 3.14; 4.13	3.7; 4.9, 13, 21	3.12
ἔσχατος		3.1	
**ἑτεροδιδασκαλέω	1.3; 6.3		
ἕτερος	1.10	2.2	
ἑτοιμάζω		2.21	
ἕτοιμος			3.1
ἔτος	5.9		
†Εὕα	2.13		
εὐαγγέλιον	1.11	1.8, 10; 2.8	
εὐαγγελιστής		4.5	
†εὐάρεστος			2.9
**Εὔβουλος		4.21	
*εὐεργεσία	6.2		
*†εὐκαίρως		4.2	
**εὐμετάδοτος	6.18		
**Εὐνίκη		1.5	
εὑρίσκω		1.17, 18	
*εὐσέβεια	2.2; 3.16; 4.7, 8; 6.3, 5, 6, 11	3.5	1.1
*εὐσεβέω	5.4		
**εὐσεβῶς		3.12	2.12
εὐχαριστία	2.1; 4.3, 4		
†εὔχρηστος		2.21; 4.11	
Ἔφεσος	1.3	1.18; 4.12	
ἐφίστημι		4.2, 6	
ἔχω	(14)	1.3, 3, 13; 2.17, 19; 3.5	1.6; 2.8
ἕως	4.13		
ζάω	3.15; 4.10; 5.6	3.12; 4.1	2.12
ζηλωτής			2.14
**Ζηνᾶς			3.13
ζητέω		1.17	
*ζήτησις	6.4	2.23	3.9
ζυγός	6.1		
*ζωγρέω		2.26	
ζωή	1.16; 4.8; 6.12, 19	1.1, 10	1.2; 3.7
*ζῳογονέω	6.13		

	1 Timothy	2 Timothy	Titus
ἤ	1.4; 2.9, 9; 5.4, 19	3.4	1.6; 3.12
ἡγέομαι	1.12; 6.1		
ἤδη	5.15	2.18; 4.6	
*ἡδονή			3.3
ἡμεῖς	1.1, 1, 2, 12, 14; 2.3; 6.3, 14, 17	1.2, 7, 8, 9, 9, 9, 10, 14; 2.12	(15)
ἡμέρα	5.5	1.3, 12, 18; 3.1; 4.8	
ἡμέτερος		4.15	3.14
*†ἤπιος		2.24	
**ἤρεμος	2.2		
ἡσυχία	2.11, 12		
*†ἡσύχιος	2.2		
θάνατος		1.10	
θέλημα		1.1; 2.26	
θέλω	1.7; 2.4; 5.11	3.12	
θεμέλιος	6.19	2.19	
**θεόπνευστος		3.16	
θεός	1.1, 2, 4, 11, 17; 2.3, 5, 5; 3.5, 15, 15; 4.3, 4, 5, 10; 5.4, 5, 21; 6.1, 11, 13, 17	1.1, 2, 3, 6, 7, 8; 2.9, 14, 15, 19, 25; 3.17; 4.1	1.1, 1, 2, 3, 4, 7, 16; 2.5, 10, 11, 13; 3.4, 8
**θεοσέβεια	2.10		
Θεσσαλονίκη		4.10	
*θήριον			1.12
†θλίβω	5.10		
*θνήσκω	5.6		
**'Ιαμβρῆς		3.8	
**'Ιάννης		3.8	
ἴδιος	2.6; 3.4, 5, 12; 4.2; 5.4, 8; 6.1, 15	1.9; 4.3	1.3, 12; 2.5, 9
**ἱεροπρεπής			2.3
†ἱερός		3.15	
'Ιησοῦς	1.1, 1, 2, 12, 14, 15, 16; 2.5; 3.13; 4.6; 5.21; 6.3, 13, 14	1.1, 1, 2, 9, 10, 13; 2.1, 3, 8, 10; 3.12, 15; 4.1	1.1, 4; 2.13; 3.6
ἱκανός		2.2	
*'Ικόνιον		3.11	
*ἱματισμός	2.9		
ἵνα	(15)	1.4; 2.4, 10; 3.17; 4.17	(13)
**'Ιουδαϊκός			1.14
ἵστημι		2.19	

	1 Timothy	2 Timothy	Titus
καθαρίζω			2.14
καθαρός	1.5; 3.9	1.3; 2.22	1.15, 15, 15
καθίστημι			1.5
καθώς	1.3		
καί	(92)	(68)	(36)
καιρός	2.6; 4.1; 6.15	3.1; 4.3, 6	1.3
κἀκεῖνος		2.12	
κακία			3.3
*†κακοπαθέω		2.9; 4.5	
κακός	6.10	4.14	1.12
*κακοῦργος		2.9	
καλέω	6.12	1.9	
**καλοδιδάσκαλος			2.3
καλός	1.8, 18; 2.3; 3.1, 7, 13; 4.4, 6, 6; 5.10, 25; 6.12, 12, 13, 18, 19	1.14; 2.3, 7	2.7, 14; 3.8, 8, 14
καλῶς	3.4, 12, 13; 5.17		
καρδία	1.5	2.22	
καρπός		2.6	
**Καρπός		4.13	
κατά	1.1, 11, 18; 5.19, 21; 6.3	1.1, 8, 9, 9; 2.8; 4.3, 14	1.1, 1, 3, 4, 5, 9; 3.5, 7
**καταλέγομαι	5.9		
καταργέω		1.10	
**κατάστημα			2.3
**καταστολή	2.9		
**καταστρηνιάω	5.11		
*†καταστροφή		2.14	
**καταφθείρω		3.8	
καταφρονέω	4.12; 6.2		
*†κατηγορία	5.19		1.6
**καυστηριάζομαι	4.2		
κεῖμαι	1.9		
**κενοφωνία	6.20	2.16	
†κέρδος			1.11
κήρυγμα		4.17	1.3
*†κῆρυξ	2.7	1.11	
κηρύσσω	3.16	4.2	
**Κλαυδία		4.21	
κληρονόμος			3.7
†κλῆσις		1.9	
**κνήθω		4.3	
κοινός			1.4
†κοινωνέω	5.22		
**κοινωνικός	6.18		
κοπιάω	4.10; 5.17	2.6	
Κόρινθος		4.20	
*κοσμέω	2.9		2.10

	1 Timothy	2 Timothy	Titus
*†κοσμικός			2.12
**κόσμιος	2.9; 3.2		
κόσμος	1.15; 3.16; 6.7		
κράτος	6.16		
**Κρήσκης		4.10	
*Κρῆτες			1.12
*Κρήτη			1.5
κρίμα	3.6; 5.12		
κρίνω		4.1	3.12
κρίσις	5.24		
*κρίτης		4.8	
κρύπτω	5.25		
†κτίζω	4.3		
*†κτίσμα	4.4		
κυριεύω	6.15		
κύριος	1.2, 12, 14; 6.3, 14, 15	1.2, 8, 16, 18, 18; 2.7, 19, 19, 22, 24; 3.11; 4.8, 14, 17, 18, 22	
κωλύω	4.3		
λαλέω	5.13		2.1, 15
λαμβάνω	4.4	1.5	
λαός			2.14
λατρεύω		1.3	
λέγω	1.7; 2.7; 4.1; 5.18	2.7, 18	2.8
*λείπω			1.5, 13
*†λέων		4.17	
*λίαν		4.15	
**Λίνος		4.21	
λογίζομαι		4.16	
**λογομαχέω		2.14	
**λογομαχία	6.4		
λόγος	1.15; 3.1; 4.5, 6, 9, 12; 5.17; 6.3	1.13; 2.9, 11, 15, 17; 4.2, 15	1.3, 9; 2.5, 8; 3.8
*†λοιδορία	5.14		
λοιπός	5.20	4.8	
†Λοῦκας		4.11	
†λουτρόν			3.5
*Λύστρα		3.11	
*λυτρόω			2.14
**Λωΐς		1.5	
μακάριος	1.11; 6.15		2.13
Μακεδονία	1.3		
†μακροθυμία	1.16	3.10; 4.2	
μάλιστα	4.10; 5.8, 17	4.13	1.10
μᾶλλον	1.4; 6.2	3.4	
**μάμμη		1.5	

	1 Timothy	2 Timothy	Titus
μανθάνω	2.11; 5.4, 13	3.7, 14, 14	3.14
*†μαργαρίτης	2.9		
Μάρκος		4.11	
μαρτυρέω	5.10; 6.13		
*μαρτυρία	3.7		1.13
μαρτύριον	2.6	1.8	
μάρτυς	5.19; 6.12	2.2	
**ματαιολογία	1.6		
**ματαιολόγος			1.10
μάταιος			3.9
†μάχη		2.23	3.9
*μάχομαι		2.24	
μέγας	3.16; 6.6	2.20	2.13
*μελετάω	4.15		
μέλλω	1.16; 4.8; 6.19	4.1	
**μεμβράνα		4.13	
μέν		1.10; 2.20; 4.4	
μένω	2.15	2.13; 3.14; 4.20	
*†μέντοι		2.19	
†μεσίτης	2.5		
μετά	1.14; 2.9, 15; 3.4;	2.10, 22; 4.11, 11,	2.15; 3.10, 15, 15
	4.3, 4, 14; 6.6, 21	22, 22	
*μεταλαμβάνω		2.6	
**μετάλημψις	4.3		
μετάνοια		2.25	
μέχρι	6.14	2.9	
μή	(24)	1.7; 2.5, 14; 4.16	(13)
μηδέ	1.4; 5.22; 6.17	1.8	
μηδείς	4.12; 5.14, 21, 22;		2.8, 15; 3.2, 13
	6.4		
**μηδέποτε		3.7	
μηκέτι	5.23		
*μήποτε		2.25	
μήτε	1.7, 7		
μήτηρ	5.2	1.5	
**μητρολῴας	1.9		
*†μιαίνω			1.15, 15
*Μίλητος		4.20	
μιμνήσκομαι		1.4	
μισέω			3.3
μισθός	5.18		
†μνεία		1.3	
μνημονεύω		2.8	
μόνον	5.13	2.20; 4.8	
μόνος	1.17; 6.15, 16	4.11	
**μονόομαι	5.5		
†μόρφωσις		3.5	
*†μῦθος	1.4; 4.7	4.4	1.14
μυστήριον	3.9, 16		

	1 Timothy	2 Timothy	Titus
†μωρός		2.23	3.9
Μωϋσῆς		3.8	
†ναυαγέω		1.19	
νεκρός		2.8; 4.1	
νέος	5.1, 2, 11, 14		2.4, 6
*νεότης	4.12		
**νεόφυτος	3.6		
**νεωτερικός		2.22	
**νηφάλιος	3.2, 11		2.2
†νήφω		4.5	
**Νικόπολις			3.12
*†νίπτω	5.10		
†νοέω	1.7	2.7	
*†νομή		2.17	
νομίζω	6.5		
*νομικός			3.9, 13
**νομίμως	1.8	2.5	
*νομοδιδάσκαλος	1.7		
νόμος	1.8, 9		
**νοσέω	6.4		
*νοσφίζομαι			2.10
†νουθεσία			3.10
νοῦς	6.5	3.8	1.15
νῦν	4.8; 6.17	1.10; 4.10	2.12
νύξ	5.5	1.3	
**ξενοδοχέω	5.10		
*ξύλινος		2.20	
ὁ, ἡ, τό	(157)	(149)	(61)
†ὀδύνη	6.10		
οἶδα	1.8, 9; 3.5, 15	1.12, 15; 2.23; 3.14, 15	1.16; 3.11
†οἰκέω	6.16		
†οἰκεῖος	5.8		
οἰκία	5.13	2.20; 3.6	
**οἰκοδεσποτέω	5.14		
οἰκονομία	1.4		
οἰκονόμος			1.7
οἶκος	3.4, 5, 12, 15; 5.4	1.16; 4.19	1.11
**οἰκουργός			2.5
οἶνος	3.8; 5.23		2.3
†οἶος		3.11, 11	
†ὄλεθρος	6.9		
ὀλίγος	4.8; 5.23		
ὅλος			1.11
ὁμολογέω	6.12		1.16

	1 Timothy	2 Timothy	Titus
†ὁμολογία	6.12, 13		
**ὁμολογουμένως	3.16		
†ὀνειδισμός	3.7		
**'Ονησίφορος		1.16; 4.19	
ὄνομα	6.1	2.19	
ὀνομάζω		2.19	
ὄντως	5.3, 5, 16; 6.19		
ὀπίσω	5.15		
ὁράω	3.16		
ὀργή	2.8		
**ὀργίλος			1.7
*†ὀρέγομαι	3.1; 6.10		
**ὀρθοτομέω		2.15	
ὅς, ἥ, ὅ	(22)	(19)	1.2, 3, 10, 11, 13; 2.1, 14; 3.5, 6
*ὅσιος	2.8		1.8
ὅσος	6.1	1.18	
ὅστις, ἥτις, ὅτι	1.4; 3.15; 6.9	1.5; 2.2, 18	1.11
†ὀστράκινος		2.20	
ὅταν	5.11		3.12
ὅτε		4.3	3.4
ὅτι	1.8, 9, 12, 13, 15; 4.1, 4, 10; 5.12; 6.2, 2, 7	1.5, 12, 15, 16; 2.23; 3.1, 15	3.11
οὐ, οὐκ	1.9; 2.7, 12, 14; 3,5; 5.8, 13, 18, 25	(12)	3.5
οὐδέ	2.12; 6.7, 16		
οὐδείς	4.4; 6.7, 16	2.4, 14; 4.16	1.15
οὖν	2.1, 8; 3.2; 5.14	1.8; 2.1, 21	
οὗτος	(18)	(11)	1.5, 13; 2.15; 3.8, 8
οὕτως		3.8	
παγίς	3.7; 6.9	2.26	
†πάθημα		3.11	
†παιδεία		3.16	
παιδεύω	1.20	2.25	2.12
*†παλιγγενεσία			3.5
πάντοτε		3.7	
παρά		1.13, 18; 2.2; 3.14; 4.18	
†παράβασις	2.14		
παραγγελία	1.5, 18		
παραγγέλλω	1.3; 4.11; 5.7; 6.13, 17		
παραγίνομαι		4.16	
*παραδέχομαι	5.19		
παραδίδωμι	1.20		

	1 Timothy	2 Timothy	Titus
**παραθήκη	6.20	1.12, 14	
*παραιτέομαι	4.7; 5.11	2.23	3.10
παρακαλέω	1.3; 2.1; 5.1; 6.2	4.2	1.9; 2.6, 15
παράκλησις	4.13		
*παρακολουθέω	4.6	3.10	
παρατίθημι	1.18	2.2	
παραχειμάζω			3.12
παρέχω	1.4; 6.17		2.7
παριστάνω		2.15; 4.17	
**πάροινος	3.3		1.7
παρρησία	3.13		
πᾶς	(23)	(18)	(14)
πάσχω		1.12	
πατήρ	1.2; 5.1	1.2	1.4
**πατρολῴας	1.9		
Παῦλος	1.1	1.1	1.1
*πειθαρχέω			3.1
πείθω		1.5, 12	
πειρασμός	6.9		
πέμπω			3.12
περί	1.7, 19; 6. 4, 21.	1.3; 2.18; 3.8	2.7, 8; 3.8
*περίεργος	5.13		
*περιέρχομαι	5.13		
*περιΐστημι		2.16	3.9
**περιούσιος			2.14
**περιπείρω	6.10		
*περιποιέομαι	3.13		
περιτομή			1.10
*†περιφρονέω			2.15
*Πιλᾶτος	6.13		
πιστεύω	1.11, 16; 3.16	1.12	1.3; 3.8
πίστις	1.2, 4, 5, 14, 19, 19; 2.7, 15; 3.9, 13; 4.1, 6, 12; 5.8, 12; 6.10, 11, 12, 21	1.5, 13; 2.18, 22; 3.8, 10, 15; 4.7	1.1, 4, 13; 2.2, 10; 3.15
πιστός	1.12, 15; 3.1, 11; 4.3, 9, 10, 12; 5.16; 6.2, 2	2.2, 11, 13	1.6, 9; 3.8
**πιστόω		3.14	
πλανάω		3.13, 13	3.3
†πλάνος	4.1		
†πλάσσω	2.13		
**πλέγμα	2.9		
πλείων		2.16; 3.9	
**πλήκτης	3.3		1.7
πληρόω		1.4	
πληροφορέω		4.5, 17	
πλούσιος	6.17		
†πλουσίως	6.17		3.6

	1 Timothy	2 Timothy	Titus
πλουτέω	6.9, 18		
πλοῦτος	6.17		
πνεῦμα	3.16; 4.1, 1	1.7, 14; 4.22	3.5
ποιέω	1.13; 2.1; 4.16; 5.21	4.5	3.5
*ποικίλος		3.6	3.3
πόλις			1.5
πολλάκις		1.16	
πολύς	3.8, 13; 6.9, 10,12	2.2; 4.14	1.10; 2.3
*†πολυτελής	2.9		
πονηρός	6.4	3.13; 4.18	
*Πόντιος	6.13		
πορεύομαι	1.3	4.10	
**πορισμός	6.5, 6		
†πόρνος	1.10		
ποτέ			3.3
**Πούδης		4.21	
πούς	5.10		
**πραγματεία		2.4	
**πραϋπαθία	6.11		
†πραΰτης		2.25	3.2
†πρέπω	2.10		2.1
*πρεσβυτέριον	4.14		
*πρεσβύτερος	5.1, 2, 17, 19		1.5
πρεσβύτης			2.2
**πρεσβῦτις			2.3
Πρίσκα (-ιλλα)		4.19	
πρό		1.9; 4.21	1.2
*προάγω	1.18; 5.24		
**πρόγονος	5.4	1.3	
*†πρόδηλος	5.24, 25		
*προδότης		3.4	
πρόθεσις		1.9; 3.10	
†προΐστημι	3.4, 5, 12; 5.17		3.8, 14
†προκοπή	4.15		
προκόπτω		2.16; 3.9, 13	
**πρόκριμα	5.21		
†προνοέω	5.8		
προπέμπω			3.13
*προπετής		3.4	
πρός	1.16; 3.14; 4.7, 8, 8	2.24; 3.16, 16, 16, 16, 17; 4.9	1.16; 3.1, 2, 12, 12
προσδέχομαι			2.13
*προσέρχομαι	6.3		
προσεύχομαι	2.8		
προσευχή	2.1; 5.5		
προσέχω	1.4; 3.8; 4.1, 13		1.14
**πρόσκλισις	5.21		
*προσμένω	1.3; 5.5		

	1 Timothy	2 Timothy	Titus
†πρότερος	1.13		
†προφητεία	1.18; 4.14		
προφητής			1.12
πρῶτον	2.1; 3.10; 5.4	1.5; 2.6	
πρῶτος	1.15, 16; 2.13; 5.12	4.16	
*πυκνός	5.23		
πῶς	3.5, 15		
**ῥητῶς	4.1		
ῥίζα	6.10		
ῥύομαι		3.11; 4.17, 18	
Ῥώμη		1.17	
σάρξ	3.16		
Σατανᾶς	1.20; 5.15		
σεαυτοῦ	4.7, 16, 16; 5.22	2.15; 4.11	2.7
†σεμνός	3.8, 11		2.2
**σεμνότης	2.2; 3.4		2.7
**σκέπασμα	6.8		
σκεῦος		2.20, 21	
*†σοφίζω		3.15	
*†σπαταλάω	5.6		
†σπένδομαι		4.6	
σπέρμα		2.8	
†σπουδάζω		2.15; 4.9, 21	3.12
σπουδαίως		1.17	3.13
*†στερεός		2.19	
†στέφανος		4.8	
*†στεφανόω		2.5	
στόμα		4.17	
**στόμαχος	5.23		
†στρατεία	1.18		
στρατεύομαι	1.18	2.4	
*στρατιώτης		2.3	
**στρατολογέω		2.4	
**στυγητός			3.3
†στῦλος	3.15		
σύ	(14)	(20)	1.5, 5; 2.1, 15; 3.8, 12, 15
**συγκακοπαθέω		1.18; 2.3	
†συζάω		2.11	
†συμβασιλεύω		2.12	
†συναποθνήσκω		2.11	
συνείδησις	1.5, 19; 3.9; 4.2	1.3	1.15
σύνεσις		2.7	
†σφραγίς		2.19	
σῴζω	1.15; 2.4, 15; 4.16	1.9; 4.18	3.5
*σωματικός	4.8		

	1 Timothy	2 Timothy	Titus
**ὑπερπλεονάζω	1.14		
ὑπό	6.1	2.26	
ὑπόκρισις	4.2		
ὑπομένω		2.10, 12	
*ὑπομιμνήσκω		2.14	3.1
*†ὑπόμνησις		1.5	
ὑπομονή	6.11	3.10	2.2
**ὑπόνοια	6.4		
†ὑποταγή	2.11; 3.4		
ὑποτάσσω			2.5, 9; 3.1
†ὑποτίθημι	4.6		
**ὑποτύπωσις	1.16	1.13	
†ὑποφέρω		3.11	
*†ὕστερος	4.1		
**ὑψηλοφρονέω	6.17		
**φαιλόνης		4.13	
φανερός	4.15		
†φανερόω	3.16	1.10	1.3
†φαῦλος			2.8
φέρω		4.13	
φεύγω	6.11	2.22	
†φθόνος	6.4		3.3
**φιλάγαθος			1.8
**φίλανδρος			2.4
*φιλανθρωπία			3.4
**φιλαργυρία	6.10		
*φιλάργυρος		3.2	
**φίλαυτος		3.2	
φιλέω			3.15
**φιλήδονος		3.4	
**Φίλητος		2.17	
**φιλόθεος		3.4	
*φιλόξενος	3.2		1.8
**φιλότεκνος			2.4
*φιμόω	5.18		
**φλύαρος	5.13		
φόβος	5.20		
**φρεναπάτης			1.10
**φροντίζω			3.8
**Φύγελος		1.15	
φυλάσσω	5.21; 6.20	1.12, 14; 4.15	
φῶς	6.16		
φωτίζω		1.10	
*†χαλεπός		3.1	
**χαλκεύς		4.14	
χαρά		1.4	
χάριν	5.14		1.5, 11

	1 Timothy	2 Timothy	Titus
χάρις	1.2, 12, 14; 6.21	1.2, 3, 9; 2.1; 4.22	1.4; 2.11; 3.7, 15
†χάρισμα	4.14	1.6	
*χειμών		4.21	
χείρ	2.8; 4.14; 5.22	1.6	
*χείρων	5.8	3.13	
χήρα	5.3, 3, 4, 5, 9, 11, 16, 16		
χρεία			3.14
χράομαι	1.8; 5.23		
**χρήσιμος		2.14	
†χρηστότης			3.4
Χριστός	1.1, 1, 2, 12, 14, 15, 16; 2.5; 3.13; 4.6; 5.11, 21; 6.3, 13, 14	1.1, 1, 2, 9, 10, 13; 2.1, 3. 8. 10; 3.12, 15; 4.1	1.1, 4; 2.13; 3.6
χρόνος		1.9	1.2
χρύσιον	2.9		
*†χρυσοῦς		2.20	
χωρίς		2.8; 5.21	
ψεύδομαι	2.7		
**ψευδολόγος	4.2		
**ψευδώνυμος	6.20		
†ψεύστης	1.10		1.12
ὦ	6.11, 20		
ὡς	5.1, 1, 2, 2	1.3; 2.3, 9, 17; 3.9	1.5, 7
ὡσαύτως	2.9; 3.8, 11; 5.25		2.3, 6
**ὠφέλιμος	4.8, 8	3.16	3.8

INDEX OF ANCIENT WRITERS AND SOURCES

856

INDEX OF AUTHORS

This list does not include references to the authors of commentaries cited in the Commentary other than in the Introduction.